The Tax Law of Private Foundations

Sixth Edition

Update Service

BECOME A SUBSCRIBER!

Did you purchase this product from a bookstore?

If you did, it's important for you to become a subscriber. John Wiley & Sons, Inc. may publish, on a periodic basis, supplements and new editions to reflect the latest changes in the subject matter that you *need to know* in order to stay competitive in this ever-changing industry. By contacting the Wiley office nearest you, you'll receive any current update at no additional charge. In addition, you'll receive future updates and revised or related volumes on a 30-day examination review.

If you purchased this product directly from John Wiley & Sons, Inc., we have already recorded your subscription for this update service.

To become a subscriber, please call 1-877-762-2974 or send your name, company name (if applicable), address, and the title of the product to:

mailing address: **Supplement Department**
John Wiley & Sons, Inc.
10475 Crosspoint Blvd.
Indianapolis, IN 46256

e-mail: subscriber@wiley.com
fax: 1-800-605-2665
online: www.wiley.com

For customers outside the United States, please contact the Wiley office nearest you:

Professional & Reference Division
John Wiley & Sons Canada, Ltd.
90 Eglinton Ave. E. Suite 300
Toronto, Ontario M4P 2Y3
Canada
Phone: 416-236-4433
Phone: 1-800-567-4797
Fax: 416-236-8743
Email: canada@wlley.com

John Wiley & Sons, Ltd.
European Distribution Centre
New Era Estate
Oldlands Way
Bognor Regis, West Sussex
PO22 9NQ, UK
Phone: (0)1243 779777
Fax: (0)1243 843 123
Email: customer@wlley.co.uk

John Wiley & Sons Australia, Ltd.
42 McDougall Street
Milton, Queensland 4064
AUSTRALIA
Phone: 61-7-3859-9755
Fax: 61-7-3859-9715
Email: aus-custservice@wiley.com

John Wiley & Sons (Asia) Pte., Ltd.
1 Fusionopolis Walk
#07-01 Solaris South Tower
SINGAPORE 138628
Phone: 65-6302-9838
Fax: 65-6265-1782
Customer Service: 65-6302-9800
Email: asiacart@wiley.com

+ website

The **Tax Law** of **Private Foundations**

Sixth Edition

Shane T. Hamilton, Bruce R. Hopkins

WILEY

Copyright © 2024 by John Wiley & Sons, Inc. All rights reserved.

Published by John Wiley & Sons, Inc., Hoboken, New Jersey.
Published simultaneously in Canada.

No part of this publication may be reproduced, stored in a retrieval system, or transmitted in any form or by any means, electronic, mechanical, photocopying, recording, scanning, or otherwise, except as permitted under Section 107 or 108 of the 1976 United States Copyright Act, without either the prior written permission of the Publisher, or authorization through payment of the appropriate per-copy fee to the Copyright Clearance Center, Inc., 222 Rosewood Drive, Danvers, MA 01923, (978) 750-8400, fax (978) 750-4470, or on the web at www.copyright.com. Requests to the Publisher for permission should be addressed to the Permissions Department, John Wiley & Sons, Inc., 111 River Street, Hoboken, NJ 07030, (201) 748-6011, fax (201) 748-6008, or online at http://www.wiley.com/go/permission.

Trademarks: Wiley and the Wiley logo are trademarks or registered trademarks of John Wiley & Sons, Inc. and/or its affiliates in the United States and other countries and may not be used without written permission. All other trademarks are the property of their respective owners. John Wiley & Sons, Inc. is not associated with any product or vendor mentioned in this book.

Limit of Liability/Disclaimer of Warranty: While the publisher and author have used their best efforts in preparing this book, they make no representations or warranties with respect to the accuracy or completeness of the contents of this book and specifically disclaim any implied warranties of merchantability or fitness for a particular purpose. No warranty may be created or extended by sales representatives or written sales materials. The advice and strategies contained herein may not be suitable for your situation. You should consult with a professional where appropriate. Further, readers should be aware that websites listed in this work may have changed or disappeared between when this work was written and when it is read. Neither the publisher nor authors shall be liable for any loss of profit or any other commercial damages, including but not limited to special, incidental, consequential, or other damages.

For general information on our other products and services or for technical support, please contact our Customer Care Department within the United States at (800) 762-2974, outside the United States at (317) 572-3993 or fax (317) 572-4002.

Wiley also publishes its books in a variety of electronic formats. Some content that appears in print may not be available in electronic formats. For more information about Wiley products, visit our web site at www.wiley.com.

Library of Congress Cataloging-in-Publication Data is Available:

ISBN 9781394214754 (Cloth)
ISBN 9781394214778 (ePDF)
ISBN 9781394214761 (ePub)

Cover Design: Wiley
Cover Image: © Tim Messick/Getty Images

Contents

A Letter to the Reader   xix

Preface   xxi

Book Citations   xxvii

1 Introduction to Private Foundations   1
- § 1.1 Private Foundations: Unique Organizations 2
- § 1.2 Definition of Private Foundation 4
- § 1.3 Background 7
- § 1.4 Private Foundation Tax Law Primer 10
  - (a) Introduction 11
  - (b) General Operational Requirements 11
  - (c) Disqualified Persons 12
  - (d) Self-Dealing Rules 12
  - (e) Mandatory Payout Rules 13
  - (f) Excess Business Holdings Rules 14
  - (g) Jeopardizing Investments Rules 14
  - (h) Taxable Expenditures Rules 15
  - (i) Tax on Investment Income 16
  - (j) Termination of Private Foundation Status 16
  - (k) Charitable Giving Rules 16
  - (l) Unrelated Business Rules 17
- § 1.5 Definition of Charity 17
- § 1.6 Operating for Charitable Purposes 19
- § 1.7 Organizational Rules 22
- § 1.8 Private Foundation Law Sanctions 24
  - (a) Sanctions (a Reprise) 25
  - (b) Self-Dealing Sanctions as Pigouvian Taxes 25
  - (c) Self-Dealing Sanctions: Taxes or Penalties? 26
  - (d) Abatement 31
  - (e) Potential of Overlapping Taxes 31
  - (f) Influence on Subsequent Law 32
- § 1.9 Statistical Profile 33
- § 1.10 Private Foundations and Law 50 Years Later 33

2 Starting, Funding, and Governing a Private Foundation   39
- § 2.1 Alternatives to Private Foundations 40
- § 2.2 Advantages of Private Foundations 42

CONTENTS

§ 2.3 Choice of Organizational Form 46
§ 2.4 Funding a Foundation 47
§ 2.5 Estate Planning Principles 49
    (a) Decedents' Estates 50
    (b) Estate and Gift Tax Considerations 50
§ 2.6 Foundations and Planned Giving 51
    (a) Introduction to Planned Giving 51
    (b) Charitable Remainder Trusts 52
    (c) Other Planned Giving Vehicles 53
    (d) Interrelationships with Private Foundation Rules 54
§ 2.7 Acquiring Recognition of Tax-Exempt Status 55
    (a) Form 1023 56
    (b) 27-Month Rule 59
    (c) IRS Determination Letters Recognizing Exempt Status 61
    (d) Administrative Procedures Where Recognition Denied 64
    (e) Declaratory Judgment Procedures Where Recognition Denied 67
    (f) Recognition of Foreign Organizations 70
    (g) Exemption for State Purposes 71
§ 2.8 Governance 72
    (a) IRS Entry into Nonprofit Governance 73
    (b) Concept of Nonprofit Governance 74
    (c) Nonprofit Governance Standards 76
    (d) Early IRS Attempts at Nonprofit Governance Regulation 80
    (e) Federal Tax Law as to Board Composition 81
    (f) IRS's Use of Private Benefit Doctrine 82
    (g) IRS's Ruling Policy 84

3 Types of Private Foundations   **87**

§ 3.1 Private Operating Foundations 87
    (a) Direct Charitable Distributions 88
    (b) Grants 92
    (c) Individual Grant Programs 93
    (d) Income Test 96
    (e) Asset, Endowment, or Support Test 99
        (i) Asset Test 99
        (ii) Endowment Test 102
        (iii) Support Test 103
    (f) Compliance Period 104
    (g) Advantages and Disadvantages of Private Operating Foundations 106
    (h) Conversion to or from Private Operating Foundation Status 107
§ 3.2 Exempt Operating Foundations 109
§ 3.3 Conduit Foundations 109

CONTENTS

§ 3.4 Common Fund Foundations 111
§ 3.5 Research and Experimentation Funds 112
§ 3.6 Nonexempt Charitable Trusts 114
§ 3.7 Split-Interest Trusts 116
§ 3.8 Foreign Private Foundations 119

4 Disqualified Persons   **123**
§ 4.1 Substantial Contributors 124
    (a) General Rules 124
    (b) 2 Percent Test 125
    (c) Terminating Substantial Contributor Status 126
§ 4.2 Foundation Managers 127
§ 4.3 Certain 20 Percent Owners 128
§ 4.4 Family Members 130
§ 4.5 Corporations or Partnerships 131
§ 4.6 Trusts or Estates 132
§ 4.7 Private Foundations 132
§ 4.8 Governmental Officials 133
§ 4.9 Termination of Disqualified Person Status 135

5 Self-Dealing   **137**
§ 5.1 Private Inurement Doctrine 140
§ 5.2 Private Benefit Doctrine 143
§ 5.3 General Definition of Self-Dealing 151
§ 5.4 Sale, Exchange, Lease, or Furnishing of Property 154
    (a) Sales 154
    (b) Transactions by Agents 156
    (c) Exchanges 157
    (d) Leasing of Property 158
    (e) Furnishing of Goods, Services, or Facilities 159
    (f) Co-Owned Property 162
    (g) Coinvestments 166
§ 5.5 Loans and Other Extensions of Credit 168
    (a) Gifts of Indebted Property 170
    (b) Interest-Free Loans 171
§ 5.6 Payment of Compensation 173
    (a) Definition of Personal Services 174
    (b) Definition of Compensation 177
    (c) Definition of Reasonable 180
    (d) Finding Salary Statistics 184
    (e) Excess Executive Compensation Tax 185
        (i) General Rules and Definitions 186
        (ii) Compensation from Related Organizations 187
        (iii) Exceptions to Covered Employee Status 188

CONTENTS

    (f) Commissions or Management Fees 190
    (g) Expense Advances and Reimbursements 191
    (h) Bank Fees 192
§ 5.7 Indemnification and Insurance 194
    (a) Noncompensatory Indemnification and Insurance 195
    (b) Compensatory Indemnification and Insurance 196
    (c) Fringe Benefit Rules and Volunteers 197
§ 5.8 Uses of Income or Assets by Disqualified Persons 199
    (a) Securities Transactions 200
      (i) Summary of Law 200
      (ii) Representative Case 201
    (b) Other Transactions Involving Manipulation 203
    (c) Payment of Charitable Pledges 203
    (d) For the Benefit of Transactions 204
    (e) Incidental or Tenuous Benefits 206
    (f) Memberships 212
    (g) Benefit Tickets 213
    (h) Other Acts 213
§ 5.9 Sharing Space, People, and Expenses 214
    (a) Determining What the Private Foundation Can Pay 215
    (b) Office Space and Personnel 215
    (c) Group Insurance 218
    (d) Public Facilities 218
§ 5.10 Payments to Government Officials 218
§ 5.11 Indirect Self-Dealing 220
    (a) Transactions with Controlled Entities 221
    (b) Concept of *Control* 222
    (c) Transactions and the Control Element 224
    (d) Exceptions 225
    (e) Fraudulent Investment Schemes 227
§ 5.12 Estate Administration Exception 228
    (a) Concept of the *Expectancy* 228
    (b) Estate Administration Exception—General Rules 230
    (c) Determining Fair Market Value 233
§ 5.13 Early Terminations of Charitable Remainder Trusts 235
§ 5.14 Additional Exceptions 237
    (a) Certain Corporate Organizations or Reorganizations 237
    (b) Transitional Rules (Savings Provisions) 238
§ 5.15 Issues Once Self-Dealing Occurs 239
    (a) Self-Dealing Excise Taxes 240
      (i) Initial Taxes 240
      (ii) Additional Taxes 243
      (iii) Termination Tax 243

CONTENTS

    (iv) Limitation on Abatement 243
    (v) Advice of Counsel 244
  (b) Amount Involved 244
    (i) Use of Money or Other Property 244
    (ii) Compensation 245
    (iii) Exceptions Predicated on Fair Market Value 246
  (c) Date of Valuation 246
  (d) Correcting the Transaction 247
    (i) Sales by the Foundation 248
    (ii) Sales to the Foundation 249
    (iii) Loans 250
    (iv) Use of Property by Disqualified Person 250
    (v) Use of Property by Private Foundation 251
    (vi) Unreasonable Compensation 251
  (e) Court Jurisdiction as to Tax 251

6 Mandatory Distributions 255

 § 6.1 Mandatory Distribution Requirement 256
  (a) Purpose and Policy 256
  (b) Distributable Amount 257
 § 6.2 Minimum Investment Return 258
  (a) General Calculation 258
  (b) Investment Assets 259
  (c) Future Interests or Expectancies 260
  (d) Exempt Function Assets 261
  (e) Acquisition Indebtedness 265
 § 6.3 Determining Fair Market Value 267
  (a) Cash 267
  (b) Readily Marketable Securities 267
  (c) Other Assets 270
  (d) Assets Held for Partial Year 272
  (e) Investment Frauds 272
 § 6.4 Qualifying Distributions 273
  (a) General Definition and Rules 273
  (b) Charitable Grants in General 275
  (c) Grants to Controlled Organizations and Other Foundations 276
    (i) Definition of Control 277
    (ii) Redistribution Rule 278
  (d) Grantor Reliance Standards 279
    (i) General Rules 279
    (ii) Grants to Certain Supporting Organizations 282
    (iii) No IRS Determination Letter 284
    (iv) Charities Under a Group Ruling 285

CONTENTS

        (e)   Grants to Foreign Organizations   286
        (f)   Direct Charitable Expenditures   289
            (i)   Exempt Function Assets   289
            (ii)   Administrative Expenses   290
        (g)   Set-Asides   292
            (i)   Suitability Test Set-Asides   294
            (ii)   Cash Distribution Test Set-Asides   296
            (iii) Court Order Set-Asides   299
§ 6.5   Excise Taxes on Failure to Distribute Income   300
        (a)   Undistributed Income   300
        (b)   Ordering Rule for Qualifying Distributions   300
        (c)   Excess Qualifying Distributions   301
        (d)   Excise Taxes on Undistributed Income   303
        (e)   Valuation Mistakes   304
        (f)   Exception for Certain Accumulations   305
§ 6.6   History of the Mandatory Distribution Requirement   305

7 Excess Business Holdings   311

§ 7.1   General Rules   311
        (a)   Definition of Business Enterprise   312
        (b)   Passive Income Businesses   313
        (c)   Certain Investment Partnerships   315
        (d)   Percentage Limitations   317
§ 7.2   Permitted and Excess Holdings   319
        (a)   General Rules   319
        (b)   Partnerships, Trusts, and Proprietorships   321
        (c)   Constructive Ownership   322
        (d)   Disposition Periods   322
§ 7.3   Functionally Related Businesses   327
§ 7.4   Philanthropic Businesses   332
§ 7.5   Rules Applicable to Certain Supporting Organizations   332
§ 7.6   Rules Applicable to Donor-Advised Funds   333
§ 7.7   Excise Taxes on Excess Holdings   333

8 Jeopardizing Investments   337

§ 8.1   General Rules   338
        (a)   Defining Jeopardy   339
        (b)   Contributed Assets   343
§ 8.2   Prudent Investments   344
        (a)   Evaluating Investment Alternatives   346
        (b)   Facing the Unknown   348
        (c)   Risk versus Return   349
        (d)   Total Return Investing   350
        (e)   Reporting of Income   351

CONTENTS

        (f)   Measuring Investment Return   351
        (g)   Mission-Related Investments   352
§ 8.3   Program-Related Investments   353
§ 8.4   Investment Frauds   359
        (a)   Background   359
        (b)   NYSBA Report   360
§ 8.5   Excise Taxes on Jeopardizing Investments   362
        (a)   Initial Taxes   362
        (b)   When a Manager Knows   363
        (c)   Reliance on Outside Advisors   364
        (d)   Additional Taxes and Removal from Jeopardy   365

9 Taxable Expenditures   369
§ 9.1   Legislative Activities   372
        (a)   Law Applicable to Charities Generally   373
        (b)   Law Applicable to Private Foundations   374
        (c)   Grants to Charities That Lobby   376
        (d)   Nonpartisan Study of Social Issues   378
        (e)   Self-Defense Exception   380
§ 9.2   Political Campaign Activities   381
        (a)   Law Applicable to Charities Generally   381
        (b)   Law Applicable to Private Foundations   382
        (c)   Voter Registration Drives   383
§ 9.3   Grants to Individuals   384
        (a)   Definition of Grant   384
        (b)   Individual Grants for Charitable or Other Permitted Purposes   384
        (c)   Disaster Relief and Other Assistance Grants   386
        (d)   Individual Grants for Travel, Study, or Other Similar Purposes   392
            (i)   Scholarships and Fellowships   393
            (ii)   Employer-Related Scholarship Programs   394
            (iii)   Prizes and Awards   399
            (iv)   Grants for Specific Objectives or to Enhance Skills   400
        (e)   Individual Grant Procedures   402
            (i)   Objective and Nondiscriminatory Basis for Selection   403
            (ii)   Grantee Reporting Requirements   405
            (iii)   Monitoring, Supervision, and Investigation Requirements   406
            (iv)   Recordkeeping Requirements   408
        (f)   IRS Approval of Grant Procedures   408
            (i)   Requests for Advance IRS Approval   409
            (ii)   Deemed IRS Approval   410
            (iii)   Impact of IRS Approval on Future Grants   411
        (g)   Individual Grant Intermediaries and Earmarking   412

CONTENTS

§ 9.4 Grants to Public Charities   415
    (a) Types of Public Charity Grantees   415
    (b) Grantor Reliance Standards   416
    (c) Intermediary and Secondary Grantees   417

§ 9.5 Grants to Exempt Operating Foundations   419

§ 9.6 Grants to Foreign Organizations   419
    (a) General Rules   419
    (b) Good Faith (Equivalency) Determinations   420
    (c) Canadian and Mexican Organizations   422
    (d) Anti-Terrorist Financing Guidelines   423

§ 9.7 Expenditure Responsibility   424
    (a) General Rules   424
    (b) Pre-Grant Inquiry   426
    (c) Grant Terms   428
    (d) Reports from Grantees   429
    (e) Grantee's Books and Records   430
    (f) Reports to IRS   431
    (g) Foundation's Recordkeeping Requirements   432
    (h) Grantee Diversions   432

§ 9.8 Spending for Noncharitable Purposes   435

§ 9.9 Excise Tax on Taxable Expenditures   440
    (a) Initial and Additional Taxes   440
    (b) Tax on Managers   441
    (c) Paying the Tax   442
    (d) Correcting the Expenditure   443

10 Tax on Net Investment Income   445

§ 10.1 Rate of Tax   446

§ 10.2 Payment of Tax   448

§ 10.3 Planning Opportunities to Reduce the Tax   448

§ 10.4 Calculating Taxable Net Investment Income   450
    (a) Gross Investment Income   450
    (b) Capital Gains and Losses   451
        (i) Exceptions, Adjustments, and Exclusions   451
        (ii) Basis   453
        (iii) Wash Sales   454
        (iv) Ponzi Scheme Losses   454
    (c) Interest and Annuities   455
    (d) Dividends   455
    (e) Rent   456
    (f) Royalties   456
    (g) Estate or Trust Distributions   456
    (h) Partnership and S Corporation Income   459

CONTENTS

§ 10.5 Reductions to Gross Investment Income   460
    (a) Deductions Allowed   460
    (b) Deductions Not Allowed   462
§ 10.6 Foreign Foundations   464
§ 10.7 Exemption from Tax on Investment Income   465

11 Unrelated Business Activity   467

§ 11.1 General Rules   468
    (a) Overview   468
    (b) Trade or Business Income   469
    (c) Substantially Related Activity   471
    (d) Regularly Carried On   474
    (e) Real Estate Activities   475
§ 11.2 Exceptions   477
    (a) Royalties   479
    (b) Rents   480
    (c) Research   483
    (d) Nonbusiness Activities   484
§ 11.3 Rules Specifically Applicable to Private Foundations   485
    (a) Business Enterprises   486
    (b) Permitted Businesses   488
    (c) Partnerships and S Corporations   489
    (d) Community Foundations' Grant-Making Services   491
    (e) Provision of Technical Assistance   494
§ 11.4 Unrelated Debt-Financed Income Rules   495
    (a) Acquisition Indebtedness   495
    (b) Related-Use Exceptions   499
    (c) Includible Income   500
§ 11.5 Calculating and Reporting the Tax   501
    (a) General Rules   501
    (b) Bucketing Rule   502
    (c) Tax Rates   505
    (d) Tax Computation and Reporting Rules   506
    (e) Penalties and Additions to Tax   507
    (f) Statute of Limitations   508

12 Tax Reporting and Administration Issues   509

§ 12.1 Form 990-PF   510
    (a) Annual Form 990-PF Filing Requirement   510
    (b) Key Form 990-PF Disclosures   510
    (c) Reporting Changes on Form 990-PF   512
        (i) Changes in Activities   512
        (ii) Changes in Governing Documents   512
        (iii) Name and Address Changes   513

CONTENTS

        (d)   Other Changes   513
            (i)   Change in Annual Accounting Period (Tax Year)   513
            (ii)   Change in Accounting Method   514

§ 12.2   Form 990-PF Penalties   515
        (a)   Daily Delinquency Penalty   515
        (b)   Form 990-PF Statute of Limitations   516
        (c)   Reasonable Cause   518
        (d)   Amended Returns   521

§ 12.3   Public Disclosure and Inspection of Returns   521
        (a)   Disclosure of Returns to the Public   521
        (b)   Disclosure of Returns to State Officials   524

§ 12.4   Reporting and Payment of Excise Taxes   525
        (a)   Reporting and Payment on Form 4720   525
        (b)   Additions to Tax and Penalties   527
        (c)   Abatement   529
        (d)   Form 4720 Statute of Limitations   533
        (e)   Closing Agreements   536

§ 12.5   Determination Letters and Letter Rulings   537
        (a)   Form 8940 Miscellaneous Determination Requests   538
        (b)   Letter Rulings   539
        (c)   Reliance on Determinations and Rulings   540

§ 12.6   IRS Examinations of Private Foundations   541
        (a)   Types of Examinations   542
        (b)   General IRS EO Examination Practices and Procedures   543
        (c)   Achieving Positive Results   545

§ 12.7   Revocation of Tax-Exempt Status   546
        (a)   Automatic Revocation for Non-Filing   546
        (b)   Retroactive Revocation   547
        (c)   IRS Administrative Appeal Procedures   548
        (d)   Contesting Revocation in Court   549
        (e)   Consequences of Revocation   550

13 Termination of Foundation Status   553

§ 13.1   Voluntary Termination   556
§ 13.2   Involuntary Termination   557
§ 13.3   Transfer of Assets to a Public Charity   558
        (a)   General Rules   558
        (b)   Restrictions and Conditions on Transfer   561
            (i)   Acceptable Restrictions and Conditions   562
            (ii)   Unacceptable Restrictions and Conditions   564
        (c)   Reservation of Right to Direct Distributions   565
            (i)   Factors Indicating a Permissible Reservation   566
            (ii)   Factors Indicating an Impermissible Reservation   566

CONTENTS

§ 13.4 Operation as a Public Charity 567
    (a) General Rules 567
    (b) Initial Notice 569
    (c) Advance Ruling Requests 570
    (d) Final Notice 572

§ 13.5 Mergers, Split-Ups, and Transfers Between Foundations 573
    (a) General Rules 573
    (b) Complete Asset Transfers to Controlled Foundations 576
    (c) Complete Asset Transfer to Non-Controlled Foundations 581
    (d) Transfers of Significant but Not All Assets 583

§ 13.6 Termination of Trusts Treated as Private Foundations 585
§ 13.7 Termination Tax 586
§ 13.8 Abatement 588

14 Charitable Giving Rules   589

§ 14.1 Concept of Gift 589
§ 14.2 Basic Rules 592
    (a) Percentage Limitations 593
    (b) Estate and Gift Tax Deductions 595

§ 14.3 Gifts of Appreciated Property 595
§ 14.4 Deduction Reduction Rules 597
    (a) Capital Gain Property Deduction Rule 597
    (b) Other Deduction Reduction Rules 597

§ 14.5 Qualified Appreciated Stock Rule 599
§ 14.6 Special Gift Situations 601
    (a) Donors' Creations 601
    (b) Bargain Sales 601
    (c) Intellectual Property 602
    (d) Vehicles 602
    (e) Use of Property 603
    (f) Services 603
    (g) Conservation Property 603

§ 14.7 Administrative Considerations 604
    (a) Recordkeeping Rules 604
    (b) Substantiation Rules 604
    (c) Disclosure Rules 608
    (d) Appraisal Rules 609
    (e) Doctrine of Substantial Compliance 611
    (f) Reporting Requirements 612
    (g) State Fundraising Regulation 612

15 Public Charities   613

§ 15.1 Advantages of Public Charity Status 614
§ 15.2 Statutory Categories of Public Charities 616

CONTENTS

§ 15.3   Public Institution Charities   617
  (a)   Churches and Similar Entities   618
  (b)   Educational Institutions   619
  (c)   Hospitals   621
  (d)   Medical Research Organizations   621
  (e)   Agricultural Research Organizations   622
  (f)   Public College Support Foundations   623
  (g)   Governmental Units   623

§ 15.4   Donative Publicly Supported Charities   624
  (a)   General Rules   625
  (b)   Two Percent Limitation   626
  (c)   Support Test   628
  (d)   Facts and Circumstances Test   631
  (e)   Community Foundations   633

§ 15.5   Service Provider Publicly Supported Charities   635
  (a)   Support Test   636
  (b)   Investment Income Test   639
  (c)   Unusual Grants   641
      (i)   Unusual Grant Factors   641
      (ii) Safe Harbor Criteria   646
      (iii) Requests for Advance IRS Rulings   646

§ 15.6   Supporting Organizations   647
  (a)   Organizational Test   649
  (b)   Operational Test   650
  (c)   Specified Public Charities   652
  (d)   Required Relationships   656
  (e)   Type I: Operated, Supervised, or Controlled By   656
  (f)   Type II: Supervised or Controlled in Connection With   657
  (g)   Type III: Operated in Connection With   658
      (i)   Overview   658
      (ii)   Notification Requirement   659
      (iii) Responsiveness Test   659
      (iv)   Types of Type III Supporting Organizations   660
      (v)   Integral Part Test—Functionally Integrated Type III Organizations   660
      (vi)   Integral Part Test—Nonfunctionally Integrated Type III Organizations   662
      (vii) Pending Regulation Projects   666
  (h)   Contributions from Controlling Donors   668
  (i)   Excess Benefit Transactions Rules   669
  (j)   Limitation on Control   669
  (k)   Excess Business Holdings Rules   672
  (l)   Noncharitable Supported Organizations   673
  (m)   Use of For-Profit Subsidiaries   674

CONTENTS

§ 15.7 Change of Public Charity Category 675
    (a) From § 509(a)(1) to § 509(a)(2) or Vice Versa 675
    (b) From § 509(a)(3) to § 509(a)(1) or § 509(a)(2) 675
    (c) From § 509(a)(3) Type III to § 509(a)(3) Type I or II 675
    (d) IRS Recognition of Change in Public Charity Status 676
§ 15.8 Termination of Public Charity Status 677
§ 15.9 Relationships Created for Avoidance Purposes 678

16 Donor-Advised Funds   679

§ 16.1 Basic Definitions 681
§ 16.2 General Concept of a Gift 682
§ 16.3 Types of Donor Funds 684
§ 16.4 Donor-Advised Fund Litigation 687
    (a) Exemption Challenges 687
    (b) Donor Challenges 689
    (c) Charitable Deduction Challenges 690
§ 16.5 Public Charity Status of Funds 692
§ 16.6 Interrelationship of Private Foundation Rules 693
§ 16.7 Statutory Criteria 694
§ 16.8 Studies 699
    (a) Treasury Study 699
    (b) Congressional Research Service Study 701
§ 16.9 Tax Regulations 704
    (a) The Ever-Pending Regulations Project 704
    (b) 2017 IRS Notice 705
    (c) Comments on IRS Notice 707
§ 16.10 Proposed Legislation 713

17 Company Foundations   717

§ 17.1 Company Foundation Overview 717
§ 17.2 Reasons for Establishment of a Company Foundation 719
§ 17.3 Private Inurement Doctrine 719
§ 17.4 Private Benefit Doctrine 720
§ 17.5 Disqualified Persons Rules 721
§ 17.6 Self-Dealing Rules 722
    (a) Payment of Compensation and Reimbursements 722
    (b) Sharing of Facilities 723
    (c) Provision of Tangible Benefits 725
    (d) Grantmaking 726
    (e) Incidental and Tenuous Benefits 727
    (f) Corporate Reorganizations and Stock Transfers 731
§ 17.7 Other Private Foundations Rules 732
    (a) Mandatory Payout Rules 732
    (b) Excess Business Holdings Rules 732

  (c) Jeopardizing Investments Rules 733
  (d) Taxable Expenditures Rules 733
  (e) Economic Returns 734
§ 17.8 Excess Executive Compensation Tax Exceptions 734
  (a) Limited Hours Exception 734
  (b) Nonexempt Funds Exception 736

About the Authors   739

About the Online Resources   741

Index   743

A Letter to the Reader

It is with a heavy heart that we relay the news to you that Bruce Richard Hopkins, JD, LLM, SJD, passed away on October 31, 2021. Bruce's love for the law and writing resulted in a wonderful relationship with Wiley that lasted for over 30 years. Throughout that time, Bruce penned more than 50 books as well as writing *Bruce R. Hopkins' Nonprofit Counsel* (a newsletter published monthly for 40 years). Bruce's texts are practical guides about nonprofits written for both lawyers *and* laypeople, many of which are considered vital to law libraries across the country. The ideas just kept flowing.

Beloved by many, Bruce was often referred to as the "Dean of Nonprofit Law." His teaching muscle was built over a period of 19 years as a Professional Lecturer in Law at George Washington University National Law Center. Later, as a Professor from Practice at the University of Kansas School of Law, Bruce exercised his generative spirit by teaching and mentoring younger colleagues. Always the legal scholar, he could brilliantly take complicated concepts and distill them down into easily understood principles for beginners, seasoned colleagues, and those unfamiliar with the subject matter. He was a presenter and featured speaker, both nationally and internationally, at numerous conferences throughout his career, among them Representing and Managing Tax-Exempt Organizations (Georgetown University Law Center, Washington, DC) and the Private Foundations Tax Seminar (El Pomar Foundation, Colorado Springs, Colorado). He practiced law in Washington, DC, and Kansas City, Missouri, for over 50 years, receiving numerous awards and various forms of recognition for his efforts.

Bruce will be dearly missed, not solely for his contributions to the Wiley catalog, but because he was a wonderful person loved and respected by all of us at Wiley and by all those he encountered.

Preface

Private foundations, although constituting a relatively small portion of the charitable community, are burdened with extensive federal tax law requirements that belie their numbers and that substantially regulate and circumscribe their operations. This body of law has steadily grown since its inception as a considerable portion of the Tax Reform Act of 1969. *The Tax Law of Private Foundations* attempts to both capture and summarize the law pertaining to these unique forms of tax-exempt organizations and to provide guidance for complying with it.

As a charitable entity, a private foundation is an organization described in section 501(c)(3) of the Internal Revenue Code (the "Code"). Of course, this, in turn, means that nearly all of the considerable law embodied in and around that section is applicable to private foundations. However, stimulated by a variety of abuses, perceived and otherwise, the law in this area includes a collection of additional statutory requirements in the form of rules applicable only to private foundations. These rules are the main subject of this book.

Many lawyers and accountants who practice in the exempt organizations field have little or no involvement with private foundations. With their exempt clients being public charities or other types of nonprofit organizations, this is understandable; these practitioners have no reason to master the private foundation rules. As private foundations proliferate, existing ones grow, and the law becomes more encompassing. Consequently, successful understanding of the private foundation rules becomes increasingly important for all tax practitioners. Indeed, as the law in the charitable area evolves, some of these rules have been extended outside the private foundation realm, with emphasis in that regard on supporting organizations and donor-advised funds.

There is more to this dimension of the matter. For the first few decades of their existence, the tax laws specifically applicable to private foundations had no real practical relationship to the tax laws pertaining to public charities. (Two exceptions of note are the laws concerning functionally related businesses and voter registration projects.) With respect to the self-dealing rules, however, this dichotomy has changed with the advent of the intermediate sanctions imposed on excessive compensation. In this area, much of the private foundation law pertaining to self-dealing has been grafted onto the public charity rules. This extension of private foundation law into the public charity context amounts to more than the concept of *self-dealing* informing the concept of the *excess benefit transaction*: the law concerning *corrections*, the *amount involved*,

PREFACE

and the *highest fiduciary standards* is also now a part of public charity law. For those advising public charities in this area, this book should be helpful.

Earlier, it was said that this book endeavors to "capture" the tax law concerning private foundations. This, in fact, is an impossible task and an elusive goal. The reason for this lies in the inherent nature of the "law" in this field. While the foundation law is framed by detailed statutes and regulations, much of the guidance in this area is technically not law at all, but rather is found in the thousands of private determinations issued by the Internal Revenue Service: private letter rulings, technical advice memoranda, chief counsel memoranda, and the like. These documents tumble out of the IRS, seemingly by the tons, every month. They infuse the law of private foundations with its dynamism, keeping it flowing, changing, and expanding. Although the field has now surpassed 50 years of age (a milestone briefly reflected upon in Chapter 1), the IRS is still initiating—and in some instances, reversing—its policy determinations in the area.

Compliance with these rules is critical to the preservation of a private foundation's tax-exempt status and the avoidance of the various excise taxes imposed on rule violations. This book thoroughly explores these rules. It seeks to dispel the myth that private foundations are difficult, if not impossible, to manage. What can be fascinating about the study of private foundations is the broad latitude of operation actually allowed and the room for creativity in planning and operating them.

The rules are detailed in six Internal Revenue Code sections concerning self-dealing, mandatory distributions, excess business holdings, jeopardizing investments, taxable expenditures, and the excise tax on net investment income. The foundation and its managers are subject to a variety of excise taxes if the rules are violated, as are those who participate in transactions the law deems to be self-dealing. Some advisors discourage the creation of private foundations because of this potential liability. Except for the excise taxes on self-dealing, however, the sanctions can be abated if the failure to meet a requirement is due to reasonable cause. Thus, there has been significant easing of the strict liability nature of these rules as initially designed by Congress. Caution cannot be thrown to the wind, but potential foundation creators shouldn't be needlessly afraid of incurring excise taxes.

The one unforgivable constraint placed on private foundations prohibits self-dealing, namely, financial transactions between the foundation and its creators, funders, insiders, and certain of their relatives. This rule is applied without regard to the amount of economic benefit received by the foundation. The Code, on the one hand, states that these acts are absolutely prohibited and lists six comprehensive types of transactions that are forbidden. The Code, on the other hand, also lists eight exceptions to the general rule; the tax regulations add a few more exceptions. So again, while the rules appear draconian,

PREFACE

there is room to maneuver. More recently, the IRS has been more liberal in interpreting and applying these exceptions and permitted transactions that, according to the Code, are self-dealing. When, for example, sharing office space with its creators saves the foundation money as a practical matter, the IRS has approved transactions that on their face constitute self-dealing based upon a literal reading of the Code. A glance at the subtopics of Chapter 5 provides a clue to the broad range of transactions that entail exceptions and thus are permitted.

To ensure private foundation assets are expended for charitable purposes (rather than accumulated), a private foundation must meet certain payout requirements to avoid an excise tax. An amount equal to at least 5 percent of the value of a foundation's investment assets must be paid out annually for charitable purposes. Advisors seeking to assist a private foundation in conserving its endowment must understand which assets are included in the calculation and which are excluded. When and how the assets that comprise the payout base are valued also impacts the results. The authors of this Code provision recognized a foundation would not necessarily always distribute the precisely calculated amount. Thus, a carryover of excess distributions to future years is permitted. In its early years, and later under appropriate circumstances, a foundation can delay or set aside a portion of its annual required payout for up to five years. These matters are covered in Chapter 6.

A foundation must pay an annual excise tax of 1.39 percent on its net investment income. Although the tax rate is modest, foundations may take advantage of certain tax planning opportunities to eliminate the tax with respect to certain assets. For example, as explained in Chapter 10, a foundation that distributes substantially appreciated property to a public charity (in satisfaction of the foundation's annual payout requirement) may be able to eliminate the tax on the built-in capital gain on those assets. The separate income tax on the unrelated business activities of private foundations is the subject of Chapter 11.

While state law generally imposes fiduciary obligations on foundation managers with respect to the investment and expenditure of their institutional (charitable funds), the Code imposes an excise tax on private foundations and their managers that purchase or hold investments in a manner that jeopardizes the foundation's ability to fulfill its exempt purposes. In many respects, the tax regulations concerning jeopardizing investments are woefully antiquated. What was perceived to be a jeopardizing investment in 1970, when these regulations were written—such as purchasing puts, calls, and straddles with respect to marketable securities—is now an accepted strategy in modern portfolio theory. As discussed in Chapter 8, the IRS, at least in private rulings, has begun to accept investment strategies that under a literal application of the tax regulations could be seen as jeopardy investments.

PREFACE

When a private foundation, in combination with its creators, funders, and certain family members and related entities, own more than 20 percent of a business enterprise, the foundation generally is deemed to have excess business holdings. Permitted holdings of business enterprises vary according to the form of ownership, type of entity, and other variables discussed in Chapter 7, and a foundation has five years to dispose of any excess holdings received as a gift or inheritance. Certain exceptions apply, the principal one being that the ownership limitation does not apply to a so-called functionally related business that accomplishes a charitable purpose, such as a low-income housing project.

A private foundation may spend its income and distribute its assets for a variety of charitable purposes. While most foundations make grants to churches, schools, hospitals, museums, and broadly supported charitable organizations, a foundation also may conduct its own charitable programs. Certain constraints on a foundation's expenditures, enforced by an excise tax on such taxable expenditures, are laid out in Chapter 9. These taxable expenditures include amounts paid to support or oppose a candidate for elective office, to influence legislation (in other words, to lobby), to make grants to individuals for travel or study (unless limited for certain permitted purposes and awarded under procedures the IRS approves in advance), and to make grants to noncharitable organizations or other private foundations (unless certain evaluation, documentation, reporting, and recordkeeping requirements are met). Thus, while the taxable expenditure excise tax regime places constraints on certain grants to individuals and organizations, it does not prohibit them outright. A private foundation that is well informed regarding the give and take in these rules will find itself with more options for grant-making activities than those less knowledgeable, and it will be able to protect itself from potential excise tax liability by observing the formalities imposed by these rules.

The myriad excise taxes private foundations face and their attendant compliance obligations (some might say burdens) prompt many foundation managers to ask how they might terminate their private foundation status. This exit, however, is blocked by yet another tax—a termination tax—that requires a private foundation to repay the government for the lifetime tax benefits received by it and its substantial contributors (or the value of all its net assets, if lower). As explained in Chapter 13, there are ways to avoid this extreme tax, basically either by transferring all the foundation's assets to one or more established public charities or operating itself as a public charity for five years. The various categories of public charities are explored in Chapter 15, which is of importance not only in this regard but also in terms of compliance with the rules for making mandatory qualifying distributions (discussed in Chapter 6) and avoiding taxable expenditures (discussed in Chapter 9).

PREFACE

The introductory chapters of this book provide a primer on private foundation basics; consider alternatives (such as donor-advised funds) to private foundations; outline the advantages offered by private foundations; offer considerations for the formation and funding of a foundation; describe the process for applying for recognition of tax-exempt status with the IRS (that is, by preparing and filing Form 1023), and discuss an available court remedy if exemption recognition is unduly delayed or denied. The various types of private foundations, including the private operating foundation, are discussed in Chapter 3, as well as certain trusts that are treated as private foundations for certain purposes. A private foundation's ongoing compliance obligations are discussed in Chapter 12, including its obligations to annually file (now, electronically) and publicly disclose Form 990-PF and to report certain changes in activities to the IRS or seek IRS preapproval of others (now done almost entirely utilizing Form 8940, which was revised and expanded in 2023). The self-reporting and payment of the private foundation excise taxes (on Form 4720), the potential for abatement of these taxes, IRS examinations, and the ways that revocation of tax-exempt status may occur and be contested are also covered in Chapter 12.

A glance at recent publications, such as the IRS's annual report for tax-exempt organizations and the annual priority guidance plan issued by the Department of Treasury and the IRS, reveals that private foundations are largely out of the federal government's sights these days. Obviously, the leaders and managers of private foundations will likely see this as good news. Yet there are regulatory and congressional rumblings for changes in this area of the law (to keep the lawyers and accountants engaged and happy), chiefly around the ways in which private foundations interact with donor-advised funds. Perhaps they will manifest themselves in legislation or at least finally in regulations (which the IRS claims to have been working on since 2007) in the donor-advised fund area—matters that are discussed in Chapter 16.

Every book summarizing a body of law has to have a cutoff date as to what developments to include. This edition covers events through the middle of 2023. Such a limitation is always frustrating, inasmuch as there have been important developments since that period. As noted, because the law in this field is so dynamic, there is no way to "capture" it in its entirety; the best that can be done is to summarize it as of a particular point in time. These subsequent and ongoing developments are certain to provide ample material for the first supplement to this edition.

* * *

John Wiley & Sons has provided enormous support in the preparation of this book. Thanks are extended to Martha Cooley and Robin Sarantos for their assistance in conjunction with the first edition, to Susan McDermott

PREFACE

and Louise Jacob for their help with the second edition, to Susan and Natasha A. S. Wolfe in connection with the preparation of the third edition, to Lia Ottaviano, Claire New, and Mary Daniello for their assistance in connection with the fourth edition, to Brian T. Neill, Vicki Adang, and Abirami Srikandan for their help with the fifth edition, and to Brian T. Neill, Venkatasubramanian Chellian, and Gabriella Mancuso for their hard work and invaluable help in connection with this edition. I have had rewarding experiences on other occasions working with the editors at Wiley, and the support received in connection with this book is par for the course.

But there is no amount of gratitude that can be expressed greater than that owed to our late mentor, colleague, and dear friend, Bruce R. Hopkins. Without him this book would not exist, nor would so many others that have helped chronicle, define, and refine the field of nonprofit law. One shudders to think of what state the field would be in today had we not been graced with his wisdom, humor, intellect, and kind and generous spirit. I hope, in my own humble way, to support carrying on his legacy.

SHANE T. HAMILTON

Book Citations

Throughout this book, the following books by Bruce R. Hopkins (in one instance, as co-author), all published by John Wiley & Sons, are referenced in this way:

1. *The Law of Fundraising, Sixth Edition* (2022): *Fundraising.*
2. *The Law of Tax-Exempt Organizations, Twelfth Edition* (2019): *Tax-Exempt Organizations.*
3. *The Tax Law of Charitable Giving, Sixth Edition* (2021): *Charitable Giving.*
4. *Tax-Exempt Organizations and Constitutional Law: Nonprofit Law as Shaped by the U.S. Supreme Court* (2012): *Constitutional Law.*

The first and second of these books are annually supplemented.

CHAPTER ONE

Introduction to Private Foundations

§ 1.1 Private Foundations: Unique Organizations 2
§ 1.2 Definition of Private Foundation 4
§ 1.3 Background 7
§ 1.4 Private Foundation Tax Law Primer 10
  (a) Introduction 11
  (b) General Operational Requirements 11
  (c) Disqualified Persons 12
  (d) Self-Dealing Rules 12
  (e) Mandatory Payout Rules 13
  (f) Excess Business Holdings Rules 14
  (g) Jeopardizing Investments Rules 14
  (h) Taxable Expenditures Rules 15
  (i) Tax on Investment Income 16
  (j) Termination of Private Foundation Status 16
  (k) Charitable Giving Rules 16
  (l) Unrelated Business Rules 17
§ 1.5 Definition of Charity 17
§ 1.6 Operating for Charitable Purposes 19
§ 1.7 Organizational Rules 22
§ 1.8 Private Foundation Law Sanctions 24
  (a) Sanctions (a Reprise) 25
  (b) Self-Dealing Sanctions as Pigouvian Taxes 25
  (c) Self-Dealing Sanctions: Taxes or Penalties? 26
  (d) Abatement 31
  (e) Potential of Overlapping Taxes 31
  (f) Influence on Subsequent Law 32
§ 1.9 Statistical Profile 33
§ 1.10 Private Foundations and Law 50 Years Later 33

Of the almost two million tax-exempt charitable organizations in the United States,[1] only about 90,000 of them are classified, for federal tax purposes, as private foundations.[2] The isolation of private foundations for purposes of government regulation makes private foundations unique.

---

1. The IRS Data Book, 2022 (Pub. 55-B) informs that there are, as of the federal government's fiscal year 2022 (ending September 30, 2022), nearly 2 million tax-exempt organizations in the United States, almost 1.5 million of which are recognized charitable and similar organizations (including private foundations), plus 108,654 nonexempt charitable trusts and split-interest trusts and 221 apostolic entities. This number of charitable organizations does not include religious organizations that are not required to seek recognition of tax exemption.
2. National Philanthropic Trust, "2022 Donor-Advised Fund Report" (Nov. 2022) 35.

§ 1.1 PRIVATE FOUNDATIONS: UNIQUE ORGANIZATIONS

The federal tax law segregates private foundations from other charitable entities, these other entities being generically referred to as *public charities*. Congress legislated the difference between private foundations and public charities by means of the Tax Reform Act of 1969; in so doing, it triggered a chain of reactions and developments in the tax law that shows no sign of abating. In a move that made life more complicated for nearly all in the charitable community, the federal tax law presumes that all charitable organizations are private foundations. (The burden of proving non–private foundation status rests with each charitable organization; the process of rebutting the presumption is part of the procedure for filing for recognition of tax-exempt status.)[3]

Certainly, the regulatory regime imposed on private foundations is unique. There is no category of tax-exempt organization that is subject to anything like the compliance burdens that comprise the sweep of Chapter 42 of the Internal Revenue Code. Even the origin of this legislation is unique. The mood of Congress was very anti–private foundation during the course of its endeavors in this regard in the years leading up to the 1969 legislation, with the nation's legislature dismayed at the findings presented to it by the Department of the Treasury in a 1965 report and by a series of congressional hearings.[4] The animosity toward, sometimes hostility against, private foundations that motivated members of Congress and the staff at that time is reflected in the legislation that quickly took shape that year.

When Congress targeted privately funded charities and gave them special status, the following sections were added to the Internal Revenue Code. These sections have operational constraints that govern the conduct of private foundations and impose excise taxes for failures to adhere to the rules.

- IRC § 4940—Tax on Investment Income
- IRC § 4941—Taxes on Self-Dealing
- IRC § 4942—Taxes on Failure to Distribute Income
- IRC § 4943—Taxes on Excess Business Holdings
- IRC § 4944—Taxes on Investments That Jeopardize Charitable Purpose
- IRC § 4945—Taxes on Taxable Expenditures

---

3. Internal Revenue Code of 1986, as amended, section (IRC §) 508(b). The procedure for filing for recognition of tax-exempt status is the subject of § 2.7.
4. See § 1.3.

INTRODUCTION TO PRIVATE FOUNDATIONS

- IRC § 4946—Disqualified Persons
- IRC § 4947—Application of Taxes to Certain Nonexempt Trusts
- IRC § 4948—Foreign Private Foundations
- IRC § 507—Termination of Private Foundation Status

Sanctions for failure to comply with the private foundation rules potentially include a tax (called the *Chapter 42 taxes*) on both the foundation and its disqualified persons, loss of tax exemption, and repayment of all tax benefits accrued during the life of the foundation for its funders and itself. Under certain circumstances, these taxes can be abated if the violation was due to reasonable cause, rather than for willful and intentional reasons, and if the violation is properly corrected.[5]

Notwithstanding the turbulence within their legal setting, private foundations are a viable and valuable type of nonprofit organization. They are also unique in that they are often used to accomplish the personal philanthropic goals of individuals. Some professional advisors discourage the formation of private foundations because of the complexity of the regulatory rules underlying and surrounding them. There is no question that the foundation rules are often more complicated than those applicable to public charities and other forms of exempt organizations. The addition of the donor-advised fund rules and the reformation of the Type III supporting organization rules by the Pension Protection Act of 2006, however, has narrowed the differences between those two types of charitable entities and private foundations. Many operational constraints and procedural requirements formerly only applicable to private foundations now also apply to donor-advised funds[6] and Type III supporting organizations.[7] Nevertheless, the creation and operation of a private foundation can be a rewarding experience.

Private foundations are ideal charitable vehicles for many funders. An individual can create a foundation qualified for tax exemption and be its sole trustee or director, retaining absolute control. Commonly, a donor and their family members comprise the governing board of a private foundation, although financial and other transactions between them and the foundation are tightly constrained by the tax law.

Funders who wish to be flexible in their grant-making programs may prefer a private foundation for a similar reason. While an annual grant payout requirement must be adhered to, there is considerable latitude in the design of its charitable programs. The foundation can maintain its own programs

---

5. IRC § 4962. See § 12.4(c).
6. See § 16.7.
7. See § 15.6(g).

rather than fund others; this entity is the *private operating foundation*. Here, a funder can establish the foundation, hire a staff, and work to further their own charitable purposes.

Another potential advantage is the fact that family members or other disqualified persons can be paid reasonable compensation in the form of director or trustee fees for their services on the organization's governing board. These persons can also be paid salaries for services rendered in their capacity as staff members. Those who learn the rules and plan well to adhere to them need not allow the tax law excise taxes to serve as a deterrent to the creation of a private foundation.

Finally, a private foundation can serve as an ideal income and estate planning device for individuals with charitable interests. The classic example is a philanthropist who has publicly traded stock that is highly appreciated in value. A private foundation can be created, the securities contributed to the foundation and sold by that entity, and the philanthropist may claim a charitable contribution deduction based on the full fair market value of the stock and avoids taxation of the capital gain. The foundation can retain the stock and endeavor to expand its base of principal, and essentially spend only the income from its investments for its charitable purposes.

Philanthropists who make charitable bequests can create private foundations to receive a portion of the bequest while they are living. Contributions to the foundations made during the donor's lifetime are deductible, thereby increasing the estate by reducing income tax. The property gifted to the private foundation and the undistributed income accumulating in the private foundation are not subject to estate tax. A private foundation can also be the remainder interest beneficiary of a charitable remainder trust created during the donor's lifetime. This approach usually results in more after-tax money for the foundation and other beneficiaries.

This unique entity known as a private foundation is thus both heavily regulated by a body of extensive and complex law and a very useful charitable planning vehicle. To achieve the optimum in charitable giving and granting by means of a private foundation, the management and advisors to the foundation must master this body of law. The pages that follow are intended to be a guide to that end.

§ 1.2 DEFINITION OF PRIVATE FOUNDATION

Essential to an understanding of the special federal tax rules applicable to private foundations is the tax law definition of the term private foundation. The federal tax law defines the term *private foundation* as a domestic or foreign charitable organization, other than one of the four categories of entities

INTRODUCTION TO PRIVATE FOUNDATIONS

collectively known as *public charities*.[8] Thus, one way to view a private foundation is as a charitable organization[9] that does not qualify as a form of public charity.

Each U.S. and foreign charitable organization is presumed to be a private foundation; this presumption is rebutted by a showing that the entity is a church, school, hospital, medical research organization, agricultural research organization, publicly supported charity, supporting organization, or organization that tests for public safety.[10] That is, by operation of law, if a charitable organization cannot be classified as a public charity, it is (or becomes) a private foundation.[11]

Despite the absence of a generic definition of the term, a private foundation essentially is a tax-exempt organization that has these characteristics: (1) it is a charitable organization, (2) it is funded from one source (usually an individual, a family, or a business), (3) its ongoing revenue is derived from investments (in the nature of an endowment fund),[12] and (4) it makes grants to other charitable organizations rather than operating its own program (unless it is a private operating foundation).[13] Congress could have crafted an affirmative definition of the term *private foundation*, using these criteria, but the statutory scheme enacted in 1969 was, as noted, developed in a strenuously anti-private foundation environment and the "definition" was thus devised in a manner to make it as encompassing as possible. (Indeed, the statutory definition is actually one of what a private foundation *is not*, rather than a definition of what a private foundation *is*.)

If a charitable organization was a private foundation on October 9, 1969, or becomes a private foundation on any subsequent date, it will be treated as

---

8. IRC § 509(a); Reg. § 1.509(a)-1. The requirements to establish public charity status are the subject of Chapter 15.
9. That is, an organization that is tax-exempt pursuant to IRC § 501(a) as an organization described in IRC § 501(c)(3).
10. IRC § 509(a)(1)-(4).
11. IRC § 508(b); IRS Revenue Procedure (Rev. Proc.) 2023-5, 2023-1 I.R.B. 265 § 7.04(2). Even though these rules have been in existence for over 50 years, there still is confusion surrounding them. This phenomenon was reflected in a decision by a federal court of appeals, which twice misstated the law as to private foundations and public charities, first by incorrectly stating that "a tax-exempt organization is not automatically classified as a private foundation," and second by erroneously declaring that if "a section 501(c)(3) organization does not meet the distinct requirements provided by section 509(a), the organization is treated as public charity" (Stanbury Law Firm, P.A. v. Internal Revenue Service, 221 F.3d 1059 (8th Cir. 2000)).
12. While private foundations may receive a consistent flow of ongoing donations, most do not.
13. The *private* aspect of a private foundation, then, principally reflects the nature of its financial support as well as the nature of its governance.

§ 1.2 DEFINITION OF PRIVATE FOUNDATION

a private foundation for all periods thereafter even though it may also qualify as some other type of tax-exempt organization, unless its private foundation status is terminated.[14] In other words, a charitable organization in existence on October 9, 1969, cannot hope to avoid private foundation status by claiming it also qualifies as, for example, a social welfare organization.[15] Likewise, if an organization created after October 9, 1969, obtains recognition from the IRS as a public charity, and later loses this status and becomes reclassified as a private foundation, it cannot claim non-private-foundation status thereafter by claiming status as a social welfare organization.

In contrast, a private foundation created after October 9, 1969, may apply and be recognized as a social welfare organization if it qualifies as such and did not previously seek recognition from the IRS as a charitable organization.[16] This is because charitable organizations created after October 9, 1969, are not considered "described in section 501(c)(3)" unless they notify the IRS and apply for recognition of exemption.[17] Thus, the presumption of private foundation status[18] is inapplicable to post-1969 organizations that do not apply for exemption;[19] such organizations likewise are not covered as organizations "described in section 501(c)(3)" in the definition of a private foundation.[20]

If an organization was a private foundation on October 9, 1969, and it is subsequently determined that it no longer qualifies as a charitable entity, it will continue to be treated as a private foundation (until it terminates such status).[21] In other words, an organization cannot shed its private foundation status by changing its governing instrument and operating as a taxable entity.

If circumstances change, or if its creators wish it, a private foundation can terminate its private foundation status. This happens most frequently where the organization's level or mix of funding is such that it can qualify as a publicly supported charity or where the organization converts to a supporting organization.[22] A private foundation may terminate its private foundation status by distributing all its assets to a public charity and dissolving itself or by merging into one or more other private foundations.[23]

---

14. IRC § 509(b); Reg. § 1.509(b)-1(a). The private foundation termination rules are the subject of Chapter 13.
15. IRC § 501(c)(4).
16. E.g., Priv. Ltr. Rul. 200846041.
17. IRC § 508(a). Organizations created prior to October 9, 1969, are not subject to this notice and application requirement for exempt status (*id.*).
18. Under IRC § 508(b).
19. IRS General Counsel Memorandum (Gen. Couns. Mem.) 37485.
20. IRC § 509(a).
21. Reg. § 1.509(b)-1(b).
22. See § 13.4. As to the requirements to qualify as a publicly supported charity or supporting organization, see Chapter 15.
23. See Chapter 13.

§ 1.3 BACKGROUND

Private foundations have long been much-maligned entities, not only in the federal tax laws but within society at large. Their history, which is extensive, is rich with many successes and strewn with few abuses.[24] They are vehicles for some of the most humanitarian and progressive acts, yet whenever a list of tax reforms is compiled, private foundations, and/or the tax law rules that apply to them, always seem to attract much attention.

A private foundation is a unique breed of tax-exempt organization, in that while it is recognized as charitable, educational, or the like, it is usually controlled and supported by a single source, for example, one donor, a family, or a company. This one characteristic, which the Internal Revenue Service has recognized as an indirect but nonetheless qualifying means of support of charity,[25] has spawned several criticisms, including alleged irresponsive governance and inadequate responses to perceived needs. Private foundations are similarly chastised for being elitist, playthings of the wealthy, and havens for "do-gooders" assuaging their inner needs by dispensing beneficence to others.[26]

More serious criticisms of private foundations are that they further various tax inequities, are created for private rather than philanthropic purposes, and do not actually achieve charitable ends.[27] As will be developed in subsequent chapters, nearly all the abuses—apocryphal or otherwise—involving private foundations were eradicated as the result of the enactment of the Tax Reform Act of 1969.[28]

The origins of private foundations are traceable to the genesis of philanthropy. Foundations as legal entities were recognized in the Anglo-Saxon legal system and were fostered in the United States by the law of charitable trusts. Charitable endowments in America are essentially creatures of common law, although amply sustained in statutory laws concerning taxes, corporations, decedents' estates, trusts, and property.[29] The modern American foundation is of relatively recent vintage, dating back to the mid-nineteenth century. Many of

---

24. Wormser, *Foundations: Their Power and Influence* (Sevierville, TN: Catholic House Books, 1993); Andrews, *Philanthropic Foundations* (New York: Russell Sage Foundation, 1956).
25. IRS Revenue Ruling (Rev. Rul.) 67-149, 1967-1 C.B. 133.
26. E.g., Branch, "The Case Against Foundations," *Washington Monthly* 3 (July 1971).
27. E.g., Stern, *The Great Treasury Raid* (New York: Random House, 1964), 242–246. *Cf.* Stern, *The Rape of the Taxpayer* (New York: Random House, 1973).
28. As one court stated, Congress enacted these rules "to put an end, as far as it reasonably could, to the abuses and potential abuses associated with private foundations." (Mannheimer Charitable Trust, Hans S. v. Commissioner, 93 T.C. 35, 39 (1989)).
29. Fremont-Smith, *Foundations and Government, State and Federal Law* (New York: Russell Sage Foundation, 1965), especially Chapter 1.

§ 1.3 BACKGROUND

the well-known foundations are reflective of the great fortunes established at the advent of the 1900s. Foundations proliferated after World War II, in large part because of favorable economic conditions and tax incentives. More recently, private foundations founded and funded by those successful in the realm of technology are being added to the list of the nation's largest charities.

Private foundations were not defined in the Internal Revenue Code (nor in any other federal statute) until 1969—though not because of Congress's lack of interest in them. They were investigated, for example, by the "Walsh Committee" (the Senate Industrial Relations Committee) from 1913 to 1915 for allegedly large stockholdings, by the "Cox Committee" (House Select Committee to Investigate and Study Educational and Philanthropic Foundations) in 1952, by Representative B. Carroll Reece in 1954 (the House Special Committee to Investigate Tax-Exempt Foundations and Comparable Organizations) for alleged support of subversives, and by Representative Wright Patman throughout the 1960s for allegedly tending more to private interests than public benefit.

Prior to enactment of the Tax Reform Act of 1969, a private foundation generally was recognized as a charitable organization to which contributions could be made that were deductible in an amount up to 20 percent of an individual donor's adjusted gross income, in contrast to contributions to churches, schools, hospitals, and other public charities, which were deductible to the extent of 30 percent of the individual donor's adjusted gross income.[30]

This 30 percent/20 percent dichotomy was introduced in the federal tax law in 1954, when Congress acted in recognition of the fact that there are distinctive differences among charitable organizations. In that year, Congress permitted an extra 10 percent deduction (from 20 percent to 30 percent) for contributions to churches, educational institutions, and hospitals, and enacted other provisions in their favor. In 1964, the privileged class of 30 percent organizations was expanded to include other public and publicly supported organizations, and a five-year carryover of excess contributions was added for gifts to these organizations.

By the mid-1960s, the likelihood that alleged private foundation abuses would eventually result in statutory modifications was on the increase. A *Treasury Report on Private Foundations*, issued in 1965,[31] emphasized the view that there was a need for more public involvement in the operation of philanthropic institutions that benefit from preferential treatment under the tax laws. Failing direct public involvement, this report stated that there should be an assurance through other means (namely, governmental regulation) that funds set aside for

---

30. IRC § 170(b)(1) (pre-1969 Act).
31. Treasury Department Report on Private Foundations, Committee on Finance, United States Senate, 89th Cong., 1st Sess. (1965).

appropriate charitable purposes will find their way promptly into the hands of those institutions where there is assurance of public control and operation.

Congress, having become convinced that there were problems concerning charitable organizations that needed remedy, believed that these problems were especially prevalent in the case of organizations in the 20 percent deduction category. On the other hand, it was also apparent that most organizations in the 30 percent deduction group were not implicated in these problems.

Congressman Patman's and others' inquiries culminated in the extensive foundation provisions of the Tax Reform Act of 1969,[32] which introduced the first statutory definition of the term *private foundation*. Yet a more expressive definition is: ". . .a nongovernmental, nonprofit organization, with funds and program managed by its own trustees or directors, and established to maintain or aid social, educational, charitable, religious, or other activities serving the common welfare."[33]

Controversy persists over the appropriate role for foundations in America—or whether they should exist at all. Foundations are attacked by some as too uninvolved in current issues and problems and by others as too effective in fomenting social change. The federal government is now spending billions of dollars in the realms of health, education, and welfare, formerly the domain of private philanthropy. Recent years have also borne witness to intensified drives for tax reform, tax equality, and tax simplification. These and other developments have made the tax treatment for private foundations and their donors even more vulnerable.

Notwithstanding a variety of anti-foundation developments in the regulatory context, Congress and the executive branch of the federal government have, on occasion, affirmed their support for private foundations. For example, the Department of the Treasury had this to say about the value of foundations:

> Private philanthropy plays a special vital role in our society. Beyond providing for areas into which government cannot or should not advance (such as religion), private philanthropic organizations can be uniquely qualified to initiate thought and action, experiment with new and untried ventures, dissent from prevailing attitudes, and act quickly and flexibly.

---

32. Andrews, *Patman and Foundations: Review and Assessment* (New York: Foundation Center, 1968); Myers, "Foundations and Tax Legislation," VI *Bull. of Found. Lib. Center* (No. 3) 51 (1965). Following a preliminary survey in 1961, Rep. Patman caused publication of "Tax Exempt Foundations and Charitable Trusts: Their Impact on Our Economy," Chairman's Report to (House) Select Committee on Small Business, First Installment, 87th Cong., 1st Sess. (1962). Six additional installments were published over the period 1963 to 1968.
33. The Foundation Center, *The Foundation Directory*, 4th ed. (1971), vii.

Private foundations have an important part in this work. Available even to those of relatively restricted means, they enable individuals or small groups to establish new charitable endeavors and to express their own bents, concerns, and experience. In doing so, they enrich the pluralism of our social order. Equally important, because their funds are frequently free of commitment to specific operating programs, they can shift the focus of their interest and their financial support from one charitable area to another. They can, hence, constitute a powerful instrument for evolution, growth, and improvement in the shape and direction of charity.[34]

Private foundations are an integral component of a society that values individual responsibility and private efforts for the public good. One organization championing private foundations advances the following rationale:

Foundations have the particular characteristic of serving as sources of available capital for the private philanthropic service sector of our society in all its range and variety. They thus help make possible many useful public services that would in most cases otherwise have to be provided by tax monies. They offer "the other door on which to knock," without which many volunteer activities would not be initiated and others could not be continued. They are there to respond both to new ideas and [to] shifting social needs with a freedom and flexibility that is not common to or easy for government agencies. Finally, as centers of independent thought and judgment in their own right, they help support freedom of thought, experimentation, and honest criticism directed at pressing needs of the society, including even the scrutiny and evaluation of governmental programs and policies.[35]

The great regulatory surge that swept over private foundations has largely subsided as the regulators have moved on to focus on other types of nonprofit organizations. The federal tax laws applicable to foundations remain complex, but, for the most part, the foundation community has learned to coexist with them. Nonetheless, it must be conceded that, as the U.S. Tax Court observed (and subsequent chapters indicate), "classification as a private foundation is burdensome."[36]

§ 1.4 PRIVATE FOUNDATION TAX LAW PRIMER

Private foundations are a type of charitable organization, exempt from federal income tax. As such, they are subject to the rules applicable to charitable

---

34. Treasury Department Report on Private Foundations, Committee on Finance, United States Senate, 89th Cong., 1st Sess. (1965), 5 (also 12-13).
35. Council on Foundations, Report and Recommendations to the Commission on Private Philanthropy and Public Needs on Private Philanthropic Foundations (1974), 1–8.
36. Friends of the Society of Servants of God v. Commissioner, 75 T.C. 209, 212 (1980).

INTRODUCTION TO PRIVATE FOUNDATIONS

organizations generally. In addition, private foundations are subject to detailed and stringent rules.

(a) Introduction

The federal tax law pertaining to private foundations was enacted as part of the Tax Reform Act of 1969.[37] The ensuing years have not brought much substantive change in the overall statutory framework. These years, however, have brought many pages of tax regulations, hundreds of private letter rulings, and a considerable number of court opinions.

Private foundation statutory law has inspired similar rules for public charities, most notably the intermediate sanctions rules,[38] some of the supporting organizations rules,[39] and the donor-advised fund rules.[40] Recently, Congress has grafted some of the private foundation rules onto the public charity rules, such as application of the excess business holdings[41] rules to donor-advised funds[42] and application of these rules to supporting organizations.[43]

(b) General Operational Requirements

Private foundations must apply for recognition of tax-exempt status;[44] must file annual information returns with the IRS;[45] must meet a special organizational test;[46] must satisfy certain disclosure requirements;[47] may receive deductible charitable contributions (albeit usually within more stringent limitations than public charities);[48] must adhere to the general rules imposed on tax-exempt charities, such as the general organizational test, the operational test, the private inurement doctrine, the private benefit doctrine, the limitation on legislative activities, and the prohibition on political campaign activities;[49] must comply with a battery of unique laws, where the sanctions include imposition of one or more excise taxes (most of which are subject to abatement

---

37. IRC Chapter 42 (IRC §§ 4940–4948).
38. IRC § 4958. See *Tax-Exempt Organizations*, Chapter 21.
39. See § 15.6.
40. See § 16.7.
41. See Chapter 7.
42. See § 16.7.
43. See § 15.6(k).
44. See § 2.7.
45. See § 12.1(a).
46. See § 1.7.
47. See § 12.3.
48. See Chapter 14.
49. See *Tax-Exempt Organizations* §§ 4.3, 4.5, and Chapters 20, 22, and 23, respectively.

§ 1.4 PRIVATE FOUNDATION TAX LAW PRIMER

provisions);[50] must pay an excise tax on net investment income;[51] and must comply with the unrelated business rules.[52]

(c) Disqualified Persons

A variety of persons are considered disqualified persons with respect to a private foundation. These persons are generally equivalent to insiders in connection with the private inurement doctrine.[53]

Disqualified persons with respect to private foundations are (1) substantial contributors, that is, the creator of the foundation if it is a charitable trust or a person that has contributed more than $5,000 to the foundation where the gift amount is in excess of 2 percent of the donee's total support during its existence as measured at the time of the contribution; (2) foundation managers, that is, a foundation trustee, director, officer, or an individual with similar powers or responsibilities; (3) an owner of more than 20 percent of a business where the entity is a substantial contributor; (4) a member of the family of an individual referenced in the foregoing three categories; (5) a corporation, partnership, trust, or estate in which any of the persons referenced in the foregoing four categories have more than a 35 percent ownership or other interest; (6) another private foundation (but only for purposes of the excess business holdings rules); and (7) a government official (but only for purposes of the self-dealing rules).[54]

(d) Self-Dealing Rules

The self-dealing rules essentially prohibit, by means of excise taxes and a correction requirement, financial transactions between a private foundation and a disqualified person.[55]

Generally, self-dealing transactions are (1) sales, exchanges, or leasing of property between a private foundation and a disqualified person; (2) lending of money or other extension of credit between a private foundation and a disqualified person; (3) furnishing of goods, services, or facilities between a private foundation and a disqualified person; (4) payment of compensation, or payment or reimbursement of expenses, by a private foundation to a disqualified person; and (5) payment by a private foundation to a governmental official (with exceptions).[56]

---

50. See § 12.4(c).
51. See Chapter 10.
52. See Chapter 11.
53. See *Tax-Exempt Organizations* § 20.3.
54. See Chapter 4.
55. See Chapter 5.
56. See § 5.3.

INTRODUCTION TO PRIVATE FOUNDATIONS

There are exceptions to these general rules, including (1) payment of compensation by a private foundation to a disqualified person for certain personal services, where the compensation is reasonable and is in furtherance of the foundation's exempt purposes; (2) certain lending and furnishing arrangements without interest or other charge, when done in furtherance of charitable purposes; and (3) certain transactions occurring during the administration of a decedent's estate.[57]

These rules are underlain by a series of excise taxes, beginning with an initial tax on an act of self-dealing equal to 10 percent of the amount involved. Another excise tax is imposed on a foundation manager equal to 5 percent of the amount involved, subject to a $20,000 per act maximum tax. If the act of self-dealing is not corrected, an additional tax may be imposed on (1) a self-dealer equal to 200 percent of the amount involved; and (2) a foundation manager equal to 50 percent of the amount involved (subject to a $20,000 per act maximum tax). Where more than one self-dealer or foundation manager is liable for the tax with respect to any one act of self-dealing, the tax liability is joint and several. Abatement of the initial tax on self-dealing is not available, although the tax will not apply to a foundation manager whose participation in the act of self-dealing is not willful and is due to reasonable cause.[58]

(e) Mandatory Payout Rules

The private foundation mandatory payout rules are designed to cause foundations to spend currently rather than indefinitely accumulate income and assets.[59]

A private foundation is generally required to pay out for charitable purposes an amount equal to 5 percent of its noncharitable assets; this involves the concepts of minimum investment return and distributable amount. The amount distributed must be in the form of a qualifying distribution, which can involve a set-aside.[60]

An initial tax is imposed on a private foundation equal to 30 percent of undistributed income. An additional tax may be imposed on a foundation equal to 100 percent of undistributed income. There is a correction requirement.[61] Tax abatement is potentially available.[62]

---

57. See § 5.4-5.6, 5.12.
58. See § 5.15(a).
59. See Chapter 6.
60. See § 6.4.
61. See § 6.5.
62. See § 12.4(c).

§ 1.4 PRIVATE FOUNDATION TAX LAW PRIMER

(f) Excess Business Holdings Rules

The excess business holdings rules are designed to prevent the control of a for-profit business by a private foundation, alone or in conjunction with its disqualified persons.[63]

A private foundation is generally prohibited, by application of excise taxes, from having excess business holdings, which generally means more than a 20 percent interest in a business; where control of the business is elsewhere, the threshold amount is 35 percent. The holdings of disqualified persons are taken into account in calculating these percentages; a 2 percent de minimis rule considers only the foundation's holdings.[64]

An initial tax on a private foundation's excess business holdings is imposed, equal to 10 percent of the value of the holdings. An additional tax may be imposed equal to 200 percent of the value of excess business holdings. There is a correction requirement. Tax abatement is potentially available.[65]

(g) Jeopardizing Investments Rules

The jeopardizing investments rules imposed on private foundations can be viewed as a federal tax law codification of traditional prudent investment principles. These rules parallel state laws under which the managers of a private foundation have a fiduciary responsibility to safeguard its assets on behalf of its charitable constituents.[66]

A private foundation is subject to an excise tax if it invests an amount in a manner that would jeopardize the carrying out of an exempt purpose. There is no per se type of jeopardizing investment. An investment jeopardizes exempt purposes of a private foundation where its foundation managers failed to exercise ordinary business care and prudence, at the time the investment was made, in providing for the short-term and long-term financial needs of the foundation in connection with the conduct of its charitable programs.[67]

These rules are inapplicable to program-related investments, the primary purpose of which is to achieve charitable objectives and no significant purpose of which is the production of income or appreciation in the value of property.[68]

An initial tax is imposed on a private foundation in the amount of 10 percent of the jeopardizing investment. An initial tax is imposed on foundation managers in the amount of 10 percent of the investment, when they

---

63. See Chapter 7.
64. See § 7.2.
65. See § 12.4(c).
66. See Chapter 8.
67. See § 8.1.
68. See § 8.3.

INTRODUCTION TO PRIVATE FOUNDATIONS

knowingly participated in it, subject to a $10,000 per investment maximum tax. An additional tax in the amount of 25 percent may be imposed on a private foundation. There is an additional tax on foundation managers, subject to a $20,000 per investment maximum tax. There is a correction requirement.[69] Tax abatement is potentially available.[70]

(h) Taxable Expenditures Rules

The taxable expenditures rules place limitations on the types of grants private foundations are permitted to make.[71]

A private foundation makes a taxable expenditure if it pays or incurs an amount to carry on propaganda or otherwise attempts to influence legislation. These rules may be triggered if a foundation makes a grant to a public charity that attempts to influence legislation or if the foundation makes the expenditure directly. A private foundation may, however, engage in nonpartisan analysis, study, or research, as well as make expenditures that are protected by the self-defense exception.[72]

A private foundation makes a taxable expenditure if it pays or incurs an amount to influence the outcome of a public election, although the funding of certain voter registration drives is permitted.[73] A foundation makes a taxable expenditure if it makes certain types of grants to individuals without first seeking IRS approval.[74] A foundation makes a taxable expenditure when it makes a grant, loan, or a program-related investment, for charitable purposes, to an entity other than a public charity (or a Type III nonfunctionally integrated supporting organization), unless it exercises expenditure responsibility.[75] A foundation makes a taxable expenditure if it pays or incurs an amount for a noncharitable purpose.[76] Special rules apply in connection with grants to foreign charities.[77]

An initial excise tax of 20 percent is imposed on a private foundation's taxable expenditure. An initial tax of 5 percent is imposed on a foundation manager who agreed to the making of the expenditure, absent reasonable cause, subject to a per-expenditure maximum tax of $10,000. An additional tax may be imposed on a private foundation at the rate of 100 percent. An additional

---

69. See § 8.5.
70. See § 12.4(c).
71. See Chapter 9.
72. See § 9.1.
73. See § 9.2.
74. See § 9.3.
75. See §§ 9.4, 9.7.
76. See § 9.8.
77. See § 9.6.

tax may be imposed on a foundation manager at the rate of 50 percent, subject to a per-expenditure maximum tax of $20,000. There is a correction requirement.[78] Tax abatement is potentially available.[79]

(i) Tax on Investment Income

Generally, a private foundation is required to pay an excise tax of 1.39 percent on its net investment income.[80] This tax is not imposed on exempt operating foundations.[81]

(j) Termination of Private Foundation Status

Termination rules apply to private foundations, designed to prevent a foundation from ceasing to be a charitable organization so that it can use its funds and assets for noncharitable purposes.[82]

A private foundation's status may be voluntarily terminated by transfer of all of its income and assets to one or more public charities or if the foundation becomes a public charity.[83] A foundation's status may be involuntarily terminated if it engages in willful, flagrant, or repeated acts (or failures to act) giving rise to one or more of the private foundation excise taxes; a foundation in this circumstance would be liable for a termination tax.[84]

Special rules apply when a private foundation transfers assets to another private foundation pursuant to a liquidation, merger, redemption, recapitalization, or other adjustment.[85]

(k) Charitable Giving Rules

Generally, contributions to private foundations give rise to a federal income tax charitable contribution deduction.[86]

There are percentage limitations on the deductibility, for federal income tax purposes, of gifts by individuals to charitable organizations. These limitations are more stringent for gifts to private nonoperating foundations than is the case with respect to gifts to public charities: (1) 30 percent of adjusted gross income in instances of gifts of cash (as contrasted with 60 percent for

---

78. See 9.9.
79. See § 12.4(c).
80. See Chapter 10.
81. See § 10.7.
82. See Chapter 13.
83. See §§ 13.3, 13.4.
84. See §§ 13.2, 13.7.
85. See § 13.5.
86. See Chapter 14.

such gifts to public charities) and (2) 20 percent of adjusted gross income in instances of gifts of property (as contrasted with 30 percent for such gifts to public charities).[87]

Generally, a contribution of property that has appreciated in value to a charitable organization gives rise to a charitable deduction based on the property's fair market value. This type of gift to a private foundation, however, generally is deductible only to the extent of the donor's basis in the property, although there is an exception for gifts of qualified appreciated securities.[88]

Gifts to private foundations are subject to the general rules for all charitable gifts as to recordkeeping, substantiation, appraisal, disclosure, and reporting requirements.[89] These gifts also qualify for the gift and estate tax charitable deductions.[90]

(I) Unrelated Business Rules

Private foundations are subject to the unrelated business income tax rules.[91] Because of the excess business holdings rules, however, private foundations are limited in their ability to directly conduct an unrelated trade or business or to invest in pass-through entities that conduct unrelated businesses.[92] The excess business holdings rules exclude from the definition of business enterprise any activity that derives at least 95 percent of its gross income from passive sources, such as interest, dividends, royalties, rent, and capital gains.[93] This exclusion ties in with the modifications (exceptions) applicable in the unrelated business context.[94]

§ 1.5 DEFINITION OF CHARITY

A private foundation must be operated for charitable purposes. For the most part, this means that a foundation must confine its grant-making and other programs to charitable ends. One of the many responsibilities, then, of private foundation management is to be certain that each of the foundation's grantees, or its programs, qualify under one or more rationales for being charitable.

The federal tax law definition of the term *charitable* is based on English common law and trust law precepts. Federal income tax regulations recognize

---

87. See § 14.2(a).
88. See §§ 14.3-14.5.
89. See § 14.7.
90. See § 14.2(b).
91. See Chapter 11.
92. See Chapter 7.
93. See § 7.1(b).
94. See § 11.2.

§ 1.5 DEFINITION OF CHARITY

this fact by stating that the term is used in its "generally accepted legal sense."[95] At the same time, court decisions continue to expand the concept of *charity* by introducing additional (more contemporary) applications of the term. As one court observed, evolutions in the definition of the word *charitable* are "wrought by changes in moral and ethical precepts generally held, or by changes in relative values assigned to different and sometimes competing and even conflicting interests of society."[96]

The term *charitable* in the federal income tax setting, in the more technical sense, embraces a variety of purposes and activities. These include relief of the poor and distressed or of the underprivileged, the advancement of religion, advancement of education, advancement of science, lessening of the burdens of government, community beautification and maintenance, promotion of health, promotion of social welfare, promotion of environmental conservancy, advancement of patriotism, care of orphans, maintenance of public confidence in the legal system, facilitating student and cultural exchanges, and promotion and advancement of amateur sports.[97]

Charitable organizations, as that term is used in the most encompassing manner, includes *educational* organizations. In addition to institutions such as schools, colleges, universities, museums, and libraries, educational organizations are those that (1) provide instruction or training of individuals in a variety of subjects for the purpose of improving or developing their capabilities or (2) instruct the public on subjects useful to the individual and beneficial to the community.[98]

Religious organizations are part of the community of charitable organizations. These entities are churches and other membership and non-membership religious organizations. For reasons of constitutional law, the terms *religion* and *religious* cannot be accorded a definition applied by governmental agencies.[99]

Scientific organizations are, for the most part, those that engage in scientific research. Entities that are scientific in nature may have as their primary purpose the dissemination of scientific information by such means as publications and conferences. These organizations may also be considered educational in nature.[100]

There are many additional types of tax-exempt organizations other than those that are charitable in nature. Other exempt organizations (often ones that private foundations will encounter) include title-holding corporations,[101]

---

95. Income Tax Regulations (Reg.) § 1.501(c)(3)-1(d)(2).
96. Green v. Connelly, 330 F. Supp. 1150, 1159 (D.D.C. 1971), *aff'd sub nom.* Coit v. Green, 404 U.S. 997 (1971).
97. Reg. § 1.501(c)(3)-1(d)(2). See *Tax-Exempt Organizations*, Chapter 7.
98. Reg. § 1.501(c)(3)-1(d)(3). See *Tax-Exempt Organizations*, Chapter 8.
99. See *Tax-Exempt Organizations*, Chapter 10.
100. Reg. § 1.501(c)(3)-1(d)(5). See *Tax-Exempt Organizations*, Chapter 9.
101. That is, entities described in IRC § 501(c)(2) and (25). See *Tax-Exempt Organizations* § 19.2.

INTRODUCTION TO PRIVATE FOUNDATIONS

social welfare organizations,[102] labor organizations,[103] business and professional associations,[104] social clubs,[105] fraternal organizations,[106] veterans' organizations,[107] and political organizations.[108]

§ 1.6 OPERATING FOR CHARITABLE PURPOSES

A private foundation, as is the case with all tax-exempt charitable organizations, must meet a standard for qualification as a charitable organization, referred to as the *operational test*.[109] This test requires that the private foundation operate *exclusively* to accomplish one or more of the purposes referenced in the Internal Revenue Code: religious, charitable, scientific, testing for public safety, literary, or educational purposes, or to foster national or international amateur sports competition, or for the prevention of cruelty to children or animals.[110] The term *exclusively* for purposes of the operational test does not literally mean exclusively, but rather means *primarily*.[111] Consequently, the conduct of some amount of nonexempt activity, such as unrelated business activity, is permitted for organizations qualifying for tax exemption as charitable organizations.

The operational test also provides that an organization is not operated exclusively for exempt purposes if its net earnings inure in whole or in part to the benefit of private shareholders or individuals.[112] Simply stated, a private foundation may not operate to accomplish the private purposes or serve the private interests of its founders, those who control it, those who fund it, or their families—these persons are termed *disqualified persons*.[113]

---

102. That is, entities described in IRC § 501(c)(4). See *Tax-Exempt Organizations*, Chapter 13.
103. That is, entities described in IRC § 501(c)(5). See *Tax-Exempt Organizations* § 16.1.
104. That is, entities described in IRC § 501(c)(6). See *Tax-Exempt Organizations*, Chapter 14.
105. That is, entities described in IRC § 501(c)(7). See *Tax-Exempt Organizations*, Chapter 15.
106. That is, entities described in IRC § 501(c)(8) and (10). See *Tax-Exempt Organizations* § 19.4.
107. That is, organizations described in IRC § 501(c)(19). See *Tax-Exempt Organizations* § 19.11.
108. That is, organizations described in IRC § 527. See *Tax-Exempt Organizations*, Chapter 17.
109. Reg. § 1.501(c)(3)-1(c)(1). A private foundation had its tax-exempt status revoked for failing to engage in any exempt activities over a long period of time (Community Education Foundation v. Commissioner, 112 T.C.M. 637 (2016), appeal dismissed due to lack of representation by legal counsel).
110. IRC § 501(c)(3). An expenditure for the purpose of testing for public safety is not considered a charitable purpose under the taxable expenditure rules; therefore, a private foundation, unlike a public charity, is effectively precluded from being operated to accomplish this purpose by the taxable expenditure rules (see § 9.8).
111. Reg. § 1.501(c)(3)-1(c)(1); see *Tax-Exempt Organizations* § 4.4.
112. Reg. § 1.501(c)(3)-1(c)(2).
113. See Chapter 4. A strange and troublesome opinion from the U.S. Tax Court was based on the operational test. On that occasion, the court held that an organization cannot

§ 1.6 OPERATING FOR CHARITABLE PURPOSES

A qualifying private foundation promotes the general welfare of society. Evidence for satisfaction of this operational test is found not only in the nature of the foundation's activities but also in its sources of financial support, the constituency for whom it operates, and the nature of its expenditures. The presence of a single nonexempt program, if substantial in nature, will destroy the exemption regardless of the number or importance of the truly exempt purposes.[114]

The benefit to an individual participating in a foundation's programs is acceptable when the activity itself is considered a charitable pursuit. Examples of these benefits are the advancement a student receives from attending college and the relief from suffering experienced by a sick person. The standards of permissible individual benefit are different for certain of the eight categories of charitable purpose, and the distinctions are sometimes vague and not necessarily logical. For example, promoting amateur sports competition is treated as an exempt purpose, but maintaining an athletic facility that restricts its availability to less than the entire community is not charitable.[115] A sports club serving only its individual members is not charitable,[116] but a fitness center promoting health and available to the general public may qualify as a charitable organization.[117] Visiting a museum or attending a play is recognized as educational, but attending a semiprofessional baseball game is not.[118]

To prove that its programs benefit the public, rather than private individuals, a private foundation often must be found to benefit an indefinite class of persons—a charitable class—rather than a particular individual or a limited group of individuals. It may not be "organized or operated for the benefit of private interests such as designated individuals, the creator's family, shareholders of the organization or persons controlled, directly or indirectly, by

---

qualify for tax-exempt status as a charitable or educational entity because its activities and those of its founder, sole director, and officer are essentially identical (Salvation Navy, Inc. v. Commissioner, 84 T.C.M. 506 (2002)). The court wrote that the affairs of the organization and this individual are "irretrievably intertwined," so that the "benefits" of tax exemption would "inure" to the individual personally (*id.* at 508). Many charities engage in activities that their founders would otherwise personally undertake, and they are under the direct control of these individuals; this is typical of a private foundation.

114. Better Business Bureau of Washington, D.C. v. United States, 326 U.S. 279, 284 (1945).
115. Rev. Rul. 67-325, 1967-2 C.B. 113.
116. I Media Sports League, Inc. v. Commissioner, 52 T.C.M. 1092 (1986).
117. E.g., IRS Private Letter Ruling (Priv. Ltr. Rul.) 8935061. An important issue in these private rulings is whether fees charged limit the availability of the facility to the general public—a characteristic required to prove that the organization operates for charitable purposes.
118. Hutchinson Baseball Enterprises, Inc. v. Commissioner, 73 T.C. 144 (1979), *aff'd*, 696 F.2d 757 (10th Cir. 1982); Wayne Baseball, Inc. v. Commissioner, 78 T.C.M. 437 (1999).

INTRODUCTION TO PRIVATE FOUNDATIONS

such private interests."[119] Thus, a trust established to benefit an impoverished retired minister and his wife cannot qualify.[120] Likewise, a fund established to raise money to finance a medical operation, rebuild a house destroyed by fire, or provide food for a particular person does not benefit a charitable class. An organization formed by merchants to relocate homeless persons from a downtown area was found to serve the merchant class and promote their interests, rather than those of the homeless or the citizens.[121] In explaining the meaning of the word *charitable*, the regulations also deem federal, state, and local governments to be charitable entities by stipulating that relieving their burdens is a form of charitable activity qualifying for tax exemption.[122]

A charitable organization may benefit a comparatively small group of individuals if the group is not limited to identifiable individuals. The class need not be indigent, poor, or distressed.[123] A scholarship fund for a college fraternity that provided school tuition for deserving members was ruled to be a tax-exempt foundation,[124] but a trust formed to aid destitute or disabled members of a particular college class was deemed to benefit a limited class. The "general law of charity recognizes that a narrowly defined class of beneficiaries will not cause a charitable trust to fail unless the trust's purposes are personal, private, or selfish as to lack the element of public usefulness."[125] Criteria for selection of eligible beneficiaries should be followed, and evidence used to choose eligible individuals—case histories, grade reports, financial information, recommendations from specialists, and the like—should be maintained.

A genealogical society tracing the migrations to and within the United States of persons with a common name was found to qualify as a tax-exempt social club, rather than a charity. Although there was educational merit in the historical information compiled, the private interest of the family group was held to predominate.[126] If membership in the society is open to all and its focus is educational—presenting lectures, sponsoring exhibitions, publishing a

---

119. Reg. § 1.501(c)(3)-1(d)(1)(iii).
120. Carrie A. Maxwell Trust, Pasadena Methodist Foundation v. Commissioner, 2 T.C.M. 905 (1943).
121. Westward Ho v. Commissioner, 63 T.C.M. 2617 (1992).
122. Reg. § 1.501(c)(3)-1(d)(2); see *Tax-Exempt Organizations* § 7.7 for a discussion of standards for qualifying as "lessening the burdens of government."
123. Consumer Credit Counseling Service of Alabama, Inc. v. United States, 78-2 U.S.T.C. ¶ 9468 (D.C.1979), but See El Paso del Aquila Elderly v. Commissioner, 64 T.C.M. 376 (1992) (making burial insurance available at cost for the elderly is a charitable activity only if distress is relieved, by allowing indigents to participate, and the community as a whole benefits).
124. Rev. Rul. 56-403, 1956-2 C.B. 307.
125. Gen. Couns. Mem. 39876.
126. Callaway Family Association, Inc. v. Commissioner, 71 T.C. 340 (1978); Rev. Rul. 67-8, 1967-1 C.B. 142.

geographic area's pioneer history—it may be classified as charitable.[127] In contrast, a society limiting its membership to one family and compiling research data for family members individually cannot qualify for tax exemption.[128]

§ 1.7 ORGANIZATIONAL RULES

One of the fundamental requirements in the law pertaining to tax-exempt organizations, particularly charitable ones, is that these organizations must be *organized* for one or more tax-exempt purposes. This is known as the *organizational test*.[129]

The organizational test for charitable organizations, in general, emphasizes two requirements. One focuses on the organization's statement of purposes, requiring language that articulates a charitable end and forbidding language that may empower the organization to engage, to more than an insubstantial extent, in noncharitable activities or to pursue noncharitable purposes.[130] The other mandates a *dissolution clause*, which directs the passage of the organization's assets and net income, in the event of its dissolution or liquidation, for charitable ends, usually by causing transfer of the assets and income to one or more other charitable organizations.[131]

There is, however, a separate and additional organizational test for private foundations. A private foundation cannot be exempt from federal income tax (nor will contributions to it be deductible as charitable gifts) unless its governing instrument or the provisions of state law applicable to it include provisions, the effects of which are to require distributions at such time and in such manner as to comply with the annual payout rules and prohibit the foundation from engaging in any act of self-dealing, retaining any excess business holdings, making any jeopardizing investments, or making any taxable expenditures.[132] Generally, these provisions must be in the foundation's articles of organization[133] and not merely in its bylaws.[134]

The provisions of the governing instrument of a private foundation or applicable state law must require or prohibit, as the case may be, the foundation to act or refrain from acting so that the foundation, and any foundation managers or other disqualified persons with respect to the foundation, will

---

127. Rev. Rul. 80-301, 1980-2 C.B. 180.
128. Rev. Rul. 80-302, 1980-2 C.B. 182.
129. Reg. § 1.501(c)(3)-1(b).
130. Reg. § 1.501(c)(3)-1(b)(1).
131. Reg. § 1.501(c)(3)-1(b)(2).
132. IRC § 508(e)(1); Reg. § 1.508-3(a). See Chapters 5–9.
133. See § 2.3.
134. Reg. § 1.508-3(c).

INTRODUCTION TO PRIVATE FOUNDATIONS

not be liable for any of the private foundation excise taxes.[135] The governing instrument of a nonexempt split-interest trust[136] must contain comparable provisions with respect to any of the applicable private foundation excise taxes.[137]

Specific reference in the governing instrument to the appropriate sections of the Internal Revenue Code is generally required, unless equivalent language is used that is deemed by the IRS to have the same full force and effect. A governing instrument that contains only language sufficient to satisfy the requirements of the organizational test for charitable organizations in general, however, does not meet the specific requirements applicable with respect to private foundations, regardless of the interpretation placed on the language as a matter of law by a state court.[138] A governing instrument of a private foundation does not meet these organizational requirements if it expressly prohibits the distribution of capital or corpus.[139]

A private foundation's governing instrument is deemed to conform with the requisite organizational requirements if valid provisions of state law have been enacted that require the foundation to act or refrain from acting so as not to subject it to any of the private foundation excise taxes or that treat the required provisions as being contained in the foundation's governing instrument.[140] The IRS ruled as to which state statutes contain sufficient provisions in this regard.[141]

Any provision of state law is presumed to be valid as enacted and, in the absence of state law provisions to the contrary, applies with respect to any private foundation that does not specifically disclaim coverage under state law (either by notification to the appropriate state official or by commencement of judicial proceedings).[142] If a state law provision is declared invalid or inapplicable with respect to a class of foundations by the highest appellate court of the state involved or by the U.S. Supreme Court, the foundations covered by the determination must meet the private foundation organizational requirements within one year from the date on which the time for perfecting an application for review by the Supreme Court expires. If this application

---

135. Reg. § 1.508-3(b)(1). Rev. Rul. 70-270, 1970-1 C.B. 135, contains sample governing instrument provisions.
136. See § 3.7.
137. Reg. § 1.508-3(b)(1). Rev. Rul. 74-368, 1974-2 C.B. 390, contains sample governing instrument provisions.
138. Reg. § 1.508-3(b)(1).
139. Reg. § 1.508-3(b). In one instance, a charitable testamentary trust was found to have violated the private foundation organizational rules because the trust instrument required the trust to accumulate, rather than distribute, income; a state court ordered modification of the instrument to provide for the requisite distribution of the foundation's income (Estate of Barnes, 74-1 U.S.T.C. ¶ 9241 (Court of Common Pleas of Lancaster County, Pa. (1973)).
140. Reg. § 1.508-3(d)(1).
141. Rev. Rul. 75-38, 1975-1 C.B. 161.
142. Reg. § 1.508-3(d)(2)(i).

is filed, these requirements must be met within one year from the date on which the Supreme Court disposes of the case, whether by denial of the application for review or decision on the merits.[143] If a provision of state law is declared invalid or inapplicable with respect to a class of foundations by a court of competent jurisdiction, and the decision is not reviewed by the highest state appellate court or the Supreme Court, and the IRS notifies the general public that the provision has been declared invalid or inapplicable, then all private foundations in the state involved must meet these organizational requirements, without reliance on the statute to the extent declared invalid or inapplicable by the decision, within one year from the date the notice is made public.[144] These rules do not apply to a foundation that is subject to a final judgment entered by a court of competent jurisdiction, holding the law invalid or inapplicable with respect to the foundation.[145]

In one case, a charitable trust created by will in 1967 had its trust instrument amended by court order to enable the trust, a private foundation, to comply with the organizational requirements.[146] In a similar case, the trustees of a private foundation were permitted by a state court to modify a trust document to facilitate compliance by the foundation with these organizational rules.[147]

§ 1.8 PRIVATE FOUNDATION LAW SANCTIONS

The federal tax rules pertaining to private foundations are often characterized in summaries as if they are typical laws, in the sense of prescriptions governing human behavior. This is not the case; these rules, comprising portions of the Internal Revenue Code, are tax provisions. Thus, this body of law states that, if a certain course of conduct is engaged in (or, perhaps, not engaged in), imposition of one or more excise taxes will be the (or a) result. For example, there is no rule of federal tax law that states that a private foundation may not engage in an act of self-dealing;[148] rather, the law is that an act of self-dealing will trigger one or more excise taxes and other sanctions.[149]

---

143. Reg. § 1.508-3(d)(2)(ii).
144. Reg. § 1.508-3(d)(2)(iii).
145. Reg. § 1.508-3(d)(2)(iv).
146. Matter of Jeanne E. Barkey, 71-1 U.S.T.C. ¶ 9350 (Surrogate Court of New York County, N.Y. (1971)).
147. William Wikoff Smith trust estate, "The W. W. Smith Foundation," 72-1 U.S.T.C. ¶ 9271 (Court of Common Pleas Montgomery County, Orphans' Court Div., Pa. (1971)).
148. State law, however, may contain such a rule. E.g., Neb. Rev. Stat. § 21-1916.
149. Even the IRS occasionally gets this wrong. For example, in a private letter ruling, the IRS stated that certain payments by a private foundation to disqualified persons "would be acts of self-dealing that are prohibited by Chapter 42 of the Internal Revenue Code" (Priv. Ltr. Rul. 201703003).

(a) Sanctions (a Reprise)

Because of the nature of this statutory tax law structure, a person subject to an excise tax does not merely pay it and continue with the transaction and its consequences, as is the case with nearly all federal tax regimes. This structure weaves a series of spiraling taxes from which the private foundation, and/or disqualified persons with respect to it, can emerge only by paying one or more excise taxes and correcting (undoing) the transaction involved, or all of the foundation's income and assets to the IRS in the form of a termination tax.[150]

The private foundation rules collectively stand as sanctions created by Congress for the purpose of curbing what was perceived as a range of abuses being perpetrated through private foundations by those who control or manipulate them. These provisions comprise a substantial part of Chapter 42 of the Internal Revenue Code.

(b) Self-Dealing Sanctions as Pigouvian Taxes

In the self-dealing context, two excise taxes are imposed on self-dealers—the initial tax[151] and the additional tax.[152] The first tax has a rate of 10 percent; the second a rate of 200 percent. There are also taxes on foundation managers where there is knowing participation in the self-dealing transaction (a scienter requirement).[153] The foundation self-dealing tax subjects the entire amount involved in a self-dealing transaction to tax. Also, the initial self-dealing tax cannot be abated by the IRS.[154] And there is a correction feature, by which the self-dealer is required to pay back the amount involved to the foundation.[155]

What has come to be known as the *Pigouvian tax* is the brainchild of English economist Arthur Cecil Pigou (1879–1959), a contributor to modern welfare economics. He introduced the concept of *externality* and the belief that externality (social problems) can be corrected by imposition of a tax. A commentator wrote that Pigouvian taxes "aim to regulate behavior by placing a small tax, usually in the form of a uniform excise tax, on the activity to be regulated because of the harm it produces for members of the public."[156]

---

150. See § 13.7.
151. IRC § 4941(a)(1).
152. IRC § 4941(b)(1).
153. IRC § 4941(a)(2), (b)(2).
154. IRC § 4962(b).
155. IRC § 4941(e)(3).
156. Aprill, "The Private Foundation Excise Tax on Self-Dealing: Contours, Comparisons, and Character," 17 *Pitt. L. Rev.* 297 (Spring 2020) ("Aprill Article").

§ 1.8 PRIVATE FOUNDATION LAW SANCTIONS

Does the federal self-dealing tax regime constitute one or more Pigouvian taxes? On the face of it, the answer would seem to be yes.[157] This commentator nicely observed that the self-dealing taxes "have the Pigouvian impulse to protect the public from harm by imposing an excise tax."[158] Despite this impulse, however, three reasons were posited why the self-dealing taxes are not Pigouvian in nature. One, the additional excise tax rate of 200 percent is not "small." Two, the initial tax subjects the entire amount involved in a self-dealing transaction to tax, "even if the transaction benefits the foundation," so that, in those circumstances, the requisite "social costs" are not involved.[159] Third, a Pigouvian tax assumes uniform social costs across all individuals and firms; the commentator mused whether "differences between large and small foundations, between corporate and family foundations, local and national foundations, old and new foundations, etc. should shape the applicable excise tax rules."[160]

Yet, it is understandable why one, perhaps not an economist, would conclude that the self-dealing taxes are Pigouvian in nature, if only because the initial tax cannot be abated and because of the correction requirement. The U.S. Supreme Court stated the general rule about a tax: "Imposition of a tax nonetheless leaves an individual with a lawful choice to do or not do a certain act, so long as he is willing to pay a tax levied on that choice."[161]

(c) Self-Dealing Sanctions: Taxes or Penalties?

Federal constitutional law differentiates between a tax and a penalty—at least conceptually. This distinction may be drawn in determining whether the exaction passes constitutional muster. A dramatic illustration of this point occurred when a bare majority of the U.S. Supreme Court upheld the constitutionality of the Patient Protection and Affordable Care Act (the "Affordable Care Act") on the basis of Congress's taxing power, construing the health insurance individual mandate (or shared-responsibility payment) as a tax, after the decision was made that the mandate could not be justified as constitutional pursuant to the Commerce Clause.[162] On that occasion, however, the Court observed that "Congress's ability to use its taxing power to influence conduct is not without limits."[163]

---

157. This is because of the inherent purpose of these taxes, which is to regulate behavior, with the sanctions more in the nature of penalties than taxes (see § 1.8(c)).
158. Aprill Article at 329.
159. *Id.* at 328.
160. *Id.*
161. National Federation of Independent Businesses v. Sebelius, 567 U.S. 519, 574 (2012).
162. *Id.* The Taxing Clause is the subject of U.S. Constitution Article I § 8. For a detailed summary of this opinion, see *Constitutional Law* § 4.8.
163. National Federation of Independent Businesses, *supra* note 161 at 572.

INTRODUCTION TO PRIVATE FOUNDATIONS

In this opinion, the fact that there is a difference between a tax and a penalty was raised, but not resolved. The Court wrote that "there comes a time in the extension of the penalizing features of the so-called tax when it loses its character as such and becomes a mere penalty with the characteristics of regulation and punishment."[164] Also, the Court stated that, "[i]n distinguishing penalties from taxes, this Court has explained that 'if the concept of penalty means anything, it means punishment for an unlawful act or omission.'"[165] The Court concluded, having decided that the individual mandate (or shared-responsibility payment) is a tax for constitutional law purposes, wrote that "we need not here decide the precise point at which an exaction becomes so punitive that the taxing power does not authorize it."[166] It should be remembered that, even if an exaction is determined to be a penalty, the constitutionality of the statutory structure may be upheld under the Commerce Clause.[167]

In the opinion, the Court principally relied on two of its precedents in discussing what is and is not a tax. In one of these cases, decided in 1953, the Court wrote that a "federal excise tax does not cease to be valid merely because it discourages or deters the activities taxed."[168] It was stated that a tax may have a "regulatory effect" but remains a tax if it "produces revenue."[169] The Court added: "It is axiomatic that the power of Congress to tax is extensive and sometimes falls with crushing effect on businesses deemed unessential or inimical to the public welfare."[170] In the other of these cases, the Court concluded that an ostensible tax was a penalty, because the sanction imposed a heavy burden, included a scienter requirement, and was enforced by a federal agency other than the Department of the Treasury.[171]

---

164. *Id.* at 573.
165. *Id.* at 567, quoting United States v. Reorganized CF&I Fabricators of Utah, Inc., 518 U.S. 213, 224 (1996).
166. National Federation of Independent Businesses, *supra* note 161 at 573 (2012). Earlier in its opinion, the Court majority held that the payment was not a tax for statutory law purposes.
167. The shared-responsibility payment was reduced to zero, effective January 1, 2019, by enactment of the Tax Cuts and Jobs Act (Pub. L. No. 115-97, 131 Stat. 2054 (2017)). A federal court held that the entirety of the Affordable Care Act, as modified by the TCJA, is unconstitutional because it can no longer be justified as a tax and the mandate is inseverable from the Act's remaining provisions (Texas v. United States, 336 F. Supp. 3d 664 (N.D. Tex. 2018)). An appellate court agreed with the district court as to the present-day unconstitutionality of the individual mandate but remanded the case for a more detailed analysis as to severability (*id.*). The U.S. Supreme Court ended this litigation by holding that the plaintiffs lacked standing (California v. Texas, No. 19-840).
168. United States v. Kahriger, 345 U.S. 22, 28 (1953).
169. *Id.*
170. *Id.*
171. Bailey v. Drexel Furniture, 259 U.S. 20 (1922).

§ 1.8 PRIVATE FOUNDATION LAW SANCTIONS

In 1974, the Supreme Court observed that the Court in some of its early cases "drew what it saw at the time as distinctions between regulatory and revenue-raising taxes," adding "[b]ut the Court has subsequently abandoned such distinctions."[172]

Several court opinions focus on the constitutionality of the federal self-dealing law. In one of these cases, the principal contention was that the provision is an unconstitutional extension of the congressional taxing power.[173] That is, the allegation in that case was that the purpose of the statute is not to raise revenue but to regulate private foundations by imposing penalties on persons who use them for noncharitable, private purposes. The court involved rejected the contention.

The court began its analysis by observing that, in its early decisions analyzing the constitutionality of tax statutes, the Supreme Court "often drew distinctions between regulatory and revenue raising taxes."[174] The court, however, wrote that the Court "has subsequently abandoned such distinctions."[175] The court quoted a 1937 Supreme Court opinion stating that "[i]t is beyond serious question that a tax does not cease to be valid merely because it regulates, discourages, or definitely deters the activity taxed."[176] In that opinion, the Court wrote that this "principle applies even though the revenue obtained is obviously negligible"[177] "or the revenue purpose of tax may be secondary."[178] The Court also stated: "Nor does a tax statute necessarily fall because it touches on activities which Congress may not otherwise regulate."[179] The court concluded that, "[u]nder the present posture of the law, tax statutes are constitutional unless they contain provisions which are extraneous to any tax need."[180]

This court stated that "[i]t is clear that [the self-dealing statute] is constitutional as measured by the standards set forth in [the 1953 case]."[181] It continued: "Congress has seen fit, in enacting the internal revenue laws, to grant tax exempt status to certain entities" and "has allowed individuals, corporations, and estates the right to escape taxation of the amounts donated for charitable

---

172. Bob Jones University v. Simon, 416 U.S. 725, 791, n.12 (1974).
173. Rockefeller v. United States, 572 F. Supp. 9 (E.D. Ark. 1982), *aff'd per curiam*, 718 F.2d 290 (8th Cir. 1983), *cert. den.*, 460 U.S. 962 (1984).
174. *Id.* at 13, citing Hill v. Wallace, 259 U.S. 44 (1922); Bailey v. Drexel Furniture Co., 259 U.S. 20 (1922); and Helmig v. United States, 188 U.S. 605 (1903).
175. Rockefeller, *supra* note 173 at 13, quoting United States v. Sanchez, 340 U.S. 42 (1950).
176. United States v. Sanchez, 340 U.S. 42, 44–45 (1950), citing Sonzinsky v. United States, 300 U.S. 506, 513–514 (1937).
177. *Id.* at 44.
178. *Id.*, citing Hampton & Co. v. United States, 276 U.S. 394 (1928).
179. *Id.*
180. Rockefeller, *supra* note 173 at 13, citing Kahriger, *supra* note 168.
181. *Id.*

INTRODUCTION TO PRIVATE FOUNDATIONS

purposes."[182] "However," the court wrote, "when Congress observed that its legislative grace was being abused, it enacted [the self-dealing statute] to insure that its original intent in granting non-taxable status was complied with."[183] The court concluded that, "[a]lthough [the statute] has a regulatory effect on the activities of charitable organizations and might not raise any revenue, it insures that revenue will be collected under income, estate, and gift tax laws which otherwise might have gone uncollected."[184]

Another court case directly involving a private foundation regulatory provision in relation to the sanction's status as a tax is a challenge to the mandatory payout rule.[185] In that case as well, the argument was that, by enacting the provision, Congress exceeded its power to lay and collect excise taxes. The contention was that the provision does not impose a tax for constitutional law purposes but "imposes a penalty measured by a prescribed rate of return on the value of the foundation's noncharitable property even though the foundation may have no income."[186] The court rejoined that the Supreme Court "has repeatedly rejected this argument," and found that a tax may be "a legitimate exercise of the taxing power" notwithstanding that it has a "collateral regulatory purpose and effect."[187]

This court wrote that, "[b]y enacting [the mandatory payout rule] . . . Congress decided to subject tax-exempt private foundations to [the rule that the tax must be paid even though the foundation has no income] in order to deal with what it perceived to be an abuse of the foundation's tax-exemption privilege,"

---

182. *Id.*
183. *Id.*
184. *Id.* The court, in Rockefeller, decided that the first-tier self-dealing tax is a penalty for purposes of a rule concerning interest (IRC § 6601(3)). Likewise, Farrell v. United States, 484 F. Supp. 1097 (E.D. Ark. 1980); Deluxe Check Printers, Inc. v. United States, 14 Ct. Cl. 782 (1988), 15 Ct. Cl. 175 (1988), *rev'd on other issue*, 885 F.2d 848 (Fed. Cir. 1989). But see Latterman v. United States, 872 F.2d 564 (3d Cir. 1989). Two federal appellate courts rejected the argument that the self-dealing taxes are excise levies and held that these sanctions are penal in nature (Mahon v. United States (In re Unified Control Systems, Inc.), 586 F.2d 1036 (5th Cir. 1978); United States v. Feinblatt (In re Kline), 547 F.2d 823 (4th Cir. 1977)). Following a brief survey of some of this case law, in a case challenging the constitutionality of the self-dealing excise taxes, the U.S. Tax Court stated simply that it "find[s] no basis for holding any of the provisions of section 4941 unconstitutional (Estate of Reis v. Commissioner, 87 T.C. 1016, 1020 (1986)).
185. Stanley O. Miller Charitable Fund v. Commissioner, 89 T.C. 1112 (1987). See Chapter 6.
186. *Id.* at 1119.
187. *Id.* at 1120, citing the discussion in Sanchez, *supra* note 175, at 44–45, of the Court's decisions in Sonzinsky, *supra* note 176, Hampton, *supra* note 178, and Magnano Co. v. Hamilton, 292 U.S. 40, 47 (1934). The court also rejected the taxpayer's other arguments that the mandatory payment tax is a direct tax in violation of Art. 1, sec. 9; that the tax violates the Sixteenth Amendment; and that this form of taxation involves denial of due process in violation of the Fifth Amendment (inasmuch as a private foundation is given the choice to forfeit its tax-exempt status and thereby avoid having to make mandatory payouts).

§ 1.8 PRIVATE FOUNDATION LAW SANCTIONS

in that "[w]hile donors to the exempt private foundation could receive substantial current tax benefits from their contributions, charity might receive no current benefits because the foundation invested in growth assets that produce no current income but are expected to increase in value."[188] Although the court did not expressly so state, private foundations in this circumstance are required to dip into principal to make the required distribution.

The legislative history of the self-dealing rules is replete with references to the sanctions as penalties. The report of the House Committee on Ways and Means accompanying its version of the 1969 tax legislation states that the "permissible activities of private foundations . . . are substantially tightened to *prevent* self-dealing between the foundations and their substantial contributors."[189] The committee added that it "has determined to generally *prohibit* self-dealing transactions and provide a variety and graduation of sanctions."[190] In this report, there are numerous references to these sanctions as constituting "prohibitions" or arising out of "prohibited" conduct. Identical or similar language appears in the report of the Senate Committee on Finance in connection with its version of the 1969 legislation.[191] This continues to be the view of Congress on this topic, as reflected in a report issued by the Ways and Means Committee in 1996 referring to the private foundation rules as a "penalty regime."[192]

A commentator, following a review of the case law, wrote that the "character" of the self-dealing and similar private foundation provisions "as a tax or a penalty seems uncertain" under the Supreme Court opinion upholding the Affordable Care Act.[193] It is pointed out that the Court's most recent discussion of what constitutes a penalty "turns, at least in part, not on the purpose of or motive for an assessment, but on its level—whether it imposes a heavy burden."[194] Here are the features posed for such a "heavy burden" under the self-dealing regime: (1) the imposition of the first-tier level of taxation on the entire amount of a self-dealing transaction, rather than just the amount by which the foundation is harmed; (2) the second-tier tax rate of 200 percent, which "gives a disqualified person little if any meaningful choice of whether or not to pay

---

188. Stanley O. Miller Charitable Fund v. Commissioner, 89 T.C. 1112, 1122 (1987).
189. H.R. Rep. No. 91-413, pt.1, at 4 (1969) (emphasis added).
190. *Id.*, Part IV, at 21 (emphasis added).
191. S. Rep. No. 91-552 (1969).
192. H.R. Rep. No. 104-506, at 56 (1996). This observation was made in the context of a discussion of the intermediate sanctions rules applicable with respect to public charities, social welfare organizations, and certain nonprofit insurance issuers (IRC § 4958), which in many ways are structured in the same fashion as the private foundation rules. In general, *Tax-Exempt Organizations,* Chapter 21.
193. Aprill Article at 322; see National Federation of Independent Businesses, *supra* note 161.
194. Aprill Article at 322.

INTRODUCTION TO PRIVATE FOUNDATIONS

the tax"; (3) the implication of the scienter requirement in connection with the excise taxes on foundation managers who knowingly participate in a self-dealing transaction; (4) the court opinions that view the self-dealing rules as having the "regulatory purpose [of] rendering self-dealing unlawful"; and (5) the IRS's inability to abate the first-tier excise tax.[195] A sixth indicator of penalty status in this context may be the correction requirement.

This commentator concludes that "private foundation excise taxes do not fit easily into either the category of constitutional taxes or constitutional penalties."[196] As to the self-dealing taxes, the commentator writes that the "status of section 4941 is uncertain under [the Supreme Court opinion upholding the Affordable Care Act], under the private foundation cases from the 1980s, and the positions of key governmental bodies."[197] Nonetheless, a good case can be made, at least as to the self-dealing tax regime, that the sanctions amount to one or more penalties. The Pigouvian impulse tugs.

(d) Abatement

The private foundation excise tax provisions themselves do not contain an exception, or excuse, for imposition of the taxes on a private foundation for failure to comply with the specific provisions. The regulations accompanying these provisions, however, contain relief for those foundation managers who do not condone or participate in the decision to conduct a prohibited action. Until 1984, the excise tax provisions were strictly applied.[198] Congress in 1984 added statutes[199] to permit abatement of the taxes imposed on both the foundation and its managers if it is established to the satisfaction of the IRS that the taxable event was due to reasonable cause and not to willful neglect, and the event was corrected within the applicable correction period. Abatement, however, is not available with respect to the initial tax on acts of self-dealing.[200]

(e) Potential of Overlapping Taxes

Taxes under more than one provision of the private foundation excise tax regime[201] may be imposed with respect to a single transaction.[202] Indeed, a

---

195. *Id.*
196. *Id.* at 323.
197. *Id.* at 325.
198. Charles Stewart Mott Foundation v. United States, 91-2 U.S.T.C. ¶ 50,340 (6th Cir. 1991); Mannheimer Charitable Trust, Hans S. v. Commissioner, 93 T.C. 35 (1989).
199. IRC §§ 4961-4963; see § 12.4(c).
200. IRC § 4962(b).
201. IRC Chapter 42 (IRC §§ 4940-4948).
202. Rev. Rul. 77-161, 1977-1 C.B. 358 ("A given set of facts can give rise to taxes under more than one provision of chapter 42 of the Code").

§ 1.8 PRIVATE FOUNDATION LAW SANCTIONS

tax regulation states that "[i]t is not intended that the taxes imposed under Chapter 42 be exclusive."[203] For example, if a private foundation purchases a sole proprietorship in a business enterprise,[204] in addition to becoming subject to the excess business holdings tax,[205] the foundation may be liable for the jeopardizing investment tax[206] if the investment jeopardizes the carrying out of any of the foundation's exempt purposes.[207]

As an illustration of the potential for overlapping private foundation excise taxes, the IRS ruled, in a case involving private foundation loans to a disqualified person, that the loans were acts of self-dealing,[208] then added that they were also jeopardizing investments.[209]

(f) Influence on Subsequent Law

When enacted in 1969, the private foundation rules were unique. The statutory scheme devised by Congress had no precedent in the tax law. (The only other prior occasion when Congress levied a tax on otherwise tax-exempt organizations was on adoption of the tax on unrelated business income, implemented in 1950).[210] But in the immediate aftermath of enactment of the foundation rules, speculation started as to whether and to what extent this new approach might be extended to other tax-exempt organizations, principally public charities.

Since then, Congress has proved adept at extending some of the private foundation law to other types of tax-exempt charitable entities. For example, aspects of the excess business holdings rules were subsequently extended to certain supporting organizations[211] and to donor-advised funds.[212] The private foundation self-dealing rules heavily influenced the shaping of the excess benefit transaction rules.[213] Indeed, the very concept of underlying regulatory rules with a system of excise taxes, initiated with Chapter 42, is reflected in the excess benefit transaction rules,[214] public charity lobbying rules,[215] public

---

203. Reg. § 53.4944-1(a)(2)(iv).
204. See § 7.2(b).
205. See § 7.7.
206. See § 8.5.
207. Reg. § 53.4944-1(a)(2)(iv). See § 8.1(a).
208. See § 5.5.
209. Priv. Ltr. Rul. 201326019. See § 8.1(a) (as to jeopardizing investments).
210. See Chapter 11.
211. See § 7.5, 15.6(k).
212. See § 7.6, 16.7.
213. IRC § 4958. See *Tax-Exempt Organizations*, Chapter 21.
214. *Id.*
215. *Id.*, Chapter 22.

charity political campaign activities rules,[216] and the donor-advised fund statutory law.[217]

Thus, private foundations law set in motion the use of a tax scheme that has been utilized since and undoubtedly will be used again. But the amount of interpretative law built up around these statutory rules is most extensive with respect to private foundations.

§ 1.9 STATISTICAL PROFILE

There are about 90,000 private foundations in the United States, thus accounting for a small percentage of tax-exempt charitable organizations in the sector. As of 2017, foundations held over $1 trillion in assets or about 1 percent of the net worth in the United States overall. Yet, on the basis of data for 2018, it is estimated that all nonprofit organizations had a collective net worth of $6.7 trillion; therefore, private foundations account for over one-seventh of assets held in the nonprofit sector.[218]

§ 1.10 PRIVATE FOUNDATIONS AND LAW 50 YEARS LATER

Notwithstanding the passage of more than 50 years, the statutory tax law regulating private foundations that was enacted in 1969—the infamous IRC Chapter 42—has not changed much. There have, of course, been some revisions, but the basic framework remains in place. There are several reasons for this phenomenon, one of them being the excellent craftsmanship that was employed when the initial statutory regime was formulated. This body of law is tough and comprehensive, although, five decades later, it is probably unnecessarily rigid and inequitable in places.

Parallel to the endurance of this statutory scheme has been the steady growth of the private foundation community. Today, there are, as noted, about 90,000 private foundations; all of the metrics reflect steady expansion: the sheer numbers of them, asset size, grant amounts, and the like. Foundations have persisted, notwithstanding this heavy mantle of statutory excise taxes (that essentially amount to prohibitions or affirmative requirements).[219]

---

216. *Id.*, Chapter 23.
217. See § 16.7.
218. These data are collected in Steuerle and Soskis, "Taxes and Foundations: A 50th Anniversary Overview," published by the Tax Policy Center, Urban Institute, and Brookings Institution (Feb. 8, 2020) (Steuerle & Soskis Paper). A subsequent report stated that there are nearly 2 million tax-exempt organizations in the United States (IRS Data Book, 2022 (Pub. 55-B) at 30).
219. See § 1.8. Two commentators nicely portrayed the Act as a "regulatory fusillade" on private foundations (Steuerle & Soskis Paper at 21).

§ 1.10 PRIVATE FOUNDATIONS AND LAW 50 YEARS LATER

This endurance and growth were not anticipated in all quarters in the immediate aftermath of enactment of the Tax Reform Act of 1969.[220] A chronicler of this 50-year period[221] collected some predictions issued in those early years. In one, two commentators characterized the effect of the Act as Congress having "thrown out the charitable baby with the dirty bathwater," "encouraging the abandonment" of private foundations, "interfering with their effective operation, attacking their involvement in major social problems and prohibiting what are in essence equitable transactions."[222] In another, the forecast was that "[a]ll of the odds seem stacked against" the growth of foundations, "given the range of disincentives built into the law."[223] Yet, private foundations have proved resilient and remain a major force in contemporary philanthropy.[224]

There have, however, been two generally unanticipated consequences of enactment of Chapter 42. Since 1969, Congress has adapted the rules enacted to reform the conduct of private foundations to apply to other types of tax-exempt charitable entities.[225]

The other unanticipated consequence of enactment of the private foundation tax laws is the rise of alternative entities. The most notable aspect of this development has been, and continues to be, the prodigious rise of the donor-advised fund.[226] For a variety of reasons, donor-advised funds often are used in lieu of private foundations, including the absence of a need to create and sustain a governing board, apply for recognition of exempt status, file annual information returns, and be subject to the mandatory payout rules, not to mention the lack of sufficient financial resources to warrant the formation and operation of a private foundation.[227]

The other primary alternative to the private foundation is the tax-exempt social welfare organization.[228] In this context, the concept of *social welfare* is commensurate with the "common good and general welfare" and "civic betterments and social improvements."[229] This concept is certainly broader than

---

220. See § 1.3.
221. Orol, "The Failures and the Future of Private Foundation Governance," 46 *ACTEC L. Jour.* (No. 2) 185 (Spring 2021) (Orol Article).
222. Goldstein and Sharpe, "Private Charitable Foundations After Tax Reform," 56 *A.B.A.J.* 447, 452 (May 1970).
223. Wadsworth, "Private Foundations and the Tax Reform Act of 1969," 39 *Law & Contemp. Probs.* 255, 262 (1975).
224. As one observer stated the matter, the "overwhelming consensus is that foundations have thrived in spite of, and not because of, the Tax Reform Act" (Orol Article at 210).
225. See, e.g., § 1.8(f).
226. See Chapter 16.
227. See § 2.1 and Chapter 16; *Tax-Exempt Organizations* § 11.8; *Charitable Giving* § 21.4.
228. This type of entity is exempt from tax under IRC § 501(a) as an organization that is described in IRC § 501(c)(4). See *Tax-Exempt Organizations*, Chapter 13.
229. Reg. § 1.501(c)(4)-1(a)(2)(i).

INTRODUCTION TO PRIVATE FOUNDATIONS

the concept of what is *charitable*.[230] A federal income tax charitable contribution deduction is not likely to be available in instances of transfers to social welfare organizations but donors may nonetheless make gifts to these entities, including gifts of appreciated property,[231] and avail themselves of the exclusion of such gifts from the federal gift tax.[232] These entities are not required to file for recognition of exemption,[233] may engage in political campaign activities, and are not subject to private foundation laws concerning self-dealing,[234] mandatory payouts, excess business holdings limitations, and the like. Donors, it is said, "are flocking to 501(c)(4) organizations."[235]

The previously referenced chronicler asserts that the "large number of existing private foundations and the significant value of their holdings mask a deep-seated and growing frustration with the restrictions imposed by the [Tax Reform] Act that threatens to dethrone the private foundation from its historical primacy in the field of private philanthropy."[236] It is contended that the combination of various issues in play, discussed below, has "precipitate[d] the decline of private foundations in favor of substantially—and arguably, troubling—less restrictive alternatives, which are largely structured in ways that make it less likely that they will achieve the type of broad-ranging social benefit that private foundations have historically fostered."[237]

This analysis concluded that there is a "lack of public confidence in the regulatory regime" applicable to private foundations.[238] Five reasons are given for this development: (1) The "single most significant source of the rules' negative consequences is their undue complexity," which (ostensibly) leads to "an explosion in administrative costs" due to legal fees;[239] (2) the dramatic decrease in IRS guidance in the private foundation field;[240] (3) many of the private foundation laws are bright-line rules that, while easier to administer, lead to over-inclusiveness in the form of unnecessary and often unfair penalties;[241]

---

230. See § 1.6.
231. See § 14.3.
232. A transfer of money or other property to tax-exempt organizations described in IRC § 501(c)(4), (5), or (6), for the use of such organizations, is not treated as a transfer by gift for purposes of the federal gift tax (IRC § 2501(a)(6)). See *Charitable Giving* § 6.2(g).
233. These organizations are, however, required to timely file a notice with the IRS (IRC § 506(a); see *Tax-Exempt Organizations* § 26.13).
234. These organizations are, however, subject to the excess benefit transactions law (IRC § 4958(e)).
235. Orol Article at 229.
236. *Id.* at 186.
237. *Id.* at 187.
238. *Id.* at 213.
239. *Id.* at 213-215.
240. *Id.* at 215-216.
241. *Id.* at 216-219.

§ 1.10 PRIVATE FOUNDATIONS AND LAW 50 YEARS LATER

(4) Congress and the public remain skeptical of private foundations, in part because of ongoing "undercurrents of anxiety about wealth," foundations' "control over charitable priorities," some well-publicized abuses, and (sometimes) lack of efficacy of the foundation laws;[242] and (5) the previously discussed rise in alternatives to private foundations.[243]

This chronicler is of the view that what is needed is a "clean slate for foundation governance,"[244] that is, foundation regulation. This is because the rules are "hopelessly complicated and penalize behavior that is not only not harmful but may in fact be beneficial for philanthropy."[245] In this regard, particular focus is placed on the self-dealing rules. Your authors are of the view that such a "clean slate" is unlikely for the foreseeable future and that, while the self-dealing and other foundation rules are indeed complex, the state of affairs is not so dire as to be "hopeless." The foundation community appears to have largely learned to accommodate the rules, advised by far more lawyers who are proficient in private foundation law than was the case many years ago. There is, however, room for more flexibility and equity in the private foundation self-dealing rules, and the IRS should be accorded authority to abate the self-dealing taxes.

This analysis raises the matter of the private foundation net investment income excise tax. As is well known, this tax was originally touted as an "audit fee," the purpose of which was to fund IRS oversight of private foundations and other components of the charitable sector—an outcome that never materialized. (It has never been clear as to why this earmarking of funds has never occurred.)[246] The analysis calls for reinstatement of this tax as an audit fee, with that law change unleashing a "cascade of benefits," including removal of bright-line rules in the self-dealing law and enabling foundations to "engage in certain behavior that is now penalized but would ultimately be beneficial charitable causes."[247] Of course, an alternative is to repeal the tax, perhaps freeing up more funds for charitable purposes. In any event, the attitude in

---

242. *Id.* at 219-225.
243. *Id.* at 225-230.
244. *Id.* at 230.
245. *Id.*
246. Two commentators dismiss this "audit fee" rationale as a mere "excuse," asserting that the true purpose of this tax is an "attack . . . on institutions thought to be controlled by the wealthy or benefiting an elite" (Steuerle & Soskis Paper at 27). The same may be said for the excise tax on college and university endowments (IRC § 4968; *Tax-Exempt Organizations* § 11.9(b)). One analysis states that, absent the audit-fee rationale, "it is difficult to justify the tax at all" (Orol Article at 233).
247. Orol Article at 234.

INTRODUCTION TO PRIVATE FOUNDATIONS

Congress about funding the IRS is shifting; the agency may soon have additional billions of dollars to spend on examinations and other forms of tax law enforcement.

Another area that is said to need improvement is IRS enforcement of the private foundation rules. It is common knowledge that the IRS is presently lacking in resources in this regard. The nation, however, appears to be entering an era of higher income taxes, increased funding of the IRS, and greater focus on audits of wealthy individuals. There is a correlation between this point and the prior one: "A more robust and well-resourced [IRS] audit function would allow us to move away from the bright-line rules that have proven to be overbroad and exceedingly complex."[248] One approach, as the chronicler noted, would be to return to the original concept of earmarking the funds generated by the tax on private foundations' net income for audits of foundations (and perhaps other categories of tax-exempt organizations).

This review of 50 years of experience with the private foundation tax laws observed that Congress "has the opportunity to retool the private foundation regulatory regime to ensure that private foundations maintain their place of primacy in private philanthropy and continue to deliver [their] socially-beneficial results."[249] Such a revision of this regulatory regime, however, is certainly not imminent. Indeed, the trend appears to be to leave the private foundation laws as they are and extend them to other exempt entities or create new forms of comparable regulation (such as in the case of donor-advised funds).

---

248. *Id.* at 230.
249. *Id.* at 237.

CHAPTER TWO

Starting, Funding, and Governing a Private Foundation

§ 2.1 Alternatives to Private Foundations 40
§ 2.2 Advantages of Private Foundations 42
§ 2.3 Choice of Organizational Form 46
§ 2.4 Funding a Foundation 47
§ 2.5 Estate Planning Principles 49
    (a) Decedents' Estates 50
    (b) Estate and Gift Tax Considerations 50
§ 2.6 Foundations and Planned Giving 51
    (a) Introduction to Planned Giving 51
    (b) Charitable Remainder Trusts 52
    (c) Other Planned Giving Vehicles 53
    (d) Interrelationships with Private Foundation Rules 54
§ 2.7 Acquiring Recognition of Tax-Exempt Status 55
    (a) Form 1023 56
    (b) 27-Month Rule 59
    (c) IRS Determination Letters Recognizing Exempt Status 61
    (d) Administrative Procedures Where Recognition Denied 64
    (e) Declaratory Judgment Procedures Where Recognition Denied 67
    (f) Recognition of Foreign Organizations 70
    (g) Exemption for State Purposes 71
§ 2.8 Governance 72
    (a) IRS Entry into Nonprofit Governance 73
    (b) Concept of Nonprofit Governance 74
    (c) Nonprofit Governance Standards 76
    (d) Early IRS Attempts at Nonprofit Governance Regulation 80
    (e) Federal Tax Law as to Board Composition 81
    (f) IRS's Use of Private Benefit Doctrine 82
    (g) IRS's Ruling Policy 84

Starting a private foundation generally involves creating an entity under state law, applying to the IRS for recognition of tax-exempt status, applying to state authorities for exemption from state taxes, and funding the foundation. Before deciding to create a private foundation, however, a donor should consider the advantages and disadvantages of a private foundation and the availability of alternatives for attaining the donor's philanthropic and tax planning goals.

§ 2.1 ALTERNATIVES TO PRIVATE FOUNDATIONS

It is almost always more advantageous for a charitable organization, when possible, to obtain and maintain public charity status rather than be classified as a private foundation. As an initial matter, with respect to funding the organization, the allowable charitable contribution deductions for gifts to private foundations are more limited than those to public charities.[1] And unlike almost all public charities, a private foundation must pay an excise tax annually on its net investment income.[2] For donors desiring privacy, the ability of a public charity to withhold the identity of their donors from public disclosure also may be desirable; private foundations, in contrast, must disclose the identity of their contributors on their annual returns and may not redact their names from copies made available for public disclosure.[3]

Perhaps most importantly, however, public charities are not subject to the *operational constraints* imposed by the excise taxes imposed by the private foundation rules. A private foundation cannot buy or sell property, nor enter into financial transactions (called *self-dealing*) with its directors or trustees, officers, contributors, or their family members, under most circumstances regardless of whether the compensation paid is reasonable or the transaction is otherwise advantageous to the foundation.[4] A private foundation's annual spending for grants to other organizations and charitable projects must meet a minimum distribution requirement.[5] A public charity has no specific spending requirement, other than those imposed by its funders. Holding more than 20 percent of a business enterprise, including interests owned by board members and contributors, is generally prohibited for private foundations, as are jeopardizing investments.[6] No such limitations are placed on public charities under the federal tax laws (other than sponsoring organizations of donor-advised funds, as discussed later). State laws, however, impose requirements regarding the prudent management of charitable funds that must be adhered to, and the management and investment of such funds must be consistent with generally applicable state law fiduciary duties.[7] Lastly, limitations are placed on a private foundation's expenditures, including certain special preapproval and "expenditure responsibility" requirements with respect to

---

1. See § 14.2, 14.4.
2. IRC § 4940; see Chapter 10. The overwhelming majority of public charities do not pay a tax on their net investment income; however, such a tax is imposed on certain colleges and universities (IRC § 4968).
3. See § 12.3(a).
4. IRC § 4941; see Chapter 5.
5. IRC § 4942; see Chapter 6.
6. IRC § 4943-4944; see Chapters 7 and 8.
7. See § 8.2.

certain grants to individuals and grants to foreign and noncharitable organizations, respectively.[8]

A charitable organization that expects to receive its support from a single family or corporation, or a limited number of financial supporters, is unlikely to qualify as a public charity, and therefore will be classified as a private foundation, unless it is structured as a supporting organization.[9] Qualifying a charitable organization as a supporting organization, however, will require the donor to cede a certain amount of meaningful control to the public charities that are supported by the supporting organization, which may make the supporting organization undesirable compared to a private foundation.

The most frequently availed of alternative to a private foundation is the donor-advised fund.[10] A donor-advised fund is not a separate entity, but rather an account at an established public charity (a *sponsoring organization*) over which the donor has advisory privileges. Because the sponsoring organization is a public charity, a sponsoring organization administering donor advised funds is not subject to the various excise taxes (and corresponding operational constraints) previously discussed that are imposed on a private foundation—other than the excess business holdings rules.[11]

In contrast, the most significant disadvantage of a donor-advised fund in comparison to a private foundation is the donor's lack of control over the donated assets. The donor is required to cede full legal ownership of any donated assets to the sponsoring organization but retains the right to make recommendations as to the disposition of those assets, subject to the internal grant policies and procedures established by the sponsoring organization. As a practical matter, donor grant recommendations are always followed if they comply with the sponsoring organization's grant guidelines, and therefore the donor essentially has the same control over grants made from the donor-advised fund as it would over grants made by a private foundation controlled by the donor (although the sponsoring organization may restrict grants to foreign and other types of organizations).

Although sponsoring organizations charge a fee for the administration of a donor-advised fund, the fee is typically less than the tax on net investment income that would have to be paid by a private foundation. Investment gains on the net assets contributed by the donor accrue to the donor's account, and

---

8. IRC § 4945; see Chapter 9.
9. See § 15.6.
10. See Chapter 16.
11. See § 16.7. Additionally, although a donor-advised fund is not subject to the taxable expenditure rules imposed on private foundations (see Chapter 9), distributions from donor-advised funds to natural persons are taxable distributions, as are distributions to organizations (other than public charities) unless the donor-advised fund exercises expenditure responsibility (see § 9.7) with respect to the distribution (see § 16.7).

thereby increase the funds available to make future grants, just as in the case of a private foundation, albeit tax free. Typically, the donor is also given some discretion as to how the assets in their account are invested, again within the investment limitations and guidelines adopted by the sponsoring organization. As with a private foundation, a donor receives an up-front charitable contribution deduction in the tax year in which assets are contributed to a donor-advised fund, but such contributions are not subject to the same limitations as those imposed on contributions to private foundations.[12] The sponsoring organization's gift acceptance guidelines, however, may restrict the types of assets it will accept for donation (such as stock in closely held corporations or land).

Thus, a donor-advised fund may be an attractive alternative to establishing a separate entity where the private foundation's sole activity will be to make grants to other charitable organizations, and the donor is agreeable to ceding legal control over the donated assets, having limited input into investment decisions regarding such assets, and does not need to avail themselves of the advantages that a private foundation offers. A donor-advised fund is a particularly attractive alternative to a private foundation when the assets to be contributed are not significant, are readily marketable, and therefore do not justify the time and expense of creating and maintaining a private foundation.

The administrative costs of creating and maintaining a private foundation include state filing fees for creating the entity, fees for filing an IRS application for recognition of tax-exempt status, and legal, accounting, and employee costs related to the foregoing. There are also legal, accounting, and employee costs related to ongoing compliance with state nonprofit law requirements (conducting an organizational meeting, conducting annual board meetings, preparing meeting minutes and bylaws, prudently managing and monitoring investments, and the like) and federal tax law requirements (principally, maintaining adequate books and records and accounting systems, paying quarterly estimated taxes, filing an annual Form 990-PF return, and complying with specific grant-making requirements).

§ 2.2 ADVANTAGES OF PRIVATE FOUNDATIONS

The bulk of the pages in this book are concerned with the myriad restrictions, limitations, disadvantages, administrative costs, and actual and potential excise taxes that accompany private foundation status. There are, however, certain advantages and benefits to a private foundation, as opposed to making charitable gifts to a public charity or to a donor-advised fund.

---

12. See §§ 14.2, 14.4.

These advantages depend on the specific goals and needs of the foundation's principal funder(s).

Governance and Control. The governing body of a public charity is typically drawn from the public. In certain circumstances, a lack of sufficient independence among a public charity's board members may lead to unwanted scrutiny or loss of an organization's tax-exempt or public charity status. In contrast, it is permitted, and commonplace, for a private foundation's board members to be related by family or business relationships. Many state jurisdictions allow a substantial contributor to a private foundation to be its sole member and appoint and remove directors or trustees of the foundation during their lifetime. A self-perpetuating board composed of family members or corporate employees is also likely to continue to elect family members or corporate employees as board members.

The price for this allowable "control" over a private foundation, of course, is that the tax laws impose greater restrictions on the operations of a private foundation as compared to those of a public charity. As a former IRS Commissioner once observed:

> I recognize that in some cases, founders, major donors and family members may and should hold key governance positions in a private foundation, including as officers, directors and trustees. In fact, this is often a distinguishing characteristic of a private foundation as compared to a public charity.... Congress recognized this difference and the potential for absence of independence in many private foundations. It has, therefore, allowed for greater control by the original donor to a private foundation in exchange for the application of a fairly precise set of restrictions on behavior.[13]

A substantial contributor to a private foundation also may exert a greater degree of control and direction over the foundation's grants than a donor to a donor-advised fund. Although, in practice, donor advice regarding grants from a donor-advised fund is almost always followed, the donor cedes legal control over the donated funds and has no say in the overall grant-making policies of the organization that sponsors the donor-advised fund. Thus, the donor is bound by these policies, which may restrict a donor's ability to recommend grants to certain organizations, such as foreign organizations and supporting organizations, or that support certain controversial causes that may be important to the donor. A private foundation, in contrast, can adopt its own grant-making policies (provided they comply with any restrictions imposed by the tax law).[14]

---

13. Prepared Remarks of Commissioner of Internal Revenue Douglas H. Shulman at the Council on Foundations 2010 Annual Conference (Apr. 24, 2010).
14. See Chapter 9.

§ 2.2 ADVANTAGES OF PRIVATE FOUNDATIONS

A donor is also limited in their ability to control how the assets in their donor advised fund accounts are invested. And although the tax law places limitations on a private foundation's ability to own a business enterprise,[15] some ownership is allowed, which may be appealing to a donor wishing to keep some control over, or continuing relationship with, a particular business enterprise.

Intergenerational Benefits. Private foundations provide a platform for the training of the next generation of leaders, both in a family and a corporate context, and from both a business and philanthropic perspective. Board service educates family members on the responsibilities of wealth and the benefits of philanthropy; it educates corporate employees on the importance of the role of charitable giving as a component of overall corporate citizenship. As a small business itself, a private foundation provides a proving ground for the next generation of business leaders, who may serve as officers or employees of the foundation. A private foundation may pay a reasonable salary to family members or company employees who work for the foundation, provided they are qualified, and their services are necessary for carrying out the foundation's charitable purposes.[16]

Estate Planning. A private foundation can be created during a donor's lifetime to provide a destination for a significant portion of the assets in the donor's estate. Because an estate enjoys an unlimited deduction for the amount of all bequests, legacies, devises, or transfers to charitable organizations,[17] substantial (if not all) estate tax liability can be eliminated by establishing a private foundation to receive estate assets. And a significant degree of control over those assets can be maintained by the decedent's family members, notwithstanding the various restrictions on the use and deployment of such assets by the federal tax law.

Branding and Reputation. A private foundation can bear the name of its family or company founder, thereby helping to preserve a family legacy for generations to come or helping to enhance a company's reputation as an organization committed to being a responsible and philanthropic corporate citizen. A donor-advised fund can bear the name of its donor as well, but as an account within a larger charitable organization, a donor-advised fund is not as easily promoted as a stand-alone charitable arm of the donor.

Although in most cases the board of a private foundation will be controlled by the family or employees of the donor, the public perception of independence of charitable goals from family or corporate goals may be enhanced by creating a separate private foundation to further charitable aims. Credibility

---

15. See Chapter 7.
16. See § 5.6.
17. IRC § 2055(a)(2).

STARTING, FUNDING, AND GOVERNING A PRIVATE FOUNDATION

in this regard may be enhanced further if the foundation has a clearly defined mission that is narrowly tailored to achieve a specific charitable purpose that must be adhered to notwithstanding the current whims of family members or corporate management. (However, a private foundation's separate philanthropic brand can be aligned to a significant degree with the donor's philanthropic mission and vision.)

Because a private foundation must meet a payout requirement year after year, creating a private foundation with a meaningful endowment also evidences a long-term commitment to philanthropy by the donor.

Facilitating Consistent Giving. A private foundation allows a company or family to maintain consistent levels of annual charitable giving regardless of fluctuations in a company's financial performance or a family's income in a particular year. In high-income years, large donations may be made to the private foundation, and in low-income years, small (or no) donations may be made, but the foundation can give consistently in lean years by drawing on the donations made in lush years. (A donor-advised fund likewise facilitates consistent annual giving.)

Centralized and Separate Giving. A private foundation allows a donor to centralize their charitable giving. A donor obviously may make additional charitable gifts outside of a private foundation, but a foundation offers the donor a way to deflect charitable requests from the donor personally. The foundation thereby provides the donor with a level of insulation when such requests are made (by referring grant requests to the donor's foundation) and, perhaps more importantly, when they are rejected. A private foundation with a clearly defined mission also allows for more unified giving to specific causes and purposes. A private foundation provides a vehicle for adding formality and focus to corporate and family giving.

International Grantmaking. In general, a charitable contribution deduction is not allowed for contributions or gifts to or for the use of an organization that is not "created or organized in the United States."[18] A contribution to a domestic foundation, however, is eligible for a charitable contribution deduction,[19] and the recipient private foundation may make grants to foreign organizations for charitable purposes.[20] Similarly, the recipient foundation may make grants to noncharitable organizations for which a charitable contribution deduction is not allowed (such as trade associations and social welfare organizations) for charitable purposes.[21]

---

18. IRC § 170(c)(2)(A).
19. See Chapter 14.
20. See § 9.6.
21. A private foundation must, however, exercise expenditure responsibility over such grants (see § 9.7).

Tax-Favorable Endowment Growth. Private foundations are subject to a low tax rate on their investment and capital gain income.[22] Thus, once funds are contributed to a foundation, they can grow in a tax-favorable manner, subject to the annual payout rules[23] and the net investment income excise tax.

§ 2.3 CHOICE OF ORGANIZATIONAL FORM

For the most part, the federal tax law does not mandate a specific organizational form for entities to qualify for tax-exempt status. There is no required form for private foundations. The federal law provision describing the exemption criteria for charitable organizations[24] refers to organizations that constitute a "corporation, community chest, fund, or foundation." Except for the word *corporation*, however, these terms do not connote organizational forms. Thus, in determining the organizational form for a private foundation, the statutory law is of no utility, inasmuch as it refers only to *foundation* (or fund).

Generally, the form choices for nonprofit organizations, including private foundations, in relation to tax exemption are nonprofit corporation, trust (lifetime or testamentary), unincorporated association, and limited liability company.[25] Whatever the form, the organization is usually created by means of a set of *articles of organization*.[26]

An unincorporated association usually is a membership entity, the articles of organization of which are termed a *constitution*. This form is not suitable for private foundations, nor as a general matter is the limited liability company. Thus, nearly all private foundations are constituted as trusts or nonprofit corporations.

Traditionally, private foundations have been created as trusts, particularly where their founders are individuals. A trust established during a founder's (grantor's) lifetime is known as an *inter vivos trust*; one created by means of an individual's will is a *testamentary trust*. For a testamentary trust, a section of the creator's will constitutes the articles of organization. With a lifetime trust, the articles of organization will be in the form of a *declaration of trust* (where the grantor establishes the trust in a document stating the fact of the trust) or a *trust agreement* (where the grantor contracts with a person, such as a financial institution, to be the trustee of the trust). Some choose to create a trust because their governance provisions often cannot be changed without judicial approval.

---

22. See Chapter 10.
23. See Chapter 6.
24. That is, organizations described in IRC § 501(c)(3) and exempt from federal income taxation by reason of IRC § 501(a).
25. Rev. Proc. 82-2, 1982-1 C.B. 367.
26. Reg. § 1.501(c)(3)-1(b)(2).

While the trust form is still used today, it is more common—and outside the estate context, generally preferable—to establish a private foundation as a nonprofit corporation. The principal reason for this is the limitation on personal liability, for directors (trustees) and officers, that the corporate form affords under state law. Unlike a trust, the nonprofit corporation's *articles of incorporation* commonly can be changed by existing directors. This type of entity almost always has a set of operational rules, usually termed its *bylaws*, which can also be changed by existing directors.

There are other considerations in this regard as well, being matters of state law. Some states have less regulatory oversight over charitable trusts than nonprofit corporations. Thus, for example, the trust organizing document may not have to be filed with the state and/or the state may not have annual reporting requirements. Therefore, a state's regulatory environment may offer greater privacy, perhaps anonymity, to those who operate a private foundation in trust form. State law may permit one trustee of a trust, where three directors of a corporation may be required. All of these factors, of course, should be assessed and weighed when selecting the form of a private foundation in a particular state.

In some instances, such as where the foundation is established as a testamentary trust, the trustee or trustees are given the discretionary authority by the grantor (decedent) to, after the grantor's death, convert the trust to the corporate form.

§ 2.4 FUNDING A FOUNDATION

Most private foundations are initially funded by contributions from the individuals or for-profit companies that create them. As discussed, private foundations are *private* in nature because they are funded from one source—usually an individual, family, or corporation. Some private foundations receive subsequent and ongoing annual contributions from the original donor, and other persons or entities related to the donor, following the founding gift. A significant, and in many cases, the sole, source of support for private foundations is income derived from the investment of contributed funds. Less commonly, a public charity ceases to conduct fundraising activities or fails to qualify as a supporting organization, and consequently becomes a private foundation.

A private foundation created by one or more individuals may be established during their lifetimes or by means of their estates. That is, a private foundation can be created entirely by one or more lifetime gifts, or it can be created wholly in testamentary form. A private foundation may be funded by an individual during their lifetime by means of a planned gift of a partial

§ 2.4 FUNDING A FOUNDATION

interest in property rather than an outright gift; a planned gift may also be made on a testamentary basis.[27]

Some foundations are established as a blend of these approaches: the foundation is initially created and funded by an individual during their lifetime, and additional assets are subsequently contributed to the foundation from the individual's estate. Family members and other persons or entities related to the creator of a foundation may also provide additional funding, again either during their lifetimes and/or by means of their estates.

There are no limitations in the law as to the amount that can be contributed to a private foundation or the number of persons who may donate to a foundation.[28] However, the amount of contributions made to private foundations that an individual may deduct for federal income tax purposes as a charitable contribution in a single tax year is more limited, as compared to those made to a public charity.[29] In the case of a corporation, the total charitable contribution deductions for any tax year (other than certain conservation contributions) may not exceed 10 percent of the corporation's taxable income, regardless of whether they are made to a private foundation or public charity.[30]

Private foundations may be funded with money or property; this property can include securities, artwork, real estate, and other assets. There are limitations in this regard as to gifts of property, however. For example, a gift of a business enterprise to a private foundation could cause problems in relation to the rules on excess business holdings, although special rules extend the time that a private foundation has to dispose of contributed excess holdings.[31] As another illustration, a gift of property with indebtedness could be an act of self-dealing or generate unrelated business income.[32]

As another example, assume a married couple wants to leave 1,000 acres of farmland to a private foundation on their death and wishes to stipulate that the property cannot be developed or broken up into small parcels. Several issues must be considered in making such a gift. The excess business holdings rules[33] effectively prohibit the foundation from operating the farm as a business itself, although it can convert the land to passive investment property by renting the land to someone else to farm or could establish programs to

---

27. See § 2.6.
28. If an organization receives a sufficiently broad base of economic support from a variety of donors, it may qualify as a publicly supported charity rather than a private foundation. See § 15.4.
29. See § 14.2, 14.4.
30. IRC § 170(b)(2).
31. See § 7.2(d).
32. See Chapters 5 and 11.
33. See Chapter 7.

devote the property to agricultural research or another charitable purpose. As investment property, the full fair market value of the farmland would be includible in the foundation's asset base for calculating its annual mandatory charitable distribution requirement. If rental income, less associated expenses, is minimal, and the foundation has few other income-producing assets, the foundation may have insufficient funds to satisfy its mandatory annual payout requirement and therefore find itself subject to excise taxes.[34]

One of the primary benefits of the federal tax rules concerning charitable giving is that a donor generally may deduct the full fair market value of a gift of property in the tax year in which the gift is made. Thus, the value of any appreciation in the property (the amount exceeding the donor's tax basis), which would be taxed if the property were sold, is not subject to the capital gains tax if the property is instead donated. Gifts of appreciated property to a private foundation, however, generally are deductible only to the extent of the donor's basis in the property. As with a gift to a public charity, a donor is not subject to capital gains tax on the amount of appreciation in property donated to a private foundation. Unlike a gift to a public charity, however, the amount of the donor's charitable contribution deduction generally is reduced by the amount of such appreciation. This limitation on the deductibility of gifts of appreciated property to a private foundation applies to most types of appreciated property—such as land, collectibles, partnership interests, or closely held company stock.[35]

There is an important exception to this limitation on the deductibility of gifts of appreciated property to a private foundation, which is that gifts of most publicly traded securities to a private foundation are deductible at their full fair market value. This exception applies only to donations of long-term capital gain stock and is not available for donations of publicly traded stock to the extent they exceed 10 percent in value of all the stock of the corporation (taking into account all prior contributions of such stock by the donor or any member of their family).[36]

§ 2.5 ESTATE PLANNING PRINCIPLES

Private foundations are often created out of decedents' estates. One mechanism to accomplish this is the establishment, by will, of a testamentary trust. This trust survives not only the decedent but also the estate of the decedent. (As noted earlier, often the trustee or trustees are given the authority to convert

---

34. See Chapter 6.
35. See § 14.4.
36. See § 14.5. Other limitations on charitable contribution deductions to private foundations are discussed in more detail in Chapter 14.

§ 2.5 ESTATE PLANNING PRINCIPLES

the trust to a nonprofit corporation.) Another approach is to create a nonprofit corporation to receive the money and/or property to be transferred to the foundation as a bequest.

(a) Decedents' Estates

The assets bequeathed and/or devised by a decedent for a charitable foundation remain in the estate until transferred at the appropriate time from the estate to the foundation. Until this transfer occurs, the assets are those of the estate, not the foundation. This can have certain advantages, such as exclusion of the assets from the asset base used to compute the annual minimum payout amount,[37] protection from certain self-dealing excise taxes,[38] and avoidance of the net investment income excise tax that applies to the assets of private foundations.[39]

An estate can be a disqualified person with respect to a private foundation.[40] This means, for example, there is a potential for an act of self-dealing between the two entities.[41] For instance, the purchase of assets of an estate, directly or indirectly, by a private foundation may be self-dealing.[42]

(b) Estate and Gift Tax Considerations

Estate planning, by necessity, takes into account the federal estate tax[43] and the federal gift tax.[44] The gift tax may be imposed on transfers of money or property during the donor's lifetime, while the estate tax is levied on transfers at death.[45] These taxes are separate from the federal income tax.

Unlike the federal income tax charitable giving rules,[46] there is no limitation with respect to estate tax deductibility as to the amount that can pass to a charitable organization from a decedent's estate. Thus, if desired, the entirety of an estate may be transferred to a private foundation (or other charitable

---

37. Reg. § 53.4942(a)-2(c)(2)(ii). If the period of administration of an estate is unduly prolonged, however, the estate may be considered terminated for federal income tax purposes (Reg. § 1.641(b)-3(a)), in which instance assets of the estate destined for the private foundation will be deemed then held by the foundation (Reg. § 53.4942(a)-2(c)(2)(ii)). In general, see § 6.2(c).
38. See § 5.12.
39. See Chapter 10.
40. See § 4.6.
41. See Chapter 5.
42. Reg. § 53.4941(d)-1(b)(3); Rockefeller v. United States, 572 F. Supp. 9 (E.D. Ark. 1982), aff'd, 718 F.2d 290 (8th Cir. 1983).
43. IRC § 2001.
44. IRC § 2501.
45. In general, see *Charitable Giving* §§ 6.2-6.4.
46. See Chapter 14.

STARTING, FUNDING, AND GOVERNING A PRIVATE FOUNDATION

organization), with a full deduction for the value of the assets devoted to charity.[47] Often, however, the decedent's estate entails a range of specific bequests, as well as assets for a foundation.

§ 2.6 FOUNDATIONS AND PLANNED GIVING

A planned gift is generally the most sophisticated type of contribution made to a charitable organization. It is often made with property that has appreciated in value rather than with money. For the most part, private foundations can be the recipients of planned gifts.

There are two basic types of planned gifts. One type is a gift made during the donor's lifetime using a trust or other agreement. The other type is a gift made by means of a will; the gift comes out of a decedent's estate, as a bequest or devise.

(a) Introduction to Planned Giving

Planned giving,[48] usually perceived as the most complex among categories of charitable giving, rests on a very simple precept: conceptually, an item of property has within it an *income interest* and a *remainder interest*.

The income interest in an item of property is a function of the income generated by the property. The remainder interest within an item of property is the projected value of the property, or the property produced by reinvestments, at a future date. The value of these interests is measured by the value of the property, the age of the donor(s), the amount and frequency of payment of the income interest, and the period of time that the income interest will exist. The actual computation is made by means of actuarial tables, usually those promulgated by the Department of the Treasury.

Most charitable gifts of the planned gift variety are made by use of a *split-interest trust*. This is the mechanism by which the two interests are conceptually separated. These gifts usually involve gifts of remainder interests and frequently utilize the vehicle of the *charitable remainder trust*. This is certainly the case with private foundations, inasmuch as a remainder interest given by means of pooled income funds is not available to private foundations.[49] Private foundations may be the recipients of *charitable gift annuities*, however.[50]

---

47. IRC § 2055(a).
48. See, in general, *Charitable Giving*, Part Three.
49. The law as to pooled income funds requires, *inter alia*, that a qualified fund be maintained at all times by certain categories of public charities (IRC § 642(c)(5)(A)). See, in general, *Charitable Giving*, Chapter 11.
50. See, in general, *Charitable Giving*, Chapter 12.

§ 2.6 FOUNDATIONS AND PLANNED GIVING

(b) Charitable Remainder Trusts

It is common for a private foundation to be initially funded by means of a charitable remainder trust, which is a form of split-interest trust. Likewise, it is often the case that an existing private foundation is made the beneficiary of a charitable remainder trust. In either instance, the remainder trust is established as a separate legal entity and, by means of the trust, a remainder interest in the property transferred is created for the ultimate benefit of the private foundation.[51]

A charitable remainder trust basically is just that: The entity is a trust that is a vehicle by means of which a charitable remainder interest destined for charity is created.[52] Each charitable remainder trust is arranged specifically for the particular circumstances of the donor(s), with the remainder interest in the gift property designated for one or more charitable organizations.

A charitable remainder trust must provide for a specified distribution of income, at least annually, to or for the use of one or more beneficiaries (at least one of which is not a charity). The flow of income must be for life or for a term of no more than 20 years, with an irrevocable remainder interest to be held for the benefit of the charitable organization or paid over to it. Again, usually noncharitable (often individual) beneficiaries are the holders of the income interest and the charitable organization has the remainder interest.

How the income interests in a charitable remainder trust are ascertained depends on whether the trust is a *charitable remainder annuity trust* (where income payments are a fixed amount, an annuity) or a *charitable remainder unitrust* (where income payments are an amount equal to a percentage of the annually determined fair market value of the assets in the trust).

All categories of charitable organization—public charities and private foundations—are eligible to be remainder beneficiaries of charitable remainder trusts.

Conventionally, once the income interest expires, the assets in a charitable remainder trust are distributed to the charitable organization that is the remainder beneficiary. If the assets, or a portion of them, are retained in the trust, the trust will be classified as a private foundation, unless it can become qualified as a public charity.

One common pattern in this regard is a charitable remainder trust created during the lifetime of a married couple. A private foundation is established and nominally funded. This foundation is made the remainder interest

---

51. The assets in a charitable remainder trust are not part of the asset base of a beneficiary private foundation for mandatory payout purposes (see Chapter 6) while they are in the trust (Reg. § 53.4942(a)-2(c)(2)(i)).
52. IRC § 664. See, in general, *Charitable Giving*, Chapter 10.

beneficiary of the remainder trust. The income interest beneficiaries of the trust are the married individuals, who have the interest jointly; the income interest continues for the benefit of the survivor of the two. On the death of the second to die, the assets in the trust are transferred to the private foundation. This approach can also be affected by means of a charitable remainder trust created by will of a married individual. The income interest is established for the benefit of the surviving spouse; at their death, the trust assets are transferred to the private foundation.

Another common approach is to utilize a charitable remainder trust in conjunction with a funded, operational private foundation. One or more individuals can establish a remainder trust at any time, for the purpose of creating a remainder interest in the trust for the foundation. Again, the trust may be established during the lifetime of the donor(s) or by means of a will.

For purposes of many of the private foundation rules, a charitable remainder trust is treated as a private foundation.[53]

(c) Other Planned Giving Vehicles

Most forms of planned giving have a common element: The donor transfers to a charitable organization the remainder interest in a property, and one or more noncharitable beneficiaries retain the income interest. A reverse sequence may occur, however—and that is the essence of the *charitable lead trust*. These trusts are frequently utilized in conjunction with private foundations.

The property transferred to a charitable lead trust is apportioned into an income interest and a remainder interest. The income interest in the property is created for the benefit of a private foundation or other charitable organization, either for a term of years or for the life of an individual (or the lives of more than one individual).[54] The remainder interest in the property is reserved to return, at the expiration of the income interest (the end of the *lead period*), to the donor or some other noncharitable beneficiary or beneficiaries; often the property passes from one generation (the donor's) to another.

The charitable lead trust can be used to accelerate into one year a series of charitable contributions that would otherwise be made annually. There may be, then, a single-year deduction for the "bunched" amount of charitable gifts.

Another form of planned giving is the *charitable gift annuity*. A form of fundraising popular with some public charities, it is infrequently used by private foundations. The annuity is based on an agreement between the donor and

---

53. IRC § 4947(a)(2). See § 3.7.
54. The assets in a charitable lead trust are not part of the asset base of a beneficiary private foundation for mandatory payout purposes (see Chapter 6) while they are in the trust (Reg. § 53.4942(a)-2(c)(2)(iii)). See, in general, *Charitable Giving*, Chapter 14.

§ 2.6 FOUNDATIONS AND PLANNED GIVING

donee; there is no use of a split-interest trust. The donor agrees to make a gift and the donee agrees, in return, to provide the donor (and/or someone else) with an annuity.

With one payment, the donor is engaging in two transactions: the purchase of an annuity and the making of a charitable gift. The sum in excess of the amount necessary to fund the annuity is the charitable gift portion; the gift gives rise to a charitable contribution deduction. Because of this duality in the transaction, the charitable gift annuity transfer constitutes a *bargain sale*.

Gifts of life insurance (whole life) may be made to charitable organizations, including private foundations. If the life insurance policy is fully paid up, the donor will receive a charitable contribution deduction for the cash surrender value or the replacement value of the policy. If premiums are still being paid, the donor receives a charitable deduction for the premium payments made during the tax year. For the deduction to be available, however, the donee charitable organization must be both the beneficiary and the owner of the insurance policy.

There is some uncertainty as to whether a gift of a life insurance policy to a charitable organization is valid (and thus enforceable and deductible), because of the necessity of *insurable interest*—the owner and beneficiary of the policy must be more economically advantaged with the insured alive rather than dead. In many instances, a charitable organization is advantaged by having a donor of a life insurance policy alive: they may be a key volunteer (such as a trustee or officer) or a potential donor of other, larger gifts.

(d) Interrelationships with Private Foundation Rules

Any contemplated planned gift to a private foundation should, before it is consummated, be evaluated in the context of the federal tax rules uniquely applicable to foundations. For example, the gift should not be made if it would entail an act of self-dealing.[55] Revenue from income-producing property, and untaxed appreciation if sold, will likely be subject to the excise tax on net investment income.[56]

There are limitations on the extent of business holdings that can be held at any point in time by a private foundation.[57] These rules are pertinent where the planned gift involves a transfer of stock or other type of business holding to a private foundation, because this may cause the foundation to have taxable excess business holdings. There is a special rule by which excess business holdings acquired by a private foundation by gift may be retained by a

---

55. See Chapter 5.
56. See Chapter 10.
57. See Chapter 7.

foundation for a five-year period before the excess holdings rules take effect.[58] In addition, the IRS has the authority to allow an additional five-year period for the disposition of excess business holdings in the case of an unusually large gift, a bequest of diverse business holdings, or holdings with complex corporate structures, under certain circumstances.[59]

A planned gift may cause a private foundation to have a jeopardizing investment.[60] Although the tax on jeopardizing investments does not apply to investments originally made by another person who later transfers them as gifts to a private foundation,[61] subsequent investment practices by the foundation involving transferred assets may create a jeopardizing investment. For example, the IRS ruled that the contribution of a whole-life insurance policy to a private foundation eventuated in a jeopardizing investment, because instead of surrendering the policy for its cash value, the foundation continued to pay the policy premiums and interest on a policy loan to the point that the amount it was paying was greater than the insurance proceeds it would derive upon the death of the insured.[62]

§ 2.7 ACQUIRING RECOGNITION OF TAX-EXEMPT STATUS

A private foundation is a tax-exempt organization, by reason of being a charitable entity. As is the case for nearly all exempt charitable organizations, private foundations are required to seek recognition of exempt status from the IRS.[63] By contrast, as a general rule, an organization desiring exempt status pursuant to any other provision of federal tax law may (but is not required to) secure recognition of that exemption from the IRS.

The IRS does not grant tax-exempt status to an organization. Whether a nonprofit organization is entitled to tax exemption, on an initial or continuing basis, is a matter of law. Thus, it is Congress that, by statute, defines the categories of organizations that are eligible for federal income tax exemption,[64] and it is Congress that determines whether a category of tax exemption should be continued.[65] Congress, then, defines the types of entities eligible for exempt status, while the function of the IRS is to *recognize* exempt status where appropriate. Consequently, when a private foundation or other organization makes

---

58. IRC § 4943(c)(6). See § 7.2(d).
59. IRC § 4943(c)(7). See § 7.2(d).
60. See Chapter 8.
61. Reg. § 53.4944-1(a)(2)(ii).
62. Rev. Rul. 80-133, 1980-1 C.B. 258.
63. IRC § 508(a).
64. E.g., HCSC-Laundry v. United States, 450 U.S. 1 (1981).
65. E.g., Maryland Savings-Share Insurance Corp. v. United States, 400 U.S. 4 (1970).

§ 2.7 ACQUIRING RECOGNITION OF TAX-EXEMPT STATUS

application to the IRS for a ruling or determination as to exempt status, it is requesting the IRS to recognize that exemption, which (if the organization is correct) has already been granted by the federal tax laws.

If a tax-exempt private foundation, that is a U.S. business entity classified as a corporation, changes its form or place of organization, it is not required to file a new application for recognition of exemption as long as it continues to carry out the same purposes.[66]

(a) Form 1023

An organization seeking recognition of exemption as a charitable organization, including a private foundation, generally is required to file an application with the IRS for recognition of exemption. For private foundations, this application is on either Form 1023-EZ or Form 1023.[67] These forms must be submitted to the IRS electronically online at www.pay.gov,[68] along with the required user fee.[69]

The Form 1023-EZ is a streamlined version of the Form 1023 application for recognition for tax-exempt status. While private foundation applicants are not precluded from using this form, the form is not of much utility to most private foundations as it is available only to organizations with limited annual gross receipts and assets.[70] Specifically, to be eligible to file Form 1023-EZ, a private foundation must have projected annual gross receipts of $50,000 or less in the current tax year and the next two years, annual gross receipts of $50,000 or less in each of the past three years for which it was in existence, and total assets the fair market value of which does not exceed $250,000.[71] Most other categories of charitable organizations are not eligible to use it at all, such as private operating foundations, foreign charitable organizations, supporting organizations, sponsoring organizations, schools, and hospitals.[72]

---

66. Rev. Proc. 2018-15, 2018-9 I.R.B. 379.
67. Rev. Proc. 2023-5, 2023-1 I.R.B. 265 §§ 4.02, 6.03. In general, *Tax-Exempt Organizations*, Chapter 26.
68. Rev. Proc. 2023-5, 2023-1 I.R.B. 265 §§ 4.02, 15.02.
69. Currently, $275 for Form 1023-EZ and $600 for Form 1023 (Rev. Proc. 2023-5, 2023-1 I.R.B. 265 at App. A (Schedule of User Fees)).
70. A donor contemplating creating a private foundation with the limited amount of revenues and total assets required to file Form 1023-EZ would likely be better served by creating a donor-advised fund account at a sponsoring organization, thereby avoiding the administrative and compliance costs of establishing and maintaining a private foundation as well as avoiding the net investment income tax and mandatory distribution requirements imposed on private foundations (but not donor-advised funds). See § 2.1 and Chapter 16.
71. Rev. Proc. 2023-5, 2023-1 I.R.B. 265 § 6.05(1). For purposes of this eligibility requirement, a good faith estimate of the fair market value of the organization's assets is sufficient (*id.*).
72. *Id.* § 6.05(2).

Another potential limitation of Form 1023-EZ for a private foundation is that, unlike Form 1023, it does not include a mechanism for a foundation to obtain advance approval from the IRS for its individual grant procedures.[73] A private foundation that intends to make grants to individuals for travel, study, or similar purposes[74] may submit with its Form 1023 a completed Schedule H (*Organizations Providing Scholarships, Fellowships, Educational Loans, or Other Educational Grants to Individuals and Private Foundations Requesting Advance Approval of Individual Grant Procedures*) to seek advance approval of its individual grant procedures. A private foundation submitting Form 1023-EZ that is also requesting advance approval of individual grant procedures, however, must submit separately a completed Form 8940 requesting such approval, along with an additional user fee.[75]

In general, every charitable organization is presumed to be a private foundation unless it is able to rebut the presumption. The rebuttal process entails the filing of the requisite notice with the IRS,[76] which is accomplished by filing Form 1023. The form does not require the filing organization to demonstrate how it qualifies as a public charity;[77] rather, it simply asks the applicant to check a box declaring whether it is either a private foundation or a public charity of one type or another.[78] Information to allow the IRS to monitor ongoing qualification for public charity status is submitted on Schedule A of Form 990. A charitable organization that expects to receive its support from a single family or corporation or a limited number of financial supporters will be unable to rebut the presumption and therefore, will be classified as a private foundation.[79]

A private foundation that engages directly in the active conduct of charitable or other exempt activities, as opposed to carrying out these activities indirectly by providing grants to individuals or other organizations, and wants to be classified as a private operating foundation, may request that it be so classified as part of the Form 1023 application.[80] The foundation must describe how it meets the requirements for private operating foundation status,[81] including

---

73. See § 9.3(e), (f).
74. See § 9.3(d).
75. Instructions for Form 1023-EZ; see § 9.3(f). Currently, this separate user fee is $2,500 (Rev. Proc. 2023-5, 2023-1 I.R.B. 265 § 4.02(6)(c) and App. A (Schedule of User Fees)). Thus, it is more cost effective for a private foundation that knows it needs to obtain advance approval of its individual grant procedures to file Form 1023 rather than Form 1023-EZ.
76. IRC § 508(a), (b).
77. See Chapter 15.
78. Form 1023, Part VII, line 1.
79. See § 1.2.
80. Form 1023, Part VII, line 1c.
81. See § 3.1.

§ 2.7 ACQUIRING RECOGNITION OF TAX-EXEMPT STATUS

how it meets the income test and either the assets test, the endowment test, or the support test (or, if the foundation has been in existence for less than one year, how it is likely to satisfy these requirements for private operating foundation status).[82]

Unlike other charitable organizations, a private foundation's exempt status is conditioned on its governing instrument including certain provisions that prohibit violation of the private foundation rules.[83] The effects of these provisions must be to require the foundation to make sufficient qualifying distributions each year,[84] and to prohibit the foundation from engaging in any act of self-dealing,[85] from retaining any excess business holdings,[86] from making any jeopardizing investments,[87] and from making any taxable expenditures.[88] Following the Tax Reform Act of 1969, the majority of states enacted legislation that imposes these requirements on private foundations automatically, and private foundations formed in these states generally are deemed to satisfy these requirements even if they do not in fact appear in a foundation's organizational documents.[89] Accordingly, Form 1023 requires a private foundation to confirm that its organizing document includes these provisions or that it relies on state law to meet this organizational requirement.[90]

To receive a favorable determination letter recognizing the organization as tax-exempt, a private foundation's application for recognition of exemption must be complete.[91] A completed Form 1023 application is one that (1) is

---

82. Form 1023, Part VII, line 1d. A private operating foundation could conceivably operate a facility for low-income, elderly, or handicapped persons, which would require it also to submit a completed Schedule F (Low Income Housing) with its Form 1023. The questions on this schedule embody the legal requirements applicable to charities providing this type of housing (Rev. Rul. 79-18, 1979-1 C.B. 152 and Rev. Rul. 81-61, 1981-1 C.B. 355 (elderly); Rev. Rul. 70-585, 1970-2 C.B. 115; Housing Pioneers, Inc. v. Commissioner, 65 T.C.M. 2191 (1993), *aff'd* (9th Cir. 1995); Rev. Proc. 96-32, 1996-1 C.B. 717 (low-income housing)).
83. IRC § 508(e); see § 1.7.
84. IRC § 4942; see Chapter 6.
85. IRC § 4941(d); see Chapter 5.
86. IRC § 4943; see Chapter 7.
87. IRC § 4944; see Chapter 8.
88. IRC § 4945; see Chapter 9.
89. Reg. § 1.508-3(d); Rev. Rul. 75-38, 1975-1 C.B. 161. Specifically, a private foundation's governing instrument is deemed to conform with the IRC § 508(e) requirements if valid provisions of state law have been enacted that require it to act or refrain from acting so as comply with these requirements, or that treat the required provisions as contained in the foundation's governing instrument, and the foundation has not disclaimed (where permitted) coverage under state law (Reg. § 1.508-3(d)). Appendix B to Form 1023 provides a list of states that have adopted legislation satisfying the requirements of IRC § 508(e) relating to private foundation governing instruments.
90. Form 1023, Part VII, line 1a.
91. Rev. Proc. 2023-5, 2023-1 I.R.B. 265 § 6.03.

signed by an authorized individual under penalties of perjury, (2) includes the organization's employer identification number, (3) includes the financial information requested by Form 1023 and its instructions, (4) includes a detailed narrative statement of proposed activities, including each fundraising activity, and a narrative description of anticipated receipts and contemplated expenditures, (5) includes a copy of the organizing or enabling document (with evidence, in the case of a corporation, that it was filed with, and approved by, an appropriate state official), (6) includes a copy of the organization's bylaws or similar governing rules (if any), and (7) is accompanied by the correct user fee.[92]

A private foundation that has submitted a completed application can check the IRS's current processing times for applications on the IRS's website.[93]

(b) 27-Month Rule

A private foundation that desires recognition as a tax-exempt charitable organization as of the date of its formation is required to notify the IRS that it is applying for recognition of tax exemption on that basis within 27 months from the end of the month in which it was organized.[94] Thus, where the IRS recognizes the tax exemption of a private foundation that files within this prescribed time, the exemption is effective retroactively, as of the date the organization was created. Otherwise, the recognition of tax exemption as a charitable organization by the IRS will be effective only on a prospective basis from the IRS receipt date (assuming a favorable determination).[95]

An organization is considered *organized* on the date it becomes a charitable entity (its date of formation).[96] In determining the date on which a corporation is organized for purposes of this exemption recognition process, the IRS looks to the date the entity came into existence under the law of the state in which it was incorporated, which usually is the date its articles of incorporation were filed in the appropriate state office.[97] This date is not the date the organizational meeting was held, bylaws were adopted, or actual operations began.[98] The IRS

---

92. *Id.* § 6.06(1).
93. https://www.irs.gov/charities-non-profits/charitable-organizations/wheres-my-application-for-tax-exempt-status.
94. IRC § 508(a). The statute does not fix the time for giving this notice, but rather leaves it to the IRS's discretion to set through regulations. Reg. § 1.508-1(a)(2)(i) states this rule in terms of a 15-month filing period. The IRS provided an automatic 12-month extension of time for this filing (Reg. § 301.9100-2(a)(2)(iv)), thereby converting it to a 27-month period.
95. Rev. Proc. 2023-5, 2023-1 I.R.B. 265 § 6.08(1), (2); e.g., Priv. Ltr. Rul. 8518067.
96. Reg. § 1.508-1(a)(2)(iii).
97. Rev. Rul. 75-290, 1975-2 C.B. 215.
98. *Id.*

§ 2.7 ACQUIRING RECOGNITION OF TAX-EXEMPT STATUS

considers the date of formation of an unincorporated association to be the date that its organizing document was adopted by the signatures of at least two individuals; of a trust (other than a trust formed by a will), the date the trust was funded (or the date that noncharitable interests expired if the trust agreement provides for any noncharitable interests); and of a trust formed by a will, the date of death or the date any noncharitable interests expired.[99]

If the IRS requires an applicant organization to make a non-substantive amendment to a governing instrument, that action is not taken into account for purposes of the 27-month rule.[100] Non-substantive amendments include correction of a clerical error in the instrument or the addition of a dissolution clause where the activities of the organization prior to the determination letter are consistent with the requirements for exemption.[101] Where a substantive amendment is made to the governing instrument, recognition of exemption is effective as of the date specified in the determination letter.[102]

The IRS has general discretionary authority, upon a showing of good cause, to grant a reasonable extension of a time fixed by the tax regulations for making an election or application for relief with respect to the federal income tax law.[103] This discretionary authority may be exercised where the time for making the election or application is not expressly prescribed by statute, and it is shown to the satisfaction of the IRS that the taxpayer acted reasonably and in good faith and that granting the extension will not jeopardize the interests of the federal government.[104] The IRS acknowledged that it may exercise this discretionary authority to extend the time for satisfaction of the 27-month notice requirement.[105]

Regulations delineate the information and representations that must be furnished when requesting an extension of the 27-month notice requirement and some factors that will be taken into consideration in determining whether an extension of this nature will be granted.[106] The factors to be considered include the organization filed Form 1023 before the IRS discovered its failure to file; the organization failed to file because of intervening events beyond its control; the organization exercised reasonable diligence, but was not aware of the filing requirements (with the complexity of the organization's filing and

---

99. Instructions for Form 1023 (Jan. 2020) at 7.
100. Rev. Proc. 2023-5, 2023-1 I.R.B. 265 § 6.08(5)(b).
101. Id.
102. Id. § 6.08(5)(a).
103. Reg. § 301.9100-1(c).
104. Reg. § 301.9100-3(a).
105. Rev. Proc. 2023-5, 2023-1 I.R.B. 265 § 6.08(3). Also Rev. Proc. 84-47, 1984-1 C.B. 545 § 4; Rev. Rul. 80-259, 1980-2 C.B. 192. As noted, the notice period is not fixed by statute, but rather by regulation (see *supra* note 94).
106. Reg. § 301.9100-3(a).

its experience in these matters taken into consideration); the organization reasonably relied on written advice from the IRS; and the organization reasonably relied on the advice of a qualified tax professional who failed to file or advise it to file Form 1023.[107]

A request for this extension is built into the Form 1023 application for recognition of exemption.[108] An organization requesting an extension must submit a completed Schedule E (*Effective Date*), which affords the organization an opportunity to explain why it did not file within 27 months of formation, how it acted reasonably and in good faith, and how granting an earlier effective date will not prejudice the interests of the government. To demonstrate that the organization acted reasonably and in good faith, it is suggested that a filing organization requesting relief include an explanation of the events that led to the failure to timely file and to the discovery of the failure, and a description of any reliance on the advice of a qualified tax professional (including details concerning the engagement and responsibilities of the professional as well as the extent to which the organization relied on the professional). To demonstrate that the interests of the government will not be prejudiced if the extension is granted, it is suggested that the filing organization provide an explanation of the effect the grant of an extension to file would have on its aggregate tax liability.

An organization's eligibility to receive deductible charitable contributions is also governed by the 27-month rule. Thus, where a private foundation or other charitable organization timely files the application for recognition of tax exemption, and the determination letter or ruling ultimately is favorable, the ability to receive deductible charitable gifts is effective as of the date the organization was formed.

There are statutory exceptions to the 27-month rule, but they are of no general applicability to private foundations.[109]

(c) IRS Determination Letters Recognizing Exempt Status

The IRS annually promulgates rules by which a determination letter may be issued to a private foundation, or other organization, in response to the filing

---

107. Reg. § 301.9100-3(b); Instructions for Form 1023 (Jan. 2020) at 22.
108. Form 1023, Part VIII.
109. Churches, their integrated auxiliaries, interchurch organizations, local units of a church, and conventions or associations of churches are not required to file for recognition of tax exemption (IRC § 508(c)(1), (2)). In addition, this notice requirement is inapplicable to organizations the gross receipts of which in each tax year are normally not more than $5,000 (IRC § 508(c)(1)); however, this exception is not available to private foundations. Another exception is for organizations covered by a group exemption (see *Tax-Exempt Organizations* § 26.11); however, private foundations are not permitted to be included in these groups.

§ 2.7 ACQUIRING RECOGNITION OF TAX-EXEMPT STATUS

of an application for recognition of tax-exempt status.[110] A *determination letter* is a written statement issued by the IRS's Exempt Organizations Determination function or Independent Office of Appeals in response to an application for recognition of exemption or other determination, including private foundation/public charity status, under the jurisdiction of the Director, EO Rulings and Agreements.[111]

A determination letter recognizing exempt status will be issued by the IRS to an organization, where its application and supporting documents establish that it meets the requirements of the category of exemption that it claimed as provided in the Internal Revenue Code and other related law.[112]

Exempt status for a newly created organization will be recognized by the IRS in advance of operations where the entity's proposed activities are described in sufficient detail to permit a conclusion that the organization will clearly meet the pertinent statutory requirements. A mere restatement of purposes or a statement that proposed activities will be in furtherance of the organization's purposes does not satisfy this requirement. An applicant organization has the burden of proof in this regard; thus, it must fully describe the activities in which it expects to engage, including the standards, criteria, procedures, or other means adopted or planned for carrying out the activities, the anticipated sources of receipts, and the nature of contemplated expenditures.[113] The IRS, generally supported by the courts, usually will refuse to recognize an organization's tax-exempt status unless the entity tenders sufficient information regarding its operations and finances.[114] An organization is considered to have made the required "threshold showing," however, where it describes its activities in sufficient detail to permit a conclusion that the entity intends to engage primarily in exempt activities, particularly where it answered all of the questions propounded by the IRS.[115]

One court concluded that an organization failed to meet its burden of proof as to its eligibility for tax exemption because it did not provide a "meaningful explanation" of its activities to the IRS.[116] Another organization suffered the

---

110. Currently, Rev. Proc. 2023-5, 2023-1 I.R.B. 265. Determination letters and rulings issued in response to requests initiated by a private foundation based on subsequent changes in its activities (rather than in response to an application for initial recognition of exempt status and private foundation status) are the subject of § 12.5.
111. Rev. Proc. 2023-5, 2023-1 I.R.B. 265 § 1.01(5).
112. *Id.* § 6.07(1).
113. *Id.* § 6.07(2)(a).
114. E.g., The Basic Unit Ministry of Alma Karl Schurig v. United States, 511 F. Supp. 166 (D.D.C. 1981).
115. E.g., The Church of the Visible Intelligence That Governs the Universe v. United States, 83-2 U.S.T.C. ¶ 9726 (Ct. Cl. 1983).
116. Public Industries, Inc. v. Commissioner, 61 T.C.M. 1626, 1629 (1991).

same fate inasmuch as it offered only "vague generalizations" of its ostensibly planned activities.[117] By contrast, the court, in another instance, observed that although the law "requires that the organization establish reasonable standards and criteria for its operation as an exempt organization," the standard does not necessitate "some sort of metaphysical proof of future events."[118]

When the representatives of a would-be tax-exempt organization fail to submit its books and records to the IRS, an inference arises that the facts, if disclosed, would not support the organization's claim that it meets the requirements for exemption.[119] A court concluded that an organization's failure to respond "completely or candidly" to many of the inquiries of the IRS precluded it from receiving a determination as to its tax-exempt status.[120]

Where the organization cannot demonstrate, to the satisfaction of the IRS, that its proposed activities will qualify it for tax exemption, the IRS generally will issue a proposed adverse determination letter.[121]

A determination letter recognizing tax exemption ordinarily will not be issued if an issue involving the organization's exempt status is pending in litigation or is under consideration within the IRS.[122] The same outcome arises where the application is based on alternative plans of proposed transactions or on hypothetical situations.[123]

An application for recognition of tax exemption may be withdrawn, on the written request of an authorized representative of the organization, at any time prior to the issuance of an initial adverse determination letter or ruling. Where an application is withdrawn, it and all supporting documents are retained by the IRS.[124] The IRS may consider the information submitted in connection with the withdrawn request in a subsequent examination of the organization, or in connection with a subsequent application submitted by the organization.[125]

---

117. Pius XII Academy, Inc. v. Commissioner, 43 T.C.M. 634, 636 (1982).
118. American Science Foundation v. Commissioner, 52 T.C.M. 1049, 1051 (1986).
119. E.g., New Concordia Bible Church v. Commissioner, 49 T.C.M. 176 (1984) (*app. dis.*, 9th Cir. (1985)). Also, Chief Steward of the Ecumenical Temples and the Worldwide Peace Movement and His Successors v. Commissioner, 49 T.C.M. 640 (1985); Basic Bible Church of America, Auxiliary Chapter 11004 v. Commissioner, 46 T.C.M. 223 (1983).
120. National Association of American Churches v. Commissioner, 82 T.C. 18, 32 (1984). Also, United Libertarian Fellowship, Inc. v. Commissioner, 65 T.C.M. 2178 (1993); Church of Nature in Man v. Commissioner, 49 T.C.M. 1393 (1985); LaVerdad v. Commissioner, 82 T.C. 215 (1984).
121. Rev. Proc. 2023-5, 2023-1 I.R.B. 265 § 6.07(2)(a)(iii).
122. *Id.* § 3.02(2).
123. *Id.* § 3.02(6).
124. *Id.* § 8.01(1).
125. *Id.* § 8.01(2).

§ 2.7 ACQUIRING RECOGNITION OF TAX-EXEMPT STATUS

A private foundation that has been issued an IRS determination letter recognizing it as a tax-exempt charitable organization will be listed in the IRS's *Tax Exempt Organization Search* database,[126] and in the IRS's *Exempt Organizations Business Master File Extract* (EO BMF) database,[127] as eligible to receive tax-deductible contributions. Copies of favorable determination letters issued in 2014 and later are available on *Tax Exempt Organization Search*.[128]

A private foundation ordinarily may rely on a favorable IRS determination letter as to its tax-exempt status unless there is a material change in facts, it was based on any omission or inaccurate material information submitted by the foundation, or there is a change in law.[129] For a determination letter on tax-exempt status, a *material change in facts* includes a change in the character, the purpose, or the method of operation of the organization that is inconsistent with the organization's tax-exempt status.[130] Inaccurate *material information* includes an incorrect representation or attestation as to the foundation's organizational documents, its exempt purpose, its conduct of prohibited and restricted activities, or its eligibility to file Form 1023-EZ.[131] A *change in law* includes the enactment of legislation, a decision of the Supreme Court of the United States, the issuance of temporary or final regulations, and the issuance of a revenue ruling, revenue procedure, or other statement published in the Internal Revenue Bulletin.[132]

Determination letters may be reviewed by IRS EO Determinations Quality Assurance to assure uniform application of the statutes, tax treaties, regulations, court opinions, or guidance published in the Internal Revenue Bulletin.[133] If such a post-determination review concludes, based on the information contained in the existing application file, that an IRS determination letter was issued in error, the matter will be referred to EO Examinations for consideration.[134]

(d) Administrative Procedures Where Recognition Denied

The filing of an application for recognition of tax-exempt status with the IRS may lead to denial of the requested recognition, resulting in an adverse

---

126. https://www.irs.gov/charities-non-profits/tax-exempt-organization-search.
127. https://www.irs.gov/charities-non-profits/exempt-organizations-business-master-file-extract-eo-bmf.
128. Rev. Proc. 2023-5, 2023-1 I.R.B. 265 § 13.02(1).
129. *Id.* § 11.01. Outside of the context of making charitable grants to other organizations (see § 9.4(b)), a private foundation generally may not rely on, use, or cite as precedent a determination letter issued to another taxpayer (IRC § 6110(k)(3); Rev. Proc. 2023-5, 2023-1 I.R.B. 265 § 11.02(1)).
130. *Id.* § 11.02(2).
131. *Id.* § 11.02(3).
132. *Id.* § 12.01.
133. *Id.* § 11.03(1).
134. *Id.* § 11.03(2); see § 12.6.

determination letter. Under IRS procedures,[135] a private foundation is given an opportunity to appeal (protest) the following types of proposed adverse determinations: (1) the initial qualification of the organization as a tax-exempt entity,[136] (2) the initial qualification of the organization as a charitable entity,[137] (3) the classification or reclassification of the organization as a public charity or a private foundation,[138] or (4) the classification of the organization as a private operating foundation.[139]

If the IRS concludes that the organization does not satisfy the requirements for a favorable determination letter and the letter is one of the four types for which an opportunity for appeal (protest) is available, the IRS will issue a proposed adverse determination letter. This letter will include a detailed discussion of the basis for the IRS's conclusion and advise the organization of its opportunity to appeal (protest) the decision and request a conference with the IRS Independent Office of Appeals.[140]

To appeal (protest) a proposed adverse determination letter, the organization must submit a statement of the facts, law, and arguments in support of its position (that is, a protest) within 30 days from the date of the proposed adverse determination letter. The organization must also state whether it wishes a conference with the Independent Office of Appeals.[141] If an organization does not timely submit a protest, a final adverse determination letter will

---

135. Rev. Proc. 2023-5, 2023-1 I.R.B. 265 § 9.02.
136. That is, an organization exempt from tax by reason of IRC § 501(a).
137. That is, an organization described in IRC § 170(c)(2).
138. See Chapter 15.
139. See § 3.1. IRS procedures previously provided that an organization could not administratively appeal an adverse determination letter that was issued based on technical advice. The IRS changed these procedures in 2014 to allow organizations to appeal an adverse determination based on technical advice if it falls within one of these four types of determinations. As part of the Protecting Americans from Tax Hikes Act of 2015 (Pub. L. No. 114-113, div. Q, tit. IV, § 404, 129 Stat. 2242, 3118), Congress enacted IRC § 7123(c) to effectively codify this change by requiring the IRS to provide procedures under which an organization may request an administrative appeal of these four types of adverse determinations (Staff of Joint Comm. on Tax'n, 114th Cong., General Explanation of Tax Legislation Enacted in 2015 324-325 (Comm. Print 2016)).
140. Rev. Proc. 2023-5, 2023-1 I.R.B. 265 § 9.03. If EO Determinations concludes that an organization does not meet the requirements for a favorable determination on an issue that is not one of the four types for which an opportunity for appeal (protest) is available, for example, advance approval of a private foundation's individual grant procedures (see § 9.3(f)) or that a grant is an unusual grant (see § 15.5(c)), the IRS generally will advise the organization of its adverse position (Rev. Proc. 2023-5, 2023-1 I.R.B. 265 § 9.11). The IRS will afford the organization the opportunity to submit additional information or withdraw the request before issuing an adverse determination letter, which will include a detailed discussion of the basis for the IRS's conclusion. The organization is precluded from appealing (protesting) this type of adverse determination letter (*id.*).
141. *Id.* § 9.04.

§ 2.7 ACQUIRING RECOGNITION OF TAX-EXEMPT STATUS

be issued to the organization. This letter will provide information about the disclosure of the proposed and final adverse letters.[142]

If an organization timely submits a protest of a proposed adverse determination letter, EO Determinations will review the protest. If it determines that the organization meets the requirements for approval of its request, it will issue a favorable determination letter. If, however, EO Determinations maintains its adverse position after reviewing the protest, it will forward the case file to the Independent Office of Appeals.[143]

If new information is raised in the protest or during consideration by the Independent Office of Appeals, the matter may be returned to EO Determinations for further consideration. As a result of its review of the new information, EO Determinations may issue a favorable determination letter, rebuttal letter, or new proposed adverse determination letter. If a rebuttal letter is issued, EO Determinations will forward the case to the Independent Office of Appeals. If a new proposed adverse determination letter is issued, the organization must submit a protest of the new proposed adverse determination letter to have the Independent Office of Appeals consider the issue.[144]

The Independent Office of Appeals will consider the organization's protest submitted in response to a proposed adverse determination letter. If the Independent Office of Appeals agrees with the proposed adverse determination, it will issue a final adverse determination or, if a conference was requested, contact the organization to schedule the conference. At the end of the conference process, which may entail submission of additional information, the Independent Office of Appeals will generally issue a final adverse determination letter or a favorable determination letter. If the Independent Office of Appeals believes that a tax exemption or public charity issue is not covered by published precedent or that there is nonuniformity, the Independent Office of Appeals must request technical advice from the Office of Associate Chief Counsel (Employee Benefits, Exempt Organizations, and Employment Taxes).[145]

An organization may withdraw its appeal (protest) before the IRS issues a final adverse determination letter. On receipt of a withdrawal request, the IRS will complete processing of the case in the same manner as if an appeal (protest) had not been received. An organization that withdraws an appeal (protest) is not considered to have exhausted its administrative remedies for declaratory judgment purposes.[146]

---

142. *Id.* §§ 9.05, 13.04.
143. *Id.* § 9.06.
144. *Id.* § 9.08.
145. *Id.* § 9.07. As to the matter of technical advice, see Rev. Proc. 2023-2, 2023-1 I.R.B. 120.
146. Rev. Proc. 2023-5, 2023-1 I.R.B. 265 § 9.09. The declaratory judgment procedure rules are the subject of § 2.7(e).

STARTING, FUNDING, AND GOVERNING A PRIVATE FOUNDATION

The opportunity to appeal a proposed adverse determination letter and the conference rights are inapplicable to matters where delay would be "prejudicial to the interests" of the IRS, such as in cases involving fraud, jeopardy, or imminence of expiration of the statute of limitations, or where immediate action is necessary to protect the interests of the federal government.[147]

(e) Declaratory Judgment Procedures Where Recognition Denied

A denial of recognition of tax-exempt status may be appealed by the organization, once all administrative remedies are exhausted, to the courts in a declaratory judgment action.[148] Jurisdiction over these cases is vested in the U.S. District Court for the District of Columbia, the U.S. Court of Federal Claims, and the U.S. Tax Court.[149]

Of specific relevance to private foundations, these rules create a remedy in a case of actual controversy involving a determination by the IRS with respect to the initial qualification or continuing qualification of an entity as (1) a charitable organization for tax exemption purposes[150] and/or charitable contribution deduction purposes,[151] (2) a public charity,[152] or (3) a private operating foundation.[153] The remedy is available in the case of a failure by the IRS to make a determination as respects one or more of these issues.[154] The remedy is pursued in one of the three previously noted courts, which is authorized to "make a declaration" with respect to these issues.[155]

---

147. Rev. Proc. 2023-5, 2023-1 I.R.B. 265 § 9.10.
148. IRC § 7428; see generally *Tax-Exempt Organizations* § 27.5(b).
149. IRC § 7428(a); Rev. Proc. 2023-5, 2023-1 I.R.B. 265 § 10.01. The U.S. Tax Court is the only one of these courts where this type of a declaratory judgment case can be pursued without the services of a lawyer; these *pro se* cases will be dismissed for that reason in the other two courts (e.g., Point of Wisdom No. 1 v. United States, 77 A.F.T.R. 2d 986 (D.D.C. 1996)). Jury trials are not available in these types of cases (The Synanon Church v. United States, 83-1 U.S.T.C. ¶ 9230 (D.D.C. 1983)).
150. That is, an organization described in IRC § 501(c)(3) and exempt from federal income taxation by reason of IRC § 501(a). Reasoning that the question as to whether a trust is a charitable trust within the meaning of IRC § 4947(a)(1) (see § 3.6) is "inextricably related" to the issue of whether it is qualified under IRC § 501(c)(3), the Tax Court held that it has declaratory judgment jurisdiction to decide the IRC § 4947(a)(1) issue (Allen Eiry Trust v. Commissioner, 77 T.C. 1263 (1981)).
151. IRC § 170(c)(2).
152. IRC § 509(a). See Chapter 15.
153. IRC § 7428(a)(1). As to private operating foundations, see § 3.1.
154. IRC § 7428(a)(2). Thus, the rulings and determination letters in cases subject to the declaratory judgment procedure of IRC § 7428 are those issued pursuant to the procedures currently stated in Rev. Proc. 2023-5, 2023-1 I.R.B. 265. The withdrawal of an application for recognition of tax exemption is not a failure to make a determination under IRC § 7428(a)(2) (*id*. § 10.04(2)).
155. IRC § 7428(a)(1).

§ 2.7 ACQUIRING RECOGNITION OF TAX-EXEMPT STATUS

A *determination* within the meaning of these rules is a final decision by the IRS, by means of a determination letter, which holds that the organization is not tax-exempt, is a public charity under a status other than the one requested, is not a private operating foundation, or is a private foundation.[156] The term does not encompass an IRS ruling passing on an organization's proposed transactions, in that this type of ruling does not constitute a denial or revocation of an organization's tax-exempt status, nor does it jeopardize the deductibility of contributions to it; thus, absent a final determination, a declaratory judgment is premature.[157] In the course of issuance of a favorable determination letter recognizing an organization's tax-exempt status, the IRS not infrequently conditions its ruling on the organization's agreement to not engage in a particular activity. A court held that this type of favorable final ruling does not constitute the requisite adverse determination.[158]

Prior to utilizing the declaratory judgment procedure, an organization must have exhausted all administrative remedies available to it within the IRS.[159] Under a *270-day rule*, for the first 270 days after a request for a determination is made, an organization is deemed to not have exhausted its administrative remedies, assuming a determination has not been made during that period.[160] After this 270-day period has elapsed, the organization may initiate an action for a declaratory judgment.[161] An action may also be initiated if the IRS makes an adverse determination during this jurisdictional period. In either event, all actions under these rules must be initiated within 90 days after the date on which the final determination by the IRS is made.[162]

---

156. Rev. Proc. 2023-5, 2023-1 I.R.B. 265 § 10.02.
157. *Id.* § 10.03. New Community Senior Citizen Hous. Corp. v. Commissioner, 72 T.C. 372 (1979).
158. AHW Corp. v. Commissioner, 79 T.C. 390 (1982).
159. In The Sense of Self Soc'y v. United States, 79-2 U.S.T.C. ¶ 9673 (D.D.C. 1979), the court ruled that the organization failed to exhaust its administrative remedies because it did not respond to the IRS's "repeated" requests for information. Cf. Change-All Souls Hous. Corp. v. United States, 671 F.2d 463 (Ct. Cl. 1982). The refusal by an organization to turn records over to the IRS, during the pendency of a contest of an IRS summons, however, cannot be considered a failure to exhaust administrative remedies that could result in a loss of declaratory judgment rights (Church of World Peace, Inc. v. Internal Revenue Service, 715 F.2d 492 (10th Cir. 1983)).
160. IRC § 7428(b)(2). Rev. Proc. 2023-5, 2023-1 I.R.B. 265 § 10.06(2).
161. The 270-day period will not be considered to have started prior to the date a completed application is submitted to the IRS (*id.*). If the IRS requests additional information from an organization, the period beginning on the date the IRS requests additional information until the date the information is submitted to the IRS will not be counted for purposes of the 270-day period (*id.*).
162. IRC § 7428(b)(3). E.g., Metropolitan Community Serv., Inc. v. Commissioner, 53 T.C.M. 810 (1987).

Exhaustion of administrative remedies means taking, in a timely manner, all reasonable steps to secure a determination from the IRS, including (1) the filing of a completed application for recognition of exemption[163] or a request for a determination of public charity or private foundation status;[164] (2) in appropriate circumstances, requesting relief with respect to an extension of time for making an election or application for relief from tax;[165] (3) the timely submission of all additional information requested by the IRS necessary to perfect an application for recognition of exemption or request for determination of public charity or private foundation status; and (4) exhaustion of all appeals within the IRS.[166]

According to the IRS, an organization cannot be deemed to have exhausted its administrative remedies prior to the earlier of (1) the completion of the foregoing steps and the issuance by the IRS of a final determination letter by certified or registered mail, or (2) the expiration of the 270-day period in a case where the IRS has not issued a final determination letter and the organization has taken, in a timely manner, all reasonable steps to secure a determination letter.[167]

Further, the IRS stated that the foregoing steps "will not be considered completed until the Service has had a reasonable time to act on an appeal."[168] (As noted, nonetheless, once the statutory 270 days have elapsed, the action can be initiated, without regard to the pace of the IRS in relation to these steps.)

The U.S. Tax Court adopted procedural rules for these types of declaratory judgment actions.[169] The single most significant feature of these rules is the decision of the court to generally confine its role to a review of the denial by the IRS of a request for a determination of tax exemption based solely on the facts contained in the administrative record, that is, not to conduct a trial *de novo* at which new evidence may be adduced.[170] Thus, in one case, the court refused to

---

163. See § 2.7(a).
164. See § 12.5(a).
165. Reg. § 301.9100-1.
166. Rev. Proc. 2023-5, 2023-1 I.R.B. 265 § 10.05.
167. *Id.* § 10.06.
168. *Id.* § 10.07. The U.S. District Court for the District of Columbia held that it lacks subject matter jurisdiction in these cases until the IRS makes an adverse determination or the 270-day period (commenced by the filing of a substantially completed application for recognition of exemption) has elapsed (New York County Health Servs. Review Org., Inc. v. Commissioner, 80-1 U.S.T.C. ¶ 9398 (D.D.C. 1980)).
169. Rules of Practice and Procedure, U.S. Tax Court, Title XXI.
170. *Id.*, Rule 217(a). In rare instances, the U.S. Tax Court has allowed supplementation of the administrative record in a denial-of-exemption case (e.g., First Libertarian Church v. Commissioner, 74 T.C. 396 (1980)). The U.S. District Court for the District of Columbia appears more willing to review facts beyond the administrative record (e.g., Freedom Church of Revelation v. United States, 588 F. Supp. 693 (D.D.C. 1984); Incorporated

§ 2.7 ACQUIRING RECOGNITION OF TAX-EXEMPT STATUS

permit information orally furnished to IRS representatives during a conference at the administrative level to be introduced in evidence during the pendency of the case before it.[171] Likewise, it was held that the administrative record may consist only of material submitted by either the applicant organization or the IRS, so that materials submitted by third parties are inadmissible.[172]

The U.S. District Court for the District of Columbia and the U.S. Court of Federal Claims generally follow the Tax Court's approach to processing these declaratory judgment cases.

An organization's fate before a court may well depend on the quality of the contents of the administrative record. The applicant organization generally controls what comprises the administrative record. Even when the record includes responses to IRS inquiries, it is the organization that decides the phraseology of the answers and what, if anything, to attach as exhibits. It is, therefore, important that the administrative record be carefully constructed, particularly in instances where there is a reasonable likelihood that an initial determination case will be unsuccessful at the IRS level and thus ripen into a declaratory judgment case.

(f) Recognition of Foreign Organizations

A charitable organization located anywhere in the world can seek recognition of its tax-exempt status from the IRS. Foreign private foundations with investments in U.S. companies must pay a 4 percent excise tax on the dividends, interest, rents, and royalties earned on its investments.[173] The tax is withheld by the investment company.[174] The rate of withholding on a nonexempt foreign charity is, however, made at the normal rate for taxpaying entities, which is 30 percent.[175] A foreign charity that can satisfy one of the tests for qualification as a public charity[176] may seek recognition of that status if it plans to seek funding from U.S. private foundations. Expenditure responsibility agreements are not required for gifts to a foreign charity with an IRS determination of its public charity status.[177]

Trustees of the Gospel Worker Soc'y v. United States, 510 F. Supp. 374 (D.D.C. 1981), aff'd, 672 F.2d 894 (D.C. Cir. 1981), cert. den., 456 U.S. 944 (1982)). This approach does not apply where the exemption has been revoked (see § 12.7(d)).
171. Houston Lawyer Referral Serv., Inc. v. Commissioner, 69 T.C. 570 (1978). Also Church in Boston v. Commissioner, 71 T.C. 102 (1979).
172. Church of Spiritual Technology v. United States, 90-1 U.S.T.C. ¶ 50,097 (Ct. Cl. 1989).
173. See § 10.6.
174. IRC § 1443(b).
175. Gen. Couns. Mem. 38840 (unless a tax treaty provides an exemption).
176. See Chapter 15.
177. See §§ 9.4(b), 9.6.

STARTING, FUNDING, AND GOVERNING A PRIVATE FOUNDATION

The United States–Canadian income tax treaty provides for reciprocal recognition of exemption for religious, scientific, literary, educational, or charitable organizations. The diplomatic notes signed in 1980 when the treaty was approved directed the "Competent Authorities" to review the other country's procedures and requirements for recognition of exemption and to avoid requiring filings that duplicate effort. The agreement provided that the United States would study the Canadian rules for determining qualification to see if they are compatible with U.S. rules. Almost 20 years later, the IRS announced it had entered into a mutual agreement for reciprocal recognition of exempt status.[178]

Accordingly, every Canadian charity that has received a Notification of Registration from the Canada Revenue Agency, and whose revocation has not been revoked, is now automatically recognized in the United States as a charitable organization without filing Form 1023. Unfortunately, all Canadian organizations are presumed to be private foundations unless the organization submits a request to the IRS that it be listed as a charitable organization (in the IRS's *Tax Exempt Organization Search* database for organizations eligible to receive tax-deductible charitable contributions)[179] or be classified as a public charity. This request is submitted using Form 8940 (along with a completed Schedule K thereto).[180]

(g) Exemption for State Purposes

Many states allow exemption from some or all of their income, franchise, licensing fees, property, sales, or other taxes to religious, charitable, and educational organizations and various other nonprofit organizations. The process for obtaining such exemptions varies with each state and locality. Each newly created private foundation should obtain current information and forms directly from the appropriate state or local authorities in conjunction with seeking recognition of federal tax exemption.

Under Texas state law, by way of example, a private foundation that has an IRS determination letter recognizing it as a charitable organization[181] exempt

---

178. IRS Notice 99-47, 1999-36 I.R.B. 344.
179. https://www.irs.gov/charities-non-profits/tax-exempt-organization-search.
180. Form 8940 must be submitted electronically at www.pay.gov; no user fee is required for this type of request (Rev. Proc. 2023-5, 2023-1 I.R.B. 265 §§ 4.02(6), 7.02, and App. A (Schedule of User Fees), as modified by Rev. Proc. 2023-12, 2023-17 I.R.B. 768 §§ 3.01, 3.03, 3.10). The requesting organization must upload a copy of its Canadian Notification of Registration and a completed Form 8833 (Treaty-Based Return Position Disclosure Under Section 6114 or 7701(b)) with its submission (Instructions for Form 8940 (Apr. 2023), Schedule K).
181. That is, an organization described in IRC § 501(c)(3).

from federal income taxes is exempt from state franchise (essentially, income) taxes and from taxes on goods and services purchased for use by the foundation.[182] Thus, a private foundation that has been granted federal tax exemption as a charitable organization will be granted an exemption from Texas sales and franchise tax by operation of state law. To claim its exemption from these state taxes, a private foundation need only file a one-page form with the Texas Comptroller of Public Accounts,[183] and include a copy of its IRS determination letter.

Most other states automatically grant exemptions from income and sales tax when federal exemption has been granted. The exemptions from sales tax, however, typically are limited to purchases by the organization; in most cases, the organization is still required to collect and remit sales tax when it makes sales.

§ 2.8 GOVERNANCE

For reasons that remain unknown, in 2007, the IRS publicly decided to become active in the realm of nonprofit governance. Historically, the matter of regulation of nonprofit organizations has been nearly exclusively the province of state law.

What the IRS did, as a consequence of its sudden plunge into nonprofit governance regulation, is immediately concoct a huge body of agency-mandated requirements. The IRS quickly introduced the equivalent of a massive federal regulation by revamping the annual information return filed by most of the larger tax-exempt organizations (Form 990). The agency exponentially expanded this annual return, in considerable part by adding many questions and other references to various aspects of nonprofit governance. Embedded in this return are references to over 30 types of policies, procedures, practices, and protocols.

These developments sparked the formation of a new industry, with lawyers, accountants, and other types of consultants clambering to prepare these documents and advise their clients as to the meaning and use of them. It is difficult to estimate the expense of money and time associated with compliance with these IRS requirements since 2008.

Federal regulation of nonprofit governance is principally focusing on public charities. The IRS currently is not evaluating private foundations from the

---

182. Texas Tax Code Secs. 151.310(a)(2), 171.063(a)(1). In contrast, organizations that qualify for exemption from state taxes based on their federal exemption are not exempt from hotel occupancy tax because Texas's hotel occupancy tax law does not recognize any federal exemptions (Texas Tax Code Sec. 156.102).
183. Texas Comptroller of Public Accounts, Form AP-204.

standpoint of governance.[184] That stance can change, of course; it may do so in the context of revision and expansion of the content of the annual information return filed by private foundations.[185]

(a) IRS Entry into Nonprofit Governance

The initial federal tax statutory law concerning tax exemption for nonprofit charitable organizations was enacted in 1913. Ninety-four years after this statutory law was created, the IRS decided it had regulatory jurisdiction over the governance of nonprofit, tax-exempt organizations, principally public charities.[186]

This change in policy did not come about by reason of the enactment of a statute, promulgation of a regulation, issuance of a revenue ruling, court order, or the like. There was no directive from Congress of any type to the Treasury Department or the IRS requiring the IRS to leap into the nonprofit governance regulatory fray. To adopt language from the U.S. Supreme Court, there is "not a word" in the legislative history of any statute giving the IRS authority of any nature remotely suggesting it assume responsibility for the regulation of nonprofit organizations' governance.[187]

One of the most dramatic and consequential events in the development of contemporary nonprofit law occurred on April 26, 2007, when the then-Tax Exempt Government Entities (TE/GE) commissioner gave the first of his speeches on the subject of nonprofit governance. On that occasion, he conceded that, for the IRS to propound and enforce good governance principles, the agency would have to go "beyond its traditional spheres of activity." The rationale for this move by the IRS was said to be that a "well-governed organization is more likely to be compliant [with the federal tax law], while poor governance can easily lead an exempt organization into trouble." For example, he spoke of "an engaged, informed, and independent board of directors accountable to the community [that the tax-exempt organization] serves."[188]

---

184. There is no principled basis for this distinction. The IRS's ruling policy is based on the private benefit doctrine (see § 2.8(f)). The private benefit doctrine (see § 5.2) is applicable to both private foundations and public charities.
185. See § 12.1.
186. This is not, however, the IRS's record in this regard. The tax return preparer regulations, that were found by two courts to be outside the range of the IRS's jurisdiction, were promulgated in 2011; the underlying statute was enacted in 1884 (Loving v. Internal Revenue Service, 917 F. Supp. 2d 67 (D.D.C. 2013), aff'd, 742 F.3d 103 (D.C. Cir. 2014); Ridgely v. Lew, 55 F. Supp. 3d 89 (D.D.C. 2014)).
187. Community Television of Southern California v. Gottfried, 459 U.S. 498, 509-510 (1983).
188. There is no basis in law for the general notion that, to be tax-exempt, a charitable organization governing board must be "accountable to the community."

§ 2.8 GOVERNANCE

Later that year, the commissioner stated that "[w]hile a few continue to argue that governance is outside our jurisdiction, most now support an active IRS that is engaged in this area."[189] He added that IRS involvement in this area is "not new"; the agency has been "quietly but steadily promoting good governance for a long time."[190]

(b) Concept of Nonprofit Governance

Many elements converge to encompass the concept of governance of nonprofit organizations, usually public charities.[191] Fundamentally, of course, the governance of nonprofit organizations focuses on the manner in which they are governed (from a structural standpoint), who does the governing, and the duties and responsibilities of those doing the governing. These elements of nonprofit governance are essentially a matter of state law, principally the states' nonprofit corporation statutes.

This structure is normally provided for in an organization's articles of organization.[192] This document, for a nonprofit corporation, will be its articles (or certificate) of incorporation; for a trust, its declaration of trust or trust agreement; for an unincorporated association, its constitution; and for a limited liability company, its operating agreement.

The articles of organization will likely stipulate the nature of the governing board—board of directors or board of trustees (collectively, directors), how the directors are selected, the size of the board (that is, the number of its members), the terms of the directors and whether they can be reelected, any term limits, and the manner of their removal (if necessary) from office. The selection of directors can involve innumerable possibilities and combinations; common models include the self-perpetuating board, boards comprised of members who serve in an ex officio capacity, board members elected by the organization's membership (or comparable constituency), or

---

189. No evidence was provided then or since in support of that observation. About one year after that statement was made, an IRS advisory committee stated that there is "little or no empirical evidence to date that supports the efficacy of any specific governance practices by nonprofit organizations, much less compliance with the requirements for maintaining tax exemption."
190. No evidence has been provided in support of that declaration either. Lawyers practicing in the nonprofit field on a fulltime basis for many years were wholly unaware of this promotional effort. There is no known public instance of IRS involvement in nonprofit governance before 2007.
191. This concept is often expressed in the shorter phrase *nonprofit governance*.
192. Reg. § 1.501(c)(3)-1(b)(2).

combinations of the foregoing. State law usually addresses the matter of board size. Most states require a minimum of three directors. A few states permit one-director boards.

A set of articles of organization should state the purpose of the organization, perhaps including one or more statements as to how that purpose is to be advanced, and contain a provision decreeing how the organization's assets and net income will be distributed in the event of the entity's dissolution or liquidation (known as a *dissolution clause*).

Another governance document is important, particularly in the case of a nonprofit corporation or a nonprofit unincorporated association—an organization's bylaws. This document should spell out the nature of the organization's officer structure (including description of positions), its committees, the holding of meetings (directors' and, if there are members, members'), and a statement limiting the liability of directors and officers. The bylaws may expand on the organization's purposes and programs, although the bylaws ought not be broader than the organization's articles in this regard. The bylaws may have something to say about the qualifications of directors and/or their compensation by the organization.

A nonprofit organization may have several other documents pertaining to its governance, such as a mission statement, a code of ethics, an employees' manual, and a collection of board resolutions. Plus, of increasing importance are board-approved policies. These are separate documents; the IRS has identified over 30 of these policies for nonprofit entities. Of course, not all policies are suitable for all organizations.

The basic policies that a nonprofit organization, particularly a public charity, would be likely to consider are a conflict-of-interest policy, a whistleblower policy, a document retention and destruction policy, an investment policy, and a travel expense and reimbursement policy. Charitable organizations that engage in considerable fundraising might consider a gift acceptance policy. Organizations that accept gifts of conservation easements might have a policy as to that practice. Organizations that engage in joint ventures with for-profit entities may have a policy pertaining to those arrangements. Nonprofit hospitals are required to have various policies, including a community needs assessment policy, a financial assistance policy, and a billing and collections policy.

Nonprofit governance, however, embraces far more than organizational structure and documentation. Also encompassed by that concept is the matter of board duties, responsibilities, and liability. For charitable organizations, this is a wide-ranging matter of fiduciary duties and responsibilities for board members and officers. Today, this is almost completely the realm of state law, both statutory and case law.

(c) Nonprofit Governance Standards

The law has little to say about nonprofit governance standards. The principles of nonprofit governance are largely found in standards promulgated by nonprofit watchdog agencies. These standards, principally applicable to public charities, vary in mission, scope, and content.

In some quarters, the philosophy underlying the concept of governance of nonprofit organizations is changing. The traditional role of the nonprofit board has been high-level oversight of the organization's operations, finances, and policy determinations. Implementation of policy and management has historically been the responsibilities of the officers and key employees.

An emerging view, sometimes patronizingly referred to as best practices, imposes on members of nonprofit boards greater responsibilities and functions (and thus potentially greater liability), intended to immerse the board more deeply in the affairs of management. This new view is nicely reflected in the characterization of the contemporary nonprofit board in the one item of legislation passed by Congress addressing the matter of nonprofit governance, which is the American National Red Cross governance statute: the governance and strategic oversight board.[193]

Charitable organizations, particularly those that engage in fundraising, often become subject to standards set and enforced by one or more watchdog agencies. These agencies, while not promulgators of law, can have a powerful impact on public perception of charitable organizations and their ability to successfully generate gifts and grants.[194]

Standards-setting for nonprofit organizations began in 1971, when the Council of Better Business Bureaus established a division called the Philanthropic Advisory Service (PAS). The PAS monitored and reported on charitable organizations that solicit contributions and grants nationwide. The primary function of the PAS was to promote ethical standards and protect consumers. The PAS standards covered five basic areas of nonprofit operations: public accountability, use of funds, solicitation and other informational materials, fundraising practices, and governance.

The PAS standards have been superseded by the Wise Giving Alliance (WGA) standards. The WGA was formed in 2001, a product of the merger of the National Charities Information Bureau (another early charitable watchdog agency) and the CBBB Foundation. The WGA is affiliated with the CBBB.

---

193. American National Red Cross Governance Modernization Act of 2007, Pub. L. No. 110-26, 110th Cong., 1st Sess. (2007), § 2(a)(5); 36 U.S.C. § 300101.

194. This is because these agencies, in addition to authoring standards, write reports about charitable organizations and rate them. An unfavorable report or rating can severely damage the reputation of a charity, precluding successful fundraising.

Other nonprofit governance standards are administered by entities such as the Evangelical Council for Financial Accountability, the Standards for Excellence Institute, the American Institute of Philanthropy, Charity Navigator, and the Council on Foundations. The U.S. Department of the Treasury issued a package of best practices, in the form of antiterrorist financing guidelines, as has the Committee for Purchase from People Who Are Blind or Severely Disabled.

Perhaps the most extensive of these sets of best practices was published by the Independent Sector in 2007, in the form of its Panel on the Nonprofit Sector's "Principles for Good Governance and Ethical Practice." These principles, somewhat revised in 2015, are organized under the four basic categories of legal compliance and public disclosure, effective governance, strong financial oversight, and responsible fundraising. A case can be made that these principles, while not flawless, are the best of them.

The panel stated that an organization must have a governing body that is "responsible for reviewing and approving the organization's mission and strategic direction, annual budget and key financial transactions, compensation practices, and fiscal and governance policies." The board, it was stated, "bears the primary responsibility for ensuring that a charitable organization fulfills its obligations to the law, its donors, its staff and volunteers, its clients, and the public at large." The board "must protect the assets of the organization and provide oversight to ensure that its financial, human and material resources are used appropriately to further the organization's mission." The board, the panel said, "also sets the vision and mission for the organization and establishes the broad policies and strategic direction that enable the organization to fulfill its charitable purpose."

The board of an organization, the panel stated, "should meet regularly enough to conduct its business and fulfill its duties." Regular board meetings provide the "chief venue for board members to review the organization's financial situation and program activities, establish and monitor compliance with key organizational policies and procedures, and address issues that affect the organization's ability to fulfill its charitable mission." The panel observed: "While many charitable organizations find it prudent to meet at least three times a year to fulfill basic governance and oversight responsibilities, some with strong committee structures, including organizations with widely dispersed board membership, hold only one or two meetings of the full board each year."

The board of an organization, said the panel, "should establish its own size and structure, and review these periodically." The board "should have enough members to allow for full deliberation and diversity of thinking on governance and other organizational matters." Except for small organizations, "this generally means that the board should have at least five members."

Nonetheless, the panel noted that the "ideal size of a board depends on many factors, such as the age of the organization, the nature and geographic scope of its mission and activities, and its funding needs."

The board of an organization should, the panel said, include members with the "diverse background (including, but not limited to, ethnic, racial and gender perspectives), experience, and organizational and financial skills necessary to advance the organization's mission." Boards of charitable organizations "generally strive to include members with expertise in budget and financial management, investments, personnel, fundraising, public relations and marketing, governance, advocacy, and leadership, as well as some members who are knowledgeable about the charitable organization's area of expertise or programs, or who have a special connection to its constituency." Some organizations "seek to maintain a board that respects the culture of and reflects the community served by the organization." An organization should, the panel stated, "make every effort" to ensure that at least one member of the board has "financial literacy."

The panel stated that a "substantial majority of the board of a public charity, usually meaning at least two-thirds of the members, should be independent." "Independent" members are those who are not compensated by the organization, do not have their compensation determined by individuals who are compensated by the organization, do not receive material financial benefits from the organization (except as a member of the charitable class served by the organization), or are not related to or residing with any of the foregoing persons. An individual who is not independent is, in the view of the panel, potentially in violation of the directors' duty of loyalty, which requires the directors to "put the interests of the organization above their personal interests and to make decisions they believe are in the best interest of the nonprofit." The panel declared that it is "important to the long-term success and accountability of the organization that a sizeable majority of the individuals on the board be free of financial conflicts of interest."

The board should, said the panel, "hire, oversee, and annually evaluate the performance of the chief executive officer of the organization, and should conduct such an evaluation prior to any change in that officer's compensation," unless a multiyear contract is in force or the change consists solely of routine adjustments for inflation or the cost of living. The panel stated that "[o]ne of the most important responsibilities of the board . . . is to select, supervise, and determine a compensation package that will attract and retain a qualified chief executive." The organization's governing documents should require the full board to evaluate the executive's performance and approve their compensation.

The board of an organization that has paid staff, the panel stated, "should ensure that the positions of chief staff officer, board chair, and board treasurer are held by separate individuals." Organizations without paid staff should ensure that the positions of board chair and treasurer are held separately. The panel was of the view that "[c]oncentrating authority for the organization's governance and management practices in one or two people removes valuable checks and balances that help ensure that conflicts of interest and other personal concerns do not take precedence over the best interests of the organization."

The board, said the panel, "should establish an effective, systematic process for educating and communicating with board members to ensure that they are aware of their legal and ethical responsibilities, are knowledgeable about the programs and [other] activities of the organization, and can carry out their oversight functions effectively." The panel observed that all board members "should receive oral and written instruction regarding the organization's governing documents, finances, program activities, and governing policies and practices." Encompassed by this principle is the thought that board members should receive agendas and background materials well in advance of board meetings.

Board members, the panel stated, "should evaluate their performance as a group and as individuals no less frequently than every three years, and should have clear procedures for removing board members who are unable to fulfill their responsibilities." The panel noted that a "regular process of evaluating the board's performance can help to identify strengths and weaknesses of its processes and procedures and to provide insights for strengthening orientation and educational programs, the conduct of board and committee meetings, and interactions with board and staff leadership." The board "should establish clear guidelines for the duties and responsibilities of each member, including meeting attendance, preparation[,] and participation; committee assignments; and the kinds of expertise board members are expected to have or develop in order to provide effective governance."

The board, the panel continued, "should establish clear policies and procedures setting the length of terms and the number of consecutive terms a board member may serve." The matter of term limits continues to be controversial. The panel stated the view in favor of term limits as follows: "Some organizations have found that such limits help in bringing fresh energy, ideas and expertise to the board through new members." The contrary view: "Others have concluded that term limits may deprive the organization of valuable experience, continuity and, in some cases, needed support provided by board members."

The board, said the panel, should review the "organizational and governing instruments no less frequently than every five years." This process will "help boards ensure that the organization is abiding by the rules it has set for itself and determine whether changes need to be made to those instruments." The board may elect to delegate some of this deliberation to a committee; if so, the "full board should consider and act upon the committee's recommendations."

§ 2.8 GOVERNANCE

The board, the panel stated, "should establish and review regularly the organization's mission and goals and should evaluate, no less frequently than every five years, the organization's programs, goals and [other] activities to be sure they advance its mission and make prudent use of its resources." Every board should "set strategic goals and review them annually." The panel noted that, "[b]ecause organizations and their purposes differ, it is incumbent on each organization to develop its own process for evaluating effectiveness." At a minimum, "interim benchmarks can be identified to assess whether the work is moving in the right direction."

Board members, the panel said, are "generally expected to serve without compensation, other than reimbursement for expenses incurred to fulfill their board duties." An organization that provides compensation to its board members should use "appropriate comparability data" to determine the amount to be paid, document the decision, and provide full disclosure to anyone, on request, of the amount of and rationale for the compensation. Board members of charitable organizations are responsible for "ascertaining that any compensation they receive does not exceed to a significant degree the compensation provided for positions in comparable organizations with similar responsibilities and qualifications." It is the view of the panel that board members "of public charities often donate both time and funds to the organization, a practice that supports the sector's spirit of giving and volunteering."

In his famous speech in 2007, where he announced the IRS's entry into nonprofit governance regulation, the then-TE/GE commissioner referred to "commonly accepted standards of good governance."[195] They do not exist. As one observer concluded, these watchdog agencies have "proliferated" and each of them has its "own approach and mission."[196]

(d) Early IRS Attempts at Nonprofit Governance Regulation

One of the principal ways the IRS regulates in the realm of nonprofit governance is by means of the annual information return filed by the largest tax-exempt organizations—the Form 990. This document was thoroughly revamped by the IRS, launching the new version beginning with filing year 2008. Primarily, the portion of the revised return pertaining to governance is in its Part VI.[197] This element of the return and its accompanying instructions is the closest counterpart to an IRS set of rules pertaining to nonprofit governance. This part contains questions about governance matters and references

---

195. See § 2.8(a).
196. Wilhelm, "Charity Under Scrutiny," XV *Chron. of Phil.* (No. 4) 22 (Nov. 28, 2002).
197. The importance of this part is reflected in the fondness of IRS officials in referring to it as the "crown jewel" of the Form 990.

to several governance policies. These governance-related questions are not part of the Form 990-PF return required to be filed by private foundations, but this does not preclude an IRS agent from pursuing such questions during an examination of a private foundation.

In early 2007, the IRS tried to advance its own set of nonprofit good governance principles. These principles did not add anything to the existing governance principles, were poorly drafted, and drew considerable ridicule. They were jettisoned in early 2008.

In 2009, the IRS made public a governance check sheet that its examination agents had been using to gather data about the governance practices of public charities, accompanied by a set of instructions.

The IRS, in 2014, made public the materials it had been using for the training of its agents in the field of nonprofit governance, for their edification in reviewing applications for recognition of exemption and annual information returns, and during examinations. For the most part, these materials did not contain anything new in relation to what the IRS had been saying about its positions on governance issues.

In 2012, the IRS made public the results of a study it undertook to prove its assertion that well-governed tax-exempt organizations were more likely to be compliant with the federal tax law. Basically, all this study shows is that exempt organizations that are knowledgeable about the federal tax law are more likely to be in compliance with that body of law. The IRS said that it was planning on future studies of this nature but, to date, the results of any such study have not been made public.

(e) Federal Tax Law as to Board Composition

There are six instances where the federal tax statutory and regulatory law addresses the matter of the composition and/or structure of the governing boards of tax-exempt organizations.

The most detailed of these federal tax rules is a body of statutory law pertaining to the membership of nonprofit boards in circumstances where the organization is seeking to qualify as a tax-exempt credit counseling organization.[198] Statutory law also provides that supporting organizations[199] may not be controlled by one or more disqualified persons[200] (other than its managers and supported organization(s)).[201]

---

198. IRC § 501(q).
199. See § 15.6.
200. See Chapter 4.
201. IRC § 509(a)(3)(C).

§ 2.8 GOVERNANCE

As to federal tax regulatory law concerning nonprofit governance, one way for an organization to qualify as a donative-type, publicly supported charity is to satisfy a facts-and-circumstances test, one of the elements of which is that the organization have a representative governing body (that is, a board that represents the broad interests of the public).[202]

Publicly supported charitable organizations, in computing their public support, are able to exclude unusual grants; one of the requirements for this exclusion is that the organization has a representative governing body.[203] Tax-exempt healthcare institutions must meet a community benefit standard, which includes a requirement that they have governing boards that are representative of their communities.[204] One of the requirements for tax exemption of public interest law firms is that the firm have a governing board that is representative of the public.[205]

(f) IRS's Use of Private Benefit Doctrine

As noted, the IRS's ruling policy is predicated on the private benefit doctrine. In the principal case on point, a nonprofit corporation sought recognition by the IRS of tax exemption and classification as a church.[206] The entity's governing instruments stated that the corporation has two classes of members. The first of these classes were the voting members, which consisted of the members of the entity's board of directors. The second class (of nonvoting members), termed associate members, were individuals who made contributions to the organization. The members of the board of directors consisted of three individuals, all members of the same family. As the trial court stated the matter, this family "thus completely controlled [the organization's] operations and were in a position, as the only voting members, to perpetuate that control."[207]

This organization was not forthcoming in providing factual information as to its eligibility for tax exemption to the IRS, which ultimately ruled that the entity was organized and operated for private benefit, and thus was not exempt. Because of the organization's lack of candor, the court construed most

---

202. Reg. § 1.170A-9(f)(3)(v). See § 15.4(d).
203. Reg. §§ 1.170A-9(f)(6)(iii), 1.509(a)-3(c)(4)(viii). See §§ 15.4(c) and 15.5(a), (c).
204. Rev. Rul. 69-545, 1969-2 C.B. 117.
205. Rev. Proc. 92-59, 1992-2 C.B. 411.
206. Bubbling Well Church of Universal Love, Inc. v. Commissioner, 74 T.C. 531 (1980), aff'd, 670 F.2d 104 (9th Cir. 1981). Despite its age, *Bubbling Well Church* derives much of its potency from the fact that it is the most frequently cited opinion by the IRS in support of its position as to application of the private benefit doctrine in the nonprofit governance context.
207. Bubbling Well Church of Universal Love, Inc. v. Commissioner, 74 T.C. 531, 532 (1980).

STARTING, FUNDING, AND GOVERNING A PRIVATE FOUNDATION

of the facts against it, applying the rule that a failure to disclose gives rise to a logical inference that the facts, if disclosed, would show that the organization did not meet the requirements for exemption. The court held that the entity failed to show that it "was not operated for the private benefit of the . . . family."[208]

The court wrote that this family "was not subject to any outside interference or influence in the control of [its] affairs," so that the family, "without challenge, could dictate [the organization's] program and operation, prepare its budget, and spend its funds, and could continue to do so indefinitely."[209]

The court also stated that, "[w]hile this domination of [the entity] by the three [family members], alone may not necessarily disqualify it for exemption, it provides an obvious opportunity for abuse of the claimed tax-exempt status."[210] The court added: These circumstances call for "open and candid disclosure of all facts bearing upon [the entity's] organization, operations, and finances so that the Court, should it uphold the claimed exemption, can be assured that it is not sanctioning an abuse of the revenue laws."[211]

The trial court held that this organization "has not shown that no part of its net earnings inure[s] to the benefit of [this] family or that [the organization] was not operated for the private benefit of" the family.[212]

A court of appeals essentially reiterated this lower court's findings. The appellate court stated that the organization "failed to show that no part of its net income inured to the benefit of private individuals."[213] The court of appeals added that it "agree[d] with the [lower court] that the potential for abuse created by the [family's] control of the church required open and candid disclosure of facts bearing on the exemption application."[214]

The import of this decision is that domination of a public charity by a family does not necessarily disqualify it from tax exemption. Rather, this type of fact situation calls for a higher level of scrutiny, requiring an organization to be "open and candid" to be certain there is no abuse of the federal tax laws. In its ruling policy zeal, however, the IRS on occasion misconstrues what the courts said in this case. Thus, the IRS wrote that private inurement is "indicated by the fact that the board members consist of the same family and control all aspects of the program."[215] Also, the agency stated that the "undue

---

208. Id. at 539.
209. Id. at 535.
210. Id.
211. Id.
212. Id. at 539.
213. Bubbling Well Church of Universal Love, Inc. v. Commissioner, 670 F.2d 104, 105 (9th Cir. 1981).
214. Id.
215. Priv. Ltr. Rul. 201302040.

control of the organization by a related board causes the organization to serve private interests."[216] Likewise, the IRS wrote that a "small group of individuals . . . have [sic] exclusive control over the management of [an organization's] funds and operations" and "as a result of this exclusive control [the entity's] founders benefit."[217]

(g) IRS's Ruling Policy

Two categories of IRS private letter rulings dominate the agency's policy regarding nonprofit governance. One category of these rulings concludes that the existence of a small board, usually of a public charity, inherently provides a private benefit. The other category of these rulings holds that a board, again usually of a public charity, dominated by related individuals is likewise inherently a manifestation of private benefit. These two notions are frequently combined in a ruling because of the existence of a small board dominated by or perhaps consisting solely of related individuals.

One such ruling held that an organization could not qualify as a tax-exempt charitable entity in part because it had a board of directors consisting of two individuals; unwarranted private benefit was automatically found.[218] Soon thereafter, the IRS began insisting that boards of charitable organizations include members who are "representative of the community"; private benefit was said to be present in the absence of that governance feature.[219] This position quickly evolved into one requiring an independent board[220] having a "majority of directors representing the community."[221] Of course, one-individual boards do not qualify under this policy.[222] On occasion, the IRS restates this policy as requiring "public oversight" of a charity's board.[223] The IRS even finds private benefit in situations where there is no public oversight of a church.[224] In one instance, the IRS, as a condition of exemption, forced an organization to expand its board from one individual to three unrelated individuals.[225]

As to the second category of these rulings, the IRS ruled early on that an organization could not qualify as a tax-exempt charitable entity because

---

216. Priv. Ltr. Rul. 201325017.
217. Priv. Ltr. Rul. 201421022.
218. Priv. Ltr. Rul. 200736037, reissued as Priv. Ltr. Rul. 200737044.
219. E.g., Priv. Ltr. Rul. 200828029.
220. E.g., Priv. Ltr. Rul. 201252021.
221. E.g., Priv. Ltr. Rul. 201436050.
222. E.g., Priv. Ltr. Rul. 201525014.
223. E.g., Priv. Ltr. Rul. 201242014.
224. E.g., Priv. Ltr. Rul. 201325017.
225. Priv. Ltr. Rul. 201541013.

of private benefit, where all the board members were members of the same family.[226] A president of an organization engaged in many forms of private inurement; all this happened, the IRS concluded, because the organization had a "family-based" governing board.[227] A majority of related individuals is seen by the IRS as constituting per se evidence of violation of the private benefit doctrine.[228] Structures where a three-individual board includes two individuals married to each other are deemed by the IRS to entail private benefit, precluding exemption.[229] The IRS ruled that an organization was unduly controlled by members of a family, causing private benefit, where the governing body consisted of the president's "family members or professional friends."[230]

It is the view of the authors that the foregoing rulings are incorrect, as not reflecting the true state of the law. Occasionally, the IRS issues a ruling on the matter of private benefit and governance that is correct. For example, the IRS wrote: "While an organization will not be denied exemption merely because it is controlled by related individuals, such a situation provides an obvious opportunity for abuse and calls for an open and candid disclosure of [the] organization and [its] operations."[231]

If these ruling policies were applied to private foundations, there would be few tax-exempt foundations. There would not be any exempt family foundations.[232]

---

226. E.g., Priv. Ltr. Rul. 200916035.
227. Priv. Ltr. Rul. 201113041.
228. E.g., Priv. Ltr. Rul. 201203025.
229. E.g., Priv. Ltr. Rul. 201801014.
230. Priv. Ltr. Rul. 201209011.
231. Priv. Ltr. Rul. 201332013. This ruling reflects a correct reading of the *Bubbling Well Church* case. See § 2.8(f)).
232. A case can be made that the IRS lacks the authority or jurisdiction to regulate in the field of nonprofit governance, utilizing the analytical construct set forth in City of Arlington, Texas v. Federal Communications Commission, 133 S. Ct. 1863 (2013). A district court opinion strongly suggests that is the law (California Independent System Operator Corp. v. Federal Energy Regulatory Commission, 372 F.3d 395 (D.C. Cir. 2004)). A case on appeal may provide insight as to the scope of the IRS's jurisdiction (Steele v. United States, 260 F. Supp. 3d 52 (D.D.C. 2017)). In general, Hopkins, *Ultra Vires: Why the IRS Lacks the Jurisdiction and Authority to Regulate Nonprofit Governance* (Clark, NJ: Talbot Pub. Co., 2017); Hopkins, "IRS Regulation of Nonprofit Governance: A Critique," 30 *Tax'n of Exempts* (No. 1) 4 (July/Aug. 2018).

CHAPTER THREE

Types of Private Foundations

§ 3.1 **Private Operating Foundations** 87
   (a) Direct Charitable Distributions 88
   (b) Grants 92
   (c) Individual Grant Programs 93
   (d) Income Test 96
   (e) Asset, Endowment, or Support Test 99
      (i) Asset Test 99
      (ii) Endowment Test 102
      (iii) Support Test 103
   (f) Compliance Period 104
   (g) Advantages and Disadvantages of Private Operating Foundations 106
   (h) Conversion to or from Private Operating Foundation Status 107

§ 3.2 **Exempt Operating Foundations** 109
§ 3.3 **Conduit Foundations** 109
§ 3.4 **Common Fund Foundations** 111
§ 3.5 **Research and Experimentation Funds** 112
§ 3.6 **Nonexempt Charitable Trusts** 114
§ 3.7 **Split-Interest Trusts** 116
§ 3.8 **Foreign Private Foundations** 119

The federal tax law definition of the term *private foundation* embraces all charitable entities other than those that are classified as public charities.[1] Most private foundations are nonoperating (essentially, grantmaking) entities; however, there are several other varieties of private foundations. Moreover, certain nonexempt trusts and foreign entities are subject to some or all of the private foundation rules.

§ 3.1 PRIVATE OPERATING FOUNDATIONS

Private operating foundations have long been recognized as nonpublicly supported organizations that devote most of their earnings and much of their assets directly to the conduct of their tax-exempt purposes. This special type

---

1. See § 1.2.

§ 3.1 PRIVATE OPERATING FOUNDATIONS

of foundation is essentially a blend of a private foundation and a public charitable organization. A private operating foundation is a charitable organization that makes qualifying distributions directly for the active conduct of activities constituting the charitable or other exempt purpose or function for which it was organized.[2] A private operating foundation must use its qualifying distributions "itself, rather than by or through one or more grantee organizations which receive such qualifying distributions directly or indirectly from such foundation."[3]

In other words, a private operating foundation makes its required charitable expenditures by sponsoring and managing its own programs rather than making grants to other organizations. For any year in which it qualifies as a private operating foundation, it is excluded from the excise tax on the failure to make qualifying distributions imposed on nonoperating private foundations.[4] Typically, a private operating foundation is an endowed institution operating a museum, a library, or some other charitable pursuit not included in the specific list of organizations that qualify as public charities without regard to their sources of support (generally churches, schools, hospitals, and certain medical research organizations).[5] Many private operating foundations are privately funded entities created by one or more individuals of means with strong ideas about the charitable objectives they want to accomplish through self-initiated projects, such as feeding the poor or preserving a wildlife and wetlands area.

A private operating foundation is subject to an annual distribution requirement that it distribute a calculated amount annually for its own charitable programs. The required distribution amount is measured under a dual system testing its income levels and the character of its assets or sources of its revenues.[6] Of particular significance for some funders, donations made to a private operating foundation are subject to the more generous contribution deduction limitations allowed for gifts made to public charities.[7]

(a) Direct Charitable Distributions

The most significant attribute of a private operating foundation is that the entity has a substantive exempt function, other than grantmaking. To be considered as operating, the foundation must spend a specified annual amount on one or more projects in which it is significantly involved in a continuing

---

2. IRC § 4942(j)(3)(A).
3. Reg. § 53.4942(b)-1(b)(1).
4. IRC § 4942(a)(1), (j)(3).
5. See Chapter 15.
6. See § 3.1(d), (e).
7. See § 3.1(g).

and sustainable fashion. Further, the requisite involvement is, as a general rule, evident where the foundation's expenditures are made directly to vendors, employees, and contractors. A private operating foundation purchases goods and services that advance its purposes rather than providing funding indirectly for such expenses through an intermediary organization. A private operating foundation is in this way unlike a nonoperating private foundation that makes grants to other charitable organizations. It must also make required annual charitable distributions, but it does so in a different manner. The requisite involvement is present where payments to accomplish the private operating foundation's charitable, educational, or similar tax-exempt purpose are made directly and without the assistance of an intervening organization or agency.

A typical private operating foundation maintains a staff of program specialists, researchers, teachers, administrators, or other personnel needed to supervise, direct, and carry out its programs on a continuing basis. The staff can be partly or wholly comprised of volunteers.[8] Depending on the scope and type of the foundation's activities, its funders and (or) its board of trustees can constitute its staff if their work involvement is substantive.

A private operating foundation typically acquires and maintains assets used in its programs, such as buildings, collections of specimens and art objects, or research laboratories. Qualifying direct expenditures also include the purchase of books and publications, supplies, computer programs, and other project supplies, such as food to feed the poor. This type of foundation might pay for travel and equipment used in connection with an archeological study. It might hire an architect to plan and design a historical restoration project, buy and restore buildings, and subsequently maintain the buildings and open them for public viewing. The costs of administering the programs, such as telephone, insurance, professional advisors, occupancy, and other expenses necessary to conduct the programs, are also treated as direct expenses of the foundation's programs.

Expenditures related to administration of the foundation's investment assets are not treated as direct program disbursements. These expenses may include management, custody, or trustee fees, salary and related costs of personnel whose time is partly or wholly devoted to handling investment properties, office space, equipment, supplies, and other facility costs associated with such personnel, real estate operating expenses (rental income properties), professional fees (a geologist and/or a lawyer to evaluate a proposed royalty agreement), market timing service, subscriptions and fees for information services, and any other costs directly connected with maintaining and conserving the foundation's investment assets. Expenses attributable to both

---

8. E.g., Priv. Ltr. Rul. 201821005 (concerning administration of a charitable loan program).

§ 3.1 PRIVATE OPERATING FOUNDATIONS

program and investment-management activities, such as the executive director's salary and office space, must be allocated on a reasonable and consistently applied basis.[9] Payment of the investment excise tax is treated as a direct program expenditure.[10]

Optimally, a private operating foundation is identified in the public eye with and by its projects. Classic examples of suitable organizational focus include operating a museum, conducting scientific research, and promoting historical restoration by publishing monographs, sponsoring lectures on the subject, and purchasing, restoring, and maintaining historic buildings. Two contrasting examples found in the regulations illustrate the concept of active programs:[11]

- Nonoperating foundation activities: A foundation is created to improve conditions in a particular urban ghetto. The foundation spends 10 percent of its income to make a survey of urban ghetto problems (an active disbursement) and grants 90 percent of its income to other nonprofit organizations doing ghetto rehabilitation projects (inactive or passive).

- Operating foundation activities: The same foundation spends 10 percent of its income on surveying the ghetto problems. Instead of granting funds to other organizations, the foundation spends its other income to maintain a staff of social workers and researchers who analyze its surveys and make recommendations as to methods for improving ghetto conditions. The foundation makes grants to independent social scientists to assist in these analyses and recommendations. The foundation publishes periodic reports indicating the results of its surveys and recommendations. The foundation makes grants to social workers and others who act as advisors to nonprofit organizations, as well as small business enterprises, functioning in the community.

Using a facts and circumstances approach, the regulations provide other examples of actively conducted, or self-initiated, programs:

Teacher training program: An entity is formed to train teachers for institutions of higher education. Fellowships are awarded to students for graduate study leading to advanced degrees in college teaching. Pamphlets encouraging prospective college teachers and describing the private operating foundation's activity are widely circulated. Seminars

---

9. Reg. § 53.4942(b)-1(b)(1).
10. Reg. § 53.4942(b)-1(b)(3).
11. Reg. § 53.4942(b)-1(d).

TYPES OF PRIVATE FOUNDATIONS

attended by fellowship recipients, foundation staff and consultants, and other interested parties, are held each summer, and papers from the conference are published. Despite the fact that a majority of the organization's money is spent on fellowship payments, the program is sufficiently comprehensive to qualify as an active project.

Medical research organization: An organization is created to study heart disease. Physicians and scientists apply to conduct research at the medical research organization's center. Its professional staff evaluates the projects, reviews progress reports, supervises the projects, and publishes the resulting findings.

Historical reference library: A library organization is established to hold and care for manuscripts and reference material relating to the history of the region in which it is located. In addition, it makes a limited number of annual grants to enable postdoctoral scholars and doctoral candidates to use its library. Sometimes, but not always, the operating foundation can obtain the rights to publish the scholar's work.

Set-asides: Funds set aside for a specific future project involving the active conduct of its tax-exempt activities will qualify as a direct expenditure.[12] An example of qualification involved a private operating foundation organized to restore and perpetuate wildlife and game animals on the North American continent. It acquired and planned to convert a portion of the new land into an extension of its existing wildlife sanctuary and the remainder into a public park under a four-year construction contract. Payments were made mainly during the last two years.[13] In such a case, the requirements for the amounts set aside must be satisfied to be counted as qualifying distributions.[14] For a newly created entity, a plan to set aside funds for a qualifying activity can be sufficient for classification of the organization as a private operating foundation.[15]

Limited liability company: A private operating foundation was ruled able to retain that status notwithstanding expansion of its activities to include control over and management of, by means of a single-member limited liability company,[16] a component of a public charity.[17]

---

12. IRC § 4942(g)(2); Reg. § 53.4942(b)-1(b)(1).
13. Rev. Rul. 74-450, 1974-2 C.B. 388.
14. See § 6.4(g).
15. Gen. Couns. Mem. 39442.
16. A single-member limited liability company is an entity that is generally disregarded for federal tax purposes (see *Tax-Exempt Organizations* § 4.1(b)).
17. Priv. Ltr. Rul. 200431018.

§ 3.1 PRIVATE OPERATING FOUNDATIONS

Specifically, this foundation assumed responsibility for administering a school of a tax-exempt university. The IRS concluded that qualifying distributions (from the foundation through the company to the university) constituted distributions directly for the active conduct of activities furthering the foundation's exempt purpose, thereby enabling the foundation to satisfy the income test.[18] The agency also ruled that the foundation's use of its assets to operate the program through the limited liability company satisfied the endowment test and that the revenue (including tuition and fees) derived from operation of the university's program may be treated as support from the general public for purposes of the support test.[19]

(b) Grants

While one or more other charities may be involved in some manner, the private operating foundation must expend a prescribed amount of its funds on its own direct charitable programs rather than by or through one or more grantee organizations. The regulations provide that qualifying distributions are not made by a foundation directly for the active conduct unless such distributions are used by the foundation itself rather than by or through one or more grantee organizations.[20]

A grant to another organization is presumed to be indirect conduct of exempt activity, even if the activity of the grantee organization helps the operating foundation accomplish its goals and its own exempt purposes.

This prohibition against mere distributions to grantees and the requirement of significant involvement by the private operating foundation in its programs nearly deprived one organization of private operating foundation status but for a liberal construction by the IRS of the rules. A private foundation (a trust) that operated a cultural center formed a corporation to act in a fiduciary capacity on its behalf in conducting the operations of the center. An amount equal to substantially all of the foundation's net income was turned over each year to the corporation and disbursed in the operation of the center. The corporation held income and property from the foundation as a fiduciary and not as an absolute owner. The IRS ruled that the corporation was not a grantee organization that received qualifying distributions from the trust but was a trustee of the trust, thereby enabling the private foundation to qualify as a private operating foundation.[21]

---

18. See § 3.1(d).
19. See § 3.1(e)(iii).
20. Reg. § 53.4942(b)-1(b).
21. Rev. Rul. 78-315, 1978-2 C.B. 271.

A private foundation that was originally created to operate residential living quarters for seniors changed its focus. It converted a former living space into a senior citizens' center to serve as a central intake and assessment point for identifying and addressing the needs of seniors in the area.[22] Part of the space was rented at a reduced rate to program partners, namely, other tax-exempt organizations that provided services to senior citizens. The remaining space was used for foundation programs benefiting the elderly: support group meeting rooms, training and placement center, resources and information room, and classrooms. The foundation reimbursed the partners for expenses incurred in assisting the foundation with its own or jointly operated programs. The foundation sought approval of its ongoing classification as a private operating foundation. The IRS found rental of space on a low-cost basis and partnering programs with other exempt organizations to be an actively conducted program.

As another example of program-related investments, the IRS ruled that a private foundation made such an investment when it invested in a for-profit company, the purpose of which was to encourage the creation of jobs and economic development in a region targeted for this purpose by a state government,[23] and when a private foundation made loans and other investments for the purpose of promoting economic development in a foreign country.[24]

A private operating foundation is not, however, prohibited from making grants to other organizations. Grants of this nature simply are not counted in calculating satisfaction of the income test.[25] So long as it distributes the requisite annual amount for the programs it actively conducts, a private operating foundation may, in addition, make grants to other organizations. Administrative expenses attributable to both active programs and grants to other organizations should be allocated on a reasonable basis between the two types of programs in presenting financial information on Form 990-PF to evidence qualification as a private operating foundation.

(c) Individual Grant Programs

Payments to individuals in connection with a scholarship program, a student loan fund, a minority business enterprise capital fund, or similar charitable effort may be classified as a distribution for the active conduct of a private operating foundation's tax-exempt purposes.[26] To qualify as a direct program

---

22. Priv. Ltr. Rul. 9723047.
23. Priv. Ltr. Rul. 199943044.
24. Priv. Ltr. Rul. 199943058.
25. See § 3.1(d).
26. Reg. § 53.4942(b)-1(b)(2)(i).

§ 3.1 PRIVATE OPERATING FOUNDATIONS

activity, the facts and circumstances surrounding the making or awarding of the grants must indicate that they are an integral part of, and essentially necessary to, accomplishing an active program in which the foundation is *significantly involved*. Merely selecting, screening, and investigating applicants for grants and scholarships is insufficient to support operating foundation status. When the grant recipients perform their work or studies solely for their own purposes, such as in the pursuit of a doctoral degree, or exclusively under the direction of some other organization, the grants are not considered as a direct qualifying expenditure.

A significantly involved foundation has a focused exempt mission or purpose. The regulations state that the test of whether individual grants are direct program expenditures is qualitative rather than strictly quantitative. To explain the meaning of this suggestion, the regulations provide that, although a foundation's grant to one or more grantee organizations or individuals might be in support of its own active programs, these grants are considered as indirect rather than direct (active) distributions. In one instance, a foundation was found to maintain a significant involvement in its ongoing attempt to ameliorate poverty in a rural area. The fund assisted needy young people in a county by providing scholarships, finding them summer jobs, getting students involved with local civic affairs, and other activities designed to educate and improve the circumstances of young people and make it possible for them to remain in the area.[27] The fact that a foundation screened, investigated, and tested the applicants to make sure they complied with academic and financial requirements set for scholarship recipients was insufficient activity to constitute an educational program.[28] Evaluating their needs and providing counseling and financial aid prior to referral of needy individuals to another agency was, on the other hand, deemed an active program.[29]

Even though grant or scholarship payments are not counted in calculating qualification for the income test,[30] the administrative expenses of screening and investigating grants (as opposed to the grants or scholarships themselves) may be counted as active program expenditures.[31]

Significant involvement of the operating foundation and its staff exists when the individual grants are a part of a comprehensive program. The regulations provide two examples of these programs.[32] In one, the foundation's purpose is

---

27. The Miss Elizabeth D. Leckie Scholarship Fund v. Commissioner, 87 T.C. 250 (1986).
28. Reg. § 53.4942(b)-1(d), Example (10).
29. Priv. Ltr. Rul. 9203004.
30. See § 3.1(d).
31. Reg. § 53.4942(b)-1(b)(2)(i).
32. Reg. § 53.4942(b)-1(b)(2)(ii).

TYPES OF PRIVATE FOUNDATIONS

to relieve poverty and human distress, and its exempt activities are designed to ameliorate conditions among the poor, particularly during national disasters. The foundation provides food and clothing to these indigents, without the assistance of an intervening organization or agency, under the direction of a salaried or voluntary staff of administrators, researchers, and other personnel who supervise and direct the activity.

In the second example, an operating foundation develops a specialized skill or expertise in scientific or medical research, social work, education, or the social sciences. A salaried staff of administrators, researchers, and other personnel supervises and conducts the work in its particular area of interest. As part of the program, the foundation awards grants, scholarships, or other payments to individuals to encourage independent study and scientific research projects and to otherwise further their involvement in its field of interest. The foundation sponsors seminars, conducts classes, and provides direction and supervision for the grant recipients. Based on these facts, the individual grants are treated as active and thus qualify under the income test.

A third example of *significant involvement* was provided when the IRS considered a situation involving a private operating foundation with the mission of conducting educational programs assisting underserved and impoverished individuals. The foundation built the capacity of providers by enhancing their financial sustainability and operational effectiveness. It provided technical assistance to policymakers to support early learning providers, offered technical assistance to enhance use of best practices in childhood development, and conducted research. The foundation proposed to operate a loan program in furtherance of its charitable and educational purposes, including making loans to service providers who cannot qualify for commercial loans; loans may also be made to intermediaries and for-profit entities. Loans to service providers would involve below-market interest rates or be interest-free; loans to for-profit organizations would have below-market rates. The IRS concluded that this foundation would maintain significant involvement in the active programs in support of which the loans would be made. The IRS noted that the foundation employed full-time experts in education and related areas, and funded consultants who specialize in assisting service providers and intermediaries who would receive training, knowledge-sharing, data collection, and educational materials to facilitate capacity-building. The foundation would be involved in the structuring of loans, oversee operations of partners funded with loans, and otherwise plan "substantive elements" with respect to the loan program.[33]

---

33. Priv. Ltr. Rul. 201821005.

§ 3.1 PRIVATE OPERATING FOUNDATIONS

(d) Income Test

To qualify as a private operating foundation, a foundation must satisfy numerical tests intended to ensure that it conducts its exempt activities directly, rather than by supporting other organizations. The two categories of tests are:

1. *Income Test:* This test requires that a specific amount be spent on directly conducted charitable programs determined by either its actual income or hypothetical minimum investment return.
2. *Asset, Endowment, or Support Test:* One of three tests regarding its assets and sources of revenues apply as described in the next subsection.

The *income test* gauges whether a private operating foundation has spent sufficient funds on its own programs or direct charitable distributions. As a general concept, the foundation need not actually (or in an accounting sense) trace the source of funds it uses to satisfy this test. Qualifying distributions that count toward meeting the income test may be made from current or accumulated income, including capital gains, or from current or accumulated contributions;[34] they can be made in cash or property.[35] In determining satisfaction of the income test, the foundation computes its adjusted net income,[36] its minimum investment return,[37] and its qualifying distributions.[38]

Adjusted net income is calculated using this formula:

$$A - B - C - D + E = \text{Adjusted net income}$$

- A = Gross income for the year, including investment income such as dividends, interest, short-term capital gains, royalties; fees, tuition, product sales, and other revenues from charitable activities, including short-term gains from the sale of charitable- and unrelated-use assets; income from a functionally related business and program-related investments; other unrelated trade or business income; and tax-exempt interest.

- B = Long-term capital gains from sale of assets held for investment, for charitable use, and for conduct of an unrelated business. The tax basis for property received by the foundation as a gift is equal to the tax basis of the donor.

---

34. Reg. § 53.4942(b)-1(c).
35. Reg. § 53.4942(a)-(3).
36. IRC § 4942(f); Reg. § 53.4942(a)-2(d).
37. IRC § 4942(e); see § 6.2 and Part IX of Form 990-PF (2022).
38. See § 6.4 and Part XIII of Form 990-PF (2022).

TYPES OF PRIVATE FOUNDATIONS

- C = Gifts, grants, and contributions received, including income distributed from an estate (unless the estate is treated as terminated for federal tax purposes because its administration has been prolonged for tax avoidance reasons).

- D = Ordinary and necessary expenses paid or incurred for the production or collection of amounts treated as gross income for this purpose, including the management, conservation, or maintenance of property held for the production of this income. Depreciation is allowed and computed on a straight-line basis; cost depletion (no percentage) is permitted. Salaries, rents, taxes, repairs, and other expenses of operating income-producing properties are included, as are expenses associated with tax-exempt interest. Where a foundation expense is related both to income production and program activities, only that portion directly attributable to includible income is deducted, following some reasonable and consistent allocation method. Direct program disbursements reduce adjusted net income to the extent of income produced by the program.

- E = Additions to the current year spending requirement are made for any recovery or refund of amounts treated as a qualifying distribution in a previous year, including proceeds of the sale of assets to the extent their purchase cost was treated as a qualifying distribution in a prior year. The addition is limited to the lower of the actual sales price or the amount previously reported as a qualifying distribution. A previously set-aside obligation is added back or increases the distributable amount if plans change or the funds are no longer needed for the purposes for which the set-aside was allowed and treated as a distribution in a past year.[39]

Over the years, a few IRS rulings have clarified the amounts includible in adjusted net income.

- Bond premium amortization is permitted.[40]

- Annuity, IRA, and other employee benefit plan payments are includible to the extent that the amount exceeds the value of the right to receive the payment on the decedent's date of death.[41]

- Capital gain dividends paid or credited for reinvestment by a mutual fund are not included, because they are considered long-term.[42]

---

39. Reg. § 53.4942(a)-2(d)(4); see § 3.1(a).
40. Rev. Rul. 76-248, 1976-1 C.B. 363; IRC § 171.
41. Rev. Rul. 75-442, 1975-2 C.B. 448.
42. Rev. Rul. 73-320, 1973-2 C.B. 385; IRC § 852(b)(3)(B).

§ 3.1 PRIVATE OPERATING FOUNDATIONS

Minimum investment return for this purpose is the same as for a nonoperating private foundation; it equals 5 percent of the average fair market value of the foundation's noncharitable or investment assets, not including its charitable-use assets.

Qualifying distributions of a private operating foundation are defined by the federal tax law in the same fashion as for a nonoperating foundation. To complete Part XIII, where the private operating foundation tests are presented, a distinction must be made between expenditures eligible to be classified as directly expended for the active conduct of a foundation's charitable programs and those distributions that are made indirectly either by grant to another organization or to an individual.[43]

Nonoperating foundations are required to distribute a minimum investment return amount.[44] Under the definition for private operating foundations, the amount that must be annually expended for the active conduct of charitable activities equals substantially all, meaning 85 percent, of the lesser of its:

- Adjusted net income (ANI), or

- Minimum investment return (MRI) (essentially results in a 4.25 percent payout if this factor applies).

A special rule applies to a private operating foundation that makes grants to other organizations in addition to its active-program expenditures.[45] The rule applies if two conditions exist: (1) the foundation's adjusted net income is higher than its minimum investment return, and (2) its total qualifying distributions exceed minimum investment return but are less than adjusted net income. To meet the income test and qualify as a private operating foundation, a foundation in that circumstance must meet a test that requires it to spend at least 85 percent of its adjusted net income for its own projects. Effectively, indirect grants to other organizations are not counted at all in meeting the distribution requirements and can be paid only in addition to substantially all of the foundation's adjusted gross income. This rule is intended to prevent

---

43. See § 3.1(a), (b).
44. See § 6.2.
45. Reg. § 53.4942(b)-1(a)(1)(ii). A special caveat was added to IRC § 4942(j)(3) when the test was revised to permit a foundation distributing a lower income amount to qualify as an operating foundation. A cryptic sentence was added to the end of the subsection, reading: "Notwithstanding the provisions of subparagraph (A) [the revised income test], if the qualifying distributions of an organization for the taxable year exceed the minimum investment return for the taxable year, clause (ii) of this subparagraph [permitting the minimum investment return be the test if it is lower] shall not apply unless substantially all of such qualifying distributions are made directly for the active conduct."

TYPES OF PRIVATE FOUNDATIONS

a private operating foundation from reducing its expenditures on its active programs to a lower minimum investment return level while expending the balance of its distributions in the form of grants to other organizations. Importantly, this rule does not prohibit grants to other organizations; it simply raises the required payout when ANI is higher than MIR.

In summary, to satisfy the income test, a private foundation must annually expend an amount equal to substantially all (85 percent) of the lesser of its adjusted net income or its minimum investment return in the form of qualifying distributions directly for the active conduct of its tax-exempt activities.

A private operating foundation must, in addition to satisfying the income test, meet one of the three other tests regarding its assets and sources of revenue, as described next. The tests must be fulfilled within specific time frames. One of the tests, the *endowment test*, requires a private operating foundation to normally make qualifying distributions directly for the active conduct of its charitable activities equal to at least $66\frac{2}{3}$ percent of its minimum investment return, which equals $3\frac{1}{3}$ percent of the minimum investment return (possibly less than required by the alternative income test described earlier).

(e) Asset, Endowment, or Support Test

A private operating foundation must also meet one of three alternative tests, an asset, endowment, or support test, for each year or three out of four average years.[46] Just like the income test that imposes a requirement that the private operating foundation spend the majority of its income for active programs, these tests determine whether the foundation's assets and income therefrom are so devoted.

(i) Asset Test. The first of the three tests, the asset test, requires that substantially all (meaning at least 65 percent) of the private operating foundation's assets be active-use assets of any of these types:[47]

- Program assets devoted directly to the active conduct of its tax-exempt activities, to functionally related businesses, or to a combination of both.

- Stock of a corporation that is controlled by the private operating foundation, the assets of which are 65 percent or more so devoted.

- Partly assets, described in the first category, and partly stock, described in the second category.

---

46. See § 3.1(f).
47. IRC § 4942(j)(3)(B); Reg. § 53.4942(b)-2(a)(1)(i).

§ 3.1 PRIVATE OPERATING FOUNDATIONS

An asset, to qualify under this test, must be used by the organization directly for the active conduct of its tax-exempt purpose(s). The determination of a particular asset's character in this regard is, however, a question of fact. The concepts applied in identifying these exempt function and dual-use assets are the same as those used to identify assets excluded in calculating a foundation's minimum investment return.[48] To the extent assets are used directly for the active conduct of the foundation's exempt activities, they are counted for this test.[49] Thus, an asset may be apportioned between its exempt and nonexempt use. For example, if the foundation's building is used 50 percent for active programs and their administration, with the other 50 percent rented to tenants not involved in the programs, one-half of the value would be treated as qualifying for the asset test. The basis of the allocation is the fair rental value of the two portions rather than the respective square footage.[50] An asset that is used 95 percent or more of the time for exempt functions can be fully counted as a qualifying asset.[51] Assets held for the production of income, investment, or other similar purpose, such as stocks and bonds, interest-bearing notes, endowment funds, or leased real estate, are generally not considered as devoted to the active conduct of the foundation's programs and are not counted. Conversely, these assets are counted for purposes of the endowment test and form the basis on which the minimum investment return is calculated.

Classic examples of active-use assets include the art collections of a museum, performance halls and studios of a music conservatory, and the laboratories and library of a research organization. Intangible assets, such as patents, copyrights, and trademarks, are also counted if used in connection with active programs.

A *functionally related business* is a department or separate entity that sells goods or renders services that accomplish the foundation's tax-exempt purposes.[52] Although a functionally related business may produce profits the foundation uses to pay for other exempt activities, its primary purpose must be to advance the foundation's charitable, educational, or other exempt purposes. A museum gift shop and a library's bookstore that sell educational materials are examples of functionally related businesses operated alongside the exempt activities. For example, a wholly owned, separately incorporated taxable entity that holds lodging facilities and other accommodations for rental to visitors to the foundation's historical area can qualify as a functionally related business. Its value would be taken into account in calculating the asset test. The income from the property is included in adjusted net income required to be distributed.

---

48. See § 6.2(d).
49. Reg. § 53.4942(b)-2(a)(2)(i).
50. Rev. Rul. 82-137, 1982-2 C.B. 303.
51. *Id.*
52. See §§ 6.2(d), 7.3.

TYPES OF PRIVATE FOUNDATIONS

The foundation may treat property it acquires for future active-program use as a qualifying asset even though it is rented, in whole or part, during the reasonable period of time it takes to make arrangements to use or otherwise ready the property for active use. One year is generally considered a reasonable time frame.

Rental property provided to tenants that serves to accomplish an exempt purpose (e.g., housing for low-income families, studio spaces for community art groups, or a hotel adjacent to the foundation's historical village) may be treated as an active-use asset in a specific circumstance—the rent is essentially below the prevailing market rate. The property is treated as an active-use asset if the rental income derived from the property is less than the amount that would be required to be charged in order to recover the cost of purchasing the property and annual upkeep and maintenance expenses, such as insurance and painting. Although the regulations provide no specific time frame permitted for the cost recovery, the number of years in which a prudent investor buying similar property in the same area would expect to recoup the investment should be acceptable. The equipment necessary to maintain a computerized database of information on endangered species, accessible on the Internet for a fee to those studying this subject, could also qualify under this test, dependent on the fee levels.

Conversely, loans receivable from members of a charitable class (students or minority business owners) or funds placed on deposit with a lending institution to guarantee these loans are not treated as actively used assets.[53] Even though the making of the loan itself is considered an active program expense, the loan itself, as an interest-bearing receivable, is not to be treated as devoted to active use. Similarly, program-related investments that produce investment income would not be treated as active-conduct assets. If the rate of interest is below market, a foundation might argue that the rule pertaining to below-market rental property be applied.

Funds set aside, or earmarked for specific active program expenditures in the future, are essentially treated as investment assets, so set-aside reserves are specifically not treated as active-use assets. Assets either acquired or disposed of during the year, and therefore held for less than a full year, are only partly includible in the asset test calculations. The included amount is the fractional part calculated by multiplying the asset's value times the ratio of the number of days in the year the assets were held, divided by 365 or 366.[54]

The asset test is calculated based on, as a general rule, the fair market value of the assets[55] and following the rules for determining the annual minimum

---

53. Reg. § 53.4942(b)-2(a)(2)(ii).
54. Reg. § 53.4942(b)-2(a)(3).
55. Reg. § 53.4942(b)-2(a)(4).

§ 3.1 PRIVATE OPERATING FOUNDATIONS

investment return.[56] Certain active-use assets, according to the regulations, may not necessarily be capable of valuation using standard methods. Examples of these assets include art objects, historical buildings, and botanical gardens. Where the foundation can demonstrate that these special-purpose assets are not readily marketable, the asset's historical cost, unadjusted for depreciation, is the amount included to calculate satisfaction of the asset test.

(ii) Endowment Test. A private operating foundation satisfies the endowment test when it normally expends its funds, in the form of qualifying distributions, directly for the active conduct of its tax-exempt activities, in an amount equal to at least two-thirds of its minimum investment return.[57] Thus, this payout requirement obligates the private operating foundation to distribute annually an amount equal to:

$$3\frac{1}{3}\% \left(\frac{2}{3} \text{ of } 5\%\right) \text{ of the value of investment (nonactive-use) assets}$$

The endowment test specifies a lower percentage than the income test, which requires at least 4.25 percent (85 percent × 5 percent) of the value of investment assets be distributed. Assume a private operating foundation has $10 million of investment assets at year-end. To satisfy the endowment test, it must spend $333,333 on active program expenditures. To satisfy the income test, this foundation must spend the lower of $425,000 (85 percent of 5 percent of $1 million), or 85 percent of its adjusted net income. Assume its adjusted net income is lower and equals $250,000. Based on these facts, it would be required by the income test to spend only $212,500 (85 percent of $250,000) on programs. Because its adjusted net income is lower than the minimum investment return, its distributions for endowment test purposes will exceed the amount required for income test purposes. Conversely, if its adjusted net income was greater than the minimum investment return, say $600,000, the direct expenditures required by the income test would automatically allow it to satisfy the endowment test.

The endowment test applies to determine qualification for foundations holding investment assets that amount to more than 35 percent of their total assets or, conversely, to a foundation with program or active-use assets equaling less than 65 percent of its total assets, as required to meet the asset test. Correspondingly, such a foundation's programs would typically be service intensive or product oriented, such as those of a self-help provider, educational

---

56. The valuation rules discussed in § 6.3 and applied for calculation of the minimum investment return are also used for this purpose.
57. Reg. § 53.4942(b)-2(b)(1).

TYPES OF PRIVATE FOUNDATIONS

publisher, or performing arts foundation that would normally have modest amounts of program assets in relation to its investment assets. The concept of expenditures directly for the active conduct of tax-exempt activities under the endowment test is the same as that under the income test.[58] The foundation is not required to trace the source of these expenditures to determine whether they were derived from investment income or from contributions.

An organization that, on May 26, 1969, and at all times after that date and before the close of the tax year involved, operated and maintained, as its principal functional purpose, facilities for the long-term care, comfort, maintenance, or education of permanently and totally disabled persons, elderly persons, needy widows, or children qualifies as an operating foundation if the organization meets the requirements of the endowment test.[59] This rule applies only for purposes of the foundation distributions to this type of organization and means they are determined as if the organization is not a private operating foundation (unless it meets a definition of a public or publicly supported charity or otherwise qualifies as a private operating foundation).

(iii) Support Test. The third alternative test imposes three concurrent tests, all of which must be met. The private operating foundation applying this test must satisfy each of these requirements:[60]

- Substantially all (85 percent) of its support (other than gross investment income) is normally received from the general public and from at least five tax-exempt organizations that are not disqualified persons[61] in respect to each other or the recipient private operating foundation.

- Not more than 25 percent of its support (other than gross investment income) is normally received from any one of these organizations.

- Not more than 50 percent of its support is normally received from gross investment income.

The support received by an organization from any one tax-exempt organization may be counted toward satisfaction of the support test only if the organization receives support from at least four other exempt organizations. The regulations permit an organization to receive support from five exempt organizations and no support from the general public, although the statute appears to

---

58. Reg. § 53.4942(b)-1(b)(1); see § 3.1(d).
59. IRC § 4942(j)(5).
60. IRC § 4942(j)(3)(B)(iii).
61. IRC § 4946(a)(1)(H), discussed in Chapter 4.

§ 3.1 PRIVATE OPERATING FOUNDATIONS

require both.[62] Support received from an individual, trust, or corporation (other than a tax-exempt organization) is taken into account as support from the general public only to the extent that the total amount received from any sources (including attributed sources) during the compliance period does not exceed 1 percent of the organization's total support (other than gross investment income) for the period. Support from a governmental unit, however, while treated as being from the general public, is not subject to this 1 percent limitation.[63]

Organizations meeting the support test have often developed an expertise in a particular area and thus are able to attract charitable contributions and grants from other foundations to enable them to sustain programs in their areas of specialization. Support received from related parties[64] is added to apply the 1 percent limitation so that their combined support is treated as if one person provided it.

(f) Compliance Period

The income test and either the asset, endowment, or support test are applied each year for a four-year period that includes the current and past three years, although the methods may be alternated as respects a subsequent tax year.[65] The private operating foundation has a choice of two methods to calculate its compliance with the tests for each year:

1. All four years can be aggregated, that is, the distributions for four years are added together. The private operating foundation must use only one of the asset, endowment, or support tests for this aggregate test.
2. For three of the four years, the private operating foundation meets the income test and any one of the asset, endowment, or support tests.

Although a private operating foundation has a choice of methods, the same method must be applied for purposes of calculating its income test and its asset, endowment, or support test for each year. There is no requirement in the regulations or the Internal Revenue Code that the foundation choosing to apply the three-out-of-four-year method must make up any deficiency of active distributions in the one year they fail to meet the tests.[66] A private foundation that applies the aggregate method for measuring its qualification is essentially allowed to carry forward excess distributions from one year.

---

62. Reg. § 53.4942(b)-2(c)(2)(iii). Support for this purpose is defined by IRC § 509. See §§ 15.4(c), 15.5(a).
63. Reg. § 53.4942(b)-2(c)(2)(iv).
64. As defined in IRC § 4946(a)(1)(C)-(G).
65. Reg. § 53.4942(b)-3(a).
66. See Priv. Ltr. Rul. 9509042.

TYPES OF PRIVATE FOUNDATIONS

Use of the three-out-of-four-year method, however, eliminates the benefit, or carryover, of any excess distributions from a prior year.

If the private operating foundation fails to qualify for a year, it is treated as a nonoperating private foundation for that year. It can return to private operating foundation classification as soon as it again qualifies under both the income test and the asset, endowment, or support test. Importantly, distributions during that year would have to satisfy both the test for a nonoperating private foundation status and its restored private operating foundation status. The tax on the failure to make qualifying distributions[67] does not apply to private operating foundations, and the deficiency of distributions need not be corrected.

New organizations generally are expected to meet the tests in their first year. Once a new organization satisfies the test in the first year, it continues to qualify for its second and third tax years of existence only if it satisfies the dual tests described above by the aggregation method for all the years it has been in existence.[68]

A special rule allows the new foundation to be treated as qualifying if such organization has made a good faith determination that it is likely to satisfy both tests. If application for recognition of exemption is made prior to the completion of the proposed private operating foundation's first fiscal year, the IRS will accept the organization's assertion, based on a good faith determination that it plans to qualify.[69]

Generally, the status of grants or contributions made to a private operating foundation is not affected until notice of a change of status of the organization is communicated to the public. This is not the case, however, if the grant or contribution was made after (1) the act or failure to act that resulted in the organization's inability to satisfy the requirements of one or more of the previously mentioned tests, and the grantor or contributor was responsible for or was aware of the act or failure to act, or (2) the grantor or contributor acquired knowledge that the IRS had given notice to the organization that it would be deleted from classification as a private operating foundation.[70] A grantor or contributor will not be deemed to have the requisite responsibility or awareness under the first of the aforementioned categories, however, if the grantor or contributor made their grant or contribution in reliance on a written statement by the grantee organization containing sufficient facts to the effect that the grant or contribution would not result in the inability of the grantee organization to qualify as a private operating foundation.[71]

---

67. IRC § 4942(a).
68. Reg. § 53.4942(b)-3(b).
69. Reg. § 53.4942(b)-3(b)(2).
70. Reg. § 53.4942(b)-3(d)(1).
71. Reg. § 53.4942(b)-3(d)(2).

(g) Advantages and Disadvantages of Private Operating Foundations

Private operating foundations have certain advantages.

Contribution Deduction Limits Are Preferential. The percentage limits for charitable deductions are higher for private operating foundations than for private foundations and are the same as the deductions permitted for public charities. A full 50 percent of an individual's adjusted net income can be sheltered by cash contributions to an operating foundation, as compared with the 30 percent of one's adjusted net income that can be deducted for cash gifts to a nonoperating private foundation.

A deduction is permitted, as a general rule, for the appreciation component of all types of property donated to a private operating foundation. The deduction for a gift of real estate, artwork, or other similar property to a nonoperating private foundation is generally limited to the donor's tax basis in the property.[72] A special exception permits a deduction for the full fair market value of readily marketable securities.[73] With or without the exception, a gift of property to a private operating foundation is fully deductible, subject to the 30 percent limitation on capital gain property.[74]

Distribution Amount May Be Lower. The minimum distribution requirement for an operating foundation may be lower than for nonoperating private foundations. In some cases, given a sufficient return on investment, a private operating foundation can accumulate a higher endowment over the years.

Because a private operating foundation is required to meet the income tests described above for the active conduct of charitable purposes, it is not subject to the same minimum payout requirements imposed on nonoperating private foundations.[75] Moreover, a private operating foundation can be the recipient of grants from a nonoperating private foundation without having to spend the funds within the following year, with the funds nevertheless qualifying as expenditures of income by the donating foundation for purposes of its mandatory distribution requirements.

The income test requires an operating foundation to distribute only the 85 percent of the lower of its adjusted net income or its minimum investment return. Where the adjusted net income is less than the minimum investment return, the endowment test would require it pay out only 66-⅔ percent of its minimum investment return.[76]

---

72. IRC § 170(e)(1)(B)(ii). See § 14.4(a).
73. IRC § 170(e)(5). See § 14.5.
74. See § 14.2(a).
75. See Chapter 6.
76. See § 3.1(d), (e).

TYPES OF PRIVATE FOUNDATIONS

The primary disadvantage of a private operating foundation is the loss of the one-year time delay afforded to nonoperating private foundations in meeting the minimum distribution requirement. For each year, a private foundation calculates a minimum distribution requirement based on 5 percent of the average value of its investment assets for that year and has until the end of the next succeeding year to make qualifying distributions in that amount. The private operating foundation, instead, must meet the income test and the asset, endowment, or support test each year as of the last day of the particular year or cumulatively for three out of the four years then ended. The need to sustain self-initiated programs and manage the staff or volunteers that conduct the active projects is for some a disadvantage, or certainly a requirement that can be an obligation some funders wish to avoid.

(h) Conversion to or from Private Operating Foundation Status

Any foundation may move from nonoperating foundation status to operating foundation status (or vice versa) if, after changing its operations or mix of assets, it meets the applicable tests. An IRS advance ruling is not required for a private foundation to convert to an operating foundation or, conversely, for an operating foundation to become a nonoperating private foundation. Without a new determination letter, however, the IRS will not recognize the entity's new operating foundation status in its records.[77] Because charitable contributions to private operating foundations are subject to higher percentage limitations,[78] seeking an updated IRS determination letter may be advisable from a donor-relations and fundraising perspective.

A nonoperating private foundation desiring a new determination letter from the IRS classifying it as an operating foundation may request one by filing Form 8940 along with the required user fee.[79] The foundation must submit with the form a completed Form 990-PF, Part XIII (Private Operating Foundations) to demonstrate to the IRS that it meets the requisite financial tests for qualification as a private operating foundation,[80] and provide (on Schedule G to Form 8940) a listing and description of its distributions that details whether its distributions are used directly for the active conduct of its own programs

---

77. Rev. Proc. 2023-5, 2023-1 I.R.B. 265 § 7.04(4).
78. See § 14.2(a).
79. Form 8940 must be submitted electronically at www.pay.gov; the user fee for this type of request is currently $550 (Rev. Proc. 2023-5, 2023-1 I.R.B. 265 §§ 4.02(6), 7.02 and App. A (Schedule of User Fees), as modified by Rev. Proc. 2023-12, 2023-17 I.R.B. 768 §§ 3.01, 3.03).
80. See § 3.1(d), (e).

§ 3.1 PRIVATE OPERATING FOUNDATIONS

or activities and a description of any adverse impact if the organization does not receive operating foundation status.[81]

Converting from nonoperating to operating foundation status (or vice versa) will have an impact on the cumulative qualifying distribution tests. An operating foundation must meet its minimum distribution requirements within the year; a nonoperating foundation, one year later. Thus, an operating foundation converting to a nonoperating private foundation gains a one-year grace period; converting to an operating foundation accelerates the required distributions.

The effective date for conversion to operating foundation status is not clearly set out in the Internal Revenue Code or in the regulations. As noted, the income, asset, endowment, and support tests are applied by reference to a four-year compliance period.[82] The IRS concluded that "a private foundation that has been in existence for at least four years and has not heretofore qualified for operating foundation status may satisfy the operating foundation requirements by showing that it has met the income test and one of the three alternative tests over a four-year period." Further, such a foundation will be "considered an operating foundation effective the final year of the four-year period."[83] A foundation was able to qualify in the year of its conversion by receiving approval for a single, but substantial, set-aside to operate a facility to assist persons with limited employability due to temporary or permanent disabilities.[84] Despite the fact that it could not meet the tests during its first through third years, it met the test on an aggregate basis of all four years.

The four-year time frame for a change in classification established by the regulations can be frustrating to foundations' donors who wish to take advantage of the higher charitable deduction percentage limitations for donations to private operating foundations. A donation of noncash assets, such as land or art, will not be eligible for the more generous deduction limitations afforded to a private operating foundation until the end of the four-year compliance period.[85]

---

81. Instructions for Form 8940 (Apr. 2023), Schedule G, Section 2. If the organization is changing from public charity to private foundation status it must also explain how it fails the donative publicly supported charity support test (see § 15.4(c)) and the service provider publicly supported charity support test (see § 15.5(a)).
82. See § 3.1(f).
83. "Private Operating Foundations," Topic N, IRS Exempt Organization Continuing Professional Education Text for FY 1984 (citing Reg. § 53.4942-3(a)).
84. Priv. Ltr. Rul. 9108001. A set-aside for summer enrichment program scholarships was approved by the IRS (Priv. Ltr. Rul. 9018033).
85. See §§ 3.1(g), § 14.2(a).

§ 3.2 EXEMPT OPERATING FOUNDATIONS

Certain private foundations qualify as *exempt operating foundations*.[86] These entities are exempt from the tax on private foundations' net investment income[87] and from the requirement that grants to them must be the subject of expenditure responsibility,[88] which constitutes the meaning of the term *exempt* in this context.

In general, an exempt operating foundation is one that qualifies as a private operating foundation, has been publicly supported for at least 10 years, has a board of directors that is representative of the public and most of whom are not disqualified individuals, and does not have an officer who is a disqualified individual.[89]

§ 3.3 CONDUIT FOUNDATIONS

A private foundation (other than an operating foundation) becomes a *conduit foundation* for any year in which it makes qualifying distributions,[90] which are treated[91] as distributions out of corpus,[92] in an amount equal in value to 100 percent of contributions received in the year involved, whether as cash or property.[93] To enable the donor to claim a charitable deduction, the distributions must be made not later than the 15th day of the third month after the close of the private foundation's tax year in which the contributions were received, and the private foundation must not have any remaining undistributed income for the year. The point is any current-year qualifying distributions are first offset against the amount required to be paid out based on the prior year's calculations. In a sense, the conduit-type private foundation is not a separate category of private foundation but is instead a term used to refer to a treatment given a particular type of contribution to a private foundation.

---

86. IRC § 4940(d).
87. See § 10.7.
88. See § 9.5.
89. IRC § 4940(d)(2). See § 10.7.
90. IRC § 4942(g), other than IRC § 4942(g)(3). In general, see Chapter 6.
91. This treatment is after the application of IRC § 4942(g)(3). This means that every contribution described in IRC § 4942(g)(3) received by the conduit foundation in a particular tax year must be distributed by it by the 15th day of the third month after the close of that year in order for any other distribution by the foundation to be counted toward the 100 percent requirement (see § 6.4(c)(ii)).
92. IRC § 4942(h).
93. IRC § 170(b)(1)(F)(ii); Reg. § 1.170A-9(g)(1).

§ 3.3 CONDUIT FOUNDATIONS

A foundation may be a conduit foundation for only that year when it receives a donation for which the donor desires a higher deduction limitation. A conduit foundation is sometimes referred to as a "pass-through foundation" because it usually receives but does not keep and instead redistributes donations. As discussed below, a foundation with an excess distributions carryover may use the excess to satisfy the redistribution requirement. Status as a conduit foundation applies on a year-by-year basis. The election to treat the gifts as being made out of corpus does not impact the succeeding year's distributions.

The qualifying distribution may be of the contributed property itself, the proceeds of the sale of contributed property, or cash or other assets of the foundation of equal value. In making the calculation in satisfaction of the 100 percent requirement, the amount of this fair market value may be reduced by any reasonable selling expenses incurred by the foundation in the sale of the contributed property. An excise tax, however, will be due on any gain from the sale.

This tax is not imposed if the property is redistributed rather than sold.[94] Moreover, at the choice of the private foundation, if the contributed property is sold or distributed within 30 days of its receipt by the private foundation, the amount of the fair market value is either the gross amount received on the sale of the property (less reasonable selling expenses) or an amount equal to the fair market value of the property on the date of its distribution to a public charity.[95]

Excess distribution carryovers[96] can also be counted as a qualifying distribution by a conduit foundation.[97] The regulations allow a foundation to elect to treat as a current distribution out of corpus any amount distributed within one of the five prior tax years, which was treated as a distribution out of corpus, and not availed of for any other purpose.

A conduit foundation must attach a statement to Form 990-PF for the year in which it treats distributions as being made out of corpus for purposes of permitting a donor to claim a full fair market deduction.

These distributions are treated as made first out of contributions of property and then out of contributions of cash received by the private foundation in the year involved. The distributions cannot be made to an organization controlled directly or indirectly by the private foundation or by one or more disqualified persons[98] with respect to the private foundation or to a private foundation that is not a private operating foundation.

---

94. See § 10.4(b).
95. Reg. § 1.170A-9(g)(2)(iv).
96. See § 6.5(c).
97. Reg. § 53.4942(a)-3(c)(2)(iv).
98. See Chapter 4.

TYPES OF PRIVATE FOUNDATIONS

The contributor must obtain adequate records or other sufficient evidence from the private foundation showing that the private foundation made the qualifying distributions.[99] The value of the contributed property will be included in the calculation of the foundation's distributable amount for the period of time it holds the property between receipt of the gift and redistribution of either the property itself, cash equal to the fair market value of the property, or proceeds of sale of the property.[100] To offset what might appear to be an unfair result, the foundation may retain any income earned on the property during the time it holds the gift. The donor receives a charitable deduction for a gift of this nature, as if the gift were to a public charity, assuming the special rule is elected; the IRS can exercise its discretionary authority to grant relief to extend the time needed to make the election.[101]

§ 3.4 COMMON FUND FOUNDATIONS

Another special type of nonoperating private foundation is one that pools contributions received in a common fund but allows the donor or their spouse (including substantial contributors)[102] to retain the right to designate annually the organizations to which the income attributable to the contributions is given (as long as the organizations qualify as certain types of entities that are not private foundations)[103] and to designate (by deed or will) the organizations to which the corpus of the contributions is eventually to be given. Moreover, this type of private foundation must pay out its adjusted net income to public charities by the 15th day of the third month after the close of the tax year in which the income is realized by the fund, and the corpus must be distributed to these charities within one year after the death of the donor or their spouse.[104]

In the sole instance of the IRS to publicly rule on the status of a private foundation as a common fund private foundation, the IRS considered a tax-exempt trust that was operated, supervised, and controlled by the distribution committee of a community trust.[105] Its function was to receive and pool

---

99. Reg. § 1.170A- 9(g)(1), Examples (1) and (2); also Priv. Ltr. Rul. 200311033. See § 6.4(c)(ii).
100. See § 6.1(b).
101. The IRS granted an extension of time to a private foundation to make an election under the conduit foundation rules, which is to be timely done by filing an amended annual information return and the requisite statement (Reg. § 301.9100-1), after the firm that prepared the return for the year involved discovered that its calculation of excess distribution carryovers was incorrect (Priv. Ltr. Rul. 201831007).
102. See § 4.1.
103. IRC § 509(a)(1).
104. IRC § 170(b)(1)(F)(iii).
105. See § 15.4(e).

contributions and to distribute its income to public and publicly supported charities. Every donor had the right to designate the charitable recipients of the trust's income and of the corpus of the fund attributable to their contribution. All of the other requirements of the common fund foundation rules were satisfied in this instance, and, therefore, the IRS concluded that the trust qualified as a common fund private foundation.[106] (Were it not for the fact that the donors had the right to designate the recipients, the trust would have qualified as a supporting organization[107] and not as a private foundation.)

Contributions to this type of private foundation qualify for the 50 percent and 30 percent limitations on the charitable deduction.[108]

§ 3.5 RESEARCH AND EXPERIMENTATION FUNDS

One of the purposes of Congress in enacting the Economic Recovery Tax Act of 1981 was to provide incentives for an increase in the conduct of research and experimentation. Consequently, a tax credit was created for certain research and experimental expenditures paid in carrying on a trade or business.[109] The tax credit is allowable to the extent that current-year expenditures exceed the average amount of research expenditures in a base period (generally, the preceding three tax years). Subject to certain exclusions, the term *qualified research* used for purposes of the tax credit is the same as that used for purposes of the deduction rules for research expenses.[110]

Research expenditures qualifying for this tax credit consist of two basic types: in-house research expenses and contract research expenses. In-house research expenditures are those for research wages and supplies, along with certain lease or other charges for research use of computers, laboratory equipment, and the like. Contract research expenditures are 65 percent of amounts paid to another person (for example, a research firm or university) for research.

A tax credit is also available for 65 percent of an amount paid by a corporation to a qualified organization for basic research to be performed by the recipient organization, where the relationship is evidenced by a written

---

106. Rev. Rul. 80-305, 1980-2 C.B. 71.
107. See § 15.6(f), (j).
108. IRC §§ 170(b)(1)(A)(vii), 170(b)(1)(F)(iii); see § 14.2(a).
109. IRC § 41.
110. A taxpayer may elect to currently deduct the amount of research or experimental expenditures incurred in connection with the taxpayer's trade or business or may elect to amortize certain research costs over a period of at least 60 months (IRC § 174). These rules apply to the costs of research conducted on behalf of the taxpayer by a research firm, university, or the like.

TYPES OF PRIVATE FOUNDATIONS

research agreement. (This research is a form of contract research.) The term *basic research* means "any original investigation for the advancement of scientific knowledge not having a specific commercial objective, except that such term shall not include (A) basic research conducted outside the United States, and (B) basic research in the social sciences or humanities."[111]

For purposes of the rules concerning basic contract research, a *qualified organization* is either (1) an institution of higher education[112] that is a tax-exempt educational organization,[113] or (2) any other type of charitable, educational, scientific, or similar tax-exempt organization[114] that is organized and operated primarily to conduct scientific research and is not a private foundation.[115]

A special provision allows certain funds organized and operated exclusively to make basic research grants to institutions of higher education to be considered as qualifying organizations, even though the funds do not themselves perform the research. To qualify, a fund must be a charitable, educational, scientific, or similar tax-exempt organization, not be a private foundation, be established and maintained by an organization that is a public or publicly supported charity and was created prior to July 10, 1981, and make its grants under written research agreements. Moreover, a fund must elect to become this type of qualified fund; by making the election, the fund becomes treated as a private foundation, except that the investment income excise tax[116] is not applicable.[117]

Thus, Congress has created a category of organizations that, because of the nature of their programs (rather than the nature of their support or degree of public involvement), are regarded as private foundations. Apparently, this status as a private foundation continues only as long as the fund makes the qualified basic research grants, and the fund can revert to a form of public charity when and if it ceases making the grants.

---

111. IRC § 41.
112. IRC § 3304(f).
113. IRC § 170(b)(A)(ii). See § 15.3(b).
114. IRC § 501(c)(3).
115. One of the questions thus posed by this provision is whether private operating foundations (see *supra* § 3.1) are eligible to participate in this contract research program. Certainly these types of foundations that conduct their own research should be qualified organizations for this purpose, notwithstanding the general prohibition against the involvement of private foundations (IRC § 41(e)(6)(B)(iii)). By contrast, for purposes of the provision allowing an estate and gift tax charitable contribution deduction for the transfer of a work of art to a qualified charitable organization, irrespective of whether the copyright therein is simultaneously transferred to the charitable organization, a private operating foundation is expressly included as a qualified organization (IRC § 2055(e)(4)(D)) even though "private foundations" are excluded.
116. IRC § 4940. See Chapter 10.
117. Once this election is made, it can be revoked only with the consent of the IRS.

§ 3.6 NONEXEMPT CHARITABLE TRUSTS

Many of the private foundation rules are applicable to nonexempt trusts, in which all or part of the unexpired interests are devoted to one or more charitable purposes—certain *charitable trusts* and *split-interest trusts*.[118] The basic purpose of this requirement is to prevent these trusts from being used to avoid the requirements and restrictions applicable to private foundations.[119]

For certain purposes,[120] a nonexempt charitable trust is treated as an organization that is a charitable entity. This type of trust[121] is a trust that is not tax-exempt, all of the unexpired interests in which are devoted to one or more charitable purposes, and for which a charitable deduction is allowed.[122]

This rule for charitable trusts usually applies to trusts in which all unexpired interests consist only of charitable income and remainder interests (regardless of whether the trustee is required to distribute corpus to, or hold corpus in trust for the benefit of, any remainder beneficiary) or to trusts in which all unexpired interests consist of charitable remainder interests, where the trustee is required to hold corpus in trust for the benefit of any charitable remainder beneficiary. An estate from which the executor or administrator is required to distribute all of the net assets (free of trust) to charitable beneficiaries is generally not considered to be a charitable trust during the period of estate administration or settlement. However, in the case of an estate from which the executor or administrator is required to distribute all of the net assets (free of trust) to charitable beneficiaries, if the estate is considered terminated for federal income tax purposes,[123] then the estate will be treated as a charitable trust between the date on which the estate is considered terminated and the date on which final distribution of all of the net assets is made to the charitable beneficiaries. Similarly, in the case of a trust in which all of the unexpired interests are charitable remainder interests that have become entitled to distributions of corpus (free of trust) upon the termination of all intervening noncharitable interests, if after the termination of the intervening interests the trust is considered terminated for federal income tax purposes,[124] the trust will be treated as a charitable trust, rather than a split-interest trust,[125] between the date on which the trust is considered terminated and the date

---

118. IRC § 4947.
119. Reg. § 53.4947-1(a). E.g., the discussion in Peters v. United States, 624 F.2d 1020 (Ct. Cl. 1980).
120. IRC §§ 507-509 (except IRC § 508(a)-(c)), 4940-4948.
121. IRC § 4947(a)(1).
122. The deduction is that allowed by IRC §§ 170, 545(b)(2), 642(c), 2055, 2106(a)(2), or 2522. Reg. § 53.4947-1(b)(1).
123. Reg. § 1.641(b)-3(a).
124. Reg. § 1.641(b)-3(b).
125. See § 3.7.

on which final distribution (free of trust) of all of the net assets is made to the charitable remainder beneficiaries.[126]

As noted, a nonexempt charitable trust is treated as a charitable organization. As discussed, an organization that is a charitable entity is a private foundation unless it meets the requirements of one or more rules by which private foundation classification is avoided.[127] Therefore, a nonexempt charitable trust is considered to be a private foundation unless it meets one of these requirements. A nonexempt charitable trust that was originally a private foundation and subsequently became qualified as a public charity must first terminate its private foundation status[128] before it can be excluded from private foundation status as a public charity.[129] A nonexempt charitable trust seeking to be initially classified as a supporting organization must also request a determination letter.[130]

The regulations accompanying these statutory rules[131] state that, for these purposes, the term *charitable* includes not only the conventional tax law meaning of the term[132] but the meaning for governmental purposes[133] as well. A court held that the government cannot validly enforce this broadened definition and that a trust that was established in part to further "public" purposes is not an "exclusively charitable" entity and thus not subject to the private foundation requirements.[134]

Not every trust with charitable beneficiaries constitutes a nonexempt charitable trust. The IRS occasionally rules that a trust will not be treated as a private foundation by virtue of these rules.[135]

As noted, this type of trust, all of the unexpired interests of which are devoted to charity, is treated as a charitable organization if a charitable deduction was allowed for gifts to it.[136] Therefore, it is not qualified as tax-exempt until it seeks recognition of its tax-exempt status by filing Form 1023.[137] Until it

---

126. Reg. § 53.4947-1(b)(2). By enactment of legislation in 1980 (P.L. 96-603, 96th Cong., 2d Sess. (1980)), Congress subjected nonexempt charitable trusts to the same reporting and disclosure requirements as are imposed on tax-exempt charitable organizations. Also Reg. § 1.6012-3(a)(7).
127. See §§ 1.2, 15.2.
128. See Chapter 13.
129. Rev. Rul. 76-92, 1971-1 C.B. 92.
130. Rev. Proc. 2023-5, 2023-1 I.R.B. 265 § 3.01(11) and Instructions for Form 8940, Schedule F; see § 12.5(a).
131. Reg. § 53.4947-1(a).
132. IRC § 170(c)(2).
133. IRC § 170(c)(1).
134. Hammond v. United States, 84-1 U.S.T.C. ¶ 9387 (D. Conn. 1984), *aff'd*, 764 F.2d 88 (2d Cir. 1985).
135. E.g., Priv. Ltr. Rul. 9742006.
136. IRC § 4947(a)(1). See *supra* note 122.
137. IRC 508(a); effective retroactively to date of creation of the trust if the application is filed within 27 months of its creation.

files for exemption, it is a taxable entity. Unless it was created prior to 1970 or meets the organizational provision described below, the charitable contribution deduction of a nonexempt charitable trust is limited to 50 percent of its income in calculating its taxable income.[138] Thus, even if, pursuant to its governing instrument, it pays out all of its income to another charitable organization, half of its income is taxed when it files Form 1041.

A nonexempt charitable trust is subject to all of the rules applicable to private foundations.[139] It must file Form 990-PF[140] and pay an excise tax on its net investment income.[141] Additionally, it must file Form 1041 and pay income tax if it has any taxable income. An unlimited deduction, rather than the 50 percent of income limit, applies to nonexempt trusts that meet the organizational rules for qualifying as a private foundation.[142] Form 1041 need not be filed if the trust has no taxable income under Subtitle A of the Code.[143] When the IRS receives Form 990-PF from a nonexempt trust, it customarily requests that the trust file Form 1023 to establish its tax-exempt status.

The IRS, from time to time, issues rulings classifying a trust as a nonexempt charitable trust.[144]

§ 3.7 SPLIT-INTEREST TRUSTS

Certain of the private foundation rules likewise apply to nonexempt split-interest trusts.[145] A *split-interest trust* is a trust that is not tax-exempt, not all of the unexpired interests in which are devoted to one or more charitable purposes, and that has amounts in trust for which a charitable deduction was allowed.[146] This type of trust is subject to the termination rules, the organizational requirements to the extent applicable, the self-dealing rules, the excess

---

138. IRC § 642(c)(6) refers to IRC § 170 limitations.
139. See Chapters 4-10.
140. IRC § 6033(d). See § 12.1.
141. IRC § 4940(b). See Chapter 10.
142. Under IRC § 642(c)(1), an income tax deduction is allowed for any amount of a trust's gross income paid or permanently set aside for charitable purposes, without limitation, pursuant to the terms of the governing instrument. Certain trusts created before October 10, 1969, are also eligible for an unlimited deduction for amounts (including income) the governing instrument requires to be permanently set aside for charitable purposes (IRC § 642(c)(2)).
143. Rev. Proc. 83-32, 1983-1 C.B. 723.
144. E.g., Priv. Ltr. Rul. 200043051.
145. IRC § 4947(a)(2).
146. See *supra* note 122. The IRS ruled that an ordinary complex trust (IRC § 661 et seq.) was not a split-interest trust simply because the trust proposed to make income distributions to charitable organizations (Priv. Ltr. Rul. 200714025).

TYPES OF PRIVATE FOUNDATIONS

business holdings rules, the jeopardizing investments rules, and the taxable expenditures rules, as if it were a private foundation.[147]

The foregoing rule is inapplicable to any amounts payable under the terms of a split-interest trust to income beneficiaries, unless a charitable deduction was allowed[148] with respect to the income interest of any beneficiary.[149] The rule is inapplicable to any assets held in trust (together with the income and capital gains derived from the assets), other than assets held in trust with respect to which a charitable deduction was allowed,[150] if the other amounts are segregated from the assets for which no deduction was allowable.[151] For these purposes, a trust with respect to which amounts are segregated must separately account for the various income, deductions, and other items properly attributable to each segregated asset in the books of account and separately to each of the beneficiaries of the trusts.[152] If any amounts held in trust are segregated, the value of the net assets for purposes of the termination rules[153] is limited to the segregated amounts.[154] The foregoing is inapplicable to any amounts transferred in trust before May 27, 1969.[155]

In the case of a trust created before May 27, 1969, the trust can avoid the private foundation rules if it can establish that it is a split-interest trust rather than a charitable trust. The issue in this instance is likely to be whether there is a noncharitable beneficiary of the trust. One opinion concerned a pre-1969 trust that was established to run a business following the owner's death, with income made available to both the company and a private foundation; the court gave an expansive reading to the term *beneficial interest*, writing that it means any right given by a trust instrument to receive a benefit from the trust in some contingency.[156] In that case, the company was held to be a noncharitable beneficiary of the trust, causing the trust to thus be a split-interest trust and not subject to the private foundation requirements.

---

147. Reg. § 53.4947-1(c)(1). For these rules, see Chapters 13, 1, 5, 7, 8, and 9, respectively.
148. See *supra* note 122.
149. IRC § 4947(a)(2)(A); Reg. § 53.4947-1(c)(2). In one instance, the IRS ruled that, because "no [charitable] deduction has ever been taken (allowed)," a charitable remainder unitrust was not subject to these split-interest trust rules, although the IRS added that, for future tax years, the burden will be on the trust to keep records to show, through the life of the unitrust, that none of the possible charitable deductions is "ever taken" (Priv. Ltr. Rul. 201713002).
150. See *supra* note 122.
151. IRC § 4947(a)(2)(B); Reg. § 53.4947-1(c)(3).
152. IRC § 4947(a)(3); Reg. § 53.4947-1(c)(3).
153. IRC § 507(c)(2), (g). See Chapter 13.
154. Reg. § 53.4947-2(a).
155. IRC § 4947(a)(2)(C); Reg. § 53.4947-1(c)(5).
156. Hammond v. United States, 84-1 U.S.T.C. ¶ 9387 (D. Conn. 1984), *aff'd*, 764 F. 2d 88 (2d Cir. 1985).

§ 3.7 SPLIT-INTEREST TRUSTS

The termination tax rules[157] do not apply to a split-interest trust by reason of a payment to a beneficiary that is directed by the terms of the governing instrument of the trust and is not discretionary with the trustee or, in the case of a discretionary payment, by reason of, or following, the expiration of the last remaining charitable interest in the trust.[158] Thus, the IRS ruled that a distribution by a charitable lead annuity trust,[159] following all annuity payments to two charities, of the remaining trust assets to the remainder beneficiaries (all disqualified persons with respect to the trust) would not constitute an act of self-dealing.[160]

Notwithstanding the foregoing, the excess business holdings rules[161] and the jeopardizing investment rules[162] do not apply to a split-interest trust if:

- All the income interest[163] (and none of the remainder interest) of the trust is devoted solely to one or more charitable purposes, and all amounts in the trust for which a charitable deduction was allowed[164] have an aggregate value (at the time the deduction was allowed) of not more than 60 percent of the aggregate fair market value of all amounts in the trust (after the payment of estate taxes and all other liabilities), or

- A charitable deduction was allowed under one of these provisions for amounts payable under the terms of the trust to every remainder beneficiary but not to any income beneficiary.[165]

An estate from which the executor or administrator is required to distribute all of the net assets in trust or free of trust to both charitable and noncharitable beneficiaries is generally not considered to be a split-interest trust during the period of estate administration or settlement.[166] When the estate is terminated, it is treated as a split-interest trust (or, if applicable, a charitable trust) between the date on which the estate is considered terminated and the date on which final distribution of the net assets to the last remaining charitable beneficiary is made.[167]

Once all of the noncharitable interests in a split-interest trust expire, the trust becomes a (nonexempt) charitable trust.[168]

---

157. IRC § 507(a). See Chapter 13.
158. Reg. § 53.4947-1(e).
159. See *Charitable Giving*, Chapter 14.
160. Priv. Ltr. Rul. 202021001.
161. See Chapter 7.
162. See Chapter 8.
163. Reg. § 53.4947-2(b)(2)(i).
164. See *supra* note 122.
165. IRC § 4947(b)(3); Reg. § 53.4947-2(b)(1). The term *income beneficiary* is defined in Reg. § 53.4947-2(b)(2)(ii).
166. Reg. § 53.4947-1(c)(6)(i).
167. Reg. § 53.4947-1(c)(6)(ii).
168. E.g., Priv. Ltr. Rul. 8220101.

TYPES OF PRIVATE FOUNDATIONS

Not every trust with charitable beneficiaries constitutes a split-interest trust. The IRS occasionally rules that a trust will not be treated as a private foundation by virtue of these rules.[169]

§ 3.8 FOREIGN PRIVATE FOUNDATIONS

In lieu of the tax on the net investment income of private foundations,[170] there is, for each tax year, on the gross investment income[171] derived from sources within the United States,[172] by every foreign organization that is a private foundation for the year, a tax equal to 4 percent of income.[173] A *foreign organization*, for these purposes, means any organization that was not created or organized in the United States or any U.S. possession, or under the law of the United States, any state, the District of Columbia, or any possession of the United States.[174]

Whenever a tax treaty exists between the United States and a foreign country, and a foreign private foundation subject to these rules is a resident of that country or is otherwise entitled to the benefits of the treaty, if the treaty provides that any item or items of gross investment income are exempt from income tax, the item or items need not be taken into account by the private foundation in computing the foreign foundation tax.[175] Thus, Canadian private foundations, exempt from the Canadian income tax and qualifying under the rules for charitable organizations generally, are exempt from the foreign private foundation tax by virtue of the U.S.–Canada Income Tax Convention.[176] The United States–Canadian income tax treaty presumes that Canadian charities that can qualify as public charities are to be treated as private foundations unless they seek recognition of public charity status.[177] Nonetheless, a foreign charitable organization (private or public) is required to file Form 990 or 990-PF only when its U.S. source gross income exceeds $25,000 and it has significant U.S. activity.[178] By contrast, a Belgian foundation, which derived only interest income from the United States, was ruled to not be exempt from the foreign private foundation tax because neither

---

169. E.g., Priv. Ltr. Rul. 9742006.
170. See Chapter 10.
171. IRC § 4940(c)(2). Also Rev. Rul. 72-244, 1972-1 C.B. 282.
172. IRC § 861.
173. IRC § 4948(a).
174. Reg. § 53.4948-1(a)(1). Also, IRC § 170(c)(2)(A).
175. Reg. § 53.4948-1(a)(3).
176. Rev. Rul. 74-183, 1974-1 C.B. 328.
177. See § 2.7(f).
178. Rev. Proc. 94-17, 1994-1 C.B. 579.

§ 3.8 FOREIGN PRIVATE FOUNDATIONS

the U.S.–Belgium Income Tax Convention nor the Treaty of Friendship, Establishment, and Navigation with the Kingdom of Belgium provides the requisite exemption.[179]

The termination tax[180] and notice requirements[181] of the special organizational rules[182] and the excise taxes imposed on domestic private foundations[183] are inapplicable to any foreign organization that, from the date of its creation, has received substantially all (i.e., at least 85 percent) of its support (other than gains from sale of capital assets) from sources outside the United States.[184] For this purpose, gifts, grants, contributions, or membership fees directly or indirectly from a U.S. person[185] are from sources within the United States.[186]

A foreign private foundation seeking recognition of exemption as a charitable entity satisfied this 85 percent–support test. This test, however, is not an independent basis for exemption; to obtain recognition as a charitable entity, an organization in this circumstance must meet all the applicable statutory requirements. This foreign foundation could not be so recognized, in part because it failed the organizational test.[187] The foundation's defense, which failed to persuade the IRS, was that the law of the country under which it is organized did not allow alteration of its purposes, so it could not amend its articles of organization to comply with the test.[188] The organization filed a petition with the U.S. Tax Court for a declaratory judgment,[189] disputing the IRS's interpretation of the organizational test and its contention that the foundation's obligation to pay an annual annuity to the spouse of the foundation's founder is a violation of the private inurement doctrine[190] and thus the operational test.[191] This case was settled, with the court entering an order that

---

179. Rev. Rul. 76-330, 1976-2 C.B. 488; Rev. Rul. 77-289, 1977-2 C.B. 490.
180. See § 13.7.
181. See § 2.7(b).
182. See § 1.7.
183. See Chapters 5-9.
184. IRC § 4948(b).
185. IRC § 7701(a)(30).
186. Reg. § 53.4948-1(b).
187. See § 1.7.
188. Priv. Ltr. Rul. 201947020. The relevant foreign law is based on Stiftung principles, a body of nonprofit law that was largely developed during the Roman Empire and spread throughout Europe.
189. IRC § 7428. See § 2.7(e).
190. See § 5.1.
191. See § 1.6.

the foundation qualified as an exempt organization[192] and was classified as a foreign private foundation.[193]

A foreign organization that can qualify for classification as a public charity can be excused from the rules pertaining to private foundations. A foreign public charity can seek a determination of its qualification as a public charity by filing an application for recognition of exemption.[194] Though it does not become eligible to receive donations deductible for U.S. income tax purposes,[195] it will receive proof of its eligibility to receive deductible donations for gift and estate tax purposes. If it wishes to seek funding from U.S. private foundations, it will also have proof that it qualifies as a public charity so that foundation grantees need not exercise expenditure responsibility over grants made to the foreign organization.[196] Finally, the foreign organization can claim exemption from the withholding tax on any U.S. source investment income that will be paid at the normal rate of 4 percent absent proof of exemption.[197]

Nonetheless, a foreign private foundation is not regarded as a tax-exempt organization if it has engaged in a *prohibited transaction*.[198] A *prohibited transaction*[199] is any act or failure to act (other than in respect to the minimum investment return requirements)[200] that would subject the private foundation or a disqualified person[201] in respect to it to a penalty in respect to any private foundation excise tax liability[202] or a termination tax[203] if the private foundation were a domestic private foundation.[204]

---

192. That is, one described in IRC § 501(c)(3).
193. The Joachim Herz Stiftung v. Commissioner, Docket No. 21039-19X, order entered Jan. 18, 2022.
194. Rev. Rul. 66-177, 1966-1 C.B. 132; Form 1023 is discussed in § 2.7(a).
195. IRC § 170(c).
196. See § 9.7.
197. Gen. Couns. Mem. 38840.
198. IRC § 4948(c)(1).
199. IRC § 4948(c)(2).
200. IRC § 4942(e); see § 6.2.
201. See Chapter 4.
202. IRC § 6684. This provision provides that if any person becomes liable for a private foundation excise tax (other than the IRC § 4940 net investment income or 4948(a) gross investment income taxes) by reason of any act or failure to act which is not due to reasonable cause and either (1) such person has theretofore been liable for tax under Chapter 42, or (2) such act or failure to act is both willful and flagrant, then such person shall be liable for a penalty equal to the amount of such tax (*id.*; Reg. § 301.6684-1(a)).
203. See § 13.7.
204. See Reg. § 53.4948-1(c)(2). E.g., Priv. Ltr. Rul. 201808010.

§ 3.8 FOREIGN PRIVATE FOUNDATIONS

A foreign private foundation will be denied exemption from taxation for all tax years beginning with the tax year during which it is notified by the IRS that it has engaged in a prohibited transaction.[205] In the case of an act or failure to act, before giving notice the IRS will warn the foreign private foundation that the act or failure to act may be treated as a prohibited transaction. The act or failure to act will not, however, be treated as a prohibited transaction if it is corrected within 90 days after the issuing of the warning. The organization may, in respect to the second tax year following the tax year in which it was given a prohibited transaction notice, apply for tax exemption. If the IRS is satisfied that the organization will not knowingly again engage in a prohibited transaction, the organization will be so notified in writing. In that case, the organization will not, in respect to tax years beginning with the tax year in respect to which a claim for tax exemption is filed, be denied exemption from taxation by reason of any prohibited transaction that was engaged in before the date on which notice was given.[206]

No gift, bequest, legacy, devise, or transfer will give rise to a charitable contribution deduction if made to a foreign private foundation in two circumstances. One circumstance is where the transaction occurred after the date on which the IRS published notice that it notified the organization that it engaged in a prohibited transaction. The other is where the transaction took place in a tax year of the organization for which it is not exempt from taxation because it engaged in a prohibited transaction.[207]

---

205. IRC § 4948(c)(3).
206. Reg. § 53.4948-1(c)(3).
207. IRC § 4948(c)(4), Reg. § 53.4948-1(d).

CHAPTER FOUR

Disqualified Persons

§ 4.1 Substantial Contributors 124
    (a) General Rules 124
    (b) 2 Percent Test 125
    (c) Terminating Substantial Contributor Status 126
§ 4.2 Foundation Managers 127
§ 4.3 Certain 20 Percent Owners 128
§ 4.4 Family Members 130
§ 4.5 Corporations or Partnerships 131
§ 4.6 Trusts or Estates 132
§ 4.7 Private Foundations 132
§ 4.8 Governmental Officials 133
§ 4.9 Termination of Disqualified Person Status 135

A fundamental concept in the federal tax laws relating to private foundations is that of the *disqualified person*. An understanding of the meaning of this term is essential to comprehending the scope of the rules defining acts of self-dealing[1] and the excess business holdings rules,[2] and affects aspects of other private foundation rules as well. Generally speaking, a disqualified person is a person[3] (including an individual, corporation, partnership, trust, estate, or other private foundation) standing in one or more relationships with respect to a private foundation, its managers, and its founders.[4]

---

1. See Chapter 5.
2. See Chapter 7.
3. Within the meaning of IRC § 7701(a)(1).
4. The facts of an IRS private letter ruling serve as an illustration of the many ways a person can be a disqualified person with respect to a private foundation (Priv. Ltr. Rul. 201433021). The term *disqualified person* is defined somewhat differently in connection with the intermediate sanctions rules that apply to public charities and social welfare organizations (IRC § 4958(f); see *infra* note 71).

§ 4.1 SUBSTANTIAL CONTRIBUTORS

(a) General Rules

The first category of disqualified persons is a substantial contributor to a private foundation.[5] The term *substantial contributor* means any person who contributed or bequeathed an aggregate amount of more than the higher of $5,000 or 2 percent of the total contributions and bequests received by the private foundation before the close of its tax year in which the contribution or bequest is received by the private foundation from that person.[6] In the case of a trust, the term substantial contributor also means the creator of the trust without regard to amounts donated;[7] additionally, it includes a decedent, even at the point in time preceding the transfer of any property from the estate to the private foundation.[8]

Although the term *person* generally is construed to mean and include an individual, a trust, estate, partnership, association, company, or corporation,[9] which includes nonprofit corporations and other types of entities that are tax-exempt, special rules apply in determining whether a person is a substantial contributor. The term substantial contributor does not include a governmental unit.[10] For purposes of the private foundation rules in Chapter 42,[11] the term substantial contributor does not include most charitable organizations that are not private foundations,[12] or an organization wholly owned by a public charity.[13] Moreover, for purposes of the self-dealing rules,[14] the term does not include any charitable organization, including another private foundation,[15] because to require inclusion of charitable organizations for this purpose would preclude private foundations from making large grants to or otherwise dealing with other private foundations.[16]

---

5. IRC § 4946(a)(1)(A), (a)(2).
6. IRC § 507(d)(2)(A); Reg. § 1.507-6(a)(1).
7. Id.
8. Rockefeller v. United States, 572 F. Supp. 9 (E.D. Ark. 1982), *aff'd*, 718 F.2d 290 (8th Cir. 1983), *cert. den.*, 466 U.S. 962 (1984).
9. IRC § 7701(a)(1).
10. Reg. § 1.507-6(a)(1). As to the definition of governmental unit, IRC § 170(c)(1).
11. IRC §§ 4940-4948.
12. Specifically, organizations described in IRC § 509(a)(1), (2), or (3). See Chapter 15.
13. Reg. §§ 1.507-6(a)(2), 53.4946-1(a)(7).
14. See Chapter 5.
15. Reg. §§ 1.507-6(a)(2), 53.4946-1(a)(8). For these purposes, a charitable organization is an organization described in IRC § 501(c)(3), other than an organization that tests for public safety (IRC § 509(a)(4); see § 15.2).
16. Reg. § 1.507-6(a)(2). This exception also applies to IRC § 4947(a)(1) trusts (see § 3.6) (Rev. Rul. 73-455, 1973-2 C.B. 187).

DISQUALIFIED PERSONS

For purposes of determining substantial contributor status, the term *contribution* includes (1) charitable contributions,[17] (2) bequests, legacies, and devises, and transfers for public, charitable, and religious uses,[18] and (3) any payment of money or transfer of property without adequate consideration.[19] Where payment is made or property transferred as consideration for admissions, sales of merchandise, performance of services, or furnishing of facilities to the donor, whether all or any part of such payment or transfer qualifies as a charitable contribution determines whether and to what extent such payment or transfer constitutes a contribution for purposes of determining substantial contributor status.[20]

(b) 2 Percent Test

The $5,000/2 percent of total contributions and bequests threshold for determining substantial contributor status is calculated on an annual and cumulative basis as of the last day of each tax year of a private foundation. Thus, in determining whether the $5,000/2 percent threshold is exceeded by a particular person, both the total contributions and bequests received by a private foundation, and the aggregate of such amounts contributed and bequeathed by such person, are determined as of the last day of each tax year.[21] A donor becomes a substantial contributor as of the first date when the private foundation receives from the donor an amount sufficient to make the donor a substantial contributor, even though the determination of the percentage of total contributions and bequests represented by a given donor's contributions and bequests is not made until the end of the foundation's tax year.[22] There is no authority for exclusion of unusual grants in calculating aggregate contributions for purposes of identifying substantial contributors.[23]

---

17. Within the meaning of IRC § 170(c).
18. Within the meaning of IRC §§ 2055 or 2106(a)(2).
19. Reg. § 1.507-6(c)(1).
20. *Id.*
21. Reg. § 1.507-6(b)(1). Generally, except for valuation purposes, all contributions and bequests made before October 9, 1969, are deemed to have been made on that date (IRC § 507(d)(2)(B)(ii); Reg. § 1.507-6(b)(1)).
22. Reg. § 1.507-6(b)(1). However, as noted, the determination as to substantial contributor status is not made until the last day of the tax year. Therefore, contributions and bequests made subsequent to those of the donor in question, but within the same tax year, may operate to keep the donor out of substantial contributor status even though that status was temporarily obtained at an earlier date during the tax year. If such additional contributions or bequests are not forthcoming, however, the donor will be a substantial contributor as of that earlier date.
23. IRC § 507(d)(2); Reg. § 1.507-6.

§ 4.1 SUBSTANTIAL CONTRIBUTORS

Each contribution or bequest is valued at its fair market value on the date received by the private foundation.[24] An individual is treated as making all contributions and bequests made by their spouse during the period of their marriage.[25] Additionally, any bequest or devise is treated as having been made by the decedent's surviving spouse for purposes of determining substantial contributor status.[26]

In the only court decision on the point, the U.S. Tax Court concluded that the self-dealing rules[27] did not apply to certain transactions involving a private foundation because the ostensible disqualified person did not meet (albeit barely) the 2 percent test for establishing substantial contributor status.[28] This outcome, which turned in part on the court's valuation of the property involved (which was necessary to establish whether the value of what the individual transferred exceeded the 2 percent threshold), enabled this individual to escape $2.7 million in taxes and penalties.

(c) Terminating Substantial Contributor Status

In general, once a person becomes a substantial contributor to a private foundation, the person remains a substantial contributor forever,[29] even though the person might not be so classified if the determination were first made at a later date.[30] For example, even though the aggregate contributions and bequests of a person become less than 2 percent of the total received by a private foundation (for example, because of subsequent contributions and bequests by other persons), such person generally will remain a substantial contributor with respect to the foundation.[31]

A limited exception applies under which a person's status as a substantial contributor will cease with respect to any private foundation as of the close of any tax year of such foundation if: (1) the person (and any related persons) did not make any contributions to the private foundation during the 10-year period ending at the close of such tax year; (2) neither the person, nor any related person, was a foundation manager of the private foundation during such 10-year period; and (3) the aggregate contributions made by the person (and any related persons) are determined by the IRS "to be insignificant when

---

24. IRC § 507(d)(2)(B)(i); Reg. § 1.507-6(c)(2).
25. IRC § 507(d)(2)(B)(iii); Reg. § 1.507-6(c)(3).
26. Reg. § 1.507-6(c)(3).
27. See Chapter 5.
28. Graham v. Commissioner, 83 T.C.M. 1137 (2002).
29. IRC § 507(d)(2)(B)(iv).
30. Reg. § 1.507-6(b)(1).
31. Id.

compared to the aggregate amount of contributions to such foundation by one other person."[32] For purposes of satisfying the third requirement, appreciation on contributions while held by the private foundation is taken into account.[33] The term *related person* for purposes of this exception means any other person who would be a disqualified person by reason of their relationship to such person, and in the case of a corporate donor includes the officers and directors of the corporation.[34]

§ 4.2 FOUNDATION MANAGERS

Another category of disqualified persons is a *foundation manager*,[35] defined as an officer, director, or trustee of a private foundation, or an individual having powers or responsibilities similar thereto.[36] An individual is considered an *officer* of a private foundation if they are specifically so designated under the constitutive documents of the private foundation (for example, its articles of incorporation or bylaws) or they regularly exercise general authority to make administrative or policy decisions on behalf of the private foundation.[37] A person who has authority merely to make recommendations pertaining to administrative or policy decisions, but lacks authority to implement them without approval of a superior, is not considered a foundation manager.[38] In one case, however, the IRS determined that employees of a bank that was the trustee of a private foundation were foundation managers because "they [were] free, on a day-to-day basis, to administer the trust and distribute the funds according to their best judgment."[39]

Independent contractors, such as lawyers, accountants, and investment managers and advisors, acting in that capacity, are also not foundation managers.[40]

Even if an employee lacks the authority to be classified as a foundation manager on an overall basis, they can be treated as a foundation manager in respect to a particular act (or failure to act) over which they do have authority or responsibility.[41] An employee who is considered a foundation manager with respect to a particular act or failure to act solely by reason of this rule,

---

32. IRC § 507(d)(2)(C)(i).
33. *Id.*
34. IRC § 507(d)(2)(C)(ii).
35. IRC § 4946(a)(1)(B).
36. IRC § 4946(b)(1); Reg. § 53.4946-1(f)(1).
37. Reg. § 53.4946-1(f)(2).
38. *Id.*
39. Rev. Rul. 74-287, 1974-1 C.B. 327.
40. *Id.*
41. IRC § 4946(b)(2); Reg. § 53.4946-1(f)(1)(ii).

however, is not considered a disqualified person for purposes of the other references to disqualified persons in the statute.[42]

§ 4.3 CERTAIN 20 PERCENT OWNERS

An owner of more than 20 percent of the total combined voting power of a corporation, the profits interest of a partnership, or the beneficial interest of a trust or unincorporated enterprise, any of which is (during the ownership) a substantial contributor to a private foundation, is a disqualified person.[43]

The term *combined voting power*[44] includes voting power represented by holdings of voting stock, actual or constructive,[45] but does not include voting rights held only as a director or trustee.[46] Thus, for example, an employee stock ownership trust[47] that held 30 percent of the stock of a corporation that was a substantial contributor to a private foundation on behalf of the corporation's participating employees (who direct the manner in which the trust votes the shares) was held to have merely the voting power of a trustee and not the ownership of the stock, and thus to not be a disqualified person in respect to the private foundation.[48]

The term *voting power* includes outstanding voting power but does not include voting power obtainable but not obtained, such as voting power obtainable by converting securities or nonvoting stock into voting stock, by exercising warrants or options to obtain voting stock, or voting power that will vest in preferred stockholders only if and when the corporation has failed to pay preferred dividends for a specified period of time or has otherwise failed to meet specified requirements.[49]

The profits interest[50] of a partner is equal to the partner's distributive share of income of the partnership as determined under special federal tax rules.[51]

---

42. Reg. § 53.4946-1(f)(4). Thus, for example, an employee of a private foundation may be considered a foundation manager with respect to a specific act of self-dealing over which they had authority, and therefore be subject to the excise tax with respect to that act of self-dealing (see Chapter 5), but not otherwise be a disqualified person with respect to other transactions between the private foundation and the employee.
43. IRC § 4946(a)(1)(C).
44. IRC § 4946(a)(1)(C)(i).
45. See IRC § 4946(a)(3).
46. Reg. § 53.4946-1(a)(5).
47. IRC § 4975(e).
48. Rev. Rul. 81-76, 1981-1 C.B. 516.
49. Reg. § 53.4946-1(a)(6).
50. IRC § 4946(a)(1)(c)(ii).
51. IRC §§ 707(b)(3), 4946(a)(4); Reg. § 53.4946-1(a)(2).

DISQUALIFIED PERSONS

The term *profits interest* includes any interest that is outstanding but not any interest that is obtainable but has not been obtained.[52]

A person's *beneficial interest in a trust* is determined in proportion to the actuarial interest of the person in the trust.[53] The term beneficial interest includes any interest that is outstanding but not any interest that is obtainable but has not been obtained.[54]

The *beneficial interest in an unincorporated enterprise* (other than a trust or estate)[55] includes any right to receive a portion of distributions from profits of the enterprise or, in the absence of a profit-sharing agreement, any right to receive a portion of the assets (if any) upon liquidation of the enterprise, except as a creditor or employee. A right to receive distribution of profits includes a right to receive any amount from the profits other than as a creditor or employee, whether as a sum certain or as a portion of profits realized by the enterprise. Where there is no agreement fixing the rights of the participants in an enterprise, the fraction of the respective interests of each participant therein is determined by dividing the amount of all investments or contributions to the capital of the enterprise made or obligated to be made by the participant by the amount of all investments or contributions to capital made or obligated to be made by all of them.[56]

Certain attribution, or *constructive ownership*, rules apply when determining the combined voting power of a corporation, profits interest of a partnership, or beneficial interest of a trust, estate, or unincorporated enterprise. When determining the combined voting power of a corporation,[57] stock owned directly or indirectly by or for a corporation, partnership, estate, or trust is considered as being owned proportionately by or for its shareholders, partners, or beneficiaries.[58] An individual is considered as owning the stock owned by members of their family.[59] Any stockholdings that have been counted once (whether by reason of actual or constructive ownership) in applying these rules are not counted a second time.[60] Ownership of profits

---

52. Reg. § 53.4946-1(a)(6).
53. Reg. § 53.4946-1(a)(4).
54. Reg. § 53.4946-1(a)(6).
55. IRC § 4946(a)(1)(C)(iii).
56. Reg. § 53.4946-1(a)(3).
57. IRC § 4946(a)(1)(c)(i), (a)(1)(E).
58. IRC §§ 267(c)(1), 4946(a)(3); Reg. § 53.4946-1(d)(1).
59. IRC § 267(c)(2), (4). IRC § 267(c)(4), however, is modified by IRC § 4946(a)(3) to define family members consistently with the definition of family members in IRC § 4946(d) (Reg. § 53.4946-1(d)(1)(i); see § 4.4). Stock constructively owned by an individual by reason of the application of IRC § 267(c)(2) is not treated as owned by them if they are described in IRC § 4946(a)(1)(D) but not also in IRC § 4946(a)(1)(A), (B), or (C) (Reg. § 53.4946-1(d)(1)).
60. Reg. § 53.4946-1(d)(1)(ii).

interests in a partnership[61] or beneficial interests in a trust, estate, or unincorporated enterprise[62] are subject to essentially the same attribution rules that apply to stockholdings.[63]

In one instance, involving three national trade associations that elected the directors of a private foundation, the 30 local association members of one of the three national associations (which thus is a federation of associations), and another national association controlled by the three associations, the IRS held that the private foundation could make grants to the local associations without committing an act of self-dealing, even though the controlled national association was a substantial contributor and the federation of associations held more than 20 percent of the combined voting power of the controlled association, inasmuch as the federation of associations had no ownership interest in its local association members and they were not otherwise disqualified persons in respect to the private foundation.[64]

For purposes of the excess business holdings rules[65] only, the term *disqualified person* does not include an employee stock ownership plan,[66] in respect to grandfathered business holdings acquired pursuant to a pre-1969 will.[67]

§ 4.4 FAMILY MEMBERS

Another category of disqualified persons is a member of the family of an individual who is a substantial contributor, a foundation manager, or one of the previously discussed 20 percent owners.[68] The term *member of the family* is defined to include only an individual's spouse, ancestors, children, grandchildren, great-grandchildren, and the spouses of children, grandchildren, and great-grandchildren.[69] Thus, these family members are themselves disqualified persons.

---

61. IRC § 4946(a)(1)(c)(ii), (a)(1)(F).
62. IRC § 4946(a)(1)(c)(iii). Although 20 percent owners of the beneficial interest of a trust or unincorporated enterprise are disqualified persons, 20 percent owners of the beneficial interest of an estate are not (*id.*). Constructive ownership of beneficial interests in an estate is significant, however, for purposes of determining whether an estate is a disqualified person under the 35 percent ownership rule (IRC § 4946(a)(1)(G); see § 4.6).
63. Reg. § 53.4946-1(e).
64. Priv. Ltr. Rul. 8525075.
65. See Chapter 7.
66. IRC § 4975(e)(7).
67. IRC § 4943(d)(4).
68. IRC § 4946(a)(1)(D).
69. IRC § 4946(d).

DISQUALIFIED PERSONS

A legally adopted child of an individual is treated for these purposes as a child of the individual by blood.[70] A brother, sister, aunt, or uncle of an individual is not, for these purposes, a member of the family.[71]

Thus, in one instance, the IRS ruled that sale of property to a disqualified person with respect to a private foundation did not result in direct or indirect self-dealing, the latter avoided in part because of the rule that brothers and sisters are not disqualified persons, as a result of that relationship, in this context.[72] In another case, conversion of a trust, treated as a private foundation, from nongrantor to grantor status did not entail self-dealing because the parties involved, being siblings, were not disqualified persons.[73]

§ 4.5 CORPORATIONS OR PARTNERSHIPS

A corporation is a disqualified person if more than 35 percent of the total combined voting power in the corporation is owned by substantial contributors, foundation managers, 20 percent owners, or members of the family of any of these individuals.[74]

The phrase *combined voting power* includes the voting power represented by holdings of voting stock, actual or constructive, but does not include voting rights held only as a director or trustee.[75] Employing that rule, the IRS concluded that stock held in a voting trust, which was related to a bank and held stock of a company for a private foundation and other entities, was excludable in computing the 35 percent threshold because it was being held by the trust only in a fiduciary capacity (thereby enabling the IRS to rule that the company was not a disqualified person with respect to the foundation and that proposed stock redemptions would not be acts of self-dealing).[76]

A partnership is a disqualified person if more than 35 percent of the profits interest in the partnership is owned by substantial contributors, foundation managers, 20 percent owners, or members of the family of any of these individuals.[77]

---

70. Reg. § 53.4946-1(h).
71. *Id*. In the intermediate sanctions context, by contrast, individuals who are siblings are included in the definition of *disqualified person* (IRC § 4958(f)(1)(B), (4)).
72. Priv. Ltr. Rul. 201510050. Under the indirect self-dealing rules, there may be control if a disqualified person, together with another person who may be a disqualified person because of a relationship with a disqualified person, may, by aggregating their votes or positions of authority with that of a foundation, require the organization to engage in a transaction (see § 5.11(b)). In this case, that test was not met because the disqualified person and other related person involved were brother and sister.
73. Priv. Ltr. Rul. 201730012.
74. IRC § 4946(a)(1)(E).
75. Reg. § 53.4946-1(a)(5).
76. Priv. Ltr. Rul. 200750020.
77. IRC § 4946(a)(1)(F).

The constructive ownership rules that apply in determining 20 percent owners also apply for purposes of applying the 35 percent rule to corporations and partnerships.[78]

§ 4.6 TRUSTS OR ESTATES

A trust or estate is a disqualified person if more than 35 percent of the beneficial interest in the trust or estate is owned by substantial contributors, foundation managers, 20 percent owners, or members of the family of any of these individuals.[79] The constructive ownership rules that apply in determining 20 percent owners also apply for purposes of applying the 35 percent rule to trusts and estates.[80]

It is the position of the chief counsel of the IRS that an estate is not a disqualified person with respect to a trust funded by the estate solely because the estate is a continuation of the decedent who was a disqualified person. Where the disqualified person-decedent's children and grandchildren (thus, also disqualified persons)[81] are beneficiaries of trusts funded by the estate and these beneficial interests are more than 35 percent of the beneficial interest in the estate, however, the estate is a disqualified person.[82]

§ 4.7 PRIVATE FOUNDATIONS

A private foundation may be a disqualified person with respect to another private foundation but only for purposes of the excess business holdings rules.[83] The disqualified person private foundation must be effectively controlled,[84] directly or indirectly, by the same person or persons (other than a bank, trust company, or similar organization acting only as a foundation manager) who control the private foundation in question, or must be the recipient of contributions substantially all of which were made, directly or indirectly, by substantial contributors, foundation managers, 20 percent owners, and members of their families who made, directly or indirectly, substantially all of the contributions to the private foundation in question.[85] One or more persons

---

78. IRC § 4946(a)(3), (4). See text accompanied by *supra* notes 57-63.
79. IRC § 4946(a)(1)(G).
80. IRC § 4946(a)(4). See text accompanied by *supra* notes 57-63.
81. See § 4.4.
82. Gen. Couns. Mem. 39445.
83. IRC § 4946(a)(1)(H). See Chapter 7.
84. Reg. § 1.482-1(a)(3).
85. Reg. § 53.4946-1(b)(1).

DISQUALIFIED PERSONS

are considered to have made *substantially all* of the contributions to a private foundation for these purposes if the persons have contributed or bequeathed at least 85 percent of the total contributions and bequests that have been received by the private foundation during its entire existence, where each person has contributed or bequeathed at least 2 percent of the total.[86]

§ 4.8 GOVERNMENTAL OFFICIALS

A governmental official may be a disqualified person with respect to a private foundation but only for purposes of the self-dealing rules.[87] The term *governmental official* means (1) an elected public official in the U.S. Congress or executive branch, (2) presidential appointees to the U.S. executive or judicial branches, (3) certain higher-compensated or ranking employees in one of these three branches, (4) House of Representatives or Senate employees earning at least $15,000 annually, (5) elected or appointed public officials in the U.S. or District of Columbia governments (including governments of U.S. possessions or political subdivisions or areas of the United States) earning at least $15,000 annually, (6) elected or appointed public officials in the executive, legislative, or judicial branch of a state, the District of Columbia, a U.S. possession, or political subdivision or other areas of the foregoing, receiving gross compensation at an annual rate of at least $20,000, (7) the personal or executive assistant or secretary to any of the foregoing, or (8) a member of the IRS Oversight Board.[88]

In defining the term *public office* for purposes of the fifth category of governmental officials, this term must be distinguished from mere public employment. Although holding a public office is one form of public employment, not every position in the employ of a state or other governmental subdivision[89] constitutes a public office. Although a determination as to whether a public employee holds a public office depends on the facts and circumstances of the case, the essential element is whether a significant part of the activities of a public employee is the independent performance of policy-making functions. Several factors may be considered as indications that a position in the executive, legislative, or judicial branch of the government of a state, possession of the United States, or political subdivision or other area of any of the foregoing, or of the District of Columbia, constitutes a public office. Among the factors to be considered, in addition to that already set forth, are that the office is created by Congress, a state constitution, or a state legislature, or by a municipality or

---

86. Reg. § 53.4946-1(b)(2).
87. IRC § 4946(a)(1)(I). See Chapter 5.
88. IRC § 4946(c).
89. IRC § 4946(c)(5).

§ 4.8 GOVERNMENTAL OFFICIALS

other governmental body pursuant to authority conferred by Congress, state constitution, or state legislature, and the powers conferred on the office and the duties to be discharged by the official are defined either directly or indirectly by Congress, a state constitution, or a state legislature, or through legislative authority.[90]

For example, a lawyer appointed by a state's attorney general to perform collection services on a part-time basis for the attorney general's office was held not to be a governmental official.[91] Likewise, the IRS ruled that the holder of the office of county attorney is not a governmental official for these purposes.[92] Similarly, an individual appointed by the president of the United States to serve as director of an entity was ruled not to be a government official because of their status as a special government employee (based on the number of days of employment).[93] By contrast, a chief administrative officer serving a city's mayor was ruled to be a government official.[94]

In a rather astounding private letter ruling, the IRS concluded that a state district court judge was not a government official for purposes of these rules.[95] The agency was moved to reach this conclusion because of a state statute providing that district court judges must apply existing law to the facts of each case; by statute, these judges cannot write new law or policy and must apply the law as created by the state's legislature or appellate courts. The IRS held that the judge in this instance "does not exercise significant independent policy-making powers, even though he may independently perform his duties as a government employee."[96] Quite appropriately, soon after this ruling was issued, it was revoked.[97]

Further, in applying the rules concerning the fifth category of governmental officials, the $15,000 amount is the individual's *gross compensation*.[98] This term refers to all receipts attributable to public office that are includible in gross income for federal income tax purposes. For example, an elected member of a state legislature may receive a salary of less than $15,000 each year,

---

90. Reg. § 53.4946-1(g)(2).
91. E.g., Priv. Ltr. Rul. 8508097.
92. Priv. Ltr. Rul. 8533099.
93. Priv. Ltr. Rul. 9804040.
94. Priv. Ltr. Rul. 200605014.
95. Priv. Ltr. Rul. 200542037.
96. It is almost impossible for a judge to write an opinion without creating "new law," despite what a state statute may stipulate; the likelihood that a given case will have a precisely applicable precedent is remote. Being human, a judge is not a legal opinion-crunching automaton. This ruling suggested that, in the absence of such a statute, a state district court judge would be a governmental official for this purpose; it also indicated that state appellate court judges are government officials.
97. Priv. Ltr. Rul. 200604034.
98. IRC § 4946(c)(5).

DISQUALIFIED PERSONS

but also receive an expense allowance that, when added to the salary, results in a total amount of more than $15,000 per year; where the expense allowance is a fixed amount given to each legislator regardless of actual expenses and there is no restriction on its use and no requirement that an accounting for its use be made to the state, the expense allowance is part of the legislator's gross compensation and the legislator becomes a disqualified person.[99]

A private foundation maintained a director-initiated grant program (enabling directors to direct grants that are not processed through the usual staff review system) and a matching gifts program (with respect to gifts by directors and staff). These director-initiated grants could not be made to fulfill a director's charitable pledge or if the director receives a benefit. One of the foundation's directors was a government official. The IRS ruled that this individual's participation in these programs did not entail any payments to the director and that none of these payments constituted compensation to this individual.[100]

§ 4.9 TERMINATION OF DISQUALIFIED PERSON STATUS

It is certainly possible for a person that is a disqualified person with respect to a private foundation to terminate their status as a disqualified person. There is, however, little law on the point. In one instance, a corporation made an exchange offer to a private foundation concerning certain shares of the corporation's nonvoting stock. This corporation was once a disqualified person with respect to the foundation solely because an individual who was a manager of the foundation[101] owned more than 35 percent of the total combined voting power of the corporation.[102] Five years before the exchange occurred, the foundation manager resigned that position. The IRS ruled that the resignation of the foundation manager terminated the status of the corporation as a disqualified person with respect to the private foundation, noting that all aspects of the exchange occurred after the separation of the foundation manager and that they were not connected with the proposed exchange while serving in that capacity.[103] This ruling gave the impression that some reasonable period of time had to pass to cause the termination of disqualified person status to be respected.

---

99. Rev. Rul. 77-473, 1977-2 C.B. 421.
100. Priv. Ltr. Rul. 200605014. Thus, this director's participation in these programs was ruled to not amount to self-dealing (see § 5.8(e)).
101. See § 4.2.
102. See § 4.5.
103. Rev. Rul. 76-448, 1976-2 C.B. 368. Thus, this exchange was able to take place without causing an act of self-dealing under IRC § 4941(d)(1)(A). See § 5.4(c).

§ 4.9 TERMINATION OF DISQUALIFIED PERSON STATUS

That impression was erased, years later, when the IRS concluded that an individual was not a foundation manager (or any other type of disqualified person) with respect to a private foundation, in connection with a prospective sale of businesses by the foundation, even though the individual resigned from the foundation's board of directors the day before they bid on the assets.[104] They had been an employee of one of the principal businesses for 25 years and were the chief operating officer of it for many of those years. Even after they retired, they were persuaded to become reinvolved in corporate management, as a consultant to a newly formed holding company, because of their knowledge and expertise. They were overseeing the process of selling the businesses until they decided to be a bidder. Nonetheless, several factors led the IRS to its conclusion that this individual would not exercise undue influence over the sale of the assets, including an open bidding process, evaluation of bids by a bank and an investment firm, supervision of the sale by a court, and approval of the transaction by the attorney general of the state involved. The ruling enabled this individual, should their bid prevail, to acquire the businesses from the foundation without engaging in one or more acts of self-dealing.[105]

The IRS ruled that two trustees of a private foundation, who resigned their positions over three years beforehand, were no longer disqualified persons with respect to the foundation, so that an exchange of property that was about to occur would not constitute self-dealing.[106] The transaction was an exchange of houses, one of which was owned by one of the former trustees. The IRS emphasized that these individuals were not disqualified persons in any other capacity, the house would be used for exempt purposes, and there were no discussions about the proposed exchange while they served as trustees. As a result of the exchange of houses, this former trustee may become a substantial contributor to the foundation, thus again becoming a disqualified person with respect to it.[107] Nonetheless, the transaction would not be self-dealing because the disqualified person status arose only as a result of the transaction.[108]

---

104. Priv. Ltr. Rul. 199943047.
105. This ruling may be contrasted with Rev. Rul. 80-207, 1980-2 C.B. 193, discussed in § 15.6(j), text accompanied by note 369.
106. Priv. Ltr. Rul. 201130008.
107. See § 4.1.
108. Reg. § 53.4941(d)-1(a). See § 5.3.

CHAPTER FIVE

Self-Dealing

§ 5.1 Private Inurement Doctrine 140
§ 5.2 Private Benefit Doctrine 143
§ 5.3 General Definition of Self-Dealing 151
§ 5.4 Sale, Exchange, Lease, or Furnishing of Property 154
    (a) Sales 154
    (b) Transactions by Agents 156
    (c) Exchanges 157
    (d) Leasing of Property 158
    (e) Furnishing of Goods, Services, or Facilities 159
    (f) Co-Owned Property 162
    (g) Coinvestments 166
§ 5.5 Loans and Other Extensions of Credit 168
    (a) Gifts of Indebted Property 170
    (b) Interest-Free Loans 171
§ 5.6 Payment of Compensation 173
    (a) Definition of Personal Services 174
    (b) Definition of Compensation 177
    (c) Definition of Reasonable 180
    (d) Finding Salary Statistics 184
    (e) Excess Executive Compensation Tax 185
        (i) General Rules and Definitions 186
        (ii) Compensation from Related Organizations 187
        (iii) Exceptions to Covered Employee Status 188
    (f) Commissions or Management Fees 190
    (g) Expense Advances and Reimbursements 191
    (h) Bank Fees 192

§ 5.7 Indemnification and Insurance 194
    (a) Noncompensatory Indemnification and Insurance 195
    (b) Compensatory Indemnification and Insurance 196
    (c) Fringe Benefit Rules and Volunteers 197
§ 5.8 Uses of Income or Assets by Disqualified Persons 199
    (a) Securities Transactions 200
        (i) Summary of Law 200
        (ii) Representative Case 201
    (b) Other Transactions Involving Manipulation 203
    (c) Payment of Charitable Pledges 203
    (d) For the Benefit of Transactions 204
    (e) Incidental or Tenuous Benefits 206
    (f) Memberships 212
    (g) Benefit Tickets 213
    (h) Other Acts 213
§ 5.9 Sharing Space, People, and Expenses 214
    (a) Determining What the Private Foundation Can Pay 215
    (b) Office Space and Personnel 215
    (c) Group Insurance 218
    (d) Public Facilities 218
§ 5.10 Payments to Government Officials 220
§ 5.11 Indirect Self-Dealing 218
    (a) Transactions with Controlled Entities 221
    (b) Concept of *Control* 222

SELF-DEALING

- (c) Transactions and the Control Element 224
- (d) Exceptions 225
- (e) Fraudulent Investment Schemes 227

§ 5.12 **Estate Administration Exception** 228
- (a) Concept of the *Expectancy* 228
- (b) Estate Administration Exception—General Rules 230
- (c) Determining Fair Market Value 233

§ 5.13 **Early Terminations of Charitable Remainder Trusts** 235

§ 5.14 **Additional Exceptions** 237
- (a) Certain Corporate Organizations or Reorganizations 237
- (b) Transitional Rules (Savings Provisions) 238

§ 5.15 **Issues Once Self-Dealing Occurs** 239
- (a) Self-Dealing Excise Taxes 240
  - (i) Initial Taxes 240
  - (ii) Additional Taxes 243
  - (iii) Termination Tax 243
  - (iv) Limitation on Abatement 243
  - (v) Advice of Counsel 244
- (b) Amount Involved 244
  - (i) Use of Money or Other Property 244
  - (ii) Compensation 245
  - (iii) Exceptions Predicated on Fair Market Value 246
- (c) Date of Valuation 246
- (d) Correcting the Transaction 247
  - (i) Sales by the Foundation 248
  - (ii) Sales to the Foundation 249
  - (iii) Loans 250
  - (iv) Use of Property by Disqualified Person 250
  - (v) Use of Property by Private Foundation 251
  - (vi) Unreasonable Compensation 251
- (e) Court Jurisdiction as to Tax 251

Tax-exempt charitable organizations, including private foundations, are subject to the federal tax law rules prohibiting private inurement and unwarranted private benefit.[1] Particularly in the case of private inurement, the law imposes standards of reasonableness with respect to transactions involving members of the board and other insiders with respect to the charitable organization, entailing payment of compensation, provision of services, purchases and sales, loans, rental arrangements, and other transfers of income or assets. The sanctions for violation of either of these doctrines are the revocation or denial of exempt status and loss of the ability to attract tax-deductible contributions.

Congress, in 1969, decided that, with respect to private foundations, these two doctrines were insufficient. Among the practices Congress found troublesome were loans and stock bailouts between certain privately funded organizations and their creators and creator's families. Prior law permitted these transactions as long as they were reasonable,[2] such as charging a reasonable rate of interest or payment of fair market value. Nevertheless, Congress believed that private foundations were being used as pocketbooks for funds not necessarily available from other sources, so it proceeded to eliminate

---

1. See §§ 5.1, 5.2.
2. IRC § 503 (repealed).

SELF-DEALING

self-interested financial activity between a private charity and those who are insiders with respect to it. As the following excerpt from the 1969 legislative history indicates, the arm's-length approach embodied in the prior law was deemed no longer sufficient, resulting in the enactment of self-dealing rules:

> Arm's-length standards have proved to require disproportionately great enforcement efforts, resulting in sporadic and uncertain effectiveness of the provisions. On occasion the sanctions are ineffective and tend to discourage the expenditure of enforcement effort. On the other hand, in many cases the sanctions are so great in comparison to the offense involved that they cause reluctance in enforcement, especially in view of the element of subjectivity in applying arm's-length standards. Where the Internal Revenue Service does seek to apply sanctions in such circumstances, the same factors encourage extensive litigation and a noticeable reluctance by the courts to uphold severe sanctions.
>
> Consequently, as a practical matter, prior law did not preserve the integrity of private foundations. Also, the Congress concluded that compliance with arm's-length standards often does not in itself prevent the use of a private foundation to improperly benefit those who control the foundations. This is true, for example, where a foundation (1) purchases property from a substantial donor at a fair price, but does so in order to provide funds to the donor who needs cash and cannot find a ready buyer; (2) lends money to the donor with adequate security and at a reasonable rate of interest, but at a time when the money market is too tight for the donor to readily find alternate sources of funds; or (3) makes commitments to lease property from the donor at a fair rental when the donor needs such advance leases in order to secure financing for construction or acquisition of the property.
>
> To minimize the need to apply subjective arm's-length standards, to avoid the temptation to misuse private foundations for noncharitable purposes, to provide a more rational relationship between sanctions and improper acts, and to make it more practical to properly enforce the law, the [Tax Reform] Act [of 1969] generally prohibits self-dealing transactions and provides a variety and graduation of sanctions. This is based on the belief by the Congress that the highest fiduciary standards require complete elimination of all self-dealing rather than arm's-length standards.[3]

Any determination that the excise tax with respect to self-dealing is to be imposed requires the existence of three elements: a private foundation,[4] a disqualified person,[5] and an act of self-dealing between the two.[6] It is usually immaterial whether a self-dealing transaction results in a benefit or a detriment

---

3. Staff of Joint Comm. on Internal Revenue Tax'n, 91st Cong., 2d Sess., General Explanation of the Tax Reform Act of 1969 30-31 (Comm. Print 1970).
4. See § 1.2.
5. See Chapter 4.
6. Thus, for example, transactions between a private foundation and a fund are not acts of self-dealing, where the fund is not a separate legal entity (Priv. Ltr. Rul. 8623080).

to the private foundation.[7] A self-dealing transaction does not include a transaction between a private foundation and a disqualified person, however, where the disqualified person status arises only as a result of the transaction.[8]

Notwithstanding enactment of the self-dealing rules, the private inurement and private benefit doctrines remain applicable with respect to private foundations. Thus, for example, if self-dealing is pervasive and ongoing, the tax-exempt status of a private foundation can be revoked.[9] Likewise, even if an exception to the self-dealing rules is applicable, the private inurement and benefit doctrines may nonetheless apply.[10]

§ 5.1 PRIVATE INUREMENT DOCTRINE

The federal tax law states that no part of the net earnings of tax-exempt charitable organizations, including private foundations, may inure to the benefit of persons in their private capacity.[11] This rule is known as the *private inurement doctrine*. Thus, this doctrine is a statutory criterion for federal income tax exemption for charitable organizations. Indeed, it is the fundamental defining principle distinguishing nonprofit organizations from for-profit organizations.[12]

The peculiarly phrased (and quite antiquated) language of the private inurement doctrine requires that the tax-exempt organization be organized and operated so that "no part of . . . [its] net earnings . . . inures to the benefit of any private shareholder or individual." This provision reads as if it were proscribing the payment of dividends. In fact, it is rare for an exempt organization to have shareholders, let alone make any payments to them.[13] The contemporary,

---

7. Leon A. Beeghly Fund v. Commissioner, 35 T.C. 490 (1960), *aff'd*, 310 F.2d 756 (6th Cir. 1962).
8. Reg. § 53.4941(d)-1(a).
9. E.g., Tech. Adv. Mem. 9335001.
10. See § 5.1, 5.2.
11. IRC § 501(c)(3); Reg. § 1.501(c)(3)-1(c)(2).
12. An oddity in this area is the fact that, in a sense, the private inurement proscription in the Internal Revenue Code is redundant and thus unnecessary, in that this proscription is inherent in the concept of a nonprofit organization. Thus, the U.S. Supreme Court wrote that a "non-profit entity is ordinarily understood to differ from a for-profit corporation principally because it is barred from distributing its net earnings, if any, to individuals who exercise control over it, such as members, officers, directors, or trustees" (Camps Newfound/Owatonna, Inc. v. Town of Harrison, Maine et al., 520 U.S. 564, 585 (1997) (internal quotation marks omitted)). It may be noted that this proscription extends to persons other than just individuals and that, since an insider is required to have a private inurement transaction, this type of a transaction rarely occurs simply because it is with an organization's member.
13. An organization was denied recognition of exemption as a charitable entity in part because it issued voting stock providing equity interests to its shareholders, which the IRS found to be a violation of the private inurement doctrine (Priv. Ltr. Rul. 201918020).

and broad and wide-ranging, meaning of the statutory language[14] is barely reflected in its literal form and transcends the nearly century-old formulation: None of the income or assets of a charitable organization may be permitted to directly or indirectly unduly benefit an individual or other person who is in a position to exercise a significant degree of control over it.

Essentially, the doctrine forbids ways of causing the income or assets of charitable (and certain other) tax-exempt organizations to flow away from the organization (*inure*) and to one or more persons who are related to the organization (*insiders*) for nonexempt purposes. The Office of Chief Counsel of the IRS bluntly summarized the doctrine: "The inurement prohibition serves to prevent anyone in a position to do so from siphoning off any of a charity's income or assets for personal use."[15]

The essence of the private inurement rule is to ensure that the tax-exempt organization involved is serving a public interest and not a private interest. That is, to be tax-exempt, it is necessary for an organization to establish that it is not organized and operated for the benefit of private interests, such as designated individuals, the creator of the organization or their family, shareholders of the organization, persons controlled (directly or indirectly) by these private interests, or any other persons having a personal and private interest in the activities of the organization.[16]

In determining the presence of any proscribed private inurement, the law looks to the ultimate purpose of the organization. If the basic purpose of the organization is to benefit individuals in their private capacity, then it cannot be tax-exempt even though exempt activities are also performed. Conversely, incidental benefits to private individuals, such as those that are generated by reason of the organization's program activities, will usually not defeat the exemption if the organization otherwise qualifies under the appropriate exemption provision.[17]

The IRS and the courts have recognized a variety of forms of private inurement. These include: (1) excessive or unreasonable compensation (the most common form of private inurement), (2) unreasonable or unfair rental arrangements, (3) unreasonable or unfair lending arrangements, (4)

---

14. A court wrote that the "boundaries of the term 'inures' have thus far defied precise definition" (Variety Club Tent No. 6 Charities, Inc. v. Commissioner, 74 T.C.M. 1485, 1494 (1997)).
15. Gen. Couns. Mem. 39862. A gentler explication of the doctrine by the agency's lawyers was that "[i]nurement is likely to arise where the financial benefit represents a transfer of the organization's financial resources to an individual solely by virtue of the individual's relationship with the organization, and without regard to accomplishing exempt purposes" (Gen. Couns. Mem. 38459).
16. Reg. §§ 1.501(a)-1(c), 1.501(c)(3)-1(c)(1)(ii), 1.501(c)(3)-1(c)(2), 1.501(c)(3)-1(d)(1)(ii).
17. Reg. § 1.501(c)(3)-1(c)(1).

§ 5.1 PRIVATE INUREMENT DOCTRINE

provision of services to persons in their private capacity, (5) certain assumptions of liability, (6) certain sales of assets to insiders, (7) certain participations in partnerships and other joint ventures, (8) certain percentage payment arrangements, and (9) varieties of tax avoidance schemes.

A striking example of private inurement occurred in connection with the formation of a "sweat equity housing cooperative association," with the stated purpose of preserving and rehabilitating rural properties of historic value that simultaneously serve as family homes. Each board member was accorded a possessory interest in one of the entity's residential units and a possessory interest in common with other members of other real and personal property. Not surprisingly, these arrangements were ruled to constitute forms of private inurement.[18]

The doctrine of private inurement does not prohibit transactions between charitable organizations and those who have a close relationship with them. As the IRS wrote, "There is no absolute prohibition against an exempt section 501(c)(3) organization dealing with its founders, members, or officers in conducting its economic affairs."[19] Rather, the private inurement doctrine requires that these transactions be tested against a standard of *reasonableness*.[20] The standard calls for a roughly equal exchange of benefits between the parties; the law is designed to discourage what the IRS termed a "disproportionate share of the benefits of the exchange" flowing to an insider.[21]

Generally, an *insider*[22] is a person who has a unique relationship with the charitable organization, by which that person can cause application of the organization's funds or assets for the private purposes of the person by reason of the person's exercise of control or influence over, or being in a position to exercise that control or influence over, the organization.[23] The scope of the concept of the *insider* continues to be the subject of litigation.[24]

The contours of the doctrine of private inurement have been immensely influenced by the intermediate sanctions rules.[25] Indeed, in some ways, the

---

18. Priv. Ltr. Rul. 201640022.
19. Priv. Ltr. Rul. 9130002. To this group may be added directors and trustees.
20. In contrast, the private foundation self-dealing rules generally and essentially forbid these types of transactions.
21. Priv. Ltr. Rul. 9130002.
22. The federal tax law has appropriated the term from the federal securities laws that prohibit, for example, insider trading.
23. American Campaign Academy v. Commissioner, 92 T.C. 1053 (1989). It was subsequently stated that the "case law [as to private inurement] appears to have drawn a line between those who have significant control over the organization's activities and those who are unrelated third parties" (Variety Club Tent No. 6 Charities, Inc. v. Commissioner, 74 T.C.M. 1485, 1492 (1997)).
24. E.g., United Cancer Council, Inc. v. Commissioner, 165 F.3d 1173 (7th Cir. 1999), *rev'g* 109 T.C. 326 (1997). In general, see *Tax-Exempt Organizations* § 20.3.
25. See *Tax-Exempt Organizations* §§ 20.8, 21.16.

intermediate sanctions rules can be viewed as codification of the private inurement doctrine. Disqualified persons are essentially the same as insiders; excessive benefit transactions are much the same as private inurement transactions.[26] Developments in the law concerning the intermediate sanctions rules help shape the private inurement doctrine; the reverse is also the case.[27]

The sanction for violation of the private inurement doctrine is denial or revocation of the charitable organization's tax-exempt status. Because of the self-dealing rules, revocation of a private foundation's exempt status on the ground of private inurement is rare.[28] The IRS may, however, resort to application of the private inurement doctrine where there are multiple violations of the self-dealing rules and insignificant grantmaking.[29] For example, the IRS revoked the exempt status of a private foundation on private inurement grounds where it provided a disqualified person with a personal residence, without charge, where the residence was the foundation's only asset and there was little grantmaking.[30] Similarly, the IRS revoked a private foundation's tax-exempt status based on a finding of private inurement, principally in the form of the use of the organization's credit cards by disqualified persons to pay personal expenses and the provision of assistance to the sister of the foundation's secretary, who was disabled, by driving her to the doctor, taking her grocery shopping weekly, and making purchases for her. The IRS stated that "[p]roviding assistance to a relative is inurement and is not an exempt activity" and also observed that the personal use of the foundation's assets for the benefit of disqualified persons constituted self-dealing transactions.[31]

§ 5.2 PRIVATE BENEFIT DOCTRINE

The federal tax law concerning tax-exempt charitable organizations, including private foundations, imposes an *operational test*, which looks to see whether the organization is conducting programs in furtherance of its tax-exempt purposes rather than for private individuals.[32] This standard has spawned the

---

26. The intermediate sanctions rules are underlain with excise taxes, as are the self-dealing rules (see §5.15(a)), although they are imposed at different rates. Also, the intermediate sanctions rules contain exceptions that are not available in the private inurement setting.
27. Developments in both areas also help shape self-dealing law; the reverse is also the case.
28. E.g., Priv. Ltr. Rul. 202110038.
29. E.g., Priv. Ltr. Rul. 201731019, in which a foundation's exemption was revoked where it engaged in little exempt activity over the audit period.
30. Tech. Adv. Mem. 9335001.
31. Priv. Ltr. Rul. 202221020. Likewise, a privation foundation's exemption was revoked where its expenditures were for the personal benefit of its trustees, it did not make any grants, and it did not engage in any other exempt functions (Priv. Ltr. Rul. 201641023).
32. Reg. § 1.501(c)(3)-1(b). See *Tax-Exempt Organizations* § 4.5.

§ 5.2 PRIVATE BENEFIT DOCTRINE

private benefit doctrine. As one court stated the matter, the private benefit proscription "inheres in the requirement that [a charitable] organization operate exclusively for exempt purposes."[33]

This doctrine is potentially applicable with respect to all persons, including those who are not insiders; that is, the doctrine embraces benefits provided to "disinterested persons"[34] or "unrelated" persons.[35] Or, as the IRS stated the matter, the private benefit doctrine applies with respect to "all kinds of persons and groups."[36] Indeed, the IRS has written that "[t]here is general agreement that [private] inurement is a subset of private benefit."[37] Thus, the private benefit doctrine is broader than the private inurement doctrine in the sense that its applicability is not confined to situations involving organizations' insiders but has the potential to apply with respect to any person or persons.[38] The private benefit doctrine essentially is intended to prevent a charitable organization from benefiting private interests in any way, other than to an insubstantial extent. By contrast, the IRS does not recognize the concept of incidental private inurement.[39]

One of the few cases fully explicating the private benefit doctrine concerned an otherwise tax-exempt school that trained individuals for careers as political campaign professionals.[40] Nearly all of the school's graduates became employed by or consultants to organizations or candidates of a national political party. A court concluded that the school did not primarily engage in activities that accomplished educational purposes, in that it benefited private interests to more than an insubstantial extent. That is, the school was found to be substantially benefiting the private interests of the political party's entities and candidates.

---

33. Redlands Surgical Services v. Commissioner, 113 T.C. 47, 74 (1999), *aff'd*, 242 F.3d 904 (9th Cir. 2001).
34. American Campaign Academy v. Commissioner, 92 T.C. 1053, 1069 (1989).
35. Redlands Surgical Services v. Commissioner, 113 T.C. 47, 74 (1999), *aff'd*, 242 F.3d 904 (9th Cir. 2001).
36. Priv. Ltr. Rul. 200635018.
37. Priv. Ltr. Rul. 201044025.
38. It is an oddity in the law that a doctrine that is based on a few words in a regulation (the private benefit doctrine) can subsume a doctrine that is based on statutory law—indeed, a law that has been in existence for more than 110 years (the private inurement doctrine).
39. This position, while never particularly credible, is now belied by the fact that the IRS, in the public charity setting, applies the intermediate sanctions rules rather than the private inurement doctrine except in the most egregious circumstances (see *Tax-Exempt Organizations* §§ 20.8, 21.16), thereby causing many acts of private inurement to not result in revocation of tax exemption (and thus be considered forms of incidental private inurement).
40. American Campaign Academy v. Commissioner, 92 T.C. 1053 (1989).

The heart of this opinion is the analysis of the concept—neither previously nor subsequently articulated—of *primary* private benefit and *secondary* private benefit. In that setting, the beneficiaries of primary private benefit were the school's students; the beneficiaries of secondary private benefit were the employers of the graduates. The existence of this secondary private benefit was what caused this school to fail to acquire tax-exempt status.

The court accepted the IRS's argument that "where the training of individuals is focused on furthering a particular targeted private interest, the conferred secondary benefit ceases to be incidental to the providing organization's exempt purposes."[41] The beneficiaries, at the secondary level, were found to be a "select group."[42]

The school unsuccessfully presented as precedent several IRS rulings holding tax-exempt, as educational organizations, entities that provide training to individuals in a particular industry or profession.[43] The court accepted the IRS's characterization of these rulings, which was that the "secondary benefit provided in each such ruling was broadly spread among members of an industry . . . as opposed to being earmarked for a particular organization or person."[44] The court said that the secondary benefit in each of these rulings was, because of the spread, "incidental to the providing organization's exempt purpose."[45]

This court subsequently held that a nonprofit organization that audited structural steel fabricators in conjunction with a quality certification program conducted by a related trade association did not constitute a charitable organization, in part because it yielded inappropriate private benefit to the association and to the fabricators that were inspected.[46] The court wrote that the "development and administration of a quality certification program, at the request of and for the structural steel industry, would appear to be consistent with [the association's] mission as a business league."[47] It added that the "focus thus seems to be on aiding industry participants, with any benefit to the general public being merely secondary."[48] The court thus saw more than insubstantial private benefit in two contexts: the extent to which the purported charitable organization served the association's interests in

---

41. *Id.* at 1074.
42. *Id.* at 1076.
43. E.g., Rev. Rul. 75-196, 1975-1 C.B. 155; Rev. Rul. 72-101, 1972-1 C.B. 144; Rev. Rul. 68-504, 1968-2 C.B. 211; Rev. Rul. 67-72, 1967-1 C.B. 125.
44. American Campaign Academy v. Commissioner, 92 T.C. 1053, 1074 (1989).
45. *Id.*
46. Quality Auditing Co. v. Commissioner, 114 T.C. 498 (2000).
47. *Id.* at 510.
48. *Id.*

§ 5.2 PRIVATE BENEFIT DOCTRINE

carrying out its role of industry betterment and the benefit accruing to the steel fabricators that requested audits and whose facilities were inspected by the organization.

The most significant of the private benefit court cases[49] concerned the matter of whole entity joint ventures, in this case a nonprofit subsidiary of a healthcare facility, where the entity places its entire operations in a venture with a for-profit entity, perhaps ceding authority over all of its resources to the co-venturer.[50] A fundamental concept in this context is control, with the IRS and the courts examining relationships between public charities and for-profit organizations to ascertain if the charity has lost control of its facilities and programs to the for-profit. Examples include relationships reflected in management agreements, leases, fundraising contracts, and, of course, partnership, limited liability company, or other joint venture agreements. In this context, it can be irrelevant if the public charity is in fact engaging substantially in exempt activities and if fees (if any) paid by the exempt organization to a for-profit entity are reasonable.

The sweeping rule of law in this regard was articulated, in one of the two most radical of these cases, by a federal court of appeals, which wrote that the "critical inquiry is not whether particular contractual payments to a related for-profit organization are reasonable or excessive, but instead whether the entire enterprise is carried on in such a manner that the for-profit organization benefits substantially from the operation of" the tax-exempt organization.[51] This opinion articulates the outer reaches of the ambit of the private benefit doctrine: the thought that there can be unwarranted private benefit, conferred on a person who is not an insider, even if the terms and conditions of the arrangement are reasonable and substantial exempt functions are occurring.

In the other of these cases, two for-profit organizations that did not have any formal structural control over the nonprofit entity, the tax exemption of which was at issue, nevertheless were found to have exerted "considerable control" over its activities.[52] The for-profit entities set fees that the nonprofit organization charged for training sessions, required the nonprofit organization to carry on certain types of educational activities, and provided management personnel paid for and responsible to one of the for-profit

---

49. Redlands Surgical Services v. Commissioner, 113 T.C. 47 (1999), *aff'd*, 242 F.3d 904 (9th Cir. 2001).
50. See *Tax-Exempt Organizations* § 31.3.
51. Church by Mail, Inc. v. Commissioner, 765 F.2d 1387, 1392 (9th Cir. 1985), *aff'g* 48 T.C.M. 471 (1984).
52. est of Hawaii v. Commissioner, 71 T.C. 1067, 1080 (1979), *aff'd*, 647 F.2d 170 (9th Cir. 1981).

organizations. Pursuant to a licensing agreement with the for-profit organizations, the nonprofit entity was allowed to use certain intellectual property for 10 years; at the end of the license period, all copyrighted material, including new material developed by the nonprofit organization, was required to be turned over to the for-profit organizations. The nonprofit organization was mandated to use its excess funds for the development of its program activities or related research. The for-profit organizations also required that trainers and local organizations sign an agreement to not compete with these activities for two years after terminating their relationship with the organizations involved.

The trial court, in this case, concluded that the nonprofit organization was "part of a franchise system which is operated for private benefit and ... its affiliation with this system taints it with a substantial commercial purpose."[53] The "ultimate beneficiaries" of the nonprofit organization's activities were found to be the for-profit corporations; the nonprofit organization was "simply the instrument to subsidize the for-profit corporations and not vice versa."[54] The nonprofit organization was held to not be operating exclusively for charitable purposes.

These two court opinions have framed this analysis. Even without formal control over the ostensible tax-exempt organization by one or more for-profit entities, the ostensible tax-exempt organization can be viewed as merely the instrument by which a for-profit organization is subsidized (benefited). The nonprofit organization's "affiliation" with a for-profit entity or a "system" involving one or more for-profit entities can taint the nonprofit organization, actually or seemingly imbuing it with a substantial commercial purpose. The result is likely to be a finding of private benefit (or, if an insider is involved, private inurement),[55] causing the nonprofit organization to lose or be denied tax-exempt status.

Matters worsen in this context where there is actual control. This is the principal message of the decision concerning whole entity joint ventures. In that case, a public charity (a subsidiary of an exempt hospital) became a co–general partner with a for-profit organization in a partnership that owned and operated a surgery center. A for-profit management company affiliated with the for-profit co–general partner managed the arrangement. The public charity's sole activity was participation in the partnership. The court termed this relationship "passive participation [by the charitable organization] in a for-profit

---

53. *Id.* at 1080.
54. *Id.*
55. The private inurement doctrine was invoked in a case concerning a charitable organization in a partnership in Housing Pioneers, Inc. v. Commissioner, 65 T.C.M. 2191 (1993).

§ 5.2 PRIVATE BENEFIT DOCTRINE

health-service enterprise."[56] The court concluded that it was "patently clear" that the partnership was not being operated in an exclusively charitable manner. The income-producing activity of the partnership was characterized as "indivisible" as between the nonprofit and for-profit organizations. No "discrete part" of these activities was "severable from those activities that produce income to be applied to the other partner's profit."[57]

The heart of this whole entity joint venture decision is this: To the extent that a public charity "cedes control over its sole activity to for-profit parties [by, in this case, entering into the joint venture] having an independent economic interest in the same activity and having no obligation to put charitable purposes ahead of profit-making objectives," the charity cannot be assured that the partnership will in fact be operated in furtherance of charitable purposes.[58] The consequence is the conferring on the for-profit party in the venture "significant private benefits."[59]

The IRS is making much of the private benefit doctrine, as two examples illustrate. The agency is of the view that private benefit is present when the founders of an otherwise tax-exempt school also are directors of a for-profit company that manages the school; the nature of the benefit is largely financial, and the IRS asserted that the educational activities of the school could be undertaken without conferring the benefit (i.e., by use of employees or volunteers).[60] The agency also believes that certain scholarship-granting foundations are ineligible for tax exemption, by reason of the private benefit doctrine, because the recipients are individuals who are participants in beauty pageants operated by tax-exempt social welfare organizations; private benefit is thought to be bestowed on the social welfare organizations because the grant programs serve to attract contestants to enter the pageants and on the for-profit entities that are corporate sponsors of the pageants.[61]

Other examples further illustrate the extent to which the IRS can apply the private benefit doctrine. A nonprofit corporation, formed to provide training

---

56. Redlands Surgical Services v. Commissioner, 113 T.C. 47, 77 (1999), *aff'd*, 242 F.3d 904 (9th Cir. 2001).
57. *Id.*
58. *Id.* at 78.
59. *Id.* This decision was a major victory for the IRS, which earlier staked out, in Rev. Rul. 98-15, 1998-1 C.B. 718, the position adopted by the court. The agency, however, did not prevail in a whole hospital joint venture case (St. David's Health Care System, Inc. v. United States, 2002-2 U.S.T.C. ¶ 50,452 (W.D. Tex. 2002), *vacated and remanded (for trial)*, 349 F.3d 232 (5th Cir. 2003) No. 101CV-046 (W.D. Tex. Mar. 4, 2004)).
60. "Private Benefit Under IRC [§] 501(c)(3)," Topic H, IRS Exempt Organizations Continuing Professional Education Text for FY 2001.
61. "Beauty Pageants: Private Benefit Worth Watching," Topic B, IRS Exempt Organizations Continuing Professional Education Text for FY 2002.

SELF-DEALING

to softball and baseball umpires, and to coordinate and schedule games and tournaments, is also involved in assigning umpires to games and promoting ethical standards among baseball officials; this entity was denied recognition of tax exemption as a charitable or educational organization, in part on the ground that it is serving the private interests of the umpires, who are paid for their services.[62] The IRS in the past has ruled that an organization with a small board of trustees or directors is inherently violating the private benefit doctrine, so that a governing board of this nature cannot qualify as an exempt charitable organization.[63]

Although tax-exempt charitable organizations may provide benefits to persons in their private capacity, benefits of this nature must—to avoid jeopardizing exempt status—be incidental both quantitatively and qualitatively in relation to the furthering of exempt purposes. To be *quantitatively incidental*, the private benefit must be insubstantial, measured in the context of the overall tax-exempt benefit conferred by the activity.[64] To be *qualitatively incidental*, private benefit must be a necessary concomitant of the exempt activity, in that the exempt objectives cannot be achieved without necessarily benefiting certain individuals privately.[65]

As an illustration of incidental private benefit, a tax-exempt charitable organization that allocated Medicaid patients to physicians in private practice was held to provide qualitatively and quantitatively incidental private benefit to the physicians, inasmuch as it was "impossible for this organization to further its exempt purposes without providing some benefit to these physicians."[66] Similarly, the IRS ruled that an exempt hospital's investment in a for-profit medical malpractice insurance company, using funds paid by its staff physicians, furthered charitable purposes and was deemed not to extend impermissible private benefit, because the investment was required for the writing of insurance for the physicians, the physicians needed the insurance to practice at the hospital, and the hospital needed the physicians to provide healthcare services to its communities.[67] Likewise, the IRS ruled that the construction and maintenance of a recreational path on an island was a charitable

---

62. Priv. Ltr. Rul. 201617012. This position by the IRS comes close to the proposition that it is a violation of the private benefit doctrine for an organization to use charitable dollars to pay compensation to individuals, either as employees or independent contractors.
63. E.g., Priv. Ltr. Rul. 201540019. See *Tax-Exempt Organizations* § 5.7(c). Were this the law (and it is not), there would be few exempt private foundations and perhaps no exempt family foundations.
64. E.g., Ginsburg v. Commissioner, 46 T.C. 47 (1966); Rev. Rul. 75-286, 1975-2 C.B. 210; Rev. Rul. 68-14, 1968-1 C.B. 243.
65. E.g., Rev. Rul. 70-186, 1970-1 C.B. 128.
66. Priv. Ltr. Rul. 9615030.
67. Priv. Ltr. Rul. 200606042.

§ 5.2 PRIVATE BENEFIT DOCTRINE

activity, with any resulting private benefit accruing to the residents of the island dismissed as incidental.[68] Further, the IRS ruled that a public charity could restore an exempt social club's historic building, where the public would be given substantial access to the facility, with the resulting private benefit to the club and its members regarded as incidental.[69]

The private benefit doctrine applies to private foundations, inasmuch as they are tax-exempt, charitable organizations. Nonetheless, there is only one known instance of application of the doctrine in the private foundation context. In that instance, an individual who was not a disqualified person with respect to the foundation desired access to the foundation's archive of valuable documents for the purpose of writing a commercial trade book about the individual who was the subject of the archive. The foundation was holding the archive to organize, preserve, and catalogue it, and ultimately transfer the archive to a public charity. The IRS ruled that although providing this individual access to the collection would not amount to self-dealing (because she was not a disqualified person), the foundation would confer impermissible private benefit to the individual: The private interests of the individual would be served by the commercial profit gained because the book would be enhanced by the information contained in the foundation-owned archive.[70]

Traditionally, the private benefit doctrine has been largely applied in cases concerning relationships between public charities and individuals. The application

---

68. Tech. Adv. Mem. 201151028.
69. Priv. Ltr. Rul. 201442066. On rare occasions, the IRS will find incidental private benefit in circumstances where the benefit may appear, to others, impermissible. For example, the IRS ruled that a public charity may provide its research results to a major for-profit global media corporation for fees, format the information specifically for the company, license rights to derivative works to the company, allow the company to use the charity's information for its internal business purposes, agree to not deliver information to the company's competitors, and agree that the company may have a perpetual license to use the information, with this package of private benefits considered incidental (Priv. Ltr. Rul. 201440023).
70. Priv. Ltr. Rul. 200114040. The IRS ruled that, when a private foundation commenced a scholarship program and collaborated in this regard with community foundations, it did not transgress the private inurement and private benefit doctrines simply because relatives of some of the directors of the community foundations received assistance (the scholarships were held to be qualifying distributions and the recipients to be members of a charitable class) (Priv. Ltr. Rul. 200332018). In contrast, unwarranted private benefit was found where a scholarship-granting organization was making grants only to members of one family (and descendants of the founder of the organization); a court condoned revocation of this entity's tax exemption (Educational Assistance Found. for the Descendants of Hungarian Immigrants in the Performing Arts, Inc. v. United States, 111 F. Supp. 3d 34 (D.D.C. 2015)).

of this doctrine, however, is being expanded to encompass arrangements between charitable organizations and for-profit entities and charitable organizations and other categories of tax-exempt organizations.[71]

The sanction for violation of the private benefit doctrine is denial or revocation of the charitable organization's tax-exempt status.

The private benefit doctrine can apply in a factual situation even where the private inurement rules or the self-dealing rules do not apply, such as where the transaction does not involve an insider or a disqualified person.[72]

§ 5.3 GENERAL DEFINITION OF SELF-DEALING

Most direct and indirect financial transactions between a private foundation and its disqualified persons are taxable as self-dealing transactions,[73] subject to certain limited exceptions.[74] If a transaction falls within the definition of self-dealing, it is usually immaterial whether the transaction results in a benefit or a detriment to the private foundation.[75] A self-dealing transaction does not, however, include one between a private foundation and a disqualified

---

71. The appellate court that reversed the U.S. Tax Court in United Cancer Council, Inc. v. Commissioner, 165 F.3d 1173 (7th Cir. 1999), *rev'g*, 109 T.C. 326 (1997), also remanded the case for reconsideration under of the private benefit doctrine. Inasmuch as the Tax Court previously held that an act of private inurement is also an act of private benefit (American Campaign Academy v. Commissioner, 92 T.C. 1053 (1989)), the United Cancer Council case was shaping up to be a significant private benefit case. The case, however, was settled before the Tax Court could rule on the application of the private benefit doctrine.
72. In Graham v. Commissioner, 83 T.C.M. 1137 (2002), the self-dealing rules were held inapplicable because the party to the transaction with a private foundation was not a disqualified person; the transaction was otherwise a self-dealing one, however, yet the IRS did not pursue revocation of the foundation's tax-exempt status because of the resulting private benefit. Likewise, the IRS ruled that the sale of a parcel of real estate to a private foundation by the nephews of the founder of the foundation was not self-dealing, in that they were not disqualified persons with respect to the foundation (Priv. Ltr. Rul. 200333030).
73. IRC § 4941(d)(1).
74. IRC § 4941(d)(2).
75. Reg. § 53.4941(d)-1(a). The concept of *reasonableness* is an essential element in the application of the personal services exception to self-dealing (see § 5.6(a)). Outside the context of this exception, however, the concept of *reasonableness* rarely is factored into the self-dealing analysis. On one occasion, however, an early termination of a charitable remainder trust (which is subject to the self-dealing rules; see § 3.7) was held to not be self-dealing because the method of allocating assets of the trust on its termination to the beneficiaries was reasonable, the income beneficiaries had life expectancies reflecting average longevity, state law allowed the early termination, and all the beneficiaries favored the early termination (Priv. Ltr. Rul. 200252092). See Rev. Rul. 2008-41, 2008-30 I.R.B. 170.

§ 5.3 GENERAL DEFINITION OF SELF-DEALING

person where the disqualified person status arises only as a result of such transaction.[76]

Six acts of self-dealing between a private foundation and a disqualified person are referenced in the statute. As a general rule, the transactions cannot occur, without taxation, directly between a private foundation and one or more of its insiders, nor indirectly through an entity controlled by such disqualified persons or by the foundation.[77] These transactions are (1) sale, exchange, or leasing of property; (2) lending of money or other extension of credit; (3) furnishing of goods, services, or facilities; (4) payment of compensation (or payment or reimbursement of expenses); (5) transfer to, or use by or for the benefit of, a disqualified person of any income or assets of the foundation; and (6) agreement to pay a government official.[78]

Statutory *special rules* provide certain limited exceptions to the self-dealing transactions described above, as follows:

- Transfer of indebted real or personal property to a private foundation is permitted if the foundation does not assume a mortgage or similar debt, or if it takes the property subject to a debt placed on the property by the disqualified person before the 10-year period ending on the date of gift.[79]

- A disqualified person may make a loan that is without interest or other charge to a private foundation if the funds are used exclusively for the foundation's tax-exempt purposes.[80]

- Offering a no-rent lease or furnishing free use of a disqualified person's goods, services, or facilities to a private foundation is permitted, as long as they are used exclusively for tax-exempt purposes.[81]

---

76. Reg. § 53.4941(d)-1(a). For example, the bargain sale of property (see *Charitable Giving* § 7.18) to a private foundation is not a direct act of self-dealing if the seller becomes a disqualified person with respect to the foundation only by reason of being a substantial contributor (see § 4.1) as a result of the bargain element of the sale (Reg. § 53.4941(d)-1(a)).
77. It is often said that these acts of self-dealing are "prohibited." Indeed, even the IRS has stated that "[a]cts of self-dealing . . . are prohibited by Chapter 42 of the Internal Revenue Code" (Priv. Ltr. Rul. 201703003). That view is inaccurate. These acts can be taxed, and subjected to correction requirements and to reporting rules, but nothing in the Code or any other federal law "prohibits" them. State law, however, may prohibit self-dealing involving a private foundation.
78. IRC § 4941(d)(1).
79. IRC § 4941(d)(2)(A); see § 5.5(a).
80. IRC § 4941(d)(2)(B); see § 5.5(b).
81. IRC § 4941(d)(2)(C); see § 5.4(d), (e).

- Furnishing a disqualified person with goods, facilities, or services that the private foundation regularly provides to the general public is not self-dealing if conditions and charges for the transaction are the same as those for the public.[82]
- A private foundation may pay reasonable compensation to, and pay or reimburse the expenses of, a disqualified person (other than a government official), if the amounts are for personal services and are reasonable and necessary to carry out the foundation's exempt purposes.[83]
- Proceeds of a corporate liquidation, merger, redemption, recapitalization, or other corporate adjustment, organization, or reorganization can be received by a private foundation if all securities of the same class as that held by the foundation are subject to the same terms and such terms provide for receipt by the foundation of no less than fair market value.[84]
- Certain scholarship, travel, and pension payments by a private foundation to elected or appointed federal and state government officials are not considered self-dealing.[85]

In addition to the special rules provided in the statute, the regulations provide other limited exceptions to the statutory categories of self-dealing transactions. For example, certain business transactions between an organization controlled by the private foundation and its disqualified persons are excluded from the definition of *indirect self-dealing*, as are certain grants to an uncontrolled intermediary organization that plans to use the funds to make payments to governmental officials, and certain transactions arising in the normal and customary course of a retail business engaged in with the public.[86] Certain transactions during administration of an estate or revocable trust in which the private foundation has an interest or expectancy are also excluded from the definition of indirect self-dealing under the regulations.[87]

The self-dealing rules also do not apply to any tax year within the 60-month period during which a private foundation is attempting to terminate its private

---

82. IRC § 4941(d)(2)(D); see § 5.4(e).
83. IRC § 4941(d)(2)(E); see § 5.6.
84. IRC § 4941(d)(2)(F); see § 5.14(a).
85. IRC § 4941(d)(2)(G); see § 5.10. The IRS applied many of these exceptions in the case of a private operating foundation (see § 3.1) functioning as a museum (Priv. Ltr. Rul. 201415010).
86. Reg. § 53.4941(d)-1(b)(1), (2), (6); see § 5.11(d).
87. Reg. § 53.4941(d)-1(b)(3); see § 5.12.

foundation status by operating as a public charity and satisfies the requirements for public charity status.[88]

The regulations also provide several transitional rules rendering the self-dealing rules inapplicable to various pre-1969 and other transactions.[89]

The specific statutory rules defining taxable acts of self-dealing, and the various exceptions thereto, are described in detail in the sections that follow.

§ 5.4 SALE, EXCHANGE, LEASE, OR FURNISHING OF PROPERTY

The sale, exchange, lease, or furnishing of property between a private foundation and a disqualified person with respect to the foundation generally constitutes self-dealing.[90]

(a) Sales

Thus, for example, the sale of incidental supplies by a disqualified person to a foundation or the sale of stock by a disqualified person to a foundation for a bargain price is an act of self-dealing, regardless of the amount paid.[91] Likewise, the sale of stock or other securities by a disqualified person to a private foundation in a bargain sale is an act of self-dealing regardless of the amount paid for such stock or other securities.[92]

A private foundation's purchase of a mortgage held by its bank trustee that was a disqualified person was found to be self-dealing, even though the rate was much more favorable than would otherwise have been available; the self-dealing occurred because the bank (disqualified as a trustee) was selling its own property, not simply handling the purchase of an investment instrument from an independent source.[93] Conversely, even though the same banking institution served as trustee for both parties, a sale to a foundation by a testamentary trust (which was not disqualified in relation to the foundation)

---

88. Reg. § 1.507-2(e)(2); see § 13.4; e.g., Priv. Ltr. Rul. 199911054. Also, the self-dealing rules do not apply with respect to amounts payable by a split-interest trust (see § 3.7) to its income beneficiaries for which a charitable deduction was allowed (Reg. § 53.4947-1(c)(2)(i)). Indeed, the self-dealing rules are not implicated where a charitable remainder trust (see § 3.6) is declared void and the assets returned to the donor (e.g., Priv. Ltr. Rul. 9816030).
89. Reg. § 53.4941(d)-4; see § 5.14(b).
90. IRC § 4941(d)(1)(A).
91. Reg. § 53.4941(d)-2(a)(1).
92. *Id.* As to bargain sales generally, see *Charitable Giving* § 7.18.
93. Rev. Rul. 77-259, 1977-2 C.B. 387.

SELF-DEALING

was not self-dealing.[94] A sale to the bank itself by either party would be self-dealing, however, because the bank is disqualified as to both parties, even though neither trust is related to the other trust.

The sale by a private foundation to an unrelated party of an option to buy shares in a corporation that is a disqualified person in regard to the foundation is not self-dealing, even though the exercise of the option by the foundation would be.[95]

A disqualified person's transfer of property to a private foundation in return for cancellation of the disqualified person's indebtedness to the foundation is regarded by the IRS as a sale of the property by the disqualified person to the foundation and thus an act of self-dealing.[96]

An installment sale may be an act of self-dealing either as a sale of property[97] or an extension of credit.[98]

The transfer of real or personal property by a disqualified person to a private foundation is treated as a sale or exchange for these purposes if the private foundation assumes a mortgage or similar lien that was placed on the property prior to the transfer, or takes the property subject to a mortgage or similar lien that a disqualified person placed on the property within the 10-year period ending on the date of transfer.[99] A *similar lien* includes, but is not limited to, deeds of trust and vendors' liens, but does not include any other lien if it is insignificant in relation to the fair market value of the property transferred.[100]

If a transaction is not a sale or exchange between a private foundation and a disqualified person, it will not be an act of self-dealing (unless some other definition of the term applies).[101] In one instance, the IRS ruled that, where the previously undivided interests of a foundation and disqualified person trusts in parcels of real estate are divided on a pro rata basis in accordance with the fair market value of the common interests surrendered and the separate interests received, the division of the properties will not constitute a sale or exchange of the properties, so that the partition will not amount to an act of

---

94. Rev. Rul. 78-77, 1978-1 C.B. 378.
95. Priv. Ltr. Rul. 8502040.
96. Rev. Rul. 81-40, 1981-1 C.B. 508.
97. IRC § 4941(d)(1)(A).
98. IRC § 4941(d)(1)(B).
99. IRC § 4941(d)(2)(A). Also Reg. § 53.4941(d)-2(a)(2); Harold and Julia Gershman Family Foundation v. Commissioner, 83 T.C. 217 (1984); Rev. Rul. 78-395, 1978-2 C.B. 270.
100. By reason of the Tax Reform Act of 1984 § 312, the self-dealing rules do not apply with respect to certain sales by the Wasie Foundation, as described in Wasie v. Commissioner, 86 T.C. 962 (1986).
101. E.g., Priv. Ltr. Rul. 201718002.

§ 5.4 SALE, EXCHANGE, LEASE, OR FURNISHING OF PROPERTY

self-dealing.[102] In another case, a contribution by disqualified persons of units in a limited liability company to a private foundation was ruled to not be self-dealing, because liabilities placed on the company did not constitute a similar lien (in that they were insignificant), so that the transfer did not constitute a sale or exchange;[103] this characterization of the transaction facilitated a side-stepping of the rule that the sale of securities by a disqualified person to a foundation in a bargain sale is self-dealing.[104]

A contribution to a private foundation by a person who is a disqualified person with respect to the private foundation is not an act of self-dealing.[105]

Certain purchases or sales of securities by a private foundation through a stockbroker that follow normal trading procedures on a stock exchange or recognized over-the-counter market, however, do not constitute acts of self-dealing. For this self-dealing exception to apply, (1) the transaction must be a purchase or sale of securities by a private foundation through a stockbroker, where normal trading procedures on a stock exchange or recognized over-the-counter market are followed, (2) neither the buyer nor the seller of the securities, nor the agent of either, knows the identity of the other party involved, and (3) the sale is made in the ordinary course of business and does not involve a block of securities larger than the average trading volume of the stock over the previous four weeks.[106]

(b) Transactions by Agents

The fact that an intermediary person or agent handles the transaction does not circumvent the rules, and self-dealing occurs when a disqualified person buys private foundation property from an agent through whom the foundation is selling property. In a case involving an art object consigned to a commercial art auction house, the purchase of the object by a disqualified person constituted self-dealing.[107] Similarly, the leasing of property to a disqualified person

---

102. Priv. Ltr. Rul. 200350022. In this ruling, the IRS relied on Rev. Rul. 56-437, 1956-2 C.B. 507 (holding that the severance of a joint tenancy in stock of a corporation, under a state's partition statute, and the issuance of separate stock certificates in the names of each of the joint tenants was a nontaxable exchange).
103. Priv. Ltr. Rul. 201012050.
104. Reg. § 53.4941(d)-2(a)(1); see text accompanied by *supra* note 92.
105. E.g., Priv. Ltr. Rul. 8234149.
106. Reg. § 53.4941(a)-1(a)(1). This exception does not apply, however, to a transaction involving a dealer who is a disqualified person acting as a principal or to a transaction which is an act of self-dealing pursuant to IRC § 4941(d)(1)(B) and Reg. § 53.491(d)-2(c)(1) (Reg. § 53.4941(a)-1(a)(1)).
107. Rev. Rul. 76-18, 1976-1 C.B. 355.

by a management company resulted in self-dealing when the foundation controlled the manager's actions through a retained veto power.[108]

(c) Exchanges

An exchange of property, such as the transfer of shares of stock in payment of an interest-free loan, is tantamount to a sale or exchange.[109] Similarly, a transfer to a private foundation by a disqualified person of real estate, the fair market value of which equals the amount of a loan made by the foundation to the disqualified person,[110] is an act of self-dealing.[111] On the other hand, a transfer of real estate in satisfaction of a pledge to pay cash or readily marketable securities was held not to be a sale or exchange because the pledge was not legally enforceable[112] and because a gratuitous pledge is not considered an extension of credit before the date of maturity.[113] Essentially, self-dealing does not result from this type of a transfer because it is a gift.[114]

The IRS ruled that a split-dollar life insurance arrangement, involving a private foundation and its chief executive officer, included as part of a comprehensive compensation package, would not entail self-dealing.[115] The premiums to be paid by the executive and the private foundation will be sent directly to the insurance company; the IRS ruled that this would not be an exchange of property between the parties. The arrangement would permit the executive to assign their rights under the agreement to another party, such as an irrevocable life insurance trust. The IRS ruled that an assignment by this executive of their rights under the insurance arrangement, and the assignee's exercise of the rights and assumptions of obligations under the agreement, would not involve a sale, exchange, or other transfer of property between the executive and the private foundation.[116]

An exchange of a private foundation's securities in a reorganization or merger of a corporation that is a disqualified person is not necessarily an act of self-dealing. If all of the securities of the same class as those held by the

---

108. Priv. Ltr. Rul. 9047001.
109. Rev. Rul. 77-379, 1977-2 C.B. 387.
110. A loan of this nature is also self-dealing (see § 5.5).
111. Rev. Rul. 81-40, 1981-1 C.B. 508.
112. See § 5.8(c).
113. See § 5.5.
114. Tech. Adv. Mem. 8723001.
115. Priv. Ltr. Rul. 200020060.
116. The IRS also ruled that this split-dollar insurance arrangement is not the type of insurance arrangement that is subject to IRC § 170(f)(10) or IRS Notice 99-36, 1999-26 I.R.B. 3 (concerning certain forbidden charitable split-dollar life insurance plans).

§ 5.4 SALE, EXCHANGE, LEASE, OR FURNISHING OF PROPERTY

foundation (prior to the transaction) are subject to the same, or uniform, terms and the foundation receives full fair market value for its securities, prohibited self-dealing does not occur.[117]

The partition of property held as tenants-in-common with a disqualified person did not produce reportable gain nor constitute self-dealing for a private foundation.[118] Without having explicitly said so, the IRS does not deem a partition as a prohibited sale or exchange. The foundation had received an undivided interest in the unproductive property as a gift from the disqualified person. Local law prohibited a nonprofit corporation from holding unproductive property, and the foundation wanted to make the property marketable by creating a divided interest.

(d) Leasing of Property

The leasing of property between a private foundation and a disqualified person generally constitutes self-dealing.[119] The leasing of property by a disqualified person to a private foundation without charge, however, is not an act of self-dealing. A lease is considered to be without charge even though the private foundation pays its portion of janitorial services, utilities, or other maintenance costs, as long as the payment is not made directly or indirectly to a disqualified person.[120]

As an example of permitted rent-free use, assume a private foundation borrows at no cost an art object from its creator to display in the foundation's museum. The foundation pays the maintenance and insurance on the object directly to the vendors. Thus, the foundation is essentially allowed to pay the disqualified person's costs of owning the art object during the time the works are on public display. The reason for permitting this arrangement is that the public benefits: Art that is otherwise not available can now be seen. On the other hand, placement of a foundation's art in its creator's home, away from public view, would be self-dealing.[121] Displaying art on the creator's property that is open to the public has been permitted, but only because the foundation's collection was displayed throughout the city, primarily on public lands, as part of a comprehensive outdoor museum program.[122]

---

117. Reg. § 53.4941(d)-3(d)(1); see 5.14(a).
118. E.g., Priv. Ltr. Rul. 8038049; see § 5.4(f).
119. IRC § 4941(d)(1)(A); Reg. § 53.4941(d)-2(b)(1).
120. Reg. § 53.4941(d)-2(b)(2).
121. Rev. Rul. 74-600, 1974-2 C.B. 385.
122. Tech. Adv. Mem. 9221002. But see Tech. Adv. Mem. 8824001 for the opposite result when, because sculptures were placed on a disqualified person's private residential grounds not physically open to the public but available only for viewing from the street, self-dealing was ruled to have occurred.

A private foundation desired to dispose of ranch land it had owned for over 30 years to acquire other income-producing property to carry out its grant programs. An engineer advised that the foundation would maximize the ranch's value by developing the property—a process expected to take considerable time and requiring someone to live on the ranch during its development. The IRS approved a plan for the foundation to lease to its executive vice president, for a nominal sum, 1 percent of the ranch acreage, on which he would, at his expense, construct a residence. The lease provided for the foundation to pay the officer the then fair market value of any improvements upon the termination of the lease. The primary purpose of the transaction was to "ensure the foundation's interests in the ranch were safeguarded." The IRS decided that although the officer and his wife were disqualified persons, the duties were reasonable and necessary to accomplishing the foundation's purposes, and therefore the lease and subsequent payment to the officer would not result in self-dealing.[123]

A foundation's rental of a charter aircraft from a charter aircraft company, which is itself a disqualified person, was found to be an act of self-dealing.[124] Donating use of the airplane to the foundation, however, would be allowed. As long as the airplane is used for bona fide foundation business, the foundation can directly pay a third party for fuel or hangar rental in the city visited, as long as the goods and services are purchased from an independent party.[125] Thus, the IRS ruled that disqualified persons may, without engaging in an act of self-dealing, lend works of art to a private foundation, inasmuch as the loan was without charge.[126]

(e) Furnishing of Goods, Services, or Facilities

As a general rule, self-dealing includes any direct or indirect furnishing of goods, services, or facilities between a private foundation and disqualified persons.[127] The law, however, also contains special rules, one of which allows the furnishing without charge of a disqualified person's goods, services, or facilities to the private foundation as long as they are used exclusively for tax-exempt purposes.[128] Thus, the use of office space, an automobile, an auditorium, laboratory

---

123. Priv. Ltr. Rul. 9327082.
124. Rev. Rul. 73-363, 1973-2 C.B. 383. Reg. § 53.4941(d)-2(d)(1).
125. See § 5.9.
126. Priv. Ltr. Rul. 200014040. Likewise, where a lease by a private foundation of property for charitable purposes was guaranteed by a disqualified person, the guarantee was characterized by the IRS as the provision of services without charge (Priv. Ltr. Rul. 199950039).
127. IRC § 4941(d)(1)(C).
128. IRC § 4941(d)(2)(C).

§ 5.4 SALE, EXCHANGE, LEASE, OR FURNISHING OF PROPERTY

and office supplies, telephone equipment, and the like can be donated.[129] The foundation must require and actually use the donated property in conducting its charitable programs. The permitted furnishing is considered as *without charge*, even though the foundation pays for transportation, insurance, maintenance, and other costs it incurs in obtaining or using the property, so long as the payment is not made directly or indirectly to the disqualified person.[130]

Another special exception permits a foundation to furnish a disqualified person with exempt function goods, facilities, or services that the private foundation regularly provides to the public, such as a park, a museum, or a library. Such furnishing is not self-dealing if the conditions and charges made to the public are at least on as favorable a basis as the goods or services are made available for the disqualified person's use.[131] This exception is intended to apply to functionally related facilities,[132] such as a public park that a substantial number of persons, other than disqualified persons, use. A director of a private foundation that operates a museum, for example, could pay the normal price for their admission into an exhibition and to purchase a book in the museum bookstore.

For example, the IRS ruled that the use of a private foundation's meeting room by a disqualified person was not an act of self-dealing inasmuch as the room was made available to the disqualified person on the same basis that it was made available to the general public and was functionally related to the performance of a tax-exempt purpose of the private foundation.[133] Similarly, the IRS held that it was not an act of self-dealing for a museum, which was a private foundation, to allow a corporation, which was a disqualified person with respect to the private foundation, to use its private road for access to the corporation's headquarters. The road was made available to the general public on a comparable basis, a substantial number of (nondisqualified) persons actually used the road, and the use of the road as an entrance to the museum was functionally related to the private foundation's tax-exempt purpose. The corporation had agreed to maintain the road, although that did not entitle it to any special privileges with respect to the use of the road.[134] In another instance, however, because the rental of office space to disqualified persons did not contribute importantly to a private foundation's tax-exempt purpose of conducting agricultural research and experimentation, the rental was held

---

129. E.g., Priv. Ltr. Rul. 9805021 (use of foundation's facility for overnight stays by disqualified person when done to carry out the foundation's business).
130. Reg. § 53.4941(d)-2(d)(3).
131. IRC § 4941(d)(2)(D); Reg. § 53.4941(d)-3(b).
132. IRC § 4941(j)(4). See §§ 6.2(d), 7.3.
133. Rev. Rul. 76-10, 1976-1 C.B. 355.
134. Rev. Rul. 76-459, 1976-2 C.B. 369.

to be self-dealing, even though the disqualified persons conducted business activities in the same subject area of the private foundation's research.[135] Likewise, the IRS concluded that self-dealing occurred when a disqualified person lived rent-free in a manor house as a resident curator of a historic plantation, which was a national historic landmark, because the private foundation that owned and operated the property insufficiently made the grounds open to the public.[136]

Although the special exceptions in the statutory law do not address the point, the regulations expand this exception to allow a foundation to furnish goods, services, or facilities to its managers in recognition of their services as employees.[137] The value of the services or goods must be reasonable and necessary to the performance of their tasks in carrying out the exempt purposes of the foundation. Whether or not reportable as taxable income, the value of facilities and goods provided must not, when added to other amounts provided to a manager, cause them to receive excessive compensation. Accordingly, the IRS found that the furnishing of living quarters in a historical district to a substantial contributor (who worked 25 to 35 hours a week overseeing the complex and managing the foundation's financial affairs) was not self-dealing, again, because the value of the personal living quarters when combined with other compensation was reasonable.[138]

Providing a residence to a private foundation's president and his wife, who also served as the foundation's treasurer, on foundation property while they supervised the development of a retreat, conference, and ministry center was found to serve the foundation's exempt purposes.[139] The couple was said to be uniquely qualified to manage the project because they had shaped the ministry's vision and the president was a civil engineer familiar with the zoning and other local property law. Once the project was complete, a retreat-center director would be hired and the disqualified persons would move out. Because their overall compensation, including the value of the rent-free housing, was reasonable and their services were integral to the accomplishment of the exempt mission, the IRS concluded that impermissible self-dealing would not result from this furnishing of housing.

A trust created to promote open space, recreation, and education on a reserve did not commit acts of self-dealing when its work impacted land partly owned by its disqualified persons. The reserve is owned 54 percent by a company that

---

135. Rev. Rul. 79-374, 1979-2 C.B. 387.
136. Tech. Adv. Mem. 9646002, revoking Priv. Ltr. Rul. 8651087. Indeed, the transgression was found to amount to unwarranted private benefit (see § 5.2).
137. Reg. § 53.4941(d)-2(d)(2).
138. Priv. Ltr. Rul. 8948034.
139. Priv. Ltr. Rul. 199913040.

was a substantial contributor to the foundation, 31 percent by a political subdivision, and 15 percent by other public and private owners.[140] The trust had extensive plans to produce a comprehensive plan for the reserve, to study its habitat and wildlife, to promote stewardship, to conduct public education activities, and to facilitate educational and recreational public access to the reserve. Due to the public nature of the project, the IRS decided any direct or indirect transfer to, or use of, foundation assets by the disqualified person (developer) was incidental and tenuous.[141]

A museum classified as a private operating foundation, functioning in accordance with a 99-year, no-rent lease (with a 25-year extension option) with a disqualified person, sought a ruling that self-dealing would not occur in connection with a proposed amendment to the lease to build a second museum building with a 100-year expected useful life, increase the acreage to which the museum had access, use roads on the disqualified person's portion of the property for public access to the museum, house maintenance and landscape equipment in a shed located on the disqualified person's property, and reimburse for services provided by two of the disqualified person's employees; a favorable ruling was issued.[142]

(f) Co-Owned Property

Mere co-ownership of a property by a private foundation and its disqualified person(s) does not, in and of itself, constitute self-dealing. Therefore, a private foundation can receive and hold a gift or bequest of an undivided interest in property from its disqualified person(s). The difficulty is that only the

---

140. Priv. Ltr. Rul. 200527020. Though not provided in the facts of the ruling, the reserve seems to be a very large tract of land that includes subdivisions developed by the disqualified person.
141. Citing Example 1 in Reg. § 53.4941(d)-2(f)(9), which deems a foundation's work to improve a ghetto in which the disqualified persons own property yielded only incidental benefit. An IRS private letter ruling illustrates the blending of some of these rules. Although self-dealing generally includes the furnishing of goods between a private foundation and a disqualified person, this type of furnishing is allowed if it is without charge. Pursuant to this exception, a foundation was permitted to borrow an art collection from a disqualified person trust and display it to the public (Priv. Ltr. Rul. 201346011). The exception also extended to the provision of exhibit space to the foundation (see § 5.4(d)). Compensation paid to those providing "special technological services" for the conservation of exhibits, being "similar to the services an anthropologist or archeologist would provide with respect to artifacts," were held eligible for the personal services exception (see § 5.6(a)). Participation by other disqualified persons in certain event activities was held to not be self-dealing because of the incidental benefit exception (see § 5.8(e)).
142. Priv. Ltr. Rul. 201415010.

SELF-DEALING

foundation can *use the property* because the statute specifically prohibits the use of any foundation income or assets by its disqualified persons.[143] Essentially, a foundation may hold and use co-owned property, but the disqualified person co-owner can only hold, but cannot use or otherwise reap any benefit from, the property. Private letter rulings illustrate why limited use or shared ownership can still be of some advantage to persons holding this type of an interest. In one case, an individual and his spouse owned an extensive art collection that they planned to bequeath to a museum they were creating. On the husband's death, the private foundation museum and the spouse became joint tenants holding an undivided interest in each object in the art collection. The IRS would not permit the spouse to display a small portion of the co-owned objects in her home and strictly applied the statute to prohibit her use of the art.[144] The IRS nonetheless permitted the spouse to display a portion of the art works in her home, holding that the spouse's "private use of the small percentage of her separate property art works not loaned to you [the museum] at any one time will not constitute an act of self-dealing." The ruling, by stipulating that only her separate property could be displayed in her home, indirectly concluded that her tenant-in-common interest in the extensive art collection could not be displayed in her home.[145]

In this case, the spouse and the foundation asked the IRS to approve an agreement that the foundation has the "duty, and will make all expenditures necessary, to insure and adequately care for, maintain, conserve, and provide security for [the spouse's] separate property art works and the art works held by you and [the spouse] as tenants-in-common as long as they are on your premises or are otherwise in [the foundation's] possession." Similarly, the spouse bore the cost of insuring and maintaining art works that were in her possession. The ruling adopted a policy regarding sharing of property and stated that:

> [I]nsuring the art works in your [museum] custody affords you protection against the risk of financial loss in the event the works are damaged or destroyed. As in the supplemental submissions to your ruling request, it is more economical for you to obtain a single policy covering all art works in your possession rather than a multiplicity of separate short-term policies covering different sets of art works that may be displayed from time to time in your museum. While [the spouse] may receive a benefit from your being the policy holder, the benefit will not be consequential in a financial sense since [the spouse] will pay the portion of the insurance premium

---

143. IRC § 4941(d)(1)(E).
144. Priv. Ltr. Rul. 8842045.
145. Gen. Couns. Mem. 39770 was more specific in holding that no portion of the co-owned art could be displayed in this individual's home.

§ 5.4 SALE, EXCHANGE, LEASE, OR FURNISHING OF PROPERTY

attributable to her private use and enjoyment of her separate property art works. Therefore, such benefits as may accrue to [the spouse] from your obtaining the insurance policy are merely incidental or tenuous benefits. Finally, the loan of art work from [the spouse] furthers your educational and charitable purposes of having available these items for public display, and any benefit to [the spouse] from your payment of transportation, maintenance, or insurance is merely incidental to the achievement of this charitable and educational goal.[146]

Loan of a trustee's historic artifact collection and library to a private operating foundation in relation to which he was a disqualified person, without charge, was deemed to not constitute self-dealing. Office and display space in the disqualified person's building was to be donated, along with office equipment, furniture, supplies, accounting services, and other general and administrative services. The museum was open three days a week for the public and conducted educational programs. The disqualified person was to pay for capital expenses that improve artifacts, specialized conservation tasks, and expenses for betterment of collections, while the museum was to pay for certain low-level conservation tasks, and repairs, preservation, and safekeeping costs. The "without-charge" exception was ruled to apply.[147]

In another illustration, two private foundations, one a museum, borrowed works of art from their disqualified person. The IRS ruled that self-dealing did not occur when the art was stored in a museum while on loan to the foundation and the museum. Storage of personally owned works of art at the museum's facility while on loan to the foundation or the museum was held to not be self-dealing.[148]

A gift to a private foundation of an undivided interest in property the donor planned to subsequently sell did not result in self-dealing.[149] The donor relinquished all rights to use the improved real estate and retained only the right to inspect the property. Expenses were to be shared proportionately between the donor and the foundation. On subsequent sale of the co-owned property, the proceeds were divided proportionately. Self-dealing did not result from the gift, from holding the property jointly, or from the eventual sale by the foundation to an independent party.

Participation in a condominium association, as compared to owning an undivided interest in property, was found by the IRS to not constitute an act of self-dealing, and importantly, the disqualified persons could use their

---

146. See §§ 5.8(e), 5.9.
147. Priv. Ltr. Rul. 201346011.
148. Priv. Ltr. Rul. 201423032.
149. Priv. Ltr. Rul. 7751033.

separately owned spaces.[150] The private foundation, which focuses on acquisition, display, and distribution of works of fine art, wished to acquire an art gallery space. Its creators purchased a warehouse building that was converted to a condominium consisting of five units. The largest unit was donated (free of encumbrances) to the foundation plus an undivided interest in the common areas and parking lot. Another unit was donated to the foundation to be used as an investment rental property. The remaining three units, comprising only 15 percent of the total square footage, were retained to be used as offices for the disqualified persons. The offices would also be available, plus a secretary/receptionist, free of charge to the foundation.

In this instance, common costs, such as maintenance, repairs, and operational (presumably utilities and janitorial) costs, were to be shared on an "objective basis according to the respective square footage of each owner's unit." Though not said to be a requirement in the decision, the foundation owned a majority of the building's square footage and, thereby, voting control of the association. If instead this foundation had been given an undivided interest in 85 percent of the property, the disqualified persons would not have been able to use the property.

The restrictions on use have also been found to include the making of improvements to a property. In one instance, a foundation jointly held property bequeathed to it by the co-owner's spouse prior to 1969, so she was permitted to receive income on her undivided share under the transitional rule. The co-owners wanted to make substantial improvements in the property to enhance its income-producing potential. Despite the fact the foundation and the spouse were to carefully divide the income and costs on a strict proportional basis, the IRS ruled that the improvement of the co-owned property would result in self-dealing and that the transitional rule could no longer apply.[151]

In another instance, sharing the cost of improvements to a residence in which the foundation had a remainder interest with the life tenant (spouse of donor), who was over 90 years old, was found not to result in self-dealing. The IRS noted that the repairs were capital in nature and necessary to maintain the condition of the property, which was a valuable foundation asset. Payment of the entire cost of improvement by the foundation could have been considered an impermissible use of foundation assets by its disqualified person; payment of its actuarially determined share of the cost was not. The ruling did not mention the fact that the relationship was not technically one of co-ownership; the tenant was not occupying foundation property. Finally, any benefit was found to be tenuous and incidental due to the life tenant's age.[152]

---

150. Priv. Ltr. Rul. 200014040.
151. Priv. Ltr. Rul. 8038049.
152. Priv. Ltr. Rul. 200149040.

§ 5.4 SALE, EXCHANGE, LEASE, OR FURNISHING OF PROPERTY

(g) Coinvestments

Although the use of co-owned property by a disqualified person is an act of self-dealing, the IRS has taken the position that the "holding and use of separate interests in a limited partnership is not the use of jointly owned property."[153] Instead of donating an undivided interest in a shopping center, two donors transferred property to and became general partners in a limited partnership. Then they gave a freely transferable limited partnership interest to an independent corporate trustee to hold in a charitable remainder trust.[154] The IRS ruled that the holding and subsequent sale of the limited partnership interest by the trust would not be an act of self-dealing, provided the independent trustee did not act in concert with the donors so as to benefit them when disposing of the limited partnership interests.

The IRS has permitted other types of passive investment holdings that might be considered self-dealing based on a literal reading of the rules. For example, the IRS characterized the co-ownership of real property in one instance an *investment relationship*. A foundation and its disqualified persons each received their ownership by gift, held property as tenants in common, and had separate interests in a 40-year lease on the property. Because there was no sale, lease, or transfer of the property between the private foundation and its disqualified persons, self-dealing did not occur as to the holding of the property. As for the lease, the private foundation received its portion of the rental payment directly, thereby "precluding its interest in the lease from being used by a disqualified person."[155]

A private foundation's purchase of limited partnerships and interests in limited liability companies, in which an investment fund managed by the foundation trustees and investment advisor also invested, was not considered by the IRS to be self-dealing because there was no direct or indirect transfer of assets to or for the use of disqualified persons. The factors on which the IRS based its approval were that (1) the foundation and the funds would not pool their investments to meet any minimum investment requirement, (2) the funds' investment return would not vary based on the foundation's investments, (3) the foundation's investment would not affect the cost of the funds' investment, (4) the funds would not advertise the foundation's participation in or connection to the investment or use it to attract other investors, (5) unrelated parties controlled and operated the partnerships and limited liability

---

153. E.g., Priv. Ltr. Rul. 9114025.
154. This type of a trust is treated as a private foundation under IRC § 4947(a)(2); see §§ 2.6(b), 3.7.
155. Priv. Ltr. Rul. 9651037.

companies, and (6) the foundation trustee would not receive additional fees from the foundation attributable to these investments.[156]

The primary focus in evaluating a coinvestment situation is whether the disqualified persons receive more than an incidental or tenuous benefit by having the foundation invest in the same investment vehicle. In one instance, the following benefits were said to accrue to both the foundation and its disqualified persons that invested together in the same investment fund: (1) reduction of administrative costs, (2) obtaining access to investments and investment funds that might otherwise be unavailable to the individual partners, (3) facilitating diversification of the assets for all partners, and (4) obtaining economies of scale and cost savings as well as greater negotiating power through a coinvestment model. In the case of any fees or expenses of third-party investment managers based on a percentage of assets managed, the foundation would pay the lowest possible percentage and the disqualified persons would pay the remaining higher fees. The IRS ruled that any benefits the disqualified persons received from the private foundation's participation in the investment would be incidental and tenuous. Also, the private foundation's coinvestment was held not to be a transfer to, or use by or for the benefit of, the private foundation's income or assets by any disqualified person.[157]

Similarly, the IRS ruled that a private foundation's investment alongside a disqualified person in an investment fund did not result in an act of self-dealing where the private foundation would not have been able to invest in the fund absent the investment by the disqualified person. The disqualified person's costs would not be lowered because of the foundation's investment. Further, unlike the foundation, the disqualified person would not be able to invest in any investment fund which it could not otherwise invest in, because the disqualified person would contribute at least the minimum required amount to each investment fund regardless of the foundation's investment. Therefore, any benefit to the disqualified person in the transactions was deemed to be incidental and tenuous.[158]

No self-dealing was found when a limited liability company (the Land LLC) formed by three unrelated private foundations leased its land to a limited liability company (the Building LLC) owned by disqualified persons with respect to the foundations.[159] The key to this conclusion was the fact that each of the disqualified persons owned less than 35 percent of the Building LLC. The leasing did not result in self-dealing because the Building LLC was

---

156. Priv. Ltr. Rul. 9844031.
157. Priv. Ltr. Rul. 200551025.
158. Priv. Ltr. Rul. 9448047; also Priv. Ltr. Rul. 9533041.
159. Priv. Ltr. Rul. 200517031.

§ 5.5 LOANS AND OTHER EXTENSIONS OF CREDIT

therefore not a disqualified person. The carefully constructed arrangement was intended to give the foundations access to the management skills of their disqualified persons that would enable the foundations to invest in real estate at relatively low risk.

Conversely, self-dealing was found to occur if a foundation and its disqualified persons were to jointly develop two tracts of land that they already co-owned 50/50. The foundation had received its one-half interest through an inheritance. The planned development was to be extensive and require substantial additional investment by the co-owners for such items as utilities, streets, drainage, and construction of buildings to be rented after completion. Costs would be paid one-half by each owner, and future profits were to be shared equally. The use of foundation income and assets for the proposed development was deemed self-dealing. The IRS further stated that "it is immaterial whether or not a transaction itself results in a benefit or a detriment to the private foundation."[160]

The consequences of transactions during the life of the partnership or joint venture deserve careful attention when the partnership or venture itself is a disqualified person[161] and other disqualified persons are also partners. Although the IRS has ruled favorably with respect to such arrangements, there has been very little consideration of the transactions throughout the life and on dissolution of the entity. It seems clear that proportional distributions of income to all partners should not represent a sale or exchange that creates self-dealing,[162] but special allocations could. Redemption of the foundation's interest could also result in self-dealing. If the terms for redemption apply equally to all partners, the IRS has concluded that the corporate redemption exception could apply.[163]

Guidance regarding private foundation investing in partnerships in which disqualified persons are also partners is one of the longstanding projects identified in the Department of the Treasury's Priority Guidance Plan.[164]

§ 5.5 LOANS AND OTHER EXTENSIONS OF CREDIT

The lending of money or other extension of credit between a private foundation and a disqualified person generally constitutes an act of self-dealing.[165]

---

160. Priv. Ltr. Rul. 8038049.
161. IRC § 4946(a)(1)(E). Subsequent capital contributions by a private foundation in exchange for a larger partnership interest will be acts of self-dealing if the partnership is a disqualified person at the time of such subsequent contribution (Priv. Ltr. Rul. 9705013).
162. E.g., Priv. Ltr. Rul. 200420029.
163. IRC § 4941(d)(2)(F); Priv. Ltr. Rul. 9237032; Field Serv. Adv. 200015007.
164. Department of the Treasury, 2023-2024 Priority Guidance Plan (Sept. 29, 2023).
165. IRC § 4941(d)(1)(B).

The lending cannot be direct or indirect, and the fact that the rate of interest is better than the foundation could otherwise receive does not eliminate the self-dealing.[166] Even if a circuitous route is taken so that the first borrower is not a disqualified person, indebtedness between the foundation and a disqualified person is prohibited. For example, if an unrelated third party purchases property subject to a mortgage payable to a private foundation, and thereafter resells the property to a disqualified person that assumes the mortgage or takes the property subject to it, self-dealing occurs with the second sale.[167]

The transfer of a disqualified person's obligation to a private foundation results in self-dealing if the foundation becomes a creditor under the note, even if the transfer is made by an unrelated third party.[168] However, the IRS ruled that a private foundation's ownership of nonvoting interests in a newly formed LLC would not constitute an act of self-dealing under section 4941, notwithstanding that the primary asset of the LLC was a promissory note the obligor of which is a disqualified person to the foundation.[169] Because the private foundation did not itself hold the note, any direct payments the foundation received in connection with the transaction would be made from the LLC (as distributions in respect to the foundation's nonvoting units in the LLC) and not by a disqualified person; therefore, there was no direct act of self-dealing.[170]

In the instance of a self-dealing transaction that is a loan, an additional self-dealing transaction is deemed to occur on the first day of each tax year in the taxable period after the tax year in which the loan occurred.[171]

A loan by a private foundation to an individual, before they become a foundation manager (and thus a disqualified person),[172] may not be an act of

---

166. Priv. Ltr. Rul. 9222052.
167. Reg. § 53.4941(d)-2(c)(1).
168. *Id*. If the estate administration exception applies to the transaction (Reg. § 53.4941(d)-1(b)(3); see § 5.12(b)), however, a private foundation's receipt and holding of a note, the obligor of which is a disqualified person, is not an act of self-dealing (Reg. § 53.4941(d)-2(c)(1)).
169. Priv. Ltr. Rul. 202101002.
170. *Id*. The IRS further ruled that this transaction would not constitute indirect self-dealing because, as the holder of nonvoting units, the private foundation did not control the LLC or have the power to compel distributions from the LLC (see § 5.11). The IRS will no longer issue rulings on whether an act of self-dealing occurs when a private foundation owns or receives an interest in an LLC or other entity that owns a promissory note issued by a disqualified person (Rev. Proc. 2023-3, 2023-1 I.R.B. 144 § 3.01(130)). The IRS previously explained that it has placed these transactions on its "no-rule" list while it reviews its prior ruling position on them and their "proper tax treatment" (Rev. Proc. 2021-40, 2021-38 I.R.B. 426).
171. See § 5.15(a)(i).
172. See Chapter 4.

§ 5.5 LOANS AND OTHER EXTENSIONS OF CREDIT

self-dealing, because the self-dealing rules do not apply, in that the disqualified person status arose only following completion of the negotiation of the compensation package.[173] Where the loan principal remains outstanding once the individual becomes a disqualified person, however, an act of self-dealing occurs;[174] indeed, as noted, an act of self-dealing takes place in each year in which there is an uncorrected extension of credit.[175]

To the extent motivated by charitable intent and unsupported by consideration, the making of a promise, pledge, or similar arrangement to a private foundation by a disqualified person, whether evidenced by an oral or written agreement, a promissory note, or other instrument of indebtedness, is not an extension of credit before the date of maturity.[176]

(a) Gifts of Indebted Property

A transfer of indebted real or personal property to a private foundation is considered an impermissible sale or exchange if the foundation assumes a mortgage or similar lien that was placed on the property prior to the transfer, or takes the property subject to a mortgage or similar lien that the disqualified person placed the loan on the property within a 10-year period ending on the date of the transfer.[177] The date on which the loan is made, not when the loan or line of credit was approved, is the date from which the 10-year exception is measured. It is normally the date a lien is actually placed on the property, even though the loan is part of a multiphase financing plan started more than 10 years before the transaction.[178]

In one instance, a disqualified person transferred to a private foundation a parcel of real property that was subject to a lien placed on the property by the disqualified person within the 10-year period ending on the transfer date. When the property was originally acquired, the lien created by the deed of trust executed in conjunction with the purchase of the property was placed on the property prior to the 10-year period. Within the 10-year period, however, the disqualified person obtained another loan, and the lien created by the deed of trust executed in conjunction with this new loan was placed on the land

---

173. Priv. Ltr. Rul. 9530032. See text accompanied by *supra* note 8.
174. Priv. Ltr. Rul. 9530032. Previously, the IRS ruled that there was no self-dealing in these circumstances because the loan was created before the individual became a disqualified person (Priv. Ltr. Rul. 9343033). This ruling was reconsidered (Priv. Ltr. Rul. 9417018), however, and thereafter revoked (Priv. Ltr. Rul. 9530032).
175. See § 5.15(a)(i).
176. Reg. § 53.4941(d)-2(c)(3). E.g., Tech. Adv. Mem. 8723001.
177. IRC § 4941(d)(2)(A).
178. Rev. Rul. 78-395, 1978-2 C.B. 270.

within the 10-year period. The IRS said that, for purposes of the self-dealing rules, "it [did] not matter that the taxpayer placed the second lien on the property as part of a multi-phased financing program begun more than 10 years before the date of transfer."[179]

The IRS accords these rules broad application, as evidenced by its determination that the contribution to a private foundation by a disqualified person of a life insurance policy subject to a policy loan was an act of self-dealing. This conclusion rested on the analysis that a life insurance policy loan is sometimes characterized as an advance of the proceeds of the policy, with the loan and the interest on it considered charges against the property, rather than amounts that must be paid to the insurer.[180] The IRS concluded that the effect of the transfer was essentially the same as the transfer of property subject to a lien, in that the transfer of the policy relieved the donor of the obligation to repay the loan, pay interest on the loan as it accrues, or suffer continued diminution in the value of the policy. Application of the self-dealing rules to this type of transaction was completed by a finding that the amount of the loan was significant in relation to the value of the policy.[181]

A future obligation to pay expenses to maintain gifted property is not indebtedness for this purpose. A loan by a foundation to a trustee's client is self-dealing because the transaction confers benefit on the trustee by providing service to the trustee's client.[182]

A gift of stock in a rental property holding company that was indebted to the substantial contributor was ruled not to result in self-dealing. The loan was made for business reasons prior to the transfer of the shares and the foundation is not personally obligated.[183]

(b) Interest-Free Loans

The lending of money or other extension of credit without interest or other charge (determined without regard to the imputed interest rules) by a disqualified person to a private foundation is permitted if the proceeds of the loan are used exclusively in carrying out the foundation's exempt activities.[184] Thus, the making of a promise, pledge, or similar arrangement to a private foundation by a disqualified person, whether evidenced by an oral or written

---

179. *Id.* at 270.
180. E.g., Dean v. Commissioner, 35 T.C. 1083 (1961).
181. Rev. Rul. 80-132, 1980-1 C.B. 255.
182. Tech. Adv. Mem. 8719004.
183. Priv. Ltr. Rul. 8409039.
184. IRC § 4941(d)(2)(B); Reg. § 53.4941(d)-2(c)(2).

§ 5.5 LOANS AND OTHER EXTENSIONS OF CREDIT

agreement, a promissory note, or other instrument of indebtedness, to the extent motivated by charitable intent and unsupported by consideration, is not an *extension of credit* before the date of maturity.[185]

Limited advances and reimbursements of expenses are permitted for foundation managers.[186] Additionally, in certain circumstances, a disqualified person's payment of expenses on behalf of a foundation may be considered an interest-free loan to the foundation. If expense advances are treated as loans without charge and are paid in connection with its exempt activities, a foundation can repay the loan and thereby make a reimbursement. Although the regulations on their face would appear to prohibit a foundation's reimbursement of expenses a disqualified person incurs on the foundation's behalf,[187] the IRS has permitted reimbursement in circumstances where the transaction clearly allows the foundation to better accomplish its exempt purposes.[188]

This exception is effectively voided where a private foundation repays or cancels the debt by transferring property other than cash (e.g., securities) to repay the loan. The IRS takes the position that the transfer, when viewed together with the making of the loan, is tantamount to a sale or exchange of property between the foundation and the disqualified person, and thus constitutes an act of self-dealing.[189]

An individual who was a disqualified person with respect to a private foundation made an interest-free loan to a tax-exempt school to enable it to complete construction, purchase furniture and other materials, and hire staff; this individual also was the school president. The private foundation planned to make a grant to the school with the understanding that the school would use the funds to repay the loan. The IRS ruled that the making of this grant would not constitute self-dealing because the prospective grant was "unrestricted," in that the school "may" repay the loan, the proceeds of which were used for exempt purposes.[190] The disqualified person was said to have "no control" over the school to compel it to repay his loan; the school was characterized by

---

185. Reg. § 53.4941(d)-2(c)(3). E.g., Priv. Ltr. Rul. 200232036 (concerning the role of a private foundation as a conduit in paying premiums on a term life insurance policy on the life of a disqualified person) and Priv. Ltr. Rul. 200112064 (concerning the pledge by a disqualified person corporation to a private foundation of an option to purchase shares of the corporation's stock).
186. See § 5.6(g).
187. Reg. § 53.4941(d)-2(d).
188. The IRS permitted reimbursements in connection with a foundation's sharing of facilities and personnel as discussed in § 5.9.
189. See § 5.4(a), (c).
190. Priv. Ltr. Rul. 200443045.

the IRS as being "under no [legal] requirement to use the loan to repay" the disqualified person lender.[191]

§ 5.6 PAYMENT OF COMPENSATION

The payment of compensation by a tax-exempt charitable organization triggers potential application of various bodies of the federal tax law. Most of these areas of the law require that this type of compensation be reasonable. For example, the doctrine of private inurement,[192] applicable to private foundations, incorporates this requirement when compensation is paid to insiders, as does the doctrine of private benefit,[193] also applicable to private foundations, when compensation is paid to anyone. The sanction for violation of either doctrine can be loss of tax-exempt status. The intermediate sanctions rules,[194] while not formally applicable to foundations, entail much law on the subject that can also inform this matter of payment of compensation by charitable entities, including whether the compensation is reasonable. The sanctions in this context are the imposition of excise taxes on disqualified persons.

The payment of compensation, including payment or reimbursement of expenses, by a private foundation to a disqualified person generally constitutes an act of self-dealing.[195] An extremely important and frequently used exception to the general rule allows payment of compensation to a disqualified person for personal services rendered in carrying out foundation affairs, except in the case of a government official. The performance of personal services must be reasonable and necessary to carry out the tax-exempt purposes of the foundation, and the total amount of the compensation paid, including reimbursements, must not be excessive.[196] Thus, for this exception to be

---

191. This position of the IRS may be contrasted with its diametrically opposite position in the charitable gift substantiation area. In that context, the IRS successfully asserted that an *expectation* or an *understanding* on the part of a donor amounts to a *service* for purposes of these substantiation requirements (e.g., Addis v. Commissioner, 118 T.C. 528 (2002), *aff'd*, 374 F.3d 881 (9th Cir. 2004), *cert. den.*, 543 U.S. 1151 (2005)). These decisions not only erroneously cast an expectation or understanding as the equivalent of *consideration* for purposes of the substantiation rules (IRC § 170(f)(8)), they inappropriately graft language from the charitable split-dollar insurance plan rules (IRC § 170(f)(10)) onto the substantiation rules.
192. See § 5.1.
193. See § 5.2.
194. IRC § 4958. See *Tax-Exempt Organizations*, Chapter 21.
195. IRC § 4941(d)(1)(D); Reg. § 53.4941(d)-2(e).
196. IRC § 4941(d)(2)(E); Reg. § 53.4941(d)-3(c).

§ 5.6 PAYMENT OF COMPENSATION

available, the compensation must be for personal services, the compensation must be reasonable, and the compensation must be necessary for the advancement of the private foundation's exempt purposes.

(a) Definition of Personal Services

The term *personal services* is not defined by statute or regulations; the boundaries of this exception are not precisely drawn. The IRS observed that the personal services exception is a "special rule that should be strictly construed," for, if not, the "fabric woven by Congress to generally prohibit insider transactions [involving private foundations] would unravel."[197] Examples in the regulations make it clear that the services of lawyers and investment managers, as such, are personal services. This exception is available irrespective of whether the person who receives the compensation (or payment or reimbursement) is an individual; thus, personal services can be provided by a corporation, partnership, or other type of service provider.[198]

In one example in the regulations, two partners in a 10-partner law firm served as trustees of a private foundation. These lawyers and the firm are disqualified persons. The firm provides legal services for the foundation. Assuming the services are reasonable and necessary for carrying out the foundation's exempt purposes, and assuming that the amount paid for these services is not excessive, these services are personal services and do not constitute impermissible self-dealing.[199] Similarly, the IRS ruled that unwarranted self-dealing did not occur when a foundation paid reasonable legal fees awarded by a court to a lawyer representing one of the foundation's managers; the lawsuit was filed against the other managers to require them to carry out the foundation's charitable program and was necessary to accomplish the foundation's exempt purposes.[200]

In another illustration provided in the regulations, a manager of a private foundation owns an investment counseling business. This individual manages the foundation's investment portfolio, for which he receives reasonable compensation. The payment of this compensation to this disqualified person is not an impermissible act of self-dealing.[201] A third illustration concerns a commercial bank that serves as a trustee for a private foundation. This bank also maintains the foundation's checking and savings accounts and rents a safety deposit box to the foundation. The use of the funds by the bank and the

---

197. Priv. Ltr. Rul. 9325061, *aff'd*, Priv. Ltr. Rul. 9404032.
198. Reg. § 53.4941(d)-3(c)(1).
199. Reg. § 53.4941(d)-3(c)(2), Example (1).
200. Rev. Rul. 73-601, 1973-2 C.B. 385.
201. Reg. § 53.4941(d)-3(c)(2), Example (2).

payment of compensation by the foundation to the bank for the performance of these services, which are reasonable and necessary to the carrying out of the foundation's exempt purposes, are not impermissible acts of self-dealing if the compensation is not excessive.[202]

In the last of these illustrations, a substantial contributor to a private foundation owns a factory that manufactures microscopes. This person contracts with the foundation to manufacture 100 microscopes for the foundation. Even if the foundation uses the microscopes in furtherance of its exempt purposes and even if the compensation paid by the foundation is reasonable, any payment under this contract by the foundation constitutes an act of self-dealing, inasmuch as such payments are not compensation paid for the performance of personal services.[203]

The term *personal services* includes the services of a broker serving as agent for a private foundation but not the services of a dealer who buys from the private foundation as a principal and sells to third parties.[204]

There is one court decision on the point, based on the foregoing illustrations, holding that the services encompassed by this exception are confined to those that are "essentially professional and managerial in nature."[205] That case involved the provision of janitorial services, which were ruled to not be professional and managerial in nature.

A wide range of services provided by disqualified person banks and other financial institutions is covered by this exception. The IRS ruled that the management and investment of the funds of two private foundations by the trust department of a financial institution were personal services.[206] Likewise, the personal services exception was held to encompass investment counseling, financial planning, custodial, legal, and accounting services provided by a bank.[207] Further, a bank assisting a private foundation in connection with its securities-lending program was held to not be engaged in prohibited self-dealing by reason of the personal services exception.[208]

This exception, however, is by no means confined to financial institutions. IRS rulings refer to disqualified person corporations, partnerships, and limited liability companies that provide personal services to private foundations.

---

202. *Id.*, Example (3).
203. *Id.*, Example (4).
204. Reg. § 53.4941(d)-3(c)(1). This exception was ruled to apply with respect to services provided by disqualified persons in connection with the sale of a private foundation's artwork (Priv. Ltr. Rul. 9011050).
205. Madden, Jr. v. Commissioner, 74 T.C.M. 440, 449 (1997).
206. Priv. Ltr. Rul. 9503023.
207. Priv. Ltr. Rul. 9114036.
208. Priv. Ltr. Rul. 200501021.

§ 5.6 PAYMENT OF COMPENSATION

These services include management of real estate,[209] cash and debt management,[210] other forms of investment management,[211] other types of financial services,[212] coordination of tax matters,[213] accounting services,[214] types of administrative services,[215] and other types of management services.[216] The IRS permitted a management company to provide services to a private foundation under these rules, notwithstanding the fact that the company was owned by a disqualified person.[217] Services provided by employees of private foundations, such as selection of grant projects, can be encompassed by the exception.[218]

The IRS ruled that payments for services provided by a disqualified person, by means of two disregarded entities,[219] to a private foundation to enable it to offer "charitable consulting" services and investment services to the foundation and other charities would not be acts of self-dealing because the payments are encompassed by the personal services exception.[220] This ruling stated that these services are necessary to carry out the exempt purposes of the foundation, without any analysis of the point; they may be unrelated businesses.[221]

---

209. E.g., Priv. Ltr. Rul. 200326039. The IRS ruled that the following array of services performed for a private foundation holding a portfolio of commercial and residential rental properties qualified for the personal services exception: identification and analysis of potential real estate acquisitions; contract negotiations; cash management; debt management including budgeting; negotiation of financing; review of loan agreements and expenditures; accounting; supervision of property operations and inspections; advertising; leasing and lease negotiations; goodwill relations with tenants and communities; interface with municipalities and compliance with new ordinances; collection of rents; supervision and administration of a risk-management program; supervision of personnel and human resources; supervision and administration of legal and tax services and other incidental and ancillary activities associated with the ownership of passive rental real property; and services relating to the disposition of property (Priv. Ltr. Rul. 200637041).
210. E.g., Priv. Ltr. Rul. 200315031.
211. E.g., Priv. Ltr. Rul. 9237035.
212. E.g., Priv. Ltr. Ruls. 200116047, 200217056.
213. E.g., Priv. Ltr. Rul. 9703031.
214. E.g., Priv. Ltr. Rul. 9702036.
215. E.g., Priv. Ltr. Rul. 200228026.
216. E.g., Priv. Ltr. Rul. 9238027. The distinctions in this area turn more on what is *managerial* than what is *professional*. For example, while janitorial services are not protected by this exception, services that constitute the management of janitorial services are within the exception (e.g., Priv. Ltr. Rul. 200326039).
217. Priv. Ltr. Rul. 200238053.
218. E.g., Priv. Ltr. Rul. 199927046.
219. See *Tax-Exempt Organizations* § 4.1(b).
220. Priv. Ltr. Rul. 201937003.
221. See Chapter 11.

By contrast, the IRS ruled that maintenance, repair, janitorial, cleaning, landscaping, and similar "operational" services do not qualify for this exception.[222] Similarly, services by a general contractor, brokerage for the sale and leasing of real property, insurance brokerage, and certain marketing and advertising services were held to not constitute personal services.[223]

A topic that is rarely discussed in the law is the matter of compensation paid to the members of the board of trustees of a private foundation for their services as such. This is a common practice; the assumption seems to be that services of this nature constitute *personal services*. An IRS ruling concerned compensation paid to trustees who performed services normally provided by officers and outside professionals, as well as services in fields such as investments, personnel, and grant-making. Noting that these trustees' fees were less than those charged by financial institutions for similar services, the agency ruled that the fees were reasonable and thus the payment of them was not self-dealing.[224] This ruling assumed—but does not hold—that the services to be provided by these trustees were personal services. The matter of compensation of private foundation trustees who serve solely in that capacity has not been addressed by a court decision or IRS ruling.[225]

(b) Definition of Compensation

The term *compensation* in this setting generally means a salary or wage, any bonuses, fringe benefits, retirement benefits, and the like. Occasionally, however, other economic benefits are treated as compensation for purposes of application of the self-dealing rules. For example, under certain circumstances, the

---

222. Priv. Ltr. Rul. 200315031. In one instance, the IRS concluded that secretarial services were embraced by the personal services exception (Priv. Ltr. Rul. 9238027), yet on another occasion, the agency required a private foundation to provide an amended services agreement that specifically precluded such services (Priv. Ltr. Rul. 200217056). The provision of secretarial services by a disqualified person to a private foundation is generally regarded as self-dealing (see § 5.9(a)).
223. Priv. Ltr. Rul. 9325061.
224. Priv. Ltr. Rul. 200135047.
225. Nonetheless, the IRS ruled that the trustees of a private foundation may cause the foundation's trust agreement to be amended to eliminate a trust termination date and extend the duration of the trust indefinitely, thereby concomitantly elongating the period of time they serve and receive compensation, without engaging in self-dealing (Priv. Ltr. Rul. 200343026); that a private foundation may compensate its board members for their participation in a conference sponsored by the foundation (Priv. Ltr. Rul. 200324056); and that a private foundation may compensate its foundation managers for attendance at board meetings (Priv. Ltr. Rul. 200007039).

§ 5.6 PAYMENT OF COMPENSATION

value of an indemnification by a private foundation of a foundation manager, or the payment by a foundation of the premiums for an insurance policy for a foundation manager, must be treated as compensation so as to avoid self-dealing. Likewise, the IRS ruled that a split-dollar life insurance arrangement established by a private foundation for the benefit of a key employee was a form of compensation to the employee.[226] By contrast, when the self-dealing rules are explicit in prohibiting a particular type of transaction between a private foundation and a disqualified person, the rules cannot be sidestepped by treating the value of the economic benefit provided as part of the disqualified person's total (reasonable) compensation.[227]

This topic is accorded more expansive treatment in the intermediate sanctions setting. In that context, the term *compensation* generally includes all economic benefits provided by a charitable organization, to or for the use of a person, in exchange for the performance of services.[228] These benefits include (but are not limited to) (1) all forms of cash and noncash compensation, including salary, fees, bonuses, severance payments, and certain deferred compensation; (2) the payment of liability insurance premiums for, or the payment or reimbursement by the organization of, (a) any penalty, tax, or expense of correction owed in connection with the intermediate sanctions rules, (b) any expense not reasonably incurred by the person in connection with a civil judicial or civil administrative proceeding arising out of the person's performance of services on behalf of the organization, or (c) any expense resulting from an act, or failure to act, with respect to which the person has acted willfully and without reasonable cause; and (3) all other compensatory benefits, whether or not included in gross income for income tax purposes, including payments to welfare benefit plans, such as plans providing medical, dental, life insurance, severance pay, and disability benefits, and both taxable and nontaxable fringe benefits (other than certain fringe benefits),[229] including expense allowances or reimbursements (other than expense reimbursements

---

226. Priv. Ltr. Rul. 200020060.
227. See § 5.7(b). For example, a loan by a private foundation to a disqualified person is an act of self-dealing (see § 5.5). The self-dealing rules cannot be avoided by regarding the value of this type of loan as compensation (Priv. Ltr. Rul. 9530032, revoking Priv. Ltr. Rul. 9343033). By contrast, this characterization of a loan as compensation is permissible in the case of a public charity dealing with an insider. Under the intermediate sanctions rules, however, this practice is impermissible when done in hindsight, in that an economic benefit cannot be treated as consideration for the performance of services unless the organization clearly indicated its intent to so treat the benefit (IRC § 4958(c)(1)(A); see *Tax-Exempt Organizations* § 21.4(c)).
228. Reg. § 53.4958-4(b)(1)(ii)(B).
229. That is, those described in IRC § 132.

SELF-DEALING

pursuant to an accountable plan),[230] and the economic benefit of a below-market loan.[231]

In a compliance questionnaire sent in 2008 to about 400 tax-exempt colleges and universities,[232] the IRS provided a comprehensive list of types of remuneration that may be paid to executives of tax-exempt organizations, including private foundations: salary; bonus; contributions to employee benefit plans (e.g., health benefit plans); incentives (short-term and long-term); contributions to life, disability, and/or long-term care insurance; split-dollar life insurance (where the organization pays the premiums); loans or other extensions of credit (in the case of forgone interest or debt forgiveness); stock or stock options (equity-based compensation); severance or change-of-control payments; personal use of the organization's credit card (where there is no reimbursement); personal use of the organization's owned or leased vehicles; personal travel for the individual and/or spouse/other family member (where there is no reimbursement); expense reimbursements pursuant to a nonaccountable plan; value of organization-provided housing and utilities; value of organization-provided vacation home; personal services provided at individual's residence (e.g., housekeeper, lawn service, maintenance or repair services); other personal services provided (e.g., legal, financial, retirement services); payment of health and/or social club dues; personal use of organization's aircraft or boat; first-class travel;[233] scholarship and/or fellowship grants (if taxable); executive fringe benefits;[234] contributions to deferred compensation plans; and any other form of compensation.

The determination as to whether any of these items is included in the gross income of a disqualified person for federal income tax purposes is made on the basis of standard federal tax principles, irrespective of whether the item is taken into account for purposes of determining the reasonableness of compensation.[235]

---

230. Reg. § 1.62-2(c).
231. IRC § 7872(e)(1). This inventory of the elements of compensation is in Reg. § 53.4958-4(b)(1)(ii)(B). In a case that should be of interest to private foundations that employ one or more children of the foundation's founders, the court assigned the income paid to such children employed by a public charity to their parents for federal income tax purposes, because the parents exercised "complete dominion and control" over the bank accounts in which the payments were deposited (Ray v. Commissioner, 116 T.C.M. 331, 335 (2018)). The court ruled that a "fundamental principle of income taxation is that income is taxable to the person who earns it" and that the "'true earner' of income is the person or entity who controlled the earning of such income, rather than the person or entity who received the income" (id. at 335-336).
232. Form 14018, Compliance Questionnaire Colleges and Universities (Sept. 2008).
233. Payment of first-class travel, however, is not a form of compensation.
234. Other than IRC § 132 fringe benefits.
235. Reg. § 53.4958-4(b)(1)(ii)(C).

§ 5.6 PAYMENT OF COMPENSATION

(c) Definition of Reasonable

The self-dealing regulations lack a definition of the phrase *reasonable compensation*, but instead direct a foundation to consult the body of law pertaining to the deductibility of compensation as a business expense to determine whether pay is excessive. In application of that law, a private foundation has the burden of showing that a compensation package is equal to "such amount as would ordinarily be paid for like services by like enterprises under like circumstances."[236] A private foundation that compensates disqualified persons is well advised, however, to follow developments regarding the excess benefit transactions rules, which are applicable with respect to public charities. These rules impose excise taxes on persons receiving, and in some instances approving of, excessive compensation.[237]

An excess benefit, in the public charity context, occurs when the economic benefit paid by the charitable organization to a disqualified person exceeds the value of the consideration received—such as for services performed or property transferred. Similarly, self-dealing occurs when a private foundation pays unreasonable compensation to a disqualified person.

Although the excess benefit transactions rules are somewhat different from the self-dealing rules, many of the terms are the same. The excess benefit transactions rules contain criteria for assessing the reasonableness of compensation that can be applied in the private foundation setting. These elements are contained as part of a unique feature of the excess benefit transactions rules: a rebuttable presumption that compensation (and other transactions) is reasonable.[238] Pursuant to that presumption, relevant information as to reasonableness of compensation includes (1) compensation levels paid by similarly situated organizations, both taxable and tax-exempt for functionally comparable positions, (2) the availability of similar services in the geographic area of the tax-exempt organization, (3) current compensation surveys compiled by independent firms, and (4) actual written offers from similar institutions competing for the services of the disqualified person.[239]

---

236. Reg. § 1.162-7(b)(3).
237. The intermediate sanctions rules follow the same formula as is used in the business expense deduction rules (Reg. § 53.4958-4(b)(1)(ii)(A)). This alchemy used in determining the reasonableness of compensation is termed an "accumulation and assessment of data as to comparability" (Reg. § 53.4958-6(c)(2)). The IRS wrote that "exemption from federal income tax of an organization is not jeopardized where agreements on compensation are entered into through negotiations conducted at arm's-length and are not considered to be excessive based on a person having similar responsibilities and comparable duties" (Priv. Ltr. Rul. 200944055). See, in general, *Tax-Exempt Organizations*, Chapter 21.
238. Reg. § 53.4958-6.
239. Reg. § 53.4958-6(c)(2)(i).

SELF-DEALING

The IRS previously has also identified the following factors to use in setting an individual's compensation:[240] the compensation levels paid by similar organizations, the level of the individual's education and experience, the specific responsibilities of the position involved, the individual's previous salary or compensation package, similar services in the same geographic or metropolitan area, the number of the organization's employees, and the organization's annual budget and/or gross revenue and assets.

The IRS also identified the following sources to be used in obtaining comparability data as to an individual's compensation: published surveys of compensation paid by similar organizations, Internet research on compensation paid by similar organizations, telephone survey(s) of compensation paid by similar organizations, use of an outside expert hired to provide a report on comparable compensation data, a report prepared by an expert compensation analyst employed by the organization involved, written offers of employment from similar organizations, and annual information returns filed by similar organizations.[241]

Courts develop criteria as to the reasonableness of compensation; often the cases involve for-profit employers. This is because a payment of compensation, to be deductible as a business expense,[242] must be an outlay that is ordinary and necessary. The concepts of reasonable and ordinary and necessary are essentially identical.[243] There is inherent tension in this context, however, in that the "judges of the Tax Court are not equipped by training or experience to determine the [reasonableness of] salaries of corporate officers; no judges are."[244]

A private foundation may decide to utilize the services of an independent consulting firm in determining the reasonableness of compensation for one or more of its employees. If it does, the foundation should be certain that the company is reputable, should consider the cost (fees and expenses), should obtain the report as a draft and have it reviewed and if necessary edited by competent legal counsel, and should verify (or have the lawyer do so) that all relevant criteria are identified and discussed in the report. The foundation

---

240. Form 14018, Compliance Questionnaire Colleges and Universities (Sept. 2008).
241. *Id.*
242. IRC § 162.
243. Rapco, Inc. v. Commissioner, 85 F.3d 950 (2d Cir. 1996).
244. Exacto Spring Corp. v. Commissioner, 196 F.3d 833, 835 (7th Cir. 1999). In one case, the U.S. Tax Court found that the reasonable compensation for an executive for a year was $98,000; revisiting the case following a partial reversal, the court concluded that the reasonable compensation amount for the same executive and year was $500,000 (E. J. Harrison and Sons, Inc. v. Commissioner, 86 T.C.M. 240 (2003), *rev'd, and remanded to* 2005-2 U.S.T.C. ¶ 50,493 (9th Cir. 2005), *on rem.*, 91 T.C.M. 1301 (2006), *aff'd*, 2008-1 U.S.T.C. ¶ 50,244 (9th Cir. 2008)).

§ 5.6 PAYMENT OF COMPENSATION

should be careful to avoid the phenomenon "created [by some consultants] by their willingness to use their resumes and their skills to advocate the position of the party who employs them without regard to objective and relevant facts, contrary to their professional obligations."[245]

To prove that compensation is reasonable applying these concepts, a foundation must show that the pay is equal to "such amount as would ordinarily be paid for like services by like enterprises under like circumstances."[246] For example, an annual salary 75 percent higher than the average for private foundations of comparable size listed in one of the Council on Foundations' *Foundation Management Reports*, which also represented 35 percent of the foundation's grant expense, was found to be excessive and an act of self-dealing.[247] The factors used in evaluating whether private inurement has occurred[248] are also relevant in determining whether compensation paid by a private foundation is reasonable for purposes of the self-dealing rules.

A foundation attempting to show that compensation is not excessive for the work performed can consider these points:

- Is the amount of any payment for personal services excessive or unreasonable?[249]

- Are the payments ordinary and necessary to carry out the exempt purposes of the foundation?[250]

- What are the individual's responsibilities and duties? Is there a written job description, a contract for services, or personnel procedures?

- Is the person qualified for the position through experience, education, or other special expertise?[251]

- How much time is devoted to the position?

- Are time sheets or other evidence of time devoted to the foundation's work maintained?

---

245. Boltar, LLC v. Commissioner, 136 T.C. 326 (2011). This observation by the court pertained to appraisers but applies equally in this setting.
246. Reg. § 1.162-7(b)(3).
247. Priv. Ltr. Rul. 9008001.
248. In general, see *Tax-Exempt Organizations* § 20.4.
249. The Labrenz Foundation v. Commissioner, 33 T.C.M. 1374 (1974).
250. Enterprise Railway Equipment Company v. United States, 161 F. Supp. 590 (Ct. Cl. 1958). This case concerned a commercial business but is cited by the IRS as an example of application of the IRC § 162 standards for the reasonableness of salaries paid by exempt organizations.
251. B.H.W. Anesthesia Foundation, Inc. v. Commissioner, 72 T.C. 681 (1979).

SELF-DEALING

To evaluate compensation accurately, not only salary must be considered but all benefits, including deferred compensation, fringe benefits, contribution to pension or profit-sharing plans,[252] housing or automobile allowances, directors' and officers' liability insurance,[253] expense reimbursements, club memberships, and compensation paid to family members.[254]

- How does the compensation structure for an individual compare with those of organizations of similar size and similar activities? Employees and consultants serving a charitable organization can be provided compensation commensurate with that paid by for-profit businesses.[255]

- To evaluate the reasonableness of compensation accurately, a private foundation should take into account all economic benefits provided.[256]

- How does the individual's compensation package compare with those of other members of the staff and the organization's overall budget?

- Are there sharp increases (spikes) in compensation levels?[257]

- Be cautious with large bonuses.[258]

- Salary increases may successfully be cast as payments, in whole or in part, for prior years' services, where the individual was undercompensated in those years.[259] Documentation is critical to the success of this position.

- Is compensation percentage-based or otherwise in commission form? This is not likely to occur in the foundation context, but contingent compensation arrangements have been upheld in the courts where the compensation is reasonable and the conditional nature of the compensation is beneficial to the organization (e.g., percentage-based fundraising compensation).[260] It usually is prudent to place a cap on this form of compensation.[261]

---

252. Rev. Rul. 74-591, 1974-2 C.B. 385.
253. See § 5.7 regarding indemnification of disqualified persons and payments of liability insurance premiums.
254. E.g., John Marshall Law School v. United States, 81-2 U.S.T.C. ¶ 8514 (Ct. Cl. 1981).
255. The House Committee on Ways and Means report accompanying the intermediate sanctions legislation states that "an individual need not necessarily accept reduced compensation merely because he or she renders services to a tax-exempt, as opposed to a taxable, organization" (H.R. Rep. 104-506, at 56 n.5 (1996)).
256. John Marshall Law School v. United States, 81-2 U.S.T.C. ¶ 8514 (Ct. Cl. 1981).
257. Miller and Son Drywall, Inc. v. Commissioner, 196 F.3d 833 (7th Cir. 1999).
258. Haffner's Service Stations, Inc. v. Commissioner, 326 F.3d 1 (1st Cir. 2003).
259. Reg. § 53.4958-4(a)(1); Devine Brothers, Inc. v. Commissioner, 85 T.C.M. 768 (2003).
260. National Foundation, Inc. v. United States, 87-2 U.S.T.C. ¶ 9602 (Ct. Cl. 1987).
261. People of God Community v. Commissioner, 75 T.C. 1053 (1989).

§ 5.6 PAYMENT OF COMPENSATION

- The law in the nonprofit context does not openly take into account, in assessing the reasonableness of compensation, the leadership skills of an individual in advancing the cause of an organization. In a for-profit business case, the court portrayed an executive as the "locomotive" of the company, observing that the business would not have succeeded without this executive's "devotion, dedication, intelligence, foresight, and skill."[262] In another instance, a court wrote that an executive was the "driving force" behind the company's success, recognizing the executive's "dedication and hard work."[263] Likewise, a court concluded that two executives (related parties) were "absolutely integral" to a company's "successful performance, a performance that included remarkable growth in revenues, assets, and gross profits" during the tax years at issue.[264]

- The emergence of nonprofit governance principles and practices is informing this subject. A private foundation may consider adoption of a compensation policy. Ideally, an interested party should abstain from voting on their compensation.

A court opinion provides another version of the IRS's standards for determining reasonable compensation. A private foundation with about $200,000 in assets paid its sole trustee annual compensation of $45,000 and furnished him with two automobiles and a fully equipped office. An expert witness for the IRS testified that the compensation for this individual should range from $1,450 to $2,000 during the years at issue, based on a formula to determine annual trustee compensation of $4 to $5 per $1,000 of foundation assets, plus 5 percent of foundation income. The court found the compensation to be self-dealing and also revoked the tax-exempt status of the foundation on the ground of private inurement.[265]

(d) Finding Salary Statistics

Comparative information is extremely useful, and sometimes critical, in evaluating the reasonableness of the compensation of a disqualified person. The most appropriate comparison is made with similar foundations in the same field of endeavor (e.g., a grant-making foundation with a similar amount of endowment, another private operating foundation that operates a library, or a medical foundation conducting competitive research projects).

---

262. Beiner, Inc. v. Commissioner, 88 T.C.M. 297, 324, 325 (2004).
263. Multi-Pak Corp. v. Commissioner, 99 T.C.M. 1567, 1579 (2010).
264. H.W. Johnson, Inc. v. Commissioner, 111 T.C.M. 1418, 1414 (2016).
265. Kermit Fischer Foundation v. Commissioner, 59 T.C.M. 898 (1990).

Perhaps the easiest way to secure reliable compensation information is to inspect the annual information returns filed by comparable foundations. Form 990-PF is required to be made available on request at each foundation's office and can be viewed on the Internet.[266] All forms of compensation paid to each officer, director, trustee, and foundation manager must be presented for each of these persons, along with their title and average amount of time devoted to the position each week. In addition, similar information is reported for the five highest-paid foundation employees and the five highest-paid independent contractors. For this purpose, a person paid more than $50,000 is highly paid. In some cases, the comparable organization might be a public charity, in which case the Form 990 would be reviewed; it contains similar information.

The Council on Foundations annually publishes a *Grantmaker Salary and Benefits Report* for its members, which contains private foundation compensation levels by grant maker type, foundation type, asset size, and geographic location. Exponent Philanthropy annually publishes a *Foundation Operations and Management Report*, a comprehensive survey of salaries and benefits for foundations with smaller staffs. A foundation may also find a survey containing information pertinent to its own area or state published by associations of regional or affinity grant-makers.

(e) Excess Executive Compensation Tax

Even where compensation paid to certain private foundation executives for personal services is reasonable and necessary, such that it is not an act of self-dealing subject to the excise tax on self-dealing, the portion of such compensation that exceeds $1 million will be subject to a separate excise tax on excess tax-exempt executive compensation.[267] This excise tax is imposed at the corporate income tax rate[268] on remuneration (including certain payments

---

266. See § 12.3(a), www.guidestar.org, and https://www.irs.gov/charities-non-profits/search-for-tax-exempt-organizations. The Guidestar Nonprofit Compensation Report provides detailed information indexed by job category, gender, geography, type of nonprofit, budget size, state, and more. National, state, and regional reports are also available.
267. IRC § 4960, added by the Tax Cuts and Jobs Act (Pub. L. No. 115-97, § 13602(a), 131 Stat. 2054, 2157-59 (2017)). If the excess compensation subject to this tax is also unreasonable compensation, then a compensation package will attract both this tax (imposed on the foundation) and a self-dealing tax (imposed on the self-dealer). Most private foundations (and related nonexempt organizations) are unaffected by this body of law simply because they do not pay any employees remuneration at the level that triggers the tax.
268. IRC § 11. Currently, 21 percent.

§ 5.6 PAYMENT OF COMPENSATION

contingent on an employee's separation from employment) in excess of $1 million paid by an applicable tax-exempt organization to a covered employee.[269]

(i) General Rules and Definitions. An *applicable tax-exempt organization*[270] includes any tax-exempt organization.[271] Thus, private foundations are applicable tax-exempt organizations for purposes of the excess executive compensation tax. A *covered employee* is an individual who is one of the five highest-compensated employees of an applicable tax-exempt organization for a tax year or was a covered employee for a preceding year (beginning in 2017).[272] The regulations contain rules for identifying these five highest-compensated individuals.[273]

Whether an employee is a covered employee is determined separately for each tax-exempt organization. An employee may be a covered employee of more than one exempt organization in a related group of organizations for a year. Once an employee is a covered employee of an exempt organization, the employee continues to be a covered employee of the entity.[274]

---

269. IRC § 4960(a). For purposes of determining liability for and the amount of this excise tax, any excess parachute payment paid to a covered employee is added to the remuneration paid to such employee (IRC § 4960(a)(2)). A *parachute payment* generally is any payment in the nature of compensation to or for the benefit of a covered employee if the payment is contingent on the employee's separation from employment and the aggregate present value of the payments in the nature of compensation to or for the benefit of the individual that are contingent on the separation equals or exceeds an amount equal to three times a base amount (IRC § 4960(c)(5)(B); Reg. § 53.4960-3(a)(1)). There are exclusions, such as compensation for medical services (IRC § 4960(c)(5)(C)(iii); Reg. § 53.4960-3(a)(2)(iii)), and payments to an individual who is not a highly compensated employee within the meaning of IRC § 414(q) (IRC § 4960(c)(5)(C)(iii); Reg. § 53.4960-3(a)(2)(iv)). An *excess parachute payment* is an amount equal to the excess of a parachute payment over the portion of the base amount allocated to the payment (IRC § 4960(c)(5)(A); Reg. § 53.4940-4(b)(2)). The regulations address the requirement of involuntary separation from employment (Reg § 53.4960-3(e)), summarize when a payment is contingent (Reg. § 53.4960-3(d)), and provide a three-times-base-amount test and rules as to calculation of excess parachute payments (Reg. § 53.4960-3(g)-(l)).
270. IRC § 4960(c)(1).
271. That is, any organization that is tax-exempt by reason of IRC § 501(a).
272. IRC § 4960(c)(2); Reg. § 53.4960-1(d)(1).
273. Reg. § 53.4960-1(d)(2)(i). For purposes of this tax, *remuneration* generally includes wages (as defined in IRC § 3401(a)), other than a designated Roth contribution (as defined in IRC § 402A(c)), and deferred compensation required to be included in gross income under IRC § 457(f) (IRC § 4960(c)(3)(A); Reg. § 53.4960-2(a)(1)). Remuneration does not include the portion of any remuneration paid to a licensed medical professional for medical or veterinary services (IRC § 4960(c)(3)(B); Reg. §§ 53.4960-1(g), -2(a)(2)).
274. Reg. § 53.4960-1(d); T.D. 9938, 86 Fed. Reg. 6196, 6198 (2021).

The employer paying the excess compensation is liable for the excise tax,[275] and where related persons have compensated the same covered employee, the tax is prorated among the entities paying compensation.[276]

(ii) Compensation from Related Organizations. Compensation of a covered employee by a related person or organization is taken into account for these purposes.[277] Another entity is a *related person* or a *related organization* if the entity controls or is controlled by the tax-exempt organization, is controlled by one or more persons that control the tax-exempt organization, or is a supporting organization[278] or a supported organization[279] with respect to the tax-exempt organization.[280]

The regulations generally utilize the definition of *control* that applies when determining controlling organizations in the unrelated business income setting.[281] A person controls a stock corporation if they own, by vote or value, more than 50 percent of the stock in the corporation.[282] A person or governmental entity generally controls a nonstock organization if more than 50 percent of the trustees or directors of the nonstock organization are either representatives of, or directly or indirectly controlled by, the person or governmental entity (the *representative test*). A person or governmental entity controls a trustee or director of a nonstock organization if the person or governmental entity has the power (either at will or at regular intervals) to remove such

---

275. IRC § 4960(b).
276. IRC § 4960(c)(4)(C). For example, if remuneration paid during a year by more than one employer to a covered employee is taken into account in determining the tax imposed on excess remuneration, then each employer is liable for the tax in an amount that bears the same ratio to the total tax as the amount of compensation paid by the employer bears to the total amount of compensation involved (Reg. § 53.4960-4(c)(1)). The regulations provide additional rules regarding when compensation is paid, the entity that is liable for the excise tax and how that tax is calculated, both as to excess remuneration and excess parachute payments, and the allocation of liability for the tax among related organizations (Reg. § 53.4960-4).
277. IRC § 4960(c)(4)(A).
278. IRC § 509(a)(3); see § 15.6.
279. IRC § 509(f)(3); see § 15.6.
280. IRC § 4960(c)(4)(B); Reg. § 53.4960-1(i)(1).
281. IRC § 512(b)(13)(D) (see *Tax-Exempt Organizations* §§ 29.4, 30.6(b), notes 81-83); Reg. § 53.4960-1(i)(2)(ii)-(iv).
282. Reg. § 53.4960-1(i)(2)(ii). Inasmuch as ownership of more than 50 percent of a business enterprise by a private foundation is generally an excess business holding (see § 7.1), the excess business holdings rules generally preclude a private foundation from controlling a stock corporation, unless it has obtained the business holdings within a five-year period (see § 7.2(d)).

§ 5.6   PAYMENT OF COMPENSATION

trustee or director and designate a new one.[283] There is also a control test for brother-sister arrangements.[284] Constructive ownership rules[285] apply when determining control.[286]

(iii) Exceptions to Covered Employee Status. An issue is whether for-profit businesses are subject to this excise tax because their executives are volunteer officers at a related exempt organization, such as a company-sponsored private foundation. This issue arises from the way an applicable tax-exempt organization's five highest-compensated employees may be identified. Generally, an *employee* is an individual performing services if the relationship between the individual and the person for whom the individual performs services is the legal relationship of employer and employee, including common-law employees. An employee generally also includes an officer of a corporation. However, an officer of a corporation who as such does not perform any services or performs only minor services and who neither receives, nor is entitled to receive, any remuneration is not considered to be an employee of the corporation solely due to the individual's status as an officer of the corporation.[287] A director of a corporation (or an individual holding a substantially similar position in a corporation or other entity) in the individual's capacity as such is not an employee of the corporation.[288]

The regulations include two pertinent exceptions to the definition of the terms *employee* and *covered employee* and the rules for identifying the five highest-compensated employees. These exceptions are intended to ensure that certain employees of a related nonexempt entity providing services as employees of an exempt organization, such as to a company-sponsored private foundation, are not treated as one of the five highest-compensated employees of the exempt organization, provided certain conditions related to their remuneration or hours of service are met.[289]

The first of these exceptions is the *limited hours exception*, which entails two requirements. For purposes of determining an exempt organization's five

---

283. Reg. § 53.4960-1(i)(2)(v).
284. Reg. § 53.4960-1(i)(2)(vi).
285. IRC § 318.
286. Reg. § 53.4960-1(i)(2)(vii).
287. Reg. § 53.4960-1(e)(1); Reg. §31.3401(c)-1.
288. Reg. § 53.4960-1(e)(2); Reg. §31.3401(c)-1(f). These principles apply by analogy to a trustee of any arrangement classified as a trust for federal tax purposes in Reg. § 301.7701-4(a) (Reg. § 53.4960-1(e)(3)).
289. T.D. 9938, 86 Fed. Reg. 6196, 6199 (2021).

highest-paid employees for a year, an individual is disregarded if neither the exempt organization nor a related exempt organization paid remuneration to the individual for services the individual performed as an employee of the exempt organization during the year. Also, to be disregarded, the individual must have performed services as an employee of the exempt organization and any related exempt organizations for no more than 10 percent of the total hours the individual worked as an employee of the exempt organization and any related organizations during the year. The second element of this exception is deemed met if the employee performed no more than 100 hours of service as an employee of the exempt organization and any related exempt organization during the year.[290]

The other exception is the *nonexempt funds exception*, which has three requirements. First, neither the exempt organization, nor any related exempt organization, nor any taxable related organization controlled by the exempt organization or by one or more related exempt organizations, either alone or together with the exempt organization, paid remuneration to the individual for services the individual performed as an employee of an exempt organization during the year and the preceding year. Second, the individual performed services as an employee of the exempt organization and any related exempt organizations for not more than 50 percent of the total hours worked as an employee of the exempt organization and any related organizations during the year and the preceding year. Third, no related organization that paid remuneration to the individual during the year and the preceding year provided services for a fee to the exempt organization, a related exempt organization, or a taxable related organization controlled by the exempt organization or by one or more related exempt organizations, either alone or together with the exempt organization, during the year and the preceding year.[291]

The limited hours and nonexempt funds exceptions thus exclude certain employees who may be employees under common law from being treated as one of an applicable tax-exempt organization's five highest-compensated employees.[292]

---

290. Reg. § 53.4960-1(d)(2)(ii); see § 17.8(a).
291. Reg. § 53.4960-1(d)(2)(iii); see § 17.8(b).
292. Additionally, a limited-services exception allows an individual to be disregarded for these purposes where the tax-exempt organization paid less than 10 percent of the individual's total compensation for services performed as an employee of the exempt organization and all related organizations during the year (Reg. § 53.4960-1(d)(2)(iv)). This exception, however, is not of much utility in the private foundation context inasmuch as it requires that the exempt organization have at least one related exempt organization.

§ 5.6 PAYMENT OF COMPENSATION

(f) Commissions or Management Fees

Compensation based on a percentage of sales of a private foundation's goods or property or the value of the property managed is permitted as long as the amount of the commission or fee is not so excessive as to be considered unreasonable. The regulations cite an investment counselor as an example of a disqualified person who can be paid in this manner.[293] This regulation does not specify the fashion in which the counselor's fee is to be calculated. Instead, the concepts discussed earlier are applied to measure what is reasonable. Particularly when paying this type of compensation, a foundation should become familiar with the market in which similar property is normally sold. The commission range for the sale of art versus securities exemplifies the need to document comparative pricing. Although the commission charged by a fine arts dealer can range between 10 percent and 50 percent of the selling price, a commission of less than 1 percent is charged for the sale of marketable securities through an established brokerage company.

The IRS ruled that commissions paid by a private foundation to art dealers who were also disqualified persons with respect to the foundation were not acts of self-dealing. The foundation stated that it would pay these disqualified persons the same or lower commissions charged by other broker-agents who sold similar artworks, and would use the following *comparability factors* as a means of determining reasonable compensation for the personal services to be rendered: commissions charged by nondisqualified persons for selling the same artist's work; commissions paid by the artist during his lifetime to persons who were now disqualified persons and to others, for selling his art; commissions that agents charge to sell art of the same school and period as the artist; and commissions that were received by agents who sell art generally in the foundation's geographic area.[294]

In another private ruling, concerning the brokerage commissions paid to a related-party investment manager, the IRS deemed the amount to be customary and normal for the industry. Total compensation, including the normal transaction fees, plus 50 percent of the account's annual equity value increases in excess of 15 percent, was found to be reasonable, because it was comparable with practices in the industry.[295]

---

293. Reg. § 53.4941(d)-3(c)(2), Example (2).
294. Priv. Ltr. Rul. 9011050.
295. Priv. Ltr. Rul. 9237035. In a situation involving services provided to maintain a historic site, the personal services were found by the IRS to be compensated at a reasonable rate, which was a "rate consistent with and no greater than the rates charged to its other clients" (Priv. Ltr. Rul. 9307026). The IRS was thus incorrect in ruling that a commission-based compensation arrangement was private inurement because a limit was not placed on the compensation, where the IRS did not address whether the compensation amount was reasonable (Priv. Ltr. Rul. 201820019).

(g) Expense Advances and Reimbursements

Advances that are "reasonable in relation to the duties and expense requirements of a foundation manager" are permitted.[296] Cash advances should not ordinarily exceed $500, according to the regulations. When a foundation chooses to exceed this $500 threshold, appropriate documentation should be gathered. Such a report could reflect the number of days and details of expected expenses. To mitigate the amount needed as an advance, the foundation can also purchase airline tickets and lodging hotels directly. For extended travel time or trips to places where it is not secure to carry cash, the foundation might obtain and allow disqualified persons to use a credit card. Personal use of the card, of course, should be prohibited. If the advance is to cover anticipated out-of-pocket current expenses for a reasonable period, such as a month, self-dealing will not occur when the foundation makes an advance, when the foundation replenishes the funds upon receipt of supporting vouchers from the manager, or if the foundation temporarily adds to the advance to cover extraordinary expenses anticipated to be incurred in fulfillment of a special assignment, such as long-distance travel.

Thus, the IRS ruled that the payment by a private foundation of legal fees, which were not excessive, awarded by a court to the lawyer for one of the private foundation's managers (and thus a disqualified person), who had initiated litigation against the other managers to require them to carry on the private foundation's charitable program, did not constitute an act of self-dealing, inasmuch as the service performed by the manager in filing the suit was reasonable and necessary to carry out the private foundation's tax-exempt purpose.[297]

A subset of this question arises when a disqualified person expends funds on behalf of the foundation and wishes to be reimbursed. For example, a disqualified person buys office supplies or writes a grant check on behalf of the foundation. Reasonable and necessary expenses incurred by a disqualified person to perform a professional service for a foundation, such as a translation fee for a legal document in connection with a foundation grant to a foreign organization, can also be reimbursed. An architect's charges might include blueprints. Expenses paid by the disqualified person in these circumstances can be classified as loans, bearing no interest, from the disqualified person to the foundation. Complete documentation, of course, should evidence the

---

296. Reg. § 53.4941(d)-3(c)(1).
297. Rev. Rul. 73-613, 1973-2 C.B. 385. A pension paid by a private foundation to one of its directors (a disqualified person), whose total compensation including the pension was not excessive, was not an act of self-dealing (Rev. Rul. 74-591, 1974-2 C.B. 385).

§ 5.6 PAYMENT OF COMPENSATION

nature of the expenditure and the fact that it advanced the exempt purposes of the foundation.

Expenses of travel and meals incurred in connection with conducting foundation affairs can also be paid or reimbursed. A foundation with directors and personnel in different locations, for example, can pay for the cost of travel to attend a meeting in one of the locations. The expense of site visits to potential grantees can be paid. When a foundation pays such expenses on behalf of its disqualified persons, a written policy should describe the terms for reimbursement and documentation required should be developed. For example, it is prudent for a foundation to adopt a policy against payment of lavish traveling expenses. Limiting the reimbursement to prevailing per diem rates published by the IRS might be considered. Full and complete reports of the expenditures, along with descriptions of the nature of the work performed, meetings held, or other foundation business that necessitated the travel, should be compiled to document the expenditure.

Reimbursement for vehicle mileage should be made based on the prevailing standard mileage rates. Beginning January 1, 2014, the rate was 56 cents per mile for business miles driven and 14 cents for service to a charitable organization. The level of reimbursement by a private foundation would depend, therefore, on the person's position in the foundation. A compensated employee, director, or trustee would be reimbursed at the higher rate. A volunteer director or person working on foundation programs on a pro bono basis would receive the lower rate.

The documentation process and required reports are referred to as an *accountable plan*. Amounts paid under an accountable plan are not reported as compensation to the person being reimbursed.[298] Importantly, these expenses are also not reported as compensation for purposes of completing Form 990-PF, Part VII.

(h) Bank Fees

Banks and trust companies frequently serve as trustees for private foundations and, in this role, often face the possibility of self-dealing. Certain general banking functions that a bank performs for all of its customers can be performed for the private foundations for which it serves as trustee without amounting to self-dealing.[299] Taking into account a fair interest rate for the use

---

298. Reg. § 1.162-2(c)(4).
299. Reg. § 53.4941(d)-2(c)(4).

SELF-DEALING

of the funds by the bank, reasonable compensation can be paid. The *general banking services* that are permitted are:

- Checking accounts, as long as the bank does not charge interest on any overdrafts. Payment of overdraft charges not exceeding the bank's cost of processing an overdraft have been ruled to be acceptable;[300]
- Savings accounts, as long as the foundation may withdraw its funds on no more than 30 days' notice without subjecting itself to a loss of interest on its money for the time during which the money was on deposit; and
- Safekeeping activities.[301]

Thus, for example, a private foundation may pay a commercial bank that serves as a trustee for the foundation reasonable compensation for maintaining the foundation's checking and savings accounts and renting it a safety deposit box.[302] The IRS has applied this general banking services exception to a foundation's investment in a money market fund established by a bank (disqualified person) consisting of short-term liquid investments, including certificates of deposit purchased from the bank. The IRS concluded that the exception applied because the private foundation was permitted to withdraw its funds from the money market account on no more than thirty-days' notice without subjecting itself to a loss of interest on its money for the time during which the money was on deposit.[303]

Transactions outside the scope of these three relationships may be troublesome. For example, if a private foundation left excess funds, which were not earning interest, in a bank that is a disqualified person, self-dealing generally would occur.[304] Nonetheless, the IRS ruled that a non-interest-bearing clearing account arrangement between a private foundation and a disqualified person bank, being a "common business practice for trust departments," was protected by this exception.[305] A bank trustee's purchase of securities owned by independent parties for a foundation's account is not self-dealing, but purchase of the bank's own mortgage loans would be.[306] The purchase of

---

300. Rev. Rul. 73-546, 1973-2 C.B. 384.
301. Reg. § 53.4941(d)-2(c)(4).
302. *Id.* Reg. § 53.4941(d)-3(c)(2), Example (3).
303. Priv. Ltr. Rul. 7850011.
304. Rev. Rul. 73-595, 1973-2 C.B. 384.
305. Priv. Ltr. Rul. 200727018.
306. Rev. Rul. 77-259, 1977-2 C.B. 387.

certificates of deposit by a foundation is unacceptable should the certificates provide for a reduced rate of interest if they are not held to the full maturity date.[307]

By contrast, the IRS ruled that a bank assisting a private foundation in connection with its securities-lending program will not be engaged in prohibited self-dealing by reason of this banking services exception. The foundation had an investment trustee (a bank with trust administration services) that was charged with generally managing and investing the foundation's assets. The IRS observed that the investment trustee, in arranging securities loans for this foundation, is acting merely as the foundation's agent; the bank and its affiliates are not borrowers as part of this program.[308]

§ 5.7 INDEMNIFICATION AND INSURANCE

It is common for a private foundation to provide officers' and directors' liability insurance to, or to indemnify, foundation managers in connection with civil proceedings arising from the managers' performance of services for the foundation. The general rule is that indemnification by a private foundation, or the provision of insurance for the purpose of covering the liabilities of an individual in their capacity as a manager of the foundation, is not self-dealing. Moreover, the amounts expended by a private foundation for insurance or indemnification generally are not included in the compensation of the disqualified person for purposes of determining whether the disqualified person's compensation is reasonable.

Indemnification payments and insurance coverage are divided into noncompensatory and compensatory categories. This body of law is a component of the general statutory scheme by which transfers to, or use by or for the benefit of, a disqualified person of the income or assets of a private foundation generally constitute self-dealing.[309]

---

307. Rev. Rul. 77-288, 1977-2 C.B. 388. By reason of the Tax Reform Act of 1984 § 312, the self-dealing rules do not apply to certain financing involving the Wasie Foundation, as described in Wasie v. Commissioner, 86 T.C. 962 (1986).
308. Priv. Ltr. Rul. 200501021.
309. See § 5.8. The tax regulation was amended in this regard in 1995 (T.D. 8639). Previously, the provision of insurance for the payment of private foundation taxes by a private foundation for a foundation manager was self-dealing unless the premium amounts were included in the compensation of the manager (prior Reg. § 53.4941(d)-2(f)(1)). Also, previously, the regulations provided that the indemnification of certain expenses by a private foundation for a foundation manager's defense in a judicial or administrative proceeding involving private foundation taxes was not, under certain circumstances, self-dealing (prior Reg. § 53.4941(d)-2(f)(3)). The IRS interpretations of these prior rules

(a) Noncompensatory Indemnification and Insurance

Self-dealing does not occur, as a general rule, when a private foundation indemnifies a foundation manager with respect to the manager's defense in any civil judicial or civil administrative proceeding arising out of the manager's performance of services (or failure to perform services) on behalf of the foundation. This indemnification may be against all expenses (other than taxes, including any of the private foundation taxes, penalties, or expenses of correction) and can include payment of lawyers' fees, judgments, and settlement expenditures. The following conditions must exist, however, for the indemnification to not be considered self-dealing: (1) the expenses must be reasonably incurred by the manager in connection with the proceeding, and (2) the manager must not have acted willfully or without reasonable cause with respect to the act or failure to act that led to the proceeding or liability for a private foundation tax.[310]

Likewise, the self-dealing rules do not apply to the payment of premiums for insurance to cover or to reimburse a foundation for this type of indemnification payment.[311] These payments are viewed as expenses for the foundation's administration and operation, rather than compensation for the manager's services. An indemnification or payment of insurance of this nature is not regarded as part of the compensation paid to the manager in the context of determining whether the compensation is reasonable for purposes of the private foundation rules.[312] The IRS ruled that this exception to the self-dealing rules was available in connection with service by some of the managers of a private foundation as trustees of charitable remainder trusts as to which the foundation was the remainder interest beneficiary.[313]

---

are contained in Rev. Rul. 82-223, 1982-2 C.B. 301 (concerning indemnification or insurance for coverage of foundation managers for liabilities arising under state law concerning mismanagement of funds; self-dealing found where foundation indemnified a foundation manager for an amount paid in settlement); Rev. Rul. 74-405, 1974-2 C.B. 384 (concerning insurance provided for foundation managers against liability for claims under the federal securities laws in connection with their role in preparing the registration statement and prospectus for a public offering of securities); Priv. Ltr. Rul. 8503098 (holding that indemnification and insurance against foundation tax liability and state mismanagement law liability was not self-dealing); Priv. Ltr. Rul. 8202082 (stating that the rules in the regulations, as to indemnification and insurance, apply with respect to all civil proceedings). There was confusion in this area of the law, occasioned in part by inconsistent rulings from the IRS.

310. Reg. § 53.4941(d)-2(f)(3)(i).
311. Reg. § 53.4941(d)-2(f)(3)(ii).
312. Id.
313. Priv. Ltr. Rul. 200649030.

§ 5.7 INDEMNIFICATION AND INSURANCE

(b) Compensatory Indemnification and Insurance

The indemnification of a foundation manager against payment of taxes, and the associated defense, is considered to be part of the manager's compensation. This type of payment by a private foundation is an act of self-dealing, unless, when the payment is added to other compensation paid to the manager, the total compensation is reasonable. A *compensatory expense* of this nature includes payment of any of the following: (1) any penalty, tax (including a private foundation tax), or expense of correction that is owed by the foundation manager; (2) any expense not reasonably incurred by the manager in connection with a civil judicial or civil administrative proceeding arising out of the manager's performance of services on behalf of the foundation; or (3) any expense resulting from an act or failure to act with respect to which the manager has acted willfully and without reasonable cause.[314]

Likewise, the payment by a private foundation of the premiums for an insurance policy providing liability insurance to a foundation manager for any of these three categories of expenses is an act of self-dealing, unless when the premiums are added to other compensation paid to the manager the total compensation is reasonable for purposes of the private foundation rules.[315] If the total compensation is not reasonable, the foundation will have engaged in an act of self-dealing. These payments are viewed as being exclusively for the benefit of the managers, not the private foundation.

A private foundation is not engaged in an act of self-dealing if the foundation purchases a single insurance policy to provide its managers both noncompensatory coverage and compensatory coverage, as long as the total insurance premium is allocated and each manager's portion of the premium attributable to the compensatory coverage is included in that manager's compensation for purposes of determining reasonable compensation.[316]

The term *indemnification* includes not only reimbursement by the foundation for expenses that a foundation manager has already incurred or anticipates

---

314. Reg. § 53.4941(d)-2(f)(4)(i).
315. Reg. § 53.4941(d)-2(f)(4)(ii).
316. Reg. § 53.4941(d)-2(f)(5). Comments on these regulations in proposed form included the thought that allocation of insurance premiums should not be required, because doing so places an undue burden on private foundations. In deciding to retain the allocation provision in the final regulations, the IRS—in the preamble to the regulations—once again articulated its view of this body of law: "The self-dealing rules were meant to discourage foundations from relieving managers of penalties, taxes and expenses of correction, as well as expenses ultimately resulting from the manager's willful violation of the law. A rule that did not require an allocation to determine whether the disqualified person's compensation is reasonable for purposes of [IRC] chapter 42 could have the opposite effect" (60 Fed. Reg. 65566 (1995)).

incurring, but also direct payment by the foundation of these expenses as the expenses arise.[317]

(c) Fringe Benefit Rules and Volunteers

The determination as to whether any amount of indemnification or insurance premium is included in a manager's gross income for individual income tax purposes is made on the basis of general federal tax law principles and without regard to the treatment of the amount for purposes of determining whether the manager's compensation is reasonable for self-dealing purposes.[318] Any property or service that is excluded from income under the de minimis fringe benefit rules[319] may be disregarded for purposes of determining whether the recipient's compensation is reasonable under the private foundation rules.[320]

The IRS adopted amended regulations concerning certain fringe benefits[321] relating to the exclusion from gross income of benefits known as *working condition fringe benefits*,[322] which clarified the treatment, in this regard, of bona fide volunteers who perform services for private foundations and other tax-exempt organizations. These regulations, which do not directly address the self-dealing aspects of this matter, apply with respect to volunteers (including directors and trustees) who provide services to exempt organizations and who receive directors' and officers' liability insurance and/or indemnification protection from these organizations.

The federal tax law excludes certain fringe benefits from an individual's gross income.[323] Generally, these fringe benefits are excludable by those who are employees, whether these individuals are compensated or working as volunteers (where the tax-exempt organization has the right to direct or control the volunteers' services). For certain purposes, the term *employee*[324] includes

---

317. Reg. § 53.4941(d)-2(f)(6).
318. Reg. § 53.4941(d)-2(f)(7).
319. IRC § 132(a)(4).
320. The IRS announced that employees' use of cell phones for business purposes is a working condition fringe benefit and that use of these phones for personal purposes is a de minimis fringe benefit (Notice 2011-72, 2011-38 I.R.B. 407).
321. IRC § 132.
322. A working condition fringe benefit is any property or service provided to an employee of an employer to the extent that, if the employee were paid for the property or service, the amount paid would be allowable as a business expense deduction (IRC § 162) or a depreciation deduction (IRC § 167) (IRC § 132(d); Reg. § 1.132-5(a)(1)).
323. IRC § 132(a), encompassing (in addition to working condition fringe benefits [see *supra* note 322]) "no-additional-cost services," "qualified employee discounts," and "de minimis fringe" benefits.
324. Reg. § 1.132-1(b).

§ 5.7 INDEMNIFICATION AND INSURANCE

independent contractors. For other purposes,[325] however, independent contractors are not treated as employees. Thus, bona fide volunteers, like their paid counterparts, could not (prior to the adoption of these regulations) exclude no-additional-cost services from their gross income (unless there was an employer-employee relationship, which was unlikely).[326] That is, although volunteers who were employees could exclude from gross income these fringe benefits, and all volunteers (including independent contractors) could exclude de minimis fringe benefits, the language of the regulations relating to working condition fringes did not encompass bona fide volunteers.

The difficulty in this connection regarded the business expense deduction rules. An individual engaged in carrying on a trade or business has the requisite profit motive for business expense deduction purposes. An individual who performs services as a bona fide volunteer, however, does not have a profit motive and thus cannot claim an expense deduction for amounts incurred in connection with the volunteer work. For example, the value of directors' and officers' insurance provided to a volunteer was not excludable as a working condition fringe benefit, even though the same insurance coverage is excludable from the income of a paid employee or director who has a profit motive. The amended regulations are designed to eliminate this distinction, that is, to ensure that, like their paid counterparts, bona fide volunteers may exclude working condition fringe benefits—including directors' and officers' liability insurance—from their gross income.

The regulations provide that, solely for these purposes, a bona fide volunteer (including a director or officer) who performs services for a tax-exempt organization[327] (or for a governmental unit) is deemed to have a profit motive for purposes of the business expense deduction.[328] An individual is a *bona fide volunteer* only if the total value of the benefits provided with respect to the volunteer services is substantially less than the total value of the volunteer services the individual provides to the organization.[329] The value of liability insurance coverage (or indemnification for liability) is deemed to be substantially less than the value of an individual's volunteer services to the organization, provided that the insurance coverage is limited to acts performed in the discharge of official duties or the performance of services on behalf of the tax-exempt organization (or government) employer.[330]

---

325. IRC § 132(a)(1) concerning no-additional-cost services (IRC § 132(b)) and (2) concerning qualified employee discounts (IRC § 132(c)).
326. IRC § 132(a).
327. That is, an organization that is tax-exempt pursuant to IRC § 501(a).
328. Reg. § 1.132-5(r)(1), (2).
329. Reg. § 1.132-5(r)(3)(i).
330. Reg. § 1.132-5(r)(3)(ii).

As noted, these regulations do not directly address the self-dealing aspects of this issue. The preamble accompanying these regulations, however, states that "like other tax-exempt organizations, private foundations need not allocate portions of D & O insurance premiums to individual directors or officers or include any such allocable amounts" as reportable compensation, "provided such amounts are excludable from gross income under the[se] final regulations," and that "whether or not such allocable amounts need to be treated as compensation for the limited purpose" of the self-dealing rules, "no employer should issue [compensation tax form] 1099 or W-2 for any such amount that is excludable from gross income as a working condition fringe benefit." Consequently, while a foundation manager still must (to avoid the self-dealing rules) be certain that this form of compensation is reasonable, the amount involved is excludable from the manager's gross income.

The IRS ruled that a private foundation may amend its articles of incorporation, in conformity with a change in state law, to limit the liability of volunteers who are not directors without engaging in an act of self-dealing.[331] In this ruling, it was concluded that the limitation of nondirector volunteers (principally officers and committee chairs) "is essential in acquiring and retaining capable volunteers who are necessary" to the carrying out of the foundations' exempt function; this situation was held to fall within the "reasonable and necessary" exception.[332]

§ 5.8 USES OF INCOME OR ASSETS BY DISQUALIFIED PERSONS

The transfer to, or use by or for the benefit of, a disqualified person of the income or assets of a private foundation generally constitutes self-dealing.[333] For example, disqualified persons with respect to a private foundation had

---

331. Priv. Ltr. Rul. 9440033.

332. This body of law is not confined to instances involving insurance and indemnification; the principles may be applicable in analogous circumstances. For example, a private foundation acquired partnership interests from a decedent's estate and thereafter engaged in various transactions to avoid receiving unrelated debt-financed income (see § 11.4). This foundation sought rulings from the IRS, including one that its payment of the legal and accounting costs for preparing and obtaining the rulings would not be self-dealing. The IRS so ruled, inasmuch as the rulings benefited the foundation to a "large extent" (Priv. Ltr. Rul. 9719041). The IRS analogized these payments to reimbursements to a private foundation for indemnification of a foundation manager with respect to the manager's defense in a civil administrative proceeding arising out of the manager's performance of services for reasonable compensation (Reg. § 53.4941(d)-2(f)(3)).

333. IRC § 4941(d)(1)(E).

§ 5.8 USES OF INCOME OR ASSETS BY DISQUALIFIED PERSONS

assets in an investment company that had a collateralization obligation used to satisfy margin requirements. The foundation also had investment assets placed with the same company, which were taken into account in determining the disqualified persons' compliance with the collateralization requirement. This was found by the IRS to constitute self-dealing, as being use of the foundation's assets for the benefit of disqualified persons.[334]

As this and subsequent examples illustrate, the IRS has an expansive view of the scope of this provision. In one instance, the IRS observed that this prohibition is intended to be "extremely broad."[335]

(a) Securities Transactions

(i) Summary of Law. The purchase or sale of stock or other securities by a private foundation is an act of self-dealing under these rules, if the purchase or sale is made in an attempt to manipulate the price of the stock or other securities to the advantage of a disqualified person.[336]

An issue on which the IRS has not directly ruled concerns the sale of stock or other securities by a private foundation in a redemption (where the purchasing corporation is not a disqualified person)[337] or in a secondary public offering (where the offering would not take place but for the involvement of the private foundation), where one or more disqualified persons desire to also participate in the securities transaction. To allow the disqualified person(s) to participate in the transaction would be an act of self-dealing under these rules, either as an attempt to manipulate the price of the stock to the advantage of the disqualified persons or to otherwise use the assets of the foundation for the benefit of the disqualified persons. In one instance, a public offering of stock made to enable a private foundation to sell its shares,

---

334. Tech. Adv. Mem. 9627001.
335. Tech. Adv. Mem. 9825001. Yet, on that occasion, the IRS held that the purchase by a charitable remainder trust (see § 3.7) of deferred annuity contracts from a commercial life insurance company, where the named annuitants were disqualified persons, did not constitute self-dealing under these rules because, under the facts (including an assignment of the disqualified person's interest in the policy to the trust), the disqualified persons did not receive any present value under the policies.
336. Reg. § 53.4941(d)-2(f)(1).
337. As discussed in § 5.14(a), an exception from the self-dealing rules is available for certain redemptions and other corporate transactions where the purchasing corporation is a disqualified person.

SELF-DEALING

where disqualified persons were excluded from the transaction, was ruled not to be an act of self-dealing.[338]

(ii) Representative Case. The facts of a court case offer an illustration of this type of securities manipulation for the benefit of disqualified persons.[339] At issue in this case, however, was the extent to which the amount of an estate's charitable contribution deduction had to be reduced because of post-death intrafamily manipulations that caused property of considerably lesser value than that originally bequeathed to pass to the private foundation that was established by the decedent.

An individual and family members owned a C corporation (Corporation). This individual was the majority shareholder of the Corporation. She created a trust (Trust), to which her entire estate was willed. She also created a private foundation (Foundation), to which the bulk of her estate, consisting primarily of the Corporation's voting and nonvoting stock, was to be transferred from the Trust. One of her sons was the sole trustee of the Trust and the Foundation. This individual died. An appraisal for purposes of determining the date-of-death fair market value of the decedent's property valued her Corporation stock at about $14 million.

Numerous events occurred after the decedent's death but before the bequeathed property was transferred to the Foundation. Seven months after the death, the Corporation elected S corporation status. The Corporation agreed to redeem all the bequeathed shares from the Trust. The redemption agreement was modified, with the Corporation agreeing to redeem all the voting stock and about two-thirds of the nonvoting shares. In exchange for the redemption, the Trust received short-term and long-term promissory notes. Simultaneous with the redemption, three of the decedent's sons purchased additional shares in the Corporation. The Foundation received contributions of the two notes and the nonredeemed nonvoting shares in the Corporation.

The date-of-death value of the Corporation's voting shares was $1,824 per share; the value of the nonvoting stock was $1,733 per share. The value of the voting shares, for purposes of the redemption and stock purchases, was set

---

338. Priv. Ltr. Ruls. 9016003, 9114025 (where the sale of limited partnership interests by charitable remainder trusts was held not to constitute an act of self-dealing as long as the trustee of the trusts acted independently of the disqualified persons holding similar interests); Priv. Ltr. Rul. 8944007 (where the managers of a private foundation were precluded from dealing in a corporation's stock during the planning and implementation of a stock redemption; the stock transaction was ruled not to be an act of self-dealing).
339. Dieringer v. Commissioner, 146 T.C. 117 (2016), *aff'd*, 917 F.3d 1135 (9th Cir. 2019).

§ 5.8 USES OF INCOME OR ASSETS BY DISQUALIFIED PERSONS

at $916 per share; the value of the nonvoting stock was set at $870 per share. The appraisal of the voting stock included discounts for lack of control and lack of marketability. The appraisal of the nonvoting stock included those two discounts, plus another for lack of voting power.

The estate claimed a charitable contribution deduction in excess of $18 million, including the date-of-death valued Corporation stock. By notice of deficiency, the IRS reduced the charitable deduction to reflect the value of the notes and nonvoting stock received by the Foundation (about $6 million), thus increasing the estate tax owed. The IRS argued that the manner in which the appraisals were obtained and the redemption of the decedent's controlling interest at a minority interest discount indicated that the sons never intended to effectuate the decedent's testamentary plan.

The court of appeals stated that valuation of a gross estate is typically done as of the date of death. Yet, the court added, there is "no uniform rule for all circumstances."[340] Also, "[c]ertain deductions not only permit consideration of post-death events, but require them."[341] Quoting from another case, the court stated that the "proper administration of the charitable deduction cannot ignore such differences in the value actually received by the charity."[342] "This rule," stated the appellate court, "prohibits crafting an estate plan or will so as to game the system and guarantee a charitable deduction that is larger than the amount actually given to charity."[343]

The court found that one of the sons "manipulated the charitable deduction so that the Foundation only received a fraction of the charitable deduction claimed by the [e]state."[344] The charitable deduction reduction rule, the court wrote, "extends to situations where the testator would be able to produce an artificially low valuation by manipula[tion], which includes the present situation."[345]

It is not known why this case was structured as one concerning the amount of the estate tax charitable deduction rather than one involving indirect self-dealing. Certainly, a compelling case can be made that, under these facts, this is more properly an indirect self-dealing case.[346]

---

340. *Id.* at 1142.
341. *Id.* at 1143.
342. *Id.*
343. *Id.* at 1143–1144.
344. *Id.* at 1144.
345. *Id.*
346. See § 5.11. A set of commentators has asserted that this case was wrongly decided, in that the estate tax charitable deduction should have been allowed at the estate tax value, and that the case should have been prosecuted as an indirect self-dealing case. Specifically, they wrote that the self-dealing tax "should have been imposed on the corporation and/or the decedent's children who [as disqualified persons] wound up

(b) Other Transactions Involving Manipulation

A disqualified person may also engage in an act to manipulate the price (or value) of other types of property owned by a private foundation to the disqualified person's advantage. Such manipulation can lead to self-dealing with respect to any type of property, not only securities.

In a rare application of these rules outside the context of a securities transaction, the IRS ruled that a purchase of artwork by a director of a private foundation from an artist whose work was on public display as the result of funding by a grantee of the foundation was not self-dealing as a transfer of foundation assets for the benefit of a disqualified person. The foundation did not earmark the use of these grants and did not have any role in the selection of secondary grantees. The director obtained an appraisal stating that the fair market value of the artwork was not more than the amount paid for it. The IRS concluded that this was not a scheme to enable the director to purchase the artwork at a below-fair-market-value price. That is, the IRS determined that this was not an attempt by a disqualified person to manipulate the price of the work of art to the advantage of a disqualified person.[347]

(c) Payment of Charitable Pledges

Self-dealing in the form of use of a private foundation's assets for the benefit of a disqualified person occurs if the foundation makes a grant that satisfies the disqualified person's legally enforceable pledge to pay the amount. Where this type of pledge qualifies as a debt under local law, payment of the pledge by the foundation relieves the person or company of its obligation and constitutes self-dealing.[348] Payment of church membership dues for a disqualified person was found, for example, to be self-dealing when the membership provided a personal benefit to the individual.[349] Similarly, the IRS ruled that the payment of

---

      acquiring the stock redeemed at what was essentially a bargain price." Fox, Blattmachr, & Gans, "Ninth Circuit Affirms Dieringer v. Com'r; Post-Death Redemption of Stock Bequeathed to Private Foundation Reduces Estate Tax Charitable Deduction; A Flawed Result Because Taxpayer Apparently Spared Section 4941 Self-Dealing Penalty," Steve Leimberg's Charitable Planning Email Newsletter Archive Message # 281 (April 23, 2019).

347. Priv. Ltr. Rul. 202035002.
348. Reg. § 53-4941(d)-2(f)(1). A disqualified person, however, as trustee of a private foundation, can cause the entity to make a grant as its obligation; that, of course, is not self-dealing. An instance of this involved a series of grants mandated by disqualified persons with respect to a private foundation and two charitable lead trusts; the IRS determined that each of these grants entails an obligation running from grantor to grantee, not an obligation of a disqualified person personally (Priv. Ltr. Rul. 201421023).
349. Rev. Rul. 77-160, 1977-1 C.B. 351.

§ 5.8 USES OF INCOME OR ASSETS BY DISQUALIFIED PERSONS

pledges by a private foundation, which were legally binding before the foundation was created, was self-dealing.[350] The foundation was established by several corporations to serve as a conduit for their contributions. Part of the foundation's initial funding was received on the condition that the foundation use the funds to pay certain charitable pledges that the corporations had previously made.

This would seem to be a harsh rule, where the foundation was established and funded solely for the purpose of satisfying the charitable pledges of the sponsoring corporations—the funds involved, after all, came from the corporations, which could have paid the pledges directly. A more lenient view was adopted by the IRS in 1995, holding that the use of assets of a private foundation, contributed to it specifically for the purpose of satisfying the charitable pledges of sponsoring corporations (which are disqualified persons), was not self-dealing in that the resulting benefit to the corporations was incidental and tenuous.[351] On reconsideration, however, the IRS realized that the assets, once transferred to the foundation under any circumstances, became charitable property in the foundation's hands that cannot be used for the benefit of disqualified persons—and revoked the 1995 ruling,[352] concluding that the pledge payments were self-dealing.[353]

The making of a promise, pledge, or similar arrangement to a private foundation by a disqualified person, whether evidenced by an oral or written agreement, a promissory note, or other instrument of indebtedness, to the extent motivated by charitable intent and unsupported by consideration, is not an extension of credit before the date of maturity.[354]

Modification of a disqualified person's charitable pledge to a foundation prior to its maturity is also acceptable. The IRS looked at the case of a foundation that operated both with current contributions from its substantial contributor and with loans made by a bank against pledges made periodically by that person. When the disqualified person reduced his current promised payments before their maturity, but pledged a larger amount later, self-dealing was held to not occur.[355]

(d) For the Benefit of Transactions

An act of self-dealing can occur where a benefit is not provided *to* a disqualified person. This type of an act can take place where a private foundation engages in a transaction with a person (or persons) who is not a disqualified

---

350. Priv. Ltr. Rul. 8128072.
351. Priv. Ltr. Rul. 9540042.
352. Priv. Ltr. Rul. 9610032.
353. Priv. Ltr. Rul. 9703020.
354. Reg. § 53.4941(d)-2(c)(3).
355. Tech. Adv. Mem. 8723001.

SELF-DEALING

person, where the income or assets of a private foundation are utilized *for the benefit of* a disqualified person (or persons).[356]

For example, where a lawyer who was the sole trustee of a private foundation caused the foundation to make a loan to an individual (who was not a disqualified person) who had substantial dealings with the lawyer and his law firm, the lending transaction amounted to an act of self-dealing because the loan enhanced the lawyer's reputation in the view of his client and thus provided an economic benefit to him.[357]

Likewise, a bank, which extended credit to large corporations and tax-exempt organizations, where notes were to be purchased by private foundations for which the bank acted as trustee (and thus was a disqualified person), was held to be engaging in a substantial activity that enhanced the reputation of the bank and significantly increased its goodwill, so that the transactions were (or would be) acts of self-dealing.[358] Similarly, marketing benefits provided to a disqualified person by means of a transaction of this nature could entail self-dealing.[359]

Consequently, it is not enough to analyze a transaction to determine if one or more disqualified persons were directly provided a benefit by a private foundation; the analysis needs to continue to see if some advantage was provided for the benefit of a disqualified person. This concept is in the intermediate sanctions rules' definition of an *excess benefit transaction*, so developments in that setting will inform this aspect of the self-dealing rules. Yet, in one instance, the IRS concluded that a benefit was not provided to disqualified persons, and thus the transaction was not an excess benefit transaction, without also analyzing whether one or more benefits were provided for the use of disqualified persons (even though the agency concluded that the "main benefit" flowing to them was "intangible public benefit," which presumably akin to enhanced reputation and increased goodwill").[360] A similar ruling was issued in the self-dealing rules setting.[361]

Likewise, the IRS analyzed a situation where a private foundation proposed to lease excess parking space in a garage it owns to tenants in an adjoining building owned by a disqualified person. The IRS concluded that self-dealing would not take place because the disqualified person will not be involved in a leasing transaction.[362] The agency, however, did not discuss the

---

356. IRC § 4941(d)(1)(E). Thus, the author of an IRS private letter ruling missed the mark in writing that the self-dealing rules do "not apply to any transactions between a private foundation and a person who is not a disqualified person" (Priv. Ltr. Rul. 201745001).
357. Tech. Adv. Mem. 8719004; Gen. Couns. Mem. 39632.
358. Gen. Couns. Mem. 39107.
359. Priv. Ltr. Rul. 9726006.
360. Priv. Ltr. Rul. 200335037.
361. Priv. Ltr. Rul. 200123072.
362. Priv. Ltr. Rul. 201301015.

§ 5.8 USES OF INCOME OR ASSETS BY DISQUALIFIED PERSONS

issue as to whether this leasing arrangement nonetheless would confer a benefit on the disqualified person; if it did, self-dealing would take place (unless the benefit was incidental).

(e) Incidental or Tenuous Benefits

The fact that a disqualified person receives an incidental or tenuous benefit from the use by a private foundation of its income or assets will not, by itself, make the use an act of self-dealing.[363] The IRS ruled that an incidental or tenuous benefit occurs when the general reputation or prestige of a disqualified person is enhanced by public acknowledgment of some specific donation by such person, when a disqualified person receives some other relatively minor benefit of an indirect nature, or when such a person merely participates to a wholly incidental degree in the fruits of some charitable program that is of broad public interest to the community.[364]

Thus, the public recognition a person may receive, arising from the charitable activities of a private foundation to which the person is a substantial contributor, is not in itself the product of an act of self-dealing.[365] For the same reason, a private foundation grant to a tax-exempt hospital for modernization, replacement, and expansion was deemed not to be an act of self-dealing even though two of the trustees of the private foundation served on the board of trustees of the hospital.[366] Similarly, a contribution by a private foundation to a public charity does not constitute an act of self-dealing notwithstanding the fact that the contribution is conditioned on the agreement of the public charity to change its name to that of a substantial contributor to the private foundation.[367] The right of a corporate foundation official (or any corporate employee) to recommend grants to be made by the corporation's foundation in their name provides an intangible benefit that does not result in self-dealing unless the foundation is satisfying an obligation of the employee. Likewise, a program that matches employee gifts with a gift from the corporate foundation

---

363. Reg. § 53.4941(d)-2(f)(2).
364. Rev. Rul. 77-331, 1977-2 C.B. 388.
365. Reg. § 53.4941(d)-2(f)(2). A closely held corporation's donation of its debentures, representing 14 percent of the value of its net assets, to a private foundation, managed by the corporation's employees and shareholders for the promotion of charitable activities in the locality of the corporation and for which it receives public recognition, was not a constructive dividend to the shareholders (Rev. Rul. 75-335, 1975-2 C.B. 107). Cf. Rev. Rul. 68-658, 1968-2 C.B. 119.
366. Rev. Rul. 75-42, 1975-1 C.B. 359. The IRS also ruled that a grant by one private foundation to another private foundation is not an act of self-dealing even though a bank served as the sole trustee of both private foundations (Rev. Rul. 82-136, 1982-2 C.B. 136).
367. Rev. Rul. 73-407, 1973-2 C.B. 383.

is an intangible and incidental benefit to an employee. Similarly, a foundation grant made in honor of a disqualified person's child, relative, or any other person does not result in self-dealing.

A grant by a private foundation to a university to establish an educational program providing instruction in manufacturing engineering is not an act of self-dealing, although a disqualified person corporation intends to hire graduates of the program and encourage its employees to enroll in the program, as long as the corporation does not receive preferential treatment in recruiting graduates or enrolling its employees.[368] In still another of these situations, the IRS ruled that the loan program of a private foundation that provided financing to publicly supported organizations for construction projects in disadvantaged areas did not result in acts of self-dealing merely because some contractors and subcontractors involved in the construction projects, their suppliers, and employees of those involved may have had ordinary banking and business relationships with a bank that was a disqualified person with respect to the private foundation.[369] Moreover, a private foundation was able to assume and operate a charitable program previously conducted by a for-profit company, which was a disqualified person with respect to the foundation, as a public service, without engaging in prohibited self-dealing, because the benefit to the company was incidental.[370] In an illustration of what may be the outer reaches of this exception, the IRS ruled that impermissible self-dealing will not occur when a private foundation establishes, funds, and operates an educational institute that has a name similar to that of a company owned by disqualified persons with respect to the foundation, which will plan the programs of the institute.[371]

A park open to the public created adjacent to a corporation's plant reception area was found to further an exempt purpose. The company retained the right to "continued use of its identifying symbol in its advertising and public relations programs in connection with the establishment of the park." The IRS decided the benefit to be derived from the corporation's gifts, which include maintenance and operation costs, flow principally to the general public through access to and use of the park. Though the words "incidental and tenuous" were not used, the ruling concluded no private benefit (by analogy no self-dealing) inured to the company.[372] A similar result was reached for a replica of an early American village named after its corporate supporter.[373] Addressing the same issue from another vantage point, the IRS decided grants

---

368. Rev. Rul. 80-310, 1980-2 C.B. 319.
369. Rev. Rul. 85-162, 1985-2 C.B. 275.
370. Priv. Ltr. Rul. 9614002.
371. Priv. Ltr. Rul. 199939049.
372. Rev. Rul. 66-358, 1966-2 C.B. 218.
373. Rev. Rul. 77-367, 1977-2 C.B. 193.

§ 5.8 USES OF INCOME OR ASSETS BY DISQUALIFIED PERSONS

paid by a private foundation to match a gift made personally by a director were not self-dealing. The fact that the director was a government official did not change the conclusion.[374]

Other instances of incidental benefits in the private foundation setting include the transfer to and use by a disqualified person (a limited liability company) of an asset of a private foundation, the asset being the foundation's contractual rights pertaining to certain charitable activities.[375] As another example, the programs of a private foundation concerning public healthcare education and publication and distribution of a booklet of statistics and a physicians' reference book were ruled to not involve prohibited self-dealing, in that the benefits provided to a disqualified person company were incidental and tenuous.[376] Likewise, a bank, a trustee of a private foundation, sold its investment management division to another bank; because the amount of foundation assets formerly managed by the first bank's division was insubstantial in relation to the total assets sold and because the assets of the foundation invested in the funds involved are insubstantial in relation to the total assets of the foundation, the IRS ruled that the fee payment by one bank to the other, reflecting the foundation's investment, will involve an incidental and tenuous benefit and thus not impermissible self-dealing.[377] Similarly, the IRS ruled that a private foundation established to promote public awareness and appreciation of a type of art could display certain works of this art in a shopping center owned by disqualified persons with respect to the foundation, without engaging in impermissible self-dealing because the display was in furtherance of exempt purposes, only a small amount of art will be displayed, the displayed art otherwise would be held in storage, and none of the art is identified with any disqualified persons.[378]

The IRS ruled, however, that the guarantee of loans made to disqualified persons under a student loan guarantee program established by a private foundation for the children of its employees constituted an act of self-dealing.[379] The program was operated by a public charity, which received a $10,000 grant from the private foundation and agreed to guarantee $100,000 in loans to the children, including the children of a few of the private foundation's employees who were disqualified persons with respect to it. In so ruling, the IRS based its position on the general rule that the indemnification (of a lender) or guarantee (of repayment) by a private foundation with respect to a loan

---

374. Priv. Ltr. Rul. 200605014.
375. Priv. Ltr. Rul. 199950039.
376. Priv. Ltr. Rul. 200309027, as amended by Priv. Ltr. Rul. 200316042.
377. Priv. Ltr. Rul. 200620029.
378. Priv. Ltr. Rul. 201029039.
379. Rev. Rul. 77-331, 1977-2 C.B. 388.

to a disqualified person is treated as a use, for the benefit of the disqualified person, of the income or assets of the private foundation, as is a private foundation grant or other payment that satisfies the legal obligation of a disqualified person.[380] Moreover, the IRS held that this use of the private foundation's income and assets involved more than an incidental or tenuous benefit for the disqualified persons involved because an act of self-dealing occurred each time a loan involving a disqualified person was made.[381]

A private foundation grant to a private tax-exempt school with the expectation, but with no binding obligation, that the school will use the funds to repay a loan made to a disqualified person in relation to the foundation was found not to result in self-dealing.[382]

A company foundation's disaster and financial relief program provided, according to the IRS, more than an incidental benefit to its sponsoring corporation, and thus resulted in acts of self-dealing.[383] Although there was some public benefit resulting from the foundation's provision of assistance in times of disaster or financial crisis, the IRS was not assured that selection of beneficiaries solely among employees of a particular employer served the best interests of the public. Instead, according to the agency, the foundation served the "private interests of [the corporation] and its subsidiaries who utilize such benefit programs to recruit and retain a more stable and productive workforce." Because the beneficiaries were a designated or limited group—employees of the company—they did not constitute a charitable class and the foundation could not qualify for tax exemption as a charitable entity. For the same reasons, the disbursements made by the foundation were said to be taxable expenditures[384] of benefit to the company officials and owners. Because the benefit to the company was more than incidental and tenuous, the grants distributed by the foundation also resulted in acts of self-dealing. Additionally, the expenditures did not constitute qualifying distributions[385] because they did not serve a charitable purpose. While the implications in the private foundation setting are not clear, the IRS ruled that a corporation with a large number of employees may maintain a payroll deduction plan for the purpose of collecting contributions for a public charity, which is not controlled by the corporation, and which makes grants and loans to the corporation's employees with a demonstrated need.[386]

---

380. Reg. § 53.4941(d)-2(f)(1).
381. An act of self-dealing did not take place when a public charity paid fees to a bank for services as trustee of its pooled income fund (Priv. Ltr. Rul. 8226159).
382. Priv. Ltr. Rul. 200443045.
383. Priv. Ltr. Rul. 199914040, revoking Priv. Ltr. Rul. 9516047.
384. See § 9.8.
385. See § 6.4.
386. Priv. Ltr. Rul. 200307084.

§ 5.8 USES OF INCOME OR ASSETS BY DISQUALIFIED PERSONS

The designation of one-fifth of the office space in a building for use as a personal office for a private foundation's 90-year-old donor was found to be incidental and tenuous use by the donor. An office building was to be constructed on land she planned to contribute to the foundation. Although this transaction technically constituted self-dealing, the IRS generously concluded that, inasmuch as the donor's health was such that it was unlikely she would live long enough to use the space, the potential use of the space did not have a value.[387]

The goodwill enjoyed by a corporation from recognition of its sponsorship of public television programs is considered an incidental benefit.[388] Likewise, a grant by a private foundation for charitable purposes, where a consequence of the grant was a likely increase in the value of adjacent land owned by a disqualified person, was found to not be impermissible self-dealing because it conferred only an incidental and tenuous benefit.[389] Similarly, a grant by a private foundation as part of a project to renovate a public library site, where two disqualified persons owning adjacent property might economically benefit, where a bank trustee might benefit as a lending institution, and where another disqualified person might benefit by being a member of the management committee of a limited liability company that was the major funder of the project, was held to not be impermissible self-dealing, because any resulting benefits would be merely incidental and tenuous.[390]

A foundation was created to continue to produce public service television programs of interest to senior citizens for broadcast on a cable television network owned by its creator and her family.[391] The network had previously funded the programs. The plan was to hire an independent producer with no relationship to the family, at fair market, under a requirement that the content be educational and charitable, to assist the creator in developing the programs. The creator would provide her services for free. The foundation would not receive any advertising or other commercial revenue from the broadcasts and the network was prohibited, with exceptions for bonus advertisers, from marketing advertising spots for the program. The ruling request asserted that broadcast over the cable network was absolutely essential to most effectively communicate the information provided in the programs to its target audience.

The IRS found that self-dealing did not occur for two reasons: The foundation creator was donating her services, and the production company was not

---

387. Priv. Ltr. Rul. 9604006.
388. Priv. Ltr. Rul. 8644003.
389. Priv. Ltr. Rul. 9819045. A significant element in this ruling, however, was the fact that the foundation's grant was not a substantial part of the overall funding of the project.
390. Priv. Ltr. Rul. 200129041.
391. Priv. Ltr. Rul. 200425051.

a disqualified person. Presumably (though not stated) the new foundation did not assume any binding obligations of the creator and her family. Further, the television programs were made available to the public and would be made available to other cable networks. Due to the educational nature of the programs, the costs were deemed direct charitable expenses and, therefore, qualifying distributions[392] that were not taxable expenditures.[393] Although it may be suggested that self-dealing occurred when the network and family members were relieved of paying for the program out of their own pockets, the IRS did not address the question. The agency also did not consider whether any more than incidental benefits were provided to the family and its network.

A company-related private foundation was establishing a program to provide on-the-job training and education for the benefit of at-risk and underserved youth living in its community. The foundation modeled its program on a similar program operated by the company; it utilized company resources in its program. The company hosted program participants without charge at its facilities, contributing employee time and other resources. It donated supervision, training, and mentoring; it provided office supplies and training materials. The company placed participants in a "sponsorship department" at its facilities. The foundation will not make any distributions to the company, which agreed to not hire or make an offer to hire any foundation program participants for a period of years following completion of the program. The IRS ruled that the conduct by this foundation of this program did not involve any acts of self-dealing, in part because the benefits to the company were incidental and tenuous.[394]

The IRS has not issued any private or published rulings on the personal use of mileage accumulated on a foundation credit card. In 2002, the IRS admitted there were numerous technical and administrative issues relating to the

---

392. See § 6.4.
393. See § 9.8.
394. Priv. Ltr. Rul. 201718002. This ruling appears correct as to the lack of self-dealing, although previous IRS rulings have found private benefit (see § 5.2) based on fewer substantive benefits than those provided in this case. But there is a huge trap here, potentially imperiling the tax-exempt status of private foundations and other charitable entities. It is the ruling position of the IRS that the conduct of a program by a nonprofit organization that is similar to a program conducted by a related for-profit company is a violation of the operational test and/or substantive evidence of commerciality and thus will preclude or lead to revocation of exemption. For example, a nonprofit entity was denied recognition of exemption because it was operating the "same program" and providing the same "educational services as a related for-profit company; the parties' operations were dismissed by the IRS as being "virtually indistinguishable" (Priv. Ltr. Rul. 201714031). Indeed, whether the parties are related may be irrelevant. Thus, the IRS held that an exempt organization "should not duplicate services or facilities provided by commercial entities" (Priv. Ltr. Rul. 201801014).

timing and valuation of such usage. Due to the unresolved issues, the IRS has not "pursued a tax enforcement program with respect to promotional benefits such as frequent flyer miles."[395] The announcement said the IRS would not assert that any taxpayer has understated their federal tax liability by reason of the receipt or personal use of frequent flyer miles or other in-kind promotional benefit attributable to the taxpayer's business or official travel. Last, any future guidance on the taxability of these benefits will be applied prospectively.

From time to time, the IRS issues private letter rulings concerning benefits that are or are not forms of incidental or tenuous benefit.[396] Occasionally the facts are such that an involvement of a private foundation in a transaction does not confer any benefit on a disqualified person with respect to the foundation.[397]

(f) Memberships

A private foundation engages in an act of self-dealing when it pays membership dues or fees on behalf of a disqualified person and thereby relieves them of that obligation. The benefit to the person is then direct and economic in nature, not tenuous or incidental. In one instance, a foundation paid its trustee's church dues, thereby enabling them to maintain their membership in and otherwise participate in the religious activities of the congregation. The dues payment was ruled to constitute self-dealing, with the IRS concluding the foundation's payment of the dues "result[ed] in a direct economic benefit to the disqualified person because that person would have been expected to pay the membership dues had they not been paid by the foundation."[398]

It is common for grant recipient organizations to identify their contributors as members eligible for special privileges. When a private foundation makes this type of grant, the individual trustees or other foundation representatives are sometimes involuntarily provided these member benefits. The question is whether the individual can accept these benefits as a representative of the foundation. The IRS, in the church ruling cited above, observed that the benefits provided by reason of the church membership might be described as incidental or tenuous. Nonetheless, self-dealing occurs where a personal obligation is satisfied on behalf of the disqualified person. Some foundations

---

395. Ann. 2002-18, 2002-1 C.B. 621.
396. E.g., Priv. Ltr. Rul. 9619027.
397. E.g., Priv. Ltr. Rul. 200148071.
398. Rev. Rul. 77-160, 1977-1 C.B. 351, 352, Cf. Rev. Rul. 70-47, 1970-1 C.B. 49; Rev. Rul. 68-432, 1968-2 C.B. 104.

have adopted a policy of disclaiming membership privileges; others specifically require that their disqualified persons pay their own memberships to avoid the issue.

(g) Benefit Tickets

Self-dealing was found when a joint purchase of benefit tickets was made by sharing the ticket cost. The private foundation paid for the portion of the ticket that was deductible as a charitable contribution; the disqualified person paid that part of the ticket price allocable to the fair market value of the dinner, entertainment, and other benefits provided to contributors in connection with the fundraising event.[399]

The IRS held that self-dealing occurred because the benefits were more than tenuous or incidental. To be able to attend the benefit, foundation representatives would have been required to individually pay the full ticket price. Thus, they reaped direct economic benefit to the extent that the foundation paid that portion of the ticket, and self-dealing occurred. Some foundations, however, argue that it is appropriate for their managers to attend fundraising events as representatives of the foundation to evidence their support and that private benefit does not result.

There is no easy answer to this question of foundation purchases of tickets, where foundation representatives attend the event. As a practical matter, if the representatives truly want to attend the event (such as because of the nature of the entertainment, the popularity of a speaker, or to invite their friends), the payment and attendance is probably self-dealing. Conversely, if the representatives do not want to attend the event and are doing so only out of obligation, payment by the foundation for the tickets is probably not self-dealing.

(h) Other Acts

The indemnification of a lender or guarantee of repayment by a private foundation with respect to a loan to a disqualified person is treated as a use for the benefit of a disqualified person of the income or assets of the foundation.[400]

The IRS ruled that a private foundation committed an act of self-dealing when it placed paintings owned by it in the residence of a substantial contributor.[401] Likewise, self-dealing was found when a private foundation permitted the placement of its sculpture on the private property of a disqualified

---

399. Priv. Ltr. Rul. 9021066.
400. Reg. § 53.4941(d)-2(f)(1).
401. Rev. Rul. 74-600, 1974-2 C.B. 385.

person.[402] A court held, however, that the making of a charitable contribution to a private foundation by one of its trustees, on the condition that any nondeductible portion of the gift would be returned to them, was not an act of self-dealing, nor was its return.[403]

It is relatively common for the IRS to allow reformation of a charitable remainder trust to enable the trust to be converted to a type envisioned by the donor or donors at the outset but that was incorrectly prepared (due to what the IRS generously describes as a scrivener's error).[404] Occasionally, the IRS rules that this type of trust revision does not entail self-dealing.[405]

The IRS also issues rulings concerning divisions of charitable remainder trusts.[406] Occasionally, the IRS rules that this type of trust division does not entail self-dealing.[407]

In one instance, a judicial reformation of a trust reduced the amount of trust assets to be received by a private foundation and increased the amount of assets to be received by disqualified persons (seemingly self-dealing). The IRS ruled, however, that, inasmuch as all interested parties consented to the reformation, as did the state's attorney general, self-dealing did not occur.[408]

§ 5.9 SHARING SPACE, PEOPLE, AND EXPENSES

As a practical matter, many private foundations are operated alongside their creators, whether these are corporations or family groups. At least until a foundation achieves a certain volume of assets with consequential grant activity (and perhaps thereafter), rental of a separate office and engagement of staff is beyond the foundation's reasonable economic capability, particularly when these expenditures take funds away from grant-making activity.

---

402. Gen. Couns. Mem. 39741. Indeed, this private benefit was found to be sufficiently egregious to warrant revocation of the foundation's tax-exempt status.
403. Underwood v. United States, 461 F. Supp. 1382 (N.D. Tex. 1978). Presumably, the returned portion of the original gift becomes gross income to the donor recipient in the year of the restoration, pursuant to the "tax benefit rule." E.g., Rosen v. Commissioner, 71 T.C. 226 (1978) aff'd, 80-1 U.S.T.C. ¶ 9138 (1st Cir. 1980).
404. See *Charitable Giving* § 10.4(i).
405. E.g., Priv. Ltr. Rul. 200850046. See § 3.7.
406. See *Charitable Giving* § 10.6.
407. E.g., Priv. Ltr. Ruls. 200831029-200831031.
408. Priv. Ltr. Rul. 201432025. This is a most reasonable approach, the only snag being that the IRS lacks the authority to excuse acts of self-dealing just because all parties involved agree to the transaction or arrangement.

(a) Determining What the Private Foundation Can Pay

The law is not particularly clear as to when a private foundation can pay for its portion of the expenses in a sharing situation involving disqualified persons. The law prohibits the "furnishing of goods, services, or facilities" between (to or from) a foundation and a disqualified person.[409] The types of property intended to be covered by this rule include office space, automobiles, auditoriums, secretarial help, meals, libraries, publications, laboratories, and parking lots.[410]

When Congress imposed these strict rules in 1969, it provided a transitional period until 1980, during which existing contractual sharing arrangements could be phased out.[411] Subsequently, the IRS in private letter rulings relaxed what initially looked like an absolute prohibition on any arrangements in which a foundation and its creators and funders share the expenses of space, staff, and the like.

(b) Office Space and Personnel

A number of private foundations sought and received approval for shared office space and personnel. In one IRS ruling, it was held that self-dealing did not occur when a private foundation rented contiguous space with a common reception area (which constituted sharing), but with separate offices, from its disqualified person. Separate leases were entered into, and the disqualified persons did not receive any benefit in the form of reduced rent because of the foundation's rental of the related space.[412] In another ruling, a foundation and a disqualified person together bought a duplicating machine and hired a shared employee. Time records were kept to determine each entity's share of the cost of the machine and the allocable time of the employee. Because "nothing was paid directly or indirectly to" the disqualified person and there was "independent use" by the foundation that was measurable and specifically paid for to outside parties, self-dealing was held to have not resulted from what certainly appears to have been a "sharing arrangement," supposedly phased out and consequentially prohibited by the self-dealing rules.[413]

Similarly, the IRS condoned a "time-sharing arrangement" of a disqualified person's management company's employees. The basis for the favorable ruling was the fact that the law permits a foundation to pay reasonable

---

409. IRC § 4941(d)(1)(C).
410. Reg. § 53.4941(d)-2(d)(1).
411. Reg. § 53.4941(d)-4(d).
412. Priv. Ltr. Rul. 8331082.
413. Tech. Adv. Mem. 7734022; Priv. Ltr. Rul. 8824010.

§ 5.9 SHARING SPACE, PEOPLE, AND EXPENSES

compensation to a disqualified person for the performance of personal services necessary to carry out its exempt purposes. Interestingly, and perhaps more important, the IRS found that the benefit to the management company in being relieved from paying a percentage of the salaries of its employees was incidental and tenuous.[414]

The IRS approved cost and property sharing arrangements between members of a group including (1) a public charity that will, for no rent, lease its half-interest in a historical site and associated personal property to a foundation, (2) a foundation whose creators also own the other half-interest, (3) a private operating foundation created by the same disqualified persons to preserve and operate this site, and (4) a business corporation owned more than 35 percent by disqualified persons (making it a disqualified person in relation to both foundations) that would furnish security services and maintenance and repair the site and its utilities. The private foundation would be billed and pay its share of costs directly to unrelated parties if possible. The agency wrote that "[o]therwise, each owner will pay an allocable share of utility costs, using reasonable methods of allocation."[415] The IRS also concluded that a foundation can pay a disqualified person corporation for personal security services it renders if they are reasonable and necessary to its operation of the site. Easements for use of a disqualified person's property granted to a foundation also did not result in self-dealing, because the foundation's exempt purpose of operating the site was served and rent was not charged.

Another office space arrangement between a foundation and its creators was approved, with slightly different language to permit the sharing.[416] "As long as any payments for the use are made directly to the vendor on a proportional basis," "the IRS ruled, self-dealing does not take place. Separate employment contracts were to be entered into with shared employees. Checks in payment of the respective share of employee group insurance were deposited into a joint bank account, from which premiums were paid to the insurer. The telephone system was jointly purchased. Separate maintenance agreements were entered into and separately paid for the foundation's and the disqualified person's respective shares of the equipment. Usage records would be maintained to evidence the portions. Payment of a private foundation's share of costs directly to an independent vendor was not required in a situation where the expenses were paid directly by a condominium association.

A private foundation's payment of the direct flight costs associated with its use of a disqualified person's airplane was found to not be self-dealing.[417]

---

414. Priv. Ltr. Rul. 9226067.
415. Priv. Ltr. Rul. 9307026.
416. Priv. Ltr. Rul. 9312022.
417. Priv. Ltr. Rul. 9732031.

SELF-DEALING

The foundation did not pay any portion of the disqualified person's maintenance or acquisition costs or relieve the disqualified person of a financial obligation. The airplane use was considered to "further the [private foundation's] exempt purposes by facilitating meetings among various individuals active in its charitable, scientific, and educational programs."[418]

Different and safer terminology was used to secure IRS approval for payment to a disqualified person's family management corporation for rendering accounting, tax, and asset management services.[419] The corporation operated on a cost-recovery basis to serve the business needs of "family assets held in trusts, foundations, and partnerships." While the arrangement is essentially a sharing one, the IRS ruled payment of a fee based on costs was reasonable compensation for services rendered and not an act of self-dealing.[420]

The addition of a supporting organization to the mix of private foundation and disqualified person expense-sharing arrangements was approved by the IRS.[421] The ruling concluded that the participation of two private foundations, along with two disqualified persons with respect thereto, in an arrangement providing for joint utilization of office space among the parties was not an act of self-dealing. The lessor was one of the supporting organizations, which was not a disqualified person to either foundation; moreover, expenses were allocated to the foundations and disqualified persons on fair market terms, based on detailed records of their actual usage.

The IRS allowed disqualified persons and a private foundation to each own office units in a condominium office building and to share common costs on an allocable basis, but only because the disqualified persons used their offices solely for charitable purposes.[422]

A private foundation conducted an Internet-based education and training program providing educational services to teachers and students nationwide. A for-profit company, which is a disqualified person with respect to this foundation, had a charitable program using innovative technologies, strategies, and employee time and talent, to improve the education of youth. The foundation is among the educational entities served by the company's employees. Guidelines established by the company ban discussion of the company's business activities when engaging in the programs; both entities strive to keep the identities of their respective programs separate and distinct. The IRS ruled that the conduct of the two programs will not constitute self-dealing.[423]

---

418. Thus, these outlays also did not constitute taxable expenditures (see § 9.8).
419. Priv. Ltr. Rul. 9019064.
420. Due to the exception in IRC § 4941(d)(2)(E).
421. Priv. Ltr. Rul. 200421010.
422. Priv. Ltr. Rul. 200014040.
423. Priv. Ltr. Rul. 200536027.

(c) Group Insurance

Group insurance policies present similar sharing situations. Corporate and other conglomerate groups funding private foundations have been allowed to include their private foundation employees in a common health insurance policy. The foundation pays directly for the premiums allocable to its employees, or reimburses the company. As discussed above, direct payment is strongly preferred, but if it is impossible, the IRS may allow reimbursement. The rationale is found in the *Special Rules*, which provide that the lending of money by a disqualified person to a private foundation will not be an act of self-dealing if the loan is without interest or other charge and if the proceeds of the loan are used exclusively for the foundation's tax-exempt purposes.[424]

(d) Public Facilities

A private foundation that operates a museum, maintains a wildlife preserve, produces an educational journal, or engages in comparable programs is faced with the decree that it not furnish goods, services, or facilities to its insiders. Taken literally, the rule prevents disqualified persons from visiting the sites, purchasing the journal, and similar interrelationships. A foundation's furnishing of goods, services, or facilities normally open to the public, to a disqualified person, however, falls within another of the useful exceptions to the general rules. This type of activity is not self-dealing under the following circumstances: (1) the property involved is functionally related to the exercise or performance by the foundation of its charitable, educational, or other purpose or function forming the basis for its exemption; (2) the number of persons (other than the disqualified persons) who use the facility is substantial enough to indicate that the general public is genuinely the primary user; and (3) the terms for disqualified person usage are not more favorable than the terms under which the general public acquires or uses the property.[425]

§ 5.10 PAYMENTS TO GOVERNMENT OFFICIALS

The statutory law generally prohibits a payment by a private foundation to a government official.[426] There are, nonetheless, a number of exceptions.

---

424. IRC § 4941(d)(2)(B).
425. Reg. § 53.4941(d)-3(b)(2). Also see § 5.4(e) for examples of particular circumstances in which a private foundation is permitted to use facilities of a disqualified person and vice versa.
426. IRC § 4941(d)(1)(F). The definition of the term *government official* for these purposes is the subject of § 4.8.

SELF-DEALING

An agreement by a private foundation to make any payment of money or other property to a government official generally constitutes self-dealing, unless the agreement is to employ a government official for a period after termination of their government service and they are terminating their service within a 90-day period.[427] An individual who otherwise meets the definition of government official is treated as a government official while on leave of absence from the government without pay.[428]

Certain de minimis payments to government officials are permitted, as follows:[429]

- A prize or award that is not includible in gross income,[430] if the government official receiving the prize is selected from the general public. (The prize must be paid over to a charitable institution.)
- A scholarship or fellowship grant that is excludable from gross income[431] and that is to be utilized for study at a qualified educational organization[432] (but only for tuition, fees, and books).[433]
- Certain types of pension plans and annuity payments.[434]
- Any contribution or gift (other than a contribution or gift of money) to, or services or facilities made available to, a government official, if the aggregate value of such gifts, contributions, services, and facilities provided total no more than $25 in any calendar year.
- Government employee training program payments.
- Reimbursement of the actual cost of travel, including meals and lodging, solely within the United States for attendance at a charitable function, not to exceed 125 percent of the prevailing per diem rate.

---

427. *Id.*
428. Reg. § 53.4941(d)-2(g).
429. IRC § 4941(d)(2)(G); Reg. § 53.4941(d)-3(e).
430. The rules in this regard are the subject of IRC § 74(b).
431. The rules in this regard are the subject of IRC § 117(a).
432. That is, an entity described in IRC § 170(b)(1)(A)(ii). Reg. § 53.4941(d)-3(e) refers to "an educational institution described in section 151(e)(4)"; however, a subsequent amendment to IRC §§ 4941(d)(2)(G)(ii) and 4945(g)(1) replaced "educational institution described in section 151(e)(4)" with "educational organization described in section 170(b)(1)(A)(ii)," effective for tax years beginning after December 31, 1976 (Pub. L. 94-455, § 1901(b)(8)(H), 90 Stat. 1520, 1795 (1976)).
433. IRC § 4941(d)(2)(G); Reg. § 53.4941(d)-3(e). For this purpose, the definition of scholarships and fellowships is that in the federal tax law prior to the amendment of the income tax exclusion of IRC § 117 in 1986, by reason of § 1001(d)(1)(A) of the Technical and Miscellaneous Revenue Act of 1988.
434. E.g., Priv. Ltr. Rul. 9510073.

With regard to the last item, the exception operates only with respect to expenses for travel from one point in the United States to another point in the United States.[435] Consequently, reimbursement by a private foundation for travel expenses incurred by a member of Congress it selects to participate in a conference it cosponsors in a foreign country constitutes an act of self-dealing.[436] Taking the position that the term *United States* is used only in a geographical sense in this context, the IRS ruled that the Commonwealth of Puerto Rico is not a "point in the United States."[437]

The payment or reimbursement, by a private foundation to a government official, of traveling expenses for travel solely from one point to another in the United States is not self-dealing as long as the payment or reimbursement does not exceed the actual cost of the transportation involved plus an amount for all other traveling expenses not in excess of 125 percent of the maximum amount payable for like travel by employees of the United States government.[438] The amendment of this law superseded the per diem rates previously used by the IRS.[439]

§ 5.11 INDIRECT SELF-DEALING

As noted, there are two categories of self-dealing transactions involving private foundations: direct and indirect.[440] The Internal Revenue Code and the tax regulations do not contain a unitary definition of the term *indirect self-dealing*. This is the case inasmuch as the IRS believed (and still does) that it was not "feasible to draft a comprehensive definition [of indirect self-dealing]

---

435. Reg. § 53.4941(d)-3(e)(7).
436. Rev. Rul. 74-601, 1974-2 C.B. 385.
437. Rev. Rul. 76-159, 1976-1 C.B. 356.
438. IRC § 4941(d)(2)(G)(vii). This maximum amount is the subject of 5 U.S.C. § 5702(a).
439. Rev. Rul. 77-251, 1977-2 C.B. 389. At the time of this ruling, the per diem rate for like travel was $35. The IRS ruled in a situation involving a private foundation that wanted to provide a $50 per diem allowance (plus reimbursement of actual transportation costs) for a government official traveling from Washington, D.C., to New York City, to participate in a three-day seminar. The law (5 U.S.C. § 5702(c)) provides for an allowance of up to $50 for travel to "high-rate geographical areas," which includes New York City. Reasoning that because Congress referred only to the general reimbursement rules and not to this particular provision when it enacted the self-dealing rules, the IRS held that the private foundation could pay a per diem allowance of only $43.75 (125 percent of $35) and not the desired $50. Thus, without engaging in self-dealing, a private foundation may reimburse a government official for their actual costs of travel plus 125 percent of the "Federal Travel Rate Prescribed Maximum per Diem Rates for CONUS" ("coterminous United States"). This change in this aspect of the self-dealing rules is discussed in Priv. Ltr. Rul. 8911063.
440. See § 5.3.

because of the great variety of possible situations which could be called 'indirect self-dealing.'"[441]

Nonetheless, two types of acts of indirect self-dealing are recognized. One of these types of acts of indirect self-dealing is a transaction between a disqualified person with respect to a private foundation and an entity controlled by the foundation. Another type of indirect self-dealing act is a sale or exchange of property to or with a disqualified person with respect to a private foundation while the property is held by an estate or trust in which the foundation has an interest or vested expectancy. The U.S. Tax Court suggested that "[t]here may exist other ways to engage in self-dealing through organizations that are related to the private foundation."[442]

From time to time, the IRS issues private letter rulings as to whether a transaction or arrangement constitutes an indirect act of self-dealing.[443]

(a) Transactions with Controlled Entities

Here is an illustration of an act of indirect self-dealing involving a transaction between a disqualified person with respect to a private foundation and an entity controlled by the foundation. Private foundation P owns the controlling interest of the voting stock of corporation X; as a result of this interest, P elects a majority of the board of directors of X. Two of the foundation managers, A and B, who are also directors of X, form corporation Y for the purpose of building and managing a country club. A and B receive 40 percent of Y's stock, making Y a disqualified person with respect to P.[444] In order to finance construction and operation of the country club, Y receives

---

441. Gen. Couns. Mem. 39445, which references a memorandum dated December 5, 1972, from then-Commissioner of Internal Revenue Johnnie M. Walters to the Assistant Secretary for Tax Policy (T.D. 7270, LR-1611). The IRS observed that "[t]ransactions between a disqualified person and an organization not controlled by the private foundation are not indirect acts of self-dealing *in most cases*" (emphasis added) and that the Code and tax regulations "do not systematically define all manner of 'indirect' self-dealing; instead, the facts and circumstances must be considered in each case" (Tech. Adv. Mem. 200727019). On another occasion, the IRS wrote that a trust's dealings with respect to a private foundation's "interest or expectancy *could* [not would] result in indirect self-dealing if the 'estate administration' exception to indirect self-dealing . . . is not met" (emphasis added), perhaps suggesting there may be some other exception to indirect self-dealing (Priv. Ltr. Rul. 201849009). In any event, it is the position of the IRS that the concept of indirect self-dealing is to be broadly construed (e.g., Priv. Ltr. Rul. 8942054).
442. Moody v. Commissioner, 69 T.C.M. 2517, 2529 (1995). The court in Moody applied the control test in the regulations (discussed *infra*) and concluded that the private foundation involved did not control a company under the facts of the case.
443. E.g., Priv. Ltr. Rul. 200620030.
444. See § 4.5.

§ 5.11 INDIRECT SELF-DEALING

a loan from X. The making of the loan by X to Y constitutes an indirect act of self-dealing.[445]

The first self-dealing case concerning the private foundation rules to be decided by a court involved acts of indirect self-dealing.[446] An individual wholly owned corporation A; the corporation transferred two encumbered properties to corporation B, which was a wholly owned subsidiary of private foundation P, of which this individual was a trustee. The individual was a foundation manager of P and thus a disqualified person with respect to P.[447] Corporation A was also a disqualified person because the individual owned more than 35 percent of the total combined voting power in the corporation.[448] The court held that sale of one of these properties by corporation A to corporation B constituted an act of indirect self-dealing.[449] (Transfer of the other property was deemed not an act of self-dealing because, as to that property, A was acting merely as a nominee for B.) Another act of self-dealing was found by reason of the fact that, even though the properties conveyed were encumbered, B paid the full purchase price for them, with the understanding that either the individual or A would satisfy the outstanding mortgage on the properties; the court held that the failure by A to immediately satisfy the liabilities on receipt of the funds from B gave rise to an implied loan to A from foundation P in the amount of the outstanding mortgage liabilities.[450]

(b) Concept of *Control*

For purposes of the rules concerning indirect self-dealing, an organization is *controlled* by a private foundation if the foundation or one or more of its foundation managers may, by aggregating their votes or positions of authority, require the organization to engage in a transaction which, if engaged in with the private foundation, would constitute self-dealing.[451] Additionally, an organization is considered controlled by a private foundation in the case of what would be a self-dealing transaction between the organization and a disqualified person if the person, together with one or more persons who are disqualified persons by reason of the person's relationship with the disqualified person, may, by aggregating their votes or positions of authority with that of the foundation, require the foundation to engage in

---

445. Reg. § 53.4941(d)-1(b)(8), Example (1). See § 5.5.
446. Adams v. Commissioner, 70 T.C. 373 (1978), *aff'd* (unpublished opinion), 688 F.2d 813 (2d Cir. 1982).
447. See § 4.2.
448. See § 4.5.
449. See § 5.4(a).
450. See § 5.5.
451. Reg. § 53.4941(d)-1(b)(5).

such a transaction.[452] An organization is considered controlled by a private foundation, or by a foundation and disqualified persons, if the persons are in fact able to control the organization (even if their aggregate voting power is less than 50 percent of the total voting power of the organization's governing body) or if one or more of the persons has the right to exercise veto power over the actions of the organization that are relevant to any potential acts of self-dealing.[453]

In a case in which a private foundation owned 35 percent of the voting stock of a corporation and a foundation manager owned the remaining 65 percent of the stock but did not hold a position of authority in the corporation by virtue of being a foundation manager, the IRS ruled that the foundation did not control the corporation for self-dealing purposes because it did not have the right to exercise veto control over the actions of the corporation and had no authority over the corporation's actions (other than that represented by its stock ownership).[454] The phrase *combined voting power* includes the voting power represented by holdings of voting stock, actual or constructive, but does not include voting rights held only as a director or trustee.[455]

In a court case, an individual, a trustee of a private foundation and a director of a for-profit corporation, incurred a large bill at a hotel owned by the corporation, which was 50 percent owned by the foundation (permissible at the time)[456] and 50 percent by a family trust. The foundation was billed for these expenses; the foundation refused to reimburse the individual for the expenses because there was no business purpose for them. Following the filing of bankruptcy by this individual, the hotel unsuccessfully sought, as part of the bankruptcy proceedings, to collect its bill from the foundation. The court concluded that the foundation or its managers acting in that capacity did not control the corporation, reasoning that (1) 50 percent ownership is

---

452. *Id.*
453. *Id.* In one instance, a trust (considered a private foundation) and its trustee (acting only in that capacity) were ruled to not have sufficient votes or positions of authority to cause a limited liability company to engage in a transaction. A power associated with nonvoting interests in the LLC as a necessary party to vote on the liquidation of the LLC was not considered equivalent to a veto power because the power could not be exercised over an action relevant to any potential act of self-dealing; therefore, the trust was ruled to not control the LLC within the meaning of the self-dealing rules (Priv. Ltr. Rul. 201907004).
454. Rev. Rul. 76-158, 1976-1 C.B. 354. In a somewhat similar situation, the IRS did not consider the holder of a power to vote on a company's liquidation, which was associated with a nonvoting interest in the company, to be the equivalent of a veto power "in that the other attributes of that interest lack any other powers with respect to operation and management" (Priv. Ltr. Rul. 201407021).
455. Reg. § 53.4946-1(a)(5).
456. See § 7.2(a).

§ 5.11 INDIRECT SELF-DEALING

ordinarily insufficient to constitute control; (2) this individual, together with others who were disqualified persons by virtue of their relationship to him (there were none), could not require the corporation to engage in self-dealing only by aggregating their influence with that of the foundation; (3) this individual lacked actual control, or veto power, over the activities of the corporation; and (4) the corporation exercised considerable independence from the individual and the foundation in seeking payment from them.[457]

The controlled organization may be any type of tax-exempt organization, such as a school, hospital, private foundation, social welfare organization, business league, or (as illustrated above) a social club. It may also be a for-profit organization.[458]

(c) Transactions and the Control Element

The IRS ruled that loans to an entity, owned 34 percent by a private foundation and 50 percent by a split-interest trust,[459] from a publicly traded company, which was a disqualified person with respect to the foundation, were not acts of indirect self-dealing because the foundation held a minority interest in the company, there were no persons who were disqualified persons by reason of an ownership relationship to the company, the trust controlled the entity without the assistance of the foundation, and the foundation did not have any veto power in connection with the company.[460]

The IRS considered the facts surrounding two proposed stock redemptions, where a private foundation would be the seller, and concluded that the foundation and/or its founder did not control the company by virtue of stock ownership or any influence over some of the company's directors, and thus that the redemptions would not be indirect self-dealing transactions.[461]

An individual who was a disqualified person with respect to a private foundation made an interest-free loan to a tax-exempt school to enable the school to complete construction, purchase furniture and other items, and hire staff; this individual also was president of the school. The private foundation planned to make a grant to the school with the understanding that the school would use the funds to repay the loan. The IRS ruled that indirect self-dealing would not occur, because the school was not controlled by the private foundation or the disqualified person. The IRS also ruled that even if the school was controlled by

---

457. Moody v. Commissioner, 69 T.C.M. 2517 (1995).
458. Reg. § 53.4941(d)-1(b)(5). A private foundation is not considered to have control over an organization merely because it exercises expenditure responsibility with respect to contributions to such organization (*id.*; see § 9.7).
459. See § 3.7.
460. Tech. Adv. Mem. 200727019.
461. Priv. Ltr. Rul. 200750020.

SELF-DEALING

the foundation, there would not be indirect self-dealing in that the grant funds were not "earmarked" for the use or benefit of a disqualified person, inasmuch as the school had "ultimate control" of the grant funds and would "not be bound to use any of the contributed [granted] funds for repayment of the loan."[462]

In a similar circumstance, a grant by a private foundation to a public charity to construct and operate a performing arts center was ruled to not entail indirect self-dealing, notwithstanding the fact that the underlying land was to be purchased from a disqualified person with respect to the foundation, in the absence of any earmarking of grant funds for the land purchase. The grant was made to an intermediate entity, namely, a supporting organization[463] that was not controlled by the foundation or its disqualified persons, nor was the supported organization.[464]

The IRS, however, deviated from this interpretation of the law, ruling that a grant by a private foundation to a public charity was an indirect act of self-dealing because, relying on a statement by the foundation (that had no binding legal efficacy), the public charity would transfer the grant property to a for-profit company owned by a disqualified person with respect to the foundation, and because this disqualified person also controlled the grantee public charity.[465] In so ruling, the IRS overlooked the facts that it had earlier found the grant to be a qualifying distribution[466] and that the grant was unrestricted so that the public charity was free to transfer the property as it wished. The IRS, because of the control of the grantee by the disqualified person, concluded that the grantee was merely an "intermediary," with the grant earmarked for the ultimate recipient, namely, the company.[467] This ruling appears to be incorrect, with the control factor trumped by the fact that the grant was unrestricted. If the property involved had value and the public charity transferred it to the for-profit company without adequate compensation, that would be an excess benefit transaction[468] or a private inurement issue;[469] the self-dealing rules, however, would not be implicated.

(d) Exceptions

The term *indirect self-dealing* does not include a transaction between a disqualified person and an organization controlled by a private foundation if

---

462. Priv. Ltr. Rul. 200443045.
463. See § 15.6.
464. Priv. Ltr. Rul. 201642001.
465. Priv. Ltr. Rul. 201719004.
466. See § 6.4.
467. Were that the case, the grant should not have been regarded as a qualifying distribution.
468. IRC § 4958. See *Tax-Exempt Organizations*, Chapter 21.
469. See § 5.1.

§ 5.11 INDIRECT SELF-DEALING

(1) the transaction results from a business relationship that was established before the transaction constituted an act of self-dealing under the federal tax rules, (2) the transaction was at least as favorable to the foundation-controlled organization as an arm's-length transaction with an unrelated person, and (3) either (a) the foundation-controlled organization could have engaged in the transaction with someone other than a disqualified person only at a severe economic hardship to the organization, or (b) because of the unique nature of the product or services provided by the foundation-controlled organization, the disqualified person could not have engaged in the transaction with anyone else or could have done so only by incurring severe economic hardship.[470] This type of transaction was illustrated by the IRS's approval of transactions between a partnership controlled by a private foundation and a company owned by a close companion of a television icon; the foundation wanted the companion, who was compensated by the company, to serve on its governing board and be one of its officers; the IRS ruled that all of the elements of this grandfathering exception were satisfied.[471]

The term *indirect self-dealing* also does not include a transaction engaged in by an intermediary organization with a governmental official, where the organization is a recipient of a grant from a private foundation if (1) the foundation does not control the organization, (2) the foundation does not earmark use of the grant for any named governmental official, and (3) there does not exist an agreement, oral or written, by which the foundation may cause the selection of the governmental official by the intermediary organization. A grant by a private foundation will not constitute an indirect act of self-dealing even though the foundation has reason to believe that certain governmental officials would derive benefits from the grant, as long as the intermediary organization exercises control, in fact, over the selection process and actually makes the selection completely independently of the private foundation.[472]

A transaction between a private foundation and an organization that is not controlled by the foundation, where those who are disqualified persons with respect to the foundation[473] own less than 35 percent of the voting power of or beneficial interest in the organization, is not an act of indirect self-dealing between the foundation and a person considered to be a disqualified person solely because of the ownership interests of those persons in the organization.[474]

---

470. Reg. § 53.4941(d)-1(b)(1).
471. Priv. Ltr. Rul. 201703003.
472. Reg. § 53.4941(d)-1(b)(2).
473. That is, are disqualified persons by reason of IRC § 4946(a)(1)(A)-(D). See §§ 4.1–4.4.
474. Reg. § 53.4941(d)-1(b)(4).

Indirect self-dealing does not include any transaction between a disqualified person and an organization controlled by a private foundation or between two disqualified persons, where the foundation's assets may be affected by the transaction, if (1) the transaction arises in the normal and customary course of a retail business engaged in with the public; (2) in the case of a transaction between a disqualified person and an organization controlled by a foundation, the transaction is at least as favorable to the organization controlled by the foundation as an arm's-length transaction with an unrelated person; and (3) the total of the amounts involved in the transactions with respect to any one disqualified person in any tax year does not exceed $5,000.[475]

Indirect self-dealing does not include a transaction involving one or more disqualified persons to which a private foundation is not a party, in any case in which the foundation, by reason of certain rules,[476] could itself engage in the transaction. Thus, for example, even if a foundation has control of a corporation, the corporation may pay to a disqualified person (except for a government official)[477] reasonable compensation for personal services.[478]

As will be discussed, another exception in this context is the estate administration exception.[479]

(e) Fraudulent Investment Schemes

Private foundations' investments in Ponzi and other fraudulent investment schemes[480] raise several issues in the federal tax law context.[481] A report by the New York State Bar Association, submitted to the federal government,[482] explored these issues. This report concluded that there are no self-dealing issues "that are unique to Ponzi schemes."

The report posited a situation in which a private foundation and a disqualified person with respect to the foundation invested in a Ponzi scheme; the disqualified person thereafter withdrew from the scheme. In considering whether an indirect act of self-dealing occurred, the report concluded that if the disqualified person was a qualified investor,[483] "no act of self-dealing should arise in this situation."[484]

---

475. Reg. § 53.4941(d)-1(b)(6).
476. IRC § 4941(d)(2).
477. See § 4.8.
478. Reg. § 53.4941(d)-1(b)(7).
479. See § 5.12.
480. See § 8.4.
481. See §§ 6.3(e), 8.4, 9.8, 10.4(b)(iv).
482. See § 8.4(b).
483. Rev. Proc. 2009-20, 2009-1 C.B. 749. See § 8.4(a).
484. The report cited, as authority for this conclusion, Reg. § 53.4941(d)-1(b)(4).

§ 5.12 ESTATE ADMINISTRATION EXCEPTION

Property bequeathed or devised to a private foundation is likely to be held in an estate or trust for a period of time before the foundation takes direct title to it. While the property is in the estate or trust, the foundation has an *expectancy* or other *interest* in the property. Property of this nature may not be suitable to be held by the foundation, such as property with a lack of marketability. From an economic or business standpoint, the preferable course of action may be to sell the property to another beneficiary of the decedent involved. That approach, however, may be an act of self-dealing.

In general, where a private foundation is a residuary beneficiary of a decedent's estate or trust, transactions (such as property dispositions) that occur during the course of administration of the estate or trust with one or more disqualified persons constitute indirect self-dealing.[485] In the principal case on point, a disqualified person with respect to a charitable trust purchased property from the estate of the decedent who created the trust. The property was destined to be a substantial part of the trust corpus. The IRS concluded that the purchase was an act of self-dealing because the disqualified person did not pay the estate an amount equal to the fair market value of the property. The matter was litigated, with the trial court and the court of appeals agreeing with the IRS.[486] Another court stated that it is "clear that transactions affecting the assets of an estate generally are treated as also affecting the assets of any private foundation which, as a beneficiary of the estate, has an expectancy interest in the assets of the estate."[487]

The tax regulations, however, provide some degree of leeway, in the form of the estate administration exception to self-dealing, which allows the estate or trust to sell the property to disqualified persons in certain circumstances.

(a) Concept of the *Expectancy*

The federal tax regulations do not address the question of when a private foundation has an interest or expectancy in property held by an estate or trust. These regulations merely refer to a "private foundation's interest or expectancy in property . . . held by an estate" or trust.[488] Generally, where a

---

485. Reg. § 53.4941(d)-1(b)(3).
486. Rockefeller v. United States, 572 F. Supp. 9 (E.D. Ark.), *aff'd*, 718 F.2d 290 (8th Cir. 1983), *cert. den.*, 466 U.S. 962 (1984).
487. Estate of Reis v. Commissioner, 87 T.C. 1016, 1022 (1986). By contrast, the IRS observed that the "mere possibility that a private foundation will eventually receive property through an estate is not sufficient to make transactions involving that property subject to the self-dealing rules" (Priv. Ltr. Rul. 9222057).
488. Reg. § 53.4941(d)-1(b)(3).

charitable beneficiary has an interest or expectancy in property in an estate, the interest is in the residue. This is because the residue consists of funds or other property remaining in the estate after payment of all proper expenses, including taxes, paid in accordance with the settlor's direction.

Three IRS private letter rulings illustrate the concept of an expectancy held by a private foundation. In the facts of one of these private letter rulings, a trust was required to pay over to the executor or administrator of an estate such amounts as were deemed necessary for the payment of all estate, gift, personal property, inheritance, succession, death, and income taxes, payable by the executor or administrator, or by any beneficiary by reason of succession to the property of the decedent (other than the private foundation involved), and to pay all debts and administrative expenses of the estate and cash bequests under the decedent's will. The trust provided that "all such amounts shall be paid from the portion of the trust estate which passes to [the foundation] under" the trust agreement. This ruling explained the concept of the residue: "That portion of the trust estate, allocated for the payment of these taxes on non-charitable bequests or transfers, never becomes part of the residuary estate to be distributed to [the private foundation involved] because the residue consists only of funds left in the trust after the payment of all proper expenses, including taxes, paid pursuant to the settlor's discretion." The IRS concluded that, "accordingly, [the private foundation] would have no expectancy or interest in that portion of the assets of the estate."[489]

In the second of these rulings, the decedent's will and trust agreement contained language that was construed by the trustee to require payment of estate taxes prior to calculating the share destined for the charitable beneficiary. The charitable organization involved intended to petition the probate court to determine the appropriate construction of the will. The IRS ruled that the payment of estate taxes in accordance with the findings of the probate court is not an act of self-dealing, even though a private foundation was the residuary beneficiary, because the payment of taxes is nothing more than the payment of a claim against the estate and does not involve a transfer of the foundation's expectancy.[490]

In the third of these rulings, the decedent's will and codicils contained ambiguous language regarding the apportionment of generation-skipping

---

489. Priv. Ltr. Rul. 9307025. Similarly, in the case of a private foundation that was a residuary beneficiary of a trust, created by a disqualified person, where the trust reimbursed the estate of another disqualified person pursuant to the trust instrument using stock, the IRS ruled that the transfer was merely a "necessary expense" associated with administration of the trust. Because the foundation had no interest in the stock, there was no expectancy therein, so that an indirect act of self-dealing did not occur (Priv. Ltr. Rul. 202042007).

490. Priv. Ltr. Rul. 9246028.

§ 5.12 ESTATE ADMINISTRATION EXCEPTION

taxes. The estate obtained a court order that taxes were to be paid from the residuary interest. The estate's payment of taxes from the residuary, in accordance with the court order, was found by the IRS to not be self-dealing, notwithstanding a private foundation as the residuary beneficiary, because the payment was authorized by the will. The IRS ruled that, because the court found that the residuary interest was liable for payment of the tax, payment of the tax would not constitute self-dealing because the foundation's interest or expectancy was subject to the generation-skipping tax obligation.[491]

(b) Estate Administration Exception—General Rules

A major exception to the general rule that transactions that occur during the course of administration of the estate or trust with one or more disqualified persons constitute indirect self-dealing is the estate administration exception.[492] Pursuant to this exception, the term indirect self-dealing does not include a transaction with respect to a private foundation's interest or expectancy in property, whether or not encumbered, held by an estate or trust, regardless of when title to the property vests under local law, if (1) the administrator or executor of an estate or trustee of a trust (a) possesses a power of sale with respect to the property, (b) has the power to reallocate the property to another beneficiary, or (c) is required to sell the property under the terms of an option subject to which the property was acquired by the estate or trust; (2) the transaction is approved by the probate court having jurisdiction over the estate or by another court having jurisdiction over the estate or trust or over the private foundation involved; (3) the transaction occurs before the estate is considered terminated for federal income tax purposes or, in the case of a revocable trust, before it is considered subject to the nonexempt charitable trust rules[493] or the split-interest trust rules;[494] (4) the estate or trust receives an amount that equals or exceeds the fair market value of the foundation's interest or expectancy in the property at the time of the transaction, taking into account the terms of any option subject to which the property was acquired by the estate or trust; and (5) the transaction (a) results in the foundation receiving an interest or expectancy at least as liquid as the one it gave up, (b) results in the foundation receiving an asset related to the active carrying out of its exempt purposes, or (c) is required under the terms of any option that is binding on the estate or

---

491. Priv. Ltr. Rul. 200225037. Still another example of a private foundation's expectancy is in Priv. Ltr. Rul. 201849009.
492. Reg. § 53.4941(d)-1(b)(3).
493. See § 3.6.
494. See § 3.7.

trust.[495] This exception is confined to sales or other dispositions of property by an estate or trust.[496]

The IRS applied the estate administration exception to a foundation that has an expectancy in the form of shares of stock in a corporation formed by two disqualified persons with respect to it. A court with jurisdiction over the foundation was to determine the "fair value" of the shares in connection with sale of them to the company as of a date the court deems appropriate. This court "may determine the fair value of [the shares] to be less than the fair market value of" them. The foundation was required to represent to the IRS its understanding that the estate administration exception will be inapplicable if the court does not approve the sales transaction and/or if an amount that equals or exceeds the fair market value of the shares at the time of the transaction is not received. In essence, the IRS ruled that if the elements of the exception are satisfied, sale of the shares to the corporation will not constitute indirect self-dealing.[497]

---

495. The word *option* is not defined in the private foundation statutory law context. Elsewhere in the Internal Revenue Code, the term *option* is defined to include the "right to subscribe to or purchase any security" (IRC § 1236(e)). The term is used in another Code section (IRC § 2703) but is not defined. Tax regulations in another setting state that the word means the "right or privilege of an individual to purchase stock from a corporation by virtue of an offer of the corporation continuing for a stated period of time, whether or not irrevocable, to sell such stock at a [determined] price . . ., such individual being under no obligation to purchase" (Reg. § 1.421-1(a)(1)). An arrangement to acquire stock qualifies as an option only where the optionee has the right to obtain the stock "at his election" (Rev. Rul. 89-64, 1989-1 C.B. 91, clarifying Rev. Rul. 68-601, 1968-2 C.B. 204, which states that an arrangement constitutes an option where the stock may be acquired at the election of the optionee and "there exists no contingencies with respect to such election"). As to contingencies, see Tech. Adv. Mem. 8106008.

496. A court reviewed the constitutionality of the estate administration exception, finding it to be a constitutional tax and not arbitrary and unreasonable (Rockefeller v. United States, 572 F. Supp. 9 (E.D. Ark.), aff'd per curiam, 718 F.2d 290 (8th Cir. 1983), cert. den., 460 U.S. 962 (1984)). The principal contention was that Congress "never intended for [§] 4941 to encompass transactions between estates and disqualified persons" (572 F. Supp. at 13). The trial court seemed to accept that underlying assumption, writing about the "fact" that Congress "failed to mention the word estate in [§] 4941, or related statutes" (*id.* at 14). The court and the litigants apparently overlooked the reference in the Internal Revenue Code to estates as disqualified persons (IRC § 4946(a)(1)(G)) (see § 4.6). In any event, the court found the regulation to be "reasonable" (*id.*) and not arbitrary and vague just because it only covers sales and exchanges (*id.* at 14-15). In this case, self-dealing was found because the disqualified person did not pay fair market value for the property involved; the estate administration exception thus was not available.

497. Priv. Ltr. Rul. 201850012. Redemption of the stock of a family corporation with several living descendant owners of more than 35 percent of the total combined voting power was allowed pursuant to the estate administration exception, in a ruling replete with complex facts that give light to the usefulness of this exception (Priv. Ltr. Rul. 201448023).

§ 5.12 ESTATE ADMINISTRATION EXCEPTION

The estate administration exception is the subject of several other IRS private letter rulings. In one instance, a private foundation was being liquidated into two new private foundations as part of a plan to settle litigation between two feuding siblings. The settlement plan included reorganization of corporations, in which some of the stock was in an estate and destined for (i.e., was an expectancy of) the foundation. Because the executors of the estate (the siblings) possessed the power of sale, the probate court involved approved the transactions, the foundation was to receive liquid assets in excess of the value of the property it was giving up, and the transactions were to occur before the estate was considered terminated for federal tax purposes, the IRS ruled that the estate administration exception was applicable.[498] Thus, despite considerable benefits to the disqualified persons (the siblings)—which somewhat troubled the IRS—the transactions were not considered self-dealing. In a similar situation, the IRS ruled that this exception was available in connection with a series of transactions, pursuant to settlement of litigation, involving a reallocation of assets destined for a private foundation and disqualified persons with respect to it.[499]

One IRS ruling involved the division of properties owned by an artist's estate in order to fund a statutory one-third life estate in favor of his wife. The IRS found that self-dealing did not occur, despite the exchanges of property inherent in the settlement, where the agreement satisfied the elements of the estate administration exception.[500] In another instance, a business corporation operated to produce and promote a musician's work during his life was bequeathed to private foundations formed to perpetuate the musician's name and compositions. The gift was accompanied by a promissory note because the estate was partially insolvent. The IRS allowed this non-pro-rata distribution inasmuch as it was approved by a probate court.[501] Likewise, the IRS ruled that a private foundation's holding of a promissory note issued by a disqualified person, and its receipt of note payments from the person after the period of estate administration terminates, will not be acts of self-dealing by reason of the exception.[502]

---

498. Priv. Ltr. Rul. 200117042.
499. Priv. Ltr. Rul. 200132037.
500. Priv. Ltr. Rul. 9242042. A substitution of artwork preferred by the artist's daughters, for objects specifically bequeathed to them, however, was ruled to be self-dealing.
501. Priv. Ltr. Rul. 9308045. The IRS also ruled that operation of the business would be functionally related to the purposes of the foundations and thus not result in excess business holdings (see § 7.3).
502. Priv. Ltr. Rul. 201129049. The IRS subsequently adopted a no-rule position as to self-dealing issues involving issuance of a promissory note by a disqualified person during the administration of an estate or trust (currently, Rev. Proc. 2023-3, 2023-1 I.R.B. 144 § 3.01(130)).

Payments out of an estate's residuary funds made pursuant to settlement of a will contest were ruled to not constitute an act of self-dealing. The decedent had left his residuary estate to a private foundation. The will left nothing to his son but gave the son an option to purchase certain assets from the estate. After controversy surrounding the purchase, a settlement was reached, providing the son part of the assets and placing other assets in a charitable remainder trust for the son's benefit, with the remainder contributed to the foundation. Based on availability of the exception, the IRS ruled that self-dealing did not occur.[503] The IRS has also issued rulings in connection with settlement agreements involving property in estates and sales to disqualified persons, finding an absence of self-dealing because of the reasonableness of the settlement and its benefits to the private foundation involved, such as the cessation of litigation and more immediate access to property passing from the estate, without expressly invoking the estate administration exception.[504]

From time to time, the IRS issues private letter rulings as to circumstances where the estate administration exception applies[505] and when it is inapplicable.[506]

(c) Determining Fair Market Value

As noted, the fourth element of the estate administration exception requires that the estate or trust involved must receive an amount equaling or exceeding the fair market value of the foundation's interest or expectancy in the property at the time of the transaction.[507]

As a general principle, the fair market value of an item of property is the price at which the property would change hands between a willing buyer and a willing seller, neither being under any compulsion to buy or to sell and both having reasonable knowledge of relevant facts.[508] All relevant facts and elements of value as of the applicable valuation date must be considered in every case.[509] The fair market value of a particular item of property is not to be

---

503. Priv. Ltr. Rul. 8929087.
504. Priv. Ltr. Ruls. 201316021, 201321027. Other rulings indicate that the IRS is often of the view that will settlements are analogous to the circumstances giving rise to the application of the estate administration exception (e.g., Priv. Ltr. Rul. 200218036).
505. E.g., Priv. Ltr. Rul. 200117042.
506. E.g., Priv. Ltr. Rul. 9252042.
507. The words *at the time of the transaction* are basically redundant, inasmuch as fair market value is almost always determined at that time. For example, the exception from the self-dealing rules for transactions in connection with corporate reorganizations (see § 5.14(a)) requires receipt by the foundation of at least fair market value, with no reference to determination of the time for establishing that value (Reg. § 53.4941(d)-3(d)(1)), yet surely the valuation date must be contemporaneous.
508. E.g., Reg. §§ 1.170A-1(c)(2), 20.2031-1(b).
509. Reg. § 2031-1(b).

§ 5.12 ESTATE ADMINISTRATION EXCEPTION

determined by a forced sale price.[510] The IRS observed that "[c]ourt decisions frequently state in addition that the hypothetical buyer and seller are assumed to be able, as well as willing, to trade and to be well-informed about the property and concerning the market for such property."[511]

A determination of fair market value is a question of fact; it will depend on the circumstances in each case.[512] Valuation of property is "not a precise science."[513] The IRS stated that a "sound valuation will be based upon all the relevant facts, but the elements of common sense, informed judgment, and reasonableness must enter into the process of weighing those facts and determining their aggregate significance."[514]

For example, the IRS stated that the "[v]aluation of securities is, in essence, a prophesy as to the future and must be based on facts available at the required date of appraisal." The agency added that the "prices of stocks which are traded in volume in a free and active market by informed persons best reflect the consensus of the investing public as to what the future holds for the corporations and industries represented." By contrast, "[w]hen a stock is closely held, is traded infrequently, or is traded in an erratic market, some other measure of value must be used." In many instances, the IRS noted, the "next best measure may be found in the prices at which the stocks of companies engaged in the same or similar line of business are selling in a free and open market."[515]

The value of stocks is the fair market value per share on the applicable valuation date.[516] Where actual sale prices and bona fide bid and asked prices are lacking, the fair market value of a share of stock is to be determined by taking into consideration the company's net worth, prospective earning power and dividend-paying capacity, and other relevant factors.[517] Some of these "other relevant factors" are enumerated in the tax regulations.[518] The IRS has amplified the factors to be considered in valuing shares of the stock of closely held corporations (or other situations where market quotations are either unavailable or are of such scarcity that they do not reflect the fair market value).[519]

---

510. Id.
511. Rev. Rul. 59-60, 1959-1 C.B. 237.
512. E.g., Goldstein v. Commissioner, 89 T.C. 535 (1987).
513. Kiva Dunes Conservation, LLC v. Commissioner, 97 T.C.M. 1818, 1821 (2009).
514. Rev. Rul. 59-60, 1959-1 C.B. 237.
515. Id.
516. E.g., Reg. § 20.2031-2(a).
517. E.g., Reg. § 20.2031-2(f)(2).
518. Reg. § 20.2031-2(f).
519. Rev. Rul. 59-60, 1959-1 C.B. 237.

SELF-DEALING

These factors, while not all-inclusive, are "fundamental and require careful analysis in each case." The factors are (1) the nature of the business and the history of the enterprise from its inception, (2) the economic outlook in general and the condition and outlook of the specific industry in particular, (3) the book value of the stock and the financial condition of the business, (4) the earning capacity of the company, (5) the company's dividend-paying capacity, (6) whether the enterprise has goodwill or other intangible value, (7) sales of the stock and the size of the block of stock to be valued, and (8) the market price of stocks of corporations engaged in the same or similar line of business having their stocks actively traded in a free and open market, either on an exchange or over the counter.[520]

As the foregoing makes clear, the determination of the value of stock is based on an understanding of all the relevant facts. It is usually prudent for sellers and buyers to retain the services of an independent, competent appraiser, who will ascertain the appropriate business valuation approach and apply the requisite factors in determining the per-share fair market value of the stock involved. Fair market value cannot be ascertained simply pursuant to a negotiation between the parties. That value must be based on the above-referenced standards that have developed in the law. Thus, for compliance with the estate administration exception from the private foundation self-dealing rules, the value of stock and other property must be determined in accordance with the foregoing principles articulated by the Department of the Treasury, the IRS, and courts.[521]

§ 5.13 EARLY TERMINATIONS OF CHARITABLE REMAINDER TRUSTS

A charitable remainder trust[522] may be terminated sooner than is provided in the trust instrument. There are several reasons for the premature termination of this type of trust, such as a desire to transfer the trust assets earlier to the remainder interest beneficiary,[523] or an income beneficiary's dissatisfaction with the level of income payments.[524]

The IRS tends to scrutinize proposed early terminations of charitable remainder trusts. The principal concern is that the early termination will result in greater allocation of the trust assets to the income beneficiary, to the

---

520. *Id.*
521. Also § 6.3.
522. See §§ 2.6(b), 3.7.
523. E.g., Priv. Ltr. Rul. 200304025.
524. E.g., Priv. Ltr. Rul. 200208039.

§ 5.13 EARLY TERMINATIONS OF CHARITABLE REMAINDER TRUSTS

detriment of the charitable remainder interest beneficiary, than would be the case if the termination instead occurred at the initially prescribed time.[525] The self-dealing rules potentially apply to the transaction.[526]

Nonetheless, in appropriate circumstances, the IRS will permit an early termination of a charitable remainder trust. The elements the agency reviews are whether (1) the trustee will be distributing to the income and remainder interest beneficiaries lump sums equal to the present value of the irrespective interests as of the termination date, (2) the income and remainder interests are vested, (3) all income beneficiaries are of full legal capacity, (4) all of the beneficiaries favor early termination, (5) any of the income beneficiaries has a medical condition that is expected to result in a shorter period of longevity for the beneficiary,[527] (6) the trust instrument prohibits early termination, and (7) state law (and/or state regulatory authorities) permits early termination.

The self-dealing rules apply except with respect to amounts payable under the terms of such trust to income beneficiaries.[528] The trust instrument may be silent on the point, but state law allowing early terminations of trusts may be considered implied terms of the instrument. Also, the early termination may not be discretionary with the trustee.[529] The foregoing factors are taken into account in the self-dealing context, with early termination of a charitable remainder trust, where a private foundation is the remainder interest beneficiary, found not to be impermissible self-dealing when the method of allocating assets of the trust on its termination was reasonable, the income beneficiaries had life expectancies reflecting average longevity, state law allowed the early termination, and all the beneficiaries favored the early termination.[530] The IRS, from time to time, issues private letter rulings as to early terminations of charitable remainder trusts.[531]

Notwithstanding the foregoing, the IRS appears to be reevaluating its position as to whether an early termination of a charitable remainder trust,

---

525. An early termination of a charitable remainder trust would, if the terms of the transfers were not reasonable, deprive the charitable remainder beneficiaries of the benefit to which it is entitled, inconsistent with the charitable contribution deduction allowed to the donor or donors.
526. See § 3.7.
527. It is the practice of the IRS to require an affidavit from a physician stating that the income beneficiary does not have a medical condition that would unduly shorten the beneficiary's life.
528. IRC § 4947(a)(2)(A).
529. Reg. § 53.4947-1(e).
530. This, then, is one of the few instances in which the concept of reasonableness is factored into a self-dealing law analysis.
531. E.g., Priv. Ltr. Rul. 200124010. In one instance, the income interest was also sold to the remainder interest beneficiary (Priv. Ltr. Rul. 200310024).

SELF-DEALING

where the remainder interest beneficiary is a private foundation, constitutes self-dealing.[532]

§ 5.14 ADDITIONAL EXCEPTIONS

(a) Certain Corporate Organizations or Reorganizations

Additional exceptions to the self-dealing rules are available. The principal exception in this group is the one for certain corporate organizations or reorganizations. Any transaction between a private foundation and a corporation that is a disqualified person with respect to the private foundation is not an act of self-dealing if the transaction is engaged in pursuant to a liquidation, merger, redemption, recapitalization, or other corporate adjustment, organization, or reorganization.[533] For this exception to apply, however, all the securities of the same class as that held (prior to the transaction) by the private foundation must be subject to the same terms, and the terms must provide for receipt by the private foundation of no less than fair market value.[534] For example, the IRS ruled that this transaction exception is available with respect to a reorganization,[535] where there is only one class of voting stock involved and the shares received will reflect a market value as determined by independent investment bankers.[536] As another illustration, the fact that the redemption offer by a company was limited to a fixed dollar amount and the fact that a redemption offer by a related company was in tandem with the other offer was ruled by the IRS to not detract from the uniform nature of the second offer.[537]

A court held that acts of self-dealing took place when a company, which was a disqualified person with respect to a private foundation, redeemed shares from a private foundation under a treasury share acquisition program; because officers and directors of the company were excluded from participation in the redemption, the requirement of the exception that *all* securities involved in a redemption must be subject to the same terms was found not to have been met.[538] This decision was reversed on appeal, however, with the appellate court holding that this *same terms* rule does not

---

532. E.g., Priv. Ltr. Rul. 200614032, revoking Priv. Ltr. Rul. 200525014. See Rev. Rul. 2008-41, 2008-30 I.R.B. 170.
533. IRC § 4941(d)(2)(F).
534. Reg. § 53.4941(d)-3(d).
535. IRC § 368(a)(1)(C).
536. Priv. Ltr. Rul. 7847049.
537. Priv. Ltr. Rul. 201624001.
538. Deluxe Check Printers, Inc. v. United States, 88-1 U.S.T.C. ¶ 9311 (Cl. Ct. 1988).

§ 5.14 ADDITIONAL EXCEPTIONS

require a corporation that is a disqualified person to include in a redemption program the shares held by its officers and directors, reasoning that this result was in harmony with the federal securities law's impact on shareholding insiders.[539]

(b) Transitional Rules (Savings Provisions)

Further, the Tax Reform Act of 1969 contains five "savings provisions"[540] or transitional rules rendering the self-dealing rules inapplicable to various pre-1969 and other transactions.[541]

One of these provisions embodied in the 1969 Act excluded from the proscriptions of the self-dealing rules the disposition of a private foundation's excess and non-excess business holdings,[542] owned by the private foundation on May 26, 1969, to a disqualified person, where the private foundation was required to dispose of the property in order to avoid the taxes on excess holdings,[543] the private foundation received an amount that at least equaled the fair market value of the property, and (in the case of nonexcess holdings) the transaction occurred before January 1975.[544] This exception was allowed in recognition of the fact that in the case of many closely held companies, the only ready market for a foundation's holdings is one or more disqualified persons.

This transitional rule concerning the disposition of holdings owned by a private foundation on May 26, 1969, does not have an effective date, as illustrated by a situation where the holdings were not excess holdings as of 1969, so that the exception was not then available, but subsequently became excess holdings. For example, where at least 95 percent of the income of a corporation, wholly owned by a private foundation and its disqualified persons on May 26, 1969, consisted of rents from real property, thus constituting passive income,[545] the corporation was not considered a business enterprise[546] so that the holdings could not be excess holdings. Years later, less than 95 percent of the corporation's gross income was being derived from real property rentals, with the balance coming from the leasing of equipment to unrelated third parties, causing the corporation to become a business enterprise and thus

---

539. Deluxe Corporation v. United States, 885 F.2d 848 (Fed. Cir. 1989). The IRS elected to not further appeal this decision (AOD 1990-08).
540. Tax Reform Act of 1969 § 101(1)(2).
541. Reg. § 53.4941(d)-4.
542. See § 7.2.
543. IRC § 4943.
544. Tax Reform Act of 1969 § 101(1)(2)(B); Rev. Rul. 75-25, 1975-1 C.B. 359.
545. IRC § 512(b)(3).
546. IRC § 4943(d)(3)(B).

allowing the excess holdings to be sold to disqualified persons pursuant to the exception, inasmuch as all of the other requirements of the transitional rule were met.[547]

Another transitional rule adopted in 1969[548] enabled a private foundation to lease (through 1979) property under certain circumstances to a disqualified person without violating the self-dealing rules.

Congress, in 1980, created a permanent exemption from the self-dealing rules for office space leasing arrangements between a private foundation tenant and a disqualified person, where (1) the lease was pursuant to a binding contract in effect on October 9, 1969, even though it had been renewed, (2) at the time of execution the lease was not a prohibited transaction,[549] (3) the space was leased to the private foundation on a basis no less favorable than that on which the space would be made available in an arm's-length transaction, and (4) the leased space was in a building in which there were tenants who were not disqualified persons with respect to the private foundation. These rules are effective for tax years beginning after December 31, 1979.[550]

To enable private foundations to sell property presently being leased to a disqualified person at its maximum value, Congress in 1976 devised another transitional rule allowing a private foundation to dispose of nonexcess property to a disqualified person if at that time it is leasing substantially all of the property under the lease transitional rule and it receives an amount that at least equals the property's fair market value.[551] This rule applied to dispositions occurring before January 1, 1978, and after October 4, 1976.

§ 5.15 ISSUES ONCE SELF-DEALING OCCURS

The rules concerning self-dealing—like the other private foundation rules—are enforced by excise taxes that may be regarded as sanctions for what Congress has characterized as wrongful conduct. One court described these sanctions as follows: "The language of the [Tax Reform] Act [of 1969], its legislative history, the graduated levels of the sanctions imposed, and the almost confiscatory level of the exactions assessed, convince us that the exactions in question were intended to curb the described conduct through pecuniary punishment."[552]

---

547. Rev. Rul. 86-53, 1986-1 C.B. 326.
548. Tax Reform Act of 1969 § 101(1)(2)(C).
549. Under former IRC § 503 (which was subsequently repealed).
550. IRC § 4941(d)(2)(H); Reg. § 53.4941(d)-2(b)(3).
551. Tax Reform Act of 1969 § 101(1)(2)(F).
552. In re Unified Control Systems, Inc., 586 F.2d 1036, 1039 (5th Cir. 1978). See § 1.8(c).

§ 5.15 ISSUES ONCE SELF-DEALING OCCURS

(a) Self-Dealing Excise Taxes

There are three taxes that are potentially applicable in the self-dealing context: the initial tax,[553] the additional tax,[554] and the termination tax.[555] Although the termination tax is imposed on the private foundation, these initial and additional taxes apply only to self-dealers (that is, to disqualified persons engaging in acts of self-dealing) and to foundation managers under certain circumstances.

(i) Initial Taxes. An *initial tax* of 10 percent of the amount involved is imposed on each act of self-dealing between a private foundation and a disqualified person. Any disqualified person (other than a foundation manager acting only in that capacity) who participates in the act of self-dealing is liable to pay this initial excise tax.[556] In any case in which this initial tax is imposed on a self-dealer, any foundation manager that participated in the act of self-dealing, knowing that it is such an act, is also subject to an initial tax of 5 percent of the amount involved. This initial *foundation manager tax* is not imposed if the foundation manager's participation is not willful and is due to reasonable cause.[557] A foundation manager that is also acting as a self-dealer may be liable for both taxes.[558]

A foundation manager is treated as *participating* in an act of self-dealing in any case in which they engage or take part in the transaction or direct any person to do so.[559] In this context, the term *participation* includes silence or inaction on the part of a foundation manager where they are under a duty to speak or act, as well as any affirmative action by the manager. A foundation manager is not considered to have participated in an act of self-dealing, however, where they have opposed the act in a manner consistent with the fulfillment of their responsibilities to the private foundation.[560]

Participation by a foundation manager is deemed *willful* if it is voluntary, conscious, and intentional. No motive to avoid the restrictions of the law or the incurrence of any tax is necessary to make the participation willful. Participation by a foundation manager is not willful, however, if they do not know that the transaction in which they are participating is an act of self-dealing.[561]

---

553. IRC § 4941(a). This tax is also known as a *first-tier tax* (IRC § 4963(a); Reg. § 53.4963-1(a)).
554. IRC § 4941(b). This tax is also known as a *second-tier tax* (IRC § 4963(b); Reg. § 53.4963-1(b)).
555. IRC § 507(c).
556. IRC § 4941(a)(1); Reg. § 53.4941(a)-1(a)(1).
557. IRC § 4941(a)(2); Reg. § 53.4941(a)-1(b)(1).
558. Reg. § 53.4941(a)-1(a)(1); Rev. Rul. 78-76, 1978-1 C.B. 377.
559. Reg. § 53.4941(a)-1(a)(3).
560. Reg. § 53.4941(a)-1(b)(2).
561. Reg. § 53.4941(a)-1(b)(4).

SELF-DEALING

A foundation manager's participation is due to *reasonable cause* if they have exercised their responsibility on behalf of the foundation with ordinary business care and prudence.[562]

An individual is considered to have participated in a transaction *knowing* that it is an act of self-dealing only if they: (1) have actual knowledge of sufficient facts so that, based solely on those facts, the transaction would be an act of self-dealing; (2) are aware that the act under these circumstances may violate the self-dealing rules; and (3) negligently fails to make reasonable attempts to ascertain whether the transaction is an act of self-dealing, or they are in fact aware that it is this type of act. The term knowing does not mean "having reason to know." Evidence tending to show that an individual has reason to know of a particular fact or particular rule, however, is relevant in determining whether they had actual knowledge of that fact or rule. For example, evidence tending to show that an individual has reason to know of sufficient facts so that, based solely on those facts, a transaction would be an act of self-dealing is relevant in determining whether they have actual knowledge of those facts.[563]

In the case of a government official,[564] tax can be imposed only if the official, as a disqualified person, participated in the act of self-dealing knowing that it was this type of an act.[565] Otherwise, the tax is imposed on a disqualified person even though the person did not have knowledge at the time of the act that it constituted self-dealing.[566]

Until the transaction is corrected (or the taxable period otherwise closes), these initial self-dealing taxes on self-dealers and foundation managers are imposed each year rather than merely with respect to the year in which the self-dealing took place.[567] Specifically, if a transaction between a private foundation and a disqualified person concerns the leasing of property, the lending of money or other extension of credit, other use of money or property, or payment of compensation, the transaction will generally be treated as giving rise to an act

---

562. Reg. § 53.4941(a)-1(b)(5).
563. Reg. § 53.4941(a)-1(b)(3).
564. See § 4.8.
565. IRC § 4941(a)(1); Reg. § 53.4941(a)-1(a)(2). There is a (perfectly reasonable) assumption that the rule, as to reliance on advice of counsel in connection with the concept of *knowing* (see § 5.15(a)(v)), is identical in the foundation manager and government official settings. Yet the regulations are improvidently written in this regard, in that reference is made to the fact that a "person's participation in such act will ordinarily not be considered 'knowing' or 'willful' and will ordinarily be considered 'due to reasonable cause' within the meaning of section 4941(a)(2)" (Reg. § 53.4941(a)-1(b)(6)). The reference to knowing, however, in connection with government officials is in IRC § 4941(a)(1). In general, the concept of *knowing* is the same in both contexts (Reg. § 53.4941(a)-1(a)(2)).
566. Reg. § 53.4941(a)-1(a)(1).
567. IRC § 4941(a); Reg. § 53.4941(a)-1(a)(1), (b)(1); Gen. Couns. Mem. 39066.

§ 5.15 ISSUES ONCE SELF-DEALING OCCURS

of self-dealing on the day the transaction occurs, plus an act of self-dealing on the first day of each tax year (or portion of a tax year) after that date.[568]

Thus, for example, where an act of self-dealing, such as a lease, continues over a four-year period before being corrected, there are four separate acts of self-dealing, four amounts involved,[569] and four taxable periods.[570] The loan gives rise to an act of self-dealing on the date the loan occurs, plus an additional deemed act of self-dealing on the first day of each subsequent tax year until correction has been made (or the taxable period otherwise closes).[571] For each deemed act of self-dealing, the amount involved is calculated by multiplying the loan balance (including any accrued but unpaid interest), the fair market interest rate on the date the act is deemed to occur, and the period of use.[572] Although the IRS may be precluded from assessing the tax on transactions occurring in years outside the statute of limitations,[573] the amount involved for a deemed act of self-dealing is determined as of the date the deemed act occurred and is not affected by expiration of the period of limitations for an earlier act of self-dealing.[574]

The *taxable period* is, with respect to an act of self-dealing, the period beginning with the date on which the act of self-dealing occurred and ending on the earliest of the following dates: (1) the date of mailing of a notice of deficiency with respect to the initial tax,[575] (2) the date on which the tax is assessed, or (3) the date on which correction of the act of self-dealing is completed.[576]

If more than one disqualified person or foundation manager is liable for one of these initial taxes, all of them are jointly and severally liable for the tax with respect to the act of self-dealing involved.[577] If more than one foundation manager is liable for the initial foundation manager tax with respect to any one act of self-dealing, however, the maximum amount of the tax cannot exceed $20,000 for all participants.[578]

---

568. Reg. § 53.4941(e)-1(e)(1).
569. See § 5.15(b).
570. Reg. § 53.4941(e)-1(e)(1)(ii), Example (2).
571. *Id*. E.g., Priv. Ltr. Rul. 9530032.
572. Reg. § 53.4941(e)-1(e)(1)(ii), Example (2); Rev. Rul. 2002-43, 2002-28 I.R.B. 85. This revenue ruling applies to prohibited transactions under section 4975; however, it applies Reg. § 53.4941(e)-1, which governs the calculation of the amount involved for purposes of both IRC §§ 4941 and 4975.
573. See § 12.4(d).
574. Chief Couns. Adv. Mem. 202243008.
575. The basic rules as to notices of deficiency are the subject of IRC § 6212.
576. IRC § 4941(e)(1); Reg. § 53.4941(e)-1(a). Where a private foundation lends money to a disqualified person with a tax year different from that of the foundation, the disqualified person must compute the tax payable under IRC § 4941 based on their own tax year (Rev. Rul. 75-391, 1975-2 C.B. 446).
577. IRC § 4941(c)(1); Reg. § 53.4941(c)-1(a).
578. IRC § 4941(c)(2); Reg. § 53.4941(c)-1(b).

SELF-DEALING

If joint participation in a transaction by two or more disqualified persons constitutes self-dealing (such as a joint sale of property to a private foundation), the transaction is generally treated as a separate act of self-dealing with respect to each disqualified person.[579]

(ii) Additional Taxes. Where the initial tax is imposed and the self-dealing is not corrected within the taxable period, an *additional tax* of 200 percent of the amount involved is imposed on the self-dealer.[580] Any foundation manager that refuses to agree to all or part of the correction is liable for an additional tax of 50 percent of the amount involved.[581] Again, if more than one disqualified person or foundation manager is liable for one of these taxes, each is jointly and severally liable for the tax with respect to the act of self-dealing involved.[582] And if more than one foundation manager is liable for the additional foundation manager tax with respect to any one act of self-dealing, the maximum amount of the tax cannot exceed $20,000 for all participants.[583]

(iii) Termination Tax. The termination tax[584] may serve as a third-tier tax where there have been either willful repeated acts (or failures to act), or a willful and flagrant act (or failure to act), giving rise to liability for the taxes on self-dealing or the other private foundation excise taxes.[585]

(iv) Limitation on Abatement. The IRS generally has the discretionary authority to abate any initial (first-tier) taxes where a private foundation establishes to the satisfaction of the IRS that the act or omission giving rise to the tax was due to reasonable cause, was not due to willful neglect, and has been corrected within the appropriate correction period.[586] This authority does not, however, extend to the self-dealing taxes.[587]

Nonetheless, in one instance, the IRS found acts of self-dealing on an audit of a private foundation, yet worked with foundation management to revise the organization's operations so as to correct the activities that gave rise to the transgression. The IRS used its general authority to grant retroactive relief[588] for the benefit of the foundation (because tax-exempt status was also at issue) and its management on the self-dealing issues.[589]

---

579. Reg. § 53.4941(e)-1(e).
580. IRC § 4941(b)(1).
581. IRC § 4941(b)(2).
582. IRC § 4941(c)(1); Reg. § 53.4941(c)-1(a).
583. IRC § 4941(c)(2); Reg. § 53.4941(c)-1(b).
584. See § 13.7.
585. IRC § 507(a)(2); see § 13.2.
586. IRC § 4962(a); see § 12.4(c).
587. IRC § 4962(b).
588. IRC § 7805(b).
589. Tech. Adv. Mem. 9646002.

§ 5.15 ISSUES ONCE SELF-DEALING OCCURS

(v) Advice of Counsel. Although abatement is not available for the initial excise tax imposed on a self-dealer,[590] reliance on advice of counsel may provide a defense to the imposition of the initial tax on foundation managers.[591]

If a foundation manager, after full disclosure of the factual situation to legal counsel (including house counsel), relies on the advice of that counsel expressed in a reasoned written legal opinion that an act is not an act of self-dealing—even if that act is subsequently held to be self-dealing—the individual's participation in the act will ordinarily not be considered knowing or willful and will ordinarily be considered due to reasonable cause. This document provided by legal counsel is not required to be a formal *opinion letter* (as the legal profession defines that term); rather, it can be a letter or memorandum containing the views of counsel on the point or points involved.[592] A written legal opinion is considered *reasoned*, even if it reaches a conclusion that is subsequently determined to be incorrect, as long as the opinion addresses itself to the facts and applicable law. A written legal opinion is not considered *reasoned*, however, if it does nothing more than recite the facts and express a conclusion. The absence of advice of counsel with respect to an act does not, by itself, give rise to any inference that a person participated in the act knowingly, willfully, or without reasonable cause.[593]

(b) Amount Involved

The excise taxes for entering into a self-dealing transaction are generally based on the *amount involved*, which is defined as the "greater of the amount of money and the fair market value of the other property given or the amount of money and the fair market value of the other property received."[594]

(i) Use of Money or Other Property. Where a self-dealing transaction entails the use of money or other property, the amount involved is the greater of the amount paid for the use or the fair market value of the use for the period for which the money or other property is used.[595]

---

590. See § 5.15(a)(iv).
591. See § 5.15(a)(i).
592. In one instance, the IRS wrote that disqualified persons avoided self-dealing taxes because they "relied on the advice of counsel," who "reviewed and approved their activities" (Tech. Adv. Mem. 9408006).
593. Reg. § 53.4941(a)-1(b)(6).
594. IRC § 4941(e)(2); Reg. § 53.4941(e)-1(b)(1).
595. Reg. § 53.4941(e)-1(b)(2)(ii).

SELF-DEALING

Thus, if a private foundation lends money to a disqualified person at a below-market interest rate, the amount involved is the difference between the interest rate set in the transaction (and paid) and the amount that was the prevailing fair market value interest rate at the time the loan was established. For example, if this type of loan is structured using a 6 percent interest rate per annum and the fair market value of the use of the money on the date the loan commenced is 10 percent per annum, the amount involved is calculated using the 10 percent interest rate.[596]

In the case of a lease of a building by a private foundation to a disqualified person, the amount involved is the greater of the amount of rent received by the private foundation from the disqualified person or the fair market value of the building for the period the building is used by the disqualified person.[597] For example, if a disqualified person leases office space in a building owned by a private foundation for $25,000 annually but the fair market value of the space is $30,000 annually, the amount involved is $30,000.[598]

As an illustration in the case of a use, assume a disqualified person with respect to a private foundation uses an airplane owned by the foundation for a two-day trip on personal business. The disqualified person pays the foundation $500 for the use, although the fair rental use value is $3,000; the amount involved with respect to the act of self-dealing is $3,000.[599]

(ii) Compensation. In the case of compensation paid for personal services to persons other than government officials, the amount involved is the portion of the total compensation in excess of the amount that would have been reasonable.[600]

The term *compensation* in this setting generally means a salary or wage, any bonuses, fringe benefits, retirement benefits, and the like. Occasionally, however, other economic benefits are treated as compensation for purposes of application of the self-dealing rules. For example, under certain circumstances, the value of an indemnification by a private foundation of a foundation manager, or the payment by a foundation of the premiums for an insurance policy for a foundation manager, must be treated as compensation to avoid self-dealing.[601] By contrast, when the self-dealing rules are explicit as to a particular type of transaction between a private foundation and a disqualified person, the rules cannot be sidestepped simply by treating the value

---

596. Reg. § 53.4941(e)-1(b)(4), Example (2).
597. Reg. § 53.4941(e)-1(b)(2)(ii).
598. Reg. § 53.4941(e)-1(b)(4), Example (3).
599. Reg. § 53.4941(e)-1(b)(4), Example (1).
600. Reg. § 53.4941(e)-1(b)(2)(i).
601. See § 5.7(b).

§ 5.15 ISSUES ONCE SELF-DEALING OCCURS

of the economic benefit provided as part of the disqualified person's total (reasonable) compensation.[602]

(iii) Exceptions Predicated on Fair Market Value. Where a transaction would not have been an act of self-dealing had the private foundation received fair market value,[603] the amount involved is the excess of the fair market value of the property transferred by the private foundation over the amount that the foundation receives, but only if the parties made a good-faith effort to determine fair market value.[604] A good-faith effort to determine fair market value ordinarily is made, where (1) the person making the valuation is not a disqualified person with respect to the foundation and is competent to make the valuation and not in a position, whether by stock ownership or otherwise, to derive an economic benefit from the value utilized, and (2) the method utilized in making the valuation is a generally accepted method for valuing comparable property for purposes of arm's-length business transactions where valuation is a significant factor.[605]

Thus, for example, if a corporation that is a disqualified person with respect to a private foundation recapitalizes in a transaction that would be exempt from the self-dealing rules[606] but for the fact that the foundation receives new stock worth only $95,000 in exchange for the stock that it previously held in the corporation and that has a fair market value of $100,000 at the time of the recapitalization, the amount involved is $5,000 if there had been a good-faith attempt to value the stock.[607] Similarly, if an estate enters into a transaction with a disqualified person with respect to a foundation and the transaction would qualify for the estate administration exception[608] but for the fact that the estate receives less than fair market value for the property exchanged, the amount involved is the excess of the fair market value of the property the estate transfers to the disqualified person over the money and the fair market value of the property received by the estate.[609]

(c) Date of Valuation

To calculate the initial tax imposed on a sale, exchange, or lease of property, the amount involved is determined as of the date on which the self-dealing

---

602. E.g., Priv. Ltr. Rul. 9530032. See text accompanied by *supra* note 227.
603. This rule pertains to two exceptions from the self-dealing rules. See §§ 5.12(c), 5.14(a).
604. Reg. § 53.4941(e)-1(b)(2)(iii).
605. *Id.* See § 5.12(c).
606. See § 5.14(a).
607. Reg. § 53.4941(e)-1(b)(2)(iii).
608. See § 5.12.
609. Reg. § 53.4941(e)-1(b)(2)(iii).

occurred.[610] An act of self-dealing *occurs* on the date on which all the terms and conditions of the transaction and the liabilities of the parties have been fixed.[611] If the self-dealing goes uncorrected and the additional (second-tier) tax is calculated, the valuation is equal to the highest value during the period of time the self-dealing continued uncorrected.

In one case, the need to correct an act of self-dealing gave rise to a peculiar series of transactions. Upon being advised by the IRS that a sale of real estate in 1971 by a disqualified person to a private foundation was an act of self-dealing that required correction, in 1973 the private foundation sold the land back to the disqualified person for the original sale price. Immediately after this transaction, the disqualified person transferred the property to a "straw person" for the same price, who in turn sold it back to the private foundation for the same price. In 1975, the land was transferred by the private foundation to the straw person for the same price. The court involved rejected the disqualified person's assertion that the transfers in 1973 were shams and thus should be ignored for tax purposes and that any taxes applicable with respect to the 1971 transaction were barred by the statute of limitations. Instead, the court held that the 1973 transfer of the land back to the disqualified person was intended to correct the initial act of self-dealing in 1971, and thus was separate from the other 1973 transaction. The court did not, at the time, rule on the question as to whether the retransfer of the land to the private foundation in 1973 via the straw person constituted an act of self-dealing.[612]

(d) Correcting the Transaction

With respect to a self-dealing transaction, *correction* means undoing the transaction that constituted the act of self-dealing to the extent possible, but, in any case, placing the private foundation in a financial position not worse than that in which it would be if the disqualified person(s) were dealing under the highest fiduciary standards.[613] For example, where a disqualified person sells property to a private foundation for cash, correction may be accomplished by recasting the transaction as a gift by returning the cash to the foundation.[614] A correction made in accordance with these rules is not a separate act of self-dealing.[615]

---

610. IRC § 4941(e)(2)(A); Reg. § 53.4941(e)-1(b)(3).
611. Reg. § 53.4941(e)-1(a)(2).
612. Dupont v. Commissioner, 74 T.C. 498 (1980).
613. IRC § 4941(e)(3); Reg. § 53.4941(e)-1(c)(1).
614. Reg. § 53.4941(e)-1(c)(1). This is an odd formulation, particularly in tax regulations; this type of transfer is hardly in the nature of a gift, if only because the transaction is not voluntary and there is no donative intent (see *Charitable Giving* § 2.1(a)).
615. Reg. § 53.4941(e)-1(c)(1).

§ 5.15 ISSUES ONCE SELF-DEALING OCCURS

Specific rules govern the required correction in the case of sales by or to the foundation, uses of property, and compensation arrangements.[616]

(i) Sales by the Foundation. In the case of a sale of property by a private foundation to a disqualified person for cash, undoing the transaction includes rescission of the sale where possible. The amount returned to the disqualified person may not exceed the lesser of the cash received by the private foundation or the fair market value of property received by the private foundation. For these purposes, fair market value is the lesser of the fair market value at the time of the self-dealing act or the fair market value at the time of the rescission. In addition to rescission, the disqualified person must pay to the private foundation any net profits the person realized after the original sale with respect to the property the person received from the sale. Thus, for example, the disqualified person must pay to the foundation any income derived by the person from the property the person received from the original sale "to the extent such income during the correction period exceeds the income derived by the foundation during the correction period from the cash which the disqualified person originally paid to the foundation."[617]

If, however, prior to the end of the correction period, the disqualified person sells the property in an arm's-length transaction to a bona fide purchaser (that is, one that is not a disqualified person), rescission is not required. In this circumstance, the disqualified person must pay to the foundation the excess (if any) of the greater of the fair market value of the property on the date on which correction of the act of self-dealing occurs or the amount realized by the disqualified person from the sale over the amount that would have been returned to the disqualified person if rescission had been required. In addition, the disqualified person is required to pay to the foundation any net profits the person realized.[618]

---

616. If a foundation manager or government official is excused from paying an initial tax, on the ground that the person participated in the act of self-dealing unknowingly (see § 5.15(a)(i), (v)), the act nonetheless occurred, yet there would not be a basis for imposition of an initial tax. Thus, there would not be any need to correct the act because the correction requirement comes into being, in connection with an additional tax, only where the initial tax is imposed. (There is, however, nothing in the statute or tax regulations on this point, and there is no known such holding in any IRS ruling.) If, moreover, aside from that point, the transaction was a transfer or use of the income or assets of the private foundation (see § 5.8), and the benefit was incidental or tenuous (see § 5.8(e)), correction would not be required because the receipt of an incidental or tenuous benefit is not an act of self-dealing in the first instance. This would also be the outcome in any other instance where a transaction is defined to not be an act of self-dealing (as opposed to merely an exception to a self-dealing tax).
617. Reg. § 53.4941(e)-1(c)(2)(i).
618. Reg. § 53.4941(e)-1(c)(2)(ii).

SELF-DEALING

(ii) Sales to the Foundation. In the case of a sale of property to a private foundation by a disqualified person for cash, undoing the transaction includes rescission of the sale where possible. The amount received from the disqualified person in accordance with the rescission must be the greater of the cash paid to the disqualified person, the fair market value of the property at the time of the original sale, or the fair market value of the property at the time of rescission. In addition to rescission, the disqualified person must pay to the private foundation any net profits the person realized after the original sale with respect to the consideration the person realized from the sale. Thus, for example, the disqualified person must pay to the foundation any income derived by the person from the cash the person received from the original sale to the extent the income during the correction period exceeds the income derived by the foundation during the correction period from the property that the disqualified person originally transferred to the foundation.[619]

If, however, prior to the end of the correction period, the foundation resells the property in an arm's-length transaction to a bona fide purchaser (that is, one that is not a disqualified person), rescission is not required. In this circumstance, the disqualified person must pay to the foundation the excess (if any) of the amount that would have been received from the disqualified person if rescission had been required over the amount realized by the foundation on resale of the property. In addition, the disqualified person is required to pay to the foundation any net profits the person realized.[620]

Caution should be exercised when attempting to effect correction of an act of self-dealing, so that the attempt is not itself regarded as an act of self-dealing. This nearly occurred when a disqualified person, in attempting to correct a self-dealing act in the form of a loan to him from a private foundation,[621] proposed to transfer to the private foundation a parcel of real estate with a fair market value equal to the amount of the loan. The IRS held that (1) the transfer would constitute self-dealing because, since the self-dealer's indebtedness to the private foundation would be canceled, the transaction would be a sale of property by the disqualified person to the private foundation, which would be an act of self-dealing,[622] and (2) the minimum standards for an authentic correction[623] would not be met because "it [would] be generally less advantageous to the foundation to receive the property than to have the loan repaid since it may be both difficult and costly for the foundation to

---

619. Reg. § 53.4941(e)-1(c)(3)(i).
620. Reg. § 53.4941(e)-1(c)(3)(ii).
621. IRC § 4941(d)(1)(B); see § 5.5.
622. IRC § 4941(d)(1)(A); see § 5.4(a).
623. Reg. § 53.4941(e)-1(c)(4).

§ 5.15 ISSUES ONCE SELF-DEALING OCCURS

convert the property to cash and thus restore its position." The IRS noted that a transfer of property could be an acceptable correction of a self-dealing loan transaction, where the property had substantially appreciated in value and could be readily converted into an amount of money in excess of the debt.[624]

In another example, a private foundation decided to cease operating a home for troubled children. The real estate involved, which had been improved by the foundation as part of its exempt use of the property, was being leased to the foundation by disqualified persons. Closing the home involved cancellation of the lease, which provided that improvements to the property would revert to the landlords. Generally, the transfer of the improvements to disqualified persons would be an act of self-dealing. The IRS, however, permitted the disqualified persons to pay to the foundation the greater of the fair market value of the transferred property at the date the correction occurred or the original cost of the property, thereby placing the foundation in the position of not having expended any of its charitable funds in connection with the property and preventing the disqualified persons from benefiting from the transaction.[625]

(iii) Loans. Where a loan has been made, the amount involved is the greater of the amount paid for the use of the funds (interest actually paid) or the fair market value of the use (prevailing market rate) for the period of time the money was lent.[626] To correct the self-dealing, the principal of the loan, plus the interest differential, must be repaid. For an interest-free demand loan, the fair value for use of the money would reasonably be equal to the prevailing federal short-term rate for funds. The authors have seen instances in which the foundation inadvertently paid expenses on behalf of a disqualified person, essentially making a loan that results in self-dealing. In this type of a situation, the excise tax is imposed on the interest factor, or the prevailing short-term interest rate times the amount of the expenses paid or loan advanced to the disqualified person.

(iv) Use of Property by Disqualified Person. In the case of the use by a disqualified person of property owned by a private foundation, undoing the transaction includes terminating the use. In addition, the disqualified person must pay the foundation (1) the excess (if any) of the fair market value of the use of the property over the amount paid by the disqualified person for the use until the termination, and (2) the excess (if any) of the amount that would have been paid by the disqualified person for the use of the property on or after the date of termination, for the period the disqualified person would have used the property (without regard to any further extensions or renewals

---

624. Rev. Rul. 81-40, 1981-1 C.B. 508, 509.
625. Priv. Ltr. Rul. 9601048.
626. Reg. § 53.4941(e)-1(b)(2)(ii).

of the period) if the termination had not occurred, over the fair market value of the use for the period.[627]

As to the first of these payment requirements, the fair market value of the use of property is the higher of the rate (that is, fair rental value per period in the case of use of property other than money or fair interest rate in the case of use of money) at the time of the act of self-dealing or the rate at the time of correction of the act of self-dealing. With respect to the second of these requirements, the fair market value of the use of property is the rate at the time of correction.[628]

(v) Use of Property by Private Foundation. In the case of the use by a private foundation of property owned by a disqualified person, undoing the transaction includes termination of the use of the property. In addition, the disqualified person must pay the foundation (1) the excess (if any) of the amount paid to the disqualified person for the use until the termination, over the fair market value of the use of the property, and (2) the excess (if any) of the fair market value of the use of the property for the period the foundation would have used the property (without regard to any further extensions or renewals of the period) if the termination had not occurred, over the amount that would have been paid to the disqualified person on or after the date of termination for the use for the period.[629]

In applying the first of these payment requirements, the fair market value of the use of property is the lesser of the rate at the time of the act of self-dealing or the rate at the time of correction of the act of self-dealing. With respect to the second of these requirements, the fair market value of the use of property is the rate at the time of the correction.[630]

(vi) Unreasonable Compensation. When excessive or unreasonable salaries have been paid to a disqualified person, the excess must be repaid to the foundation. Termination of the employment or independent contractor arrangement, however, is not required.[631]

(e) Court Jurisdiction as to Tax

The effectiveness of these additional taxes was temporarily in jeopardy as the result of U.S. Tax Court decisions holding that the court lacked the jurisdiction

---

627. Reg. § 53.4941(e)-1(c)(4)(i).
628. *Id.*
629. Reg. § 53.4941(e)-1(c)(5)(i).
630. *Id.*
631. Reg. § 53.4941(e)-1(c)(6).

§ 5.15 ISSUES ONCE SELF-DEALING OCCURS

to ascertain whether these taxes should be imposed. The matter first arose in 1978, in connection with the Tax Court's first self-dealing case,[632] where the court ordered the submission of briefs by the parties as to its authority to determine the 200 percent additional tax.[633] Subsequently, the court found that it did not have jurisdiction to determine whether this second-level tax should be imposed.[634]

The Tax Court reasoned that its jurisdiction[635] is generally confined to authority to redetermine the correct amount of a deficiency,[636] which is the amount by which the tax imposed (in this instance, by the various private foundation excise taxes)[637] exceeds the tax shown on the return.[638] In these cases, however, said the court, there is yet no deficiency for the court to redetermine, since the second-level tax cannot be imposed until the first-level tax is imposed and the act of self-dealing is corrected, and since the correction period does not expire until the court's decision is final.[639] By the time the second-level tax deficiency arises, the court held, the IRS has already mailed a deficiency notice as respects the act of self-dealing. But since the IRS is precluded from issuing a second deficiency notice for the same self-dealing act,[640] it is, the court held, barred from issuing a deficiency notice for a second-level tax.[641]

Legislation to resolve this unintended void in Tax Court jurisdiction was adopted by Congress in 1980.[642] Under this approach, the additional (second-tier) excise taxes will be imposed at the end of the *taxable period*, which begins with the event giving rise to the self-dealing tax and ends on the earliest of (1) the date a notice of deficiency with respect to the initial (first-tier) tax is mailed, (2) the date the initial (first-tier) tax is assessed if no deficiency notice is mailed, or (3) the date the taxable act is corrected.[643] Where the act or failure to act that gave rise to the additional (second-tier) tax is corrected within the

---

632. Adams v. Commissioner, 70 T.C. 373 (1978), *aff'd* (in an unpublished opinion), 688 F.2d 815 (Table) (2d Cir. 1982).
633. Adams v. Commissioner, 70 T.C. 466 (1978).
634. Adams v. Commissioner, 72 T.C. 81 (1979).
635. IRC § 7442.
636. IRC § 6214(a).
637. IRC Chapter 42.
638. IRC § 6211(a).
639. IRC § 4941(a)(4).
640. IRC § 6212(c).
641. Presumably, this line of reasoning also precluded Tax Court jurisdiction over cases involving similar taxes in IRC §§ 4942, 4943, 4944, 4945, 4947, 4951, and 4952. As respects IRC § 4945, the Tax Court so held (Larchmont Foundation, Inc. v. Commissioner, 72 T.C. 131 (1979)).
642. Pub. L. No. 96-596, 94 Stat. 3469.
643. IRC § 4941(e)(1); Reg. § 53.4941(e)-1.

correction period,[644] the tax will not be assessed, or if assessed will be abated, or if collected will be credited or refunded.[645] The collection period is suspended during any litigation.[646]

Subsequently, the Tax Court decided that the 1980 revisions in the statutory law modifying the additional (second-tier) tax rules are applicable to a docketed and untried case where the additional (second-tier) taxes have not been assessed.[647] The new rules apply with respect to taxes assessed after the date of enactment of the 1980 law, which was December 24, 1980; a statutory notice of deficiency was mailed to the person, alleged to be a self-dealer with a private foundation, on May 14, 1980. The court said that the litigant in the case "confused two distinct events by equating the mailing of the notice of deficiency with the assessment of the tax."[648] Noting that "no assessment can be made where a petition has been timely and validly filed in this Court until the decision of this Court becomes final,"[649] the court decided that the 1980 amendments "are applicable in this case to the second-tier taxes imposed by Section 4941 because such taxes have not been 'assessed' and the doctrine of res judicata clearly does not apply where the case has not yet been tried and decided on its merits."[650]

---

644. IRC § 4962(e); Reg. § 53.4962-1(d), (e).
645. IRC § 4961(a); Reg. § 53.4961-1.
646. IRC § 4961(c); Reg. § 53.4961-2.
647. Howell v. Commissioner, 77 T.C. 916 (1981).
648. *Id.* at 920.
649. IRC § 6213(a).
650. Howell v. Commissioner, 77 T.C. 916, 920 (1981). This opinion also rejected the contention that this interpretation of the 1980 law gave it a retroactive effect and that it is being applied in a manner in violation of due process requirements because its retroactivity was not clearly expressed by the setting of a fixed date. Also, The Barth Foundation v. Commissioner, 77 T.C. 1008 (1981); Applestein Foundation Trust v. Commissioner, 42 T.C.M. 1635 (1981); The Barth Foundation v. Commissioner, 42 T.C.M. 1580 (1981). In general, intent or motive is not required for self-dealing to be found. As the tax regulations state, the initial tax for self-dealing "shall be imposed on a disqualified person even though he had no knowledge at the time of the act that such act constituted self-dealing" (Reg. § 53.4941(a)-1(a)(1)). Also, compliance with state fiduciary law principles (see § 8.2) is not a defense for self-dealing. In denying a motion to compel the IRS to produce documents in an action to recover taxes imposed for acts of self-dealing, a court held that the language of IRC § 4941 and the regulations thereunder are "unambiguous" (Deluxe Check Printers, Inc. v. United States, 84-2 U.S.T.C. ¶ 9647 (Ct. Cl. 1984)). Another court held that the IRC § 4941 taxes are constitutional, in that they are not an impermissible extension of congressional taxing power (under U.S. Const. Art. 1 § 8, clause 1) nor a transgression of states' rights (U.S. Const., Tenth Am.), and that the underlying regulations are consistent with the statute, are reasonable, are not arbitrary, and are not unconstitutionally vague (Rockefeller v. United States, 572 F. Supp. 9 (E.D. Ark. 1982), *aff'd*, 718 F.2d 291 (9th Cir. 1983), *cert. den.*, 466 U.S. 962 (1984)). Also, Estate of Reis v. Commissioner, 87 T.C. 1016 (1986).

CHAPTER SIX

Mandatory Distributions

§ 6.1 **Mandatory Distribution Requirement** 256
    (a) Purpose and Policy 256
    (b) Distributable Amount 257

§ 6.2 **Minimum Investment Return** 258
    (a) General Calculation 258
    (b) Investment Assets 259
    (c) Future Interests or Expectancies 260
    (d) Exempt Function Assets 261
    (e) Acquisition Indebtedness 265

§ 6.3 **Determining Fair Market Value** 267
    (a) Cash 267
    (b) Readily Marketable Securities 267
    (c) Other Assets 270
    (d) Assets Held for Partial Year 272
    (e) Investment Frauds 272

§ 6.4 **Qualifying Distributions** 273
    (a) General Definition and Rules 273
    (b) Charitable Grants in General 275
    (c) Grants to Controlled Organizations and Other Foundations 276
        (i) Definition of Control 277
        (ii) Redistribution Rule 278
    (d) Grantor Reliance Standards 279
        (i) General Rules 279
        (ii) Grants to Certain Supporting Organizations 282
        (iii) No IRS Determination Letter 284
        (iv) Charities Under a Group Ruling 285
    (e) Grants to Foreign Organizations 286
    (f) Direct Charitable Expenditures 289
        (i) Exempt Function Assets 289
        (ii) Administrative Expenses 290
    (g) Set-Asides 292
        (i) Suitability Test Set-Asides 294
        (ii) Cash Distribution Test Set-Asides 296
        (iii) Court Order Set-Asides 299

§ 6.5 **Excise Taxes on Failure to Distribute Income** 300
    (a) Undistributed Income 300
    (b) Ordering Rule for Qualifying Distributions 300
    (c) Excess Qualifying Distributions 301
    (d) Excise Taxes on Undistributed Income 303
    (e) Valuation Mistakes 304
    (f) Exception for Certain Accumulations 305

§ 6.6 **History of the Mandatory Distribution Requirement** 305

§ 6.1 MANDATORY DISTRIBUTION REQUIREMENT

(a) Purpose and Policy

Prior to the enactment of the Tax Reform Act of 1969, the tax law provided that a charitable organization, including a private foundation, would lose its tax-exempt status if its aggregate accumulated income was "unreasonable in amount or duration in order to carry out the charitable, educational, or other purpose or function constituting the basis for [its] exemption. . . ."[1]

This statutory sanction was deemed ineffective by Congress with respect to private foundations, as the following indicates:

> Under prior law, if a private foundation invested in assets that produced no current income, then it needed to make no distributions for charitable purposes. As a result, while the donor may have received substantial tax benefits from his contribution currently, charity may have received absolutely no current benefit. In other cases, even though income was produced by the assets contributed to charitable organizations, no current distribution was required until the accumulations became "unreasonable." Although a number of court cases had begun to set guidelines as to the circumstances under which an accumulation became unreasonable, in many cases the determination was essentially subjective. Moreover, as was the case with self-dealing, it frequently happened that the only available sanction (loss of exempt status) either was largely ineffective or else was unduly harsh.[2]

Consequently, Congress, in enacting the Tax Reform Act of 1969, repealed this law and substituted rules imposing excise taxes on private foundations that fail to make a specified amount of distributions for charitable purposes each year.

To avoid the imposition of an excise tax,[3] private foundations are required to expend a certain amount, with respect to each tax year, for charitable purposes (whether in the form of grants to other charitable organizations or direct

---

1. Prior IRC § 504(a)(1) (repealed for tax years beginning after December 31, 1969) provided, in general, that an organization described in IRC § 501(c)(3) would be denied exemption under IRC § 501 for the tax year involved if amounts accumulated out of income during the tax year or any prior tax year and not actually paid out by the end of the tax year are unreasonable in amount or duration in order to carry out the charitable purpose or function constituting the basis for the organization's tax exemption. For instances of unreasonable accumulation, see Rev. Rul. 67-108, 1967-1 C.B. 127; Rev. Rul. 67-106, 1976-1 C.B. 126.
2. Staff of Joint Comm. on Internal Revenue Tax'n, 91st Cong., 2d Sess., General Explanation of the Tax Reform Act of 1969 36 (Comm. Print 1970); also Rev. Rul. 67-5, 1967-1 C.B. 123.
3. IRC § 4942(a), (b); see § 6.5.

charitable expenditures).[4] There are four of these mandatory distribution rules; the applicable one is dependent on the type of private foundation involved. The general mandatory distribution requirement that applies to nonoperating foundations is the subject of this chapter. The distribution rules for private operating foundations, conduit private foundations, common fund private foundations, and certain supporting organizations are discussed elsewhere.[5]

As noted, the general purpose underlying this mandatory payout requirement is to compel private foundations to make distributions for charitable purposes that are not solely dependent on a foundation's investment income. The mandatory payout requirement does not prohibit a private foundation from making investments with low- or no-current yield (such as an investment in raw land). When a private foundation invests in this manner, however, it periodically may have to sell some assets to meet the distribution requirements or distribute property for charitable purposes in satisfaction of the payout rules. Unless the value of its investments is increasing, the mandatory payout requirement will force a private foundation investing in this manner to deplete its asset base, thereby hastening the day when its investment approach causes its decline and perhaps ultimate extinction. This is one of the reasons the "death knell" provision in the Senate version of the 1969 tax legislation, by which foundations would have to terminate their existence after a stated period of years, was abandoned in favor of the mandatory distribution requirement.[6]

(b) Distributable Amount

A private foundation's mandatory distribution requirement principally is a function of the value of its noncharitable-use assets. The amount that must be annually distributed is determined by computing the private foundation's *distributable amount*, which is equal to the sum of its minimum investment return, plus certain additional amounts,[7] reduced by the sum of the foundation's unrelated business

---

4. With one exception, the federal tax law does not impose a mandatory distribution requirement on any other type of tax-exempt organization. The exception is the distribution requirement applicable to Type III nonfunctionally integrated supporting organizations (see § 15.6(g)). One court held that the IRC § 4942 taxes are constitutional, in that they are not an impermissible extension of congressional taxing power (under U.S. Const. Art. I § 8, clause 1) nor a violation of Const. Art. I § 9, the Fifth Amendment, or the Sixteenth Amendment (Stanley O. Miller Charitable Fund v. Commissioner, 89 T.C. 1112 (1987)).
5. See Chapter 3, § 6.4(c)(ii).
6. E.g., Fritchey, "Should Foundations Be Granted Immortality?" *The Washington Star*, Aug. 4, 1969, A-7; also § 8.2 for investment yield concepts.
7. These include (1) amounts received or accrued as repayments of amounts which were taken into account as a qualifying distribution for any tax year, (2) amounts received or accrued from the sale or other disposition of property to the extent that the acquisition of such property was taken into account as a qualifying distribution for any tax year, and (3) amounts set aside (see § 6.4(g)) to the extent it is determined that such amount is not necessary for the purposes for which it was set aside (IRC § 4942(f)(2)(C)).

income taxes[8] and the excise tax on net investment income[9] for that year.[10] A foundation's *minimum investment return* generally is an amount equal to 5 percent of the value of its noncharitable assets, reduced by any outstanding debt.[11] To avoid the excise tax on failure to distribute income, a foundation's distributable amount must be distributed timely in the form of one or more *qualifying distributions*.[12]

§ 6.2 MINIMUM INVESTMENT RETURN

(a) General Calculation

As noted, to avoid the excise tax on failure to distribute income, a private foundation generally must make annual qualifying distributions equal to its distributable amount. The calculation of a foundation's distributable amount depends in significant part on the foundation's minimum investment return. A foundation's *minimum investment return* generally is an amount equal to 5 percent of the average fair market value for the preceding year of its investment assets, reduced by the amount of any debt incurred to acquire the property.[13]

---

8. See Chapter 11.
9. See Chapter 10.
10. IRC § 4942(d); Reg. § 53.4942(a)-2(b)(1)(ii). For tax years beginning before January 1, 1982, a foundation's distributable amount was an amount equal to the greater of its minimum investment return or its adjusted net income (Reg. § 53.4942(a)-2(b)(1)(i)). Although the calculation of adjusted net income is no longer relevant for nonoperating foundations, it continues to apply in the context of qualifying for private operating foundation status (see § 3.1).

    The regulations defining a foundation's distributable amount also contain provisions requiring income paid or payable to a foundation by certain split-interest trusts (see § 3.7) be added to the distributable amount, notwithstanding that the statute does not (Reg. § 53.4942(a)-2(b)(2)). The U.S. Tax Court held that this provision in the regulation was an "unwarranted extension of a statutory position" (Ann Jackson Family Foundation v. Commissioner, 97 T.C. 534, 537 (1991), aff'd, 15 F.3d 917 (9th Cir. 1994)).
11. IRC § 4942(e); see § 6.2. A foundation's minimum investment return is thus a hypothetical return, created by applying the statutory rules, that bears no relationship to a foundation's actual investment returns or investment income.
12. IRC § 4942(c), (g); see § 6.4. This rule is often misstated, both in the popular literature and in court opinions. As an example of the latter, the United States Court of Appeals for the Ninth Circuit wrote that a private foundation "must give away at least 5% of its assets annually in order to retain its tax-exempt status" (Ann Jackson Family Foundation v. Commissioner, 15 F.3d 917, 921, n.10 (9th Cir. 1994), aff'g 97 T.C. 534 (1991)). The law, however, is that the distributable amount generally is an amount equal to 5 percent of the average value of the assets (the assets themselves need not be distributed) and (2) the sanction is the tax(es) for failure to meet the payout requirement (see § 6.5(d)), not revocation of tax-exempt status.
13. IRC § 4942(e)(1).

MANDATORY DISTRIBUTIONS

The 5 percent applicable percentage is reduced for a foundation with a short tax year.[14] If the foundation's tax year is less than 12 months, the percentage is calculated by multiplying the number of days in the year by 5 percent and dividing the result by 365. For example, assume a foundation is created on September 1 and chooses to close its tax year on December 31. Its minimum distribution amount for the first short year is calculated using a percentage of 1.79 percent.

Assume instead that a foundation is created on September 1 of one year, adopts a calendar year, but does not receive its first assets until March 1 of the following year. Because it has no assets for the first four months of its existence, it will have no payout requirement for its first partial year, but it would file a return. For its next (or second) year, it would have been in existence for a full year, even though it received assets in March. Thus, its payout percentage would be a full 5 percent.

The partial year allocation of the payout percentage also applies to an existing foundation that changes its year-end. Assume a foundation changes its financial reporting year-end from August 31 to December 31 by filing a short period annual information return for the four months ending in December.[15] The percentage applied to calculate its minimum distribution requirement for the next succeeding full calendar year would be 1.67 percent, as shown in the calculation above. The full 5 percent minimum distribution amount attributable to the foundation's last full year ending in August, however, would have to be distributed by the end of the foundation's short tax year (December 31).[16]

(b) Investment Assets

Because assets used (or held for use) directly in carrying out a private foundation's exempt purpose are excluded from the calculation of its minimum investment return, distinguishing investment assets from exempt function assets is essential when performing this calculation.

The minimum investment return is calculated based on the "excess of the fair market value of all assets of the foundation," other than those that represent future interests or expectations and exempt function assets.[17] Although referred to as an "investment return," neither the tax statutory law nor the regulations define the word *investment* for this purpose. Instead, all assets are included in the calculation unless they are specifically excluded. The value of these assets is reduced by a cash reserve for operations presumed to equal

---

14. Reg. § 53.4942(a)-2(c)(5)(iii).
15. See § 12.1(d)(i).
16. Rev. Rul. 74-315, 1974-2 C.B. 386.
17. Reg. § 53.4942(a)-2(c)(1)-(3), further discussed in § 6.2(c), (d).

§ 6.2 MINIMUM INVESTMENT RETURN

1½ percent of the total includible assets and acquisition indebtedness with respect to those assets.[18]

The typical private foundation investment portfolio of stocks, bonds, certificates of deposit, and rental properties forms the basis for calculating the minimum investment return. All types of funds—unrestricted, temporarily restricted, permanently restricted, deferred revenues, capital, endowment, and similar types of reserves—are included in the calculation, whether or not current income is produced by the property.

(c) Future Interests or Expectancies

Assets over which the foundation has no control and in which it essentially holds no present interest are not included in the minimum investment return calculation. These assets most often are not in the possession or under the control of the foundation, nor are they customarily included in the financial records or statements of the foundation. These future interests are:[19]

- Interests in charitable remainder trusts and other future interests in property (whether legal or equitable) created by someone other than the foundation. These interests are not included in the minimum investment return calculation until the intervening interests expire or are otherwise set apart for the foundation. If the foundation can take possession of the property at its will or to acquire it readily on giving notice, the property is included. The rules of constructive receipt for determining when a cash-basis taxpayer receives an item of income are relevant.

- The value of present interests in a trust, usually called a charitable lead trust,[20] is also excluded. Income attributable to principal placed in these trusts after May 26, 1969, is includible in the adjusted net income and impacts a private operating foundation's required distributions.[21]

- Pledges of money or other property to the foundation, irrespective of whether the pledges are legally enforceable.[22]

- Property bequeathed to the foundation is excluded while it is held by the decedent's estate. If the IRS treats the estate as terminated because

---

18. See § 6.2(d), (e).
19. Reg. § 53.4942(a)-2(c)(2).
20. See *Charitable Giving*, Chapter 14.
21. Reg. § 53.4942(a)-2(b)(2).
22. A stock option pledged to a foundation was not regarded by the IRS as an investment asset (Priv. Ltr. Rul. 8315060).

the period of administration is prolonged, the assets are treated as foundation assets from the time of the IRS determination.[23]

- Options to sell property that are not readily marketable, such as a nontransferable right to buy real estate, are excluded. Listed options to buy or sell marketable securities or other future obligations that are traded on a stock exchange that have ascertainable value, however, are included.

(d) Exempt Function Assets

Assets used (or held for use) directly in carrying out a private foundation's exempt purposes are excluded from the calculation of a foundation's minimum investment return.[24] An asset is excluded as an *exempt function asset* only if it is actually used or held for use directly by the foundation in the carrying out of its charitable or other exempt purpose(s). For example, an office building used by a private foundation's employees who manage the foundation's endowment funds is not being used directly by the foundation to carry out its exempt purposes. Likewise, assets that are held to produce income or for investment (for example, stocks, bonds, interest-bearing notes, endowment funds, or, generally [except as discussed later], leased real estate) are not exempt function assets, even though the income from such assets is used to carry out exempt purposes.[25]

Where property is used for both tax-exempt purposes and investment purposes, the value of such *dual-use property* must be allocated. Where exempt use represents 95 percent or more of the total use of the property, it is considered to be used exclusively for exempt purposes. If the exempt use of such property represents less than 95 percent of the total use, a reasonable allocation between such exempt and nonexempt use must be made.[26] For a building that is partly used by the foundation and partly rented to commercial tenants, the IRS has ruled that an allocation based on dividing the fair rental value of that portion of the building used for exempt purposes by the fair rental value of the entire building, rather than on the square footage, is appropriate.[27]

The most common types of exempt function assets excluded from the minimum investment return calculation follow.[28]

---

23. See Reg. § 1.641(b)-3, for circumstances under which the length of time for administering an estate is considered excessive.
24. IRC § 4942(e)(1)(A).
25. Reg. § 53.4942(a)-2(c)(3)(i).
26. *Id.*
27. Rev. Rul. 82-137, 1982-2 C.B. 303.
28. Reg. § 53.4942(a)-2(c)(3)(ii); also § 3.1, where the attributes of exempt function assets and direct program activities are discussed in regard to private operating foundations.

§ 6.2 MINIMUM INVESTMENT RETURN

Administrative assets, such as office furnishings, equipment, and supplies used by employees and consultants are exempt function assets, but only to the extent these assets are devoted to and used directly in the administration of the foundation's exempt activities.[29] The same property, if used by persons who manage a foundation's investment properties or endowments, is included in the minimum investment return calculation.

Real estate, including the portion of a *building* used by the foundation directly in its exempt activities.[30] Buildings of historical significance and land of environmental importance being held for ultimate use as a center for environmental and cultural conservation are examples of exempt function assets.[31] An island owned by a private foundation dedicated to preserve the natural ecosystems and historical and archaeological remains on the island was ruled by the IRS to be an exempt function asset. The island had no residential use and access was limited to invited public and private researchers.[32]

In one instance, a private foundation owned a sheep ranch and conducted educational, research, and development programs intended to enhance the quality and increase the production of range sheep in the western United States by developing and introducing into the market sheep with genetically desirable traits, and furthered educational and scientific inquiry concerning the production of sheep. It sold culled sheep to slaughterhouses, along with wool; this undertaking was operated at a significant loss. The foundation represented to the IRS that no portion of the ranch was held for the production of income or investment. The IRS ruled that the ranch was exempt function property so that the value of the property was not taken into account in determining the foundation's minimum investment return.[33]

In what may be the most controversial private letter ruling on this topic, the IRS ruled that a private operating foundation may exclude the value of a parcel of undeveloped land in computing its minimum investment return purposes because maintenance of the land in its natural state enhanced security for the charitable programs of the foundation and thus was being used directly in carrying out the foundation's tax-exempt purposes. This foundation's exempt activities consisted of maintenance of a historic residence, a visitor and garden center, cottages, and buildings for administrative offices, collections and archives, operations, security, wetlands, and storage. The undeveloped land is said in the ruling to defend foundation guests and employees in cases where "physical, biological, radiological, chemical, and

---

29. Reg. § 53.4942(a)-2(c)(3)(ii)(a).
30. Reg. § 53.4942((a)-2(c)(3)(ii)(b).
31. Priv. Ltr. Rul. 200136029.
32. Rev. Rul. 75-207, 1975-1 C.B. 361.
33. Priv. Ltr. Rul. 201315031.

human threats may avail themselves." The undeveloped land also provided a study site for schools conducting conservation education programs and was said to serve conservation purposes by contributing to sustainable conservation that improved the health of the community's ecosystem.[34]

Any *property leased* by a private foundation in carrying out its exempt purposes at no cost (or at a nominal rent) to the lessee or for a program-related purpose[35] is also considered to be an exempt function asset, such as the leasing of renovated apartments to low-income tenants at a low rental as part of the lessor foundation's program for rehabilitating a blighted portion of a community. For this purpose, the regulations do not contain a definition of the term *nominal*.[36] Land leased by a private foundation to a government instrumentality for nominal or no cost so that the instrumentality could harvest hay from property to feed livestock at its historic working farm park was considered by the IRS to qualify as an exempt function asset under this rule.[37]

In one instance, a private foundation received, by bequest, intellectual property used in connection with television programming and related educational services directed to the promotion of emotional and intellectual development of children. The foundation desired to license the property, on a no-royalty basis, to a public charity in furtherance of its charitable and educational purposes. The public charity agreed to pay any expenses necessary to protect and defend the property. The IRS ruled that the value of this intellectual property may be excluded from the foundation's asset base for purposes of computing its minimum investment return.[38]

Physical facilities used in a foundation's exempt activities are exempt function assets. Examples include paintings or other works of art owned by the foundation which are on public display, fixtures and equipment in classrooms, research facilities and related equipment which under the facts and circumstances serve a useful purpose in the conduct of such activities.[39] Thus, paintings loaned by a private foundation for display in museums, universities, and similar institutions are exempt function assets.[40]

---

34. Priv. Ltr. Rul. 201829003.
35. Within the meaning of IRC § 4944(c).
36. Reg. § 53.4942(a)-2(c)(3)(ii)(f). The asset test for private operating foundations, however, does define a rental property leased to carry out an exempt purpose. That definition states the property is considered to be exempt property if the rent is less than the amount that would be required to be charged in order to recover the cost of property purchase and maintenance.
37. Priv. Ltr. Rul. 201419017.
38. Priv. Ltr. Rul. 200414050.
39. Reg. § 53.4942(a)-2(c)(3)(ii)(c).
40. Rev. Rul. 74-498, 1974-2 C.B. 387.

§ 6.2   MINIMUM INVESTMENT RETURN

Reasonable cash balances necessary to cover current administrative expenses and other normal and current disbursements directly connected with a private foundation's exempt activities are excluded from the minimum investment return calculation. One and one-half percent of the included investment assets is presumed to be a reasonable cash balance, even if a smaller cash balance is actually maintained.[41] If the facts and circumstances indicate that the foundation needs to maintain a higher amount of cash to cover its expenses and disbursements, the foundation can claim a higher amount, but it must attach an explanation to its Form 990-PF supporting its position.[42]

An asset acquired by a private foundation for *future use in an exempt activity* may be treated as an exempt function asset where the foundation establishes to the satisfaction of the IRS that the asset's immediate use for an exempt purpose is not practical and the foundation has definite plans to commence using the asset in an exempt activity within a reasonable period of time. A private foundation may lease property acquired for future exempt use for a limited period of time during which arrangements are made for its conversion to the use for which it was acquired, provided such income-producing use of the property does not exceed a reasonable period of time (generally, limited to one year).[43]

A private foundation's interest in a program-related investment,[44] or in a functionally related business, is also excluded from the minimum investment return calculation.[45] A *functionally related business* is a trade or business that is not an unrelated trade or business,[46] or an activity that is carried on within a larger aggregate of similar activities or within a larger complex of other endeavors that is related (aside from the need of the organization for income or funds or the use it makes of the profits derived) to the exempt purposes of a private foundation.[47] For example, a restaurant and hotel operated

---

41. Reg. § 53.4942(a)-2(c)(3)(ii)(e), (iv).
42. Instructions for Form 990-PF (2022), Part IX, line 4.
43. Reg. § 53.4942(a)-2(c)(3)(i). Where the income-producing use continues beyond a reasonable period of time, and the acquisition of the property was taken into account as a qualifying distribution (see § 6.4), the property is treated as disposed of as of the time the income-producing use becomes unreasonable. If the property later is used by the foundation directly in carrying out its exempt purposes, a qualifying distribution in the amount of its then fair market value will be deemed to have been made as of the time such exempt use begins (Reg. § 53.4942(a)-2(c)(3)(i)).
44. As defined in IRC § 4944(c); see § 8.3.
45. Reg. § 53.4942(a)-2(c)(3)(ii)(d).
46. See § 11.1.
47. Reg. § 53.4942(a)-2(c)(3)(iii)(a); see § 7.3. An example of such a program-related investment is a private foundation's participation in the acquisition, planning, development, construction, marketing, and servicing of a low-income housing project (Priv. Ltr. Rul. 7823072).

within a larger community of historic value open to the public is a functionally related business, as is the publishing of a medical journal notwithstanding that revenue from advertising space sold in the journal may be subject to unrelated business income tax, because both activities are carried on within a larger complex of activities related to exempt purposes.[48] Because a business for which substantially all the work is performed by volunteers without compensation is excluded from the definition of an unrelated trade or business,[49] the business is treated as a functionally related business and assets used in the business are excluded for the minimum investment return calculation.[50]

A private foundation's ownership of stock in a corporation engaging in curatorial activities and management of the legacy of an artist (the foundation's founder) was considered by the IRS to be a functionally related business. The corporation was formed by an artist during his lifetime to house his artistic enterprise. This corporation acquired and stored the materials used by the artist in the creation of his artwork; handled the creation, fabrication, shipment, storage, and insurance of this work; and managed its sale, reproduction, and licensing. After the artist died, all of the stock of this corporation was to be transferred to a private operating foundation established by the artist. The function of the corporation would change to curatorial activities and management of the artist's legacy. The foundation would use these resources to increase public exposure and understanding of the broad scope of this artist's work, advance scholarship of his work, and encourage artists' involvement in civic issues by showing that they can change the world. The IRS ruled that this corporation was a functionally related business and that the value of the foundation's interest in the corporation would be excluded in calculating its minimum investment return.[51]

(e) Acquisition Indebtedness

In calculating the minimum investment return, a reduction in includible assets is allowed for the amount of any acquisition indebtedness with respect to such assets[52] without regard to the tax year in which the indebtedness was incurred.[53] In general, acquisition indebtedness is the unpaid amount of (1) the indebtedness incurred by a private foundation in acquiring or improving property, (2) the indebtedness incurred before the acquisition or improvement

---

48. Reg. § 53.4942(a)-2(c)(3)(iii)(b).
49. IRC § 513(a)(1); see § 11.2(d).
50. Rev. Rul. 76-85, 1976-1 C.B. 357.
51. Priv. Ltr. Rul. 201323029.
52. Determined under IRC § 514(c).
53. IRC § 4942(e)(1)(B); Reg. § 53.4942(a)-2(c)(1)(i).

§ 6.2 MINIMUM INVESTMENT RETURN

of property if the indebtedness would not have been incurred but for such acquisition or improvement, and (3) the indebtedness incurred after the acquisition or improvement of property if the indebtedness would not have been incurred but for such acquisition or improvement and the incurrence of such indebtedness was reasonably foreseeable at the time of such acquisition or improvement.[54]

Some foundations with significant portfolios of marketable securities enter into security lending transactions to enhance the return on those investment assets. The foundation lends its securities to a financial institution, which in return customarily provides the foundation with cash collateral equal to the value (or more) of the securities. The foundation retains its right to receive dividends or interest from the securities and also is entitled to invest the cash it holds as collateral. This obligation to return collateral security is not treated as acquisition indebtedness.[55]

A private foundation, pursuant to a securities lending and guaranty agreement with a bank, loaned certain securities in its investment portfolio to approved borrowers. The bank served as the custodian in these transactions, receiving collateral, which it invested in commingled cash management funds. The foundation could not acquire access to, sell, or pledge this collateral, which was to be returned to the borrower, except in the case of a default. On termination of a lending arrangement, the foundation was entitled to receive back from the borrower either the original securities or securities identical to those loaned. The foundation, as compensation, received a percentage of the earnings on the collateral.

The private foundation's auditors determined that, for financial statement purposes, the private foundation's transfers of securities to the bank in conjunction with the securities lending transactions must be disclosed on the foundation's financial statements by means of offsetting asset and liability entries on the balance sheet. Thus, the foundation reflects the collateral received and the corresponding obligation to return it pursuant to these transactions as assets and liabilities on its financial statements.

The IRS ruled that this foundation, in computing its minimum investment return, did not have to include as an asset the collateral received in

---

54. IRC § 514(c)(1); see § 11.4(a).
55. IRC § 514(c)(8)(C). Because there is no acquisition indebtedness, there is no debt-financed property, which means the exclusion from unrelated business taxable income under IRC § 512(b)(1) for payments with respect to securities loans applies to this type of securities lending transaction. For these purposes, *payments with respect to securities loans* include all amounts received with respect to a security transferred by the owner to another person including income from collateral security for such loan (IRC § 512(a)(5)(iii)).

MANDATORY DISTRIBUTIONS

connection with its securities lending program, inasmuch as the collateral amount was offset by the requirement to return the collateral on termination of the lending transaction.[56]

§ 6.3 DETERMINING FAIR MARKET VALUE

To calculate its minimum investment return, a private foundation must determine the aggregate fair market value of all of its investment assets.

(a) Cash

Cash is valued by taking the average of the cash on hand at the beginning and end of each month.[57] This prevents a private foundation from easily manipulating its cash balance. The calculation of average cash balances adds together the 24 beginning and ending month-end balances for all accounts and divides the result by 24. Thus, funds that are not on hand on either of such days will be excluded from the cash balance computation.[58]

(b) Readily Marketable Securities

Securities for which market quotations are readily available must be valued monthly, using any reasonable and consistent method.[59] Securities include common and preferred stocks, bonds, and mutual fund shares.[60] Market quotations are considered readily available for securities: (1) listed on the New York Stock Exchange, the American Stock Exchange, or any city or regional exchange in which quotations appear on a daily basis, including foreign securities listed on a recognized foreign national or regional exchange; (2) regularly traded in a national or regional over-the-counter market, for which published quotations are available; and (3) locally traded, provided quotations can readily be obtained from established brokerage firms.[61]

For purposes of allowing a charitable contribution deduction for the fair market value of donated shares (rather than limiting the deduction to the donor's basis in the shares),[62] the IRS concluded that stock traded on

---

56. Priv. Ltr. Rul. 200329049.
57. Reg. § 53.4942(a)-2(c)(4)(ii).
58. Priv. Ltr. Rul. 8909037.
59. Reg. § 4942(a)-2(c)(4)(i)(a).
60. Reg. § 53.4942(a)-2(c)(4)(v).
61. Reg. § 4942(a)-2(c)(4)(i)(a).
62. See § 14.4, 14.5.

the Over-the-Counter Bulletin Board is stock that is regularly traded in the national or regional over-the-counter market, for which published quotations are available. The IRS noted "the ease with which anyone can access current and historical market quotations on the OTCBB internet site and other financial internet sites."[63] Likewise, securities traded on OTCBB should constitute readily marketable securities for monthly valuation purposes.

The quotation system can be one of a variety of methods, again, as long as a consistent pattern is followed. The following examples are given in the regulations: (1) the classic method, averaging the high and low quoted price on a particular day each month, which could be the first, fifth, last, or any other day; (2) a formula averaging the first, middle, and last day closing prices for each month; and (3) the average of the bid and asked price for over-the-counter stocks or funds on a consistent day, using the nearest day if no quote is available on the regular day.[64]

In the case of securities that are held in trust for, or on behalf of, a private foundation by a bank or other financial institution which values such securities periodically by use of a computer, a foundation may determine the correct value of such securities by use of such computer pricing system, provided the IRS has accepted the computer pricing system as a valid method for valuing securities for federal estate tax purposes.[65] The regulations do not provide further guidance on how such IRS acceptance is obtained, and there is no other published IRS guidance on the topic. Thus, before relying on this rule, a private foundation would be advised to obtain written confirmation from the financial institution that its computer pricing system has been accepted by the IRS as a valid valuation method for federal estate tax purposes.

Blockage discounts of up to 10 percent are permitted to reduce the valuation of securities when a foundation can show that the quoted market prices do not reflect fair market value for one or more of the following reasons: (1) the block of securities is so large in relation to the volume of actual sales on the existing market that it could not be liquidated in a reasonable time without depressing the market, (2) sales of the securities are few or sporadic in nature, and the shares are in a closely held corporation, or (3) the sale of the securities would result in a forced or distress sale because the securities cannot be offered to the public without first being registered with the SEC.[66]

---

63. Priv. Ltr. Rul. 200702031.
64. Reg. § 53.4942(a)-2(c)(4)(i)(e).
65. Reg. § 4942(a)-2(c)(4)(i)(d).
66. IRC § 4942(c)(2); Reg. § 53.4942(a)-2(c)(4)(i)(c).

MANDATORY DISTRIBUTIONS

Essentially, a foundation is permitted to use the price at which the securities could be sold by an underwriter outside the normal market. The blockage rule recognizes that if the securities to be valued represent a controlling interest, either actual or effective, in a going business, the price at which other lots change hands may have little relation to the true value of the securities. The IRS concluded that a foundation that did not previously use a blockage discount in valuing its securities but currently wished to do so, and do so retroactively, may recompute its minimum investment return and distributable amounts for the years that are still open under the statute of limitations.[67]

Unlisted securities in which no one "makes a market," so that price quotations are not available, are valued annually like other assets described below, and are not subject to the 10 percent limitation on value reduction due to blockage.[68] An exception to annual valuation of unlisted securities applies, however, in the case of a private foundation that owns voting stock of an issuer of unlisted securities and has, alone or together with disqualified persons or another private foundation, effective control[69] of the issuer. In this situation, to the extent that the issuer's assets consist of shares of listed securities issues, such assets shall be valued monthly (like readily marketable securities) based on market quotations and any blockage discount (if appropriate). Thus, for example, suppose a private foundation and a disqualified person together own all of the unlisted voting stock of a holding company, which in turn holds a portfolio of securities that are listed on the New York Stock Exchange. In determining the net worth of the holding company, the underlying portfolio securities must be valued monthly by reference to market quotations unless the blockage discount rule applies.[70]

---

67. Priv. Ltr. Rul. 9233031.
68. The IRS initially took the position in a letter ruling that securities that are restricted from trade on an exchange because of the federal securities laws are not securities for which market quotations are readily available and thus are other assets that may be valued annually without limitation on the use of a blockage discount (Priv. Ltr. Rul. 7933084). This ruling was later revoked, however, without meaningful explanation, thus creating some uncertainty regarding the valuation of restricted securities (Priv. Ltr. Rul. 8029109). The initial ruling relied on guidelines promulgated by the IRS for the valuation of securities that cannot be immediately sold because they are restricted from sale pursuant to the federal securities laws (Rev. Rul. 77-287, 1977-2 C.B. 319; also Rev. Rul. 78-367, 1978-2 C.B. 249). Subsequently, the IRS ruled that stock that was not registered on an exchange and was subject to voting and transferability restrictions was subject to the provisions regarding the valuation of other assets (see § 6.3(c)), not the provisions governing the valuation of securities for which market quotations are readily available (Priv. Ltr. Rul. 8650091).
69. Within the meaning of Reg. § 53.4943-3(b)(3)(ii).
70. Reg. § 53.4942(a)-2(c)(4)(iv)(a).

§ 6.3 DETERMINING FAIR MARKET VALUE

(c) Other Assets

The fair market value of assets other than cash, marketable securities, and common trust fund interests[71] must be determined annually.[72] For purposes of the foregoing, commonly accepted methods of valuation must be used in making an appraisal.[73] Valuations made in accordance with the estate tax valuation principles[74] constitute acceptable methods of valuation.[75]

The annual determination of fair market value may be made by employees of the private foundation or by any other person, without regard to whether the person is a disqualified person with respect to the foundation. A valuation made in this regard, if accepted by the IRS, is valid only for the tax year for which it is made. Thus, a new valuation made in accordance with this rule is required for the succeeding tax year.[76] In the case of an asset that is required to be valued on an annual basis, the asset may be valued as of any day in the private foundation's tax year, provided the foundation follows a consistent practice of valuing the asset as of that date in all tax years.[77]

In the case of an interest in real property, a private foundation has the option to determine the fair market value of the property, including any improvements, on a five-year basis rather than on an annual basis. This value must be determined by means of a certified, independent appraisal made in writing by a qualified person who is neither a disqualified person with respect to nor an employee of the private foundation involved. The certification must state that, in the opinion of the appraiser, the values placed on appraised assets were ascertained in accordance with valuation principles regularly employed in making appraisals of the property using all reasonable valuation methods. If these requirements are met, the valuation may be used by the foundation for the tax year in which it is made and for each of the succeeding four tax years. A valuation properly made pursuant to this five-year rule may be replaced by

---

71. Annual valuation is not required with respect to a participating interest in a common trust fund (as defined in IRC § 584) established and administered under a plan providing for the periodic valuation of participating interests during the fund's tax year and the reporting of such valuations to participants (Reg. § 53.4942(a)-2(c)(4)(iii)). The foundation's interest in such a fund may be based upon the average of the valuations reported to the foundation during its tax year (*id.*).
72. Reg. § 53.4942(a)-2(c)(4)(iv)(a).
73. Reg. § 53.4942(a)-2(c)(4)(iv)(c).
74. IRC § 2031.
75. Reg. § 53.4942(a)-2(c)(4)(iv)(c).
76. Reg. § 53.4942(a)-2(c)(4)(iv)(a). The tax regulations in this context are silent as to the content of this annual valuation, although surely the valuation must be a reasoned one. Additionally, the applicable regulation makes it clear that an annual valuation may be rejected by the IRS (although there are no published IRS procedures on this point).
77. Reg. § 53.4942(a)-2(c)(4)(vi)(a).

a subsequent qualifying five-year valuation or with an annual valuation; the most recent valuation of the assets must be used in computing the foundation's minimum investment return. The valuation must be made no later than the last day of the first tax year; any subsequent five-year valuation must be similarly made. A valuation, if properly made, will not be disturbed by the IRS during the five-year period for which it applies, even if the actual fair market value of the property changes during the period.[78]

Valuations of mineral interests typically are based on reserve studies conducted by independent petroleum evaluation engineers. These studies are customarily updated every five years, as is the case with the real estate surface and buildings. It also is a common industry practice to value a mineral interest at anywhere from two to three times annual income, particularly where the annual income is relatively small and formal appraisals would be unduly expensive. In one situation, however, a court rejected the annual income approach in favor of a more sophisticated appraisal.[79]

The IRS found in two instances that real estate held in a wholly owned title holding company[80] and a limited liability partnership[81] could be valued using a qualified appraisal made every five years, according to the general rule for real estate valuation, even though the form of ownership was essentially an "other asset" required to be valued annually.

Valuation of computers, office equipment, and other tangible assets used in managing investment activity can be determined from the local newspaper's classified advertisements for used equipment, or by obtaining a quotation from a used office furniture dealer.

The value of a whole-life insurance policy is its cash surrender value.

Notes and accounts receivable are included at their net realizable value, or at their face value discounted for any uncollectible portion. Though it seems logical that a note receivable for which the foundation receives monthly principal payments that reduce the principal amount of the loan be valued on a monthly basis, the regulations provide for annual valuation.[82]

Collectibles such as gold, paintings, and gems are valued under estate tax valuation rules.

Valuation of so-called alternative investments, such as hedge funds, offshore partnerships, and stock investments, for purposes of calculating the foundation's minimum investment return, is often a challenge. Hedge funds and partnerships often hold several types of investments, including marketable

---

78. Reg. § 53.4942(a)-2(c)(4)(iv)(b).
79. Estate of Smith v. Commissioner, 65 T.C.M. 2808 (1993).
80. Priv. Ltr. Rul. 9347041.
81. Priv. Ltr. Rul. 200548026.
82. Reg. § 53.4942(a)-2(c)(4)(iv).

securities and options (which would be valued monthly if held outside of the partnership) as well as unlisted venture capital stocks. Unless the fund is itself readily marketable, such as a publicly traded partnership, the regulations require that investments in such funds and partnerships be valued annually,[83] notwithstanding that a foundation may receive valuations more than once a year (for example, quarterly).

Thus, an interest in a non-publicly traded investment partnership is valued annually in accordance with estate tax valuation principles.[84] When the terms of the partnership restrict withdrawals from the partnership or sale of the interest, the value may be less than the fair market value of the underlying assets. In considering valuation of a partnership controlled by a private foundation and its disqualified persons, the IRS observed that a "taxpayer's profits interest in a partnership is analogous to the voting stock of an issuer of unlisted securities."[85] A discount due to lack of marketability may be appropriate, without regard to the 10 percent limitation on value reduction for blockage, which applies only to securities for which market quotations are readily available.[86]

(d) Assets Held for Partial Year

An asset held by a private foundation for only part of a year is taken into account for purposes of the foundation's minimum investment return by multiplying the fair market value of the asset (as otherwise determined under the applicable regulations) by a fraction that serves to reduce the amount included to account for the partial-year holding. The numerator of this fraction is the number of days in the tax year that the foundation held the asset; the denominator is the number of days in the tax year.[87]

(e) Investment Frauds

Some private foundations faced valuation concerns in calculating their distribution requirement, given what turned out to have been a gross overvaluation of assets due to investment fraud during 2008 and before. A report from The New York State Bar Association Tax Section[88] stated that a "critical initial question" relevant to the payout rules "is whether a foundation should go

---

83. Reg. § 53.4942(a)-2(c)(4)(iv)(a).
84. IRC § 2031.
85. Priv. Ltr. Rul. 200548026.
86. *Id*. See § 6.3(b).
87. Reg. § 53.4942(a)-2(c)(4)(vii). For purposes of applying this rule in the case of a newly created private foundation, the date on which the foundation is created should be used as the first day of its first tax year, not the date on which it first receives assets.
88. See § 8.4 for additional aspects of this issue.

back in time and measure its income and asset values for prior years based on current knowledge and information or whether the foundation should view prior year income and asset values as correct and deal with Ponzi scheme losses only in the year of discovery."

This report posed questions: How are Ponzi scheme losses to be taken into account in calculating a foundation's distributable amount? How are prior year investments to be valued? May foundations amend prior year returns, in order to recalculate asset values for prior years, taking into account the fraud (theft) that was discovered in 2008 (or later)? The report observed that this amendment approach "could provide significant relief [for] a number of private foundations." If the IRS accepted this recalculation of asset values and amendment of prior year returns, it would likely generate a significant carryover of excess distributions for these foundations from these years.[89]

§ 6.4 QUALIFYING DISTRIBUTIONS

As noted, to avoid the excise tax on failure to distribute income, a private foundation generally must make annual qualifying distributions equal to its distributable amount.[90]

(a) General Definition and Rules

A *qualifying distribution* includes:[91]

1. Any amount, including reasonable and necessary administrative expenses, paid to accomplish one or more charitable or other permitted purposes,[92] other than a contribution or grant to:

   a. An organization controlled by the distributing private foundation or by one or more disqualified persons with respect to the private foundation (unless a redistribution rule is satisfied),

   b. A private foundation that is not a private operating foundation (unless a redistribution rule is satisfied),

   c. A Type III supporting organization that is not a functionally integrated Type III supporting organization,[93] or

---

89. See § 6.5(c).
90. See § 6.1(b).
91. IRC § 4942(g); Reg. § 53.4942(a)-3(a)(2).
92. That is, a purpose described in IRC § 170(c)(2)(B). An expenditure made for any other purpose is a taxable expenditure (see IRC § 4945(d)(5); see § 9.8).
93. See § 15.6(g).

§ 6.4 QUALIFYING DISTRIBUTIONS

    d. A Type I supporting organization,[94] a Type II supporting organization,[95] or a functionally integrated Type III supporting organization[96] if a disqualified person with respect to the private foundation controls the organization or a supporting organization with respect to it or if the IRS determines by regulation that a distribution to the organization otherwise is inappropriate;

2. Any amount paid to acquire an asset used or held for use directly in carrying out one or more charitable or other permitted purposes;
3. Certain set-asides;[97] and
4. Program-related investments.[98]

The amount of a qualifying distribution of property is the fair market value of such property as of the date such qualifying distribution is made. The amount of a private foundation's qualifying distributions must be determined solely on the cash receipts and disbursements method of accounting.[99]

Qualifying distributions may be paid in cash or other property. The fair market value of noncash assets or the distributable amount of dispersal is treated as a qualifying distribution.[100] Because property the foundation receives by gift retains the same tax basis as that of the donor, some private foundations have assets with a value significantly higher than the basis. These appreciated noncash assets held for investment purposes, particularly marketable securities or real estate, provide a tax-planning opportunity. The excise tax on net investment income does not include the capital gain inherent in property that is distributed. Thus, it is sometimes desirable for the foundation to grant property, rather than selling the property to raise cash to make the distribution in cash.[101]

When an asset previously used by the foundation in its own exempt activities is subsequently granted to another charity, the grant is still a qualifying distribution. If the foundation had previously considered the purchase of an asset as a qualifying distribution, only the current value of the distributed asset in excess of the purchase cost is counted as a qualifying distribution.[102]

---

94. See § 15.6(e).
95. See § 15.6(f).
96. See § 15.6(g).
97. See § 6.4(g).
98. As defined in IRC § 4944(c) (Reg. § 53.4942(a)-3(a)(2)(i); see § 8.3).
99. Reg. § 53.4942(a)-3(a)(1).
100. E.g., Priv. Ltr. Rul. 201335020.
101. Rev. Rul. 79-375, 1979-2 C.B. 389.
102. H. Fort Flowers Foundation, Inc. v. Commissioner, 72 T.C. 399 (1979).

If a private foundation uses *borrowed funds* to make expenditures for a tax-exempt purpose, a qualifying distribution is made when the grant or expense is paid, not when the debt is created nor when the debt is repaid.[103] Interest on indebtedness incurred to enable the foundation to make charitable distributions is not itself treated as a qualifying distribution.[104]

A *pledge* to make a grant in the future is not a qualifying distribution. The use of the word *paid* in the statute defining a qualifying distribution means that a distribution is counted in the year in which it is paid out in cash or property, not the year in which a grant is approved or promised.[105] Thus, a foundation that pledged a grant to a public charity in support of a museum building program could not count the grant as a qualifying distribution until the funds were actually paid. Holding the funds for a three-year period before construction begins to enable the foundation to earn interest precluded treating the funds as distributed in the year the pledge is made.[106] Sometimes such a pledge itself can qualify as a set-aside distribution.[107]

From time to time, the IRS issues private letter rulings concerning the eligibility of a distribution by a private foundation as a qualifying distribution.[108]

(b) Charitable Grants in General

Grants made directly to public charities,[109] for general support or for a wide range of specific charitable purposes, comprise by far the majority of qualifying distributions made by private foundations. A foundation may also make a qualifying distribution to a single-member limited liability company that is a disregarded entity owned solely by a public charity that is not controlled by the private foundation or one or more disqualified persons with respect to the foundation.[110]

---

103. Reg. § 53.4942(a)-3(a)(4)(i).
104. Reg. § 53.4942(a)-3(a)(4)(iii).
105. Rev. Rul. 79-319, 1979-2 C.B. 388; also Rev. Rul. 77-7, 1977-1 C.B. 354; e.g., Tech. Adv. Mem. 8839003; also Priv. Ltr. Rul. 8750006, concerning reporting deferred grant awards.
106. Rev. Rul. 79-319, 1979-2 C.B. 388.
107. See § 6.5(g).
108. E.g., Priv. Ltr. Ruls. 200041037, 201029040.
109. See Chapter 15.
110. INFO 2010-0052. As a disregarded entity generally receives the benefit of its owners tax-exempt status and public charity classification, a private foundation need not exercise expenditure responsibility over a grant to a disregarded entity of a public charity (*id.*; see §§ 9.4, 9.7). This position of the IRS was augmented by more formal guidance when the agency held that contributions to a single-member limited liability company, that is a disregarded entity, where the limited liability company is wholly owned and controlled by a U.S. charity, are deductible, with the gift treated as being made to a branch or division of the charity (Notice 2012-52, 2012-35 I.R.B. 317). See *Tax-Exempt Organizations* §§ 4.1(b)(ii), 32.4.

§ 6.4 QUALIFYING DISTRIBUTIONS

A grant by a private foundation to an unrelated private operating foundation also constitutes a qualifying distribution.[111]

Under current law, a grant to a donor-advised fund at a community foundation or other public charity constitutes a qualifying distribution, provided the grantee is not controlled by the grantor foundation or one or more disqualified persons with respect to it, notwithstanding that the private foundation's governing board retains the ability to make recommendations as to the subsequent granting of the money.[112]

A grant or other expenditure made to a noncharitable organization can be a qualifying distribution so long as the payment is made for a charitable or other permitted purpose.[113] Private foundation grants to tax-exempt social fraternities specifically earmarked for educational purposes have been condoned in a number of IRS letter rulings. One such grant was paid to build a study room in the chapter house that would contain exclusively educational equipment and furniture, along with computers linked to the university's mainframe. The private foundation was entitled to the return of any funds not so expended and retained the right to inspect the room annually.[114]

Grants to individuals for charitable purposes, such as scholarships, are also qualifying distributions.[115]

(c) Grants to Controlled Organizations and Other Foundations

A grant or contribution is not a qualifying distribution if it is made (1) to another private foundation that is not a private operating foundation, or (2) to an organization controlled by the distributing private foundation or by one

---

111. IRC § 4942(g)(1)(A)(ii). Nonetheless, unless the grantee is an exempt operating foundation (see § 10.7), the grantor private foundation must exercise expenditure responsibility over the grant (see § 9.5).
112. E.g., Priv. Ltr. Rul. 8836033. Form 990-PF asks whether a foundation made a distribution to a donor-advised fund over which the foundation or a disqualified person had advisory privileges; if it did, it is required to submit an attachment with the return stating whether the foundation treated the distribution as a qualifying distribution, and explain how the distributions will be used to accomplish an IRC § 170(c)(2)(B) purpose (Instructions for Form 990-PF (2022), Part VI-A, line 12). For a discussion of proposed legislation (and a proposal by the administration) that would prevent (or restrict) distributions to a donor-advised fund by a private foundation from being treated as qualifying distributions for purposes of meeting a foundation's annual payout requirement, see § 16.10.
113. That is, for purposes described in IRC § 170(c)(2)(B). Such grants to noncharitable organization for charitable purposes require the exercise of expenditure responsibility (see § 9.7).
114. Priv. Ltr. Rul. 9025073.
115. E.g., Leckie Scholarship Fund v. Commissioner, 87 T.C. 251, 255 n.7 (1986). Certain grants to individuals for travel, study, or other similar purposes may require preapproval by the IRS to avoid being treated as a taxable expenditure (see § 9.3).

MANDATORY DISTRIBUTIONS

or more disqualified persons with respect to the private foundation, unless a redistribution rule is satisfied.

(i) Definition of Control. For purposes of determining whether an organization is *controlled* (directly or indirectly) by a distributing foundation or one or more disqualified persons with respect to the foundation,[116] the requisite *control* exists if any of such persons may, by aggregating their votes or positions of authority, require the donee organization to make an expenditure, or prevent the donee organization from making an expenditure, regardless of the method by which the control is exercised or exercisable. Control is determined without regard to any conditions imposed upon the donee organization as part of the distribution or any other restrictions accompanying the distribution as to the manner in which the distribution is to be used unless such conditions are material restrictions or conditions that prevent the donee organization from freely and effectively employing the distributed assets.[117]

In general, it is the donee, not the distribution, that must be controlled by the distributing private foundation. Thus, the furnishing of support to an organization and the consequent imposition of budgetary procedures upon that organization with respect to such support shall not in itself be treated as subjecting that organization to the distributing foundation's control. Such budgetary procedures include expenditure responsibility requirements.[118] The controlled organization need not be a private foundation; it may be any type of exempt or nonexempt organization including a school, hospital, operating foundation, or social welfare organization.[119]

The existence of overlapping directors is insufficient to establish control for these purposes if the majority of the members of the donee organization do not have any relationship of authority with the grantor foundation.[120] In contrast, where four of the six directors of two private foundations served as trustees of a charitable trust, the foundations were considered to control the trust.[121]

If employees of a disqualified person (for example, a corporation that is itself a disqualified person with respect to a foundation) are directors of an

---

116. IRC § 4942(g)(1)(A)(i).
117. Within the meaning of Reg. § 1.507-2(a)(7); see § 13.3(b), (c). E.g., Priv. Ltr. Rul. 9014004.
118. See § 9.7.
119. Reg. § 53.4942(a)-3(a)(3).
120. E.g., Priv. Ltr. Rul. 7828012; also Priv. Ltr. Rul. 8232051 (right to appoint two of nine directors); Priv. Ltr. Rul. 8606040 (right to appoint three of eighteen directors and no veto power over decisions made by the donee's governing body); Priv. Ltr. Rul. 8812046 (right to appoint two of five directors); and Priv. Ltr. Rul. 9551037 (one of twelve directors in common).
121. Priv. Ltr. Rul. 8713056.

organization, the disqualified person's employees will be considered in determining whether one or more disqualified persons indirectly controls 50 percent or more of the voting power of the organization's governing body. Where two of an organization's four directors were also employees of a corporation that was itself a disqualified person (because more than 35 percent of its voting power is owned by a disqualified person), and one of the other four directors was a substantial contributor (and therefore a disqualified person in their own right), the IRS ruled that the organization was indirectly controlled by disqualified persons.[122]

(ii) Redistribution Rule. A grant or contribution to another nonoperating private foundation or to a controlled charitable organization may be treated as a qualifying distribution if a redistribution rule is satisfied. This *redistribution rule* requires the following requirements to be met:[123]

1. No later than the close of the first tax year after the tax year in which the contribution is received, the recipient organization makes a distribution equal to the amount of the contribution that is treated as a qualifying distribution.

2. The recipient organization treats the redistributed amount as a distribution out of corpus,[124] or it would so be treated if the recipient organization were a nonoperating private foundation.

3. The donor private foundation obtains adequate records or other sufficient evidence from the recipient organization (such as a statement by an appropriate officer, director, or trustee of the recipient organization) showing that the recipient made a redistribution in accordance with the first two requirements and indicating the name and addresses of the recipients of the redistributions and the amount received by each.[125]

---

122. Rev. Rul. 80-207, 1980-2 C.B.193. This ruling applied the control test for supporting organizations, which, similarly to the control test for qualifying distributions, provides that a supporting organization will be considered to be controlled directly or indirectly by one or more disqualified persons if the voting power of such persons is 50 percent or more of the total voting power of the organization's governing body or if one or more of such persons has the right to exercise veto power over the actions of the organization (Reg. § 1.509(a)-4(j)).
123. IRC § 4942(g)(3); Reg. § 53.4942(a)-3(c). This regulation contains five examples that should be reviewed by a foundation claiming a qualifying distribution based on a donee's redistribution of its grant.
124. IRC § 4942(h). E.g., Rev. Rul. 78-45, 1978-1 C.B. 378. Compliance with this pass-through (out-of-corpus) distribution rule is nicely illustrated in Priv. Ltr. Rul. 201719004. Also Priv. Ltr. Rul. 201437014, involving a situation where a private foundation made start-up and ongoing grants to a private operating foundation, which it controlled.
125. Reg. § 53.4942(a)-3(c)(1)(ii).

For purposes of satisfying the redistribution rule, a grantee organization may elect to treat as a current distribution out of corpus any amount distributed in a prior tax year that was treated as a distribution out of corpus,[126] provided that the amount has not been availed of for any other purpose (such as a carryover or redistribution), the corpus distribution occurred within the preceding five years, and the amount is not subsequently availed of for any other purpose. This election to use prior-year excess distributions[127] for this purpose must be made by attaching a statement to the private foundation's Form 990-PF for the tax year for which the election is to apply. This statement must contain a declaration by an appropriate foundation manager that the foundation is making this election and it must specify that the distribution was treated as a distribution out of corpus in a designated prior tax year (or years).[128]

A private foundation may also make this election to meet the redistribution requirements[129] necessary to make a charitable contribution to the foundation eligible for the 50 percent limitation on charitable contributions by an individual[130] and prevent it from being subject to the basis limitations on donations of appreciated property to a nonoperating private foundation.[131]

If all or part of the funds are not redistributed by the recipient organization by the next year-end, the grantor's distributable amount for the subsequent year must be increased. Essentially, a grant treated as qualifying in the year it is paid because of expected redistribution by the grantee is added back in the subsequent year in which the failure occurred. If more than one payment was granted, a proration is made.[132]

(d) Grantor Reliance Standards

(i) General Rules. For purposes of determining whether an organization is a public charity, a private foundation may rely upon an IRS determination letter or ruling that an organization is a publicly supported organization until the IRS publishes notice of a change of such status in the weekly *Internal Revenue Bulletin* or other IRS publication.[133] A private foundation may also rely

---

126. Reg. § 53.4942(a)-3(d)(2). See § 6.5(b).
127. See § 6.5(b), (c).
128. Reg. § 53.4942(a)-3(d)(2).
129. Under IRC § 170(b)(1)(F)(ii).
130. IRC § 170(b)(1)(a)(vii); see § 14.2(a).
131. IRC § 170(e)(1)(B)(ii); see § 14.4(a). The election is the subject of Reg. § 53.4942(a)-3(c)(2)(iv). If the election is not timely made, the IRS will, if the circumstances warrant, grant an extension of time for the election to be made (e.g., Priv. Ltr. Rul. 201336019).
132. Reg. § 53.4942(a)-3(c)(2)(i).
133. Reg. §§ 1.170A–9(f)(5)(ii), 1.509(a)-3(e)(2)(i), 1.509-7.

§ 6.4 QUALIFYING DISTRIBUTIONS

on an organization's public charity status to the extent set forth in the IRS's *Tax Exempt Organization Search* database[134] or the IRS's *Exempt Organizations Business Master File Extract* (EO BMF) database,[135] for purposes of determining whether a grant to such an organization constitutes a qualifying distribution.[136]

A private foundation may not, however, rely on an organization's determination letter or ruling, or the organization's listing in one of the IRS's online databases, if the private foundation was responsible for, or aware of, the act or failure to act that resulted in the organization's loss of classification as a public charity (or acquired knowledge that the IRS notified the organization that it would be deleted from such classification).[137]

A private foundation will not be deemed responsible for, or aware of, the act or failure to act that resulted in the loss of an organization's publicly supported classification if the foundation makes a grant in reliance upon a written statement by the grantee organization that such grant or contribution will not result in the loss of such organization's publicly supported status. The written statement must be signed by a responsible officer of the grantee organization and must set forth sufficient information, including a summary of the pertinent financial data for the five tax years immediately preceding the current tax year, to assure a reasonably prudent person that the grant will not result in the loss of the grantee organization's publicly supported status.[138]

A private foundation is not considered responsible for or aware of an act that results in the loss of a grantee's classification as a publicly supported charity due to a change in financial support if the aggregate of grants or contributions received from the private foundation is 25 percent or less of the aggregate support received by the grantee for the four tax years immediately preceding such tax year.[139] This safe harbor rule is not available to a private foundation that has the ability to exercise control over the recipient organization, or gains the ability to exercise control as a consequence of the grant.[140]

---

134. https://www.irs.gov/charities-non-profits/tax-exempt-organization-search. Historically, the IRS's eligible organization list was maintained in IRS Publication 78. In 2011, the IRS discontinued publishing the paper version of Publication 78 and began to maintain the eligible organization list solely on an electronic database. This electronic database was initially called Exempt Organizations Select Check; the name was changed to Tax Exempt Organization Search in 2018. Thus, this searchable database is the successor to Publication 78 (Rev. Proc. 2018-32, 2018-23 I.R.B. 739 § 3.01).
135. https://www.irs.gov/charities-non-profits/exempt-organizations-business-master-file-extract-eo-bmf.
136. Rev. Proc. 2018-32, 2018-23 I.R.B. 739 § 5.01.
137. Reg. §§ 1.170A–9(f)(5)(ii), 1.509(a)-3(e)(2)(i), 1.509-7; Rev. Proc. 2018-32, 2018-23 I.R.B. 739 § 5.02.
138. Reg. §§ 1.170A–9(f)(5)(iii), 1.509(a)-3(e)(2)(ii).
139. Rev. Proc. 2018-32, 2018-23 I.R.B. 739 § 7.01(1).
140. *Id.* § 7.01(4).

This safe harbor rule is also unavailable if the grantor or contributor has actual knowledge of the loss of public charity status or after the date of a public announcement by the IRS that the organization ceases to qualify as a public charity.[141]

A less rigorous safe harbor rule applies to private foundation grantors provided they do not control the recipient organization. Under this rule, a private foundation grantor will not be considered responsible for, or aware of, an act that results in a recipient organization's loss of public charity classification if the recipient organization has received a determination letter or ruling that it is either a donative publicly supported charity[142] or a service provided publicly supported charity[143] and the recipient organization is not controlled directly or indirectly by the private foundation.[144] Thus, if a grantee is a publicly supported charity that is not controlled directly or indirectly by the private foundation, the foundation need not undertake the more detailed percentage analysis of public support required by the other safe harbor rule. For these purposes, a recipient organization is controlled, directly or indirectly, by a private foundation if the private foundation and disqualified persons with respect to the private foundation, by aggregating their votes or positions of authority, may require the recipient organization to perform any act that significantly affects its operations or may prevent the recipient organization from performing such an act.[145] As with the other safe harbor rule, this rule does not apply if the private foundation has actual knowledge of the loss of classification of public charity status or after the date of a public announcement by the IRS that the organization ceases to qualify as a public charity.[146]

Additionally, a grantor or contributor will not be responsible for, or aware of, the act or failure to act that resulted in the loss of an organization's publicly supported classification if they acted in reliance on a written statement by the grantee organization that the grant or contribution would not cause the loss of such classification. This statement must be signed by a responsible officer of the organization and must set forth sufficient information, including a summary of the pertinent financial data for the five tax years immediately preceding the current tax year, to assure a reasonably prudent person that the grant or contribution would not cause loss of the organization's classification as a

---

141. *Id.* § 7.01(5). An additional safe harbor rule may be available to private foundations where the recipient organization is not controlled by the private foundation (*id.* § 7.02).
142. IRC §§ 170(b)(1)(A)(vi), 509(a)(1).
143. IRC § 509(a)(2).
144. Rev. Proc. 2018-32, 2018-23 I.R.B. 739 § 7.02(1).
145. *Id.* § 7.02(2).
146. *Id.* § 7.02(3).

§ 6.4 QUALIFYING DISTRIBUTIONS

publicly supported entity. This rule does not apply if the grantor is one of the organization's founders, creators, or foundation managers.[147]

If a reasonable doubt exists as to the effect of a private foundation's grant on a grantee charity's publicly supported status, and the grant meets the criteria for an unusual grant, a private foundation may request a determination from the IRS that the grant is an unusual grant that is excluded from the public support calculation.[148]

(ii) Grants to Certain Supporting Organizations. As noted,[149] a nonoperating private foundation may not treat as a qualifying distribution an amount paid (1) to a Type III supporting organization that is not a functionally integrated Type III supporting organization, or (2) to any other type of supporting organization[150] if a disqualified person with respect to the foundation directly or indirectly controls the supporting organization or a supported organization of the supporting organization.[151]

For purposes of determining whether an organization is a Type I, Type II, or Type III functionally or non-functionally integrated supporting organization, a private foundation may rely upon an IRS determination letter or ruling indicating a supporting organization's type until the IRS publishes notice of a change of such status in the weekly *Internal Revenue Bulletin* or other IRS publication.[152] A private foundation may also rely on an organization's supporting organization type, to the extent set forth in the IRS's *Tax Exempt Organization Search* database[153] or the IRS's *Exempt Organizations Business Master File Extract* (EO BMF) database,[154] for purposes of determining whether a grant to a supporting organization constitutes a qualifying distribution or requires expenditure responsibility.[155]

In many circumstances, especially for supporting organizations that have been in existence since before the limitations on qualifying distributions with

---

147. Reg. §§ 1.170A–9(f)(5)(iii), 1.509(a)-3(e)(2)(ii).
148. Reg. §§ 1.170A–9(f)(5)(iii), (6)(iv), 1.509(a)-3(c)(3)-(5); see § 15.5(c).
149. See § 6.4(a).
150. Supporting organizations are the subject of § 15.6.
151. IRC § 4942(g)(4)(B). As to the second element of this rule, a payment also is not a qualifying distribution if the IRS determines by regulation that the distribution "otherwise is inappropriate" (IRC § 4942(g)(4)(A)(ii)(II)). A grant that does not count as a qualifying distribution under this rule will also result in a taxable expenditure if expenditure responsibility is not exercised over the grant (see § 9.7).
152. Reg. § 1.509-7.
153. https://www.irs.gov/charities-non-profits/tax-exempt-organization-search.
154. https://www.irs.gov/charities-non-profits/exempt-organizations-business-master-file-extract-eo-bmf.
155. Rev. Proc. 2018-32, 2018-23 I.R.B. 739 § 5.01.

MANDATORY DISTRIBUTIONS

respect to supporting organizations were enacted,[156] the IRS's databases do not have specific information regarding an organization's supporting organization type. Pursuant to interim guidance issued by the IRS,[157] a grantor private foundation, acting in good faith, may rely on a written representation signed by a trustee, director, or officer of the grantee that the grantee is a Type I or II supporting organization, provided that (1) the representation describes how the grantee's trustees, directors, and/or officers are selected, and references any provision in the governing documents that establish a Type I or II relationship between the grantee and its supported organization(s); and (2) the grantor collects and reviews copies of the governing documents of the grantee and, if relevant, of the supported organization(s).

To establish that a grantee is a functionally integrated Type III supporting organization, a grantor, acting in good faith, may rely on a written representation signed by a trustee, director, or officer of the grantee that the grantee is a functionally integrated Type III supporting organization, provided that (1) the grantee's representation identifies the one or more supported organizations with which the grantee is functionally integrated; (2) the grantor collects and reviews copies of governing documents of the grantee (and, if relevant, of the supported organization(s)) and any other documents that set forth the relationship of the grantee to its supported organization(s), if the relationship is not reflected in the governing documents; and (3) the grantor reviews a written representation signed by a trustee, director, or officer of each of the supported organizations with which the grantee represents that it is functionally integrated, describing the activities of the grantee and confirming that, but for the involvement of the grantee engaging in activities to perform the functions of, or to carry out the purposes of, the supported organization, the supported organization would normally be engaged in those activities itself (see below).

As an alternative to the foregoing, a grantor may rely on a reasoned written opinion of counsel of either the grantor or the grantee concluding that the grantee is a Type I, Type II, or Type III functionally integrated supporting organization.

A private foundation considering a grant to a Type I, Type II, or Type III functionally integrated supporting organization may need to obtain a list of the grantee's supported organizations to determine whether any of the supported organizations is controlled by disqualified persons with respect to the foundation. Pursuant to the interim guidance issued by the IRS, the standards as to control in the qualifying distribution regulations[158] apply in determining

---

156. IRC § 4942(g)(4), enacted by the Pension Protection Act of 2006, P.L. 109-280, § 1244(a), 120 Stat. 780, 1107.
157. Notice 2006-109, 2006-51 I.R.B. 1121 § 3.01.
158. Reg. § 53.4942(a)-3(a)(3); e.g., Priv. Ltr. Rul. 202137007; see § 6.4(c)(i).

§ 6.4 QUALIFYING DISTRIBUTIONS

whether a disqualified person with respect to a private foundation controls a supporting organization or one of its supported organizations.[159]

(iii) No IRS Determination Letter. In certain situations, a private foundation may wish to make a grant to an organization that qualifies as a public charity but does not have a determination letter. For example, churches and their integrated auxiliaries and governmental units do not commonly receive recognition of exemption as public charities, although some seek such a letter to aid in fundraising. Some church groups have a certification issued by a national or area association of the member parishes and congregations. For example, Catholic churches, schools, and affiliated auxiliaries are listed in *The Official Catholic Directory*, which includes all entities listed under the Conference of Catholic Bishop's Group Ruling.

For a church lacking this type of documentation, a private foundation will need to gather information directly from the church to determine if the church satisfies the IRS's criteria.[160] For example, the IRS ruled that a private foundation that collected sufficient information demonstrating that a potential grantee possessed all 14 of the identifying features the IRS uses to determine whether an organization is a church for federal tax purposes could in good faith determine that the grantee was the equivalent of a public charity.[161] Therefore, the foundation could treat such grants as qualifying distributions and did not need to exercise expenditure responsibility over the grants.[162] Verifying that an entity is a political subdivision of a governmental unit[163] would involve a similar process. If, however, a private foundation cannot make a good faith determination that an organization without a determination letter

---

159. Notice 2006-109, 2006-51 I.R.B. 1121 § 3.02. The portions of Notice 2006-109, 2006-51 I.R.B. 1121, that relate to reliance for purposes of determining whether a grantee is a public charity have been superseded (Rev. Proc. 2009-32, 2009-28 I.R.B. 142, modified and superseded by Rev. Proc. 2011-33, 2011-25 I.R.B. 887, modified and superseded by Rev. Proc. 2018-32, 2018-23 IRB 739). All other parts of Notice 2006-109 remain unchanged and in effect, including the separate requirements for grantors to determine whether a grantee is a Type I, Type II, or functionally integrated Type III supporting organization and the standards for determining control by disqualified persons (Rev. Proc. 2009-32, 2009-28 I.R.B. 142).
160. See § 15.3(a).
161. Priv. Ltr. Rul. 200209055. Although the process for making a good faith determination that a grantee is the equivalent of a public charity is presented in the regulations in the context of grants to foreign organizations without determination letters (Reg. § 53.4942-3(a)(6) (see § 6.4(e)) and Reg. § 53.4945-5(a)(5) (see § 9.6(b))), this same process was applied in this ruling in the case of a domestic organization without a determination letter.
162. See §§ 6.4(e), 9.7.
163. IRC § 170(b)(1)(A)(v), (c)(1); see § 15.3(g).

MANDATORY DISTRIBUTIONS

is indeed a church or a governmental unit, it may be advisable to exercise expenditure responsibility over the grant.[164]

(iv) Charities Under a Group Ruling. Private foundations, as part of their program of making grants to public charities, may make grants to entities that have their tax-exempt and public charity status established by means of a group exemption. An organization, such as a chapter, that is affiliated with and is subject to the general supervision or control of a central organization, itself often a public charity, may be considered a tax-exempt organization (and a public charity, solely by reason of its relationship with the parent organization). Exempt status acquired in this manner is referred to as tax exemption on a group basis.[165]

Generally, private foundations do not seem to have had much difficulty when making grants to public charities encompassed by the group exemption rules, relying on central organizations' enforcement of the affiliation and supervision-or-control requirements. (The IRS assigns the public charity status of the central organization to the subordinate entities.) To confirm the public charity status of subordinate organizations, a private foundation could request documentation that the entity is indeed a subordinate of an organization with a group ruling (most issue a certificate), verify the parent organization's public charity status on one of the IRS databases,[166] and determine whether the front page of the grantee's Form 990 indicates it is a member of a group.

This situation may change. In mid-2020, the IRS issued a proposed revenue procedure setting forth updated group exemption procedures.[167] This proposal includes new procedures a central organization will be required to follow to maintain a group exemption. In understatements, the IRS recognized in the preamble accompanying this proposal that the proposal would make "substantial changes" in the existing procedures and "may" impose "additional administrative burden[s]" on central organizations. Although as a technical matter the existing revenue procedure concerning group rulings continues to apply, the IRS has stopped accepting requests for group exemption letters and will not accept any new ones until the proposed revenue procedure is finalized.[168]

---

164. See § 9.7.
165. The group exemption procedures are the subject of Rev. Proc. 80-27, 1980-1 C.B. 677. A private foundation itself is not eligible to be included as a subordinate in a group exemption letter. *Id.* § 2.04. In general, see *Tax-Exempt Organizations* § 26.11.
166. See § 6.4(d)(i).
167. Notice 2020-36, 2020-21 I.R.B. 840.
168. *Id.*

§ 6.4 QUALIFYING DISTRIBUTIONS

Private foundations making grants to entities encompassed by a group exemption, believing them to be public charities, should be more cautious once the new group exemption rules take effect. Central organizations may not be fully adhering to the new affiliation and supervision rules. The proposed rules as to control are particularly onerous (indeed, unrealistic). Thus, a private foundation that does not engage in the requisite due diligence in this regard may find itself making grants to nonexempt organizations or charitable organizations that are not public charities. Expenditure responsibility grants may be in order.[169]

(e) Grants to Foreign Organizations

A domestic tax-exempt charitable organization may further charitable and educational purposes by serving beneficiaries in foreign countries,[170] and may qualify for exemption even if all of its charitable activities are carried on in foreign countries.[171] Thus, a private foundation may make a qualifying distribution if it makes a distribution to a foreign organization[172] for appropriate purposes.[173] Under the general definition of a qualifying distribution, however, a distribution to a private foundation that is not a private operating foundation is not a qualifying distribution,[174] unless certain redistribution requirements are met.[175]

A foreign organization that does not have an IRS determination letter, but is equivalent to and would in fact qualify as a public charity or a private operating foundation (a *qualifying public charity*)[176] if it sought approval, may also be treated as a qualifying public charity for purposes of the qualifying distribution rules if the grantor private foundation makes a good faith determination that the foreign organization so qualifies (commonly called an *equivalency determination*).[177]

---

169. See § 9.7.
170. Rev. Rul. 68-117, 1968-1 C.B. 251.
171. Rev. Rul. 71-460, 1971-2 C.B. 231.
172. That is, any organization that is not described in section 170(c)(2)(A) (Reg. § 53.4942(a)-3(a)(6)(ii)(a)), including a foreign government (e.g., Priv. Ltr. Rul. 200031053).
173. That is, for one or more purposes described in IRC § 170(c)(2)(B) (IRC § 4942(g)(1)(A)).
174. IRC § 4942(g)(1)(A).
175. IRC § 4942(g)(3).
176. Specifically, a qualifying public charity for purposes of the qualifying distribution rules includes a private operating foundation (IRC § 4942(j)(3)) or a public charity described in IRC § 509(a)(1), (2), or (3), other than a disqualified supporting organization (Reg. § 53.4942(a)-3(a)(6)(i)). A disqualified supporting organization includes a nonfunctionally integrated Type III supporting organization (Reg. § 1.509(a)-4(i)) and any other supporting organization if a disqualified person of the private foundation directly or indirectly controls the supporting organization or a supported organization (IRC § 4942(g)(4)(A)).
177. Reg. § 53.4942(a)-3(a)(6)(i).

MANDATORY DISTRIBUTIONS

A determination ordinarily will be considered a good faith determination if it is based on current written advice received by a qualified tax practitioner[178] concluding that the prospective grantee is a qualifying public charity and if the foundation reasonably relied in good faith on the written advice.[179] The written advice must set forth sufficient facts concerning the operations and financial support of the grantee organization for the IRS to determine that the grantee organization is the equivalent of a qualifying public charity as of the date of the advice. Written advice is considered *current* if, as of the date of the grant payment, the relevant law on which the advice is based has not changed since the date of the written advice and the factual information on which the advice is based is from the grantee's current or prior tax year (or other applicable accounting period for foreign purposes). Written advice that a grantee met a public support test for a period of five years is treated as current for purposes of grant payments to the grantee during the first two years (or accounting periods) of the grantee immediately following the close of the five-year period.[180]

The IRS published rules by which private foundations may make good faith determinations that a foreign grantee qualifies as a qualifying public charity, so that grants to them for charitable purposes will generally be qualifying distributions.[181] Written advice that meets these guidelines—*preferred written advice*—ordinarily will be considered to contain sufficient facts concerning the foreign grantee's operations and support to enable the IRS to determine that the grantee would likely qualify as a qualifying public charity as of the date of the written advice.[182]

---

178. *A qualified tax practitioner* is a lawyer, a certified public accountant, or an enrolled agent (Reg. § 53.4942(a)-3(a)(6)(ii)(b)). To be qualified, the tax practitioner must be subject to the requirements of 31 C.F.R. Part 10, also known as "Circular 230," which sets forth rules related to practice before the IRS (*id.*).
179. *Id.* The standards for reasonable reliance are the subject of Reg. § 1.6664-4(c)(1).
180. Reg. § 53.4942(a)-3(a)(6)(i).
181. Rev. Proc. 2017-53, 2017-40 I.R.B. 263. This revenue procedure eliminates a previous "simplified procedure" (Rev. Proc. 92-94, 1992-2 C.B. 507) that allowed a private foundation to rely solely on grantee affidavits in making good faith (equivalency) determinations, without needing to obtain current written advice received from qualified tax practitioners. When rendering written advice, however, a qualified tax practitioner may rely on factual information set forth in grantee affidavits (Rev. Proc. 2017-53, *supra*, § 4.03).
182. Rev. Proc. 2017-53, 2017-40 I.R.B. 263. If an equivalency determination pursuant to these guidelines has been made with respect to a foreign grantee, the grantor private foundation need not exercise expenditure responsibility with respect to grants made to the grantee (see § 9.6(b)). These guidelines are inapplicable where the grant is a transfer of assets pursuant to a liquidation, merger, redemption, recapitalization, or other adjustment, organization, or reorganization of the foundation (Rev. Proc. 2017-53, *supra*, § 2). These reorganizations and the like are the subject of IRC § 507(b)(2) and Reg. § 1.507-3(c) (see § 13.5).

§ 6.4 QUALIFYING DISTRIBUTIONS

Even if an organization does not make a good faith (equivalency) determination with respect to a foreign organization, the IRS has indicated that a grant to the foreign organization nevertheless may constitute a qualifying distribution. The IRS ruled that a private foundation's grant to a foreign grantee will be treated as a qualifying distribution if the private foundation treats the grantee as not being described in IRC § 501(c)(3), and, hence, not a private foundation. The IRS stated that these conclusions hold true regardless of the fact that the private foundation may have the capacity to make a reasonable judgment or good faith determination with respect to the foreign organization, or may have embarked on the procedure to collect the necessary information to make a reasonable judgment or good faith determination but did not reach a definitive conclusion, or if another private foundation has made a reasonable judgment or good faith determination with respect to the foreign organization. Thus, while making a good faith (equivalency) determination is one way to qualify a distribution as a qualifying distribution, the IRS has suggested that another is for a private foundation to simply treat the foreign grantee as not being described in IRC § 501(c)(3).[183]

Essentially, the IRS reasoned that a qualifying distribution is defined as any amount paid to accomplish charitable purposes, except for a distribution made to an organization controlled by the foundation or a distribution made to another private foundation that is not an operating foundation.[184] Making an equivalency determination that a foreign grantee is a qualifying public charity is one option to establish that the foreign organization is not a private foundation. Another way, however, is for the grantor foundation not to make a determination whether the foreign grantee is a private foundation, in which case the statutory provision making distributions to a nonoperating private foundation ineligible for treatment as qualifying distributions does not apply. The IRS observed that a private foundation retains "full discretion" to elect to treat a foreign grantee that has not received an IRS determination letter as not being described in IRC § 501(c)(3) (and therefore not a private foundation) even if it may be possible for the private foundation to make a good faith determination to the contrary.[185]

---

183. Priv. Ltr. Rul. 200321023. A consequence of so doing, however, is that the grantor private foundation will be required to exercise expenditure responsibility over the grant (IRC § 4945(d)(4), (h); see § 9.7) and the grantee will be required to maintain the grant funds in a separate fund dedicated to one or more purposes described in IRC § 170(c)(2)(B) (Reg. § 53.4945-6(c); see § 9.8).
184. IRC § 4942(g)(1)(A).
185. Priv. Ltr. Rul. 200321023; also Priv. Ltr. Rul 202119002.

MANDATORY DISTRIBUTIONS

(f) Direct Charitable Expenditures

Any amount, including that portion of reasonable and necessary administrative expenses, paid to accomplish one or more charitable purposes[186] may be treated as a qualifying distribution.[187] When a foundation directly conducts its own program of charitable activities (*direct charitable activity*),[188] expenses paid directly (of the sort a private operating foundation incurs) by a nonoperating private foundation also count as qualifying distributions. There are many examples of this type of expenditure, including the costs of operating a museum or a library, running a summer camp for children, conducting research and publishing books, buying food for the hungry, and preserving historic houses.

(i) Exempt Function Assets. The purchase of assets used, or held for use, in carrying out a foundation's tax-exempt purposes (an *exempt function asset*) is treated as a qualifying distribution.[189] Thus, for example, a private foundation's purchase of real property on which it plans to build hospital facilities to be used for medical care and education is a qualifying distribution,[190] as is the purchase of an additional building to exhibit paintings by a private foundation engaged in holding paintings and exhibiting them to the public.[191] Amounts expended to make improvements on property used directly in carrying out a private foundation's exempt purposes may also be treated as a qualifying distribution.[192] Depreciation is not a qualifying distribution.[193]

Conversion of an asset previously held for investment, an active business property, or a future exempt purpose, to use as an exempt function asset is counted as a qualifying distribution. The amount of the qualifying distribution is the fair market value of the converted asset as of the date of its conversion.[194] The IRS ruled that where a private foundation adopted a plan for the exempt use of a property on July 1, 1974, and immediately proceeded to implement it, that date was the date of conversion of the property to exempt use for

---

186. IRC § 4942(g)(1)(A).
187. IRC § 4942(g)(1)(B).
188. Reg. § 53.4942(b)-1(b)(1).
189. IRC § 4942(g)(1)(B); Reg § 53.4942(a)-3(a)(2)(ii); see § 6.2(d).
190. Reg § 53.4942(a)-3(a)(8), Example (2).
191. Reg § 53.4942(a)-3(a)(8), Example (3).
192. E.g., Priv. Ltr. Rul. 8617123 (improvements to develop a camp to preserve a natural ecosystem, educate the public about wildlife, and give youngsters a chance to experience the wilderness were qualifying distributions).
193. Rev. Rul. 74-560, 1974-2 C.B. 389.
194. Reg. § 53.4942(a)-3(a)(5).

purposes of treating the conversion as a qualifying distribution. Although it was not until the middle of the following year that the property was usable for exempt purposes, the property was effectively committed to exempt use on July 1, 1974.[195]

The adoption of a plan of conversion of real property to an exempt use by a private operating foundation was considered to be a qualifying distribution, as was a transfer of land to the operating foundation by another private foundation.[196] In another example, a private foundation, rather than making grants directly to a tax-exempt university to financially salvage an educational program, acquired control over the program by means of a limited liability company, appointing a majority of the overseers of the program, purchasing program assets, and becoming responsible for funding the activity. Because the program became conducted under the authority and direction of the foundation, expenditures of the limited liability company were treated as active program expenses, enabling the foundation to qualify as a private operating foundation.[197] In a similar situation, a private foundation utilized a single-member limited liability company to acquire real estate and fund the construction of a tax-exempt school, to be operated by an unrelated party.[198]

(ii) Administrative Expenses. Reasonable and necessary administrative expenses paid to accomplish the foundation's exempt purposes may be treated as a qualifying distribution.[199] These expenses may include amounts paid for staff salaries, occupancy, office expense, and overhead, but only to the extent that they are attributable to a charitable or other exempt program or activity. For example, assume a private foundation conducted a program of educational grants for research and study and paid $20,000 for various items of overhead, 10 percent of which was attributable to the activities of the employees conducting the grant program and the other 90 percent of which was attributable to administrative expenses which were not paid to accomplish

---

195. Rev. Rul. 78-102, 1978-1 C.B. 379.
196. Priv. Ltr. Rul. 9247036.
197. Priv. Ltr. Rul. 200431018. See § 3.1.
198. Priv. Ltr. Rul. 201134023.
199. IRC § 4942(g)(1)(A); Reg § 53.4942(a)-3(a)(2)(i). In the conference committee report accompanying the Tax Reform Act of 1984, it is stated that "the mere fact that a State attorney general, or other State government official, has approved the amount of director fees or other expenditures by a foundation does not establish that such amounts or expenditures are reasonable or not excessive for purposes of any of the private foundation tax provisions" (H.R. Rep. No. 98-861, at 1087 (1984)). For a discussion of proposed legislation that would prevent certain payments of administrative expenses to a disqualified person from constituting qualifying distributions, see § 16.10.

any exempt purpose. The foundation may only treat $2,000 of the overhead expense as a qualifying distribution.[200]

Expenses associated with the management and sale of a private foundation's investment properties are paid or incurred for the production or collection of income and are not qualifying distributions.[201] The IRS concluded that payments of accounting and legal fees incurred by a private foundation to recover and maintain its income-producing assets after discovering it had been the victim of embezzlement were general administrative and investment expenses of the foundation, none of which were made to conduct any charitable program.[202] In contrast, the payment of legal fees in a suit to determine the proper beneficiary of a charitable trust was ruled to be a reasonable and necessary expense to accomplish the trust's exempt purpose and therefore a qualifying distribution.[203] Similarly, legal fees and associated expenses paid by

---

200. Reg. § 53.4942(a)-3(a)(8), Example (1). In response to Congress's conclusion that the administrative expenses of private foundations were absorbing an excessive portion of qualifying distributions, prior IRC § 4942(g)(4), added by the Tax Reform Act of 1984 § 304, placed a limitation on the extent to which grant administrative expenses could be included in determining compliance with the payout requirement. For years beginning after December 31, 1984, but not for years beginning after December 31, 1990, a private foundation was required to timely pay out, as qualifying distributions, an amount equal to 4.35 percent of its noncharitable assets as grants or contributions, expenditures directly for the active conduct by it of its tax-exempt activities, or qualified administrative expenses incurred directly in making the direct operating expenditures. Congress directed the IRS to modify the private foundation annual information return to facilitate the collection of more information about operating and nonoperating private foundations' administrative expenses (H.R. Rep. No. 98-861, at 1086 (1984)). Congress directed that, "to the extent practicable," the study is "to examine (1) the amount of qualifying distributions which actually reach charitable beneficiaries; (2) the administrative costs of such payouts; (3) the effect of the revised general definition . . . [IRC § 4942 (g)(1)(A)] on those administrative expenses which are eligible to be qualifying distributions, subject to the new limitation; and (4) the additional information provided by the revised form concerning categories and types of administrative expenses, and the basis for allocating such expenses among categories of foundation expenditures" (*id.* at 1087). On the basis of this information, the Department of the Treasury, in January 1990, submitted an analysis of the subject to the House Committee on Ways and Means and the Senate Committee. The report ("Private Foundation Grant-Making Administrative Expenses Study") concluded that this limitation on grant administrative expenses should be allowed to terminate with respect to the years beginning after December 31, 1990. The IRS concluded that the limit "was not an effective method of discouraging foundations from incurring excessive amounts of these administrative expenses" and that "computations regarding the grant-making administrative expenses limit were complex and burdensome to private foundations." Prior IRC § 4942(g)(4) was allowed to expire and is no longer applicable.
201. E.g., Priv. Ltr. Rul. 9211005.
202. Priv. Ltr. Rul. 8338002.
203. Rev. Rul. 75-495, 1975-2 C.B. 449.

§ 6.4 QUALIFYING DISTRIBUTIONS

a foundation in connection with a mediation agreement to distribute the foundation's assets to two new foundations created to resolve a dispute between two remaining directors after the death of a director were treated as a qualifying distribution.[204]

Legal, accounting, state registration, and other fees and expenses paid in connection with creation and qualification of a new private foundation as a tax-exempt organization and ensuring ongoing compliance with applicable laws can also be treated as disbursements for charitable purposes.[205]

(g) Set-Asides

Money set aside or saved for specific future charitable projects, rather than being paid out currently, may be considered to be a qualifying distribution by a private foundation for mandatory payout purposes.[206] An amount set aside in one year for a specific project that is for a tax-exempt purpose or purposes may be treated as a qualifying distribution, if payment for the project is to be subsequently made over a period not to exceed 60 months. The funds set aside are credited, for purposes of the qualifying distribution requirements, as if paid in the tax year the set-aside is made, thus reducing the amount of the mandatory payout required in that year (but not in the year actually paid).[207]

A private foundation records a set-aside on its books and records as a pledge or obligation to be paid at a future date.[208] The amount set aside does not need to reflect an accumulation of income; it needs only to be evidenced by a bookkeeping entry that will require funding out of corpus by the end of the set-aside period.[209] The amount set aside, plus income, is included in the asset base for purposes of calculating the minimum investment return.[210]

A specific project includes, but is not limited to, situations where relatively long-term grants or expenditures must be made in order to ensure the continuity of particular projects or program-related investments, or where grants are made as part of a matching-grant program.[211] The concept of this type of project may encompass, for example:

- A plan to erect a building to house a tax-exempt activity of a private foundation (e.g., a museum building in which paintings are to be hung,

---

204. Priv. Ltr. Rul. 200725043.
205. E.g., Priv. Ltr. Rul. 200610020.
206. IRC § 4942(g)(2); Reg. § 53.4942(a)-3(b)(1).
207. Id.
208. Reg. § 53.4942(a)-3(b)(8).
209. Rev. Rul. 78-148, 1978-1 C.B. 380.
210. Reg. § 53.4942(a)-3(b)(8).
211. Reg. § 53.4942(a)-3(b)(2).

even though the location of the building and architectural plans have not been finalized).

- A plan to purchase an additional group of paintings offered for sale only as a unit that requires an expenditure of more than one year's income.
- A plan to fund a specific research program that is of such magnitude as to require an accumulation prior to commencement of the research.[212]
- A plan to fund the development and improvement of a family camping facility operated by a charitable organization, where the construction of some of the facilities was unavoidably delayed.[213]
- A plan to fund a supporting organization's history exhibits, with the set-aside necessary to enable the foundation to oversee the construction process and integrate the use of proceeds from a planned issuance of bonds.[214]
- A plan for an "innovative and dynamic educational" website that will focus on "critical scientific global issues, including global warming, climate control and effects on the planet and global economics; population control, overpopulation and future diminishment of resources and relation to extinction of species; and nuclear disarmament and controlling proliferation of weapons of mass destruction."[215]
- A plan to convert newly acquired land into an extension of an existing wildlife sanctuary and the remainder into a public park, under a four-year construction contract where approximately 85 percent of the payments would not be made until years three and four.[216]

By contrast, a private foundation, which made renewable scholarships and fixed-sum research grants that usually ran for three years, proposed to set aside the full amount to be given to each grantee and make annual payments to them from a set-aside account, rather than take the payments out of its current income. The IRS ruled that the amounts were not qualifying distributions within the meaning of the set-aside rules.[217] Subsequently, however, the IRS allowed a set-aside for a scholarship grant program where the private foundation was newly created, students who would benefit from its grants could not be identified during the grant period, the request was for a one-time set-aside,

---

212. *Id.*
213. Priv. Ltr. Rul. 200327062.
214. Priv. Ltr. Rul. 200347018.
215. Priv. Ltr. Rul. 201534018.
216. Rev. Rul. 74-450, 1974-2 C.B. 388.
217. Rev. Rul. 75-511, 1975-2 C.B. 450.

§ 6.4 QUALIFYING DISTRIBUTIONS

the foundation's program did not promise future grants, and the foundation advised its grantees to not expect further funding.[218]

(i) Suitability Test Set-Asides. The most often used type of set-aside is based on the *suitability test*. This test requires a private foundation to convince the IRS that a charitable project (such as those described above) can be better accomplished by a set-aside rather than by the immediate payment of funds.[219]

A ruling from the IRS is necessary for this type of set-aside, and the private foundation must apply for the ruling before the end of the year in which the amount is set aside. The request for the ruling must include: (1) a detailed description of the specific project, including the expected costs, sources of future funding, and location of any physical facilities to be acquired or constructed as part of the project; (2) the amount of the intended set-aside; (3) a description of the amounts and dates of any planned additions to the set-aside after its initial establishment; (4) a statement of the reasons why the project can be better accomplished by a set-aside than an immediate payment of funds, and a detailed description of the project; and (5) a statement by a foundation manager that the amounts to be set aside will be paid within 60 months, or a statement showing good cause why the payment period should be extended.[220] A ruling is requested by filing Form 8940 along with the required fee.[221]

According to the IRS, a private foundation's desire to retain control over the funds so as to receive income from them is not a persuasive reason for utilizing a qualified set-aside, where the private foundation can make the grants out of current or future income.[222]

For good cause shown, the period for paying an amount set aside under the suitability test may be extended by the IRS.[223] For example, a private foundation permitted a set-aside to construct a youth camp was granted a two-year extension to pay out the funds, because of the institution of a building moratorium that caused a delay in acquiring the necessary property.[224] As another illustration, the IRS found good cause for a significant extension of time for

---

218. Priv. Ltr. Rul. 200434026.
219. IRC § 4942(g)(2)(A), (B)(i); Reg. § 53.4942(a)-3(b)(2). E.g., Priv. Ltr. Rul. 8834011.
220. Reg. § 53.4942(a)-3(b)(7)(i).
221. Form 8940 must be submitted electronically at www.pay.gov; the user fee for this type of request is currently $2,500 (Rev. Proc. 2023-5, 2023-1 I.R.B. 265 §§ 4.02(6), 7.02 and App. A (Schedule of User Fees), as modified by Rev. Proc. 2023-12, 2023-17 I.R.B. 768 §§ 3.01, 3.03). A completed Schedule A to Form 8940 also must be submitted with the request, which to is designed to obtain the information required by the regulations and other information relevant to a set-aside request.
222. Rev. Rul. 79-319, 1979-2 C.B. 388.
223. IRC § 4942(g)(2) (flush language); Reg. § 53.4942(a)-3(b)(1).
224. Priv. Ltr. Rul. 7821141.

paying funds under a set-aside, in connection with a student-debt-reduction program for science, technology, engineering, and mathematics workers who agreed to live and work for 10 years in a state.[225] Moreover, a private foundation will not incur any taxes under these rules where it disregards a set-aside ruling it received and instead adheres to the general distribution requirements.[226]

Funds set aside by a foundation for two challenge, matching-grant programs were treated as qualifying distributions.[227] The foundation pledged to match a grant to a private school and another to a charity providing social and rehabilitation services. This ruling is contrary to other private rulings that hold that a pledge is not a qualifying distribution and departs from the accepted meaning of the word *paid*.[228]

Construction of new foundation headquarters that would be mostly rented at below cost to other tax-exempt organizations;[229] redevelopment of a city block as a part of a downtown rejuvenation;[230] construction of facilities in Central America for abandoned and underprivileged children;[231] and the making of guarantees of below-market bank loans to public charities to advance charitable child-care programs, and loan deposits and interest-rate subsidy arrangements for the same purpose,[232] were ruled to constitute suitable programs for which a private foundation can set aside funds that will be treated as qualifying distributions.

The IRS ruled that a private foundation may use borrowed funds to satisfy all or portions of previously approved set-asides for a project, enabling the set-asides to continue to constitute qualifying distributions. The IRS observed that the law does not "specify or limit the source of the funds expected to be used for completion of a project, other than that it must be disclosed at the time the private foundation submits its written request for a set-aside." If a private foundation borrows money to make expenditures for a charitable purpose, a qualifying distribution out of the borrowed funds will generally be deemed to have been made only at the time that the borrowed funds are actually distributed for the exempt purpose.[233] The IRS noted that this regulation

---

225. Priv. Ltr. Rul. 201627005. The IRS also granted a private foundation an extension of time to pay out set-aside funds for the construction of a new headquarters building to administer its scholarship program due to the "lingering effects" of the COVID-19 pandemic (Priv. Ltr. Rul. 202250015).
226. Priv. Ltr. Rul. 8830070.
227. Priv. Ltr. Rul. 9524033.
228. See § 6.4(a).
229. Priv. Ltr. Rul. 199907028.
230. Priv. Ltr. Rul. 199906053.
231. Priv. Ltr. Rul. 199905039.
232. Priv. Ltr. Rul. 200043050.
233. See § 6.4(a).

§ 6.4 QUALIFYING DISTRIBUTIONS

"implicitly recognizes that expenditures for qualifying distributions may be made out of borrowed funds."[234]

Because advance approval from the IRS is required for a set-aside under the suitability test, the IRS issues many private letter rulings with respect to these requests.[235]

(ii) Cash Distribution Test Set-Asides. Another type of set-aside is based on the *cash distribution test* and may be utilized by a private foundation only in its early years.[236] It originated in 1976 in response to the general reluctance of the IRS to approve set-aside requests—a dilemma that was particularly acute for new or newly funded private foundations that were attempting to institute long-term supervised projects in the face of IRS inaction. This test applies where the specific project for which the amount is set aside will not be completed before the end of the tax year in which the set-aside is made. It requires a private foundation to distribute a *start-up period minimum amount* and a *full-payment period minimum amount*. Approval from the IRS is not required where the cash distribution approach is correctly utilized.[237]

A private foundation's *start-up period* is generally the four years following the year in which the private foundation was created.[238] The *start-up period minimum amount* that must be timely distributed, in cash or its equivalent, is at least the sum of (1) 20 percent of the private foundation's distributable amount for the first year of the start-up period, (2) 40 percent of its distributable amount for the second tax year of the start-up period, (3) 60 percent of its distributable amount for the third year of the start-up period, and (4) 80 percent of its distributable amount for the fourth year of its start-up period.[239]

Only the aggregate sum of these minimum amounts must be distributed before the end of the start-up period (end of the fourth year). There is no requirement that any portion be distributed in any particular tax year of the start-up period.[240] Under certain circumstances, distributions made during the year preceding the private foundation's start-up period and/or made within

---

234. Priv. Ltr. Rul. 201152021.
235. E.g., Priv. Ltr. Rul. 8627055.
236. IRC § 4942(g)(2)(A), (B)(ii)(I)-(III); Reg. § 53.4942(a)-3(b)(3).
237. Reg. § 53.4942(a)-3(b)(7)(ii). If a private foundation submits with its annual Form 990-PF the attachments described in the text accompanied by *infra* note 250, the IRS will be deemed to have approved a set-aside under the cash distribution test rules (*id.*; Priv. Ltr. Rul. 8423076).
238. Reg. § 53.4942(a)-3(b)(4)(i).
239. IRC § 4942(g)(2)(B)(ii)(III); Reg. § 53.4942(a)-3(b)(4)(ii).
240. Reg. § 53.4942(a)-3(b)(4)(iii).

MANDATORY DISTRIBUTIONS

5½ months following the start-up period are deemed part of the start-up period minimum amount.[241]

The years of a private foundation's existence after expiration of the start-up period are termed the *full-payment period*.[242] The *full-payment period minimum amount* that must be timely distributed, in cash or its equivalent, is at least its distributable amount determined under the general rules.[243] Moreover, a private foundation has a five-year carryover of certain distributions that are in excess of the full-payment period minimum amount.[244]

Although making the minimum distribution amounts during the start-up period satisfies the cash distribution test, the foundation will still be required to distribute the balance of any distributable amounts (calculated under the normal rules) that it did not distribute during the start-up period.[245] The reduced percentage distributions required in the start-up period are not a substitute for the requirement that a private foundation distribute its full distributable amount in those years, but merely provide the foundation with the ability to defer payment of a certain percentage of them to the full-payment period.

Specific references to a foundation's "year of . . . creation" in the statute imply that the cash-distribution test applies only to newly created private foundations.[246] The legislative history also describes the test as designed for start-up foundations and existing foundations that have recently received a sizeable influx of new assets.[247] In two private letter rulings, however, the IRS allowed a private foundation to use the cash distribution set-aside test where the foundation had been in existence well beyond its initial start-up period and had not received a sizeable influx of funding. In the first instance, cash distribution set-asides were allowed in 1986 and 1988 for a private foundation that was created in 1952.[248] Since the foundation's start-up period had long since passed, it was under the full-payment period minimum distribution

---

241. Reg. § 53.4942(a)-3(b)(4)(iv).
242. Reg. § 53.4942(a)-3(b)(5)(i).
243. IRC § 4942(g)(2)(B)(ii)(II); Reg. § 53.4942(a)-3(b)(5)(ii); see § 6.1(b).
244. IRC § 4942(g)(2)(D), (E); Reg. § 53.4942(a)-3(b)(5)(iii).
245. Reg. § 53.4942(a)-3(b)(5)(v), Example(1) illustrates this concept that distributions made during the full-payment period on account of set-asides made during the start-up period do not count toward a private foundation's qualifying distributions in the full-payment period. Where a foundation distributes $500,000 in the first year of its full-payment period, but $400,000 of this amount is on account of a set-aside made during its start-up period (and which was not previously distributed), it has only made $100,000 in qualifying distributions during the first year of its full-payment period. To avoid liability for the IRC § 4942(a) tax on undistributed income, the foundation must distribute or set aside an additional $400,000 before the end of the next tax year.
246. IRC § 4942(g)(2)(B)(ii)(II).
247. S. Rep. No. 94-938, pt. 1, at 593 (1976).
248. Priv. Ltr. Rul. 9301022.

§ 6.4 QUALIFYING DISTRIBUTIONS

requirements. Based on the facts of the ruling, it was apparent that the foundation had met its distribution requirements for purposes of the 5 percent minimum distribution test. It sought, however, and was allowed to qualify for the (now repealed) 1 percent versus 2 percent excise tax on net investment income. By making use of the cash distribution test for some grants that were not paid by the end of the foundation's tax year, the foundation was able to claim additional set-aside amounts as qualifying distributions for purposes of meeting the 1 percent excise tax requirements.

In the second ruling, the foundation wanted the ability to use the cash distribution test for multi-installment grants that covered more than one tax year.[249] By claiming set-aside amounts as qualifying distributions prior to actual disbursement of the cash, the foundation was allowed to monitor the multiyear grants and get progress reports before the foundation made further distributions to the recipient. Again, the IRS approved use of the cash distribution test for current and *future* tax years for a foundation that included years well after the foundation's start-up period had expired. Although the two private rulings allowed existing foundations to apply the cash distribution test, caution should be exercised in considering this approach.

For the first tax year involved in a cash distribution set-aside, a private foundation must submit an attachment with its Form 990-PF that includes: (1) a statement describing the nature and purposes of the specific project for which amounts are to be set aside; (2) a statement that the amounts set aside for the specific project will actually be paid for the specific project within a specified period of time that ends not more than 60 months after the date of the set-aside; (3) a statement that the project will not be completed before the end of the tax year of the private foundation in which the set-aside is made; (4) a statement showing the distributable amounts determined under the general rules for any past tax years in the private foundation's start-up and full-payment periods; and (5) a statement showing the aggregate amount of actual cash (or cash-equivalent) distributions made during each tax year in the private foundation's start-up and full-payment periods, including any distributions made during the year preceding the private foundation's start-up period that are deemed part of the start-up period minimum amount. The attachment to the Form 990-PF must include the fourth and fifth statements for the five tax years following the tax year in which the amount is set aside (or, if longer, for each tax year in any extended period for paying the amount set aside).[250] For good cause shown, the period for paying an amount set aside under the cash distribution test may be extended by the IRS.[251]

---

249. Priv. Ltr. Rul. 9129006.
250. Reg. § 53.4942(a)-3(b)(7)(ii).
251. Reg. § 53.4942(a)-3(b)(1).

MANDATORY DISTRIBUTIONS

Although advance approval of a set-aside under the cash distribution test is not required, the IRS has occasionally issued private letter rulings concerning compliance with these set-aside rules.[252]

(iii) Court Order Set-Asides. A third type of set-aside is available in the event a private foundation is involved in litigation and may not distribute income or assets because of a court order. In this situation, the foundation may seek and obtain a contingent set-aside.[253] The amount to be set aside pursuant to this rule must be equal to that portion of the private foundation's distributable amount that is attributable to the income or assets that are held in accordance with a court order and that, but for the court order precluding the distribution of the income or assets, would have been distributed.[254] However, if no portion of the private foundation's assets may be distributed while litigation is pending, then the set-aside amount may be equal to the entire portion of the private foundation's distributable amount.[255] If the litigation encompasses more than one tax year, the foundation may seek additional contingent set-asides. Any amounts set aside must actually be distributed by the last day of the tax year following the tax year in which the litigation is terminated.[256]

Amounts not distributed by the close of the tax year in which the litigation is terminated are included in gross income for purposes of determining the private foundation's adjusted gross income for that tax year.[257] In one instance, a private foundation was ensnarled in litigation over a grant-making issue and desisted from the making of distributions on the advice of legal counsel. The IRS denied its set-aside request because of the absence of a court order.[258]

As with set-asides under the suitability test, requests for advance IRS approval of a contingent set-aside based on a court order are submitted on Form 8940.[259] From time to time, the IRS issues private letter rulings in response to such requests.[260]

---

252. E.g., Priv. Ltr. Rul. 8432108.
253. Reg. § 53.4942(a)-3(b)(9).
254. *Id.* E.g., Priv. Ltr. Rul. 202211010.
255. E.g., Priv. Ltr. Rul. 200328049.
256. Reg. § 53.4942(a)-3(b)(9).
257. *Id.*; Reg. § 53.4942(a)-2(d)(2)(iii)(c).
258. Priv. Ltr. Rul. 201835014.
259. Form 8940 must be submitted electronically at www.pay.gov; the user fee for this type of request is currently $2,500 (Rev. Proc. 2023-5, 2023-1 I.R.B. 265 §§ 4.02(6), 7.02 and App. A (Schedule of User Fees), as modified by Rev. Proc. 2023-12, 2023-17 I.R.B. 768 §§ 3.01, 3.03). As with set-asides under the suitability test, a completed Schedule A to Form 8940 also must be submitted with the request, and the requesting organization must upload a copy of the court order restricting the foundation from distributing income or assets with the foundation's submission (Instructions for Form 8940 (Apr. 2023), Schedule A).
260. E.g., Priv. Ltr. Rul. 202249022.

§ 6.5 EXCISE TAXES ON FAILURE TO DISTRIBUTE INCOME

(a) Undistributed Income

The excise taxes on failure to distribute income are imposed on the undistributed income of a private foundation. A private foundation's *undistributed income* is the amount by which its distributable amount[261] for any tax year as of any time exceeds its qualifying distributions[262] made before such time out of its distributable amount.[263]

(b) Ordering Rule for Qualifying Distributions

When a private foundation has undistributed income for a prior year, it must make additional qualifying distributions in the current year to address the shortfall in prior years to avoid being liable for the initial excise tax. A qualifying distribution made during a private foundation's current tax year is applied in the following order:

- First, the qualifying distribution is treated as made out of the undistributed income of the immediately preceding tax year (if the private foundation was subject to the initial excise tax for failure to distribute income for the preceding tax year) to the extent thereof.

- Second, the qualifying distribution is treated as made out of the undistributed income for the tax year in which the qualifying distribution was made, to the extent thereof.

- Third, the qualifying distribution is treated as made out of corpus.[264]

In the case of any qualifying distribution that is not treated as made out of the undistributed income of the immediately preceding tax year under the first ordering rule above, a private foundation may elect to treat any portion of such distribution as made out of the undistributed income of a designated

---

261. See § 6.1(b).
262. See § 6.4.
263. IRC § 4942(c); Reg § 53.4942(a)-2(a).
264. IRC § 4942(h)(1); Reg. § 53.4942(a)-3(d)(1). The reference in the first ordering rule to a private foundation being "subject to" the initial excise tax (see § 6.5(d)) does not mean that the tax was imposed on the foundation in the preceding year. A private foundation is "subject to" the initial excise tax if it is classified as a private foundation. Current year qualifying distributions are first applied to reduce any prior-year undistributed income without regard to whether the initial tax was imposed on undistributed income for the preceding tax year (e.g., Reg. § 53.4942(a)-3(d)(3), Example (1); see Instructions for Form 990-PF (2022), Part XII).

MANDATORY DISTRIBUTIONS

prior tax year or out of corpus. This *election* must be made by filing a statement with the IRS during the tax year in which such qualifying distribution is made or by attaching a statement to the private foundation's Form 990-PF for the tax year in which the qualifying distribution was made. The statement must contain a declaration by an appropriate foundation manager that the foundation is making the election and specify whether the distribution is made out of the undistributed income of a designated prior tax year (or years) or is made out of corpus.[265]

A private foundation may make this election to treat a portion of the current year's distribution as made out of corpus in order to allow a foundation donor to apply a higher charitable contribution deduction percentage limitation to its donation[266] or to satisfy the redistribution rule[267] for the benefit of a grantor private foundation.

(c) Excess Qualifying Distributions

Qualifying distributions in excess of the distributable amount that remain after the ordering rules and any elections described above are applied may be carried forward for five years to reduce a foundation's distributable amount in this five-year *adjustment period*.[268] Thus, excess distributions with respect to a tax year cannot be carried over beyond the succeeding five tax years (meaning that unused excess distributions expire after the end of the adjustment period).[269]

---

265. IRC § 4942(h)(2); Reg. § 53.4942(a)-3(d)(2). If the election is made by filing a statement with the IRS, the election may be revoked in whole or in part by filing a statement with the IRS during the tax year during the tax year in which the qualifying distribution was made. This statement must contain a declaration by an appropriate foundation manager that the foundation is revoking the election and it must specify the election or part thereof being revoked (*id.*). Because the election must be revoked during the tax year in which the qualifying distribution was made, an election made by filing the required statement with Form 990-PF (which is filed after the end of the year of distribution) cannot be revoked.
266. That is, this election may also be made to meet the redistribution requirements under IRC § 170(b)(1)(F)(ii) necessary to made a charitable contribution to the foundation eligible for the 50 percent limitation on charitable contributions by an individual (IRC § 170(b)(1)(a)(vii); see § 14.2(a)) and prevent it from being subject to the basis limitations on donations of appreciated property to a nonoperating private foundation (IRC § 170(e)(1)(B)(ii); see § 14.4(a)).
267. See § 6.4(c)(ii).
268. IRC § 4942(i); Reg § 53.4942(a)-3(e).
269. Reg. § 53.4942(a)-3(e)(3). If a foundation ceases to be subject to the IRC § 4942(a)(1) initial excise tax during any tax year, for example, because it terminates its private foundation status by operating as a public charity (see § 13.4) or is treated as a private operating foundation (Reg. § 53.4942(a)-3(e)(4), Example (3)), it will lose the ability to carry forward any unused, unexpired excess qualifying distributions, even if the organization again becomes a nonoperating private foundation subject to the initial excise tax in a subsequent year (Reg. § 53.4942(a)-3(e)(3)).

§ 6.5 EXCISE TAXES ON FAILURE TO DISTRIBUTE INCOME

If additional excess qualifying distributions are created during any tax year in the adjustment period, the more recently created excess distributions will not be applied until any earlier excess qualifying distributions have been completely applied against distributable amounts during the adjustment period.[270] Thus, a first in, first out rule applies to excess qualifying distributions.

A private foundation may make an election to apply excess qualifying distributions from prior years to allow a donor to apply a higher charitable contribution deduction percentage limitation to its donation[271] or to satisfy the redistribution rule[272] for the benefit of a grantor private foundation. A private foundation making the election to apply excess qualifying distributions in this manner must attach the same statement to its Form 990-PF required for making an election under the redistribution rule.[273]

Because the adjustment period for qualifying distribution carryovers is five years, a private foundation may have excess qualifying distributions for tax years for which the statute of limitations (typically, three years) is closed. It is the IRS's position that an excess qualifying distribution relating to a closed tax year, if erroneous, may be recalculated if a private foundation uses it to reduce its distributable amount in an open year. Thus, only correct excess carryovers may be used in the computation of a private foundation's distributable amount.[274]

An operating foundation is expected to make distributions for the active conduct of its exempt activities beginning in its first year of qualification; it is not afforded the one-year delay for making qualifying distributions that applies to nonoperating private foundations. An operating foundation may calculate its required distributions using either a four-year average method, or a three-out-of-four test.[275] For an operating foundation choosing the three-out-of-four test, the required distributions must be made each year without an allowance for any carryover resulting from excess distributions (although it can fail the test in one year out of the four without losing its private operating foundation status). Application of the four-year average method essentially allows an operating foundation to carry forward excess qualifying distributions from year to year, similar to the rules for nonoperating private foundations.

---

270. Reg § 53.4942(a)-3(e)(1).
271. That is, this election may also be made to meet the redistribution requirements under IRC § 170(b)(1)(F)(ii) necessary to made a charitable contribution to the foundation eligible for the 50 percent limitation on charitable contributions by an individual (IRC § 170(b)(1)(a)(vii); see § 14.2(a)) and prevent it from being subject to the basis limitations on donations of appreciated property to a nonoperating private foundation (IRC § 170(e)(1)(B)(ii); see § 14.4(a)).
272. See § 6.4(c)(ii).
273. Reg. § 53.4942(a)-3(c)(2)(iv); see § 6.4(c)(ii).
274. Gen. Couns. Mem. 39808; Priv. Ltr. Rul. 9530033.
275. See § 3.1(f).

(d) Excise Taxes on Undistributed Income

There are three taxes that are potentially applicable when a private foundation fails to make the required mandatory distributions: the initial tax,[276] the additional tax,[277] and the termination tax.[278]

A private foundation that fails to make the required qualifying distributions is subject to an *initial tax* of 30 percent calculated based on its undistributed income. Specifically, this excise tax is imposed on the undistributed income of a private foundation for any tax year that has not been distributed before the first day of the second (or any succeeding) tax year following such tax year. Thus, a private foundation may avoid the tax if it distributes any undistributed income from one tax year by the end of the next tax year. If undistributed income from one tax year remains undistributed for more than one succeeding tax year (that is, for any year after the end of the tax year immediately following the year to which the undistributed income relates), the tax applies to each year or partial year that the failure to distribute remains uncorrected until the close of the taxable period.[279]

With respect to the undistributed income for any tax year, the *taxable period* is the period beginning with the first day of the tax year and ending on the earlier of the date of mailing of a notice of deficiency with respect to the initial tax or the date on which the initial tax is assessed.[280]

In any case in which an initial tax is imposed on the undistributed income of a private foundation for any tax year, an *additional tax* is imposed on any portion that remains undistributed at the close of the taxable period. This additional excise tax imposed is equal to 100 percent of any amount remaining undistributed at the close of the correction period.[281] The *correction period* is the period beginning on the first day of the tax year for which there was a failure to distribute income and ending 90 days after the date of mailing of a notice of deficiency with respect to the additional tax imposed on such failure. The correction period is extended by any period in which a deficiency cannot be assessed and any other period that the IRS determines is reasonable and necessary to bring about correction of the failure to distribute income.[282]

The *termination tax*[283] may serve as a third-tier tax where there have been either willful repeated acts (or failures to act), or a willful and flagrant act

---

276. IRC § 4942(a). This tax is also known as a *first-tier tax* (IRC § 4963(a); Reg. § 53.4963-1(a)).
277. IRC § 4942(b). This tax is also known as a *second-tier tax* (IRC § 4963(b); Reg. § 53.4963-1(b)).
278. IRC § 507(c); see § 13.7.
279. IRC § 4942(a); Reg. § 53.4942(a)-1(a)(1).
280. IRC § 4942(j)(1); Reg. § 53.4942(a)-1(c)(1)(i).
281. IRC § 4942(b); Reg. § 53.4942(a)-1(a)(2).
282. IRC § 4963(e).
283. See § 13.7.

§ 6.5 EXCISE TAXES ON FAILURE TO DISTRIBUTE INCOME

(or failure to act), giving rise to liability for the taxes on the failure to distribute income or the other private foundation excise taxes.[284] The regulations make clear that payment of the excise taxes for failure to distribute income is in addition to, not in lieu of, making the distribution of any undistributed income, and indicate that where the failure to do so is willful the termination tax may apply.[285]

The IRS has discretionary authority to abate or refund the excise taxes on failure to distribute income if a private foundation establishes to the satisfaction of the IRS that the failure was due to reasonable cause, was not due to willful neglect, and has been corrected within the appropriate correction period.[286]

(e) Valuation Mistakes

Where a private foundation fails to make its required annual distributions due solely to an incorrect valuation of assets, the excise tax for failure to distribute income does not apply if the following four conditions are met:[287]

1. The failure to value the assets properly was not willful and was due to reasonable cause.
2. The deficiency is distributed as a qualifying distribution by the foundation within 90 days after receipt of IRS notice of deficiency.
3. The foundation notifies the IRS that the deficiency has been distributed to correct the mistake.
4. The extra distribution made to correct the deficiency is treated as being distributed in the tax year of the deficiency.

To prove that the undervaluation was *not willful* and *due to reasonable cause*, the foundation must show it made all reasonable efforts in good faith to value the assets correctly.[288] An appraisal prepared by a qualified appraiser with no relationship to the foundation or its disqualified persons, which is based on full disclosure of the factual situation by the foundation, is ordinarily considered to establish that the undervaluation was not willful and due to reasonable cause.[289]

A private foundation notifies the IRS of a failure to distribute income based solely on an incorrect valuation of assets by disclosing on its Form 990-PF the

---

284. IRC § 507(a)(2); see § 13.2.
285. Reg. § 53.4942(a)-1(a)(3).
286. IRC § 4962; see § 12.4(c).
287. IRC § 4942(a)(2), (j)(2); Reg. § 53.4942(a)-1(b)(1)(ii).
288. Reg. § 53.4942(a)-1(b)(2).
289. Id.

year(s) to which the incorrect valuation applied. A statement must also be attached to the return explaining all the facts regarding the incorrect valuation of assets (that is, an explanation why the incorrect valuation was not willful and was due to reasonable cause) and the actions taken (or planned) to comply with the last three requirements above.[290]

(f) Exception for Certain Accumulations

The mandatory payout rules do not apply to a private foundation to the extent that its income is required to be accumulated pursuant to the mandatory terms (as in effect on May 26, 1969, and at all subsequent times) of an instrument executed before May 27, 1969, with respect to the transfer of income-producing property to the private foundation.[291] The exception to this exception, however, is that the rules are applicable where the organization would have been denied tax exemption by reason of former law if that law had not been repealed by the Tax Reform Act of 1969.[292]

The payout rules also do not apply to a private foundation that is prohibited by its governing instrument or other instrument from distributing capital or corpus to the extent the requirements of the section are inconsistent with the prohibition.[293] However, this exception applies only during the pendency of any judicial proceeding by the private foundation that is necessary to reform or to excuse it from compliance with its instrument in order to comply with the mandatory payout rules.[294] Thus, these two exceptions are of limited applicability.[295]

§ 6.6 HISTORY OF THE MANDATORY DISTRIBUTION REQUIREMENT

Of all the private foundation rules, none has been more extensively revised since its original enactment than these mandatory distribution requirements. The evolution of these revisions can be useful in understanding the purpose and mechanics of the rules in their contemporary form.

The definition of the minimum amount that must, under the general rules, be distributed by a private foundation was originally enacted in 1969 and revised in 1976 and 1981.

---

290. Instructions for Form 990-PF (2022), Part VI-B, line 2.
291. Reg. § 53.4942(a)-2(e)(1)(i).
292. Id.
293. IRC §§ 4942(b), 4942(j)(2); Reg. § 53.4942(a)-2(e)(1)(ii).
294. Reg. § 53.4942(a)-2(e)(3).
295. Rev. Rul. 77-74, 1977-1 C.B. 352.

§ 6.6 HISTORY OF THE MANDATORY DISTRIBUTION REQUIREMENT

The percentage used to determine a private foundation's minimum investment return was, at the initiation of this requirement, set at 6 percent of noncharitable assets, for tax years beginning in 1970 or 1971, in the case of a private foundation created after May 26, 1969.[296] The Department of the Treasury was authorized to adjust this rate prospectively from time to time, based on changes in money rates and investment yields, using as the standard the 6 percent rate, given rates and yields for 1969. The subsequent applicable percentages were 5.5 percent for tax years beginning in 1972,[297] 5.25 percent for 1973,[298] and 6 percent for 1974[299] and 1975.[300] The rate for 1976 and thereafter was set at 5 percent.[301]

To afford private foundations organized before May 27, 1969, an opportunity to revise their investment and payout practices, a phase-in period with respect to the 6 percent rate was instituted.[302] The minimum payout was 4.125 percent for tax years beginning in 1972,[303] 4.375 percent for tax years beginning in 1973,[304] 5.5 percent for 1974,[305] and 6 percent for 1975. The Department of the Treasury set the applicable percentage for 1976 at 6.75 percent.[306] This was, however, a dual (or alternative) distribution test, in that the amount to be distributed was the greater of a private foundation's minimum investment return (computed using the applicable year's percentage rate) or its adjusted net income.

Congress, as part of the enactment of the Tax Reform Act of 1976, lowered the private foundation mandatory distribution rate. It was lowered, for years beginning after December 31, 1975, to the greater of a foundation's adjusted net income or a minimum investment return of 5 percent;[307] this amount was reduced by any taxes on unrelated business income[308] and the excise tax on net investment income.[309] The authority in the Department of the Treasury to annually adjust the rate was eliminated; this change nullified the prospective increase in the applicable percentage for 1976 to 6.75 percent.

---

296. Reg. § 53.4942(a)-2(c)(5)(i)(a).
297. Reg. § 53.4942(a)-2(c)(5)(i)(b); Rev. Rul. 72-625, 1972-2 C.B. 604.
298. Reg. § 53.4942(a)-2(c)(5)(i)(c); Rev. Rul. 73-235, 1973-1 C.B. 519.
299. Reg. § 53.4942(a)-2(c)(5)(i)(d); Rev. Rul. 74-238, 1974-1 C.B. 326.
300. Reg. § 53.4942(a)-2(c)(5)(i)(d); Rev. Rul. 75-270, 1975-2 C.B. 449.
301. Reg. § 53.4942(a)-2(c)(5)(i)(e).
302. Reg. § 53.4942(a)-2(c)(5)(ii).
303. Reg. § 53.4942(a)-2(c)(5)(ii)(b); Rev. Rul. 72-625, 1972-2 C.B. 604.
304. Reg. § 53.4942(a)-2(c)(5)(ii)(c); Rev. Rul. 73-235, 1973-1 C.B. 519.
305. Reg. § 53.4942(a)-2(c)(5)(ii)(d); Rev. Rul. 74-238, 1074-1 C.B. 326.
306. Rev. Rul. 76-193, 1976-1 C.B. 357.
307. Reg. § 53.4942(a)-2(c)(5)(i)(e).
308. See Chapter 11.
309. Reg. § 53.4942(a)-2(b)(1)(ii). This excise tax is the subject of Chapter 10.

Thus, under the post-1969, pre-1982 regime, a private foundation had to determine its adjusted net income in computing its annual distributable amount. In this connection, the IRS ruled that repayments of principal received by a private foundation in tax years beginning after 1969 on loans made in prior years to individuals for charitable purposes were not includible in its gross income to determine its adjusted net income for these purposes; however, payments of interest on the loans were held to be items of adjusted net income.[310]

Repayments of a loan made by a private foundation need not be treated as gross income where the loan amounts were not used in meeting the private foundation's distribution obligations, and the repayments may be returned to the corpus.[311] The IRS issued two other rulings in this context. In one case, a private foundation receiving annual payments as a beneficiary of a decedent's deferred incentive compensation income plan was advised to include each payment as gross income to the extent that it exceeded the amount attributable to the value of the right to receive the payment on the decedent's date of death.[312]

In the other instance, the IRS ruled that capital gain dividends received by a private foundation from a regulated investment company[313] are excluded from the private foundation's adjusted net income because the dividends are treated statutorily as long-term capital gains.[314]

Only net short-term capital gains are included in private foundations' gross income for this purpose.[315] Thus, the amount of undistributed income is not reduced for long-term capital losses or for short-term capital losses in excess of capital gains.[316] Interest on government obligations that is normally excludible from gross income[317] is included as private foundation gross income. Generally, deductions are limited to ordinary and necessary expenses paid or incurred for the production or collection of gross income, or for the management, conservation, or maintenance of property held for the production of income. Amortizable bond premiums are deductible (to the extent permitted).[318,319]

---

310. Rev. Rul. 75-443, 1975-2 C.B. 449.
311. Rev. Rul. 77-252, 1977-2 C.B. 390.
312. Rev. Rul. 75-442, 1975-2 C.B. 448.
313. IRC § 851.
314. IRC § 852(b)(3)(B). Rev. Rul. 73-320, 1973-2 C.B. 385.
315. IRC § 4942(f)(2)(B).
316. Stanley O. Miller Charitable Fund v. Commissioner, 89 T.C. 1112 (1987).
317. IRC § 103.
318. IRC § 171.
319. Rev. Rul. 76-248, 1976-1 C.B. 353.

§ 6.6 HISTORY OF THE MANDATORY DISTRIBUTION REQUIREMENT

Imputed interest[320] is included within this concept of adjusted gross income. Some private foundations sold property, prior to the enactment of the private foundation rules in 1969, on an installment sales basis that did not call for a stated rate of interest. The Senate Finance Committee, when developing its version of the Tax Reform Act of 1976, regarded as "onerous" the fact that a private foundation had to distribute income imputed to it as the result of pre-1969 sales, thereby causing it to drastically expand its ongoing active program or forcing it to make one-time grants (which, in the case of a private operating foundation, could cause it to fail to meet the income test, in that grant-making does not constitute the "active conduct" of tax-exempt activities).[321,322]

Accordingly, in 1976 Congress changed the definition of adjusted net income for these purposes to exclude imputed interest in the case of sales made before 1969.[323] However, imputed income from pre-1969 transactions is included in the net investment income of private foundations for purposes of the net investment income tax.[324] The contemporary distribution requirement does not utilize the element of a private foundation's adjusted net income.[325] This concept of adjusted net income concept remains in the law, however, because it is used in determining whether a private foundation constitutes a private operating foundation,[326] and in calculating the annual distributable amount of a nonfunctionally integrated Type III supporting organization.[327] The term *adjusted net income* means the excess (if any) of the gross income for the tax year determined with certain income modifications over the sum of the deductions determined with certain deduction modifications.[328] Gross income does not include gifts, grants, or contributions received by a private foundation; it does include income from a functionally related business.

When Congress adopted the Economic Recovery Tax Act of 1981, it revised the private foundation mandatory distribution rules again, causing the requirement to utilize solely the minimum investment return rate of 5 percent. The law on the point was revised in 1981 because of the dramatically high interest rates paid on bonds and other debt instruments during the late 1970s. The previous requirement that private foundations distribute the entirety of their adjusted net income for charitable purposes contributed to a rapid erosion of the

---

320. IRC § 483.
321. See § 3.1.
322. S. Rep. No. 94-938, pt. 2, at 89 (1976).
323. IRC § 4942(f)(2)(D).
324. See Chapter 10.
325. See § 6.1(b).
326. See § 3.1.
327. See § 15.6(g)(vi).
328. IRC § 4942(f)(2); Reg. § 53.4942(a)-2(d)(1)-(4).

resources of private foundations and imposed an artificial, distortive pressure on the investment practices of private foundations. (By contrast, other forms of charitable and other tax-exempt organizations were able to take advantage of these high-income yields to buttress their income and asset base and combat inflation.) During these economic conditions, the income payout requirement forced private foundations to either accept damaging erosion of their assets or engage in investment considerations dictated by federal tax rules rather than prudent investing strategies. The first course of action forced a private foundation to distribute its entire income yield; the second course of action forced the foundation to skew its investment decisions to select its holdings largely from those with low current yields, frequently including relatively risky holdings such as growth stocks and commodities.

The revision of the payout rules in 1981—the use of a single percentage standard—was designed to simultaneously enable private foundations to adequately support charitable activities currently and allow them to maintain their ability to do so in the future. This law revision meant that private foundations could return to more traditional, prudent investment practices. This process usually entails the definition of specific investment objectives, a forecast of desired economic returns, and the allocation of assets over a range of investment opportunities that are most likely to achieve the desired rate of return consistent with the investor's risk tolerance and income needs. Unlike the conventional investor, however, a private foundation, in its investment program, must take into account not only the mandatory distribution requirement (both the 5 percent payout requirement and the distinction between charitable and noncharitable assets), but also the jeopardizing investment rules,[329] and the net investment income excise tax (which is imposed on net investment income, including capital gain).[330]

---

329. See Chapter 8.
330. See Chapter 10.

CHAPTER SEVEN

Excess Business Holdings

§ 7.1 General Rules 311
   (a) Definition of Business Enterprise 312
   (b) Passive Income Businesses 313
   (c) Certain Investment Partnerships 315
   (d) Percentage Limitations 317
§ 7.2 Permitted and Excess Holdings 319
   (a) General Rules 319
   (b) Partnerships, Trusts, and Proprietorships 321
   (c) Constructive Ownership 322
   (d) Disposition Periods 322
§ 7.3 **Functionally Related Businesses** 327
§ 7.4 **Philanthropic Businesses** 332
§ 7.5 **Rules Applicable to Certain Supporting Organizations** 332
§ 7.6 **Rules Applicable to Donor-Advised Funds** 333
§ 7.7 **Excise Taxes on Excess Holdings** 333

§ 7.1 GENERAL RULES

A private foundation's ability to own an active business—one that is not conducted as an exempt charitable function—generally is limited by rules concerning *excess business holdings*. The basic rule is that the combined ownership by a private foundation and those who are disqualified persons with respect to it,[1] of a business enterprise in any form—corporation, partnership, joint venture, sole proprietorship, or other type of unincorporated company—may not exceed 20 percent. There are rules enabling foundations, without incurring liability for the excise tax on excess business holdings, to receive and dispose of excess holdings when the excess is acquired by the foundation by means of a contribution or inheritance subject to limitations on purchasers imposed by the self-dealing rules.[2]

---

1. See Chapter 4.
2. See Chapter 5.

§ 7.1 GENERAL RULES

Congress placed limitations on the extent to which a business may be controlled by a private foundation because of concerns that permitting extensive business holdings had a tendency to result in the neglect of a foundation's charitable activities and could result in unfair competition. It was observed that:

> Those who wished to use a foundation's stock holdings to acquire or retain business control in some cases were relatively unconcerned about producing income to be used by the foundation for charitable purposes. In fact, they might have become so interested in making a success of the business, or in meeting competition, that most of their attention and interest was devoted to this with the result that what was supposed to be their function, that of carrying on charitable, educational, etc., activities was neglected. Even when such a foundation attains a degree of independence from its major donor, there is a temptation for its managers to divert their interest to the maintenance and improvement of the business and away from their charitable duties. Where the charitable ownership predominates, the business may be run in a way which unfairly competes with other businesses whose owners must pay taxes on the income that they derive from the businesses.[3]

(a) Definition of Business Enterprise

The term *business enterprise* is broadly defined to include the active conduct of a trade or business, including any activity that is regularly carried on for the production of income from the sale of goods or the performance of services, and that constitutes an unrelated trade or business.[4] Where an activity carried on for profit is an unrelated business, no part of it may be excluded from classification as a business enterprise merely because it does not result in a profit.[5]

A for-profit business may be started, yet not generate any income for an initial period of time. That undertaking would appear to be a business enterprise as of its commencement, inasmuch as it is carried on *for* the production of income. That is, presumably an activity cannot escape classification as a business enterprise during a start-up period in which income is not yet being produced. The tax regulations provide that, if a private foundation holds an interest that is not an interest in a business enterprise (because it meets the definition of a passive income business),[6] and the interest subsequently

---

3. Staff of Joint Comm. on Internal Revenue Tax'n, 91st Cong., 2d Sess., General Explanation of the Tax Reform Act of 1969 41 (Comm. Print 1970).
4. IRC § 4943(d)(4); Reg. § 53.4943-10(a)(1). The unrelated business income rules are the subject of Chapter 11.
5. *Id.*
6. See § 7.1(b).

becomes an interest in a business enterprise, the interest becomes an interest in a business enterprise at the time of the change in status.[7]

A bond or other evidence of indebtedness is not a holding in a business enterprise unless it is otherwise determined to be an equitable interest in the enterprise.[8] Thus, an ostensible indebtedness will be treated as a business holding if it is essentially an equity holding in disguise. A leasehold interest in real property is not an interest in a business enterprise, even if the rent is based on profits, unless the leasehold interest is an interest in the income or profits of an unrelated trade or business.[9]

Four exceptions are available from the definition of the term *business enterprise*: a trade or business of which at least 95 percent of the gross income is derived from passive sources,[10] a functionally related business,[11] a philanthropic business,[12] and a program-related investment.[13]

Thus, a private foundation, like all tax-exempt organizations, can be viewed as clusters of "businesses," with some (if not nearly all) businesses related to exempt purposes and some (perhaps) unrelated to exempt purposes. A fragmentation rule[14] is used to fractionate each business from the cluster, such as in determining whether a business is related or unrelated. The concept of fragmenting any entity into its ascertainable businesses has taken on new meaning and importance with adoption of the so-called "bucketing rule."[15]

(b) Passive Income Businesses

The term *business enterprise* does not include a trade or business at least 95 percent of the gross income from which is derived from passive sources.[16] An alternative to this passive-source gross income rule is a multiyear averaging mechanism.[17] Thus, stock in a passive holding company is not considered a holding in a business enterprise even if the company is controlled by the foundation; the foundation is treated as owning its proportionate share of any interests in a business enterprise held by the company.[18]

---

7. Reg. § 53.4943-10(d)(2)(i).
8. Reg. § 53.4943-10(a)(2).
9. *Id.*
10. See § 7.1(b).
11. See § 7.3.
12. See § 7.4.
13. See § 8.3.
14. IRC § 513(c); Reg. § 1.513-1(b).
15. See § 11.5(b).
16. IRC § 4943(d)(3)(B); Reg. § 53.4943-10(c)(1).
17. Reg. § 53.4943-10(c)(1).
18. *Id.*

§ 7.1 GENERAL RULES

The concept of *passive source income* is derived from the unrelated business rules. Thus, passive income includes items considered passive in nature for purposes of those rules,[19] including (1) dividends, interest, and annuities; (2) royalties, including overriding royalties, whether measured by production or by gross or taxable income from the property;[20] (3) rental income from real property and from personal property leased with real property, if the rent attributable to the personal property is incidental (less than 50 percent of the total rent); (4) gains or losses from sales, exchanges, or other dispositions of property other than stock in trade held for regular sale to customers; and (5) income from the sale of goods, if the seller does not manufacture, produce, physically receive or deliver, negotiate sales of, or keep inventories in the goods.[21]

Tax-exempt title-holding companies[22] can be utilized to house passive business operations.[23]

A contemporary application of these rules involves the concept of the blocker corporation. In one of its private letter rulings on the point, the IRS considered the tax law consequences of a wholly owned blocker corporation in a foreign country, formed by a private foundation for asset management and liability protection purposes.[24] At least 95 percent of this corporation's income was expected to be from passive investments; some investments are to be debt-financed. This income will be foreign personal holding company income;[25] no income will be attributable to insurance activity. The IRS ruled that (1) the Subpart F income[26] to be received by the foundation from the corporation will not be subject to the unrelated business income tax,[27] (2) the income the foundation will receive from the corporation will be dividend income and therefore excluded from unrelated business income taxation,[28] (3) the foundation's ownership of the corporation's stock is not an excess business holding because the operation is not a business enterprise,[29] and (4) the foundation's ownership of the corporation will not be a jeopardizing investment.[30]

---

19. IRC § 512(b)(1), (2), (3), (5). See § 11.2.
20. Working interests in oil and mineral properties are active businesses (e.g., Priv. Ltr. Rul. 8407095).
21. Reg. § 53.4943-10(c)(2).
22. Organizations that are tax-exempt by reason of IRC § 501(c)(2) or (25).
23. E.g., Priv. Ltr. Rul. 8840055.
24. Priv. Ltr. Rul. 201430017.
25. IRC § 954(c)(1)(A).
26. IRC §§ 951-964.
27. See Chapter 11.
28. See § 11.2.
29. See § 7.1(a).
30. See § 8.1(a).

EXCESS BUSINESS HOLDINGS

Income derived from a property may constitute both nontaxable income (because the associated activity is passive) and taxable unrelated business income.[31]

The fact that the unrelated debt-financed income rules[32] may apply to an item of passive income does not alter the character of the income as passive.[33]

(c) Certain Investment Partnerships

According to the IRS, the term *business enterprise* "may not encompass certain partnerships that engage solely in investment activities,"[34] even though less than 95 percent of the partnership's income may be derived from passive sources.[35] The matter involved the formation and operation of an investment partnership by 15 private foundations, each of which is a disqualified person with respect to the others.[36] The partnership agreement prohibits the admission of partners that are not private foundations; one of the foundations will serve as the managing general partner. An investment management company that provides services to the manager foundation is to provide investment management and administrative services to this investment partnership without charge. Each foundation's investment in and capital commitment to the investment partnership will not exceed 20 percent of the value of its investment portfolio.[37]

The purpose of this investment partnership is to enable each of these private foundations to invest in equity interests in private businesses and private equity funds not otherwise available to them and to achieve greater diversification in investments. The investments generally will be made in other (lower-tier) limited partnerships, to which this investment partnership will subscribe as a limited partner. The investment partnership's gross income from nonpassive sources (such as income from partnerships engaged in an active business) may not exceed 5 percent a year.[38]

---

31. E.g., Priv. Ltr. Rul. 201422027, involving a situation where a private foundation was gifted an apartment complex. The IRS ruled that passive rental income derived from operation of the complex (more than 95 percent of total income) was not unrelated business income because of the rental income exclusion (IRC § 512(b)(3)(i)) but that income from an onsite coin-operated laundry facility was unrelated business income.
32. IRC §§ 512(b)(4), 514. See § 11.4.
33. Reg. § 53.4943-10(c)(2).
34. Priv. Ltr. Rul. 199939046.
35. See § 7.1(b).
36. See § 4.7.
37. See § 7.1(d).
38. A foundation in this instance treats its proportionate share of income of this nature as unrelated business income and may have to pay the resulting tax if the underlying property is debt-financed (IRC § 512 (c)(1)). See § 11.4.

§ 7.1 GENERAL RULES

The partnership agreement prohibits this investment partnership from making any investments that would cause any of the foundations to be involved in jeopardy investments.[39] The partnership may not directly engage in an operating business. The agreement forbids the partnership from making any investment that would cause the combined interests of any partner and all disqualified persons with respect to that partner in any business enterprise to exceed the permitted business holdings of the partner.[40] The investment partnership will not purchase property from, sell property to, exchange property with, or lease property to or from a disqualified person with respect to any of the foundation partners.[41] The partnership will not receive credit from or extend credit to a disqualified person with respect to any of the foundation partners.[42] The partnership will not purchase or sell investments in an attempt to manipulate the price of the investments to the advantage of a disqualified person.[43]

If this investment partnership were a business enterprise, then the investment of each of the participating foundations would be an excess business holding, because the combined profits interests of each foundation and its disqualified persons would be in excess of 20 percent,[44] and the 2 percent de minimis rule[45] would be inapplicable. The IRS observed that a "strict reading" of the tax regulations would limit the concept of the passive business to organizations receiving at least 95 percent of their gross income from passive sources. Nonetheless, because the partnership's activities will consist of investing in private business, mostly as a limited partner in other limited partnerships, and because limited partnership interests "may represent passive investments," the IRS ruled that the investment partnership will not be treated as a business enterprise for purposes of the excess business holdings rules.

In a buttressing of its position, the IRS reviewed the legislative history of the excess business holdings rules.[46] The agency stated that Congress "only sought to prevent private foundations from engaging in active businesses." The IRS observed that a contrary conclusion would prevent a participating private foundation indirectly investing in limited partnership interests through the partnership, even though it could invest in such interests directly. There was, as noted, a representation that the investment partnership would not acquire more than a 20 percent interest in any limited partnership. The IRS

---

39. See Chapter 8.
40. See § 7.2(b).
41. See § 5.4.
42. See § 5.5.
43. See § 5.8(a), (b).
44. See § 7.1(d).
45. *Id.*
46. E.g., S. Rep. No. 91-552, at 2066-2072 (1969).

said that the "mere interposition" of this investment partnership "should not produce a different result."

The IRS wrote that "this is a situation that calls for the application of the constructive ownership rule." Under this rule,[47] the investment partnership will not hold an impermissible interest in any business enterprise that would result in an indirect excess business holding for any of its foundation partners. The IRS concluded that, given that the foundation partners could directly hold these interests in business enterprises, and given that the investment partnership is formed for "valid business reasons," the foundations should be allowed to form and hold interests in the partnership to achieve the same result indirectly.[48]

A foundation's limited partnership interest in the lower tier of a fund-of-funds partnership was found by the IRS to qualify for the "business enterprise" exception and thereby not to be a business holding. The IRS reasoned that limited partner distributions should also be viewed as passive source income similar to stock dividends.[49] The ruling does not consider the question of whether the income would be treated as unrelated business income.

(d) Percentage Limitations

The excess business holdings rules generally limit to 20 percent the permitted ownership of a corporation's voting stock or other interest in a business enterprise that may be held by a private foundation and all disqualified persons combined.[50] Thus, as a general rule, a private foundation and its substantial contributors, managers, their family members, and the like cannot collectively own more than 20 percent of a corporation.

Generally, ownership of a corporation is measured in terms of the extent of a person's holding of voting stock. For excess business holdings purposes, however, there is a correlation between those holdings and the underlying right, if any, to select one or more directors of the corporation involved. That is, the percentage of voting stock held by a person in a corporation is normally determined by reference to the power of stock to vote for the election of directors.[51] Treasury stock and stock that is authorized but not issued are disregarded for these purposes.[52]

---

47. See § 7.2(c).
48. This type of investment partnership has been the subject of proposed legislation, by which its tax exemption, and terms and conditions of operation, would be prescribed by statute, somewhat along the lines of IRC § 501(f), which is an exempt investment pool for schools, colleges, and universities (see *Tax-Exempt Organizations*, § 11.5).
49. Priv. Ltr. Rul. 200611034, citing Reg. § 53.4943-10(c)(2).
50. IRC § 4943(c)(2)(A); Reg. §§ 53.4943-1, 3(b)(1)(i).
51. Reg. § 53.4943-3(b)(1)(ii).
52. *Id.*

§ 7.1 GENERAL RULES

For example, a private foundation holds 20 percent of the shares of one class of stock in a corporation. That class is entitled to elect three directors. The foundation does not hold any stock in another class of the corporation's stock, which is entitled to elect five directors. The foundation is treated as holding 7.5 percent of the voting stock because the class of stock it holds has 37.5 percent of the voting power. The foundation is able to elect three of eight directors (37.5 percent); 20 percent of 37.5 percent is 7.5 percent.[53]

Where all disqualified persons with respect to a private foundation together do not own more than 20 percent of the voting stock of an incorporated business enterprise, the foundation can own any amount of nonvoting stock.[54] Equity interests that do not have voting power attributable to them are classified as nonvoting stock.[55] Stock carrying contingent voting rights is treated as nonvoting stock until the event triggering the right to vote occurs.[56] (An illustration is preferred stock that can be voted only if dividends are not paid; these shares are considered nonvoting until the voting power is exercisable.)[57]

In the case of a partnership, including a limited partnership, or a joint venture, the terms *profits interest* and *capital interest* are substituted for *voting stock* and *nonvoting stock*, respectively.[58] On at least two occasions the IRS has indicated that a private foundation's holdings as a limited partner are not equivalent to nonvoting stock.[59] In the case of a sole proprietorship, a private foundation may not have any permitted holdings.[60] For any other unincorporated business or for a trust, the term *beneficial interest* is substituted for *voting stock*, but no amount of an equivalent to nonvoting stock is allowed.[61]

If effective control of a business enterprise can be shown to the satisfaction of the IRS to be elsewhere (i.e., other than by the private foundation and its disqualified persons), a 35 percent limit may be substituted for the 20 percent limit.[62] The term *effective control* means possession of the power, whether

---

53. *Id.*
54. IRC § 4943(c)(2). An illustration of this rule is provided in Priv. Ltr. Rul. 201013072. This percentage can be as high as 35 percent if effective control lies outside the foundation and its disqualified persons (see discussion of effective control *infra*).
55. Reg. § 53.4943-3(b)(2)(i).
56. Reg. § 53.4943-3(b)(2)(ii).
57. The IRS has taken the position that the intrinsic character of stock, and not any side agreements, determines whether a stock is voting stock. For example, entering into a binding agreement (scripted on the shares and transferable to any purchaser of the shares) not to vote a private foundation's stock does not reduce excess business holdings (e.g., Priv. Ltr. Rul. 9124061).
58. Reg. § 53.4943-3(c)(2).
59. Priv. Ltr. Rul. 8407095; Gen. Couns. Mem. 39195.
60. Reg. § 53.4943-3(c)(3).
61. Reg. § 53.4943-3(c)(4).
62. IRC § 4943(c)(2)(B); Reg. § 53.4943-3(b)(3)(i).

direct or indirect, and whether or not actually exercised, to direct or cause the direction of the management and policies of a business enterprise.[63] Effective control can be achieved through ownership of voting stock, the use of voting trusts, contractual arrangements, or otherwise. It is the reality of control that is decisive rather than its form or the means by which it is exercisable. For this 35 percent rule to apply, a private foundation must demonstrate by affirmative proof that some unrelated third party, or group of third parties, does in fact exercise control over the business enterprise involved.[64]

A private foundation must, however, hold, directly or indirectly, more than 2 percent of the voting stock or other value of a business enterprise before either of these limitations becomes applicable.[65] The holdings of related private foundations[66] are aggregated for the purpose of computing this 2 percent amount,[67] so as to preclude the use of multiple private foundations as a means of converting this de minimis rule into a method of evading the excess business holdings rules.

§ 7.2 PERMITTED AND EXCESS HOLDINGS

The *permitted business holdings* of a private foundation are those that are within the previously described 20 percent or 35 percent limitations.[68] Thus, *excess business holdings* constitute the amount of stock or other interest in a business enterprise that a private foundation would have to dispose of by transferring it to a person (other than a disqualified person) in order for the remaining holdings of the foundation in the enterprise to constitute permitted holdings.[69]

(a) General Rules

When a purchase, by a disqualified person, of stock or other interest in a business enterprise creates an excess business holding, the private foundation involved has 90 days—from the date it knows, or has reason to know, of the event that caused it to have the excess holdings—to dispose of the excess

---

63. Reg. § 53.4943-3(b)(3)(ii).
64. Rev. Rul. 81-111, 1981-1 C.B. 509.
65. IRC § 4943(c)(2)(C); Reg. § 53.4943-3(b)(4). In 1991, the IRS ruled that a private foundation could split the 2 percent *de minimis* holding allotment between itself and a new private foundation formed to receive one-half of the original foundation's assets (Priv. Ltr. Rul. 9117070); following a review of the issue, however, the IRS revoked its ruling in 1993 (Priv. Ltr. Rul. 9333051).
66. See § 4.7.
67. Reg. § 53.4943-3(b)(4).
68. See § 7.1(d).
69. IRC § 4943(c)(1); Reg. § 53.4943-3(a)(1).

§ 7.2 PERMITTED AND EXCESS HOLDINGS

holdings.[70] The excise taxes[71] are not applied if the holdings are properly reduced within this 90-day period. The period can be extended to include any period during which a foundation is prevented by federal or state securities law from disposing of the excess holdings.[72]

An interest purchased by a private foundation that causes the ownership of a business holding (combined with that of disqualified persons) to exceed the permissible limits must be disposed of immediately, and the foundation is subject to tax. If the foundation had no knowledge, nor any reason to know, that its holdings had become excessive, the 90-day-period rule applies, and the tax is not assessed.[73]

Whether a private foundation is treated as knowing or having reason to know of the acquisition of holdings by a disqualified person depends on the facts and circumstances of each case. Factors to be considered are that the foundation did not discover acquisitions made by disqualified persons through the use of procedures reasonably calculated to discover the holdings, the diversity of foundation holdings, and the existence of large numbers of disqualified persons who have little or no contact with the foundation or its managers.[74]

If a private foundation disposes of an interest in a business enterprise with any material restrictions or conditions that prevent free use of or prevent disposition of the transferred shares, the foundation is treated as owning the interest until the restrictions or conditions are eliminated.[75]

These rules have a complex past. They were initiated in 1969; interests held as of that year were termed *present holdings*.[76] The excess business holdings rules did not apply to present interests; a 50 percent limitation applied or, if lower, the actual percentage of holdings.[77] If a private foundation with present holdings reduced its percentage holdings in a business enterprise, it could not thereafter increase the holdings (the *downward rachet rule*); however, if the reduction caused the holdings to fall below the 20 percent (or 35 percent) level, they could be increased to those levels.[78] Any excess ownership held at

---

70. Reg. § 53.4943-2(a)(1)(ii).
71. See § 7.7.
72. Reg. § 53.4943-2(a)(1)(iii).
73. Reg. § 53.4943-2(a)(1)(ii).
74. Reg. § 53.4943-2(a)(1)(v).
75. Reg. § 53.4943-2(a)(1)(iv). A private foundation was able to correct an excess business holding of stock by granting stock to public charities to bring its ownership of the shares to less than the 2 percent de minimis amount (see § 7.1(d)); the IRS ruled that the additional criteria accompanying a grant to one of these charities will not entail any material restrictions (Priv. Ltr. Rul. 201414031).
76. Reg. § 53.4943-4(d)(1).
77. IRC § 4943(c)(4)(A)(i). Also, Rev. Rul. 75-25, 1975-1 C.B. 359.
78. IRC § 4943(c)(4)(A)(ii); Reg. § 53.4943-4(d)(4).

that time had to be divested by the foundation, with the period of disposition (or phase) being 10, 15, or 20 years, depending on the percentage of combined ownership.[79] These rules, which played out in 1989, caused major dispositions of securities holdings by private foundations during the 1970s and 1980s. An interest received from a trust that was irrevocable as of May 26, 1969, or from a will in effect and not revised since that date remains subject to these divestiture requirements.[80]

(b) Partnerships, Trusts, and Proprietorships

The excess business holdings rules often focus on holdings in the form of stock in incorporated businesses. These rules, however, also apply with respect to holdings in unincorporated business entities, such as partnerships, joint ventures, and trusts.[81] In these contexts, the terms identifying the nature of the ownership are different. In a general or limited partnership or a joint venture, the terms *profit interest* and *capital interest* are substituted for *voting stock* and *nonvoting stock*.[82] For trusts, the term *beneficial interest* is used to define ownership.[83]

The interest of a private foundation and its disqualified persons in a partnership is determined using the federal tax law's distributive share concepts.[84] Absent a formal partnership agreement, the private foundation's ownership is measured by the portion of assets that the foundation is entitled to receive on withdrawal or dissolution, whichever is greater.[85]

For example, a private foundation owning 45 percent of a partnership is considered to own 45 percent of the property owned by the partnership; thus, if the partnership owned 50 percent of the outstanding stock of a corporation, the foundation would be treated as owning 22.5 percent of the corporation (50 percent of 45 percent). Therefore, in this example, the foundation would have excess holdings of 2.5 percent, unless the 35 percent limitation was applicable.[86] This may be the case where a foundation holds a limited partnership interest, which normally does not accord the foundation the requisite power to direct or cause the direction of the management and policies of a business enterprise.[87] A right on the part of the limited partner private foundation to

---

79. The tax law is detailed as to these procedures (IRC § 4943(c)(4)(B)-(D); Reg. § 53.4943-4).
80. IRC § 4943(c)(5); Reg. § 53.4943-5.
81. IRC § 4943(c)(3); Reg. § 53.4943-3(c)(1), (2), (4).
82. IRC § 4943(c)(3)(A); Reg. § 53.4943-3(c)(2).
83. IRC § 4943(c)(3)(C); Reg. § 53.4943-3(c)(4).
84. IRC § 704(b).
85. Reg. § 53.4943-3(c)(2).
86. See § 7.1(d).
87. Reg. § 53.4943-3(b)(3)(ii).

§ 7.2 PERMITTED AND EXCESS HOLDINGS

veto the general partner's actions may, however, constitute sufficient control to cause the 20 percent limitation to be applicable.[88]

A private foundation may not operate a business enterprise (other than a functionally related or otherwise exempted one) as a sole proprietorship,[89] because that arrangement by definition entails a 100 percent ownership.[90]

(c) Constructive Ownership

In computing the holdings of a private foundation or a disqualified person with respect to a private foundation in a business enterprise, any stock or other interest owned, directly or indirectly, by or for a corporation, partnership, estate, or trust is considered as being owned proportionately by or for its shareholders, partners, or beneficiaries.[91] Exempted from this constructive ownership rule (subject to certain exceptions) are holdings of corporations that are engaged in an active trade or business (the *myopia rule*).[92] A passive parent of an affiliated group of active businesses is treated as an active business for these purposes.[93]

Any interest in a business enterprise over which a private foundation or a disqualified person has a power of appointment, exercisable in favor of the foundation or disqualified person, is treated as owned by the foundation or disqualified person holding the power of appointment.

Stock in a split-interest trust[94] is not considered constructively owned by a private foundation where the foundation's sole relationship with the trust is that it has an income or remainder interest in it.[95]

(d) Disposition Periods

If a private foundation obtains holdings in a business enterprise *other than by purchase* by the foundation or by disqualified persons with respect to it, and the additional holdings would result in the foundation's having excess

---

88. Priv. Ltr. Rul. 9250039.
89. IRC § 4943(c)(3)(B); Reg. § 53.4943-3(c)(3).
90. If a private foundation owns a sole proprietorship and subsequently divests itself of a portion of the interest in it (so that the foundation has less than a 100 percent interest in the equity of the business enterprise), the resulting business enterprise is treated as a partnership (Reg. § 53.4943-10(e)).
91. IRC § 4943(d)(1); Reg. § 53.4943-8(a), (b), (d). A foreign private foundation (see §10.6) was held to constructively own precisely 20 percent of the voting stock of a company and thus not have an excess business holding (Priv. Ltr. Rul. 201737003).
92. Reg. § 53.4943-8(c)(1)-(3).
93. Reg. §§ 53.4943-8(c)(4), 10(c)(3).
94. See § 3.7.
95. IRC § 4943(d)(1); Reg. § 53.4943-8(b)(2).

business holdings, the foundation has five years to reduce these holdings to permissible levels.[96] This is because the excess holdings (or an increase in excess holdings) resulting from the transaction are treated as being held by a disqualified person—rather than by the foundation—during the five-year period beginning on the date the foundation obtained the holdings.

Acquisitions by gift, devise, bequest, legacy, or intestate succession are the subjects of this five-year rule,[97] as are certain increases in holdings in a business enterprise that are the result of a readjustment of the enterprise.[98] In the case of an acquisition of holdings in a business enterprise by a private foundation pursuant to the terms of a will or trust, the five-year period does not commence until the date on which the distribution of the holdings from the estate or trust occurs.[99]

A supporting organization that converted to private foundation status was allowed five years to dispose of certain wholly owned for-profit subsidiaries acquired during the time it operated as a supporting organization.[100] Because the acquisitions of stock in the subsidiaries were made during the time it was a supporting organization, the private foundation was treated as having obtained the assets by ceasing to be a public charity, not by purchase. Additional capital contributions made to the subsidiaries after the organization converted to private foundation status were not treated as additional purchases of stock because they could not result in additional stock ownership over the 100 percent already held by the foundation.

This five-year rule does not apply to any transfer of holdings in a business enterprise by one private foundation to another private foundation that is related to the first foundation.[101] The rule does not apply to an increase in the holdings of a private foundation in a business enterprise that is part of a plan by which disqualified persons will purchase additional holdings in the same enterprise during the five-year period beginning on the date of the change (e.g., for the purpose of maintaining control of the enterprise). In this situation, the increase in the private foundation's holdings is treated as caused in part by the purchase of such additional holdings.[102] The purchase of holdings

---

96. IRC § 4943(c)(6); Reg. § 53.4943-6(a)(1).
97. Reg. § 53.4943-6(a)(2).
98. Reg. § 53.4943-6(d). A *readjustment* may be a merger or consolidation; a recapitalization; an acquisition of stock or assets; a transfer of assets; a change in identity, form, or place of organization; a redemption; or a liquidating distribution (Reg. § 53.4943-7(d)(1)).
99. Reg. § 53.4943-6(b)(1). An illustration of the application of this rule is in Priv. Ltr. Rul. 201849009.
100. Priv. Ltr. Rul. 9852023.
101. Reg. § 53.4943-6(c)(1). See § 4.7.
102. Reg. § 53.4943-6(c)(2). This matter of a "plan" is not clear. For example, how is such a plan to be evidenced? Can the plan be only among disqualified persons, or is it contemplated that the private foundation involved must be part of it (the latter interpretation seemingly the most reasonable)?

§ 7.2 PERMITTED AND EXCESS HOLDINGS

by an entity whose holdings are treated as constructively owned by a private foundation, its disqualified persons, or both[103] is treated as a purchase by a disqualified person if the foundation, its disqualified persons, or both have effective control of the entity or otherwise can control the purchase. For example, if a foundation is the beneficiary of a specific cash bequest and its consent is required for the estate to make a purchase of additional business holdings using such cash, then a purchase by the estate using such cash would be treated as a purchase by a disqualified person for purposes of determining whether the five-year rule applies.[104]

If a private foundation, its disqualified persons, or both hold an interest in specific property under the terms of a will or trust, and if the foundation and/or its disqualified persons agree to the substitution of holdings in a business enterprise for the property, the holdings are regarded as a purchase by a disqualified person.[105]

When a private foundation has a program-related investment (and thus does not have an interest in a business enterprise)[106] and subsequently the investment fails to qualify as a program-related one (so that the holding becomes an interest in a business enterprise), for purposes of this five-year rule, the interest becomes one acquired other than by purchase as of the date it fails to so qualify.[107] A similar rule applies with respect to passive holdings[108] and to other circumstances in which an interest not originally a business enterprise becomes a business enterprise.[109]

The IRS has the authority to allow an additional five-year period for the disposition of excess business holdings in the case of an "unusually large gift or bequest of diverse business holdings or holdings with complex corporate structures" if:

- The private foundation establishes that diligent efforts to dispose of the holdings were made within the initial five-year period and disposition within the initial five-year period was not possible (except at a price substantially below fair market value) by reason of the size and complexity or diversity of the holdings.

---

103. See § 7.2(c).
104. Reg. § 53.4943-6(c)(3).
105. Reg. § 53.4943-6(c)(4).
106. See § 7.1(a).
107. Reg. § 53.4943-10(d)(1).
108. Reg. § 53.4943-10(d)(2)(i).
109. Reg. § 53.4943-10(d)(2)(ii).

EXCESS BUSINESS HOLDINGS

- Before the close of the initial five-year period, the private foundation submits to the IRS a plan for disposition of all of the excess business holdings involved in the extension, submits the plan to the appropriate state attorney general or similar official, and submits to the IRS any response received by the foundation from the state official to the plan during the initial five-year period.
- The IRS determines that the plan can reasonably be expected to be carried out before the close of the extension period.[110]

The IRS grants extensions of this nature to private foundations through private letter rulings.[111] By way of example, the IRS has granted the additional five-year extension in the following instances:

- An independent financial consultant developed a plan to assist a private foundation in selling its holdings in conjunction with the substantial contributor's family members who owned the same holdings.[112]
- A private foundation made "diligent and continuous" efforts to sell real estate but was impeded by the need for substantial capital improvements and conversions in order to secure a purchaser.[113]
- Disposition of the foundation's interest in a business during the initial five-year period was not feasible, and an investment banker advised the foundation that the interests in the enterprise should be able to be sold for their true value over the coming three to four years.[114]
- A private foundation had been trying to dispose of its interest in a company, received by bequest, but was unable to sell the interest during the initial five-year period because it became embroiled in litigation with a developer. Upon resolution of the litigation, the foundation represented it would make "diligent" efforts to sell the interest, including retaining a broker with the requisite expertise.[115]
- A private foundation retained the services of an investment banking firm to help it sell stock in a corporation that owned and operated a collection

---

110. IRC § 4943(c)(7).
111. E.g., Priv. Ltr. Rul. 8508114. A request for an additional five years to dispose of excess business holdings must be made in the form of a letter ruling request (see § 12.5(b)).
112. Priv. Ltr. Rul. 9115061.
113. Priv. Ltr. Rul. 200332020.
114. Priv. Ltr. Rul. 200438042.
115. Priv. Ltr. Rul. 201636021.

§ 7.2 PERMITTED AND EXCESS HOLDINGS

of retail stores and warehouses throughout multiple states. Despite significant marketing efforts, it had been unable to sell the properties due to the complex nature of the corporation and adverse marketing conditions. It had a plan to sell the properties to an employee-owned group and also a back-up plan entailing reorganization of the company and consideration of a different marketing advisor.[116]

- Despite diligent efforts, a private foundation was unable to dispose of a partial interest in a closely held company operating in a niche market with few competitors, which made the company's stock highly illiquid. As a result of these factors, there was essentially no market for a partial interest in the company and any possible disposition would require a sale of the entire company. The foundation's plan for disposing of its stock during the extended period provided that, if sale of the stock involved during the first four years of the extended period did not occur, the company would be recapitalized so that the foundation's holdings of the company's voting stock would be reduced to no more than 20 percent of the total.[117]

- Through a bequest, a private foundation received a large, but minority, interest in a corporation and an LLC. Despite diligent efforts, the foundation was unable to dispose of these interests for various reasons, including significant transfer restrictions on the interests, the complex and highly regulated nature of the industry in which the entities operated, an adversarial relationship with management of the two entities, economic issues relating to the COVID-19 pandemic, and the inability of the LLC to operate because it lacked governmental approvals. In the event the LLC was unable to obtain the regulatory approvals needed to resume operations during the extension period, the LLC would be liquidated and the foundation would receive its share of the liquidation proceeds. Otherwise, the foundation would sell the portion of its interests in both entities needed to reduce its holdings in both to (or below) the 20 percent threshold.[118]

By contrast, the IRS declined to grant a five-year extension where the stock at issue was not acquired by an unusually large gift or bequest of diverse business holdings or holdings with complex corporate structures; the private foundation did not demonstrate that it made diligent efforts to dispose of such holdings during the initial five-year period; and the foundation's marketing

---

116. Priv. Ltr. Rul. 201329027.
117. Priv. Ltr. Rul. 202040002.
118. Priv. Ltr. Rul. 202251003.

plan for the disposition of the stock, other than indicating that it would be identifying prospective buyers, did not show that it had a "sound strategy" that was focused on overcoming the problems that prevented it from selling the stock during the initial five-year period. This foundation's cause was not helped either by the fact that it increased its holdings by purchasing additional shares of stock during the initial five-year period.[119] Likewise, the extension was denied where a private foundation had excess business holdings during all or a portion of the period prior to receiving a bequest that further increased its holdings; the bequest was not an unusually large gift; the amount of its excess business holdings was not exceptionally large; it had opportunities to reduce its holdings during several stock redemptions; and other avenues to divest itself of its excess business holdings were available.[120]

Although a private foundation must also submit its disposition plan to the appropriate state attorney general or similar official, and submit to the IRS any response thereto, a failure to receive a response from such state official does not preclude the IRS from granting the extension.[121]

§ 7.3 FUNCTIONALLY RELATED BUSINESSES

The taxes on excess business holdings do not apply with respect to holdings in a *functionally related business*.[122] This type of business is not a *business enterprise*.[123] A functionally related business is a business or activity:

- The conduct of which is substantially related (aside from the mere provision of funds for the tax-exempt purpose) to the exercise or performance by the private foundation of its charitable, educational, or other tax-exempt purpose,

- In which substantially all the work is performed for the foundation without compensation,[124]

- Carried on by the foundation primarily for the convenience of its employees, members, patients, visitors, or students (such as a cafeteria or shop operated for a hospital or museum),

---

119. Priv. Ltr. Rul. 9029067.
120. Priv. Ltr. Rul. 199923057. The extension was also denied where a private foundation requested the extension before it had even received the stock from an estate that was still being probated and, consequently, had made only minimal efforts to dispose of the stock (Priv. Ltr. Rul. 9646031).
121. E.g., Priv. Ltr. Rul. 9211067.
122. IRC § 4942(j)(4); Reg. § 53.4943-10(b).
123. IRC § 4943(d)(3)(A).
124. Rev. Rul. 76-85, 1976-1 C.B. 357.

§ 7.3 FUNCTIONALLY RELATED BUSINESSES

- That consists of the selling of merchandise, substantially all of which has been received by the foundation as contributions, or
- Carried on within a larger aggregate of similar activities or within a larger complex of other endeavors that is related to the tax-exempt purposes of the foundation (other than the need to simply provide funds for these purposes).[125]

As an example of the first of these types of businesses, a private foundation proposed to build, maintain, and lease a public ice arena to promote the health and welfare of its community and to lessen the burdens of local government. This facility, which would conform to National Hockey League and college rink specifications, would include a pro shop, coffee shop, concession area, day care center, and lounge. It might also include a conference center, gymnastics facility, and an athletic medicine center. This arena would be leased to third parties at a fair rental value rate. The IRS ruled that the development, ownership, and leasing of the arena will further the foundation's charitable purposes; these activities were held to constitute a functionally related business, and therefore did not constitute a business enterprise for excess business holdings rule purposes.[126]

As another example, the IRS concluded that a music publishing company that concentrated on classical music was related to the purposes of a private foundation promoting music education and the choice of music as a career, and thus was a functionally related business.[127] Likewise, a racetrack and a campground were ruled by the IRS to constitute functionally related businesses, inasmuch as they were conducted in conjunction with a museum operated by a private foundation.[128] Similarly, a farm in a foreign country, previously conducted as a for-profit operation by the founder of a private foundation, became operated by the foundation after his death as an exempt demonstration project and thus a functionally related business.[129] Also, a grant by a private foundation to a for-profit corporation for the purpose of funding a medical malpractice reinsurance program, to enable physicians in an area to continue to practice, constituted a qualifying distribution because the reinsurance company was a functionally related business.[130]

---

125. Reg. § 53.4942(a)-2(c)(3)(iii).
126. Priv. Ltr. Rul. 200532058.
127. Priv. Ltr. Rul. 8927031.
128. Priv. Ltr. Rul. 200202077.
129. Priv. Ltr. Rul. 200343027.
130. Priv. Ltr. Rul. 200347017.

Likewise, a supporting organization[131] functioning as a qualified scholarship funding corporation made an election[132] to transfer all of its student loan notes to a taxable corporation in exchange for all of the corporation's senior stock and operated thereafter as a private foundation; the IRS ruled that the holding of this stock is a functionally related business.[133] Moreover, the IRS ruled that a taxable subsidiary of a private foundation, formed to provide consulting services to other foundations and exempt organizations about program-related and other investments, to assist in locating investors for community development venture capital funds or rural business investment companies, to provide certain asset management services, and to manage a public mutual fund to facilitate investments in public companies the business practices of which support the foundation's mission, is a functionally related business.[134] This latter ruling, however, was revoked by the IRS without explanation.[135]

In another instance, an artist created a for-profit corporation to house his "artistic enterprise." This corporation acquired and stored the materials used by the artist in the creation of his artwork; handled the creation, fabrication, shipment, storage, and insurance of this work; and managed its sale, reproduction, and licensing. The artist died; all of the stock of this corporation is to be transferred to a private operating foundation established by the artist. The function of the corporation will change to curatorial activities and management of the artist's legacy. The foundation will use these resources to increase public exposure and understanding of the broad scope of this artist's work, advance scholarship of his work, and encourage artists' involvement in civic affairs by showing that art can change the world. The IRS ruled that the operations of this corporation are a functionally related business, so that the foundation's holding of the stock will not be excess business holdings.[136]

Likewise, a private foundation owned a portion of a limited liability company, with two other members. The LLC operated a low-income housing project for the elderly, which qualified for and had been allocated low-income housing tax credits. The private foundation proposed to purchase the other two members' interests at less than fair market value, thereby becoming the sole owner of the LLC. The foundation represented that the project operated by the LLC, which would be attributed to the foundation, would meet the IRS's

---

131. See § 15.6(g).
132. IRC § 150(d)(3).
133. Priv. Ltr. Rul. 200434028.
134. Priv. Ltr. Rul. 200709065.
135. Priv. Ltr. Rul. 201006032.
136. Priv. Ltr. Rul. 201323029.

§ 7.3 FUNCTIONALLY RELATED BUSINESSES

low-income housing safe harbor standards, pursuant to which a low-income housing project is considered to further charitable purposes by relieving the poor and distressed.[137] The IRS analyzed whether the foundation's ownership of the LLC should be treated as an excess business holding. Because the activity of the LLC was substantially related to the foundation's exempt purpose, the IRS determined that the operation of the housing project was a functionally related business.[138]

In some instances, more than one definition of a *functionally related business* is used in the same context. For example, a private operating foundation was in the process of funding a community cultural center that will display traveling educational exhibits, and house a museum containing historical artifacts, other exhibits, artistic performances, an archive, a library, and an atrium. Within the center will be a gift shop, selling items affiliated with the center's programs, and a coffee shop for use by its visitors and employees, which is not designed to be a "public eating establishment." The IRS ruled that the coffee shop will be a functionally related business, in that it "will help attract visitors" to the center. The IRS also held that the gift shop will be "an activity carried on as part of the overall activities as they relate to the center's exempt educational purpose" and that as long as it is "actually operating as a functional part of the center's larger aggregate of other activities which are related to the center's exempt educational purpose," the gift shop will be a functionally related business.[139]

Although not involving a private foundation, the IRS has considered the topic of a functional part of an organization's aggregated other activities in the context of a tax-exempt professional society[140] that had as one of its core functions the publication of a journal. The journal was published under a contract with a for-profit publishing company. The society had complete responsibility for the editorial content of the journal; the publisher was solely responsible for selling advertising space in the journal. The issue before the IRS was whether the business of publishing commercial advertising was regularly carried on[141] by the society. In concluding that the advertising activities of the publisher were not attributable to the society, the IRS found that the publisher was not acting as the society's agent with respect to those activities. The IRS ruled that, "within the larger complex of publishing an exempt organization periodical, advertising activities are considered separately from the activities of

---

137. Rev. Proc. 96-32, 1996-1 C.B. 717.
138. Priv. Ltr. Rul. 201603032.
139. Priv. Ltr. Rul. 201710005.
140. An IRC § 501(c)(6) organization. See *Tax-Exempt Organizations*, § 14.1(e).
141. See § 11.1(d).

producing editorial material," leading the IRS to decide that the commercial advertising was not regularly carried on by the society.[142]

The IRS has also ruled that a private foundation can have a functionally related business in the form of a partial ownership of a for-profit business.[143] The foundation in this instance promoted the cause of music education and encouraged the choice of music as a profession. It held 80 percent of the stock of a music publishing company that concentrated its activities in the field of classical and other serious music, publishing and distributing concert music and instructional materials. This publisher published the works of little-known composers. Losses were incurred from these activities, which were subsidized by the functions of acting as a major U.S. distributor of domestic and foreign catalogs representing serious and educational music publishers.[144]

These rules may be utilized as part of a plan to eliminate excess business holdings. For example, a private foundation developed a restructuring plan to enable it to reduce its interests in the voting stock of various companies, held by a single-member limited liability company (a disregarded entity),[145] to permissible levels. The core of this plan was placement of 80 percent of this stock with public charities. The companies were recapitalized so that the foundation owned, by means of this limited liability company (considered a holding company), 100 percent of a class of stock entitled to elect 20 percent and zero percent of a class of stock entitled to elect 80 percent, of the companies' directors. The voting stock was designed so that if the private foundation or any of its disqualified persons (or anyone who becomes a disqualified person) acquires a share, it automatically converts to nonvoting stock. Additionally, owners of the voting stock were entitled to vote for only one of five directors, so that any increase in the foundation's equity in the companies would not result in an increase in voting rights. The IRS ruled that this foundation timely shed sufficient holdings in the companies' stock to avoid excess business holdings and that the holding company, owning facilities that are used for charitable purposes, is a functionally related business.[146]

---

142. Tech. Adv. Mem. 201837014.
143. Priv. Ltr. Rul. 8930047.
144. Given the development of the commerciality doctrine (see *Tax-Exempt Organizations* § 4.9) over recent years, the ongoing validity of this ruling may be in some doubt. The catalog distribution function is likely to be commercial by today's standards, if only because, presumably, the publishers were for-profit businesses. Or the IRS would assert impermissible private benefit (see § 5.2). Even so, a business more commercial in nature than this one may not qualify the partial ownership of it by a private foundation as a functionally related business.
145. See *Tax-Exempt Organizations* § 4.1(b).
146. Priv. Ltr. Rul. 200825050.

§ 7.4 PHILANTHROPIC BUSINESSES

An exception from the concept of excess business holdings is available for holdings in a philanthropic business.[147] A *philanthropic business* is a business that satisfies three tests: ownership requirements, an all-profits-to-charity distribution requirement, and independent operation requirements.

Pursuant to the ownership requirements, all the voting stock in the business enterprise must be held by the private foundation at all times during the year and none of the foundation's ownership interests in the enterprise may have been acquired by purchase.[148]

The all-profits-to-charity requirement is met if the business enterprise, no later than 120 days following the close of a year, distributes an amount equal to its net operating income for the year to the private foundation.[149]

The independent operation requirement is met if at all times during the year no substantial contributor[150] to the foundation or family member of this type of contributor[151] is a trustee, director, officer, manager, employee, or contractor of the business enterprise or is an individual with similar powers or responsibilities. Also, at least a majority of the foundation's board may not be directors or officers of the business enterprise or be family members of a substantial contributor to the foundation. Further, there cannot be an outstanding loan from the business enterprise to a substantial contributor to the foundation or a family member of this type of contributor.[152]

§ 7.5 RULES APPLICABLE TO CERTAIN SUPPORTING ORGANIZATIONS

The excess business holdings rules are applicable to Type III supporting organizations, other than functionally integrated Type III supporting organizations.[153] In applying these rules, the term *disqualified person* is defined under the intermediate sanctions rules and includes substantial contributors, related persons, and

---

147. IRC § 4943(g). This provision, created for the benefit and relief of the Newman's Own Foundation, was enacted as part of the Bipartisan Budget Act of 2018 (Pub. L. No. 115-123, div. D, § 41110, 132 Stat. 64, 159).
148. IRC § 4943(g)(2).
149. IRC § 4943(g)(3).
150. As defined in IRC § 4958(c)(3)(C).
151. As defined in IRC § 4958(f)(4).
152. IRC § 4943(g)(4). The concept of the philanthropic business does not apply with respect to deemed private foundations, namely, donor-advised funds and certain supporting organizations (IRC § 4945(e), (f)), certain charitable trusts (IRC § 4947(a)(1)), and split-interest trusts (IRC § 4947(a)(2)). IRC § 4943(g)(5).
153. IRC § 4943(f)(1), (3)(A). See § 15.6(k).

EXCESS BUSINESS HOLDINGS

any organization that is effectively controlled by the same person or persons who control the supporting organization or any organization substantially all of the contributions to which were made by the same person or persons who made substantially all of the contributions to the supporting organization.[154]

These rules also apply to a Type II supporting organization[155] if the organization accepts a contribution from a person (other than a public charity that is not a supporting organization) who controls, either alone or with family members and/or certain controlled entities, the governing body of a supported organization of the supporting organization.[156] Nonetheless, the IRS has the authority to not impose the excess business holdings rules on a supporting organization if the organization establishes that the holdings are consistent with the organization's tax-exempt status.[157]

§ 7.6 RULES APPLICABLE TO DONOR-ADVISED FUNDS

The excess business holdings rules are applicable to donor-advised funds.[158] For this purpose, the term *disqualified person* means, with respect to a donor-advised fund, a donor, a donor advisor, a member of the family of either, or a 35 percent controlled entity of any of these persons.[159]

§ 7.7 EXCISE TAXES ON EXCESS HOLDINGS

An initial excise tax is imposed on a private foundation in an instance of excess business holdings in a business enterprise for each tax year that ends during the taxable period.[160] The amount of this tax is 10 percent of the total value of all of the foundation's excess business holdings in each of its business

---

154. IRC § 4943(f)(4).
155. See § 15.6(k).
156. IRC § 4943(f)(1), (3)(B). Temporary standards for determining *control* in this context were provided by the IRS (Notice 2006-109, 2006-51 I.R.B. 1121 § 3.02).
157. IRC § 4943(f)(2). The IRS exercised this authority, holding that a nonfunctionally integrated Type III supporting organization's holdings in a development project were exempt from the excess business holdings tax; the IRS reached this result by applying factors set forth in the legislative history of the Pension Protection Act of 2006 (Staff of Joint Comm. on Tax'n, Technical Explanation of H.R. 4, the "Pension Protection Act of 2006," as Passed by the House on July 28, 2006, and as Considered by the Senate on August 3, 2006 361 (Comm. Print JCX-38-06)), which the IRS is to consider in exercising this authority (Priv. Ltr. Rul. 201645011).
158. IRC § 4943(e)(1). See § 16.7.
159. IRC § 4943(e)(2). An illustration of application of the excess business holdings rules in this context is in Priv. Ltr. Rul. 201311035 (discussed in § 16.7).
160. IRC § 4943(a)(1). This tax is also known as a *first-tier tax* (IRC § 4963(a); Reg. § 53.4963-1(a)).

§ 7.7 EXCISE TAXES ON EXCESS HOLDINGS

enterprises.[161] This tax is determined using the greatest value of the foundation's excess holdings in the enterprise during the year.[162] Form 4720 is used to calculate and report the tax due. The valuation is determined under the estate tax rules.[163]

The *taxable period* is the period beginning with the first day on which there are excess holdings and ending on the earliest of the following dates: the date on which the IRS mails a notice of deficiency with respect to the initial tax[164] in respect of the excess holdings, the date on which the excess holding is eliminated, or the date on which the initial tax in respect of the excess holdings is assessed.[165]

If the initial tax is imposed and the excess business holdings are not disposed of by the close of the taxable period, an additional tax is imposed on the private foundation.[166] The amount of this tax is 200 percent of the value of the excess business holdings.[167]

The additional taxes are imposed at the end of the taxable period. Where the act or failure to act that gave rise to the additional tax is corrected within the correction period, the tax will not be assessed, or if assessed will be abated, or if collected will be credited or refunded.[168] The *correction period* is the period beginning on the date on which the *taxable event* occurs and ending 90 days after the date of mailing of a notice of deficiency with respect to the additional tax imposed on the event, extended by any period in which a deficiency cannot be assessed[169] and any other period that the IRS determines is reasonable and necessary to bring about correction of the taxable event.[170] In this setting, a taxable event is an act or failure to act giving rise to liability for tax under the excess business holdings rules.[171] This event occurs on the first day on which there are excess business holdings.[172] *Correction* means complete elimination of the excess holdings.[173]

---

161. *Id.*; Reg. § 53.4943-2(a)(1)(i).
162. IRC § 4943(a)(2); Reg. § 53.4943-2(a)(2).
163. Reg. § 53.4943-2(a)(1)(i).
164. IRC § 6212.
165. IRC § 4943(d)(2); Reg. § 53.4943-9(a)(1).
166. IRC § 4943(b). This tax is also known as a *second-tier tax* (IRC § 4963(b); Reg. § 53.4963-1(b)).
167. *Id.*; Reg. § 53.4943-2(b).
168. IRC § 4961(a); Reg. § 53.4961-1.
169. IRC § 6213(a).
170. IRC § 4963(e)(1); Reg. § 53.4963-1(e)(1).
171. IRC § 4963(c); Reg. § 53.4963-1(c).
172. IRC § 4963(e)(2)(B); Reg. § 53.4963-1(e)(7)(ii).
173. IRC § 4963(d)(2)(B); Reg. § 53.4963-1(d)(2)(ii).

EXCESS BUSINESS HOLDINGS

The collection period is suspended during any litigation.[174]

The termination tax[175] may serve as a third-tier tax where there have been either willful, repeated acts (or failures to act), or a willful and flagrant act (or failure to act), giving rise to liability for the taxes on excess business holdings or the other private foundation excise taxes.[176]

---

174. IRC § 4961(c); Reg. § 53.4961-2.
175. See § 13.7.
176. IRC § 507(a)(2); see § 13.2.

CHAPTER EIGHT

Jeopardizing Investments

§ 8.1 General Rules 338
    (a) Defining Jeopardy 339
    (b) Contributed Assets 343
§ 8.2 Prudent Investments 344
    (a) Evaluating Investment Alternatives 346
    (b) Facing the Unknown 348
    (c) Risk versus Return 349
    (d) Total Return Investing 350
    (e) Reporting of Income 351
    (f) Measuring Investment Return 351
    (g) Mission-Related Investments 352

§ 8.3 Program-Related Investments 353
§ 8.4 Investment Frauds 359
    (a) Background 359
    (b) NYSBA Report 360
§ 8.5 Excise Taxes on Jeopardizing Investments 362
    (a) Initial Taxes 362
    (b) When a Manager Knows 363
    (c) Reliance on Outside Advisors 364
    (d) Additional Taxes and Removal from Jeopardy 365

A private foundation has limitations—albeit not particularly stringent ones—on its investment options. Generally speaking, a private foundation's assets may not be used in a way that jeopardizes their use for exempt purposes. The rationale for the rules that apply to such *jeopardizing investments* is that using a private foundation's assets in this manner prevents gifts to a foundation from being used for charitable ends, which is the justification for granting current tax benefits to donors to private foundations and to foundations themselves.[1]

Under pre-1969 law, a private foundation manager might invest the foundation's assets in warrants, commodity futures, and options, or might purchase on margin or otherwise expose the corpus of the foundation to risk of loss without being subject to sanction. The purpose, then, of these jeopardizing investment rules is to shield foundation assets from a high degree of risk, so as to maximize both capital and income available for charitable purposes. This

---

1. Staff of Joint Comm. on Internal Revenue Tax'n, 91st Cong., 2d Sess., General Explanation of the Tax Reform Act of 1969 46 (Comm. Print 1970)

body of federal law generally parallels that of state law, where the directors and trustees of private foundations have a fiduciary responsibility to safeguard a charitable entity's assets on behalf of its charitable constituency by following prudent investor standards.

§ 8.1 GENERAL RULES

A private foundation cannot, without incurring an excise tax, invest any amount (income or principal) in a manner that would jeopardize the carrying out of its tax-exempt purposes.[2] The statute is silent as to what constitutes this type of investment, other than to exclude from the concept investments that are program-related ones.[3] The regulations state, however, that an investment is considered to jeopardize the carrying out of the tax-exempt purposes of a private foundation if it is determined that the foundation managers, in making the investment, failed to exercise ordinary business care and prudence, under the facts and circumstances prevailing at the time the investment was made, in providing for the long- and short-term financial needs of the private foundation to carry out its exempt purposes.[4] Congress contemplated that the determination as to whether investments jeopardize the carrying out of a private foundation's charitable purposes is to be made as of the time of the investment, in accordance with the prudent trustee approach,[5] and not subsequently on the basis of hindsight.

A determination as to whether the making of a particular investment jeopardizes the tax-exempt purposes of a private foundation is to be made on an investment-by-investment basis, in each case taking into account the private foundation's portfolio as a whole. It is considered prudent for the foundation managers to take into account the expected returns (income and appreciation of capital), the risks of rising and falling price levels, and the need for diversification within the investment portfolio. As to this third criterion, a private foundation manager should consider the type of security involved, the type of industry, the maturity of the company, the degree of risk, and the potential for return. To avoid the imposition of the applicable excise tax, however, a careful analysis of potential investments must be made and good business judgment must be exercised.[6]

---

2. IRC § 4944(a)(1).
3. See § 8.3.
4. Reg. § 53.4944-1(a)(2)(i). Thus, where a private foundation and its managers took reasonable measures and exercised ordinary business care and prudence prior to entering into the investment, the jeopardizing investment excise taxes (see § 8.5) can be avoided (e.g., Tech. Adv. Mem. 200218038).
5. S. Rep. No. 91-552, at 46 (1969).
6. Reg. § 53.4944-1(a)(2)(i).

Once it has been ascertained that an investment does not jeopardize the carrying out of a private foundation's tax-exempt purposes, the investment is never considered to jeopardize the carrying out of exempt purposes, even though, as a result of the investment, the private foundation subsequently realizes a loss.[7]

(a) Defining Jeopardy

No category of investments is treated as a per se violation of these rules. However, the types or methods of investment that are closely scrutinized to determine whether foundation managers have met the requisite standard of care and prudence include trading in securities on margin, trading in commodity futures, investments in oil and gas syndications, the purchase of puts, calls, and straddles, the purchase of warrants, and selling short. More latitude is permissible in today's sophisticated financial markets, which were not anticipated when the regulations were written in 1970. In 1992, the American Law Institute revised its *Restatement of the Law, Trusts—Prudent Investor Rule*,[8] containing the basic rules governing the investment of trust assets. This update is a useful guide that reflects modern investment concepts and practices. The *prudent investor rule* recognizes that return on investment is related to risk, that risk includes the risk of deterioration of real return owing to inflation, and that the risk/return relationship must be taken into account in managing trust assets.

The IRS ruled that a whole-life insurance policy that was contributed to a private foundation resulted in a jeopardizing investment. The policy was subject to a policy loan by the donor (the insured) who at the time of the gift had a life expectancy of 10 years. The private foundation did not surrender the policy for its cash value but continued to pay the annual premiums and interest due on the policy and the loan. Finding that the combined premium and interest payments were such that, by the end of eight years, the private foundation would have invested a greater amount in premiums and interest than it could receive as a return on the investment (as insurance proceeds upon the death of the insured), the IRS concluded that "the foundation managers, by investing at the projected rate of return prevailing at the time of the investment, failed to exercise ordinary business care and prudence in providing for the long-term and short-term financial needs of the foundation in carrying out its exempt purposes." Therefore, under the circumstances, the IRS held that each payment made by the private foundation for a premium on the policy and interest on the policy loan was a jeopardizing investment.[9]

---

7. *Id.*
8. American Law Institute Publishers, St. Paul, Minn. See § 8.2.
9. Rev. Rul. 80-133, 1980-1 C.B. 258.

§ 8.1 GENERAL RULES

In a hospital reorganization,[10] the IRS considered whether the for-profit subsidiaries of a supporting organization converting to private foundation status were in jeopardy. There seemed to be no question that the closely held insurance company, health maintenance organization, and practice management company were risky ventures. The IRS's answer to whether the now-private foundation would be considered to have made the investments was no. The for-profit subsidiaries were created by the supporting organization before it became a private foundation, so there was no liability for the excise tax on jeopardizing investments. Under excess business holdings provisions, the shares would, however, be required to be distributed.[11]

The purchase of gold stocks to protect a portfolio as a hedge against inflation was not treated as jeopardizing, despite a net loss of $7,000 on a $14,500 investment. The private foundation involved bought the shares over three years; it made money on one block and lost on two others. The ruling noted that the foundation had realized $31,000 in gains and $23,000 in dividends during the same period on its whole portfolio. The portfolio performance as a whole was found to enable the foundation to carry out its purposes, and the investments were found not to be jeopardizing.[12] Selling options against the foundation's portfolio in a "covered option trading" program is considered to be a prudent way to enhance yield without risk. Conceivably, failure to conduct this type of program could be considered to create a jeopardizing investment.

A "managed commodity trading program" was found to give diversity to a private foundation's marketable security portfolio and not to be a jeopardizing investment. Since commodity futures have little or no correlation to the stock market, the added diversity may provide less risk for the foundation's overall investment. The foundation proposed to invest 10 percent of its portfolio.[13]

In one case, the manager of a private foundation invested the entire corpus of the foundation in a Bahamian bank without inquiring into the integrity of the bank. Unknown to the manager was the fact that the bank's license to do business had been revoked, as had its charter. Interest payments to the foundation were irregular. The IRS concluded, and a court agreed, that the investment was a jeopardizing one.[14] In another case, investment of nearly all of a foundation's assets in a single partnership was ruled not to be a jeopardizing investment because the partnership's assets were diversified.[15]

---

10. Priv. Ltr. Rul. 9852023.
11. See § 7.2(d).
12. Priv. Ltr. Rul. 8718006.
13. Priv. Ltr. Rul. 9237035.
14. Thorne v. Commissioner, 99 T.C. 67 (1992).
15. Priv. Ltr. Rul. 200318069.

In connection with a ruling holding that a private foundation's ownership of a blocker corporation was not a jeopardizing investment, the IRS observed that the foundation's managers determined that its foreign investments can be better managed, result in a more tax-efficient structure, and enhance the foundation's ability to fulfill its charitable mission by means of the corporation, and that the foundation worked closely with its investment advisors in making this determination.[16]

An investment in a limited partnership trading in the futures and forward markets was found not to be a jeopardizing investment, notwithstanding that the foundation invested an unspecified, but "significant," amount of its total assets in the partnership.[17] The examining IRS agent had argued the foundation could have received a better return with less risk in another investment vehicle. Nonetheless, the IRS National Office found that the foundation managers took reasonable measures and exercised *ordinary business care and prudence* prior to entering into the partnership based on these facts: (1) foundation managers were actively involved in establishing the partnership and choosing the four different advisors to make allocations to counterbalance the investments; (2) special conditions were negotiated that allowed the foundation to withdraw its funds at any time on written notice prior to the end of the normal term of the partnership; (3) two separate legal opinions concluding the establishment of the partnership was not a jeopardizing investment had been secured and relied upon by the foundation prior to making the investment; and (4) there was no relationship among the foundation, its managers, or the chosen investment advisors that would have been furthered by the investment.

Although the foundation invested a significant amount of its assets and may have received a better return with less risk in another investment vehicle, the IRS observed that neither of these elements is necessarily dispositive of whether a jeopardizing investment was made. The facts at the time the investment was made must be considered, and an investment is not a jeopardizing investment "merely because the end result is not as beneficial to the financial interests of a private foundation as another investment might have been." Even though a substantial portion of the foundation's assets was invested in the partnership, the regulations list diversification as only one of the factors to be considered.[18] Whether something is a jeopardizing investment hinges on whether the foundation managers exercised ordinary business care and prudence. This determination, the IRS concluded, "should be made on an investment-by-investment inquiry based on the prevailing facts and circumstances taking into account the foundation's portfolio as a whole."

---

16. Priv. Ltr. Rul. 201430017.
17. Tech. Adv. Mem. 200218038.
18. Reg. § 53.4944-1(a)(2)(i).

§ 8.1 GENERAL RULES

The IRS considered a situation where a private foundation wanted to accept a contribution of a working interest in an oil and gas exploration and development venture. There was no public market for sale of this interest; any liquidation of it would entail sale to the other investors in the project at a substantial discount. Additionally, the project had been highly profitable and the foundation's interest would represent only 1 percent of the venture. The interest was not itself a jeopardizing investment because the foundation received it without consideration, or in other words, did not make an investment.[19] The foundation was, however, subject to calls for capital and payment of expenses in connection with its interest. The IRS did not consider the question of whether such amounts paid by the foundation subsequent to the gift might result in a jeopardizing investment.

The IRS ruled that "approval of an investment procedure governing investments to be made in the future is not possible."[20] This position reflects the fact that advance approval of investment procedures would constitute a determination prior to the investment, would not be on an investment-by-investment basis, and would necessarily preclude application of the "prudent trustee" approach.

The IRS, however, will rule as to a *currently proposed investment*. In one instance, the IRS ruled that *nontraditional investments* by a private foundation in four partnerships would not be jeopardizing investments. The first of these partnerships invested primarily in distressed real estate, particularly defaulted or under-secured mortgage loans; the second was a hedge fund that invested strictly in U.S. stocks, used very low leverage, and employed a variety of investment vehicles (such as futures and forwards); the third engaged in the trading of a diverse group of commodity interests, such as agriculture products, energy products, metals, currencies, financial instruments, and stock indices; and the fourth was formed to provide a broad range of capital to support the growth of small- to medium-sized energy companies, such as oil and gas enterprises. The IRS's conclusion that the foundation's investments in each of these partnerships was not a jeopardizing investment was based on the facts that the amount of the investment in each partnership would be only 1 percent of the foundation's investment portfolio, there was a diversity of investments among the partnerships, and the investments were based on professional advice. The IRS also approved of this foundation's investment in a market neutral fund that invested in long and short portfolios.[21]

---

19. Priv. Ltr. Rul. 200621032.
20. Rev. Rul. 74-316, 1974-2 C.B. 389.
21. Priv. Ltr. Rul. 9451067.

In general, if a private foundation changes the form or terms of an investment, it is considered to have entered into a new investment on the date of the change. Thus, a determination as to whether the change in the investment causes the investment to be a jeopardizing one is made as of that time.[22]

The IRS occasionally issues private letter rulings as to whether an investment constitutes a jeopardizing investment.[23]

(b) Contributed Assets

The jeopardizing investment rules do not apply to investments made by a person who later transferred them as gifts to a private foundation.[24] Further, these rules do not apply to an investment that is acquired by a private foundation solely as a result of a corporate reorganization.[25] If a foundation furnishes any consideration to a person in connection with this type of transfer, the foundation is treated as having made an investment in the amount of the consideration. Moreover, these rules are inapplicable to investments made before January 1, 1970, unless the form or terms of the investments are later changed or they are exchanged for other investments.[26] Essentially, the foundation is not treated as having made the investment. Though the excess business holding rules might require disposition of such investment, the excise tax on jeopardizing investments is not imposed.

In one instance, an estate (the decedent being the founder of a foundation) proposed to gratuitously transfer assets to the foundation. The IRS ruled that since the foundation, in acquiring these assets, was not incurring any obligation to use its resources in the future in connection with maintenance of these assets and (at least with respect to one of the assets) it would be "in a position in which it only [stood] to gain and [had] nothing to lose," the jeopardy investment rules would not be implicated.[27]

The private foundation rules are not exclusive. For example, if a private foundation purchases a sole proprietorship in a business enterprise, it may be liable for tax under the excess business holdings rules[28] as well as the rules pertaining to jeopardizing investments.[29]

---

22. Reg. § 53.4944-1(a)(2)(iii).
23. E.g., Priv. Ltr. Rul. 200637041.
24. Reg. § 53.4944-1(a)(2)(ii)(a).
25. Reg. § 53.4944-6.
26. Reg. § 53.4944-1(a)(2)(ii)(b). The corporate reorganization must be one described in IRC § 368(a).
27. Priv. Ltr. Rul. 9614002.
28. See § 7.1.
29. Reg. § 53.4944-1(a)(2)(iv).

§ 8.2 PRUDENT INVESTMENTS

The jeopardizing investment rules do not exempt or relieve any person from compliance with any federal or state law imposing any obligation, duty, responsibility, or other standard of conduct with respect to the operation or administration of an organization or trust to which this body of law applies. Nor does any state law exempt or relieve any person from any obligation, duty, responsibility, or other standard of conduct provided in these rules.[30] In choosing prudent investments, foundation managers must take into account their need to meet the mandatory charitable distribution rules.[31]

The managers of a private foundation's investments can be guided by the *prudent investor* rules in evaluating proposed investments for jeopardy. An investment policy following these rules should theoretically prevent the making of a jeopardizing investment. These standards are compiled by the American Bar Association and were formerly referred to as the *prudent man rules*.[32]

These standards state that "a trustee is under a duty to the beneficiaries to invest and manage the funds of the trust as a prudent investor would, in light of the purposes, terms, distribution requirements, and other circumstances of the trust."[33] The *business judgment rule* requires essentially the same standard for nonprofit corporations and trustees in regard to the management of endowment funds and restricted gifts or bequests.[34]

The prudent investor rules have been codified and adopted by many states. The Uniform Prudent Investor Act was finalized in 1995 and is applicable to trusts. The Uniform Management of Institutional Funds Act (UMIFA) was finalized in 1972 to apply incorporated and unincorporated charitable organizations and certain government organizations. Most of the states adopted this standard. In 2006, the National Conference of Commissioners on Uniform State Laws approved a Uniform Prudent Management of Institutional Funds Act (UPMIFA) to replace UMIFA. A major goal of UPMIFA is to apply the same standards for the management and investment of charitable funds to those organized as a trust, a nonprofit corporation, or any other type of entity. As of 2012, Mississippi became the 51st state or territory to approve.

---

30. Reg. § 53.4944-1(a)(2)(i).
31. See Chapter 6. As investment returns vary throughout the years since 1969, the annual payout percentage has varied. In response to the increase in returns during the late 1990s, there were suggestions to raise the rate; in 2002, there were requests that it be reduced.
32. *Prudent Investor Rules*, Restatement of the Law of Trusts adopted by The American Law Institute at Washington, D.C., May 18, 1990, St. Paul, Minn.: American Law Institute Publishers.
33. *Id.*, p. 8.
34. Overton, ed., *Guidebook for Directors of Nonprofit Corporations*, Nonprofit Corporations Committee, Section of Business Law, American Bar Association, p. 41.

UPMIFA requires that the organization consider both the charitable purposes of the institution and the purposes of the fund, subject to the intent expressed by the donor, adhering to the following standards: (1) the person responsible for managing and investing an institutional fund must manage and invest the fund in good faith and with the care an ordinarily prudent person in a like position would exercise under similar circumstances, (2) managers are subject to the duty of loyalty imposed by other laws, and (3) the institution may incur only reasonable costs in relation to the fund assets, purposes of the institution, and the skills available to the institution, and (4) the institution must diversify its investments unless special circumstances exist in which the purposes of the fund are better serviced without diversification.

UPMIFA eliminates the concept of historic dollar value. Instead the institution can set an appropriate level of expenditures and accumulation as it deems prudent for the uses, benefits, purposes, and duration for which the endowment fund is established.

The tax rules suggest an investment-by-investment approach.[35] According to the IRS, the "prudent trustee" approach of the regulations could be viewed as neither entirely consistent with nor entirely inconsistent with the Prudent Investor Rule and the UMIFA.[36] Private letter rulings issued by the IRS acknowledge the prudent nature of diversification[37] and the need to consider each investment's relationship to the whole to reach this goal. Foundation officials must acknowledge the inconsistency between the tax and local law and take both into account in meeting their obligation to prudently invest the foundation's funds.

The predecessor prudent man rule was first set forth in 1830, and directed trustees to "observe how men of prudence, discretion, and intelligence manage their own affairs, not in regard to speculation, but in regard to the permanent disposition of their funds, considering the probable income, as well as the probable safety of the capital to be invested."[38] The facts and circumstances of each investor (the foundation) must be taken into account in choosing appropriate investments. The foundation's financial managers must familiarize themselves with basic investment strategies and terms reflected

---

35. See § 8.1.
36. "Public Charity Classification and Private Foundation Issues: Recent Emerging Significant Developments," Topic P, IRS Exempt Organization Continuing Professional Education Text for FY 2000.
37. The IRS, on one occasion, observed: "Generally, diversification is a prudent strategy for management of investment assets" (Priv. Ltr. Rul. 200433028).
38. Harvard College v. Amory, 26 Mass (9 Pick) 446, 461 (1830). In 1959, the rule was changed to direct trustees "to make such investment and only such investments as a prudent man would make of his own property having in view the preservation of the estate and the amount and regularity of the income to be derived."

§ 8.2 PRUDENT INVESTMENTS

in modern investment concepts and practices. Unless the trustees or directors individually possess expertise and time to manage an investment with care, skill, and caution (avoiding jeopardy), they have a duty to delegate management of these funds. The fees charged by professional investment managers are often modest when viewed in relation to the possibility of enhanced yield over a period of time and protection from excise taxes that can be imposed if investment decisions are found to jeopardize the foundation's capital.

(a) Evaluating Investment Alternatives

A foundation's financial managers must evaluate how to invest the foundation's funds in a prudent manner that balances the short- and long-term needs of the foundation and avoids jeopardizing investments. Depending on the answers to the following questions, the managers might prudently keep only a portion of the foundation's assets in cash-type interest-bearing accounts. Alternatively, the foundation might be fully invested in bonds, equities, real estate, and alternative investments. The questions that can form the basis for investment decisions include:

1. *What rate of return should the foundation target on its investments?* The mandatory distribution rules generally require a nonoperating private foundation to pay out annually (in cash or other assets) an amount equal to 5 percent of the fair market value of its investment assets.[39] Thus, without regard to other factors, such as a goal to expand programs or to allow the principal to keep pace with inflation, a private foundation needs to achieve at least a 5 percent current return on its investment to avoid using principal to make annual qualifying distributions.

2. *Should the foundation use a total return investment policy?*[40] How a foundation answers this question is related to its answer to the first question. A foundation investing for a *total return* defines its income to include dividends, rent, interest, and other current payments plus an increase in the value of its asset or minus a decline in value. Such a foundation would expect to make grant payments with its dividends and its capital gains. Since the total return method typically embodies capital gains, this policy can have a modest excise tax advantage if the foundation distributes the appreciated property rather than sell it to make cash distributions.[41]

---

39. See Chapter 6.
40. See § 8.2(d).
41. See § 10.3.

3. *For what length of time can the funds be invested?* The foundation's future liquidity needs must be projected. To choose prudent investments, the foundation must know when or if funds might be needed to meet its annual distribution requirements, to buy a needed asset, or to meet some other financial obligation or program goal. Many investment partnerships, hedge funds, and funds of funds are not readily marketable. Some have a "lock-up period" of one or more years during which the foundation may not withdraw funds. For a foundation with these illiquid investment assets or real estate, this question is particularly relevant. The value of illiquid investments is included in the calculation of a foundation's annual distributable amount even if the property yields no current income. In this situation, it is likely necessary that the foundation's other investment assets bear a return that is above the minimum needed to meet the payout requirement.

4. *Can the foundation afford a loss in its principal?* The answer to this question measures the level of risk the foundation perceives prudent. The higher the risk of loss, the higher the expected return will be on a particular investment.[42] Thus, a foundation must balance the prospect of a higher return on a riskier investment with the possibility that it may lose its original (*principal*) investment, and with the need to make its annual qualifying distributions. The possibility that an investment might decline (instead of increase as anticipated) is not necessarily evidence that the investment is a jeopardizing one. The issue is primarily managing the foundation's ability to meet its financial obligations.

5. *How secure are the foundation's funding sources?* Though many private foundations are endowed, some foundations are dependent (partly or fully) on new funding to conduct their programs. Each foundation must evaluate the stability of its funding sources to project the level of contingency (or emergency) reserves it may require. Suppose a foundation that sponsors ongoing programs receives annual funding from family members of its creators that are dependent on their income level and consequentially allowed contribution deductions. Assume further that the foundation commonly makes annual disbursements that exceed the required amount and, in some years, in excess of its current annual funding plus the income from its investment. Such a foundation might prudently maintain its funds in investments with a low risk of loss in principal value (since the funds might be needed at a time when the value is low).

---

42. See § 8.2(c).

§ 8.2 PRUDENT INVESTMENTS

6. *Is the foundation's staff capable of overseeing the investments?* Absent a Midas touch, special talents and training are required to successfully manage a fully diversified investment portfolio. This question has two different aspects. As evidenced by stock market fluctuations over the years, stock values are unpredictable. A foundation's financial managers must evaluate their own knowledge and experience and consider the need to engage outside professional investment managers. In questioning an investment that resulted in a loss, the fact that the foundation engaged a qualified independent manager might establish reasonable cause for the abatement of an excise tax.[43]

7. *How will economic conditions impact the investment?* Fixed money investments, such as certificates of deposit and U.S. Treasury obligations, fluctuate in value in relation to the prevailing interest rate and overall economic factors, but have a determinable value if held to maturity (the original principal invested can be expected to be returned). Conversely, the value of common stocks, real estate, and tangibles rises or falls in relation to a multitude of factors, including a specific company's earnings, investor mood, and inflationary or deflationary conditions. The foundation must project expected economic conditions to properly diversify its investments.

Many private foundations are choosing to place some of their investment assets in "alternative investments," such as hedge funds and offshore partnerships. These investments embody a number of tax and legal considerations not present in a portfolio of marketable securities.

(b) Facing the Unknown

A healthy dose of skepticism and an appreciation of the uncertainty that abounds is important for a foundation attempting to avoid jeopardizing investments. As one writer noted in describing the Federal Reserve Board's deliberations about the interest rate, "no word seems to appear more frequently in the transcripts than *uncertainty*."[44] The financial markets in which a foundation must choose to place its funds are influenced daily by international forces beyond its control. Who knows whether the stock market will go up, whether a global stock fund will sustain its yield, or whether the U.S. dollar will go up against the Japanese yen? The significant declines in the equity markets accompanied by a drastic decline in interest rates during 2001–2002

---

43. See § 12.4(c).
44. Uchitelle, "At the Fed It Looks Like Deja Vu, Again," *New York Times*, July 2, 1995.

evidence the need for great caution in making decisions about future market performance.

Diversification is an important technique designed to manage the unknown. A prudently balanced investment portfolio contains a variety of financial instruments—stocks, bonds, real estate, and so on. The mix of investments assumes that some go up, some go down, and in the long run the averages will provide a desirable stream of income. It is not necessarily conservative or prudent to maintain all the funds invested in fixed-money or interest-bearing securities or all in equities. To conserve the principal in its original dollar amount, inviolate and permanent into perpetuity, may not necessarily be safeguarding the fund for the donor's intentions. It should be remembered that fixed-return investments do have some inherent risk; in 1994 some bond values fell more than 10 percent as the interest rates changed quickly. Conversely, during 2001 and 2002, the market value of some fixed-money obligations rose 10 percent in response to interest rate declines.

The investment alternatives available to a foundation are the same as those available to a for-profit investor. Because the foundation pays a modest excise tax on its income, certain choices, such as municipal bonds or deferred annuities, may not be suitable.

A classically diversified investment portfolio would contain some investments in each of the categories. What portion of the total investments is held in each category depends on the foundation's risk tolerance and life phase, as discussed in the following sections. Suppose a foundation has $1 million to invest permanently. If the board adopts a conservative approach, it might invest $100,000 in short-term cash and bonds, $400,000 in long-term bonds, $500,000 in common stocks, and nothing in real estate, gold, or commodities, such as oil.

The investments within each category might be further diversified. A fixed-money portfolio, for example, would have debt instruments with staggered maturity dates and credit ratings, since fixed-return investments can also fluctuate in value and have inherent risk of loss. The $400,000 in the preceding example might include $133,000 of 5-year bonds, $133,000 of 7-year bonds, and $133,000 of 30-year bonds. Similarly, a common stock portfolio would include stock of companies in different types of businesses—auto manufacturer, drug company, computer software, home building, banking, and so on. Professional investment managers today add commodities, minerals, venture capital, and hedge funds.

(c) Risk versus Return

A foundation must carefully identify those funds that are suitable for each category of investment type. The possibility for a higher yield or overall return

§ 8.2 PRUDENT INVESTMENTS

provided by common stock is not always worth the inherent risk of the investment. Funds received as a donation to build a museum over the next two years should earn some interest, but would not prudently be invested in technology stocks.

The relationship of risk to investment return must be understood. The reason a six-month certificate of deposit pays the lowest available interest rate is that no risk is taken. Without question, the face amount of the certificate plus a stated amount of interest will be paid (absent a bank collapse or other banking system crisis). As uncertainty about the final outcome or risk of loss increases, the yield (in theory) increases. Correspondingly, a lower yield comes with less uncertainty. The conflict between risks the foundation is willing (or reasonably able) to take and the return on investment needed to pay its annual charitable disbursements is the same as for individuals and for-profit companies. Note that the jeopardy to principal is thought to increase from bottom to top. Some advisors, however, recommend a mixture of the lowest- to highest-risk investments to achieve diversification that ultimately achieves a higher yield.

(d) Total Return Investing

The financial markets expect low dividend yields equal to a small portion of a company's annual income. This *current return* is accepted to allow the corporation to reinvest most of its earnings in expansion and conglomeration. The desired result is a consequential appreciation in underlying value of the securities. Investors today anticipate annual income will be earned from a combination of dividends and interest, plus gains resulting from appreciation in the value of the underlying security. The objective is to achieve what is called *total return* on the capital invested. What formerly was treated as an addition to the principal—the appreciation in value of the asset(s)—is now treated as income under this theory of investing.

The trend toward following a total return concept for endowment funds was encouraged by the Ford Foundation as early as 1969.[45] In a study, Ford concluded, "We find no authoritative support in the law for the widely held view that the realized gains on endowment funds can never be spent. Prudence would call for the retention of sufficient gains to maintain purchasing power in the face of inflation and to guard against potential losses, but subject to the standards which prudence dictates, the expenditure of gains

---

45. Cary and Bright, *The Law and the Lore of Endowment Funds: A Report to the Ford Foundation* (New York: Ford Foundation, 1969). The study was commissioned to examine the law governing the endowment funds of colleges and universities with the goal of conveying new knowledge and informed commentary about charitable investments to strengthen the efforts of the institutions to improve their endowment income.

should lie within the discretion of the institution's directors." The study investigated whether "the directors of an educational institution are circumscribed by the law or are free to adopt the investment policy they regard as soundest for their institution, unhampered by legal impediments, prohibitions or restrictions."

(e) Reporting of Income

According to financial analysis theories, long-term investment income may be reported for financial purposes in at least four different ways. The term *realized* is used to denote capital gain or loss from transactions that actually occurred. Realized capital gain is the excess of actual sales proceeds over the amount paid for a security. *Unrealized* capital gain is the hypothetical gain calculated assuming securities still held as investments were sold on the report date. Measures of investment income include:

1. *Current return method.* Using this method, actual interest, dividends, rents, and royalties paid are treated as income (called *unrestricted* for accounting purposes). Any realized or unrealized gains or losses are added back to or subtracted from the principal fund (unrestricted or restricted).

2. *Overall return method.* This method classifies the current return (identified in the preceding item) plus realized capital gains and losses (those resulting from actual sales of the investment asset) as operating (unrestricted) income.

3. *Total return method.* This method reports overall return actually received, plus or minus unrealized gains and losses, as unrestricted income.

4. *Constant return.* Based on a historical average amount, a fixed annual percentage of the value of the investment pool is treated as unrestricted income.

(f) Measuring Investment Return

For some investments, the return, or income earned, is easy to calculate. A certificate of deposit pays a fixed yield (or returns a fixed amount) to its purchaser. Others are more complicated. The basic formula for an asset, the value of which may fluctuate, arrives at income by dividing the current income received in a year—the interest paid or accrued, dividends, capital gain distributions or other profit share (for partnership), plus the increase in value of the underlying investment less any decrease in value. The return, or yield, is then determined by dividing the income by the value of the investment at the beginning of the period.

§ 8.2 PRUDENT INVESTMENTS

Fixed-money investments whose principal values fluctuate with the prevailing interest rates require an additional step. They are often purchased at what is called a *premium* (paying $102 for a $100 bond) or *discount* (paying $95 for a $100 bond). When a premium is paid, the stated yield on the bond is usually higher than the prevailing rate. Conversely, a bond selling at a discount is likely paying a lower percentage than the current rate. Each year the bond is held, a ratable portion of the premium or discount is added to or deducted from income to reflect the true yield. Similarly, a bond originally purchased with a coupon interest rate of 8 percent does not yield 8 percent in a year when its principal value declines 2 percent; instead, it yields 6 percent.

Professional investment managers and mutual funds governed by the Securities and Exchange Commission must conform to similar unified standards for reporting investment yield.

(g) Mission-Related Investments

The IRS published guidance on the application of the jeopardizing investment rules to investments that are made by private foundations for charitable purposes.[46] This development is inapplicable to program-related investments.[47]

Pursuant to the tax regulations, an investment made by private foundation is not considered a jeopardizing investment if, in making the investment, the foundation managers exercise ordinary business care and prudence (under the circumstances prevailing at the time of the investment) in providing for the long-term and short-term financial needs of the foundation in carrying out its exempt purposes.[48] Although the regulations list some factors that managers generally consider when making investment decisions, the regulations do not provide an exhaustive list of facts and circumstances that may properly be considered.

When exercising ordinary business care and prudence in deciding whether to make an investment, foundation managers may consider all relevant facts and circumstances, including the relationship between an investment and the foundation's charitable purposes. Foundations are not required to select only investments that offer the highest rate of return, the lowest risks, or the greatest liquidity as long as the foundation managers exercise the requisite ordinary business care and prudence under the facts and circumstances prevailing at the time of the investment.

---

46. Notice 2015-62, 2015-39 I.R.B. 411.
47. See § 8.3.
48. Reg. § 53.4944-1(a)(2)(i). See § 8.1.

§ 8.3 PROGRAM-RELATED INVESTMENTS

A *program-related investment* is not considered a jeopardizing investment.[49] A program-related investment is an investment, the primary purpose of which is to accomplish one or more charitable purposes, and no significant purpose of which is the production of income or the appreciation of property.[50] The regulations add a third characteristic, in that no purpose of the investment may be the furthering of substantial legislative or any political activities.[51] Conspicuously absent from the elements of the program-related investment is the proscription on private inurement,[52] simply because private individuals necessarily benefit from the investment, albeit in the course of achieving a larger (charitable) purpose.

An investment is considered as made primarily to accomplish one or more charitable purposes if it significantly furthers the accomplishment of a private foundation's tax-exempt activities and if the investment would not have been made but for the relationship between the investment and the activities.[53] An investment in a functionally related business[54] is considered as made primarily to accomplish one or more charitable purposes.[55] In determining whether a significant purpose of an investment is the production of income or the appreciation of property, it is relevant to determine whether investors for profit would be likely to make the investment on the same terms as the private foundation. The fact, however, that an investment produces significant income or capital appreciation is not, in the absence of other factors, conclusive evidence of this type of significant purpose.[56] A program-related investment can be made by investment in a limited liability company.[57]

Illustrations of program-related investments include low-interest or interest-free loans to needy students; high-risk investments in nonprofit, low-income housing projects; low-interest loans to small businesses owned by

---

49. Reg. § 53.4944-3(a)(1).
50. IRC § 4944(c); Reg. § 53.4944-3(a)(1).
51. Reg. § 53.4944-3(a)(1)(iii). Also, IRC § 170(c)(2)(D). See §§ 9.1, 9.2. The regulations provide that an investment shall not be considered as a substantial involvement in an attempt to influence legislation if the recipient of the investment appears before or communicates to any legislative body with respect to legislation or proposed legislation of direct interest to the recipient, as long as the expenses associated with those activities are deductible as a business expense (Reg. § 53.4944-3(a)(2)(iv)). The rules as to deductibility of these types of expenses have been, however, significantly narrowed (IRC § 162 (e)).
52. IRC § 170(c)(2)(C). See § 5.1.
53. Reg. § 53.4944-3(a)(2)(i).
54. See § 7.3.
55. Reg. § 53.4944-3(a)(2)(ii). See § 1.5.
56. Reg. § 53.4944-3(a)(2)(iii).
57. E.g., Priv. Ltr. Rul. 199910066.

§ 8.3 PROGRAM-RELATED INVESTMENTS

members of economically disadvantaged groups, where commercial funds at reasonable interest rates are not readily available; investments in businesses in deteriorated urban areas under a plan to improve the economy of the area by providing employment or training for unemployed residents; and investments in nonprofit organizations combating community deterioration.

Likewise, the IRS ruled that low-interest-rate loans by a private foundation, established to aid the blind in securing employment, which are made to blind persons who desire to establish themselves in business but who are unable to obtain funds through commercial sources, constitute program-related investments.[58] The following examples from the tax regulations and IRS rulings illustrate the concept:[59]

- A small business enterprise, X, is located in a deteriorated urban area and is owned by members of an economically disadvantaged minority group. Conventional sources of funds are unwilling or unable to provide funds to the enterprise. A private foundation makes a below-market-interest-rate loan to the enterprise to encourage economic development.

- The private foundation described in the previous instance allows an extension of X's loan in order to permit X to achieve greater financial stability before it is required to repay the loan. Since the change is not motivated by attempts to enhance yield, but by an effort to encourage success of an exempt project, the altered loan is also considered to be program related.

- Assume instead that a commercial bank will loan X money if it increases the amount of its equity capital. A private foundation's purchase of X's common stock to accomplish the same purposes as the loan described earlier is a program-related investment.

- Assume instead that substantial citizens own X, but continued operation of X is important for the economic well-being of the low-income persons in the area. To save X, a private foundation lends X money at below-market rates to pay for specific projects benefiting the community. The loan is program related.

- A private foundation wants to encourage the building of a plant to provide jobs in a low-income neighborhood. The foundation lends the building funds at below-market rates to SS, a successful commercial company that is unwilling to build the plant without this inducement. Again, the loan is program related.

---
58. Rev. Rul. 78-90, 1978-1 C.B. 380.
59. Reg. § 53.4944-3(b), as to first five bullet points.

JEOPARDIZING INVESTMENTS

- A loan program established to make low-interest-rate loans to blind persons unable to obtain funds through commercial sources constitutes a program-related investment.[60]
- Land purchased for land conservation, wildlife preservation, and the protection of open and scenic spaces is program related.[61]
- Investment in a for-profit company, the purpose of which is to encourage the creation of jobs in a region targeted for this purpose by a state government.[62]
- Loans and investments to promote economic development in a foreign country, which has a low standard of living, energy and food shortages, and natural disasters.[63]
- A series of low-interest or interest-free loans to organizations in the media field (most of which, if not all, were for-profit businesses), located principally in Central and Eastern Europe and the former Soviet Union, Latin America, Southeast Asia, and Africa, for the purpose of speeding the institution-building process toward open societies and democratic systems.[64]
- A foundation's investment in a for-profit venture capital fund limited to achieving environmental and economic development goals, subject to environmental guidelines and oversight, accomplishes an exempt purpose. The foundation supports biodiversity and sustainability and believes there is a link between economic development and reduction of poverty and conservation of the biological resources on which nearly all economics are based. Therefore, the foundation's fund investment qualified as a program-related one. The investment was not thereby jeopardizing and the expenditure was not a taxable one.[65]
- Loans by a private foundation to promote development and construction of housing in a downtown area were ruled to be program-related investments.[66]
- Operation of a farm in a foreign country, previously conducted as a for-profit operation by the founder of a private foundation, that became operated by the foundation after his death as an exempt demonstration project and thus a program-related investment.[67]

---

60. Rev. Rul. 78-90, 1978-1 C.B. 380.
61. Priv. Ltr. Rul. 8832074.
62. Priv. Ltr. Rul. 199943044.
63. Priv. Ltr. Rul. 199943058.
64. Priv. Ltr. Rul. 200034037.
65. Priv. Ltr. Rul. 200136026.
66. Priv. Ltr. Rul. 200331005.
67. Priv. Ltr. Rul. 200343027.

§ 8.3 PROGRAM-RELATED INVESTMENTS

- A grant by a private foundation to a for-profit medical malpractice reinsurance company was held to be a program-related investment because it promoted health by enabling physicians to continue to practice in or locate to a community.[68]

- To stimulate participation of private industry to discover interventions for the developing world, a private foundation will grant funding to commercial companies. Proposals must evidence research that will achieve a charitable objective, a strategy for making the results readily available at affordable prices to those without access, an evaluation of ownership and resulting intellectual property rights, and an outline of a global access plan. Grant recipients must have a reasonable strategy and principles for managing innovation for the purpose of facilitating the future availability and affordability in the developing world. The results of early-stage research were found impractical or unreasonable to be published and made available to the general public. The ruling finds the expense will constitute a qualifying distribution.[69] It also notes expenditure responsibility[70] will occur. There is no mention of terms for returning the "investment"; the ruling refers to the payments as "transactions," and also refers to "making of grants, contracts, or program-related investments."

- Investments by a private foundation in an angel investment fund for businesses owned by members of disadvantaged groups in low-income communities were held to be program-related investments.[71]

- Royalty interest held by a private foundation, arising out of a research agreement with a tax-exempt hospital, pursuant to which the foundation makes grants to the hospital, was held to qualify as a program-related investment; the royalty interest will arise if the hospital or its licensing affiliate receives payments in return for the use of any invention resulting from the funded research.[72]

- Pledging of marketable securities as collateral in support of issuance of a bond for the benefit of a tax-exempt hospital that is building an acute care hospital.[73]

---

68. Priv. Ltr. Rul. 200347014.
69. Priv. Ltr. Rul. 200603031.
70. See § 9.7.
71. Priv. Ltr. Rul. 200610020.
72. Priv. Ltr. Rul. 201145027.
73. Priv. Ltr. Rul. 201442061.

The applicable tax regulations were expanded to provide additional guidance as to what constitutes program-related investments.[74] This guidance offers nine additional examples[75] illustrating that an activity conducted in a foreign country furthers a charitable purpose if the activity would further a charitable purpose if conducted in the United States, such as scientific research and enhancement of the environment; the exempt purposes served by a program-related investment are not limited to situations involving economically disadvantaged individuals and deteriorated urban areas; the recipients of program-related investments need not be within a charitable class if they are the instruments for furthering an exempt purpose; a potentially high rate of return does not automatically prevent an investment from qualifying as a program-related investment; program-related investments can be achieved through a variety of investments, including loans to individuals, tax-exempt organizations, and for-profit entities, and equity investments in for-profit organizations; a credit enhancement arrangement, such as a guarantee and reimbursement arrangement, may qualify as a program-related investment; and the acceptance by a private foundation of an equity position in conjunction with making a loan does not necessarily prevent the investment from qualifying as a program-related investment.

Another illustration of a program-related investment was provided when the IRS considered a situation involving a private operating foundation with the mission of conducting educational programs assisting underserved and impoverished individuals. The foundation proposed to operate a loan program in furtherance of its charitable and educational purposes, including making loans to service providers who cannot qualify for commercial loans; loans may also be made to intermediaries and for-profit entities. Loans to service providers would involve below-market interest rates or be interest-free; loans to for-profit organizations would have below-market rates. The IRS concluded that this foundation would maintain significant involvement in the active programs in support of which the loans will be made. The IRS noted that the foundation employed full-time experts in education and related areas, and funded consultants who specialize in assisting service providers and intermediaries who would receive training, knowledge-sharing, data collection, and educational materials to facilitate capacity-building. The foundation would be involved in the structuring of loans, oversee operations of partners funded with loans, and otherwise plan "substantive elements" with respect to the loan program. The loans would not have a significant purpose of income production or appreciation of property.[76]

---

74. T.D. 9762, 81 Fed. Reg. 24014 (2016).
75. Reg. § 53.4944-3(b), Examples 11-19.
76. Priv. Ltr. Rul. 201821005.

§ 8.3 PROGRAM-RELATED INVESTMENTS

In another instance, a private foundation's proposed loan to a limited liability partnership established in a foreign country to enable the borrower to loan funds to various arts organizations in that country (in alignment with the foundation's mission), with all loans at below-market interest rates, was ruled by the IRS to be a program-related investment.[77] This loan arrangement would be orchestrated in conjunction with a network of other creditors providing similar loans to the same borrower simultaneously, pursuant to an "intercreditor" agreement, which outlined the order for drawing on the loans, determined the order of loan repayments, and committed all lending to charitable purposes. The foundation would be a mezzanine lender in that its repayment rights would be subordinate to at least one other lender.

Once it has been determined that an investment is a program-related one, it does not cease to qualify as this type of investment, provided that any changes in the form or terms of the investment are made primarily for tax-exempt purposes and not for any significant purpose involving the production of income or the appreciation of property. A change made in the form or terms of a program-related investment for the prudent protection of a private foundation's investment ordinarily will not cause the investment to cease to qualify as program-related.[78] Under certain circumstances, a program-related investment may cease to be this type of investment because of a critical change in circumstances, such as where it is serving an illegal purpose or the private purpose of the foundation or its managers. An investment that ceases to be a program-related one because of a critical change in circumstances will not subject the foundation to the tax on jeopardizing investments before the thirtieth day after the date on which the foundation (or any of its managers) has actual knowledge of the critical change in circumstances.

An investment that jeopardizes the carrying out of a private foundation's tax-exempt purposes is considered to be removed from jeopardy when the foundation sells or otherwise disposes of the investment and the proceeds therefrom are not themselves investments that jeopardize the carrying out of exempt purposes.[79]

A program-related investment constitutes a qualifying distribution for a private foundation.[80] Expenditure responsibility must be exercised for most program-related investments and reports made to the IRS on Form 990-PF throughout the life of the investment.

A program-related investment made with a low-profit limited liability company also requires an expenditure responsibility agreement because an L3C

---

77. Priv. Ltr. Rul. 202123004.
78. Reg. § 53.4944-3(a)(3).
79. IRC § 4944(e)(2); Reg. § 53.4944-5(b).
80. See § 6.4.

is not a public charity. An L3C is a hybrid nonprofit/for-profit organization designed to facilitate investments by private foundations in social programs that advance a charitable mission. Unlike a tax-exempt charitable organization, an L3C may distribute its after-tax profits to its investors or owners. In April 2008, Vermont was the first state to recognize this form of organization, followed by Michigan in January 2009 and Wyoming in February 2009.

Loan programs referred to as *recoverable grants* are treated by some advisors as program-related investments and by others as grants. These grants are most commonly made in support of affordable housing, neighborhood centers in low-income areas, and community development initiatives. The Council on Foundations suggests: "Recoverable grants are grants that function as interest-free loans. They are made by foundations from their grantmaking budget, and are entered on the books as 'recoverable grants.' If repayment is not received, they are converted to grant status."[81]

Expenditure responsibility agreements are not, however, required for investments placed with public charities. For example, a loan to a public school at a low or no-interest rate would qualify as a program-related investment, but expenditure responsibility would not be required because of the borrower's public charity status.[82]

§ 8.4 INVESTMENT FRAUDS

The federal tax law essentially is silent on the consequences in law of private foundations' investments in fraudulent schemes, such as Ponzi schemes.

(a) Background

There are several issues in this regard, most of them brought to light as a result of several foundations' investments by means of the Bernard L. Madoff Investment Securities firm. Mr. Madoff admitted to running a Ponzi scheme through his investment firm, involving losses, concerning foundations and other entities, in excess of $50 billion. According to a report referenced in a major newspaper article, at least 147 foundations invested with the Madoff firm.[83] One foundation invested $958 million with the Madoff firm—virtually all of its assets; three other foundations lost $244 million, $199 million, and

---

81. Freeman and the Council on Foundations, *Handbook on Private Foundations*, published by the Foundation Center in 1993.
82. See § 9.4.
83. Browning, "For Investing with Madoff, Private Foundations Could Face Tax Fines," *New York Times*, Feb. 12, 2009, at B4.

$178 million. One of the federal tax law issues of the day is whether some of these investments constitute jeopardizing investments. As this article stated the matter, some foundations "bet the farm—which some tax lawyers say could signal the lack of due diligence and fiduciary responsibility."[84]

A tax law assistant to Senator Charles Grassley, the then ranking member of the Senate Finance Committee, said, a few weeks before this article was published, that members of the boards of private foundations may be liable for jeopardizing investment taxes in situations where their foundations invested with the Madoff firm.[85] She noted that some charitable organizations decided not to invest with Madoff after engaging in due diligence, raising the question as to whether those who invested with his company violated the jeopardy investment standard. Brushing aside the argument that these foundations and other investors were defrauded, she said that "[w]ith respect to charities that apparently have had to close their doors or stop issuing grants because of the losses on their Madoff investments, it would seem hard to argue that these investments did not jeopardize the carrying on of their exempt purpose."

The IRS published general guidance to taxpayers who invested in Ponzi schemes. One element of this guidance is that an individual investor in a Ponzi scheme is entitled to a theft loss deduction in the year the fraud is discovered.[86] The other component of the guidance is a safe-harbor approach for taxpayers to claim a theft loss for Ponzi scheme investments. To avail themselves of this safe harbor, taxpayers must agree not to file amended returns.[87]

(b) NYSBA Report

The Tax Section of the New York State Bar Association submitted a report to the Department of the Treasury and the IRS in response to the government's request for assistance in identifying and addressing issues confronting private foundation investors in Ponzi schemes and other frauds.[88]

The NYSBA report identified the relevant issues that private foundations and the IRS need to address in this context. One of the questions posed was whether IRS guidance should impose a single approach that foundations must follow in resolving issues arising from Ponzi scheme investments or whether

---

84. Id.
85. Bureau of Nat'l Affairs interview with Theresa Pattera, Daily Tax Report (no. 16) G-2 (Jan. 28, 2009).
86. Rev. Rul. 2009-9, 2009-14 I.R.B. 735.
87. Rev. Proc. 2009-20, 2009-1 C.B. 749, as modified by Rev. Proc. 2011-58, 2011-50 I.R.B 849.
88. Letter and accompanying report submitted to the Treasury Department and the IRS, dated May 7, 2009, reproduced in *Daily Tax Report*, May 11, 2009, TaxCore. This letter observed that this IRS guidance "is not aimed at exempt organizations and does not squarely address the issues facing private foundations."

JEOPARDIZING INVESTMENTS

IRS guidance should give foundations a choice of actions. The report's initial conclusion was that "there are too many differences between foundations (multibillion-dollar foundations vs. small family foundations; foundations with minor losses from a Ponzi scheme vs. foundations with all or most of their assets lost in a Ponzi scheme, etc.) to come out with a one-size-fits-all approach." Also: "Different institutions inevitably will have different needs and administrative capabilities for dealing with Ponzi scheme losses."

As this report observed, private foundations with losses from Ponzi scheme investments "face many difficult reporting and compliance issues for which there is little or no precedent or guidance." The report treats these issues as falling into two categories. One set of these issues concerns the measurement of income and asset values.

This matter arises in two settings: calculation of the required payout amount[89] and determination of net investment income for purposes of the excise tax on that income.[90] The second category of issues "address or relate to the foundation's process for making the Ponzi scheme investment in the first place." Here, the critical question "is whether making the investment involved some prohibited conduct that should be punished by the imposition of a penalty excise tax." The principal issue in this area is whether one or more of the jeopardizing investments rules were transgressed. Of secondary importance are the self-dealing rules[91] and the taxable expenditures rules.[92]

The NYSBA report stated that application of the jeopardizing investment rules in the Ponzi scheme context is a "key issue" for foundations that made investments of this nature.

The first issue posed by the NYSBA report was: What are the standards to be applied to Ponzi scheme investments that appeared legitimate at the time the investment was made? The report states that, inasmuch as jeopardy investment determinations are not to be based on hindsight, "it would appear that if a foundation or a foundation manager conducted proper due diligence, there should be no penalty." Then: "The key question is what constitutes adequate due diligence" under the circumstances of Ponzi scheme investments. After sketching some of the pertinent factors, the report observed that "frauds are structured and documented in ways to avoid detection and so by definition a Ponzi scheme may not be discovered by a foundation that conducts reasonable diligence."[93]

---

89. See § 6.3(e).
90. See § 10.4(b)(iv).
91. See § 5.11(e).
92. See § 9.8.
93. This view is buttressed by the IRS's position that these schemes involve thefts (see § 8.4(a)).

§ 8.5 EXCISE TAXES ON JEOPARDIZING INVESTMENTS

The second issue is: Is placement of a substantial portion or all of a foundation's assets with one fund manager (who represents that its investments are prudent and diversified) an indication of a jeopardizing investment? The report concluded that the examples in the existing jeopardizing investments regulations are "outdated" and thus "do not provide helpful guidance for private foundations in today's market." Stating that the "better view" may be that investing with one manager "is not per se a jeopardizing investment if the foundation uses due diligence in selecting and monitoring the manager and its actual investments, the report concluded that "[h]aving clear guidance on what constitutes a jeopardizing investment would be helpful to foundation managers."

The third issue (actually a cluster of issues) assumes that a Ponzi scheme investment is a jeopardizing investment. Question: How many years may the IRS go back to impose the excise tax(es)? Question: If the Ponzi scheme investment is exchanged for cash, where the cash continues to be the subject of a clawback obligation, does the jeopardizing investments rules taxable period continue?[94] The report stated that it is "unclear" as to how these issues should be resolved.

What about discovery of the Ponzi scheme? Does that mean that the investment was actually removed from jeopardy?[95] The tax regulations appear to treat the investment as removed from jeopardy when the foundation actively does something to change, exchange, or dispose of the investment. Therefore, the report observes, in a Ponzi scheme situation, which is "discovered and collapses on its own, it is unclear whether the foundation has disposed of a jeopardizing investment."

§ 8.5 EXCISE TAXES ON JEOPARDIZING INVESTMENTS

(a) Initial Taxes

If a private foundation invests any amount in a manner as to jeopardize the carrying out of any of its tax-exempt purposes, an initial tax is imposed on the private foundation on the making of the investment, at the rate of 10 percent of the amount so invested for each tax year or part thereof in the taxable period.[96]

The *taxable period* is the period beginning with the date on which the amount is invested in a jeopardizing manner and ending on the earliest of the following dates: (1) the date on which the IRS mails a notice of deficiency with

---

94. See § 8.5(a).
95. See § 8.5(d).
96. IRC § 4944 (a)(1), Reg. § 53.4944-1(a)(1). This tax is also known as a *first-tier tax* (IRC § 4963 (a); Reg. § 53.4963-1(a)).

respect to the initial tax[97] imposed on the foundation, (2) the date on which the initial tax is assessed, or (3) the date on which the amount invested is removed from jeopardy.[98]

In any case in which this initial tax is imposed, a tax is also imposed on the participation of any foundation manager in the making of the investment, knowing that it is jeopardizing the carrying out of any of the private foundation's tax-exempt purposes, equal to 5 percent of the amount so invested for each tax year of the private foundation (or part of the tax year) in the taxable period.[99] With respect to any one jeopardizing investment, the maximum amount of this tax is $10,000.[100] Managers found liable under these rules are jointly and severally liable for the tax.[101] This tax, which must be paid by any participating foundation manager, is not imposed where the participation is not willful and is due to reasonable cause.[102]

The IRS has the discretionary authority to abate this initial tax where the private foundation establishes that the violation was due to reasonable cause and not to willful neglect, and timely corrects the violation.[103]

(b) When a Manager Knows

A foundation manager is considered to have participated in the making of an investment *knowing* that it is a jeopardizing one only if the manager:

- Has actual knowledge of sufficient facts so that, based solely on those facts, the investment would be a jeopardizing one,

- Is aware that the investment under these circumstances may violate the federal tax law rules governing jeopardizing investments, and

- Negligently fails to make reasonable attempts to ascertain whether the investment is a jeopardizing one, or is in fact aware that it is a jeopardizing investment.[104]

The word *knowing* does not mean "having reason to know." Evidence tending to show that a foundation manager has reason to know of a particular fact or particular rule is relevant, however, in determining whether they had

---

97. IRC § 6212.
98. IRC § 4944(e)(1); Reg. § 53.4944-5(a).
99. IRC § 4944(e)(1); Reg. § 53.4944-1(b)(1).
100. IRC § 4944(d)(2); Reg. § 53.4944-4(b).
101. IRC § 4944(d)(1); Reg. § 53.4944-4(a).
102. IRC § 4944(a)(2); Reg. § 53.4944-1(b)(1).
103. IRC § 4962; see § 12.4(c).
104. Reg. § 53.4944-1(b)(2)(i).

actual knowledge of the fact or rule. Evidence tending to show that a foundation manager has reason to know of sufficient facts so that, based solely on the facts, an investment would be a jeopardizing one is relevant in determining whether the manager has actual knowledge of the facts.[105] Thus, the pertinent facts and circumstances are examined to find out why the manager did not know of the relevant facts or law. To be excused of tax liability, the foundation manager essentially must be ignorant of the pertinent facts or law.

For example, the board of trustees of a private foundation may consist of 10 members, three of whom comprise a finance committee. The written investment policy of the foundation provides that the board approves investment decisions proposed by the finance committee, based on the advice of independent counselors. Those members of the board who are not on the finance committee should not be expected to be aware of details discussed in finance committee meetings.

A foundation manager's participation in the making of a jeopardizing investment is *willful* if it is voluntary, conscious, and intentional. A motive to avoid the restrictions of the law or the incurrence of a tax is not necessary to make this type of participation willful. A foundation manager's participation in a jeopardizing investment, however, is not willful if the manager does not know that it is a jeopardizing investment.[106]

A foundation manager's actions are due to reasonable cause if the manager has exercised their responsibility on behalf of the foundation with ordinary business care and prudence.[107] The *participation* of any foundation manager in the making of an investment consists of any manifestation of approval of the investment.[108] Clearly, a vote as a board member to approve an investment is participation. Board members who do not attend meetings but allow investment decisions may be derelict as to their fiduciary responsibility, but their inability to participate in the investment decision and resulting lack of knowledge may shield them from the tax. If members of the board of directors receive a board information packet revealing the investment under scrutiny, they have the requisite knowledge; however, the tax applies only if they participate in the approval.

(c) Reliance on Outside Advisors

If, after full disclosure of the factual situation to legal counsel (including in-house counsel), a foundation manager relies on the advice of that counsel, expressed in a reasoned written legal opinion, that a particular investment

---

105. *Id.*
106. Reg. § 53.4944-1(b)(2)(ii).
107. Reg. § 53.4944-1(b)(2)(iii).
108. Reg. § 53.4944-1(b)(2)(iv).

JEOPARDIZING INVESTMENTS

would not jeopardize the carrying out of any of the foundation's exempt purposes, the foundation manager's participation in the investment will ordinarily not be considered knowing or willful, and will ordinarily be considered due to reasonable cause. This is the case even where the investment is subsequently held to be a jeopardizing one.[109] A lawyer is not qualified to opine on the appropriateness of an investment as such. Thus, a legal opinion from a lawyer must address a situation where, as a matter of law, the investment is excepted from classification as a jeopardizing investment, such as because it is a program-related investment.

A written legal opinion is considered *reasoned*, even if it reaches a conclusion that is subsequently determined to be incorrect, as long as the opinion addresses itself to the facts and applicable law. A written legal opinion will not be considered reasoned if it does nothing more than recite the facts and express a conclusion. The absence of advice of legal counsel or qualified investment counsel with respect to an investment, however, does not, by itself, give rise to any inference that a foundation manager participated in the investment knowingly, willfully, or without reasonable cause.

Likewise, if a foundation manager, after full disclosure of the factual situation to qualified investment counsel, relies on the advice of that counsel, the foundation manager's participation in failing to provide for the long- and short-term financial needs of the foundation will ordinarily not be considered knowing or willful, and will be considered due to reasonable cause. For this rule to apply, the advice must have been derived in a manner consistent with generally accepted practices of individuals who are qualified investment counsel and expressed in writing that a particular investment will provide for these financial needs of the foundation. Again, this is the case even where the investment is subsequently held to be a jeopardizing one.[110]

(d) Additional Taxes and Removal from Jeopardy

An additional tax is imposed in any case in which the initial tax is imposed and the investment is not removed from jeopardy during the taxable period.[111] An investment that jeopardizes the carrying out of exempt purposes is considered to be removed from jeopardy when the investment is sold or otherwise disposed of, and the proceeds from the sale or other disposition are not investments that jeopardize the carrying out of exempt purposes.[112] Correction of a jeopardizing investment may be difficult—if not impossible—where the asset

---

109. Reg. § 53.4944-1(b)(2)(v).
110. *Id.*
111. IRC § 4944(b)(1); Reg. § 53.4944-5(d).
112. IRC § 4944(e)(2); Reg. § 53.4944-5(b).

§ 8.5 EXCISE TAXES ON JEOPARDIZING INVESTMENTS

is not marketable. An effort to maximize available funds from the investment may help to avoid the additional tax.

A change by a private foundation in the form or terms of a jeopardizing investment results in the removal of the investment from jeopardy if, after the change, the investment no longer jeopardizes the carrying out of the foundation's exempt purposes. The making of one jeopardizing investment by a foundation and a subsequent change by the foundation of the investment for another jeopardizing investment generally is treated as only one jeopardizing investment. A jeopardizing investment cannot be removed from jeopardy by a transfer from a private foundation to another foundation that is related to the transferor foundation[113] unless the investment is a program-related investment in the hands of the transferee foundation.[114]

This additional tax, which is to be paid by the foundation, is at the rate of 25 percent of the amount of the investment.[115] Where this tax is imposed and a foundation manager refuses to agree to part or all of the removal of the investment from jeopardy, a tax is imposed on the manager at the rate of 5 percent of the amount of the investment.[116] With respect to any one investment, the maximum amount of this tax is $20,000.[117] Where more than one foundation manager is liable for an additional tax with respect to any one jeopardizing investment, all of the managers are jointly and severally liable for the tax.[118]

Where the act or failure to act that gave rise to the additional tax is corrected within the correction period, the tax will not be assessed, or if assessed will be abated, or if collected will be credited or refunded.[119] The *correction period* is the period beginning on the date on which the *taxable event* occurs and ending 90 days after the date of mailing of a notice of deficiency with respect to the additional tax imposed on the event, extended by any period in which a deficiency cannot be assessed[120] and any other period that the IRS determines is reasonable and necessary to bring about correction of the taxable event.[121] In this setting, a taxable event is an act or failure to act giving rise to liability for

---

113. See § 4.7.
114. Reg. § 53.4944-5(b).
115. IRC § 4944(b)(1); Reg. § 53.4944-2(a). This tax is also known as a *second-tier tax* (IRC § 4963 (b); Reg. § 53.4963-1(b)).
116. IRC § 4944(b)(2); Reg. § 53.4944-2(b). This tax cannot be imposed until the individual involved has received adequate notice and had an opportunity to remove a jeopardizing investment (Thorne v. Commissioner, 99 T.C. 67 (1992)).
117. IRC § 4944(d)(2); Reg. § 53.4944-4(b).
118. IRC § 4944 (d)(1); Reg. § 53.4944-4(b).
119. IRC § 4961(a); Reg. § 53.4961-1.
120. IRC § 6213(a).
121. IRC § 4963(e)(1); Reg. § 53.4963-1(e)(1).

tax under the jeopardizing investment rules.[122] This event occurs on the date a jeopardizing investment takes place.[123] *Correction* means removing the investment from jeopardy.[124]

The collection period is suspended during any litigation.[125]

The termination tax[126] may serve as a third-tier tax where there have been either willful repeated acts (or failures to act), or a willful and flagrant act (or failure to act), giving rise to liability for the taxes on jeopardizing investments or the other private foundation excise taxes.[127]

---

122. IRC § 4963(c); Reg. § 53.4963-1(c).
123. IRC § 4963(e)(2)(D); Reg. § 53.4963-1(e)(7)(iv).
124. IRC § 4963(d)(2)(C); Reg. § 53.4963-1(d)(2)(iii).
125. IRC § 4961(c); Reg. § 53.4961-2.
126. See § 13.7.
127. IRC § 507(a)(2); see § 13.2.

CHAPTER NINE

Taxable Expenditures

§ 9.1 **Legislative Activities** 372
  (a) Law Applicable to Charities Generally 373
  (b) Law Applicable to Private Foundations 374
  (c) Grants to Charities That Lobby 376
  (d) Nonpartisan Study of Social Issues 378
  (e) Self-Defense Exception 380
§ 9.2 **Political Campaign Activities** 381
  (a) Law Applicable to Charities Generally 381
  (b) Law Applicable to Private Foundations 382
  (c) Voter Registration Drives 383
§ 9.3 **Grants to Individuals** 384
  (a) Definition of Grant 384
  (b) Individual Grants for Charitable or Other Permitted Purposes 384
  (c) Disaster Relief and Other Assistance Grants 386
  (d) Individual Grants for Travel, Study, or Other Similar Purposes 392
    (i) Scholarships and Fellowships 393
    (ii) Employer-Related Scholarship Programs 394
    (iii) Prizes and Awards 399
    (iv) Grants for Specific Objectives or to Enhance Skills 400
  (e) Individual Grant Procedures 402
    (i) Objective and Nondiscriminatory Basis for Selection 403
    (ii) Grantee Reporting Requirements 405
    (iii) Monitoring, Supervision, and Investigation Requirements 406
    (iv) Recordkeeping Requirements 408
  (f) IRS Approval of Grant Procedures 408
    (i) Requests for Advance IRS Approval 409
    (ii) Deemed IRS Approval 410
    (iii) Impact of IRS Approval on Future Grants 411
  (g) Individual Grant Intermediaries and Earmarking 412
§ 9.4 **Grants to Public Charities** 415
  (a) Types of Public Charity Grantees 415
  (b) Grantor Reliance Standards 416
  (c) Intermediary and Secondary Grantees 417
§ 9.5 **Grants to Exempt Operating Foundations** 419
§ 9.6 **Grants to Foreign Organizations** 419
  (a) General Rules 419
  (b) Good Faith (Equivalency) Determinations 420
  (c) Canadian and Mexican Organizations 422

■ 369 ■

TAXABLE EXPENDITURES

§ 9.7
(d) Anti-Terrorist Financing Guidelines 423
Expenditure Responsibility 424
(a) General Rules 424
(b) Pre-Grant Inquiry 426
(c) Grant Terms 428
(d) Reports from Grantees 429
(e) Grantee's Books and Records 430
(f) Reports to IRS 431
(g) Foundation's Recordkeeping Requirements 432

(h) Grantee Diversions 432
§ 9.8 **Spending for Noncharitable Purposes** 435
§ 9.9 **Excise Tax on Taxable Expenditures** 440
(a) Initial and Additional Taxes 440
(b) Tax on Managers 441
(c) Paying the Tax 442
(d) Correcting the Expenditure 443

The federal tax law regards private foundations as trusts that must serve public ends and their trustees as stewards of charitable assets that must be solely devoted to advancement of these purposes. Consequently, the activities for which private foundations may expend their funds are restricted by limitations that are far more stringent than those applicable to charitable organizations generally. In effect, these rules impose a standard that forbids a private foundation to incur any expenditure for a variety of purposes or functions. Other types of tax-exempt organizations can engage in some amount of nonexempt activity without loss of exempt status or other sanction, but private foundations are not accorded any such leeway. Impermissible expenditures are termed *taxable expenditures*. The private foundation and some, if not all, of its disqualified persons are subject to an excise tax, and loss of the foundation's exemption may also result, if any amount is paid or incurred for one of the following categories of *taxable expenditures*:

1. To carry on propaganda or otherwise attempt to influence legislation.
2. To influence the outcome of any specific election, or to carry on any voter registration drive (except efforts of at least five states in scope).
3. As a grant to an individual for travel, study, or other similar purpose.
4. As a grant to an organization unless:
   - It is a public charity, either as one of the institutional types or as a publicly supported charity,
   - It is a supporting organization, other than a non–functionally integrated supporting organization[1] or any other supporting organization controlled by a disqualified person,[2]

---

1. IRC § 4942(g)(4)(A)(i). See § 15.6(g).
2. IRC § 4942(g)(4)(A)(ii). See § 15.6(j).

- It is an exempt operating foundation,[3]
- The private foundation making the grant exercises expenditure responsibility,[4] or
5. For noncharitable purposes.[5]

These prohibitions apply where a private foundation either directly makes the expenditure itself for the impermissible activity or makes a grant to an organization (usually a public charity) with the funds targeted for an impermissible expenditure by the grantee. The taxable expenditures rules, like so many of the other private foundation rules, were enacted as part of the Tax Reform Act of 1969. Prior to that legislation, the only sanctions available in response to legislative, political, or other activity deemed inappropriate for private foundations were revocation of tax exemption and denial of charitable donee status—sanctions the IRS is usually reluctant to deploy. Moreover, it was thought that the standards under prior law as to the permissible level of activities were so vague as to encourage subjective application of the sanctions.

One summary of the rationale for these rules stated:

> In recent years [before 1969], private foundations had become increasingly active in political and legislative activities. In several instances called to the Congress's attention, funds were spent in ways clearly designed to favor certain candidates. In some cases, this was done by financing registration campaigns in limited geographical areas. In other cases contributions were made to organizations that then used the money to publicize the views, personalities, and activities of certain candidates. It also appeared that officials of some foundations exercised little or no control over the organizations receiving the funds from the foundations.[6]

Additionally, "prior law did not effectively limit the extent to which foundations could use their money for 'educational' grants to enable people to take vacations abroad, to have paid interludes between jobs, and to subsidize the preparation of materials furthering specific political viewpoints." Congress therefore concluded that more effective limitations, and more effective sanctions, should be placed on the distribution of tax-deductible and tax-exempt funds by private persons, and that grant-making foundations "should take substantial

---

3. IRC § 4940(d)(2). See § 10.7.
4. See § 9.7.
5. IRC § 4945(d).
6. Staff of Joint Comm. on Internal Revenue Tax'n, 91st Cong., 2d Sess., General Explanation of the Tax Reform Act of 1969 48 (Comm. Print 1970).

responsibility for the proper use of the funds they give away." "Accordingly, the Congress determined that a tax should be imposed on expenditures by private foundations for activities that should not be carried on by exempt organizations (such as lobbying, electioneering, and 'grass roots' campaigning)."[7]

More than any other aspect of the private foundation rules, the taxable expenditures rules reflect the nearly unbridled anti–private foundation emotionalism that gripped Congress as it legislated in this area in 1969. Several of these provisions are directly traceable to specific events that fomented the legislators' unhappiness, many of which came to widespread public attention in the wake of the testimony early in 1969 by Ford Foundation president McGeorge Bundy before the House Committee on Ways and Means.[8] The restrictions on individual grants trace their heritage to the "travel and study awards" that the Ford Foundation made to staff assistants to Senator Robert F. Kennedy following his assassination.[9] The rules concerning private foundations' involvement in public elections and voter registration drives are a reflection of the Ford Foundation financing of voter registration projects, including a grant to Cleveland CORE, travel grants to members of Congress, and the school decentralization experiments in New York (the subject of citywide teachers' strikes),[10] and of the spending interests of the Frederick W. Richmond Foundation at the time Mr. Richmond was seeking election to Congress.[11] These and similar incidents triggered many critical commentaries on private foundations in the general media,[12] which added to the reaction against private foundations in Congress.

§ 9.1 LEGISLATIVE ACTIVITIES

The federal tax law limits the extent to which a private foundation, as a charitable organization, may engage in attempts to influence legislation without endangering its tax exemption. These undertakings are often referred to as *lobbying activities*. Private foundations are subject to an overlay of additional, more stringent, laws in this regard. It is often critical for a private foundation to understand the lobbying activities permitted by a public charity or charities to which it makes grants. Despite the severity of these rules, however,

---

7. *Id.*
8. "Many in Congress Ready to Tax All Foundations, Curb Their Operations," *Wall Street Journal*, Feb. 28, 1969, at 1.
9. E.g., "5 RFK Aides Defend Grants," *Washington Post*, Feb. 27, 1969, at G1.
10. E.g., "Ford Fund Hints No Retreat on Financing of Disputed Projects, No Fear on Taxes," *Wall Street Journal*, March 3, 1969, at 12.
11. "Rooney Cites Tax-Free Aid Used by Foe," *Washington Star*, Feb. 19, 1969, at A-1.
12. E.g., White, "Congress Girding to Reduce Vast Power of Foundations," *Washington Post*, Feb. 22, 1969, at A-15; McGrory, "Stylist Bundy Sprinkles Snow," *Washington Star*, Feb. 2, 1969, at A-3.

private foundations can support programs involving public policy and social advocacy issues so long as the activities do not involve attempts to influence legislation. Educational and scientific efforts involving these subjects are not necessarily legislative efforts, even if the problems are of a type with which the government would be ultimately expected to deal.[13]

(a) Law Applicable to Charities Generally

No substantial part of the activities of a charitable organization may consist of carrying on propaganda or otherwise attempting to influence legislation.[14] The term *legislation* means action by Congress, a state legislature, a local council or similar governing body, or the public in a referendum, initiative, constitutional amendment, or similar procedure.[15] It also includes a proposed treaty required to be submitted by the president to the Senate for its advice and consent, from the time the president's representative begins to negotiate its position with the prospective parties to the treaty.[16]

One definition of the term *influence legislation* is any attempt (1) to influence any legislation through an attempt to affect the opinion of the general public or any segment of it, or (2) to influence any legislation through communication with any member or employee of a legislative body or with any government official or employee who may participate in the formulation of the legislation.[17] Another is (1) to contact, or urge the public to contact, members of a legislative body for the purpose of proposing, supporting, or opposing legislation, or (2) to advocate the adoption or rejection of legislation.[18] The word *substantial* in this setting is essentially undefined, although it is measured by the expenditures of money, time spent, and other facts and circumstances of the particular organization's activities.[19] A charitable organization that engages in legislative activities to a substantial extent is an *action organization* and thus cannot qualify as or remain federally tax-exempt.[20]

This rule as to lobbying is termed the *substantial part test*. Public charities that engage in extensive lobbying, and their management, can become subject to an excise tax under the substantial part test.[21] Most public charities can elect[22]

---

13. There are exceptions. See § 9.1(d).
14. IRC § 501(c)(3). In general, see *Tax-Exempt Organizations*, Chapter 22.
15. IRS § 4911(e)(2); Reg. §§ 1.501(c)(3)-1(c)(3)(ii), 56.4911-2(d)(1)(i).
16. Reg. § 56.4911-2(d)(1)(i).
17. IRC § 4911(d)(1).
18. Reg. § 1.501(c)(3)-1(c)(3)(ii).
19. E.g., The Nationalist Movement v. Commissioner, 102 T.C. 558 (1994), *aff'd*, 37 F.3d 216 (5th Cir. 1994).
20. Reg. § 1.501(c)(3)-1(c)(3).
21. IRC § 4912.
22. IRC § 501(h).

§ 9.1 LEGISLATIVE ACTIVITIES

an alternative set of rules that have the advantage of specifically measuring allowable lobbying; this package of rules[23] is known as the *expenditure test*. This test allows a charitable organization to spend stated percentages for lobbying, but taxes any excess lobbying outlays. Many of the rules pertaining to private foundations in this area are the same as those formulated as part of the expenditure test for public charities.

Charitable organizations that engage in lobbying may also have to comply with the Lobbying Disclosure Act of 1995,[24] which in part utilizes some of these federal tax rules.

(b) Law Applicable to Private Foundations

A private foundation may not, without incurring an excise tax, pay or incur any amount to carry on propaganda or otherwise attempt to influence legislation.[25] To do so would be to make a taxable expenditure. Thus, though private foundations are subject to the general test of *substantiality* applicable to charitable organizations as a condition of tax exemption, they are also subject to more specific prohibitions.

Two types of lobbying are embraced by these rules: (1) an attempt to influence legislation through communication with any member or employee of a legislative body or with any other governmental official or employee who may participate in the formulation of legislation,[26] (2) an attempt to influence any legislation through an attempt to affect the opinion of the public or any segment of it.[27] The first type of lobbying is direct lobbying; the second type is indirect, or grassroots, lobbying.

An expenditure is an attempt to influence legislation if it is for a direct lobbying communication or a grassroots lobbying communication.[28] A *direct lobbying communication* means an attempt to influence legislation through communication with (1) a member or employee of a legislative body, or (2) a government official or employee (other than a member or employee of a legislative body) who may participate in the formulation of the legislation, but only if the principal purpose of the communication is to influence legislation.[29] Moreover, to be a direct lobbying communication, it must refer to specific legislation and reflect a view on that legislation.[30]

---

23. IRC § 4911.
24. 2 U.S.C. §§ 1601–1602.
25. IRC § 4945(d)(1); Reg. § 53.4945-2(a)(1).
26. IRC § 4945(e)(2).
27. IRC § 4945(e)(1).
28. Reg. § 53.4945-2(a)(1).
29. Reg. § 56.4911-2(b)(1)(i).
30. Reg. § 56.4911-2(b)(1)(ii).

TAXABLE EXPENDITURES

The phrase *specific legislation* means (1) legislation that has been introduced in a legislative body or a specific legislative proposal that the organization supports or opposes, and (2) in the case of a referendum, ballot initiative, constitutional amendment, or other measure that is placed on the ballot by petitions signed by a required number or percentage of voters, an item becomes specific legislation when the petition is first circulated among voters for signature.[31]

A *grassroots lobbying communication* is an attempt to influence any legislation through an attempt to affect the opinions of the general public or any segment of it.[32] To be a grassroots lobbying communication, the communication must refer to specific legislation, it must reflect a view on the legislation, and it must encourage its recipient to take action with respect to the legislation.[33] The phrase *encouraging recipient to take action* with respect to legislation means that the communication specifically (1) states that the recipient should contact a legislator, staff member, or other government official; (2) gives the address, telephone number, or similar information about the individual(s) to be contacted; (3) provides some material to facilitate the contact (such as a petition or postcard); or (4) identifies one or more legislators who will vote on the legislation as opposing the communication's view of the legislation, being undecided with respect to it, being the recipient's representative in the legislature, or being a member of the committee or subcommittee that will consider the legislation.[34]

A private foundation and its founder were held liable, by the U.S. Tax Court, for excise taxes as the result of cumulative taxable expenditures for producing and broadcasting radio messages that were ruled to be attempts to influence legislation.[35] As a foundation manager, the founder agreed to the making of the expenditures. The court further determined that, because the taxable expenditures were not timely corrected, the foundation and its founder were liable for additional taxes.[36] The messages, plus newspaper advertisements, were held to be direct lobbying expenditures because they were targeted at a state ballot initiative, where the voters constitute the legislative body.[37] The court held that a communication is subject to excise taxation if it refers to a ballot measure "by name or, without naming it, employs terms widely used in connection with the measure or describes the content or effect of the measure."[38] The foundation's argument that the communications

---

31. Reg. § 56.4911-2(d)(1)(ii).
32. Reg. § 56.4911-2(b)(2)(i).
33. Reg. § 56.4911-2(b)(2)(ii).
34. Reg. § 56.4911-2(b)(2)(iii).
35. Parks Found. v. Commissioner, 145 T.C. 278 (2015), *aff'd*, 717 Fed. Appx. 712 (9th Cir. 2017).
36. See § 9.9.
37. Reg. § 56.4911-2(b)(1)(iii).
38. Parks Found. v. Commissioner, 145 T.C. 278, 309 (2015).

at issue constituted nonpartisan analysis, study, or research,[39] and thus were not forms of lobbying, was rejected by the court.

This decision was affirmed, with the appellate court stating that these communications "distorted the facts presented to the public or omitted supporting facts entirely," adding that "[m]any of the communications also used inflammatory or disparaging terms seemingly directed at producing an emotional response to the messages' content, rather than promoting an objective assessment of issues of public concern."[40]

(c) Grants to Charities That Lobby

A general support grant by a private foundation to a public charity that conducts lobbying activities is not a taxable expenditure to the extent that the grant is not *earmarked* to be used to influence legislation.[41] The word *earmarked* means an agreement, oral or written, that the grant will be used for specific purposes.[42] Whether the public charity has elected to measure its permissible lobbying under the expenditure test is irrelevant.

A grant by a private foundation to fund a specific project of a public charity is not a taxable expenditure to the extent that the grant is not earmarked for a legislative purpose and the amount of the grant (aggregated with other grants by the foundation for the same project in the same year) does not exceed the amount budgeted, for the year of the grant, by the grantee for activities of the project that are not attempts to influence legislation.[43] There are rules for multiyear grants.

In this connection, the private foundation may rely on budget documents or other sufficient evidence supplied by the prospective grantee—unless the foundation doubts or reasonably should doubt the accuracy or reliability of the documents.[44] Again, whether the public charity has elected to be under the expenditure test is irrelevant.

---

39. Reg. § 53.4945-2(d)(1)(i).
40. Parks Foundation v. Commissioner, 717 Fed. Appx. 712, 713–714 (9th Cir. 2017).
41. Reg. § 53.4945-2(a)(6)(i). These rules were written in the aftermath of adoption of the final regulations (in 1990) underlying the expenditure test enacted in 1976. It was thought that, as a consequence of this body of law, the scope and extent of lobbying by public charities would increase. These prospects gave the private foundation community pause; there was fear that the legislative activities of a grantee public charity electing under the expenditure test would be attributed to the grantor private foundation, causing a taxable expenditure. (The likelihood of this result was present before enactment of the expenditure test, but it was heightened following the introduction of that test and the foundation community's perception of it.)
42. Reg. § 53.4945-2(a)(5)(i).
43. Reg. § 53.4945-2(a)(6)(ii).
44. Reg. § 53.4945-2(a)(6)(iii).

TAXABLE EXPENDITURES

The prohibition against electioneering and lobbying, though absolute for the foundation itself, does not apply to foundation officials acting on their own behalf. Although officials are closely identified with the foundation they have created or direct, the rules do not constrain acts of individuals acting as such. In these situations, it is prudent for the officials to overtly state that they are not acting on behalf of the foundation, and foundation monies or facilities should never be used to advance a candidate or promote legislative initiatives.[45]

If the public charity grantee loses its tax exemption because of excessive lobbying, the private foundation grantor will not be considered as having made a taxable expenditure if it was unaware of the revocation and does not control the grantee.[46] A private foundation may want to protect itself from any question about whether it pays for lobbying by specifically requiring, as part of its grant agreement, that its public charity grantees agree not to do so. For grantees significantly involved in public affairs, it is prudent for a private foundation to retain documentation reflecting the portion of the grantee's budget spent on lobbying, although these precautions are not required by law.

A private foundation does not make a taxable expenditure merely because it makes a grant on the condition that the grantee obtain a matching support appropriation from a governmental body.[47]

A private foundation does not make a taxable expenditure when it pays or incurs expenditures in connection with carrying on discussions with officials of government bodies as long as (1) the subject of the discussions is a program that is jointly funded by the foundation and the government or is a new program that may be so jointly funded, (2) the discussions are undertaken for the purpose of exchanging data and information on the subject matter of the program, and (3) the discussions are not undertaken by foundation managers in order to make any direct attempt to persuade governmental officials or employees to take particular positions on specific legislative issues other than the program.[48]

An amount paid or incurred by a recipient of a program-related investment[49] in connection with an appearance before or communication with a legislative body, with respect to legislation or proposed legislation of direct interest to the grantee, is not attributed to the investing foundation as long as the foundation did not earmark the funds for legislative activities and the

---

45. The IRS provided examples of voter education versus electioneering and instances where an individual may speak personally rather than as a representative of an organization (Rev. Rul. 2007-41, 2007-1 C.B. 1421). Additionally, IRS Publication 1828, *Tax Guide for Churches and Religious Organizations*, contains guidelines for determining when a minister represents themself rather than the church.
46. Reg. § 53.4945-2(a)(7)(i).
47. Reg. § 53.49452(a)(3).
48. *Id.*
49. See § 8.3.

§ 9.1 LEGISLATIVE ACTIVITIES

recipient was allowed a business expense deduction for the expenditure.[50] There is no business expense deduction for lobbying unless it is done at the local level.[51]

A private foundation is highly unlikely to have a membership base; if it does, communications to members must be tested against the rules concerning direct lobbying communications.[52] A private foundation may make a grant to an electing public charity earmarked for a communication from the public charity to its members; where special rules[53] apply, the grant is not a taxable expenditure.[54] A grant to a nonelecting public charity for a communication to its members must be tested against the rules concerning direct lobbying communications.

(d) Nonpartisan Study of Social Issues

Sponsoring discussions or conferences, conducting research, and publishing educational materials about matters of broad social and economic subjects, such as human rights or war, are appropriate and permissible activities for a private foundation. These topics are often the subject matter of legislation, involve public controversy, and raise the possibility that a private foundation will be treated as conducting prohibited legislative activity. A private foundation is safe in sponsoring discussions on such topics and examining these issues, however, as long as the activity constitutes engaging in nonpartisan analysis, study, or research and making available the results of the work to the general public, a segment of the public, or to governmental bodies, officials, or employees.[55] Examinations and discussions of societal problems are not necessarily direct nor grassroots lobbying communications, even where the problems are of the type with which government would be expected to deal ultimately.[56] Thus, expenditures in connection with public discussion or communications with members of legislative bodies or governmental employees that concern an issue currently being considered by a legislative body are not taxable expenditures, as long as

---

50. Reg. § 53.4945-2(a)(4).
51. IRC § 162(e)(2).
52. Reg. § 53.4945-2(a)(2).
53. Reg. § 56.4911-5. Under these rules, in certain instances, expenditures for a membership communication are not regarded as lobbying expenditures (even where the expenditures would be lobbying expenditures if the communication was with nonmembers). In other instances, expenditures for a membership communication are treated as direct lobbying expenditures even though they would be grassroots lobbying expenditures if the communication was with nonmembers. There is a set of more lenient rules that apply for communications that are directed only to members, and one for communications that are directed primarily to members.
54. Reg. § 53.4945-2(a)(2).
55. IRC § 4945(e); Reg. § 53.4945-2(d)(1)(i).
56. Reg. § 53.4945-2(d)(4).

the discussion does not address itself to the merits of a specific legislative proposal, nor directly encourage recipients to take action with respect to legislation.

The phrase *nonpartisan analysis, study, or research* means an independent and objective exposition or study of a particular subject matter.[57] This definition embraces an activity that is considered educational;[58] this means the exposition can advocate a particular position or viewpoint as long as there is a sufficiently full and fair exposition of the pertinent facts to enable an individual or the public to form an independent opinion or conclusion. A foundation could, for example, issue a communiqué distributing the results of a study reaching the conclusion that oil tankers should have double hulls to lessen the possibility of oil spills, so long as the information forming the basis for the viewpoint is unbiased.

Normally, a publication or a broadcast is evaluated on a presentation-by-presentation basis. If a publication or a broadcast is one of a series prepared or supported by a private foundation and the series as a whole meets the standards of this exception, however, any individual publication or broadcast within the series will not result in a taxable expenditure even though the individual broadcast or publication does not, by itself, meet the standards. Whether a broadcast or a publication is part of a series will ordinarily depend on all the facts and circumstances of each particular situation.[59]

As to the *making available test*, a private foundation can do this by distributing reprints of articles and reports, conferences, meetings, and discussions, and by dissemination to the news media and other public forums. These communications, however, may not be confined to or be directed solely toward those who are interested in one side of a particular issue.[60]

Subsequent use of nonpartisan analysis, study, or research in grassroots lobbying (usually by a public charity grantee) may cause publication of the results to become a grassroots lobbying communication and thus not shielded from this exception.[61] There are rules detailing how this can occur, where the materials are *advocacy communications or research materials*.[62] In this connection, there is a primary purpose test, with a "safe harbor" rule to facilitate it.[63] A foundation grant is converted to a taxable expenditure under the *subsequent use rule*, however, only where the foundation's primary purpose in making the

---

57. Reg. § 53.4945-2(d)(1)(ii).
58. Reg. § 1.501(c)(3)-1(d)(3). See *Tax-Exempt Organizations* §§ 7.8, 8.1.
59. Reg. § 53.4945-2(d)(1)(iii).
60. Reg. § 53.4945-2(d)(1)(iv).
61. Reg. § 53.4945-2(d)(1)(v)(A).
62. Reg. § 56.4911-2(b)(2)(v). These are materials that refer to and reflect a view on specific legislation but do not, in their initial format, contain a direct encouragement for recipients to take action with respect to legislation.
63. Reg. § 56.4911-2(b)(2)(v)(C), (E).

grant is for lobbying or where the foundation knows (or should know) that the public charity's primary purpose in preparing the communication to be funded by the grant is for use in lobbying.[64]

A communication that reflects a view on specific legislation is not within this exception if the communication directly encourages the recipient to take action with respect to the legislation.[65] A communication can encourage the recipient to take action with respect to legislation, but not do so *directly*,[66] thereby preserving this exception.[67]

Amounts paid or incurred in connection with providing technical advice or assistance to a governmental body, a governmental committee, or a subdivision of either, in response to a written request from that entity (but not just from an individual member of it), do not constitute taxable expenditures.[68] The response to the request must be available to every member of the requesting entity. The offering of opinions or recommendations ordinarily is shielded by this exception if the opinions or recommendations are specifically requested by the entity or are directly related to the requested materials.[69]

(e) Self-Defense Exception

The taxable expenditures rules do not apply to any amount paid or incurred in connection with an appearance before or communication with any legislative body with respect to a possible decision of that body that might affect the existence of the foundation, its powers and duties, its tax-exempt status, or the deductibility of contributions to it.[70] Under this exception, known as the *self-defense exception*, a foundation may communicate with anyone (legislature, committees, individual legislators, staff members, or executive branch representatives) as long as the communication is confined to the permitted subjects. An expenditure to initiate legislation will not be a taxable expenditure if the legislation concerns *only* matters that are the permitted ones listed above. It is not enough, however, that the legislation merely relate to the scope of the foundation's program activities in the future.

Examples of the type of legislative proposal that threatens a foundation's existence or its powers include a rule that would require the inclusion of outside directors on a foundation's governing body, a provision that would restrict the power of a foundation to engage in transactions with certain

---

64. Reg. § 53.4945-2(d)(1)(v)(B).
65. Reg. § 53.4945-2(d)(1)(vi).
66. Reg. § 56.4911-2(b)(2)(iv).
67. Reg. § 53.4945-2(d)(1)(vi).
68. IRC § 4945(e)(2); Reg. § 53.4945-2(d)(2)(i).
69. Reg. § 53.4945-2(d)(2)(ii).
70. IRC § 4945(e)(2); Reg. § 53.4945-2(d)(3)(i).

related persons, a change in permitted holdings for excess business holding purposes that would cause the foundation to have a self-dealing transaction, and proposal to limit the life of a foundation to a term certain.

Examples of the type of legislative proposal that is not considered to threaten the life or powers of the foundation include: an appropriation bill to decrease government funding for programs that the foundation normally funds that would place a financial burden on the foundation by increasing demand for its support by grantees conducting such programs, and a proposal for a state to assume certain responsibilities for nursing care of the aged that are currently performed by a foundation that believes that it and other private organizations can better accomplish the job.

§ 9.2 POLITICAL CAMPAIGN ACTIVITIES

A private foundation, as a charitable organization, is basically forbidden by the federal tax law to engage, without jeopardizing its tax-exempt status, in political campaign activities. There are more specific rules in this regard for private foundations. It can be important for a private foundation to know the applicability of the federal tax laws relating to political campaign activities as they apply to the public charity or charities to which it makes grants.

(a) Law Applicable to Charities Generally

A charitable organization, whether public charity or private foundation, may not participate in or intervene in (including the publishing or distributing of statements) any political campaign on behalf of or in opposition to any candidate for public office.[71] Activities that constitute *participation or intervention* in a political campaign, for or against a candidate, include the publication or distribution of written or printed statements or the making of oral statements on behalf of or in opposition to a candidate.[72] For example, a charitable organization making political campaign statements in its fundraising literature transgresses these rules.[73] These activities also embrace campaign contributions and the provision of facilities and other resources to political candidates (although that type of support is likely to also be a violation of federal or state campaign finance laws).

The term *candidate for public office* means an individual who offers themselves, or is proposed by others, as a contestant for an elective public office, whether the office be national, state, or local.[74] As to the word *campaign*, a

---

71. IRC § 501(c)(3). In general, see *Tax-Exempt Organizations*, Chapter 23.
72. Reg. § 1.501(c)(3)-1(c)(3)(iii).
73. E.g., Tech. Adv. Mem. 9609007.
74. Reg. § 1.501(c)(3)-1(c)(3)(iii).

§ 9.2 POLITICAL CAMPAIGN ACTIVITIES

federal court observed that "a campaign for a public office in a public election merely and simply means running for office, or candidacy for office, as the word is used in common parlance and as it is understood by the man in the street."[75] While these rules lack a definition of the term *public office*, that term is defined in the context of defining disqualified persons;[76] this is a facts-and-circumstances determination that focuses on whether a significant part of the activities of a public employee is the independent performance of policy-making functions.[77]

A charitable organization that engages in political campaign activities is an *action organization* and thus cannot qualify as or remain federally tax-exempt.[78] Public charities that engage in political campaign activities, and their management, can become subject to excise taxes.[79] Moreover, a public charity in this circumstance can have its tax year involved immediately terminated and taxes assessed on an accelerated basis,[80] and willful and repeated violations may result in a court-imposed injunction pursued by the IRS.[81]

Charitable organizations that engage in *political* activities (which may not be political campaign activities) may become ensnared in the political organizations rules, whereby the expenditures involved are taxed.[82]

(b) Law Applicable to Private Foundations

In general, a private foundation may not pay or incur any amount to influence the outcome of any specific public election or carry on, directly or indirectly, any voter registration drive.[83] To do so would be to make a taxable expenditure.

A grant by a private foundation to a public charity is not a taxable expenditure, however, if the grant is not earmarked[84] for political campaign activities.[85] Thus, if a public charity were to use foundation funds for a political campaign activity under these circumstances, no portion of the grant would be a taxable expenditure, assuming no agreement, oral or written, by which

---

75. Norris v. United States, 86 F.2d 379, 382 (8th Cir. 1936), *rev'd on other grounds*, 300 U.S. 564 (1937).
76. See § 4.8.
77. Reg. § 53.4946-1(g)(2)(i).
78. Reg. § 1.501(c)(3)-1(c)(3).
79. IRC § 4955.
80. IRC § 6852.
81. IRC § 7409.
82. IRC § 527(f)(1).
83. IRC § 4945(d)(2); Reg. § 53.4945-3(a)(1).
84. See § 9.1(c).
85. Reg. §§ 53.4945-2(a)(5)(i), -3(a)(1).

the foundation may cause the grantee organization to engage in the prohibited activity.[86]

A private foundation is considered to be influencing the outcome of a specific public election if it participates or intervenes, directly or indirectly, in any political campaign on behalf of or in opposition to any candidate for public office.[87] The phrase *participation or intervention* in a political campaign includes: publishing or distributing written or printed statements or making oral statements on behalf of or in opposition to a candidate for public office, paying salaries or expenses of campaign workers, conducting or paying the expenses of conducting a voter registration drive limited to the geographic area covered by the campaign, and making a campaign contribution for the benefit of a candidate for public office (which may also be a campaign financing law violation).

(c) Voter Registration Drives

The taxable expenditure rule as to political campaign activities is inapplicable to any amount paid or incurred by a tax-exempt charitable organization, including a private foundation, where (1) its activities are nonpartisan, not confined to one specific election period, and are carried on in at least five states; (2) substantially all (at least 85 percent) of its income is expended directly for the active conduct of its exempt function activities; (3) substantially all of its support (other than gross investment income)[88] is received from tax-exempt organizations, the general public, governmental units, or any combination of these sources, as long as no more than 25 percent of this support is received from any one exempt organization and as long as no more than one-half of its support is received from gross investment income, with these computations made on the basis of the most recent five tax years of the organization;[89] and (4) contributions to the organization for voter registration drives are not subject to conditions that they may be used only in specified states, possessions of the United States, or political subdivisions or other areas of any of these jurisdictions, or the District of Columbia, or that they may be used in only one specific election period.[90]

---

86. Reg. § 53.4945-2(a)(5)(i).
87. Reg. § 53.4945-3(a)(2). To the extent a tax is imposed on a private foundation's participation or intervention in any political campaign on behalf of or in opposition to any candidate for public office under IRC § 4955(a), such expenditure will not also be treated as a taxable expenditure (IRC § 4955(e)).
88. IRC § 509(e).
89. IRC § 4945(f), penultimate sentence.
90. IRC § 4945(f); Reg. § 53.4945-3(b)(1), (3).

An advance ruling may (but is not required to) be obtained as to the status of an organization under these rules for its first year of operation by filing Form 8940 (and a completed Schedule B thereto), along with the required fee.[91] Where these requirements are satisfied, an amount paid or incurred by a private foundation for the activity is not a taxable expenditure.[92]

§ 9.3 GRANTS TO INDIVIDUALS

(a) Definition of Grant

Not every payment by a private foundation to an individual constitutes a grant. The term *grant* does not include payments for personal services, such as salaries, consultant fees, and reimbursement of travel and other expenses incurred on behalf of the foundation if paid to persons (regardless of whether the persons are individuals) working on a private foundation project.[93] A private foundation can, without engaging in grant making, hire persons to assist it in planning, evaluating, or developing projects and program activity by consulting, advising, or participating in conferences organized by the foundation.[94] Persons hired to develop model curricula and educational materials are not considered grant recipients.[95] Likewise, a private foundation can retain the services of an individual to manage the implementation of its grant programs, with the payments treated as compensation for personal services rather than grants.[96]

(b) Individual Grants for Charitable or Other Permitted Purposes

A private foundation grant to an individual will result in a taxable expenditure if it is for "travel, study, or other similar purposes,"[97] unless certain IRS preapproval requirements are met.[98] IRS preapproval need not be sought, however, for grants to individuals falling outside the definition of individual grants for travel, study, or other similar purposes. For example, if a private

---

91. IRC § 4945(f); Reg. § 53.4945-3(b)(4). Form 8940 must be submitted electronically at www.pay.gov; the user fee for this type of request is currently $2,500 (Rev. Proc. 2023-5, 2023-1 I.R.B. 265 §§ 4.02(6), 7.02 and App. A (Schedule of User Fees), as modified by Rev. Proc. 2023-12, 2023-17 I.R.B. 768 §§ 3.01, 3.03).
92. IRC § 4945(f), last sentence; Reg. § 53.4945-3(b)(1), (2).
93. Reg. § 53.4945-4(a)(3)(i). *Cf.* Westward Ho v. Commissioner, 63 T.C.M. 2617 (1992).
94. Reg. § 53.4945-4(a)(2).
95. Rev. Rul. 74-125, 1974-1 C.B. 327.
96. Priv. Ltr. Rul. 200408033.
97. IRC § 4945(d)(3); see § 9.3(d).
98. IRC § 4945(g); see § 9.3(f).

TAXABLE EXPENDITURES

foundation makes grants to indigent individuals to enable them to purchase furniture, such grants are not taxable expenditures even if the preapproval requirements are not met.[99]

All private foundation grants, however, regardless of whether they are subject to the preapproval requirements, must be made for a religious, charitable, scientific, literary, or educational purpose, or to foster national or international amateur sports competition, or for the prevention of cruelty to children or animals (that is, for a charitable or other permitted purpose).[100] A private foundation grant that is not made for a charitable or other permitted purpose will result in a taxable expenditure.[101] For example, a private foundation's purchase and distribution of gifts to underprivileged children during a holiday season furthers the charitable purpose of relief of the poor and distressed and thus will not result in a taxable expenditure.[102] Similarly, a private foundation may make grants to individuals for disaster relief or emergency hardship assistance, but the grant recipients must be members of a charitable class, such as needy or distressed individuals, and private foundations are restricted in their ability to provide assistance to employees of a particular employer.[103]

In one instance, the IRS ruled that private foundation grants to pay the educational loan debt of ministers were taxable expenditures. Because the grant program was not directed to either financially needy ministers or to any specific objective, such as a commitment by the minister to remain in the ministry, the IRS could not be certain that the program was sufficiently tailored to achieve a permitted exempt purpose (specifically, the advancement of religion).[104]

For grants to individuals not subject to the specific reporting and recordkeeping requirements applicable to individual grants for travel, study, or other similar purposes,[105] a private foundation should follow the general recordkeeping requirements that apply to charitable organizations that make distributions to individuals. Pursuant to these requirements, a private foundation should maintain adequate records and case histories that show the name and address of each recipient of aid; the amount distributed to each; the purpose for which the aid was given; the manner in which the recipient was selected and the relationship, if any, between the recipient and any disqualified person[106] with respect to the foundation.[107] These records must be

---

99. Reg. § 53.4945-4(a)(3)(i).
100. IRC § 170(c)(2)(B); Rev. Rul. 76-460, 1976-2 C.B. 371.
101. IRC § 4945(d)(5); see § 9.8.
102. Priv. Ltr. Rul. 9252031.
103. See § 9.3(c).
104. Priv. Ltr. Rul. 199927047.
105. See § 9.3(d).
106. IRC § 4946(a)(1). See Chapter 4.
107. Rev. Rul. 56-304, 1956-2 C.B. 306.

§ 9.3 GRANTS TO INDIVIDUALS

sufficiently detailed to demonstrate that the selection of grantees was made in an objective and nondiscriminatory manner and that the grants were made in furtherance of a charitable or other permitted purpose.[108]

(c) Disaster Relief and Other Assistance Grants

Legislation enacted in 2001 introduced rules for provision of assistance by charitable organizations to individuals who are victims of terrorism.[109] Pursuant to this enactment, charitable organizations that make payments to individuals by reason of the death, injury, wounding, or illness of an individual incurred as a result of the September 11, 2001, attacks, or as the result of an attack involving anthrax occurring on or after September 11, 2001, and before January 1, 2002, are not required to make a specific assessment of need for the payments to be considered made for charitable purposes. The grantor organization must make the payments in good faith using a reasonable and objective formula that is consistently applied.

A summary of this legislation, prepared by the staff of the Joint Committee on Taxation,[110] provided examples of these rules.[111] This analysis addressed the matter of the provision of disaster relief assistance by a private foundation controlled by an employer where those who are assisted are employees of the employer. It articulated this standard: "If payments in connection with a qualified disaster are made by a private foundation to employees (and their family members) of an employer that controls the foundation, the presumption that the charity acts consistently with the requirements of section 501(c)(3) applies if the class of beneficiaries is large or indefinite and if recipients are selected based on an objective determination of need by an independent committee of

---

108. A court upheld the IRS's denial of recognition of tax-exempt status to an organization that made grants purportedly "to assist the poor who were in need of food, clothing, shelter, and medical attention," because the organization failed to furnish any documented criteria "for the selection process of a deserving recipient, the reason for specific amounts given, or the purpose of the grant" (The Church in Boston v. Commissioner, 71 T.C. 102, 106-107 (1978)). The organization's only documentation was a list of grants that included the name of the recipient, the amount of the grant, and a designation of "either unemployment, moving expenses, school scholarship, or medical expense" as the "reason" for the grant (*id.* at 107). The court held that this information "clearly" precluded the IRS "from determining whether the grants were made in an objective and nondiscriminatory manner and whether the distribution of such grants was made in furtherance of an exempt purpose" (*id.*).
109. Victims of Terrorism Tax Relief Act of 2001, Pub. L. No. 107-134, § 111(a), 115 Stat. 2427 (2001), enacting, inter alia, an exclusion from gross income for qualified disaster relief payments (IRC § 139(a)).
110. Staff of Joint Comm. on Tax'n, Technical Explanation of the Victims of Terrorism Tax Relief Act of 2001 17 (Comm. Print JCX-93-01).
111. See *Tax-Exempt Organizations* § 7.2(b).

TAXABLE EXPENDITURES

the private foundation, a majority of the members of which are persons other than persons who are in a position to exercise substantial influence over the affairs of the controlling employer (determined under principles similar to those in effect under section 4958)."[112] A qualified disaster means a disaster that results from a terroristic or military action, a presidentially declared disaster, an accident involving a common carrier, and any other event that the IRS determines is catastrophic.[113] This legislative history stated that the IRS is expected to reconsider its ruling position, in connection with private foundations and disaster relief programs, in light of this paradigm.

The IRS returned to this matter of disaster relief programs provided by charitable organizations when it issued a publication, initially in 2005 and revised at the close of 2014.[114] In this publication, the IRS states that charitable organizations may provide disaster relief assistance to individuals in the form of funds, services, or goods to ensure that victims have the basic necessities, such as food, clothing, housing (including repairs), transportation, and medical assistance (including psychological counseling). The type of aid that is appropriate is dependent on each individual's needs and resources. The assistance may be for the short term, such as food, clothing, and shelter, but not for the long term if an individual has adequate financial resources. The publication states that individuals who are "financially needy or otherwise distressed are appropriate recipients of charity." Examples given are individuals who are temporarily in need of food or shelter when stranded, injured, or lost because of a disaster; temporarily unable to be self-sufficient as a result of a sudden and severe personal or family crisis, such as victims of violent crimes or physical abuse; in need of long-term assistance with housing, childcare, or educational expenses because of a disaster; and in need of counseling because of trauma experienced as a result of a disaster or a violent crime.[115]

---

112. The reference to "section 4958" is to the intermediate sanctions rules. See *Tax-Exempt Organizations*, Chapter 21.
113. IRC § 139(c). The president of the United States, on March 13, 2020, declared the COVID-19 pandemic to be a national emergency under the Robert T. Stafford Disaster Relief and Emergency Assistance Act, thereby triggering application of the federal tax disaster relief law, enabling employers to provide financial assistance to employees and their family members by means of charitable organizations, including private foundations.
114. Pub. 3833, *Disaster Relief: Providing Assistance Through Charitable Organizations* (Dec. 2014), hereafter "IRS Pub. 3833."
115. Past pronouncements of the IRS (incorrectly) indicated that an individual must be shown to be financially needy to receive disaster relief. For example, in a summary of the federal tax law concerning international grantmaking by charitable organizations, the IRS suggested that to be an eligible recipient of financial assistance in the disaster relief context, an individual must be "needy"; the word *distressed* was not used (Chief Couns. Adv. Mem. 200504031). Assistance may be provided to those who are distressed, however, irrespective of their financial condition. See *Tax-Exempt Organizations* § 7.2(b).

§ 9.3 GRANTS TO INDIVIDUALS

Disaster assistance may be provided to businesses to achieve these charitable purposes: aid individual business owners who are financially needy or otherwise distressed, combat community deterioration,[116] and lessen the burdens of government.[117] A tax-exempt charitable organization can accomplish a charitable purpose by providing disaster assistance to a business if the assistance is a "reasonable means" of accomplishing a charitable purpose and any "benefit to a private interest" is incidental to the accomplishment of a charitable purpose.

The IRS guidelines invoke a *needy or distressed* test. They state that, generally, a disaster relief or emergency hardship organization must make a "specific assessment" that a potential recipient of aid is financially or otherwise in need. Individuals do not have to be "totally destitute" to be financially needy, the IRS stated, "they may merely lack the resources to obtain basic necessities." Yet, the IRS continued, "charitable funds cannot be distributed to individuals merely because they are victims of a disaster." Therefore, a charitable organization's decision about how its funds will be distributed must be based on an objective evaluation of the victims' needs at the time the grant is made.

These guidelines state that a charity may provide crisis counseling, rescue services, or emergency aid (such as blankets or hot meals) in the immediate aftermath of a disaster without a showing of financial need. That is, provision of these services to the distressed in the immediate aftermath of a disaster serves a charitable purpose regardless of the financial condition of the recipients. However, the IRS guidelines state that "as time goes on and people are able to call upon their individual resources, it may become increasingly appropriate for charities to conduct individual financial needs assessments." Said the IRS: "While those who may not have the resources to meet basic living needs may be entitled to such assistance, those who do not need continued assistance should not use charitable resources."

The IRS states that an individual who is eligible for assistance because the individual is a victim of a disaster or emergency hardship has "no automatic right" to a charitable organization's funds. For example, a charitable organization that provides disaster or emergency hardship relief does not have to make an individual whole, such as by rebuilding the individual's uninsured home destroyed by a flood or replacing an individual's income after the individual becomes unemployed as the result of a civil disturbance. This "issue," the IRS writes, is "especially relevant when the volume of contributions received in response to appeals exceeds the immediate needs." The IRS states that a charitable organization "is responsible for taking into account the charitable

---

116. See *Tax-Exempt Organizations* § 7.11.
117. See *id.* § 7.7.

TAXABLE EXPENDITURES

purposes for which it was formed, the public benefit of its activities, and the specific needs and resources of each victim when using its discretion to distribute its funds."

The IRS guidelines address the matter of charitable organizations' documentation obligations. The rule is that a charitable organization in this context must maintain "adequate records" to show that the organization's payments further its charitable purposes and that the victims served are "needy or distressed." Moreover, these charities are required to maintain "appropriate records" to show that they have made distributions to individuals after making "appropriate needs assessments" based on the recipients' financial resources and their physical, mental, and emotional well-being.

The IRS states that this documentation should include a complete description of the assistance provided; the costs associated with provision of the assistance; the purpose for which the aid was given; the charity's objective criteria for disbursement of assistance under each program; how the recipients were selected; the name and address of, and the amount distributed to, each recipient; any relationship between a recipient and directors, officers, and/or key employees of, or substantial contributors to, the charitable organization; and the composition of the selection committee approving the assistance.

With respect to short-term emergency aid, the IRS guidelines recognize that charities providing that type of assistance are only expected to maintain records showing the type of assistance provided; the criteria for disbursing assistance; the date, place, and estimated number of victims assisted; the charitable purpose intended to be accomplished; and the cost of the aid. By contrast, organizations that are distributing longer-term assistance are required to keep the more detailed records.

The IRS publication discusses employer-sponsored assistance programs involving charitable entities aimed at helping employees cope with the consequences of a disaster or facing other emergency hardships. The IRS notes that the types of benefits a charitable organization can provide through an employer-sponsored assistance program depend on whether the charity is a public charity,[118] a donor-advised fund,[119] or a private foundation.

With respect to public charities, this guidance states that "[b]ecause public charities typically receive broad financial support from the general public," their operations are generally more transparent and are subject to greater public scrutiny. Accordingly, the IRS states, public charities may provide a "broader range of assistance" to employees than can be provided by donor-advised funds or private foundations. The IRS writes that an employer can establish an employer-sponsored public charity to provide assistance programs to

---
118. See Chapter 15.
119. See Chapter 16.

§ 9.3 GRANTS TO INDIVIDUALS

respond to any type of disaster or other employee emergency hardship situations, as long as the employer involved does not exercise "excessive control" over the public charity. Generally, the IRS observes, employees contribute to the public charity, and rank and file employees constitute a "significant portion" of the organization's governing board.

The IRS states that "[t]o ensure the program is not impermissibly serving the related employer," the public charity must meet the following requirements: (1) the class of beneficiaries must constitute a charitable class, (2) the recipients must be selected on the basis of an "objective determination of need," and (3) the recipients must be selected by an independent selection committee or adequate substitute procedures must be in place to ensure that any benefit to the employer is incidental and tenuous. As to this third requirement, the public charity's selection committee is independent if a majority of its members consists of persons who are not in a position to exercise substantial influence over the affairs of the employer.

If these requirements are met, the public charity's payments to the employer-sponsor's employees and their family members in response to a disaster or emergency hardship are presumed to be made for charitable purposes and not to result in taxable compensation to the employees.

As to donor-advised funds, the IRS observes that, in general, grants cannot be made from the funds to individuals. The agency notes, however, its recognition of an exception for certain employer-related funds established to benefit employees and their family members who are victims of a qualified disaster.[120]

Specifically, a donor-advised fund can make grants to employees and their family members where (1) the fund serves the single identified purpose of providing relief from one or more qualified disasters; (2) the fund serves a charitable class; (3) recipients of grants are selected on the basis of an objective determination of need; (4) the selection of recipients of grants is made using either an independent selection committee or adequate substitute procedures to ensure that any benefit to the employer is incidental and tenuous; (5) no payment is made from the fund to or for the benefit of any trustee, director, or officer of the sponsoring organization, public charity, or member of the fund's selection committee; and (6) the fund maintains adequate records to demonstrate the recipients' need for the disaster assistance provided. The selection

---

120. Notice 2006-109, 2006-2 C.B. 1121. This exception is made pursuant to statutory authority granted to the IRS to exempt funds from treatment as donor-advised funds if the fund is advised by a committee not directly or indirectly controlled by the donor or any person appointed or designated by the donor for the purpose of advising with respect to distributions from such fund (and any related parties), or if such fund benefits a single identified charitable purpose (IRC § 4966(d)(2)(C)).

TAXABLE EXPENDITURES

committee is considered independent if a majority of its members consists of individuals who are not in a position to exercise substantial influence over the employer's affairs.

Where private foundations are concerned, the IRS guidelines acknowledge that private foundations may make need-based distributions to victims of disasters or to the poor or distressed. Although the IRS previously ruled that such programs conferred a significant (and impermissible) private benefit on the sponsoring companies,[121] the IRS guidelines recognize that, after the September 11 attacks, "Congress took the position that employer-sponsored private foundations should be able to provide assistance to employees in certain situations."

Accordingly, current IRS policy is that employer-sponsored private foundations may provide financial assistance to employees or family members affected by a qualified disaster,[122] as long as certain safeguards are in place to ensure that the assistance is serving charitable purposes rather than the employer's business purposes. Employer-sponsored private foundations may not, however, make payments to employees or their family members affected by nonqualified disasters or other emergency hardship situations.[123]

The IRS will presume that payments in response to a qualified disaster made by a private foundation to employees or their family members of an employer that is a disqualified person with respect to the foundation are consistent with the foundation's charitable purposes if (1) the class of beneficiaries is "large or indefinite" (that is, is a charitable class), (2) the recipients are selected on the basis of an "objective determination of need," and (3) the selection is made using either an independent selection committee or "adequate substitute procedures" so as to ensure that any benefit to the employer is incidental and tenuous.[124] A foundation's selection committee is independent if a

---

121. During the early 1990s, the IRS issued several private letter rulings that concluded that payments to employees by a company-sponsored private foundation pursuant to emergency employee hardship assistance or disaster relief programs were made for a charitable purpose; constituted qualifying distributions; and did not constitute either acts of self-dealing or taxable expenditures (e.g., Priv. Ltr. Rul. 9314058 (employee hardship assistance program); Priv. Ltr. Rul. 9516047 (employee disaster and hardship assistance program); and Priv. Ltr. Rul. 9544023 (disaster relief program)). By the late 1990s, however, the IRS was receiving an increasing number of ruling requests involving these types of programs adopted by company-sponsored private foundations for the sole benefit of persons with a current or former employment relationship with the company. In 1999, after reexamining its prior ruling position with respect to such programs, the IRS reversed its position and revoked several of its earlier rulings (e.g., Priv. Ltr. Rul. 199914040, revoking Priv. Ltr. Rul. 9516047; Priv. Ltr. Rul. 199917077, revoking Priv. Ltr. Rul. 9544023; and Priv. Ltr. Rul. 199917079, revoking Priv. Ltr. Rul. 9314058).
122. IRC § 139.
123. IRS Pub. 3833 at 18.
124. See § 5.8(e).

majority of the members of the committee consists of persons who are not in a position to exercise substantial influence over the affairs of the employer.

If these requirements are met, the private foundation's payments in response to a qualified disaster are treated as made for charitable purposes. The payments do not result in acts of self-dealing merely because the recipient is an employee, or family member of an employee, of the employer.[125] This presumption does not apply to payments that would otherwise constitute self-dealing, such as payments made to or for the benefit of individuals who are trustees, directors, or officers of the private foundation.[126]

In this publication, the IRS states that, even if a private foundation fails to meet all the requirements of this presumption, "other procedures and standards may be considered to constitute adequate substitutes to ensure that any benefit to the employer is incidental and tenuous, where all the facts and circumstances are taken into account." By contrast, even if a foundation satisfies the presumption, the IRS reserves the right to review the facts and circumstances to ensure that any benefit to the employer is merely incidental and tenuous. For example, a program "may not be used to induce employees to follow a course of action sought by the employer or designed to relieve the employer of a legal obligation for employee benefits."

The IRS has issued private letter rulings consistent with its position taken in these guidelines. In one of the first, a private foundation provided non-employer-related financial assistance grants to victims or families of victims of a natural disaster, violence, or terrorist acts of war; victims of discrimination, social injustice, or persecution; and impoverished artists. The IRS ruled that these grants were qualifying distributions as long as the assistance was confined to "impoverished individuals with desperate financial needs."[127]

Conversely, the IRS ruled that a private foundation's financial assistance program was not a charitable undertaking because a substantial portion of the charitable class to be aided consisted of employees of a related for-profit corporation, thus causing unwarranted private benefit and self-dealing involving the private foundation that would be conducting the program.[128]

(d) Individual Grants for Travel, Study, or Other Similar Purposes

A grant to an individual for "travel, study, or other similar purposes" is not a *taxable expenditure* if the grant is awarded on an objective and nondiscriminatory

---

125. These payments are not taxable compensation to the employees (IRC § 139(a)).
126. In the publication, the IRS extends this rule to members of the selection committee, although they may not be disqualified persons (see Chapter 4).
127. Priv. Ltr. Rul. 200634016.
128. Priv. Ltr. Rul. 200926033.

TAXABLE EXPENDITURES

basis pursuant to a procedure approved in advance by the IRS and it is demonstrated to the satisfaction of the IRS that:

1. the grant constitutes a scholarship or fellowship grant that is excluded from gross income[129] and is to be used for study at an educational organization[130] that normally maintains a regular faculty and curriculum and normally has a regularly organized body of students in attendance at the place where the educational activities are carried on,[131]
2. the grant constitutes a prize or award that is excluded from gross income,[132] provided the recipient of the prize or award is selected from the general public,[133] or
3. the purpose of the grant is to achieve a specific objective, produce a report or other similar product, or improve or enhance a literary, artistic, musical, scientific, teaching, or other similar capacity, skill, or talent of the grantee.[134]

(i) Scholarships and Fellowships. For the first of these grant categories, the broader definition of an excludable *scholarship* grant found in the federal income tax law before its amendment in 1986 is used, which embraces payments for tuition, fees, living expenses, and allowances for travel, research, clerical help, or equipment.[135] Without discussing the specifics of this definition, the IRS approved the amendment of a private foundation's fellowship grant program to include payments for infant and childcare. The existing program granted funds for equipment, supplies, graduate student support,

---

129. As provided by IRC § 117(a) before its amendment in 1986; see text accompanied by *infra* note 135.
130. IRC § 170(b)(1)(A)(ii).
131. IRC § 4945(g)(1).
132. IRC § 74(b), without regard to IRC § 74(b)(3).
133. IRC § 4945(g)(2).
134. IRC § 4945(g)(3). Also Reg. § 53.4945-4(a)(3)(ii).
135. The Tax Reform Act of 1986 revised the IRC § 117 exclusion, so that it is available only for qualified scholarships, which are grants for tuition and fees required for enrollment or attendance, and fees, books, supplies, and equipment required for courses of instruction, thereby leaving outside the reach of the exclusion payments for room and board. However, Congress, in narrowing the scope of the IRC § 117 exclusion, did not intend to correspondingly narrow the scope of the private foundation individual grant rules. That is, in this context, it is the pre-1986 scholarship and fellowship rules that are applicable. The IRS, from the outset of this matter, recognized that the pre-1986 rules remain applicable in the private foundation individual grant setting (Notice 87-31, 1987-1 C.B. 475), as did the staff of the Joint Committee on Taxation (Staff of Joint Comm. on Tax'n, 99th Cong., General Explanation of the Tax Reform Act of 1986 42 n.21 (Comm. Print 1987)). This clarity was subsequently incorporated into the Internal Revenue Code (IRC § 4945(g)(1)).

§ 9.3 GRANTS TO INDIVIDUALS

technical and secretarial services, travel, summer salary, and salary offset for released time from teaching. Provision of childcare funds was intended to enhance the ability of young women fellows to continue to do research work at universities and encourage more women scientists and engineers. The IRS's ruling was based on the understanding that childcare would be provided to enable the fellows to pursue their research and not for the personal or family needs of the individual.[136]

The IRS ruled that grants by a private foundation to college students who plan to adhere to a "moral commitment" to teach in a particular state after graduation did not require IRS preapproval as scholarship grants. Because the foundation could reasonably expect the recipients to render substantial services in return for its grants, by teaching in the state after graduation, the grants did not meet the statutory requirements for scholarships excludable from gross income as scholarships,[137] even though the conditions upon which they are awarded are not legally enforceable.[138] The IRS further ruled, however, that these grants are included within the third category of grants requiring IRS preapproval, because the purpose of the grants is to achieve a specific objective and they also serve to improve or enhance the recipients' teaching skills.[139] Similarly, the IRS ruled that an educational loan is not a scholarship or fellowship grant, but is an individual grant including within the third category of grants requiring IRS preapproval.[140]

(ii) Employer-Related Scholarship Programs. Additional requirements and IRS guidelines apply to scholarships or fellowships made pursuant to an employer-related grant program. An *employer-related grant program* is a program that limits grant recipients to some or all of the employees of a particular employer or their children, or otherwise gives them a preference or priority over others in being selected as grantees.[141] A scholarship program that provides scholarships to the children of deceased or retired employees of a particular employer is therefore an employer-related grant program.[142]

---

136. Priv. Ltr. Rul. 9116032.
137. Within the meaning of IRC § 117(a).
138. Rev. Rul. 77-44, 1977-1 C.B. 355. This position stems from the insistence of the IRS that a tax-excludable scholarship cannot exist where there is a requirement of a substantial quid pro quo from the recipient (e.g., Bingler v. Johnson, 394 U.S. 741 (1969); Rev. Rul. 73-256, 1973-1 C.B. 56, as modified by Rev. Rul. 74-540, 1974-2 C.B. 38; Miss Georgia Scholarship Fund, Inc. v. Commissioner, 72 T.C. 267 (1979)).
139. *Id.*
140. Rev. Rul. 77-434, 1977-2 C.B. 420.
141. Rev. Proc. 76-47, 1976-2 C.B. 670.
142. Rev. Rul. 79-365, 1979-2 C.B. 389.

In contrast, a company-related private foundation's scholarship program that is open to all students in the community on an equal basis, and which does not give children of employees of the company any preference or priority over others, is not an employer-related grant program.[143]

Grants made by a private foundation under an employer-related grant program to an employee or an employee's family member may be subject to additional requirements or restrictions depending on whether the grants are scholarships or fellowships, employee hardship assistance grants, or qualified disaster relief grants. If such programs do not adhere to these requirements or restrictions, grants made under the programs will be taxable expenditures.

To be excluded from the definition of a taxable expenditure as a scholarship or fellowship (subject to preapproval from the IRS),[144] an educational grant made by a private foundation to the employees of a particular employer, or to the employees' children, must fall outside the so-called pattern of employment. In other words, the purpose of the educational grant program may not be to provide extra compensation, an employment incentive, or an employee fringe benefit to the employees. This requires that sufficient non-employment-related conditions are placed on the program to ensure that the preferential treatment derived from employment does not continue to be of any significance beyond an initial qualifier.

The IRS has promulgated guidelines for use in preapproving employer-related scholarship programs. If the following eight conditions are met, the IRS will assume that scholarship or fellowship grants awarded under such a program to employees, their children, or both, will fall outside the pattern of employment and will not be taxable expenditures:

1. The scholarship plan must not be used by the employer, the foundation, or the organizer of it, to recruit employees or to induce continued employment.

2. The selection committee must be wholly made up of persons totally independent from the private foundation, its organizer, and the employer concerned, not including former employees, and preferably including persons knowledgeable about education.

3. Identifiable minimum requirements for grant eligibility must be established. Employees or children of employees must meet the minimum

---

143. Rev. Rul. 79-131, 1979-1 C.B. 368.
144. IRC § 4945(g)(1).

§ 9.3 GRANTS TO INDIVIDUALS

standards for admission to an educational organization[145] for which the grants are available and are reasonably expected to attend such an organization. Eligibility should not depend on employment-related performance, although up to three years of service for the parent (employee) can be required.

4. Selection criteria must be based on substantial objective standards, such as prior academic performance, tests, recommendations, financial need, and personal interviews, and unrelated to job performance.

5. A grant may not be terminated because the recipient or parent (employee) terminates employment. If the grant award is subject to annual review to continue support for a subsequent year, the recipient cannot be ineligible for renewal because the individual or their parent is no longer employed.

6. The courses of study for which grants are available must not be limited to those of particular benefit to the employer.

7. The terms of the grant and course of study must serve to allow recipients to obtain an education in their individual capacities solely for their personal benefit and must not include any commitments, understandings, or obligations of future employment.

8. The program must satisfy either a percentage test or a facts and circumstances test. Under the percentage test, in the case of a program that awards grants to children of employees, the number of grants awarded in any year may not exceed 25 percent of eligible employee children who applied for a grant in that year and were considered by the selection committee, or 10 percent of the number of employees' children who were eligible for a grant in that year (whether or not they submitted an application). In the case of a program that awards grants to employees, the number of grants awarded in any year may not exceed 10 percent of eligible employees who were considered by the selection committee in selecting grant recipients for that year. Renewals of grants awarded in prior years are not considered in determining the number of grants awarded in a current year and grants awarded to children of employees and those awarded to employees are considered as having been

---

145. That is, an organization described in IRC § 170(b)(1)(A)(ii). Rev. Proc. 76-47, 1976-2 C.B. 670 and Rev. Proc. 85-51, 1985-2 C.B. 717, refer to "an educational institution described in section 151(e)(4)"; however, a subsequent amendment to IRC §§ 4941(d)(2)(G)(ii) and 4945(g)(1) replaced "educational institution described in section 151(e)(4)" with "educational organization described in section 170(b)(1)(A)(ii)," effective for tax years beginning after December 31, 1976 (Pub. L. 94-455, § 1901(b)(8)(H), 90 Stat. 1520, 1795 (1976)).

awarded under separate programs even if they are administered under the same program.[146]

These conditions also apply to employer-related educational loan programs.[147] If these conditions are satisfied, the IRS will assume that employer-related educational loans are made on an objective and nondiscriminatory basis and thus are not taxable expenditures.

If a private foundation's employer-related program includes both educational loans and scholarship or fellowship grants, the percentage tests apply to the total number of individuals receiving combined grants of scholarships, fellowships, and educational loans.[148]

Provided all the other conditions are met, the failure of an employer-related educational grant or loan program to satisfy the percentage test will not necessarily disqualify the program if the facts and circumstances demonstrate that the primary purpose of the program is not to provide extra compensation or another employment incentive (in the case of an educational grant program) or further the private interests of the employer (in the case of an educational loan program), but rather is to educate recipients in their individual capacities.[149] For example, the IRS ruled that educational grants

---

146. Rev. Proc. 76-47, 1976-2 C.B. 670, as clarified by Rev. Proc. 81-65, 1981-1 C.B. 690 and Rev. Proc. 85-51, 1985-2 C.B. 717, and amplified by Rev. Proc. 94-78, 1994-2 C.B. 833. Rev. Proc. 85-51, *supra*, provides additional guidance regarding how many employees' children may be counted as eligible for a scholarship or loan for purposes of applying the 10 percent (of eligible employees' children) test. Under this guidance, a private foundation may include as eligible only those children with respect to whom the foundation receives a written statement, or for whom information is maintained sufficient to demonstrate, other than by statistical or sampling techniques, that they meet the foundation's eligibility requirements and (1) they are enrolled in or have completed a course of study preparing them for admission to an educational institution at the level for which the scholarships or loans are available, have applied or intend to apply to such an institution, and expect, if accepted, to attend such an educational institution in the immediately succeeding academic year, or (2) they currently attend an educational institution for which the scholarships or loans are available but are not in the final year for which an award may be made (*id.*). In Rev. Proc. 94-78, *supra*, the IRS announced a rounding convention to be used in connection with these percentage tests, permitting a rounding up of the number of allowable grants provided the number otherwise is at least four.
147. Educational loans that are limited to furtherance of the recipient's education at an educational institution described in IRC § 170(b)(1)(A)(ii) are individual grants to obtain a "specific objective" within the meaning of IRC § 4945(g)(3) (Rev. Rul. 77-434, 1977-2 C.B. 420).
148. Rev. Proc. 80-39, 1980-2 C.B. 772, as clarified by Rev. Proc. 81-65, 1981-1 C.B. 690 and Rev. Proc. 85-51, 1985-2 C.B. 717, and amplified by Rev. Proc. 94-78, 1994-2 C.B. 833.
149. Rev. Proc. 76-47, 1976-2 C.B. 670 (educational grant programs); Rev. Proc. 80-39, 1980-2 C.B. 772 (educational loan programs).

§ 9.3 GRANTS TO INDIVIDUALS

made by a private foundation without regard to the percentage test are not taxable expenditures where they are made only to employees and children of employees who are killed or seriously injured from a qualified disaster.[150] The IRS stated that this requirement for eligibility provides sufficient assurance that the primary purpose of the grant is to educate recipients in their individual capacities, outside of any pattern of employment. Therefore, the program met the facts and circumstances test and was not required to satisfy the percentage test.[151]

Notwithstanding the first of these conditions, the IRS subsequently indicated its understanding "that for an employer-related educational grant or loan program to fulfill its intended purpose, it is necessary to inform the eligible employees of its availability."[152] Thus, the IRS stated that a private foundation's employer-related grant or loan program may be publicized in the employer's newsletter if the private foundation is "clearly identified" as the grantor of the awards.[153] The IRS also stated that "making public announcements of the grants or loans in the employer's newsletter" is permitted if the private foundation or the independent selection committee is "clearly identified" as the grantor of the awards.[154]

An individual grant program administered by a company-related private foundation thus may be able to qualify for exemption from treatment as taxable expenditures where the grants are scholarships or fellowships used for study at a qualified educational organization and the grants satisfy these guidelines.[155] Even if the grants cannot meet those requirements, they may avoid classification as taxable expenditures by constituting grants made to achieve a specific objective, produce a product, or improve or enhance some capacity, skill, or talent of the grantees.[156]

Because IRS preapproval of such programs is mandatory, the IRS has issued many private letter rulings reviewing and approving (or denying approval of) employer-related scholarship and loan programs under these guidelines.[157]

---

150. IRC § 139(c).
151. Rev. Rul. 2003-32, 2003-1 C.B. 689. Also, Rev. Rul. 86-90, 1986-2 C.B. 184.
152. Rev. Proc. 81-65, 1981-2 C.B. 690.
153. Id.
154. Id.
155. IRC § 4945(g)(1). Not surprisingly, the IRS declined to approve a private foundation's employer-related grant program that did not meet any of these guidelines (Priv. Ltr. Rul. 202207010).
156. IRC § 4945(g)(3); Beneficial Foundation, Inc. v. United States, 85-2 U.S.T.C. ¶ 9601 (Cl. Ct. 1985); see § 9.3(d)(iii).
157. E.g., Priv. Ltr. Rul. 8807002.

(iii) Prizes and Awards. To constitute a *prize or award* that falls within the second category of individual grants identified in the statute,[158] the recipient must be selected from the general public,[159] must be selected without any action on their part to enter the contest or proceeding, and may not be required to render substantial future services as a condition of receiving the prize or award.[160] The prize or award must also be made primarily in recognition of past achievements of the recipient in religious, charitable, scientific, educational, artistic, literary, or civic fields.[161] A private foundation need not require the recipient of the prize or award to transfer it to a governmental unit or a charitable organization in order for the prize or award to qualify for the exception to the private foundation individual grant rules.[162] This requirement must, however, be met for the recipient to exclude the prize or award from their gross income.[163]

A prize or award by a private foundation to an individual granted in recognition of past achievements of the recipient in the religious, charitable, scientific, educational, artistic, literary, or civic fields will not be considered a grant "for travel, study, or other similar purposes," however, if it is not intended to finance any future activities of the recipient and no conditions are imposed on the manner in which the award funds may be expended by the recipient.[164] Awards for past achievement meeting these criteria are not considered grants for travel, study, or other similar purposes in the first instance; therefore, they will not constitute taxable expenditures even if the IRS preapproval requirements are not met.[165] Indeed, current IRS policy in this regard provides that the IRS will not issue advance approval for these types of grant-making programs.[166] Thus, a private foundation's proposed grant program awarding a medal and cash honorarium in recognition of outstanding acts of community

---

158. IRC § 4945(g)(2).
159. *Id.*
160. IRC § 74(b).
161. Reg. § 1.74-1(b)(1).
162. IRC §§ 74(b)(3), 4945(g)(2).
163. IRC § 74(b)(3).
164. Rev. Rul. 75-393, 1975-2 C.B. 451; Rev. Rul. 76-460, 1976-2 C.B. 371; Rev. Rul. 77-380, 1977-2 C.B. 419. These rulings also indicate that an award for past achievement that meets these criteria and therefore falls outside the definition of a grant for travel, study, or other similar purpose does not need to meet the requirement (for IRC § 4945(g)(2) purposes) that the recipient of the prize or award must be selected without any action on their part to enter the contest or proceeding.
165. *Id.*; Reg. § 53.4945-4(a)(3)(i).
166. Internal Revenue Manual 7.20.3.3.6.2. If a private foundation submits a request for advance approval of this type of grant-making procedure, the IRS will inform the foundation that it does not process such requests and close the case (*id.*).

§ 9.3 GRANTS TO INDIVIDUALS

service was determined not to require IRS preapproval, because the awards were made in recognition of past achievements, were not intended to finance any future activity of the recipient, and no conditions were imposed on the manner in which the cash could be expended.[167]

In contrast, if an award for past achievement is earmarked by the private foundation to pay for subsequent travel by the award recipient, the award will represent a grant to an individual for travel, and the IRS preapproval requirements for awards and prizes must be met.[168] Similarly, if an award for past achievement is required to be used for study at an educational organization, the award will represent a grant to an individual for study, and the IRS preapproval requirements for scholarships must be met.[169] Thus, an award by a private foundation to the winner of a local science fair required IRS preapproval where the use of the award funds was earmarked for the recipient's college education.[170] Likewise, IRS preapproval was required for a grant-making program providing awards in recognition of achievements in addressing world problems, such as climate change or inequality, where the award recipients were required to use the award funds for travel, study, or toward ongoing projects in these areas.[171]

(iv) Grants for Specific Objectives or to Enhance Skills. The types of individual grants included within the third category requiring IRS preapproval, that is, grants to achieve a specific objective, produce a report or other similar product, or improve or enhance a literary, artistic, musical, scientific, teaching or other similar capacity, skill or talent of the grantee,[172] can be quite expansive.[173] Indeed, after finding that educational loans "do not readily fit" the

---

167. Priv. Ltr. Rul. 8327094. Other examples of private foundation programs meeting these criteria and therefore not requiring IRS preapproval include awards made to the person who has written the best work of literary criticism during the preceding year (Rev. Rul. 75-393, 1975-2 C.B. 451); to the winner of a competition conducted among students attending schools specializing in teaching a special craft (Rev. Rul. 76-460, 1976-2 C.B. 371); to the person whose work represents the best example of investigative reporting on matters concerning the federal government (Rev. Rul. 77-380, 1977-2 C.B. 419); to basketball coaches, based on overall win/loss records, grade point averages of the teams, and total community service hours of the players (Priv. Ltr. Rul. 200327060); and to a scientist or other individual for practical accomplishments in the field of commercial space activities (Priv. Ltr. Rul. 200349007).
168. Rev. Rul. 77-380, 1977-2 C.B. 419.
169. *Id.* As to the IRS preapproval requirements for scholarships, see § 9.3(f).
170. Rev. Rul. 76-461, 1976-2 C.B. 371.
171. Priv. Ltr. Rul. 202250018.
172. IRC § 4945(g)(3).
173. The phrase "other similar purposes" is not defined in the statute or regulations, but certainly includes the purposes described in IRC § 4945(g)(3) (Gen. Couns. Mem. 36223).

grant categories for scholarships and fellowships, or prizes and awards, the IRS concluded that "they must be to achieve a specific objective or otherwise qualify within the meaning of [the third grant category] in order to avoid being taxable expenditures."[174] The IRS went on to state that the term "specific objective" and the other purposes described in the third grant category requiring IRS preapproval "were employed to describe those individual grants that are made for purposes sufficiently narrow and definite to ensure that recipients are authorized to expend the funds only in furtherance of charitable purposes."[175]

Within this third category of grants, the IRS approved in advance a private foundation's program to make grants to choreographers and composers to produce one or more ballets; to designers to produce one or more works of art relating to dancing; to ballet masters and teachers to encourage scholarship; to dancers and others engaged in serious pursuit of an aspect of ballet for study at a recognized school or study under a recognized teacher to enhance their skill; and to writers to produce an article, nonfiction or other writing in the field of dancing.[176]

The IRS also approved a private foundation's grant program that funded sabbaticals and professional development for chief executives of public charities. These grants were in the form of stipends for living and travel expenses. The foundation also provided grants in the form of additional compensation for the chief executives' second-in-command or interim leadership team of senior managers who were acting chief executives or executive teams during the sabbatical.[177]

As another example, the IRS provided advance approval of grant procedures to a private foundation that was formed to foster national and international sports competition by supporting and developing Tai Kwon Do, martial arts, and "anti-violence students, instructors, educators, and leaders through education, experience, training, and opportunities." The foundation's program provided grants to individuals for the purpose of development of, travel to, or participation in martial arts, self-defense, and anti-violence training programs, classes, workshops, seminars, tournaments, demonstrations, or certification courses on local, regional, national, or international levels, or development of informational and instructional publications and other forms of communication.[178]

---

174. Rev. Rul. 77-434, 1977-2 C.B. 420.
175. *Id.*
176. Priv. Ltr. Rul. 8237084.
177. Priv. Ltr. Rul. 201541011.
178. Priv. Ltr. Rul. 201610022.

§ 9.3 GRANTS TO INDIVIDUALS

In a capacious interpretation of an individual grant to obtain a specific objective, the IRS approved in advance a private foundation grant program providing support to public charities and certain small businesses to enable them to transition their products or service offerings to online operations. To be eligible for a grant, an entity was required to have a certain annual operating budget, a certain number of employees, and a need for assistance in moving its functions online. Small business grantees were further required to be located within the city limits of an economically depressed area, inhabited mainly by low-income, minority, or other disadvantaged groups, and have experienced difficulty in obtaining conventional financing due to its minority composition or due to prevailing economic conditions. Under the program, the private foundation directly paid information technology service providers to oversee these transitions and hired contractors to oversee the program and work directly with the participating entities. The organizations involved had access to on-call support from the foundation's team and other support in the form of virtual office hours, training administered through IT firms, coaching from foundation staff, and workshops pertaining to specific IT matters.[179]

(e) Individual Grant Procedures

Once a private foundation chooses to make grants to individuals that are subject to the IRS preapproval process, it must adopt procedures for its grant program that comply with the IRS's preapproval requirements. To secure advance approval of grants to individuals for travel, study, or similar purposes,[180] a private foundation must demonstrate to the satisfaction of the IRS that:

- Its grant procedure includes an objective and nondiscriminatory selection process.

- The procedure is reasonably calculated to result in performance by grantees of the activities that the grants are intended to finance.

---

179. Priv. Ltr. Rul. 202114024. These payments to individuals may not be *grants* to begin with. Grants do not ordinarily include payments, such as consultants' fees, to individuals for personal services in assisting a foundation in planning, evaluating, or developing projects or areas of program activity by consulting or advising (see § 9.3(a)). Perhaps the view is that the IT providers are assisting the public charities and small businesses involved, rather than the foundation.
180. IRC § 4945(g); Reg. § 53.4945-4(c)(1).

- The private foundation plans to obtain reports to determine whether the grantees have performed the activities that the grants are intended to finance.[181]

No single procedure or set of procedures is required. Procedures may vary depending on factors such as the size of the private foundation, the amount and purpose of the grants, and whether one or more recipients are involved.[182]

(i) Objective and Nondiscriminatory Basis for Selection. In order for a private foundation to establish that its grants to individuals for study, travel, or other similar purposes are made on an *objective and nondiscriminatory basis*, the grants must be awarded in accordance with a program that, if it were a substantial part of the foundation's activities, would be consistent with (1) the existence of the private foundation's tax-exempt status, (2) the allowance of deductions to individuals for contributions to it, and (3) three additional requirements, relating to candidates for grants, the criteria for selection of potential grantees, and the persons making selections.[183]

In general, *candidates for grants* must be selected from a *group* of potential candidates, and the criteria for defining this group of candidates must be reasonably related to the purposes of the grant. The group must also be sufficiently broad so that the giving of grants to members of the group would be considered to fulfill a charitable purpose,[184] which means that ordinarily the group must be sufficiently large to constitute a *charitable class*. Selection from a group is not required, and reasonable restrictions may be imposed on the group of potential grantees, where taking into account the purposes of the grant, one or several persons are selected because they are exceptionally qualified to carry out the grant purposes or it is otherwise evident that the grantee selected is particularly calculated to effectuate the charitable purpose of the grant rather than to benefit particular persons or a particular class of persons. For example, selection of a qualified research scientist to work on a particular project will not violate this requirement merely because the private foundation selects the scientist from a group of three who are experts in the field.[185]

---

181. Reg. § 53.4945-4(c)(1).
182. *Id.*
183. Reg. § 53.4945-4(b)(1).
184. That is, a purpose described in IRC § 170(c)(2)(B).
185. Reg. § 53.4945-4(b)(2).

§ 9.3 GRANTS TO INDIVIDUALS

The requirement of a sufficiently broad group of grant candidates is satisfied, for example, where a private foundation awards 20 annual scholarships to members of a certain ethnic minority living within a state, where all members of the ethnic minority group (other than disqualified persons to the foundation) are eligible to apply for the scholarships and there are an estimated 400 potentially eligible applicants.[186] The IRS also found this requirement was satisfied in the case of private foundation grant programs providing scholarships to the children and grandchildren of members of an association,[187] and to students at a tax-exempt boarding school, notwithstanding the fact that this school was an all-boys institution.[188] A group of girls and boys, however, with at least one-quarter Finnish blood, living in two particular towns, was found to be a discriminatory group and not sufficiently broad.[189] Likewise, a plan that gave preference to family members and relatives of the trust's creator, if their qualifications were substantially the same as an unrelated party, was found to be discriminatory.[190]

The *selection criteria* used to choose grantees from within the group of potential grantees must be related to the purposes of the grant. Thus, for example, criteria used for selecting scholarship recipients might include (but not be limited to) prior academic performance, performance on tests designed to measure ability and aptitude for college work, recommendations from instructors, financial need,[191] and the conclusions which the selection committee might draw from a personal interview as to the individual's motivation,

---

186. Reg. § 53.4945-4(b)(5), Example (2). In contrast, a scholarship program established for students attending two named universities failed to qualify for the estate tax charitable contribution deduction because an additional criterion was that the grantees have the same surname as the decedent; inasmuch as there are only about 600 families in the United States with that surname, the IRS concluded that a charitable class was not present (i.e., that the group of potential grantees was too small) and denied the charitable deduction (Priv. Ltr. Rul. 9631004).
187. Priv. Ltr. Rul. 201919018.
188. Priv. Ltr. Rul. 200603029.
189. Priv. Ltr. Rul. 7851096.
190. Rev. Rul. 85-175, 1985-2 C.B. 276. One private foundation administered a scholarship program, one of the criteria of which was that recipients had to be related to trustees of the foundation! For that and other reasons, its tax-exempt status was retroactively revoked (Priv. Ltr. Rul. 201022030).
191. While financial need may be considered in selecting scholarship recipients, it is by no means a mandatory requirement (Rev. Rul. 76-340, 1976-2 C.B. 370). A trust for educational purposes is charitable even though the persons to be educated are not limited to the poor. Such a trust is charitable because it advances or promotes education, which is a charitable purpose itself. Therefore, the fact that recipients of scholarships are selected based on merit (scholastic ability) without regard to financial need is consistent with the existence of a private foundation's tax-exempt status under IRC § 501(c)(3) (Rev. Rul. 69-257, 1969-1 C.B. 151; Rev. Rul. 76-340, 1976-2 C.B. 370).

character, ability, and potential.[192] With respect to private foundation grants made to achieve a specific objective; produce a report; or improve or enhance a capacity, skill, or talent of the grantee, the IRS approved the following selection criteria: potential benefit of the proposed activities to the community and specific population to be served, capacity of the individual to achieve the result, adequacy of proposed financial and time budgets for achieving the desired result, evidence of cooperation and coordination with other organizations and individuals working in the same field, likelihood of ongoing support from other sources for the program, and other factors indicating that the program will accomplish the foundation's charitable purposes.[193]

Grant recipients may be chosen by a single person, or by a *selection committee*, but in either case the person or persons making the selection should not be in a position to derive a private benefit, directly or indirectly, if certain potential grantees are selected over others.[194]

As noted, additional conditions and requirements must be satisfied to obtain IRS preapproval of an employer-related scholarship program.[195]

(ii) Grantee Reporting Requirements. Generally, with respect to any scholarship or fellowship grant, a private foundation must make arrangements to receive a report of the grantee's work in each academic period. A report of the grantee's courses taken (if any) and grades earned (if any) in each academic period must be received at least once annually and verified by the educational organization. For grantees whose work does not involve classes but only the preparation of research papers or projects, such as a doctoral thesis, the foundation must receive a brief report at least once annually, which must be approved by the faculty members supervising the grantee or another school official. On completion of a grantee's study, a final report must also be obtained.[196]

These reporting requirements will be considered satisfied with respect to scholarship or fellowship grants under the following circumstances: (1) the grants are made pursuant to an approved plan;[197] (2) the private foundation

---

192. Reg. § 53.4945-4(b)(3). Thus, the IRS ruled that scholarship grants made to individuals by a private foundation based on academic standing, financial need, personal history, the cost of the programs of study to be pursued, and sources of income available to the applicant other than the foundation's scholarship grant, were not taxable expenditures (Rev. Rul. 76-340, 1976-2 C.B. 370).
193. Priv. Ltr. Rul. 200009053.
194. Reg. § 53.4945-4(b)(4).
195. See § 9.3(d)(ii).
196. Reg. § 53.4945-4(c)(2).
197. IRC § 4945(g)(1).

pays the grants to an educational organization;[198] and (3) the educational organization agrees to use the grant funds to defray the recipient's expenses or to pay the funds (or a portion of them) to the recipient only if the recipient is enrolled at the educational organization and their standing at the educational organization is consistent with the purposes and conditions of the grant.[199]

With respect to grants made to achieve a specific objective; produce a report; or improve or enhance a capacity, skill, or talent or the grantee, a private foundation must require reports on the use of the funds and the progress made by the grantee toward achieving the purposes for which the grant was made. These reports must be made at least once annually and upon completion of the funded undertaking. This final report must describe the grantee's accomplishments and contain an accounting of the funds received.[200]

(iii) Monitoring, Supervision, and Investigation Requirements. Where the requisite reports or other information (including the failure to submit the reports) indicates that all or any part of a grant is not being used in furtherance of the purposes of the grant, the private foundation has a *duty to investigate*. While conducting its investigation, the private foundation must withhold further payments to the extent possible until any delinquent reports have been submitted.[201] In cases in which the grantor private foundation determines that any part of a grant has been used for improper purposes and the grantee has not previously diverted grant funds to any use not in furtherance of a purpose specified in the grant, the private foundation will not be treated as having made a taxable expenditure solely because of the diversion as long as the private foundation:

1. Is taking all reasonable and appropriate steps either to recover the grant funds or to ensure restoration of the diverted funds and the dedication of other grant funds held by the grantee to the purposes being financed by the grant, and

---

198. That is, an organization described in IRC § 170(b)(1)(A)(ii). Reg. § 53.4945-4(c)(5) refers to "an educational institution described in section 151(e)(4)"; however, a subsequent amendment to IRC §§ 4941(d)(2)(G)(ii) and 4945(g)(1) replaced "educational institution described in section 151(e)(4)" with "educational organization described in section 170(b)(1)(A)(ii)," effective for tax years beginning after December 31, 1976 (Pub. L. 94-455, § 1901(b)(8)(H), 90 Stat. 1520, 1795 (1976)).
199. Reg. § 53.4945-4(c)(5).
200. Reg. § 53.4945-4(c)(3).
201. Reg. § 53.4945-4(c)(4)(i).

TAXABLE EXPENDITURES

2. Withholds any further payments to the grantee after the grantor becomes aware that a diversion may have taken place, until it has received the grantee's assurances that future diversions will not occur and requires the grantee to take extraordinary precautions to prevent future diversions from occurring.[202]

All *reasonable and appropriate steps* may include appropriate legal action, but need not include a lawsuit if it is unlikely funds would be recouped in satisfaction of a judgment.[203]

If a private foundation is treated as having made a taxable expenditure in these circumstances, then the amount of the taxable expenditure is the amount of the diversion plus any further payments to the grantee, unless the foundation takes the steps described in the first of the preceding two requirements. If the foundation complies with the first requirement but not the second, however, the amount of the taxable expenditure is limited to the amount of the further payments.[204]

In cases where a grantee has previously diverted funds received from a grantor private foundation and the grantor foundation determines that any part of a grant has again been used for improper purposes, the private foundation is not treated as having made a taxable expenditure solely by reason of the diversion so long as the private foundation again meets the two requirements listed earlier. In this instance, the private foundation also must withhold further funds until the diverted funds are, in fact, recovered or restored.[205]

If a private foundation is treated as having made a taxable expenditure in a case where a grantee has previously diverted grant funds, then the amount of the taxable expenditure is the amount of the diversion plus the amount of any further payments to the grantee, unless the private foundation complies with the first of the two preceding requirements. If the private foundation meets the first requirement, but fails to withhold further payments until the second requirement is met and the diverted funds are in fact recovered or restored, the amount of the taxable expenditure is the amount of the further payments.[206]

The foregoing supervision requirements will be considered satisfied with respect to scholarship or fellowship grants under the following circumstances: (1) the grants are made pursuant to an approved plan;[207] (2) the

---

202. Reg. § 53.4945-4(c)(4)(ii).
203. Reg. § 53.4945-4(c)(4)(iv).
204. Reg. § 53.4945-4(c)(4)(ii).
205. Reg. § 53.4945-4(c)(4)(iii).
206. *Id.*
207. IRC § 4945(g)(1).

§ 9.3 GRANTS TO INDIVIDUALS

private foundation pays the grants to an educational organization;[208] and (3) the educational organization agrees to use the grant funds to defray the recipient's expenses or to pay the funds (or a portion of them) to the recipient only if the recipient is enrolled at the educational organization and their standing at the educational organization is consistent with the purposes and conditions of the grant.[209]

(iv) Recordkeeping Requirements. A private foundation must retain records pertaining to grants to individuals for travel, study, or other similar purposes. These records must include all information obtained to evaluate the qualification of potential grantees, identification of grantees (including any relationship that would make the grantee a disqualified person with respect to the private foundation),[210] the amount and purpose of each grant, and any information obtained by the private foundation to comply with the grantee reporting and monitoring, supervision, and investigation requirements.[211]

The IRS declined to approve one private foundation's grant procedures in part because the foundation did not require scholarship applications and instead relied on correspondence and notes of conversations. The IRS deemed this informal level of documentation to be insufficient to ensure compliance with the recordkeeping requirements applicable to grants to individuals for travel, study, or other similar purposes.[212]

(f) IRS Approval of Grant Procedures

The requirement to seek advance IRS approval of grants to individuals for travel, study, or other similar purposes is a mandatory, substantive provision of federal law, rather than a mere ministerial filing requirement.[213] Thus, a private foundation's failure to seek IRS preapproval of its individual grant procedures, when required, may result in significant liability for the excise tax on taxable expenditures.[214]

---

208. That is, an organization described in IRC § 170(b)(1)(A)(ii). Reg. § 53.4945-4(c)(5) refers to "an educational institution described in section 151(e)(4)"; however, a subsequent amendment to IRC §§ 4941(d)(2)(G)(ii) and 4945(g)(1) replaced "educational institution described in section 151(e)(4)" with "educational organization described in section 170(b)(1)(A)(ii)," effective for tax years beginning after December 31, 1976 (Pub. L. 94-455, § 1901(b)(8)(H), 90 Stat. 1520, 1795 (1976)).
209. Reg. § 53.4945-4(c)(5).
210. IRC § 4946(a)(1). See Chapter 4.
211. Reg. § 53.4945-4(c)(6).
212. Priv. Ltr. Rul. 7951102.
213. John Q. Shunk Association v. United States, 85-2 U.S.T.C ¶ 9830 (S.D. Ohio 1986).
214. One court held that a private foundation that awarded scholarships without first obtaining approval of its grant-making procedures and that subsequently received retroactive

TAXABLE EXPENDITURES

(i) Requests for Advance IRS Approval. A request for advance IRS approval of a private foundation's grant procedures may be submitted in connection with a private foundation's initial application for recognition of tax-exempt status,[215] or, if the foundation has already been recognized as tax-exempt by the IRS, by submitting Form 8940, along with the required fee.[216]

A request for advance IRS approval of a foundation's grant procedures must fully describe the foundation's procedures for awarding grants and for ascertaining that the grants are used for the proper purposes. Specifically, the request must contain (1) a statement describing the selection process that is sufficiently detailed for the IRS to determine whether the grants are made on an objective and nondiscriminatory basis; (2) a description of the terms and conditions under which the foundation ordinarily makes these grants that is sufficient to enable the IRS to determine whether the grants awarded under the procedures would meet the preapproval requirements for either scholarships or fellowships, prizes or awards, or to grants to achieve a specific objective, produce a report, or improve or enhance a capacity, skill or talent or the grantee; (3) a detailed description of the private foundation's procedure for exercising supervision over grants; and (4) a description of the foundation's procedures for review of grantee reports, for investigation where diversion of grant funds from their proper purposes is indicated, and for recovery of diverted grant funds.[217]

---

approval of the procedures is nonetheless liable for the initial excise tax imposed by IRC § 4945(a)(1) (see § 9.9(a)), in that the corrective measures taken relieved the private foundation only from liability for the additional tax imposed by IRC § 4945(b) (German Society of Maryland, Inc. v. Commissioner, 80 T.C. 741 (1983)). Another court apparently was of the view that approval of a private foundation's grant program procedures is automatically retroactive where the features of the program have not changed (The Addison H. Gibson Foundation v. United States, 91-1 U.S.T.C. ¶ 50,178 (W.D. Pa. 1991), *aff'd in unpub. opinion* (3rd Cir. 1992)).

In one instance, the IRS determined that a private foundation's failure to obtain advance approval of an employer-related scholarship program caused grants made under the program to be subject to the excise tax on taxable expenditures for the year under examination as well as subsequent years (Tech. Adv. Mem. 9825004). As the program also failed to meet the applicable percentage test guidelines (Rev. Proc. 76-47, 1976-2 C.B. 670), it is unclear whether the IRS might have been more lenient if the program had otherwise been compliant. Additionally, if the matter had been identified and corrected by the foundation, rather than by the IRS on examination, the foundation may have had a basis on which to request abatement of the tax (Priv. Ltr. Rul. 201940013; see § 12.4(c)).

215. By completing and submitting Schedule H to Form 1023.
216. Form 8940 must be submitted electronically at www.pay.gov; the user fee for this type of request is currently $2,500 (Rev. Proc. 2023-5, 2023-1 I.R.B. 265 §§ 4.02(6), 7.02 and App. A (Schedule of User Fees), as modified by Rev. Proc. 2023-12, 2023-17 I.R.B. 768 §§ 3.01, 3.03).
217. Reg. § 53.4945-4(d)(1). Schedule C to Form 8940 (Apr. 2023) is designed to obtain this and other information relevant to a request for IRS preapproval of a private foundation's grant procedures.

§ 9.3 GRANTS TO INDIVIDUALS

Because IRS preapproval is mandatory for grants for travel, study, or other similar purpose, the IRS frequently issues rulings preapproving (or denying) requests for preapproval of private foundations' grant-making procedures.[218]

(ii) Deemed IRS Approval. If a private foundation properly submits a request for advance approval of its grant procedures and does not receive notification from the IRS within 45 days that the procedures are unacceptable, the grant procedures will be considered approved from the date of submission until any receipt of actual notice from the IRS that the grant procedures are unacceptable.[219]

Recognition of a private foundation as a tax-exempt charitable organization does not in itself constitute approval of the foundation's grant procedures, but the submission of a full and complete request for approval of grant procedures in connection with a foundation's application for recognition of exemption will start the running of the 45-day period.[220] Thus, if a private foundation does not receive notification from the IRS regarding its grant procedures by the 45th day after submission of its exemption application, the private foundation's procedures are considered to have been approved from the date of its application.[221]

After the 45-day period passes, it is possible that a private foundation may begin making grants in accordance with its grant procedures, and then subsequently receive notification from the IRS that the procedures do not conform to the statutory requirements. In this situation, a grant made after notification by the IRS that the private foundation's individual grant procedures are unacceptable is a taxable expenditure,[222] but a grant made prior to the adverse notice is not a taxable expenditure. Even where the grant is structured in multiple payments of a fixed amount, payments of the installments remaining after the notification will not result in taxable expenditures; such payments are considered merely the satisfaction of the private foundation's obligation under a grant that were deemed approved. A renewal of a grant made during the prenotification period would, however, be a taxable expenditure; this type

---

218. E.g., Priv. Ltr. Rul. 7830122.
219. Reg. § 53.4945-4(d)(3).
220. Rev. Rul. 86-77, 1986-1 C.B. 334. This rule applies even if a private foundation does not complete Schedule H to Form 1023 or specifically request advance approval as part of its exemption application (Internal Revenue Manual 7.20.3.2.2(5)) as long as the foundation makes a full and complete disclosure of its grant procedures in its exemption application that contains the information required by Reg. § 53.4945-4(d) (see text accompanied by *supra* note 217).
221. Rev. Rul. 86-77, 1986-1 C.B. 334.
222. Reg. § 53.4945-4(d)(3).

of payment would be within the discretion of the private foundation, and, thus, a new grant.[223]

(iii) Impact of IRS Approval on Future Grants. The approval procedure is intended to be a one-time approval of a system of standards, procedures, and follow-up designed to result in grants that meet the IRS advance approval requirements. Thus, the approval applies to a subsequent grant program provided that the procedures under which it is conducted do not "differ materially" from those described in the request.[224]

Examples of changes the IRS has found were not *material changes* include changing the scholarship award check to be made payable jointly to the student and the school;[225] eliminating limitations on the amount of scholarships and the number of years they may run and broadening the range of schools for which scholarship students may enroll;[226] instead of scholarships being provided by the private foundation directly, distributing annual lump sum amounts to a university to be allocated and distributed by it as scholarships in amounts and to recipients determined by the university;[227] changing wholly owned subsidiaries to 90 percent owned subsidiaries for purposes of determining eligibility of employees' children for scholarships; expanding courses of study to include master's degree programs (and modifying the duration of and reporting requirements for such scholarships as compared to those previously approved for undergraduate programs); announcing scholarship awards in an employer's newsletter, provided the private foundation is identified as the grantor of the awards; increasing the amount of the scholarship award to reflect increased educational costs; and changing the payee of the award from the school to the third-party administrator of the scholarship program, for disbursement to the school or the grantee, as appropriate.[228]

A change in the use of fellowship grant funds to allow recipients to use them for childcare was considered a material change but was approved by the IRS.[229] In the case of one employer-related scholarship program,[230] the IRS characterized the following changes as material: an expansion of the group of

---

223. Rev. Rul. 81-46, 1981-1 C.B. 514.
224. Reg. § 53.4945-4(d)(1).
225. Priv. Ltr. Rul. 8110040.
226. Priv. Ltr. Rul. 8206144.
227. Priv. Ltr. Rul. 8109063. Note that this "change" might more appropriately have been characterized as a separate program qualifying for an exception to the preapproval requirement as a grant to an intermediary (see § 9.3(g)).
228. Priv. Ltr. Rul. 8302090.
229. Priv. Ltr. Rul. 9116032.
230. See § 9.3(d)(ii).

eligible applicants to include children of active, full-time, permanent employees of the employer and its affiliates worldwide; a change in the definition of eligible employees to include those in lower compensation bands; and the inclusion of foreign educational institutions meeting the definition of an educational organization[231] in the list of eligible educational organizations. The IRS observed that the first two changes furthered a charitable purpose by increasing the number of eligible applicants and that the private foundation was committed to ensuring that any foreign organizations met the definition of an educational organization. The IRS also described a decrease in the total maximum annual number of awards, and a reduction in the annual award amount, as material changes but went on to observe that these changes are not part of the criteria for IRS approval of the employer-related program and therefore did not prevent the private foundation from obtaining approval.[232]

A *renewal* of a grant that was made pursuant to a procedure preapproved by the IRS does not require further preapproval if (1) the grantor has no information indicating that the original grant is being used for any purpose other than that for which it was made, (2) any reports due at the time of the renewal decision pursuant to the terms of the original grant have been furnished, and (3) any additional criteria and procedures for renewal are objective and nondiscriminatory.[233] Recognizing "that it would be burdensome and unnecessary for the foundation to repeat the original grant-making procedures for every renewal unless it has knowledge that the original grant was misused or that the requirements of the original grant have not been met," this rule is intended to provide "a simplified procedure for renewals when the full and proper grant-making procedures have been followed in making the original grant."[234] An extension of the period over which a grant is to be paid is not itself regarded as a grant or a renewal of a grant.[235]

(g) Individual Grant Intermediaries and Earmarking

For private foundations wishing to avoid the administrative burden and cost of applying for approval and disbursing scholarships directly, an alternative is to fund a grant program at an independent public charity. A grant by a private foundation to another organization, which the grantee organization uses to

---

231. That is, an organization described in IRC § 170(b)(1)(A)(ii).
232. Priv. Ltr. Rul. 201308031. This ruling's description of these two additional changes as material is unfortunate insofar as they would appear to, in fact, be immaterial.
233. Reg. § 53.4945-4(a)(3)(iii).
234. Rev. Rul. 81-46, 1981-1 CB 514.
235. Reg. § 53.4945-4(a)(3)(iii).

TAXABLE EXPENDITURES

make payments to an individual for travel, study, or other similar purposes, is not regarded as a grant by the foundation to the individual grantee if (1) the foundation does not earmark the use of the grant for any named individual and (2) there does not exist an agreement, oral or written, by which the grantor foundation may cause the selection of the individual grantee by the grantee organization. A grant is not regarded as a grant by the private foundation to an individual grantee, even though the foundation has reason to believe that certain individuals will derive benefits from the grant, so long as the grantee organization exercises control, in fact, over the selection process and actually makes the selection completely independently of the foundation.[236]

A grant by a private foundation to a public charity that the public charity uses to make individual grants is not regarded as a grant by the foundation to the individual grantee (regardless of the application of the rules in the preceding paragraph) if the grant is made for a project that is supervised by the public charity that also controls the selection of the individual grantee. This rule applies regardless of whether the name of the individual grantee is first proposed by the private foundation, but only if there is an objective manifestation of control by the public charity over the selection process. Essentially, the selection need not be made completely independently of the foundation.[237] If, however, a private foundation makes grants for scholarships to a public charity that is controlled by the foundation, the grants are treated as if made directly to the individual recipients of the scholarships.[238]

An illustration of these rules was provided in the case of a private foundation that made grants to vocational high schools (all operating educational organizations), in a certain geographical area, to be used to purchase the basic tools of a trade for students to enable them to better learn their trades and to enter into those trades upon graduation. Because the individual grant recipients were selected by representatives of the private foundation rather than the schools, the grants were deemed to be made directly to the individual students. Since the purpose of the grants was to aid needy and talented students in the completion of their vocational education, the grants were to individuals for study or similar purposes and constituted taxable expenditures unless the private foundation's grant-making procedures satisfied the requirements for IRS preapproval of individual grants.[239]

These rules were also applied in the case of a private foundation program whereby the private foundation made grants to a public charity in partial funding of a scholarship program, with the stipulation that the grants be expended

---
236. Reg. § 53.4945-4(a)(4)(i).
237. Reg. § 53.4945-4(a)(4)(ii).
238. E.g., Priv. Ltr. Rul. 200209061.
239. Rev. Rul. 77-212, 1977-1 C.B. 356.

§ 9.3 GRANTS TO INDIVIDUALS

on behalf of children of employees of a particular company who were finalists as determined by the public charity. As a variation of this program, a similar approach required that any excess funds be made available as grants to the next most highly rated children of employees of the company, even though they were not finalists. The IRS concluded that the grants were amounts paid to individuals for study and were taxable expenditures unless made pursuant to a procedure approved in advance by the IRS. The exception for foundation grants to public charities was deemed inapplicable, in that the public charity did not select the scholarship recipients completely independently of the private foundation and merely functioned as an evaluator of the grant program of the private foundation.[240]

The IRS has issued various other private letter rulings concerning the application of these individual grant intermediary rules.[241]

If a private foundation makes a grant to a governmental agency[242] and the grant is earmarked for use by an individual for travel, study, or other similar purposes, the grant is not subject to the taxable expenditure rules if the agency (rather than the private foundation) satisfies the IRS in advance that its grant-making program is in furtherance of a charitable purpose, requires that the individual grantee submit suitable reports to it, and requires that the agency investigate jeopardized grants in a manner substantially similar to the general rules concerning investigation of jeopardized grants.[243] The IRS was satisfied that this exception applied, and approved a private foundation's scholarship grant procedures, where the grants were made to a school district, the school district selected the grant recipients, agreed to investigate jeopardized grants, and required that individual grantees to submit reports on their academic progress.[244]

A grant by a private foundation to an individual, which meets the requirements of these general rules yet qualifies for an exception, is a taxable expenditure only if (1) the grant is earmarked to be used for any legislative, electioneering, or noncharitable activity,[245] or is earmarked to be used in a manner that would violate the rules concerning grants to individuals or the expenditure responsibility requirement;[246] (2) there is an agreement, oral or written, whereby the grantor private foundation may cause the grantee to

---

240. Rev. Rul. 81-217, 1981-2 C.B. 217.
241. E.g., Priv. Ltr. Rul. 8826029.
242. That is, an entity described in IRC § 170(c)(1).
243. Reg. § 53.4945-4(a)(4)(iii). See § 9.3(e)(ii) (as to the report requirement) and 9.3(e)(iii) (as to the investigation requirement).
244. Priv. Ltr. Rul. 7944027.
245. IRC § 4945(d)(1), (2), and (5). See §§ 9.1, 9.2.
246. IRC § 4945(d)(3) and (4). As to expenditure responsibility, see § 9.7.

engage in any prohibited activity and the grant is in fact used in a manner that violates these rules; or (3) the grant is made for a noncharitable purpose.[247]

§ 9.4 GRANTS TO PUBLIC CHARITIES

The federal tax law pertaining to private foundations favors making grants to public charities, rather than to other types of organizations or to individuals. The clearest evidence of this bias is the exemption of grants to public charities from the expenditure responsibility requirements.[248] Furthermore, if grant funds are not earmarked for proscribed purposes, grants to public charities may be exempt from the individual grant and lobbying expense rules that would otherwise be applicable if the foundation made the grant itself for such purposes.[249]

Because of the favoritism the tax rules show to private foundation grants to public charities, most private foundations prefer to make grants to public charities. A private foundation, however, may make a grant to accomplish a charitable or other permitted purpose to any type of organization, including a nonexempt organization, if the grant is made for charitable or other permitted purposes and the private foundation complies with the expenditure responsibility rules.[250]

(a) Types of Public Charity Grantees

The concept of *public charity* embraces charitable organizations that are in one of five categories:

1. § 509(a)(1) *public institutions*, such as churches, universities, colleges, schools, hospitals, medical research organizations, agricultural research organizations, and governmental units and agencies,[251] which are considered to be public because of the activities they conduct.

2. § 509(a)(1) or (2) publicly supported entities, either *donative charities* or *service provider charities*,[252] because they receive revenues from many sources.

---

247. Reg. § 53.4945-4(a)(5).
248. IRC § 4945-2(d)(4)(A)(i), (ii). As to expenditure responsibility, see § 9.7.
249. See §§ 9.1(c), 9.3(g).
250. See §§ 9.7, 9.8.
251. See § 15.3. An Indian tribal government is treated as a state for purposes of the Chapter 42 excise taxes applicable to private foundations (IRC § 7871(a)(7)(B)). For more information on tribal governments, visit Native American Philanthropy's website at www.nativephilanthropy.org.
252. See §§ 15.4, 15.5.

§ 9.4 GRANTS TO PUBLIC CHARITIES

3. § 509(a)(3) *supporting organizations classified as Type I or II* that exist to benefit one or more other public charities.[253]

4. § 509(a)(3) *supporting organizations classified as Type III functionally integrated*[254] because they conduct active programs on behalf of one or more other public charity.

5. § 509(a)(3) *supporting organizations classified as Type III nonfunctionally integrated*[255] that exist to benefit one or more other public charities (now treated for some purposes as private foundations).

Grants to the first four categories of public charities listed above and to *exempt operating foundations*[256] do not require the granting private foundation to exercise expenditure responsibility. A grant to an instrumentality of a foreign government is considered to be a grant to a public charity that does not require expenditure responsibility, as long as it is made for charitable purposes.[257] Likewise, an instrumentality of a U.S. political subdivision is treated as a grant to a public charity that does not require expenditure responsibility.[258]

A grant to a nonfunctionally integrated Type III supporting organization,[259] or to any other type of supporting organization if a disqualified person with respect to the foundation directly or indirectly controls the supporting organization or a supported organization of the supporting organization, requires the grantor private foundation to exercise expenditure responsibility[260] to prevent the grant from being treated as a taxable expenditure.[261] Additionally, such a grant does not count as a qualifying distribution.[262]

(b) Grantor Reliance Standards

For purposes of determining whether an organization is a public charity, or its supporting organization type, a private foundation may rely upon an IRS determination letter or ruling that an organization is a publicly supported

---

253. See § 15.6(e), (f).
254. See § 15.6(g)(v).
255. See § 15.6(g)(vi).
256. See § 10.7.
257. Reg. § 53.4945-5(a)(4).
258. Rev. Rul. 81-125, 1981-1 C.B. 515. The IRS reasoned that if a grant to an instrumentality of a foreign government is treated as a grant to a public charity, a grant to an instrumentality of a domestic political subdivision should likewise be treated as a grant to a public charity (*id.*).
259. See § 15.6(g).
260. See § 9.7.
261. IRC § 4945(d)(4)(A)(ii).
262. See § 6.4(c).

organization until the IRS publishes notice of a change of such status in the weekly *Internal Revenue Bulletin* or other IRS publication.[263] A private foundation may also rely on an organization's public charity status or supporting organization type, to the extent set forth in the IRS's *Tax Exempt Organization Search* database[264] or the IRS's *Exempt Organizations Business Master File Extract* (EO BMF) database,[265] for purposes of determining whether a grant to such an organization constitutes a qualifying distribution[266] or requires expenditure responsibility.[267]

A private foundation may not rely on an organization's determination letter or ruling, or the organization's listing in one of the IRS's online databases, if the private foundation was responsible for, or aware of, the act or failure to act that resulted in the organization's loss of classification as a publicly supported organization (or acquired knowledge that the IRS notified the organization that it would be deleted from such classification).[268]

Additional due diligence may be required before making a grant to an organization that does not have a determination letter, such as a church or governmental unit,[269] and for charitable organizations under a group ruling.[270] Expenditure responsibility grants may be advisable in cases in which questions remain as to a grantee's public charity status.[271]

(c) Intermediary and Secondary Grantees

A grant by a private foundation to a grantee organization which the grantee organization uses to make payments to another organization (the secondary grantee) is not considered a grant by the private foundation to the secondary

---

263. Reg. §§ 1.170A–9(f)(5)(ii), 1.509(a)-3(e)(2)(i), 1.509-7.
264. https://www.irs.gov/charities-non-profits/tax-exempt-organization-search. Historically, the IRS's eligible organization list was maintained in IRS Publication 78. In 2011, the IRS discontinued publishing the paper version of Publication 78 and began to maintain the eligible organization list solely on an electronic database. This electronic database was initially called Exempt Organizations Select Check; the name was changed to Tax Exempt Organization Search in 2018. Thus, this searchable database is the successor to Publication 78 (Rev. Proc. 2018-32, 2018-23 I.R.B. 739 § 3.01).
265. https://www.irs.gov/charities-non-profits/exempt-organizations-business-master-file-extract-eo-bmf.
266. See § 6.4(d).
267. Rev. Proc. 2018-32, 2018-23 I.R.B. 739 § 5.01.
268. Reg. §§ 1.170A–9(f)(5)(ii), 1.509(a)-3(e)(2)(i), 1.509-7; Rev. Proc. 2018-32, 2018-23 I.R.B. 739 § 5.02. As to circumstances under which a private foundation will not be deemed responsible for, or aware of, the act or failure to act that resulted in the loss of an organization's public charity classification, see § 6.4(b).
269. See § 6.4(d)(iii).
270. See § 6.4(d)(iv).
271. See § 9.7.

§ 9.4 GRANTS TO PUBLIC CHARITIES

grantee if the foundation does not earmark the use of the grant for any named secondary grantee and there does not exist an agreement, oral or written, whereby such grantor foundation may cause the selection of the secondary grantee by the organization to which it has given the grant. This rule applies even though such foundation has reason to believe that certain organizations would derive benefits from such grants so long as the original grantee organization exercises control, in fact, over the selection process and actually makes the selection completely independently of the private foundation.[272] If, however, the private foundation earmarks the grant for the use of the secondary grantee, and the secondary grantee is not a public charity, the foundation will need to exercise expenditure responsibility with respect to the grant to avoid the grant constituting a taxable expenditure.[273]

If a private foundation makes a grant to a government agency[274] and such grant is earmarked for use by another organization, the granting foundation need not exercise expenditure responsibility with respect to such grant if the government agency satisfies the IRS in advance that its grant-making program is in furtherance of a charitable or other permitted purpose,[275] and the governmental agency exercises expenditure responsibility over the grant.[276] With respect to the reports to the IRS that are required to be made under expenditure responsibility rules, however, the granting foundation, not the governmental agency, makes such reports, unless the grant is earmarked for use by an exempt operating foundation or a public charity (other than a non-functionally integrated Type III supporting organization or any other type of supporting organization if a disqualified person with respect to the foundation directly or indirectly controls the supporting organization or a supported organization of the supporting organization).[277] Thus, for example, this exception was found to apply, and a private foundation was not required to exercise expenditure responsibility (other than the making of the required reports to the IRS on its Form 990-PF) over grants made to an agency of a state government. These grants were earmarked for use in educating and counseling eligible dropout youths through a contractual arrangement between the agency and a private for-profit corporation that operates as an educational clinic and the agency exercised expenditure responsibility over the grants.[278]

---

272. Reg. § 53.4945-5(a)(6).
273. See § 9.7. Thus, a *look-through rule* applies when the private foundation earmarks its grant in an oral or written manner.
274. That is, an organization described in IRC § 170(c)(1).
275. That is, a purpose described in IRC § 170(c)(2)(B).
276. Reg. § 53.4945-5(a)(6)(ii).
277. Id.
278. Priv. Ltr. Rul. 8311046.

§ 9.5 GRANTS TO EXEMPT OPERATING FOUNDATIONS

In addition to grants to organizations that are public charities,[279] private foundations may make grants to exempt operating foundations, without having to exercise expenditure responsibility.[280]

As an erroneous IRS ruling amply illustrated, this can be treacherous territory because of potential confusion between private operating foundations[281] and exempt operating foundations. The basic rule is that a standard grant-making foundation may make a grant to an exempt operating foundation without having to exercise expenditure responsibility over the grant, but a private foundation grant to a private operating foundation is an expenditure responsibility grant unless the grantee qualifies as an exempt operating foundation.

In this ruling, the IRS mistakenly held that a standard private foundation may make a grant to a private operating foundation, without having to exercise expenditure responsibility, and not make a taxable expenditure because the prospective grantee, as a private operating foundation, automatically qualified as an exempt operating foundation.[282] The IRS stated: "The proposed grant will be made to [g]rantee, which has been recognized as an operating foundation . . . and *as such*, qualifies as an exempt operating foundation."[283] This *as such* was the source of the problem, inasmuch as qualification as a private operating foundation does not automatically result in exempt operating status. Rather, that status is only one of five criteria used in defining an exempt operating foundation.[284] Thus, the IRS's holding that the proposed grant will not be a taxable expenditure by the grantor was inaccurate because the proposed grantee was not an exempt operating foundation. This matter was rectified by means of a subsequent ruling, where the facts were changed to make the grant an expenditure responsibility grant.[285]

§ 9.6 GRANTS TO FOREIGN ORGANIZATIONS

(a) General Rules

One tax advantage to a private foundation funding foreign projects is the ability of U.S. taxpayers to deduct (as charitable contributions) gifts made to the private foundation that would not be deductible if made to the foreign charity

---

279. See § 9.4(a).
280. IRC § 4945(d)(4)(A)(iii). Exempt operating foundations are the subject of § 10.7.
281. Private operating foundations are the subject of § 3.1.
282. Priv. Ltr. Rul. 201652004.
283. Emphasis added.
284. IRC § 4940(d)(2)(A).
285. Priv. Ltr. Rul. 201724001.

§ 9.6 GRANTS TO FOREIGN ORGANIZATIONS

directly.[286] Provided the private foundation exercises control and discretion as to the use of the funds raised, the fact that the funds are raised for projects outside the United States does not render contributions to the U.S. foundation in support of a foreign project nondeductible.[287] Thus, for example, the IRS ruled that contributions to a U.S. foundation were deductible for U.S. income tax purposes, notwithstanding that they were raised to build a basketball arena in a foreign country, because the domestic foundation's board of directors exercised discretion and control over the funds raised.[288]

If, however, a private foundation makes a grant to a foreign organization,[289] and the grantee does not have an IRS determination letter recognizing it as an exempt operating foundation or a public charity, or is otherwise treated as one under the taxable expenditure rules,[290] a private foundation will be required to exercise expenditure responsibility with respect to the grant.[291]

A foreign government and any agency or instrumentality thereof is treated as a public charity for this purpose, as long as any grant is made exclusively for charitable purposes.[292] Certain international organizations also qualify as public charities, such as the World Health Organization, the United Nations, the International Bank for Reconstruction and Development, the International Monetary Fund, and others designated by the president.[293]

(b) Good Faith (Equivalency) Determinations

A foreign organization that does not have an IRS determination letter, but that is equivalent to and would in fact qualify as a public charity or an exempt operating foundation (a *qualifying public charity*)[294] if it sought approval, may

---

286. IRC § 170(a), (c)(2); Rev. Rul. 63-252, 1953-2 C.B. 101; Rev. Rul. 66-79, 1995-1 C.B. 48; Rev. Rul. 75-65, 1975-1 C.B. 79.
287. Rev. Rul. 63-252, 1953-2 C.B. 101; Rev. Rul. 66-79, 1995-1 C.B. 48; Chief Couns. Adv. Mem. 200504031.
288. Priv. Ltr. Rul. 9129040.
289. That is, any organization that is not described in section 170(c)(2)(A) (Reg. § 53.4942(a)-5(a)(5)(ii)(a)).
290. See § 9.4(a), 9.6(b).
291. See § 9.7.
292. Reg. § 53.4945-5(a)(4)(iii).
293. *Id.* The international organizations are designated by executive order under 22 U.S.C. § 288.
294. Specifically, a *qualifying public charity* for purposes of the taxable expenditure rules includes an exempt operating foundation (IRC § 4940(d)(2)) or a public charity described in IRC § 509(a)(1), (2), or (3), other than a disqualified supporting organization (Reg. § 53.4945-5(a)(5)(i)). A disqualified supporting organization includes a non-functionally integrated Type III supporting organization (Reg. § 1.509(a)-4(i)) and any other supporting organization if a disqualified person of the private foundation directly or indirectly controls the supporting organization or a supported organization (IRC § 4942(g)(4)(A)).

TAXABLE EXPENDITURES

also be treated as a qualifying public charity for purposes of the taxable expenditure rules. A foreign organization may be so treated, and therefore expenditure responsibility may be avoided, if the grantor private foundation makes a good-faith determination that the foreign organization qualifies.

A determination ordinarily will be considered a good-faith determination if it is based on current written advice received by a qualified tax practitioner concluding that the prospective grantee is a qualifying public charity and if the foundation reasonably relied in good faith[295] on the written advice. The written advice must set forth sufficient facts concerning the operations and financial support of the grantee organization for the IRS to determine that the grantee organization is the equivalent of a qualifying public charity as of the date of the advice. Written advice is considered *current* if, as of the date of the grant payment, the relevant law on which the advice is based has not changed since the date of the written advice and the factual information on which the advice is based is from the grantee's current or prior tax year or (or other applicable accounting period for foreign tax purposes). Written advice that a grantee met a public support test for a period of five years is treated as current for purposes of grant payments to the grantee during the first two years (or accounting periods) of the grantee immediately following the close of the five-year period.[296]

A *qualified tax practitioner* is a lawyer, a certified public accountant, or an enrolled agent.[297]

The IRS published rules by which private foundations may make good-faith determinations that foreign grantees are qualifying public charities, so that grants to them, if made for charitable or other permitted purposes,[298] will not require expenditure responsibility in order to not be taxable expenditures.[299]

---

295. *Id*. The standards in this regard are the subject of Reg. § 1.6664-4(c)(1).
296. Reg. § 53.4945-5(a)(5)(i).
297. Reg. § 53.4945-5(a)(5)(ii)(b). To be qualified, the tax practitioner must be subject to the requirements of 31 C.F.R. Part 10 (also known as "Circular 230," which sets forth rules related to practice before the IRS) (*id*.).
298. That is, for one or more purposes described in IRC § 170(c)(2)(B) (IRC § 4945(d)(5); see § 9.8).
299. Rev. Proc. 2017-53, 2017-40 I.R.B. 263. This revenue procedure eliminates a previous "simplified procedure" (Rev. Proc. 92-94, 1992-2 C.B. 507) that allowed a private foundation to rely solely on grantee affidavits in making good faith (equivalency) determinations, without needing to obtain current written advice received from qualified tax practitioners. When rendering written advice, however, a qualified tax practitioner may rely on factual information set forth in grantee affidavits (Rev. Proc. 2017-53, *supra*, § 4.03). These guidelines are inapplicable where the grant is a transfer of assets pursuant to a liquidation, merger, redemption, recapitalization, or other adjustment, organization, or reorganization of the foundation (Reg. § 53.4945-6(c)(2)(ii); Rev. Proc. 2017-53, *supra*, § 2). These reorganizations and the like are the subject of IRC § 507(b)(2) and Reg. § 1.507-3(c) (see § 13.5).

§ 9.6 GRANTS TO FOREIGN ORGANIZATIONS

Written advice that meets these guidelines—*preferred written advice*—ordinarily will be considered to contain sufficient facts concerning the foreign grantee's operations and support to enable the IRS to determine that the grantee would likely qualify as a qualifying public charity as of the date of the written advice.[300]

(c) Canadian and Mexican Organizations

The treaty between Canada and the United States provides that Canadian charities are given reciprocal classification under U.S. rules.[301] However, unless the Canadian organization provides sufficient information to the IRS to establish its public charity status, it is presumed to be a private foundation.[302] Expenditure responsibility can be exercised to avoid classification of a grant to a Canadian charity presumed to be a private foundation as a taxable expenditure. A grant to a Canadian charitable organization that has not sought classification as a public charity, however, may not be treated as a qualifying distribution unless the money is passed through for a charitable purpose[303] or the private foundation makes a good faith determination that the Canadian recipient is a qualifying public charity.[304]

The treatment of grants made by a U.S.-based private foundation to a charitable organization in Mexico is governed by the U.S.-Mexico Income Tax Convention[305] and an accompanying protocol.[306] These two countries recognize each other's public charities on a reciprocal basis, for purposes of tax exemption and public charity status. Thus, a U.S. private foundation can, if the Mexican authorities have granted the requisite authorization to a Mexican

---

300. Rev. Proc. 2017-53, 2017-40 I.R.B. 263 § 4.01. A grant for permitted purposes made to a foreign organization for which an equivalency determination pursuant to these guidelines has been made will also constitute a qualifying distribution (see § 6.4(e)).
301. Convention Between the U.S. and Canada With Respect to Taxes on Income and on Capital, signed on September 26, 1980, as amended by protocols, the most recent signed on July 29, 1997.
302. IRS Notice 99-47, 1999-2 C.B. 391. The classification of foreign organizations as publicly supported charities is determined by applying the same rules that apply to domestic organizations, discussed in Chapter 15 (Rev. Rul. 75-435, 1975-2 C.B. 215). The information required for a Canadian charity to establish its public charity status is provided to the IRS by submitting Form 8940 (see § 2.7(f)).
303. See § 6.4(c)(ii) for a discussion of the redistribution rule.
304. See § 6.4(e).
305. Convention and Protocol Between the Government of the U.S. and the Government of the United Mexican States for the Avoidance of Double Taxation and the Prevention of Fiscal Invasion With Respect to Taxes on Income, effective as of January 1, 1994 (Art. 22).
306. Paragraph 17 of the Protocol.

charity, treat that charity as a public charity for expenditure responsibility and other purposes. A U.S. private foundation, however, must request proof of that status from the Mexican charity.[307]

(d) Anti-Terrorist Financing Guidelines

Although not expressly required by the taxable expenditure rules, an additional consideration for a private foundation making grants to foreign organizations is implementing adequate procedures to ensure grant funds do not aid persons identified by the government as terrorists in violation of the U.S. Patriot Act.[308] The U.S. Treasury Department issued voluntary guidelines for an organization conducting programs in foreign countries to consider when adopting such procedures.[309]

These guidelines are intended to assist charitable organizations in developing a risk-based approach to guard against the threat of diversion of charitable funds for use by terrorists and their support networks. They are, however, voluntary and do not supersede or modify current or future applicable legal requirements. Given the risk-based nature of the guidelines, they explicitly recognize that certain aspects will not be applicable to every charitable organization, charitable activity, or circumstance. The guidelines further acknowledge that certain exigent circumstances (such as catastrophic disasters) may make application of the guidelines difficult. In such cases, the guidelines recommend that charitable organizations maintain a risk-based approach that includes all prudent and reasonable measures that are feasible under the circumstances.[310]

Importantly, adherence to the guidelines does not excuse a private foundation from compliance with any local, state, or federal law or regulation, nor does it release any person from or constitute a legal defense against any civil or criminal liability for violating any such law or regulation. Thus, adherence to the guidelines will not preclude any criminal charge, civil fine, or other action by Treasury or the Department of Justice against persons who engage

---

307. INFO 2003-0158. Specifically, a private foundation should request either a copy of a letter granting the special authorization to the Mexican charity from the Mexican Ministry of Finance and Public Credit or a copy of the current list of the Mexican charities that have obtained the authorization, as published in the Mexican Official Gazette (*id.*).
308. Executive Order 13224 bans humanitarian aid to Specially Designated Nationals and Blocked Persons.
309. "U.S. Department of the Treasury Anti-Terrorist Financing Guidelines: Voluntary Best Practices for U.S.-Based Charities" (Nov. 2005).
310. *Id.* at 2.

in prohibited transactions with persons appearing on the master list of Specially Designated Nationals (the SDN List).[311]

§ 9.7 EXPENDITURE RESPONSIBILITY

(a) General Rules

As noted, the term *taxable expenditure* also includes any amount paid or incurred by a private foundation as a grant, loan, or program-related investment[312] to an organization other than an exempt operating foundation or certain types of public charities (or organizations treated as such),[313] unless the private foundation exercises expenditure responsibility with respect to the grant.[314] A private foundation is considered to be exercising *expenditure responsibility* if it exerts all reasonable efforts and establishes adequate procedures to (1) see that the grant is spent solely for the charitable or other permitted purpose for which it was made, (2) obtain full and complete reports from the grantee on how the funds were spent, and (3) make full and detailed reports with respect to the expenditures to the IRS.[315]

More specifically, to fulfill its expenditure responsibility obligations, a private foundation must: (1) conduct a pre-grant inquiry concerning the grantee organization;[316] (2) enter into a written grant agreement with the grantee organization specifying the purpose of the grant funds and including various provisions specified by IRS regulations;[317] (3) obtain annual reports from the grantee organization on the use of the funds until all funds have been expended by the grantee, and a final report once all grant funds have been expended;[318] (4) make annual reports to the IRS on the foundation's IRS Form 990-PF containing specific information required by IRS regulations;[319] and

---

311. *Id*. The master SDN List is an integrated listing of designated parties with whom U.S. persons are prohibited from providing services or conducting transactions and whose assets are blocked (*id*. at 9 n.9). The SDN List, and other lists maintained by the Office of Foreign Asset Controls (OFAC), is searchable in the OFAC website (https://sanctionssearch.ofac.treas.gov/).
312. See § 8.3.
313. See §§ 9.4(a), 9.6(b).
314. IRC § 4945(d)(4); Reg. § 53.4945-5(a)(1). For these rules to apply, the payment involved must be a *grant*, rather than, for example, the payment of administrative expenses (e.g., Priv. Ltr. Rul. 200019044).
315. IRC § 4945(h); Reg. § 53.4945-5(b)(1).
316. Reg. § 53.4945-5(b)(2).
317. Reg. § 53.4945-5(b)(3), (4).
318. Reg. § 53.4945-5(c).
319. Reg. § 53.4945-5(d).

(5) take appropriate action to address any diversion of funds by the grantee organization for improper purposes.[320] Expenditure responsibility does not, however, require a private foundation to be an insurer of the activity of an organization to which it makes a grant.[321]

Thus, to ensure accountability for grants and program-related investments by private foundations, due diligence and recordkeeping requirements are more stringent when a grant is made to another private foundation (including a private operating foundation), a nonfunctionally integrated Type III supporting organization, any other type of supporting organization if a disqualified person with respect to the foundation directly or indirectly controls the supporting organization or a supported organization of the supporting organization, an organization that is tax-exempt for reasons other than being a charitable organization, or a for-profit business. Grants to these types of organizations are not prohibited, so long as they are made for charitable or other permitted purposes,[322] and the grantor private foundation exercises expenditure responsibility.

For example, the IRS ruled that a private foundation may make a grant for scientific purposes to another private foundation, which in turn will make grants to a third private foundation, without endangering its tax-exempt status and without making any taxable expenditures, where the first and third of these foundations adhered to the expenditure responsibility requirements.[323] The IRS also ruled that a private foundation grant to a tax-exempt social club[324] to fund a program of educational seminars and speakers was not a taxable expenditure where the foundation exercised expenditure responsibility over the grant.[325] In another instance, the IRS ruled that a private foundation grant to a social fraternity's title-holding organization[326] to build a study room in its chapter house was not a taxable expenditure where the foundation exercised expenditure responsibility over the grant. The facility contained exclusively educational equipment and furniture, along with computers linked to the university's mainframe, and had the effect of reducing the cumulative burden on the university's own such facilities.[327]

---

320. Reg. § 53.4945-5(e).
321. Reg. § 53.4945-5(b)(1).
322. See § 9.8.
323. Priv. Ltr. Rul. 201143022.
324. An organization described in IRC § 501(c)(7).
325. Priv. Ltr. Rul. 8220080.
326. An organization described in IRC § 501(c)(2).
327. Priv. Ltr. Rul. 9025073. Another example of this type of grant was a grant by a private foundation to a local house corporation for a chapter of a national fraternity, which is a tax-exempt social organization, for the purpose of renovating the educational areas of a chapter house (Priv. Ltr. Rul. 9306034).

§ 9.7 EXPENDITURE RESPONSIBILITY

A grantor private foundation does not have to exercise expenditure responsibility with respect to amounts granted to organizations pursuant to the previously discussed voter registration drive rules,[328] grants to intermediary grantees that are not earmarked by the private foundation for secondary grantees,[329] and certain grants to government agencies that are earmarked for secondary grantee organizations and with respect to which the government agency agrees to exercise expenditure responsibility.[330] A grantor private foundation also does not have to exercise expenditure responsibility with respect to grants made to foreign organizations for which the foundation has made a good faith equivalency determination pursuant to published IRS procedures.[331]

When one private foundation that has expenditure responsibility grants outstanding merges into another private foundation, the surviving foundation must exercise expenditure responsibility with respect to these grants.[332]

These expenditure responsibility rules have been given strict construction by the U.S. Tax Court, which, in concluding that a private foundation's grants failed all of them, wrote that they reflect a "Congressional determination to leave no loophole by imposing strict and detailed conditions to make sure that a private foundation's grants would not be used for proscribed purposes."[333]

(b) Pre-Grant Inquiry

Before making a grant for which expenditure responsibility is required, the grantor private foundation must conduct a pre-grant inquiry with respect to the grantee organization. A *pre-grant inquiry* is a limited inquiry directed at obtaining enough information to give a reasonable person assurance that the grantee will use the grant for the proper purposes.[334] The inquiry should concern itself with matters such as:

- The identity, prior history, and experience (if any) of the grantee organization and its managers. Is the grantee capable of accomplishing the grant purposes?

---

328. Reg. § 53.4945-5(a)(1). See § 9.2(c).
329. See § 9.4(c).
330. Id.
331. Rev. Proc. 2017-53, 2017-40 I.R.B. 263; see §§ 6.4(e), 9.6(b).
332. Priv. Ltr. Rul. 9331046. See § 13.5.
333. Mannheimer Charitable Trust, Hans S. v. Commissioner, 93 T.C. 35, 51 (1989). The foundation argued unsuccessfully that all of its internal documents, meeting transcriptions, and actual observations of the activities amounted to the exercise of expenditure responsibility. Despite the facts and the foundation's argument that its failure to report was due to an oversight, the court upheld the assessment of the excise tax on taxable expenditures.
334. Reg. § 53.4945-5(b)(2)(i).

- Information about the management, activities, and practices of the grantee organization, obtained either through the private foundation's prior experience and association with the grantee or from other readily available sources.[335]

The scope of the inquiry is expected to vary depending on the size and purpose of the grant, the period over which the grant is to be paid, and the private foundation's prior experience with the grantee. If the proposed grantee has previously received an expenditure responsibility grant, made proper use of the grant funds, and successfully satisfied all of the expenditure responsibility reporting requirements, no further pre-grant inquiry is ordinarily required.[336]

The pre-grant inquiry requirement was determined to be satisfied with respect to a proposed grant to a newly created social welfare organization for a proposed program to combat drug abuse by establishing neighborhood clinics in certain ghetto areas of a city. The organization had no previous history of administering grants and its officials had no experience in administering programs of this nature. In inquiring about the officials of the organization, the private foundation's managers discovered that one of the organization's officials had an arrest record, but also determined that the official was fully rehabilitated after having been convicted of a narcotics violation. In the opinion of the foundation's managers, the officials of the potential grantee, including the ex-convict, were well qualified to conduct this program because they are members of the communities in which the clinics are to be established and are more likely to be trusted by drug users in these communities than are outsiders. Under these circumstances, the private foundation was considered to have satisfied the pre-grant inquiry requirement.[337]

The pre-grant inquiry was also determined to be satisfied, where the proposed grant recipient conducted a research fellowship program for years and had received many grants from other foundations to support the program. Another foundation that supports the grantee informed the private foundation that it was satisfied that its grants have been used for the purposes for which they were made. Under these circumstances, the grantor private foundation was considered to have enough information that a reasonable man would require to assure that the grant would be used for proper purposes.[338]

In the case of a grant to an organization such as a split-interest trust,[339] which is required by its governing instrument to make payments to a

---

335. Id.
336. Reg. § 53.4945-5(b)(2)(i) and (ii), Example (2).
337. Reg. § 53.4945-5(b)(2)(ii), Example (1).
338. Reg. § 53.4945-5(b)(2)(ii), Example (3).
339. See § 3.7.

specified public charity, a less-extensive pre-grant inquiry is required than in the case of a private foundation that has discretion regarding potential grant recipients.[340]

(c) Grant Terms

To satisfy the expenditure responsibility requirements, a private foundation must also require an officer, director, or trustee of the grant recipient to sign a written commitment (essentially, a grant agreement) that, in addition to stating the charitable purposes to be accomplished,[341] obligates the grantee to (1) repay any portion of the amount granted that is not used for the purposes of the grant; (2) submit full and complete annual reports on the manner in which the funds are spent and the progress made in accomplishing the purposes of the grant; (3) maintain records of the receipts and expenditures, and make its records available to the grantor at reasonable times; and (4) not use any of the funds to carry on propaganda or otherwise to attempt to influence legislation, to influence the outcome of any specific public election, or to carry on, directly or indirectly, any voter registration drive, to make any grant to an individual or organization, or to undertake any activity for any noncharitable purpose, to the extent that use of the funds would be a taxable expenditure if made directly by the private foundation.[342]

The agreement must also clearly specify the purposes of the grant. These purposes may include contributing for capital endowment, for the purchase of capital equipment, or for general support, provided that neither the grants nor the income from them may be used for noncharitable purposes.[343]

Program-related investments.[344] In addition to the foregoing requirements, the recipient of program-related investment funds must also agree to (1) repay the funds not invested in accordance with the agreement, but only to the extent permitted by applicable law concerning distributions to holders of equity interests; (2) at least once a year during the existence of the program-related investment, submit financial reports of a type ordinarily required by commercial investors under similar circumstances, and a statement that it has complied with the terms of the investment; and (3) maintain books and records of a type normally required by commercial investors.[345]

Program-related investments often provide financing for projects of a business nature, such as real estate development or scientific research.

---

340. Reg. § 53.4945-5(b)(2)(i).
341. That is, any of the purposes specified in IRC § 170(c)(2)(B).
342. Reg. § 53.4945-5(b)(3)(i)-(iv).
343. Reg. § 53.4945-5(b)(3); e.g., Priv. Ltr. Rul. 199952092.
344. See § 8.3.
345. Reg. § 53.4945-5(b)(4).

TAXABLE EXPENDITURES

Presumably, funds expended by these projects might not necessarily be considered charitable expenditures if the foundation paid the expenses itself. Therefore, the expenditure responsibility agreement for such investments does not have to contain a requirement that the grantee not use the funds to engage in any activity for any purpose other than a charitable or other permitted purpose. For purposes of avoiding the excise tax on jeopardizing investments, however, the primary purpose of the program-related investment must be to accomplish a charitable or other permitted purpose.[346]

Foreign grants. With respect to a grant to a foreign organization that requires expenditure responsibility to be exercised, the terms required to be included in the written grant agreement will be deemed satisfied if the agreement imposes restrictions on the use of the grant substantially equivalent to the limitations imposed on a domestic private foundation. These restrictions "may be phrased in appropriate terms under foreign law" or custom and "ordinarily will be considered sufficient" if the grantor obtains an affidavit or opinion of counsel (of the grantor or grantee), or written advice of a qualified tax practitioner, stating that, under foreign law or custom, the agreement imposes restrictions on the use of the grant substantially equivalent to the restrictions imposed on a domestic private foundation.[347]

(d) Reports from Grantees

In the case of expenditure responsibility grants, except with respect to certain capital endowment grants, the grantor private foundation must require reports on the use of the funds, compliance with the terms of the grant, and progress made by the grantee toward achieving the purposes for which the grant was made. The grantee must make the reports as of the end of its annual accounting period within which the grant or any portion of it is received and all subsequent periods until the grant funds are expended in full or the grant is otherwise terminated. The reports must be furnished to the grantor within a reasonable period of time after the close of the annual accounting period of the grantee for which the reports are made. Within a reasonable period of time after the close of its annual accounting period during which the use of the grant funds is completed, the grantee must make a final report with respect to all expenditures made from the funds (including salaries, travel, and supplies) and indicating the progress made toward the goals of the grant. The grantor need not conduct any independent verification of the reports unless it has reason to doubt their accuracy or reliability.[348]

---

346. Reg. § 53.4944-3(a)(1)(i). See § 8.3.
347. Reg. § 53.4945-5(b)(5). See § 9.6.
348. Reg. § 53.4945-5(c)(1).

§ 9.7 EXPENDITURE RESPONSIBILITY

If a private foundation makes a *capital endowment grant* to another tax-exempt private foundation, that is, a grant for endowment, for the purchase of capital equipment, or for other capital purposes, the grantor foundation must also require reports from the grantee on the use of the principal and any income from the grant funds. At a minimum, the grantee must make these reports annually for its fiscal year in which the grant was received and the immediately succeeding two years. However, if it is reasonably apparent to the grantor that, before the end of the second succeeding tax year, neither the principal, the income from the grant funds, nor the equipment purchased with the grant funds has been used for any purpose that would result in liability for a taxable expenditure, the grantor foundation may then allow the discontinuance of the reports.[349] A court held that this rule applies only to a capital endowment grant from one private foundation to another; otherwise, reporting must be made for the full duration of a grant or for the life of a program-related investment.[350]

A private foundation that distributes part of its assets to another private foundation in a termination distribution also has a duty to exercise expenditure responsibility indefinitely. This responsibility ceases when the foundation disposes of all of its assets.[351]

(e) Grantee's Books and Records

A tax-exempt private foundation grantee, or the recipient of a program-related investment, need not segregate grant funds nor separately account for them on its books unless either is required by the grantor private foundation.[352]

If neither practice is followed, grants received within a year are deemed to be expended before grants received in a succeeding year, and expenditures of grants received within any year must be prorated among all the grants. In accounting for grant expenditures, grantees that are private foundations may make the necessary computations on a cumulative annual basis (or, where appropriate, as of the date on which the computations are made). These rules are to be applied in a manner consistent with the available records of the grantee and with the grantee's treatment of qualifying distributions. The records of expenditures, as well as copies of the reports submitted to the grantor, must be kept for at least four years after completion of the use of the grant funds.[353]

---

349. Reg. § 53.4945-5(c)(2).
350. Charles Stewart Mott Foundation v. United States, 938 F.2d 58 (6th Cir. 1991).
351. Reg. §§ 53.4945-5(b)(7), 1.507-3(a)(7), (8). See Chapter 13.
352. Reg. § 53.4945-5(c)(3)(i).
353. Id.

TAXABLE EXPENDITURES

For an expenditure responsibility grantee that is not a tax-exempt private foundation or the recipient of a program-related investment, either the separate fund rule or reasonable judgment rule (for foreign grantees that do not have an IRS ruling or determination letter) applicable to grants to noncharitable organizations must be followed.[354]

(f) Reports to IRS

A private foundation making expenditure responsibility grants must provide specific information, as part of its Form 990-PF annual information return, for each tax year in which any such grants are made. This information must also be provided on any subsequent return with respect to each expenditure responsibility grant for which any amount or any report is outstanding at any time during the tax year.[355]

Program-related investments must be reported for the life of the loan or for as many years as the investment is outstanding.[356] If a grantee's report contains the required information, the reporting requirement with respect to that grant may be satisfied by submission with the foundation's return of the actual report received from the grantee.[357]

These reports must include, with respect to each grant, the name and address of the grantee, the date and amount of the grant, the purpose of the grant, the amounts expended by the grantee (based on the most recent report received from the grantee), whether, to the knowledge of the grantor private foundation, the grantee has diverted any funds from the purpose of the grant, the dates of any reports received from the grantee, and the date and results of any verification of the grantee's reports undertaken by or at the direction of the grantor private foundation.[358]

In making these reports, a private foundation may rely on adequate records or other sufficient evidence supplied by the grantee showing, to the extent applicable, the information that the foundation must report to the IRS.[359]

---

354. Reg. §§ 53.4945-5(c)(3)(ii), -6(c). See §§ 6.4(e) and 9.8.
355. Reg. § 53.4945-5(d)(1). With respect to any grant made to another private foundation for endowment or other capital purposes, the grantor must provide the required information only for the tax years for which the grantor must require a report from the grantee under the rules concerning capital grants to private foundations (Reg. § 53.4945-5(c)(2)), typically the grant year plus two subsequent years (see § 9.7(d)).
356. Reg. § 53.4945-5(b)(4)(ii), (d)(1). A private foundation was held liable for the tax on taxable expenditures where it failed to submit reports to the IRS for the full duration of a program-related investment as required by this rule (Charles Stewart Mott Foundation v. United States, 938 F.2d 58 (6th Cir. 1991)).
357. Reg. § 53.4945-5(d)(1).
358. Reg. § 53.4945-5(d)(2).
359. Reg. § 53.4945-5(c)(4).

§ 9.7 EXPENDITURE RESPONSIBILITY

Other sufficient evidence includes a statement by an appropriate trustee, director, or officer of the grantee.[360]

(g) Foundation's Recordkeeping Requirements

In addition to the information included on the annual information return, a grantor private foundation must make available to the IRS, at the foundation's principal office, a copy of the agreement as to each expenditure responsibility grant made during the year, a copy of each report received during the year from each grantee on any expenditure responsibility grant, and a copy of each report made by the grantor's personnel or independent auditors of any audits or other investigations made during the year with respect to any expenditure responsibility grant.[361]

Data contained in these reports, where the reports are received by a private foundation after the close of its accounting year but before the due date of its annual information return for that year, need not be reported on that return, but may be reported on the grantor's information return for the year in which the reports are received from the grantee.[362]

In the interest of efficiency and to streamline its operations, a private foundation asked the IRS if it was acceptable to maintain its grant-making activity records solely in electronic form.[363] Grant requests and correspondence and reports to and from grantees would be transmitted and stored electronically. Grant agreements would be signed by both the foundation and grantee officials. The state in which the foundation operated permitted the use of electronic records and signatures in most contracts and other writings of legal significance, plus the origination and maintenance of all books and records for tracking investments, charitable activities, and all other matters. The IRS determined that the private foundation's originating and maintaining of its books and records in electronic form satisfied both the general federal tax law recordkeeping requirements[364] and the expenditure responsibility requirements.[365]

(h) Grantee Diversions

A diversion of grant funds (including the income from the funds in the case of an endowment grant) by an expenditure responsibility grantee to any use not

---

360. Id.
361. Reg. § 53.4945-5(d)(3).
362. Reg. § 53.4945-5(d)(4).
363. Priv. Ltr. Rul. 200324057, citing Rev. Rul. 71-20, 1971-1 C.B. 392, and Rev. Proc. 98-25, 1998-1 C.B. 689, as well as the Electronic Signatures Act of 2000.
364. IRC § 6001.
365. See § 9.7(a).

TAXABLE EXPENDITURES

in furtherance of a purpose specified in the grant may result in the diverted portion of the grant being treated as a taxable expenditure of the grantor.[366]

A grantee's failure to use any portion of the grant funds as indicated in the original budget projection is not treated as a diversion, however, if the use to which the funds are committed is consistent with the purpose of the grant as stated in the grant agreement and does not result in a violation of the required terms of the agreement.[367]

Additionally, a grantor will not be treated as having made a taxable expenditure solely by reason of a diversion by the grantee, if the grantor meets the requirements of one of the two following exceptions.[368] The first exception applies to situations in which the grantor private foundation determines that any part of a grant has been used for improper purposes but the grantee has not previously diverted grant funds. In these situations, the private foundation will not be treated as having made a taxable expenditure solely by reason of the diversion as long as the private foundation can show that it (1) is taking all reasonable and appropriate steps either to recover the grant funds or to ensure the restoration of the diverted funds and the dedication of the other grant funds held by the grantee to the purposes being financed by the grant, and (2) withholds any further payments to the grantee after it becomes aware that a diversion may have taken place, until it has received the grantee's assurances that future diversions will not occur and requires the grantee to take extraordinary precautions to prevent future diversions.[369]

If a private foundation is treated as having made a taxable expenditure in this type of situation, then, unless the private foundation meets the requirements of the first of these conditions, the amount of the taxable expenditure is the amount of the diversion[370] plus the amount of any further payments to the same grantee. If the private foundation complies with the requirements of this first condition, however, but not the requirements of the second, the amount of the taxable expenditure is the amount of the further payments.[371]

The second exception applies to situations in which a grantee has previously diverted funds received from a grantor private foundation, and the grantor foundation determines that any part of a grant has again been used for improper purposes. In these situations, the private foundation will not be treated as having made a taxable expenditure solely by reason of the diversion

---

366. Reg. § 53.4945-5(e)(1)(i).
367. Id.
368. Reg. § 53.4945-5(e)(1)(ii).
369. Reg. § 53.4945-5(e)(1)(iii).
370. For example, the income diverted in the case of an endowment grant, or the rental value of capital equipment for the period it is diverted (id.).
371. Id.

§ 9.7 EXPENDITURE RESPONSIBILITY

as long as the private foundation can show that it has (1) complied with the two conditions above applicable to first-time diversions of funds, and (2) withholds future payments until the diverted funds are in fact recovered or restored. Additionally, if, in fact, some or all of the diverted funds are not so restored or recovered, then the foundation must take all reasonable and appropriate steps to recover *all* of the grant funds.[372]

If a private foundation is treated as having made a taxable expenditure in this circumstance, then, unless the private foundation meets the requirements of the first of these conditions, the amount of the taxable expenditure is the amount of the diversion plus the amount of any further payments to the same grantee. If the private foundation complies with the first requirement, however, but fails to withhold further payments until the second requirement is met, the amount of the taxable expenditure is the amount of the further payments.[373]

As to either of these scenarios, the phrase *all reasonable and appropriate steps* includes legal action where appropriate, but need not include a lawsuit if the action would in all probability not result in the satisfaction of execution on a judgment.[374]

A failure by the grantee to make the required expenditure responsibility reports (or the making of inadequate reports) will result in treatment of the grant as a taxable expenditure by the grantor unless the grantor has made the grant in accordance with the general expenditure responsibility requirements, has complied with the applicable reporting requirements, makes a reasonable effort to obtain the required report, and withholds all future payments on the grant and on any other grant to the same grantee until the report is furnished.[375] In addition, a grant that is subject to the expenditure responsibility requirements is considered a taxable expenditure of the grantor private foundation if the grantor fails to make the requisite pre-grant inquiry, fails to make the grant in accordance with a written agreement containing the required grant terms, or fails to report to the IRS.[376]

While "reaffirm[ing] the central purpose of the expenditure responsibility rules—to ensure that private foundation grants will be properly used by the recipient organization solely for tax-exempt purposes," the House-Senate conferees, in finalizing the Tax Reform Act of 1984, expressed concern about any "unduly burdensome or unnecessary requirements in some respects (which may operate to deter grants by some foundations to newly formed,

---

372. Reg. § 53.4945-5(e)(1)(iv).
373. *Id.*
374. Reg. § 53.4945-5(e)(1)(v).
375. Reg. § 53.4945-5(e)(2).
376. Reg. § 53.4945-5(e)(3).

community-based foundations)."[377] Accordingly, the conference report directed the Department of the Treasury "to review its expenditure responsibility regulations for purposes of modifying any requirements which are found to be unduly burdensome or unnecessary" and, specifically, to modify the required grantor private foundation reports to the IRS.[378] Nevertheless, the expenditure responsibility regulations have not been revised.

From time to time, the IRS issues rulings as to whether a private foundation has complied with the expenditure responsibility requirements.[379]

§ 9.8 SPENDING FOR NONCHARITABLE PURPOSES

The term *taxable expenditure* includes any amount paid or incurred by a private foundation for any *noncharitable purpose*.[380] The purposes that are considered charitable under this rule are those that are religious, charitable, scientific, literary, or educational, the fostering of national or international sports competition, and the prevention of cruelty to children or animals (but not testing for public safety).[381] Thus, ordinarily, only an expenditure for an activity that, if it were a substantial part of the organization's total activities, would cause loss of tax exemption is a taxable expenditure.[382] A private foundation can make a grant to a public charity and earmark the funds for a specific project and not make a taxable expenditure as long as the project itself constitutes a charitable undertaking.[383]

In one instance, the IRS ruled that grants made under a proposed grant program to relieve ministers of educational debt did not further charitable purposes, and therefore were taxable expenditures, where the minister grantees were not required to document the actual use of the funds and there was no requirement that the minister grantees show financial need or evidence

---

377. H.R. Rep. No. 98-851, at 1091 (1984).
378. *Id*. The conferees also directed the Treasury Department to report to the House Committee on Ways and Means and the Senate Committee on Finance on its review and modifications.
379. E.g., Priv. Ltr. Rul. 8717024.
380. IRC § 4945(d)(5); Reg. § 53.4945-6(a).
381. That is, the charitable and other exempt purposes encompassed by IRC § 170(c)(2)(B) (which do not include testing for public safety).
382. Reg. § 53.4945-6(a). E.g., Rev. Rul. 80-97, 1980-1 C.B. 257, where the IRS held that an unrestricted grant from a private foundation to a cemetery company exempt by reason of IRC § 501(c)(13) was a taxable expenditure because the grantee is not described in IRC § 170(c)(2)(B), even though contributions to it are deductible under IRC § 170(c)(5). Also, Gladney v. Commissioner, 745 F.2d 955 (5th Cir. 1984), where the court held that the transfer of assets to noncharitable recipients upon dissolution of an organization, where the IRC § 507 termination rules were not satisfied, constituted a taxable expenditure.
383. E.g., Tech. Adv. Mem. 9240001.

§ 9.8 SPENDING FOR NONCHARITABLE PURPOSES

of a commitment to remain in the ministry. Under these circumstances, the IRS concluded that there was no reasonable assurance that the grants would advance, or were otherwise related to the advancement of, religion or to any other exempt purpose and it was uncertain that the program was "sufficiently tailored" to achieve the advancement of religion.[384]

Expenditures not treated as taxable expenditures under these rules are purchases of investments to obtain income to be used in furtherance of charitable purposes, reasonable expenses with respect to such investments, payment of taxes, any expenses that qualify as deductions in the computation of unrelated business income tax,[385] any payment that constitutes a qualifying distribution[386] or an allowable deduction pursuant to the net investment income tax rules,[387] reasonable expenditures to evaluate, acquire, modify, and dispose of program-related investments,[388] and business expenditures by the recipient of a program-related investment.[389] Conversely, expenditures for unreasonable administrative expenses—including compensation, consultants' fees, and other fees for services rendered—are ordinarily taxable expenditures, unless the private foundation can demonstrate that the expenses were paid or incurred in the good-faith belief that they were reasonable and that the payment or incurrence of the expenses in the amounts involved was consistent with ordinary business care and prudence.[390] The determination as to whether an expenditure is unreasonable is dependent on the facts and circumstances of the particular case.[391]

For example, the IRS ruled that a private foundation's grants to improve students' ability to manage their finances and invest for their future financial security were qualifying distributions rather than taxable expenditures.[392]

---

384. Priv. Ltr. Rul 199927047.
385. See § 11.5.
386. See § 6.4.
387. See § 10.5.
388. See § 8.3.
389. Reg. § 53.4945-6(b)(1).
390. Reg. § 53.4945-6(b)(2). E.g., Kermit Fischer Foundation v. Commissioner, 59 T.C.M. 898 (1990) (payment of unreasonable compensation). In Rev. Rul. 82-223, 1982-2 C.B. 301, the IRS held that a private foundation may, without making a taxable expenditure, indemnify and/or purchase insurance to cover its managers for liabilities arising under state law concerning mismanagement of funds, as long as the payments are treated as part of the foundation manager's compensation and the compensation is reasonable, but that the private foundation would make a taxable expenditure if it indemnified a foundation manager for an amount paid in settlement of a state proceeding. The IRS ruled that a private foundation may amend its articles of incorporation, in conformity with a change in state law, to limit the personal liability of volunteers who are not directors, without making a taxable expenditure (Priv. Ltr. Rul. 9440033).
391. Reg. § 53.4945-6(b)(2).
392. Priv. Ltr. Rul. 201830003.

The students involved were required to be high-achieving individuals with financial need residing in counties with less-than-average median household income. In finding that these grants served a charitable purpose, as opposed to a private one, the IRS primarily relied on a ruling concluding that a fund used by students as an adjunct to their course of instruction to obtain knowledge and experience in security portfolio management contributes to the students' education.[393] As another illustration, the IRS ruled that a private foundation's grant to fund a religious journalism project constituted a qualifying distribution and was not a taxable expenditure.[394] The intent of the project was to produce fair, accurate, and objective articles that explain the religious convictions, practices, and dynamics behind news events. In this instance, the pivotal issue was not private benefit but commerciality.[395] The IRS ruled that this project was educational in that it would increase understanding of various religions and the role that religion plays in society. The IRS observed that the prospective grantee would rely on members of its staff and contributing authors who are experts in the fields of religious news gathering to "ensure that the preparation of the content will conform to non-commercial educational purposes."[396]

A court held that the return of monies to an individual by a private foundation that the foundation should not have received and was not entitled to keep is not an "amount paid or incurred" by a private foundation for purposes of these rules.[397] Relying on this case, the IRS ruled that payments made by a private foundation to a trust, as to which the foundation was the sole beneficiary, to cover trust claims and expenses, would not be taxable expenditures because the foundation was returning funds to which it was not entitled in the first instance.[398] The foundation had requested acceleration of distributions of trust assets to it before the trustees of the trust knew the full extent of potential claims against and liabilities of the trust. The trustees, facing personal liability, were willing to accelerate distributions to the foundation if it indemnified them. The foundation agreed to refund monies to the trustees should any claims or liabilities as to the trust materialize.

An investment may subsequently be discovered to be a Ponzi scheme or other fraud.[399] A report submitted to the government by the New York State Bar Association[400] concluded that an outcome such as this "may be indicative

---

393. Rev. Rul. 68-16, 1968-1 C.B. 246.
394. Priv. Ltr. Rul. 201851003.
395. As to the commerciality doctrine, see *Tax-Exempt Organizations* § 4.9.
396. It is a non sequitur to state that, simply because this organization's writers are "experts" in their field, the content they produce will "conform to . . . noncommercial purposes."
397. Underwood v. United States, 461 F. Supp. 1382 (N.D. Tex. 1978).
398. Priv. Ltr. Rul. 201745001.
399. See § 8.4.
400. See § 8.4(b).

§ 9.8 SPENDING FOR NONCHARITABLE PURPOSES

of a failure of [due] diligence or business judgment, but does not indicate the foundation's purpose was not to earn a profit." As to whether this type of an amount paid constitutes a taxable expenditure, this report observed that "it is not at all clear that there is any benefit in stretching the statute to punish a foundation for an investment in a Ponzi scheme where there has been no self-dealing and where the investment was not a jeopardizing investment, based on facts known at the time the investment was made." The report posed three questions in the taxable expenditures context, pertaining to fictitious income reported and reinvested in the arrangement. One, are these amounts considered paid or incurred for taxable expenditure law purposes? Two, are amounts paid, as investment advisory or management fees, in connection with investments in a fraudulent investment scheme, considered taxable expenditures when paid to the operator of the fraudulent arrangement or to a person unaware of the fraud who invested the private foundation's funds in the scheme? Three, what criteria are to be applied in evaluating the reasonableness of the expenses?

An expenditure may be made for a charitable or other permitted purpose even though the expenditure constitutes an act of self-dealing.[401] In one instance, a private foundation made a loan to a disqualified person to generate income to be used solely for the private foundation's charitable purposes—an act of self-dealing.[402] Because the loan was, however, made to the disqualified person at a reasonable rate of interest, was adequately secured, and otherwise met prudent investment standards, and was designed solely to provide income for the private foundation's charitable purposes, the IRS concluded that it was not a taxable expenditure.[403]

A grantee need not itself be a charitable organization[404] as long as the purpose of the private foundation's grant is a charitable or other permitted purpose.[405] Since a private foundation is not permitted to make an expenditure for a noncharitable purpose, however, a private foundation may not make a grant to an organization other than a charitable organization[406] unless the making of the grant itself constitutes a direct charitable act or the making of a program-related investment, or the grantor is reasonably assured that the

---

401. See Chapter 5.
402. IRC § 4941(d)(1)(B).
403. Rev. Rul. 77-161, 1977-1 C.B. 358. In this ruling, the IRS observed that "a given set of facts can give rise to taxes under more than one provision of Chapter 42 of the Code," citing Reg. § 53.4944-1(a)(2)(iv).
404. For purposes of this rule, an organization described in IRC § 170(c).
405. Reg. § 53.4945-6(a).
406. For purposes of this rule, an organization described in IRC § 501(c)(3), or an organization treated as an IRC § 509(a)(1) organization under Reg. § 53.4945-5(a)(4) (Reg. § 53.4945-6(c)(1)).

grant will be used exclusively for charitable purposes.[407] In a reversal of its approval of a company foundation employee relief program, the IRS provided a comprehensive review of the sanctions that can result when a private foundation is found to have made a noncharitable expenditure. This ruling discusses the interaction between the self-dealing, mandatory payout, and tax expenditures rules.[408]

If a private foundation makes a grant (which is not a transfer of assets pursuant to a liquidation, merger, redemption, recapitalization, or other adjustment, organization, or reorganization)[409] to an organization other than a charitable one,[410] the grantor can be reasonably assured that the grant will be used exclusively for charitable purposes only if the grantee organization agrees to maintain and, during the period in which any portion of the grant funds remains unexpended, continuously maintains the grant funds (or other assets transferred) in a separate fund dedicated to one or more charitable purposes.[411] If a private foundation makes a transfer of assets (other than as part of a direct charitable act or as a private foundation) pursuant to one of the previously referenced adjustments or reorganizations, to any person, the transferred assets are not considered used exclusively for charitable purposes unless the assets are transferred to a charitable fund or organization.[412]

A foreign organization that does not have a ruling or determination letter that it is a charitable organization is treated as a charitable organization for purposes of these rules if, in the reasonable judgment of a foundation manager of the grantor private foundation, the grantee organization is a charitable organization. The term *reasonable judgment* is given its generally accepted legal sense within the outlines developed by judicial decisions in the law of trusts.[413] Where a private foundation makes a good faith determination that a foreign organization is the equivalent of a qualifying public charity in accordance with published IRS procedures, a foundation manager will be considered to have exercised reasonable judgment in this regard, and a grant to such an organization need not be maintained in a separate fund.[414]

---

407. Reg. § 53.4945-6(c)(1).
408. Priv. Ltr. Rul. 199914040.
409. See IRC § 507(b)(2), which is the subject of § 13.5.
410. For purposes of this rule, a charitable organization is one described in IRC § 501(c)(3) other than IRC § 509(a)(4); see Chapter 15.
411. Reg. § 53.4945-6(c)(2)(i).
412. Reg. § 53.4945-6(c)(3). For purposes of this rule, a charitable fund or organization is one described in IRC § 501(c)(3) other than IRC § 509(a)(4) (see Chapter 15) or one that is treated as so described in IRC § 4947(a)(1) (see § 3.6).
413. Reg. § 53.4945-6(c)(2)(ii).
414. Rev. Proc. 2017-53, 2017-40 I.R.B. 263 § 3.01, 3.02; see § 9.6(b).

§ 9.9 EXCISE TAX ON TAXABLE EXPENDITURES

(a) Initial and Additional Taxes

An initial excise tax is imposed on each taxable expenditure of a private foundation, which is to be paid by the foundation at the rate of 20 percent of the amount of each taxable expenditure.[415] An initial excise tax is also imposed on any foundation manager that agreed to the making of a taxable expenditure by a private foundation, equal to 5 percent of the amount involved up to a maximum of $10,000.[416] This initial tax on a manager is imposed only where the foundation initial tax is imposed, the manager knows that the expenditure to which they agree is a taxable expenditure, and the agreement is willful and not due to reasonable cause.[417]

An additional excise tax is imposed in any case in which an initial tax is imposed on a private foundation because of a taxable expenditure and the expenditure is not timely corrected.[418] This additional tax is to be paid by the private foundation and is at the rate of 100 percent of the amount of each taxable expenditure.[419] In any case in which an additional tax has been levied on a private foundation, an additional tax is also imposed on a foundation manager if the foundation manager refused to agree to part or all of the correction of the expenditure.[420] This additional tax, which is at the rate of 50 percent of the amount of the taxable expenditure, is to be paid by the foundation manager.[421] Where a taxable event is corrected within the correction period, any additional tax imposed with respect to the event is abated.[422]

The termination tax[423] may serve as a third-tier tax where there have been either willful repeated acts (or failures to act), or a willful and flagrant act (or failure to act), giving rise to liability for the taxes on taxable expenditures or the other private foundation excise taxes.[424]

---

415. IRC § 4945(a)(1). This tax is also known as a *first-tier tax* (IRC § 4963(a); Reg. § 53.4963-1(a)).
416. IRC § 4945(a)(2), (c)(2).
417. Reg. § 53.4945-1(a)(2)(i).
418. IRC § 4945(b)(1). This tax is also known as a *second-tier tax* (IRC § 4963(b); Reg. § 53.4963-1(b)).
419. IRC § 4945(b)(1); Reg. § 53.4945-1(b)(1).
420. IRC § 4945(b)(2); Reg. § 53.4945-1(b)(2).
421. *Id.*
422. IRC § 4961; see § 12.4(c).
423. See § 13.7.
424. IRC § 507(a)(2); see § 13.2.

(b) Tax on Managers

The 5 percent tax with respect to any particular expenditure applies only to those foundation managers who are authorized to approve, to exercise discretion in recommending approval of, or who agreed to the making of the expenditure by the foundation and to those foundation managers who are members of a group (such as the foundation's board of directors or trustees) that is so authorized.[425]

The *agreement* of a foundation manager to the making of a taxable expenditure consists of any manifestation of approval of the expenditure that is sufficient to constitute an exercise of the foundation manager's authority to approve, or to exercise discretion in recommending approval of, the making of the expenditure by the foundation, whether or not the manifestation of approval is the final or decisive approval on behalf of the foundation.[426]

A foundation manager is considered to have agreed to an expenditure, *knowing* that it is a taxable one, only if they (1) have actual knowledge of sufficient facts so that, based solely on those facts, the expenditure would be a taxable one; (2) is aware that the expenditure under these circumstances may violate the federal tax law governing taxable expenditures; and (3) negligently fails to make reasonable attempts to ascertain whether the expenditure is a taxable one, or they are in fact aware that it is such an expenditure. While the term *knowing* does not mean "having reason to know," evidence tending to show that a foundation manager has reason to know of a particular fact or particular rule is relevant in determining whether they had actual knowledge of that fact or rule.[427]

A foundation manager's agreement to a taxable expenditure is *willful* if it is voluntary, conscious, and intentional. No motive to avoid the restrictions of the law or the incurrence of any tax is necessary to make an agreement willful. A foundation manager's agreement to a taxable expenditure is not willful, however, if they do not know that it is a taxable expenditure.[428] A foundation manager's actions are *due to reasonable cause* if they have exercised their responsibility on behalf of the private foundation with ordinary business care and prudence.[429]

If a foundation manager, after full disclosure of the factual situation to legal counsel (including house counsel), relies on the *advice of counsel* expressed in a

---

425. Id.
426. Reg. § 53.4945-1(a)(2)(ii).
427. Reg. § 53.4945-1(a)(2)(iii).
428. Reg. § 53.4945-1(a)(2)(iv).
429. Reg. § 53.4945-1(a)(2)(v).

§ 9.9 EXCISE TAX ON TAXABLE EXPENDITURES

reasoned written legal opinion that an expenditure is not a taxable one (or that expenditures conforming to certain guidelines are not taxable ones), although the expenditure is subsequently held to be a taxable one, the foundation manager's agreement to the expenditure will ordinarily not be considered knowing or willful and will ordinarily be considered due to reasonable cause. This rule also applies with respect to an opinion that proposed reporting procedures concerning an expenditure will satisfy the taxable expenditure rules, even though the procedures are subsequently held to not satisfy the rules, and to grants made with provisions for such reporting procedures that are taxable solely because of such inadequate reporting procedures. A written legal opinion is considered *reasoned* even if it reaches a conclusion that is subsequently determined to be incorrect as long as the opinion addresses the facts and applicable law. By contrast, a written legal opinion is not a reasoned one if it merely recites the facts and expresses a conclusion. The absence of advice of counsel with respect to an expenditure, however, does not alone give rise to an inference that a foundation manager agreed to the making of the expenditure knowingly, willfully, or without reasonable cause.[430]

Where more than one foundation manager is liable for an excise tax with respect to the making of a taxable expenditure, all the foundation managers are jointly and severally liable for the tax.[431] The maximum aggregate amount collectible as an initial tax from all foundation managers with respect to any one taxable expenditure is $10,000, and the maximum aggregate amount so collectible as an additional tax is $20,000.[432] The additional excise taxes are imposed at the end of the *taxable period*, which begins with the date on which the taxable expenditure occurs and ends on the earliest of the date a notice of deficiency with respect to the initial tax is mailed or the date the initial tax is assessed if no deficiency notice is mailed.[433]

(c) Paying the Tax

The initial tax on taxable expenditures is calculated and reported on IRS Form 4720.[434] The IRS has the discretionary authority to abate this initial tax where the private foundation establishes that the violation was due to reasonable cause and not to willful neglect, and timely corrects the violation.[435]

---

430. Reg. § 53.4945-1(a)(2)(vi).
431. IRC § 4945(c)(1); Reg. § 53.4945-1(c)(1).
432. IRC § 4945(c)(2).
433. IRC § 4945(i)(2); Reg. § 53.4945-1(e)(1).
434. See § 12.4(a).
435. IRC § 4962; see § 12.4(c).

(d) Correcting the Expenditure

As noted, to avoid the imposition of the additional tax, a taxable expenditure must be corrected during the correction period. The *correction period* is the period beginning on the date on which the *taxable event* occurs and ending 90 days after the date of mailing of a notice of deficiency with respect to the additional tax imposed on the event.[436] This period is extended by any period in which a deficiency cannot be assessed[437] and any other period that the IRS determines is reasonable and necessary to bring about correction of the taxable event.[438] In this setting, a taxable event is an act or failure to act giving rise to liability for tax under the taxable expenditures rules.[439] This event occurs on the date on which the act or failure to act giving rise to the liability occurred.[440]

In general, *correction* of a taxable expenditure is accomplished by recovering part or all of the expenditure to the extent recovery is possible. Where full recovery cannot be accomplished, correction entails any additional corrective action that the IRS may prescribe. This additional corrective action is to be determined by the circumstances of each case and may include requiring that any unpaid funds due the grantee be withheld, that no further grants be made to the grantee, periodic (such as quarterly) reports from the foundation (in addition to other reports that may be required) with respect to all of its expenditures,[441] improved methods of exercising expenditure responsibility, and improved methods of selecting recipients of individual grants. The IRS may prescribe other measures in a particular case. The private foundation making the expenditure is not under any obligation to attempt to recover the expenditure by legal action if the action would in all probability not result in the satisfaction of execution on a judgment.[442]

If the expenditure is taxable only because the private foundation fails to obtain full and complete reports from the grantee,[443] or fails to make full and detailed reports to the IRS,[444] correction may be accomplished by obtaining or making the report in question. Additionally, if the expenditure is taxable only

---

436. IRC § 4963(e)(1); Reg. § 53.4963-1(e)(1).
437. IRC § 4963(e)(1)(A); Reg. § 53.4963-1(e)(2). The rules as to non-assessment of a deficiency are those of IRC § 6213(a).
438. IRC § 4963(e)(1)(B); Reg. § 53.4963-1(e)(3).
439. IRC § 4963(c); Reg. § 53.4963-1(c).
440. IRC § 4963(e)(2)(B); Reg. § 53.4963-1(e)(7)(iv).
441. These reports must be equivalent in detail to those the private foundation is required to file with the IRS (see § 9.7(f)).
442. Reg. § 53.4945-1(d)(1).
443. See § 9.7(d).
444. See § 9.7(f).

§ 9.9 EXCISE TAX ON TAXABLE EXPENDITURES

because of a failure to obtain a full and complete report and an investigation indicates that grant funds were not diverted to a use not in furtherance of a purpose specified in the grant, correction may be accomplished by exerting all reasonable efforts to obtain the report in question and reporting the failure to the IRS, even though the report is not finally obtained.[445]

Where an expenditure is taxable under the rules concerning grants to individuals only because the private foundation failed to obtain advance approval of procedures with respect to grants to individuals for travel, study, or other similar purposes,[446] correction may be accomplished by obtaining approval of the grant-making procedures and establishing to the satisfaction of the IRS that grant funds have not been diverted to any use not in furtherance of a purpose specified in the grant, the grant-making procedures instituted would have been approved if advance approval of the procedures had been properly requested, and where advance approval of grant-making procedures is subsequently required, the approval will be properly requested.[447]

Where the act or failure to act that gave rise to the additional tax is corrected within the correction period, the tax will not be assessed, or if assessed will be abated, or if collected will be credited or refunded.[448] The collection period is suspended during any litigation.[449]

The termination taxes may serve as a third-tier tax where there have been either willful repeated acts (or failures to act), or a willful and flagrant act (or failure to act), giving rise to liability for the taxes on taxable expenditures or the other private foundation excise taxes.[450]

---

445. Reg. § 53.4945-1(d)(2).
446. See § 9.3(d)-(f).
447. Reg. § 53.4945-1(d)(3).
448. IRC § 4961(a); Reg. § 53.4961-1; see § 12.4(c).
449. IRC § 4961(c); Reg. § 53.4961-2; see § 12.4(c).
450. See IRC § 507(a)(2), (c) and §§ 13.2, 13.7.

CHAPTER TEN

Tax on Net Investment Income

§ 10.1 Rate of Tax 446
§ 10.2 Payment of Tax 448
§ 10.3 Planning Opportunities to Reduce the Tax 448
§ 10.4 Calculating Taxable Net Investment Income 450
    (a) Gross Investment Income 450
    (b) Capital Gains and Losses 451
        (i) Exceptions, Adjustments, and Exclusions 451
        (ii) Basis 453
        (iii) Wash Sales 454
        (iv) Ponzi Scheme Losses 454
    (c) Interest and Annuities 455
    (d) Dividends 455
    (e) Rent 456
    (f) Royalties 456
    (g) Estate or Trust Distributions 456
    (h) Partnership and S Corporation Income 459
§ 10.5 Reductions to Gross Investment Income 460
    (a) Deductions Allowed 460
    (b) Deductions Not Allowed 462
§ 10.6 Foreign Foundations 464
§ 10.7 Exemption from Tax on Investment Income 465

Private foundations are one of the few types of tax-exempt organizations that are required to pay a tax on investment income.[1] The revenue derived from this tax is intended to offset the cost of enforcing the sanctions imposed on private foundations and other exempt organizations. As one analysis stated, private foundations are to "share some of the burden of paying the cost of government, especially for more extensive and vigorous enforcement of the

---

1. IRC § 4940. Three other types of tax-exempt organizations are required to pay an investment income tax: social clubs (described in IRC § 501(c)(7)), political organizations (described in IRC § 527), and homeowners associations (described in IRC § 528); this tax is paid as an unrelated business income tax. Furthermore, under certain circumstances, all tax-exempt organizations, including private foundations, are subject to the unrelated business income tax on investment income to the extent that the income is derived from debt-financed property (IRC § 514). Until 2017, only private foundations, however, were required pay a tax on investment income that is the subject of a statute solely on this point. For tax years beginning after December 31, 2017, however, IRC § 4968 imposes an excise tax of 1.4 percent on the net investment income of certain private colleges and universities. Net investment income for purposes of this tax is determined "under rules similar to the rules of" IRC § 4940(c) (IRC § 4968(c)).

tax laws relating to exempt organizations."[2] To preserve the concept that private foundations are exempt entities, this tax is cast as an excise tax rather than an income tax.[3]

Indeed, the tax was intended to be in the nature of an audit fee.[4] These taxes are not actually earmarked for auditing and supervising foundations but are mingled with the general federal revenues.

§ 10.1 RATE OF TAX

An excise tax is imposed on the net investment income of all domestic tax-exempt private foundations for each tax year.[5] This tax is also imposed on private operating foundations[6] and nonexempt wholly charitable trusts.[7] When adopted in 1969, this tax was set at 4 percent; because the receipts from this tax exceeded the actual costs of the enforcement efforts of the IRS, the tax was reduced to 2 percent in 1978,[8] and a 1 or 2 percent rate was effective for post-1984 years

---

2. Staff of Joint Comm. on Internal Revenue Tax'n, 91st Cong., 2d Sess., General Explanation of the Tax Reform Act of 1969 29 (Comm. Print 1970)
3. It has been held that the application of this tax does not violate equal protection rights (Williams Home, Inc. v. United States, 540 F. Supp. 310 (W.D. Va. 1982)).
4. H.R. Rep. No. 91-413, at 18 (1969); S. Rep. No. 91-552, at 27 (1969). Because the tax imposed by IRC § 4940(a) is an excise tax, rather than an income tax, the tax is not treated as a covered tax under U.S. income tax treaties unless a treaty expressly provides otherwise (Rev. Rul. 84-169, 1984-2 C.B. 216).
5. See § 10.2; IRC § 4940(a); Reg. § 53.4940-1(a). In one case, however, a private law enacted by Congress in 1875 was found to exempt a private foundation from the IRC § 4940 excise tax (Trustees of the Louise Home v. Commissioner, 46 T.C.M. 1494 (1983)).
6. See § 3.1.
7. See § 3.6.
8. Subsequent to enactment of the Tax Reform Act of 1969, which set the administration tax on private foundations at 4 percent for each tax year beginning after December 31, 1969 (through 1977), representatives of the private foundation community urged reduction of the private foundation tax to the actual level of the cost of auditing and supervision, and an earmarking of the receipts for these purposes. The late Representative Wright Patman, a longtime foe of private foundations, proposed the establishment of an account in the Treasury for excise tax revenues, with at least 50 percent of the receipts to be used by the IRS for supervision of private foundations and the remainder for the states for independent oversight of private foundations' activities (H.R. 5728, 93rd Cong., (1973)). This approach, however, was never seriously entertained. The Senate version of the Tax Reform Act of 1976 would have lowered the private foundation net investment income tax to 2 percent, but that approach was not taken at that time, because Congress lowered the mandatory payout percentage to a flat 5 percent (see Chapter 6) and did not want to have too much legislation favorable to private foundations in one tax act. The reduction in the private foundation net investment income tax to 2 percent was delayed until adoption of the Revenue Act of 1978.

ending on or before December 20, 2019.[9] For tax years beginning after December 20, 2019, this tax is imposed at a single rate of 1.39 percent.[10]

The tax is also imposed on any private foundation that is not exempt from tax if the tax on net investment income plus any unrelated business income tax[11] exceeds the normal corporate or trust income tax it would pay.[12] The purpose of this latter tax is to ensure that a private foundation will not attempt to reduce its tax liability by intentionally losing its tax-exempt status.

Notwithstanding the reduction of the excise tax rate in 1978, the tax-law-writing committees of Congress remained concerned that the IRS devote adequate resources to the administration of the law of tax-exempt organizations.[13] This is relevant in this context, because this tax was instituted to ensure the availability of these resources. In 1974, Congress made a permanent authorization of appropriations to further ensure the availability of sufficient resources to administer this law.[14] However, the change in the private foundation tax rate does not affect the amount of that permanent authorization.

In discussing this law change, the tax committees expressed their expectation that the IRS will annually report to Congress on (1) the extent to which audits are conducted as to the tax liabilities of tax-exempt organizations, (2) the extent to which examinations are made as to the continued qualification of exempt organizations for their exempt status, (3) the extent to which IRS personnel are given initial and refresher instruction in the relevant portions of the law and administrative procedures, (4) the extent to which the IRS cooperates with and receives cooperation from state officials with regard to supervision of tax-exempt organizations, (5) the costs of maintaining the programs at levels that would produce proper compliance with the laws,

---

9. Deficit Reduction Act of 1984. For tax years beginning after 1984 and on or before December 20, 2019, the excise tax rate on a private foundation's net investment income was reduced to 1 percent for each year during which the foundation's qualifying distributions (see Chapter 6) equaled a hypothetical distribution amount, based upon the past five-year average qualifying distributions, plus 1 percent of net investment income (prior IRC § 4940(e)). Essentially, the reduction in the rate of tax was permitted for a foundation if its current-year distributions exceed its payout percentage for the past five years times the average fair market value of its current-year investment assets, plus half of the normal 2 percent tax. Thus, in effect, under prior law a foundation could choose to distribute 1 percent of its investment income to charitable recipients rather than to the U.S. Treasury.
10. This law change was occasioned by enactment of the Taxpayer Certainty and Disaster Tax Relief Act of 2019, enacted as part of the Further Consolidated Appropriations Act, 2020 (Pub. L. No. 116-94, div. Q, tit. III, § 206, 133 Stat. 2534, 3246).
11. See Chapter 11.
12. IRC § 4940(b); Reg. § 53.4940-(b).
13. H.R. Rep. No. 95-842 (1978), to accompany H.R. 112, which is the original legislation containing the private foundation excise tax reduction that was made part of the Revenue Act of 1978.
14. Employee Retirement Income Security Act of 1974 (Pub. L. No. 93-406, § 1052, 88 Stat. 829, 952).

§ 10.3 PLANNING OPPORTUNITIES TO REDUCE THE TAX

(6) the amounts requested by the executive branch for the maintenance of the programs, and (7) the reasons for any difference between the needed funds and the requested amounts. In addition, these committees required the IRS to notify Congress "of any administrative problems that [are] experienced in the course of this enforcement of the internal revenue laws with respect to exempt organizations."[15]

§ 10.2 PAYMENT OF TAX

The net investment tax is calculated each year on Form 990-PF (Part V). A private foundation must make quarterly payments of estimated net investment income tax. IRS Form 990-W provides a worksheet for figuring the quarterly estimated tax. These quarterly estimated tax payments must be made electronically using the Electronic Federal Tax Payment System,[16] and separate penalties are imposed for the failure to pay estimated tax when due[17] or to deposit quarterly estimated taxes electronically.[18] IRS Form 2220 is used to calculate the amount of any estimated tax penalty and must be attached to the private foundation's Form 990-PF when filed. A separate addition to tax will apply if the private foundation fails to pay any net investment income tax that is due but still unpaid by the due date for its Form 990-PF.[19]

§ 10.3 PLANNING OPPORTUNITIES TO REDUCE THE TAX

Given its low rate, the excise tax on net investment income has become a generally accepted cost of retaining control over funds donated to a private foundation. Although the tax is imposed at a low rate, a tax planning opportunity nevertheless exists to reduce the amount of tax paid on property with built-in capital gain. If a private foundation distributed such property as a qualifying distribution—for example, as a grant to a public charity—paying the net investment income excise tax on the gain can be avoided.

---

15. H.R. Rep. No. 95-842 (1978); S. Rep. No. 94-938, at 598-599 (1976).
16. Reg. § 1.6301-1. A private foundation may enroll in, and make payments through, EFTPS at www.eftps.gov.
17. IRC § 6655.
18. IRC § 6656.
19. Because Form 990-PF serves as an excise tax return for the net investment income tax (Gen. Couns. Mem. 36506), an addition to tax for failure to file a tax return will also apply if Form 990-PF is not timely filed (*id.*; see § 12.4(b)).

TAX ON NET INVESTMENT INCOME

According to the Council on Foundations,[20] a typical private foundation invests its assets for *total return*.[21] Under this investment philosophy, a security portfolio, on average, often is composed of securities with low current income payments and an expectation for underlying appreciation in the value of the securities, typified by common stocks. It is expected that capital gains will be regularly earned as portfolio holdings are sold in response to market changes. When the desired result—capital gain—occurs, this capital gain is subject to the net investment income excise tax.

A foundation with a 2 percent current dividend and interest yield on its total return portfolio will lack the liquidity needed to meet its annual requirement to pay out approximately 5 percent of the average fair market value of its assets for the previous year in the form of qualifying distributions.[22] Thus, a foundation with such a portfolio will need to use capital gain property to meet part of its payout requirement. If appreciated property is distributed to permitted grantees, rather than sold to generate cash to make a distribution, the capital gain earned on the appreciated property is not subject to the net investment income excise tax. For purposes of this tax, a distribution of property that is a qualifying distribution[23] is not treated as a sale or other disposition of property.[24]

For example, assume that a foundation needs to make qualifying distributions of $500,000 by the end of its current tax year to avoid the private foundation excise tax on failure to distribute income.[25] Assume further that the foundation has $500,000 of appreciated securities with a basis of $100,000. If the foundation distributes the appreciated securities to qualifying grantees, rather than first selling the stock and distributing the cash, the foundation will save $5,560 in net investment income tax ($400,000 gain x 1.39 percent tax rate).

Readily marketable securities are the most suitable for distributing to charitable grantees because of the ease with which they can be converted to cash (or be retained by the grantee as part of its own investment portfolio). Inasmuch as almost all of a foundation's gains are taxed,[26] however, this planning opportunity may also apply to grants of other appreciated property, such as art objects, historic houses, and other types of assets that might be used by the grantee in furtherance of its own exempt purposes, rather than having to

---

20. Council on Foundations, *Foundation Management Report*, 8th ed. (Washington, DC: 1996).
21. See § 8.2(d).
22. See § 6.4.
23. Under IRC § 4942(g); see § 6.4.
24. Reg. § 53.4940-1(f)(1).
25. See § 6.5.
26. See § 10.4(b).

be liquidated by the grantee. If the grantee needs to liquidate the property distributed by a private foundation, it may be appropriate for the foundation to gross up the amount of the grant to account for the costs of liquidating the distributed asset.

A private foundation may also use appreciated property to meet the redistribution requirements[27] necessary to make a charitable contribution to the foundation eligible for the 50 percent limitation on charitable contributions by an individual[28] and prevent it from being subject to the basis limitations on donations of appreciated property to a nonoperating private foundation.[29] For a redistribution to "not be treated as a sale or other disposition of property" so that the built-in gain in the property may be excluded from the net investment income excise tax,[30] the redistribution must be a qualifying distribution,[31] and the redistribution rule must be satisfied (including the requirement that the distribution be made out of corpus).[32] A foundation can also use any excess distribution carryovers to satisfy this requirement.[33]

§ 10.4 CALCULATING TAXABLE NET INVESTMENT INCOME

The excise tax is imposed on net investment income for each tax year. A private foundation's net investment income is the amount by which the sum of its gross investment income and net capital gain exceeds the allowable deductions.[34]

(a) Gross Investment Income

The term *gross investment income* means the gross amount of income from interest, dividends, rents, payments with respect to securities loans, and royalties, but not including any such income to the extent included in computing the unrelated business income tax.[35]

Gross investment income also includes income that is from sources that are similar to interest, dividends, and the like.[36] The somewhat vague word

---

27. Under IRC § 170(b)(1)(F)(ii).
28. IRC § 170(b)(1)(a)(vii); see § 14.2(a).
29. IRC § 170(e)(1)(B)(ii); see § 14.4.
30. Reg. § 53.4940-1(f)(1).
31. IRC § 4942(g); see § 6.4.
32. IRC § 4942(g)(3); see § 6.4(c)(ii).
33. See § 6.5(c).
34. IRC § 4940(c)(1); Reg. § 53.4940-1(c)(1), (2).
35. IRC § 4940(c)(2); Reg. § 53.4940-1(d); e.g., Priv. Ltr. Rul. 201441018. As to the computation of the unrelated business income tax, see § 11.5.
36. IRC § 4940(c)(2); Reg. § 53.4940-1(d).

similar is intended to expand the definition to include income from peripheral security transactions that do not produce dividends or interest, such as options to sell (a put) or buy (a call) securities, commodity transactions, derivatives, and other investments not anticipated when the excise tax law was written. These similar items also include income from notional principal contracts,[37] annuities, and other substantially similar income from ordinary and routine investments,[38] and, with respect to capital gain net income, capital gains from appreciation, including capital gains and losses from the sale or other disposition of assets used to further an exempt purpose.[39]

The income is reportable using the method of accounting normally used by the foundation for financial statement purposes, with certain exceptions as discussed in the following paragraphs.[40] Income of the specified types that is produced by both investment assets and exempt function assets is taxed.[41] Therefore, interest income from student loans or dividends from a program-related corporate stock are included.

(b) Capital Gains and Losses

(i) Exceptions, Adjustments, and Exclusions. There are four exceptions to, or adjustments in connection with, the general rule that essentially all capital gains are taxed, including those resulting from the sale of exempt function assets. In the case of property held by a private foundation on December 31, 1969, and continuously thereafter to the date of its disposition, the basis for determining gain is deemed to be no less than the fair market value of the property on December 31, 1969.[42] Another exception is that gain or loss from the disposition of property is not taken into account for this purpose if the

---

37. As defined in Reg. § 1.863-7 or regulations issued under IRC § 446.
38. Reg. §§ 1.512(b)-1(a)(1), 53.4940-1(d)(1).
39. Staff of Joint Comm. on Tax'n, Technical Explanation of H.R. 4, the "Pension Protection Act of 2006," as Passed by the House on July 28, 2006, and as Considered by the Senate on August 3, 2006 324 (Comm. Print JCX-38-06). The Pension Protection Act of 2006 amended the IRC § 4940 definition of gross investment income, to include items of income that are "similar to" the items already enumerated therein, including "with respect to capital gain net income, capital gains from appreciation, including capital gains and losses from the sale or other disposition of assets used to further an exempt purpose" (*id.*).
40. Reg. § 53.4940-1(c).
41. Reg. § 53.4940-1(d)(1).
42. IRC § 4940(c)(4)(B). This exception is, of course, dated and of little vitality today (other than for private foundations holding appreciated property on December 31, 1969). Its concept, nonetheless, was reinvigorated when the Department of the Treasury and the IRS announced that the calculation of net investment income for purposes of the tax on college and university endowment income includes a rule that the basis of property for determining this income is set as of December 31, 2017 (Notice 2018-55, 2018-26 I.R.B. 773).

§ 10.4 CALCULATING TAXABLE NET INVESTMENT INCOME

gain or loss is taken into account in computing unrelated business income tax.[43] A third exception provides for a nontaxable exchange, stating:

> Except to the extent provided by regulation, under rules similar to the rules of section 1031 (including the exception under subsection (a)(2) thereof), no gain or loss shall be taken into account with respect to any portion of property used for a period of not less than 1 year for a purpose or function constituting the basis of the private foundation's exemption if the entire property is exchanged immediately following such period solely for property of like kind which is to be used primarily for a purpose or function constituting the basis for such foundation's exemption.[44]

A fourth adjustment provides that net losses from sales or other dispositions of property are only allowed to the extent of gains from such sales or other dispositions and no capital loss carryovers or carrybacks are allowed.[45] For purposes of these rules, there is no distinction between long- and short-term gains and losses, except for private operating foundations.[46] For example, both short- and long-term mutual fund capital gain dividends are classified as capital gain, not dividends.[47] The limitation on capital losses makes it advisable for a private foundation to review its current year investment results prior to its year end so as to take steps, if possible, to avoid loss of the tax benefit from any capital losses.

Certain types of gains are excluded from excise taxation:

- Gain inherent in appreciated property distributed as a grant to another charity.[48] The reason is that distribution of property for charitable purposes is not considered a sale or other disposition for purposes of this tax.

- Gain from disposition of excess business holdings held on December 31, 1969 (or received as a bequest under a trust irrevocable on May 26, 1969)

---

43. IRC § 4940(c)(4)(A); see Chapter 11. A similar rule operates for nonexempt charitable trusts described in IRC § 4947(a)(1) (Rev. Rul. 74-497, 1974-2 C.B. 383; see § 3.6).
44. IRC § 4940(c)(4)(D).
45. IRC § 4940(c)(4)(C); Reg. § 53.4940-1(f)(3). The legislative history of the Pension Protection Act of 2006 (see *supra* note 39) indicates that capital losses from the disposition of exempt function assets may be used to offset capital gains from the disposition of investment assets (but only to the extent of capital gains).
46. For private operating foundation purposes, net short-term gains defined by IRC § 1222(5), but not long-term or IRC § 1231 gains, are treated as adjusted gross income, but losses do not reduce income (Reg. § 53.4942(a)-2(d)(2)(ii)).
47. Rev. Rul. 73-320, 1973-2 C.B. 385.
48. Reg. § 53.4940-1(f)(1); see § 10.3.

TAX ON NET INVESTMENT INCOME

and sold to or redeemed by a disqualified person to reduce the holdings pursuant to the excess business holdings rules.[49]

- Gain realized in a merger or corporate reorganization ruled to be tax free.[50]
- Distributions of capital gains from a charitable lead trust.[51]

(ii) Basis. A foundation is to follow the tax rules in subchapter O of the Internal Revenue Code for purposes of determining gain or loss on the sale or other disposition of property.[52] The basis for calculating gain or loss on a purchased asset is equal to the amount paid by a private foundation for the assets to acquire or construct it, less any allowable depreciation or depletion. Assets acquired by gift, on the other hand, retain the donor's, or a carryover, basis and asset holding period. Therefore, there is no "step up" in the basis of gifted assets. The generally applicable income tax rules[53] are used to determine the carryover basis amount.[54] The basis of inherited property is equal to its value as reported on the federal estate tax return,[55] which ordinarily is its value on the date of the decedent's death.

For a sale of stock traded on an established securities market, a private foundation includes the sales proceeds in income the year that includes the trade date (not the date the proceeds are received). Thus, where a foundation places a sale order on stock with its broker on December 31, 1992, but does not deliver the stock certificates or receive the proceeds from the sale until January 8, 1993, the year of disposition and realization is 1992.[56]

Appreciation of assets held by a newly classified private foundation attributable to the time it was a supporting organization may not necessarily be subject to the net investment income excise tax.[57] A healthcare conglomerate asked the IRS to consider the issue concerning its reorganization. The parent supporting organization planned to sell its assets—charitable health centers, a publicly traded health maintenance organization, a for-profit physician

---

49. Reg. § 53.4940-1(d)(3); Priv. Ltr. Rul. 8214023.
50. IRC § 368 or other provision of IRC Subchapter C. E.g., Priv. Ltr. Rul. 8730061.
51. Tech. Adv. Mem. 9724005.
52. Reg. § 53.4940-1(f)(2).
53. IRC § 1015.
54. Reg. § 53.4940-1(f)(2).
55. Form 706.
56. Rev. Rul. 93-84, 1993-2 C.B. 225; also, Rev. Rul. 66-97, 1966-1 C.B. 190. A private foundation that has used the settlement date may need to consider whether a change to use of the trade date is a change in its accounting method to be reported (see § 12.1(d)(ii)). It may be sufficient for the foundation to simply disclose the change in an attachment to its annual information return.
57. Priv. Ltr. Rul. 9852023.

§ 10.4 CALCULATING TAXABLE NET INVESTMENT INCOME

practice management group, and insurance subsidiary—over a period of years, in a plan to convert itself into a grant-making private foundation. Although the federal tax law does not contain any rule regarding the basis of assets of a converted public charity, the IRS privately adopted a generous position. It allowed a step-up of basis to fair market value on the date a public charity was converted to a private foundation. Essentially, it treated the built-in gains as if they had been realized during the period the organization was a public charity (and therefore free of the excise tax). The ruling cited the transition rule allowing a step-up to value as of December 31, 1969, when the excise tax was first imposed, as the rationale for not requiring recognition of gain realized while the now-private foundation was classified as a supporting organization.[58]

(iii) Wash Sales. A private foundation is subject to limitations on certain capital loss transactions called wash sales.[59] A wash sale is a security sale that results in a loss occurring within 30 days before or after a purchase of the same security. Because net capital losses are not deductible against other investment income, it is advisable for the timing of losses and gains to be coordinated in view of both of these rules. Gains from security sales are not subject to the wash sale limitation, providing an opportunity to realize a gain to offset losses (that cannot be deducted) and immediately repurchase the security. A comparison of tax savings with the costs of the sale should be made.

(iv) Ponzi Scheme Losses. A loss from criminal fraud or embezzlement in a transaction entered into for profit (for example, an investment in a Ponzi scheme) is considered to be a theft loss, and thus is an ordinary (not a capital) loss. In reaching the conclusion that such losses are ordinary (rather than capital) losses, the IRS stated: "The character of an investor's loss related to fraudulent activity depends, in part, on the nature of the investment." Thus, a loss sustained from the worthlessness or other disposition of stock acquired on the open market for investment results in a capital loss, even if the decline is attributable to fraudulent activities of the corporation's officers. The distinction between a capital and ordinary loss in the circumstance rests on the intention of the company officials, namely, whether they had the specific intent to deprive the shareholder of money or property. When the officials intended to, and did, deprive the investors of money by criminal acts, the loss results from a theft and is therefore an ordinary loss, not a capital loss.[60]

---

58. See §§ 7.2(d) (concerning associated issues involving excess business holdings), 8.1(a) (regarding acquisition of jeopardizing investments).
59. IRC § 1091.
60. Rev. Rul. 2009-9, 2009-14 I.R.B. 735; also, Rev. Rul. 77-17, 1977-1 C.B. 44; see § 8.4(a).

(c) Interest and Annuities

Interest income is included in gross investment income if it is earned on the following types of obligations and investments:

- Bank savings or money market accounts, certificates of deposit, commercial paper, and other temporary cash investment accounts.
- Commercial paper, U.S. Treasury bills, notes, bonds, and other interest-bearing government obligations, and corporate bonds.
- Interest on student loans receivable,[61] on mortgage loans to purchasers in low-income housing projects, and loans to minority business owners as a program-related investment.
- Payments with respect to securities loans.[62]

Interest income need not be imputed on a no- or low-interest-bearing loan made and held for exempt purposes (essentially those loans classified as program-related investments).[63]

Municipal bond interest paid by state and local governments is excluded and is not taxed, even though it is included in adjusted income for private operating foundations. Expenses relating to such income are not deductible.[64]

In one instance, the IRS acknowledged that distributions from an annuity to a private foundation may constitute gross investment income, but found that there was no gross investment income in that instance because the decedent's basis in the annuity was greater than the fair market value of the annuity on the date of the decedent's death. Accordingly, the foundation would not be subject to the net investment income excise tax when it received distributions from the decedent's annuity.[65]

(d) Dividends

Dividends that are taxable include dividends paid on all types of securities, whether listed and marketable or privately held and unmarketable; mutual fund dividends (not including the portion reported as capital gain); for-profit

---

61. Reg. § 53.4940-1(d)(1).
62. Payments with respect to securities loans (IRC § 512(a)(5)) are excluded from unrelated business taxable income (IRC § 512(b)(1)) and therefore are included in gross investment income for purposes of the excise tax on net investment income (IRC § 4940(c)(2)).
63. Reg. § 1.7872-5T(b)(11); program-related investments are the subject of § 8.3.
64. IRC § 4940(c)(5).
65. Priv. Ltr. Rul. 200425027. As to the treatment of distributions from an estate for net investment income excise tax purposes generally, see § 10.4(g).

§ 10.4 CALCULATING TAXABLE NET INVESTMENT INCOME

subsidiary dividends; and corporate liquidating distributions classified as dividends,[66] but not including payments on complete redemption of shares that are classified as capital gains.[67]

The redemption of stock from a private foundation to the extent necessary for it to avoid the excess business holdings tax[68] is a sale or exchange not equivalent to a dividend, and the proceeds will not be taxed as investment income.[69] Similarly, a conversion of shares of a corporation owned by a private foundation for shares of another corporation, where the conversion occurs pursuant to a tax-free corporate reorganization,[70] does not result in net investment income.[71] Dividends on paid-up insurance policies that were donated to a private foundation, however, constitute net investment income.[72]

(e) Rent

Amounts paid in return for the use of real or personal property, commonly called rent, are taxable—whether the rental is related or unrelated to the private foundation's exempt activities.[73] The portion of rental income from debt-financed rental property includible in unrelated business income is excluded from the net investment income excise tax.[74]

(f) Royalties

Payments received in return for assignments of mineral interests owned by a foundation, including overriding royalties, are taxed. Only cost, not percentage, depletion is permitted as an expense. Royalty payments received in return for use of a private foundation's intangible property, such as the foundation's name or a publication containing a literary work commissioned by the foundation, are also taxable.

(g) Estate or Trust Distributions

Net investment income is to be determined under the principles of subtitle A of the Internal Revenue Code (except to the extent inconsistent with the net

---

66. IRC § 302(b)(1).
67. E.g., Priv. Ltr. Rul. 8001046.
68. See § 7.2(d).
69. Rev. Rul. 75-336, 1975-2 C.B. 110.
70. IRC § 368.
71. Priv. Ltr. Rul. 7847049.
72. Priv. Ltr. Rul. 8449069.
73. Reg. § 53.4940-1(d)(1).
74. IRC §§ 514(a)(1), 4940(c)(2).

TAX ON NET INVESTMENT INCOME

investment income excise tax rules).[75] The treatment of income received by an estate or trust and distributed to a beneficiary, in the hands of the beneficiary, is governed by subchapter J of subtitle A of the Internal Revenue Code (which contains provisions generally applicable to estates, trusts, and beneficiaries). Under the provisions of subchapter J, a beneficiary is generally required to include in gross income amounts distributed by a trust or estate,[76] and the amounts distributed have the same character in the beneficiary's hands as in the hands of the distributing estate or trust.[77] Such amounts are not included in income, however, if they qualify for the deduction for amounts paid or permanently set aside for a charitable purpose.[78] Further, a distribution to a private foundation from an estate, or from a nonexempt charitable or split-interest trust,[79] generally does not retain its character in the hands of the distributee private foundation for purposes of computing the net investment income excise tax.[80]

Accordingly, where an estate or trust reports an amount to be distributed to a private foundation as income, and avails itself of the charitable deduction for amounts paid or permanently set aside for a charitable purpose, the income reported by the estate or trust does not retain its character (as income) once distributed to the private foundation. Thus, this income is excluded from the private foundation's gross investment income for purposes of the net investment income excise tax.[81] Such income is therefore not taxable to either the estate or trust or the private foundation. This is true even if the income earned by the estate is recognized for financial purposes because the foundation follows the accrual method of accounting.[82]

The general rule that a distribution of income from an estate or trust is not taxed when it is received by a private foundation does not apply, however, where the estate or trust does not report the income. Thus, where a private foundation received Series E U.S. savings bonds from an estate, and no part of the periodic increase in the value of the bonds was reported as income by the estate or the decedent,[83] the private foundation was required to include in its gross investment income the interest income received upon its redemption

---

75. IRC § 4940(c)(1); Reg. § 53.4940-1(c)(1).
76. IRC § 662(a).
77. IRC § 662(b).
78. IRC § 663(a)(2). IRC § 642(c) allows a deduction from taxable income for estates, and certain trusts, of amounts which pursuant to the terms of the taxpayer's governing instrument are, during the tax year, paid or permanently set aside for a charitable or other purpose specified in IRC § 170(c).
79. IRC § 4947(a)(1), (2); see §§ 3.6, 3.7.
80. Reg. § 53.4940-1(d)(2).
81. E.g., Priv. Ltr. Rul. 8909066.
82. Priv. Ltr. Rul. 200224035.
83. IRC § 454.

§ 10.4 CALCULATING TAXABLE NET INVESTMENT INCOME

of the bonds.[84] Thus, where a private foundation was a named beneficiary of a Keogh account, and the income in the account was not reported by the decedent or their estate, the private foundation was subject to the net investment income excise tax on the proceeds of the account that were in excess of the contributions made to the account.[85] The private foundation does not recognize income for purposes of the net investment income excise tax when it receives such an asset, however, but only when it actually receives the income or disposes of the asset.[86]

The current regulations also provide for a different result with respect to distributions from a split-interest trust,[87] stating that the income of such a trust attributable to transfers in trust after May 26, 1969, retains its character in the hands of a distributee private foundation for purposes of the net investment income excise tax (unless such income is otherwise taken into account).[88,89] Thus, under this regulation, income distributions from a split-interest trust are included in a private foundation's net investment income. After studying the application of this regulation to distributions from various types of trusts and estates, the Treasury Department and the IRS concluded that the disparate treatment of distributions from split-interest trusts for purposes of the net investment income excise tax "is no longer appropriate." Therefore, until further guidance is promulgated, income distributions from trusts will not retain their character in the hands of a distributee private foundation for purposes of determining a private foundation's net investment income.[90]

---

84. Rev. Rul. 80-118, 1980-1 C.B. 254.
85. Priv. Ltr. Rul. 9633006. In other instances, the IRS has taken the view that proceeds of a donor's individual retirement account received by a private foundation on the donor's death constituted deferred compensation income that was not of a type similar to the types of income listed in the statute (that is, dividends, interest, and the like); therefore, these retirement account proceeds were not includible in the foundation's gross investment income (Priv. Ltr. Ruls. 9838028, 200003055, 200425027). In the third of these letter rulings, however, an estate tax charitable deduction was allowed for the value of the retirement accounts contributed to the foundation, so the income was reported by the decedent's estate (Priv. Ltr. Rul. 200425027). The IRS has also ruled that proceeds of this nature constitute income in respect of a decedent (IRC § 691) to the recipient private foundation (Priv. Ltr. Rul. 9818009).
86. Priv. Ltr. Rul. 9341008.
87. IRC § 4947(a)(2).
88. Because of the application of IRC § 671.
89. Reg. § 53.4940-1(d)(2). A court invalidated a special rule in another regulation (Reg. § 53.4942(a)-2(b)(2)) requiring a private foundation to increase its distributable amount by the income portion of distributions from a split-interest trust (*Ann Jackson Family Foundation v. Commissioner*, 15 F.3d 917 (9th Cir. 1994), *aff'g* 97 T.C. 534 (1991); see § 6.1(b)). The special rule for split-interest trusts in Reg. § 53.4940-1(d)(2), however, remains unchallenged.
90. Notice 2004-35, 2004-19 I.R.B. 889. The IRS previously concluded that distributions to a private foundation of capital gains, unlike gross investment income, of a split-interest

TAX ON NET INVESTMENT INCOME

(h) Partnership and S Corporation Income

When a private foundation buys, or is given, an interest in a partnership, its proportionate share of interest, dividends, rents, royalties, and capital gains earned by the partnership is included in its gross investment income. Items of partnership income retain the same character in a foundation's hands; thus, certain items of income may be subject to the net investment income excise tax and others to the unrelated business income tax, depending on their character. A partnership is required to provide Form K-1 to its partners each year to report their share of income earned by the partnership. A partnership must provide on Form K-1 any information needed to allow a tax-exempt partner, including a private foundation, to calculate any unrelated business taxable income. Rentals from indebted real estate are the most common type of unrelated income distributed from partnerships.[91]

As in the case of a partnership, a tax-exempt shareholder, including a private foundation, is taxed on its proportionate share of the S corporation's items of income. Unlike a partnership, however, all items of income from a subchapter S corporation reported to a private foundation on Form K-1 are subject to the unrelated business income tax, rather than the net investment income excise tax, even if the character of the income in the hands of the corporation is interest, dividends, rent, or royalties.[92]

---

trust are not taxable under IRC § 4940 (Priv. Ltr. Rul. 9724005). The rationale for this position is that net investment income of a private foundation is determined under the principles of IRC subtitle A (income taxes), except to the extent inconsistent with the provisions of IRC § 4940 (IRC § 4940(c)(1); Reg. § 53.4940-1(c)(1)). A charitable lead trust is a *complex trust* because its terms require distributions to charity; thus, the amount includible in gross income and the character of distributions to a private foundation are determined by IRC § 662. Distributions to charity pursuant to the governing instrument are excluded from the income of the beneficiaries (IRC §§ 642(c), 663(a)(2)). Therefore, capital gain distributions from a charitable lead trust to a private foundation are not includible in a private foundation's net investment income under general trust taxation principles. For purposes of the net investment income tax, the term *gross investment income* is defined in Reg. § 53.4940-1(d). *Capital gains and losses* are defined in Reg. § 53.4940-1(f). The first of these regulations provides that the income of a split-interest trust retains its character in the hands of a distributee private foundation, but that distributions from these trusts do not otherwise retain their character (Reg. § 53.53.4940-1(d)(2)). (That is, the distributions are treated as contributions rather than income to the private foundation.) There is no counterpart provision in the second of these regulations. Thus, the IRS was of the view that the retention-of-character concept does not apply to capital gains.

91. See § 11.4.
92. IRC § 512(e); e.g., Priv. Ltr. Rul. 201441018.

§ 10.5 REDUCTIONS TO GROSS INVESTMENT INCOME

For purposes of computing net investment income, there is allowed, as a deduction from gross investment income, all the ordinary and necessary expenses paid or incurred for the production or collection of gross investment income and for the management, conservation, or maintenance of property held for the production of income.[93] These expenses include that portion of a private foundation's operating expenses that is paid or incurred for the production or collection of gross investment income.[94] A private foundation's operating expenses include compensation of officers; other salaries and wages of employees; outside legal, accounting, and other professional fees; interest; and rent and taxes on property used in the private foundation's operations (but not the net investment income excise tax).[95]

Where a private foundation's officers or employees engage in activities on behalf of the private foundation for both investment purposes and for tax-exempt purposes, compensation and salaries paid to them must be allocated between the investment activities and the tax-exempt activities, also referred to as functions.[96] All other operating expenses of a private foundation are subject to allocation where paid or incurred for investment, program services, and foundation administration.[97]

(a) Deductions Allowed

The following deductions from gross investment income are permitted:

- Depreciation using a straight-line method calculated over the estimated useful life of the property; accelerated systems are not allowed.[98]

- Cost, but not percentage, depletion.[99]

- Investment management or counseling fees, except the portion allocable to tax-exempt interest.[100]

- Legal, accounting, and other professional fees allocable to investment income activity. A private foundation can ask its advisors to render

---

93. IRC § 4940(c)(3)(A).
94. Reg. § 53.4940-1(e)(1).
95. Reg. § 53.4940-1(e)(1).
96. Reg. § 53.4940-1(e)(1), (2)(iv).
97. Julia R. & Estelle L. Foundation, Inc. v. Commissioner, 70 T.C. 1 (1978), *aff'd*, 598 F.2d 755 (2d Cir. 1979).
98. IRC §§ 167, 4940(c)(3)(B)(i).
99. IRC § 4940(c)(3)(B)(ii).
100. IRC §§ 265 and 4940(c)(2).

TAX ON NET INVESTMENT INCOME

billings specifically identifying this type of an allocation based on time actually spent or another reasonable basis.[101]

- Taxes, insurance, maintenance, and other direct and specifically identifiable costs paid for property producing rental or royalty income, and an allocable part of these costs for administrative offices. Space rental is similarly treated.

- A proportionate part of operating expenses, including director, trustee officer, and staff fees, salaries and associated costs, occupancy costs, office and clerical costs, meetings, dues, administrative fees, and bank trustee fees.

- An allocable portion of expenses paid or incurred incident to a charitable program that produces investment income is deductible to the extent of the income earned.[102]

- Bond premium amortization that is deductible.[103]

- Allocable portion of cost of setting up the foundation.

The basis to be used for calculating the deduction for depreciation or depletion for purposes of the net investment income excise tax is the basis determined under the normal rules of subchapter O of the Internal Revenue Code.[104] Special rules apply to assets held by a foundation before 1969 when it began to claim depreciation or depletion for the first time in 1970.[105]

When a project or asset produces or is operated to produce income, the deductions associated with the activity must be allocated between the exempt and investment uses.[106] With these joint-purpose activities, however, the primary motivation for undertaking the project (investment or program) must be

---

101. Rev. Rul. 75-410, 1975-2 C.B. 446.
102. Reg. § 53.4940-1(e)(2)(iv); Priv. Ltr. Rul. 8047007.
103. Rev. Rul. 76-248, 1976-1 C.B. 353. This deduction is pursuant to IRC § 171.
104. Subject to the provisions of IRC § 4940(c)(3)(B), and without regard to IRC § 4940(c)(4)(B), relating to the basis for determining gain, or IRC § 362(c) (Reg. § 53.4940-1(e)(2)(iii)).
105. Reg. § 53.4940-1(e)(2)(iii). In the case of a private foundation that held royalty interests in oil and gas properties, which (prior to 1970) did not claim a depletion deduction, and which recorded depletion on its books using the percentage method (of IRC § 613), the IRS advised the private foundation to determine the basis of its depletable property as of January 1, 1970, and reduce its basis in the property by an amount equal to the potential cost depletion (as provided by IRC § 611; e.g., Beal Foundation v. United States, 76-1 U.S.T.C. ¶ 9149 (W.D. Tex. 1975), aff'd, 559 F.2d 359 (5th Cir. 1977)). Because the private foundation did not claim any depletion deduction on this royalty interest, however, the IRS held that the private foundation did not have to further reduce the basis by the amount of the percentage of depletion recorded on its books (Reg. § 53.4940-1(e)(2)(iii); Rev. Rul. 79-200, 1979-2 C.B. 364).
106. Reg. § 53.4940-1(e)(1)(ii).

§ 10.5 REDUCTIONS TO GROSS INVESTMENT INCOME

determined. When the expenses are incurred in connection with an exempt-function project, the regulations provide that allocable expenses are deductible only to the extent of the gross investment income from the project. For example, where rental income is incidentally realized from historic buildings held open to the public, deductions for amounts paid or incurred for the production of such income is limited to the amount of rental income includible as gross investment income during the tax year.[107]

The general rule allowing deductions against gross investment income does not reference Internal Revenue Code sections,[108] although certain portions of the regulations do.[109] Inasmuch as an expense allocation method is not prescribed, a foundation is free to use any reasonable method consistently (from year to year). The concepts and rules applicable to deductible expenses for unrelated business income tax purposes can be used as a guideline.[110] The manner in which the allocations are made should be documented.

(b) Deductions Not Allowed

Not every expenditure associated with the receipt of income by a private foundation is deductible in determining net investment income. There must be a *nexus* or an *integral relationship* between the expenses and the earning of gross investment income. Thus, IRS ruled that interest expense to borrow funds to lend interest free to another exempt organization was not an investment expense for purposes of calculating this excise tax.[111] The loan was not intended to, and did not, produce gross income; therefore, the interest paid was an administrative rather than an investment expense. A suitable nexus between the gross investment income and interest expense was lacking because the borrowed funds were used to make a grant with no intention of receiving income in return. In contrast, a suitable nexus was found with respect to interest expense incurred by a private foundation on a debt underlying a bond issue while the bond proceeds, destined for use in furthering charitable purposes, were temporarily invested.[112]

---

107. Reg. § 53.4940-1(e)(2)(iv).
108. E.g., IRC §§ 62, 162, 165, or 212.
109. Reg. § 53.4940-1(c)(2) states that the provisions of IRC §§ 103 and 265 are applicable for interest on certain government obligations and related expenses; Reg. § 53.4940-1(d)(3) refers to IRC § 301 for reporting distributions in redemption of stock; Reg. § 53.4940-1(f)(2) states that the basis for purposes of calculating capital gains and losses is determined under part II of Subchapter O.
110. See § 11.5.
111. Rev. Rul. 74-579, 1974-2 C.B. 383; Gen. Couns. Mem. 35554.
112. Indiana University Retirement Community, Inc. v. Commissioner, 92 T.C. 891 (1989). The court distinguished the situation from that of Rev. Rul. 74–579, 1974-2 C.B. 383, in which "the proceeds of the loan were not a source of investment income."

TAX ON NET INVESTMENT INCOME

A court held that a trustee's termination fee paid by private foundation that was the sole beneficiary of the trust not allowable as a deduction against gross investment income because it was a distribution expense of the trust having nothing to do with production or collection of any specific item of income of the foundation. This court also held that the foundation could not deduct unused deductions from the final trust return (customarily deductible to a noncharitable beneficiary)[113] against its gross investment income.[114]

Other examples of expenses that are not deductible from gross investment income follow.

- Charitable distributions and administrative expenses associated with grant-making programs are not deductible as investment expense.[115] Similarly, expenses of charitable programs directly conducted by the foundation are not deductible.

- Purchases of exempt-function assets, depreciation of their cost, and cost of their maintenance, repair, or conservation are not deductible except to the extent of taxable revenues from the assets.[116]

- A charitable deduction[117] is not permitted, and net operating losses incurred in a preceding year do not carry forward from year to year.[118]

- The allocable portion of expenses of an exempt-function income-producing property, or activity, in excess of the income produced therefrom and reportable as investment income is not deductible.[119]

- Expenses allocable to taxable unrelated business income are not deductible.[120] (Such income is not included in gross investment income in the first place.)[121]

- The special corporation deductions, including the dividends received deduction, are not allowed.[122]

---

113. IRC § 642(h)(2).
114. Lettie Pate Whitehead Foundation, Inc. v. United States, 606 F.2d 534 (5th Cir. 1979).
115. Julia R. and Estelle L. Foundation, Inc. v. Commissioner, 70 T.C. 1 (1978), *aff'd*, 598 F.2d 755 (2d Cir. 1979).
116. Historic House Museum Corp. v. Commissioner, 70 T.C. 12 (1978). The purchase of these types of assets may be treated as a qualifying distribution (see § 6.5(b)).
117. IRC §§ 170, 642(c).
118. Reg. § 53.4940-1(e)(1)(iii).
119. The excess expense is, however, treated as a qualifying distribution (see § 6.4(a)).
120. Reg. § 53.4940-1(e)(1)(i).
121. See § 10.4(a).
122. Reg. § 53.4940-1(e)(1)(iii); Staff of Joint Comm. on Internal Revenue Tax'n, 91st Cong., 2d Sess., General Explanation of the Tax Reform Act of 1969 29 (Comm. Print 1970).

§ 10.6 FOREIGN FOUNDATIONS

Foreign private foundations are generally taxed at a rate of 4 percent on their U.S. source[123] gross investment income.[124] Tax treaties with some foreign countries, including Canada, provide an exemption from the tax.[125] The excise tax must be specifically mentioned in a tax treaty for an exemption to apply.[126]

In an unusual instance, a foreign private foundation owned an investment portfolio held in an investment fund in the United States. The IRS issued this foundation a ruling that, when the fund becomes a disregarded entity, its income and assets will be reported as income and assets of the foundation, with the income exempt from federal income tax. The foundation, however, will be required to take this income into account in determining its U.S. source gross income subject to this 4 percent excise tax.[127]

Though the excise tax is applied to all investment income earned by a foreign private foundation, those that receive substantially all (at least 85 percent) of their support (other than capital gains) from sources outside the United States are not subject to the other excise taxes imposed on domestic private foundations.[128] The notice requirements and termination tax[129] are also inapplicable.[130]

The U.S. source investment income of foreign organizations, both privately and publicly supported, is subject to a 4 percent tax withholding requirement.[131] Because they are ineligible to receive deductible contributions and have no U.S. source taxable income, foreign charities do not normally seek recognition of exempt status for U.S. purposes. To avoid the withholding tax, however, and to more easily receive grants from private foundations,[132] a foreign organization that can qualify as a public charity due either to its activities or to its sources of support might wish to apply for recognition of its public character.[133] A nonexempt charitable organization is subject to normal income tax withholding on its foreign-source U.S. income.

This body of law is the substitute, for foreign organizations, for the conventional net investment income excise tax applicable to private foundations.[134]

---

123. IRC § 861.
124. IRC § 4948(a); Reg. § 53.4948-1(a)(1). Gross investment income is defined in IRC § 4940(c)(2) (see § 10.3(a)).
125. Rev. Rul. 74-183, 1974-1 C.B. 328.
126. Reg. § 4948-1(a)(3); Rev. Rul. 84-169, 1984-2 C.B. 216.
127. Priv. Ltr. Rul. 201808010.
128. See Chapters 5-9.
129. See §§ 2.7, 13.7.
130. IRC § 4948(b).
131. IRC § 1443(b).
132. See § 9.6.
133. The process of seeking recognition of exemption is discussed in § 2.7.
134. See § 10.1.

TAX ON NET INVESTMENT INCOME

This law does not, however, affect the category of U.S. tax exemption under which a foreign organization can be classified. For example, a foreign private foundation receiving 84 percent of its support from sources outside the United States could be recognized as an exempt social welfare organization,[135] assuming it was not in existence on October 9, 1969.[136] This type of foreign private foundation however, could not be recognized as an exempt social welfare organization if it were in existence on that date.[137]

A foreign private foundation that receives at least 85 percent of its financial support from sources outside the United States, other than gross investment income, cannot be tax-exempt under U.S. law if it engaged in a prohibited transaction.[138] The term *prohibited transaction* means an act or failure to act (other than with respect to the minimum investment return rules)[139] that would subject the foreign foundation or a disqualified person with respect to it to liability for a penalty for violating one or more of the private foundation rules[140] or for a termination tax,[141] if the foreign organization were a U.S. organization.[142] For example, a foreign private foundation received a ruling that it was in compliance with the excess business holdings rules and thus avoided engaging in a prohibited transaction.[143]

§ 10.7 EXEMPTION FROM TAX ON INVESTMENT INCOME

A private foundation that qualifies as an *exempt operating foundation* is exempt from the tax on net investment income.[144] To be an exempt operating foundation for any year, a private foundation must have the following characteristics:

1. It qualifies as a private operating foundation.[145]

---

135. See § 1.2.
136. *Id.*
137. E.g., Priv. Ltr. Rul. 200846041.
138. IRC § 4948(c)(1); Reg. § 53.4948-1(c)(1).
139. IRC § 4942(e). See §§ 6.1, 6.2.
140. IRC § 6684. This provision provides that if any person becomes liable for a private foundation excise tax (other than the IRC § 4940 net investment income or 4948(a) gross investment income taxes) by reason of any act or failure to act which is not due to reasonable cause and either (1) such person has theretofore been liable for tax under Chapter 42, or (2) such act or failure to act is both willful and flagrant, then such person shall be liable for a penalty equal to the amount of such tax (*id.*; Reg. § 301.6684-1(a)).
141. See § 13.7.
142. IRC § 4948(c)(2); Reg. § 53.4948-1(c)(2).
143. Priv. Ltr. Rul. 201737003.
144. IRC § 4940(d)(1).
145. See § 3.1.

§ 10.7 EXEMPTION FROM TAX ON INVESTMENT INCOME

2. It has been publicly supported for at least 10 years.[146]
3. At all times during the year involved, the governing body of the private foundation consisted of individuals of whom at least 75 percent were not *disqualified individuals*,[147] and was broadly representative of the general public.
4. At no time during the tax year did the private foundation have an officer who was a disqualified individual.[148]

The purpose of this exemption is to eliminate this tax liability for organizations that are inherently not private foundations, such as museums and libraries.[149]

Also (although, in a sense, this is not really an "exemption"), a private foundation that is on the accrual method of accounting is not required to recognize income, for purposes of the tax on net investment income, received by a trust containing assets destined for the foundation, where the foundation lacks control over the assets.[150]

---

146. IRC § 4940(d)(3)(A). See §§ 15.4, 15.5.
147. Namely, substantial contributors (see § 4.1) and certain related persons. IRC § 4940(d)(3)(B)-(E).
148. IRC § 4940(d)(2). An organization claiming to be an exempt operating foundation must obtain an IRS determination letter to that effect to be exempt from the tax on net investment income (Rev. Proc. 2023-5, 2023-1 I.R.B. 265 § 7.04(4)). This request is made by submitting Form 8940 electronically at www.pay.gov; the user fee for this type of request is currently $550 (Rev. Proc. 2023-5, 2023-1 I.R.B. 265 §§ 4.02(6), 7.02 and App. A (Schedule of User Fees), as modified by Rev. Proc. 2023-12, 2023-17 I.R.B. 768 §§ 3.01, 3.03). Also, Instructions for Form 8940 (Apr. 2023), Part II and Schedule G (reclassification of private foundation status).
149. H.R. Rep. No. 98-861, at 1084 (1984).
150. Priv. Ltr. Rul. 200224035.

CHAPTER ELEVEN

Unrelated Business Activity

§ 11.1 **General Rules** 468
   (a) Overview 468
   (b) Trade or Business Income 469
   (c) Substantially Related Activity 471
   (d) Regularly Carried On 474
   (e) Real Estate Activities 475

§ 11.2 **Exceptions** 477
   (a) Royalties 479
   (b) Rents 480
   (c) Research 483
   (d) Nonbusiness Activities 484

§ 11.3 **Rules Specifically Applicable to Private Foundations** 485
   (a) Business Enterprises 486
   (b) Permitted Businesses 488
   (c) Partnerships and S Corporations 489
   (d) Community Foundations' Grant-Making Services 491
   (e) Provision of Technical Assistance 494

§ 11.4 **Unrelated Debt-Financed Income Rules** 495
   (a) Acquisition Indebtedness 495
   (b) Related-Use Exceptions 499
   (c) Includible Income 500

§ 11.5 **Calculating and Reporting the Tax** 501
   (a) General Rules 501
   (b) Bucketing Rule 502
   (c) Tax Rates 505
   (d) Tax Computation and Reporting Rules 506
   (e) Penalties and Additions to Tax 507
   (f) Statute of Limitations 508

The unrelated business rules constitute a significant component of the general federal tax law for tax-exempt organizations.[1] These rules impact private foundations on a more limited basis, however, because of the tax law rules concerning excess business holdings,[2] which essentially bar foundations from actively engaging in an unrelated business. Nonetheless, certain aspects of the unrelated business income rules are applicable to private foundations.

A private foundation may receive unrelated business income, for example, from a permitted minority interest in a partnership. During the period of time a private foundation is allowed to dispose of an excess business interest, it might receive business income. Those private operating foundations that

---

1. In general, *Tax-Exempt Organizations*, Chapters 24 and 25.
2. See Chapter 7.

charge fees or sell the products of their programs must determine whether this income-producing activity qualifies as a permitted functionally related business activity. A private foundation may have a mortgaged rental property. Finally, the exceptions to these rules are important to all private foundations because, according to the literal definition, investment income is unrelated business income.

§ 11.1 GENERAL RULES

Taxation of a tax-exempt organization's unrelated business income is based on the concept that the approach is a more effective and workable sanction for enforcement of this aspect of the tax law. Rather than deny or revoke the exempt status, the law requires an otherwise tax-exempt organization to pay tax on certain types of income.

(a) Overview

This body of law is fundamentally simple: The unrelated business income tax applies only to business income that arises from an activity conducted by a tax-exempt organization—technically known as a *trade or business*—that is unrelated to the organization's exempt purposes. The purpose of the unrelated business income tax is to place an exempt organization's business activities on the same tax basis as the nonexempt business endeavors with which they compete.[3]

The term *unrelated trade or business* means any trade or business, the conduct of which is not substantially related to the exercise or performance of the exempt purpose or function of the tax-exempt organization carrying on the trade or business. The conduct of a trade or business is not substantially related to an organization's tax-exempt purpose solely because the organization needs the income or because the profits derived from the business are used for its exempt purposes.

Absent one or more exceptions,[4] gross income of a tax-exempt organization subject to the tax on unrelated income—and most exempt organizations are—is includible in the computation of unrelated business taxable income if the income is from a trade or business, the trade or business is regularly carried on, and the conduct of the business is not substantially related to the organization's performance of its tax-exempt purposes.[5]

---

3. Reg. § 1.513-1(b).
4. See § 11.2.
5. Reg. § 1.513-1(a).

(b) Trade or Business Income

To have unrelated business income, a private foundation must first be found to be engaging in a *trade or business*, defined to include any activity carried on for the production of income from the sale of goods or performance of services.[6] The U.S. Tax Court held that a *business* is conducted with "continuity and regularity" and in a "competitive manner similar to commercial enterprises."[7] Voluntary contributions and grants paid to the foundation with donative intention are, by contrast, not business income. A foundation does, however, receive business income when it invests its assets in return for interest, dividends, rents, or royalties. Although embodied in the definition of a business, income received from passive investments is exempt from the unrelated business income tax.[8]

A few foundations use their assets to conduct an active business in which services and goods are provided to accomplish their exempt purposes. Private foundations operate museums, publish educational materials, manage low-income housing projects, and conduct other programs that, according to the literal definition, constitute a trade or business.[9] These foundations require visitors to pay admission fees, to pay tuition to attend educational seminars, and to pay rent and other forms of business income. This chapter considers situations when this income becomes unrelated business income subject to income tax.

Some courts have embellished the definition of a business with another criterion, which is that an activity, to be considered a business for tax purposes, must be conducted with a *profit motive*.[10] Under this test, an activity conducted simply to produce some revenue, but without an expectation of producing a profit (similar to that considered under the hobby loss rules), is not a business.[11] If an activity is carried on in a manner similar to that of a commercial business, it may constitute a trade or business.[12]

---

6. IRC § 513; Reg. § 1.513-1(b).
7. National Water Well Association, Inc. v. Commissioner, 92 T.C. 75, 84 (1989).
8. See § 11.2. The IRS ruled that a tax-exempt university was not engaged in unrelated business when it enabled charitable remainder trusts, as to which it was trustee and remainder interest beneficiary, to participate in the investment return generated by the university's endowment fund, inasmuch as the university was not receiving any economic return by reason of the arrangements (e.g., Priv. Ltr. Rul. 200703037).
9. See § 3.1.
10. IRC § 513(c); Reg. § 1.513-1(b).
11. West Virginia State Medical Association v. Commissioner, 882 F.2d 123 (4th Cir. 1989), *aff'g* 91 T.C. 651 (1988).
12. IRC § 513(c); Reg. § 1.513-1(b); Better Business Bureau v. United States, 326 U.S. 279, 283 (1945); Scripture Press Foundation v. United States, 285 F.2d 800 (Ct. Cl. 1961); Greater United Navajo Development Enterprises, Inc. v. Commissioner, 74 T.C. 69 (1980).

§ 11.1 GENERAL RULES

Historically, the IRS almost always prevailed on the issue as to whether an activity rose to the level of a trade or business. One of the rare exceptions to this phenomenon is a federal court of appeals decision in 1996. On that occasion, where the appellate court held that a tax-exempt organization must carry out extensive activities over a substantial period of time for the activities to be considered a business, the court ruled that an income-producing activity was not a business for unrelated business purposes.[13] In other instances, courts have regarded an economic activity of a tax-exempt organization as something less than a *business*, relying on an absence of competition and lack of profits.[14]

An organization regularly operating an investment service business, even though its customers were other tax-exempt organizations, was also not found to qualify for tax exemption because providing investment services on a regular basis for a fee is a trade or business ordinarily carried on for profit.[15] Similarly, because a conference center was operated in a commercial manner on a break-even basis, it was also denied exemption.[16] It organized and sponsored more than 600 educational conferences a year in areas as diverse as civil and human rights, international relations, public policy, the environment, medical education, mental health, and disability. Twenty percent of the events were held for government clients, 50 percent for nonprofit and/or educational clients, and 30 to 40 percent for other users, including a large number of weddings and other private events. Only a few of the events were financially subsidized with lower prices. The court stated that, "as it is clear from the facts that plaintiff engages in conduct of both a commercial and exempt nature, the question whether it is entitled to tax-exempt status turns largely on whether its activities are conducted primarily for a commercial or for an exempt purpose" and decided the former was the case.[17]

The IRS is empowered to fragment a tax-exempt organization's operations, run as an integrated whole, into its component parts in search of one or more unrelated businesses. That is, an activity does not lose identity as a trade or business merely because it is carried on within a larger aggregate of similar activities or within a larger complex of other endeavors that may, or may not, be related to the exempt purposes of the organization.[18] This *fragmentation*

---

13. American Academy of Family Physicians v. United States, 91 F.3d 1155 (8th Cir. 1996).
14. Laborer's International Union of North America v. Commissioner, 82 T.C.M. 158 (2001); Vigilant Hose Company of Emmitsburg v. United States, 2001-2 U.S.T.C. ¶ 50,458 (D. Md. 2001).
15. Rev. Rul. 69-528, 1969-2 C.B. 127; Gen. Couns. Mem. 34369.
16. Airlie Foundation v. Internal Revenue Service, 283 F. Supp. 2d 58 (D.D.C. 2003).
17. *Id*. at 64.
18. IRC § 513(c); Reg. § 1.513-1(b).

rule enables the IRS to ferret out unrelated business activity that is conducted with, or as a part of, related business activity. The rule is intended to prevent exempt organizations from hiding unrelated business activities within a cluster of related ones.

The operation of a typical museum shop is a classic example of a related business that can be fragmented and found to embody an unrelated segment. The shop itself is undoubtedly a trade or business, often established with a profit motive and operated in a commercial manner. While the books and art reproductions sold serve an educational purpose, the souvenirs and handicrafts that also are often sold are not necessarily treated as educational. The fragmentation rule requires that all items sold be analyzed to identify the educational items from which the profit is not taxable, and the unrelated souvenir items that may not only be taxable but also impermissible under the excess business holdings rules.[19] Likewise, the IRS applied the fragmentation rule to determine when the making and sales of caskets by an exempt monastery were and were not unrelated business.[20]

The IRS also uses the fragmentation rule in the context of the provision of services by tax-exempt organizations. For example, the IRS determined that the use of the golf course of a university by its students and employees was not unrelated business, while use of the course by alumni of the university, members of its President's Club, other major donors, and guests of these individuals was unrelated business.[21] As another example, the IRS used the fragmentation rule to differentiate between related and unrelated educational and religious tours conducted by a tax-exempt organization.[22]

Where an activity carried on for profit constitutes an unrelated trade or business, no part of the business may be excluded from that classification merely because it does not result in profit.[23]

(c) Substantially Related Activity

Generally, gross income derives from unrelated trade or business if the regular conduct of the trade or business that produces the income is not substantially related to the purposes for which tax exemption was recognized.[24] This requirement necessitates an examination of the relationship between the business activities that generate the particular income in question—the

---

19. See Chapter 7.
20. Priv. Ltr. Rul. 200033049.
21. Tech. Adv. Mem. 9645004; see § 11.3(b).
22. Tech. Adv. Mem. 9702004.
23. IRC § 513(c); Reg. § 1.513-1(b).
24. IRC § 513(a); Reg. § 1.513-1(d)(1).

§ 11.1 GENERAL RULES

activities, that is, of producing or distributing the goods or performing the services involved—and the accomplishment of the organization's tax-exempt purposes.[25] The fact that an organization uses revenue for one or more exempt purposes does not make the underlying business activity a related one.[26]

A trade or business is related to an organization's tax-exempt purposes only where the conduct of the business activity has a causal relationship to the achievement of its tax-exempt purpose(s) and the relationship is a substantial one.[27] Thus, for the conduct of a trade or business from which a particular amount of gross income is derived to be substantially related to the purposes for which tax exemption is granted, the conduct must contribute importantly to the accomplishment of the particular organization's exempt purposes. If the activity does not accomplish an exempt purpose, the income from the sale of the goods or the performance of the services is not derived from the conduct of related trade or business. The finding of such a causal relationship depends, in each case, on the facts and circumstances involved.[28] The following are examples of related income-producing activities that a private foundation might conduct: Sale of educational materials and publications, sale of tickets for a cultural performance or lecture, conference or seminar fees, scientific research consultations or publications, student academic counseling fees, sale of museum admission tickets, and art exhibition loan charges.

The size and extent of the activities involved are considered in relation to the nature and extent of the tax-exempt function that they purport to serve.[29] If an organization conducts related activities on a larger scale than is reasonably necessary for performance of the functions, the gross income attributable to that portion of the activities in excess of the needs of tax-exempt functions constitutes unrelated business income. For example, a college was found to emphasize "revenue maximization" in the promotion of rock concerts in its multipurpose college auditorium to the exclusion of other considerations, indicating that the trade or business was not operated as an integral part of educational programs and that the activity, therefore, failed the substantially related test.[30] This type of income is not derived from the production or distribution of goods or the performance of services that contribute importantly to the accomplishment of any tax-exempt purpose of the organization.[31] The sale of literature, evaluation equipment, and instructional tapes on use of

---

25. Reg. § 1.513-1(d)(1).
26. IRC § 513(a).
27. Reg. § 1.513-1(d)(2).
28. Id.
29. Reg. § 1.513-1(d)(3).
30. Priv. Ltr. Rul. 9147008.
31. Id.

devices designed to measure the extent of a child's developmental deficiencies was ruled to produce related income to an organization devoted to helping children.[32]

Gross income derived from charges for the performance of exempt functions constitutes gross income from the conduct of a *related trade or business*.[33] For revenues to be treated as *related*, the service or product resulting from exempt functions must ordinarily be sold in substantially the same state they were in on completion of the exempt functions.[34] If, however, a product is utilized or exploited in further business endeavors, beyond those reasonably appropriate or necessary for disposition in the state it is in on completion of tax-exempt functions, the gross income derived from these endeavors is considered to be derived from the conduct of unrelated business.[35]

An asset or facility necessary to the conduct of tax-exempt functions and so used may also be utilized in a commercial endeavor. This is called a *dual use* arrangement. An illustration of this type of use is museum gallery space rented out for private parties in the evening. The mere fact that the gallery is used during the day for educational exhibits does not, by itself, make the income from the commercial rental related income. The test, instead, is whether the rental to private individuals contributes importantly to the accomplishment of the museum's tax-exempt purposes or qualifies for the rental exception.[36]

Activities carried on by an organization in the performance of exempt functions may generate goodwill or other intangibles that are capable of being exploited in commercial endeavors. Where an organization exploits an intangible such as its mailing list or logo, in a commercial fashion, the mere fact that the resultant income depends in part on an exempt function of the organization does not make it related income. In these cases, unless the commercial activities themselves contribute importantly to the accomplishment of an exempt purpose, the income that they produce is gross income from the conduct of unrelated business.[37] Another example of exploitation is advertising in a foundation's periodical that contains reports from a drug abuse study it conducted.[38]

---

32. Priv. Ltr. Rul. 9851052. Likewise, the operation of a guest house, used only by attendees at conferences conducted by a private operating foundation (see § 3.1), was ruled to be a related business (Priv. Ltr. Rul. 200030027).
33. Reg. § 1.513-1(d)(4)(i).
34. Reg. § 1.513-1(d)(4)(ii).
35. *Id.*
36. Reg. § 1.513-1(d)(4)(iii); if unrelated see § 11.2(b) for a rental income exception that depends on the level of service the organization provides to the tenant.
37. Reg. § 1.513-1(d)(4)(iv); see § 11.2(a) for a royalty income exception.
38. Reg. § 1.512(a)-1(d)(1), (f).

(d) Regularly Carried On

To be taxable, an unrelated business must be *regularly carried on*.[39] In determining whether a particular business is regularly carried on by a tax-exempt organization, consideration must be given to the frequency and continuity with which the activities that are productive of the income are conducted and the manner in which they are pursued.[40] This requirement is applied in light of the purpose of the unrelated business income tax, which, as noted, is to place tax-exempt organization business activities on the same tax basis as the nonexempt business endeavors with which they compete. Thus, specific business activities of a tax-exempt organization will ordinarily be deemed to be *regularly carried on* if they manifest a similar frequency and continuity, and are pursued in a manner similar to comparable commercial activities of nonexempt organizations.[41]

Where income-producing activities are of a kind normally conducted by nonexempt commercial organizations on a year-round basis, their conduct by a tax-exempt organization over a period of only a few weeks does not constitute the regular carrying on of a trade or business.[42] Where income-producing activities are of a kind normally undertaken by nonexempt commercial organizations only on a seasonal basis, however, the conduct of the activities by a tax-exempt organization during a significant part of the season ordinarily constitutes the regular conduct of trade or business.[43]

In determining whether intermittently conducted activities are regularly carried on, the manner in which the activities are conducted must be compared with the manner in which commercial activities are normally pursued by nonexempt organizations. In general, exempt organization business activities that are engaged in only discontinuously or periodically are not considered regularly carried on if they are conducted without the competitive and promotional efforts typical of commercial endeavors.[44] Sales that are systematically and consistently promoted and carried on are deemed to be regularly carried on.[45]

Certain intermittent income-producing activities, such as a benefit golf tournament, occur so infrequently that neither their recurrence nor the manner of their conduct will cause them to be regarded as a business activity that is regularly carried on.[46] Likewise, activities are not regarded as regularly carried on merely because they are conducted on an annually recurrent basis.[47]

---

39. IRC § 512(a)(1).
40. Reg. § 1.513-1(c)(1).
41. *Id.*
42. Reg. § 1.513-1(c)(2)(i).
43. *Id.*
44. Reg. § 1.513-1(c)(2)(ii).
45. *Id.*
46. E.g., Priv. Ltr. Rul. 200128059.
47. Reg. § 1.513-1(c)(2)(iii).

When a museum rented an airplane to a company to use for testing purposes, the IRS contended that the personal property rents paid by the company were taxable unrelated business income. A court disagreed with the IRS's position, held that the lease was not a business regularly carried on, and agreed with the museum that the transaction was a "one-time, completely fortuitous lease of unique equipment."[48]

(e) Real Estate Activities

A tax-exempt organization may acquire real property under a variety of circumstances and for a variety of reasons. The acquisition may be by purchase or by contribution and be undertaken to advance exempt purposes or to make an investment. The activity may be, or may be seen as being, part of dealings in the ordinary course of a business. Where exempt functions are not involved, the dichotomy becomes whether the exempt organization is a passive investor or is a dealer in property. Often the issue arises when the property, or portions of it, is being sold; is the exempt organization liquidating an investment or selling property to customers in the ordinary course of business?

The elements to take into account in this evaluation are many. One is the purpose for which the property was acquired. Others are the length of time the property was held, the purpose for which the property was held, the proximity of the sale to the purchase of the property, the activities of the exempt organization in improving and disposing of the property, and the frequency, continuity, and size of the sales of the property.

In the absence of use of the property for exempt functions, the factor of frequency of sales tends to be the most important of the criteria.[49] Even in this context, the activity may not be characterized as a business if the sales activity results from unanticipated, externally introduced factors that make impossible the continued preexisting use of the property. The IRS places emphasis on the presence of and the reasons for improvements on the land.

The exception from unrelated income taxation for capital gain,[50] which interrelates with these rules, is not available when the property is sold in circumstances in which the exempt organization is a dealer in the property. Where dealer status exists or is imposed, the property is considered to be property sold in the ordinary course of business, giving rise to ordinary income.

The standard followed in making these determinations, as to whether property is held primarily for sale in the ordinary course of business or is held for investment, is a primary purpose test. In this setting, the word *primary* has

---

48. Museum of Flight Foundation v. United States, 99-1 U.S.T.C. ¶ 50,311 (D. Wash. 1999).
49. In part, this is due to the regularly carried on test (see § 11.1(d)).
50. See § 11.2.

§ 11.1 GENERAL RULES

been interpreted to mean "of first importance" or "principally."[51] Applying this standard, the IRS ruled that ordinary income would not result unless a "sales purpose" is "dominant."[52]

In a typical instance, the IRS reviewed a proposed sale of certain real estate interests held by a public charity. In this case, substantially all of the property was received by bequest and had been held for a significant period of time. The decision was made to sell the property (liquidate the investment) due to the enactment of legislation adverse to the investment, so as to receive fair market value. Availability of the property for sale was not advertised to the public. Applying the primary purpose test, the IRS concluded that the proposed sales did not involve property held primarily for sale to customers in the ordinary course of business.[53]

By contrast, a charitable organization purchased real estate, divided it into lots, and improved the lots. The project evolved into the equivalent of a municipality. Lots were sold to the public pursuant to a marketing plan involving real estate companies. The IRS concluded that the subdivision, development, and sale of the lots was a business that was regularly carried on, "in a manner that is similar to a for-profit residential land development company." The organization advanced the argument that the land development and sales were done in furtherance of exempt purposes, by attracting members who participate in its educational programs.[54] But the IRS concluded that the relationship between the sales of lots for single-family homes and the organization's goal of increasing program attendance was "somewhat tenuous." Therefore, the IRS held that the resulting sales income was unrelated business income.[55] The IRS, however, approved exclusion of gain on the sale of farmland owned by an orphanage. The sales were expected to involve as many as nine separate parcels over a period of several years. The organization characterized its proposed marketing as "patient and passive" without improvements being made to enhance the sale to developers. The fact that the property would not be advertised through real estate brokers was also noted as a fact evidencing the nonbusiness nature of the sales activity.[56] In a comparable instance, a "liquidity challenged" charitable trust that wanted to sell leased fee interests in three condominium properties was held by the IRS to be able to utilize the capital gain exclusion; the underlying land was acquired by the trust by gift nearly 100 years before the proposed transaction, and most

---

51. Malat v. Riddell, 383 U.S. 569 (1966).
52. Priv. Ltr. Rul. 9316032.
53. Id.
54. An argument of this nature was successful in Junaluska Assembly Housing, Inc. v. Commissioner, 86 T.C. 1114 (1986).
55. Tech. Adv. Mem. 200047049.
56. Priv. Ltr. Rul. 200210029.

of the land had been maintained to produce rental income in support of the trust's exempt activities.[57]

Even if the primary purpose underlying the acquisition and holding of real property is advancement of exempt purposes, the IRS may apply the fragmentation rule[58] in search of unrelated business. As the IRS stated the matter in one instance, a charitable organization "engaged in substantial regularly carried on unrelated trade [or] business as a component of its substantially related land purchase activity."[59] The IRS looked to substantial and frequent sales of surplus land that were not intended for exempt use, and found that those sales were unrelated businesses. The same factors were used to reach that conclusion as are used in the general context, such as the sale of land shortly after its purchase and the extent of improvements.

§ 11.2 EXCEPTIONS

A variety of types of income or activities is exempt from taxation under the unrelated business income rules, though some of these exceptions are of little or no utility to private foundations.

The fact that forms of passive income are exempt from unrelated business income taxation, however, is significant to private foundations.[60] This type of income is exempt from unrelated income taxation by virtue of a host of what are euphemistically termed *modifications*.[61] For private foundations, the following types of income that are protected by the passive income modifications are the most pertinent:

- Dividends, interest, payments with respect to securities loans, amounts received or accrued as consideration for entering into agreements to make loans, income from notional principal contracts, annuities, and other substantially similar income from ordinary and routine investments.[62]

- Royalties, including overriding royalties, whether measured by production or by gross or taxable income from a property.[63]

---

57. Priv. Ltr. Rul. 200728044.
58. See § 11.1(b).
59. Priv. Ltr. Rul. 200119061.
60. See § 7.1(b).
61. IRC § 512(b). These items of income and capital gain are likely, however, to be subject to the excise tax on net investment income (see Chapter 10).
62. IRC § 512(b)(1); Reg. § 1.512(b)-1(a)(1). Inclusions of subpart F income (IRC § 951(a)(1)(A)) and inclusions of global intangible low-taxed income (IRC § 951A(a)) are treated in the same manner as dividends (Reg. § 1.512(b)-1(a)(1)).
63. IRC § 512(b)(2); Reg. § 1.512(b)-1(b).

§ 11.2 EXCEPTIONS

- Rents from real property and rents from personal property leased with real property (where the rent from personal property is incidental to the total rent).[64]

- Capital gains and gains recognized from the lapse or termination of options to buy or sell securities.[65]

In one instance, amounts realized from the disposition of timber on timberland owned by a private foundation were held to be excludible capital gain,[66] because of a special rule treating this type of economic gain or loss as capital in nature.[67] Some sales of property that may appear to yield capital gain may not, in fact, if it is determined that the sales amount to an activity of selling property to customers in the ordinary course of business.[68] The IRS developed factors to consider in making this determination: the purpose for which the property was acquired; the cost of the property to be sold; the frequency, continuity, and size of the sales; the activities of the owner in the improvement and disposition of the property; the extent of improvements made to the property; the proximity of the time of sale in relation to the date of purchase; the purpose for which the property was held; and the prevailing market conditions.[69]

A private foundation received, out of its founder's estate, accounts receivable in connection with legal services provided by the founder. The foundation was not involved in any activities that gave rise to these legal fees. The IRS ruled that receipt of the receivables was passive income, not subject to unrelated business income taxation.[70]

Income that is passive in nature may nonetheless be subject, in whole or in part, to unrelated income taxation where the income is debt-financed income[71] or the income is derived from a controlled corporation.[72]

As to the latter, the rule applies where there is the appropriate degree of control of the subsidiary by the parent. This type of control requires the ownership of stock possessing more than 50 percent of the total combined voting

---

64. IRC § 512(b)(3)(A)(i); Reg. § 1.512(b)-1(c)(2)(i), (ii).
65. IRC § 512(b)(5); Reg. § 1.512(b)-1(d).
66. Priv. Ltr. Rul. 9252028.
67. IRC § 631(b).
68. E.g., Priv. Ltr. Rul. 9619068 (where a community foundation was able to sell its interests in developed real estate without participating in a commercial business of sales to customers).
69. E.g., Priv. Ltr. Rul. 9619069.
70. Priv. Ltr. Rul. 201626004.
71. IRC § 512(b)(4); Reg. § 1.512(b)-1(a)(2). See § 11.4.
72. IRC § 512(b)(13); Reg. § 1.512(b)-1(1)(1). These rules are inapplicable to the payment of dividends.

UNRELATED BUSINESS ACTIVITY

power of all classes of stock entitled to vote and more than 50 percent of the total number of shares of all other classes of stock of the corporation.[73]

(a) Royalties

The exception for royalties has proven to be the most contentious of these exclusions for forms of passive income. The IRS and the U.S. Tax Court have different views concerning the scope of this exception. The Tax Court defined a royalty as a payment for the use of valuable intangible property rights; it rejected the thought that a royalty must be passive in nature to be excludible from unrelated income taxation.[74] Thus, for example, it is the view of that court that certain payments for the use of mailing lists constitute royalties.[75] It also extended its rationale in this regard to revenue derived from the use of affinity credit cards.[76] The IRS, by contrast, was of the view that when an exempt organization performs services to or for the benefit of the payor, or otherwise is actively involved in the activity that generates the income—such as a partnership or in maintaining a membership list—the entity is participating in a joint venture, so that the exclusion is unavailable. For some time, the IRS continued to insist that the only royalties that are statutorily excluded from unrelated business income are those that are forms of investment income or otherwise are passive in nature.[77]

One court of appeals is of the view that the Tax Court's definition of the term is too broad, in that a royalty "cannot include compensation for services rendered by the owner of the property."[78] This position is a compromise between the approach of the Tax Court and that of the IRS on the point. Thus, the appellate court wrote that, to the extent the IRS "claims that a tax-exempt organization can do nothing to acquire such fees, "the agency is "incorrect."[79] Yet the court continued, "to the extent that. . .the exempt organization involved appears to argue that a 'royalty' is any payment for the use of a property right—such as a copyright—regardless of any additional services that are

---

73. IRC § 368(c). The tax regulations extend this definition of control to "non-stock" organizations (Reg. § 1.512(b)-1(1)(4)(i)(b)).
74. This view was first articulated in Disabled American Veterans v. Commissioner, 94 T.C. 60 (1990), *rev'd on other grounds*, 942 F.2d 309 (6th Cir. 1991).
75. Sierra Club, Inc. v. Commissioner, 65 T.C.M. 2582 (1993); Disabled American Veterans v. Commissioner, 94 T.C. 60 (1990), *rev'd on other grounds*, 942 F.2d 309 (6th Cir. 1991). These cases involve situations where the statutory exclusion for mailing list revenue is unavailable (see text accompanied by *infra* note 110).
76. Sierra Club, Inc. v. Commissioner, 103 T.C. 307 (1994).
77. E.g., Tech. Adv. Mem. 9509002.
78. Sierra Club, Inc. v. Commissioner, 86 F.3d 1526, 1532 (9th Cir. 1996).
79. *Id.* at 1535.

§ 11.2 EXCEPTIONS

performed in addition to the owner simply permitting another to use the right at issue, we disagree."[80] Following this and subsequent defeats, the IRS, by the end of 1999, instructed its agents to cease attempts to apply its definition of the term *royalty* in cases of this nature.

Mineral royalties are excluded from taxation, whether measured by production or by gross or taxable income from the mineral property. Where, however, a tax-exempt organization owns a working interest in a mineral property, even if it is relieved of its share of the development costs by the terms of any agreement with an operator, income received from the interest is not excluded from taxation. Payments in discharge of mineral production payments are treated in the same manner as royalty payments for the purpose of computing unrelated business taxable income. To the extent that the carve-out is treated as a loan, the portion of each production payment that is the equivalent to interest is excluded as interest for purposes of unrelated business income taxation.[81]

(b) Rents

As noted, rents from real property are generally excluded from unrelated business taxable income. Rents from personal property leased with real property are also excluded provided the rent attributable to the personal property is incidental (i.e., no more than 10 percent).[82] For example, if rent attributable to personal property leased with real property is determined to be $3,000 per year, and the total rent from all property leased is $10,000 per year, then the $3,000 amount is not excluded from the computation of unrelated business taxable income.[83] If more than 50 percent of the total rent is attributable to the personal property leased, however, none of the rent (including the amount attributable to the real property leased) is excludible from the computation

---

80. *Id*. The U.S. Court of Appeals for the Ninth Circuit affirmed the opinion in Sierra Club, Inc. v. Commissioner, 65 T.C.M. 2582 (1993), because of the organization's minimal involvement in the royalty generation process. By contrast, this court reversed and remanded Sierra Club, Inc. v. Commissioner, 103 T.C. 307 (1994) for a trial of the case in light of the appellate court's revised definition of the term *royalty*. Even with that revised definition, however, the Tax Court held that the affinity card payments were royalties (Sierra Club, Inc. v. Commissioner, 77 T.C.M. 1569 (1999)); the government elected not to appeal this decision. Also, New Jersey Council of Teaching Hospitals v. Commissioner, 149 T.C. 466 (2018); Oregon State University Alumni Association, Inc. v. Commissioner; Alumni Association of the University of Oregon, Inc. v. Commissioner, 99-2 U.S.T.C. ¶ 50,879 (9th Cir. 1999).
81. Reg. § 1.512(b)-1(b).
82. IRC § 512(b)(3)(A)(ii); Reg. § 1.512(b)-1(c)(2)(ii)(b).
83. Reg. § 1.512(b)-1(c)(2)(ii)(b).

of UBI under section 512(b)(3).[84] Thus, for example, if the rent attributable to personal property leased with real property is determined to be $5,500 per year, and the total rent from all property leased is $10,000 per year, then none of the $10,000 rent is excluded from the computation of unrelated business taxable income.[85]

Moreover, rental income is not excluded where the determination of the amount of the rent depends, in whole or in part, on the income or profits derived by any person from the property leased (other than an amount based on a fixed percentage or percentages of gross receipts or sales).[86] Further, in the view of the IRS, the exclusion for rent is unavailable in the case of payments for the use or occupancy of rooms and other space where services are rendered to the occupants that are primarily for their convenience and are other than those usually or customarily rendered in connection with the rental of rooms or other space for occupancy only.[87] Thus, apartment rentals are normally excluded, while hotel room rentals are included.

Examples of rentals that have been deemed to involve the provision of services and thereby treated as unrelated business income not excludible as passive rents include:

- The storage of trailers, campers, motor homes, boats, and cars in the exhibition halls not being used during winter months by an exempt agricultural organization was found to involve the provision of services on a level that caused the resulting fees to be unrelated business income.[88]

- Substantial services were found to be provided to corporate and business patrons who rented a museum's facilities for receptions in the evenings. The services provided included maintenance and security personnel and liquor service (because the museum held the license).

---

84. IRC § 512(b)(3)(B)(i); Reg. §§ 1.512(b)-1(c)(2)(iii)(a).
85. Reg. § 1.512(b)-1(c)(4), Example (3).
86. IRC § 512(b)(3)(B)(ii); Reg. § 1.512(b)-1(c)(2)(iii)(b). A classic illustration of the lines to be drawn in this area is the litigation over the issue of sharecrop lease arrangements; the courts have held that the income from these arrangements received by tax-exempt organizations is rent within the scope of the exclusion, rather than income generated out of a joint venture that is not in furtherance of exempt purposes (e.g., Harlan E. Moore Charitable Trust v. United States, 812 F. Supp. 130 (C.D. Ill. 1993), aff'd, 9 F.3d 623 (7th Cir. 1993); Trust U/W Emily Oblinger v. Commissioner, 100 T.C. 114 (1993); Independent Order of Odd Fellows Grand Lodge of Iowa v. United States, 93-2 U.S.T.C. ¶ 50, 448 (S.D. Iowa 1993); White's Iowa Manual Labor Institute v. Commissioner, 66 T.C.M. 389 (1993)).
87. Reg. § 1.512(b)-1(c)(5).
88. Tech. Adv. Mem. 9822006. Also Tech. Adv. Mem. 9853001. This type of fee-for-service income is not rent (Tech. Adv. Mem. 199901002).

§ 11.2 EXCEPTIONS

The IRS was not convinced that the rentals served an exempt purpose in finding the programs were primarily social- or business-oriented and included such items as cocktails, dinner-dances, awards presentations, and holiday celebrations. While there was some educational benefit to the attendees of viewing exhibits, they were ancillary to the events' principal purpose.[89] The IRS noted that the holding would be different if the request was for the organization to create an educational event in its space, with the food and services provided only incidentally.

- Sharecrop arrangements for farmland owned by a foundation may or may not be treated as excludible from unrelated business income under the rent exception. The method for calculating the rent and risk inherent in the agreement is determinative. The issue is whether the foundation is a joint venturer participating in the farming operations. The following factors were considered in court cases on the subject:[90]
  - The organization is not involved in the day-to-day operation of the farm; it simply provides the land and buildings.
  - The organization bears no risk of loss from accidents.
  - The organization is not required to contribute to any losses from the operation, but pays only an agreed portion of the operating expenses (in one case 50 percent).
  - The rent is equal to a fixed percentage of the gross sale of the crop or a fixed amount, not a percentage of net profits.[91]

Parking lot rental presents a similar situation. Rental of the bare real estate to another party that operates the lot (where the foundation has no relationship or responsibility to the parkers) clearly produces passive rental income.[92] If the foundation provides some services to the operator, the passive income exclusion may not apply.

Operation of a parking lot for the benefit of employees and persons participating in an exempt organization's functions, rather than disinterested persons, may be a related activity.[93] A parking rate structure "not consistent with commercially operated for-profit facilities in the same metropolitan area" was found to reflect an organization's desire to provide a necessary service to the public.

---

89. Priv. Ltr. Rul. 9702003.
90. See the court opinions referenced in *supra* note 86.
91. IRC § 512(b)(3)(A)(ii).
92. Priv. Ltr. Rul. 9301024.
93. IRC § 513(a)(2); Priv. Ltr. Rul. 9401031.

UNRELATED BUSINESS ACTIVITY

The rules as to rental income, as applicable to private foundations, were nicely illustrated by a situation in which a private foundation had a significant expectancy in the assets of a limited liability company that included an apartment complex. The services provided to tenants of the apartment units were limited to necessary and customary maintenance and utility services. The maintenance staff provided janitorial and related services only for the common areas. Tenants were responsible for paying for their own gas and electric services, and for their share of water, sewer, and garbage services. An independent company provided security services. Apartment units were unfurnished; they contained only the usual kitchen and laundry appliances, as to which separate rent was not charged.[94] None of this rent was based in whole or in part on the income or profits derived by any person from the leased property. The LLC's real property was subject to a mortgage.[95] The IRS ruled that the payments from tenants received by the LLC (and indirectly by the foundation) were rent from real property excludible from unrelated business income, except to the extent attributable to debt-financed property.[96]

(c) Research

Any income derived from research performed for any person is excluded from the unrelated business tax, where the organization is operated primarily for the purpose of carrying on fundamental research, the results of which are freely available to the public.[97] Likewise, income derived from research for the federal government (including any of its agencies or instrumentalities) or a state government (or a political subdivision of it), is also excluded.[98]

Critical to the scope of this exclusion is the meaning of the term *research*. As noted, the exclusion emphasizes *fundamental* (or basic) research; it usually is not available for applied research.[99] For example, scientific research does not include activities ordinarily carried on incidental to commercial operations, such as the testing or inspection of materials or products or the designing or construction of equipment or buildings.[100] Also illustrative is the case of an organization that

---

94. The portion of rent attributable to these appliances was said to be minimal (i.e., "well below" 5 percent of the total rent).
95. See § 11.4.
96. Priv. Ltr. Rul. 201849009.
97. IRC § 512(b)(9); Reg. § 1.512(b)-1(f)(3).
98. IRC § 512(b)(7); Reg. § 1.512(b)-1(f)(1).
99. Reg. § 1.501(c)(3)-1(d)(5)(i).
100. Reg. § 1.501(c)(3)-1(d)(5)(ii). In one case, this type of activity was described as "generally repetitive work done by scientifically unsophisticated employees for the purpose of determining whether the item tested met certain specifications, as distinguished from testing done to validate a scientific hypothesis" (Midwest Research Institute v. United States, 554 F. Supp. 1379, 1386 (W.D. Mo. 1983), *aff'd*, 744 F.2d 635 (8th Cir. 1984)).

§ 11.2 EXCEPTIONS

tested drugs for commercial pharmaceutical companies, which was held to not qualify for tax exemption as a scientific organization because the testing was regarded as principally serving the private interests of the manufacturers.[101] Likewise, an organization that inspected, tested, and certified safety shipping containers used in the transport of cargo, and engaged in related research activities, was found to not be engaged in scientific research because the activities were incidental to commercial or industrial operations.[102]

(d) Nonbusiness Activities

Income may be excluded from unrelated business income taxation because the nature of the activity that produced the income is not similar to that of activities conducted by businesses. Exclusions of this nature that can be of relevance to a private foundation are:

- Income derived from a business in which substantially all of the work in carrying it on is performed for the organization without compensation (in other words, by volunteers).[103]

- Income from a business that sells merchandise, substantially all of which has been received by the organization as contributions.[104]

- Income from a business conducted primarily for the convenience of the organization's students, patients, members, officers, or employees.[105]

- Income from the conduct of entertainment at certain fairs and expositions.[106]

- Income from the conduct of certain convention activities and trade shows.[107]

- Income from the conduct of qualified bingo games.[108]

---

101. Rev. Rul. 68-373, 1968-2 C.B. 206.
102. Rev. Rul. 78-426, 1978-2 C.B. 175.
103. IRC § 513(a)(1); Reg. § 1.513-1(e)(1).
104. IRC § 513(a)(3); Reg. § 1.513-1(e)(3).
105. IRC § 513(a)(2); Reg. § 1.513-1(e)(2). This exclusion is extensively analyzed in New Jersey Council of Teaching Hospitals v. Commissioner, 149 T.C. 466 (2018). The IRS ruled that an educational institution's provision of living quarters for its students is an activity protected from taxation by the convenience doctrine (Priv. Ltr. Rul. 200625035); this ruling is incorrect, however, inasmuch as the provision of housing by an educational institution to its students is a related business (see *Tax-Exempt Organizations* § 24.5(a)), and thus there is no need to rely on an exception from the unrelated business rules.
106. IRC § 513(d)(1).
107. *Id.*; Reg. § 1.513-3.
108. IRC § 513(f); Reg. § 1.513-5.

- Income from the distribution of certain low-cost articles incidental to the solicitation of charitable contributions.[109]
- Income from the exchange or rental of mailing lists with or to other charitable organizations.[110]
- Payments from a business sponsor that are acknowledged in a fashion that does not contain quantitative or qualitative language are treated as contributions rather than unrelated advertising business income.[111] Even if the "thank you" is limited to the permissible language, an acknowledgment printed in the monthly newsletter is treated as producing unrelated income.

§ 11.3 RULES SPECIFICALLY APPLICABLE TO PRIVATE FOUNDATIONS

From a tax law standpoint, the principal reason that private foundations have minimal entanglement with the unrelated business income rules is the limitation on excess business holdings.[112] For tax-exempt organizations generally, it is common for an unrelated business to be conducted by the organization itself, as one of its many activities. When an exempt organization does that, it is operating the business function as a sole proprietorship; the exempt organization is the sole "owner" of the business enterprise.[113] A private foundation cannot, however, "own" 100 percent of a business operated as a sole proprietorship.[114] Therefore, because of this rule, a private foundation generally cannot engage in an unrelated business activity.[115]

---

109. IRC § 513(h).
110. Id.
111. Reg. §§ 1.513(i)(2)(a); 1.513-4(c).
112. See Chapter 7.
113. A sole proprietorship is any business enterprise (see § 11.3(a)) that is actually and directly owned by a private foundation, in which the foundation has a 100 percent equity interest, and that is not held by a corporation, trust, or other business entity for the foundation (Reg. § 53.4943-10(e)).
114. IRC § 4943(c)(3)(B); Reg. 53.4943-3(c)(3).
115. Some exempt organizations participate in unrelated business activity by means of partnerships. The principles of the excess business holdings rules apply, however, to holdings by a private foundation by means of a partnership, joint venture, or other business enterprise that is not incorporated (IRC § 4943(c)(3)). See § 7.2(b). As noted, for a proprietorship owned by a private foundation to be a sole proprietorship, the foundation must have a 100 percent interest in the equity of the business enterprise. Thus, if a private foundation sells an interest in a sole proprietorship, the business enterprise becomes treated as a partnership (Reg. § 53.4943-10(e)).

§ 11.3 RULES SPECIFICALLY APPLICABLE TO PRIVATE FOUNDATIONS

(a) Business Enterprises

The concept of the *business enterprise* is integral to the excess business holdings rules. In general, that term means the active conduct of an unrelated trade or business, including any activity that is regularly carried on for the production of income from the sale of goods or the performance of services.[116] Where an activity carried on for profit constitutes an unrelated business, no part of the business may be excluded from the classification of a business enterprise merely because it does not result in a profit.[117]

There are several ways in which a private foundation can, without adverse tax consequences, engage in a business (or businesslike) activity. These ways are founded on the concept that the activity does not constitute a *business enterprise*.

The principal way to engage in allowable and nontaxable business activity is to engage in a business activity in which at least 95 percent of the gross income of the business is derived from *passive sources*.[118]

Gross income from passive sources includes the items excluded under the modification rules for dividends, interest, payments with respect to securities loans, amounts received as consideration for entering into agreements to make loans, annuities, royalties, rents, capital gains, and gains from the lapse or termination of options to buy or sell securities.[119] For example, a private foundation held, as an investment, a fee ownership interest in several thousand acres of timberland and received capital gain pursuant to timber cutting contracts; the IRS ruled that the foundation's ownership of the timberland was not a business enterprise, inasmuch as at least 95 percent of the gross income from the property was capital gain.[120]

There are two refinements as to these rules: A bond or other evidence of indebtedness does not constitute a holding in a business enterprise, unless the bond or evidence of indebtedness is otherwise determined to be an equitable interest in the enterprise.[121] A leasehold interest in real property does not constitute an interest in a business enterprise, even though rent payable under the

---

116. Reg. § 53.4943-10(a)(1).
117. *Id.* This language, and that of the previous sentence, is identical to that defining a trade or business in the unrelated business income setting (see § 11.1(b)).
118. IRC § 4943(d)(3)(B); Reg. § 53.4943-10(c)(1). These types of undertakings are discussed in § 7.1(b). Also see Priv. Ltr. Rul. 199952086 in which a charitable remainder unitrust's wholly owned foreign subsidiary's distributive share of U.S. partnership's income was found not to be unrelated business income. Conversely, gain from the sale of an interest in a partnership that held indebted real estate was treated as gain subject to the unrelated business income tax.
119. IRC § 4943(d)(3), last sentence; Reg. § 53.4943-10(c)(2). See § 11.2.
120. Priv. Ltr. Rul. 9252028.
121. Reg. § 53.4943-10(a)(2).

UNRELATED BUSINESS ACTIVITY

lease is dependent, in whole or in part, on the income or profits derived by another person from the property, unless the leasehold interest constitutes an interest in the income or profits of an unrelated business.[122]

Thus, as long as the income is generated as one or more forms of these or other types of passive activity, the income will not—as a general rule—be taxed as unrelated business income. Therefore, this exception usually shields most forms of investment income from the unrelated business income tax.

Consequently, as a general proposition, a private foundation may freely invest in (or receive as a contribution and retain) securities without becoming subject to the unrelated business income rules. The same is generally true with respect to rental property, although the income may be taxed if the rental property is used in an active business operation, if the rent is based on the lessee's net income or profits, or if the property is indebted. As to royalties, as long as the income is passive in nature, it is not taxable; otherwise, availability of the exclusion is dependent on the extent of services provided by the tax-exempt organization.[123]

Gross income from passive sources also includes income from the sale of goods (including charges or costs passed on at cost to purchasers of the goods or income received in settlement of a dispute concerning or in lieu of the exercise of the right to sell the goods) if the seller does not manufacture, produce, physically receive or deliver, negotiate sales of, or maintain inventories in the goods.[124] For example, where a corporation purchases a product under a contract with the manufacturer, resells it under contract at a uniform markup in price, and does not physically handle the product, the income derived from that markup meets the definition of passive income.[125] By contrast, income from individually negotiated sales, such as those made by a broker, would not meet the definition, even if the broker did not physically handle the goods.[126]

If, in a year, less than 95 percent of the income of a trade or business is from passive sources, a private foundation may, in applying this 95 percent test, substitute for the passive source gross income in the year, the average gross income from passive sources for the 10 years immediately preceding the year in question.[127] Thus, stock in a passive holding company is not to be considered a holding in a business enterprise even if the company is controlled by the foundation; instead, the foundation is treated as owning its proportionate share of any interests in a business enterprise held by the company.[128]

---

122. Id.
123. See § 11.2(a).
124. IRC § 4943(d)(3), last sentence.
125. Reg. § 53.4943-10(c)(2).
126. Id.
127. Reg. § 53.4943-10(c)(1).
128. Id.

§ 11.3 RULES SPECIFICALLY APPLICABLE TO PRIVATE FOUNDATIONS

A private foundation should be cautious when attempting to maximize the value of real property that it holds, whether it is property originally invested in by the foundation or acquired by gift. A private foundation can own or have an expectancy interest in this type of property for years, then be tempted to improve it, sell it, or otherwise generate maximum value for the holding. A plan of maximizing value may have been initiated while the property was held by a prior owner, such as a donor or property in an estate that was protected by the estate administration exception.[129] The private foundation may want to continue that plan or initiate one of its own; its trustees may believe that, as a matter of prudent management of assets, that is the proper course of conduct. Nonetheless, unless the property is being (or will be) used for exempt purposes, the foundation should be wary about being classified, for tax purposes, as a dealer in the property. This classification not only raises difficult unrelated business issues—it also entails excess business holdings issues.[130]

(b) Permitted Businesses

There are two other ways in which a private foundation can, without adverse tax consequences, actively engage in a business activity: (1) operate a functionally related business that accomplishes its exempt purposes, such as a research institute or publication program[131] or (2) own business holdings that include *program-related investments*,[132] which are related undertakings.[133]

Passive income from a *controlled entity* is generally taxable as unrelated business income.[134] Generally, a private foundation cannot own a subsidiary because of the excess business holdings rules.[135] A private foundation may, however, be able to own a controlled organization that generates passive income.[136] For some time, a private foundation could avoid unrelated income taxation in this context either by owning less than 80 percent of the interest in the subsidiary (often an impracticality) or by sharing ownership of the subsidiary with another foundation. For example, two private foundations could

---

129. See § 5.12.
130. See Chapter 7.
131. IRC § 4943(d)(3)(A); Reg. § 53.4943-10(b). For example, the IRS ruled that a low-income housing program for the elderly, operated by a private foundation by means of a disregarded limited liability company, was a functionally related business in that it relieved the poor and distressed (Priv. Ltr. Rul. 201603032). The law as to functionally related businesses is discussed elsewhere (see § 7.3).
132. As defined in IRC § 4944(c). See § 8.3.
133. Reg. § 53.4943-10(b).
134. IRC § 512(b)(13).
135. See Chapter 7.
136. See § 7.1(b).

each own 50 percent of the subsidiary. Or one foundation could own all of the stock entitled to vote (common stock), and the other foundation could own all of the stock of another class (such as nonvoting preferred stock). Tax avoidance on either of these bases was, however, eliminated by a change in the law in 1997, which reduced the control standard to a more than 50 percent test and introduced an indirect control rule.[137]

These exceptions may be obviated where a private foundation incurred debt to acquire or improve a property.[138] That is, the resulting income may be taxed, in whole or in part, as unrelated business income, notwithstanding the fact that it is passive income. (This type of income nonetheless retains its character as passive income for purposes of the excess business holdings rules.)[139]

(c) Partnerships and S Corporations

A private foundation's share of unrelated business income from a partnership, whether or not distributed or paid to the foundation, flows through to and retains its character as unrelated business income received by the foundation.[140] If the partnership conducts a trade or business that is unrelated to the foundation's exempt purpose, the foundation's share of the business income, less associated deductions, must be reported as unrelated business taxable income on Form 990-T and income tax be paid on the income. Alternatively, where a partnership's trade or business activities are substantially related to a private foundation's exempt purposes,[141] the foundation will not be subject to unrelated business income tax on its distributive share of the partnership's income.[142] Additionally, the exceptions and modifications pertaining to passive income apply to exclude the foundation's share of interest or other passive income distributed by the partnership. This rule applies to foundations that are general and limited partners.[143] The instructions for Form 1065 filed by partnerships require that the entity provide sufficient information to tax-exempt partners to allow them to correctly report unrelated income items. In the authors' experience, however, such information is sometimes found lacking or confusing.

Financial advisors to institutional investors have created sophisticated forms of investment vehicles in recent years. Some trade securities, some

---

137. IRC § 512(b)(13)(D). The indirect control rule utilizes the constructive ownership rules in IRC § 318.
138. See § 11.4.
139. Reg. § 53.4943-10(c)(2).
140. IRC § 512(c)(1).
141. Reg. § 1.513-1(d)(2).
142. Rev. Rul. 2004-51, 2004-22 I.R.B. 974.
143. Service Bolt Nut Co. Profit Sharing Trust v. Commissioner, 724 F.2d 519 (6th Cir. 1983), aff'g 78 T.C. 812 (1982).

§ 11.3 RULES SPECIFICALLY APPLICABLE TO PRIVATE FOUNDATIONS

buy rental buildings, some buy security hedges, and some invest in venture capital. The income tax rules pertaining to the character of income earned are sometimes complex. Those that invest in real estate (both partnerships and real estate investment trusts) commonly distribute income attributable to indebted property that may be taxable as unrelated income.[144] A partnership that elects to use the mark-to-market rules[145] for security trading reports the income on line 1 of Form K-1, "ordinary income from trade or business," to its partners although it actually has realized short-term capital gain. This type of income is not, however, treated as unrelated business income to a foundation (and other tax-exempt organizations).[146] Dividends, interest, payments with respect to securities loaned, annuities, income from notional principal contracts, or other substantially similar income from ordinary and routine investment[147] are modified or excluded from unrelated business income. Income from the sale of property "other than stock in trade or other property of a kind which would properly be included in the inventory of the organization if on hand at the close of the tax year" is also excluded.[148] Thus, the gain or loss is specifically excluded from the computation of unrelated business income unless the partnership is a dealer in securities. Additionally, gain from the lapse or termination (sale) of options to buy or sell securities written in connection with the organization's investment activity is excluded from unrelated business income.[149]

As to distributions from publicly traded partnerships, the partnership's income is fragmented to allow each type of income to flow through to the tax-exempt partner according to the general rule. Thus, partnership income or loss retains its character as either taxable business income or passive investment income in the hands of the tax-exempt partner.[150] A *publicly traded partnership* is one for which interests in it are traded on an established securities market or are readily tradable on a secondary market.[151]

Tax-exempt charitable organizations are eligible to be shareholders of an S corporation.[152] Stock in an S corporation, however, represents an interest in an unrelated trade or business.[153] Unlike a partnership, all of the income distributed to an exempt organization by an S corporation flows through to it

---

144. See § 11.4.
145. IRC § 475.
146. Reg. § 1.512(b)-1(d)(1), (2).
147. Reg. § 1.512(b)-1(a)(1).
148. Reg. § 1.512(b)-1(d)(1).
149. Reg. § 1.512(b)-1(d)(2).
150. IRC § 512(c)(2).
151. IRC § 469(k)(2).
152. IRC § 1361(c)(6).
153. IRC § 512(e).

as unrelated business income, including passive income otherwise modified from tax. Gain or loss on the sale of S corporation shares is also treated as unrelated business income. Thus, whenever possible, a foundation's investment in an entity that will produce significant amounts of passive income should preferably be held in partnership form.

(d) Community Foundations' Grant-Making Services

The IRS held that the sale of grant-making services by a community foundation[154] to charitable organizations in its community is a related business, while the sales of administrative and clerical services to them are unrelated businesses.[155]

In furtherance of its grantmaking, a community foundation engaged in various internal grant management and administrative functions, including undertaking research of potential grantees, designing and operating strategic grant-making programs, exercising proper oversight over the grants made, and numerous routine administrative, accounting, and clerical tasks necessary for the daily operation of the organization. The sources of funding of the foundation's grants were component funds and certain affiliated noncomponent funds, the latter being supporting organizations, pooled income funds, and other split-interest trusts.

This community foundation proposed to sell its internal grant management and administrative services to other grant-making charities, primarily private foundations, that operate independently in the community and lacked the staff, expertise, or resources to conduct their own internal grant-making functions. The foundation's goal in providing these services was to educate and assist these entities to enable them to provide more efficient support to the citizens of the community and ultimately for them to establish cooperative relationships with the community foundation that would maximize the pool of charitable resources available for the strategic funding of community-based programs. The foundation advised the IRS that education would be a core component of all the services it intended to sell and that every participating entity would receive, on a continuing basis, instruction and educational materials from it on tactics for strategic and effective grant-making in the community.

---

154. See § 15.4(e).
155. Priv. Ltr. Rul. 200832027. The law as to the sale of services by tax-exempt organizations, in the unrelated business setting, is summarized in *Tax-Exempt Organizations* § 24.5(k). In essence, the general sale of services (such as consulting services) to the public is an unrelated business, while the sale of services to related parties is disregarded for purposes of tax law analysis.

§ 11.3 RULES SPECIFICALLY APPLICABLE TO PRIVATE FOUNDATIONS

The foundation intended to charge a reasonable fee based on its staff's hourly rate in providing the services. Each participating charitable organization would be required to execute a sales contract with the community foundation, pursuant to which it becomes an "enrollee organization." This contract would include a menu of core organizational functions that the foundation agreed to perform for the enrollee organization. Although the community foundation would generally contract only with organizations located and operating in this community, it conceded that exceptions may be made where an organization is located elsewhere but retains it to administer funds to be distributed within the community.

The following services were proposed to be sold to enrollees: (1) assistance with establishment of a grant-making program (such as development of guidelines and procedures for reviewing requests); (2) review and evaluation of grant requests and preparation of written reports on findings (including the conduct of site visits and pregrant inquiries to obtain information necessary to evaluate proposals); (3) preparation of research in specific grant-making areas of interest and/or identification of nonprofit organizations conducting programs in interest areas; (4) design and/or maintenance of a system of monitoring funded programs; (5) identification of opportunities for collaboration with other funders; (6) handling day-to-day inquiries from potential grant recipients; (7) printing checks for approved grants and expenses and balancing an enrollee's checking account; (8) organization and staffing of board and grant committee meetings; and (9) tracking of grant applications and grants awarded and generating related reports.

The IRS ruled that these proposed services constitute the conduct of a variety of businesses that will be regularly carried on.[156] The focus thus was on the question of whether these businesses will be substantially related to the community foundation's exempt purpose.[157] The IRS's analysis began with a review of the primary objective of the unrelated business rules, which is to eliminate unfair competition by placing the unrelated business activities of tax-exempt organizations on the same tax basis as the nonexempt business endeavors with which they compete.[158]

Review by the IRS of the "foundation management industry" as a whole revealed that there are "dozens of for-profit companies that provide services similar to those [the community foundation] intends to sell." These companies provide a "diverse array of services," which the IRS enumerated in great detail, ranging from grant-making services to check-writing and reconciliation services. The agency concluded that these services are "nearly identical

---

156. See § 11.1(d).
157. See § 11.1(c).
158. See *Tax-Exempt Organizations* § 24.1.

to those you propose to sell and that you are in direct competition with the for-profit foundation management industry."

Nonetheless, wrote the IRS, the "fact that commercial entities may also provide similar services, in and of itself, is not determinative as to whether a particular service is or is not substantially related to exempt functions." The agency said that if the provision of a service "contributes importantly to benefiting the charitable class served by an organization's activities, the commercial nature of the service should not be controlling." If, however, "commercial alternatives are available, the argument that a service is substantially related to an organization's exempt function because the organization is uniquely qualified to provide a particular service to help charitable organizations address unmet charitable needs in the community served by the organization would be difficult to sustain."

The IRS classified the proposed services as grantmaking, administrative, and clerical. The grant-making services, said the IRS, are those referenced in the first five items listed above. These services were ruled to be those that contribute importantly to the accomplishment of the community foundation's exempt purpose. By providing this package of services, the foundation was said to be able to "uniquely coordinate" the enrollees' grant-making activities for the benefit of the community, provide advice about unmet charitable needs in the community, and provide advice about how to effectively advance those needs. Noting that "similar services are available from the for-profit foundation management industry," the IRS wrote that the community foundation's grant-making services are "uniquely tailored" to enable it to achieve its exempt purpose "effectively and efficiently." These services, therefore, were related businesses.

The IRS characterized the services in the fourth item listed above as administrative services (this class of service is classified twice and differently). The "skill set required to conduct these activities is not," stated the IRS, "unique" to the charitable sector. These activities are "conducted throughout the business community on a daily basis by individuals such as office administrators, personnel managers, and executive assistants." The IRS characterized the sixth through ninth items above as clerical services. These activities are said to require office staff "trained in general office procedures, including word processing, data entry, and bookkeeping entries." These are the functions of "secretaries, receptionists, and bookkeepers." The IRS held that the administrative and clerical services do not contribute importantly to accomplishment of the community foundation's exempt purposes. Some of these services, which are "generic and routine commercial services," amount, it was said, to "back office administration."

Another element of the law that the IRS considered is the inquiry as to whether an activity is conducted on a scale larger than is reasonably necessary

§ 11.3 RULES SPECIFICALLY APPLICABLE TO PRIVATE FOUNDATIONS

to achieve an organization's tax-exempt purpose.[159] The IRS wrote that an organization's income will be subject to the unrelated business income tax where the activities generating the income are not "narrowly tailored" to the accomplishment of exempt purposes. The community foundation's grant-making services were found to be so narrowly tailored; the administrative and clerical services were not. As to the latter, the proposed sales of these services are activities that "encompass a wide range of services and are too broadly conducted." This is a separate rationale for concluding that these activities are unrelated businesses.

The IRS noted that if the community foundation provided these administrative and clerical services at substantially below its cost to charitable organizations, such as by charging 15 percent of its costs and subsidizing 85 percent of its costs to deliver these services,[160] the resulting income would not be taxable. None of the foundation's services were to be provided at substantially below cost, however.

The IRS reminded the community foundation that it must make a reasonable allocation of the fees it receives from the enrollee organizations, and of the expenses involved, as between the related and unrelated business activities.[161]

(e) Provision of Technical Assistance

A private operating foundation's program of providing "technical assistance" to neighborhood nonprofit organizations and government agencies was held by the IRS to not be an unrelated business (and not the type of activity giving rise to excise taxation under the excess business holdings rules).[162]

In this situation, the private operating foundation furthered its charitable purpose through collection, analysis, interpretation, and sharing of data concerning a metropolitan region to improve community decision-making. Some of this information was made available to the public by means of the foundation's website. The foundation also offered technical assistance to an array of nonprofit organizations and government agencies. The foundation

---

159. *Id.* § 24.4(b).
160. E.g., Rev. Rul. 72-369, 1972-2 C.B. 245. See, e.g., *Tax-Exempt Organizations* § 7.13.
161. See § 11.5(a), (b). This ruling is inconsistent, in many ways, with the general precepts of the commerciality doctrine, which places great emphasis on exempt organizations' program activities that are in direct competition with counterpart for-profit entities (see *Tax-Exempt Organizations* § 4.9). No court has made the IRS's distinction among program, administrative, and clerical functions. Also, the notion that the charitable entities purchasing the services are members of a charitable class is inconsistent with the IRS's position in similar circumstances (*id.* § 7.13). Further, the IRS often seizes on fee-charging as a basis for asserting nonexempt activity (*id.* § 24.2(e)).
162. Priv. Ltr. Rul. 201701002. The excess business holdings rules are the subject of Chapter 7.

represented to the IRS that it administers an extensive screening process to ensure that each project it agrees to undertake for one of these organizations will provide information and insight to advance its mission. Information provided to what the foundation termed its "clients" was added to the foundation's repository for use in other projects.

This foundation previously absorbed the costs of providing this technical assistance. To engage in more projects that will bring in valuable new data and identify research questions not previously explored, the foundation proposed to charge a "reasonable fee" for assistance requests. The foundation represented that this pricing was set to be in alignment with its clients' ability to pay.

The IRS concluded that the foundation's technical assistance services are substantially related to the performance of its exempt functions because the projects generate research data that serve its charitable ends and provide new data for the foundation's use. Further, it was noted that this assistance enabled client organizations to perform their charitable activities. Thus, the IRS ruled that these activities do not constitute an unrelated business.

§ 11.4 UNRELATED DEBT-FINANCED INCOME RULES

The modifications exempting passive investment income, such as dividends and rent, from the unrelated business income tax do not apply to the extent that the investment is made with borrowed funds, that is, the purchase is *debt-financed*. A classic example of a permitted foundation investment impacted by this rule is a rental building financed with a mortgage.

(a) Acquisition Indebtedness

The term *debt-financed property* means, with certain exceptions, property that is held to produce income (usually dividends, interest, or rent) and with respect to which there is an *acquisition indebtedness* at any time during the tax year (or during the preceding 12 months if the property is disposed of during the year).[163] "Acquisition indebtedness," with respect to debt-financed property, means the unpaid amount of the indebtedness incurred by the foundation in acquiring or improving the property, before any acquisition or improvement of the property if the indebtedness would not have been incurred but for the acquisition or improvement of the property, and after the acquisition or improvement of the property if the indebtedness would not have been incurred but for the acquisition or improvement, and the

---

163. IRC § 514(b)(1).

§ 11.4 UNRELATED DEBT-FINANCED INCOME RULES

incurring of the indebtedness was reasonably foreseeable at the time of the acquisition or improvement.[164]

If property is acquired by a private foundation subject to a mortgage or other similar lien, the indebtedness thereby secured is considered an acquisition indebtedness incurred by the organization when the property is acquired, even though the organization did not assume or agree to pay the indebtedness.[165] In the case of mortgaged property acquired as a result of a bequest or devise, however, the indebtedness secured by this type of mortgage is not treated as an acquisition indebtedness during the 10-year period following the date of acquisition.[166] A like rule applies with respect to mortgaged property received by gift, where the mortgage was placed on the property more than five years before the gift and the property was held by the donor more than five years before the gift.[167] In order to qualify for these exclusions, the foundation must not agree to pay the indebtedness on the gifted or bequeathed property.[168] Indebted property not producing any recurrent annual income but held to produce appreciation in underlying value is subject to this rule; thus, the capital gains are taxable.[169]

---

164. IRC § 514(c)(1). The word *indebtedness* is not defined in this setting. In other contexts (e.g., the deduction for interest paid on indebtedness (IRC § 163(a)), courts have held that indebtedness is an unconditional and legally enforceable obligation for the payment of money (e.g., Autenreith v. Commissioner, 115 F.2d 856 (3rd Cir. 1940); Kovtun v. Commissioner, 54 T.C. 331 (1970), *aff'd per curiam*, 448 F.2d 1268 (9th Cir. 1971)). The IRS supplements this definition by borrowing from the law concerning the bad debt deduction (IRC § 166), which provides that a debt must be a fixed or determinable sum of money (Reg. § 1.166-1(c)). E.g., Priv. Ltr. Rul. 201740002 (where the IRS held that, although a private foundation's participation in a rezoning agreement obligated it to reimburse a developer for its portion of rezoning costs and pay the developer a fee in the event of successful completion of the rezoning, the agreement did not create an unconditional and legally enforceable obligation for payment of a fixed or determinate sum of money, so that the foundation was found to not have incurred indebtedness and thus an acquisition indebtedness did not arise).
165. IRC § 514(c)(2)(A).
166. IRC § 514(c)(2)(B). An interest in an LLC was held by a trust formed for the benefit of the trustor's surviving spouse. The IRS observed that the distribution of the trust's interest in the LLC to the foundation after the spouse's death would be a devise from the spouse. Thus, the IRS ruled, any indebtedness secured by mortgages against real property owned by the LLC would not be treated as acquisition indebtedness during a period of 10 years following the date of acquisition by the foundation of any interest in the company, provided that the foundation did not assume and agree to pay the indebtedness secured by the mortgage and did not make any payment for the equity in the property (Priv. Ltr. Rul. 201849009).
167. *Id.*
168. See, e.g., Priv. Ltr. Rul. 9241064.
169. Reg. § 1.514(b)-1(a).

Income from a short sale of publicly traded stock through a broker is not considered unrelated debt-financed income for an exempt organization.[170] Essentially, the transaction does not involve borrowing to acquire an asset, but instead to sell. The code applies to indebtedness incurred to acquire or improve property. Though it does not seem entirely logical, the ruling describes an exempt organization that "borrows 100 shares of a stock and sells the shares." The broker retains the sales proceeds, plus $250x cash and any income earned on the proceeds, as collateral for the organization's obligation to return the borrowed shares. Although the short sale creates an obligation, it does not create acquisition indebtedness.[171]

The same type of reasoning may be applied to a line of credit secured by the foundation's investment portfolio. Assume, for example, that expected proceeds from an asset sale are delayed, and the foundation prefers not to sell its securities to meet its payroll or pledged grants. The proceeds of a margin loan are not used to acquire an income-producing asset, but rather to provide working capital to pay for operating expenses. It could be argued that the loan is equivalent to acquisition because it allows the organization not to sell its investments temporarily. Technically, however, no purchase occurs. The IRS labels such indebtedness as "transitory" and part of a "routine investment program" falling short of acquisition indebtedness.[172]

Some foundations with depressed portfolios beginning in 2008 chose to obtain "transitory" indebtedness. A decision to borrow funds to be able to meet the foundation's mandatory payout requirements is not treated as acquisition of the asset the foundation is choosing not to sell. It is important that the foundation records, such as in minutes of the finance committee or trustees, document the purpose for the borrowing.[173]

Similarly, a foundation may hold assets that it does not wish to, or cannot, sell for a number of reasons. When a foundation fully invests its assets in equity securities, the cash flow from dividends may not provide sufficient cash to meet its minimum distribution requirements.[174] If a foundation in these circumstances borrows money to meet its obligations, rather than selling its shares, it could be considered to have borrowed the money to keep the shares. In general, securities purchased on margin by a tax-exempt organization constitute debt-financed property,[175] and borrowing against securities on margin

---

170. Rev. Rul. 95-8, 1995-1 C.B. 107.
171. Deputy v. du Pont, 300 U.S. 488, 497-98 (1940).
172. Priv. Ltr. Ruls. 8721107, 9644063.
173. Priv. Ltr. Ruls. 8721107, 9644063, and 200235042.
174. See Chapter 6.
175. E.g., Henry E. & Nancy Horton Bartels Trust for the Benefit of the University of New Haven v. United States, 209 F.3d 147 (2d Cir. 2000).

§ 11.4 UNRELATED DEBT-FINANCED INCOME RULES

is generally deemed a jeopardizing investment.[176] If the foundation instead holds an unmarketable asset, such as real estate, that it is unable to sell, the debt should not be associated with the property.

Not every debt that is associated with a property is an acquisition indebtedness. Payment obligations may not be debts incurred for the purpose of acquiring or carrying property to which the debt-financed property provisions apply but may be incurred by a private foundation (or other exempt organization) solely for convenience in administering an exempt organization's exempt function and/or as part of ordinary and routine activities undertaken in the administration of investment properties. For example, an exempt investment fund with participants confined to exempt entities proposed to establish with a bank a short-term credit facility in order to ensure its ability to pay redemption proceeds on a timely basis in the infrequent circumstances that its cash reserve was depleted. The IRS ruled that this "transitory indebtedness" amounted to "temporary payment obligations" that were incurred for the organization's convenience in administering the fund's exempt function and to minimize adverse effects stemming from settlement delays.[177] (There is, however, no exemption from the debt-financed property rules for short-term borrowings as such.)

This ruling position of the IRS is based on a revenue ruling concerning application of the unrelated business rules to securities lending programs engaged in by tax-exempt organizations.[178] Under the facts of that ruling, an exempt organization transferred, for temporary periods, securities from its investment portfolio to a brokerage house in order to enable the brokerage house to cover short sales. As part of its compensation for the securities-lending, the organization received cash equal to the value of the securities as collateral, which it had the right to invest and retain the income therefrom but which it was required to repay on return of the securities. This ruling holds that the securities lending program does not give rise to unrelated business income because "Congress did not intend for ordinary and routine investment activities [of an exempt organization] in connection with its securities portfolio to be treated as the conduct of a trade or business."[179] Further, this ruling states that the organization would not have debt-financed income as a result of the lending program because the organization had not "incurred indebtedness for the purpose of making additional investments," although it had clearly incurred debt because it had the right in the interim to invest

---

176. See § 8.1(a).
177. Priv. Ltr. Rul. 200010061.
178. Rev. Rul. 78-88, 1978-1 C.B. 163.
179. *Id.* at 164.

UNRELATED BUSINESS ACTIVITY

and retain the income from the cash received as "collateral" and the ultimate obligation to repay the money.[180]

A private foundation or other type of tax-exempt organization may be a partner in a partnership or a member of a limited liability company that acquires assets with borrowed funds. The investments of the partnership or limited liability company are attributed to the exempt organization, as discussed, so that the exempt organization is regarded as owning its share of the debt-financed property. Consequently, part of the foundation's (or other organization's) distributive share of income from a partnership or similar entity may constitute debt-financed income.

(b) Related-Use Exceptions

Acquisition indebtedness does not include indebtedness with respect to property where substantially all (at least 85 percent) of its use is related to the exercise or performance by the organization involved of its exempt purpose or, if less than substantially all of its use is related, to the extent that its use is related to exempt purposes.[181] For example, proceeds received by a private foundation from loans do not constitute taxable income from debt-financed property where the funds will be distributed, in the forms of grants, by the foundation for charitable purposes.[182] Further, acquisition indebtedness does not include an obligation to pay a qualified charitable gift annuity.[183]

Also excepted from treatment as debt-financed property are the following types of properties: (1) property to the extent the income is derived from research activities;[184] (2) property to the extent that its use is in a business exempted from tax because substantially all the work is performed without compensation;[185] (3) property to the extent that its use is in a business carried on primarily for the convenience of the organization's members, students, patients, officers, or employees;[186] (4) property to the extent that its use is in a business that is the selling of merchandise, substantially all of which was

---

180. Id. The IRS referred, in the private letter ruling, to these borrowings as "transitory indebtedness" and "short-term" borrowings. This element was not present in the revenue ruling, which referred to "ordinary and routine investment activities." It would seem that the use of the funds determines whether the debt is acquisition indebtedness, rather than the time period in which the debt is outstanding.
181. IRC § 514(c)(4).
182. Priv. Ltr. Rul. 200432026.
183. IRC § 514(c)(5).
184. See § 11.2(c).
185. See § 11.2(d).
186. Id.

§ 11.4 UNRELATED DEBT-FINANCED INCOME RULES

donated to the organization;[187] and (5) property to the extent that its income is already subject to tax as income from the conduct of an unrelated trade or business.[188]

The *neighborhood land rule* provides another exemption from the debt-financed property rules for interim income from neighborhood real property acquired for a tax-exempt purpose. This rule states that where an exempt organization acquires real property for the principal purpose of using the land in the performance of its exempt functions commencing within 10 years of the time of acquisition, the property will not be treated as debt-financed property for tax purposes as long as the property is in the neighborhood of other property owned by the exempt organization, which is used for exempt ends, and the organization does not abandon its intent to use the land in an exempt manner within the 10-year period.[189] This rule applies after the first 5 years of the 10-year period only if the exempt organization satisfies the IRS that future use of the acquired land in furtherance of its exempt purposes before the expiration of the period is reasonably certain. This process is to be initiated by a timely filing of a ruling request,[190] although the IRS may provide administrative relief[191] in a situation where a ruling request was not timely submitted.[192]

(c) Includible Income

In computing the unrelated business taxable income of a private foundation (or any other tax-exempt organization), there must be included with respect to each debt-financed property that is unrelated to the organization's exempt function—as an item of gross income derived from an unrelated trade or business—an amount of income from the property, subject to tax in the proportion in which the property is financed by the debt. Basically, deductions are allowed with respect to each debt-financed property in the same proportion.[193]

The average acquisition indebtedness equals the arithmetic average of each month or partial month of the tax year. The average-adjusted basis is similarly calculated, and only straight-line depreciation is allowed.

---

187. Id.
188. IRC § 514(b)(1).
189. IRC § 514(b)(3)(A).
190. Reg. § 1.514(b)-1(d)(1)(iii).
191. Reg. § 301.9100-1(a).
192. E.g., Priv. Ltr. Rul. 9603019.
193. IRC § 514(a)(1).

§ 11.5 CALCULATING AND REPORTING THE TAX

Unrelated business taxable income means the gross income derived by a tax-exempt organization from an unrelated trade or business, regularly carried on by the organization, less business deductions that are directly connected with the carrying on of the business.[194] For purposes of this determination, gross income and business deductions are computed with certain modifications.[195]

(a) General Rules

Generally, to be directly connected with the conduct of an unrelated business, an item of deduction must have a *proximate and primary relationship* to the carrying on of that business.[196] Expenses, depreciation, and similar items attributable solely to the conduct of an unrelated business are proximately and primarily related to that business and therefore qualify for deduction to the extent that they meet the requirements of relevant provisions of the federal income tax law.[197]

Where facilities and/or personnel are used both to carry on tax-exempt activities and to conduct unrelated trade or business, the expenses, depreciation, and similar items attributable to the facilities and/or personnel (such as overhead and items of salary) must be allocated between the two uses on a reasonable basis.[198] Despite the statutory rule that an expense must be directly connected with an unrelated business, the regulations merely state that the portion of the expense allocated to the unrelated business activity is, where the allocation is on a "reasonable basis," proximately and primarily related to the business activity. Once an item is proximately and primarily related to a business undertaking, it is allowable as a deduction in computing unrelated business income in the manner and to the extent permitted by the federal income tax law generally.[199]

Gross income may be derived from an unrelated trade or business that exploits a tax-exempt function. Generally, in these situations, expenses, depreciation, and similar items attributable to the conduct of the exempt function are not deductible in computing unrelated business taxable income. Since the items are incident to a function of the type that is the chief purpose of

---

194. IRC § 512(a)(1).
195. See § 11.2.
196. IRC § 512(a)(1); Reg. § 1.512-1(a).
197. Reg. § 512(a)-1(b). The business expense deduction rules are the subject of IRC § 162; the depreciation rules are in IRC § 167.
198. Reg. § 1.512(a)-1(c). See *Tax-Exempt Organizations* § 25.7.
199. *Id.*

§ 11.5 CALCULATING AND REPORTING THE TAX

the organization to conduct, they do not possess a proximate and primary relationship to the trade or business. Therefore, they do not qualify as being directly connected with that business.[200]

(b) Bucketing Rule

The federal tax law generally does not limit the number of unrelated businesses that tax-exempt organizations may have. Provided it does not cause it to run afoul of the excess business holdings rules,[201] a private foundation may therefore hold an interest in one or more unrelated businesses (for example, through one or more limited partnership interests).

Pursuant to the bucketing rule, however, if a private foundation is engaged in two or more unrelated businesses, unrelated business taxable income must first be computed separately with respect to each business.[202]

Generally, a private foundation identifies each of its separate unrelated businesses using the first two digits of the North American Industry Classification System code that most accurately describe the unrelated business.[203] The NAICS two-digit code must identify the unrelated business in which the private foundation engages, directly or indirectly, and not activities the conduct of which is substantially related to the exercise or performance by it of its exempt purpose or function.[204] These codes must be reported only once.[205] A private foundation must allocate deductions between or among separate unrelated businesses using an existing method.[206]

---

200. Reg. § 1.512(a)-1(d).
201. See Chapter 7.
202. IRC § 512(a)(6), added by the Tax Cuts and Jobs Act (TCJA) (Pub. L. No. 115-97, § 13702(a), 131 Stat. 2054 (2017)). This law, also called the "silo" rule, is generally effective for tax years beginning after 2017. In an attempt to achieve parity with taxable employers who cannot deduct certain transportation-related fringe benefit expenses, including parking provided to employees, the TCJA also added a provision taxing such benefits as unrelated business income (IRC § 512(a)(7)). In response to widespread criticism from the tax-exempt sector, this provision was retroactively repealed by the Taxpayer Certainty and Disaster Tax Relief Act of 2019, enacted as part of the Further Consolidated Appropriations Act, 2020 (Pub. L. No. 116-94, div. Q, tit. III, § 302, 133 Stat. 2534, 3248).
203. Reg. § 1.512(a)-6(b)(1).
204. Reg. § 1.512(a)-6(b)(2).
205. Reg. § 1.512(a)-6(b)(3). A private foundation that later changes the identification of a separate unrelated business must report the change in the tax year of the change in accordance with IRS forms and instructions and provide the reason for the change (Reg. § 1.512(a)-6(a)(3)).
206. Reg. § 1.512(a)-6(f). This method is the subject of Reg. § 1.512(a)-1(c). The IRS is in the process of modifying these regulations (Department of the Treasury, 2023-2024 Priority Guidance Plan (Sept. 29, 2023)).

UNRELATED BUSINESS ACTIVITY

Most forms of passive income, such as dividends, interest, annuities, rents, royalties, and capital gains, are excluded from unrelated business income taxation.[207] Investment activities that generate unrelated business income are subject to one of two sets of rules. Investments in qualifying partnership interests,[208] qualifying S corporation interests,[209] and debt-financed property or properties[210] are collectively regarded as one separate business.[211] Other investment activities must be treated as separate businesses and be separately identified using the applicable NAICS two-digit code for each business.[212]

A *qualifying partnership interest* (QPI) excludes any interest in a general partnership, regardless of the private foundation's percentage interest.[213] An interest in a limited partnership is a QPI if the private foundation holds, directly or indirectly, an interest in the partnership where that interest meets a de minimis test or a participation test.[214] Pursuant to a look-through rule, if a private foundation holds a direct interest in a limited partnership, which itself is not a QPI because it does not meet one of these tests, any partnership in which the foundation holds an indirect interest through the directly held (non-QPI) partnership interest may be a QPI if the indirectly held partnership interest meets the de minimis test or the participation test.[215]

A limited partnership interest is a QPI under the *de minimis test* if the private foundation holds, directly or indirectly, no more than 2 percent of the profits interest and no more than 2 percent of the capital interest of the partnership during the foundation's tax year with which or in which the partnership's tax year ends.[216] A limited partnership interest is a QPI under the *participation test* if the private foundation holds, directly or indirectly, no more than 20 percent of the capital interest in the partnership during the foundation's tax year with which or in which the partnership's tax year ends and the foundation does not

---

207. See § 11.2.
208. Reg. § 1.512(a)-6(c)(2).
209. Reg. § 1.512(a)-6(c)(2).
210. See § 11.4.
211. Reg. § 1.512(a)-6(c)(1).
212. Reg. § 1.512(a)-6(b)(1).
213. Reg. § 1.512(a)-6(c)(8)(ii).
214. Reg. § 1.512(a)-6(c)(2)(i).
215. Reg. § 1.512(a)-6(c)(2)(ii). An organization that has a limited partnership interest meeting the requirements above concerning direct or indirect interests in a tax year may designate that partnership interest as a QPI by including its share of partnership gross income (and directly connected deductions) with the gross income (and such deductions) from its other investment activities in accordance with IRS forms and instructions (Reg. § 1.512(a)-6(c)(2)(iii)).
216. Reg. § 1.512(a)-6(c)(3).

§ 11.5 CALCULATING AND REPORTING THE TAX

significantly participate in the partnership.[217] A private foundation is considered to significantly participate in a partnership if (1) the foundation, by itself, may require the partnership to perform, or may prevent the partnership from performing (other than through a unanimous voting requirement or through minority consent rights), any act that significantly affects the operations of the partnership; (2) any of the foundation's officers, directors, trustees, or employees have rights to participate in the management of the partnership at any time; (3) any of the foundation's officers, directors, trustees, or employees have rights to conduct the partnership's business at any time; or (4) the foundation, by itself, has the power to appoint or remove any of the partnership's officers or employees or a majority of directors.[218]

For purposes of the de minimis test, a private foundation's profits interest in a limited partnership is determined in the same manner as its distributive share of partnership taxable income.[219] For purposes of the de minimis test and the participation test, in the absence of a provision of the partnership agreement, a private foundation's capital interest in a partnership is determined on the basis of its interest in the assets of the partnership that would be distributed to it on its withdrawal from the partnership or on liquidation of the partnership, whichever is greater.[220]

For purposes of both tests, a private foundation must determine its percentage interest by taking the average of the foundation's percentage interest at the beginning and the end of the partnership's tax year (or if held for less than a year, the percentage interest held at the beginning and end of the period of ownership within the partnership's tax year).[221] When determining its average percentage interest in a limited partnership for purposes of these tests, a private foundation may rely on the Schedule K-1 (Form 1065) it receives from the partnership if the form lists the foundation's percentage profits interest or its percentage capital interest, or both, at the beginning and end of the year.

---

217. Reg. § 1.512(a)-6(c)(4)(i). When determining a private foundation's percentage interest in a partnership for purposes of the percentage test, the interests of a controlled entity (IRC § 512(b)(13)(D)) in the same partnership are taken into account (Reg. § 1.512(a)-6(c)(4)(ii)).
218. Reg. § 1.512(a)-6(c)(4)(iii).
219. Reg. § 1.512(a)-6(c)(5)(i).
220. Reg. § 1.512(a)-6(c)(5)(ii). The preamble to the bucketing rule regulations notes that these rules for determining a private foundation's profits and capital interests in a partnership are consistent with longstanding rules in Reg. § 53.4943-3(c)(2) (see § 7.2(b)) for purposes of a private foundation's determination of whether it has excess business holdings (85 Fed. Reg. 77952, 77962 n.4 (2020)).
221. Reg. § 1.512(a)-6(c)(5)(iii). A limited partnership interest that fails to meet the de minimis test or the participation test because of an increase in percentage interest in the private foundation's current tax year may be treated, for the tax year of the change, as meeting the requirements of the test it met in the prior tax year under certain circumstances (Reg. § 1.512(a)-6(c)(6)).

UNRELATED BUSINESS ACTIVITY

A private foundation may not rely on the form, however, to the extent that any information about the foundation's percentage interest is not specifically provided.[222]

Where a private foundation owns stock in an S corporation, the interest is treated as an interest in a separate unrelated business for purposes of the bucketing rule unless it meets the definition of a *qualifying S corporation interest*.[223] Rules similar to those that apply in determining whether a limited partnership interest is a QPI apply for purposes of determining whether an interest in an S corporation is eligible to be aggregated with other qualified investment activities for purposes of the bucketing rule, namely, substituting "stock ownership" in place of "profits interests" and "capital interests" where used in the de minimis and participation tests.[224]

If a private foundation controls another entity,[225] all specified payments[226] from the controlled entity are treated as gross income from a separate unrelated business for purposes of the bucketing rule.[227] If a private foundation receives specified payments from two controlled entities, the payments from each controlled entity are treated as separate unrelated businesses.[228]

The total unrelated business taxable income of a private foundation with more than one unrelated business is the sum of the unrelated business taxable income computed with respect to each unrelated business, less a charitable contribution deduction,[229] a net operating loss deduction for losses arising in tax years beginning before January 1, 2018,[230] and the specific deduction.[231]

(c) Tax Rates

The unrelated business income tax rates payable by most tax-exempt organizations, including private foundations that are not trusts, are the corporate rates.[232] Private foundations and other exempt organizations that are trusts are subject to the trust income tax rates.[233]

---

222. Reg. § 1.512(a)-6(c)(5)(iv).
223. Reg. § 1.512(a)-6(e).
224. Reg. § 1.512(a)-6(e)(2).
225. IRC § 512(b)(13)(D).
226. IRC § 512(b)(13)(C).
227. Reg. § 1.512(a)-6(d)(1).
228. *Id*.
229. IRC § 512(b)(10), (11).
230. See IRC §§ 172, 512(b)(6). The bucketing rule regulations contain additional rules pertaining to net operating losses, including the coordination of pre-2018 NOLs and post-2017 NOLs (Reg. § 1.512(a)-6(h)).
231. Reg. § 1.512(a)-6(g)(1). The specific deduction is provided under IRC § 512(b)(12).
232. IRC § 11(b).
233. IRC § 1(e).

§ 11.5 CALCULATING AND REPORTING THE TAX

The federal tax on unrelated business taxable income is correlated to the basic federal income tax. The current rate of tax imposed on corporations is 21 percent,[234] thereby causing the corporate rate for unrelated business taxable income to be 21 percent.[235] The top tax rate imposed on a trust is 39.6 percent.[236]

(d) Tax Computation and Reporting Rules

A private foundation is required to file Form 990-T (Exempt Organization Business Income Tax Return) electronically for each tax year in which it has gross income from an unrelated business of $1,000 or more.[237] The due date for the return is the 15th day of the 5th month after the end of the foundation's tax year (which is May 15th for a calendar-year organization).[238]

Gross income from an unrelated trade or business must be reported, along with associated deductions.[239] In addition to deductions directly connected with conduct of an unrelated trade or business, a filing organization is entitled to a specific deduction of $1,000 in calculating its unrelated business taxable income,[240] except for the purpose of computing a net operating loss deduction.[241] A charitable contribution deduction equal to 10 percent of a tax-exempt corporation's net income and 50 percent of a trust's income is allowed for grants paid to other charitable organizations.[242]

In reflection of the bucketing rule,[243] an organization with more than one unrelated trade or business should complete and attach a separate schedule to report income and allowable deductions for each separate unrelated trade or business[244]

---

234. IRC § 11(b)(D).
235. IRC § 511(a)(1), (2)(A).
236. IRC §§ 1(e), 511(b). A nonexempt charitable trust that is treated as a private foundation (IRC § 4947(a)(1)) is not subject to the unrelated business income tax (IRC § 511(b)(2)). However, under the general tax law rules applicable to trusts, a trust's deduction for amounts paid or permanently set aside for a charitable purpose (IRC § 642(c)) is reduced by the amount allocable to the trust's unrelated business income (IRC § 681(a)), thereby causing the trust's unrelated business income to be taxed under the trust rules (IRC § 641(a); see Gen. Couns. Mem. 35816).
237. IRC § 6011(a), (h); Reg. §§ 1.6012-2(e), 301.6011-10. The electronic filing requirement applies to tax years beginning after July 1, 2019 (Pub. L. No. 116-25, § 3101(d)(1), 133 Stat. 981, 1015 (2019)). See § 12.3(a) for public inspection and disclosure requirements applicable to Form 990-T.
238. IRC § 6072(e); Reg. § 1.6072-2(c).
239. Form 990-T (2022), Part I.
240. IRC § 512(b)(12).
241. IRC §§ 172, 512(b)(6).
242. IRC § 512(b)(10), (11).
243. See § 11.5(b).
244. Form 990-T (2022), Schedule A.

and report the sum of the income and deductions from all schedules on the face of the return.[245]

(e) Penalties and Additions to Tax

An organization must pay quarterly estimated tax if it expects its unrelated business income tax for the year to be $500 or more.[246] An addition to tax applies in the case of a failure to pay estimated tax,[247] and a penalty is imposed for failure to deposit estimated tax on time.[248] Additions to tax for failure to file and failure to pay may also be assessed if a private foundation does not timely file its Form 990-T and pay its tax liability by the due date (including extensions).[249] Interest is also charged on any unpaid tax based on an underpayment rate established by statute.[250]

An accuracy-related penalty may also be imposed if an underpayment of unrelated business income tax is attributable to negligence or disregard of rules or regulations or if there is a substantial understatement of income tax required to be shown on the return.[251] The penalty is equal to 20 percent of the amount of the understatement.[252] For purposes of this penalty, negligence includes any failure to make a reasonable attempt to comply with the tax laws, and disregard includes any careless, reckless, or intentional disregard.[253] A substantial understatement of tax occurs if the amount of the understatement exceeds the greater of 10 percent of the tax required to be shown on the return for the tax year, or $5,000.[254] These accuracy-related penalties do not apply to any portion of an underpayment if it is shown that there was a reasonable cause for such portion and that the taxpayer acted in good faith with respect to such portion.[255]

---

245. Form 990-T (2022), Part I.
246. IRS Form 990-W (Estimated Tax on Unrelated Business Taxable Income for Tax-Exempt Organizations) contains a worksheet used to determine the amount of estimated tax payments required.
247. IRC § 6655(a), (g)(3).
248. IRC § 6656; Reg. § 1.6302-1.
249. IRC § 6651(a)(1), (2); see § 12.4(b). If an organization fails to file a Form 990-T in electronic form (see text accompanied by *supra* note 237), the organization has failed to file the return for purposes of the IRC § 6651 addition to tax for failure to file a return (Reg. § 301.6011-10(b)).
250. IRC §§ 6601, 6621.
251. IRC § 6662(a), (b)(1)-(2).
252. IRC § 6662(a). There is no stacking of accuracy-related penalty components; thus, if a portion of an underpayment of tax required to be shown on a return is attributable both to negligence and a substantial understatement of income tax, the maximum accuracy-related penalty is 20 percent of such portion (Reg. § 1.6662-2(c)).
253. IRC § 6662(c).
254. IRC § 6662(d)(1)(A).
255. IRC § 6664(c)(1); see § 12.2(c).

(f) Statute of Limitations

If a private foundation files an unrelated business income tax return, the statute of limitations for the IRS to assess additional unrelated business income tax is three years.[256] A six-year statute of limitations applies if the return omits an amount of gross income that exceeds 25 percent of the amount of gross income shown on the return.[257] And if no return is filed, the statute of limitations typically does not begin to run at all.[258]

Construing a provision relating to the filing of an exempt organization return in good faith where the filing organization is later determined to be taxable,[259] however, the U.S. Tax Court held that the filing of a Form 990 in good faith starts the running of the statute of limitations with respect to the tax on unrelated business income even if no Form 990-T is filed.[260] The IRS subsequently agreed to follow this decision, but only in situations where the taxpayer has disclosed sufficient facts on Form 990 to apprise the IRS "of the potential existence of unrelated business taxable income."[261] To meet the IRS's "sufficient facts" requirement, the return must state the nature of the income-producing activity with sufficient specificity to enable the IRS to determine whether the income is from an activity related to the organization's exempt purpose, and the return must disclose the gross receipts from this activity.[262] On the other hand, if sufficient facts are not disclosed, the IRS takes the position that the filing of a Form 990 does not start the running of the period of limitations with respect to the unrelated business income tax.[263]

---

256. IRC § 6501(a).
257. IRC § 6501(e)(1).
258. IRC § 6501(c)(3).
259. IRC § 6501(g)(2).
260. California Thoroughbred Breeders Association v. Commissioner, 47 T.C. 335 (1966), acq. in result only, 1969-1 C.B. 21.
261. Rev. Rul. 69-247, 1969-1 C.B. 303.
262. Id.
263. Id.; Rev. Rul. 62-10, 1962-1 C.B. 305.

CHAPTER TWELVE

Tax Reporting and Administration Issues

§12.1 **Form 990-PF** 510
   (a) Annual Form 990-PF Filing Requirement 510
   (b) Key Form 990-PF Disclosures 510
   (c) Reporting Changes on Form 990-PF 512
      (i) Changes in Activities 512
      (ii) Changes in Governing Documents 512
      (iii) Name and Address Changes 513
   (d) Other Changes 513
      (i) Change in Annual Accounting Period (Tax Year) 513
      (ii) Change in Accounting Method 514

§ 12.2 **Form 990-PF Penalties** 515
   (a) Daily Delinquency Penalty 515
   (b) Form 990-PF Statute of Limitations 516
   (c) Reasonable Cause 518
   (d) Amended Returns 521

§12.3 **Public Disclosure and Inspection of Returns** 521
   (a) Disclosure of Returns to the Public 521
   (b) Disclosure of Returns to State Officials 524

§ 12.4 **Reporting and Payment of Excise Taxes** 525
   (a) Reporting and Payment on Form 4720 525
   (b) Additions to Tax and Penalties 527
   (c) Abatement 529
   (d) Form 4720 Statute of Limitations 533
   (e) Closing Agreements 536

§ 12.5 **Determination Letters and Letter Rulings** 537
   (a) Form 8940 Miscellaneous Determination Requests 538
   (b) Letter Rulings 539
   (c) Reliance on Determinations and Rulings 540

§ 12.6 **IRS Examinations of Private Foundations** 541
   (a) Types of Examinations 542
   (b) General IRS EO Examination Practices and Procedures 543
   (c) Achieving Positive Results 545

§ 12.7 **Revocation of Tax-Exempt Status** 546
   (a) Automatic Revocation for Non-Filing 546
   (b) Retroactive Revocation 547
   (c) IRS Administrative Appeal Procedures 548
   (d) Contesting Revocation in Court 549
   (e) Consequences of Revocation 550

§12.1 FORM 990-PF

(a) Annual Form 990-PF Filing Requirement

A private foundation is required to file an annual return with the IRS on Form 990-PF regardless of its annual gross receipts.[1] Although this return is primarily an information return, it is also used to calculate any net investment income tax due and payable by a private foundation and therefore in this respect is also an income tax return.[2] The return is due by the 15th day of the 5th month following the end of the private foundation's tax year (which is May 15 for a calendar-year taxpayer).[3]

Form 990-PF must be filed electronically for all tax years beginning after July 1, 2019.[4]

A private foundation may request an automatic six-month extension of time to file its Form 990-PF.[5] When it files for an extension, however, a private foundation must pay any net investment income tax that is unpaid as of the original Form 990-PF due date.[6]

(b) Key Form 990-PF Disclosures

Form 990-PF requires a private foundation to provide a detailed analysis of its annual revenues and expenses (Part I); a current balance sheet, showing both book and market value as of the end of the year (Part II); an analysis of changes in net assets or fund balances (Part III); capital gains and losses and other investment income for purposes of calculating the excise tax on net investment income (Parts IV and V); statements regarding activities, which may identify certain areas of noncompliance by the private foundation (Part VI-A); statements regarding activities for which the private foundation may be

---

1. IRC § 6033(a)(1); Reg. § 1.6033-2(a)(2). The exemption from filing an annual Form 990 series return for organizations normally having annual gross receipts of not more than $50,000 does not apply to private foundations. Rev. Proc. 2011-15, 2011-3 I.R.B. 322 § 3.01. Consequently, the requirement for such an organization to instead file a Form 990-N (e-Postcard) likewise does not apply (*id.* at § 3.03).
2. See § 10.2.
3. Reg. § 1.6033-2(e).
4. IRC § 6033(n), enacted as part of the Taxpayer First Act (Pub. L. No. 116-25, § 3101(a), 133 Stat. 981, 1015 (2019)); Reg. § 301.6033-4. An addition to tax (see § 12.4(b)) may apply if Form 990-PF is submitted on paper instead of electronically (Reg. § 301.6033-4(b)).
5. Reg. § 1.6081-9(a). A request for an extension is made on IRS Form 8868 (Application for Automatic Extension of Time to File an Exempt Organization Return) (Reg. § 1.6081-9(b)(1)). The request must be filed on or before the original Form 990-PF due date (Reg. § 1.6081-9(b)(2)).
6. Reg. § 1.6081-9(b)(4).

required to file Form 4720 (and therefore may also be liable for one or more of the excise taxes applicable to private foundations) (Part VI-B); compensation paid to officers, directors, trustees, foundation managers, and to the private foundation's five highest-paid employees and five highest-paid independent contractors (Part VII); a summary of the private foundation's four largest direct charitable activities and two largest program-related investments, along with related expenses (Part VIII); and details regarding the private foundation's minimum investment return, distributable amount, qualifying distributions, undistributed income, and excess distributions carryover to the next tax year (Parts IX – XII).

By statute, a private foundation is required to disclose on Form 990-PF (Part XIV) the names and addresses of its foundation managers[7] who are substantial contributors,[8] or who own 10 percent or more of the stock of any corporation, or an equally large portion of a partnership or other entity, of which the private foundation has a 10 percent or greater interest.[9]

Private foundations are also required by statute to include on Form 990-PF an itemized list of grants and contributions paid during the year or approved for future payment (Part XIV).[10] The list of grants and contributions must show the amount of each grant or contribution, the name and address of the recipient, any relationship between any individual recipient and the foundation's managers or substantial contributors, and a concise statement of the purpose of each such grant or contribution.[11] A private foundation is not required, however, to disclose the name and address of any grant or contribution recipient who is not a disqualified person and who receives, as an indigent or needy person, one or more charitable gifts or grants from the private foundation that do not, in the aggregate, exceed $1,000 during the year.[12]

A separate schedule to Form 990-PF is required to be completed only by private operating foundations (Part XIII).

All private foundations must provide on Form 990-PF an analysis of their income-producing activities and indicate whether those activities constitute unrelated business income, are eligible for an exclusion from unrelated business income, or are related to the private foundation's exempt purposes (Part XV-A). For activities that are related to its exempt purposes, a private foundation must provide an explanation of how each activity contributed importantly

---

7. Within the meaning of IRC § 4946(b).
8. Within the meaning of IRC § 507(d)(2); that is, persons who have contributed more than 2 percent of the total contributions received by the foundation before the close of any tax year, but only if they have contributed more than $5,000.
9. IRC § 6033(c); Reg. § 1.6033-3(a)(4).
10. IRC § 6033(c); Reg. § 1.6033-3(a)(2).
11. Id.
12. Reg. § 1.6033-3(a)(2).

to the accomplishment of the private foundation's exempt purposes (Part XV-B). Interestingly, this level of explanation, and therefore scrutiny, of a private foundation's basis for excluding income from unrelated business income is not required of public charities filing Form 990.

If a private foundation engaged in transfers of cash or other assets, or certain other listed transactions or asset-sharing arrangements with a noncharitable exempt organization,[13] the private foundation is required to identify the name of the organization, the type of transfer or other transaction or asset-sharing arrangement, and the amount involved (Part XVI). If the private foundation is directly or indirectly affiliated with one or more such organizations, it must also disclose the name of the organization and provide a description of the relationship.

(c) Reporting Changes on Form 990-PF

(i) Changes in Activities. When a private foundation changes its activities or governing documents, it must report these changes to the IRS on its Form 990-PF for the year in which the change occurred. Form 990-PF specifically asks whether a private foundation has engaged in any activities that have not previously been reported to the IRS. If it has, the foundation is required to attach a detailed description of the activities.

Although this puts the IRS on notice that the private foundation has changed its activities, as a legal matter it does not preclude the IRS from later examining those activities and proposing excise taxes or revocation of tax-exempt status based on those activities. If a private foundation wants assurance that changes in its activities will not result in excise tax liability or adversely affect its tax-exempt status, it must seek a determination letter or private letter ruling from the IRS on the matter.[14]

(ii) Changes in Governing Documents. Form 990-PF also specifically asks whether a foundation has made any changes, not previously reported to the IRS, in its governing instrument, articles of incorporation, or bylaws, or other similar instruments. If it has, the foundation is required to provide the IRS with a conformed copy of the changes with the return.[15] Because Form 990-PF

---

13. That is, an organization described in IRC § 527 or in IRC § 501(c) other than IRC § 501(c)(3).
14. See § 12.5.
15. A *conformed copy* of a private foundation's organizational document is one that agrees with the original document and all its amendments. Unsigned copies must be accompanied by a written declaration signed by an officer authorized to sign for the organization, certifying that they are complete and accurate copies of the original documents (Instructions for Form 990-PF (2022), Part VI-A, line 3).

is required to be filed electronically, the foundation must mail the conformed copy to the IRS at the appropriate address provided in the Form 990-PF instructions.

(iii) Name and Address Changes. Name and address changes can be reported by checking these boxes on the first page of Form 990-PF and using the new name or address on the return. The IRS should automatically update its Business Master File database to reflect name and address changes reported on Form 990-PF, although this process may be delayed due to IRS resource constraints. A private foundation may seek an affirmation letter from the IRS EO Determinations Office showing its new name and address.[16] It also may, but is not required to, report a name change to the IRS by filing a form.[17]

(d) Other Changes

(i) Change in Annual Accounting Period (Tax Year). As an organization exempt from tax, a private foundation may follow a simplified procedure to change its annual accounting period (tax year). In general, a private foundation may do so by timely filing a Form 990-PF with the appropriate Internal Revenue Service Center for the short period for which a return is required and indicate on the short-year Form 990 that a change of accounting period is being made.[18] The short-year Form 990 must be filed by the 15th day of the 5th month following the close of the short period,[19] unless a request for extension is filed.[20]

For example, assume that a calendar-year foundation wishes to change its tax year to a fiscal year spanning July 1 to June 30. A return is filed, reporting financial transactions for the short-period year (the six months ending June 30 of the year of change). The June 30 return would be due to be filed by November 15, the normal due date for a full-year return ending June 30.

Where a private foundation has previously changed its annual accounting period at any time within the 10 calendar years ending with the calendar year that includes the beginning of the short period resulting from the change of an

---

16. https://www.irs.gov/charities-non-profits/exempt-organizations-affirmation-letters.
17. Form 8822-B. Although the filing of this form is optional for reporting name changes, filing is mandatory within 60 days of a change in a private foundation's responsible party for purposes of the trust fund recovery penalty (on withholding and employment taxes) (Instructions for Form 8822-B (Dec. 2019)). A private foundation's *responsible party* is a person who has a level of control over, or entitlement to, the funds or assets in the foundation that, as a practical matter, enables the person, directly or indirectly, to control, manage, or direct the entity and the disposition of its funds and assets (Instructions for Form SS-48 (Dec. 2019)).
18. Rev. Proc. 85-58, 1985-2 C.B. 740 § 3.01.
19. *Id*. § 3.02.
20. The extension is requested by filing Form 8868. E.g., Tech. Adv. Mem. 200824029.

annual accounting period, this simplified procedure is not available. Instead, the foundation must file IRS Form 1128 (Application to Adopt, Change, or Retain a Tax Year) with the appropriate Internal Revenue Service Center and with its timely-filed Form 990. The Form 1128 must be filed by the 15th day of the 5th month following the close of the short period, not including extensions,[21] and no earlier than the day following the end of the short-year period.[22] A user fee of $5,000 must accompany the copy filed with the Service Center.[23]

When a private foundation changes its tax year, its minimum distribution requirements are calculated for the short tax year, applying a percentage prorated for the number of days in the short tax year. For example, the percentage for a six-month year ending June 30 would be 2.48 percent, or 5 percent times 181/365.[24] The full 5 percent minimum distribution amount attributable to the foundation's last full year ending in December, however, would have to be distributed by the end of the foundation's short tax year (June 30).[25]

(ii) Change in Accounting Method. Generally accepted accounting principles recommend that the accrual method of accounting be used for financial statement reporting; thus, a certified public accountant cannot issue a clean or unqualified opinion on financial statements prepared on a cash receipts and disbursements basis. Because it is simpler, however, many foundations in their early years use the cash method, which is an acceptable method for purposes of filing Form 990-PF and for reporting to most boards and contributors. As a private foundation matures, however, it may desire to change to the accrual method of accounting in order to receive an audited financial statement.

To complicate matters, the cash method is required for calculating annual payout requirements and for reporting charitable donations and qualifying distributions on Form 990-PF.[26]

Once a taxpayer, including a tax-exempt private foundation, adopts an accounting method for federal income tax purposes, the taxpayer must generally request the IRS's consent before it can change its accounting method. In most cases, a taxpayer requests consent to change an accounting method by filing a Form 3115 (Application for Change in Accounting Method).[27] Depending upon the specific accounting method change being requested, however, a private foundation may qualify for automatic consent. If the

---

21. Rev. Proc. 85-58, 1985-2 C.B. 740 § 3.03.
22. Instructions for Form 1128 (Nov. 2017) at 2.
23. Rev. Proc. 2023-1, 2023-1 I.R.B. 1, App. A (Schedule of User Fees).
24. Reg. § 53.4942(a)-2(c)(5)(iii).
25. Rev. Rul. 74-315, 1974-2 C.B. 386; see § 6.2(a).
26. See § 6.4.
27. See generally Rev. Proc. 2015-13, 2015-5 I.R.B. 419.

automatic consent procedures apply and a foundation follows them, it does not have to wait for formal approval by the IRS before applying the new accounting method.[28]

For example, a private foundation that has adopted an accounting method for an item of income from an unrelated trade or business must generally request consent before it can change its method of accounting for that item in any subsequent year (regardless of whether gross income from the unrelated trade or business is greater than or equal to $1,000 in the subsequent year). Alternatively, if a private foundation has not yet adopted an accounting method for an item of income or deduction, a change in how the entity reports the item is not a change in accounting method. In this case, filing a Form 3115 is not required.[29]

§ 12.2 FORM 990-PF PENALTIES

(a) Daily Delinquency Penalty

A daily delinquency penalty applies if Form 990-PF is not filed on time (including any extension of time for filing the return obtained by the private foundation), or if the private foundation fails to include any of the information required to be shown on the Form 990-PF or reports incorrect information.[30] This penalty is equal to $20 per day, or $100 per day for a private foundation with annual gross receipts exceeding $1,000,000 in any year.[31] The penalty is capped with respect to any one return at the lesser of $10,000 or 5 percent of the private foundation's gross receipts for the year, or $50,000 for a private foundation with annual gross receipts exceeding $1,000,000 in any year.[32]

If a private foundation fails to file a Form 990-PF in electronic form, the foundation will be considered to have failed to file the return for purposes of the imposition of the daily delinquency penalty.[33]

The IRS may also make a "written demand" on any private foundation subject to the daily delinquency penalty "specifying therein a reasonable future date by which the return shall be filed" or the missing or incorrect information furnished to the IRS. If any "person," presumably a foundation

---

28. See generally Rev. Proc. 2022-14, 2022-7 I.R.B. 502, or its successor, for a list of accounting method changes that generally qualify for automatic consent.
29. Instructions for Form 990-PF (2022), General Instruction I.
30. IRC § 6652(c)(1)(A).
31. Id.
32. Id. These amounts are adjusted for inflation, and are $12,000, $60,000, and $1,208,500, respectively, for returns required to be filed in 2024 (IRC § 6652(c)(7); Rev. Proc. 2022-38, 2022-45 I.R.B. 445 § 3.53).
33. Reg. § 301.6033-4(b).

manager, fails to comply with such a demand before the date specified in the demand, that person is subject to a $10 penalty for each day the failure continues. The maximum penalty imposed on all persons for failures with respect to any one Form 990-PF is $5,000.[34]

(b) Form 990-PF Statute of Limitations

In general, the statute of limitations during which the IRS may assess the daily delinquency penalty is three years from the due date of the return or the date on which the return is actually filed, whichever is later.[35]

If the Form 990-PF for a tax year omits "material information," the IRS takes the position that this is tantamount to not filing a return at all, and therefore the statute of limitations does not begin to run with respect to that tax year.[36] Thus, the daily delinquency penalty may be asserted at any time with respect to such return.[37] On the other hand, if the Form 990-PF includes all material information but omits nonmaterial information, then the typical three-year statute of limitations will apply to the return.[38]

With respect to Form 990-PF, the IRS considers the following information to be "material":

- The fair market value of the private foundation's assets at the end of the year (Line I).

---

34. IRC § 6652(c)(1)(B). Adjusted for inflation (IRC § 6652(c)(7)), the maximum penalty under this section is $6,000 for returns required to be filed in 2024 (Rev. Proc. 2022-38, 2022-45 I.R.B. 445 § 3.53).

    The requirement that the initial determination of a penalty assessment be personally approved in writing by the immediate supervisor of the IRS individual making the determination does not apply to this penalty or to the daily delinquency penalty because these penalties are automatically calculated through electronic means (IRC § 6751(b)(2)(B); Grace Foundation v. Commissioner, 108 T.C.M. 513 (supervisory approval not required for the delinquency penalty for failure by a tax-exempt organization to file an annual return)). Under proposed regulations, however, this penalty will no longer be considered automatically calculated through electronic means if an organization responds to a computer-generated notice proposing a penalty, challenges the penalty, and an IRS employee works the case (Prop. Reg. § 301.6751(b)-1(a)(3)(vi)). This is because where an organization's response questions the validity of the penalty or the adjustments to which the penalty relates, and an examiner considers the response, any subsequent assessment of the penalty would not be based solely on the automatic calculation of the penalty by the computer program. Instead, it would be at least partially based on a decision by an IRS employee as to whether the penalty is appropriate (88 Fed. Reg. 21564, 21569 (2023)).
35. IRC § 6501(a).
36. IRC § 6501(c)(3); Rev. Rul. 77-162, 1977-1 C.B. 400; Gen. Couns. Mem. 39861 (Sept. 26, 1991).
37. Id.
38. IRC § 6501(a); Gen. Couns. Mem. 39861 (Sept. 26, 1991).

- The analysis of total revenues and expenses of the foundation (all columns), the compensation of officers, directors, and trustees, and adjusted net income (Part I).

- The analysis of the total assets and liabilities of the private foundation at the end of the year (Part III).

- The answers to the questions of whether there was any attempt by the private foundation to influence any legislation or to participate or intervene in any political campaign; whether there was a liquidation, termination, dissolution, or substantial contraction during the year; and whether the foundation is claiming private operating foundation status (Part VI-A).

- The list of states to which the foundation reports or is registered, and the schedule identifying any persons who became substantial contributors to the foundation (Part VI-A).

- Information related to acts of self-dealing; information regarding taxes on failure to distribute income; information on taxes on excess business holdings; information on investments which jeopardize the foundation's charitable purpose; and information on taxes on taxable expenditures (Part VI-B).

- The list of, and compensation paid to, all officers, directors, trustees, and foundation managers, the five highest-paid employees, and the five highest-paid independent contractors for professional services (Part VII).

- The calculations of the minimum investment return (Part IX), the distributable amount (Part X), the total amount of qualifying distributions (Part XI), and undistributed income (Part XII).

- All the information required to be reported on Form 990-PF by a private operating foundation (Part XIII).[39]

A six-year statute of limitations applies if the Form 990-PF omits an amount of net investment income tax in excess of 25 percent of the amount of tax

---

39. Gen. Couns. Mem. 36506 (Dec. 8, 1975); Gen. Couns. Mem. 38760 (Jun. 29, 1981). Although the IRS considers the reasons for the materiality of these items to be an "administrative matter and not a legal one," the IRS Office of Chief Counsel has advised that "if the materiality of these items is questioned by a taxpayer or subsequently made the subject of litigation, the [IRS] should be prepared to substantiate why it considers such items to be material" (Gen. Couns. Mem. 36506, *supra*). See also Blount v. Commissioner, 86 T.C. 383 (1980) (an individual return omitting taxpayer's Form W-2 was "complete" for purposes of applying three-year statute of limitations); Gen. Couns. Mem. 39805 (Sept. 27, 1989) (concluding that the decision in Blount, *supra*, requires a reconsideration of whether the items designated in Gen. Couns. Mem. 36506, *supra*, are still material).

reported on the return."[40] In the case of the net investment income tax, however, the normal three-year statute of limitations will apply if a private foundation discloses in its return (or in a schedule or statement attached thereto) the nature, source, and amount of any income giving rise to the omitted net investment income tax.[41]

(c) Reasonable Cause

The daily delinquency penalties will not apply if a private foundation can show that the failure to file a Form 990-PF or include correct and complete information is due to reasonable cause.[42] The private foundation bears the burden of establishing reasonable cause.[43] To establish reasonable cause, the private foundation must make an affirmative showing of reasonable cause in the form of a written statement, containing a declaration by the appropriate person (or in their absence by any officer, director, or trustee of the organization) that the statement is made under penalties of perjury, setting forth all the facts alleged as reasonable cause.[44] The "appropriate person" means any officer, director, trustee, employee, member, or other individual whose duty it is to perform the act in respect of which the violation occurs.[45]

Neither the statute nor the regulations defines what constitutes reasonable cause for abatement of the daily delinquency penalty. However, authorities related to establishing reasonable cause for the avoidance of the accuracy-related penalties on understatements provide the most likely legal framework.[46]

---

40. IRC § 6501(e)(3); Reg. § 301.6501(e)-1(c)(1).
41. Reg. § 301.6501(e)-1(c)(3)(i). If such a disclosure is made, the net investment income tax arising from the adequately disclosed income is counted as reported on the return in computing whether the private foundation has omitted more than 25 percent of the tax reported on its return (*id.*).
42. IRC § 6652(c)(5). A private foundation is deemed to have reasonable cause for failure to comply with the requirements of IRC § 6033 for filing of returns and payment of taxes until 90 days after it is issued a letter containing a determination of private foundation status from the IRS, thereby immunizing it from application of the IRC § 6652 penalty with respect to a tax year for which, prior to the due date for filing Form 990-PF, the organization has filed notice (on Form 1023) claiming not to be a private foundation (Rev. Proc. 79-8, 1979-1 C.B. 487).
43. West Side Tennis Club v. Commissioner, 111 F.2d 6 (2d Cir.1940); Hale v. Commissioner, T.C. Memo 2010-229, 44 T.C.M. 1116.
44. Treas. Reg. § 301.6652-2(f).
45. Treas. Reg. § 301.6652-2(d)(1).
46. Accuracy penalties (IRC § 6662) apply to underpayments attributable to, among other things, negligence or disregard of rules or regulations, substantial understatements of income tax, and substantial valuation misstatements. IRC § 6664(c) provides an exception for the portion of any underpayment if it is shown that there was a reasonable cause for such portion and that the taxpayer acted in good faith.

For purposes of the accuracy-related penalties, whether a taxpayer acted with reasonable cause is determined on a case-by-case basis, taking into account all pertinent facts and circumstances, with the most important factor generally being "the extent of the taxpayer's effort to assess the taxpayer's proper tax liability."[47] "Circumstances that may indicate reasonable cause and good faith include an honest misunderstanding of fact or law that is reasonable in light of all the facts and circumstances, including the experience, knowledge and education of the taxpayer."[48] For example, a bankruptcy court found that a trustee had reasonable cause for failing to file a return and an extension to file where ongoing litigation made it impossible for the trustee to determine the amount of taxes due or the amount of estimated taxes that was required to be paid upon filing of an extension.[49]

Reliance on professional advice does not necessarily constitute reasonable cause, but will if, under all the circumstances, such reliance was reasonable and the taxpayer acted in good faith.[50] A taxpayer's "education, sophistication and business experience will be relevant in determining whether the taxpayer's reliance on tax advice was reasonable and made in good faith."[51] Minimum requirements that must be met for reliance on the opinion or advice of a professional to be considered reasonable cause are: (1) the advisor was a competent professional who had sufficient expertise to justify reliance (that is, the taxpayer did not know, or should not have known, that the advisor lacked knowledge in the relevant aspects of federal tax law); (2) the advice was based on all pertinent facts and circumstances and the tax law as it relates to the matter involved, including the taxpayer's purpose for entering into the transaction and for structuring it in a particular manner; and (3) the advice was based on reasonable factual or legal assumptions and did not unreasonably rely on the representations, statements, findings, or agreements of the taxpayer or any other person.[52]

In evaluating whether reasonable cause exists, courts often examine whether a taxpayer acted with "ordinary business care and prudence" when relying on professional advice. The U.S. Supreme Court wrote:

> When an accountant or attorney advises a taxpayer on a matter of tax law, such as whether a liability exists, it is reasonable for the taxpayer to rely on that advice. Most taxpayers are not competent to discern error in the

---

47. Reg. § 1.6664-4(b)(1).
48. *Id.*
49. In re Molnick's, Inc., 95-1 U.S.T.C. ¶ 50,209 (Bankr. C.D. Cal. 1995).
50. Reg. § 1.6664-4(b)(1).
51. Reg. § 1.6664-4(c)(1).
52. *Id.*; see also Neonatology Assoc., P.A. v. Commissioner, 115 T.C. 43, 99 (2000), *aff'd*, 299 F.3d 221 (3d Cir. 2002).

substantive advice of an accountant or attorney. To require the taxpayer to challenge the attorney, to seek a "second opinion," or to try to monitor counsel on the provisions of the Code himself would nullify the very purpose of seeking the advice of a presumed expert in the first place . . . . "Ordinary business care and prudence" does not demand such actions.[53]

"When a corporate taxpayer selects a competent tax expert, supplies him with all necessary information, and requests him to prepare proper tax returns, . . . the taxpayer has done all that ordinary business care and prudence can reasonably demand."[54]

To be sure, there are limitations to the reasonable cause defense in the context of reliance on a competent tax return preparer. "Even if all data is furnished to the preparer, the taxpayer still has a duty to read the return and make sure all income items are included."[55] This does not mean, however, that a taxpayer must "duplicate the work of his return preparer, or that any omission of an income item in a return prepared by a third party is necessarily fatal to a finding of reasonable cause and good faith . . . ."[56] Thus, a court conceded that "the reasonable cause defense may be available to a taxpayer who conducts a review of his third-party prepared return with the intent of ensuring that all income items are included, and who exerts effort that is reasonable under the circumstances, but who nonetheless fails to discover an omission of an income item."[57]

A private foundation that pays another person, such as a management services company, for the services of its officers, directors, trustees, foundation managers, or highest-paid employees is no longer considered to have reasonable cause for purposes of the daily delinquency penalty if it reports a bulk compensation amount paid to a management services company on Form 990-PF.[58] Rather, in accordance with the Form 990-PF instructions, it must report the compensation paid to each person who provided services to the private foundation on behalf of that management company as if the private foundation had paid them directly.

---

53. United States v. Boyle, 469 U.S. 241, 251 (1985).
54. Haywood Lumber & Mining Co. v. Commissioner, 178 F.2d 769, 771 (2d Cir. 1950).
55. Magill v. Commissioner, 70 T.C. 465, 479-80 (1978), aff'd, 651 F.2d 1233 (6th Cir. 1981).
56. Woodsum v. Commissioner, 136 T.C. 585, 595-96 (2011).
57. *Id*. at 596. In this case, the court found that the taxpayer's review of their return did not reflect the exertion of a reasonable effort under the circumstances where he failed to discover the omission of $3.4 million of income; thus, the court held that reasonable cause did not exist for the omission of this income notwithstanding taxpayer's reliance on a tax return preparer to whom the taxpayer gave an information return reporting the income (*id*.).
58. Ann. 2021-18, 2021-52 I.R.B. 910, revoking Ann. 2001-33, 2001-1 C.B. 1137.

(d) Amended Returns

If a taxpayer subsequently discovers an amount of net investment income tax was omitted from a previously filed Form 990-PF, regulations in other contexts indicate that the taxpayer "should, if within the period of limitation, file an amended return and pay any additional tax due."[59] However, a taxpayer has no obligation to file an amended return, and the IRS is not required to accept an amended return.[60] Such acceptance is within the IRS's discretion,[61] although in practice the IRS typically does accept the filing of an amended return. The filing of an amended return, assuming it is accepted by the IRS, does not extend the statute of limitations.[62]

Because there is no obligation to file an amended return, most private foundations do not amend a Form 990-PF subsequently found to be in error unless the return omits or misstates material information. If there is such an omission or misstatement, filing an amended return is typically prudent to avoid an open-ended statute of limitations for that tax year.[63] Filing an amended return before the IRS discovers a material omission or misstatement may also help support a private foundation's reasonable cause defense to the imposition of the daily delinquency penalty.[64] In the event a private foundation chooses not to file an amended Form 990-PF, the correct and complete information should be reported on the following year's return.

§12.3 PUBLIC DISCLOSURE AND INSPECTION OF RETURNS

(a) Disclosure of Returns to the Public

A private foundation must make its Forms 990-PF and Forms 990-T, if any, available for public inspection during regular business hours at its principal office, and at any regional or district office that has three or more employees.[65] Regional or district offices subject to the requirement are further limited to any office that has full- or part-time employees whose aggregate number of paid hours per week are at least 120.[66] An office is exempted from the requirement if the only services provided at the site further exempt purposes (such

---

59. Reg. §§ 1.451-1(a), 1.461-1(a)(3).
60. Badaracco v. Commissioner, 464 U.S. 386, 393 (1984).
61. Colvin v. Commissioner, 95 A.F.T.R.2d 1079 (5th Cir. 2005).
62. Zellerbach Paper Co. v. Helvering, 293 U.S. 172 (1934); National Refining Co. v. Commissioner, 1 B.T.A. 236 (1924).
63. See § 12.2(b).
64. See § 12.2(c).
65. IRC § 6104(d)(1)(A)(i), (ii). This disclosure regime likewise applies to returns filed by nonexempt private foundations and nonexempt charitable trusts (IRC § 6104(d)(8)).
66. Reg. § 301.6104(d)-1(b)(5).

§12.3 PUBLIC DISCLOSURE AND INSPECTION OF RETURNS

as day care, health care, or scientific or medical research) and the site does not serve as an office for management staff, other than managers who are involved solely in managing the exempt activities at the site.[67]

The public inspection requirement does not apply to returns, including amended returns, that are more than three years old.[68] The three-year period is calculated based on the date the return is required to be filed, including any filing extensions, or the date it is actually filed, whichever is later.[69] An amended return must be made available for three years from the date it is filed.[70] The public inspection requirement also applies to a private foundation's application for recognition of exemption, any papers submitted in support of its application, and any letter or other document issued by the IRS with respect to its application, including but not limited to its determination letter (collectively, its "application materials").[71] If the IRS has not yet recognized a private foundation as exempt, then its application materials are not (yet) subject to disclosure.[72] Unlike public charities, a private foundation is required to disclose the names and addresses of its contributors in response to a request for public inspection of its returns or application materials and may not redact their names from copies made available for public disclosure.[73]

Unless one of two exceptions applies,[74] a private foundation must also provide copies of these returns and application materials upon request, without charge other than a reasonable fee for any reproduction and mailing costs.[75] If the request is made in person, the requested copies must be provided "immediately"; if made in writing, the private foundation must provide the copies within 30 days.[76]

One exception to the requirement to provide copies applies if the IRS determines, upon application by the private foundation, that such request is

---

67. Id.
68. IRC § 6104(d)(2).
69. Reg. § 301.6104(d)-1(b)(4)(iii).
70. Id.
71. IRC § 6104(d)(1)(A)(iii). An exception to these inspection and disclosure rules as they pertain to application materials applies if the private foundation filed its application before July 15, 1987, and it did not have a copy of the application on that date (Reg. § 301.6104(d)-1(b)(3)(iii)(B)).
72. Reg. § 301.6104(d)-1(b)(3)(iii)(A).
73. IRC § 6104(d)(3)(A); Reg. § 301.6104(d)-1(b)(3)(iii)(C); Reg. § 301.6104(d)-1(b)(4)(ii). Form 990-PF requires a private foundation to indicate whether any persons became substantial contributors during the tax year, and if so, attach a schedule listing their names and addresses (Form 990-PF (2022), Part VI-A).
74. IRC § 6104(d)(4).
75. IRC § 6104(d)(1)(B); Reg. § 301.6104(d)-1(d)(3) (defining a "reasonable fee" for providing copies).
76. IRC § 6104(d)(1).

part of a harassment campaign and that compliance with such request is not in the public interest.[77] A private foundation may disregard, without seeking a determination from the IRS that the request is part of a harassment campaign, any request for copies beyond the first two received within any 30-day period, or the first four received within any one-year period, from the same individual or the same address.[78]

The other exception to the requirement to provide copies applies with respect to returns and application materials that the private foundation makes widely available. A private foundation may make its returns and application materials *widely available* by posting them on a webpage that it establishes and maintains, or by having the document posted, as part of a database of similar documents of other tax-exempt organizations, on a webpage established and maintained by another entity. The webpage must clearly inform readers that the document is available and provide instructions for downloading it; be posted in a format that exactly reproduces the document as originally filed with the IRS; and permit the document to be accessed, downloaded, viewed, and printed for free and without the need for specialized computer hardware of software (other than readily available, free software).[79] Currently, both Guidestar.org and the IRS's *Tax-Exempt Organization Search* database[80] post copies of Forms 990-PF that satisfy these requirements; however, application materials, other than determination letters, are not similarly posted.[81] If a private foundation has posted its returns and application materials on its own website, or is relying on a third-party website, to make its returns or application materials widely available, it must notify any individual requesting a copy where the documents are available (including the web address). If the request is made in person, the organization must provide this notice immediately; if made in writing, the notice must be provided within seven days of receiving the request.[82] This exception only applies to requests for copies; a private foundation must nevertheless make the document available for public inspection at its offices as described above.[83]

A daily delinquency penalty applies with respect to any failure to meet the public inspection or copying requirements for returns or application materials. With respect to returns, this penalty is equal to $20 per day, up to a

---

77. IRC § 6104(d)(4); Reg. § 301.6104(d)-3.
78. Reg. § 301.6104(d)-3(c).
79. Reg. § 301.6104(d)-2.
80. https://www.irs.gov/charities-non-profits/tax-exempt-organization-search.
81. Beginning December 31, 2021, the publicly available data provided by the IRS from electronically filed Forms 990 in a machine-readable format is to be found solely in its *Tax-Exempt Organization Search* database (IR-2021-250 (Dec. 16, 2021)).
82. Reg. § 301.6104(d)-2(d).
83. Reg. § 301.6104(d)-2(a).

§12.3 PUBLIC DISCLOSURE AND INSPECTION OF RETURNS

maximum of $10,000 per any one return.[84] With respect to application materials, this penalty is equal to $20 per day, with no maximum.[85] As with the daily delinquency penalties for failure to file a Form 990-PF, these disclosure-related penalties will not apply if the private foundation can show that the failure to comply was due to reasonable cause.[86] An additional penalty of $5,000 applies in the case of any willful failure to comply with the public inspection or copying requirements.[87]

Although there is no private right of action to compel the production of a private foundation's returns or application materials, one court observed that "current IRS regulations offer the public a mechanism for complaining to the IRS" if a foundation fails to comply with the public disclosure and inspections rules.[88] If a private foundation denies an individual's request for inspection or a copy of its returns or application materials, the individual may "alert" the IRS "to the possible need for enforcement action" by providing a statement to the IRS that describes the reason why the individual believes the denial was in violation of the inspection or copying requirements.[89]

(b) Disclosure of Returns to State Officials

A private foundation is required to list on its annual Form 990-PF (Part VI-A) all states to which the private foundation reports in any fashion concerning its organization, assets, or activities, or with which the private foundation has registered (or which it has otherwise notified in any manner) that it intends to be, or is, a charitable organization or a holder of property devoted to a charitable purpose.[90] At the same time a private foundation files its Form 990-PF with the IRS, it must also furnish a copy to the Attorney General of any state included on this list, the state in which its principal office is located, and the state in which it was incorporated or created. Upon request, a copy of Form 990-PF must also be furnished to the Attorney General or other appropriate state officer of any state.[91] A copy of Form 4720, if any, filed by the private foundation for the year must also be attached to any Form 990-PF required to be sent to a state officer.[92]

---

84. IRC § 6652(c)(1)(C). Adjusted for inflation (IRC § 6652(c)(7)), the maximum penalty under this section is $12,000 for returns required to be filed in 2024 (Rev. Proc. 2022-38, 2022-45 I.R.B. 445 § 3.53).
85. IRC § 6652(c)(1)(D).
86. IRC § 6652(c)(5). See § 12.2(c).
87. IRC § 6685.
88. Tax Analysts v. Internal Revenue Service, 214 F.3d 179 (D.C. Cir. 2000).
89. Reg. § 301.6104(d)-1(g).
90. IRC § 6033(c)(1); Reg. § 1.6033-2(a)(2)(iv).
91. IRC § 6033(c)(2); Reg. § 1.6033-3(c). The term "appropriate state officer" is defined in IRC § 6104(c)(6)(B).
92. Reg. § 1.6033-3(c)(1)(iii).

§ 12.4 REPORTING AND PAYMENT OF EXCISE TAXES

(a) Reporting and Payment on Form 4720

The private foundation excise tax regime is largely dependent on self-enforcement by foundations that engage in taxable transactions. Form 990-PF (Part VI-B) asks a series of detailed questions regarding whether a private foundation has engaged in any activities that would give rise to the imposition of Chapter 42 excise taxes on the foundation. If a private foundation indicates that it has engaged in a taxable transaction, it will also be required to file a Form 4720.

Even if the taxable transaction reported on Form 990-PF is a self-dealing transaction for which the private foundation itself has no excise tax liability, the foundation must file a Form 4720 to report the transaction.[93] In these situations, the foundation may have incomplete information as to how to calculate the excise tax on such transactions, in which case the foundation would appear to be left to calculate the tax on the self-dealing disqualified persons or foundation managers to the best of its ability.

Form 4720 is used to figure and pay initial taxes on self-dealers, private foundations, and foundation managers, as appropriate, for self-dealing[94] (Schedule A), failure to distribute income[95] (Schedule B), excess business holdings[96] (Schedule C), investments that jeopardize charitable purpose[97] (Schedule D), taxable expenditures[98] (Schedule E), and political expenditures[99] (Schedule F). A private foundation also uses Form 4720 to report excise taxes on being a party to a prohibited tax shelter transaction[100] (Schedule J) and excess executive compensation[101] (Schedule N).

Other taxes reported on Form 4720 that are not applicable to private foundations include taxes on excess lobbying expenditures[102] (Schedule G), disqualifying lobbying expenditures[103] (Schedule H), excess benefit transactions[104]

---

93. Reg. § 53.6011-1(b).
94. IRC § 4941; see Chapter 5.
95. IRC § 4942; see Chapter 6.
96. IRC § 4943; see Chapter 7.
97. IRC § 4944; see Chapter 8.
98. IRC § 4945; see Chapter 9.
99. IRC § 4955. To the extent this tax is imposed on a political expenditure of a private foundation, such expenditure will not also be treated as a taxable expenditure (IRC § 4955(e); see § 9.2).
100. IRC § 4965.
101. IRC § 4960; see §§ 5.6(e), 17.8.
102. IRC § 4911; but see § 9.1.
103. IRC § 4912(c)(2)(C).
104. IRC § 4958.

§ 12.4 REPORTING AND PAYMENT OF EXCISE TAXES

(Schedule I), distributions of sponsoring organizations maintaining donor-advised funds[105] (Schedule K), prohibited benefits from donor-advised funds[106] (Schedule L), failure of a hospital organization to meet community health needs[107] (Schedule M), and net investment income of private colleges and universities[108] (Schedule O).

Like Form 990-PF, a private foundation must file Form 4720 electronically.[109] Because private foundations must file Form 4720 electronically, and the IRS system allows for only one taxpayer per return, a self-dealer, foundation manager, or other disqualified person who owes tax may no longer report the tax on the Form 4720 filed by the private foundation but rather must file a separate Form 4720.[110] Most self-dealers, foundation managers, or other disqualified persons who are individuals may continue to file a paper Form 4720; however, an entity must file its Form 4720 electronically if it is required to file at least 10 returns of any type during the calendar year.[111]

In general, Form 4720 is due by the due date (not including extensions) for filing a private foundation's Form 990-PF.[112] However, if the tax year of a self-dealer or other disqualified person ends on a date other than the private foundation's tax year, Form 4720 must be filed on or before the 15th day of the 5th month following the close of such person's tax year.[113] A Form 4720 must be filed for each year until the act (or failure to act) giving rise to the excise tax liability is corrected.[114] An automatic extension to file Form 4720 can be obtained by filing a separate form,[115] but any excise tax due must be paid with the filing of the extension to avoid the imposition of certain additions to tax and statutory interest.[116]

For transactions requiring correction, Form 4720 requires a private foundation or disqualified person to provide a detailed description of any correction

---

105. IRC § 4966(d)(1)(B); see § 16.7.
106. IRC § 4967; see § 16.7.
107. IRC §§ 501(r)(3), 4959.
108. IRC § 4968.
109. Form 4720, when filed by a private foundation, is part of the return required to be filed electronically under IRC § 6033 (Reg. § 301.6033-4(c)).
110. Reg. § 53.6011-1 was revised to remove the ability of a disqualified person to designate the private foundation's Form 4720 as the disqualified person's return, because joint Form 4720 submissions are no longer possible (T.D. 9972, 88 Fed. Reg. 11754 (2023)).
111. Reg. § 301.6011-12(a)(1). A "return" for these purposes is a return of "any type," including information returns (for example, Forms W-2 and Forms 1099), income tax returns, employment tax returns, and excise tax returns (Reg. § 301.6011-12(d)(3)).
112. Reg. § 53.6071-1(a).
113. Reg. § 53.6071-1(b).
114. Reg. § 53.6011-1(b).
115. Form 8868, Application for Extension of Time to File an Exempt Organization Return.
116. See § 12.4(b).

made (full or partial), and the date of each correction, or a detailed explanation of why full correction has not been made and what steps are being taken to make the correction.

Form 4720 filed by a private foundation is subject to public disclosure, whereas Form 4720 filed by a disqualified person is not.[117]

(b) Additions to Tax and Penalties

An addition to tax is imposed with respect to the failure to file a Form 4720 if one is required to be filed. The amount of this addition is equal to 5 percent of the tax required to be shown on the return for the first month the return is past due, with an additional 5 percent for each additional month (or fraction thereof) during which the failure to file continues, not to exceed 25 percent in the aggregate.[118] An addition to tax is also imposed with respect to the failure to pay a tax shown on Form 4720 when the tax is due. The amount of this addition to tax is equal to 0.5 percent of the unpaid tax for each month the tax remains unpaid, not to exceed 25 percent of the unpaid tax.[119] An addition to tax in the same amount likewise applies with respect to the failure to pay a tax required to be shown on a return, but not shown, when the tax is due (which would be the case if a Form 4720 is required to be filed, and a tax to be shown on the return, but is not).[120] Interest may also be charged on unpaid excise taxes at an underpayment rate set by statute.[121]

---

117. Reg. § 1.6033-2(a)(2)(ii)(J) clarifies that Form 4720, when filed by a private foundation, is part of the information return required under IRC § 6033 as well as a tax return required under IRC § 6011; therefore, Form 4720 filed by a private foundation is information required by IRC § 6033 and the regulations thereunder and thus is disclosable under IRC § 6104 (see § 12.3(a)), whereas Form 4720 filed by a taxpayer other than a private foundation is not information required by IRC § 6033 and the regulations thereunder and thus is not disclosable under IRC § 6104 (T.D. 7785, 46 Fed. Reg. 38507 (1981); Notice 2021-1, 2021-2 I.R.B. 315).
118. IRC § 6651(a)(1). This addition to tax also applies if Form 4720 is submitted on paper when required to be filed electronically (see § 12.4(a)) (Reg. § 301.3011.12(c)).
119. IRC § 6651(a)(2). The larger failure to file penalty will be partially offset to the extent this smaller failure to pay penalty is also imposed (IRC § 6651(c)(1)).
120. IRC § 6651(a)(3). The requirement that the initial determination of a penalty assessment be personally approved in writing by the immediate supervisor of the IRS individual making the determination does not apply to this addition to tax (IRC § 6751(b)(2)(A)).
121. See IRC §§ 6601, 6621. Relying on Latterman v. United States, 872 F.2d 564 (3d Cir. 1989), the IRS is likely to take the position that private foundation excise taxes are taxes, not penalties, and therefore that underpayment interest begins to accrue on the due date for filing Form 4720, as opposed to from the date of an IRS notice and demand for payment (as is generally the case with penalties) (see, e.g., Chief Couns. Adv. 200819017 (May 9, 2008)). But see § 1.8(c), concerning whether the self-dealing taxes are penal in nature and therefore constitute penalties, not taxes.

§ 12.4 REPORTING AND PAYMENT OF EXCISE TAXES

If a private foundation or disqualified person fails to file a Form 4720 electronically when required to do so, this is considered a failure to file the return for purposes of the imposition of the addition to tax for failure to file a return.[122]

If Form 4720 is required to be filed by a private foundation or a disqualified person but is not filed, and the IRS prepares a substitute Form 4720, the substitute Form 4720 is disregarded for purposes of the addition to tax for failure to file. That is, the substitute return is not treated as a return filed by the taxpayer and the addition to tax for failure to file will still apply. The substitute Form 4720 is treated as a return filed by the taxpayer, however, for purposes of the addition to tax for failure to pay, such that the taxpayer will also be liable for the additions to tax with respect to the taxpayer's failure to pay any unpaid amount shown on the substitute return.[123]

None of these additions to tax will be imposed if it can be shown that the failure at issue was "due to reasonable cause and not due to willful neglect."[124] The term "willful neglect" means a "conscious, intentional failure or reckless indifference."[125] For purposes of the additions to tax, if the taxpayer exercised ordinary business care and prudence and was nevertheless unable to file a return within the prescribed time, then the delay is considered to be due to a reasonable cause.[126] The taxpayer bears the burden of establishing reasonable cause.[127] As with the daily delinquency penalty that applies with respect to Form 990-PF, a taxpayer who wishes to avoid an addition to tax must make an affirmative showing of all facts alleged as a reasonable cause for their failure to file such return or pay such tax on time in the form of a written statement containing a declaration that it is made under penalties of perjury.[128]

Reasonable cause is presumed for purposes of the failure to file penalty in the case of a disqualified person liable for the initial self-dealing tax where a private foundation files a Form 4720 in good faith and such return indicates no tax liability with respect to such tax.[129] This presumption does not apply if

---

122. Reg. § 301.6011-12(c).
123. IRC § 6651(a)(2), (3), and (g); Reg. § 301.6651-1(g).
124. IRC § 6651(a).
125. United States v. Boyle, 469 U.S. 241 (1985).
126. Reg. § 301.6651-1(c)(1). For the definition of "ordinary business care and prudence," see § 12.2(c).
127. West Side Tennis Club v. Commissioner, 111 F.2d 6 (2d Cir.1940); Hale v. Commissioner, 44 T.C.M. 1116 (1982).
128. Reg. § 301.6651-1(c).
129. Reg. § 53.6651-1(b)(1).

TAX REPORTING AND ADMINISTRATION ISSUES

the disqualified person knew of facts that, if known by the private foundation, would have precluded the private foundation from filing the Form 4720 in good faith.[130]

The IRS may also seek to impose an accuracy-related penalty on an underpayment of private foundation excise taxes that is attributable to negligence or disregard of rules or regulations.[131] On the face of the statute, the accuracy-related penalty for a substantial understatement of *income* tax[132] does not apply to *excise* taxes.[133] The applicable regulations also limit the application of the accuracy-related penalty for negligence or disregard of rules and regulations to income taxes,[134] but the statute itself does not contain any such limitation.[135] Thus, the IRS is likely to apply this penalty to an understatement of excise tax that is attributable to negligence or disregard of rules or regulations on the ground that the regulations conflict with the statute.[136]

Penalties also apply in the case of a willful failure to file a Form 4720, or to supply information required by law or pay tax with respect to a Form 4720, and for willfully filing fraudulent returns or statements. These tax crimes are punishable by a fine or imprisonment, or both.[137]

(c) Abatement

The IRS has discretionary authority not to assess, or to abate or refund, any qualified first-tier tax, if a private foundation establishes to the satisfaction of the IRS that the violation: (1) was due to reasonable cause; (2) was not due to willful neglect; and (3) has been corrected within the appropriate correction period.[138] All of the initial private foundation excise taxes are *qualified first-tier taxes*, except for the initial tax on an act of self-dealing.[139] Reasonable cause for purposes of the abatement provision generally equates

---

130. Reg. § 53.6651-1(b)(2).
131. IRC § 6662(b)(1); see § 11.5(e).
132. See § 11.5(e).
133. IRC § 6662(b)(2), (d)(1)(A); Drummond v. Commissioner, 73 T.C.M. 1959 (1997).
134. Reg. § 1.6662-3(a).
135. IRC § 6662(b)(1), (c).
136. E.g., Program Manager Tech. Adv. 2007-00205.
137. IRC §§ 7203, 7206, 7207.
138. IRC § 4962(a).
139. IRC § 4962(b). Although the initial tax on the participation of a foundation manager in an act of self-dealing cannot be abated under IRC § 4962, the statutory language of IRC § 4941(a)(2) itself provides an exception to the imposition of the tax where the foundation manager's "participation is not willful and is due to reasonable cause" (*id.*).

§ 12.4 REPORTING AND PAYMENT OF EXCISE TAXES

to the exercise of ordinary business care and prudence,[140] and the taxpayer bears the burden of establishing reasonable cause.[141] The term *willful neglect* means a voluntary, conscious, intentional act or failure to act or reckless indifference.[142]

For purposes of the abatement provision, the term *correct* means reducing the amount of undistributed income to zero for the excise tax on failure to distribute income; reducing the amount of excess business holdings to zero for the excise tax on excess business holdings; and removing the investment from jeopardy for the excise tax on investments that jeopardize charitable purpose.[143] For the excise taxes on acts of self-dealing and taxable expenditures, "correct" has the same meaning as when used in the section that imposes the second-tier tax.[144]

The term *correction period* means, with respect to any taxable event, the period beginning on the date on which such event occurs and ending 90 days after the date of mailing of a notice of deficiency with respect to the second-tier tax imposed on such taxable event.[145] The correction period is extended by (1) any period in which a deficiency cannot be assessed because the time for filing a petition in Tax Court has not expired or a petition has been filed and the decision of the court has not become final, and (2) any other period that the IRS determines is reasonable and necessary to bring about correction of the taxable event.[146] If the tax is paid and a refund claim is filed, the correction period is extended during the pendency of the claim plus an additional 90 days; if within that time a suit for refund of the tax with respect to the claim is timely filed,[147] the correction period is extended until the determination in the suit for refund is final.[148]

---

140. Reasonable cause is not defined in IRC § 4962; however, regulations under certain of the private foundation excise tax provisions indicate that the standard should be "ordinary business care and prudence." See Treas. Reg. §§ 53.4941(a)-1(b)(5), 53.4944-1(b)(2)(iii), 53.4945-1(a)(2)(v); see also § 12.2(c).
141. West Side Tennis Club v. Commissioner, 111 F.2d 6 (2d Cir.1940); Hale v. Commissioner, 44 T.C.M. 1116 (1982).
142. United States v. Boyle, 469 U.S. 241 (1985). See also Treas. Reg. §§ 53.4941(a)-1(b)(4), 53.4944-1(b)(2)(ii), 53.4945-1(a)(2)(iv).
143. IRC § 4963(d)(2).
144. IRC §§ 4941(e)(3), 4945(i), 4963(d)(1).
145. IRC § 4963(e)(1).
146. *Id.* The IRS ordinarily will not exercise its discretion to extend the correction period unless adequate corrective action cannot reasonably be expected to result during the unextended correction period and the taxable event appears to have been an isolated occurrence such that similar taxable events are unlikely to occur in the future (Reg. § 53.4963-1(e)(3)).
147. IRC § 7422(g).
148. Reg. § 53.4963-1(e)(5). Reg. § 301.7422-1(a) provides rules for determining when a suit for refund is final.

The *taxable event* for these purposes is the act (or failure to act) giving rise to liability for one of the private foundation excise taxes.[149] The taxable event is treated as occurring: on the first day of the tax year for which there was a failure to distribute income; on the first day on which there are excess business holdings; or on the date on which the event occurred in the case of all other private foundation excise taxes.[150]

The U.S. Tax Court has adopted a three-part test for determining whether a taxpayer reasonably relied on professional advice, which requires a taxpayer to prove by a preponderance of the evidence that: (1) the advisor was a competent professional who had sufficient expertise to justify reliance, (2) the taxpayer provided necessary and accurate information to the advisor, and (3) the taxpayer actually relied in good faith on the advisor's judgment.[151] Applying this test, the IRS was not satisfied that a private foundation had established reasonable cause for the abatement of the excess business holdings tax where the foundation submitted no evidence that it provided necessary and accurate information to its advisors or that it had actually relied on its advisors' judgment. The IRS conceded that ignorance of the law regarding excess business holdings was sufficient to establish that the private foundation did not act with willful neglect, but it was insufficient to establish reasonable cause.[152] On the other hand, where a taxpayer relied on a written analysis of its "well-respected" tax preparer concluding that the amount of its business holdings did not constitute excess business holdings and were thus permissible, the IRS found reasonable cause for abatement.[153]

The IRS was not satisfied that reasonable cause for abatement existed where a private foundation failed to exercise expenditure responsibility over certain grants. The private foundation argued that by providing full information regarding the grants to both its legal counsel and its tax return preparer, neither of whom identified the need for the foundation to exercise expenditure responsibility, the foundation reasonably relied on their professional advice that expenditure responsibility was not required. The IRS rejected this argument on the grounds that merely providing an attorney or tax preparer

---

149. IRC § 4963(c).
150. IRC § 4963(e)(2).
151. Neonatology Associates, P.A. v. Commissioner, 115 T.C. 43, 99 (2000), *aff'd*. 299 F.3d 221 (3d Cir. 2002). The court's test is based on Reg. § 1.6664-4(c) (see § 12.2(c)).
152. Tech. Adv. Mem. 201441021. The legislative history of the abatement provision (IRC § 4962) states that a "violation" of the initial Chapter 42 private foundation excise taxes "which was due to ignorance of the law is not to qualify for abatement" (H.R. Rep. No. 98-432, pt. 2, at 1472 (1984), and S. Rep. No. 98-169, at 591 (1984)).
153. Tech. Adv. Mem. 201448032. The written advice was prepared with full knowledge of the facts, addressed the facts and the applicable law, but nevertheless reached an erroneous conclusion (*id.*).

§ 12.4 REPORTING AND PAYMENT OF EXCISE TAXES

with all the appropriate information does not constitute professional advice that exercising expenditure responsibility is unnecessary.[154] The IRS similarly found lack of reasonable cause for making required minimum distributions where a private foundation failed to provide evidence to substantiate its claim that it was advised by its accounting firm that it met the private operating foundation requirements (which it in fact did not) and thus was not required to make any minimum distributions.[155]

The IRS found that a private foundation did not have reasonable cause for the abatement of the initial tax on taxable expenditures where it made a grant, without exercising expenditure responsibility, to an organization that had filed an application for recognition of exemption but had not yet received a determination letter from the IRS recognizing it as a public charity.[156]

Although satisfying the IRS that reasonable cause for abatement exists may be a challenge in some cases, the IRS found that reasonable cause existed to abate the initial tax on failure to distribute income in the case of a non-exempt charitable trust treated as a private foundation that failed to make sufficient qualifying distributions. The trustee, who was not a sophisticated investor, relied on an accountant who was an enrolled agent and held themselves out as a tax expert to advise the trustee as to the correct return to file and other tax-related obligations. The accountant incorrectly advised the trustee to file an annual return for a trust, not a private foundation, and did not inform the trustee of the requirement to make qualifying distributions and pay net investment income tax. The IRS concluded that the trustee had no reason to question the advice of the accountant until the trustee consulted a new accountant and tax counsel, at which time the trustee filed Forms 990-PF for prior tax years and made corrective qualifying distributions. This private

---

154. Tech. Adv. Mem. 201547007. The IRS relied on Woodsum v. Commissioner, 136 T.C. 585 (2011), and Hans Mannheimer Charitable Trust v. Commissioner, 93 T.C. 35 (1989), to support this rather harsh conclusion. Its reliance on both is dubious. The omission of a substantial item of income from a taxpayer's return of which the taxpayer was most certainly aware, as was the case in Woodsum, is quite different than answering the specific questions posed on Form 990-PF that ask whether grants were made to noncharitable organizations and whether any of them failed to qualify for an exception under the applicable regulations. By the IRS's own admission, the "technical requirements underlying expenditure responsibility constitute four pages of regulations" (Tech. Adv. Mem. 201547007); therefore, reliance on a qualified return preparer to determine whether an exception was applicable with respect to grants fully disclosed to the preparer would seem immanently reasonable. Mannheimer is also inapposite insofar as its strict application of the initial tax on taxable expenditures predated the enactment of the abatement provision (IRC § 4962).
155. Tech. Adv. Mem. 201129050.
156. Tech. Adv. Mem. 201351027. The IRS noted that there was no evidence indicating that the foundation consulted with or sought professional advice before making the grants (*id.*).

foundation's case for reasonable cause was no doubt significantly bolstered, however, by the fact that the IRS had previously audited the trust and also failed to recognize it as a nonexempt charitable trust that should be treated as a private foundation required to make qualifying distributions.[157]

The IRS also found reasonable cause for abatement of the tax on taxable expenditures where a private foundation neglected to obtain IRS preapproval of its scholarship program. The private foundation followed the requirements in the applicable regulations to correct its failure to obtain advance approval,[158] including seeking approval after the fact and showing that its grant-making procedures met all applicable statutory and regulatory requirements[159] in prior years except for the failure to obtain advance approval.[160]

On occasion, the IRS will abate, or decline to abate, private foundation excise taxes without providing any detailed explanation or analysis.[161]

Although abatement of first-tier (initial) private foundation excise taxes is discretionary, abatement of all second-tier (additional) private foundation excise taxes (including interest, additions to the tax, and additional amounts) is mandatory if correction occurs during the correction period.[162]

Where reasonable cause can be established for abatement of an excise tax reported on Form 4720, a separate form is filed to request abatement, refund, or relief from payment of the tax.[163]

(d) Form 4720 Statute of Limitations

In general, the statute of limitations during which the IRS may assess one of the private foundation excise taxes is three years from the due date of the return or the date on which the return is actually filed, whichever is later.[164]

---

157. Tech. Adv. Mem. 201423035. Reliance on the accountant was also sufficient to establish that the private foundation had not acted with willful neglect (*id.*).
158. Reg. § 53.4945-1(d)(3); see § 9.9(d).
159. IRC § 4945(g); Reg. § 53.4945-4(c)(1).
160. Priv. Ltr. Rul. 201940013. In another instance, the IRS concluded that scholarship grants should be treated as taxable expenditures where preapproval was not sought and the private foundation's program did not meet the guidelines for employer-related programs, including the percentage test (see § 9.3(d)(ii)), for the year under examination and subsequent years (Tech. Adv. Mem. 9825004). In this instance, however, the issue was identified by the IRS on examination as opposed to being identified, and corrected, proactively by the private foundation.
161. E.g., Tech. Adv. Mem. 9424004 (initial IRC § 4943 tax not abated); Tech. Adv. Mem. 200347023 (initial IRC §§ 4942-4945 taxes abated); and Tech. Adv. Mem. 200452037 (initial IRC § 4945 tax abated).
162. IRC § 4961(a). If the tax has already been collected, then the IRS is required to credit or refund it as an overpayment (*id.*).
163. Form 843, Claim for Refund and Request for Abatement.
164. IRC § 6501(a).

§ 12.4 REPORTING AND PAYMENT OF EXCISE TAXES

A six-year statute of limitations applies, however, if the return "omits an amount of such tax properly includible thereon which exceeds 25 percent of the amount of such tax reported thereon."[165]

If a taxpayer subsequently discovers an amount of excise tax was omitted from a previously filed Form 4720, regulations in other contexts indicate that the taxpayer "should, if within the period of limitation, file an amended return and pay any additional tax due."[166] However, a taxpayer has no obligation to file an amended return, and the IRS is not required to accept an amended return.[167] Such acceptance is within the IRS's discretion,[168] although in practice the IRS typically does accept the filing of an amended return. The filing of an amended return, assuming it is accepted by the IRS, does not extend the statute of limitations.[169]

If an amended Form 4720 reporting the correct amount of tax is filed before the due date for the original return, the amended return will be treated as the original return.[170] A timely filed amended return will thus effectively cure an initial omission of tax of greater than 25 percent and the three-year statute of limitations will apply. An amended return filed after the due date for the original return, on the other hand, will not cure a greater than 25 percent omission of tax on the original return and the extended six-year period will apply.[171] Any amount shown as additional tax on an amended return filed after the due date of the return will be treated as an amount reported on the return for purposes of computing the amount of any excise tax deficiency.[172]

The extended six-year statute of limitations does not apply to the private foundation excise taxes required to be reported on Form 4720 if the transaction giving rise to such tax is disclosed in the return, or in a statement attached to the return, "in a manner adequate to apprise the [IRS] of the existence and nature of such item."[173] In the case of private foundation excise taxes required to be reported on Form 4720, the "return" referred to in these rules is the Form

---

165. IRC § 6501(e)(3); Reg. § 301.6501(e)-1(c)(1).
166. Reg. §§ 1.451-1(a), 1.461-1(a)(3).
167. Badaracco v. Commissioner, 464 U.S. 386, 393 (1984).
168. Colvin v. Commissioner, 95 A.F.T.R.2d 1079 (5th Cir. 2005).
169. Zellerbach Paper Co. v. Helvering, 293 U.S. 172 (1934); National Refining Co. v. Commissioner, 1 B.T.A. 236 (1924).
170. Haggar Co. v. Helvering, 308 U.S. 389 (1940). If the original return was false or fraudulent, then no statute of limitations applies (IRC § 6501(c)(1)), and a subsequently filed nonfraudulent return will not cause the statute of limitations to start running (Badaracco v. Commissioner, 464 U.S. 386 (1984)).
171. Goldring v. Commissioner, 20 T.C. 79 (1953).
172. Reg. § 301.6211-1(a).
173. IRC § 6501(e)(3); Reg. § 301.6501(e)-1(c)(3)(ii).

990-PF filed by the private foundation for the year in which the transaction (or failure to act) giving rise to the excise tax took place.[174]

A court rejected an IRS argument that the failure to file a Form 4720 is tantamount to reporting zero excise tax, and, thus, the omission of any amount of properly includible excise tax exceeds 25 percent of the amount reported (that is, zero), triggering the six-year statute of limitations. The court noted that, under applicable regulations, if a private foundation files a Form 990-PF and answers the questions on Form 990-PF with respect to the potential application of the private foundation excise taxes, the filing of the Form 990-PF constitutes the filing of a return with respect to any such act, "even though the foundation incorrectly answered such questions."[175] The private foundation, in this case, responded to the questions on Form 990-PF related to the issue of self-dealing,[176] and affirmatively indicated that it did not engage in the acts of self-dealing listed on the return (and therefore was not required to file a Form 4720). The court held that this constituted adequate disclosure for purposes of applying the three-year, not the six-year, statute of limitations.[177]

In the case of the excise tax for failure to distribute income, a special statute of limitations rule applies to excise tax deficiencies attributable to contributions made to another nonoperating private foundation that are not distributed by the recipient foundation in the form of a qualifying distribution by the close of the first tax year after the year of receipt.[178] If the recipient private foundation fails to make the prescribed distribution, the applicable statute of limitations is extended by an extra year (essentially to account for the extra year the recipient private foundation has to distribute the contribution from the contributing private foundation).[179] Another special rule applies to excise tax deficiencies attributable to a failure of a set-aside to satisfy the cash distribution test.[180] This special rule extends the statute of limitations by two years for the tax year to which the amount set aside relates.[181]

If the IRS has assessed a private foundation excise tax, and the legitimacy of that assessment is not timely challenged by the taxpayer administratively or in court, the IRS may collect the tax by levy or by a proceeding in court within 10 years after the assessment of the tax.[182] The statute of limitations on

---

174. IRC § 6501(l)(1) (formerly IRC § 6501(n)).
175. Reg. § 301.6501(n)-1(a)(1).
176. See Form 990-PF (2022), Part VI-B.
177. Cline v. Commissioner, 55 T.C.M. 540 (1988); see also Thoburn v. Commissioner, 95 T.C. 132, 149 n.16 (1990).
178. IRC § 4942(g)(3). In general, see §§ 3.3, 6.4(c)(ii).
179. IRC § 6501(l)(2).
180. See § 6.4(g)(ii).
181. IRC § 6501(l)(3).
182. IRC § 6502(a).

§ 12.4 REPORTING AND PAYMENT OF EXCISE TAXES

collection is suspended, and the IRS is prohibited from collecting a second-tier tax, during the pendency of judicial proceedings conducted to determine a taxpayer's liability for a second-tier tax.[183]

If a taxpayer has filed a Form 4720, has paid one or more excise taxes, and wishes to challenge the liability for the tax in court, it must file a refund claim within three years from the time the return was filed or two years from the time the tax was paid, whichever is later.[184] The "return" for purposes of calculating this filing period is not Form 4720, however, but rather the private foundation's Form 990-PF for the year in which the act (or failure to act) giving rise to the tax liability occurred.[185]

(e) Closing Agreements

Where a private foundation has self-identified prior transactions giving rise to excise taxes, and reasonable cause exists for the abatement of some or all of these taxes, it may be advisable for the foundation to approach the IRS and request a closing agreement resolving its excise tax liability in lieu of filing Forms 4720.

A closing agreement is a contractual agreement between the IRS and a taxpayer on a specific issue or liability.[186] A closing agreement is final and conclusive unless fraud, malfeasance, or misrepresentation of a material fact can be shown.[187] A closing agreement may be entered into when it is advantageous to have a matter permanently and conclusively closed or when a taxpayer can show that there are good reasons for an agreement and that making the agreement will not prejudice the interests of the government.[188]

Not every matter is appropriate for resolution through a closing agreement. For example, where the first-tier self-dealing tax is at issue, and the self-dealing violations are numerous or willful and flagrant, such that the private foundation has concerns regarding involuntary termination of its private foundation status,[189] a closing agreement might be appropriate. If only the self-dealing tax liability is at issue, however, the IRS is unable to abate the tax even if reasonable cause exists and therefore will not enter into a closing agreement. The private foundation and disqualified person(s) have no choice in this situation but to file Form 4720 and pay the tax. Where an abatable tax is at issue, however, such as where a private foundation has made taxable

---

183. IRC § 4961(c); Reg. § 53.4961-2.
184. IRC § 6511(a).
185. IRC §§ 6511(f), 6501(l)(1); Reg. § 301.6511(f)-1.
186. Closing agreements are entered into under the authority granted in IRC § 7121.
187. IRC § 7121(b); Reg § 301.7121-1(c).
188. Reg § 301.7121-1(a).
189. IRC § 507(a)(2); see § 13.2.

TAX REPORTING AND ADMINISTRATION ISSUES

expenditures, the IRS may be willing to negotiate a private foundation's liability for the applicable excise tax if the foundation can show reasonable cause for abatement. Depending on the magnitude of the issue, a closing agreement may provide a private foundation with more certainty than filing Form(s) 4720, requesting abatement on the return, and hoping for the best as these returns work their way through the IRS's enigmatic processing system.

In the case of voluntary taxpayer-initiated (walk-in) closing agreement requests, the IRS will informally discuss the possibility of a closing agreement on an anonymous (no-names) basis with the taxpayer's representative.[190] This allows a private foundation to ascertain whether the IRS believes a closing agreement is viable before identifying itself and making a formal closing agreement request.

To initiate a formal closing agreement request, a private foundation should send a letter to the IRS Exempt Organizations Closing Agreement Coordinator for Examinations (EOCAC), containing the following information: (1) why a closing agreement is appropriate; (2) the advantages to the foundation and how the government will sustain no disadvantages; (3) a detailed description of the method proposed for correcting non-compliant activities (which must be completely corrected before the IRS will enter into a closing agreement); (4) a narrative description of each step of the correction method, providing specific information to support the suggested method; (5) how the taxpayer will achieve future compliance; (6) the foundation's proposed methodology to calculate any tax, interest, and penalty, for the tax period(s); and (7) an explanation of the facts, legal analysis, and proposed terms of the closing agreement.[191]

§ 12.5 DETERMINATION LETTERS AND LETTER RULINGS

If a private foundation wants assurance that changes in its activities will not result in excise tax liability or adversely affect its tax-exempt status, it must seek a determination letter or private letter ruling from the IRS on the matter. The IRS annually issues procedures for obtaining determination letters[192] and

---

190. Internal Revenue Manual 4.75.25.1.5(3), 4.75.25.10(8).
191. Internal Revenue Manual 4.75.25.10.1(3). The address for the EOCAC is available on the IRS Charities and Nonprofits webpage (https://www.irs.gov/charities-and-nonprofits) under the "Charity and Nonprofit Audits: Closing Agreements" topic.
192. Currently, Rev. Proc. 2023-5, 2023-1 I.R.B. 265, and Form 8940 (Apr. 2023) (Request for Miscellaneous Determination) and Instructions. Determination letters issued in response to applications for initial recognition of exempt status and private foundation status (rather than in response to subsequent changes in a private foundation's activities) are the subject of § 2.7.

§ 12.5 DETERMINATION LETTERS AND LETTER RULINGS

letter rulings.[193] A determination letter or letter ruling as to changes in a private foundation's activities usually must be obtained in advance of any such changes.[194]

(a) Form 8940 Miscellaneous Determination Requests

Certain changes in a private foundation's activities require it to obtain a determination letter from the IRS. For example, proposed changes in a private foundation's activities that involve grants to individuals for travel, study, or other similar purposes require preapproval from the IRS in the form of a determination letter.[195] IRS preapproval through a determination letter is also required if a private foundation wants to treat funds set aside for future projects as a current-year qualifying distribution under the suitability test.[196] A foundation claiming to be an exempt operating foundation must obtain a determination letter from the IRS recognizing such status to be exempt from the tax on net investment income.[197] A nonexempt charitable trust seeking to be initially classified or reclassified as a supporting organization must also request a determination letter.[198]

Seeking a determination letter is optional for other changes in a private foundation's activities or circumstances, including converting from nonoperating to operating foundation status,[199] conducting voter registration activities,[200] and operating as a public charity for purposes of voluntarily terminating its private foundation status.[201] A charitable organization that

---

193. Currently, Rev. Proc. 2023-1, 2023-1 I.R.B. 1. This revenue procedure provides instructions, a sample letter ruling format, and checklists for submitting ruling requests to the IRS.
194. The IRS will issue a letter ruling on completed transactions if the letter ruling request is submitted before the return is filed for the year in which the transaction is completed (Rev. Proc. 2023-1, 2023-1 I.R.B. 1 § 5.14).
195. See § 9.3(f).
196. See § 6.4(g)(i).
197. Rev. Proc. 2023-5, 2023-1 I.R.B. 265 § 7.04(4). See § 10.7.
198. Rev. Proc. 2023-5, 2023-1 I.R.B. 265 § 3.01(11) and Instructions for Form 8940 (Apr. 2023), Schedule F. See §§ 3.1 (as to private operating foundations), 3.6 (as to nonexempt charitable trusts).
199. Rev. Proc. 2023-5, 2023-1 I.R.B. 265 § 7.04(4). Although a private foundation may qualify as an operating foundation without a new determination letter, the IRS will not recognize such status in its records without a new determination letter (id.; see § 3.1(h)).
200. See § 9.2(c).
201. See § 13.4. Although an advance ruling to this effect is optional, a private foundation must notify the IRS, using Form 8940, of its intent to voluntarily terminate its private foundation status by operating as a public charity for a continuous 60-month period prior to the commencement of such period, and notify the IRS at the end of such period (again, using Form 8940) that it has met the public charity requirements during such period (id.).

erroneously determined that it was a private foundation and wishes to correct the error may request a determination letter classifying it as a public charity by showing that it continuously met the public support test.[202]

Determination letters on the matters described above may be sought by filing a Form 8940 (Request for Miscellaneous Determination) with the IRS, along with the appropriate fee, which varies depending on the type of request.[203] The information that must be submitted with the form in support of the request also depends on the type of request and is set forth in the instructions for the form.

A private foundation may not appeal an adverse determination letter on these matters to the IRS Independent Office of Appeals, other than an adverse determination letter as to private operating foundation status or reclassification of a nonexempt charitable trust as a supporting organization.[204]

(b) Letter Rulings

For proposed changes in activities that fall outside the determination letter categories for which Form 8940 is required, a private foundation may, but is not required to, seek a letter ruling from the IRS addressing the impact of the activities on the foundation's excise tax liability, unrelated business income tax liability, or its tax-exempt status.

The IRS ordinarily will not issue a letter ruling if, at the time of the request, the identical issue is involved in the private foundation's return for an earlier period and that issue is being examined by the IRS, is being considered by the IRS Independent Office of Appeals, or is pending in litigation in a case involving the taxpayer or a related party (such as a disqualified person).[205] Nor will the IRS generally issue a letter ruling on an issue that it cannot readily resolve before the promulgation of a regulation or other published guidance.[206]

Additionally, the IRS annually publishes a list of specific issues on which it will not rule.[207] Issues on this "no rule" list that are relevant to private foundations include whether a transaction meets the requirements of the estate administration exception to self-dealing in cases in which a disqualified

---

202. Rev. Proc. 2023-5, 2023-1 I.R.B. 265 § 7.04(3). See § 15.8(d). The matter of a public charity becoming a private foundation is the subject of § 15.8.
203. The user fees for these matters currently range from $550 to $2,500 (Rev. Proc. 2023-5, 2023-1 I.R.B. 265, App. A (Schedule of User Fees)). Form 8940 must be submitted electronically at www.pay.gov (id. §§ 4.02(6), 7.02, as modified by Rev. Proc. 2023-12, 2023-17 I.R.B. 768 §§ 3.01, 3.03, 3.11).
204. Rev. Proc. 2023-5, 2023-1 I.R.B. 265 §§ 9.02, 9.11.
205. Rev. Proc. 2023-1, 2023-1 I.R.B. 1 § 6.01.
206. Id. at § 6.09.
207. Rev. Proc. 2023-3, 2023-1 I.R.B. 144.

§ 12.5 DETERMINATION LETTERS AND LETTER RULINGS

person issues a promissory note in exchange for property of an estate or trust, and whether an act of self-dealing occurs when a private foundation owns or receives an interest in a limited liability company or other entity that owns a promissory note issued by a disqualified person.[208] The IRS also will not issue a letter ruling on whether changes in a private foundation's activities or operations will affect or jeopardize its exempt status, but will issue a ruling on whether a specific activity furthers an exempt purpose.[209] Thus, where a letter ruling is sought on the impact of a change in activities on exempt status, care is advised when fashioning the precise question on which the ruling is sought.

Requesting a letter ruling can be costly, both in terms of preparation time (which may involve professional fees) and the hefty fee charged by the IRS for submitting a ruling request.[210] Where a letter ruling involves the potential tax liability of both the foundation and a disqualified person with respect to the same transaction, however, a reduced user fee will apply to the request for a substantially identical letter ruling by one of the parties.[211]

(c) Reliance on Determinations and Rulings

A private foundation may rely on an IRS determination letter issued in response to a request submitted on Form 8940 to the same extent and subject to the same limitations as an IRS determination letter as to tax-exempt status.[212]

A private foundation may not rely on a letter ruling issued to another private foundation (or to any other taxpayer); likewise, a disqualified person may not rely on a private letter ruling issued to a private foundation and vice versa.[213] If a private foundation receives a favorable letter ruling from the IRS, it may generally rely in the letter ruling to avoid the imposition of taxes or revocation of its tax-exempt status based on the transaction(s)

---

208. Rev. Proc. 2023-3, 2023-1 I.R.B. 144 § 3.01(130), (131). See §§ 5.5, 5.12(b).
209. Rev. Proc. 2023-3, 2023-1 I.R.B. 144 § 3.01(80). The IRS will also not issue a new determination letter confirming a private foundation is still recognized under IRC § 501(c)(3) under current facts (Rev. Proc. 2023-5, 2023-1 I.R.B. 265 § 3.02(7)).
210. Currently, $38,000 (Rev. Proc. 2023-1, 2023-1 I.R.B. 1, App. A (Schedule of User Fees)). Reduced user fees of $3,000 and $8,500 apply for a private foundation or disqualified person with gross income of less than $250,000 and with gross income between $250,000 and $1 million, respectively (*id.*). Lower user fees also apply for letter rulings pertaining to changes in tax year, changes in accounting method, or requests for extensions of time to make a regulatory election (*id.*).
211. Rev. Proc. 2023-1, 2023-1 I.R.B. 1 § 15.07(2). To avoid a potential act of self-dealing, the private foundation, not the disqualified person, should pay the reduced fee (currently, $3,800).
212. Rev. Proc. 2023-5, 2023-1 I.R.B. 265 § 11.01; see § 2.7(c).
213. Rev. Proc. 2023-1, 2023-1 I.R.B. 1 § 11.02; IRC § 6110(k)(3).

TAX REPORTING AND ADMINISTRATION ISSUES

covered by the letter ruling, but limitations apply.[214] A letter ruling issued on a particular transaction represents a holding of the IRS on that transaction only; it will not apply to a similar transaction in the same year or any other year.[215] The IRS may retroactively revoke a letter ruling if there has been a misstatement or omission of controlling facts; the facts at the time of the transaction are materially different from the controlling facts on which the letter ruling was based; or the transaction involves a continuing action or series of actions and the controlling facts change during the course of the transaction.[216] Where the IRS proposes to revoke or modify a letter ruling for other (non-fact-based) reasons, it generally will not do so retroactively provided that there has been no change in the applicable law; the letter ruling was originally issued for a proposed transaction; and the taxpayer directly involved in the letter ruling acted in good faith in relying on the letter ruling, and revoking or modifying the letter ruling retroactively would be to the taxpayer's detriment.[217]

Where the IRS finds a letter ruling to be in error or not in accord with its current views, or there has been a change in the applicable law, it may retroactively revoke or modify the letter ruling for all years open under the statute of limitations.[218] The IRS may exercise its discretionary authority to limit the retroactive effect of the revocation or modification, and a taxpayer may request that the IRS exercise its discretion to do so.[219]

§ 12.6 IRS EXAMINATIONS OF PRIVATE FOUNDATIONS

IRS examinations (also known as audits) of private foundations focus primarily on potential liability for the various private foundation excise taxes but also encompass liability for the unrelated business income tax and continuing eligibility for tax-exempt status.[220] In extreme cases, an IRS examination may lead to the involuntary termination of private foundation status.

---

214. Rev. Proc. 2023-1, 2023-1 I.R.B. 1 § 11.01.
215. Rev. Proc. 2023-1, 2023-1 I.R.B. 1 § 11.07.
216. Rev. Proc. 2023-1, 2023-1 I.R.B. 1 § 11.05.
217. Rev. Proc. 2023-1, 2023-1 I.R.B. 1 § 11.06.
218. Rev. Proc. 2023-1, 2023-1 I.R.B. 1 § 11.04. Changes in law for this purpose include the enactment of legislation, a decision of the U.S. Supreme Court, the issuance of temporary or final (but not proposed) regulations, and the issuance of a revenue ruling, revenue procedure, notice, or other statement published in the Internal Revenue Bulletin (*id.*).
219. This discretionary authority is granted to the IRS under IRC § 7805(b). Procedures for requesting relief under this provision are the subject of Rev. Proc. 2023-1, 2023-1 I.R.B. 1 § 11.11.
220. See generally *Tax-Exempt Organizations* § 27.6.

§ 12.6 IRS EXAMINATIONS OF PRIVATE FOUNDATIONS

(a) Types of Examinations

EO Examinations currently conducts two types of examinations (or audits): field examinations and office or correspondence examinations. If the initial contact letter received by a private foundation sets up an appointment for an IRS agent to visit the foundation's premises, the IRS is conducting a *field examination*. A field examination is conducted at the foundation's office, the office of an authorized representative of the foundation, or a local IRS office. In most cases, the IRS will ask that the examination take place where the foundation's books and records are located because the essence of any examination is a review of an organization's books and records. In certain circumstances, an examination may involve the questioning of relevant third parties.

There are two types of field examinations: a general program examination and a Team Examination Program (TEP) examination. A *general program examination* is typically conducted by a single IRS revenue agent who will visit the foundation's location. A *TEP examination* is generally reserved for large, complex organizations, and typically involves a team of specialized revenue agents, as well as coordination between IRS functions and other governmental agencies.[221]

If the initial contact letter received by a private foundation instead asks the foundation to submit documents to an IRS office by mail, the IRS is conducting a *correspondence examination*. A correspondence examination is (at least initially) limited in scope and focuses on only one or two items on a return. An EO specialist typically conducts the examination through letters and phone calls with the Foundation's officers or authorized representative(s). A correspondence audit can, however, expand and become a field examination, particularly if more complex issues are identified during the correspondence examination or the foundation does not respond to the IRS agent's requests for information and documents.

A private foundation may also receive a letter from the IRS indicating that it is conducting a compliance check or asking it to complete a questionnaire. Neither a compliance check nor a compliance check questionnaire constitutes an IRS examination, as neither directly relates to determining a tax liability for any particular period.

A *compliance check* is a limited review conducted by the IRS to determine whether an organization is adhering to recordkeeping and information reporting requirements and whether its activities are consistent with its stated tax-exempt purpose. It is a review of information and tax forms that an organization is required to file or maintain (for example, Forms 990-PF, 990-T, 940, 941, W-2, 1099, or W-4). The IRS's stated purpose of a compliance check is to

---

221. FS-2008-14.

TAX REPORTING AND ADMINISTRATION ISSUES

help educate organizations about their reporting requirements and to increase voluntary compliance.[222]

There is no penalty for failure, or refusal, to participate in a compliance check. If a private foundation declines to participate, however, the IRS has the option of opening a formal examination. On the other hand, participation in the compliance check offers no assurances a private foundation will not be examined, as the IRS may also commence a formal examination based on the foundation's responses to the compliance check.[223]

(b) General IRS EO Examination Practices and Procedures

The IRS is authorized by statute to conduct an examination of a taxpayer's books and records to determine tax liability.[224] Examination procedures for exempt organizations, including private foundations, are set out in the IRS's *Tax-Exempt Organizations Examination Procedures*, a part of the *Internal Revenue Manual*.[225] Prior to 2020, the *Internal Revenue Manual* also included information on audit guidelines and techniques for exempt organizations. After 2019, however, this information was removed from the *Internal Revenue Manual*, reserving it for procedural guidance. To retain this information, the IRS initially created *Audit Technique Guides* (ATGs), but in 2021 began publishing *Technical Guides* (TGs) and will continue publishing them until all the topics in the ATGs and other relevant tax-exempt status matters are covered in TGs. The TGs are intended, in part, to serve as a research aid and training tool for Exempt Organizations (EO) specialists conducting examinations,[226] and they recommend specific examination techniques.

Many of the TGs currently published by the IRS and available on its website[227] are of specific relevance to private foundations, including *Introduction to Private Foundations and Special Rules, Private Operating Foundations, Termination of Private Foundation Status, Taxes on Net Investment Income, Excise Taxes on Self-Dealing, Taxes on Foundation Failure to Distribute Income, Taxes on Excise Business Holdings, Excise Taxes on Investments Which Jeopardize Charitable Purposes, Excise Taxes on Taxable Expenditures, Disqualified Persons, Application of Taxes on Denial of Exemption to Certain Foreign Organizations*.

---

222. Pub. 4386, *Compliance Checks* (Apr. 2006).
223. *Id.*
224. IRC § 7602.
225. Internal Revenue Manual, Part 4, Chapter 4.75.
226. Pub. 5729, *Exempt Organizations Technical Guide TG 0: Technical Guide Overview* (Dec. 2022).
227. https://www.irs.gov/charities-non-profits/audit-technique-guides-atgs-and-technical-guides-tgs-for-exempt-organizations.

§ 12.6 IRS EXAMINATIONS OF PRIVATE FOUNDATIONS

The IRS primarily selects exempt organization returns for examination by applying a data-driven approach. In its 2019 fiscal year, the IRS used data to select almost 70 percent of its examinations of Form 990 returns. Almost half of these examinations were selected using models that score returns for potential noncompliance.[228] The IRS also pursues referrals received from internal and external sources that allege noncompliance by exempt organizations.

An IRS revenue agent will typically request the following documents to begin a field examination: a private foundation's governing instruments (articles of incorporation, charter, or constitution, including all amendments; and bylaws, including all amendments); pamphlets, brochures, and other printed literature describing the foundation's activities; and copies of the foundation's Forms 990-PF for the years before and after the year under examination. For at least the year under examination (and potentially those before and after), the IRS will typically request minutes of meetings of the board of directors or trustees and any standing committees or councils; all books and records of assets, liabilities, receipts, and disbursements; an auditor's report, if any; copies of other federal tax returns filed and any related workpapers (for example, Form 990-T for unrelated business taxable income); and copies of employment tax returns and any related workpapers (for example, Forms W-2, W-3, 941, 1096, and 1099).[229] Many of these documents and records may also be requested by the IRS during a correspondence examination.

During an opening conference with the foundation's officers or representatives, the revenue agent will explain the audit plan and the reason the foundation has been selected for examination. The revenue agent usually conducts a comprehensive interview and tours the foundation's facilities to gain a basic understanding of the foundation's purposes and activities.

The examination of a private foundation is multifaceted and includes a review of its operation and activities to verify the existence of an exempt purpose, as well as a review of financial records. The length of the examination will depend upon a variety of factors, such as the size of the foundation, the complexity of its activities, and the issues that may arise during the examination. Some examinations can be completed in just a few days; others can last for a year or more.

When auditing a private foundation's return, IRS examiners will review any letter ruling issued to the private foundation to determine whether (1) the conclusions stated in the letter ruling are properly reflected in the return; (2) the representations upon which the letter ruling was based reflect an accurate

---

228. U.S. Government Accountability Office, "Tax Exempt Organizations: IRS Increasingly Uses Data in Examination Selection, but Could Further Improve Selection Processes" (GAO-20-454) (June 2020).
229. FS-2008-14

statement of the controlling facts; (3) the transaction was carried out substantially as proposed; and (4) there has been any change in the law that applies to the period during which the transaction was consummated. If the examiner finds that the letter ruling should be revoked or modified, it must route its findings and conclusions to the Office of Associate Chief Counsel (Employee Benefits, Exempt Organizations, and Employment Taxes) as a request for technical advice. Otherwise, the examiner is to apply the letter ruling when determining the private foundation's tax liability.[230]

A field examination typically concludes with a closing conference. The revenue agent will discuss the examination with the foundation's representatives, and if necessary, furnish a report explaining proposed adjustments to the foundation's returns or exempt status. If the revenue agent and the foundation's representatives disagree on the findings, the organization may request a meeting with the revenue agent's manager to discuss the disagreement. If the manager cannot resolve the differences, the foundation may protest (appeal) its case to the IRS Independent Office of Appeals.[231]

(c) Achieving Positive Results

There are four rules for achieving positive results in an IRS examination:

1. *Assign a contact person:* One individual should be identified as the lead contact on behalf of the exempt organization through whom all answers are to be funneled. If an outside professional is involved in the examination, they may be this contact.

2. *The less said the better:* Answer only the specific question asked. Do not provide more information than is requested. The examiner should be given specific answers to specific questions. They should not be allowed to go through the organization's file cabinets. Whenever possible, the foundation should produce documents and other information only in response to a written document request from the examiner.[232]

3. *Do not answer a question if you are unsure of its import:* Problem issues should be identified ahead of time, and the materials to be furnished to the IRS should be organized for presentation in the most favorable light. New materials, reports, or summaries of information found lacking can be prepared to better reflect the foundation's purposes and

---

230. Rev. Proc. 2023-1, 2023-1 I.R.B. 1 § 11.03. Procedures for requesting technical advice are the subject of Rev. Proc. 2023-2, 2023-1 I.R.B. 120.
231. See § 12.7(c).
232. IRS Form 4564.

accomplishments. If you are unsure of the answer to any question, say that you are not sure and that you will find out. Make a list for further consideration, consult a professional, or simply become better prepared to present the best picture of the organization.

4. *Expect the best from the examiner:* The IRS agents who examine exempt organizations are knowledgeable, experienced, cooperative (usually), and sympathetic with the spirit of the nonprofit community. They perceive their purpose as different from that of income tax examiners. Their examination often can be a positive experience for an organization. It can validate the foundation's compliance with the tax laws and can sometimes help foundation staff to understand why in fact the foundation is exempt. Another very useful aspect is the reminder it serves of the need to document and preserve a clear record of accomplishments, both from a financial and a philosophical standpoint.

§ 12.7 REVOCATION OF TAX-EXEMPT STATUS

A private foundation's tax-exempt status may be revoked automatically for failure to file Forms 990-PF for three consecutive years. Additionally, the IRS may revoke a private foundation's tax-exempt status as the result of an examination for any number of substantive reasons, including private inurement, substantial private benefit, substantial unrelated business (or other nonexempt) activities, or because the private foundation has engaged in repeated acts giving rise to one or more private foundation excise taxes.[233] The IRS may also revoke a private foundation's tax exempt status where there has been a material change in the foundation's activities that is inconsistent with tax-exempt status, a change in law, or where the conclusion reached in the foundation's original determination letter is no longer in accord with the IRS's position.

(a) Automatic Revocation for Non-Filing

If a private foundation fails to file a Form 990-PF for three consecutive years, its tax-exempt status will be automatically revoked on and after the due date for the filing of the third Form 990-PF. The IRS is required to publish and maintain a list of any organization the status of which is so revoked. The IRS is also required to notify a private foundation if the IRS has no record that

---

233. See Chapters 5–9.

a private foundation has filed a Form 990-PF for two consecutive years and inform the private foundation that automatic revocation will occur if it fails to file a Form 990-PF by the due date for the next Form 990-PF required to be filed.[234]

If a private foundation's tax-exempt status is automatically revoked in this manner, the private foundation must apply to the IRS to have its tax-exempt status reinstated.[235] If the private foundation can provide satisfactory evidence of reasonable cause for its failure to file, the IRS has the discretion to reinstate the private foundation's tax-exempt status retroactively to the date of revocation.[236] The IRS has published specific procedures for applying for reinstatement of an organization's tax-exempt status following an automatic revocation, which in most cases require an organization to submit a statement of reasonable cause for the organization's failure to file the required returns.[237]

A private foundation may not, however, bring a declaratory judgment action to reinstate its tax-exempt status after it has been automatically revoked.[238] Further, a private foundation that has had its tax-exempt status automatically revoked does not have an opportunity for reconsideration of the revocation by the IRS Independent Office of Appeals.[239]

(b) Retroactive Revocation

The IRS has broad discretion whether to revoke a private foundation's tax-exempt status prospectively or retroactively. The exercise of this discretion is reviewable by the courts only for its abuse.[240] Where a private foundation has filed a Form 990-PF in good faith based on a determination that it is

---

234. IRC § 6033(j)(1). The notification requirement in IRC § 6033(j)(1)(A) appears to be separate from, and not a condition precedent to, automatic revocation under IRC § 6033(j)(1)(B) (Field Att'y Advice 20221101F (Feb. 23, 2022)). The IRS's failure to satisfy this notification requirement, however, would presumably be a factor in a private foundation's establishing reasonable cause for reinstatement of its tax-exempt status (discussed *infra*).
235. IRC § 6033(j)(2).
236. IRC § 6033(j)(3).
237. Rev. Proc. 2014-11, 2014-3 I.R.B. 411. Form 1023-EZ may only be used under certain streamlined retroactive reinstatement procedures for small organizations or reinstatement of tax-exempt status from the postmark date of the application (Rev. Proc. 2023-5, 2023-1 IRB 265 § 6.05(3)).
238. IRC § 7428(b)(4); see § 12.7(d).
239. Rev. Proc. 2023-5, 2023-1 IRB 265 § 12.02.
240. Automobile Club of Mich. v. Commissioner, 353 U.S. 180 (1957); Dixon v. United States, 381 U.S. 68(1965). See *Tax-Exempt Organizations* § 27.3.

§ 12.7 REVOCATION OF TAX-EXEMPT STATUS

tax-exempt, however, a three-year statute of limitations will apply to such retroactive revocation.[241]

If there is a material change in facts inconsistent with the conclusion of a private foundation's original determination letter, revocation of tax-exempt status will ordinarily take effect as of the date of the change (subject to the statute of limitations).[242] A material change includes a change in the character, the purpose, or the method of operation of the organization that is inconsistent with the organization's tax-exempt status.[243] Thus, the IRS retroactively revoked the tax exemption of a private foundation that failed to make any grants for charitable purposes during its existence, to pay any tax on its net investment income, to pay penalties for late filing of its annual information returns, and to respond to inquiries from the IRS and state officials.[244]

A determination letter may also be retroactively revoked if there has been a change in the applicable law.[245] Under current IRS procedures, "applicable law" for these purposes would appear to include only enactment of legislation or ratification of a tax treaty; a decision of the U.S. Supreme Court; the issuance of temporary or final (but not proposed) regulations; and the issuance of a revenue ruling, revenue procedure, or other statement published in the Internal Revenue Bulletin.[246]

An organization may request relief from retroactive revocation or modification of a determination letter.[247] If a determination letter is no longer in accord with the IRS's position and such relief is granted, ordinarily the revocation will be effective no earlier than the date on which the original determination letter is revoked.[248]

(c) IRS Administrative Appeal Procedures

The administrative procedures to protest and appeal the revocation of a determination letter to the IRS Independent Office of Appeals generally are the same as those followed in connection with proposed denials of recognition

---

241. IRC § 6501(g)(2). This provision states that if an organization determines in good faith that it is an exempt organization and files a return as such—for example, a Form 990-PF—but is thereafter held to be a taxable organization, the Form 990-PF shall be deemed the return of the organization for purposes of applying the 3-year statute of limitations under IRC § 6501. See *Tax-Exempt Organizations* § 27.4.
242. Rev. Proc. 2023-5, 2023-1 I.R.B. 265 § 12.05(2).
243. Rev. Proc. 2023-5, 2023-1 I.R.B. 265 § 11.02(2).
244. Priv. Ltr. Rul. 201021029.
245. Rev. Proc. 2023-5, 2023-1 I.R.B. 265 § 12.03(2).
246. *Id.* at §§ 11.02(4), 12.01.
247. This relief is provided pursuant to IRC § 7805(b). Rev. Proc. 2023-5, 2023-1 I.R.B. 265 at § 12.04.
248. *Id.* at § 12.05(3).

of exemption,[249] except, as noted, in the case of automatic revocation of tax-exempt status for failure to file Form 990-PF for three years.[250]

(d) Contesting Revocation in Court

A private foundation may contest a final adverse determination revoking its tax-exempt status, finding that it does not continue to qualify as a public charity (thereby reclassifying it as a private foundation), or finding that it does not continue to qualify as a private operating foundation, by filing a declaratory judgment action in the U.S. Tax Court, the U.S. Court of Federal Claims, or the U.S. District Court for the District of Columbia.[251] A declaratory judgment action pursuant to these procedures may not, however, be brought with respect to a revocation of tax-exempt status, by operation of law, occasioned by a failure to file an annual information return for three consecutive years.[252]

As with an IRS final adverse determination as to initial qualification for tax-exempt or private foundation status, a private foundation must exhaust its administrative remedies before filing a declaratory judgment action contesting the revocation of its tax-exempt status.[253] A declaratory judgment action must be filed within 90 days of the date the adverse determination letter is mailed to the foundation.[254] Unlike a denial of initial determination of tax-exempt status, a declaratory judgment action brought to challenge a revocation of tax-exempt status is not confined to a review of the facts contained in the administrative record.[255]

A private foundation may also be able to challenge a *proposed* revocation of its tax-exempt status if it has submitted a written protest to the proposed revocation and has completed the administrative appeal process. In one case, an exempt charitable organization received a letter in which the IRS proposed to revoke its public charity status; in response, it filed a written protest. After the IRS failed to respond to the organization's protest for 900 days, it filed

---

249. *Id.* at § 12.03; see § 2.7(d).
250. Rev. Proc. 2023-5, 2023-1 I.R.B. 265 at § 12.03; see § 12.7(a).
251. IRC § 7428(a). See *Tax-Exempt Organizations* § 27.5(b). Conventional declaratory judgment suits are of no avail in this setting, because the Declaratory Judgment Act (26 U.S.C. § 2201) expressly excludes controversies over federal taxes from its purview (*e.g.*, Ecclesiastical Order of the Ism of Am, Inc. v. Internal Revenue Service, 725 F.2d 398 (6th Cir. 1984); Mitchell v. Riddell, 401 F.2d 842 (9th Cir. 1968), *cert. den.*, 394 U.S. 456 (1969); In re Wingreen Co., 412 F.2d 1048 (5th Cir. 1969); Jolles Foundation, Inc. v. Moysey, 250 F.2d 1966 (2d Cir. 1957)).
252. IRC § 7428(b)(4); as to the automatic revocation of tax-exempt status by law for failure to file annual information returns, see § 12.7(a).
253. IRC § 7428(b)(2). As to the exhaustion of administrative remedies, see § 2.7(e).
254. IRC § 7428(b)(3).
255. Rules of Practice and Procedure, U.S. Tax Court, Title XXI, Rule 217(a). See § 2.7(e).

§ 12.7 REVOCATION OF TAX-EXEMPT STATUS

a petition for a declaratory judgment (under the 270-day rule).[256] The court found that the written protest constituted a request for a determination and that the IRS had failed to make a determination in the statutorily allotted time period.[257]

Where a private foundation's corporate status has been suspended under state law, however, it will be unable to initiate or prosecute a declaratory judgment action. A court dismissed a private foundation's challenge to the IRS's revocation of its tax-exempt status because its corporate powers and privileges were suspended at the time it filed its petition for a declaratory judgment.[258]

To protect the financial status of an allegedly charitable organization during the litigation period, the law provides for circumstances under which contributions made to the organization during that period are deductible[259] even though the court ultimately decides against the organization.[260] Basically, this relief can be accorded only where the IRS is proposing to revoke, rather than initially deny, an organization's charitable status. The total deductions to any one organization from a single donor, to be so protected during this period, however, may not exceed $1,000.[261] Where an organization ultimately prevails in a declaratory judgment case, however, this $1,000 limitation on deductibility becomes inapplicable, so that all gifts are fully deductible within the general limitations of the charitable deduction rules.[262] This benefit is not available to any individual who was responsible, in whole or in part, for the actions (or failures to act) on the part of the organization that were the basis for the revocation of tax-exempt status.[263]

(e) Consequences of Revocation

A private foundation that has its tax-exempt status revoked, whether automatically for failure to file Form 990-PF for three consecutive years or as the result of an IRS examination or other administrative procedure, will continue to be classified as a private foundation. A nonexempt private foundation can

---

256. As to the 270-day rule, see § 2.7(e).
257. J. David Gladstone Foundation v. Commissioner, 77 T.C. 221 (1981).
258. XC Foundation v. Commissioner, T.C. Memo. 2023-3.
259. IRC § 170(c)(2).
260. IRC § 7428(c)(1).
261. IRC § 7428(c)(2)(A).
262. See § 14.2.
263. IRC 7428(c)(3). To inform potential donors of this protection for their contributions made during the litigation period, the IRS publishes, in the *Internal Revenue Bulletin*, the names of organizations that are challenging, under IRC § 7428, the revocation of their status as organizations entitled to receive deductible charitable contributions (Ann. 85-169, 1985-48 I.R.B. 40).

TAX REPORTING AND ADMINISTRATION ISSUES

only terminate its private foundation status by complying with the specific statutory private foundation termination provisions.[264]

Thus, in addition to continuing to file Form 990-PF, a nonexempt private foundation will be required to file either Form 990-PF and either Form 1120 (if a corporation) or Form 1041 (if a trust) and pay any applicable income taxes.[265] A private foundation that has had its tax-exempt status revoked will be liable for the net investment income tax[266] in addition to income taxes only if the sum of the net investment income tax (computed as if the foundation were exempt) and the unrelated business income tax[267] (that would have been imposed if the foundation were exempt) exceeds the amount of income tax imposed on the foundation for the tax year at issue.[268]

Unless and until its private foundation status is terminated, a foundation that has lost its tax-exempt status will also continue to be subject to the private foundation excise taxes.[269]

---

264. IRC § 507. See Chapter 13.
265. E.g., Priv. Ltr. Rul. 202305014.
266. IRC § 4940.
267. IRC § 511(a).
268. IRC § 4940(b).
269. See Chapters 5–9.

CHAPTER THIRTEEN

Termination of Foundation Status

§ 13.1 Voluntary Termination 556
§ 13.2 Involuntary Termination 557
§ 13.3 Transfer of Assets to a Public Charity 558
  (a) General Rules 558
  (b) Restrictions and Conditions on Transfer 561
    (i) Acceptable Restrictions and Conditions 562
    (ii) Unacceptable Restrictions and Conditions 564
  (c) Reservation of Right to Direct Distributions 565
    (i) Factors Indicating a Permissible Reservation 566
    (ii) Factors Indicating an Impermissible Reservation 566

§ 13.4 Operation as a Public Charity 567
  (a) General Rules 567
  (b) Initial Notice 569
  (c) Advance Ruling Requests 570
  (d) Final Notice 572
§ 13.5 Mergers, Split-Ups, and Transfers Between Foundations 573
  (a) General Rules 573
  (b) Complete Asset Transfers to Controlled Foundations 576
  (c) Complete Asset Transfer to Non-Controlled Foundations 581
  (d) Transfers of Significant but Not All Assets 583
§ 13.6 Termination of Trusts Treated as Private Foundations 585
§ 13.7 Termination Tax 586
§ 13.8 Abatement 588

Congress, in its deliberations that concluded with the Tax Reform Act of 1969, decided that private foundations should not be able to receive tax benefits in exchange for the promise of use of their assets for charitable purposes and, subsequently, avoid the carrying out of these responsibilities. The consequence was enactment of IRC § 507. This statutory provision imposes an onerous termination tax on any private foundation that has committed willful repeated acts or a single willful and flagrant act (or failure(s) to act) and permits the IRS to involuntarily require such a private foundation to terminate.

TERMINATION OF FOUNDATION STATUS

The following is an explanation of the rationale underlying the private foundation termination provisions:

> Under prior law, an organization was exempt if it met the requirements of the code, whether or not it sought an "exemption certificate" from the Internal Revenue Service.
>
> If an organization did not continue to meet the requirements for exemption, if it committed certain specifically prohibited acts . . . or if it dealt in certain prohibited ways with its accumulated earnings . . . it lost its exempt status. This loss of exempt status might relate back to the time the organization first violated the code's requirements. However, if the violation occurred after the contributions had been made to the organization, no deductions were disallowed to such contributors. Also, the organization's income tax exemption was not disturbed for years before the organization's first violation. . . .
>
> Congress was concerned that in many cases under prior law the loss of exempt status would impose only a light burden on many foundations. This was true in those circumstances, for example, where the foundation had already received sufficient charitable contributions to provide its endowment and where the foundation could retain its exemption as to its current income by qualifying under an exemption category other than § 501(c)(3).[1]

The private foundation termination provisions provide the framework for a variety of mergers, consolidations, conversions, and other structural changes desirable for some private foundations.

The statutory scheme distinguishes between two distinct types of terminations:

Type 1. This type of termination[2] renders the foundation subject to a termination tax[3] unless the IRS permits abatement.[4] The law pertains to two circumstances under which a private foundation might go out of existence as follows:

1. An *involuntary termination* initiated by the IRS for reasons of repeated and flagrant violations of the private foundation excise taxes.[5]

---

1. Staff of Joint Comm. on Internal Revenue Tax'n, 91st Cong., 2d Sess., General Explanation of the Tax Reform Act of 1969 54-55 (Comm. Print 1970).
2. IRC § 507(a).
3. IRC § 507(c); see § 13.7.
4. IRC § 507(g); see § 13.8.
5. IRC § 507(a)(2); see § 13.2.

TERMINATION OF FOUNDATION STATUS

2. A private foundation that has operated in accordance with the foundation rules can notify the IRS of its intention to terminate its existence (a *voluntary termination*) and request abatement of the termination tax.[6]

Type 2. Under this type of termination,[7] a private foundation ceases to be classified as a private foundation under one of two different circumstances:

1. A private foundation transfers all of its assets to one or more organizations that qualify as certain statutorily designated types of public charities.[8]
2. Based on its intention to reform its sources of support and/or the nature of its activities, a private foundation qualifies as a public charity. This type of foundation must notify the IRS that it is seeking what is called a *60-month termination*.[9]

Unless the IRS initiates an involuntary termination, or the rules applicable to terminating distributions to public charities apply, a private foundation is not treated as having terminated for purposes of the termination tax rules unless it gives notification of its intent to do so.[10] It has been held that the notice element in the termination requirements is reflective of Congress's intent in 1969 to provide the IRS and appropriate state officials with a means to gain more and ongoing information about the activities of private foundations.[11]

A foundation must carefully follow the rules for ending its existence because missteps can be costly. The *termination tax* is equal to the lower of (1) the aggregate tax benefits resulting from the tax-exempt status of the foundation, or (2) the value of the net assets of the foundation.[12]

The statutory scheme for private foundation terminations also provides rules with respect to a private foundation's transfer of all or part of its assets to one or more other private foundations pursuant to a liquidation, merger, redemption, recapitalization, or other adjustment, organization, or reorganization.[13] A private foundation that engages in this type of transaction is not treated as having terminated unless it voluntarily gives the requisite notice to the IRS.[14]

---

6. IRC § 507(a)(1); see § 13.7.
7. IRC § 507(b).
8. IRC § 507(b)(1)(A); see § 13.3.
9. IRC § 507(b)(1)(B); see § 13.4.
10. Reg. § 1.507-1(b)(7).
11. Gladney v. Commissioner, 745 F.2d 955 (5th Cir. 1984), *cert. den.*, 474 U.S. 923 (1985).
12. IRC § 507(c).
13. IRC § 507(b)(2); see § 13.5.
14. Reg. §§ 1.507-1(b)(6), 1.507-3(d); see § 13.1.

§ 13.1 VOLUNTARY TERMINATION

A private foundation may wish to end its existence or change its classification as a private foundation for a number of reasons. Some foundations are created and have charter provisions that provide they exist for a fixed number of years. Second-generation trustees may choose to divide up a private foundation's assets into several foundations so each can manage their own. A foundation's mission may be accomplished by spending its assets to buy a historic building and donating the site to a preservation society. In a rare circumstance, there could be some action[15] that would be impermissible if the organization remains a private foundation. These organizational changes are referred to as *voluntary terminations*.

The language of the statute starts with the pronouncement that a private foundation can only terminate its private foundation status if it gives advance notice to the IRS of its intention to do so and either pays the termination tax or secures IRS abatement of such tax.[16] An organization may terminate its private foundation status without incurring the draconian termination tax, however, if it distributes all of its net assets to one or more permitted types of public charities, or if it notifies the IRS that it is terminating its private foundation status and itself operates as a public charity for a continuous period of 60 calendar months.[17]

If a private foundation transfers all or part of its assets to one or more private foundations (or one or more private foundations and one or more public charities, or to an organization operated for testing for public safety) pursuant to a liquidation, merger, redemption, recapitalization, or other adjustment, organization, or reorganization, the transferor private foundation will not have accomplished a voluntary termination.[18]

Voluntary termination of private foundation status does not relieve a private foundation, or any disqualified person[19] with respect to the private foundation, of liability for any of the private foundation excise taxes with respect to acts or failures to act prior to termination or for any additional taxes imposed for failure to correct the acts or failures to act.[20] If any liability for a private foundation excise tax is incurred by a private foundation before or in connection with a transfer, transferee liability may be applied against the transferee organization for payment of the taxes.[21]

---

15. The self-dealing rules of IRC § 4941 prohibit, for example, the purchase or sale of an asset by a private foundation to its insiders and vice versa; see § 5.4.
16. IRC § 507(a)(1).
17. IRC § 507(b)(1)(A), (B); see §§ 13.3, 13.4.
18. Reg. § 1.507-1(b)(6); see § 13.5.
19. See Chapter 4.
20. Reg. § 1.507-1(b)(2).
21. Reg. § 1.507-1(b)(8).

TERMINATION OF FOUNDATION STATUS

An organization that erroneously determined that it was a private foundation but actually qualified and has continued to qualify as a public charity may request a retroactive reclassification as a public charity instead of voluntarily terminating private foundation status. The organization must demonstrate that it has continuously qualified as a public charity.[22]

To voluntarily terminate its private foundation status, an organization must submit a statement (notice) to the Manager, Exempt Organizations Determinations, Tax Exempt and Government Entities Division (TE/GE), of its intent to terminate its private foundation status.[23] Such statement must set forth in detail the computation and amount of the termination tax.[24] Unless the organization requests abatement of such tax,[25] full payment of such tax must be made at the time the statement is filed. An organization may request the abatement of the entire termination tax or may pay any part thereof and request abatement of the unpaid portion of the amount of tax assessed.[26] If the organization requests abatement of the termination tax and such request is denied, the organization must pay such tax in full upon notification by the IRS that such tax will not be abated.[27]

§ 13.2 INVOLUNTARY TERMINATION

A private foundation's private foundation status may be involuntarily terminated if the IRS notifies the organization that because of willful, flagrant, or repeated acts or failures to act giving rise to one or more of the private foundation excise taxes, the organization is liable for the termination tax.

Under the involuntary termination rule, the phrase *willful repeated acts (or failures to act)* means at least two acts or failures to act that are voluntary,

---

22. The request is made by filing Form 8940 electronically at www.pay.gov, along with a $550 user fee (Rev. Proc. 2023-5, 2023-1 I.R.B. 265 §§ 4.02(6), 7.02 and App. A (Schedule of User Fees), as modified by Rev. Proc. 2023-12, 2023-17 I.R.B. 768 §§ 3.01, 3.03). Also, Instructions for Form 8940 (Apr. 2023), Part II, line 1 and Schedule G (reclassification of private foundation status).
23. Reg. § 1.507-1(b)(1); Rev. Rul. 2002-28, 2002-1 C.B. 941; Rev. Rul. 2003-13, 2003-1 C.B. 305. This statement (notice) is to be sent to an address provided in the Instructions for Form 990-PF. A submission of a Form 990-PF marked "Final" does not constitute the requisite notice of termination of private foundation status (Rev. Rul. 2003-13, 2003-1 C.B. 305).
24. IRC § 507(c); see § 13.7.
25. IRC § 507(g); see § 13.8.
26. Reg. § 1.507-1(b)(1).
27. *Id.*

conscious, and intentional.[28] This type of an act (or failure to act) is one that is voluntarily, consciously, and knowingly committed in violation of any of the private foundation rules[29] and that appears to a reasonable person to be a gross violation of the rules.[30] An act or failure to act may result in termination of the private foundation's private foundation status, even though the tax is imposed on the foundation's managers rather than on the private foundation itself. A failure to timely correct the act or acts, or failures to act, that gave rise to liability for tax under any of the private foundation rules, may be a willful and flagrant act (or failure to act).[31]

No motive to avoid legal restrictions or the incurrence of tax is necessary to make an act or failure to act willful. A private foundation's act or failure to act is not willful, however, if the private foundation, or its manager if applicable, does not know that the act or failure to act is an act of self-dealing, a taxable expenditure, or other act or failure to act giving rise to liability for one or more of the private foundation taxes.[32]

§ 13.3 TRANSFER OF ASSETS TO A PUBLIC CHARITY

(a) General Rules

A private foundation, with respect to which there has not been any act or acts described in the involuntary termination rules,[33] may terminate its private foundation status by distributing all of its net assets to one or more publicly supported organizations and institutions specifically identified in the applicable statute,[34] each of which has been in existence and so described for a continuous period of at least 60 calendar months immediately preceding

---

28. IRC § 507(a)(2); Reg. § 1.507-1(c)(1). In addition to this form of termination, the IRS may attempt a jeopardy assessment under IRC § 6861, which in this context is likely, on challenge (IRC § 7429), to be abated by a court (e.g., George F. Harding Museum v. United States, 674 F. Supp. 1323 (N.D. Ill. 1987)).
29. Other than IRC §§ 4940 (Chapter 10) or 4948 (§ 3.8).
30. Reg. § 1.507-1(c)(2).
31. Reg. § 1.507-1(c)(4).
32. Reg. § 1.507-1(c)(5).
33. See § 13.2.
34. That is, one or more organizations described in section 170(b)(1)(A) other than in clauses (vii) and (viii) (IRC § 507(b)(1)(A); see §§ 15.3, 15.4). The regulations clarify that the reference to "other than in clauses (vii) and (viii)" refers only to an organization that is described solely in one of those subsections of IRC § 170(b)(1)(A); thus, an organization described in another subsection of IRC § 170(b)(1)(A) is not precluded from being a permitted recipient organization merely because it also appears to meet the description of one of the organizations specifically excluded by reference in the statute (Reg § 1.507-2(a)(3)).

TERMINATION OF FOUNDATION STATUS

the distribution.[35] The IRS ruled that, in measuring this 60-month period, the recipient organization may be an organization that has been in existence for less than 60 months where (1) it was formed as a result of a consolidation of two organizations, both of which would have qualified as eligible public or publicly supported entities and would have been in existence for the requisite 60 months had the consolidation not occurred, and (2) the successor organization was formed for the same purposes and carried on the same activities as the two consolidating organizations.[36]

A private foundation seeking to terminate its private foundation status under these rules may rely on a ruling or determination letter issued to a potential distributee that the distributee is a permitted public charity.[37]

If a private foundation distributes all its net assets to one or more public charities, at least one of which is not a specifically permitted publicly supported organization or institution,[38] then this rule will not apply and the distributions will not cause the private foundation to terminate its private foundation status (unless it gives the notice and follows the process required to effectuate an involuntary termination).[39] As a practical matter, however, a private foundation may expand the range of permitted charitable organizations and institutions to include service provider publicly supported organizations[40] and supporting organizations,[41] by first distributing all of its assets to one or more of these organizations and then giving notice of voluntary termination to the IRS at least one day later.[42] Although the termination tax would technically apply in such a scenario, the amount of the tax would be zero because the private foundation would have no assets on the day it provides notice.[43] The IRS confirmed the viability of this termination-tax-free strategy in a ruling that considered the transfer of all of a private foundation's assets to four different types of charitable organizations.[44]

---

35. IRC § 507(b)(1)(A). A private foundation that transfers a portion, but not all, of its assets to one or more permitted public charities will not be terminated under this rule (e.g., Priv. Ltr. Rul. 200719012).
36. Rev. Rul. 75-289, 1975-2 C.B. 215.
37. Reg. § 1.507-2(a)(2).
38. That is, an organization that has been described in IRC § 509(a)(1) (see §§ 15.3, 15.4) for fewer than 60 calendar months immediately preceding the distribution, a service provider publicly supported organization described in IRC § 509(a)(2) (see § 15.5), or a supporting organization described in IRC § 509(a)(3) (see § 15.6).
39. Reg. § 1.507-1(b)(7); Rev. Rul. 2003-13, 2003-1 C.B. 305. As to involuntary terminations, see § 13.1.
40. That is, organizations described in IRC § 509(a)(2); see § 15.5.
41. That is, organizations described in IRC § 509(a)(3); see § 15.6.
42. Rev. Rul. 2003-13, 2003-1 C.B. 305.
43. *Id.*; Reg. § 1.507-7(a), (b).
44. Rev. Rul. 2003-13, 2003-1 C.B. 305.

§ 13.3 TRANSFER OF ASSETS TO A PUBLIC CHARITY

An organization that terminates its private foundation status by transferring all its assets to one or more permitted public charities remains subject to the private foundation rules until the required distribution of all of its net assets has been completed.[45] Therefore, a private foundation terminating under these rules should retain sufficient income or assets to pay any private foundation excise taxes for which it may be liable and pay such taxes when due.[46] In most situations, only the net investment income tax[47] for the portion of the tax year prior to the distribution will be applicable (although the distribution of assets to one or more public charities will not itself give rise to taxable net investment income). Because the distribution of assets must be made to public charities to qualify under these rules, the distribution will not result in excess business holdings, or constitute a self-dealing transaction, jeopardizing investment, or taxable expenditure, or require the exercise of expenditure responsibility. Further, provided the distributions are not made to organizations controlled directly or indirectly by the distributing private foundation, or by one or more disqualified persons with respect thereto, the distributions will be qualifying distributions.[48]

It is possible that a private foundation may transfer all or part of its assets to one or more public charities,[49] and one or more of the transferee organizations subsequently may lose its public charity status and become a private foundation. If such a loss of public charity status occurs within a period of three years from the date of such transfers, then the transfers will be treated as a transfer pursuant to a liquidation, merger, redemption, recapitalization, or other adjustment, organization, or reorganization and the rules applicable to such transfers[50] will apply to any such transferee organization from the date on which any such transfer was made to it.[51]

A private foundation terminating in this manner is not required to notify the IRS and does not incur a termination tax, thereby obviating the need to request any abatement.[52] Although notification is not required, a private foundation that terminates its private foundation status under these rules must include a statement with its Form 990-PF that describes the asset transfer(s) and the date on which the final distribution of assets was made. In addition to this statement, a private foundation must also attach to the return a certified copy of the liquidation plan, board resolution, or similar documentation

---

45. Reg. § 1.507-2(a)(4).
46. Rev. Rul. 2003-13, 2003-1 C.B. 305.
47. IRC § 4940; see Chapter 10.
48. Rev. Rul. 2003-13, 2003-1 C.B. 305.
49. For purposes of this rule, organizations described in IRC § 509(a)(1), (2), or (3).
50. That is, the rules applicable to IRC § 507(b)(2) transfers; see § 13.5.
51. Reg. § 1.507-3(e).
52. Reg. § 1.507-2(a)(1).

TERMINATION OF FOUNDATION STATUS

(if there is any), a list of the names and addresses of all recipient organizations, and an explanation of the nature and fair market value of the assets distributed to each recipient.[53]

An organization that remains in existence after terminating its private foundation status under these rules must file an application for recognition of exemption[54] (unless exempt from that requirement) if it wishes to be regarded as a charitable organization, since it is treated as a newly created organization.[55]

Although a ruling with respect to this type of termination is not required, the IRS occasionally issues rulings as to terminations of private foundation status involving a transfer of assets to one or more public charities.[56]

(b) Restrictions and Conditions on Transfer

A private foundation meets the requirement that it "distribute all of its net assets" to one or more permitted public charities only if it transfers all of its right, title, and interest in and to all of its net assets to such organizations.[57] Therefore, to effectuate this type of transfer, a transferor private foundation may not impose any *material restrictions or conditions* that prevent the transferee public charity from freely and effectively employing the transferred assets, or the income derived from the assets, in furtherance of its tax-exempt purposes.

Whether or not a particular condition or restriction imposed on a transfer of assets is *material* must be determined from all of the facts and circumstances of the transfer.[58] Some of the more significant facts and circumstances to be considered in making this determination are whether the transferee public charity is the owner in fee of the assets it receives from the private foundation, whether the assets are held and administered by the public charity in a manner consistent with one or more of its tax-exempt purposes, whether the governing body of the public charity has the ultimate authority and control over the assets and the income derived from them, and whether and to what extent the governing body of the public charity is organized and operated so as to be independent from the transferor.[59]

---

53. Instructions for Form 990-PF (2022), General Instruction T. A private foundation terminating in this manner must also check the box on the first page of Form 990-PF to indicate that its private foundation status was terminated under IRC § 507(b)(1)(A).
54. See § 2.7(a).
55. Rev. Rul. 74-490, 1974-2 C.B. 171.
56. E.g., Priv. Ltr. Rul. 200123069.
57. Reg. § 1.507-2(a)(7)(i).
58. *Id.*
59. *Id.*

§ 13.3 TRANSFER OF ASSETS TO A PUBLIC CHARITY

Whether a governing body is "independent from the transferor" for these purposes is also to be determined from all of the facts and circumstances.[60] Some of the more significant facts and circumstances to be considered are (1) whether, and to what extent, members of the governing body are individuals selected by the transferor private foundation or its disqualified persons, or are themselves disqualified persons; (2) whether, and to what extent, members of the governing body are selected by public officials acting in their capacities as such; and (3) how long a period of time each member of the governing body may serve. In the case of a transfer to a community trust, the community trust satisfies the third factor if its governing body is comprised of members who may serve a period of not more than 10 consecutive years; and upon completion of a period of service (beginning before or after the date of transfer), no member may serve again within a period consisting of the lesser of 5 years or the number of consecutive years the member has immediately completed serving.[61]

(i) Acceptable Restrictions and Conditions. The presence of some or all of the following four factors is not considered to prevent the transferee from freely and effectively employing the transferred assets, or the income derived from them, in furtherance of its tax-exempt purposes:

1. The transferred assets are maintained in an identifiable or separate fund that is given a name or other designation that is the same as or similar to that of the transferor private foundation or otherwise memorializes the creator of the private foundation or their family.

2. The income and assets of the separate fund are to be used for a designated purpose or for one or more particular public charities, and the use is consistent with the charitable, educational, or other basis for the tax-exempt status of the public charity.

3. Some or all of the principal of the separate fund is not to be distributed for a specified period, provided that the public charity is the legal and equitable owner of the fund and the public charity's governing body exercises ultimate and direct authority and control over the fund. An example of such an arrangement is a fund to endow a chair at a university or a medical research fund at a hospital.

4. The transferor private foundation transfers property the continued retention of which by the transferee is required by the transferor, but only if such retention is important to the achievement of charitable or other similar purposes in the community because of the peculiar features

---

60. Reg. § 1.507-2(a)(7)(ii).
61. *Id.*

TERMINATION OF FOUNDATION STATUS

of such property. A private foundation's transfer of a woodland preserve subject to a requirement that it be maintained by the transferee public charity as an arboretum for the benefit of the community is an example of such an acceptable restriction on transfer. A restriction on the disposition of an investment asset or the distribution of income is not, however, an acceptable restriction on transfer.[62]

Thus, for example, a private foundation's transfer of all its net assets to a university on the condition that the university uses the income and principal to endow a chair at the university named after the private foundation's creator is an acceptable restriction on the use of the transferred assets. Although the transferred assets are to be used for a specified purpose by the university, this purpose is in furtherance of the university's tax-exempt educational purposes.[63] Similarly, a private foundation's transfer of all its net assets to a public institution engaged in cancer research on the condition that the recipient keep the assets in a separate fund, and use the income and principal to further cancer research, is an acceptable restriction on the use of the transferred assets. Although the assets may be used only for a limited purpose, this purpose is consistent with and in furtherance of the recipient's tax-exempt purposes.[64]

In one instance, a private foundation proposed to provide an endowment to fund the operating expenses of a public charity, including those for construction of a facility. The funds were to be paid to an escrow agent, who would hold the funds until certain conditions were satisfied. The purpose for establishment of the endowment, before construction took place, was to assure bond holders and contributors that funds would be available to support the entity. In finding the restrictions not to be "material," the IRS observed that the private foundation had given up any right to control use of the funds in the grantee's possession, other than through the restrictions set forth in the escrow agreement; the private foundation retained no right of reversion or other interest in the transferred assets; ultimate distribution of the funds would occur within a reasonable period of time; and the ultimate grantee was a public charity.[65]

---

62. Reg. § 1.507-2(a)(7)(iii).
63. Reg. § 1.507-2(a)(7)(v), Example (2). Although the use of the name of the foundation's creator for the chair is an acceptable restriction on the use of the transferred assets, the imposition of conditions on investment or reinvestment of the principal or income would not be an acceptable restriction (*id.*).
64. Reg. § 1.507-2(a)(7)(v), Example (1). This example also notes that, prior to the transfer, the private foundation's activities consisted of making grants to hospitals and universities to further research into the causes of cancer, thereby illustrating that making terminating distributions to public charities with the same or similar purposes as the distributing foundation is both expected and accepted.
65. Priv. Ltr. Rul. 9014004.

§ 13.3 TRANSFER OF ASSETS TO A PUBLIC CHARITY

(ii) Unacceptable Restrictions and Conditions. The presence of any of the following factors is considered to prevent the transferee from freely and effectively employing the transferred assets, or the income derived from them, in furtherance of its tax-exempt purposes:

1. The transferor private foundation, a disqualified person with respect to it, or any person or committee designated by, or pursuant to the terms of an agreement with, such a person (collectively, the "grantor") reserves the right, directly or indirectly, to name the persons to which the transferee public charity must distribute,[66] or to direct the timing of these distributions[67] as, for example, by a power of appointment.

2. The terms of the transfer agreement, or any express or implied understanding between the transferor and the transferee, require the public charity to take or withhold action with respect to the transferred assets that is not designed to further one or more of the tax-exempt purposes of the public charity, and the action or withholding of action would, if performed by the transferor private foundation with respect to the assets, have subjected the transferor to one or more of the private foundation excise taxes.[68]

3. The public charity assumes leases, contractual obligations, or liabilities of the transferor private foundation, or takes the assets of the transferor private foundation subject to such liabilities (including obligations under commitments or pledges to grantees of the transferor private foundation), for purposes inconsistent with the purposes or best interests of the public charity.[69]

4. The transferee public charity is required by any restriction or agreement (other than a restriction or agreement imposed or required by law or regulatory authority), express or implied, to retain any securities or other investment assets transferred to it by the private foundation. Where transferred assets consistently produce a low annual return of income, the IRS will examine carefully whether the transferee is required by any such restriction or agreement to retain such assets.

---

66. Other than by designating particular IRC § 509(a)(1), (2), or (3) organizations in the instrument of transfer.
67. Other than by direction in the instrument of transfer that some or all of the principal, as opposed to specific assets, not be distributed for a specified period, such as in the case of an endowed chair at a university (see Reg. § 1.507-2(a)(7)(iii)(C)).
68. Other than with respect to the minimum investment return requirement of IRC § 4942(e). See Chapter 6.
69. Other than the payment of the private foundation's Chapter 42 taxes incurred prior to the transfer to the public charity to the extent of the value of the assets transferred.

TERMINATION OF FOUNDATION STATUS

5. An agreement is entered into between the transferor private foundation and the transferee public charity in connection with the transfer of securities or other property that grants directly or indirectly to the transferor private foundation or any disqualified person with respect thereto a right of first refusal to purchase the transferred securities or other property, when and if disposed of by the public charity, unless the securities or other property were purchased or otherwise received by the transferor private foundation subject to the right of first refusal prior to October 9, 1969.

6. An agreement is entered into between the transferor private foundation and the transferee public charity that establishes irrevocable relationships with respect to the maintenance or management of assets transferred to the public charity, such as continuing relationships with banks, brokerage firms, investment counselors, or other advisors with regard to the investments or other property transferred to the public charity.[70]

7. Any other condition is imposed on action by the public charity that prevents it from exercising ultimate control over the assets received from the private foundation for purposes consistent with its tax-exempt purposes.[71]

Thus, for example, a private foundation was found not to have made a terminating transfer of all its assets to a public charity where, under the terms of the transfer agreement, the transferred assets were required to be retained in their present form for a period of 20 years, or until the date of the creator's death if it occurred earlier.[72]

(c) Reservation of Right to Direct Distributions

With respect to the first of the unacceptable restrictions and conditions on transfer above—the reservation of a right to direct distributions—an impermissible reservation of such a right will be considered to exist where the only criterion considered by the public charity in making a distribution of income or principal from a grantor's fund is advice offered by the grantor. In other circumstances, the IRS will examine carefully whether the seeking of advice by the transferee public charity from, or the giving of advice by, any grantor after the assets have been transferred constitutes an indirect impermissible reservation of a right to

---

70. Other than a relationship with a trustee, custodian, or agent for a community trust acting as such.
71. Reg. § 1.507-2(a)(7)(iv).
72. Reg. § 1.507-2(a)(7)(v), Example (4).

direct the distributions. Whether there is an impermissible reservation of such a right is to be determined based on all the facts and circumstances.[73]

(i) Factors Indicating a Permissible Reservation. The presence of some or all of the following factors indicates that an impermissible reservation of a right to direct distributions does not exist:

1. The staff of the public charity has independently evaluated whether the grantor's advice is consistent with specific charitable needs most deserving of support by the recipient public charity (as determined by it).

2. The public charity has promulgated guidelines enumerating specific charitable needs consistent with the charitable purposes of the public charity, and the grantor's advice is consistent with these guidelines.

3. The public charity has instituted an educational program publicizing these guidelines to potential donors and other members of the public.

4. The public charity distributes funds in excess of amounts distributed from the grantor's fund to the same or similar types of organizations or charitable needs as those recommended by the donor.

5. The solicitations for funds by the public charity state that the public charity will not be bound by advice offered by the grantor.[74]

(ii) Factors Indicating an Impermissible Reservation. The presence of some or all of the following four factors indicates that an impermissible reservation of a right to direct distributions exists:

1. The manner in which the public charity solicits funds states or implies that the grantor's advice will be followed, or the public charity engages in a pattern of conduct that creates such an expectation.

2. The advice of the grantor (whether or not restricted to a distribution of income or principal from the grantor's trust or fund) is limited to distributions of amounts from the grantor's fund and the public charity has not (i) conducted an independent investigation evaluating whether the grantor's advice is consistent with the public charity's charitable needs, and (ii) promulgated guidelines consistent with the charitable needs of the public charity.[75]

---

73. Reg. § 1.507-2(a)(7)(iv)(A)(1).
74. Reg. § 1.507-2(a)(7)(iv)(A)(2).
75. That is, the first two factors in text accompanied by *supra* note 74 are not present.

TERMINATION OF FOUNDATION STATUS

3. Only the advice of the grantor as to distributions of the grantor's fund is solicited by the public charity, and no procedure is provided for considering advice from persons other than the grantor with respect to the fund.

4. For the year involved and all prior years the public charity follows the advice of all grantors with respect to their funds substantially all of the time.[76]

Thus, for example, a private foundation was found not to have made a terminating transfer of all its assets to a public charity where, under the terms of the transfer agreement, the transferee public charity was required to distribute the income to public charities designated by the creator of the transferor private foundation, and the public charity's governing body had no authority during the creator's lifetime to vary the creator's direction.[77]

§ 13.4 OPERATION AS A PUBLIC CHARITY

(a) General Rules

A private foundation, as to which there have not been any act or acts described in the involuntary termination rules, can voluntarily terminate its private foundation status by operating as a public charity if the organization:

- Meets the requirements to be classified as a public institution, a publicly supported charity, or a supporting organization,[78] for a continuous period of 60 calendar months beginning with the first day of any tax year,

- Properly notifies the IRS before the commencement of the 60-month period that it is terminating its private foundation status, and

- Properly establishes immediately after the expiration of the 60-month period that it has complied with the requirements of the rules for classification of one of the types of public charities identified above.[79]

---

76. Reg. § 1.507-2(a)(7)(iv)(A)(3).
77. Reg. § 1.507-2(a)(7)(v), Example (4).
78. That is, the requirements of either IRC § 509(a)(1), (2), or (3) (see §§ 15.3-15.6).
79. IRC § 507(b)(1)(B); Reg. § 1.507-2(b)(1).

§ 13.4 OPERATION AS A PUBLIC CHARITY

A private foundation that terminates its private foundation status under these rules by operating as a public charity does not incur a termination tax and, therefore, an abatement of the tax is not required.[80] It is not required to file a new application for recognition of tax exempt status,[81] and the statutory presumption that it is a private foundation[82] will not apply.[83] It is also not necessary to file a final return[84] when an organization terminates its private foundation status in this manner.[85] A private foundation that satisfies these rules continuously during the 60-month period is treated as a public charity for the entire 60-month period.[86]

A private foundation that fails to terminate by operating as a public charity for a continuous 60-month period is not considered to have given notice of intent to terminate its private foundation status under the voluntary termination rules.[87] Thus, a private foundation that fails to operate continuously as a public charity after giving notice of its intent to terminate by doing so will remain a private foundation. It generally will be treated as a private foundation for the entire 60-month period for purposes of the excise taxes applicable to private foundations. However, it will be treated as a public charity for such purposes for any tax year during the 60-month period in which it meets the requirements for public charity status. Similarly, grants or contributions to such an organization will be treated as made to a private foundation for purposes of the charitable contribution deduction rules, and the qualifying distribution and taxable expenditure rules, except for any tax year during the 60-month period in which it meets the public charity requirements. For purposes of determining whether such an organization satisfies the publicly supported charity requirements with respect to a specific tax year in the 60-month period, the calculation of public support is made over the period beginning with the start of the 60-month period and ending with the last day of the tax year being tested. The organization will not be treated as a publicly supported organization for any tax year during the 60-month period solely by reason of having met one of the public support tests for the preceding year.[88]

---

80. Reg. § 1.507-2(b)(2).
81. IRC § 508(a).
82. IRC § 508(b).
83. Reg. § 1.507-2(b)(6).
84. IRC § 6043(b).
85. Reg. § 1.507-2(b)(6).
86. Reg. § 1.507-2(e)(1).
87. Reg. § 1.507-2(b)(2); as to the voluntary termination rules, see § 13.1.
88. Reg. § 1.507-2(e)(2)(i), (ii). Any tax year during the 60-month period for which the private foundation organization meets the requirements for public charity status is excluded from the computation of its aggregate tax benefit (Reg. § 1.507-2(e)(2)(iii); see § 13.7).

TERMINATION OF FOUNDATION STATUS

(b) Initial Notice

A private foundation notifies the IRS that it intends to terminate its private foundation status by operating as a public charity by filing Form 8940 before the beginning of the 60-month period.[89]

The submission of Form 8940 serves as the required statement of a private foundation's intent to terminate its private foundation status.[90] Other information required to be provided on Form 8940 to meet the notification requirement includes the name and address of the private foundation, the date the organization's regular tax year begins, and (on Schedule I) the Internal Revenue Code section(s) under which it seeks public charity classification[91] and the date the 60-month termination period begins.[92] If Form 8940 is submitted prior to the beginning of the 60-month period, but is incomplete, it will be considered a timely notification if the private foundation supplies the necessary additional information at the request of, and within the additional time period allowed by, the IRS.[93]

A private foundation that gives notice of its intent to terminate under these rules is required to continue to file Form 990-PF for each year during the 60-month period. A private foundation that is only giving notice to the IRS of its intent to terminate, and not requesting an advance ruling, is not required to complete and submit Form 872-B agreeing to extend the statute of limitations for paying the excise tax on net investment income. If it chooses not to do so, however, it must continue to pay this tax until after the end of the 60-month period.[94]

---

89. Reg. § 1.507-2(b)(1)(ii); Rev. Proc. 2023-5, 2023-1 I.R.B. 265 § 4.02(6), as modified by Rev. Proc. 2023-12, 2023-17 I.R.B. 768 § 3.01); Instructions for Form 8940 (Apr. 2023), Part II and Schedule I. Form 8940 must be submitted electronically at www.pay.gov (*id.*). No user fee is required for merely providing this notice (Rev. Proc. 2023-5, 2023-1 I.R.B. 265 § 14.03 and App. A (Schedule of User Fees), as modified by Rev. Proc. 2023-12, 2023-17 I.R.B. 768 § 3.04).
90. Reg. § 1.507-2(b)(3)(ii); Instructions for Form 8940 (Apr. 2023), Schedule I.
91. If classification is sought under IRC § 509(a)(1), the organization also must indicate the type of IRC § 170(b)(1)(A) entity it expects to be.
92. Reg. § 1.507-2(b)(3); Instructions for Form 8940 (Apr. 2023), Schedule I.
93. Reg. § 1.507-2(b)(5).
94. Reg. § 1.507-2(b)(7); Instructions for Form 8940 (Apr. 2023), Schedule I. If a consent to extend the statute of limitations is not filed, but the private foundation subsequently meets the requirements to be treated as a publicly supported charity over the 60-month period, it may submit a refund claim for the net investment income tax paid during this period (Reg. § 1.507-2(e), Example (1)). To be able to file a claim for refund, however, the foundation and the IRS must agree to extend the statute of limitation for the first tax year in the 60-month period (to avoid the statute of limitations expiring for that year, thereby precluding the refund claim) (*id.*). For consequences where a consent to extend the statute of limitation is filed with a notice to terminate, but it is subsequently determined that the net investment income tax is due because the foundation did not complete a successful termination by operating as a public charity, see § 13.4(c).

§ 13.4   OPERATION AS A PUBLIC CHARITY

In one instance, a private foundation filed the requisite notice with the IRS that it was terminating its private foundation status by operating as a public or publicly supported charity for a continuous 60-month period beginning with the first day of its next tax year. In conjunction with that notice, filed on February 1, the private foundation also gave notice that it was changing its annual accounting period from a calendar year to a fiscal year beginning April 1. The IRS ruled that the private foundation could begin the 60-month period required for termination of its private foundation status with its tax year beginning April 1, rather than postpone the commencement of that period to January 1.[95]

(c)   Advance Ruling Requests

The IRS is authorized to issue an advanced ruling that an organization can be expected to satisfy the requirements of these rules during a 60-month termination period where that expectation is reasonable.[96] In determining whether a private foundation can reasonably be expected to meet the necessary requirements for the 60-month period, the basic consideration is whether its organizational structure, current or proposed programs or activities, actual or intended method of operation, and current or projected sources of support are such as to indicate that the organization is likely to satisfy the requirements for public charity status during the 60-month period. All pertinent facts and circumstances are considered in making this determination.[97]

An advance ruling is not required, but if desired is requested by filing Form 8940, along with the required fee.[98] In addition to the information that must be provided when submitting a notice of intent to terminate its private foundation status,[99] a private foundation that requests an advance ruling must describe (on Schedule H) how its organizational structure (taking into account any revisions made prior to the beginning of the 60-month period), current or proposed programs or activities, actual or intended method of operation, and current or projected sources of support are such that it is likely to satisfy the requirements of its intended public charity classification during the 60-month period. A private foundation is required to complete additional

---

95. Rev. Rul. 77-113, 1977-1 C.B. 151.
96. Reg. § 1.507-2(d)(1).
97. Reg. § 1.507-2(d)(2).
98. Form 8940 must be submitted electronically at www.pay.gov; the user fee for this type of request is currently $550 (Rev. Proc. 2023-5, 2023-1 I.R.B. 265 §§ 4.02(6), 7.02 and App. A (Schedule of User Fees), as modified by Rev. Proc. 2023-12, 2023-17 I.R.B. 768 §§ 3.01, 3.03).
99. See § 13.4(b).

TERMINATION OF FOUNDATION STATUS

schedules if it intends to qualify as a supporting organization (Schedule F) or a public institution (Schedule L through Schedule P). For certain public charity classifications,[100] it is also required to upload copies of its governing instruments, bylaws, and amendments when submitting an advance ruling request on Form 8940.[101]

A private foundation must also submit a completed Form 872-B with its advance ruling request to extend the statute of limitations to assess the excise tax on net investment income for any tax year within the advance ruling period. The statute of limitations for each tax year within the advance ruling period must be extended for a period of four years after the filing of Form 990 or Form 990-PF for the last tax year within the 60-month period within the advance ruling period. In contrast to a private foundation that is only giving notice to the IRS of its intent to terminate, submission of a completed Form 872-B is a mandatory condition of receiving an advance ruling.[102]

If a private foundation obtains an advance ruling that it can be expected to satisfy the requirements for public charity status during the 60-month period, contributors may rely on that ruling until the IRS publishes notice that the advance ruling is being revoked (such as by publication in the Internal Revenue Bulletin).[103] In contrast, a private foundation obtaining an advance ruling cannot rely on such a ruling. Consequently, if the foundation does not pay the net investment income tax for any tax year(s) during the 60-month period, and it is subsequently determined that such tax is due because the foundation did not complete a successful termination by operating as a public charity, the foundation also will be liable for statutory interest[104] on the amount of any unpaid tax.[105]

---

100. That is, where the organization's public charity status is based on IRC § 170(b)(1)(A)(iii) as a medical research organization, IRC § 170(b)(1)(A)(iv), or IRC § 509(a)(3).
101. Instructions for Form 8940 (Apr. 2023), Schedule H.
102. Reg. § 1.507-2(d)(5); Instructions for Form 8940 (Apr. 2023), Part II and Schedule H.
103. Reg. § 1.507-2(d)(3). A grantor or contributor may not rely on such an advance ruling, however, if the grantor or contributor was responsible for, or aware of, the act or failure to act that resulted in the organization's failure to meet the requirements for public charity status or acquired knowledge that the IRS had given notice to such organization that its advance ruling would be revoked. Prior to receiving a grant or contribution that may cause the grantee to fail to meet the requirements for public charity status, the grantee may request a ruling from the IRS whether such grant or contribution may be made without such failure. If a favorable ruling is issued, the grantor or contributor may rely on the ruling with respect to the grant or contribution that is the subject of the ruling (*id.*).
104. IRC § 6601.
105. Reg. § 1.507-2(d)(4). Any failure to pay the tax during the 60-month period (or prior to the revocation of the advance ruling) will be considered to be due to reasonable cause; therefore, the IRC § 6651 addition to tax with respect to the IRC § 4940 tax will not apply (*id.*; see § 12.4(b)). Thus, this is one advantage to obtaining an advance ruling as compared to simply giving notice of intent to terminate.

§ 13.4 OPERATION AS A PUBLIC CHARITY

The IRS ruled that a private foundation may be given an advance ruling that it can be expected to operate as a supporting organization where the only organization it supports has commenced a 60-month termination period and has received a favorable advance ruling. The supported organization received an advance ruling on the basis that it could reasonably be expected to operate as a public charity during its 60-month termination period. Therefore, the IRS reasoned, the supporting organization could be given an advance ruling that it can reasonably be expected to be supporting a public charity during its own 60-month termination period.[106]

(d) Final Notice

Whether or not a private foundation obtains an advance ruling, a private foundation that has completed the 60-month termination period is required, within 90 days after the end of this period, to provide the IRS with information sufficient for the IRS to make a determination that the foundation qualifies as a public charity.[107] This information is submitted on Form 8940, along with the appropriate user fee.[108]

The information to be submitted with Form 8940 (on Schedule J) includes (1) a complete description of the organization's current operations pertinent to the public charity status, as well as any changes during the 60-month period; and (2) in certain instances, copies of the organization's governing instrument, bylaws, and amendments.[109] An organization qualifying as a publicly supported charity must also upload a completed copy of Form 990 or 990-EZ, Schedule A, Part II (for donative publicly supported charities) or Part III (for service provider publicly supported charities), as applicable. An organization is required to complete additional schedules if it qualifies as a supporting organization (Schedule F) or a public institution (Schedule L through Schedule P).

---

106. Rev. Rul. 78-386, 1978-2 C.B. 179. The IRS ruled that a private operating foundation (*see* § 3.1) could be expected to qualify as a publicly supported charity by reason of the facts-and-circumstances test (see § 15.4(d)) (Priv. Ltr. Rul. 200623068). In another instance, the IRS ruled that a private foundation could be converted to an educational organization (see § 15.3(b)) (Priv. Ltr. Rul. 200620036).
107. Reg. § 1.507-2(b)(4), (c).
108. Form 8940 must be submitted electronically at www.pay.gov; the user fee for this type of request is currently $550 (Rev. Proc. 2023-5, 2023-1 I.R.B. 265 §§ 4.02(6), 7.02 and App. A (Schedule of User Fees), as modified by Rev. Proc. 2023-12, 2023-17 I.R.B. 768 §§ 3.01, 3.03).
109. This requirement is applicable only where the organization's public charity status is based on IRC § 170(b)(1)(A)(iii) as a medical research organization, IRC § 170(b)(1)(A)(iv), or IRC § 509(a)(3).

TERMINATION OF FOUNDATION STATUS

If Form 8940 is submitted within 90 days after the end of the 60-month period but is incomplete, it will be considered to have been timely submitted if the private foundation supplies the necessary additional information at the request of, and within the additional time period allowed by, the IRS.[110]

If information is furnished establishing a successful termination, then, for the final year of the termination period, the organization should comply with the Form 990 filing requirements for the type of public charity it has become. This applies even if the IRS has not confirmed that the organization has terminated its private foundation status by the time the return for the final year of the termination is due (or would be due if a return were required). The organization will be allowed a reasonable period of time to file any private foundation returns required (for the last year of the termination period) but not previously filed if it is later determined that the organization did not terminate its private foundation status. Interest on any tax due will be charged from the original due date of Form 990-PF, but additions to tax[111] will not be assessed if Form 990-PF is filed within the period allowed by the IRS.[112]

§ 13.5 MERGERS, SPLIT-UPS, AND TRANSFERS BETWEEN FOUNDATIONS

(a) General Rules

When one private foundation "transfers its assets to another private foundation, pursuant to any liquidation, merger, redemption, recapitalization, or other adjustment, organization, or reorganization," the transferee (recipient) foundation is not treated "as a newly created organization."[113] Furthermore, the transferor foundation engaging in such a transaction will not have involuntarily terminated its private foundation status, unless it chooses to notify the IRS of its intent to voluntarily terminate such status.[114] A common use of this *private foundation reformation* rule is to transfer assets of a private foundation to one or more other private foundations in a division of assets because the trustees of the original foundation are not getting along; as the IRS discreetly

---

110. Reg. § 1.507-2(b)(5).
111. Under IRC § 6651 and 6652 (see § 12.4(b)).
112. Instructions for Form 990-PF (2022), General Instruction U.
113. IRC § 507(b)(2). Termination of a private foundation can involve this rule and one of the other termination scenarios. In one instance, a foundation transferred all its assets to a private operating foundation and a public charity (a museum); the transfer of assets to the transferee foundation was ruled by the IRS to be subject to this rule, while the transfer to the public charity was not (it was subject to the rules summarized in § 13.3) (Priv. Ltr. Rul. 201435016).
114. Reg. § 1.507-1(b)(6), (7).

§ 13.5 MERGERS, SPLIT-UPS, AND TRANSFERS BETWEEN FOUNDATIONS

stated the matter in one case, the "charitable interests" of the trustees of a foundation have "diverged," with the foundation thus finding it "difficult" to "develop a unified approach to grant making."[115] Another somewhat frequent use of this rule is in connection with mergers; in one instance, the IRS applied it in connection with a proposed merger of a private operating foundation and a nonoperating private foundation controlled by the same individuals, where the operating foundation would be the surviving entity.[116]

For purposes of this private foundation reformation rule, the terms "other adjustment, organization, or reorganization" in the statute include any partial liquidation or any other significant disposition of assets to one or more private foundations other than transfers for full and adequate consideration or distributions out of current income.[117] A "significant disposition of assets" includes any disposition (or series of related dispositions) by a private foundation to one or more private foundations of 25 percent or more of the fair market value of the net assets of the transferor foundation at the beginning of the tax year in which the transfers occur.[118]

Thus, when 25 percent or more of a foundation's assets are transferred to one or more other private foundations, or the private foundation reformation rule otherwise applies to a transfer of assets to one or more other private foundations, the transferee private foundation(s) will not be treated as a newly created organization.[119] Consequently, the transferee private foundation(s) are treated as possessing the following "attributes and characteristics" of the transferor.[120] First, a transferee private foundation succeeds to the transferor's aggregate tax benefit in an amount equal to the amount of the transferor's aggregate tax benefit multiplied by a fraction the numerator of which is the fair market value of the assets (less encumbrances) transferred to such transferee and the denominator of which is the fair market value of the assets of the transferor (less encumbrances) immediately before the transfer.[121] When the transferee private foundation is not effectively controlled, directly or indirectly, by the same person or persons who effectively control the transferor private foundation, however, the transferee foundation will not succeed to an aggregate tax benefit in excess of the fair market value of the assets transferred at the time of the transfer.[122] Second, any person who is a substantial contributor with

---

115. Priv. Ltr. Rul. 201130006.
116. Priv. Ltr. Rul. 201321024.
117. Reg. § 1.507-3(c)(1). For these purposes, a distribution out of current income includes any distribution described in IRC § 4942(h)(1)(A) and (B) (*id.*).
118. Reg. § 1.507-3(c)(2).
119. Reg. § 1.507-3(a)(1).
120. *Id.*
121. Reg. § 1.507-3(a)(2)(i).
122. Reg. § 1.507-3(a)(2)(ii).

TERMINATION OF FOUNDATION STATUS

respect to the transferor foundation prior to the transfer shall be treated as a substantial contributor with respect to each transferee foundation, regardless of whether such person meets the $5,000 2 percent test[123] with respect to the transferee at any time.[124] Third, if the transferor private foundation incurs liability for one or more of the taxes imposed under Chapter 42 (or any penalty resulting therefrom) prior to, or as a result of, making the transfer, in any case where transferee liability applies, each transferee foundation shall be treated as receiving the transferred assets subject to such liability to the extent that the transferor foundation does not satisfy such liability.[125] Additionally, the transferee foundation's holding period for purposes of the excess business holdings rules includes the time the transferred assets were held by both the transferor and the transferee.[126]

In determining whether a transferee private foundation is *effectively controlled*, directly or indirectly, by the same person or persons who effectively control a transferor private foundation, control is defined to include any kind of control, direct or indirect, whether legally enforceable and however exercisable or exercised. It is the reality of the control which is decisive, not the form or the mode of its exercise.[127]

If a private foundation transfers all of its net assets to one or more private foundations that are effectively controlled by the same person(s), the transferee private foundation will be treated as if it were the transferor private foundation for purposes of the private foundation rules.[128] However, where proportionality is appropriate, such a transferee foundation will be treated as if it were the transferor in the proportion that the fair market value of the assets (less encumbrances) transferred to such transferee bears to the fair market value of the assets (less encumbrances) of the transferor immediately before the transfer.[129]

If a private foundation was organized as a corporation, has its corporate status administratively revoked, and cannot be reinstated as a corporation, its board of directors can create a successor transferee corporation. For federal tax purposes, the transferor foundation will remain in existence as a corporation, being deemed under the check-the-box regulations to be an association

---

123. IRC § 507(d)(2); see § 4.1.
124. Reg. § 1.507-3(a)(3).
125. Reg. § 1.507-3(a)(4).
126. Reg. § 1.507-3(a)(6).
127. Reg. § 1.482-1(a)(3), now redesignated as Reg. § 1.482-1A(a)(3), as cross-referenced in Reg. § 1.507-3(a)(2)(ii). Priv. Ltr. Rul. 199920045 provides an example of the application of these principles to determine effective control in the context of one private foundation's transfer of assets to two newly formed private foundations.
128. Specifically, for purposes of §§ 507-509 and 4940-4948.
129. Reg. § 1.507-3(a)(9)(i).

§ 13.5 MERGERS, SPLIT-UPS, AND TRANSFERS BETWEEN FOUNDATIONS

taxable as a corporation.[130] The foundation that lost its status as a corporation under state law can terminate its private foundation status pursuant to the federal tax law by utilizing the reorganization approach.[131]

Although a ruling with respect to a liquidation, merger, redemption, recapitalization, or other adjustment, organization, or reorganization transaction involving private foundations is not required, the IRS frequently issues private letter rulings concerning these types of private foundation reformation transactions.[132]

(b) Complete Asset Transfers to Controlled Foundations

The IRS addressed three types of private foundation reformations involving commonly controlled private foundations.[133] The ruling described the filing obligations and excise tax issues that arise when a private foundation transfers assets to one or more other private foundations. The ruling is based on the following assumptions, the last of which limits the applicability of the ruling to commonly controlled foundations: (1) all of the foundations involved are classified as tax-exempt organizations, are treated as private foundations, and are not private operating foundations; (2) none of the foundations involved has committed willful and flagrant acts, or failures to act, giving rise to tax under Chapter 42 so as to be subject to the termination tax; (3) the private foundations have not involuntarily terminated[134] or terminated by transferring their assets to one or more public charities;[135] (4) the transferor foundation has existing expenditure responsibility grants requiring future monitoring and reports; and (5) all of the foundations, both the transferor(s) and transferee(s), are effectively controlled, directly or indirectly, by the same persons.

The ruling considers the reporting requirements and factors that carry over to the successor foundations in the following three situations:

Situation 1: A private foundation, due to the divergent interests of its current directors, distributes all of its remaining assets in equal shares to three other private foundations. Pursuant to the plan of dissolution, the foundation satisfies all of its outstanding liabilities, causes the recipient foundations to satisfy its existing expenditure responsibility reporting

---

130. Reg. § 301.7701-2(b)(2), 3(c)(v).
131. Priv. Ltr. Rul. 200607027.
132. E.g., Priv. Ltr. Rul. 8629062.
133. Rev. Rul. 2002-28, 2002-1 C.B. 941. Due to the complicated nature of the issues involved, the IRS limited this ruling to private foundation transformations. See § 13.3 for discussion of a subsequent ruling on transfers of foundation assets to public charities.
134. See § 13.2.
135. See § 13.3.

TERMINATION OF FOUNDATION STATUS

requirements, and, after all of its assets are transferred, files articles of dissolution with the appropriate state authority.

Situation 2: The trustees of a private foundation trust create a nonprofit corporation to carry on the trust's charitable activities, which the trustees have determined can be accomplished more effectively by operating in corporate form. All of the trust's assets and liabilities are transferred to the new nonprofit corporation.

Situation 3: Two private foundations that confine their grant-making activities to programs in the particular city in which they are located transfer all their assets and liabilities to a newly formed private foundation.

In this ruling, the IRS considered the transferor private foundation's termination notice requirements and tax return filing obligations, the implications under the private foundation excise tax provisions, and the implications for the transferor's aggregate tax benefit resulting from the transfers under all three situations.

The IRS first concluded that if a private foundation transfers all of its assets to one or more private foundations, it is not required to notify the IRS of its plans to terminate its private foundation status and pay the termination tax. Advance IRS notification is not required when a private foundation voluntarily makes a significant disposition of its assets to one or more private foundations. A transfer of all of a private foundation's assets to one or more private foundations, other than transfers for full and adequate consideration or distributions out of current income, constitutes a significant disposition of assets subject to the private foundation reformation rule.[136] Thus, in Situations 1, 2, and 3, described above, no termination occurs unless the transferor voluntarily gives notice of its intent to terminate.[137] The fact that a private foundation dissolves under state law has no effect on whether it has terminated its private foundation status for federal tax purposes.

If a foundation chooses to provide notice to the IRS of its intent to terminate voluntarily, it is subject to the termination tax unless it requests and receives abatement of the tax.[138] If the foundation has no assets on the day it provides notice, however (for example, it provides notice at least one day after it transfers all of its assets), the termination tax will be zero. (This is so even if the foundations involved are not effectively controlled by the same person(s).)[139]

---

136. IRC § 507(b)(2); Reg. § 1.507-3(c)(1), (2).
137. Reg. §§ 1.507-1(b)(6), 1.507-3(d).
138. Reg. § 1.507-7(a), (b)(1).
139. E.g., Priv. Ltr. Rul. 200204039.

§ 13.5 MERGERS, SPLIT-UPS, AND TRANSFERS BETWEEN FOUNDATIONS

Next, the IRS considered a private foundation's tax return filing obligations after it transfers all of its assets to one or more transferee private foundations and its legal existence is dissolved, or it continues to exist in a dormant condition. A private foundation that has disposed of all of its assets and terminates its private foundation status must file a Form 990-PF for the tax year of the disposition and must comply with any expenditure responsibility reporting obligations on such return. A private foundation that has disposed of all of its assets, but does not terminate its private foundation status, continues to be treated as a private foundation. It must file a Form 990-PF for the tax year of the disposition and must comply with any expenditure responsibility reporting obligations on such return.[140] It does not, however, need to file returns in the following tax years if it does not have equitable title to any assets and does not engage in any activity.[141] If, in later tax years, it receives additional assets or resumes activities, it must resume filing a Form 990-PF for those tax years in which it has assets or activities.

A transferor foundation that engages in a liquidation, dissolution, termination, or substantial contraction must attach a statement describing the transaction to its Form 990-PF for the year in which the transaction occurs.[142] A certified copy of the liquidation plan or resolutions (if any), a schedule of the names and addresses of all recipients of assets, and an explanation of the nature and fair market value of the assets distributed to each recipient must also be attached to the return. If the foundation has ceased to exist, the "Final return" box on the first page of Form 990-PF must be checked.[143]

The IRS then considered the implications for a private foundation's aggregate tax benefit when it transfers all of its assets to one or more private foundations that are effectively controlled by the same person(s). Regardless of whether the transferor foundation provides notice of its intent to terminate, the transferee foundations are treated as possessing the aggregate tax benefit of the transferor foundations.[144] In Situation 1, because there are multiple transferee foundations, each transferee foundation succeeds to the transferor foundation's aggregate tax benefit in proportion to the assets transferred to each.[145]

Finally, the IRS considered the implications under the various private foundation excise tax provisions where a private foundation transfers all of

---

140. The expenditure responsibility requirements of the transferor and transferee foundation, respectively, are discussed below in connection with the IRC § 4945 implications of these transaction(s).
141. Reg. §§ 1.507-1(b)(9), -3(a)(10).
142. IRC § 6043(b).
143. Instructions for Form 990-PF (2022), General Instruction T.
144. Reg. § 1.507-3(a)(1), (2)(i). For the definition of *aggregate tax benefit*, see § 13.7.
145. Reg. § 1.507-3(a)(2)(i).

its assets to one or more private foundations that are effectively controlled by the same person(s).

Section 4940 Implications. In all three situations considered in the ruling, the transfers do not constitute investments of the transferor for purposes of the net investment income tax;[146] therefore, the transfers do not give rise to net investment income subject to the tax.[147] Additionally, because each transferor foundation transfers all of its assets to one or more private foundations effectively controlled by the same person(s), any excess net investment income tax paid by the transferor may be used by the transferees to offset the transferees' tax liability.

In Situation 1, where there are three transferee foundations, proportionality is appropriate, and each transferee foundation will succeed to one-third of any excess net investment income tax paid by the transferor foundation.[148] Because it may be challenging as an administrative matter to get the IRS to recognize a transfer of tax deposits from one entity to another, a transferee foundation in this situation may be better off simply requesting a refund of its share of any tax paid by the transferor. When underpayment penalties will not result, it would be better still to avoid this issue by causing the final return to reflect a tax liability rather than a tax overpayment.

Section 4941 Implications. The transfers do not constitute self-dealing in any of the three situations considered in the ruling because the transferee foundations are tax-exempt charitable organizations. Tax-exempt charitable organizations are not treated as disqualified persons for purposes of the self-dealing rules;[149] therefore, there is no transaction between a foundation and a disqualified person that could give rise to an act of self-dealing.[150]

Section 4942 Implications. The transfers are not qualifying distributions of the transferor foundation in any of the three situations considered in the ruling. Because the foundations are effectively controlled by the same person(s), the transferee foundations are treated as though they were the transferor for purposes of the qualifying distributions rules,[151] and a private foundation cannot make a qualifying distribution to itself.[152]

---

146. Also Tech. Adv. Mem. 200613038.
147. See Chapter 10.
148. Reg. § 1.507-3(a)(9)(i).
149. Reg. § 53.4946-1(a)(8); see § 4.1(a).
150. See Chapter 5.
151. Reg. § 1.507-3(a)(9)(i).
152. The transferor private foundation does not, however, need to separately meet the IRC § 4942 distribution requirements for the tax year in which it makes an IRC § 507(b)(2) transfer of all or part of its net assets to another private foundation effectively controlled by the same person(s) (e.g., Priv. Ltr. Rul. 202328004). Reg. § 1.507-3(a)(9)(i) operates to override the general rule to the contrary in Reg. § 1.507-3(a)(5). See § 13.5(c).

§ 13.5 MERGERS, SPLIT-UPS, AND TRANSFERS BETWEEN FOUNDATIONS

Additionally, in Situations 2 and 3, each transferee foundation assumes all obligations with respect to the transferor's undistributed income,[153] if any, and reduces its own distributable amount by the transferor foundation's excess qualifying distributions.[154] In Situation 1, where there are three transferee foundations, proportionality is appropriate;[155] therefore, each transferee foundation becomes responsible for one-third of the transferor foundation's undistributed income and succeeds to one-third of its excess qualifying distributions, if any, which the transferee foundation may use to reduce its own distributable amount.[156]

Section 4943 Implications. Because the foundations involved in all three situations considered in the ruling are effectively controlled by the same person(s), the disqualified persons, including substantial contributors, of both the transferor and transferee foundations are treated as disqualified persons of the transferee in determining whether the transferee has excess business holdings.[157] In addition, the transferee's holding period for purposes of the excess business holdings rules includes the time the transferred assets were held by both the transferor and the transferee.[158]

Section 4944 Implications. None of the asset transfers considered in the ruling constitute investments by the transferor private foundation; therefore, the transfers do not constitute investments jeopardizing the transferor foundation's exempt purposes. If any of the transferred assets constituted a jeopardizing investment prior to transfer, however, the transferee would be subject to any related pre-transfer excise tax liability to the extent not satisfied by the transferor,[159] as well as ongoing excise tax liability if the transferee does not dispose of the jeopardizing investment.[160]

Section 4945 Implications. In all three situations considered in the ruling, the transferor foundation is required to exercise expenditure responsibility[161] over the transferor's outstanding grants until the transferor disposes of all of its assets. The transferor must also meet the Form 990-PF expenditure responsibility reporting requirements for the outstanding grants for the year in which the transfers are made. Subsequently, during any period in which the

---

153. Within the meaning of IRC § 4942(c).
154. Under IRC § 4942(i).
155. Reg. § 1.507-3(a)(9)(i).
156. Rev. Rul. 78-387, 1978-2 C.B. 270. As to a private foundation's distributable amount, see § 6.1(b).
157. IRC § 4943; see Chapter 7.
158. Reg. § 1.507-3(a)(6).
159. Reg. § 1.507-3(a)(4).
160. See § 8.5(a).
161. Under IRC § 4945(d)(4) or (h); see § 9.7.

transferor foundation has no assets, the transferor foundation is not required to exercise expenditure responsibility over any outstanding grants.[162]

With respect to the transfers to the transferee foundations, there are no expenditure responsibility requirements that must be exercised by the transferor private foundation because the (effectively controlled) transferee foundations are treated as the transferor foundation rather than as recipients of expenditure responsibility grants.[163] The transferee foundations assume expenditure responsibility for all the transferor's outstanding grants.[164] In Situation 1, because one of the transferee foundations agreed to exercise expenditure responsibility for all of the transferor foundation's outstanding grants, the other two transferee foundations have no expenditure responsibility obligations over the transferor foundation's grants. In the absence of such an agreement, however, each of the three transferee foundations would be required to exercise expenditure responsibility with respect to all of the transferor foundation's outstanding grants.[165]

(c) Complete Asset Transfer to Non-Controlled Foundations

Subsequent to the foregoing, the IRS issued private letter rulings to two private foundations with identical exempt purposes, where, to realize administrative cost savings and eliminate duplication of efforts, one of the foundations planned to transfer all of its assets to the other, then dissolve.[166] These private foundations were not effectively controlled by the same person(s). This transaction resulted in the following rulings:

1. The transfer of assets is a transfer subject to the private foundation reformation rule,[167] and therefore is not a voluntary termination.[168] Thus, the transferor foundation is not liable for the termination tax.[169]

2. Because the asset transfer is subject to the private foundation reformation rule, the transferee foundation will not be treated as a "newly created organization."[170]

---

162. Reg. § 1.507-3(a)(7).
163. Reg. § 1.507-3(a)(9)(i) and (iii), Example 2. For an example of a subsequent application by the IRS of the conclusions reached in Rev. Rul. 2002-28, 2002-1 C.B. 941, see Priv. Ltr. Rul. 200421010.
164. Reg. § 1.507-3(a)(9)(i).
165. Reg. § 1.507-3(a)(9)(i) and (iii), Example 2.
166. Priv. Ltr. Ruls. 201013065 and 201013066.
167. IRC § 507(b)(2); see § 13.5(a).
168. See § 13.1.
169. See § 13.7.
170. IRC § 507(b)(2); Reg. § 1.507-3(a)(1).

§ 13.5 MERGERS, SPLIT-UPS, AND TRANSFERS BETWEEN FOUNDATIONS

3. The asset transfer will not adversely affect the tax-exempt status of either the transferor foundation or the transferee foundation.

4. The transferee foundation will succeed to the "aggregate tax benefit" of the transferor foundation, but not in excess of the fair market value of the assets transferred (because the foundations are not effectively controlled by the same person(s)).[171]

5. Inasmuch as the transferred assets will not constitute investment income,[172] the receipt of these assets will not be investment income to the transferee foundation and it will not be liable for the net investment income tax with respect to its receipt of the transferred assets. If the transferor foundation is liable for the net investment income tax (for the period prior to the transfer of the assets) and this liability is not satisfied, the transferee foundation will receive the transferred assets subject to this liability and will be required to satisfy it.[173] If the transferor foundation is entitled to a refund of the net investment income tax, the right to the refund will be included in the transferred assets, but the transferee foundation may not use it to offset its liability for the tax (because it is not effectively controlled by the same person(s) that control the transferor foundation).[174]

6. The asset transfer will not constitute an act of self-dealing because, as tax-exempt charitable organizations, neither private foundation is a disqualified person with respect to the other.[175]

7. For the tax year in which the asset transfer occurs, the transferor foundation must comply with the annual qualifying distribution requirements.[176] No part of the transfer of the assets will constitute a qualifying distribution for the transferor foundation, except to the extent that the transferee foundation makes a timely redistribution of such assets that it treats as a distribution out of corpus.[177]

8. The asset transfer will not result in a jeopardizing investment by either the transferor or transferee foundation.[178]

---

171. Reg. § 1.507-3(a)(2)(i), (ii). For the definition of *aggregate tax benefit*, see § 13.7.
172. As defined in IRC § 4940(c)(2).
173. Reg. § 1.507-3(a)(4).
174. Reg. § 1.507-3(a)(9)(i).
175. Reg. § 53.4946-1(a)(8); see § 4.1(a).
176. IRC § 4942(g)(1)(A); Reg. § 1.507-3(a)(5).
177. IRC § 4942(g)(3); Reg. § 1.507-3(a)(5); see § 6.4(c)(ii).
178. IRC § 4944; see Chapter 8. This ruling mischaracterizes the asset transfer as a program-related investment (IRC § 4944(c)); however, as a gratuitous transfer of all right and title in the transferred assets, without consideration or obligation of repayment, it is not an investment in the first instance.

TERMINATION OF FOUNDATION STATUS

9. The asset transfer itself will not be a taxable expenditure by the transferor foundation.[179] As to any obligation the transferor foundation has to exercise expenditure responsibility[180] at the time of the transfer, the transferee foundation will not be required to exercise expenditure responsibility. (Because the foundations are not effectively controlled by the same person(s), the transferee foundation will not be treated as the transferor foundation for purposes of Chapter 42.)[181] Nor will the transferor foundation have any ongoing requirements to exercise expenditure responsibility after the asset transfer, other than to comply with the expenditure responsibility information reporting requirements[182] for the tax year of the transfer.[183]

10. The transferor foundation will be required to file a Form 990-PF for the tax year in which it transfers the assets to the transferee foundation. If, however, after the assets transfer, the transferor foundation does not have legal or equitable title in any assets and does not engage in any activity, it is not required to file a Form 990-PF for any year following the year of the transfer.[184] The transferor will also have to file certain information with its Form 990-PF for the year of transfer because the transfer constitutes a liquidation, dissolution, termination, or substantial contraction of assets.[185]

(d) Transfers of Significant but Not All Assets

Where a private foundation makes a significant disposition (that is, 25 percent or more) of its assets to one or more other private foundations[186] but does not transfer all of its net assets to them, the transferee foundation(s) will not be treated as the transferor foundation for purposes of all of the private foundation rules.[187] The transferee foundation(s) will, however, be treated as possessing the following attributes and characteristics of the transferor foundation:

- The aggregate tax benefit of the transferor foundation in an amount equal to the amount of such aggregate tax benefit multiplied by a fraction the

---

179. IRC § 4945(d); see Chapter 9.
180. See § 9.7.
181. Reg. § 1.507-3(a)(7), (9)(i).
182. Under IRC § 4945(h)(3).
183. Reg. § 1.507-3(a)(7).
184. Reg. § 1.507-1(b)(9).
185. See text accompanied by *supra* notes 142-143.
186. Reg. § 1.507-3(c)(2).
187. That is, Reg. § 1.507-3(a)(9)(i) applies only where a private foundation transfers *all* of its net assets to one or more private foundations that are effectively controlled by the same person(s).

§ 13.5 MERGERS, SPLIT-UPS, AND TRANSFERS BETWEEN FOUNDATIONS

numerator of which is the fair market value of the assets (less encumbrances) transferred to such transferee and the denominator of which is the fair market value of the assets of the transferor (less encumbrances) immediately before the transfer. If the transferee foundation is not effectively controlled by the same person(s) as the transferor, the amount of the transferor's aggregate tax benefit to which the transferee succeeds will not exceed the fair market value of the assets transferred at the time of the transfer.[188]

- Any person who is a substantial contributor with respect to the transferor foundation prior to the transfer shall be treated as a substantial contributor with respect to each transferee foundation, regardless of whether such person meets the $5,000 2 percent test[189] with respect to the transferee at any time.[190]

- If the transferor private foundation incurs liability for one or more of the taxes imposed under Chapter 42 (or any penalty resulting therefrom) prior to or as a result of making the transfer, in any case where transferee liability applies, each transferee foundation shall be treated as receiving the transferred assets subject to such liability to the extent that the transferor foundation does not satisfy such liability.[191]

- The transferee's holding period for purposes of the excess business holdings rules includes the time both the transferor and the transferee held the assets.[192]

The implications under the other private foundation excise tax provisions are the same as where a private foundation transfers all of its assets to one or more private foundations that are not effectively controlled by the same person(s).[193] Where the transferor does not dispose of all of its assets, however, it is required to exercise expenditure responsibility with respect to any asset transfer it makes to another private foundation (unless and until it eventually disposes of all of its assets).[194]

---

188. Reg. § 1.507-3(a)(2).
189. IRC § 507(d)(2); see § 4.1.
190. Reg. § 1.507-3(a)(3).
191. Reg. § 1.507-3(a)(4).
192. Reg. § 1.507-3(a)(6).
193. See § 13.5(c).
194. E.g., Priv. Ltr. Rul. 201435016.

§ 13.6 TERMINATION OF TRUSTS TREATED AS PRIVATE FOUNDATIONS

For certain purposes, nonexempt charitable trusts[195] and split-interest trusts[196] are treated as private foundations. Like any other private foundation, a nonexempt charitable trust that was originally a private foundation, but subsequently meets the requirements to be classified as a public charity, must first terminate its private foundation status pursuant to the notice and 60-month termination period rules[197] before it will be treated as a public charity.[198]

A payment by a nonexempt charitable trust or a split-interest trust to a beneficiary that is required by the terms of the trust's governing instrument and is not discretionary with the trustee or, in the case of a discretionary payment, by reason of, or following, the expiration of the last remaining charitable interest in the trust, does not result in the termination of the trust's private foundation status.[199] Accordingly, such a distribution will not subject the trust to the termination tax.[200] Further, once the entire charitable income interest has been paid from a split-interest trust, the private foundation termination provisions will no longer apply to the trust because it no longer retains any amounts for which a charitable deduction was allowed.[201]

Thus, for example, where the governing instrument of a nonexempt charitable trust requires it to distribute all of its assets to another charitable organization after 15 years, a terminating distribution in accordance with this provision will not be considered to be a termination of the trust's private foundation status.[202] Similarly, a final distribution required to be made from a charitable remainder annuity trust to a charitable organization upon the death of the lifetime beneficiary will also not be considered a termination of the trust's private foundation status,[203] nor will a final payment to a charitable

---

195. IRC § 4947(a)(1); see § 3.6.
196. IRC § 4947(a)(2); see § 3.7.
197. See § 13.4.
198. Rev. Rul. 76-92, 1971-1 C.B. 92.
199. Reg. § 53.4947-1(e)(1). The regulations state that "the provisions of section 507(a) shall not apply" to a nonexempt charitable trust or a split-interest trust making such a payment (*id*).
200. See § 13.7.
201. Reg. § 53.4947-1(e)(2), Example (2). Specifically, the provisions of IRC § 4942(a)(2) cease to apply to the trust following such a distribution; therefore, IRC § 507 no longer applies (*id*.; e.g., Priv. Ltr. Rul. 8637123).
202. Reg. § 53.4947-1(e)(2), Example (1).
203. Reg. § 53.4947-1(e)(2), Example (3).

organization from a charitable lead annuity trust in accordance with the terms of the trust.[204]

The IRS, from time to time, issues rulings that distributions from nonexempt charitable and split-interest trusts will not be a termination of the trust's private foundation status.[205]

§ 13.7 TERMINATION TAX

There is imposed on each organization, the private foundation status of which is terminated under the voluntary or involuntary termination rules,[206] a tax equal to the lower of (1) the amount that the organization substantiates by adequate records or other corroborating evidence as the *aggregate tax benefit* resulting from the tax-exempt status of the organization as a charitable entity, or (2) the value of the net assets of the organization.[207] The aggregate tax benefit resulting from the tax-exempt status of a private foundation is the sum of:

1. Aggregate increases in income, estate, and gift taxes that would have been imposed with respect to all substantial contributors[208] to the private foundation if deductions for all contributions made by the substantial contributors to the private foundation after February 28, 1913, had been disallowed.

2. Aggregate increases in income taxes that would have been imposed with respect to the income of the foundation for tax years beginning after December 31, 1912, if it had not been exempt from tax (or if a trust, the amount by which its income taxes were reduced because it was permitted to deduct charitable contributions in excess of 20 percent of its taxable income).

3. Any amounts succeeded to from transferor private foundations.[209]

4. Interest on the foregoing increases in tax from the first date on which each increase would have been due and payable to the date on which the organization ceases to be a private foundation.[210]

---

204. Reg. § 53.4947-1(e)(2), Example (2).
205. E.g., Priv. Ltr. Rul. 201930017.
206. See §§ 13.1, 13.2.
207. IRC § 507(c); Reg. § 1.507-4(a). Private foundations that make transfers described in IRC § 507(b)(1)(A) (see § 13.3) or IRC § 507(b)(2) (see § 13.5) are not subject to the termination tax imposed with respect to such transfers unless the voluntary or involuntary termination provisions of IRC § 507(a) become applicable (Reg. § 1.507-4(b)).
208. See § 4.1.
209. IRC § 507(b)(2); Reg. §1.507-3(a)(2); see § 13.5.
210. IRC § 507(d); Reg. § 1.507-5(a).

In computing the amount of the aggregate increases in tax under the first of these items, all deductions attributable to a particular contribution for income, estate, or gift tax purposes must be included. Thus, the aggregate tax benefit in respect to a single contribution may exceed the fair market value of the property transferred.[211]

With respect to the amount of the tax benefit as stated in the second of these items in the case of a trust, one court found the provision "ambiguous."[212] Specifically, the applicable law describes the tax benefit of a trust as including the aggregate increases in tax that would be imposed if "deductions under section 642(c) . . . had been limited to 20 percent of the taxable income of the trust (computed without the benefit of section 642(c) but with the benefit of section 170(b)(1)(A))."[213] The court concluded that the provision requires a two-step calculation. The first step is to apply the pertinent charitable contribution deduction rule, which is the charitable deduction available to individuals for up to 50 percent of the donor's contribution base.[214] The second step is to apply a deduction of 20 percent of the trust's taxable income, rather than the full (100 percent) deduction normally allowed,[215] against the trust income remaining after the charitable deduction. This interpretation thus produces a 60 percent (50 percent plus 20 percent of 50 percent) deduction, which in turn produces the amount retained by the trust in calculating the tax benefit to be recaptured. Pursuant to this reading of the statute, this portion of the termination tax equals 40 percent of the value of the trust's deduction, namely, the 100 percent deduction taken by the trust minus the 60 percent deduction the trust can retain.

In computing the value of the net assets of a private foundation, the amount of the value is determined at whichever time the value is higher: the first day on which action is taken by the organization that culminates in its ceasing to be a private foundation or the date on which it ceases to be a private foundation.[216] In the case of a voluntary termination, the first of these dates is the date the organization submitted notice it was terminating its private foundation status; in the case of an involuntary termination, it is the date a willful and flagrant act, failure to act, or a series of repeated acts or failures to act first occurred.[217]

The term *net assets* means the gross assets of a private foundation reduced by all its liabilities, including appropriate estimated and contingent liabilities (such as any private foundation excise taxes or winding-up expenses).[218]

---

211. Reg. § 1.507-5(b).
212. Peters v. United States, 80-2 U.S.T.C. ¶ 9510 (Ct. Cl. 1980).
213. IRC § 507(d)(1)(B)(ii).
214. IRC § 170(b)(1)(A). See § 14.2(a).
215. IRC § 642(c).
216. IRC § 507(e); Reg. § 1.507-7(a).
217. Reg. § 1.507-7(b).
218. Reg. § 1.507-7(d).

§ 13.8 ABATEMENT

The IRS has the discretion to abate an unpaid portion of the assessment of a termination tax or any liability with respect to the tax if a private foundation distributes all of its net assets to one or more eligible public or publicly supported organizations, each of which has been in existence and so described for a continuous period of at least 60 calendar months, or if the private foundation gives effective assurance to the IRS that its assets will be used for charitable purposes.[219]

Abatement of the unpaid portion of the assessment of a termination tax will occur only where the IRS determines that there will be vigorous enforcement of state laws sufficient to ensure implementation of the private foundation excise tax provisions and ensure that the assets of the private foundation are preserved for charitable or other exempt purposes.[220] The appropriate state officer has one year from the date of notification[221] that a notice of deficiency of termination tax has been issued to advise the IRS that corrective action has been initiated (by the state officer or a recipient public or publicly supported charity) pursuant to state law as may be ordered or approved by a court of competent jurisdiction.[222] On receipt of certification from the state officer that corrective action has been taken, the IRS may abate the termination tax assessment, unless the IRS determines that the action is not sufficiently corrective, in which case action on the assessment and collection of the tax may be suspended until corrective action[223] is obtained, or assessment and collection of the tax may be resumed.[224]

---

219. IRC § 507(g); Reg. § 1.507-9(a).The IRS ruled that it did not have the discretion to abate the termination tax where a private foundation did not transfer of all its net assets to eligible public charities before the foundation submitted its notice of intent to terminate (Priv. Ltr. Rul. 200124024; see § 13.4(a), (b)).
220. Reg. § 1.507-9(b)(1).
221. IRC § 6104(c).
222. Reg. § 1.507-9(b)(2).
223. Reg. § 1.507-9(c).
224. Reg. § 1.507-9(b)(3).

CHAPTER FOURTEEN

Charitable Giving Rules

§ 14.1 Concept of Gift   589
§ 14.2 Basic Rules   592
    (a) Percentage Limitations   593
    (b) Estate and Gift Tax Deductions   595
§ 14.3 Gifts of Appreciated Property   595
§ 14.4 Deduction Reduction Rules   597
    (a) Capital Gain Property Deduction Rule   597
    (b) Other Deduction Reduction Rules   597
§ 14.5 Qualified Appreciated Stock Rule   599
§ 14.6 Special Gift Situations   601
    (a) Donors' Creations   601
    (b) Bargain Sales   601
    (c) Intellectual Property   602
    (d) Vehicles   602
    (e) Use of Property   603
    (f) Services   603
    (g) Conservation Property   603
§ 14.7 Administrative Considerations   604
    (a) Recordkeeping Rules   604
    (b) Substantiation Rules   604
    (c) Disclosure Rules   608
    (d) Appraisal Rules   609
    (e) Doctrine of Substantial Compliance   611
    (f) Reporting Requirements   612
    (g) State Fundraising Regulation   612

Federal law provides an income tax charitable contribution deduction. Pursuant to this deduction, individuals who itemize deductions, as well as corporations, can deduct, subject to varying limitations, an amount equal to the value of a contribution made to a qualified charitable donee.[1]

§ 14.1 CONCEPT OF GIFT

Integral to the concept of the charitable contribution deduction is the fundamental requirement that money or property paid or otherwise transferred to a charitable organization be transferred pursuant to a transaction that constitutes a gift. Just because money is paid or property is transferred to a charitable, educational, scientific, religious, or like organization does not necessarily mean that the payment or transfer is a gift. Consequently, when a university's

---

1. IRC § 170(a)(1).

§ 14.1 CONCEPT OF GIFT

tuition, a hospital's healthcare fee, or an association's dues are paid, there is no gift; thus, a charitable deduction does not arise as a result of the payment. These are situations in which there is an absence of a gift because the payor or transferor received a material quid pro quo in exchange for the transfer.

Basically, the concept of the word *gift* has two elements: It is a transfer that is voluntary and is motivated by something other than the receipt of consideration.[2] For example, the federal tax regulations promulgated in amplification of the business expense deduction rules state that a transfer is not a contribution when it is made "with a reasonable expectation of financial return commensurate with the amount of the donation."[3] Thus, the tax regulations also provide that a contribution is a "voluntary transfer of money or property that is made with no expectation of procuring financial benefit commensurate with the amount of the transfer."[4] The IRS stated that, "[w]here consideration in the form of substantial privileges or benefits is received in connection with payments by patrons of fund-raising activities, there is a presumption that the payments are not gifts."[5]

In an oft-quoted passage, the U.S. Supreme Court observed that a gift is a transfer motivated by "detached or disinterested generosity."[6] Likewise, the Court referred to a gift as a transfer made "out of affection, respect, admiration, charity or like impulses."[7] The Court also wrote that a "payment of money [or transfer of property] generally cannot constitute a charitable contribution if the contributor expects a substantial benefit in return."[8] The Court further stated that an exchange having an "inherently reciprocal nature" was not a gift, even if the recipient was a charitable entity.[9]

Thus, as these definitions indicate, a transfer that causes the transferor to receive a substantial quid pro quo in exchange for the amount or value transferred cannot qualify as a gift. This concept of the quid pro quo in the charitable

---

2. *Consideration* is a contract law concept referring to something received, usually goods and/or services, in return for a payment. When payments are made to receive something of approximate value in exchange, the transaction is in the nature of a contract, rather than a gift. For example, in the public charity setting, an excess benefit transaction is defined as a transaction in which an economic benefit is provided by the charitable organization to or for the benefit of a disqualified person if the value of the economic benefit provided exceeds the value of the consideration, such as the performance of services, received by the organization for providing the benefit (IRC § 4958(c)(1)(A)).
3. Reg. § 1.162-15(b).
4. Reg. § 1.170A-1(c)(5). Also, Reg. § 1.170A-1(h)(1).
5. Rev. Rul. 86-63, 1986-1 C.B. 88.
6. Commissioner v. Duberstein, 363 U.S. 278, 285 (1960), quoting from Commissioner v. LoBue, 351 U.S. 243, 246 (1956).
7. Robertson v. United States, 343 U.S. 711, 714 (1952).
8. United States v. American Bar Endowment, 477 U.S. 105, 116-117 (1986).
9. Hernandez v. Commissioner, 490 U.S. 680, 692 (1989).

contribution context gained national attention when the Department of the Treasury and the IRS used it to combat the efforts in some states to circumvent the $10,000 limit on the deductibility of state and local taxes[10] by substituting an increased charitable deduction for a disallowed state and local tax deduction. Final regulations were issued, providing rules stating the lack of availability of federal income tax charitable contribution deductions when a transfer of money or other property is made pursuant to one of these SALT cap "workarounds."[11] The general rule is that when a taxpayer receives or expects to receive a state or local tax credit in return for a payment to a charitable organization, the receipt of the tax benefit constitutes a quid pro quo that may preclude a full charitable deduction. That is, the amount otherwise deductible as a charitable contribution generally must be reduced by the amount of the state or local tax credit received or expected to be received.[12]

As an example of this body of law, a grant of a conservation easement to a county was considered to be part of a quid pro quo transaction because the transferor of the easement, a real estate developer, expected a substantial benefit in the form of an increase in value of the surrounding residential lots by reason of use of the eased property as a park.[13] As another illustration, the dedication of real property to a city was held to be part of a quid pro quo transaction because the purpose of the transfer was to cause the city to approve a planned community development plan, with the expectation of approval of a subsequent plan.[14]

Another body of law looks at this matter of a gift from a different perspective, namely, the intent of the payor or transferor. As an illustration, the U.S. Tax Court denied an estate tax deduction because a trust, funded by the estate from which the gifts were made, was modified solely to preserve the estate tax charitable deduction.[15] The Tax Court, however, has since abjured the donative-intent test. In a more recent holding, the court preserved most of the donors' charitable contribution deduction for noncash gifts, in the process rejecting the government's argument that the deduction should be denied in full on the ground that the donors lacked the requisite donative intent.[16] The court stated that in assessing whether a transaction constitutes a "quid pro quo exchange,"

---

10. IRC § 164(b)(6). This provision was added to the IRC by the Tax Cuts and Jobs Act (Pub. L. No. 115-97, § 11042, 131 Stat. 2054 (2017)). This limitation applies to tax years beginning after December 31, 2017, and before January 1, 2026.
11. T.D. 9864, 84 Fed. Reg. 27513 (2019).
12. Reg. § 1.170A-1(h)(3)(i)-(v).
13. Wendell Falls Development, LLC v. Commissioner, 115 T.C.M. 1197 (2018), supplemented by 116 T.C.M. 504 (2018).
14. Triumph Mixed Use Investments LLC v. Commissioner, 115 T.C.M. 1329 (2018).
15. Estate of La Meres v. Commissioner, 98 T.C. 294 (1992).
16. McGrady v. Commissioner, 112 T.C.M. 688 (2016).

it "give[s] most weight to the external features of the transaction, avoiding imprecise inquiries into taxpayers' subjective motivations."[17]

A corollary of these rules is that a single transaction can be partially a gift and partially a consideration-based transaction, so that when a charitable organization is the payee or transferee, only the gift portion gives rise to a charitable deduction.[18]

Not every economic benefit occasioned by a transfer defeats the availability of a charitable deduction. Thus, an economic benefit that is incidental does not disturb the deductible amount. Indeed, in a sense, every charitable contribution made by a donor who itemizes tax deductions gives rise to a quid pro quo because of the economic value, in the form of reduction of tax owed, provided by the resulting charitable deduction. Yet, the jurisprudence is clear that the tax benefit resulting from a federal or state charitable deduction is not regarded as a type of return benefit that reduces or eliminates the deduction.[19] Were the law otherwise, there would be few deductible charitable gifts.

Thus, a *charitable contribution* is a gift to or for the use of a qualified charitable entity, such as a private foundation.[20]

§ 14.2 BASIC RULES

The extent of the income tax charitable deduction is dependent in part on whether the charitable donee is a public charity or a private foundation.[21] Another basic element in determining whether, or the extent to which, a contribution to charity is deductible is the nature of the property contributed: capital gain property or ordinary income property.[22] Other distinctions may

---

17. *Id.* at 693. The nadir in this regard was reached when the court ruled that payments to a charitable organization were not deductible as charitable gifts, because the substantiation requirements (see § 14.7(b)) were not met, in that there was an undisclosed return benefit in the form of an "expectation" that the charity would use the funds to purchase an insurance policy which included a death benefit to one of the donors (Addis v. Commissioner, 118 T.C. 528 (2002), *aff'd*, 374 F.3d 881 (9th Cir. 2004), *cert. den.*, 543 U.S. 1151 (2005)).
18. See §14.6(b).
19. The U.S. Tax Court rejected the government's assertion that donative intent was not present in a case because the donor "desired the tax benefits flowing from a charitable contribution" (Davis v. Commissioner, 109 T.C.M. 1451, 1459 (2015)). Also McLennan v. United States, 91-1 U.S.T.C. ¶ 50,230 (Cl. Ct. 1991), *aff'd*, 994 F.2d 839 (Fed. Cir. 1993); Sheppard v. United States, 361 F.2d 972 (Cl. Ct. 1966) (taxpayer entitled to deduction even though donation was made for the exclusive purpose of obtaining a tax benefit).
20. IRC § 170(c). The IRS stated that a contribution to a single-member limited liability company, which is a disregarded entity for federal tax purposes, where the company is wholly owned and controlled by a U.S. charitable organization, is deductible, with the gift treated as being to a branch or a division of the charity (Notice 2012-52, 2012-35 I.R.B. 317).
21. See § 15.2.
22. See § 14.3.

be made between current giving or planned giving, between gifts of money and gifts of property, and between outright gifts, partial interest gifts, and gifts by means of a trust.[23] The amount of a qualified charitable contribution of an item of property is normally based on its fair market value (with no tax imposed on the increase, if any, over what the donor paid for the property, or the capital gain).[24]

A charitable deduction for a contribution of less than the donor's entire interest in the property—a gift of a *partial interest*—including the right to use the property, generally is denied.[25] There are exceptions for certain gifts of interests in trust,[26] and gifts of an outright remainder interest in a personal residence or farm, gifts of an undivided portion of one's entire interest in a property, and qualified conservation contributions.[27]

The general rule is that there is no charitable deduction for a contribution of a remainder interest in property unless it is in trust and the trust is a charitable remainder trust (annuity trust or unitrust) or pooled income fund.[28] Other charitable gifts of remainder interests may be made by means of the charitable gift annuity.[29] Contributions of income interests in property may be made by means of charitable lead trusts.[30]

(a) Percentage Limitations

The deductibility of charitable contributions for a tax year can be restricted by percentage limitations, which in the case of individuals are a function of the donor's *contribution base*. For nearly all individuals, the contribution base is the same as adjusted gross income.[31] These percentage limitations, which are more stringent in the case of most nonoperating private foundations, are:

- 60 percent of contribution base for gifts of cash to public charities.[32]
- 50 percent of contribution base for gifts of ordinary income property to public charities.[33]

---

23. A charitable contribution by means of a trust may be deductible pursuant to IRC § 642(c)(1). In general, *Charitable Giving* § 7.21.
24. E.g., Campbell v. Prothro, 209 F.2d 331 (5th Cir. 1954). Other factors affecting the deductibility of charitable gifts are discussed in *Charitable Giving* § 2.6.
25. IRC § 170(f)(3)(A).
26. IRC § 170(f)(2)(A).
27. IRC § 170(f)(3)(B). Qualified conservations contributions are defined in IRC § 170(h)(1).
28. IRC § 170(f)(2)(A). See § 2.6(b).
29. See § 2.6(c).
30. *Id.*
31. IRC § 170(b)(1)(H).
32. IRC § 170(b)(1)(G).
33. IRC § 170(b)(1)(A).

§ 14.2 BASIC RULES

- 30 percent of contribution base for contributions of long-term capital gain property to public charities.[34]

- 30 percent of contribution base for contributions of cash and ordinary income property to nonoperating private foundations.[35]

- 50 percent of contribution base for contributions of capital gain property to public charities, where the amount of the contribution is reduced by all of the unrealized appreciation in the value of the property.[36]

- 20 percent of contribution base for contributions of capital gain property to nonoperating private foundations and charitable organizations other than public charities.[37]

For purposes of these percentage limitations, private operating foundations,[38] conduit foundations,[39] and common fund foundations[40] are treated the same as public charities.[41]

When an individual makes charitable contributions that exceed the percentage limitations for the year, generally the excess may be carried forward and deducted in subsequent years, up to five.[42]

Deductible charitable contributions by corporations in a tax year may not exceed 10 percent of its taxable income.[43] A corporation using the accrual method of accounting can elect to treat a charitable contribution as having been paid in a tax year if it is actually paid during the first 2½ months of the following year.[44] Special rules apply as to the deductibility of corporate gifts of inventory,[45] of scientific property used for research,[46] and of computer equipment and technology for elementary or secondary school purposes.[47]

---

34. IRC § 170(b)(1)(C)(i).
35. IRC § 170(b)(1)(B)(i).
36. IRC § 170(b)(1)(C)(iii).
37. IRC § 170(b)(1)(D)(i).
38. See § 3.1.
39. See § 3.3.
40. See § 3.4.
41. IRC § 170(b)(1)(A), (A)(vii), (F).
42. IRC §§ 170(d)(1), (b)(1)(C)(ii), (b)(1)(B), (b)(1)(D)(ii), (b)(1)(G)(ii).
43. IRC § 170(b)(2).
44. IRC § 170(a)(2).
45. IRC § 170(e)(3). In the case of certain donations of inventory to private operating foundations, the donor is permitted to deduct half the amount of any short-term appreciation, but only to the extent it does not exceed twice the amount of the taxpayer's basis in the donated property (*id*).
46. IRC § 170(e)(4).
47. IRC § 170(e)(6).

CHARITABLE GIVING RULES

There are carryover rules in this context.[48] The making of a charitable gift by a business corporation is not considered to be an act outside the entity's corporate powers as long as the general interests of the corporation and its shareholders are advanced.[49]

(b) Estate and Gift Tax Deductions

There are charitable contribution deductions in the estate and gift context as well. A charitable estate tax deduction is allowed for the value of all transfers from a decedent's estate to or for the use of charitable organizations.[50] A charitable gift tax deduction is available for transfers by gift to or for the use of charitable organizations.[51] The extent of these charitable deductions is not dependent on whether the charitable donee is a public charity or a private foundation; percentage limitations do not apply to these deductions.[52]

§ 14.3 GIFTS OF APPRECIATED PROPERTY

A charitable gift of property to a private foundation or other charitable organization may involve an outright gift of the property or of a partial interest in the property. The property may be personal property or real property, tangible property or intangible property. The gift may be limited by one or more of the percentage rules or entail a reduction of the otherwise deductible amount.[53] The income tax rules, or the estate and gift tax rules, may be involved.

In the case of a charitable contribution of property, a key determinant in the amount of the charitable deduction often is the fair market value of the property. As a general rule, the fair market value of an item of property is the price at which the property would change hands between a willing buyer and a willing seller, neither being under any compulsion to buy or sell and both having reasonable knowledge of relevant facts.[54] The IRS amplified this rule, holding that the "most probative evidence of fair market [value] is the price at which similar quantities of . . . [the property] are sold in arm's-length transactions."[55] The IRS also determined that the fair market value of gift property is

---

48. IRC § 170(d)(2).
49. As to percentage limitations generally, see *Charitable Giving*, Chapter 5.
50. IRC § 2055.
51. IRC § 2522.
52. In general, *Charitable Giving* §§ 6.2-6.4.
53. See § 14.2(a), 14.4.
54. Reg. § 1.170A-1(c)(2).
55. Rev. Rul. 80-69, 1980-1 C.B. 55.

§ 14.3 GIFTS OF APPRECIATED PROPERTY

determined by reference to the "most active and comparable marketplace at the time of the donor's contribution."[56] The fair value of property is frequently the subject of litigation.[57]

Inasmuch as the charitable deduction for a gift of property is often based on the fair market value of the property, a donor can be economically benefited where the property has increased in value since the date on which the donor acquired the property. Property in this condition has *appreciated* in value; it is known as *appreciated property*. Where certain requirements are satisfied, a donor is entitled to a charitable deduction based on the full fair market value of the property.[58]

This rule—allowance of the charitable deduction based on the full value of an item of property—is one of the rules in the tax law that is most beneficial to donors. This is particularly the case when it is considered that the donor in this circumstance is not usually required to recognize any gain on the transfer. The gain is the amount that would have been recognized had the donor sold the property; it is sometimes referred to as the *appreciation element*.

The ability of a donor to take a charitable deduction for a contribution of property based on the fair market value of the property is dependent on several factors. Chief among these are the nature of the property contributed, the tax classification of the charitable donee, and the use to which the charitable donee puts the property.

As to the first of these factors, the federal tax law categorizes items of property as long-term capital gain property, short-term capital gain property, and ordinary income property.

An item of *long-term capital gain property* is a capital asset that has appreciated in value that, if sold, would result in long-term capital gain.[59] One feature of this type of property is that the owner must hold it for at least 12 months.[60] Property that is deductible on the basis of its fair market value is long-term capital gain property. Other property is *ordinary income property* or *short-term capital gain property*; this is property that, if sold, would give rise to ordinary income or short-term capital gain, respectively. Charitable deductions for donations of ordinary income property and short-term capital gain property are limited to the donor's tax basis in the donated property.[61]

---

56. Rev. Rul. 80-233, 1980-2 C.B. 69.
57. E.g., Hilborn v. Commissioner, 85 T.C. 677 (1985); Droz v. Commissioner, 71 T.C.M. 2204 (1996).
58. IRC § 170(a); Reg. § 1.170A-(c)(1).
59. IRC § 170(b)(1)(C)(iv).
60. IRC §§ 1(h), 1223.
61. See § 14.4(a).

§ 14.4 DEDUCTION REDUCTION RULES

In the federal income tax scheme relating to deductible charitable giving, there are several deduction reduction rules. One of them is unique to private foundations.

(a) Capital Gain Property Deduction Rule

The deduction reduction rule that is unique to private foundations is this: When a charitable gift of capital gain property is made, the amount of the charitable deduction that would otherwise be determined must be reduced by the amount of gain that would have been long-term capital gain if the property contributed had been sold by the donor at its fair market value, determined at the time of the contribution.[62] This rule does not apply, however, with respect to a gift to a private operating foundation, a conduit foundation, or a common fund foundation.[63]

Where this rule applies, the charitable deduction that would otherwise be determined must be reduced by the amount of the unrealized appreciation in value. The charitable deduction under these rules is confined to the basis in the property. This rule applies irrespective of whether the donor is an individual or a corporation, irrespective of whether the charitable contribution is made to or for the use of a charitable organization, and to a gift of property prior to application of one or more of the appropriate percentage limitations.

(b) Other Deduction Reduction Rules

Other deduction reduction rules may apply:

1. In the case of a contribution of ordinary income property or short-term capital gain property, regardless of whether it is made to a private foundation or a public charity, the donor must reduce the deduction by the amount of any gain.[64]

2. A donor who makes a gift of long-term capital gain tangible personal property to a public charity must reduce the deduction by the amount of gain that would have been recognized had the donor sold the property

---

62. IRC § 170(e)(1)(B)(ii); Reg. § 1.170A-4(b)(2)(i).
63. IRC § 170(e)(1)(B)(ii), by cross-reference to the three types of private foundations referenced in IRC § 170(b)(1)(F). See §§ 3.1, 3.3, and 3.4, respectively.
64. IRC § 170(e)(1)(A); Reg. § 1.170A-4(a)(1).

§ 14.4 DEDUCTION REDUCTION RULES

at its fair market value, where the use of the property by the charitable donee is not related to its tax-exempt purposes.[65]

3. The tax benefit arising from charitable contributions of tangible personal property, with respect to which a fair market value charitable contribution is claimed and that is not used for charitable purposes, must, in general, be recovered.[66] This recapture rule applies to *applicable property*, which is tangible personal property that has appreciated in value that has been identified by the donee organization as being for a use related to the donee's exempt purpose or function and for which a charitable deduction of more than $5,000 has been claimed.[67] If a donee organization disposes of applicable property within three years of the contribution of the property—an *applicable disposition*[68]—the donor is subject to an adjustment of the tax benefit. If the disposition occurs in the tax year of the donor in which the contribution was made, the donor's deduction generally is confined to the basis in and not the fair market value of the property. If the disposition occurs in a subsequent year, the donor must include as ordinary income for the year in which the disposition occurs an amount equal to the excess (if any) of (1) the amount of the deduction previously claimed by the donor as a charitable contribution with respect to the property, over (2) the donor's basis in the property at the time of the contribution.[69] There is no adjustment of this tax benefit, however, if the donee organization makes a certification to the IRS by written statement signed under penalties of perjury by an officer of the organization.[70]

4. A deduction reduction rule similar to the second one applies in the case of a charitable contribution of a patent, copyright, trademark, trade name, trade secret, know-how, software, or similar property, or applications or registrations of this type of property.[71]

5. A deduction rule similar to the second one applies in the case of a charitable contribution of a taxidermy property that is contributed by the person who prepared, stuffed, or mounted the property, or by any person who paid or incurred the cost of the preparation, stuffing, or mounting.[72]

---

65. IRC § 170(e)(1)(B)(i)(I); Reg. § 1.170A-4(b)(2)(ii). The concept of *unrelated use* is discussed in Chapter 11.
66. IRC § 170(e)(1)(B)(i)(II).
67. IRC § 170(e)(7)(C).
68. IRC § 170(e)(7)(B).
69. IRC § 170(e)(7)(A).
70. IRC § 170(e)(7)(D).
71. IRC § 170(e)(1)(B)(iii).
72. IRC § 170(e)(1)(B)(iv).

§ 14.5 QUALIFIED APPRECIATED STOCK RULE

The deduction reduction rule does not apply in the case of a contribution of qualified appreciated stock.[73] That is, where this exception is applicable, the charitable deduction for a contribution of stock to a private foundation is equal to the fair market value of the stock at the time of the gift.

Basically, the term *qualified appreciated stock* means any stock for which (as of the date of the contribution) market quotations are readily available on an established securities market and that is long-term capital gain property.[74]

It is the view of the IRS that stock that cannot be sold or exchanged by reason of the securities law rules confining sales of control stock to small portions[75] cannot qualify as qualified appreciated stock.[76] The IRS also initially ruled that stock traded by means of the Over-the-Counter Bulletin Board Service is not qualified appreciated stock because market quotations are not readily available, in that they can be obtained only by consulting a broker, subscribing to a service, or obtaining a copy of the one newspaper that lists the stock.[77] The IRS later ruled, however, that stock to be contributed to a private foundation was qualified appreciated stock because the market quotations for the stock were readily available on the OTCBB due to accessibility to the information on Internet sites.[78]

In the sole case on the point, a court held that stock contributed to a private foundation did not give rise to a charitable contribution deduction based on its fair market value because the stock did not constitute qualified appreciated stock.[79] The stock involved was that of a bank holding company. The shares were not listed on the New York Stock Exchange, the American Stock Exchange, or any city or regional stock exchange, nor were the shares regularly traded in the national or any regional over-the-counter market for which published quotations are available. The shares were not those of a

---

73. IRC § 170(e)(5)(A).
74. IRC § 170(e)(5)(B). The requirement that market quotations be readily available on an established securities market has the same meaning for the purpose of defining qualified appreciated stock and in determining when securities are publicly traded for the purpose of exempting a donor from the substantiation requirements of Reg. § 1.170A-13(c)) (Todd v. Commissioner, 118 T.C. 334, 345 (2002)). Reg. § 1.170A-13(c)(7)(xi) describes the circumstances in which the market quotations requirement is met for purposes of exempting contributions of certain publicly traded securities from these substantiation requirements.
75. Securities and Exchange Commission Rule 144.
76. Priv. Ltr. Rul. 9247018, *aff'd*, Priv. Ltr. Rul. 9320016.
77. Priv. Ltr. Rul. 9504027.
78. Priv. Ltr. Rul. 200702031.
79. Todd v. Commissioner, 118 T.C. 334 (2002).

§ 14.5 QUALIFIED APPRECIATED STOCK RULE

mutual fund. A brokerage firm occasionally provided a suggested share price based on the bank's net asset value. The procedure for someone wishing to purchase or sell shares of the corporation was to contact an officer of the bank or a local stock brokerage firm specializing in the shares. An attempt would be made to match a potential seller with a potential buyer; the shares were not sold frequently. The court held that the stock could not constitute qualified appreciated stock because the market quotations requirement was not satisfied.

Further, qualified appreciated stock does not include any stock contributed to a private foundation to the extent that the amount of stock contributed (including prior gifts of stock by the donor) exceeds 10 percent (in value) of all of the outstanding stock of the corporation.[80] In making this calculation, an individual must take into account all contributions made by any member of their family.[81] The fact that a private foundation disposed of qualified appreciated stock is irrelevant in making this computation.[82]

In applying this limitation with respect to future contributions of qualified appreciated stock, the values of prior contributions of the same stock are based on the value of the stock at the time of the original contributions. That is, for this purpose, the prior contributions of stock are not revalued each time there is another contribution of the same stock.

From time to time, the IRS issues private letter rulings as to stock that constitutes qualified appreciated stock[83] and stock that does not so qualify.[84] With respect to the first category, the IRS held that stock contributed to a private foundation by a single-member limited liability company (a disregarded entity) was qualified appreciated stock, thereby giving rise to a fair market value deduction for the two individuals who were the managers of the LLC, where one of these individuals was the sole trustee of the foundation and the settlor and trustee of a trust that was the LLC's member.[85]

---

80. IRC § 170(e)(5)(C)(i). This rule is applicable only in the case of a contribution to which IRC § 170(e)(1)(B)(ii) applies (see text accompanied by *supra* notes 62-63) but for this rule. These rules are, of course, rules in the income tax charitable contribution context. Therefore, a stock contribution to a private foundation by an estate is not subject to the 10 percent limitation, because that gift would presumably give rise to an estate tax charitable deduction but not an income tax charitable deduction (Priv. Ltr. Rul. 200112022).
81. IRC § 170(e)(5)(C)(ii). The term *member of the family* means an individual's brothers and sisters (whether by whole or half blood), spouse, ancestors, and lineal descendants (IRC § 267(c)(4)).
82. Priv. Ltr. Rul. 200112022.
83. E.g., Priv. Ltr. Rul. 199925029 (mutual fund shares are qualified appreciated stock).
84. E.g., Priv. Ltr. Rul. 199915053.
85. Priv. Ltr. Rul. 201848005.

§ 14.6 SPECIAL GIFT SITUATIONS

The federal tax law includes a variety of requirements concerning types of charitable gifts. Some of these rules are not particularly applicable in the private foundation setting.

(a) Donors' Creations

An individual may make a contribution to a charitable organization of an item of property that was created by the donor, such as a painting or a manuscript. The charitable deduction for this type of gift is not based on the property's fair market value; the deduction is confined to the donor's cost basis in the property.

This tax law result is occasioned by the rule that requires a reduction in the charitable contribution deduction created by a gift of property by an amount equal to the amount of gain that would not have been long-term capital gain had the property been sold by the donor at its fair market value at the time of the contribution.[86] The federal tax law excludes from the definition of the term *capital asset* a "copyright, a literary, musical, or artistic composition, a letter or memorandum, or similar property," held by (1) an individual "whose personal efforts created such property," (2) "in the case of a letter, memorandum, or similar property, a taxpayer [person] for whom such property was prepared or produced," or (3) a person "in whose hands the basis of such property is determined, for purposes of determining gain from a sale or exchange, in whole or in part by reference to the basis of such property in the hands of a person described in either of the foregoing two categories."[87]

(b) Bargain Sales

A *bargain sale* is a transfer of property to a charitable organization when the transaction is in part a sale or exchange of the property and in part a charitable contribution of the property.[88] Basically, a bargain sale is a sale of an item of property to a charitable organization at a price that is less than the fair market value of the property; the amount equal to the fair market value of the property, less the amount of the sales price, is treated as a contribution to the charitable organization.[89]

---

86. See § 14.4(a).
87. IRC § 1221(3).
88. Reg. § 1.170A-4(c)(2)(ii).
89. E.g., Stark v. Commissioner, 86 T.C. 243 (1986).

§ 14.6 SPECIAL GIFT SITUATIONS

There must be allocated to the contribution portion of the property that element of the adjusted basis of the entire property that bears the same ratio to the total adjusted basis as the fair market value of the contributed portion of the property bears to the fair market value of the entire property. Also, for these purposes, there must be allocated to the contributed portion of the property the amount of gain that is not recognized on the bargain sale but that would have been recognized if the contributed portion of the property had been sold by the donor at its fair market value at the time of its contribution to the charitable organization.[90]

(c) Intellectual Property

The charitable contribution deduction for contributions of patents, copyrights, and other intellectual property in the year of the gift is confined to the lesser of the donor's basis in the property or its fair market value.[91] To the extent the property produces income in subsequent years, additional deductible gifts may be deemed to occur, but not if the initial donation is made to a nonoperating private foundation.[92] A donee receiving this type of contribution must file a form with the IRS and provide the donee with a copy each year following the gift to report any income it receives by reason of the property.[93]

(d) Vehicles

The charitable deduction for a gift of an automobile, boat, or airplane valued in excess of $500 is limited to the proceeds of sale received by the donee charity, unless the charity retains the vehicle for its exempt use or makes repairs.[94]

---

90. IRC § 1011(b); Reg. § 1.1011-2(a)(1). A bargain sale is an act of self-dealing, however, if engaged in between a disqualified person and a private foundation (see § 5.4(a)). As to bargain sales generally, see *Charitable Giving* § 7.18.
91. IRC § 170(e)(1)(B)(iii).
92. IRC § 170(m)(9). Gifts of intellectual property donated to private operating foundations (see § 3.1), conduit private foundations (see § 3.3), and common fund private foundations (see § 3.4), however, may be eligible for additional deductible gifts in post-contribution years based on income from the donated property pursuant to the rules of IRC § 170(m).
93. IRC § 6050L(b), (c); Reg. § 1.6050L-2. The form is Form 8899 and it must be filed with the IRS and provided to the donor by the last day of the first full month following the close of the donee's tax year (Reg. § 1.6050L-2(c), (d)). Form 8899 is not required to be filed for tax years that begin more than 10 years after the date of contribution, or tax years that begin after the expiration of the legal life of the donated property, or any year in which the donated intellectual property produced no income (Reg. § 1.6050L-2(a)).
94. IRC § 170(f)(12).

CHARITABLE GIVING RULES

Only if the charity keeps the vehicle for use in its charitable programs, referred to as a *significant intervening use*, or makes material improvements to the vehicle, may the deduction be equal to the vehicle's fair market value.[95]

(e) Use of Property

A person may contribute to a charitable organization a right to use an item of property. Examples of this type of gift are a contribution by an owner of an office building of the rent-free use of office space to a charitable organization for a period of time and a contribution by an owner of vacation property of the right to use the property for a time period. There is, however, no federal income tax charitable deduction for this type of gift.[96]

The reason for the lack of a deduction for a gift of this nature is the fact that the contribution is of a partial interest in the property;[97] this is not one of the forms of partial interests the gift of which gives rise to a charitable deduction.[98] Also, because the donor of a right to use an item of property rarely takes the value of the use of the property into income as imputed rent, to allow a charitable deduction in this circumstance would be to allow a double deduction.

(f) Services

An individual may contribute their services to a charitable organization. A federal income tax charitable deduction is not, however, available for this type of contribution.[99] Again, because the donor of services rarely takes the value of them into income as imputed income, to allow a charitable deduction for the contribution of the services to a charitable organization would be to allow a double deduction.

(g) Conservation Property

Special federal tax rules pertain to contributions to charity of real property or interests in real property (such as easements) for conservation purposes. These rules are an exception to the general rule that there is no charitable contribution deduction for contributions of partial interests in property.[100] This exception is the qualified conservation contribution.[101] These gifts, however,

---

95. *Id.*
96. Reg. § 1.170A-7(a)(1).
97. IRC § 170(f)(3)(A).
98. *Id.*, last sentence.
99. Reg. § 1.170A-1(g).
100. IRC § 170(f)(3)(A).
101. IRC § 170(f)(3)(B)(iii).

§ 14.7 ADMINISTRATIVE CONSIDERATIONS

to be deductible, must be given to qualified organizations, which does not include private foundations.[102]

§ 14.7 ADMINISTRATIVE CONSIDERATIONS

The federal tax law contains many requirements to which donors to private foundations (or other tax-exempt charitable organizations) must adhere as a condition of receiving a charitable deduction for their contributions. Chief among these rules are the mandates for gift recordkeeping, substantiation, disclosure, appraisal, and reporting.

(a) Recordkeeping Rules

As to any type of monetary gift, the donor must, as a condition of a charitable deduction, maintain a bank record or a written communication from the donee showing the name of the donee organization, the date of the contribution, and the amount of the contribution.[103] Some charitable organizations elect to provide this information to their donors as a matter of donor relations. Likewise, some charities, in providing this information, include the information required pursuant to the substantiation rules in the same letter, irrespective of the amount of the contribution. These considerations, however, are of less concern to donee private foundations because the substantiation rules almost always apply.

(b) Substantiation Rules

A charitable contribution deduction is generally not allowed for a noncash charitable contribution of less than $250 by an individual, partnership, S corporation, or C corporation that is a personal service corporation or closely held corporation, unless the donor maintains for each contribution a receipt from the donee organization showing the name and address of the donee, the date of the contributions, a description of the property, and, in the case of securities, the name of the issuer, the type of security, and whether the securities are publicly traded.[104]

---

102. IRC § 170(h)(3).
103. IRC § 170(f)(17); Reg. § 1.170A-15(a)(1).
104. Reg. § 1.170A-16(a)(1). In certain instances where obtaining a receipt is impracticable, reliable written records may be substituted (Reg. § 1.170A-16(a)(2)).

CHARITABLE GIVING RULES

A federal income tax charitable contribution deduction is not available in the case of a charitable contribution of $250 or more unless the donor substantiates the contribution by a *contemporaneous written acknowledgment* from the donee charitable organization.[105] This written acknowledgment of the gift must provide the amount of any money contributed, a description of any property contributed, and a statement as to whether the charitable donee provided any goods or services in consideration for the gift.[106] A written acknowledgment is *contemporaneous* if it is obtained by the donor on or before the earlier of (1) the date the donor files the original return for the tax year in which the contribution is made, or (2) the due date, including extensions, for filing the donor's original return for that year.[107]

In situations where the charity has provided goods or services[108] to the donor in consideration[109] for making the contribution, this contemporaneous written acknowledgment must include a good faith estimate of the value of the goods or services.[110] Unlike the fundraising practices engaged in by many public charities, however, a private foundation is unlikely to provide any goods or services to a donor in exchange for a gift. Where the donor is a disqualified person,[111] this type of transaction would be self-dealing.[112]

Usually, a charitable donee provides the required substantiation to a donor by means of a letter or similar document. Courts are holding, however, that in the absence of a qualifying document from the donee, the requisite substantiation information can be found in another document pertaining to the

---

105. IRC § 170(f)(8); Reg. §§ 1.170A-13(f)(1), -15(a)(2). An exception is available where the goods or services consist solely of *intangible religious benefits*.
106. Reg. § 1.170A-13(f)(2). See § 16.7 for a discussion of this rule in the donor-advised fund context.
107. Reg. § 1.170A-13(f)(3). Other than subsection (f), Reg. § 1.170A-13 is largely inapplicable to contributions made after June 30, 2018, except to the extent its provisions are cross-referenced in Reg. §§ 1.170A-15 through -17 (see T.D. 9836, 83 Fed. Reg. 36417 (2018)).
108. The phrase *goods or services* means cash, property, services, benefits, and privileges (Reg. § 1.170A-13(f)(5)). Certain goods or services of insubstantial value, however, are disregarded (Reg. § 1.170A-13(f)(8), (9)).
109. A donee organization provides goods or services in *consideration* for a person's payment if, at the time the person makes the payment to the donee organization, the person receives or expects to receive, goods or services in exchange for that payment (Reg. § 1.170A-13(f)(6)). Goods or services a donee organization provides in consideration for a payment by a person include goods or services provided in a year other than the year in which the person makes the payment to the organization (*id.*).
110. Reg. § 1.170A-13(f)(7). A *good faith estimate* means a donee organization's estimate of the fair market value of any goods or services, without regard to the manner in which the organization in fact made that estimate (*id.*).
111. See Chapter 4.
112. See § 5.4(e).

§ 14.7 ADMINISTRATIVE CONSIDERATIONS

gift, such as a series of documents evidencing a bargain sale,[113] a deed,[114] or a letter signed by a government official.[115] It was held, however, that a settlement agreement between a donor and a donee cannot serve as an appropriate substantiation document.[116]

This rule is somewhat of an anomaly in the private foundation setting. It requires a written acknowledgment, often involving one individual. Suppose individual A establishes a private foundation as a trust, where A is the sole trustee. When A funds the foundation during their lifetime, A must make the requisite substantiation on a timely basis to themselves (assuming, of course, that the gift is in excess of $250, which is almost certain to be the case).[117]

This rule is applied strictly by the U.S. Tax Court, where charitable deductions involving millions of dollars can be eradicated solely because the acknowledgment document was not provided, was incomplete, or was misleading. In one case, a charitable contribution deduction, with a claimed value of $64.5 million, was held unavailable because the donee did not provide the donor with the requisite substantiation letter.[118]

More stringent substantiation requirements apply in instances of contributions of motor vehicles, boats, and airplanes, the claimed value of which exceeds $500.[119] (These types of gifts are infrequently made to private foundations.) Under these rules, the required contents of the contemporaneous written acknowledgment are more extensive, and the donor must include a copy of the acknowledgment with the appropriate tax return.[120]

---

113. Irby v. Commissioner, 139 T.C. 371 (2012).
114. E.g., Big River Development, L.P. v. Commissioner, 114 T.C.M. 239 (2017); 310 Retail, LLC v. Commissioner, 114 T.C.M. 228 (2017); Averyt v. Commissioner, 104 T.C.M. 65 (2012); Simmons v. Commissioner, 98 T.C.M. 211 (2009), aff'd, 646 F.3d 6 (D.C. Cir. 2011). Where a deed of gift did not include a statement that no goods or services were received in exchange for a sizeable gift of artifacts and jewelry, however, a court held that the deed did not satisfy the contemporaneous written acknowledgment requirement (Albrecht v. Commissioner, T.C. Memo. 2022-53). Moreover, for a deed to serve as a de facto contemporaneous written acknowledgment, "the deed taken as a whole" must prove compliance with the statutory requirements; it cannot be supplemented by other documents (Keefer v. United States, 130 A.F.T.R. 2d 2022-5002 (N.D. Tex. 2022)). Silence in a deed meets these acknowledgment requirements only if the deed qualifies that the terms of the deed are the entire agreement, such as through a merger or entire agreement clause (Brooks v. Commissioner, T.C. Memo. 2022-122).
115. Crimi v. Commissioner, 105 T.C.M. 1330 (2013).
116. DiDonato v. Commissioner, 101 T.C.M. 173 (2011).
117. The U.S. Tax Court held that the substantiation rules must be complied with where the donor and the principal representative of the donee charity is the same individual (Villareale v. Commissioner, 105 T.C.M. 1464 (2013)).
118. 15 West 17th Street, LLC v. Commissioner, 147 T.C. 557 (2016).
119. IRC § 170(f)(12).
120. IRC § 170(f)(12)(A)(i), (B); Reg. § 1.170A-16(c)(4).

CHARITABLE GIVING RULES

A charitable deduction is not allowed for a noncash charitable contribution of more than $500 but not more than $5,000 by an individual, partnership, S corporation, or C corporation that is a personal services corporation or a closely held corporation unless the donor completes an IRS form and files it with the return on which the deduction is claimed.[121]

Generally, a charitable deduction is not allowed for a noncash charitable contribution of more than $5,000 unless the donor (1) substantiates the contribution with a contemporaneous written acknowledgment, (2) obtains a qualified appraisal prepared by a qualified appraiser,[122] and (3) completes an IRS form[123] and files it with the return on which the deduction is claimed.[124] A qualified appraisal is not required, however, in instances of contributions of publicly traded securities, certain intellectual property, certain vehicles, and inventory and like property.[125] In a case, a donor lost their deduction for a charitable contribution in the amount of $338,080, reflecting their undivided ownership share in an aircraft, by reason of these rules; they did not obtain the requisite acknowledgment from the donee and did not include the requisite information with the tax return involved.[126] In the case of noncash charitable contributions of more than $500,000, the foregoing three requirements must be met, and a copy of a qualified appraisal must be attached to the return on which the contribution is claimed.[127]

As noted, if the applicable substantiation requirements are not satisfied, the charitable deduction otherwise available is not allowed.[128] This deduction disallowance rule does not apply, however, if it is shown that the failure to meet the requirements is due to reasonable cause and not to willful neglect.[129]

---

121. IRC § 170(f)(11)(A), (B); Reg. § 1.170A-16(c)(2). The form is Form 8283 (Section A) (Noncash Charitable Contributions) (Reg. § 1.170A-16(c)(2), (3)). A C corporation is a *closely held corporation* if more than 50 percent of its stock is held (directly or by attribution) by five or fewer individuals (Reg. § 1.170A-13(c)(7)(i)) and is a *personal service corporation* if it is a service organization within the meaning of IRC § 414(m)(3) (Reg. § 1.170A-13(c)(7)(ii)).
122. See § 14.7(d).
123. Form 8283 (Section B).
124. IRC § 170(f)(11)(C); Reg. § 1.170A-16(d)(1).
125. Reg. § 1.170A-16(d)(2).
126. Izen, Jr. v. Commissioner, 148 T.C. 71 (2017), aff'd, 38 F.4th 459 (5th Cir. 2022), *cert. denied* (2023). To underscore the strict application the substantiation rules, the lower court's decision in this case was affirmed solely on the basis that the taxpayer's taxpayer identification number, which is specifically required by IRC § 170(f)(12)(B)(i), was not included on any of the forms or the contemporaneous written acknowledgment filed with their return (*id.*).
127. IRC § 170(f)(11)(D); Reg. § 1.170A-16(e)(1).
128. IRC § 170(f)(11)(A)(i).
129. IRC § 170(f)(11)(A)(ii)(II).

§ 14.7 ADMINISTRATIVE CONSIDERATIONS

The U.S. Tax Court ruled that a reasonable cause inquiry is "inherently a fact-intensive one, and facts and circumstances must be judged on a case-by-case basis."[130] Consequently, the tax regulations do not include a standard for determining reasonable cause in this context.[131]

A charitable deduction otherwise allowable for a gift to a donor-advised fund will be allowed only if the donor obtains a contemporaneous written acknowledgment[132] from the sponsoring organization of the fund that the organization has exclusive legal control over the contributed assets.[133]

(c) Disclosure Rules

A charitable organization must provide a written disclosure statement to donors who make a *quid pro quo contribution* in excess of $75.[134] This disclosure must inform the donor that the amount of the contribution that is deductible for federal income tax purposes is limited to the excess of any money (and the value of any property other than money) the donor contributed over the value of goods or services provided by the charity. The disclosure must also provide the donor with a good faith estimate of the value of the goods or services the donor received. The charitable organization may use any reasonable methodology in making a good faith estimate, as long as it applies the methodology in good faith.[135] A penalty is imposed on charitable organizations that do not satisfy these disclosure requirements.[136] Again, a quid pro quo

---

130. Crimi v. Commissioner, 105 T.C.M. 1330, 1353 (2013). The court concluded that the donors reasonably and in good faith relied on their long-term certified public accountant's advice that their appraisal satisfied all the legal requirements for claiming a charitable deduction. In another case, a court found that this reasonable cause standard was not met where a taxpayer did not attach a completed Form 8283 to its return or an appraisal of any kind with respect to charitable contributions of art. The taxpayer did not demonstrate that it in fact relied on advice of its tax return preparer in making these omissions (see § 12.2(c)) and, even if it did, it would not have been reasonable for them to rely on such advice under the circumstances because the taxpayer possessed "a sharp and sophisticated mind for business and dealings in fine art" (Schweizer v. Commissioner, T.C. Memo. 2022-102).
131. A standard was in these regulations in their proposed form but was omitted from the final version of the regulations because of the court's decision in Crimi v. Commissioner, 105 T.C.M. 1330, 1353 (2013) (T.D. 9836, 83 Fed. Reg. 36417, 36419 (2018)).
132. This acknowledgment is considered contemporaneous if it satisfies requirements "similar to" those described in § 14.7(b) (IRC § 170(f)(18)(B)).
133. IRC § 170(f)(18). As to other limitations on the deductibility of contributions to a donor-advised fund, see § 16.7.
134. IRC § 6115.
135. Reg. § 1.6115-(a)(1).
136. IRC § 6714.

CHARITABLE GIVING RULES

transaction is arguably prohibited self-dealing for a disqualified person.[137] Usually only a foundation conducting a public fundraising campaign, a rare instance, would be subject to this rule.

(d) Appraisal Rules

There are requirements that apply to contributions of nearly all types of non-cash property, other than publicly traded securities, where the value of the property is in excess of $5,000.[138]

In the case of real estate, artwork, interests in partnerships, and similar types of gifts to which these requirements apply, the donor must obtain a qualified appraisal and attach a completed appraisal summary (Form 8283, Section B) to the return on which the deduction is claimed.[139] The qualified appraisal must be signed and dated by the qualified appraiser no earlier than 60 days before the date of the contribution and no later than (1) the due date, including extensions, of the return on which the deduction for the contribution is first claimed; (2) in the case of a donor that is a partnership or S corporation, the due date, including extensions, of the return on which the deduction for the contribution is first reported; or (3) in the case of a deduction first claimed on an amended return, the date on which the amended return is filed.[140] A *qualified appraisal* is an appraisal document that is prepared by a qualified appraiser in accordance with generally accepted appraisal standards and meets certain other requirements.[141] The phrase *generally accepted appraisal standards* means the substance and principles of the Uniform Standards of Professional Appraisal Practice, as developed by the Appraisal Standards Board of the Appraisal Foundation.[142]

A qualified appraisal must include certain information about the contributed property, the terms of any agreement between the donor and donee as to disposition of the contributed property, the date or expected date of the contribution, certain information about the appraiser, the signature of the appraiser, the date the report was signed by the appraiser, a declaration by the appraiser, a statement that the appraisal was prepared for income tax

---

137. See discussion of incidental and tenuous benefits in § 5.8(e).
138. Reg. § 1.170A-16(d)(1), (2).
139. *Id*. A claimed charitable deduction of $33 million was disallowed because the Form 8283 attached to the donor's return left blank the line for reporting the donor's basis in the gifted property; the basis amount was about $3 million and the gift was made 17 months after the date of acquisition of the property (RERI Holdings I, LLC v. Commissioner, 149 T.C. 1 (2017)).
140. Reg. § 1.170A-17(a)(4).
141. IRC § 170(f)(11)(E)(i); Reg. § 1.170A-17(a)(1).
142. Reg. § 1.170A-17(a)(2).

§ 14.7 ADMINISTRATIVE CONSIDERATIONS

purposes, the method of valuation used to determine fair market value, and the specific basis for the valuation.[143]

Notwithstanding the foregoing, an appraisal is not a qualified appraisal for a particular contribution if the donor failed to disclose or misrepresented facts, and a reasonable person would expect that the failure or misrepresentation would cause the appraiser to misstate the value of the contributed property.[144] A donor must obtain a separate qualified appraisal for each item of property for which an appraisal is required and that is not included in a group of similar items of property.[145] If the contributed property is a partial interest,[146] the appraisal must be of the partial interest.[147] The fee for a qualified appraisal cannot be based to any extent on the appraised value of the property.[148]

A *qualified appraiser* is an individual with verifiable education and experience in valuing the type of property for which the valuation is performed. The appraiser must have (1) successfully completed professional or college-level coursework in valuing the type of property involved and have had at least two years of experience in valuing the type of property, or (2) earned a recognized appraisal designation for the type of property.[149]

These individuals are not qualified appraisers for the appraised property: (1) an individual who receives a fee based on the appraised value of the property, (2) the donor of the property, (3) a party to the transaction in which the donor acquired the property, (4) the donee of the property, (5) related parties, (6) an independent contractor who is regularly used as an appraiser by the individuals involved and who does not perform a majority of appraisals for others during the tax year, and (7) an individual who is prohibited from practicing before the IRS at any time during the three-year period ending on the date the appraisal is signed by the individual.[150]

---

143. Reg. § 1.170A-17(a)(3).
144. Reg. § 1.170A-17(a)(6).
145. Reg. § 1.170A-17(a)(7). As to items included in a group of similar items of property, see Reg. §1.170A-13(c)(7)(iii).
146. See *Charitable Giving* § 9.2.
147. Reg. § 1.170A-17(a)(12). For example, in one case, an appraiser incorrectly valued a parcel of real property rather than an easement, the subject of the gift, placed on the property (Costello v. Commissioner, 109 T.C.M. 1441 (2015)). A corollary to this rule is the rule that an appraisal must be of the gifted property. In one instance, two appraisals were held to not be qualified ones, in part because they did not appraise the correct asset; the appraisals valued the assets of a corporation where they should have valued the shares of stock of the corporation that were the subject of the gift (Estate of Evenchik v. Commissioner, 105 T.C.M. 1231 (2013)).
148. Reg. § 1.170A-17(a)(9).
149. IRC § 170(f)(11)(E)(ii), (iii); Reg. § 1.170A-17(b)(1)-(4).
150. Reg. § 1.170A-17(b)(5). An appraisal from an appraiser who has been prohibited from practicing before the IRS will be disregarded as to value but could constitute a qualified

CHARITABLE GIVING RULES

In addition, the appraiser must complete Form 8283, Section B, Part IV. More than one appraiser may appraise the property, provided that each complies with the requirements, including signing the qualified appraisal and Form 8283, Section B, Part IV.[151]

If the contribution of property involves a charitable deduction where more than $500,000 is claimed, the donor must attach a copy of the qualified appraisal to the appropriate tax return.[152]

(e) Doctrine of Substantial Compliance

The doctrine of substantial compliance first emerged in a case involving the validity of a charitable contribution deduction where donors failed to attach to their income tax returns, where the deduction was claimed, a copy of the qualified appraisal of the donated property.[153] The court found that the gift was indeed made, there was an appraisal by a qualified appraiser, and the charitable donee was a qualified one. The court concluded that the donors "met all of the elements required to establish the substance or essence of a charitable contribution, but merely failed to obtain and attach to their return a separate written appraisal containing the information specified in [the tax] regulations even though substantially all of the specified information except for the qualifications of the appraiser appeared in the [appraisal summary] attached to the return."[154] The court added: "The denial of a charitable deduction under these circumstances would constitute a sanction which is not warranted or justified."[155] The court held that these requirements were not mandatory but merely procedural or directory, so that only substantial compliance was required.

Nonetheless, this doctrine is inapplicable where the donor did not substantially comply with the requirements.[156] In one of its decisions, the U.S. Tax Court identified five categories of "fatal mistakes" that preclude application of the substantial compliance doctrine: failing to get an appraisal; failing to fill out the required appraisal summary; having someone without appraisal expertise complete the appraisal; having an appraisal prepared at the wrong time (that is, either more than 60 days before the gift or after the return was

---

appraisal if the requirements are otherwise satisfied and the donor did not have any knowledge that the signature, date, or declaration was false when the appraisal and Form 8283 (Section B) were signed by the appraiser (Reg. § 1.170A-17(a)(11)).

151. Reg. § 1.170A-16(d)(7).
152. IRC § 170(f)(11)(D); Reg. § 1.170A-16(e)(1).
153. Bond v. Commissioner, 100 T.C. 32 (1993).
154. *Id.* at 42.
155. *Id.*
156. E.g., Estate of Clause v. Commissioner, 122 T.C. 115 (2004).

§ 14.7 ADMINISTRATIVE CONSIDERATIONS

filed); and including insufficient information or inappropriate information in an appraisal or appraisal summary.[157]

The Tax Court held, however, that the recitation in the gift substantiation acknowledgment must adhere to the specific statutory requirements for there to be allowance of the charitable contribution deduction.[158] That is, the doctrine of substantial compliance is inapplicable where the statutory, as opposed to regulatory, substantiation requirements are not met.[159]

(f) Reporting Requirements

A charitable donee that sells, exchanges, consumes, or otherwise disposes of gift property, having a value of $5,000 or more, within three years after the date of the contribution of the property must file an information return[160] with the IRS.[161] This information return must contain the name, address, and taxpayer identification number of the donor and donee; a sufficient description of the property; the date of the contribution; the amount received on the disposition; and the date of the disposition.

A copy of the information return must be provided to the donor and retained by the charitable organization.

(g) State Fundraising Regulation

Nearly all states have a charitable solicitation act. Countless counties, cities, towns, and hamlets have charitable solicitation ordinances. A *charitable solicitation* act is a statute requiring a charitable organization soliciting contributions in the state to, in advance of the fundraising, register with the state. Thereafter, annual reports are required. Several other obligations may be imposed by these laws on charities, such as a bond requirement and mandatory contracts with professional fundraisers and solicitors. Charitable solicitation acts are usually under the jurisdiction of the state's attorney general. These acts are rarely applicable to private foundations, however, which, by nature, infrequently solicit charitable gifts.[162]

---

157. Mohamed v. Commissioner, 103 T.C.M. 1814, 1819 (2012).
158. Boone Operations Co., LLC v. Commissioner, 105 T.C.M. 1610 (2013).
159. Izen, *supra* note 126; Keefer, *supra* note 114; Addis v. Commissioner, 374 F.3d 881, 887 (9th Cir. 2004); French v. Commissioner, 111 T.C.M. 1241 (2016). See § 14.7(b).
160. IRS Form 8282.
161. IRC § 6050L.
162. This body of law is detailed in *Fundraising*, Chapters 3 and 4.

CHAPTER FIFTEEN

Public Charities

§ 15.1 Advantages of Public Charity Status 614
§ 15.2 Statutory Categories of Public Charities 616
§ 15.3 Public Institution Charities 617
    (a) Churches and Similar Entities 618
    (b) Educational Institutions 619
    (c) Hospitals 621
    (d) Medical Research Organizations 621
    (e) Agricultural Research Organizations 622
    (f) Public College Support Foundations 623
    (g) Governmental Units 623
§ 15.4 Donative Publicly Supported Charities 624
    (a) General Rules 625
    (b) Two Percent Limitation 626
    (c) Support Test 628
    (d) Facts and Circumstances Test 631
    (e) Community Foundations 633
§ 15.5 Service Provider Publicly Supported Charities 635
    (a) Support Test 636
    (b) Investment Income Test 639
    (c) Unusual Grants 641
        (i) Unusual Grant Factors 641
        (ii) Safe Harbor Criteria 646
        (iii) Requests for Advance IRS Rulings 646
§ 15.6 Supporting Organizations 647
    (a) Organizational Test 649
    (b) Operational Test 650
    (c) Specified Public Charities 652
    (d) Required Relationships 656
    (e) Type I: Operated, Supervised, or Controlled By 656
    (f) Type II: Supervised or Controlled in Connection With 657
    (g) Type III: Operated in Connection With 658
        (i) Overview 658
        (ii) Notification Requirement 659
        (iii) Responsiveness Test 659
        (iv) Types of Type III Supporting Organizations 660
        (v) Integral Part Test—Functionally Integrated Type III Organizations 660
        (vi) Integral Part Test—Nonfunctionally Integrated Type III Organizations 662
        (vii) Pending Regulation Projects 666
    (h) Contributions from Controlling Donors 668
    (i) Excess Benefit Transactions Rules 669
    (j) Limitation on Control 669
    (k) Excess Business Holdings Rules 672
    (l) Noncharitable Supported Organizations 673
    (m) Use of For-Profit Subsidiaries 674
§ 15.7 Change of Public Charity Category 675
    (a) From § 509(a)(1) to § 509(a)(2) or Vice Versa 675
    (b) From § 509(a)(3) to § 509(a)(1) or § 509(a)(2) 675
    (c) From § 509(a)(3) Type III to § 509(a)(3) Type I or II 675
    (d) IRS Recognition of Change in Public Charity Status 676
§ 15.8 Termination of Public Charity Status 677
§ 15.9 Relationships Created for Avoidance Purposes 678

§ 15.1 ADVANTAGES OF PUBLIC CHARITY STATUS

The significance of public charity status for a tax-exempt charitable organization[1] is primarily twofold. First, there are various federal tax law advantages to qualifying as a public charity as compared to a private foundation that must comply with the operational constraints of the private foundation rules. Second, private foundation grants to certain types of public charities are qualifying distributions[2] and are not taxable expenditures (regardless of whether the private foundation exercises expenditure responsibility over the grant).[3] Thus, an understanding of the various categories of public charities is also a fundamental element to understanding the tax law of private foundations.

§ 15.1 ADVANTAGES OF PUBLIC CHARITY STATUS

Private foundations must comply with a variety of special rules and sanctions; these constraints generally are not applicable to public charities. Therefore, it is typically preferable, when possible, to obtain and maintain public charity status. Advantages of public charities as compared to private foundations include:

- The charitable giving rules are generally more favorable for donations to public charities than private foundations.[4] The percentage limitation on deductions for charitable contributions by individuals to private foundations is 30 percent of adjusted gross income for gifts of money and 20 percent for gifts of appreciated property. In contrast, up to 60 percent of an individual's AGI can be deducted for cash gifts to public charities and 30 percent for gifts of appreciated property. For example, if an individual with an AGI of $1 million wishes to make a $500,000 charitable contribution in cash, $300,000 of the gift would be deductible in the year of the gift if made to a private foundation, but the full $500,000 would be deductible if the gift were made to a public charity.

- Appreciated property generally is not fully deductible when given to a private foundation; the amount of a charitable contribution of real estate, closely held company stock, and most other types of property to a private foundation generally is limited to the taxpayer's basis in the property. Gifts of appreciated property to a public charity, in contrast, are generally deductible at their full fair market value (provided the

---

1. That is, organizations that are described in IRC § 501(c)(3) and tax-exempt by reason of IRC § 501(a).
2. See Chapter 6.
3. See §§ 9.4 (as to grants to public charities), 9.7 (as to expenditure responsibility).
4. See § 14.2(a).

PUBLIC CHARITIES

property is long-term capital gain property).[5] The amount of a charitable contribution of shares of qualified appreciated stock to a private foundation, however, is equal to the fair market value of the shares.[6]

- An excise tax of 1.39 percent must be paid on a private foundation's net investment income.[7] There is no tax on investment income for a public charity unless the unrelated business income tax applies.[8]

- A private foundation is generally per se prohibited from buying or selling property or entering into other economic transactions with its directors, officers, contributors, or their family members (although there are certain limited exceptions to these self-dealing rules).[9] In contrast, public charities generally may enter into business transactions with their insiders, provided the compensation paid by the public charity is reasonable.[10]

- An annual Form 990-PF must be filed by private foundations regardless of revenue levels and value of assets. A return is not required for certain public types of public charities (for example, churches), and a short form or e-postcard filing is available for many others.[11]

- Private foundations may not make grants to noncharitable organizations for charitable purposes without complying with expenditure responsibility rules, which require pre-grant inquiries, written agreements, and reporting from the grantee and to the IRS.[12] These rules are not imposed on public charities.

- Lobbying activity by private foundations is generally not permitted, while a limited amount of lobbying is allowed by public charities. Absolutely no political campaign activity is permissible for private foundations or public charities.[13]

- A private foundation must make a minimum amount of charitable distributions each year (based on the value of its investment assets) in the form of grants to other organizations or spending on its own charitable projects.[14] A public charity, other than a nonfunctionally integrated

---

5. IRC § 170(e)(1)(B); see § 14.4.
6. IRC § 170(e)(5); see § 14.5.
7. See Chapter 10.
8. See Chapter 11.
9. See § 5.3.
10. IRC § 4958 (the excess benefit transactions rules); see *Tax-Exempt Organizations*, Chapter 21.
11. See § 12.1(a).
12. See § 9.7.
13. See §§ 9.1, 9.2.
14. See Chapter 6.

Type III supporting organization,[15] however, does not have a specific spending requirement (provided it maintains a level of charitable activities commensurate in scope with its resources).[16]

- Holding more than 20 percent of a business enterprise, taking into account shares owned by disqualified persons[17] as well, is generally prohibited for private foundations,[18] as are jeopardizing investments.[19] Limits of this nature are not placed on most public charities.

§ 15.2 STATUTORY CATEGORIES OF PUBLIC CHARITIES

To rebut the presumption that a tax-exempt charitable organization is, by default, a private foundation,[20] it must demonstrate that it meets one of the statutory categories of a public charity.[21]

The general statutory categories of public charities[22] are:

1. § 509(a)(1)—Organizations engaging in inherently public activity (public institutions)
2. § 509(a)(1)—Organizations principally supported by contributions and grants from the public (donative publicly supported charities)
3. § 509(a)(2)—Organizations principally supported by fee-for-service revenue (service provider publicly supported charities)
4. § 509(a)(3)—Supporting organizations
5. § 509(a)(4)—Organizations that test for public safety

There are, therefore, four general categories of charitable organizations that are *not* private foundations. These are *public institutions, publicly supported*

---

15. See § 15.6(g)(vi).
16. Rev. Rul. 64-182, 1964-1 C.B. 186; see *Tax-Exempt Organizations* § 4.7.
17. See Chapter 4.
18. See Chapter 7.
19. See Chapter 8.
20. IRC § 508(b).
21. IRC § 509(a); see § 1.2.
22. The term *public charity* is not per se defined in the Internal Revenue Code but has been defined in regulations to mean any charitable organization "that is not a private foundation" under IRC § 509(a) (e.g., Reg. § 1.501(h)-1(a)(2)). The term public charity is occasionally used in other regulations without definition (e.g., Reg. § 1.170A-9(h)(1)(iv)), perhaps with the assumption that the reader is aware of its general meaning, and sometimes is used to define a subset of the categories of public charities defined in IRC § 509(a)(1)-(4) (e.g., Reg. § 53.4945-2(a)(6)(i)).

charities, *supporting organizations*, and *organizations that test for public safety*. The organizations that comprise nearly all public charities are those that fall within the first three of these categories; that is, organizations that either have broad public support or involvement or that actively function in a supporting relationship to public or publicly supported charities.[23]

The fourth category of organizations that are not private foundations, organizations organized and operated exclusively for *testing for public safety*,[24] do not enjoy the favored status accorded to the other three categories of public charities for purposes of the private foundation rules. Private foundation grants to these organizations require expenditure responsibility.[25] According to a 1965 Department of Treasury report, these organizations are more analogous to business leagues, social welfare organizations, and similar tax-exempt groups than to private foundations.[26] As with these other types of exempt organizations, contributions to public safety testing organizations are not deductible as charitable contributions.[27]

§ 15.3 PUBLIC INSTITUTION CHARITIES

Churches, schools, colleges, universities, hospitals, medical research organizations, agricultural research organizations, and governmental units qualify as public charities by reason of the inherently public nature of their program activities. These include many of the *institutions* to be found in the charitable sector.[28]

Organizations in other categories of nonprivate foundation status may also have the attributes of institutions (such as museums and libraries), but they must qualify, if they can, under another category of public charity. The institutions that are public charities in this category are those that satisfy the requirements of at least one category of public institution. That is, these public institutions are not private foundations by reason of the nature of their programmatic activities (rather than by reason of how they are funded[29] or their relationship with one or more other tax-exempt organizations).[30]

---

23. IRC § 509(a)(1), (2), or (3); Reg. § 1.509(a)-1.
24. IRC § 509(a)(4).
25. See §§ 9.7, 9.8.
26. Treasury Department Report on Private Foundations, Committee on Finance, United States Senate, 89th Cong. (1965) at 2 n.4
27. By exclusion from the definition of charitable contribution in IRC § 170(c).
28. IRC §§ 170(b)(1)(A), 509(a)(1); Reg. §§ 1.170A- 9(a), 1.509(a)-2.
29. See §§ 15.4, 15.5.
30. See § 15.6.

§ 15.3 PUBLIC INSTITUTION CHARITIES

(a) Churches and Similar Entities

A church or a convention or association of churches is a public charity.[31] The IRS formulated criteria that it uses to ascertain whether a religious organization constitutes a *church*. Originally these criteria, unveiled in 1977, were in a list of 14 elements, not all of which needed to be satisfied. These elements include a distinct legal existence, a recognized creed, an ecclesiastical government, a distinct religious history, a literature of its own, and schools for the religious instruction of youth and preparation of its ministers.

Over the ensuing years, however, the federal tax law in this context has radically changed. In part this is due to a shift in emphasis by the IRS, which has downgraded in importance some of the criteria in the 14-element list, concluding they are common to tax-exempt organizations in general.[32] It is currently the position of the agency that, to be a church, an organization must have a defined congregation of worshippers, an established place of worship, and regular worship services.[33] Coincidentally, a major court opinion held that, for a religious entity to qualify as a church, it must meet an *associational test*.[34] This test and the contemporary IRS ruling policy are much the same. Thus, today the IRS is issuing private letter rulings finding that an organization is not a church because it did not satisfy the IRS core criteria,[35] it failed the associational test,[36] or both.[37]

The IRS ruled that a tax-exempt organization, the membership of which is composed of churches of different denominations, qualifies as an association of churches.[38] Another type of religious public charity is the integrated auxiliary of a church; in one instance, however, the IRS revoked the exempt status of an ostensible auxiliary when the agency discovered that it was formed without the knowledge of the church.[39]

---

31. IRC § 170(b)(1)(A)(i); Reg. § 1.170A-9(b). An example of a religious organization that failed to qualify as a church and constituted a private foundation appears in First Church of In Theo v. Commissioner, 56 T.C.M. 1045 (1989).
32. E.g., Priv. Ltr. Rul. 200727021.
33. E.g., Tech. Adv. Mem. 200437040.
34. Foundation of Human Understanding v. United States, 2009-2 U.S.T.C. ¶ 50,519 (U.S. Ct. Fed. Cl. (2009), *aff'd*, 614 F.3d 1383 (Fed. Cir. 2010), *cert. den.*, 562 U.S. 1286 (2011)). Thereafter, the U.S. Tax Court found a religious organization to be a church, on the basis of the traditional IRS criteria and without reference to the *Foundation of Human Understanding* opinion (Chambers v. Commissioner, 101 T.C.M. 1550 (2011)).
35. E.g., Priv. Ltr. Rul. 201242014. Because of the place-of-worship requirement, the IRS has held that an entity conducting services by means of the Internet cannot qualify as a church (e.g., Priv. Ltr. Rul. 201232034), nor can an entity that conducts its services by teleconference (e.g., Priv. Ltr. Rul. 200926049).
36. E.g., Priv. Ltr. Rul. 201232034.
37. E.g., Priv. Ltr. Rul. 201221022. In general, *Tax-Exempt Organizations* § 10.3.
38. Rev. Rul. 74-224, 1974-1 C.B. 61.
39. Priv. Ltr. Rul. 201246037.

(b) Educational Institutions

An "educational organization which normally maintains a regular faculty and curriculum and normally has a regularly enrolled body of pupils or students in attendance at the place where its educational activities are regularly carried on" is a public charity.[40] This type of institution is essentially a school; consequently it must have as its primary function the presentation of formal instruction.[41] Thus, a tax-exempt organization that has as its primary function the presentation of formal instruction, has courses that are interrelated and given in a regular and continuous manner (thereby constituting a regular curriculum), normally maintains a regular faculty, and has a regularly enrolled student body in attendance at the place where its educational activities are regularly carried on, qualifies as an educational institution that is a public charity.[42]

Educational institutions qualifying for public charity status include primary, secondary, preparatory, and high schools, and colleges and universities.[43] For purposes of the charitable contribution deduction and nonprivate foundation status, these organizations also encompass federal, state, and other public schools that otherwise qualify, although their tax exemption may be a function of their status as governmental units. An organization engaged in educational and noneducational activities (e.g., a museum operating a school) cannot achieve public charity status under the definition of an educational organization unless the latter activities are merely incidental to the former.[44] Thus, the IRS denied public charity status to an organization the primary function of which was not the presentation of formal instruction but the operation of a museum.[45]

---

40. IRC § 170(b)(1)(A)(ii).
41. Reg. § 1.170A-9(c)(1). An appellate court invalidated the requirement in the regulations that an educational organization must have as its "primary function . . . the presentation of formal instruction," but upheld the requirements in the regulations that an educational organization's primary purpose be "educational" and that its noneducational activities be merely incidental to that primary purpose (Mayo Clinic v. United States, 997 F.3d 789 (8th Cir. 2021), nonacq. 2021-47 I.R.B. 725).
42. Rev. Rul. 78-309, 1978-2 C.R. 123.
43. Examination guidelines for colleges and universities (Ann. 93-2, 1993-2 I.R.B. 39 § 342.1.) generally defined a *university* as an institution of higher learning with teaching and research facilities, comprising an undergraduate school that awards bachelor's degrees and a graduate school and professional schools that award master's or doctor's degrees. A *college* is generally referred to as a school of higher learning that grants bachelor's degrees in liberal arts or sciences; the term is also frequently used to describe undergraduate divisions or schools of a university that offer courses and grant degrees in a particular field. The term *school* is defined as a division of a university offering courses of instruction in a particular profession. In general, the term *school* is also applicable to institutions of learning at the primary and secondary levels of education.
44. Reg. § 1.170A-9(c)(1).
45. Rev. Rul. 76-167, 1976-1 C.B. 329.

§ 15.3 PUBLIC INSTITUTION CHARITIES

An organization may be regarded as presenting formal instruction even though it lacks a formal course program or formal classroom instruction. Thus, an organization that provided elementary education on a full-time basis to children at a facility maintained exclusively for that purpose, with a faculty and enrolled student body, was held to be a public charity despite the absence of a formal course program.[46] Similarly, an organization that conducted a survival course was granted public charity classification, even though its course periods were only 26 days and it used outdoor facilities more than classrooms, since it had a regular curriculum, faculty, and student body.[47] By contrast, a tax-exempt organization, the primary activity of which was providing specialized instruction by correspondence and a 5- to 10-day seminar program of personal instruction for students who completed the correspondence course, was ruled not to be an operating educational organization "since the organization's primary activity consist[ed] of providing instruction by correspondence."[48] In another instance, tutoring on a one-to-one basis in its students' homes was ruled insufficient to make a tutoring organization an operating educational entity.[49]

The fact that an otherwise qualifying organization offers a variety of lectures, workshops, and short courses concerning a general subject area, open to the general public and to its members, is not sufficient for it to acquire nonprivate foundation status as an educational institution.[50] This is because such an "optional, heterogeneous collection of courses is not formal instruction" and does not constitute a curriculum.[51] Where the attendees are members of the general public and can attend the functions on an optional basis, there is no "regularly enrolled body of pupils or students."[52] Further, where the functions are led by various invited authorities and personalities in the field, there is no "regular faculty."[53]

Even if an organization qualifies as a school or other type of "formal" educational institution, it will not be able to achieve tax-exempt status if it maintains racially discriminatory admissions policies[54] or if it benefits private

---

46. Rev. Rul. 72-430, 1972-2 C.B. 105.
47. Rev. Rul. 73-434, 1973-2 C.B. 71. Also, Rev. Rul. 79-130, 1979-1 C.B. 332; Rev. Rul. 73-543, 1973-2 C.B. 343, *clar. by* Ann. 74-115, 1974-52 I.R.B. 29; Rev. Rul. 75-215, 1975-1 C.B. 335; Rev. Rul. 72-101, 1972-1 C.B. 144; Rev. Rul. 69-492, 1969-2 C.B. 36; Rev. Rul. 68-175, 1968-1 C.B. 83.
48. Rev. Rul. 75-492, 1975-2 C.B. 80.
49. Rev. Rul. 76-384, 1976-2 C.B. 57. Also, Rev. Rul. 76-417, 1976-2 C.B. 58.
50. Rev. Rul. 78-82, 1978-1 C.B. 70.
51. Rev. Rul. 62-23, 1962-1 C.B. 200.
52. Rev. Rul. 64-128, 1964-1 (Part I) C.B. 191.
53. Rev. Rul. 78-82, 1978-1 C.B. 70.
54. Bob Jones University v. United States, 461 U.S. 574 (1983).

interests to more than an insubstantial extent.[55] As an illustration of the latter point, an otherwise qualifying school that trained individuals for careers as political campaign professionals was denied exempt status because of the secondary benefit accruing to entities of a national political party and its candidates, since nearly all of the school's graduates become employed by or consultants to these entities or candidates.[56]

(c) Hospitals

An "organization the principal purpose or functions of which are the providing of medical or hospital care or medical education or medical research, if the organization is *a hospital*," is a public charity.[57]

For public charity classification purposes, the term *hospital* includes federal government hospitals, state, county, and municipal hospitals that are instrumentalities of governmental units, rehabilitation institutions, outpatient clinics, extended care facilities, or community mental health or drug treatment centers, and cooperative hospital service organizations,[58] if they otherwise qualify. The term does not include, however, convalescent homes, homes for children or the aged, or institutions the principal purpose or function of which is to train disabled individuals to pursue a vocation,[59] nor does it include free clinics for animals.[60] For these purposes, the term *medical care* includes the treatment of any physical or mental disability or condition, whether on an inpatient or outpatient basis, as long as the cost of the treatment is deductible[61] by the person treated.[62]

(d) Medical Research Organizations

Medical research organizations directly engaged in the continuous active conduct of medical research in conjunction with a hospital can qualify as a public charity. The term *medical research* means the conduct of investigations, experiments, and studies to discover, develop, or verify knowledge relating

---

55. Reg. § 1.501(c)(3)-1(c)(1).
56. American Campaign Academy v. Commissioner, 92 T.C. 1053 (1989). In general, Hopkins, Gross, and Schenkelberg, *Nonprofit Law for Colleges and Universities: Essential Questions and Answers for Officers, Directors, and Advisors* (Hoboken, NJ: John Wiley & Sons, 2011).
57. IRC § 170(b)(1)(A)(iii).
58. Cf. Rev. Rul. 76-452, 1976-2 C.B. 60.
59. Reg. § 1.170A-9(d)(1).
60. Rev. Rul. 74-572, 1974-2 C.B. 82.
61. IRC § 213.
62. Reg. § 1.170A-9(d)(1).

to the causes, diagnosis, treatment, prevention, or control of physical or mental diseases and impairments of human beings. To qualify, an organization must have the appropriate equipment and professional personnel necessary to carry out its principal function.[63] Medical research encompasses the associated disciplines spanning the biological, social, and behavioral sciences.

To be a public charity under these rules, an organization must have the conduct of medical research as its principal purpose or function[64] and be primarily engaged in the continuous active conduct of medical research in conjunction with a hospital, which itself is a public charity. The organization need not be formally affiliated with a hospital to be considered primarily engaged in the active conduct of medical research in conjunction with a hospital. There must, however, be a joint effort on the part of the research organization and the hospital pursuant to an understanding that the two organizations will maintain continuing close cooperation in the active conduct of medical research.[65] An organization will not be considered to be "primarily engaged directly in the continuous active conduct of medical research" unless it, during the applicable computation period,[66] devotes more than one-half of its assets to the continuous active conduct of medical research or it expends funds equaling at least 3.5 percent of the fair market value of its endowment for the continuous active conduct of medical research.[67] If the organization's primary purpose is to disburse funds to other organizations for the conduct of research by them or to extend research grants or scholarships to others, it is not considered directly engaged in the active conduct of medical research.[68]

(e) Agricultural Research Organizations

An agricultural research organization is a type of public charity. This is an entity that is engaged in the continuous active conduct of agricultural research (as that term is defined in the Agricultural Research, Extension, and Teaching Policy Act of 1977) in conjunction with a land-grant college or university or a non-land-grant college of agriculture.[69] For a contribution to an agricultural research organization to qualify for the 50 percent limitation,[70] during the calendar year in which a contribution is made to the organization, the organization must have committed to spend the contribution for the research before

---

63. Reg. § 1.170A-9(d)(2)(iii).
64. Reg. § 1.170A-9(d)(2)(iv).
65. Reg. § 1.170A-9(d)(2)(vii).
66. Reg. § 1.170A-9(d)(2)(vi)(A).
67. Reg. § 1.170A-9(d)(2)(v)(B).
68. Reg. § 1.170A-9(d)(2)(v)(C).
69. IRC §§ 170(b)(1)(A)(ix), 509(a)(1).
70. IRC § 170(b)(1)(A).

January 1 of the fifth calendar year that begins after the date of the contribution. It is intended that this provision be interpreted in like manner to and be consistent with the rules applicable to medical research organizations.[71]

(f) Public College Support Foundations

Public charity status is provided for certain organizations providing support for public colleges and universities.[72] These entities are useful in attracting private giving for these institutions, with the gifts usually not subject to the direction of the particular state legislature.

Specifically, the organization must normally receive a substantial part of its support (exclusive of income received in the exercise or performance of its tax-exempt activities) from the United States and/or direct or indirect contributions from the public. It must be organized and operated exclusively to receive, hold, invest, and administer property and to make expenditures to or for the benefit of a college or university (including a land grant college or university) that is a public charity and that is an agency or instrumentality of a state or political subdivision thereof, or that is owned or operated by a state or political subdivision thereof or by an agency or instrumentality of one or more states or political subdivisions.

These expenditures include those made for any one or more of the regular functions of colleges and universities, such as the acquisition and maintenance of real property comprising part of the campus area; the construction of college or university buildings; the acquisition and maintenance of equipment and furnishings used for, or in conjunction with, regular functions of colleges and universities; or expenditures for scholarships, libraries, and student loans.[73]

Another frequently important feature of the state college- or university-related foundation is its ability to borrow money for or on behalf of the supported institution, with the indebtedness bearing tax-excludible interest.[74]

(g) Governmental Units

The United States, District of Columbia, states, possessions of the United States, and their political subdivisions are classified as governmental units.[75] An important point is that this type of a unit qualifies as a public charity without regard to its sources of support, partly because, by its nature, it is

---

71. See § 15.3(d).
72. IRC § 170(b)(1)(A)(iv).
73. Reg. § 1.170A-9(c)(2).
74. IRC § 103.
75. IRC § 170(c)(1).

responsive to all citizens.[76] The regulations do not contain an additional definition or explanation of the meaning of the term. A *governmental unit* presumably encompasses not only political subdivisions of states and the like, but also government instrumentalities, agencies, and entities referenced by similar terms. The distinction between a *political subdivision* and an *instrumentality* was made by the IRS in 1975, when it observed that a county is a political subdivision of a state and that an association of counties is a wholly owned instrumentality of the counties,[77] on the basis of criteria promulgated in 1957.[78]

An unincorporated intergovernmental cooperative organization established by an act of a state legislature on behalf of a consortium of 11 of the state's public school districts was found to be a private foundation, not a governmental unit, because its source of support was a private foundation that granted the money to undertake the curriculum research and development. Also, although the cooperative arguably was an instrumentality of the state, it had no sovereign powers, such as the right of eminent domain, the power to assess and collect taxes, or police powers. The fact that it was an integral part of a group of governmental units—the public schools by which it was established—did not make it a governmental unit.[79]

§ 15.4 DONATIVE PUBLICLY SUPPORTED CHARITIES

One way for a charitable organization to avoid private foundation status is to receive its financial support from a requisite number of sources. A publicly supported charity is the antithesis of a private foundation, in that the latter customarily derives its financial support from one source, while a publicly supported organization is primarily supported by the public. The law in this area principally concerns the process for determining *public* support.

There are essentially two ways by which a charitable organization can be supported for federal tax law purposes. One is to be an organization whose revenues come from a variety of gifts and grants from a diversity of donors—a *donative* publicly supported charity.[80] The other is to be an organization that is primarily supported by an sufficient amount of fee-for-service (exempt function) revenue, gifts, and grants—a *service provider* publicly supported charity.[81]

---

76. IRC § 170(b)(1)(A)(v); Reg. § 1.170A-9(e).
77. Rev. Rul. 75-359, 1975-2 C.B. 79.
78. Rev. Rul. 57-128, 1957-1 C.B. 311.
79. Texas Learning Technology Group v. Commissioner, 958 F.2d 122 (5th Cir. 1992).
80. IRC §§ 170(b)(1)(A)(vi), 509(a)(1).
81. IRC § 509(a)(2). See § 15.5.

The rules concerning the donative type of public charity were enacted in 1954; the rules concerning the service provider type of public charity were introduced in 1969. Thus, Congress has provided two definitions of the same type of organization (in a generic sense); although there are substantive differences between the two sets of rules, many charitable organizations are able to satisfy the requirements of both.[82]

(a) General Rules

An organization is a donative publicly supported charity if it is a charitable entity that "normally receives a substantial part of its support" (other than income from the performance of an exempt function) from a governmental unit[83] or from direct or indirect contributions from the public.[84]

Organizations that qualify as donative publicly supported charities generally are entities such as museums of history, art, or science; libraries; community centers to promote the arts; organizations providing facilities for the support of an opera, symphony orchestra, ballet, or repertory drama group; organizations providing some other direct service to the public; and organizations such as the American Red Cross or the United Givers Fund.[85]

The principal way for an organization to be a publicly supported organization under these rules is for it to normally derive at least one-third of its support from qualifying contributions and grants.[86] Thus, an organization classified as a publicly supported entity under these rules must maintain a support fraction, the denominator of which is total eligible support received during the computation period and the numerator of which is the amount of support from eligible public and/or governmental sources for the period. An organization's support is determined under the method of accounting on the basis of which the organization regularly computes its income in keeping its books.[87]

---

82. The donative type of publicly supported charity is generally perceived as the preferred category of the two. For example, only a charitable organization that satisfies the requirements of the donative public charity rules (or the rules pertaining to public institutions (see § 15.3)) may maintain a pooled income fund (IRC § 642(c)(5)(A)).
83. IRC § 170(c)(1).
84. IRC § 170(b)(1)(A)(vi). The U.S. Tax Court, faced with interpreting the regulations accompanying IRC § 170(b)(1)(A)(vi), found them "almost frighteningly complex and technical" (Friends of the Society of Servants of God v. Commissioner, 75 T.C. 209, 213 (1980)).
85. Reg. § 1.170(A)-9(f)(1)(ii). An organization otherwise qualifying as a public institution (see § 15.3) may nonetheless qualify under IRC § 170(b)(1)(A)(vi) (Rev. Rul. 76-416, 1976-2 C.B. 57).
86. Reg. § 1.170A-9(f)(2).
87. Reg. § 1.170A-9(f)(13).

§ 15.4 DONATIVE PUBLICLY SUPPORTED CHARITIES

(b) Two Percent Limitation

In general, when calculating a donative publicly supported charity's public support fraction, contributions by an individual, trust, or corporation are taken into account as support from direct or indirect contributions from the general public only to the extent that the total amount of the contributions by any such donor during the calculation period does not exceed 2 percent of the organization's total support for such period. For example, any contribution by one individual is included in full in the denominator of the public support fraction, but is included in the numerator of the fraction only to the extent that such amount does not exceed 2 percent of the denominator.[88]

In addition to individuals, public support can be derived from for-profit entities (including corporations and partnerships) and nonprofit entities (including various forms of tax-exempt organizations). For example, the IRS ruled that contributions made by a business league to a charitable organization seeking designation as a donative publicly supported charity are subject to this 2 percent limitation.[89] The 2 percent limitation is applicable to amounts received from a supporting organization.[90] It frequently happens, therefore, that private foundations are sources of public support, albeit subject to the 2 percent limitation.

The 2 percent limitation does not generally apply to support received from other donative publicly supported charities nor to support from governmental units[91]—that is, this type of support is, in its entirety, public support.[92] This includes distributions from donor-advised funds sponsored by donative publicly supported charities.[93] Certain types of public institution charities,[94] such as hospitals and churches, may also qualify as donative publicly supported charities if they also meet the public support test.[95] As with support from

---

88. Reg. § 1.170A-9(f)(6)(i).
89. Rev. Rul. 77-255, 1977-2 C.B. 74.
90. Priv. Ltr. Rul. 9203040, where the IRS also ruled that contributions to the supporting organization are not forms of support to the affiliated supported organization at the time they are made to the supporting organization. The supporting organization requirements are the subject of § 15.6. This private letter ruling also stated that the special rule by which supporting organization grants to service provider publicly supported charities retain their character as investment income (see § 15.5(b)) does not apply to these grants made to donative publicly supported charities.
91. IRC § 170(c)(1).
92. Reg. § 1.170A-9(f)(6)(i).
93. For a discussion of proposed legislation that would subject distributions from a donor-advised fund to the 2 percent limitation, see § 16.10. The Treasury Department and the IRS are considering changes to Reg. § 1.170A-9(f) to the same end (Notice 2017-73, 2017-51 I.R.B. 562 § 5).
94. See § 15.3(a)-(d).
95. Rev. Rul. 76-416, 1976-2 C.B. 57; Rev. Rul. 78-95, 1978-1 C.B. 71.

domestic governmental units, assistance from a foreign government may be considered allowable support in determining an organization's qualifications as a donative publicly supported charity.[96]

Nonetheless, the 2 percent limitation applies with respect to support received from a donative publicly supported charity or governmental unit if the support represents an amount that was expressly or impliedly earmarked by a donor or grantor to the publicly supported organization or unit of government as being for or for the benefit of the organization asserting status as a publicly supported charitable organization.[97] Earmarked contributions constitute support of the intermediary organization under these rules to the extent that they are treated as contributions to the organization under the law concerning the charitable deduction, except where the intermediary organization receives the contributions as the agent for the donor for delivery to the ultimate recipient.[98]

In applying the 2 percent limitation, all contributions made by a donor and any person or persons standing in a relationship to the donor that is described in the private foundation disqualified persons rules[99] must be combined and treated as if made by a single person.[100] The IRS considered whether contributions from a potential donor (a corporation) and distributions from a trust created by the potential donor would be treated as made by a single person under these rules. The donor possessed no beneficial interest in the trust, the trust owned no stock in the donor, and persons described in the applicable private foundation disqualified person rules owned less than 35 percent of the combined voting power of the donor. Thus, the type of disqualified person relationship between the trust and the donor necessary

---

96. Rev. Rul. 75-435, 1975-2 C.B. 215.
97. Reg. § 1.170A-9(f)(6)(v). This concept of earmarking is also reflected in the rules for service provider publicly supported charities (see § 15.5(a)) (Reg. § 1.509(a)-3(j)(1), (2)). Examples that apply in both contexts are in Reg. § 1.509(a)-3(j)(3).
98. Gen. Couns. Mem. 39748. This conclusion is based on the fact that the extent of deductibility of gifts to private foundations is not dependent on any earmarking (e.g., IRC § 170(b)(1)(F)(ii)) and, thus, that gifts to nonprivate foundations should not be treated any differently. In 1992, the IRS, in Gen. Couns. Mem. 39875, withdrew Gen. Couns. Mem. 39748. This occurred because the IRS was rethinking its position concerning *donor-directed funds* (see §§ 16.1, 16.3) and believed that the conclusion reached in the now-withdrawn general counsel memorandum was being applied in circumstances beyond those contemplated. The IRS ruled, however, that contributions to a donative publicly supported charity will constitute *support* under these rules, even though some of the contributors may designate their gifts for one of two specific projects, as long as all of the contributions are expended for the organization's exempt purposes (Priv. Ltr. Rul. 9203040).
99. IRC § 4946(a)(1)(C) through (a)(1)(G).
100. Reg. § 1.170A-9(f)(6)(i).

§ 15.4 DONATIVE PUBLICLY SUPPORTED CHARITIES

to treat them as a single person was not present for purposes of applying the 2 percent limitation.[101]

Similarly, where a private foundation formed as a nonstock, nonprofit corporation and a substantial contributor to the foundation both make donations to a public charity, these donations are not considered to be made by the same person for purposes of applying the 2 percent limitation. Neither the substantial contributor, nor any person standing in one of the identified disqualified person relationships to them, will have any ownership, profits, or beneficial interest in the private foundation; therefore, the necessary disqualified person relationship to treat them as a single person for purposes of the 2 percent limitation is lacking.[102]

Likewise, under current law, distributions from a donor-advised fund are not combined with other contributions made by a person who has advisory privileges with respect to the donor-advised fund.[103]

(c) Support Test

A matter that can be of considerable significance in enabling a charitable organization to qualify as a donative publicly supported charity is the meaning of the term *support*. For this purpose, *support* means amounts received as gifts, grants, contributions; net income from unrelated business activities; gross investment income;[104] tax revenues levied for the benefit of the organization and either paid to or expended on behalf of the organization; and the value of services or facilities (exclusive of services or facilities generally furnished to the public without charge) furnished by a governmental unit to the organization without charge.[105] All of these items are amounts that, if received by the organization, comprise the denominator of the support fraction. *Support* does not include any gain from the disposition of property that would be considered as gain from the sale or exchange of a capital asset, or the value of exemption from any federal, state, or local tax

---

101. Priv. Ltr. Rul. 9203040.
102. In general, a private foundation is treated as a disqualified person only for purposes of the excess business holdings rules (IRC § 4946(a)(1)(H)).
103. For a discussion of proposed legislation that would treat all distributions from donor-advised funds sponsored by the distributing charity as support received from one person except where the sponsoring organization identifies the donor making the contribution, see § 16.10.
104. IRC § 509(e).
105. IRC § 509(d); Reg. § 1.170A-9(f)(7)(i).

PUBLIC CHARITIES

or any similar benefit.[106] Also, funding in the form of a loan does not constitute support.[107]

Sponsorship payments that are acknowledged by the tax-exempt organization without quantitative and qualitative information so as to avoid classification as advertising revenue[108] can be treated as contributions for public support purposes.[109]

In constructing the support fraction, an organization must exclude from both the numerator and the denominator amounts received from the exercise or performance of its exempt purpose or function (*exempt function revenue*) and contributions of services for which a deduction is not allowable.[110] An organization will not be treated as meeting the support test, however, if it receives *almost all* of its support from gross receipts from related activities and an insignificant amount of its support from governmental units and the public.[111] Moreover, the organization may exclude from both the numerator and the denominator of the support fraction an amount equal to one or more qualifying unusual grants.[112]

In computing the support fraction, the organization's support that is *normally* received must be determined. This is reference to support received over a five-year period, consisting of its current tax year (the test year) plus the four tax years immediately preceding the current tax year.[113] If the requisite support is received over this period, the organization is considered to have met the one-third public support test for its current tax year and the immediately succeeding tax year.

There are several issues that can arise in computing the public support component (the numerator) of the support fraction for donative publicly supported charities, including:

- Whether or not a contribution or grant is from a qualifying publicly supported charity.[114]

---

106. IRC § 509(d).
107. E.g., Priv. Ltr. Rul. 9608039.
108. Reg. § 513-4(c)(2)(iv).
109. Reg. § 1.170A-9(f)(6)(i).
110. Reg. § 1.170A-9(f)(7)(i), (ii).
111. Reg. § 1.170A-9(f)(7)(iii).
112. Reg. § 1.170A-9(f)(6)(ii), (iii); see § 15.5(c).
113. Reg. § 1.170A-9(f)(4)(i).
114. IRC § 170(b)(1)(A)(vi) (donative publicly supported charity).

§ 15.4 DONATIVE PUBLICLY SUPPORTED CHARITIES

- Whether or not a contribution or grant from a qualifying publicly supported charity or governmental unit is a pass-through transfer from another donor or grantor.[115]

- Whether or not a "membership fee" constitutes a contribution rather than a payment for services.[116]

- Whether or not a payment pursuant to a government contract is support from a governmental unit (a grant) rather than revenue from a related activity (exempt function income).[117]

- Whether or not an organization is primarily dependent on gross receipts from related activities.[118]

---

115. See text accompanied by *supra* note 97.
116. Reg. § 1.170A-9(f)(7)(iv). E.g., The Home for Aged Men v. United States, 80-2 U.S.T.C. ¶ 9711 (N.D. W. Va. 1980), *aff'd unrep. dec.* (4th Cir. 1981), where the court found that funds provided to a home for the aged by new admittees are not membership fees but are items constituting exempt function income, with the result that the organization was determined to be a private foundation. Also, Williams Home, Inc. v. United States, 540 F. Supp. 310 (W.D. Va. 1982), where funds conveyed to a home for aged women as a condition of admission were held to not be contributions.
117. Reg. § 1.170A-9(f)(8). An amount paid by a governmental unit to an organization is not regarded as received from the exercise or performance of its tax-exempt functions (and thus can qualify as eligible support) if the purpose of the payment is primarily to enable the organization to provide a service to the direct benefit of the public, rather than to serve the direct and immediate needs of the payor (Reg. § 1.170A-9(f)(8)(ii)). In application of this rule, the IRS determined that payments by the U.S. Department of Health and Human Services to a professional standards review organization are not excludible gross receipts but are includible support, because the payments compensate the professional standards review organization for a function that promotes the health of the beneficiaries of governmental healthcare programs in the areas in which the organization operates, thus enabling the organization to be classified as an entity described in IRC § 170(b)(1)(A)(vi) (Rev. Rul. 81-276, 1981-2 C.B. 128). By contrast, Medicare and Medicaid payments to tax-exempt healthcare organizations constitute gross receipts derived from the performance of exempt functions, and thus are not includible support, because the patients control the ultimate recipients of the payments by their choice of a healthcare provider, so that they, not the governmental units, are the payors (Rev. Rul. 83-153, 1983-2 C.B. 48).
118. Reg. § 1.170A-9(f)(7)(iii). One of the similarities between a donative publicly supported charity and a state-university related foundation (see § 15.3(f)) is that both must normally receive a substantial part of their support from governmental sources and/or contributions from the public. There is a difference, however, in respect to the measurement of allowable governmental support. For purposes of publicly supported organizations (IRC § 170(b)(1)(A)(vi)), governmental sources are a state, a U.S. possession, a political subdivision of the foregoing, or the United States or the District of Columbia (IRC § 170(c)(1)), while for purposes of the state university related "foundation" (IRC § 170(b)(1)(A)(iv)), governmental sources are the United States or a state, or any political subdivision thereof. Thus, the sources of qualifying government support for an IRC § 170(b)(1)(a)(vi) entity are broader than those for an IRC § 170(b)(1)(A)(iv) organization (Rev. Rul. 82-132, 1982-2 C.B. 107).

A court held that investment income generated by an endowment fund cannot be regarded as public support, notwithstanding the fact that the endowment principal originated with public contributions.[119] This correct decision may be contrasted with one where a court failed to distinguish between investment income as public support—which it is not—and grants from trusts that are funded with investment income—which clearly constitute public support, limited perhaps by the 2 percent limitation.[120]

In making these computations, care must be taken in a situation where the organization being evaluated under these rules previously had to make changes in its operations to qualify as a charitable entity. The position of the IRS is that the rules that require, as discussed, a determination of the extent of broad public financial support in prior years "presuppose" that the organization was organized and operated exclusively for charitable purposes and otherwise qualified as a charitable entity during those years. Consequently, support received by an organization in these circumstances in one or more years in which it failed to meet the requirements for a charitable entity cannot be considered in ascertaining its status as a publicly supported charitable organization.[121]

A tax-exempt charitable organization with more than one unrelated business may aggregate its net income and net losses from all unrelated businesses for purposes of determining whether the organization is publicly supported under these rules.[122] That is, an organization may opt to not apply the bucketing rule[123] in this context.

(d) Facts and Circumstances Test

One of the defects of the donative public charity support rules is that organizations that are not private foundations in a generic sense, because they have many of the attributes of a public organization, may be classified as private

---

119. Trustees for the Home for Aged Women v. United States, 86-1 U.S.T.C. ¶ 9290 (D. Mass. 1986).
120. St. John's Orphanage, Inc. v. United States, 89-1 U.S.T.C. ¶ 9176 (Ct. Cl. 1989).
121. Rev. Rul. 77-116, 1977-1 C.B. 155. The IRS likewise asserted that support received by an organization prior to the date of the filing of its application for recognition of tax exemption, where the application was filed after the 15-month period (see § 2.5), cannot be used in ascertaining public charity status (Rev. Rul. 77-469, 1977-2 C.B. 196; Rev. Rul. 77-208, 1977-1 C.B. 153). A charitable organization filed an annual information return showing a public support ratio, by reason of IRC § 170(b)(1)(A)(vi), of 99 percent, even though virtually all of its income was derived from a trust; the IRS concluded that an incomplete return was filed for purposes of imposition of penalties (IRC §§ 6501(c)(3), 6652(c)(1)) (Tech. Adv. Mem. 200047048).
122. Reg. § 1.170A-9(f)(7)(v).
123. See § 11.5(b).

§ 15.4 DONATIVE PUBLICLY SUPPORTED CHARITIES

foundations because they cannot meet the precise mechanical one-third test. Organizations in this position include museums and libraries that principally rely on their endowments for financial support and thus have little or no need for contributions and grants. Although the statutory law is silent on the point, the tax regulations offer some relief in this regard, by means of the *facts and circumstances test*.

The history of the organization's fundraising efforts and other factors can be considered as an alternative method to the strict mathematical formula for qualifying for public support under the general donative public charity rules. This test is not available in connection with the service provider public charity rules. These factors must be present for this test to be met:[124]

- Public support must be at least 10 percent of the total support; the higher the better.

- The organization must have an active "continuous and bona fide" fundraising program designed to attract new and additional public and governmental support. Consideration will be given to the fact that, in its early years of existence, the charitable organization may limit the scope of its solicitations to those persons deemed most likely to provide seed money in an amount sufficient to enable it to commence its charitable activities and to expand its solicitation program.

- Other favorable factors must be present, such as the composition of the board, which must be representative of broad public interests; support that is derived from governmental and other sources representative of the public; facilities and programs that are made available to the public, such as those of a museum or symphony society; and programs that appeal to a broad-based public.[125]

The higher the percentage of support from public or governmental sources, the less is the burden of establishing the publicly supported nature of the organization through the other factors—and the converse is also true.

Concerning the governing board factor, the organization's nonprivate foundation status will be enhanced where it has a governing body that

---

124. Reg. § 1.170A-9(f)(3). An illustration of an organization that failed both the general rules and the facts and circumstances test appears in Collins v. Commissioner, 61 T.C. 593 (1974).
125. In a case concerning the public charity status of a home for the elderly, a court held that the practice of the home to encourage lawyers to mention to their clients the possibility of bequests to the home was inadequate compliance with the requirement of an ongoing development program (The Home for the Aged Men v. United States, 80-2 U.S.T.C. ¶ 9711 (N.D. W. Va. 1980), *aff'd unrep. dec.* (4th Cir. 1981)).

represents the interests of the public, rather than the personal or private interests of a limited number of donors. This can be accomplished by the election of board members by a broad-based membership or by having the board composed of public officials, persons having particular expertise in the field or discipline involved, community leaders, and the like.

As noted, one of the important elements of the facts and circumstances test is the availability of public facilities or services. Examples of entities meeting this requirement are a museum that holds its building open to the public, a symphony orchestra that gives public performances, a conservation organization that provides educational services to the public through the distribution of educational materials, and an old age home that provides domiciliary or nursing services for members of the public.

(e) Community Foundations

A community trust (or community foundation) may qualify as a donative publicly supported charity if it attracts, receives, and depends on financial support from members of the general public on a regular, recurring basis. Community foundations are designed primarily to attract large contributions of a capital or endowment nature from a small number of donors, with the gifts often received and maintained in the form of separate trusts or funds. They are generally identified with a particular community or area and are controlled by a representative group of persons from that community or area. Individual donors relinquish control over the investment and distribution of their contributions and the income generated from them, although donors may designate the purposes for which the assets are to be used, subject to change by the governing body of the community trust.[126]

To qualify as a publicly supported organization, a community foundation must meet the support requirements for a donative publicly supported charity. With regard to the facts and circumstances test for donative public charities,[127] the requirement of attraction of public support will generally be satisfied if a community foundation seeks gifts and bequests from a wide range of potential donors in the community or area served, through banks or trust companies, through lawyers or other professional individuals, or in other appropriate ways that call attention to the community foundation as a potential recipient of gifts and bequests made for the benefit of the community or area served. A community foundation is not required to engage in periodic, community-wide fundraising campaigns directed toward attracting

---

126. Reg. § 1.170A-9(f)(10).
127. See § 15.4(d).

§ 15.4 DONATIVE PUBLICLY SUPPORTED CHARITIES

a large number of small contributions in a manner similar to campaigns conducted by a community chest or united fund.[128]

A community foundation wants to be treated as a single entity, rather than as an aggregation of separate funds. To be regarded as a *component part* of a community foundation, a trust or fund must be created by gift or like transfer to a community foundation that is treated as a separate entity and may not be subjected by the transferor to any material restriction[129] with respect to the transferred assets.[130] To be treated as a separate entity, a community foundation must be appropriately named, be so structured as to subject its funds to a common governing instrument, have a common governing body, and prepare periodic financial reports that treat all funds held by the community foundation as its funds.[131] The governing body of a community foundation must have the power to modify any restriction on the distribution of funds where it is inconsistent with the charitable needs of the community, must commit itself to the exercise of its powers in the best interests of the community foundation, and must commit itself to seeing that the funds are invested pursuant to accepted standards of fiduciary conduct.[132]

A private foundation may make a grant to a designated fund within a community foundation or other charitable entity that maintains a donor-advised fund program.[133] A foundation may treat the grant as a qualifying distribution for purposes of its annual mandatory payout requirement,[134] even though it acquires the ability to make recommendations as to distributions to other charitable organizations from the fund.[135] This assumes, of course, that all of the appropriate requirements are satisfied, particularly the absence of prohibited material restrictions.[136] Grants of this nature are regarded as made to the community foundation and not to a separate trust fund, which, standing alone, would likely be treated as a private foundation.[137]

---

128. Reg. § 170A-9(f)(10).
129. See § 13.3(b), (c).
130. Reg. § 1.170A-9(f)(11)(ii). E.g., Priv. Ltr. Rul. 200204040.
131. Reg. § 1.170A-9(f)(11)(iii)-(vi). E.g., Priv. Ltr. Rul. 201307008, superseded by Priv. Ltr. Rul. 201322046, superseded by Priv. Ltr. Rul. 201403016.
132. Reg. § 1.170A-9(f)(11)(v).
133. Donor-advised funds are the subject of Chapter 16.
134. See § 6.4(b).
135. E.g., Priv. Ltr. Rul. 8836033.
136. See § 13.3(b), (c).
137. E.g., Priv. Ltr. Rul. 9807030. Any trust that is alleged to be a component part of a community trust, but that fails to meet the component part requirements, will instead be treated as a separate trust (subject to the provisions of IRC § 501 and IRC §§ 4947(a)(1) or 4947(a)(2), as the case may be) (Reg. § 1.170A-9(f)(12)). A nonprofit corporation or association that similarly fails the component part test will be treated as a separate entity, and, if it is described in IRC § 501(c)(3), will be treated as a private foundation unless it meets one of the exclusions from private foundation status in IRC § 509(a)(1)-(4) (*id.*).

There is nothing in the law that expressly requires a community foundation to serve only a *community*. Indeed, some community foundations operate programs nationwide. Nonetheless, the concept of community foundation (and even the term) would seem to lead to the conclusion that the grant-making activities and other programs of a community foundation should be confined to the organization's community.

§ 15.5 SERVICE PROVIDER PUBLICLY SUPPORTED CHARITIES

A charitable organization can be a publicly supported organization as a *service provider* entity.[138] Qualification as a service provider publicly supported charity is measured by sources of revenue, but there are significant differences in relation to the donative public charity rules. Unlike donative publicly supported charities, public support for a service provider public charity includes *exempt function income*—that is, gross receipts from admissions, sales of merchandise, performance of services, or furnishing of facilities, in an activity which is not an unrelated trade or business.[139] Thus, the service provider publicly support charity category typically includes organizations receiving a major portion of their support from fees and other charges for participation in the organization's exempt activities, such as museums, historical sites, day care centers, animal shelters, theaters, and educational publishers.

A two-part support test must be met to qualify under this category. First, investment income normally cannot exceed one-third of the organization's total support (the investment income test).[140] Second, more than one-third of total support normally must be received from a combination of exempt function income and gifts, grants, contributions, and membership dues received from persons other than disqualified persons with respect to the organization,[141] or from governmental units,[142] public institutions,[143] or donative publicly supported charities[144] (*permitted sources*).[145]

---

138. The U.S. Supreme Court referred to organizations of this nature as "nonprofit service provider[s]" (Camps Newfound/Owatonna, Inc. v. Town of Harrison, Maine, 520 U.S. 564, 572 (1997)).
139. IRC § 509(a)(2)(A)(ii). An organization claimed that the sale of pickle cards (a type of gambling) was revenue constituting a form of public support; the IRS not only disagreed but also found, as did a court, that the revenue was unrelated business income (Education Athletic Association, Inc. v. Commissioner, 77 T.C.M. 1525 (1999)).
140. IRC § 509(a)(2)(B); see § 15.5(b).
141. See Chapter 4.
142. IRC § 170(c)(1); see § 15.3(g).
143. See § 15.3.
144. See § 15.4.
145. IRC § 509(a)(2)(A); Reg. § 1.509(a)-3(a)(2).

§ 15.5 SERVICE PROVIDER PUBLICLY SUPPORTED CHARITIES

(a) Support Test

An organization seeking to qualify under the service provider one-third support test must construct a support fraction, with the amount of support received from permitted sources constituting the numerator of the fraction and the total amount of support received being the denominator.[146]

For purposes of calculating the denominator of the service provider public support fraction, the term *support*[147] means (in addition to the categories of public support referenced above) (1) net income from unrelated business activities,[148] (2) gross investment income,[149] (3) tax revenues levied for the benefit of the organization and either paid to or expended on behalf of the organization, and (4) the value of services or facilities (exclusive of services or facilities generally furnished to the public without charge) furnished by a governmental unit to the organization without charge. The term does not include any gain from the disposition of property that would be considered as gain from the sale or exchange of a capital asset or the value of exemption from any federal, state, or local tax or any similar benefit.[150] Also, funding in the form of a loan does not constitute support.[151] For these purposes, an organization's support is determined under the method of accounting on the basis of which the organization regularly computes its income in keeping its books.[152]

In computing the support fraction, the organization's support that is *normally* received must be determined. This is a reference to support received over a five-year period, consisting of its current tax year (the test year) plus the four tax years immediately preceding the current tax year.[153] If the requisite support is received over this period, the organization is considered to have met the one-third public support test for its current tax year and the immediately succeeding tax year. If, in an organization's current tax year, there are substantial and material changes in its sources of support (e.g., an unusually large contribution or bequest), other than changes arising from unusual grants,[154] the computation period becomes the tax year of the substantial and material changes and the four immediately preceding tax years.[155]

---

146. IRC § 509(a)(2)(A); Reg. § 1.509(a)-3(a)(2).
147. IRC § 509(d).
148. See Chapter 11.
149. IRC § 509(e).
150. IRC § 509(d).
151. E.g., Priv. Ltr. Rul. 9608039.
152. Reg. § 1.509(a)-3(k).
153. Reg. § 1.509(a)-3(c)(1)(i).
154. See § 15.5(c).
155. Reg. § 1.509(a)-3(c)(1)(ii).

PUBLIC CHARITIES

Gross receipts from related activities from any person,[156] or from any bureau or similar agency of a governmental unit, may be included in the numerator of the public support fraction in any tax year only to the extent that these receipts do not exceed the greater of $5,000 or 1 percent of the organization's support for the year.[157] Because gifts, grants, contributions, and membership fees are not subject to this limitation, it is important to distinguish them from gross receipts when calculating the public support fraction. Any payment of money or transfer of property without adequate consideration is considered a *gift* or *contribution*.[158] A *grant* is normally made to encourage the grantee organization to carry on certain programs or activities in furtherance of its exempt purposes that benefit the public;[159] in contrast, *gross receipts* generally include amounts received from an activity which is not an unrelated trade or business, if a specific service, facility, or product is provided to serve the direct and immediate needs of the payor, rather than primarily to confer a direct benefit upon the general public. Thus, payments made primarily to enable the payor to realize or receive some economic or physical benefit from the service, facility, or product provided by a service provider public charity will be treated as gross receipts.[160] To the extent the basic purpose for making a payment is to provide support for the organization rather than to purchase admissions, merchandise, services, or the use of facilities, the payment will be treated as a *membership fee* rather than gross receipts. If the organization uses membership fees as a means of selling admissions, merchandise, services, or the use of facilities to members of the general public who have no common goal or interest (other than the desire to purchase these things), then the payments for such fees will be gross receipts, not membership fees.[161]

Identifying precisely who a payor is also may be significant for purposes of arriving at a favorable public support percentage. In one instance, a nonprofit blood bank entered into agreements with hospitals it supplied with blood, by which the hospitals were responsible for collecting charges from the patients and reimbursing the blood bank. Because of the existence of an agency relationship, the amounts paid to the hospitals were treated as

---

156. The term person, as used in IRC § 509(a)(2)(A)(ii), includes IRC § 509(a)(1) organizations, so that, for example, rent paid to a tax-exempt medical center by related hospitals constitutes support subject to the $5,000/1 percent limitation (Gen. Couns. Mem. 39104).
157. Reg. § 1.509(a)-3(b)(1).
158. Reg. § 1.509(a)-3(f).
159. Reg. § 1.509(a)-3(g)(1).
160. Reg. § 1.509(a)-3(g)(2). For example, Medicare and Medicaid payments made to healthcare organizations constitute gross receipts from the conduct of a related activity rather than grants (Rev. Rul. 83-153, 1983-2 C.B. 48).
161. Reg. § 1.509(a)-3(h)(1).

though paid directly by the patients to the blood bank. Thus, each patient was considered a separate payor for purposes of the $5,000 or 1 percent support test.[162] Similarly, because Medicare and Medicaid patients control the recipients of the payments by their choice of a healthcare provider, each patient (rather than a governmental unit) is considered a payor for purposes of this support test.[163]

The phrase government *bureau or similar agency*[164] means a specialized operating (rather than policy-making or administrative) unit of the executive, judicial, or legislative branch of government, usually a subdivision of a department of government. Therefore, an organization receiving gross receipts from both a policy-making or administrative unit (e.g., the Agency for International Development, AID) and an operational unit of a department (e.g., the Bureau for Latin America, an operating unit within AID) is treated as receiving gross receipts from two agencies, with the amount from each separately subject to the $5,000 or 1 percent limitation.

Support from a disqualified person, including a substantial contributor,[165] is also excluded—in its entirety—from the numerator of the public support fraction under the service provider public charity rules. A *substantial contributor* is a person who contributes or bequeaths an aggregate amount of more than $5,000 to a charitable organization, where that amount is more than 2 percent of the total contributions and bequests received by the organization before the close of its tax year in which the contribution or bequest from the person is received.[166] Thus, transfers from a substantial contributor (or any other type of disqualified person) cannot qualify as public support under the service provider public charity rules.[167] Grants from governmental units, public institutions, and donative publicly supported charities,[168] however, are not subject to this rule, even if the grantor meets the $5,000/2 percent test for substantial contributor status,[169] unless the grant is in fact an indirect contribution that was earmarked by a disqualified person as being for the benefit of the

---

162. Rev. Rul. 75-387, 1975-2 C.B. 216.
163. Rev. Rul. 83-153, 1983-2 C.B. 48.
164. Reg. § 1.509(a)-3(i).
165. See § 4.1.
166. IRC § 507(d)(2)(A).
167. Since the concept of *disqualified person* is inapplicable in the context of the donative publicly supported charity (see § 15.4), however, a contribution from a person who would be a disqualified person under the service provider public charity rules may be, in whole or in part, public support under the donative public charity rules.
168. See §§ 15.3, 15.4.
169. Reg. § 1.509(a)-3(j). A grant from another service provider publicly supported organization that meets the substantial contributor test, however, would be excluded from the numerator of the public support fraction under this rule.

service provider publicly supported charity.[170] Thus, under current law, distributions from donor-advised funds sponsored by donative publicly supported charities are not excluded from the numerator of the public support fraction, even if a substantial contributor has advisory privileges with respect to the donor-advised fund.[171]

Sponsorship payments that are acknowledged by the tax-exempt organization without quantitative and qualitative information so as to avoid classification as advertising revenue[172] can be treated as contributions for public support purposes.[173] This parallels rules applicable in the donative publicly supported charity context.[174]

(b) Investment Income Test

To meet the *investment income test*, an organization seeking to avoid private foundation classification as a service provider publicly supported charity, must normally receive not more than one-third of its support from the sum of (1) gross investment income,[175] including interest, dividends, payments with respect to securities loans, rents, and royalties, and (2) any excess of the amount of unrelated business taxable income over the amount of the tax on that income.[176] To qualify under this test, an organization must construct a *gross investment income fraction*, with the amount of gross investment income and any unrelated income (less the tax paid on it) received constituting the numerator of the fraction and the total amount of support received being the denominator.[177] In certain instances, it may be necessary to distinguish between *gross receipts* and *gross investment income*.[178] For example, interest income earned on a portfolio of microloans that pay dividend and interest income is gross receipts from exempt function activity, not investment income for this purpose.[179]

---

170. Reg. § 1.509(a)-3(j).
171. The Treasury Department and the IRS are considering changes to Reg. § 1.509(a)-3(j) that would treat distributions from donor-advised funds as coming from the donor that funded the donor-advised fund for purposes of applying the rule excluding contributions from a substantial contributor from public support (Notice 2017-73, 2017-51 I.R.B. 562 § 5).
172. Reg. § 513-4(c)(2)(iv).
173. Reg. § 1.509(a)-3(f)(1).
174. See § 15.4(c).
175. IRC § 509(e).
176. IRC § 509(a)(2)(B).
177. Reg. § 1.509(a)-3(a)(3).
178. Reg. § 1.509(a)-3(m).
179. Priv. Ltr. Rul. 200508018.

§ 15.5 SERVICE PROVIDER PUBLICLY SUPPORTED CHARITIES

A tax-exempt charitable organization with more than one unrelated business may aggregate its net income and net losses from all unrelated businesses for purposes of determining whether the organization is publicly supported under these rules.[180] That is, an organization may opt to not apply the bucketing rule[181] in this context.

In two instances, amounts received by a service provider publicly supported charity retain their character as gross investment income (that is, are not treated as gifts or contributions) to the extent that the amounts are characterized as gross investment income in the possession of the distributing organization. This rule applies to distributions from (1) an organization seeking classification as a supporting organization[182] by reason of its support of the would-be publicly supported organization, or (2) a charitable trust, corporation, fund, or association or a split-interest trust,[183] which is required by its governing instrument or otherwise to distribute, or which normally does distribute at least 25 percent of its adjusted net income to the putative publicly supported organization, and where the distribution normally comprises at least 5 percent of the would-be publicly supported organization's adjusted net income. Where an organization, as described here, makes distributions to more than one putative service provider publicly supported charity, the amount of gross investment income deemed distributed is prorated among the distributees.[184] Further, where this type of an organization expends funds to provide goods, services, or facilities for the direct benefit of a putative service provider publicly supported charity, the amounts are treated as gross investment income to the beneficiary organization to the extent that the amounts are so characterized in the possession of the organization distributing the funds.[185]

As noted, these rules provide that an organization having or seeking nonprivate foundation status as a service provider publicly supported charity may not normally receive more than one-third of its support each tax year from a combination of gross investment income and any excess of unrelated business taxable income over the tax on that income.[186] This provision arose in 1975[187] because the Senate adopted amendments to postpone depreciation recapture where a controlled subsidiary operating an unrelated trade or

---

180. Reg. § 1.509(a)-3(a)(3)(i), (4).
181. See § 11.5(b).
182. See § 15.6.
183. IRC § 4947(a)(2). See Chapter 3.
184. Reg. § 1.509(a)-5(a)(1).
185. Reg. § 1.509(a)-5(a)(2).
186. IRC § 509(a)(2)(B)(ii).
187. Pub. L. No. 94-81, § 3, 89 Stat. 417 (1975).

business is liquidated into a parent tax-exempt corporation.[188] The Senate acted in this regard for the benefit of the Colonial Williamsburg Foundation, which liquidated a wholly owned subsidiary in 1970 so as to qualify as a publicly supported charity under these rules. The House of Representatives responded with another amendment,[189] however, to treat income from an unrelated trade or business acquired by an organization after June 30, 1975, the same as investment income for these purposes.[190] The House amendment was designed to prevent a change of form, as to the operation of an unrelated business to enable a charitable organization to convert from a private foundation to a publicly supported charity—albeit grandfathering in prior transactions such as the Colonial Williamsburg liquidation.

(c) Unusual Grants

Under the *unusual grant* rule, a contribution may be excluded from the numerator of the one-third support fraction and from the denominator of both the one-third support and one-third gross investment income fractions. When the inclusion of this type of gift in the public support calculation would cause the loss of public charity status, the exception is important. A grant is unusual if it is a substantial contribution or bequest from a disinterested party that is attracted by the publicly supported nature of the organization, is unusual or unexpected in its amount, and by reason if its size would adversely affect the status of the organization as normally being publicly supported.[191]

(i) Unusual Grant Factors. The following factors are considered in determining whether a grant (or contribution) is an unusual one; no single factor is necessarily determinative:[192]

1. Whether the grant was made by any person, or a related disqualified person,[193] who created the organization, previously contributed a substantial part of its support or endowment, or stood in a position of

---

188. IRC §§ 1245(b)(7), 1250(d)(9). See 121 Cong. Rec. 22264 (1975).
189. IRC § 509(a)(2)(B)(ii).
190. See 121 Cong. Rec. 24812 (1975). Also, Reg. § 1.509(a)-3(a)(3).
191. Reg. §§ 1.170A-9(f)(6)(ii), 1.509(a)-3(c)(3). The term *unusual grant* is somewhat of a misnomer; a better term would have been *unexpected grant*, and the term should also reflect the fact that it also applies with respect to contributions.
192. Reg. § 1.509(a)-3(c)(4). The same factors are considered in determining whether a grant or contribution to a donative publicly supported charity (see § 15.4(c)) is an unusual grant or contribution (Reg. § 1.170A-9(f)(6)(iii)).
193. For purposes of this factor, a *related disqualified person* is any person standing in a relationship to the grantor that is described in IRC § 4946(a)(1)(C)-(G). See Chapter 4.

§ 15.5 SERVICE PROVIDER PUBLICLY SUPPORTED CHARITIES

authority, such as a foundation manager,[194] with respect to the organization (that is, an *interested person*). A grant made by a disinterested person will ordinarily be given more favorable consideration than one made by an interested person. Additionally, continued direct or indirect control of the organization by the grantor, or any related disqualified person(s), will weigh against the finding of an unusual grant.

2. Whether the grant is a bequest or an inter vivos transfer, with more favorable consideration given to a bequest.

3. Whether the grant was in the form of cash, readily marketable securities, or assets which further the exempt purposes of the organization, such as a gift of a painting to a museum, with less favorable consideration given to grants in the form of property that is illiquid, difficult to dispose of, or not useful in furthering the organization's exempt activities.

4. Except in the case of a new organization, whether, prior to the receipt of the grant, the organization had an actual program of public solicitation and exempt activities and was able to attract a significant amount of public support.

5. Whether the organization may reasonably be expected to attract a significant amount of public support after the grant. Continued reliance on unusual grants to fund an organization's current operating expenses is considered evidence that the organization cannot reasonably be expected to attract future public support, and therefore a grant is more likely to be viewed as an unusual one if it provides new endowment (rather than operational) funds.

6. Whether, prior to the grant, the organization met the public support test without having to rely on any exclusions of unusual grants. Reliance on the exclusion of prior unusual grants to meet the public support test weighs against the finding of another unusual grant.

7. Whether the organization has a representative governing body.[195] Control of the organization by related parties (especially those related to the grantor) weighs against the finding of an unusual grant.

---

194. For purposes of this factor, a *foundation manager* includes an officer or director of the grantee organization or other person described in IRC § 4946(b)(1).

195. A representative governing body is one that is composed of public officials, or individuals chosen by public officials acting in their capacity as such; of persons having special knowledge in the particular field or discipline in which the organization is operating; of community leaders, such as elected officials, clergy members, and educators; or, in the case of a membership organization, of individuals elected pursuant to the organization's governing instrument or bylaws by a broadly based membership (Reg. § 1.509(a)-3(d)(3)(i)).

8. Whether any material restrictions or conditions[196] are placed on the transfer. Material encumbrances on the use of the grant funds or assets weighs against the finding of an unusual grant.

The IRS applied the unusual grant rule in the case of an organization that received a large inter vivos gift of undeveloped land from a disinterested party, with the condition that the land be used in perpetuity to further its tax-exempt purpose of preserving the natural resources of a particular town. The IRS ruled that the gift constituted an unusual grant and, thus, that the organization's nonprivate foundation status was not adversely affected, even though all of the aforementioned factors were not satisfied and the organization had previously received an unusual grant ruling. The IRS cited the following facts as being of "particular importance": The donor was a disinterested party, the organization's operating expenses were paid for primarily through public support, the gift of the land furthered the tax-exempt purpose of the organization, and the contribution was in the nature of new endowment funds because the organization was relatively new.[197]

There has been a flurry of favorable private letter rulings in recent years concerning unusual grants. In one instance, a proposed grant was ruled to constitute an unusual grant; it indeed had an unusual feature, which was that the grant request was made by an unrelated third party, without the private foundation's knowledge.[198] A bequest to a community foundation was determined to be an unusual grant where its size was unusual compared with the recipient's financial support levels, it would have adversely affected the recipient's status a public charity, the decedent had not previously contributed a substantial part of the recipient's support, and the bequest was not burdened with any material restrictions.[199] In another case, factors supporting

---

196. Reg. § 1.507-2(a)(7). The following factors are not considered to be material restrictions or conditions with respect to a grant: the grant gives the grantor naming rights; the grant is for a restricted purpose, but that purpose is consistent with the charitable or other basis for the exempt status of the grantee; the grant funds are administered in an identifiable or separate fund, distributions of principal from which are restricted for a specified period, provided the grantee is the legal and equitable owner of the fund and the grantee's governing body exercises ultimate and direct authority and control over the fund (Reg. § 1.507-2(a)(7)(iii)). In contrast, the retention by the grantor of the right to control the timing of the expenditure of grant funds (or earnings thereon) (other than a restriction on principal distributions), or the recipients of such grant funds (or earnings thereon) (other than by designation in the grant agreement of particular charitable organizations as recipients), as, for example, by a power of appointment, is considered a material restriction or condition with respect to a grant (Reg. § 1.507-2(a)(7)(iv)).
197. Rev. Rul. 76-440, 1976-2 C.B. 621.
198. Priv. Ltr. Rul. 201952009.
199. Priv. Ltr. Rul. 201507024.

§ 15.5 SERVICE PROVIDER PUBLICLY SUPPORTED CHARITIES

the finding of an unusual grant were that the prospective grantor was a disinterested party, did not exercise control over the prospective grantee, and was not a disqualified person with respect to the grantee; the prospective grantee had a public solicitation program and a representative governing body.[200] In yet another case, a private foundation's transfer of a significant amount of artwork to a public charity operating a sculpture park and museum was found to be an unusual grant; again, the prospective grantee had a fundraising effort and a representative governing body, although it had used the unusual grant exception once before.[201]

A tax-exempt charitable organization provided injured special operations combat veterans with outdoor recreational programs to, in part, encourage and foster rehabilitation, recovery, and transition. Having learned of these programs, another organization allowed this entity use of its property in furtherance of these veterans' assistance programs. The second entity decided to dissolve and distribute its remaining assets to the veterans' organization. Ruling that this assets transfer would be an unusual grant, the IRS held that the prior relationship between the entities, concerning use of the land, was "incidental" and, although there was some board overlap, the veterans' group had sufficient independent members. In so ruling, the IRS said that the transfer was in the nature of a bequest.[202]

In another ruling, the criteria for unusual grants were stretched.[203] The grantor was the founder of, and controlled, the grantee. The grantor was a tax-exempt cemetery association.[204] The IRS rationalized that the grant was part of the association's "efforts to reorganize itself and separate out charitable portions of its activities from its primary exempt function" (although the relevance of that observation is unclear). The transfer was of real estate. A majority of the association's board was said (without any stated evidence) to be "representative of the community rather than of any selfish interest" in the association and "may be expected to act in [the grantee's] best interest and not be unduly influenced by their affiliation" with the association.

As part of reorganizations of charitable entities, it is common for one charitable entity to transfer assets to a new parent or new subsidiary. Because the transfer is part of the reorganization and where the amount is unusual, the IRS typically will apply the exclusion for unusual grants to allow the transferee to disregard the amount transferred in determining its status as a publicly

---

200. Priv. Ltr. Rul. 201512004.
201. Priv. Ltr. Rul. 201516069.
202. Priv. Ltr. Rul. 201923027.
203. Priv. Ltr. Rul. 201711014.
204. That is, an organization described in IRC § 501(c)(13). See *Tax-Exempt Organizations* § 19.6.

supported entity.[205] The IRS typically reaches the same conclusion where an organization that is dissolving transfers assets or dissolution proceeds to another public charity.[206] Likewise, a terminating distribution from a private foundation to a public charity will ordinarily constitute an unusual grant.[207]

Thus, where a supporting organization was merged into a supported organization,[208] transferring cash, marketable securities, venture capital, and private equity investments, the IRS ruled that this distribution would be an unusual grant, in part because the "size and method of [the] contribution is unusual compared to [the organization's] typical level of support" and the transfer was a "one-time occurrence."[209]

Likewise, in a situation involving the reorganization of a publicly supported charity resulting in a new publicly supported charity and a new supporting organization with respect to them, the IRS ruled that transfers of assets from the original publicly supported charity to the new one, as well as payments to the new supporting organization, would qualify as unusual grants.[210] In so ruling, the IRS indicated that grants from related charitable organizations should be treated differently from grants "from outside persons" when applying the first of the unusual grant factors. The IRS also emphasized the facts that the assets transferred to the new publicly supported charity would further its charitable purposes and that it was expected to attract significant future public support, such that it would not be dependent upon a repetition of the unusual grant; similarly, the payments to the new supporting organization were "for specific start-up purposes," and therefore were not expected to recur.

From time to time, the IRS will find that a proposed grant or contribution is not an unusual one.[211] As an illustration of a proposed contribution that was not sufficiently unusual, an individual agreed to fund the construction of a new facility of a charity if the gift was classified as an unusual grant. The prospective donor had provided a majority of this entity's funding since its inception. The chair and president of the charity is the donor's spouse. The executive director of the charity is the donor's daughter. The IRS concluded that the proposed gift had not been attracted by reason of the charity's publicly supported nature but rather by the charity's historical relationship with the donor. The agency concluded that the proposed gift was "not unusual or unexpected" and that the donor "has shown a history of providing support

---

205. E.g., Priv. Ltr. Rul. 8510068.
206. E.g., Priv. Ltr. Rul. 202309021.
207. E.g., Priv. Ltr. Rul. 8019084. See § 13.3.
208. See § 15.6.
209. Priv. Ltr. Rul. 201909015.
210. Priv. Ltr. Rul. 200437036.
211. E.g., Priv. Ltr. Rul. 201240036.

§ 15.5 SERVICE PROVIDER PUBLICLY SUPPORTED CHARITIES

[to this charity], in significant amounts, to the point where the proposed [gift] of the given amount is not unusual."[212]

A private foundation proposed a grant to a public charity to provide permanent support for two of the charity's core programs. There would not be any material restrictions or conditions regarding this grant other than typical restrictions concerning the establishment and maintenance of an endowment fund. The foundation previously granted a substantial part of the charity's financial support. The IRS concluded that, due to the historical relationship between the parties, the proposed grant was not "unusual or unexpected."[213] Indeed, the IRS added, "[s]ubsequent grants from the same donor [i.e., grantor] are logically more usual and more expected."

(ii) Safe Harbor Criteria. The IRS has promulgated "safe harbor" criteria that, if satisfied, automatically cause a contribution or grant to be considered *unusual* if the gift or grant, by reason of its size, would otherwise adversely affect the recipient organization's public status. These criteria are that the (1) grant (or contribution) is not made by the organization's founder or a substantial contributor,[214] or a related person; (2) grant is not made by a person who is in a position of authority with respect to the organization, a person with the ability to exercise control over the organization, or a related person; (3) grant is in the form of cash, readily marketable securities, or exempt-function assets; (4) recipient organization has received a favorable determination letter as to its publicly supported status; (5) recipient organization is actively engaged in exempt activities; (6) grantor has not imposed material restrictions or conditions[215] in connection with the grant; (7) terms and conditions of the grant are expressly limited to underwriting no more than one year's operating expenses (if the grant is for expenses); and (8) grant is not used to finance capital items.[216] A grant would adversely affect the publicly supported status of an organization only if it otherwise meets the support test in the year being tested without taking the grant into account.[217]

(iii) Requests for Advance IRS Rulings. A request for advance approval that a prospective grant or contribution constitutes an unusual grant may (but

---

212. Priv. Ltr. Rul. 201239011.
213. Priv. Ltr. Rul. 201850023.
214. See § 4.1.
215. See § 13.3(b), (c).
216. Rev. Proc. 2018-32, 2018-23 I.R.B. 739 § 7.03(1).
217. *Id.* § 7.03(2). These rules do not preclude a potential donee or grantee organization from requesting a determination from the IRS as to whether a proposed gift or grant, with or without the characteristics, will constitute an unusual gift or grant. *Id.* § 7.03(3).

PUBLIC CHARITIES

is not required to) be sought from the IRS by filing Form 8940.[218] The following information and documentation must be submitted with the request: (1) explanations of how the grantee was selected because of its publicly supported nature; why the amount of the grant is unusual or unexpected; how the grant, due to its size, would adversely affect the grantee's status as a publicly supported organization; whether the grant was made by a disqualified person who created the grantee, previously contributed a substantial amount of its support or endowment, or stood in a position of authority, such as a foundation manager, with respect to the grantee, and whether such person(s) continue to exercise control, directly or indirectly, over the grantee; the extent to which the grantee has a representative governing body; and whether there are any material restrictions or conditions on the grant; (2) the name of the grantor, the amount of the grant, the timing of the grant payments, and the purpose(s) for which the grant funds will be used; (3) whether the grant was a bequest or an inter vivos transfer; (4) a description of the form or format of the expected grant (for example, cash, readily marketable securities, or assets that further the grantee's exempt purposes); (5) descriptions of the grantee's public solicitation programs, including how much public support it received from such efforts, how the grantee expects to attract public support following the grant, and whether the grantee was able to meet the public support test without the benefit of any exclusions of unusual grants prior to receiving the grant.[219]

The IRS regularly issues rulings in response to such requests.[220]

§ 15.6 SUPPORTING ORGANIZATIONS

Another category of charitable organization that is deemed not to be a private foundation is the *supporting organization*.[221]

Charitable supporting organizations usually are those entities that are not themselves publicly supported or qualified public institutions, but are

---

218. Reg. §§ 1.170A-9(f)(6)(iv), 1.509(a)-3(c)(5). Form 8940 must be submitted electronically at www.pay.gov; the user fee for this type of request is currently $550 (Rev. Proc. 2023-5, 2023-1 I.R.B. 265 §§ 4.02(6), 7.02 and App. A (Schedule of User Fees), as modified by Rev. Proc. 2023-12, 2023-17 I.R.B. 768 §§ 3.01, 3.03).
219. Instructions for Form 8940 (Apr. 2023), Schedule E. For the relevant unusual grant factors, see Reg. §§ 1.170A-9(f)(6)(iii), 1.509(a)-3(c)(4) and § 15.5(c)(i).
220. E.g., Priv. Ltr. Rul. 202313010.
221. IRC § 509(a)(3); Reg. § 1.509(a)-4(a). The U.S. Tax Court concluded that an organization claiming to be a supporting organization (with that status ignored by the court), that passively rented commercial real estate and distributed its net revenue to a public charity, was instead a (nonexempt) feeder organization (IRC § 502; see *Tax-Exempt Organizations* § 28.15) (CRSO v. Commissioner, 128 T.C. 153 (2007)).

§ 15.6 SUPPORTING ORGANIZATIONS

instead sufficiently related to one or more organizations that are publicly supported or are otherwise public entities so that the requisite degree of public control and involvement is deemed present. Thus, the supported (benefited) organization is usually a public charity,[222] while the organization that is not a private foundation by virtue of these rules is characterized as a supporting organization.[223] Certain types of noncharitable tax-exempt organizations may be supported organizations.[224] The supported organization generally may be a foreign organization as long as it otherwise qualifies as an eligible entity.[225]

A supporting organization must be organized, and at all times thereafter operated, exclusively for the benefit of, to perform the functions of, or to carry out the purposes of one or more eligible supported organizations.[226] Thus, if the IRS discovers that a supported organization is not a qualified one, it will revoke the organization's supporting organization status.

A supporting organization also must be operated, supervised, or controlled by one or more qualified supported organizations,[227] supervised or controlled in connection with one or more such organizations, or operated in connection with one or more such organizations.[228] These organizations are referred to as Type I, II, or III organizations, respectively.[229] However, inasmuch as Type III supporting organizations are classified as either functionally integrated Type III supporting organizations or nonfunctionally integrated Type III supporting organizations,[230] there are four types of supporting organizations.[231]

A supporting organization must not be controlled directly or indirectly by one or more disqualified persons (other than foundation managers or eligible public charitable organizations).[232]

A supporting organization may evolve out of a public or publicly supported charity.[233] To qualify as a supporting organization, a charitable organization must meet both an organizational test and an operational test.[234]

---

222. See §§ 15.3-15.5.
223. Reg. § 1.509(a)-4(a)(5).
224. See § 15.6(l).
225. Rev. Rul. 74-229, 1974-1 C.B. 142.
226. IRC § 509(a)(3)(A); Reg. § 1.509(a)-4(a)(2).
227. The term *supported organization* is defined in IRC § 509(f)(3). Also, Reg. § 1.509(a)-4(a)(6).
228. IRC § 509(a)(3)(B). Also, Reg. §§ 1.509(a)-4(a)(3), 4(f)(2).
229. The *Type III supporting organization* is defined in IRC § 4943(f)(5)(A).
230. IRC § 4943(f)(5)(B); Reg. § 1.509(a)-4(i)(1)(iii)(B), (5); see § 15.6(g).
231. In general, Reg. § 1.509(a)-4(f)(4), (g)(1)(i).
232. IRC § 509(a)(3)(C); Reg. § 1.509(a)-(a)(4). See § 15.6(j).
233. E.g., Priv. Ltr. Rul. 8825116.
234. Reg. § 1.509(a)-4(b)(1).

(a) Organizational Test

A supporting organization must be organized exclusively to support or benefit one or more eligible supported organizations.[235] Its articles of organization[236] must limit its purposes to one or more of the purposes that are permissible for a supporting organization,[237] may not expressly empower the organization to engage in activities that are not in furtherance of these purposes, must state the specified organization or organizations on behalf of which it is to be operated, and may not expressly empower the organization to operate to support or benefit any other organizations.[238]

To qualify as a supporting organization, an organization's stated purposes may be as broad as, or more specific than, the purposes that are permissible for a supporting organization. Thus, an organization formed "for the benefit of" one or more eligible organizations will meet this organizational test, assuming the other requirements of the test are satisfied.[239] Similarly, articles that state that an organization is formed to perform the publishing functions of a specified university are sufficient to comply with this test.[240] An organization that is "operated, supervised, or controlled by" (Type I) or "supervised or controlled in connection with" (Type II) one or more eligible supported organizations to carry out their purposes will satisfy these requirements if the purposes as stated in its articles of organization are similar to, but no broader than, the purposes stated in the articles of the controlling organization or organizations.[241]

An organization will not meet this organizational test if its articles of organization expressly permit it to operate to support or benefit any organization other than its supported organization or organizations. The fact that the actual operations of the organization have been exclusively for the benefit of one or more eligible supported organizations is not sufficient to permit it to satisfy this organizational test.[242]

---

235. IRC § 509(a)(3)(A).
236. Reg. § 1.501(c)(3)-1(b)(2).
237. IRC § 509(a)(3)(A).
238. Reg. § 1.509(a)-4(c)(1). The U.S. Tax Court applied these regulations in concluding that an organization was not a supporting organization because the organizational documents of the entity expressly empowered it to benefit organizations other than specified publicly supported organizations (Trust U/W of Bella Mabury v. Commissioner, 80 T.C. 718 (1983)).
239. Reg. § 1.509(a)-4(c)(2).
240. Id.
241. Id.
242. Reg. § 1.509(a)-4(c)(3).

(b) Operational Test

A supporting organization must be operated exclusively to support or benefit one or more qualified supported organizations.[243] Unlike the definition of the term *exclusively* as applied in the context of charitable organizations generally, which means *primarily*,[244] the term *exclusively* in this context means *solely*.[245]

The supporting organization must engage solely in activities that support or benefit one or more eligible supported organizations.[246] These activities may include making payments to or for the use of, or providing services or facilities for, individual members of the charitable class benefited by the supported organization.[247] A supporting organization may make a payment indirectly through another unrelated organization to a member of a charitable class benefited by a specified public or publicly supported organization, but only where the payment constitutes a grant to an individual rather than a grant to an organization.[248] The IRS ruled that a supporting organization operating for the benefit of a community college may make grants to a capital fund for advancement of a business incubator program, because the resulting educational opportunities are expected to contribute importantly to the college's teaching program.[249]

An organization is regarded as operated exclusively to support or benefit one or more supported organizations even if it supports or benefits a charitable organization, other than a private foundation, that is operated, supervised, or controlled directly by or in connection with the supported organizations,[250] or that is a state college or university.[251] An organization will not be regarded as operated exclusively to support or benefit one or more supported organizations, however, if any part of its activities is in furtherance of a purpose other than supporting or benefiting one or more supported organizations.[252]

The concept of the supporting organization includes, but is not confined to, one that pays more than a suitable amount of its income to one or more eligible supported organizations. A supporting organization may carry on a discrete program or activity that supports or benefits one or more supported

---

243. IRC § 509(a)(3)(A).
244. See § 1.6.
245. Reg. § 1.509(a)-4(e)(1).
246. Reg. § 1.509(a)-4(e)(1), (2).
247. Reg. § 1.509(a)-4(e)(1).
248. Reg. § 1.509(a)-4(e)(1). The criteria used to distinguish grants to individuals from grants to organizations are the same as those used in the private foundation taxable expenditures context (Reg. § 53.4945-4(a)(4); see Chapter 9).
249. Priv. Ltr. Rul. 200614030.
250. That is, other supporting organizations that also support or benefit one or more of the supporting organization's supported organizations.
251. Reg. § 1.509(a)-4(e)(1).
252. *Id.*

organizations. For example, a supporting organization, supportive of the academic endeavors of the medical school at a university, was used to operate a faculty practice plan in furtherance of the teaching, research, and service programs of the school.[253] As another illustration, a supporting organization with respect to an entity that provided residential placement for mentally and physically disabled adults had as its supportive programs the construction and operation of a facility to provide employment suitable to disabled persons and to establish an information center about the conditions of disabled individuals.[254] A supporting organization may also engage in fundraising activities, such as solicitations of contributions and grants, special events, and unrelated trade or business activities, to raise funds for one or more supported organizations or for other permissible beneficiaries.[255]

Thus, the operational test applicable to supporting organizations does not allow the supporting organization much leeway in engaging in activities other than those that directly support or benefit one or more eligible supported organizations. An example in the tax regulations, however, states that a supporting organization may make a "small annual general purpose" grant to a public charity that is operated in connection with the supported organization and that is engaged in activities "similar to" those carried on by the supported organization. This function is characterized in the regulations as "assist[ing] in the overall program" carried on by the supported organization.[256] Nonetheless, a grant to an organization that is not to one of the supporting organization's specified supported organizations will prevent it from complying with this test and thus from being a supporting organization,[257] unless the grant is earmarked for individual members of the charitable class benefited by the supported organization, or is to another supporting organization that supports the same supported organization(s).[258]

A supporting organization has many characteristics of a private foundation, most notably, the absence of any requirement to be publicly supported. Thus, like a private foundation, a supporting organization can be funded entirely by investment income; it can satisfy the operational test by engaging in investment activities (assuming charitable ends are being served).[259]

---

253. Priv. Ltr. Rul. 9434041, superseded by Priv. Ltr. Rul. 9442025.
254. Priv. Ltr. Rul. 9438013.
255. Reg. § 1.509(a)-4(e)(2).
256. *Id.*, Example 4.
257. *Id.*, Example 3.
258. Reg. § 1.509(a)-4(e)(1).
259. This point is illustrated by the case styled Henry E. & Nancy Horton Bartels Trust for the Benefit of the University of New Haven v. United States, 209 F.3d 147 (2d Cir. 2000). This aspect of the law does not, however, cause the investment activity to be an exempt function to the extent that the unrelated debt-financed income rules (see § 11.4) become inapplicable.

§ 15.6 SUPPORTING ORGANIZATIONS

This being the state of the law as to the supporting organization operational test, it was surprising to learn that the IRS retroactively revoked[260] the tax-exempt and public charity status of a supporting organization inasmuch as the organization never made any grants to its supported organization, stating that this failure to fund was a violation of the operational test applicable to charitable organizations[261] as a condition of exemption.[262] Both statuses were lost because, as the ruling stated the matter, the organization "failed to contribute any contributions to the intended supported organization." The IRS thus confused the general operational test, used for purposes of qualification for exemption, and the supporting organization rules. From an exemption and supporting organization status standpoint, this organization did not violate any rule. As noted, it can be a charitable purpose for an organization to hold property, including investment property, for another charitable organization; it is common, for example, for a supporting organization to hold an endowment fund. There is no general payout requirement for supporting organizations other than in the case of a nonfunctionally integrated Type III supporting organization.[263]

(c) Specified Public Charities

A supporting organization must be organized and operated exclusively to support or benefit one or more *specified* supported organizations.[264] This specification must be in the supporting organization's articles of organization, although the manner of the specification depends on which of the types of relationships with one or more eligible supported organizations is involved.[265] Generally it is expected that the articles of organization of the supporting organization will designate (i.e., *specify*) each of the specified supported organizations by name.[266] If the relationship is one of *operated, supervised, or controlled by* (Type I) or *supervised or controlled in connection with* (Type II), however, designation by name is not required as long as the articles of organization of the supporting organization require that it be operated to support or benefit one or more beneficiary organizations that are designated by class or purpose. The organizations so designated must include one or more supported organizations, as to which there is one of the foregoing two relationships (without designating the organizations by name), or public institutions or publicly supported charities

---

260. See § 12.7(b).
261. See § 1.6.
262. Priv. Ltr. Rul. 200903081.
263. See § 15.6(g).
264. IRC § 509(a)(3)(A).
265. Reg. § 1.509(a)-4(d)(1).
266. Reg. § 1.509(a)-4(d)(2)(i).

that are closely related in purpose or function to supported organizations, as to which there is one of the two relationships (again, without designating the organizations by name).[267] In contrast, if the relationship is one of *operated in connection with* (Type III), generally the supporting organization must designate the specified supported organizations by name.[268]

Where the relationship is other than *operated in connection with*, the articles of organization of a supporting organization may (1) permit the substitution of one eligible organization within a designated class for another eligible organization either in the same or a different class designated in the articles of organization, (2) permit the supporting organization to operate for the benefit of new or additional eligible organizations of the same or a different class designated in the articles of organization, or (3) permit the supporting organization to vary the amount of its support among different eligible supported organizations within the class or classes of organizations designated by the articles of organization.[269]

These rules were illustrated in the reasoning followed by the IRS in classifying a tax-exempt community trust[270] as a supporting organization. The community trust was created by a publicly supported community chest to hold endowment funds and to distribute the income from the endowment to support public or publicly supported charities in a particular geographic area. A majority of the trustees of the community trust were appointed by the governing body of the community chest. The trust was required by the terms of its governing instrument to distribute its income to public or publicly supported charities in a particular area, so that, the IRS held, even though the public or publicly supported charities were not specified by name, the trust qualified as a supporting organization because the community chest was specified by the requisite class or purpose, in that the trust was organized and operated exclusively for the benefit of this class of organizations. Inasmuch as the community chest appointed a majority of the trust's trustees, the trust was ruled to be *operated, supervised, or controlled by* the community chest so that the *specification* requirement was met.[271]

---

267. Reg. § 1.509(a)-4(d)(2)(i)(a), (b). Supporting organization classification will be denied to an organization where, after payment of a certain amount to qualified supported organizations, the supporting organization requirements would no longer be met (Rev. Rul. 79-197, 1979-2 C.B. 204).

268. Reg. § 1.509(a)-4(d)(4)(i). In one case, the U.S. Tax Court generally ignored these regulations and found compliance with the specificity requirement of IRC § 509(a)(3)(A) merely by reading the statutory provision in light of the facts of the case (Warren M. Goodspeed Scholarship Fund v. Commissioner, 70 T.C. 515 (1978)).

269. Reg. § 1.509(a)-4(d)(3).

270. Reg. § 1.170A-9(f)(11); see § 15.4(e).

271. Rev. Rul. 81-43, 1981-1 C.B. 350.

§ 15.6 SUPPORTING ORGANIZATIONS

In another case, an organization, attempting to qualify pursuant to the "supervised or controlled in connection with" category of supporting organization, was unable to satisfy the "class or purpose" test. This organization, according to its articles of incorporation, existed to conduct and support activities "for the benefit of, to perform the functions of, and/or to carry out the purposes of" other organizations "which support, promote and/or perform public health and/or Christian objectives, including but not limited to Christian evangelism, edification, and stewardship." A court of appeals agreed with the IRS and took the position that the "class or purpose" exception applies only where the class of beneficiaries is "readily identifiable."[272] The appellate court noted that, in this charitable organization's articles of incorporation, there is no "geographic limit" and no "limit by type" of supported organization.[273] The court agreed with the government that "it would be difficult, if not impossible, to determine whether the [f]oundation will receive oversight from a readily identifiable class of publicly supported organizations."[274] The organization retained its tax-exempt status but as a private foundation.

An organization that is *operated in connection with* one or more eligible supported organizations (Type III) may satisfy the specification requirement even if its articles of organization permit an eligible supported organization that is designated by class or purpose to be substituted for the supported organizations designated by name in its articles, but "only if such substitution is conditioned upon the occurrence of an event which is beyond the control of the supporting organization."[275] This type of event is stated as being one such as loss of tax exemption, substantial failure or abandonment of operations, or dissolution of the eligible supported organization or organization designated in the articles of organization.[276] In one case, the trustee of a charitable entity had the authority to substitute other charitable beneficiaries for those named in its articles whenever, in the trustee's judgment, the charitable uses had become "unnecessary, undesirable, impracticable, impossible, or no longer adapted to the needs of the public." A court held that the organization failed the organizational test and thus was a private foundation because the events that could trigger the substitution of beneficiaries were "within the trustee's control for all practical purposes" since the standard "require[d] the trustee to make a judgment as to what is desirable and what are the needs of the public."[277] The court stated

---

272. Polm Family Foundation v. United States, 644 F.3d 406, 409 (D.C. Cir. 2011).
273. *Id.* at 409-10.
274. *Id.*
275. Reg. § 1.509(a)-4(d)(4)(i)(a).
276. *Id.*
277. William F., Mable E., and Margaret K. Quarrie Charitable Fund v. Commissioner, 70 T.C. 182, 187 (1978), *aff'd*, 603 F.2d 1274 (7th Cir. 1979).

PUBLIC CHARITIES

that the organizational test is essential to qualification of entities as supporting organizations because the "public scrutiny [necessary to obviate the need for governmental regulation as a private foundation] derives from the publicly supported beneficiaries, which, in turn, oversee the activities of the supporting organization" and "this oversight function is substantially weakened if the trustee has broad authority to substitute beneficiaries and, thus, it is essential that such authority be strictly limited."[278]

A supporting organization that has one or more supported organizations designated by name in its articles of organization may have a provision in the articles that permits it to operate for the benefit of a beneficiary organization that is not a supported organization, but only if the supporting organization is currently operating for the benefit of a supported organization and the possibility of its operating for the benefit of an organization other than a supported organization is a "remote contingency."[279] Should that contingency occur, however, the supporting organization would then fail to meet this operational test.[280] Moreover, under these circumstances, the articles of organization of a supporting organization may permit it to vary the amount of its support between different designated organizations as long as it meets the requirements with respect to at least one beneficiary organization.[281]

A supporting organization will be deemed to meet the specification requirement even though its articles of organization do not designate each supported organization by name—despite the nature of the relationship—if there has been a "historic and continuing" relationship between the supporting organization and the supported organizations and, by reason of the relationship, there has developed a "substantial identity of interests" between the organizations.[282]

In general, the federal tax law is vague as to how a supported organization with respect to a supporting organization can be changed without loss of the supporting organization's public charity status. In a rare private letter ruling on the subject, the IRS ruled that a tax-exempt organization could retain its status as a supporting organization, notwithstanding a transaction in which a supported organization was substituted.[283] An exempt university caused a related support organization to become affiliated with another entity that also functions to support and benefit the university. This ruling is of limited utility

---

278. *Id.*, 70 T.C. at 190.
279. Reg. § 1.509(a)-4(d)(4)(i)(b).
280. Reg. § 1.509(a)-4(d)(4)(ii).
281. Reg. § 1.509(a)-4(d)(4)(i)(c).
282. Reg. § 1.509(a)-4(d)(2)(iv). E.g., Cockerline Memorial Fund v. Commissioner, 86 T.C. 53 (1986).
283. Priv. Ltr. Rul. 200731034.

§ 15.6 SUPPORTING ORGANIZATIONS

in planning a supporting organization substitution, however, because, under the facts of the ruling, the functions of the supporting organization remained essentially the same, and it continued to support the university indirectly.

(d) Required Relationships

As noted, to qualify as a supporting organization, an organization must be operated, supervised, or controlled by or in connection with one or more eligible supported organizations.[284] These types of relationships must be one of the following: (1) operated, supervised, or controlled by (Type I); (2) supervised or controlled in connection with (Type II); or (3) operated in connection with, one or more eligible supported organizations (Type III).[285]

Thus, if an organization does not stand in at least one of the required relationships to one or more eligible supported organizations, it cannot qualify as a supporting organization.[286] Regardless of the applicable relationship, it must be ensured that the supporting organization will be responsive to the needs or demands of one or more eligible supported organizations and that the supporting organization will constitute an integral part of or maintain a significant involvement in the operations of one or more qualified supported organizations.[287] These *responsiveness* and *integral part* requirements are more specifically defined in the federal tax regulations with respect to (Type III) supporting organizations operated in connection with one or more supporting organizations.[288]

(e) Type I: Operated, Supervised, or Controlled By

The distinguishing feature of the *operated, supervised, or controlled by* relationship between a supporting organization and one or more eligible supported organizations—a Type I supporting organization relationship—is the presence of a substantial degree of direction by one or more supported organizations over the conduct (policies, programs, and activities) of the supporting organization.[289] The requisite relationship is comparable to that of a subsidiary and a parent, where the subsidiary is under the direction of and accountable or responsible to the parent.[290]

---

284. IRC § 509(a)(3)(B).
285. Reg. § 1.509(a)-4(f)(2).
286. Reg. § 1.509(a)-4(f)(1).
287. Reg. § 1.509(a)-4(f)(3).
288. Reg. § 1.509(a)-4(i); see § 15.6(g).
289. Reg. §§ 1.509(a)-4(f)(4), (g)(1)(i).
290. Reg. § 1.509(a)-4(g)(1)(i).

This relationship is established by the fact that a majority of the officers, directors, or trustees of the supporting organization are appointed or elected by the governing body, members of the governing body, officers acting in their official capacity, or the membership of the supported organizations.[291] This relationship will be considered to exist with respect to one or more supported organizations and the supporting organization considered to operate *for the benefit of* one or more different supported organizations only where it can be demonstrated that the purposes of the former organizations are carried out by benefiting the latter organizations.[292]

A supporting organization will not qualify as a Type I entity for any tax year, however, if it accepts a contribution from a controlling donor.[293]

(f) Type II: Supervised or Controlled in Connection With

The distinguishing feature of the *supervised or controlled in connection with* relationship between a supporting organization and one or more eligible supported organizations—a Type II supporting organization relationship—is the presence of common supervision or control among the governing bodies of all organizations involved, such as the presence of common directors.[294] The requisite relationship is therefore comparable to a brother-sister corporate relationship. There must be common supervision or control by the persons supervising or controlling both the supporting organization and the supported organization(s) to ensure that the supporting organization will be responsive to the needs and requirements of the supported organization(s).[295] Therefore, in order to meet this requirement, the control or management of the supporting organization must be vested in the same individuals who control or manage the supported organizations.[296]

A supporting organization will not be considered to be in this relationship with one or more eligible supported organizations if it merely makes payments (mandatory or discretionary) to one or more named supported organizations, regardless of whether the obligation to make payments to the named beneficiaries is enforceable under state law and the supporting organization's governing instrument contains the private foundation rules provisions.[297] According to the regulations, this arrangement does not provide a sufficient

---

291. Reg. § 1.509(a)-4(g)(1)(i).
292. Reg. § 1.509(a)-4(g)(1)(ii).
293. See § 15.6(h).
294. Reg. §§ 1.509(a)-4(f)(4), (h)(1).
295. Reg. § 1.509(a)-4(h)(1).
296. *Id.*
297. IRC § 508(e)(1)(A), (B).

§ 15.6 SUPPORTING ORGANIZATIONS

connection between the payor organization and the needs and requirements of the supported organizations to constitute supervision or control in connection with these organizations.[298]

(g) Type III: Operated in Connection With

Qualification as a supporting organization by reason of the *operated in connection with* relationship—a Type III supporting organization relationship—entails the presence of the distinguishing feature by which the supporting organization is responsive to and significantly involved in the operations of one or more supported organizations.[299] A court nicely observed that this category of supporting organization involves the "least intimate" of the three types of relationships.[300] The Department of the Treasury and the IRS believe that most of the abuses concerning supporting organizations reside within this relationship. The IRS once viewed this relationship as the most tenuous one; the agency referred to these entities as "razor edge" organizations.[301] Statutory law changes enacted in 2006 and the subsequent development of tax regulations have had the effect of significantly tightening the Type III relationship.[302]

(i) Overview. An organization is a Type III supporting organization only if it meets five tests: (1) it is not disqualified by reason of the rules concerning acceptance of contributions from controlling donors,[303] (2) it does not support any foreign supported organizations,[304] (3) it satisfies a notification requirement,[305] (4) it meets a responsiveness test,[306] and (5) it meets one of two integral part tests.[307]

---

298. Reg. § 1.509(a)-4(h)(2).
299. Reg. § 1.509(a)-4(f)(4).
300. Lapham Foundation, Inc. v. Commissioner, 84 T.C.M. 586, 593 (2003), *aff'd*, 389 F.3d 606 (6th Cir. 2004).
301. "Control and Power: Issues Involving Supporting Organizations, Donor Advised Funds, and Disqualified Person Financial Institutions," Topic G, IRS Exempt Organization Continuing Professional Education Text for FY 2001, at 110.
302. Congress mandated the promulgation of regulations requiring Type III supporting organizations that are not functionally integrated Type III supporting organizations to make distributions of a percentage of either income or assets to supported organizations (Pension Protection Act of 2006, Pub. L. No. 109-280, § 1241(d), 120 Stat. 780, 1103).
303. See § 15.6(h).
304. A supporting organization is not a Type III entity if it supports any supported organization organized outside of the United States (IRC § 509(f)(1)(B); Reg. § 1.509(a)-4(i)(10)).
305. See § 15.6(g)(ii).
306. See § 15.6(g)(iii).
307. See § 15.6(g)(v), (vi). In general, Reg. § 1.509(a)-4(i)(1).

(ii) Notification Requirement. For each of its tax years, a Type III supporting organization must provide the following documents to each of its supported organizations: (1) a written notice, addressed to a principal officer of the supported organization, describing the type and amount of all of the support the supporting organization provided to the supported organization during the supporting organization's tax year immediately preceding the tax year in which the notice is provided; (2) a copy of the supporting organization's annual information return that was most recently filed as of the date the notification is provided; and (3) a copy of the supporting organization's governing documents as in effect on the date the notification is provided (unless previously provided and not subsequently amended).[308] The notification documents must be provided by the last day of the fifth calendar month following the close of the year involved and may be provided electronically.[309]

(iii) Responsiveness Test. A supporting organization meets the responsiveness test if it is responsive to the needs or demands of a supported organization.[310] Generally,[311] to meet this test, a supporting organization must satisfy two sets of requirements.

First, (1) one or more trustees, directors, or officers of the supporting organization must be elected or appointed by the trustees, directors, officers, or membership of the supported organization; (2) one or more members of the governing body of the supported organization must also be trustees, directors, or officers of, or hold other important offices in, the supporting organization; or (3) the trustees, directors, or officers of the supporting organization must maintain a close and continuous working relationship with the trustees, directors, or officers of the supported organization.[312]

---

308. Reg. § 1.509(a)-4(i)(2). For purposes of this notification requirement, a principal officer includes, but is not limited to, a person who, regardless of title, has ultimate responsibility for implementing the decisions of the governing body of a supported organization; for supervising the management, administration, or operation of the supported organization; or for managing the finances of the supported organization. Reg. § 1.509(a)-4(i)(2)(iv).
309. Reg. § 1.509(a)-4(i)(2)(ii), (iii).
310. Reg. § 1.509(a)-4(i)(3)(i).
311. There is an exception for pre–November 20, 1970, organizations (Reg. § 1.509(a)-4(i)(3)(v)). This exception requires a "historic and continuing relationship" between the parties. Other factors will likely have to be examined in connection with this exception, such as a "close and continuous" working relationship between the trustees, directors, or officers of the two organizations (Reg. § 1.509(a)-4(i)(5)(ii)) and a "significant voice" by the supported organization in the supporting organization's investment practices, the timing of grants, the manner of making grants, and in otherwise directing the use of the income or assets of the supporting organization (Reg. § 1.509(a)-4(i)(5)(iii)).
312. Reg. § 1.509(a)-4(i)(3)(ii).

§ 15.6 SUPPORTING ORGANIZATIONS

Second, the trustees, directors, or officers of the supported organization must, by reason of one of the foregoing three types of relationships, have a *significant voice* in the investment policies of the supporting organization, the timing of grants, the manner of making grants, and the selection of grant recipients by the supporting organization, and in otherwise directing the use of the income and assets of the supporting organization.[313]

(iv) Types of Type III Supporting Organizations. The federal tax law provides for two categories of Type III supporting organizations: functionally integrated Type III supporting organizations and nonfunctionally integrated Type III supporting organizations. The criteria for these types of Type III supporting organizations are found in two different integral part tests.

(v) Integral Part Test—Functionally Integrated Type III Organizations. A supporting organization meets the integral part test and thus is considered functionally integrated with a supported organization if it (1) engages in activities substantially all of which directly further the exempt purposes of one or more supported organizations, (2) is the parent of each of its supported organizations, or (3) supports a governmental supported organization.[314]

A supporting organization meets the first of these requirements if it engages in activities substantially all of which (1) directly further the exempt purposes of one or more supported organizations to which the supporting organization is responsive by performing the functions of, or carrying out the purposes of, the supported organization(s), and (2) but for the involvement of the supporting organization would normally be engaged in by the supported organization(s).[315]

Activities *directly further* the exempt purposes of one or more supported organizations only if they are conducted by the supporting organization. Holding title to and managing exempt-use assets[316] are activities that directly further the exempt purposes of a supported organization. By contrast, generally fundraising, making grants (whether to a supported organization or third parties), and investing and managing nonexempt-use assets are not activities that directly further the exempt purposes of a supported organization.[317]

The making or awarding of grants, scholarships, or other payments to individual beneficiaries who are members of the charitable class benefited by

---

313. Reg. § 1.509(a)-4(i)(3)(iii).
314. Reg. § 1.509(a)-4(i)(4)(i).
315. Reg. § 1.509(a)-4(i)(4)(ii)(A). All pertinent facts and circumstances are taken into account in ascertaining the *substantially all* requirement (Reg. § 1.509(a)-4(i)(4)(ii)(B)).
316. See § 15.6(g)(vi) for the meaning of *exempt use assets* in this context.
317. Reg. § 1.509(a)-4(i)(4)(ii)(C).

a supported organization is an activity directly furthering the exempt purposes of the supported organization if (1) the beneficiaries are selected on an objective and nondiscriminatory basis; (2) the trustees, directors, and officers of the supported organization have a significant voice in the timing of the payments, the manner of making them, and the selection of recipients; and (3) the making or awarding of the payments is part of an active program of the supporting organization that directly furthers the exempt purposes of the supported organization and in which the supporting organization maintains significant involvement.[318]

A supporting organization is the *parent of a supported organization* if the supporting organization exercises a substantial degree of direction over the policies, programs, and activities of the supported organization and a majority of the trustees, directors, and officers of the supported organization is appointed or elected, directly or indirectly, by the governing body, members of the governing body, or officers of the supporting organization.[319]

The IRS issued interim guidance for Type III supporting organizations seeking to qualify as functionally integrated entities by *supporting a governmental entity*.[320] Pursuant to this transitional rule, a supporting organization is considered functionally integrated if it (1) supports at least one supported organization that is a governmental entity to which the supporting organization is responsive[321] and (2) engages in activities for or on behalf of the governmental supported organization that perform the functions of, or carry out the purposes of, the governmental entity and that, but for the involvement of the supporting organization, would normally be engaged in by the governmental entity.[322]

---

318. Reg. § 1.509(a)-4(i)(4)(ii)(D). For these purposes, *significant involvement* is as defined in Reg. § 53.4942(b)-1(b)(2)(ii), except that "supporting organization" is substituted for "foundation" (Reg. § 1.509(a)-4(i)(4)(ii)(D)).
319. Reg. § 1.509(a)-4(i)(4)(iii).
320. Notice 2014-4, 2014-2 I.R.B. 274. The final Type III supporting organization regulations reserved a portion of the rules relating to this topic (Reg. § 1.509(a)-4(i)(4)(iv)); proposed regulations have been issued on the subject (see § 15.6(g)(vii)).
321. See § 15.6(g)(iii).
322. Notice 2014-4, 2014-2 I.R.B. 274, provided that a supporting organization may rely on these rules beginning on December 28, 2012, and until the earlier of the date final regulations on this topic are published or the first day of the organization's third tax year beginning after December 31, 2013 (*id*. § 3.01). Proposed regulations further extended this transition relief to Type III supporting organizations in existence on or before February 19, 2016, that continue to meet these requirements until the earlier of the first day of the organization's first tax year beginning after the date final regulations are published with respect to the governmental entity supporting organization rules or the first day of the organization's second tax year beginning after February 19, 2016 (Prop. Reg. § 1.509(a)-4(i)(4)(iv)(F)). Nevertheless, Instructions for Form 990 (2022), Schedule A, Part IV, Section E, line 1, indicate that organizations may continue to rely on the transitional relief provided in Notice 2014-4, 2014-2 I.R.B. 274.

§ 15.6 SUPPORTING ORGANIZATIONS

(vi) Integral Part Test—Nonfunctionally Integrated Type III Organizations. In general, a supporting organization also meets the integral part test but is considered nonfunctionally integrated, where it satisfies a distribution requirement and an attentiveness requirement.[323]

To satisfy the *distribution requirement*, a nonfunctionally integrated Type III supporting organization must, with respect to each tax year, distribute to or for the use of one or more supported organizations an amount equaling or exceeding the supporting organization's distributable amount for the year, on or before the last day of the year.[324]

The *distributable amount* for a tax year generally is an amount equal to the greater of 85 percent of the supporting organization's adjusted net income for the immediately preceding tax year or its minimum asset amount for the immediately preceding tax year, reduced by the amount of any income taxes imposed on the supporting organization during the immediately preceding tax year.[325] An organization's *adjusted net income* is determined by applying the principles of the private foundation adjusted net income rules.[326]

A supporting organization's *minimum asset amount* for its immediately preceding tax year is 3.5 percent of the excess of the aggregate fair market value of all of the organization's nonexempt-use assets in that year over the acquisition indebtedness[327] with respect to these assets.[328] This amount must be increased by (1) amounts received or accrued during the immediately preceding tax year as repayments of amounts that were taken into account by the organization to meet its distribution requirement for any tax year; (2) amounts received or accrued during the immediately preceding tax year from the sale or other disposition of property to the extent that the acquisition of the property was taken into account by the organization to meet its distribution requirement for any tax year; and (3) any amount set aside to the extent it is determined during the immediately preceding tax year that the amount is not necessary for the purposes for which it was set aside and the amount was taken into account by the organization to meet its distribution requirement for any tax year.[329]

For purposes of determining its minimum asset amount, the aggregate *fair market value* of an organization's nonexempt-use assets in the immediately preceding tax year is made using the valuation methods used by a private

---

323. Reg. § 1.509(a)-4(i)(5)(i)(A). An exception for pre-November 20, 1970, trusts (Reg. § 1.509(a)-4(i)(5)(i)(B) requires satisfaction of the rules in Reg. § 1.509(a)-4(i)(9)).
324. Reg. § 1.509(a)-4(i)(5)(ii)(A).
325. Reg. § 1.509(a)-4(i)(5)(ii)(B).
326. IRC § 4942(f); Reg. § 53.4942(a)-2(d). See § 3.1(d).
327. See § 11.4(a).
328. Reg. § 1.509(a)-4(i)(5)(ii)(C).
329. Reg. § 1.509(a)-4(i)(5)(ii)(C)(1)-(3).

foundation when calculating its minimum investment return under the mandatory distribution rules.[330] The aggregate fair market value of the assets may not be reduced by any amount that is set aside. The nonexempt-use assets of a supporting organization are all of its assets other than (1) certain future interests in the income or corpus of any real or personal property, (2) assets of an estate before their distribution, (3) present interests in certain trusts, (4) any pledge of money or property, and (5) assets that are used (or held for use) to carry out the exempt purposes of the supporting organization's supported organization(s) (known as *exempt-use assets*) by either the supporting organization or one or more supported organizations but only if the supporting organization makes the asset available to the supported organization(s) at no cost (or nominal rent) to the supported organization(s).[331]

The amount of a distribution made to a supported organization is the amount of cash distributed or the fair market value of the property distributed as of the date the distribution is made. The amount of a distribution is determined using the cash receipts and disbursements method of accounting. Distributions by a supporting organization that count toward the distribution requirement include (1) any amount paid to a supported organization to accomplish the supported organization's exempt purposes, (2) any amount paid by the supporting organization to perform an activity that directly furthers the exempt purposes of the supported organization but only to the extent the amount exceeds any income derived by the supporting organization from the activity, (3) any reasonable and necessary administrative expenses paid to accomplish the exempt purposes of the supported organization (which expressly exclude expenses incurred in the production of investment income), (4) any amount paid to acquire an exempt-use asset, and (5) any amount set aside for a specific project that accomplishes the exempt purposes of a supported organization as long as certain criteria are satisfied.[332]

---

330. Reg. §§ 1.509(a)-4(i)(8), 53.4942(a)-2(c); see § 6.2.
331. Reg. § 1.509(a)-4(i)(8). The distributable amount for the first tax year an organization is treated as a nonfunctionally integrated Type III supporting organization is zero (Reg. § 1.509(a)-4(i)(5)(ii)(D)).
332. Reg. § 1.509(a)-4(i)(6). An amount *set aside* for a specific project that accomplishes the exempt purposes of a supported organization to which the supporting organization is responsive will count toward the distribution requirement for the tax year in which the amount is set aside, but not in the year in which it is actually paid, if at the time of the set-aside, the supporting organization: (1) obtains a written statement from each supported organization whose exempt purposes the specific project accomplishes, signed under penalty of perjury by one of the supported organization's principal officers, stating that the supported organization approves the project as one that accomplishes one or more of the supported organization's exempt purposes and also approves the supporting organization's determination that the project is one that can be better accomplished

§ 15.6 SUPPORTING ORGANIZATIONS

If with respect to a tax year, an excess amount is created, the amount may be used to reduce the distributable amount in any of the five tax years immediately following the tax year in which the excess amount is created. An *excess amount* is created for a year if the total distributions made in that year that count toward the distribution requirement exceed the supporting organization's distributable amount for the year.[333]

A nonfunctionally integrated Type III supporting organization that fails to meet this distribution requirement will not be classified as a private foundation for the year in which it fails to meet the requirement if the organization establishes to the satisfaction of the IRS that the (1) failure was due solely to unforeseen events or circumstances that are beyond the organization's control, a clerical error, or an incorrect valuation of assets; (2) failure was due to reasonable cause and not to willful neglect; and (3) distribution requirement is met within 180 days after the organization is first able to distribute its distributable amount notwithstanding the unforeseen events or circumstances, or 180 days after the date the incorrect valuation or clerical error was or should have been discovered.[334]

To satisfy the *attentiveness requirement*, a nonfunctionally integrated Type III supporting organization must distribute, with respect to each tax year, at least one-third of its distributable amount to one or more supported organizations that are attentive to the operations of the supporting organization and with respect to which the supporting organization satisfies the responsiveness test.[335]

A supported organization is *attentive* to the operations of a supporting organization during a tax year if, in the year, at least one of the following requirements is satisfied:

1. The supporting organization distributes to the supported organization amounts equaling or exceeding 10 percent of the supported organization's total financial support (or the total support of a division of the

---

by such a set-aside than by the immediate payment of funds; (2) provides the written statement(s) to the IRS and establishes to the IRS's satisfaction, by meeting the approval and information requirements for private foundation set-asides under the suitability test (Reg. § 53.4942(a)-3(b)(7)(i); see § 6.4(g)(i)), that the amount set aside will be paid for the specific project within 60 months after it is set aside and that the project is one that can better be accomplished by the set-aside than by the immediate payment of funds; and (3) evidences the set-aside by the entry of a dollar amount on its books and records as a pledge or obligation to be paid at a future date or dates within 60 months of the set aside (Reg. § 1.509(a)-4(i)(6)(v)).

333. Reg. § 1.509(a)-4(i)(7).
334. Reg. § 1.509(a)-4(i)(5)(ii)(F).
335. Reg. § 1.509(a)-4(i)(5)(iii)(A). As to the responsiveness test, see § 15.6(g)(iii).

organization) received during the supported organization's last tax year ending before the beginning of the supporting organization's tax year.

2. The amount of support received from the supporting organization is necessary to avoid interruption of the conduct of a particular function or activity of the supported organization. The support is *necessary* if the supporting organization or the supported organization earmarks the support for a particular program or activity of the supported organization, even if the program or activity is not the supported organization's primary program or activity, as long as the program or activity is a substantial one.

3. Based on the consideration of all pertinent factors, including the number of supported organizations, the length and nature of the relationship between the supported organization and supporting organization, and the purpose to which the funds are put, the amount of support received from the supporting organization is a sufficient part of a supported organization's (or of one of its division's) total support to ensure attentiveness. Because the attentiveness of a supported organization normally is influenced by the amounts received from the supporting organization, the more substantial the amount involved in terms of a percentage of the supported organization's total support, the greater the likelihood that the required degree of attentiveness will be present. In determining whether the amount received from a supporting organization will ensure attentiveness, however, evidence of actual attentiveness by the supported organization is almost equally important. A supported organization is not considered to be attentive solely because it has enforceable rights against the supporting organization under state law.[336]

In determining whether a supported organization is attentive to the operations of a supporting organization, any amount received from the supporting organization that is held by the supported organization in a donor-advised fund[337] is disregarded.[338]

---

336. Reg. § 1.509(a)-4(i)(5)(iii)(B). An exception for certain pre-November 20, 1970, trusts requires, among its elements, that the trustee of the trust makes, since 1972, annual written reports to the supported organization, describing the trust's assets and income (Reg. § 1.509(a)-4(i)(9)).
337. See Chapter 16.
338. Reg. § 1.509(a)-4(i)(5)(iii)(C). A supporting organization, in the aftermath of publication of the final regulations embodying these rules, determined that "it could be run more efficiently as a private foundation"; it settled its relationship with its supported organizations and successfully converted to foundation status (Priv. Ltr. Rul. 201825004).

§ 15.6 SUPPORTING ORGANIZATIONS

(vii) Pending Regulation Projects. Several regulation projects relating to Type III supporting organizations are ongoing (either pending or in proposed form):

1. Proposed regulations have been issued to revise the responsiveness test[339] to require that a supporting organization be responsive to the needs and demands of each of its supported organizations (not just of one, as required under the current regulations).[340]

2. For charitable trusts that are supporting organizations, proposed regulations are to be issued that provide clarification regarding satisfaction of the significant voice test, where the trust instrument specifies the recipients, timing, manner, and amount of grants.[341]

3. Proposed regulations have been issued to amend the integral part rules for functionally integrated Type III supporting organizations to clarify that, for a supporting organization to qualify as the parent of each of its supported organizations,[342] the supporting organization and its supported organizations must be part of an integrated system (such as a hospital system), the supporting organization must engage in activities typical of the parent of an integrated system, and a majority of the trustees, directors, or officers of each supported organization must be appointed or elected, directly or indirectly, by the governing body, members of the governing body, or officers (acting in their official capacities) of the supported organization. Examples of activities typical of the parent of an integrated system of supported organizations include coordinating the activities of the supported organizations and engaging in overall planning, policy development, budgeting, and resource allocation for the supported organizations.[343]

4. Proposed regulations have been issued concerning functionally integrated Type III supporting organizations that support governmental supported organizations.[344] Pursuant to the proposal, this type of supporting organization (1) may support only governmental supported

---

339. See § 15.6(g)(iii).
340. Prop. Reg. § 1.509(a)-4(i)(3)(i).
341. T.D. 9605, 77 Fed. Reg. 76382, 76386 (2012).
342. See § 15.6(g)(v).
343. Prop. Reg. § 1.509(a)-4(i)(4)(iii).
344. The term *governmental supported organization* is proposed to be defined as a supported organization that is (1) a governmental unit as defined in IRC § 170(c)(1) or (2) an organization described in IRC § 170(c)(2) and (b)(1)(A) (other than in clauses (vii) and (viii)) that is an instrumentality of one or more governmental units (Prop. Reg. § 1.509(a)-4(i)(4)(iv)(B)).

organizations and (2) a substantial part of the supporting organization's total activities must be activities that directly further the exempt purposes of the governmental supported organization(s).[345] If a supporting organization supports more than one governmental organization, all of the supported organizations would have to (1) operate within the same geographic region,[346] or (2) work in close collaboration with one another to conduct a service, program, or activity that the supporting organization supports.[347] To satisfy the *close coordination or collaboration* requirement, the supporting organization would be required to maintain a letter on file from each of the supported organizations (or a joint letter) describing their collaborative or cooperative efforts with respect to the particular service, program, or activity.[348]

5. Proposed regulations have been issued to revise one of the rules concerning distributions that count toward the distribution requirement[349] to state that they include reasonable and necessary (1) administrative expenses paid to accomplish the exempt purposes of the supported organization, which do not include expenses incurred in the production of investment income or the conduct of fundraising activities (except as provided next), and (2) expenses incurred to solicit contributions that are received directly by a supported organization but only to the extent the amount of the expenses does not exceed the amount of contributions received by the supported organization as a result of the solicitation, as substantiated in writing by the supported organization.[350]

6. Proposed regulations are to be issued as to whether program-related investments may count toward the distribution requirement for non-functionally integrated Type III supporting organizations.[351]

---

345. Prop. Reg. § 1.509(a)-4(i)(4)(iv)(A).
346. The term *geographic region* is proposed to be defined as a city, county, or metropolitan area (Prop. Reg. § 1.509(a)-4(i)(4)(iv)(C)).
347. Prop. Reg. § 1.509(a)-4(i)(4)(iv)(A)(1).
348. Prop. Reg. § 1.509(a)-4(i)(4)(iv)(D). The proposed regulations provide a grandfather rule for a Type III governmental supporting organization in existence on or before February 19, 2016, that met and continues to meet the following requirements: (1) it supports one or more governmental supported organizations and only supports governmental supported organizations; (2) each of the supported organizations is designated by the supporting organization, within the meaning of Reg. § 1.509(a)-4(d)(4) (see § 15.6(c)), on or before February 19, 2016; and (3) a substantial part of the supporting organization's total activities are activities that directly further the exempt purposes of its governmental supported organization(s) (Prop. Reg. § 1.509(a)-4(i)(4)(iv)(E)).
349. See § 15.6(g)(vi).
350. Prop. Reg. § 1.509(a)-4(i)(6)(iii).
351. T.D. 9605, 77 Fed. Reg. 76382, 76390 (2012).

§ 15.6 SUPPORTING ORGANIZATIONS

7. Proposed regulations have been issued to address the definition of the term *control* in the rules concerning the relationship test for Types I or III supporting organizations in the context of contributions from controlling donors.[352] Pursuant to the proposal, the governing body of a supported organization would be considered controlled by such a person if the person, alone or by aggregating the person's votes or positions of authority, may require the governing body of the supported organization to perform any act that significantly affects its operations or may prevent the governing body of the supported organization from performing any act of that type. The governing body of a supported organization will generally be considered controlled, directly or indirectly, by these or related persons if the voting power of these persons is 50 percent or more of the total voting power of the governing body or if one or more of these persons have the right to exercise veto power over the actions of the governing body of the supported organization. All pertinent facts and circumstances, however, would be taken into consideration in determining whether one or more persons do, in fact, directly or indirectly control the governing body of a supported organization.[353]

(h) Contributions from Controlling Donors

For any tax year, a supporting organization is not a Type I or Type III entity if it accepts a contribution from a *controlling donor*, that is, a person (other than from another category of public charity)[354] who directly or indirectly controls, alone or together with family members or certain 35 percent controlled entities, the governing body of a specified publicly supported organization supported by the supporting organization.[355]

For purposes of this rule, family members are determined by applying the rules for determining disqualified persons with respect to a private foundation,[356] except that the brothers and sisters (whether by the whole or half blood) of an individual and their spouses are also included.[357] A 35 percent controlled entity is a corporation in which a controlling donor and/or their family members own more than 35 percent of the total combined voting power, a partnership in which such persons own more than 35 percent of the profits interest, and a trust or estate in which such persons own more than 35 percent of the

---

352. See § 15.6(h).
353. Prop. Reg. § 1.509(a)-4(f)(5)(ii).
354. That is, an organization described in IRC § 509(a)(1), (2), or (4). See §§ 15.2-15.5.
355. IRC § 509(f)(2); Reg. § 1.509(a)-4(f)(5)(i).
356. IRC § 4946(d); see § 4.4.
357. IRC §§ 509(f)(2)(B)(ii) and 4958(f)(4); Reg. § 1.509(a)-4(f)(5)(i)(B).

beneficial interest.[358] Constructive ownership rules similar to those for determining disqualified persons with respect to a private foundation apply.[359]

(i) Excess Benefit Transactions Rules

An excise tax is imposed on disqualified persons if they engage in one or more excess benefit transactions with public charities and social welfare organizations.[360] A grant, loan, compensation, or other similar payment (e.g., an expense reimbursement)[361] by any type of supporting organization to a substantial contributor or to certain persons related to a substantial contributor, as well as a loan provided by a supporting organization to certain disqualified persons with respect to the supporting organization, is an automatic excess benefit transaction.[362] Thus, the entire amount of the grant, loan, compensation, or other similar payment to the substantial contributor, disqualified persons, or related parties is an excess benefit.[363]

(j) Limitation on Control

A supporting organization may not be controlled directly or indirectly by one or more disqualified persons other than foundation managers and one or more supported organizations.[364] An individual who is a disqualified person with respect to a supporting organization (e.g., a substantial contributor) does not lose that status because a beneficiary public or publicly supported charity appoints or designates them to be a foundation manager of the supporting

---

358. IRC §§ 509(f)(2)(B)(iii) and 4958(f)(3); Reg. § 1.509(a)-4(f)(5)(i)(C).
359. IRC §§ 4946(a)(3), (4) and 4958(f)(3)(B); see § 4.3.
360. IRC § 4958. See *Tax-Exempt Organizations*, Chapter 21.
361. A *similar payment* does not include, for example, a payment made pursuant to a bona fide sale or lease of property with a substantial contributor (Staff of Joint Comm. on Tax'n, Technical Explanation of H.R. 4, the "Pension Protection Act of 2006," as Passed by the House on July 28, 2006, and as Considered by the Senate on August 3, 2006 358 (Comm. Print JCX-38-06) (PPA Joint Comm. Explanation).
362. IRC § 4958(c)(3). For purposes of the *similar payment* rule, the term *substantial contributor* does not include an eligible supported organization (other than a supporting organization) (IRC § 4958(c)(3)(C)(ii)). Likewise, for purposes of the loan rule, the term *disqualified person* does not include an eligible supported organization (other than a supporting organization) (IRC § 4958(c)(3)(A)(i)(II)). There was an anomaly here in that, when these rules were originally written, these exclusions failed to include the types of noncharitable organizations that qualify as supported organizations (see § 15.6(l)) (Pension Protection Act of 2006, Pub. L. No. 109-280, § 1242, 120 Stat. 780, 1104-05). This matter was remedied by subsequent legislation (Tax Technical Corrections Act of 2007, Pub. L. No. 110-172, § 3(i), 121 Stat. 2473, 2475).
363. IRC § 4958(c)(3)(A)(ii). Similar rules apply to donor-advised funds (see § 16.7).
364. IRC § 509(a)(3)(C).

§ 15.6 SUPPORTING ORGANIZATIONS

organization to serve as the representative of the public or publicly supported charity.[365]

A supporting organization is considered *controlled* if the disqualified persons, by aggregating their votes or positions of authority, may require the organization to perform any act that significantly affects its operations or may prevent the supporting organization from performing this type of an act. Generally, control exists if the voting power of these persons is 50 percent or more of the total voting power of the organization's governing body or if one or more disqualified persons have the right to exercise veto power over the actions of the organization. All pertinent facts and circumstances, including the nature, diversity, and income yield of an organization's holdings, the length of time particular securities or other assets are retained, and its manner of exercising its voting rights with respect to securities in which members of its governing body also have some interest, will be taken into consideration in determining whether a disqualified person does, in fact, indirectly control an organization.[366] Supporting organizations are permitted to establish, to the satisfaction of the IRS, that disqualified persons do not directly or indirectly control them.[367]

For example, this control element may be the difference between the qualification of an organization as a supporting organization and its qualification as a common fund private foundation. This is because the right of the donors to designate the recipients of the organization's gifts can constitute control of the organization by disqualified persons, namely, substantial contributors.[368]

In one instance, the IRS found indirect control of a supporting organization by, in effect, legislating an expanded definition of the term *disqualified person*. The matter involved a charitable organization that made distributions to a university. The organization's board of directors was composed of a substantial contributor to the organization, two employees of a business corporation of which more than 35 percent of the voting power was owned by the substantial contributors, and one individual selected by the university. None of the directors had veto power over the organization's actions. Conceding that the organization was not directly controlled by disqualified persons, the IRS said that "one circumstance to be considered is whether a disqualified person is in a position to influence the decisions of members of the organization's governing body who are not themselves disqualified persons." Thus, the IRS decided that the two directors who were employees of the disqualified person

---

365. Reg. § 1.509(a)-4(j)(1).
366. *Id*.
367. Reg. § 1.509(a)-4(j)(2).
368. Rev. Rul. 80-305, 1980-2 C.B. 71. For a discussion of *common fund foundations*, see § 3.4, and of *substantial contributors*, see § 4.1.

PUBLIC CHARITIES

corporation should be considered disqualified persons for purposes of applying the 50 percent control rule. This position, in turn, led to the conclusion that the organization was indirectly controlled by disqualified persons and, therefore, could not be a nonprivate foundation by virtue of being a qualifying supporting organization.[369]

The operation of these rules is further illustrated by two IRS rulings. One instance concerned a charitable trust formed to grant scholarships to students graduating from a particular public high school. The sole trustee of the trust was the council of the city in which the school was located, and its funds were managed by the city's treasurer. The school system was an integral part of the city's government. One of the purposes of the city, as outlined in its charter, was to provide for the education of its citizens. The IRS granted the trust classification as a supporting organization (and thereby determined it was not a private foundation),[370] using the following rationale: (1) the city, being a governmental unit,[371] was a qualified supported entity;[372] (2) because of the involvement of the city council and treasurer, the trust satisfied the requirements of the "operated, supervised, or controlled by" (Type I) relationship; (3) the organizational test was met because of the similarity of educational purpose between the trust and the city; (4) the "exclusive" operation requirement was deemed met because the trust benefited individual members of the charitable class aided by the city through its school system; and (5) the trust was not controlled by a disqualified person (other than a public or publicly supported charity).

By contrast, the IRS considered the public or publicly supported charity status of a charitable trust formed to grant scholarships to students graduating from high schools in a particular county. The scholarship recipients were selected by a committee composed of officials and representatives of the county. The trustee of the trust was a bank. The IRS denied the trust classification as a supporting organization (and thereby determined that it was a private foundation),[373] using the following rationale: (1) the high schools were qualified supported organizations;[374] (2) since the trustee was independent of the county, neither the operated, supervised, or controlled by (Type I) nor the supervised or controlled in connection with (Type II) relationship was present; (3) the integral part test of the operated in connection with (Type III) relationship was not met because of the independence of the trustee, the

---

369. Rev. Rul. 80-207, 1980-2 C.B. 193.
370. Rev. Rul. 75-436, 1975-2 C.B. 217.
371. IRC §§ 170(c)(1), (b)(1)(A)(v).
372. IRC § 509(a)(1).
373. Rev. Rul. 75-437, 1975-2 C.B. 218.
374. IRC §§ 170(b)(1)(A)(ii) or (v); 509(a)(1).

county's lack of voice in the trust's investment and grant-making policies, and the absence of the necessary elements of significant involvement, dependence on support, and sufficient attentiveness; (4) the responsiveness test of the same relationship was not met because the beneficiary organizations were not named and lacked the power to enforce the trust and compel an accounting; and (5) the trust failed the organization test because its instrument lacked the requisite statement of purpose and did not specify the publicly supported organizations.

The U.S. Tax Court demonstrated a disposition to avoid this type of stringent reading of these requirements. In finding a scholarship-granting charitable trust to be a public charity pursuant to the operated in connection with (Type III) requirements, the court ruled that it satisfied the responsiveness and integral part tests even though the school was not a named beneficiary of the trust and the funds were paid directly to the graduates rather than to the school or a school system.[375] This, a prior,[376] and a subsequent Tax Court holding[377] indicate that the courts will not be giving these exceedingly complex and intricate regulations an overly technical interpretation, but will apply them in a commonsense manner to effectuate the intent of Congress.

A supporting organization must annually demonstrate that it is not controlled, directly or indirectly, by one or more disqualified persons (other than its managers and supported organization(s)); this is done by means of a certification on its annual information return.[378]

(k) Excess Business Holdings Rules

The private foundation excess business holdings rules apply to nonfunctionally integrated Type III supporting organizations.[379] These rules also apply to a Type II supporting organization that accepts a gift or contribution from (1) a person (other than a public charity that is not another supporting organization) who directly or indirectly controls, either alone or together with family members or a 35 percent controlled entity of such person, the governing body

---

375. Nellie Callahan Scholarship Fund v. Commissioner, 73 T.C. 626 (1980).
376. Warren M. Goodspeed Scholarship Fund v. Commissioner, 70 T.C. 515 (1978).
377. Cockerline Memorial Fund v. Commissioner, 86 T.C. 53 (1986).
378. IRC § 6033(l)(3); Form 990 (2022), Schedule A, Part IV, Section A, line 9. Congress intended that supporting organizations be able to certify that the majority of the organization's governing body is composed of individuals who were selected on the basis of their special knowledge or expertise in the particular field or discipline in which the supporting organization is operating or because they represent the particular community that is served by the supported public charity(ies) (PPA Joint Comm. Explanation at 359), although no such certification currently is required on Form 990.
379. IRC § 4943(f)(1), (f)(3)(A).

of such supported organization, (2) a family member[380] of such person, or (3) a 35 percent controlled entity[381] of such person(s).[382]

(l) Noncharitable Supported Organizations

Certain tax-exempt organizations that are not charitable entities qualify as supported organizations; this means that the charitable organization that is supportive of one or more of these noncharitable entities is able to avoid classification as a private foundation on the ground that it is a supporting organization.

This point of law is contained in a rather cryptic passage in the Internal Revenue Code, which states that, for purposes of the supporting organization rules, "an organization described in paragraph (2) [§ 509(a)(2)] shall be deemed to include an organization described in section 501(c)(4) [social welfare organization], (5) [agricultural, horticultural, or labor organization], or (6) [trade, business, and professional association and other forms of business leagues] which would be described in paragraph (2) if it were an organization described in section 501(c)(3)."[383]

This provision means that a tax-exempt charitable entity may be operated in conjunction with a social welfare organization, an agricultural, horticultural, or labor organization, or a business league, and thus qualify as a supporting organization if the supported organization meets the one-third support test of the rules concerning the service provider publicly supported charity.[384] These organizations frequently meet this support requirement simply because they have a membership that pays dues. This rule is principally designed to preserve nonprivate foundation status for related "foundations" and other funds (e.g., scholarship and research funds) operated by the specified noncharitable organizations.

This type of supporting organization is often in an awkward position: it must be charitable in function to be tax-exempt[385] yet be supportive of a noncharitable entity to avoid being considered a private foundation.[386] As a charity, the supporting organization cannot be organized and operated to further

---

380. Determined under IRC § 4958(f)(4).
381. Determined under IRC § 4958(f)(3) by substituting "persons described in clause (i) or (ii) of section 509(f)(2)(B)" for "persons described in subparagraph (A) or (B) of paragraph (1)" in subparagraph (A)(i) thereof).
382. IRC §§ 509(f)(2)(B) and 4943(f)(1), (f)(3)(B).
383. IRC § 509(a), last sentence.
384. Reg § 1.509(a)-4(k). Also Rev. Rul. 76-401, 1976-2 C.B. 175.
385. E.g., Priv. Ltr. Rul. 201844013.
386. An illustration of the need to use a supporting organization, to house substantial charitable and educational activities, in connection with an exempt business league, appears in Priv. Ltr. Rul. 202017035.

the general purposes of a noncharitable organization. Thus, if the supported organization is one of the eligible noncharitable entities, the supporting organization will meet the organizational test[387] if its articles require it to carry on charitable and other permitted activities.[388] Likewise, a supporting organization of a noncharitable organization will meet the operational test[389] if it is operated in furtherance of such activities.[390]

The IRS issued an odd private letter ruling concerning an entity formed as a supporting organization with respect to a tax-exempt business league. The agency revoked the organization's exempt status, stating that the "sole purpose" of the organization was to support the league and observing that exempt business leagues "serve the private interest of [their] members and not the general public," suggesting that a supporting organization with respect to a business league cannot be exempt as a charitable entity because of inherently unwarranted private benefit, which obviously is not the law. The statutory provision allowing business leagues to be supported organizations was not referenced.[391]

(m) Use of For-Profit Subsidiaries

For a time, there was an issue as to whether a supporting organization may have a for-profit subsidiary. The difficulty was this: The law requires that a supporting organization be organized and operated *exclusively* for the benefit or other support of one or more public charities.[392] This is a literal use of the word *exclusively*: Congress meant *exclusively*, rather than merely *primarily*. The question then was whether the very use of a for-profit subsidiary would violate the *exclusively* standard and thus cause the supporting organization to lose its public charity status on that basis.

The mystery intensified when, in 1993, the IRS ruled that a charitable organization that is a supporting organization could establish and operate a wholly owned for-profit subsidiary without jeopardizing its tax-exempt status.[393] This ruling was silent, however, on the impact of the use of the subsidiary on the organization's supporting organization status. Nonetheless, three years later, the IRS ruled that a supporting organization could, without jeopardizing its public charity status, utilize a for-profit subsidiary.[394] Later

---

387. See § 15.6(a). Permitted activities other than charitable activities include those described in IRC § 170(b)(2).
388. Reg. § 1.509(a)-4(c)(2).
389. See § 15.6(b).
390. Rev. Rul. 76-401, 1976-2 C.B. 175; e.g., Priv. Ltr. Rul. 200149045.
391. Priv. Ltr. Rul. 201338059.
392. IRC § 509(a)(3)(A). See § 15.6(a), (b).
393. Priv. Ltr. Rul. 9305026.
394. Priv. Ltr. Rul. 9637051.

PUBLIC CHARITIES

in 1996, the IRS ruled as to the tax consequences of liquidation of a for-profit subsidiary into a supporting organization.[395]

Thus, unless the IRS or a court alters this policy position, it seems clear that a supporting organization may, without endangering its tax classifications, hold and otherwise utilize a for-profit subsidiary—unless it is a nonfunctionally integrated Type III supporting organization or a Type II supporting organization to which the excess business holdings rules apply.[396]

§ 15.7 CHANGE OF PUBLIC CHARITY CATEGORY

The sources of financial support of a publicly supported charity may change, causing it to fail to qualify under the category of publicly supported charity recognized in its determination letter, yet begin to qualify under another category of publicly supported charity.

(a) From § 509(a)(1) to § 509(a)(2) or Vice Versa

An organization may commence operations qualifying as a donative publicly supported charity,[397] then subsequently become qualified only as a service provider publicly supported charity, or vice versa.[398] In this circumstance, in addition to reporting the change in public charity status on its annual information return, the organization must decide whether to seek formal recognition of its new public charity status from the IRS.[399]

(b) From § 509(a)(3) to § 509(a)(1) or § 509(a)(2)

A charitable organization classified as a supporting organization[400] may receive revenues that enable it to qualify as a donative publicly supported charity or a service provider publicly supported charity.

(c) From § 509(a)(3) Type III to § 509(a)(3) Type I or II

A supporting organization that has been in existence for many years may not have been assigned a specific type of supporting organization when it received its initial IRS determination letter and may therefore wish to seek an updated

---

395. Priv. Ltr. Rul. 9645017.
396. See § 15.6(k).
397. See § 15.4.
398. See § 15.5.
399. See § 15.7(d).
400. See § 15.6.

§ 15.7 CHANGE OF PUBLIC CHARITY CATEGORY

letter from the IRS identifying its specific supporting organization type. A Type III supporting organization may also restructure its organizational documents so as to qualify instead as a Type I or Type II supporting organization.

(d) IRS Recognition of Change in Public Charity Status

The IRS annually issues procedures that address the matter of changes from one public charity status to another.[401] Under these procedures, although an organization is not required to obtain a new determination letter to *qualify* for a different public charity status, IRS records will not *recognize* the change in public charity status unless the organization obtains a new determination letter.[402] This includes determination letters as to supporting organization type,[403] whether a Type III supporting organization is functionally integrated with one or more supported organizations,[404] and whether a nonexempt charitable trust[405] can constitute a supporting organization.

A determination letter as to any of these reclassifications of public charity status may be sought by filing a Form 8940 (Request for Miscellaneous Determination) with the IRS, along with the appropriate fee.[406] The information that must be submitted with the form in support of the request depends on the type of request and is set forth in the instructions for the form.

A charitable organization that erroneously determined that it was a private foundation when it initially applied for recognition of tax-exempt status (for example, by erroneously classifying items of public support) and wishes to correct the error can request a new determination letter instead of terminating its private foundation status.[407] The organization must be able to demonstrate that it continuously met the public support tests during its first five years.[408]

---

401. Currently, Rev. Proc. 2023-5, 2023-1 I.R.B. 265.
402. *Id*. § 7.04(1).
403. See § 15.6(e)-(g).
404. See § 15.6(g)(v).
405. An IRC § 4947(a)(1) entity (see § 3.6).
406. Form 8940 must be submitted electronically at www.pay.gov; the user fee for this type of request is currently $550 (Rev. Proc. 2023-5, 2023-1 I.R.B. 265 §§ 4.02(6), 7.02 and App. A (Schedule of User Fees), as modified by Rev. Proc. 2023-12, 2023-17 I.R.B. 768 §§ 3.01, 3.03).
407. Termination of private foundation status is the subject of Chapter 13.
408. This request is also made by filing Form 8940 electronically at www.pay.gov. The user fee for this type of request is currently $550 (Rev. Proc. 2023-5, 2023-1 I.R.B. 265 §§ 4.02(6), 7.02, 7.04(3) and App. A (Schedule of User Fees), as modified by Rev. Proc. 2023-12, 2023-17 I.R.B. 768 §§ 3.01, 3.03). Also, Instructions for Form 8940 (Apr. 2023), Part II and Schedule G (reclassification of private foundation status).

§ 15.8 TERMINATION OF PUBLIC CHARITY STATUS

On occasion, a charitable organization will lose its public charity status. This usually happens when an organization ceases to constitute a publicly supported charity, with no likelihood of meeting a public support test[409] or otherwise remaining a public charity. For example, an organization might receive a series of major gifts from a small group of donors and insufficient support from other donors that cause it to cease to meet the support test to be a donative publicly supported charity. Likewise, a mature organization that has accumulated significant investment assets might receive investment income that equals more than two-thirds of its total annual revenues, thereby causing it to cease to meet the support test to be a service provider publicly supported charity. A charitable organization that no longer qualifies as a public charity becomes, by operation of law, a private foundation due to the statutory presumption to that effect.[410]

Schedule A to Form 990 prompts a formerly publicly supported organization to file Form 990-PF, rather than 990, if the organization fails one of the public support tests over the five-year testing period.[411] When it files Form 990-PF, the organization checks the box on the first page of the form indicating that the return is the initial return of a former public charity.

Beginning to file Form 990-PF, and ceasing to file Form 990, is all that is formally required to notify the IRS that a former public charity has become a private foundation. An organization that loses its public charity status may, but is not required to, obtain a new determination letter reflecting its new private foundation status.[412]

As a private foundation, of course, a former public charity becomes subject to all of the private foundation excise taxes, including payment of the tax on net investment income.[413]

---

409. See §§ 15.4(c), 15.5(a).
410. IRC § 508(b); Rev. Proc. 2023-5, 2023-1 I.R.B. 265 § 7.04(2); see § 1.2. In one instance, a supporting organization effected a conversion to private foundation status by revising its governing documents to cause it to fail the organizational and operation tests applicable to supporting organizations (see § 15.6(a), (b)) (Priv. Ltr. Rul. 9052055).
411. See §§ 15.4(c), 15.5(a).
412. Form 8940 must be submitted electronically at www.pay.gov; the user fee for this type of request is currently $550 (Rev. Proc. 2023-5, 2023-1 I.R.B. 265 §§ 4.02(6), 7.02, 7.04(2) and App. A (Schedule of User Fees), as modified by Rev. Proc. 2023-12, 2023-17 I.R.B. 768 §§ 3.01, 3.03). Also, Instructions for Form 8940 (Apr. 2023), Part II and Schedule G (reclassification of private foundation status).
413. See Chapter 10.

§ 15.9 RELATIONSHIPS CREATED FOR AVOIDANCE PURPOSES

The income tax regulations contain rules to ensure that the requirements concerning service provider publicly supported charities and supporting organizations are not manipulated to avoid private foundation status for charitable organizations. Thus, if a relationship between a would-be service provider publicly supported charity and a putative supporting organization is established or availed, and one of the purposes of the relationship is to avoid classification as a private foundation with respect to either organization, the character and amount of support received by the ostensible supporting organization will be attributed to the would-be service provider publicly supported charity for purposes of determining whether the latter meets the one-third support test and the one-third gross investment income test.[414]

If an organization seeking qualification as a service provider publicly supported charity fails to meet either the one-third support test or the one-third gross investment income test by reason of the application of the foregoing rules or the rules with respect to retained character of gross investment income, and the organization is one of the specified organizations[415] for whose support or benefit an organization seeking the qualification is operated, the would-be supporting organization will not be considered to be operated exclusively to support or benefit one or more eligible public or publicly supported organizations.[416]

For purposes of determining whether an organization meets the gross investment income test in the rules concerning the service provider publicly supported charity,[417] amounts received by the organization from an organization seeking categorization as a supporting organization, by reason of its support of the would-be publicly supported organization, retain their character as gross investment income (rather than gifts or contributions) to the extent that the amounts are characterized as gross investment income in the possession of the distributing organization. The rule is also applicable with respect to support of a would-be publicly supported organization from a charitable trust, corporation, fund, association, or similar organization that is required by its governing instrument or otherwise to distribute, or that normally does distribute, at least 25 percent of its adjusted net income to the organization and the distribution normally comprises at least 5 percent of the distributee organization's adjusted net income. (There is no similar rule in connection with the donative publicly supported charity.)

---

414. Reg. § 1.509(a)-5(b).
415. IRC § 509(a)(3)(A).
416. Reg. § 1.509(a)-5(c).
417. IRC § 509(a)(2)(B).

CHAPTER SIXTEEN

Donor-Advised Funds

§ 16.1 Basic Definitions 681
§ 16.2 General Concept of a Gift 682
§ 16.3 Types of Donor Funds 684
§ 16.4 Donor-Advised Fund Litigation 687
    (a) Exemption Challenges 687
    (b) Donor Challenges 689
    (c) Charitable Deduction Challenges 690
§ 16.5 Public Charity Status of Funds 692
§ 16.6 Interrelationship of Private Foundation Rules 693
§ 16.7 Statutory Criteria 694
§ 16.8 Studies 699
    (a) Treasury Study 699
    (b) Congressional Research Service Study 701
§ 16.9 Tax Regulations 704
    (a) The Ever-Pending Regulations Project 704
    (b) 2017 IRS Notice 705
    (c) Comments on IRS Notice 707
§ 16.10 Proposed Legislation 713

One of the most controversial entities in the realm of charitable organizations is the *donor-advised fund*. These funds are created and maintained within public charities,[1] such as community foundations, churches, and charitable gift funds. Indeed, these funds were initiated by community foundations, which have existed since the early 1900s.

Today, hundreds of community foundations and a growing number of charitable gift funds account for billions of dollars in assets and income. According to a report prepared by the National Philanthropic Trust, in 2021,

---

1. It is incontrovertible that use of a donor-advised fund amounts to avoidance of the private foundation rules. Indeed, it can be said that every public charity is a mechanism for sidestepping these rules. The point is that this is an avoidance of a set of rules in a lawful manner. The U.S. Supreme Court long ago observed: "The legal right of a taxpayer to decrease the amount of what otherwise would be his taxes, or altogether to avoid them, by means which the law permits, cannot be doubted" (Gregory v. Helvering, 293 U.S. 465, 469 (1935)). More recently, an appellate court wrote that "[w]e recognize that it is axiomatic that taxpayers lawfully may arrange their affairs to keep taxes as low as possible" (Neonatology Associates P.A. v. Commissioner, 299 F.3d 221, 232-233 (3rd Cir. 2002)).

there were 1,285,801 individual donor-advised funds, with assets totaling over $234 billion. This is double the amount of assets held by donor-advised funds in 2017. The average size of an individual DAF account is estimated to be $182,842 for 2021. In the aggregate, these donor-advised funds made total grants of $45.74 billion in 2021 and had an average payout rate of 27.3 percent (notwithstanding the lack of any mandatory federal payout minimum amount). By comparison, private foundations held over $1.3 trillion in assets and made total grants of $96.27 billion. Thus, although donor-advised funds held less the 20 percent of the amount of assets held by private foundations, the value of grants made by donor-advised funds was 48 percent of grants made by private foundations in 2021.[2]

As the number of, and charitable assets held by, donor-advised funds has grown, so too has the scrutiny and criticism of these charitable giving vehicles. Several federal tax issues are involved, all resting on the fundamental fact that the donor-advised fund can be an alternative to a private foundation. Some choose to state the matter somewhat differently, regarding donor-advised funds as a means of sidestepping or avoiding the private foundation rules—principally as a way to bypass the mandatory distribution rules that apply to private foundations.

A statutory definition of donor-advised funds and two private foundation-like excise taxes were enacted in 2006.[3] Regulations have yet to be promulgated under these provisions, but the IRS continues to mull over various approaches to regulating donor-advised funds,[4] and they are beginning to see renewed attention from Congress.[5]

---

2. National Philanthropic Trust, "2022 Donor-Advised Fund Report" (Nov. 2022). NPT's report relied on data from 995 charitable sponsoring organizations that reported assets in any year from 2015 through 2021, including 60 national charities, 607 community foundations, and 328 single-issue charities. NPT defines a *national charity* as a tax-exempt organization with a national focus in fundraising and grantmaking, including independent organizations, such as NPT, and other charitable organizations affiliated with financial institutions; a *community foundation* as a tax-exempt organization that raises funds from the public, typically a donative publicly supported charity (see § 15.4) with a long-term goal of engaging many individual donors to carry out charitable interests for the benefit of residents of a defined geographic area, typically no larger than a state; and a *single-issue charity* as a tax-exempt organization that works in a specific topic area, such as universities, faith-based charities and issue-specific charities, such as those in the environmental, social justice, or international relief arenas. One of the largest of the national charities, Fidelity Investment Charitable Gift Fund, with 182,640 individual donor-advised funds, reported that it made 2.2 million in grants in 2022, totaling $11.2 billion (Fidelity Charitable 2023 Giving Report).
3. See § 16.7.
4. See § 16.9.
5. See § 16.10.

§ 16.1 BASIC DEFINITIONS

A donor-advised fund is not a separate legal entity. Rather, as noted, it is a fund within an organization that is a public charity. This type of fund is often referred to as an *account* of the organization that sponsors the donor-advised fund.

These accounts can be in the name of an individual, family, corporation, private foundation, or cause; they can be used to facilitate anonymous gifts. They often bear the name of the contributor or the contributor's family or business. Because of its name, a donor-advised fund can appear to be a separate legal entity—seemingly a charitable organization with many of the attributes of a private foundation.

The donor-advised fund is to be contrasted with the *donor-directed fund*. In the case of a donor-directed fund, the donor or a designee of the donor retains the right to direct the investment of the fund's assets and/or to direct grants from the fund for charitable purposes. By contrast, with the donor-advised fund, the donor has the ability (but not a legal right) to make recommendations (proffer advice) as to investment policy and/or the making of grants.

The donor-advised fund has, as noted, long been a staple of community foundations.[6] Today, many other types of charitable organizations and commercial investment companies have created donor-advised funds, recognized as public charities by the IRS. As long as the use of these funds was confined to community foundations, there was no controversy;[7] the attention accorded these funds, including criticism, started when their use was extended to other public charities.

These funds can, as noted, be viable alternatives to the formation of private foundations. The individual or individuals involved may wish to avoid the responsibilities imposed by law (including annual reporting to the IRS and other foundation regulatory requirements) of operating a private foundation. With a donor-advised fund, as opposed to a private foundation, there is no need for a board of directors or trustees (with the concomitant requirements of board meetings, maintenance of meeting minutes, election and supervision of officers and employees, and the like). Contributions to these funds are deductible pursuant to the rules concerning public charities, not private foundations.

---

6. See § 15.4(e). In general, Hoyt, *Legal Compendium for Community Foundations* (Washington, DC: Council on Foundations, 1996).
7. E.g., Priv. Ltr. Rul. 9807030 (ruling that distribution of up to 10 percent of a private foundation's assets to a donor-advised fund within a community foundation, with respect to which there were no material restrictions or conditions, "is an acceptable transfer to a public charity").

Another factor may be that the amount of money or property involved is too small to warrant the establishment of a private foundation.[8]

§ 16.2 GENERAL CONCEPT OF A GIFT

One of the legal issues raised by donor-advised funds is whether the transfer to the fund constitutes a gift. That is, the question arises as to whether the transfer to the fund is incomplete, in that the donor, by reserving an ability to advise, has retained some form of "right" that precludes the transfer from being a completed gift.

There must be a gift before there can be a charitable gift. Integral to the concept of the charitable contribution deduction is the fundamental requirement that the payment of money or property to a charitable organization be pursuant to a transaction that constitutes a gift. Although the Internal Revenue Code does not define the word *gift*, the federal income tax regulations contain this definition: A *contribution* is a "voluntary transfer of money or property that is made with no expectation of procuring financial benefit commensurate with the amount of the transfer."[9] This definition reflects the observation of the United States Supreme Court, years ago, that a *gift* is a transfer motivated by "detached or disinterested generosity."[10] Any condition by which the donor retains complete dominion and control over the transferred property makes the gift incomplete.[11] An incomplete gift cannot give rise to a deductible contribution.

The Supreme Court also ruled, in the context of determining the concept of a *charitable gift*, that a "payment of money [or a transfer of property] generally cannot constitute a charitable contribution if the contributor expects a substantial benefit in return."[12] Subsequently, the Supreme Court wrote that an exchange having an "inherently reciprocal nature" is not a gift and thus cannot

---

8. See § 2.1. The Giving USA Foundation, in early 2018, published a report, researched and written by the Indiana University Lilly Family School of Philanthropy, concluding that donor-advised funds are "one of the fastest-growing giving vehicles" ("The Data on Donor-Advised Funds: New Insights You Need to Know"). During 2016, contributions to donor-advised funds amounted to $23.27 billion, an annual growth of 7.6 percent (growth in charitable giving in general during that year being 2.7 percent). This report stated: "Donor-advised funds are here to stay for the foreseeable future, and this study will be the bedrock on which future quantitative studies will be built."
9. Reg. § 1.170A-1(c)(5).
10. Commissioner v. Duberstein, 363 U.S. 278, 285 (1960), quoting from Commissioner v. LoBue, 351 U.S. 243, 246 (1956).
11. Reg. § 25.2511-2(b).
12. United States v. American Bar Endowment, 477 U.S. 105, 116-117 (1986). See § 14.1.

be a charitable gift when the recipient is a charity.[13] At the same time, when a benefit to a donor arising out of a transfer to a charitable organization is *incidental*, the benefit will not defeat the charitable deduction.[14]

Thus, a *charitable gift* can be defined as a voluntary transfer of money or property to a charitable organization without actual or anticipated receipt by the donor of more than incidental economic considerations or benefits in return. The value inherent in any economic consideration or benefit received in return, other than an incidental one, must be subtracted from the value of the total gift to determine the value (if any) of the actual gift (the deductible portion).[15]

The traditional type of donor-advised fund is that which, as noted, is a component entity of a community foundation.[16] A monumental rivalry for millions of dollars in charitable gifts is under way between community foundations and charitable gift funds, and this activity is helping to stimulate and maintain the government's interest in this area. This focus has brought intense scrutiny of donor-advised funds.

This use of charitable gift funds involves the law concerning conditional gifts. A *conditional gift* is one that is made subject to the occurrence of an event, either before (*condition precedent*) or after (*condition subsequent*). This matter concerns conditions subsequent, namely, gifts made to a charitable organization containing binding covenants on the charitable donee.

Usually, with respect to the tax consequences of conditional gifts, the only party that may be subject to any risk is the donor who is taking a full charitable deduction yet may not lawfully be allowed to do so. The tax-exempt status of the charitable donee may, however, be implicated.[17]

---

13. Hernandez v. Commissioner, 490 U.S. 680, 692 (1989).
14. E.g., Rev. Rul. 81-307, 1981-2 C.B. 78.
15. This concept is also reflected in the charitable gift substantiation rules, which require a good faith estimate of any goods or services provided to a donor in consideration of the contribution (see § 14.7(b)). The U.S. Tax Court held that contributions to a charitable organization were not deductible because the substantiation requirements were not met (Addis v. Commissioner, 118 T.C. 528 (2002), *aff'd*, 374 F.3d 881 (9th Cir. 2004), *cert. den.*, 543 U.S. 1151 (2005)). The court concluded that certain "expectations" of the donors amounted to a "service," so that the expectations had to be valued and reflected in the substantiation document for the contributions to be deductible. This is a troublesome decision in the donor-advised fund setting, inasmuch as donors to these funds clearly have an expectation that the charitable donee will give attention to and usually follow their recommendations. If this decision is correct, charitable organizations must now be ever so cautious in preparing the substantiation documents, in that they must not only value what they *provided* in exchange for the gift, they must also peer into the misty reaches of donor motivation and intent to discern what donors *expect to be provided* (and value that).
16. A donor-advised fund established within a community trust must be administered in or as a component part of the trust (Reg. § 1.170A-9(e)(1)). See § 15.4(e).
17. E.g., Fund for Anonymous Gifts v. Internal Revenue Service, 97-2 U.S.T.C. ¶ 50,710 (D.D.C. 1997), *vacated in part and remanded in part*, 194 F.3d 173 (D.C. Cir. 1999).

§ 16.3 TYPES OF DONOR FUNDS

Conditions subsequent that are not negligible can defeat the income tax charitable deduction. In one case, donors gifted real property to a charitable trust but retained control over its future occupancy and sale; the entire federal income tax charitable contribution deduction was disallowed because of these retained rights (although they were incapable of valuation).[18] The charitable deduction for a gift of a rare book collection to a charity was disallowed because the donor retained an unlimited right of access to the collection and the right to deny access to it to others.[19] An illustration of a negligible or incidental condition subsequent was a gift of theatrical materials to a public library, where the materials could not be copied or removed from the library without the donor's permission.[20]

§ 16.3 TYPES OF DONOR FUNDS

Until the enactment of legislation in 2006, the Internal Revenue Code and the income tax regulations offered only two significant methods for donors to charitable organizations to exercise any post-transfer control or direction over the use of money or property irrevocably transferred to charity for which the donor is entitled to a charitable deduction in the year of the transfer. One method is the use of a special type of private foundation that is, in essence, a donor-directed fund.[21] This entity is referred to as the common fund foundation.[22] The other method is utilization of the community foundation or community trust.[23] The community foundation regulations and another regulation concerning prohibited material restrictions[24] only allow donor designation at the time of the gift and donor advice (not donor direction) after the date of the gift. The 2006 legislation introduced a third approach in this context, introducing statutory law concerning donor-advised funds.[25]

Relevant to the concept of a charitable gift and the matter of reciprocal benefits to donors is the fact that the federal law, as noted, distinguishes between donor-advised funds and donor-directed funds. To reiterate, the latter type of fund involves an arrangement between a charitable organization and a donor whereby the donor retains one or more rights as to the subsequent investment

---

18. Darling v. Commissioner, 43 T.C. 520 (1965).
19. Rev. Rul. 77-225, 1977-2 C.B. 73.
20. Lawrence v. United States, 75-1 U.S.T.C. ¶ 9165 (C.D. Cal. 1974).
21. See § 16.1.
22. See § 3.4.
23. Reg. § 1.170A-9(e)(10); see § 15.4(e).
24. Reg. §§ 1.170A-9(e)(11)(ii)(B), 1.507-2(a)(7) (defining material restrictions and conditions); see § 13.3(b), (c).
25. See § 16.7.

DONOR-ADVISED FUNDS

and/or disposition of the subject of the gift. By contrast, a donor-advised fund does not have the feature of donor direction but allows the donor to tender advice as to subsequent investment and/or disposition of the subject of the gift.

Until 2006, there was little specific law on donor-advised funds and donor-directed funds, however. The closest reference in the Internal Revenue Code to the concept was the provision authorizing the common fund foundation; deductible charitable contributions are allowed in these circumstances.[26] This is the case even though the donor and their spouse can annually designate public charities to which the foundation must grant the income and principal of the original contribution. Thus, the common fund foundation is a type of private foundation closely comparable to a donor-directed fund.

In the case of community foundations, which hold themselves out as a bundle of donor-advised funds, a donor at the time of the gift (i.e., at the time of creation of the component fund) is permitted to designate the charitable purpose of the gift or the specific charity that will receive the income or principal, consistent with the community foundation's exempt purposes.[27] These regulations do not permit the donor to direct, aside from the original designation, which charity may receive distributions or the timing of the distributions to the charitable recipient.[28] The donor may also offer nonbinding advice to the community fund manager regarding payouts from the component fund. (When a donor offers advice of this nature, the IRS is likely to carefully examine the facts involved to determine whether the giving of the "advice" by the donor is in actuality an indirect reservation of a right to direct the distributions.)

There is, nonetheless, a determination from the IRS that is somewhat pertinent to this analysis.[29] This private letter ruling involved a private foundation, the trustees of which determined to transfer all of its assets to a community foundation, which in turn would place the assets in a donor-advised fund. (The private letter ruling does not define this term.) The private foundation would remain in existence for the sole purpose of advising the community foundation on the use of the fund for charitable purposes. The IRS ruled that the trustees' retention of this ability to make this type of recommendation in their role as "donor advisors" would not constitute a prohibited material restriction as that term is used for purposes of the private foundation termination provisions.[30]

---

26. IRC § 170(b)(1)(F)(iii); see § 3.4.
27. Reg. §§ 1.170A-9(e)(11)(B), 1.507-2(a)(7)(iii)(B).
28. Cf. Reg. § 1.507-2(a)(7)(iv)(A)(1).
29. Priv. Ltr. Rul. 8836033.
30. See § 13.3(b), (c).

§ 16.3 TYPES OF DONOR FUNDS

As noted, one of the reasons for the focus on these types of donor funds is the need for a judgment as to whether a transaction, which is otherwise a charitable gift,[31] is not, in law, a completed gift at all because the donor retains too much control over the subsequent use and disposition of the gift money or property. At least in the context of donor-advised gift funds (and thus presumably in most other donor fund contexts, including donor-directed funds), the IRS may look to the *prohibited material restrictions* criteria provided in the private foundation termination rules[32] to determine whether a completed gift has been made.

A charitable organization may terminate its private foundation status by transferring all of its income and assets to one or more public charities.[33] The regulations concerning termination of private foundation status in this manner focus on whether a grantor private foundation has transferred "all of its right, title, and interest in and to" the funds (including any property) transferred.[34] To effectuate such a transfer, a grantor private foundation "may not impose any material restriction or condition" that prevents the grantee from "freely and effectively employing the transferred assets, or the income derived therefrom, in furtherance of its exempt purposes."[35] The private foundation termination regulations provide several factors, which are not considered to prevent the public charity from freely and effectively employing the transferred asset, such as the administering the transferred assets in an identifiable or separate fund, some or all of the principal of which is not to be distributed for a specified period, if the public charity is the legal and equitable owner of the fund and its governing body exercises ultimate and direct authority and control over such fund.[36] These regulations also provide a list of various adverse factors, which if present, will be considered as preventing the grantee public charity from freely and effectively employing the transferred assets.[37] Chief among these adverse factors, and the most relevant in the donor-advised fund context, is whether the donor has reserved the right, directly or indirectly, to name the persons to which the transferee public charity must distribute, or to direct the timing of such distributions, as for example by a power of appointment.[38] Thus, a conceptual distinction between the legal right to direct donations from a donor fund and the non-binding ability to make recommendations as to disbursements from a donor fund is inherent in these regulations.

---

31. See § 16.2.
32. See § 13.3(b), (c).
33. See § 13.3(a).
34. Reg. § 1.507-2(a)(6).
35. Reg. § 1.507-2(a)(7)(i).
36. Reg. § 1.507-2(a)(7)(iii); see § 13.3(b)(i).
37. Reg. § 1.507-2(a)(7)(iv); see § 13.3(b)(ii).
38. Reg. § 1.507-2(a)(7)(iv)(A); see § 13.3(c).

The IRS ruled that a donor is entitled to a charitable contribution deduction for a gift of money or other property where the donor, or the donor's investment manager, retains the power to manage the investments in a designated account, subject to various investment-related limitations and conditions imposed on the donor's management of the account.[39]

A significant (albeit unfortunate) court opinion concerning donor-advised funds concluded that an organization that operated such a fund could not be tax-exempt as a charitable entity, although the case was more about tax fraud and private benefit.[40] Because of the fund's promotional materials, which emphasized donor self-interest rather than charitable intent, the court observed that the organization "served significant non-exempt purposes that focused primarily on providing personal, rather than public, benefits." It wrote that the organization's operations were "characterized at the least by willful neglect, and, more than likely, an active willingness to participate in a scheme designed to produce impermissible tax benefits." These materials and operations suggested, the court wrote, that the "donors in question did not truly relinquish ownership and control over the donated funds and property" but rather treated the organization as a "conduit for accomplishing the twin tax avoidance goals of building up their assets tax-free and then siphoning off the accumulated wealth to pay for personal expenditures." This case was an aberration, certainly not in the donor-advised or donor-directed mainstream; it is essentially a private benefit doctrine[41] case with unusually ugly facts.

§ 16.4 DONOR-ADVISED FUND LITIGATION

(a) Exemption Challenges

The IRS challenged the donor-advised fund technique in court; the government lost the case for reasons articulated in an opinion issued in 1987.[42] The IRS attempted to deny tax-exempt status to a public charity maintaining donor-advised funds, contending that the entity was merely an association of donors for which commercial services were being performed for fees and that the entity was violating the prohibitions on private inurement and private benefit.[43] The IRS asserted that the organization's "activities are all originated,

---

39. Priv. Ltr. Rul. 200445023.
40. New Dynamics Foundation v. United States, 2006-1 U.S.T.C. ¶ 50,286 (U.S. Ct. Fed. Cl. 2006).
41. See § 5.2.
42. National Foundation, Inc. v. United States, 13 Cl. Ct. 486 (1987).
43. See §§ 5.1 and 5.2.

§ 16.4 DONOR-ADVISED FUND LITIGATION

funded, and controlled by small related groups, by single individuals, or by families" and that "these individual donors retain full control of the funds."[44]

The court, however, found that donors to the organization "relinquish all ownership and custody of the donated funds or property" and that the organization is "free to accept or reject any suggestion or request made by a donor."[45] Indeed, the court enthused that the "goal" of the organization "is to create an effective national network to respond to many worthy charitable needs at the local level which in many cases might go unmet" and that its activities "promote public policy and represent the very essence of charitable benevolence as envisioned by Congress in enacting" tax-exempt status for charitable organizations.[46]

Ten years later, the IRS prevailed on the point.[47] The entity involved was structured much the same as the collective of donor-advised funds in the previous case. The trustee of the fund was bound by the donor's enforceable conditions as to disposition of its funds to ultimate charities. Nonetheless, the fund was ruled to not be tax-exempt as a charitable organization. The court wrote: "The manner in which the fund's investment activity would be conducted makes clear that one of the purposes of the fund is to allow persons to take a charitable deduction for a donation to the fund while retaining investment control over the donation."[48] This opinion did not differentiate between material and other restrictions.

The IRS's victory was short-lived, however. This decision was appealed, which led to settlement negotiations. The trustee of the fund agreed, as requested by the IRS, to eliminate the language in the fund's document that gave donors the control that was found by the lower court to be unwarranted private benefit.[49] Nonetheless, for more than one year, the IRS refused to grant

---

44. National Foundation, Inc. v. United States, 13 Cl. Ct. 486, 491 (1987).
45. Id. at 493.
46. Id. at 493-94.
47. Fund for Anonymous Gifts v. Internal Revenue Service, 97-2 U.S.T.C. ¶ 50,710 (D.D.C. 1997), *vacated in part and remanded in part*, 194 F.3d 173 (D.C. Cir. 1999).
48. Id.
49. The Tax Division of the Department of Justice (Tax Division) proposed that the fund's trust agreement be amended to state that the "Trustee shall only accept gifts that are free of any 'material restrictions or conditions' within the meaning of Section 1.507-2(a)(8) of the Income Tax Regulations." The Tax Division also wanted this language: "The Trustee shall establish procedures that insure complete and independent control and discretion over the Fund's assets. The Trustee agrees that it is not obligated to use or contribute [grant] donated funds in the manner requested by the donor of the funds." The fund rejected this proposal. The Tax Division then proposed the following language, to which the trustee of the fund agreed: "The Trustee may not receive any contribution, donation, gift, bequest or devise that is not a transfer of all the donor's right, title, and interest or is subject to a restriction or condition that prevents the Trustee from freely

the fund recognition of tax-exempt status, eventually causing the court of appeals, in frustration, to vacate the district court's decision and to direct that court to issue an order that the fund is an exempt charitable entity.[50]

The government was of the view that this amendment did not "sufficiently address the inadequacies" of the fund's operations. It contended that the administrative record showed that the fund would not "take complete control over the contributions." Rather, the government was of the view that the fund would "adhere to the directions of its donors regarding the investment and the ultimate distribution of the contributed funds." This amendment did not, the government asserted, prevent the fund from "providing investment services and acting as an administrative conduit for its donors' funds."[51]

(b) Donor Challenges

Two donors sued Fidelity Investments Charitable Gift Fund alleging a variety of misdeeds in administration of their contributions of 1.93 million shares of publicly traded stock to their donor-advised fund. These donors alleged that, to induce them to transfer the securities, Fidelity Charitable made certain promises as to how the block of stock would be liquidated in a gradual and sophisticated manner. They contended that these promises were broken and that Fidelity Charitable sold the stock in a negligent manner, which reduced the sales price for the stock and therefore reduced the amount of their tax deduction. Thus, this case largely concerned state law issues as to misrepresentation, breach of contract, promissory estoppel, unfair business practices, and negligence.

The trial court ruled in favor of Fidelity Charitable on all counts. It held that either the promises were kept or that there was no evidence that they were made. As to the negligence claim, the court did not determine whether Fidelity Charitable owed the donors the requisite duty of care but concluded that, even if the duty was owed, the court was not persuaded it was breached. The court noted the liquidation was "consistent" with Fidelity Charitable's

---

and effectively employing the transferred assets, or income therefrom, in furtherance of the Fund's exempt purposes. The Trustee may not receive any contribution, donation, gift, bequest or devise that is subject to any condition or term that prevents the Trustee from obtaining the ultimate authority and control over the assets, and the income derived from them, at the time of the transfer."

50. Fund for Anonymous Gifts v. Internal Revenue Service, 194 F.3d 173 (D.C. Cir. 1999). The Fund for Anonymous Gifts eventually became reorganized as a tax-exempt public charity, by ruling dated February 27, 2003, as the result of mediation with the IRS.
51. "Public Charity Classification and Private Foundations Issues: Recent Emerging Significant Developments," Topic P, IRS Exempt Organization Continuing Professional Education Text for FY 2000.

"published" policies. It found that these policies gave Fidelity Charitable "room to make judgments as to how and when to sell publicly traded shares." The donors were said to have not met their burden of proof that the applicable standard of care was violated. The court found that the liquidation "more likely than not" did not have an adverse effect on the stock's market price.[52]

The impact of this decision on the law of donor-advised funds, such as it is, is twofold. One, the opinion reinforces the point of law that money or other property transferred to a bona fide donor-advised fund is wholly owned and controlled by the sponsoring organization, notwithstanding the advisory rights retained by the donor. Two, the printed materials made available to prospective donors to donor-advised funds by the sponsoring organizations have significant legal import.

The first of these points was reinforced by a subsequent decision of the same court that found a plaintiff lacked standing to sue Schwab Charitable for its investment decisions related to the plaintiff's donor-advised fund.[53] The donor objected to Schwab Charitable's choice of investment pools (because there were less costly options available) and its payment of excessive fees for custodial and brokerage services to Charles Schwab (because the plaintiff thought Schwab Charitable could have negotiated better rates). The plaintiff's lack of standing was based on his giving up "title to and control of his donation in exchange for an immediate tax deduction," consistent with the "statutory framework."[54] The court stated that there was no authority for "the conclusion that the right to designate investments (in pre-selected funds) and donations in a donor-advised fund is a contractual or contingent property interest that gives a donor Article III standing to challenge the fund's choice of investment funds or administrative fees."[55]

(c) Charitable Deduction Challenges

A court thwarted the IRS's attempt to recast a transaction involving a donation of stock to a donor-advised fund held by Fidelity Investments Charitable

---

52. Fairbairn v. Fidelity Investments Charitable Gift Fund, 2021 WL 754534 (N.D. Cal. 2021).
53. Pinkert v. Schwab Charitable Fund, 2021 WL 2476869 (N.D. Cal. 2021), *aff'd*, 48 F.4th 1051 (2022).
54. *Id.* As to the statutory framework, the court cited the requirement in IRC § 170(f)(18)(B) that a contemporaneous written acknowledgment from the sponsoring organization of a donor-advised fund must include a statement that the organization has exclusive legal control over the funds or assets contributed (see § 16.7).
55. Pinkert v. Schwab Charitable Fund, 2021 WL 2476869 (N.D. Cal. 2021), *aff'd*, 48 F.4th 1051 (2022). The court distinguished Fairbairn, *supra* note 52, on the ground that the fund in Fairbairn allegedly broke specific promises that it made to the plaintiffs about how it would sell stock that they donated, whereas no such specific promises were allegedly made to the plaintiff in Pinkert.

DONOR-ADVISED FUNDS

Gift Fund. The donation of stock was followed by a redemption of the stock by the taxpayer's employer shortly after the donation. The IRS attempted to recast the donation to the donor-advised fund as a taxable redemption of stock followed by a donation to the donor-advised fund, thus requiring the taxpayer to recognize gain on the sale of the stock before claiming a charitable contribution deduction.[56] The taxpayer selected Fidelity Charitable based on its internal policy of immediately liquidating donated stock, but the court found that this did not alter the fact that the taxpayer transferred all of its rights in the stock to the donor-advised fund before the stock was redeemed. The court considered the application of the anticipatory assignment of income doctrine,[57] and determined it would apply only if the redemption was practically certain to occur at the time of the gift and would have occurred whether the shareholder made the gift or not. The court found that the doctrine did not apply because the redemption and the shareholder's corresponding right to income had not yet crystallized at the time of the gift.

In a subsequent case, however, the same court applied the anticipatory assignment of income doctrine to a donation of closely held appreciated stock to a donor-advised fund two days before a subsequent sale of this stock was scheduled to (and did in fact) close. "To avoid an anticipatory assignment of income on the contribution of appreciated shares of stock followed by a sale by the donee," the court wrote, "a donor must bear at least some risk at the time of contribution that the sale will not close." The court determined that transferring the shares to the donor-advised fund two days before closing "eliminated any such risk and made the sale a virtual certainty" and held that the donor recognized gain on the subsequent sale of the appreciated stock by the donor-advised fund.[58] The court echoed the sentiment of another court in remarking that "any tax lawyer worth [their] fees would not have recommended that a donor make a gift of appreciated stock" so close to the closing of a sale.[59] Although the donor was required to recognize gain on the subsequent sale of the stock, this did not preclude the donor from taking a charitable contribution deduction for the gift of the stock. The donor's failure to obtain a qualified appraisal,[60] however, did.

---

56. Dickinson v. Commissioner, T.C. Memo. 2020-128.
57. The *assignment of income doctrine* is essentially this: a taxpayer who has earned income cannot escape taxation by assigning their right to receive payment (Helvering v. Horst, 311 U.S. 112, 116 (1940).) Thus, "if stock is about to be acquired by the issuing corporation via redemption, a shareholder cannot avoid tax on the transaction by donating the stock before he receives the proceeds" (Dickinson v. Commissioner, T.C. Memo. 2020-128).
58. Estate of Scott M. Hoensheid v. Commissioner, T.C. Memo. 2023-34.
59. *Id.*, quoting Ferguson v. Commissioner, 174 F.3d 997 (9th Cir. 1999).
60. See § 14.7(d).

§ 16.5 PUBLIC CHARITY STATUS OF FUNDS

Another issue being raised by the functions of charitable organizations that maintain donor-advised funds—particularly those that maintain these funds as their sole function, such as charitable gift funds and *national foundations*[61]—is whether these entities qualify as publicly supported charities.

Community foundations, charitable gift funds, and other entities maintaining donor-advised funds to a significant extent are classified as donative publicly supported charities.[62] This is because the contributions to these organizations, albeit earmarked for donor-advised funds, are treated, in whole or in part, as public support for the charity. The IRS, however, has been fretting over the propriety of treating donor-advised funds as publicly supported charities on the theory that these charities may not be *supported* in a technical, legal sense.

When a grant is made from a donor-advised fund to a charity—which may be termed the *ultimate beneficiary*—the grant amount can be regarded (in whole or in part) as public support for the ultimate beneficiary. For some time, it was the view of the IRS that these gifts to charities maintaining donor-advised funds amounted to public support for both the "intermediate" and "ultimate" beneficiary charities.[63] As the controversy widened, however, the IRS withdrew its views on the subject.[64]

The IRS is not troubled by the concept that "earmarked" gifts are forms of public support for the "ultimate" charitable recipient. It is the treatment of these gifts as public support for the "intermediate" entity—the collective of donor-advised funds—that the IRS has said is giving it pause.[65]

The IRS's publication feigns objectivity in places, then loses even that in others. Thus, it was written: "There is no authority in the regulations or elsewhere that the earmarked funds are treated as support for the intermediary organizations as well as the ultimate recipient."[66] It is true that the law is silent on the point, but that does not necessarily mean that this dual characterization of the funds for tax purposes is inappropriate. This is particularly the case with donor-advised funds, where the gifts are not earmarked as a matter of law.[67]

---

61. A term of disparagement once promoted by certain members of congressional staff to describe these entities is *accommodation charities*.
62. See § 15.4.
63. Gen. Couns. Mem. 39748.
64. Gen. Couns. Mem. 39875.
65. "Donor Directed Funds," Topic M, IRS Exempt Organization Continuing Professional Education Text for FY 1996.
66. *Id.*
67. Nonetheless, in one set of circumstances, the IRS ruled that contributions to a donor-advised fund may be treated as support from the general public (in this instance, under IRC § 170(b)(1)(A)(vi)) to the charity that maintains the fund (Priv. Ltr. Rul. 200037053). In a second determination, the IRS reached a like conclusion (Priv. Ltr. Rul. 200150039).

This analysis posited a second approach, in that it applied the distinction between contributions to a charitable organization and those *for the use of* a charitable organization.[68] The idea is that only contributions to a charitable organization can be treated as public support, as the charity is free to use the gifts in its charitable program. The IRS essay asserts that an earmarked gift and a gift "for the use of" a charity are similar in that "both have qualities of property held in trust." That is, this view asserts that the intermediary entity is the functional equivalent of a trustee for the ultimate charity, so that these earmarked contributions ought not to be regarded as public support for the intermediate entity (the organization housing charitable gift funds).

There are fundamental problems with this approach. This analysis often fails to differentiate between donor-advised funds and donor-directed funds. Given the limited recommendatory authority associated with the former, it is not credible to assert that the arrangement involves a trust relationship. Also, it is common for donors to make restricted gifts, where the restriction is a programmatic one (such as for research or scholarships); there is no authority for a proposition that these restrictions give rise to a trust. Moreover, the statutory definition of *support*[69] does not embody this dubious dichotomy in this context between gifts to and for the use of charity.

In the IRS's first private letter ruling on the point, the agency held that the establishment by a charitable organization of a donor-advised gift fund program did not jeopardize the organization's exempt status or its public charity status.[70] In this ruling, however, the organization's public charity status was based on its being a supporting organization of a noncharitable organization (a business league);[71] thus, whether donations made to the supporting organization's donor-advised gift fund constituted public support was not at issue.

§ 16.6 INTERRELATIONSHIP OF PRIVATE FOUNDATION RULES

Of great concern to the IRS in approving tax exemption for donor-advised funds, particularly those created by for-profit financial institutions, is the potential for avoidance of the minimum distribution requirements.[72] This is one of the reasons the IRS has regarded certain donor-advised funds as

---

68. See *Charitable Giving* § 8.2.
69. IRC § 509(d).
70. Priv. Ltr. Rul. 200149045.
71. See § 15.6(l).
72. See Chapter 6.

§ 16.7 STATUTORY CRITERIA

"aggressive tax avoidance schemes."[73] Under current law, a private foundation can make a grant (qualifying distribution) to a donor-advised fund in satisfaction of the foundation's mandatory payout requirements.[74] These distribution requirements can be satisfied even though the private foundation's governing board retains the ability to make recommendations as to the subsequent granting of the money.[75] Because they qualify as public charities, however, charitable organizations administering donor-advised funds are not subject to the private foundation mandatory payout rules.

As a public charity, a sponsoring organization administering donor-advised funds is not subject to any of the other various excise taxes (and corresponding operational constraints) that are imposed on a private foundation—other than the excess business holdings rules.[76]

§ 16.7 STATUTORY CRITERIA

The Pension Protection Act of 2006 enacted a statutory definition of the term *donor-advised fund*. Essentially, it is a fund or account that is (1) separately identified by reference to contributions of one or more donors, (2) that is owned and controlled by a sponsoring organization, and (3) as to which a donor or a *donor advisor*[77] has, or reasonably expects to have, advisory privileges with respect to the distribution or investment of amounts held in the fund or account by reason of the donor's status as a donor.[78] A *sponsoring organization* is a public charity that maintains one or more donor-advised funds.[79]

A donor-advised fund does not include funds that make distributions only to a single identified organization or governmental entity.[80] A donor-advised fund also does not include certain funds where a donor or donor advisor provides advice as to which individuals receive grants for travel, study, or other similar purposes if (1) such person's advisory privileges are performed exclusively by them in their capacity as a member of a committee all of the

---

73. "Public Charity Classification and Private Foundations Issues: Recent Emerging Significant Developments," Topic P, IRS Exempt Organization Continuing Professional Education Text for FY 2000.
74. See § 6.4(b). For a discussion of proposed legislation (and a proposal by the administration) that would prevent (or restrict) distributions to a donor-advised fund by a private foundation from being treated as qualifying distributions for purposes of meeting a foundation's annual payout requirement, see § 16.10.
75. E.g., Priv. Ltr. Ruls. 8836033 and 9807030.
76. IRC § 4943(e); see § 16.7.
77. That is, any person appointed or designated by a donor.
78. IRC § 4966(d)(2)(A).
79. IRC § 4966(d)(1).
80. IRC § 4966(d)(2)(B)(i). E.g., Priv. Ltr. Rul. 201922038.

DONOR-ADVISED FUNDS

members of which are appointed by the sponsoring organization, (2) no combination of donors or donor advisors (or persons related to such persons) control, directly or indirectly, such committee, and (3) all grants from such fund or account are awarded on an objective and nondiscriminatory basis pursuant to a procedure approved in advance by the board of directors of the sponsoring organization.[81]

The IRS also has the *discretionary authority* to exempt other funds or accounts from treatment as a donor-advised fund if (1) such fund or account is advised by a committee not directly or indirectly controlled by the donor or any donor advisor (or any related parties) with respect to distributions from such fund (that is, an independent selection committee) or (2) if such fund benefits a single identified charitable purpose.[82] Exercising this authority, the IRS announced that certain employer-sponsored disaster relief assistance funds at community foundations or other publicly supported charities do not constitute donor-advised funds. To be eligible for this exclusion, a fund must meet the following requirements: (1) the fund must serve a single identified charitable purpose, which is to provide relief from one or more qualified disasters,[83] (2) the fund must serve a large or indefinite class (that is, a charitable class), (3) recipients of grants from the fund must be selected based on objective determinations of need, (4) the selection of recipients of grants from the fund must be made using either an independent selection committee or adequate substitute procedures to ensure that any benefit to the employer is incidental and tenuous,[84] (5) no payment may be made from the fund to or for the benefit of any director, officer, or trustee of the sponsoring organization of the fund, or members of the fund's selection committee, and (6) the fund must maintain adequate records that demonstrate the recipients' needs for the disaster relief assistance provided.[85]

A distribution from a donor-advised fund is a *taxable distribution* if it is to (1) a natural person,[86] (2) any other person for a noncharitable purpose, or

---

81. IRC § 4966(d)(2)(B)(ii). This procedure must be designed to ensure that all such grants meet the requirements of IRC § 4945(g)(1), (2), or (3) (*id.*; see § 9.3(d), (e)(i)).
82. IRC § 4966(d)(2)(C).
83. Within the meaning of IRC § 139(c)(1), (2), or (3).
84. The selection committee is considered independent if a majority of the members of the committee consists of persons who are not in a position to exercise substantial influence over the affairs of the employer.
85. Notice 2006-109, 2006-51 I.R.B. 1121 § 5.01. As to employer-sponsored disaster relief assistance funds, see § 9.3(c).
86. Thus, absent the IRS's exercise of its discretionary authority to exempt employer-sponsored disaster relief funds from the definition of donor-advised funds (see text accompanying previous footnote), distributions from these funds to employees or their family members (that is, to natural persons) would be taxable distributions.

§ 16.7 STATUTORY CRITERIA

(3) to any other person (even if for a charitable purpose) unless expenditure responsibility is exercised with respect to the distribution.[87] A taxable distribution does not, however, include a distribution from a donor-advised fund to most public charities,[88] the fund's sponsoring organization, or another donor-advised fund,[89] and therefore expenditure responsibility does not need to be exercised with respect to a distribution from a donor-advised fund to such an organization or fund.

A tax of 20 percent of the amount of a taxable distribution is imposed on the sponsoring organization.[90] Another tax of 5 percent is imposed on the agreement of a fund manager to the making of a taxable distribution, where the manager knew that the distribution was a taxable one.[91] The tax on fund management is subject to joint and several liability.[92] The term *fund manager* encompasses trustees, directors, officers of a sponsoring organization, or an individual with similar powers and responsibilities, and with respect to any act (or failure to act), the employees of the sponsoring organization having authority or responsibility with respect to such act (or failure to act).[93]

If a donor, donor advisor, or a person related to a donor or donor advisor,[94] provides advice as to a distribution from a donor-advised fund that results in any of those persons receiving, directly or indirectly, a benefit that is more than incidental, an excise tax equal to 125 percent of the amount of the benefit is imposed on the person who advised as to the distribution and on the recipient of the benefit.[95] Also, if a fund manager agreed to the making of the

---

87. IRC § 4966(c)(1). E.g., Priv. Ltr. Rul. 201922038. The expenditure responsibility rules are the subject of § 9.7.
88. That is, organizations described in IRC § 170(b)(1)(A), other than a *disqualified supporting organization*, which is a Type III supporting organization (other than a functionally integrated one) and any Type I and II supporting organizations if the donor or any donor advisor with respect to distributions from a donor-advised fund (and any related parties) directly or indirectly controls a supported organization of such organization (IRC § 4966(d)(4)). See § 15.6(e)-(g).
89. IRC § 4966(c)(2).
90. IRC § 4966(a)(1).
91. IRC § 4966(a)(2). This tax is limited to $10,000 per transaction (IRC § 4966(b)(2)).
92. IRC § 4966(b)(1).
93. IRC § 4966(d)(3).
94. A *related person* for these purposes (IRC § 4967(d)) includes a family member (IRC § 4958(f)(4)) of a donor or donor advisor or an entity that is a 35 percent controlled entity (IRC § 4958(f)(3)) because of such persons' ownership interests in such entity (IRC § 4958(f)(7)).
95. IRC § 4967(a)(1). The term *incidental* is not defined in this context. A summary of this legislation, however, states that "there is a more than incidental benefit if, as a result of a distribution from a donor-advised fund, a donor, donor advisor, or related person with respect to such fund receives a benefit that would have reduced (or eliminated) a charitable contribution deduction if the benefit was received as part of the contribution to the

distribution, knowing that the distribution would confer more than an incidental benefit on a donor, donor advisor, or related person, the fund manager is subject to an excise tax equal to 10 percent of the amount of the benefit.[96] Both the tax on donors, donor advisors, or related persons and the tax on fund managers is subject to joint and several liability.[97] Neither tax is imposed if a tax with respect to the distribution has been imposed pursuant to the intermediate sanctions rules.[98]

A grant, loan, compensation, or other similar payment (e.g., reimbursement of expenses) from a donor-advised fund to a person that, with respect to the fund, is a donor, donor advisor, or a person related to a donor or donor advisor automatically is treated as an excess benefit transaction for intermediate sanctions law purposes.[99] The entire amount paid to any of these persons is an excess benefit.[100] Donors and donor advisors with respect to a donor-advised fund (and related persons) are disqualified persons for intermediate sanctions law purposes with respect to transactions with the donor-advised fund (although not necessarily with respect to transactions with the sponsoring organization).[101]

The private foundation *excess business holdings rules*[102] apply to donor-advised funds.[103] For this purpose, the term *disqualified person* means, with respect to a donor-advised fund, a donor, donor advisor, member of the family of either, or a 35 percent controlled entity of any such person(s).[104]

In the facts of the first IRS private letter ruling applying this law, a charitable organization maintaining donor-advised funds was the recipient of gifts of a corporation's nonvoting stock from two brothers, founders of the

---

sponsoring organization" (Staff of Joint Comm. on Tax'n, Technical Explanation of H.R. 4, the "Pension Protection Act of 2006," as Passed by the House on July 28, 2006, and as Considered by the Senate on August 3, 2006 350 (Comm. Print JCX-38-06) (PPA Joint Comm. Explanation)). This suggests that at least one way to define the term *incidental* is to use the definition of the term in the charitable giving context where a charitable deduction is not otherwise reduced by reason of an inconsequential benefit (see § 14.1; also see *Charitable Giving* § 2.1(d)). For definitions of incidental or tenuous benefits applicable to private foundations in the self-dealing context, see § 5.8(e).

96. IRC § 4967(a)(2). The maximum amount of this tax per distribution is $10,000 (IRC § 4967(c)(2)).
97. IRC § 4967(c)(1).
98. IRC § 4967(b); see *Tax-Exempt Organizations*, Chapter 21.
99. IRC § 4958(c)(2)(A).
100. IRC § 4958(c)(2)(B). For the application of these rules in the supporting organizations context, see § 15.6(i).
101. IRC § 4958(f)(7).
102. See Chapter 7.
103. IRC § 4943(e)(1).
104. IRC § 4943(e)(2).

§ 16.7 STATUTORY CRITERIA

corporation; the gifts were placed in donor-advised funds. The brothers were disqualified persons. After these gifts and after transfer of all the voting stock of the corporation to another public charity, however, the disqualified persons owned less than 20 percent of the voting stock, causing the nonvoting stock to be permitted holdings. The second public charity was not a disqualified person with respect to the charitable donee. Thus, the sponsoring organization, including its donor-advised funds, was ruled to not have any excess business holdings.[105]

Contributions to a donor-advised fund maintained by a sponsoring organization are not eligible for a charitable deduction for federal income tax purposes if the sponsoring organization is a fraternal society, a cemetery company, or a veterans' organization.[106] Such contributions are not eligible for a charitable deduction for federal estate or gift tax purposes if the sponsoring organization is a fraternal society or a veterans' organization.[107] Such contributions are not eligible for a charitable deduction for income, estate, or gift tax purposes if the sponsoring organization is a Type III supporting organization (other than a functionally integrated Type III supporting organization).[108] With respect to each charitable contribution to a sponsoring organization to be maintained in a donor-advised fund, a donor must obtain a contemporaneous written acknowledgment from the sponsoring organization that the organization has exclusive legal control over the funds or assets contributed.[109]

A sponsoring organization is required to disclose on its annual information return the number of donor-advised funds it owns, the aggregate value of assets held in the funds at the end of the organization's tax year, and the aggregate contributions to and grants made from these funds during the year.[110] When seeking recognition of tax-exempt status,[111] a sponsoring organization must disclose whether it intends to maintain donor-advised funds. As to this latter rule, the legislative history to the donor-advised fund rules indicates that a sponsoring organization must provide information regarding its planned operation of these funds, including a description of procedures it intends to use to (1) communicate to donors and donor advisors that assets held in the funds are the property of the sponsoring organization,

---

105. Priv. Ltr. Rul. 201311035.
106. IRC § 170(f)(18)(A)(i). See *Tax-Exempt Organizations* §§ 19.4, 19.6, 19.11, respectively.
107. IRC §§ 2055(e)(5)(A)(i), 2522(c)(5)(A)(i).
108. IRC §§ 170(f)(18)(A)(ii), 2055(e)(5)(A)(ii), 2522(c)(5)(A)(ii).
109. IRC §§ 170(f)(18)(B), 2055(e)(5)(B), 2522(c)(5)(B). This requirement is in addition to other charitable giving substantiation requirements (see § 14.7(b)). A substantiation document issued in connection with a contribution to a donor-advised fund was pronounced adequate by the IRS (Chief Couns. Adv. Mem. 201736023).
110. IRC § 6033(k).
111. IRC § 508(f).

and (2) ensure that distributions from donor-advised funds do not result in more than incidental benefit to any person.[112]

Sponsoring organizations, fund managers, donors, donor advisors, or related persons liable for any of the excise taxes described above are required to file Form 4720 to report and pay these taxes.[113] Specifically in the donor-advised fund context, Form 4720 is used to calculate and pay the taxes on excess business holdings (Schedule C), excess benefit transactions (Schedule I), distributions of sponsoring organizations maintaining donor-advised funds (Schedule K), and prohibited benefits from donor-advised funds (Schedule L).

§ 16.8 STUDIES

(a) Treasury Study

The Department of the Treasury was directed by Congress to undertake a study on the organization and operation of donor-advised funds, to consider whether (1) the deductions allowed for income, estate, or gift taxes for charitable contributions to sponsoring organizations of donor-advised funds are appropriate in consideration of the use of contributed assets or the use of the assets of such organizations for the benefit of the person making the charitable contribution, (2) donor-advised funds should be required to distribute for charitable purposes a specified amount in order to ensure that the sponsoring organization with respect to the donor-advised fund is operating in a manner consistent with its tax exemption or public charity status, (3) the retention by donors to donor-advised funds of "rights or privileges" with respect to amounts transferred to such organizations (including advisory rights or privileges with respect to the making of grants or the investment of assets) is consistent with the treatment of these transfers as completed gifts, and (4) these issues are also issues with respect to other forms of charitable organizations or charitable contributions.[114]

The report focuses on both supporting organizations[115] and donor advised funds.[116] This report summarizes these two bodies of law, including the rules

---

112. PPA Joint Comm. Explanation at 350. The current version of Form 1023 does not precisely track these requirements, however, and instead asks a sponsoring organization to provide a description of its program, including the specific advice that donors may provide and to describe in detail the control it maintains (or will maintain) over the use of the funds (Form 1023 (Jan. 2020), Part IV, line 11).
113. See § 12.4(a).
114. Pension Protection Act of 2006, Pub. L. No. 109-280, § 1226, 120 Stat. 780, 1094.
115. See § 15.6. Because the analysis of the two topics is integrated in the report, the elements of it pertaining to supporting organizations are included in this summary.
116. Department of Treasury, "Report to Congress on Supporting Organizations and Donor Advised Funds" (Dec. 5, 2011).

enacted in 2006; provides a statistical analysis of supporting organizations and donor-advised funds; and answers questions posed by Congress. Overall, this report concludes that supporting organizations and donor-advised funds "play an important role in the charitable sector."

The statistics utilized by the Treasury Department are for 2006, the first year for which complete data were available for use in time for this report. Supporting organizations received $94.1 billion, had outlays of $72.5 billion, including $11.5 billion in grants, $4 billion in payments to affiliates, and $46.9 billion in program expenditures. As of the close of that year, supporting organizations had a net worth of $226.7 billion. The report observes that supporting organizations that "support organizations that provide medical and dental care for low-income households, work with hospital patients and employees, and conduct health research had the largest [amount of] revenue, expenses, and net worth."

Organizations sponsoring donor-advised funds received $59.5 billion, including $9 billion in contributions to the funds. These sponsoring organizations had total expenses of $37.7 billion, including $5.7 billion in grants paid from donor-advised fund assets, $6.8 billion in other grants made, and $20.7 billion in program expenses. These organizations had a net worth of $211.3 billion at the end of the year. The 2,398 organizations sponsoring donor-advised funds had 160,000 of them, entailing assets valued at $31.1 billion as of the end of the year.

The report notes that, beginning with 2006, the annual information return (Form 990) was redesigned, requiring sponsoring organizations to report the aggregate value of assets held in, the aggregate contributions to, and the grants from their donor-advised funds. This data, the report adds, will make it possible to calculate aggregate payout rates at the sponsoring organization level and compare the payout rates of these aggregate donor-advised funds with those of private foundations.

The report references sponsoring organizations that have a "national reach" and have as their primary role services as "intermediaries between donors and a broad range of charities providing direct charitable services by sponsoring and maintaining donor-advised funds and other similar charitable funds." These are referred to as *national donor-advised funds*. A subset of national donor-advised funds is those that are sponsored by charitable affiliates of financial institutions—given the (unfortunate) name of *commercial national donor-advised funds*.

Aggregate donor-advised funds that are commercial national donor-advised funds had an average of $424.5 million in total assets and median assets of $58.9 million. The average payout rate across all aggregate donor-advised funds in 2006 was 9.3 percent. Among the commercial national donor-advised funds, the average payout rate was 14.2 percent. This led the report to conclude that it would be "premature to recommend a distribution requirement for [donor-advised funds] at this point."

The report states that the Pension Protection Act "appears to have provided a legal structure to address abusive practices and accommodate innovations in the sector without creating undue additional burden or new opportunities for abuse."

As for public comments received by Treasury, the report observes that respondents "generally praised the relative benefits of [supporting organizations] to the supported organizations compared to the benefits that charities derive from [donor-advised funds] and private foundations." Also, "[t]here is a consensus among the respondents that [donor-advised funds] have been a helpful development for donors in the charitable sector."

The final component of this report is a collection of answers to questions posed by Congress. As to the workability of the charitable contribution deduction in these contexts, the report concludes that the charitable deduction rules "for gifts to [donor-advised funds] and [supporting organizations], which are the same as the rules for gifts to other public charities, appear to be appropriate." Concerning distribution requirements, the report states, as noted, that "it would be premature to make a recommendation regarding distribution requirements for [donor-advised funds] on the basis of this first year of reported data." The report is of the view that "it is consistent to treat donations to [donor-advised funds] and [supporting organizations] that comply with existing legal requirements as completed gifts even if the donor retains non-binding advisory rights."

The report concludes with this: "The [Pension Protection Act] enacted provisions designed to mitigate undue donor influence on [supporting organizations] and [donor-advised fund] sponsoring organizations and to increase the required transparency of these organizations. New reporting requirements will make more data available to federal and state regulators, as well as to researchers, the press, and the general public. As the effects of the [Pension Protection Act] and new regulations become clearer over time, Treasury looks forward to working with Congress to determine whether additional legislation or reporting is necessary."

(b) Congressional Research Service Study

The Congressional Research Service (CRS) also issued a report that includes statistics on donor advised funds, using data derived from Forms 990 for 2008.[117] In 2008, more than 181,000 individual donor advised fund accounts

---

117. Congressional Research Service, "An Analysis of Charitable Giving and Donor Advised Funds," Rep. No. R42595 (July 11, 2012).

were maintained. In that year, there were about 1,818 organizations maintaining at least one donor-advised fund account. Approximately one-third of organizations claiming to have donor-advised funds reported that only one fund was maintained. About one-half of all sponsoring organizations reported that five or fewer funds were held.

Thus, according to this report, a small percentage of sponsoring organizations held a large number of donor-advised fund accounts. Fifty-one organizations (about 3 percent of all sponsoring organizations) reported having 500 or more individual donor-advised funds. More than 121,000 of all fund accounts (or two-thirds of them) are maintained by organizations that have at least 500 individual accounts. The report observes that the fact that a large proportion of individual donor-advised fund accounts are maintained by a small number of sponsoring organizations explains why the number of donor-advised funds per organization (100) is "highly skewed." Also: "Since most [donor-advised fund] accounts are held by organizations maintaining multiple [fund] accounts, little is known about the characteristics of the majority of individual [fund] accounts."

For the year, sponsoring organizations reported $29.5 billion in donor-advised fund assets. On average, assets per donor-advised funds had a value of about $162,000. Nearly all donor-advised fund assets (87 percent) are held by sponsoring organizations that maintain 100 or more individual fund accounts.

Total contributions to donor-advised funds were reported to be $7.1 billion. These contributions represented approximately 3.3 percent of total individual giving. On average, sponsoring organizations received $3.9 million in contributions. The average contribution per fund account was $39,103.

Sponsoring organizations reported paying out $7 billion in grants. On average, $38,641 in grants were paid per donor-advised fund. Out of the 1,828 sponsoring organizations included in the sample, an estimated 453 did not make any grants. The organizations that sponsored donor-advised funds but did not pay grants held $280.4 million in assets in 2008.

The average payout rate across sponsoring organizations was 13.1 percent. The median payout rate was 6.1 percent; this average was said to be "skewed" by the payout rates of organizations with "unusually large payouts." Forty-three percent of sponsoring organizations had an average payout of less than 5 percent. Twenty-six percent did not report a payout.

This study included a review of 21 "commercial" organizations maintaining donor-advised funds. In 2008, 46.7 percent of individual fund accounts were maintained by these organizations. For the year, 34.3 percent of donor-advised fund assets, 39.2 percent of fund contributions, and 39.7 percent of fund grants involved "commercial" sponsoring organizations.

The average payout rate for commercial donor-advised funds was 26.5 percent. The report observed that since commercial sponsoring organizations "tend to sponsor a large number of individual accounts (2,720 on average), it is possible that there is substantial variation in payout rates across individual accounts that is masked by the aggregate nature of available payout data."

The CRS report also extensively addressed the matter of a minimum distribution requirement for donor-advised funds. It noted that the Treasury's position on a minimum payout for donor-advised funds was that it is premature to consider it based on one year of data. Yet, both the 2006 and 2008 data indicate a payout ratio in the aggregate that was higher than that of private foundations (but considerable variability in these ratios across sponsoring organizations).

The Treasury report stated that the payout rates for donor-advised funds in the aggregate in 2006 "appear to be high for most categories of [fund] sponsoring organizations." The CRS said this statement "seems to imply that observing an overall payout rate higher than that for foundations is a rationale for not imposing a minimum payout requirement" in the donor-advised fund context. The CRS, however, wrote that "there is ample reason to reject the notion that an aggregate payout ratio higher than that of private foundations provides a good rationale for not imposing such requirements on a per [fund] account basis." Yet, the CRS noted, although for sponsoring organizations maintaining a single fund account the average payout rate was 10.6 percent, over one-half of these organizations did not make any distribution and over 70 percent made a distribution of less than 5 percent. The CRS concluded that "there is likely to be substantial variation in payout rates at the individual account level across all sponsoring organizations."

The CRS report, not so subtly advocating consideration of a minimum payout rate for individual donor-advised funds, stated that a minimum rate imposed on sponsoring organizations would be "relatively meaningless," given the data. This approach, the CRS report stated, "would also create an incentive for donors who wished to accumulate funds and maintain endowments while paying little or nothing in grants to move to the larger [fund] sponsors, including commercial [donor-advised funds]."

This report also recalled that the Treasury report rejected application of private foundation rules to donor-advised funds on the ground that, as a matter of law, control of the fund is in the sponsoring organization (a public charity). The CRS report rejected this, writing that "donors appear to have actual control of grant-making because sponsoring organizations typically follow their advice." The report states that "[i]n considering this issue, one question is whether the restricted legal rights of the donor or actual practice should determine the appropriate treatment."

The report raised the issue as to whether commercial donor-advised funds and national ones lacked a charitable purpose. It noted that some have suggested "tighter regulations and greater restrictions" for these sponsors. Also referenced was, in the case of commercial donor-advised funds, a "tension" between the "needs of charitable organizations . . . and the incentive to maintain large investment accounts."

Another proposal discussed in the CRS report is the one to restrict the duration of donor-advised funds. This could be done by limiting the life of these accounts or by limiting the period of years that advisory rights would be effective. The report states that this approach "would be an alternative or perhaps addition to a payout requirement to insure that the amounts in [fund] accounts are used for charitable purposes in some reasonable time period."

The CRS report bemoaned the fact that "all reporting is done at the aggregate [donor-advised fund] sponsor level, which means there is information only by inference concerning the shares of accounts that have low or no payout ratios." It stated: "Requiring reporting on individual [fund] accounts is an option that could improve understanding of how [donor-advised funds] operate and provide better oversight."

The report stated: "Useful information that could be provided by [donor-advised fund] sponsors could include the share of their [fund] accounts that made no distributions, the share that made distributions of less than 5 [percent], or a general distribution of accounts across different payout intervals." Also: "Information on investment fees and administrative costs of managing the [donor-advised funds], separated from other costs, could also be useful." Further: "Additional information could help policy makers evaluate whether giving through [donor-advised funds] is achieving charitable giving policy goals."

The CRS report concluded by questioning whether allowing donors "to make contributions that are not immediately used for charitable purposes . . . increase[s] charitable giving per dollar of cost or decrease[s] it." Permitting contributions "to accumulate and earn a tax-free return increases the benefit to the donor and thus may increase contributions to funds or foundations, albeit at an additional cost." By "encouraging fund accumulation" instead of distributions, however, such arrangements can also reduce current charitable, "a concern that presumably motivated the minimum distribution rules for private foundations." The CRS noted that although "legal technicalities" differentiate donor-advised funds from private foundation, in practice they are "very similar." A common concern with both continues to be "how soon donations are put to charitable use."

§ 16.9 TAX REGULATIONS

(a) The Ever-Pending Regulations Project

The development of guidance to accompany the donor-advised fund statutory rules has been a dusty fixture on the Department of the Treasury Priority Guidance Plan since the 2007–2008 Plan issued following the enactment of the

Pension Protection Act of 2006. The long-standing generic reference to guidance on the excise taxes on donor-advised funds and fund management has more recently been updated to include three "priority" regulations projects: (1) regulations regarding donor-advised funds, including excise taxes on sponsoring organizations and fund management,[118] (2) regulations regarding prohibited benefits, including excise taxes on donors, donor advisors, related persons, and fund management,[119] and (3) regulations under the intermediate sanctions rules[120] regarding donor-advised funds and supporting organizations.[121] Guidance regarding the public-support computation with respect to distributions from donor-advised funds is also listed as a priority.[122] Time will tell if this separation of one regulation project into several signals a more resolute commitment on the part of Treasury and the IRS to finally propose regulations in this area.

(b) 2017 IRS Notice

A 2017 IRS notice identified "approaches" that the Treasury Department and the IRS are considering to address certain issues regarding donor-advised funds of sponsoring organizations.[123] The first issue considered is whether a distribution from a donor-advised fund to a public charity that enables a donor, donor advisor, or related person to attend or participate in an event results in them receiving a more than incidental benefit.[124] The IRS rejected a suggestion that a distribution from a donor-advised fund should be considered as conferring only an incidental benefit as long as the amount of the distribution from the donor-advised fund does not exceed the portion of the ticket cost that would be deductible as a charitable contribution deduction if paid by the donor directly and the donor separately pays for the nondeductible portion. Thus, it is anticipated that under (eventually) proposed regulations, the relief of the donor's obligation to pay the full price of a ticket to a charity-sponsored event (thereby subsidizing the donor's attendance or participation in the event) would be considered a direct benefit to the donor that is more than incidental.[125] The notice notes that a donor who wishes to receive goods or services (such as tickets to an event) offered by a charity in

---

118. IRC § 4966.
119. IRC § 4967.
120. IRC § 4958.
121. Department of the Treasury, 2023-2024 Priority Guidance Plan (Sept. 29, 2023).
122. Id.
123. Notice 2017-73, 2017-51 I.R.B. 562. For purposes of the discussion of this notice, a donor, donor advisor, or related person will collectively be referred to as a "donor."
124. For purposes of the IRC § 4967 tax.
125. The IRS has taken the same position in the self-dealing context with respect to attempts to bifurcate the costs of event tickets (see § 5.8(g)).

exchange for a contribution of a specified amount can make the contribution directly, without the involvement of a donor-advised fund. The same analysis would apply to a donor-advised fund's payment of the deductible portion of a membership fee for the benefit of a donor.[126]

For purposes of the private foundation self-dealing rules, a foundation's grant or other payment in fulfillment of the legal obligation of a disqualified person ordinarily constitutes a prohibited act of self-dealing.[127] Because of the difficulty for sponsoring organizations to differentiate between a legally enforceable pledge by an individual to a third-party charity and a mere expression of charitable intent, the Treasury Department and the IRS are of the view that the determination of whether an individual's charitable pledge is legally binding is best left to the charity receiving the distribution from a donor-advised fund because it has knowledge of the facts surrounding the pledge. Accordingly, the Treasury Department and the IRS are considering proposed regulations providing that distributions from a donor-advised fund to a charity will not be considered to result in a more than incidental benefit to a donor merely because the donor has made a charitable pledge to the same charity (regardless of whether the recipient charity treats the distribution as satisfying the pledge), provided the following requirements are met: (1) the sponsoring organization makes no reference to the existence of a charitable pledge when making the donor-advised fund distribution; (2) no donor receives, directly or indirectly, any other benefit that is more than incidental on account of the donor-advised fund distribution; and (3) a donor does not attempt to claim a charitable contribution deduction with respect to the donor-advised fund distribution,[128] even if the recipient charity erroneously sends the donor a written acknowledgment with respect to the donor-advised fund distribution.[129]

Because of the contributions they receive from the general public, sponsoring organizations typically qualify as donative publicly supported charities; therefore, distributions from their donor-advised funds ordinarily may be counted as public support in their entirety by the recipient charity. That

---

126. Notice 2017-73, 2017-51 I.R.B. 562 § 3.
127. See § 5.8(c).
128. It seems somewhat odd that this third requirement is called out in this context, in that a donor should not be attempting to claim a charitable contribution deduction with respect to any distribution *from* a donor-advised fund. The donor would have been allowed to claim such a deduction on its initial contribution *to* the donor-advised fund.
129. Notice 2017-73, 2017-51 I.R.B. 562 § 4. This special rule (if adopted in regulations) would only apply in the donor-advised context and would not be extended to the private foundation context because "the relationship between a private foundation and its disqualified persons typically is much closer" than a sponsoring organization's relationship with its donors (*id.*). Taxpayers may rely on this special rule until additional guidance is issued (*id.* § 7).

is, distributions from donor-advised funds are not subject to the 2 percent limitation on support imposed on donative publicly supported charities[130] or the limitation on support received from substantial contributors imposed on service provider publicly supported charities.[131] Thus, there is a potential for a donor whose support would otherwise be subject to one of these limitations to funnel their contribution through a donor-advised fund to "circumvent" these limitations to avoid jeopardizing the recipient's public charity status (or, stated differently, to facilitate the recipient in continuing to avoid private foundation status). In light of this "potential for abuse," and to "better reflect the degree to which . . . [a] charity receives broad support from a representative number of persons," the Treasury Department and the IRS are considering treating a distribution from a donor-advised fund, for purposes of the public support tests, as an indirect contribution from the donor(s) that funded the donor-advised fund rather than as a contribution from the sponsoring organization. Additionally, all anonymous contributions received (including a donor-advised fund distribution for which the sponsoring organization fails to identify the donor that funded the donor-advised fund) would be treated as being made by one person. Distributions from a sponsoring organization would be treated as public support without limitation only if the sponsoring organization specifies that the distribution is not from a donor-advised fund or states that no donor advised the distribution.[132]

In addition to requesting comments on these three issues, the Treasury Department and the IRS requested comments on how private foundations use donor-advised funds in support of their purposes and on whether, consistent with the purposes underlying the mandatory private foundation distribution rules,[133] a transfer of funds by a private foundation to a donor-advised fund should be treated as a qualifying distribution only if the sponsoring organization agrees to redistribute the funds for charitable purposes (or to transfer the funds to its general fund) within a certain time frame.[134]

(c) Comments on IRS Notice

The Council on Foundations, by letter to the IRS, dated May 5, 2018, expressed its concern that the proposal in the 2017 IRS notice to subject all distributions from donor-advised funds to the 2 percent limitation is "overbroad, administratively burdensome, and will serve to discourage financial support for many

---

130. See § 15.4(b).
131. See § 15.5(a).
132. Notice 2017-73, 2017-51 I.R.B. 562 § 5.
133. IRC § 4942; see Chapter 6.
134. Notice 2017-73, 2017-51 I.R.B. 562 § 6.

public charities." The Council urged the Treasury Department to "narrowly tailor any new regulations to be imposed on donor-advised fund distributions to address the very particular circumstances that could be viewed as abusive." These circumstances would be situations where a donor or donor advisor controls the public charity grantee and derives a more-than-incidental benefit as a result of the distribution.

The Council wrote that it is "generally pleased with the recognition that it is often difficult for a sponsoring organization to differentiate between a charitable pledge and a mere expression of charitable intent and appreciates the approach that would leave this determination to the grantee charity rather than to the sponsoring organization." It noted that, since passage of the Pension Protection Act of 2006, it has advised its membership that distributions from donor-advised funds should not be approved if a donor, donor advisor, or related party receives tickets to an event or other more-than-incidental benefit.

The Philanthropy Roundtable, by letter to the Treasury and IRS, dated March 5, 2018, also submitted comments in response to the notice in the form of examples that "demonstrate how important donor advised funds can be for private foundations in sustaining our nation's diverse, abundant and vibrant civil society." Donor-advised funds are, wrote the Roundtable, a "valuable tool for private foundations, which use them for a wide variety of purposes consistent with their purposes and federal law."

Here are some of the illustrations:

Safety and Security

- A private foundation makes grants to a donor-advised fund to support charities in foreign countries where the foundation has staff working in the country, accompanied by their families. Many of these countries are unstable and dangerous; the lives of the foundation's staff and family members would be in jeopardy if this foundation made the grants directly to the charities. This use of a donor-advised fund keeps the identity of the foundation private and protects the safety and well-being of those connected to it.

- A foundation makes grants to a donor-advised fund to support organizations that oppose terrorism, some of which have *fatwas* against them. This grantmaking protects the foundation's trustees from the threat of violence.

Collaboration Among Foundations

- A foundation utilizes a donor-advised fund at a community foundation as part of a collaborative effort with several other foundations that also make grants to the fund to jointly fund local economic development projects. This donor-advised fund is a vehicle that can accept and manage grants from multiple sources without the need for establishing an additional management structure for the collaboration.

- A foundation participates in multi-foundation collaborative funding efforts by making grants to donor-advised funds at community foundations, which it finds more efficient than coordinating direct grants by the participating foundations. This approach also allows grantees to have a single entity to which to report.

Support of Local Projects

- A foundation makes grants to a donor-advised fund at a community foundation in a geographic region as to which the foundation lacks significant local knowledge. This grantmaking allows the foundation to access the local knowledge and experience of the community foundation's staff.
- A foundation supports, in collaboration with other foundations, a project collecting data about city and county governments. All of these foundations fund this project at a community foundation.

Funding Outside Normal Areas

- A foundation uses a donor-advised fund when it supports organizations and projects outside of its typical areas of grantmaking.
- A foundation normally does not provide support for fundraising events. The foundation decided to make a one-time exception, funding a major fundraising event for a charity. By granting to a donor-advised fund and recommending a grant to the charity, the foundation avoided sending a signal to other charities that might encourage them to seek a similar funding exception.
- A foundation allows its board members to make discretionary grants. By keeping these gifts private by use of a donor-advised fund, unsolicited proposals from similar organizations, which might otherwise waste time and effort, are reduced.
- A foundation allocates annual grants to a donor-advised fund for innovative programs that are outside the foundation's normal grant-making procedures. The foundation established a donor-advised fund to be paid out over three years to help drive these programs.

Align Funding with Program Schedule

- A foundation made a grant to a donor-advised fund to support a large capital campaign commitment to a university. The foundation wanted to fund the commitment in a year where its investments performed well, then distribute the funds over several years as elements of the project are completed and the grant contingencies are met.

- A foundation makes grants to donor-advised funds at community foundations because this approach enables the foundation to make distribution decisions with respect to projects based on the projects' timeline and achievements rather than be constrained by the annual distribution requirement.

Maximize Funding and Efficiency

- A foundation uses a donor-advised fund to make international grants to foreign charities. This is seen as a more efficient use of charitable funds inasmuch as the fees are nominal.

- A foundation supports programming at a university's law school that provides training and professional development for federal judges. The organization providing the programming will apply for recognition of exempt status but has yet to do so. The foundation makes grants to a donor-advised fund for this funding, finding this approach more efficient and less costly than making expenditure responsibility grants.

- A foundation used a donor-advised fund to support a consumer education project sponsored by a tax-exempt business league. The foundation utilized this approach because a new organization that is administering this project has yet to receive its determination that it is a charitable organization. Again, this avenue of funding was used to avoid costly and less-efficient expenditure responsibility grants.

Instill Family Giving

- A family with a private foundation uses a donor-advised fund to encourage the next generation to be more philanthropic. The family created the fund, with their children as advisors, to provide the children with a giving vehicle. Due to the children's busy lives, this donor-advised fund turned out to be an ideal charitable giving entity enabling the children to learn about funding philanthropy and making an impact in advance of involving them directly in the management of the foundation.

- A foundation terminated and distributed its assets to a donor-advised fund to bring multiple generations of family members into the grant-making process and document and create the vision for the family's legacy in philanthropy in perpetuity, without the continuing administrative burden of the foundation. This donor-advised fund will become an endowed fund that distributes income each year to causes the family members champion.

- A foundation uses a donor-advised fund during times of economic downturn to maintain granting levels.

- A foundation created a donor-advised fund to create an endowment for an impact investment fund at a university's business school. This investment fund allows students to make investments and learn from the experience.

- A foundation allows its board members to make discretionary grants from a donor-advised fund as to which the foundation is the advisor. By keeping these grants separate from the foundation's general accounts, use of this fund makes accounting easier because the discretionary grant ledger is managed by the sponsoring organization with respect to the fund.

- A foundation allows board members to make discretionary grants, utilizing the due diligence screening capacity of a donor-advised fund sponsor to ensure that the grantees are qualified and have a mission that is aligned with that of the foundation.

The Community Foundation Public Awareness Initiative, consisting of 115 community foundations in 45 states, submitted comments in response to the notice by letter to the IRS dated March 5, 2018. This group observed that donor-advised funds "have become a vitally important philanthropic tool for [community foundations], their donors, and nonprofit organizations in our communities." It "support[ed] changes that will open up more opportunities for charitable giving" and it "oppose[d] any regulations that will discourage charitable giving by making the process more complex for donors, sponsoring organizations, and beneficiary charities to understand."

The Initiative opposes the proposal to cease allowing grants from donor-advised funds from constituting forms of public support for the grantees. It wrote that "there is no showing of evidence that the perceived abuse is so common and widespread as to justify imposing a new rule creating significant administrative burdens on grantee organizations."

The Initiative wants the forthcoming donor-advised fund regulations to allow, in the case of charitable fundraising events, donor-advised funds to make grants in the amounts that would be deductible if made directly by the donor. It also recommends a regulation that permits a donor-advised fund to pay a charitable pledge of the donor or donor advisor irrespective of the enforceability of the pledge or whether the sponsoring organization references or knows of the pledge.

The Initiative "disagree[d] with the implication by some donor-advised fund critics that if a private foundation meets a portion of its payout requirement with a grant to a donor-advised fund, this is prima facie suspect or nefarious." It added that for a private foundation to make a grant to a donor-advised fund at a community foundation "is not uncommon" but "in the vast majority of cases, these grants fulfill a genuine charitable purpose and are not meant to skirt the five percent payout requirement." The group offered a list of the "myriad ways" a private foundation may use a donor-advised fund—a set of examples along the lines of those provided by the Philanthropy Roundtable.

The Tax Section of the Bar Association of New York responded to the notice by letter dated February 28, 2018, and made four recommendations. The first recommendation was that regulations should be issued providing for a "look through" rule for the treatment of grants made by a donor-advised fund to a tax-exempt charitable organization for purposes of determining whether the grantee is publicly supported. That is, grants made from a donor-advised fund should be treated as if the grants were made by the fund's donor or donor advisor.

The second recommendation was that a grant to a donor-advised fund by a private foundation would not be considered a qualifying distribution[135] unless the fund's sponsoring organization agrees to distribute the funds for charitable purposes within a certain time frame.

The third recommendation was for a regulation that provides that a donor or donor advisor receives a more-than-incidental benefit if the donor-advised fund involved makes a grant to a public charity and, as a result, the donor or donor advisor becomes entitled to attend an event or receives membership or similar benefits that would result in the payment being a contribution that is not fully deductible if made directly by the donor.

Fourth, the NYSBA recommended that a regulation be promulgated providing that a distribution from a donor-advised fund to satisfy a donor or donor advisor's legally enforceable pledge to contribute to a charity would confer more than incidental benefit on the donor or donor advisor. The NYSBA further believes that a donor or donor advisor should be required to provide a representation or certification to the donor-advised fund or its sponsoring organization that the recommended distribution is not in satisfaction of a legally enforceable pledge. If this requirement is met, absent actual knowledge by the fund or sponsoring organization that the certification is false, the donor-advised fund or sponsoring organization would not be subject to an excise tax.

The Fidelity Investments Charitable Gift Fund, by letter to the Department of the Treasury and IRS, dated March 2, 2018, stated that the notice proposed a "complicated and unwieldy set of rules that would recharacterize grants received from sponsoring organizations." The Fund wrote that the proposed set of rules is "unwarranted" because (1) "there has [not] been any showing of abuse," (2) a sponsoring organization is a donative publicly supported charity

---

135. See § 6.4(b).

under federal tax statutory law and there is no authority for disregarding that status or for attributing grants from donor-advised funds to the donors, and (3) the "set of presumptions and rules" described in the notice are "overly burdensome on the recipient charitable organization[s], and do not yield useful information."

§ 16.10 PROPOSED LEGISLATION

Parallel bills have been introduced in both houses of Congress for the enactment of the "Accelerating Charitable Efforts Act" or the "ACE Act,"[136] which would make significant changes to the tax law applicable to donor-advised funds and the ways in which private foundations currently utilize them. These proposed changes are intended to ensure that assets held in donor-advised funds are distributed within reasonable time frames.

With respect to private foundations specifically, the ACE Act would prevent distributions to a donor-advised fund by a private foundation from being treated as qualifying distributions for purposes of meeting the foundation's annual payout requirement.[137] The ACE Act would also prevent payments of administrative expenses to a disqualified person from constituting qualifying distributions.[138] An exception would apply with respect to administrative expenses paid to a foundation manager unless that foundation manager is a member of the family of a substantial contributor to the foundation or a 20 percent owner of an entity that is a substantial contributor to the foundation.[139] To encourage accelerated charitable distributions from private foundations, exemption from the section 4940 net investment income tax[140] would be bestowed on private foundations of limited duration (25 years) or in any year in which a private foundation makes significant qualifying distributions (at least 7 percent of the value of the foundation's nonexempt-use assets). Recapture rules would apply to a private foundation of limited duration that later extends its duration beyond 25 years or makes a distribution to a disqualified private foundation (that is, one that has at least one overlapping disqualified person).

Under the ACE Act, distributions from sponsoring organizations of donor-advised funds would become subject to the 2 percent limitation, except where the sponsoring organization specifies that (1) the distribution is not from a donor-advised fund, and (2) no donor or donor advisor had advisory

---

136. S. 1981, 117th Cong. (2021); H.R. 6595, 117th Cong. (2022).
137. See § 6.4(b).
138. See § 6.4(f)(ii).
139. IRC § 4946(a)(1)(A) and (C); see §§ 4.1, 4.3.
140. See Chapter 10.

privileges with respect to the distribution.[141] Additionally, all donor-advised fund distributions from sponsoring organizations would be treated as support received from a single person except where the sponsoring organization identifies the donor making the contribution.[142]

The ACE Act would also create two new types of donor-advised funds: 15-year and 50-year donor-advised funds. With respect to a 15-year donor-advised fund, a donor generally would receive upfront tax benefits as under current law, but only if the agreement establishing the donor-advised fund provides that advisory privileges will be released within 15 years of establishment. In the case of a non-publicly traded asset (that is, any asset for which market quotations are not readily available on an established securities market as of the date of contribution), however, no deduction would be allowed until the non–publicly traded asset is sold and would be limited to the amount of the sales proceeds. The 50-year donor-advised fund is structured based on an "aligned benefit" concept whereby a donor would continue to receive capital gains and estate tax benefits upon donation but would not receive an income tax deduction until distributions are made from the fund to a charitable recipient. The 15-year and 50-year time limitations would be enforced through a 50 percent tax imposed on any contribution not distributed out of the donor-advised fund through a qualifying distribution[143] within six months of the end of the 14th or 49th tax year, depending on whether the donor-advised fund is of the 15-year or 50-year variety.

An exception would apply in the case of a qualified community foundation. A donor would be eligible to receive upfront tax benefits for contributions to a donor-advised fund owned or controlled by a qualified community foundation without being subject to the time limitations described above. This exception is limited to $1 million in donor-advised funds unless the agreement establishing the donor-advised fund requires that it make at least a 5 percent annual payout. For these purposes, a qualified community foundation is one (1) organized and operated for the purpose of understanding and serving the needs of a particular geographic community (that is no larger than four states) by engaging donors and pooling donations to create charitable funds in direct furtherance of those needs, and (2) holds at least 25 percent of its assets outside donor-advised funds.

Criticisms of the ACE Act have rolled in from inside and outside Congress. A May 18, 2022, letter signed by 14 state attorneys general criticizes the ACE

---

141. See § 15.4(b). The Treasury Department and the IRS are considering changes to Reg. § 1.170A-9(f) to the same end (Notice 2017-73, 2017-51 I.R.B. 562 § 5).
142. See § 15.4(b).
143. For these purposes, a qualifying distribution would be any distribution from the donor-advised fund that is not a taxable distribution under IRC § 4966(c)(1) (see § 16.7).

Act restrictions and warns that they "will chill donations and frustrate the ability of charities to receive funding." In a March 7, 2022, letter to their colleagues, 11 House Ways and Means Committee members opined (albeit without specific explanation as to how) that these legislative proposals would not further their goal of ensuring that charitable organizations receive funding as quickly as possible and would instead "reduce the flow of charitable dollars." An August 2, 2021, letter signed by 285 national and community organizations representing each of the 50 states expressed a similar view, again without specific explanation as to how, that the ACE Act's proposed limitations on donor-advised funds would reduce the incentive for donors to use them, "pave the way for their elimination, and sharply curtail philanthropic giving to charities and their beneficiaries." The letter also states the view that the ACE Act's provisions directed at private foundations would "restrict the useful ways that private foundations use DAFs to further their charitable missions." A June 11, 2021, letter to Congress signed by the Community Foundation Public Awareness Initiative, the Council on Foundations, Independent Sector, The Philanthropy Roundtable, and United Philanthropy Forum expressed concerns about the ACE Act and noted that "there is no data to indicate whether these measures would propel more charitable giving." On the other hand, in a September 10, 2021, letter to the California Congressional Delegation, the California Association of Nonprofits urged the members of the delegation to support the ACE Act.

One of the Biden administration's fiscal 2024 revenue proposals would "clarify" that a distribution by a private foundation to a donor-advised fund is not a qualifying distribution unless (1) the donor-advised fund distributes the funds received from the foundation by the end of the following tax year, and (2) the foundation maintains adequate records or other evidence showing that the donor-advised fund has made a qualifying distribution within this time frame. According to the Treasury Department, the failure under current law to require a donor-advised fund to make a further distribution of funds received from a private foundation within a specified period "can subvert the goal behind requiring minimum distributions" by delaying the use of these charitable funds (potentially indefinitely).[144]

---

144. U.S. Treasury Department, General Explanations of the Administration's Fiscal Year 2024 Revenue Proposals (Mar. 9, 2023) 140 ("Green Book"). The Green Book's description of this proposal as a clarification of existing law is inaccurate; indeed, the Green Book itself acknowledges that under current law "a distribution by a private foundation to a DAF is generally considered a qualifying distribution" (see § 6.4(b)) and there is "no requirement that amounts held in a DAF be distributed within any set period of time" (Green Book at 139).

CHAPTER SEVENTEEN

Company Foundations[1]

§ 17.1 Company Foundation
Overview 717
§ 17.2 Reasons for Establishment of a
Company Foundation 719
§ 17.3 Private Inurement Doctrine 719
§ 17.4 Private Benefit Doctrine 720
§ 17.5 Disqualified Persons Rules 721
§ 17.6 Self-Dealing Rules 722
    (a) Payment of Compensation and Reimbursements 722
    (b) Sharing of Facilities 723
    (c) Provision of Tangible Benefits 725
    (d) Grantmaking 726
    (e) Incidental and Tenuous Benefits 727
    (f) Corporate Reorganizations and Stock Transfers 731
§ 17.7 Other Private Foundations Rules 732
    (a) Mandatory Payout Rules 732
    (b) Excess Business Holdings Rules 732
    (c) Jeopardizing Investments Rules 733
    (d) Taxable Expenditures Rules 733
    (e) Economic Returns 734
§ 17.8 Excess Executive Compensation Tax Exceptions 734
    (a) Limited Hours Exception 734
    (b) Nonexempt Funds Exception 736

Tax-exempt charitable organizations that are affiliated with for-profit corporations, and usually controlled by them, are almost always private foundations (generically, *company foundations* or *company-sponsored foundations*). This private foundation status arises, in large part, because the related for-profit corporation typically is the sole funder of a company foundation.

§ 17.1 COMPANY FOUNDATION OVERVIEW

Among the four features of a conventional private foundation is the characteristic that it is funded from one source.[2] Because the typical foundation related to a for-profit business is financially supported only by that business entity, a company foundation usually is a private foundation. It is possible for a charitable organization that is controlled by a for-profit entity to be a public

---

1. Virginia C. Gross provided invaluable assistance in the preparation of this chapter.
2. See § 1.2.

§ 17.1 COMPANY FOUNDATION OVERVIEW

charity—most likely, a donative-type publicly supported organization[3]—but these types of affiliated charities are rare.

A company foundation is a separate legal entity[4] and must be operated primarily for charitable purposes.[5] Most frequently, a company foundation is a corporation. The governing board of a company foundation is subject to the same requirements as to duties and responsibilities that are applicable to charitable organizations generally. As noted, a company foundation is usually controlled by a for-profit business; this control element is almost always manifested in overlapping board or officer positions[6] and/or the ability of the related business entity to appoint (and remove) at least a majority of the trustees or directors of the foundation.

Thus, in several ways, a company foundation is the alter ego of the for-profit business related to it. The two organizations usually have similar names (such as the XYZ Corporation and the XYZ Foundation), and the foundation's governing board is likely to be populated with present and former executives (indeed, as noted, probably at least a majority) of the related company. The name of the for-profit company usually brings recognition to the name of a company foundation; more substantially, the charitable works of a company foundation bring positive public recognition to the for-profit company and serve as evidence of the company's commitment to advancement of charitable causes.

A company foundation (assuming it is a private foundation) is subject to all of the requirements of law imposed on private foundations. There are, however, unique aspects of private foundation law as they relate to company foundations. These aspects arise because the related for-profit business almost always is an insider for private inurement doctrine purposes[7] and a disqualified person for private foundation law purposes.[8] As to the private foundation rules, the body of law that is most likely to be applicable is that pertaining to self-dealing.[9]

---

3. See § 15.4. For example, the affiliated charitable organization could be principally funded by the employees of the related for-profit business (perhaps because it provides disaster relief grants or other employee assistance (see § 9.3(c)) that employees wish to support) or perhaps by a suitable number of members of the public.
4. See § 1.7.
5. See § 1.6.
6. For example, the chief executive officer of the related business corporation is automatically the president of the company foundation, and/or the treasurer of the business corporation is also the foundation's treasurer. Another model has the executive committee of the for-profit corporation serving as the full board of the foundation.
7. See § 17.3.
8. See § 17.5.
9. See § 17.6.

§ 17.2 REASONS FOR ESTABLISHMENT OF A COMPANY FOUNDATION

A company foundation is a legitimate recipient of the related for-profit business's contributions, which presumably are, in whole or in part, deductible by the donor.[10] The investment income generated by the company's gifts (money or other property) is not subject to income tax[11] and provides a source of additional funding of a company foundation's grants. In most instances, a company foundation serves as a vehicle for a more focused and stable charitable grant-making program than the for-profit company could achieve within itself. Additionally, a company foundation may engage in program activities that the for-profit company itself cannot conduct using deductible charitable gifts; thus, a company foundation enables the related company to use its tax-deductible contributions to engage in charitable activities such as grants to individuals[12] and foreign charities.[13]

A separate company foundation allows for increased awareness and branding of the charitable objectives of the for-profit corporation. Foundations of this type facilitate the creation and maintenance of an increased charitable asset base by means of solicitation and receipt of contributions from employees of the related for-profit business and, perhaps, contributions and grants from others. Overall, these foundations provide for a more "tax-efficient manner" of conducting a charitable grant-making program, in relation to what the related for-profit company could do on its own.

§ 17.3 PRIVATE INUREMENT DOCTRINE

Private foundations are subject to the doctrine of private inurement.[14] The various forms of private inurement are transactions or other arrangements with persons who are insiders with respect to the foundation. An insider is a person who has a unique relationship with a charitable organization, by which that person can cause application of the organization's funds or assets for the private purpose of the person by reason of the person's exercise of control or influence over, or being in a position to exercise that control or influence over, the organization. A for-profit business that is operated in tandem with a company foundation is almost certainly an insider with respect to the foundation.

---

10. IRC § 170(a)(1). See Chapter 14; *Charitable Giving* § 4.16.
11. It is, however, subject to an excise tax on its net investment income (see Chapter 10) and a tax on any unrelated business income (see Chapter 11).
12. See § 9.3.
13. See § 9.6.
14. See § 5.1.

The federal tax law does not prohibit transactions between charitable organizations and their insiders; they are, however, subject to the requirement that the terms and conditions of the transaction (or other arrangement) be reasonable. Thus, any transaction between a company's foundation and its insiders must be tested against the standard of reasonableness.

In one instance, the IRS reviewed the operations of a private foundation established and controlled by two rate-regulated utilities. The foundation made grants to a project established by the companies and a public charity. The IRS ruled that private inurement was not occurring because disqualified persons were not benefiting from the foundation's operations and that the project was serving a charitable class.[15]

Positive public recognition accorded a for-profit company due to the charitable activities of its company foundation is not the type of private benefit that is a transgression of the doctrine of private inurement.[16]

§ 17.4 PRIVATE BENEFIT DOCTRINE

Private foundations are also subject to the doctrine of private benefit.[17] This doctrine is infrequently applied in the company foundation context, however, because the self-dealing rules or the private inurement doctrine usually take precedence.

A rare instance involving the private benefit doctrine in this context concerned the Panera Bread Foundation, which operated Panera Cares Cafes. The Foundation's view was that this program provided food to the needy and provided job training to high-risk individuals and those with developmental disabilities. The IRS proposed to revoke retroactively the tax-exempt status of the Foundation, on the grounds of unwarranted private benefit and violation of the commerciality doctrine.[18] Thereafter, the Foundation filed a petition in the U.S. Tax Court seeking continuation of its exemption, noting that the cafes operating in only five of Panera's 2,000-plus stores had been closed.[19] Subsequently, the Tax Court issued a stipulated opinion enabling the Foundation to retain its exempt status.[20]

---

15. Priv. Ltr. Rul. 201436051. The IRS also ruled that these grants were not acts of self-dealing because any benefits to the companies were incidental and tenuous (see §§ 5.8(e), 17.6(e)).
16. See, e.g., *Charitable Giving* § 2.1(d).
17. See § 5.2.
18. Priv. Ltr. Rul. 201911010.
19. Panera Bread Foundation, Inc. v. Commissioner, T.C. Docket No. 5198-19X (Mar. 15, 2019).
20. Panera Bread Foundation, Inc. v. Commissioner, T.C. Docket No. 5198-19X (Mar. 24, 2020).

Private benefit is permitted if it is qualitatively and quantitatively incidental.[21] This point of law was illustrated by an IRS ruling concerning a private foundation created and solely funded by a utility providing electricity and natural gas services. The foundation proposed to make grants to governmental bodies and other public charities to offset the cost difference between the purchase of gasoline and diesel vehicles and the purchase of electric vehicles. The IRS ruled that any private benefit potentially received by the utility will be qualitatively and quantitatively incidental in relation to the public benefit generated by the grants (improvement of the environment and public health), so that the foundation's activities in this regard will not serve a private interest.[22]

§ 17.5 DISQUALIFIED PERSONS RULES

As noted, the for-profit business that is associated with a company foundation is highly likely to be a disqualified person, probably as a substantial contributor.[23] Corporations, partnerships, and/or trusts, as to which the for-profit entity has more than a 35 percent interest, are also disqualified persons with respect to a company foundation.[24] Generally, a for-profit organization affiliated with a company foundation cannot be a foundation manager with respect to the foundation, even if the for-profit entity controls the foundation, because foundation managers usually are individuals.[25]

The directors and officers of a for-profit organization that controls a company foundation are not, by statute, disqualified persons (for that reason) with respect to the foundation. If, however, the for-profit organization is significantly involved in the management of a related company foundation (an inadvisable practice),[26] the IRS might assert (the agency has yet to do so) that officers and/or employees of the company are foundation managers with respect to the foundation.[27] In one instance, the IRS determined that

---

21. See § 5.2.
22. Priv. Ltr. Rul. 202034001. This qualitatively and quantitatively incidental private benefit was also determined to be "incidental or tenuous" (within the meaning of Reg. § 53.4941(d)-2(f)(2)) and therefore to not give rise to an act of self-dealing (see § 17.6(e)).
23. See § 4.1.
24. See §§ 4.5, 4.6.
25. See § 4.2. A for-profit corporation that is a director or the trustee of a private foundation, however, is a disqualified person.
26. See *Tax-Exempt Organizations* § 29.2.
27. The IRS, in a misapplication of the law, found that the activities of a wholly owned for-profit subsidiary were attributable to a tax-exempt parent entity (causing retroactive revocation of exemption) (Priv. Ltr. Rul. 200842050). This type of attribution of activities is to be made where the parent is involved in the management of the subsidiary on a day-to-day basis; it is not to be made merely on the basis of the existence of control (unavoidable where the subsidiary is wholly owned).

employees of a bank that was the trustee of a private foundation were foundation managers, because "they [were] free, on a day-to-day basis, to administer the trust and distribute the funds according to their best judgment."[28] Also, in a determination concerning paid admissions to fundraising functions, the IRS found self-dealing in connection with a transaction involving a company's executive, not because the executive was a disqualified person but because the executive was functioning as an agent of the related company.[29]

§ 17.6 SELF-DEALING RULES

In general, self-dealing between a private foundation and a disqualified person with respect to it is essentially forbidden.[30] This prohibition thus obviously extends to transactions or other arrangements between a company foundation and the for-profit business that is related to it. (As is the case with the private inurement doctrine,[31] positive public recognition accorded a for-profit company due to the charitable activities of its company foundation is not the type of private benefit that is a transgression of the self-dealing rules.)[32]

(a) Payment of Compensation and Reimbursements

The payment of compensation by a private foundation to a disqualified person generally constitutes an act of self-dealing.[33] An important exception to this general rule allows payment of compensation by a private foundation to a disqualified person where the compensation is for personal services reasonable and necessary for advancement of the foundation's exempt purposes. It is the view of the IRS that a private foundation may, without engaging in an act of self-dealing, share the services of employees of the disqualified person, with the foundation reimbursing the disqualified person for its allocable share of the cost of the services, where the services are reasonable, necessary, and not excessive.[34] It is essential, however, for the availability of this exception, that the services be personal services, which means that the services must be professional and managerial, not merely operational, in nature.[35]

---

28. Rev. Rul. 74-287, 1974-1 C.B. 327.
29. Tech. Adv. Mem. 8449008. See § 17.6(c).
30. See § 5.3.
31. See §§ 5.1, 17.3.
32. This is a type of incidental and tenuous benefit (see § 17.6(e)).
33. See § 5.6.
34. Priv. Ltr. Rul. 7952117.
35. See § 5.6(a).

The foregoing rules also apply in connection with the payment to or reimbursement of the expenses of a disqualified person.[36]

(b) Sharing of Facilities

It is common for a company foundation to share offices and the like (such as equipment and supplies) with its related for-profit company. Yet, the general rule is that self-dealing includes the "furnishing of goods, services, or facilities" between (to or from) a private foundation and a disqualified person.[37] Nonetheless, the IRS has been rather generous in permitting shared office space and facilities.[38] Still, as a general principle, it is preferable for a company foundation (and private foundations generally) to procure goods, services, equipment, and the like from sources other than the related company (or other disqualified persons).

The furnishing of goods, services, or facilities by a disqualified person to a private foundation is not self-dealing when done without charge and where the goods, services, or facilities that are furnished are used exclusively for charitable purposes. This includes rental arrangements.[39] Thus, the for-profit business can, without causing self-dealing, allow its company foundation to use its office space and equipment without charge. By contrast, a payment of rent by a company foundation to the related for-profit company would be an act of self-dealing.

If a company foundation and a related for-profit company are to have adjoining rented office space, each entity should enter into separate lease agreements with the property owner (assuming that person is not a disqualified person with respect to the foundation). Any remodeling costs should be borne by the entity receiving the benefit of the remodeling. The cost of any remodeling benefiting both parties should be allocated equally between the two organizations or borne solely by the for-profit company. The for-profit company may allow the foundation to utilize certain of its areas, such as a lobby/reception area, library, conference rooms, kitchen, mailroom, and/or restrooms, without charge.

A company foundation and a related for-profit company may share certain office equipment owned by the company. The foundation may use this equipment without charge. Detailed records of this use could be maintained, however, to enable the company, should it choose to do so, to allocate to the foundation its share of maintenance costs for the equipment. The foundation

---

36. See § 5.6(g).
37. See § 5.4(e).
38. See § 5.9(b).
39. See §§ 5.4(d), 5.9(b).

§ 17.6 SELF-DEALING RULES

should pay its allocable share of these costs, if any, directly to the third-party service provider (assuming it is not a disqualified person with respect to the foundation). If leased equipment is shared, the foundation and company should enter into separate leases with the lessor (assuming it is not a disqualified person with respect to the foundation); the rental amounts should be based on actual use as established by detailed records. The foundation and company may jointly purchase a common telephone system; the two entities should have separate outside telephone lines and individual telephone instruments and be billed separately by the telephone company.

A company foundation and its related for-profit company may share office and certain other supplies, such as refreshments and postage. Detailed records should be maintained by the foundation with respect to such a supplies-sharing arrangement to ensure that it does not pay more than its share of the costs. The foundation should pay its share of these costs directly to the third-party vendors (assuming none of them is a disqualified person with respect to the foundation).

A company foundation and its related for-profit company may share the cost of a receptionist. This individual should be an employee of both organizations and be entitled to each entity's benefits. Each organization should enter into a contract with this individual, with compensation based on a determination of the reasonable value of the employee's services to the organization. Sharing of other employees, if any, should be in accordance with similar arrangements, unless one or more employees are paid solely by the for-profit company.

The situation may arise where, due to sick leave, vacations, and the like, support staff from one entity would render services to the other on a temporary basis. If an employee of the for-profit company provided services to a company foundation under these circumstances, the foundation should pay the employee directly for the services (unless they are provided to the foundation at no charge). Likewise, if one of the foundation's employees provided services to the company under these circumstances, the company should directly compensate the employee.

In one instance, a company foundation and its related for-profit company proposed to open a bank account for the purpose of making payments of premiums on group insurance policies or other similar benefits covering the employees of both entities. The two organizations would each deposit into this account its share of the premium payments; a single check would be drawn against the account each month for the total premium payment for each policy or other benefit. Both organizations represented to the IRS that this type of arrangement would prevent administrative difficulties that could arise on the part of the third-party provider (which was not a disqualified person with respect to the foundation) if separate checks were issued by the company and the foundation each month for each policy or other benefit. The IRS ruled that the establishment and use of this account would not constitute one or more acts of self-dealing.[40]

(c) Provision of Tangible Benefits

The provision of a tangible economic benefit to a related for-profit business by a company foundation generally constitutes an act of self-dealing. The principal exception is the incidental and tenuous benefit,[41] which in this context means an intangible, indirect promotion benefit accruing to the company as an unavoidable consequence of the conduct of the foundation's charitable activities.

For example, self-dealing would arise if a for-profit company advertised that it was sponsoring a community event, where the cost of the sponsorship was borne by its company foundation. Likewise, a company foundation that works to promote the arts would engage in self-dealing if it paid for a work of art to be placed on or near a building owned by the related for-profit company, where the artwork improved the look of the building and/or its surroundings, and thus enhanced public perception of the company and its business.

One of the rare instances of any guidance on this point pertains to the pesky matter of purchase of tickets to fundraising events.[42] In one instance (reflective of a common practice), a company foundation purchased tickets to fundraising activities sponsored by various charitable organizations. The foundation provided an individual, who was the chair of the board and chief executive officer of the related company, and his guests, with paid admission to several of the fundraising functions. This individual was not a director, officer, or employee of the foundation. He attended the events; the directors and officers of the foundation used the remaining tickets. The IRS ruled that the foundation's managers' use of the tickets was not self-dealing because their attendance at the functions was reasonable and necessary to the performance of their evaluation and oversight tasks for the foundation. By contrast, the use of the tickets by the company executive was found to be self-dealing inasmuch as the executive was attending the charitable functions as an agent of the company and not as a representative of the foundation.[43]

Company foundations cannot avoid self-dealing by paying only the charitable portion of the cost of a ticket to a fundraising event and having the related for-profit corporation pay the costs allocable to the noncharitable

---

40. Priv. Ltr. Rul. 9312022, which also pertains to the five paragraphs preceding this one.
41. See § 17.6(e).
42. See § 5.8(g).
43. Tech. Adv. Mem. 8449008.

§ 17.6 SELF-DEALING RULES

portion. The IRS ruled that this bifurcation approach results in self-dealing inasmuch as the event can be attended only by paying both portions of the ticket price. A company foundation's payment of the charitable portion, the IRS reasoned, relieved the for-profit business's obligation to pay that element of the payment, which resulted in an economic benefit to the for-profit company and thus self-dealing.[44]

(d) Grantmaking

Company foundations need to be cautious in their grant-making policies and practices, being concerned about grants that benefit, or may benefit, or may be perceived as benefiting the related for-profit company. Again, any grant from a company foundation confers a private benefit on the related company; yet this alone is insufficient to constitute self-dealing (or private inurement).[45] The related company will thus benefit, directly or indirectly, incidentally or otherwise, from each related company foundation grant. The objective obviously should be to avoid conferring an unwarranted benefit on the related company as the consequence of a company foundation grant; this is often a question of judgment. There is little law to guide a company foundation in this regard.

Company foundation programs that are among the most problematic in this regard are the making of scholarship grants to employees of the related for-profit company and disaster relief grants to this category of employees. The federal tax law in these contexts has developed largely in connection with the taxable expenditures rules.[46]

One way to cause self-dealing is by transfer of a private foundation's income or assets to a grantee under circumstances where the item is considered transferred for the benefit of a disqualified person.[47] Under this body of law, the grantee can be a qualified charity and the purpose of the grant can be furtherance of charitable purposes, yet it is still self-dealing because an inappropriate benefit was provided to a disqualified person. This is an area of considerable traps, if only because many think of self-dealing transactions as transactions directly with disqualified persons.

The IRS ruled that a grant-making program was conducted by a charitable organization in a way so as to create substantial benefits for a business interest. Grants were made to writers who produced manuscripts that a for-profit company published; substantial royalties were paid to the parties. Finding that the grants were, in substance, compensation for the writers' services, the

---

44. E.g., Priv. Ltr. Rul. 9021066.
45. See § 17.6(e).
46. See § 17.7(d).
47. See § 5.8(d).

IRS concluded that private inurement had occurred and revoked the organization's tax-exempt status.[48]

(e) Incidental and Tenuous Benefits

As referenced throughout, the self-dealing rules include an exception for incidental and tenuous benefits provided to disqualified persons.[49] This exception is critical to the functioning of company foundations; the mere existence of these entities necessarily and unavoidably confers a benefit on the related company.

One example of this type of incidental benefit is the commonality of the names of the two entities. As an illustration, a disqualified person with respect to a private foundation contributed real estate to the foundation for the purpose of building a neighborhood recreation center in an underprivileged area. As a condition of this contribution, the foundation agreed to use the disqualified person's name as part of the name of the center. Inasmuch as this benefit to the disqualified person was merely incidental, the naming of the center in this manner does not constitute self-dealing. This point carries over into the company foundation context.

As another illustration, a private foundation and a public charity entered into an agreement pursuant to which the foundation agreed to make a sizeable grant to the charity if the charity changed its name to include that of a substantial contributor to the foundation and agreed to refrain from thereafter changing its name for 100 years. The IRS ruled that the public recognition this disqualified person received from this name change was an incidental and tenuous benefit; therefore, the making of this grant was not self-dealing.[50]

Public recognition is another element usually protected by this exception. Thus, for example, a company foundation proposed to make a grant to a public charity in support of an annual educational competition organized by the charity. Participants in the competition were ninth-to-twelfth-grade students. The competition culminated in a banquet at which awards were presented to the winners. The foundation agreed to be the primary sponsor of this competition for five years; the charity agreed to rename the competition and banquet, using the name of the for-profit company that was the sole funder of the foundation. The IRS concluded that the public recognition this company was to receive as a consequence of the foundation's grant was an incidental and tenuous benefit.[51]

---

48. Rev. Rul. 66-104, 1966-1 C.B. 135. This was not a self-dealing case.
49. Reg. § 53.4941(d)-2(f)(2); see § 5.8(e).
50. Rev. Rul. 73-407, 1973-2 C.B. 383.
51. Priv. Ltr. Rul. 7817081.

§ 17.6 SELF-DEALING RULES

Additionally, the IRS considered a grant by a company foundation to a public broadcasting company for the purpose of underwriting a program, which featured credits at the beginning and close of the weekly telecast. These credits included the showing of the foundation's logo, which was identical to the related company's logo, and messages generally favorable to the company and its product line. The station published messages about the company, along with other corporate underwriters, in its viewers' guide. The IRS ruled that the television and viewing guide credits were merely an "inconsequential amount of commercial benefit."[52]

Other forms of private benefit may be shielded by this exception. Two classic IRS rulings illustrate the basic concept. In one, a for-profit corporation contributed parklands and money to a charitable organization, retaining the right to use as a brand symbol a scenic view located in the park. The IRS ruled that the tax-exempt status of the charitable organization was not jeopardized by this arrangement, in that the beneficial use of the park, subsidized by the donor, flowed principally to the public and that any identification of the donor's business interest by visitors to the park was incidental to this primary public benefit.[53] In the other ruling, a for-profit corporation provided a substantial portion of the support of a charitable organization operating a replica of a nineteenth-century village. Although the corporation benefited by having the village named after it, by having its name associated with the village in conjunction with its advertising program, and by having its name mentioned in each publication of the charitable organization, the IRS ruled that these benefits are "merely incidental to the benefits flowing to the general public," so that the exempt status of the charitable organization operating the village was not jeopardized.[54]

The incidental and tenuous benefits exception thus applies in connection with benefits received by businesses related to company foundations for grants made in the community in which the foundation and the related for-profit entity reside. For example, a grant by a private foundation to the governing body of a city for the purpose of alleviating slum conditions of one of the city's neighborhoods is not an act of self-dealing merely because a related for-profit business is located in the same geographic area where the grant will be applied.[55] In addition, a for-profit corporation that was a substantial contributor to a private foundation was found to benefit only in an incidental manner from a grant by the private foundation to a local university

---

52. Priv. Ltr. Rul. 8644003. Federal law requires these noncommercial stations to identify (albeit in a nonpromotional manner) the sponsors of broadcast segments, thus restricting the import of this ruling, which is somewhat inconsistent with the IRS's posture on other occasions where the provision of goodwill was found to be self-dealing (see § 5.8(d)).
53. Rev. Rul. 66-358, 1666-2 C.B. 218.
54. Rev. Rul. 77-367, 1977-2 C.B. 193.
55. Reg. § 53.4941(d)-2(f)(9), Example 1.

to establish an educational department in manufacturing engineering. While the for-profit business would encourage its employees to enroll in the program and would recruit graduates from the program, it would not receive any preferential treatment regarding these activities, and its employees would compete for admission to the program on an equal basis with the public. Thus, the IRS ruled this grant did not constitute an act of self-dealing.[56]

A company-related private foundation established a program to provide on-the-job training and education for the benefit of at-risk, underserved, and underexposed youth living in its community. The company operated a summer employment jobs training program for high-school- and college-age youth in the same community. The foundation modeled its program on the company's program and utilized company resources in operation of its program. Participants in the foundation's program were selected on the basis of academic performance, performance on aptitude tests, recommendations from instructors and others, financial need, and interviews. Employees and relatives of the foundation and the company were ineligible to participate. Any purchases the foundation made in connection with program operations were from independent parties. The company agreed not to hire or make an offer to hire any foundation program participants for a period of years following completion of the program. The IRS ruled that the private foundation's job training program did not entail any acts of self-dealing, in part because the benefits to the company were incidental and tenuous.[57]

Matching gift and similar programs can be shielded from self-dealing excise taxes by this exception. In one instance, a company foundation proposed to match, within certain limits, contributions to educational institutions made by full-time employees who had completed a minimum of one year of service for the related for-profit company. This foundation also proposed to provide financial assistance to any publicly supported charity on whose behalf any full-time employee of the company, with at least one year of service, has been serving as a volunteer for at least one year. Further, this foundation gave

---

56. Rev. Rul. 80-310, 1980-2 C.B. 319.
57. Priv. Ltr. Rul. 201718002. This IRS ruling may be correct as to the lack of self-dealing in these facts on the ground that the benefits to the disqualified person company were incidental. That should be the case if the facts were confined to the similarity of the programs. But there was more. The company was hosting foundation program participants at its facilities. The company was donating services, including "supervision, training and mentoring." The company placed foundation program participants in a "sponsoring department" at the company. There was a suggestion that the company may hire foundation program participants after a certain period has passed. Private foundations and other charitable organizations should be cautious in taking heart from this ruling, inasmuch as previous IRS rulings have found unwarranted private benefit (see § 5.2) on the basis of less substantive benefits than those provided in this case.

§ 17.6 SELF-DEALING RULES

particular attention to grant applications from public charities endorsed by local charities, the formation of which was encouraged by the company, that functioned in each community in which the company maintains a plant or office. The IRS ruled that, as to each of these programs, the financial benefit of the foundation's grants accrues directly and entirely to the qualified public charities and that the public recognition and goodwill enjoyed by the company as a result of the programs constituted an incidental or tenuous benefit.[58]

In another instance, a private foundation assumed payments in connection with its related company's matching gifts program. The company had a policy by which its employees were informed that certain charitable gifts they made were matched. The IRS ruled that this foundation's payments in accordance with the company's gift match program do not constitute acts of self-dealing (and will be qualifying distributions[59] and not taxable expenditures.)[60,61] The IRS was assured that the foundation will not match any gifts made by participants in the company's program prior to termination of that program and that the foundation was not taking on any obligation of the company or relieving the company of any financial burden.[62]

In a subsequent and similar situation, apparently involving the same private foundation, the IRS stated that the benefits the company will receive from this change in program administration, in the form of "favorable public recognition and good will" and a "happier and more loyal workforce," are "similar to" incidental and tenuous benefits.[63]

There is a trap here, potentially imperiling the tax-exempt status of private foundations (and other charitable entities). These rulings finding incidental and tenuous benefits are confined to the self-dealing issue. It is the ruling position of the IRS that the conduct of a program by a nonprofit organization that is similar to a program conducted by a related for-profit company is a violation of the operational test[64] and/or substantive evidence of commerciality,[65] and thus will preclude or lead to revocation of tax exemption.[66]

---

58. Priv. Ltr. Rul. 8004086. The IRS added that any "secondary intangible benefit" derived by this company in the form of "increased morale and satisfaction" is likewise an incidental or tenuous benefit.
59. See Chapter 6.
60. See Chapter 9.
61. Priv. Ltr. Rul. 201417022.
62. See § 5.8(c). The IRS recognized that the company was deriving "some benefit" because of the goodwill created by the foundation's match program but held that this element of goodwill is "merely [an] incidental benefit" for the company.
63. Priv. Ltr. Rul. 201725008.
64. See *Tax-Exempt Organizations* § 4.5(a).
65. *Id.* § 4.9.
66. E.g., Priv. Ltr. Rul. 201714031 (where a nonprofit entity was denied recognition of exemption as a charitable organization because it was operating the "same program" and

COMPANY FOUNDATIONS

A private foundation, created and solely funded by a utility providing electricity and natural gas services, proposed to make grants to governmental bodies and other public charities to offset the cost difference between the purchase of gasoline and diesel vehicles and the purchase of electric vehicles. Prospective grantees would include a governmental entity operating a city bus system and a public university. Essentially, the purpose of these grants was to subsidize the purchase of electric buses for the city. The self-dealing rules were implicated, inasmuch as the utility was a disqualified person with respect to the foundation (being a substantial contributor). The potential problem was that the purchase of the electric vehicles would result in additional sales of electricity by the utility. The IRS dismissed this issue, however, holding that the additional sales "will be negligible in comparison with [the] utility's total electricity sales and minimal in relation to the [amount of the] proposed grants." As such, any benefit to the utility from the proposed grants would be "incidental or tenuous" and, therefore, not constitute an act of self-dealing.[67]

(f) Corporate Reorganizations and Stock Transfers

Under certain circumstances, a transaction between a private foundation and a corporation that is a disqualified person with respect to the foundation is not considered self-dealing if the transaction takes place pursuant to a liquidation, merger, redemption, recapitalization, or other corporate adjustment, organization, or reorganization.[68] This exception to the self-dealing rules can be important for company foundations holding one or more forms of securities issued by the related for-profit company.

This exception is available where all securities of the same class as that held are subject to the same terms, and those terms provide for receipt by the foundation of no less than fair market value. The issuer corporation must make a bona fide offer on a uniform basis to the foundation and to all other persons who hold the securities. Compensating a company foundation with property, such as debentures, for its stock while the other holders of identical stock received cash would not be a transaction that comports with the uniform-basis rule.[69]

In one instance, a private foundation organized as a trust owned approximately 9 percent of the preferred stock of a corporation, which was a

---

providing the same "educational services" as a related for-profit company; the parties' operations were characterized by the IRS as being "virtually indistinguishable"). On another occasion the IRS observed that a tax-exempt organization "should not duplicate services or facilities provided by commercial entities" (Priv. Ltr. Rul. 201801014).
67. Priv. Ltr. Rul. 202034001.
68. See § 5.14(a).
69. Reg. § 53.4941(d)-3(d).

disqualified person with respect to the trust. Under the corporation's articles of incorporation, the corporation was annually required to invite tenders from all the holders of preferred stock to be made by a certain date. The maximum price at which the stock could be offered was $104 per share plus any accumulated or unpaid dividends. The corporation was required to accept the tender of not more than 2,400 shares, starting with tenders having the lowest prices. If more than 2,400 shares were tendered in any year, the shares to be purchased of tenders made at the same price had to be selected by lot or in another manner as the directors selected. The trustees of the trust sought to tender the trust's shares for $104 per share each year, provided that the fair market value per share equaled or was less than $104, until all of the shares held by the trust had been redeemed. The IRS held that any redemptions by the corporation of the preferred stock tendered by the trust would not constitute self-dealing, with the agency basing its holding on the fact that all of the corporation's preferred stock had to be tendered in accordance with the same terms and conditions.[70] Thus, this exception from the self-dealing rules for certain securities redemptions was satisfied.

§ 17.7 OTHER PRIVATE FOUNDATIONS RULES

The relationship between a company foundation and the related for-profit company can implicate federal tax private foundation rules other than those concerning self-dealing.

(a) Mandatory Payout Rules

In connection with the mandatory payout rules,[71] the value of any stock owned by a company foundation that was issued by the related for-profit company will be included in the foundation's asset base for purposes of calculating the required amount of qualifying distributions.[72] The foundation could satisfy some or all of its payout obligation for one or more years by distributing some or all of this stock to one or more qualifying distributees.[73]

(b) Excess Business Holdings Rules

In connection with the excess business holdings rules,[74] any stock owned by a company foundation that was issued by the related for-profit company will

---

70. Priv. Ltr. Rul. 8425080.
71. See Chapter 6.
72. See § 6.2(b).
73. See § 6.4(b).
74. See Chapter 7.

be taken into account in determining whether the foundation has permitted or excess business holdings.[75]

(c) Jeopardizing Investments Rules

In connection with the jeopardizing investments rules,[76] it is highly unlikely that stock owned by a company foundation that was issued by the related for-profit company will be considered a jeopardizing investment. This is the case at the very least because of the exception from these rules for property that is contributed to a private foundation.[77]

(d) Taxable Expenditures Rules

In connection with the taxable expenditures rules,[78] a grant by a company foundation that provides an unwarranted benefit to the related for-profit company may be considered a distribution for noncharitable purposes.[79] Company foundation programs that are among the most problematic in this regard include the making of scholarship grants to employees of the related for-profit company. The IRS developed guidelines for use by these foundations in determining whether grants of this nature are forms of qualifying distributions[80] and thus are not taxable expenditures.[81]

Another law area involving company foundations that raises taxable expenditures issues is the matter of disaster relief and hardship assistance programs involving employees of the related for-profit company. The IRS has vacillated on this topic, first approving then disapproving these programs, and then ultimately approving such programs, provided the grants under the programs are qualified disaster relief payments and not employee financial hardship assistance grants.[82] The concerns of the IRS with respect to these programs are whether a charitable class is being served,[83] whether there is private inurement or unwarranted private benefit,[84] and otherwise whether the program is designed to provide a type of welfare benefit to the employees.

---

75. See § 7.1(d).
76. See Chapter 8.
77. See § 8.1(b).
78. See Chapter 9.
79. See § 9.8.
80. See § 6.4.
81. See § 9.3(d)(ii).
82. See § 9.3(c).
83. See *Tax-Exempt Organizations* § 6.3(a).
84. See §§ 5.1, 5.2.

(e) Economic Returns

In connection with the excise tax on net investment income,[85] securities issued by the related for-profit company may be held by a company foundation; any resulting dividend and/or interest income is subject to taxation.[86] Likewise, any capital gain incurred because of a sale or other disposition of this type of stock will be subject to this tax.[87]

§ 17.8 EXCESS EXECUTIVE COMPENSATION TAX EXCEPTIONS

One of the many issues associated with the excise tax on excess tax-exempt executive compensation[88] is whether for-profit businesses are subject to this tax because their executives are volunteers at related tax-exempt organizations. This issue arises from the way an applicable tax-exempt organization's five highest-compensated employees may be identified. The issue is one of concern to for-profit businesses with related private foundations because executives that are highly paid by a company often serve as officers and directors of a related company foundation.

The tax regulations provide two pertinent exceptions to this excise tax that may apply where an officer or other employee of a private foundation is treated as an employee of a foundation even though the individual is not compensated by the foundation. Where these exceptions apply, the individual is disregarded for purposes of determining the private foundation's highest-compensated employees for a year and thus is not a covered employee. These exceptions are the *limited hours exception* and the *nonexempt funds exception*.

(a) Limited Hours Exception

The tax regulations concerning the *limited hours exception*[89] include the following two examples.

In one of these illustrations, the applicable tax-exempt organization (hereafter referenced as a private foundation) and a for-profit corporation are related. No other organizations are related to the foundation. Individual D is an employee of the corporation. As part of D's duties at the corporation, D serves as an officer of the foundation. Only the corporation paid

---

85. See Chapter 10.
86. See § 10.4(c), (d).
87. See § 10.4(b).
88. See § 5.6(e).
89. See § 5.6(e)(iii).

remuneration to D and the foundation did not reimburse the corporation for any portion of D's remuneration. During 2022, D provided services as an employee of the corporation totaling 2,000 hours and 200 hours to the foundation.

Even though D is an employee of the private foundation because D provided more than minor services as an officer, D is disregarded for purposes of determining the foundation's five highest-compensated employees for 2022. This is the case because only the corporation paid D any remuneration in 2022, and D provided services as an employee of the foundation for 200 hours, which is not more than 10 percent of the 2,200 total hours D worked as an employee of the foundation and the corporation.[90]

As to the second illustration,[91] the facts are the same as in the first illustration, except that the private foundation also provides a reasonable allowance for expenses incurred by D in performing D's duties as an officer of the foundation. This allowance is excluded from gross income because it is paid in accordance with an accountable plan.[92] Again, even though D is an employee of the private foundation because D provided more than minor services for it, D is disregarded for purposes of determining the foundation's five highest-compensated employees for 2022 because the expense allowance is excluded from wages[93] and thus is not remuneration for purposes of this excise tax.[94]

A similar example pertains to premiums paid in accordance with a directors and officers liability insurance plan.[95] In this illustration, individual C is an officer of a private foundation who performs more than minor services for the foundation. In 2022, neither this foundation nor any related organization paid remuneration to employee C. The foundation paid premiums for insurance for liability arising from C's service with the foundation; this payment is a working condition fringe benefit excluded from gross income.[96] Again, C is disregarded for purposes of the tax for 2022 because neither the foundation nor any related organizations paid C any remuneration in that year. The working condition fringe benefit does not constitute wages[97] and thus is not remuneration.[98]

---

90. Reg. § 53.4960-1(d)(3)(v), Example 5.
91. Reg. § 53.4960-1(d)(3)(vi), Example 6.
92. Reg. § 1.62-2.
93. Reg. § 31.3401(a)-4.
94. Reg. § 53.4960-2(a).
95. Reg. § 53.4960-1(d)(3)(iv), Example 4.
96. Reg. § 1.132-5.
97. IRC § 3401(a)(19).
98. Reg. § 53.4960-2(a). This matter of fringe benefits being excluded from wages is also applicable with respect to the nonexempt funds exception (see §§ 5.6(e)(iii), 17.8(b)).

§ 17.8 EXCESS EXECUTIVE COMPENSATION TAX EXCEPTIONS

(b) Nonexempt Funds Exception

The tax regulations concerning the *nonexempt funds exception*[99] include the following four examples.

In the first of these illustrations, a private foundation and a for-profit corporation are related. The foundation does not have any other related organizations and does not control the corporation. During 2022, individual E provided 2,000 hours of services as an employee of the corporation and no hours of service as an employee of the foundation. During 2023 and 2024, E provided 1,100 hours of services as an employee of the corporation and 900 hours of services as an employee of the foundation. The foundation neither paid any remuneration to E nor paid a fee for services to the corporation during any year. The limited hours exception is inapplicable to E.

E is disregarded for purposes of determining this private foundation's five highest-compensated employees for 2023 because, for 2022 and 2023, E provided services as an employee of the foundation for not more than 50 percent of the total hours E provided services as an employee of the foundation and the corporation (900 hours/4,000 hours) and the foundation neither paid any remuneration to E nor paid a fee for services to the corporation during 2022 and 2023. The same conclusion obtains for 2024 because of the no-more-than 50 percent rule (1,800 hours/4,000 hours) and the no-remuneration-or-fee rule with respect to 2023 and 2024.[100]

The second illustration is based on the facts of the first one, except that during 2022, E provided services as an employee for 2,000 hours to the corporation and for no hours to the foundation; during 2023, E provided services as an employee for no hours to the corporation and 2,000 hours to the foundation; and during 2024, E resumed employment with the corporation, so that E provided services as an employee for 2,000 hours to the corporation and no hours to the foundation.

E is disregarded for purposes of determining the foundation's five highest-compensated employees for 2023 because, for 2022 and 2023, E provided services as an employee of the foundation for not more than 50 percent of the total hours E provided services as an employee of the foundation and the corporation (2,000 hours/4,000 hours) and the foundation neither paid any remuneration to E nor paid a fee for services to the corporation during 2022 and 2023. For the same reasons, E is disregarded for 2024 with respect to the years 2023 and 2024.[101]

---

99. See § 5.6(e)(iii).
100. Reg. § 53.4960-1(d)(3)(viii), Example 8.
101. Reg. § 53.4960-1(d)(3)(ix), Example 9.

The third illustration is also based on the facts of the first one, except that, during 2022, E provided services as an employee for 2,000 hours to the corporation and for no hours to the foundation; during 2023, E provided services as an employee for 600 hours to the corporation and for 1,400 hours to the foundation; and, during 2024, E provided services as an employee for 1,400 hours to the corporation and for 600 hours to the foundation.

E is disregarded for purposes of determining the foundation's five highest-compensated employees for 2023 because, for 2022 and 2023, E provided services as an employee of the foundation for not more than 50 percent of the total hours E provided services as an employee of the foundation and the corporation (1,400 hours/4,000 hours) and the foundation neither paid any remuneration to E nor paid a fee for services to the corporation during the years 2022 and 2023. For the same reasons, E is disregarded for 2024 with respect to the years 2023 and 2024 (with the hours of services to both entities generating the ratio of 2,000 hours/4,000 hours).[102]

The fourth illustration is likewise based on the facts of the first one, except that, during 2022, E provided services as an employee for 2,000 hours to the corporation and for no hours to the foundation; during 2023, E provided services as an employee for 600 hours to the corporation and for 1,400 hours to the foundation; and, during 2024, E provided services as an employee for 1,300 hours to the corporation and for 700 hours to the foundation.

E is disregarded for purposes of determining the foundation's five highest-compensated employees for 2023 because, for 2022 and 2023, E provided services as an employee of the foundation for less than 50 percent of the total hours E provided services as an employee of the foundation and the corporation (1,400 hours/4,000 hours) and the foundation neither paid any remuneration to E nor paid a fee for services to the corporation during 2022 and 2023.

E may be a covered employee of the foundation as one of its five highest-compensated employees for 2024 because this exception is not available, and no other exception applies. For years 2023 and 2024, E provided services as an employee of the foundation for more than 50 percent of the total hours E provided services as an employee of the foundation and the corporation (2,100 hours/4,000).[103]

Three other aspects of this body of law will apply in the private foundation context. One, while the concept of an employee generally includes an officer of a corporation,[104] an officer of a corporation who as such does not

---

102. Reg. § 53.4960-1(d)(3)(x), Example 10.
103. Reg. § 53.4960-1(d)(3)(xi), Example 11.
104. Reg. § 53.4960-1(e)(1); Reg. §31.3401(c)-1; see § 5.6(e)(iii).

§ 17.8 EXCESS EXECUTIVE COMPENSATION TAX EXCEPTIONS

perform any services[105] or performs only minor services and who neither receives, nor is entitled to receive, any remuneration is not considered an employee of the corporation solely due to the individual's status as an officer of the corporation.[106] Two, a director of a corporation (or an individual holding a substantially similar position in a corporation or other entity, such as a trust) in the individual's capacity as such is not an employee of the corporation.[107] Three, an employee of a person (who is not a trustee, director, or officer, or an employee who possesses the authority commonly exercised by an officer) who is a director or trustee of a nonstock organization (or acting in that capacity) is not treated as a representative of the person if the employee does not act as a representative of the person, as long as that fact is reported to the IRS on the appropriate annual information return.[108]

---

105. It is not clear how an individual can lawfully be an officer of a corporation and not perform any services.
106. Reg. § 53.4960-1(e)(1); see § 5.6(e)(iii).
107. Reg. § 53.4960-1(e)(2), (3).
108. Reg. § 53.4960-1(i)(2)(v)(C). Generally, trustees, directors, officers, employees, or agents of a person are deemed representatives of the person (*id.*).

About the Authors

SHANE T. HAMILTON is a shareholder in Hamilton Vopelak P.C. in Coppell, Texas, and Special Counsel for tax-exempt organization matters for Miller & Chevalier Chartered in Washington, D.C. He represents nonprofit, tax-exempt organizations exclusively, with a significant concentration around company-sponsored and family-endowed private foundations. In addition to advising private foundations and other tax-exempt organizations on tax compliance and other legal matters, Mr. Hamilton also represents them before the IRS in the context of IRS examinations, protests to the IRS Independent Office of Appeals, and closing agreement and private letter ruling requests.

In addition to being the co-author of this edition of *The Tax Law of Private Foundations*, Mr. Hamilton is also the co-author, also with Bruce R. Hopkins, of the 2023 Cumulative Supplement to *The Law of Tax-Exempt Organizations, Twelfth Edition*.

Mr. Hamilton earned his JD at the University of Virginia School of Law; he also earned a BA in Economics and an MA in English Literature from the University of Virginia. He is a member of the bars of the District of Columbia, the State of Texas, and the Commonwealth of Virginia. While attending law school, he was an Executive Editor and the Tax Cite Editor of the *Virginia Tax Review*.

BRUCE R. HOPKINS was the principal in the Bruce R. Hopkins Law Firm, LLC, Kansas City, Missouri. His practice concentrated on the representation of private foundations and other categories of tax-exempt organizations, ranging over the entirety of law matters involving exempt organizations, with emphasis on the formation of nonprofit organizations, acquisition of recognition of their tax-exempt status, the private inurement and private benefit doctrines, governance, the intermediate sanctions rules, legislative and political campaign activities issues, public charity and private foundation rules, unrelated business planning, use of exempt and for-profit subsidiaries, joint venture planning, tax shelter involvement, review of annual information returns, Internet communications developments, the law of charitable giving, and fundraising law issues.

Mr. Hopkins served as Chair of the Committee on Exempt Organizations, Tax Section, American Bar Association; Chair, Section of Taxation, National Association of College and University Attorneys; and President, Planned Giving Study Group of Greater Washington, D.C. He received the

ABOUT THE AUTHORS

2007 Outstanding Nonprofit Lawyer Award (Vanguard Lifetime Achievement Award) from the American Bar Association, Section of Business Law, Committee on Nonprofit Corporations.

Mr. Hopkins was the series editor of Wiley's Nonprofit Law, Finance, and Management Series. In addition to being co-author of *The Tax Law of Private Foundations, Sixth Edition*, he was the author of *The Law of Tax-Exempt Organizations, Twelfth Edition*; *The Planning Guide for the Law of Tax-Exempt Organizations: Strategies and Commentaries*; *Bruce R. Hopkins' Nonprofit Law Library* (e-book); *Tax-Exempt Organizations and Constitutional Law: Nonprofit Law as Shaped by the U.S. Supreme Court*; *Bruce R. Hopkins' Nonprofit Law Dictionary*; *IRS Audits of Tax-Exempt Organizations: Policies, Practices, and Procedures*; *The Tax Law of Charitable Giving, Sixth Edition*; *The Tax Law of Associations*; *The Tax Law of Unrelated Business for Nonprofit Organizations*; *The Nonprofits' Guide to Internet Communications Law*; *The Law of Intermediate Sanctions: A Guide for Nonprofits*; *Starting and Managing a Nonprofit Organization: A Legal Guide, Seventh Edition*; *Nonprofit Law Made Easy*; *Charitable Giving Law Made Easy*; *Private Foundation Law Made Easy*; *650 Essential Nonprofit Law Questions Answered*; *The First Legal Answer Book for Fund-Raisers*; *The Second Legal Answer Book for Fund-Raisers*; *The Legal Answer Book for Nonprofit Organizations*; and *The Second Legal Answer Book for Nonprofit Organizations*. He was the co-author, with Thomas K. Hyatt, of *The Law of Tax-Exempt Healthcare Organizations, Fourth Edition*; with Alicia M. Beck, of *The Law of Fundraising, Fifth Edition*; with Douglas K. Anning, Virginia C. Gross, and Thomas J. Schenkelberg, of *The New Form 990: Law, Policy and Preparation*; also with Ms. Gross, of *Nonprofit Governance: Law, Practices & Trends*; and with Ms. Gross and Mr. Schenkelberg, of *Nonprofit Law for Colleges and Universities: Essential Questions and Answers for Officers, Directors, and Advisors*. He also wrote *Bruce R. Hopkins' Nonprofit Counsel*, a monthly newsletter, published by John Wiley & Sons.

Mr. Hopkins was the Professor from Practice at the University of Kansas School of Law, where he taught courses on the law of tax-exempt organizations.

Mr. Hopkins earned his JD and LLM degrees at the George Washington University, his SJD at the University of Kansas, and his BA at the University of Michigan.

About the Online Resources

The Tax Law of Private Foundations, Sixth Edition is complemented by a number of online resources. Please visit www.wiley.com/go/privatefoundations6e to download various tables in PDF format and other documents to use alongside the sixth edition. These include:

- Appendix A—Sources of the Law
- Appendix B—Internal Revenue Code Sections
- Table of Cases
- Table of IRS Revenue Rulings, Revenue Procedures, and Notices
- Table of IRS Private Determinations Cited in Text
- Table of Other IRS Private Determinations

For a list of all Wiley books by Bruce R. Hopkins, please visit www.wiley.com/go/hopkins.

Index

15-year DAFs, §16.10
20-percent owners, disqualified persons, §4.3
27-month rule, §2.7(b)
50-year DAFs, §16.10
270-day rule, §12.7(d)
§509(a)(1), donative publicly supported charities, §15.4
§509(a)(1), public institution charities, §15.3(a)
§509(a)(2), public charity category change, §15.7(a)
§509(a)(2), service provider publicly supported charities, §15.5
§509(a)(3), change of supporting organization type, §15.7(c)
§509(a)(3), public charity category change, §15.7(b)
§509(a)(3), supporting organizations, §15.6
§509(a)(4), organizations, §15.2

A

Abatement, §1.8(d), §12.2(c), §12.4(c), §13.8
  limitation, self-dealing transactions, §5.15(a)(iv)
  reasonable cause for, §§12.2(c), 12.4(c)
"Accelerating Charitable Efforts Act" (ACE Act), §16.10
Accuracy-related penalty, §11.5(e)
  application, excise taxes, §12.4(b)
  reasonable cause for abatement, §12.2(c)
Acquisition indebtedness, §§ 6.2(e), 11.4(a)
  related-use exceptions, §11.4(b)
Action organization, §9.1(a), §9.2(a)
Additional (second-tier) excise tax
  on excess business holdings, §7.7
  on jeopardizing investments, §8.5(d)
  on self-dealing transactions, §5.15(a)
  on taxable expenditures, §9.9(a)
  on undistributed income, §6.5(d)
Adjusted net income (ANI)
  calculation, §3.1(d)
  Congressional change, §6.6
  determination, §15.6(g)(vi)
  includible amounts, IRS ruling clarification, §3.1(d)
  private foundation determination, §6.6
Adjustment period, excess qualifying distributions, §6.5(c)
Administrative appeal procedures (IRS), §12.7(c)
Administrative assets, as exempt function assets, §6.2(d)
Administrative expenses, as qualifying distributions, §6.4(f)(ii)
Administrative procedures, tax-exempt status recognition (denial), §2.7(d)
Advance IRS ruling
  and court-ordered set-asides, §6.4(g)(iii)
  and individual grant procedures, §9.3(f)
  and suitability test set-asides, §6.4(g)(i)
  and termination of private foundation status, §13.4(c)
  and unusual grants, §15.5(c)(iii)
  and voter registration drives, §9.2(c)
Advice of counsel, self-dealing, §5.15(a)(v)
Advocacy communications, §9.1(d)
Affinity credit cards, usage, §11.2(a)

INDEX

Aggressive tax avoidance schemes, §16.7
Agricultural research organizations, public charity qualification, §15.3(e)
All-profits-to-charity requirement, §7.4
Amended returns (Form 990-PF), §12.2(d)
American Stock Exchange, shares (nonlisting), §14.5
Angel investment fund, private foundation investments, §8.3
Annual accounting period (tax year), Form 990-PF (change), §§ 12.1, 12.1(d)(i)
Annual form 990-PF filing requirement, §12.1(a)
Annuities, capital gains/losses, §10.4(c)
Anticipatory assignment, avoidance, §16.4(c)
Anti-terrorist financing guidelines, §9.6(d)
Applicable property
 disposition of, §14.4(b)
 recapture rule, §14.4(b)
Applicable tax-exempt organization, §5.6(e)(i)
Application for Change in Accounting Method (Form 3115), §12.1(d)(ii)
Application materials, §12.3(a)
Application to Adopt, Change, or Retain a Tax Year (Form 1128), §12.1(d)(i)
Appraisal rules, §14.7(d)
Appreciated capital asset, §14.3
Appreciated property
 deductibility, contributions of, §14.3
 and funding a foundation, §2.4
 gifts of, §14.3
 and tax on net investment income, §10.3
Appropriate person, meaning (reasonable cause), §12.2(c)
Asset (assets)
 administrative assets, §6.2(d)
 appreciation, §10.4(b)(ii)
 assets held for partial year, §6.3(d)
 charitable pledges, payment, §5.8(c)
 controlled foundations, complete asset transfers, §13.5(b)
 disqualified person, use by, §5.8
 exempt function assets, §§ 6.2(d), 6.4(f)(i)
 investment assets, §6.2(b)
 long-term capital gain property (appreciated capital asset), §14.3
 non-controlled foundations, complete asset transfers, §13.5(c)
 other assets, §6.3(c)
 significant but not all assets, transfers, §13.5(d)
 test, §3.1(e)(i)
 transactions, manipulation (involvement), §5.8(b)
 transferred assets, maintenance, §13.3(b)(i)
 transfer to public charity, termination of private foundation status, §13.3
 taxable expenditure, exception, §13.5(c)
Asset test, private operating foundation compliance period, §3.1(f)
Asset test, private operation foundation, §3.1(e)(i)
Assistance grants, §9.3(c)
Attentiveness requirement, nonfunctionally integrated Type III supporting organization, §15.6(g)(vi)
Attorney General, Form 990-PF copy (furnishing), §12.3(b)
Audit Technique Guides (ATGs), §12.6(b)
Automatic revocation, non-filing, §12.7(a)
Average acquisition indebtedness, §11.4(c)
Awards, individuals, §9.3(d)(iii)

INDEX

B

Bank fees, §5.6(h)
Bargain sales, §14.6
   evidencing, §14.7(b)
Below-market interest rates, §8.3
Beneficial interest, §4.3
   term, substitution, §7.1(d), §7.2(b)
Benefit tickets, joint purchase, §5.8(g)
Bona fide volunteer, §5.7(c)
Bond premium amortization
   and adjusted net income, §3.1(d)
   deduction allowance, net investment income tax, §10.5(a)
Bucketing rule, §11.5(b)
Business
   continuity/regularity, U.S. Tax Court opinion, §11.1(b)
   definition, §11.1(a)
   income, §§ 11.1(b), 11.2(d), 11.3(a)
   organization tax-exempt purposes, relationship, §11.1(c)
   related trade/business, conduct, §11.1(c)
   sole proprietorship, §11.3
Business enterprise
   concept, unrelated trade or business, §11.3(a)
   definition, excess business holdings, §7.1(a)
      exceptions, §7.1(a)
   exception, §7.1(c)
Business judgment rule, §8.2

C

Campaign, term (usage), §9.2(a)
Canadian organizations, private foundation grants, §9.6(c)
Candidate for public office, meaning, §9.2(a)
Capacity-building, facilitation, §8.3
Capital asset, §14.6
Capital endowment grant, §9.7(d)
Capital gain
   dividends, payment/credit, §3.1(d)
   property deduction rule, §14.4(a)
   unrelated income taxation, exception, §11.1(d)
Capital gains/losses, §10.4(b)
   basis, §10.4(b)(ii)
   dividends, §10.4(d)
   estate/trust distributions, §10.4(g)
   exceptions/adjustments/exclusions, §10(b)(i)
   interest/annuities, §10.4(c)
   partnership income, §10.4(h)
   Ponzi scheme losses, §10.4(b)(iv)
   rent, §10.4(e)
   royalties, §10.4(f)
   S Corporation income, §10.4(h)
   wash sales, §10.4(b)(iii)
Capital loss carryovers/carrybacks, allowance (disallowance), §10.4(b)(i)
Cash distribution test set-asides, §6.4(g)(ii)
Cash-type interest-bearing accounts, §8.2(a)
Cash, valuation, §6.3(a)
Charitable contribution
   administrative considerations, §14.7
   appraisal rules, §14.7
   bargain sales, §14.6(b)
   conservation property, §14.6(g)
   deductibility, §14.2(a)
   disclosure rules, §14.7(c)
   donor-created assets, §14.6(a)
   gift, equivalence, §14.1
   intellectual property, §14.6(c)
   percentage limitations, §14.(a)
   property, use, §14.6(e)
   recordkeeping rules, §14.7(a)
   reporting requirements, §14.7(f)
   services, §14.6(f)
   state fundraising regulation, §14.7(g)
   substantiation rules, §14.7(b)
   tax benefit, §14.4(b)
   vehicles, §14.6(d)
Charitable distributions, private foundation contribution minimum, §15.1

INDEX

Charitable donee
    substantiation, providing, §14.7(b)
    tax-exempt status, §16.2
Charitable gift
    concept, determination, §16.2
    definition, §16.2
    funds, §16.5
Charitable giving rules
    appraisal rules, §14.7(d)
    bargain sales, §14.6(b)
    basic rules, §14.2
        estate and gift tax
            deductions, §14.2(b)
        percentage limitations, §14.2(a)
    conservation property, §14.6(g)
    doctrine of substantial
        compliance, §14.7(e)
    general overview, §1.4(k)
    gifts of appreciated property, §14.3
        capital gain property deduction
            reduction rule, §14.4(a)
        other deduction reduced
            rules, §14.4(b)
        qualified appreciated stock
            rule, §14.5
    intellectual property, §14.6(a)
    property created by donor, §14.6(a)
    quid pro quo contributions,
        disclosure, §14.7(c)
    recordkeeping rules, §14.7(a)
    reporting requirements, §14.7(f)
    right to use of property, donation
        of, §14.6(e)
    services, §14.6(f)
    substantiation rules, §14.7(b)
    vehicles, §14.6(d)
Charitable grants, in general, §6.4(b)
Charitable pledges, payment, §5.8(c)
Charitable program, expenses
    deduction allowance, net investment
        income tax, §10.5(a)
    private operating foundations,
        §§3.1, 3.1(b)
    as qualifying distributions, §6.4(f)
Charitable purposes, operating, §1.6

Charitable remainder trusts, early
    terminations, §5.13
Charitable solicitation act, §14.7(g)
Charitable trusts, nonexempt, §3.6
Charity (charities)
    crisis counseling, providing, §9.3(c)
    defined, §1.5
    group ruling, §6.4(d)(iv)
    legislative activities, §9.1(a)
    lobbying activities, grants
        supporting, §9.1(c)
    political campaign activities,
        §9.2(a)
    recipient, §9.3(c)
Checking accounts (general banking
    service), §5.6(g)
Childcare funds, provision, §9.3(d)(i)
Churches, §15.3(a)
    criteria, §15.3
Closely held company (partial interest),
    private foundation disposition
    (inability), §7.2(d)
Closing agreements, §12.4(e)
Co-investments, §5.4(g)
Collection period, suspension, §7.7
Colonial Williamsburg
    liquidation, §15.5(b)
Combined voting power, §§ 4.3, 4.5
Commercial enterprise, business
    (relationship), §11.1(b)
Commercial national donor-advised
    funds, §16.8(a)
Commissions, §5.6(f)
Common fund foundations, §3.4
Community foundations
    donative publicly supported charity
        qualification, §15.4(e)
    grant-making services, §11.3(d)
    treatment, §15.4(e)
    utilization, §16.3
Community trust, creation, 15.6(c)
Company foundations
    establishment, reasons, §17.2
    law, requirements, §17.1
    overview, §17.1

INDEX

receptionist, cost (sharing), §17.6(b)
self-dealing rules, §17.6(b)
Company-related private foundation, on-the-job training/education provision, §17.6(e)
Compensation, §5.15(b)(ii)
  bank fees, §5.6(h)
  commissions, §5.6(f)
  correction, self-dealing, §5.15(d)(vi)
  definition, §5.6(b)
  excess executive compensation tax, §5.6(e)
    compensation from related organizations, §5.6(e)(ii)
    covered employee status, exceptions, §5.6(e)(iii)
    general rules/definitions, §5.6(e)
  expense advances, §5.6(g)
  levels, increases/spikes, §5.6(c)
  management fees, §5.6(f)
  nonprofit context, law, §5.6(c)
  package, comparison, §5.6(c)
  payment, §§ 5.6, 17.6(a)
  reasonable compensation, §5.6(c)
  reasonableness, evaluation, §5.6(c)
  reimbursements, §5.6(g)
Compensatory indemnification/insurance, §5.7(b)
Compliance, check, §12.6(a)
Conditional gift, §16.2
Condition precedent, §16.2
Conduit foundations, §§ 3.3, 14.2(a)
Conservation property (gift), §14.6(g)
Constant return, §8.2(e)
Constructive ownership rules
  compensation from related organizations, §5.6(e)(ii)
  disqualified persons, §§4.3, 4.5, 4.6
  excess business holdings, §7.2(c)
Contingent voting rights, treatment, §7.1(d)
Contributed assets, §8.1(b)
Contribution
  base, §14.2(a)
  definition, §16.2

term, meanings (substantial contributor), §4.1(a)
Control
  concept, indirect self-dealing, §5.11(b)
  definition, §§ 6.4(c)(i), 15.6(g)(vii)
Controlled foundations, complete asset transfers, §13.5(b)
  Section 4940 implications, §13.5(b)
  Section 4942 implications, §13.5(b)
  Section 4943 implications, §13.5(b)
  Section 4944 implications, §13.5(b)
  Section 4945 implications, §13.5(b)
Controlled organizations, grants, §6.4(c)
Controlling donors
  contributions, supporting organizations, §15.6(h)
  control, limitation (supporting organizations), §15.6(j)
  excess benefit transactions rules, §15.6(i)
Co-owned property, §5.4(f)
Corporate organizations, self-dealing rules (exceptions), §5.14(a)
Corporate reorganizations, §17.6(f)
  self-dealing rules, exceptions, §§5.14(a), 17.6(f)
Corporations
  deductible charitable contributions, §14.2(a)
  disqualified persons, relationship, §4.5
Correction, meaning, §§5.15(d), 7.7, 8.5(d), 9.9(d)
Correction period, §§ 5.15(e), 6.5(d), 7.7, 8.5(d)
  meaning, §12.4(c)
Cost depletion, deduction allowance, §10.5(a)
Court-order set-asides, §6.4(g)(iii)
Covered employee, §5.6(e)(i)
  status, exceptions, §5.6(e)(iii)
Credit, extensions (self-dealing), §5.5
Current return, §8.2(d)
  method, §8.2(e)

■ 747 ■

INDEX

D

Daily delinquency penalty, §§ 12.2(a), 12.3(a)
   application, §12.4(b)
Debt-financed income, §11.4(a)
Debt-financed property, term (meaning), §11.4(a)
Decedents, estates (tax considerations), §2.2(a)
Declaratory judgment action, §12.7(d)
Declaratory judgment procedures, tax-exempt status recognition denial, §2.7(e)
Deductible charitable contributions, §14.2(a)
   capital gain property deduction rule, §14.4(a)
   deduction reduction rules, §14.4
Deduction reduction rules, §§ 14.4, 14.4(b)
De minimis payments, government officials, §5.10
De minimis test
   excess business holdings (2 percent), §§1.4(f), 7.1(d)
   qualified partnership interests, §11.5(b)
Depreciation (calculation), straight-line method (usage), §10.5(a)
Detached or disinterested generosity, §§14.1, 16.2
Determination letters, §12.5
   reliance, §§6.4(d), 9.4(b), 12.5(c)
   seeking, §§2.7, 12.5(a)
Diligent and continuous efforts, §7.2(d)
Direct charitable distributions, §3.1(a)
Direct charitable expenditures, §6.4(f)
Direct lobbying
   communication, §9.1(b)
   expenditures, §9.1(b)
Disaster
   assistance, §9.3(c)
   hardship, providing, §9.3(c)
   relief, grants, §9.3(c)

Disclosure of *quid pro quo* contributions, §14.7(c)
Disclosure of returns (public), §12.3(a)
Disclosure of returns (state officials), §12.3(b)
Disposition periods, excess business holdings, §7.2(d)
Disqualified persons
   certain 20 percent owners as, §4.3
   charitable pledges, payment of, §5.8(c)
   compensation of, §5.6
   corporations as, §§4.5, 17.5
   definition, certain supporting organizations, §7.5
   and donor-advised funds, §16.7
   family members, §4.4
   foundation managers, §4.2
   general overview, § 1.4(c)
   goods/facilities/services, furnishing, §§ 5.3, 17.6(b)
   government officials as, §4.8
   incidental/tenuous benefits, §5.8(e)
   income/assets, uses by, §5.8
   loans, §§5.3, 9.8
   partnerships as, §4.5
   property use by, §5.15(d)(iv)
   and public support test, §§15.4(b), 15.5(a)
   status, termination of, §4.9
   substantial contributors, §4.1
   and supporting organizations, §15.6(j)
   term, §§ 4.3, 15.6(j), 16.7
   transactions, manipulation (involvement), §5.8(b)
   trusts or estates as, §4.6
Distributable amount, §§ 6.1(b), 15.6(c)(vi)
Distribution. *See* Qualifying distributions
   amount, reduction, §3.1(g)
   directing, right (reservation), §13.3(c)
   excess qualifying distributions, §6.5(c)
   grantor advice, limitation, §13.3(c)(ii)
   impermissible reservation, factors, §13.3(c)(ii)

permissible reservation, factors, §13.3(c)(i)
requirement, satisfaction, §15.6(g)(vi)
Diversification
　prudent nature, §8.2
　technique, importance, 8.2(b)
Diversified investment portfolio, investments, §8.2(b)
Dividends and net investment income, §10.4(d)
Doctrine of private inurement, §§5.1, 17.3
Doctrine of substantial compliance, §14.7(e)
Donative publicly supported charities, §15.4
　charitable organization qualification, support test (usage), §15.4(c)
　community foundations, §15.4(e)
　facts and circumstances test, §15.4(d)
　support fraction, §15.4(c)
　two-percent limitation, §15.4(b)
Donor-advised funds (DAFs)
　collective, §16.4
　commercial national donor-advised funds, §16.8(a)
　community foundations, §16.3
　contributions, §§ 16.7, 16.9(b)
　definitions, §16.1
　distributions, §§ 15.4(b), 16.7, 16.9(b)
　earmarking, §16.5
　excess business holdings rules, application, §7.6
　exemption challenges, §16.4(a)
　grants, §9.3(c)
　　making, §16.7
　　treatment, §16.9(c)
　IRS Notice (2017)
　　comments, §16.9(c)
　　content, §16.9(b)
　law, decision (impact), §16.4(b)
　litigation, §16.4
　maintenance, §16.7
　national donor-advised funds, §16.8(a)
　proposed legislation, §16.10
　regulations project, §16.9(c)
　studies, §16.8
　tax regulations, §16.9
　Treasury study, §16.8(a)
　usage by private foundations, §16.9(c)
Donors
　advisor, expectation, §16.7
　challenges to donor-advised funds, §16.4(b)
　contribution base, §14.2(a)
　creations, charitable contributions of, §14.6
Dual-use property, allocation, §6.2(d)
Duty to investigate, expenditure responsibility grants, §9.3(e)(iii)

E

Earmarked
　and awards for past achievement, §9.3(d)(iii)
　and donor-advised funds, §16.5
　and expenditure responsibility, §9.7(a)
　grants to government agencies, §9.4(c)
　grants to public charities
　　generally, §9.4(c)
　　for lobbying activities, §9.1(c)
　individual grant intermediaries/ earmarking, §9.3(g)
　and political campaign activities, §9.2(b)
　term, usage, §9.1(c)
Economic Recovery Tax Act (1981), Congress adoption, §6.6
Educational institutions, §15.3(b)
　public charity status, §15.3(b)
Emergency hardship, §9.3(c)
Employer-related educational loan programs, §9.3(d)(ii)
Endowment
　funds, total return concept, §8.2(d)
　test, private operating foundations, §3.1(e)(ii)
　　compliance period, §3.1(f)

INDEX

Equivalency (good faith) determinations, §§6.4(e), 9.6(b)
Estate administration exception, §5.12
    expectancy, concept, §5.12(a)
    fair market value, determination, §5.12(c)
    general rules, §5.12(b)
    requirements, §12.5(b)
Estate planning principles, §2.5
    decedent's estates, §2.2(a)
    estate considerations, §2.2(b)
    gift tax considerations, §2.2(b)
Estates
    disqualified persons, relationship, §4.6
    distributions, capital gains/losses, §10.4(g)
Excess benefit transactions rules, supporting organizations and, §15.6(i)
Excess business holdings
    business enterprise, definition, §7.1(a)
    constructive ownership rules, §7.2(c)
    disposition periods for excess holdings, §7.2(d)
    donor-advised funds, application, §7.6
    excise taxes on, §7.7
    functionally related business, exception, §7.3
    general overview, §1.4(f)
    general rules, §§ 7.1, 7.2(a)
    investment partnerships, §7.1(c)
    legislative history, IRS review, §7.1(c)
    passive income businesses, §7.1(b)
    percentage limitations, §7.1(d)
    permitted holdings, §7.2
        general rules, §7.2(a)
        partnerships, §7.2(b)
        sole proprietorships, §7.2(b)
        trusts, §7.2(b)
    philanthropic business, exception, §7.4
    supporting organizations, application, §7.5
Excess executive compensation tax, §5.6(e)
    covered employee status, exceptions, §5.6(e)(iii)
    employee, definition, §5.6(e)(iii)
    general rules, §5.6(e)(i)
    limited hours exception, §§5.6(e)(iii), 17.8(a)
    nonexempt funds exception, §§5.6(e)(iii), 17.8(b)
    related organizations, compensation from, §5.6(e)(ii)
Excess parachute payment, §5.6(e)(i)
Excess qualifying distributions, §6.5(c)
Excise taxes
    abatement of first-tier (initial) excise taxes, §12.4(c)
    excess business holdings, §7.7
    excise holdings, excise taxes, §7.7
    jeopardizing investments, §8.5
    payment, §12.4
    reporting, §12.4
    self-dealing, §5.15(a)
    taxable expenditures, §9.9
    understatement penalties, §12.4(b)
    undistributed income, §6.5(d)
Exclusively, term
    application, §15.6(b)
    literal use, §15.6(m)
Exempt activity, future use, §6.2(d)
Exempt-function assets, §§ 6.2(d), 6.4(f)(i)
    purchases, nondeductibility, §10.5
Exempt-function income-producing property, nondeductibility, §10.5(b)
Exempt-function revenue, §15.4(c)
Exempt operating foundations, §§3.2, 10.7
    private foundation grants, §9.5
    requirements, §10.7
Exempt Organization Business Income Tax Return (Form 990-T), §11.5(d)
    disclosure, §12.3(a)

INDEX

Exempt Organizations Business Master File Extract (EO BMF), §§ 6.4(d)(i), 6.4(d)(ii), 9.4(b)
Exempt Organizations Closing Agreement Coordinator for Examinations (EOCAC) (IRS), 12.4(e)
Exempt-use assets, supporting organizations, §15.6(g)(vi)
 management, §15.6(g)(v)
Expectancy
 concept, §5.12(a)
 exclusion from minimum investment return, §6.2(c)
Expenditure responsibility, §9.7
 diversion of funds by grantee, §9.7(h)
 general rules, §9.7(a)
 grantee books and records, §9.7(e)
 grantee reports, §9.7(d)
 grant terms, required, §9.7(c)
 IRS reports, §9.7(f)
 pre-grant inquiry, §9.7(b)
 private foundation recordkeeping requirements, §9.7(g)
Expense advances, §5.6(g)

F

Facilities
 furnishing, §5.4(e)
 sharing, §17.6(b)
Facts, material change, §12.7(b)
Fair market value
 assets held for partial year, §6.3(d)
 cash, §6.3(a)
 determination, §§ 5.12(c), 6.3
 exceptions, §5.15(b)(iii)
 investment frauds, §6.3(e)
 other assets, §6.3(c)
 readily marketable securities, §6.3(b)
Family members, disqualified persons (relationship), §4.4
Farmland, sharecrop arrangements, §11.2(b)
"Favorable public recognition and goodwill," §17.6(e)

Federal tax law, nonprofit board composition, §2.8(e)
Fellowships, §9.3(d)(i)
First-tier (initial) private foundation excise taxes
 abatement, §12.4(c)
 excess business holdings, §7.7
 jeopardizing investments, §8.5(a)
 self-dealing, §5.15(a)
 taxable expenditures, §9.9(a)
 undistributed income, §6.5(a)
Fixed-money investments, §8.2(f)
Foreign foundations, gross investment income taxation, §10.6
Foreign grants, §9.7(c)
Foreign organizations
 anti-terrorist financing guidelines, §§ 9.6, 9.6(d)
 foreign private foundations, §3.8
 general rules, §9.6(a)
 good faith (equivalency) determinations, §§6.4(e), 9.6(b)
 grants to, §§6.4(e), 9.6
 recognition of, §2.7(f)
 U.S. source investment income, taxation, §10.6
Foreign private foundations, §3.8
Form 990-PF, §§ 6.5(c), 6.5(e), 10.2, 12.1
 accounting method, change, §12.1(d)(ii)
 activities, changes, §12.1(c)(i)
 amended returns, §12.2(d)
 annual accounting period (tax year), change, §12.1(d)(i)
 annual Form 990-PF, private foundation filing, §15.1
 annual form, filing requirement, §12.1(a)
 changes, §12.1(d)
 reporting, §12.1(c)
 copies, providing, §12.3(a)
 daily delinquency penalty, §12.2(a)
 application, §12.4(b)
 disclosures, §12.1(b)
 filing, §§13.4(c), 15.8

INDEX

Form 990-PF (*Continued*)
    failure, §§12.3(a), 12.7(a), 12.7(e)
    resumption, §13.5(b)
    governing document changes,
        §12.1(c)(ii)
    name/address change, §12.1(c)(iii)
    penalties, §12.2
        reasonable cause for
            abatement, §12.2(c)
        reporting of private foundation status
            termination, §13.3(a)
        statute of limitations, §12.2(b)
Form 990-T (Exempt Organization
    Business Income Tax
    Return), §11.5(d)
    availability, §12.3(a)
Form 990-W, §10.2
Form 1023, §2.7(a)
Form 1041, §12.7(e)
Form 1065 (Schedule K-1), §11.5(b)
Form 1128 (Application to Adopt,
    Change, or Retain a Tax Year),
    §12.1(d)(i)
Form 2220, §10.2
Form 3115 (Application for Change
    in Accounting Method),
    §12.1(d)(ii)
Form 4720, §§ 9.9(c), 12.1(b), §§ 12.5(a),
    15.5(c)(iii)
    advance ruling request
        submission, §13.4(c)
    copy, filing, §12.3(b)
    correction, providing, §12.4(a)
    due date, §12.4(a)
    filing, §15.7(d)
    filing failure, §12.4(b)
        IRS argument, court
            rejection, §12.4(d)
    filing requirement, §12.4(b)
    payment, §12.4(a)
    reporting, §§12.4(a), 12.4(d)
    request, submission, §12.5(c)
    statute of limitations, §12.4(d)
    submission, §13.4(d)
    tax/penalties, additions, §12.4(b)

Form K-1, §11.3(c)
Foundation managers, §4.2
    agreement, components, §9.9(b)
    excise taxes on, §§5.15(a), 9.9(b)
Foundation managers, tax, §§5.15(a),
    8.5, 9.9(b)
Fragmentation rule, §11.1(b)
Fraudulent investment schemes, §5.11(e)
Fringe benefit rules, volunteer
    services, §5.7(c)
Full-payment period minimum amount,
    §6.4(g)(ii)
Functionally integrated Type III
    organizations, integral part
    test, §15.6(g)(v)
Functionally related business, §§3.1(e)(i),
    6.2(d), 7.3
    definition, usage, §7.3
Funding (DAFs), §16.9(c)
    maximization, §16.9(c)

G

Gains. *See* Capital gains/losses
    determination, §10.4(b)(ii)
    excise taxation exclusions, §10.4(b)(i)
General banking services, §5.6(g)
Generally accepted appraisal
    standards, §14.7(d)
Gifts
    administrative considerations, 14.7
    appraisal rules, §14.7(d)
    appreciated property gifts, §14.3
    bargain sales, §14.6(b)
    basic rules, §14.2
    charitable contribution,
        equivalence, §14.1
    concept, §14.1
        elements, §14.1
    conservation property, §14.6(g)
    consideration, §15.5(a)
    disclosure rules, §14.7(c)
    donors, creations, §14.6(a)
    general concept, §16.2
    intellectual property, §14.6(c)
    partial interest, §14.2

INDEX

percentage limitations, §14.2(a)
property, use, §14.6(e)
recordkeeping rules, §14.7(a)
reporting requirements, §14.7(f)
services, §14.6(f)
special gift situations, §14.6
state fundraising regulation, §14.7(g)
substantiation rules, §14.7(b)
vehicles, §14.6(d)
Gift taxes
   aggregate increases, §13.7
   considerations, §2.2(b)
   deductions, §14.2(b)
Good faith (equivalency) determinations, §§6.4(e), 9.6(b)
Goods, furnishing, §5.4(e)
Governance, §2.8
   nonprofit governance
      concept, §2.8(b)
      IRS entry, §2.8(a)
      regulation, IRS attempts, §2.8(d)
      standards, §2.8(c)
Governing documents, changes, §12.1(c)(ii)
Governmental agency, private foundation grant, §§ 9.3(g), 9.4(c)
Governmental entity, supporting organization, §15.6(c)(v)
Governmental officials, disqualified persons (relationship), §4.8
Governmental units, public charity status, §15.3(f)
Government bureau, phrase (meaning), §15.5(a)
Government officials
   de minimis payments, permission, §5.10
   private foundation payments, prohibition, §5.10
Grant-making, §§ 9.3(d)(ii), 15.5(a), 15.6(g)(v)
   activity records, electronic maintenance, §9.7(g)
   programs

      charitable distributions/ administrative expenses, nondeductibility, §10.5(b)
      IRS ruling, §17.6(d)
   services, §11.3(d)
      IRS classification, §11.3(d)
Grants, §3.1(b)
   accountability, ensuring, §9.7(a)
   charitable purposes, §9.8
   definition, §9.3(a)
   foreign grants, §9.7(c)
   prizes/awards, §9.3(d)(iii)
   procedures, IRS advance approval, §9.3(d)(iv)
   procedures, objective/ nondiscriminatory selection process, §9.3(e)
   public charity grants, §9.4
   renewal, §9.3(f)(iii)
   scholarship, §9.3(d)(i)
   skills enhancement, relationship, §9.3(d)(iv)
   specific objectives, relationship, §9.3(d)(iv)
   terms, §9.7(c)
   unusual. *See* Unusual grants.
Grassley, Charles, §8.4(a)
Grassroots lobbying communication, §9.1(b), §9.1(d)
Gross income
   derivation, §§11.1(c), 11.5(a)
   passive source derivation, §§ 7.1(a), 11.3(a)
   substantially related activity, §11.1(c)
Gross investment income, §§ 9.2(c), 10.4(a)
   collection, §10.5
   deductions
      allowance, §10.5(a)
      nonallowance, §10.5(b)
   expenses/earnings, nexus/ integral relationship, §10.5(b)
   expenses, nondeductibility, §10.5(b)

INDEX

Gross investment income (*Continued*)
    foreign foundations, gross investment income taxation, §10.6
    interest income, inclusion, §10.4(c)
    reductions, §10.5

H
High-income yields, advantage, §6.6
Historic and continuing relationship, §15.6(c)
Hospitals, public charity qualification, §15.3(c)
Housing, development/construction (promotion), §8.3

I
Imputed interest, inclusion, §6.6
Incidental/tenuous benefits, §§ 5.8(e), 17.6(e)
Income
    anticipatory assignment, avoidance, §16.4(c)
    charitable pledges, payment, §5.8(c)
    derivation, §11.2(d)
    disqualified persons uses, §5.8
    distribution
        failure, excise taxes, §6.5
        nontaxation, §10.4(g)
    passive characteristic, §11.2
    reporting, §8.2(e)
    test, §3.1(d)
    transactions, manipulation (involvement), §5.8(b)
    undistributed income, §6.5(a)
    unrelated debt-financed income rules, §11.4
        includible income, §11.4(c)
Income interest, split-interest trust, §3.7
Income-producing asset, acquisition, §11.4(a)
Income taxes
    aggregate increases, §13.7
    regulations, §§ 15.9, 16.3
    understatement, §12.4(b)
Indebted property, gifts, §5.5(a)
Indebted real/personal property, transfer, §5.3
Indemnification
    compensatory indemnification, §5.7(b)
    noncompensatory indemnification, §5.7(a)
Indirect self-dealing, §§ 5.3, 5.11
    control, concept, §5.11(b)
    exceptions, §5.11(d)
    fraudulent investment schemes, §5.11(e)
    transactions
        control element, relationship, §5.11(c)
        controlled entities, usage, §5.11(a)
Individual grant intermediaries/earmarking, §9.3(g)
Individual grant procedures, §9.3(e)
    advance IRS approval, requests, §9.3(f)(i)
    candidates, selection, §9.5(e)(i)
    deemed IRS approval, §9.3(f)(ii)
    future grants, IRS approval (impact), §9.3(f)(iii)
    grant candidates, breadth (requirement), §9.3(e)(i)
    grantee reporting requirements, §9.3(e)(ii)
    grant renewal, §9.3(f)(iii)
    IRS approval, §9.3(f)
    monitoring/supervision/investigation requirements, §9.3(e)(iii)
    reasonable and appropriate steps, §9.3(e)(iii)
    recordkeeping requirements, §9.3(e)(iv)
    selection, objective/nondiscriminatory basis, §9.3(e)(i)
Individual grants, §9.3(d)
    charitable/permitted purposes, §9.3(b)
    preapproval requirements, §9.3(e)

INDEX

prizes/awards, §9.3(d)(iii)
programs, private operating foundations, §3.1(c)
specific objective, obtaining, §9.3(d)(iv)
Individuals
compensation package, comparison, §5.6(c)
grants, §9.3
Influencing legislation (lobbying), §9.1(a)
Information, materiality (IRS consideration), §12.2(b)
Initial (first-tier) excise taxes, §9.9(a)
abatement, IRS discretionary authority, §12.4(c)
limitation on, §15.15(a)(iv)
on excess business holdings, §7.7
on jeopardizing investments, §8.5(a)
payment, §9.9(c)
on self-dealing transactions, §5.15(a)
on taxable expenditures, §9.9(a)
on undistributed income, §6.5(d)
Inspection of returns, §12.3
Institutional investors, financial advisers, §11.3(c)
Insurance
compensatory insurance, §5.7(b)
deduction allowance, §10.5(a)
noncompensatory insurance, §5.7(a)
Integral part test, §§ 15.6(g)(v), 15.6(g)(vi)
Intellectual property (gift), §14.6(c)
Interest
capital gains/losses, §10.4(c)
disposal, §7.2(d)
income, inclusion, §10.4(c)
rate, Federal Reserve Board deliberations, §8.2(b)
Interested person, term (usage), §15.5(c)(i)
Interest-free loans, §§ 5.5(b), 8.3
Intermediary grantees, §9.4(c)
Intermediate entity, §16.5
Internal Revenue Bulletin, §12.7(b)
Internal Revenue Manual, 12.6(b)

Internal Revenue Service (IRS)
abatement, discretion, §12.4(c)
administrative appeal procedures, §12.7(c)
advance IRS approval, individual grant program requests, §9.3(f)(i)
advance ruling. *See* Advance IRS ruling requests.
Audit Technique Guides (ATGs), §12.6(b)
deemed IRS approval, §9.3(f)(ii)
determination letters, §2.7(c)
absence, §§6.4(d)(iii), 9.6(b)
EO examination practices/ procedures, §12.6(b)
examiner, expectations, §12.6(c)
Exempt Organizations Business Master File Extract (EO BMF), §§ 6.4(d)(i), 6.4(d)(ii), 9.4(b)
Exempt Organizations Closing Agreement Coordinator for Examinations (EOCAC), §12.4(e)
future grants approval, impact, §9.3(f)(iii)
grant procedure approval, §9.3(f)
Independent Office of Appeals, §§ 12.5(b), 12.7(a)
Internal Revenue Manual, §12.6(b)
nonprofit governance, IRS entry, §2.8(a)
positive results, achievement (IRS examination), §12.6(c)
reports, §9.7(f)
retroactive revocation, §12.7(b)
revenue agent, field examination request, §12.6(b)
ruling policy, governance, §2.8(g)
Tax Exempt Organization Search (database), §§ 6.4(d)(i), 6.4(d)(ii), 9.4(b), 12.3(a)
Tax-Exempt Organizations Examination Procedures, §12.6(b)
Technical Guides (TGs), 12.6(b)

INDEX

Intervention, constituting, §9.2(a)
Inter vivos gift, receipt (IRS unusual grant rule), §15.5(c)(i)
Investment
   alternatives, §8.2(b)
      evaluation, §8.2(a)
   assets, §6.2(b)
   economic conditions, impact, §8.2(a)
   frauds, §§ 6.3(e), 8.4
      background, §8.4(a)
   making, §8.3
   management fees, deduction allowance, §10.5(a)
   partnerships, §7.1(c)
      partnership agreement investment prohibition, §7.1(c)
   procedure, approval, §8.1(a)
   rate of return, foundation targeting, §8.2(a)
   return, measurement, §8.2(f)
Investment-by-investment approach, §8.2
Investment-by-investment inquiry, §8.1(a)
Investment income
   generation, §15.4(c)
   test, §15.5(b)
   transferred assets, relationship, §13.5(c)
Investment income, tax on. *See* Net investment income tax
Involuntary termination, private foundation status, §13.2

J

Jeopardizing investments, §8.1(a)
   additional (second-tier) excise taxes, §8.5(d)
   foundation manager knowledge, §8.5(b)
   general overview, §1.4(g)
   general rules, §8.1
   initial (first-tier) excise taxes, §8.5(a)
   Ponzi scheme investment, comparison, §8.4(b)
   removal from jeopardy, §8.5(d)
   tax, §8.3
   willfulness, §8.5(b)
Jeopardy
   defining, §8.1(a)
   removal, §8.5(d)

K

Knowing, meaning, §8.5(b)

L

Lawyer, legal opinion (impact), §8.5(c)
Legal/accounting/professional fees, deduction allowance, §10.5(a)
Legislative activities, §9.1
Legislative proposal, examples, §9.1(e)
Letter rulings, §§ 12.5, 12.5(b)
   request, §12.5(b)
Limited hours exception, §§5.6(e)(iii), 17.8(a)
Limited liability company
   private foundation, ownership, §7.3(d)
   single-member limited liability, holdings, §7.3
Limited partnership trading, investment, §8.1(a)
Loans, §5.5
   interest-free loans, §5.5(b)
   self-dealing rules, correction, §5.15(d)(iii)
Lobbying
   activities, §9.1
   types, §9.1(b)
Lock-up period, §8.2(a)
Long-term capital gain property (appreciated capital asset), §14.3
Losses
   determination, §10.4(b)(ii)
   net capital losses, nondeductibility, §10.4(b)(iii)
   Ponzi schemes losses, §10.4(b)(iv)
Low-cost articles, income distribution, §11.2(d)

INDEX

Low-income neighborhood, jobs (providing), §8.3
Low-interest loans, §8.3
Low-profit limited liability corporation (L3C), investment facilitation, §8.3

M

Madoff, Bernard L., §8.4(a)
Managed commodity trading program, §8.1(a)
Management fees, §5.6(f)
Mandatory distribution requirement, §6.1
   distributable amount, §6.1(b)
   general overview, §1.4(e)
   history, §6.6
   purpose/policy, §6.1(a)
Marketable securities
   collateral pledge, §8.3
   distribution suitability, §10.3
   qualified appreciated stock, deduction, §14.5
Mark-to-market rules, usage, §11.3(c)
Material changes, §12.7(b)
   individual grant procedures, §9.3(f)(iii)
Material information, omission, §12.2(b)
Material restrictions/conditions, imposition (absence), §13.3(b)
Medical research organization, §3.1(a)
   public charity qualification, §15.3(d)
Medical research, term (meaning), §15.3(d)
Member of the family, definition, §4.4
Membership fee, payment treatment, §15.5(a)
Mexican organizations, private foundation grants, §9.6(c)
Minimum asset amount, §15.6(g)(vi)
Minimum distribution requirements, meeting, §11.4(a)
Minimum investment return (MIR), §§ 3.1(d), 6.2
   acquisition indebtedness, §6.2(e)
   assets held for partial year, §6.3(d)
   calculations, §12.2(b)
   cash, valuation, §6.3(a)
   exempt function assets, §6.2(d)
   future interests/expectancies, §6.2(c)
   general calculation, §6.2(a)
   investment assets, §6.2(b)
   other assets, §6.2(c)
   readily marketable securities, §6.3(b)
Ministers educational loan debt, private foundation grants payment (taxable expenditures), §9.3(b)
Miscellaneous Determination Requests (Form 8940), §12.5(a)
   request, submission, §12.5(c)
Mission-related investments, §8.2(g)
Modifications, unrelated business income tax, §11.2
Money, use, §5.15(b)(i)
Monies, return (court ruling), §9.8
Municipal bond interest (state/local government payment), exclusion/nontaxation, §10.4(c)
Myopia rule, §7.2(c)

N

National Conference of Commissioners on Uniform State Laws, UPMIFA approval, §8.2
National donor-advised funds, §16.8(a)
National foundations, §16.5
Need-based distributions, IRS guidelines, §9.3(c)
Need, objective determination, §9.3(c)
Needy test (distressed test), §9.3(c)
Neighborhood land rule, §11.4(b)
Net assets
   private foundation distribution, §13.3(a)
   term, meaning, §13.7
   value, computation, §13.7
Net capital losses, nondeductibility, §10.4(b)(iii)

INDEX

Net investment income tax
  calculation, §10.4
  capital gains/losses, §10.4(b)
    basis, §10.4(b)(ii)
    exceptions/adjustments/
      exclusions, §10.4(b)(i)
    Ponzi losses, §10.4(b)(iv)
    wash sales, §10.4(b)(iii)
  deductions, §10.5
  exemption, exempt operating
    foundation, §10.7
  general overview, §1.4(i)
  opportunities to reduce,
    planning, §10.3
  payment of tax, §10.2
  rate of tax, §10.1
  reduction, planning
    opportunities, §10.2
  taxable net investment income,
    calculation, §10.4
Net short-term capital gains,
  inclusion, §6.6
New York State Bar
  Association (NYSBA)
  recommendations, §16.9(c)
  report, §8.4(b)
New York Stock Exchange, shares
  (nonlisting), §14.5
Nominal, definition, §6.2(d)
Nonbusiness activities, §11.2(d)
Noncash charitable contribution,
  charitable deduction
  (nonallowance), §14.7(b)
Noncharitable organizations,
  private foundation grants
  (prohibition), §15.1
Noncharitable purposes
  spending, §9.8
  taxable expenditure, §9.8
Noncharitable supported
  organizations, §15.6(l)
Non-controlled foundations,
  complete asset
  transfers, §13.5(c)
Nonexempt charitable trusts, §3.6

termination of private foundation
  status, §13.6
Nonexempt funds exception, §§ 5.6(e)
  (iii), 17.8(b)
Non-exempt-use assets, aggregate fair
  market value, §15.6(c)(vi)
Non-filing, automatic
  revocation, §12.7(a)
Nonfunctionally integrated Type III
  organizations, integral part
  test, §15.6(g)(vi)
  attentiveness requirement,
    §15.6(g)(vi)
  distribution requirement,
    §15.6(g)(vi)
  excess (distribution) amounts,
    creation, §15.6(g)(vi)
  and excess business holdings
    rules, §15.6(k)
Nonpartisan analysis/study/research,
  meaning, §9.1(d)
Nonprofit governance
  board composition, federal tax
    law, §2.8(e)
  concept, §2.8(b)
  IRS entry, §2.8
  IRS ruling policy, §2.8(g)
  principles/practices,
    emergence, §5.6(c)
  private benefit doctrine, IRS
    usage, §2.8(f)
  regulation, IRS attempts, §2.8(d)
  standards, §2.8(c)
Nontaxable exchange, exceptions,
  §10.4(b)(i)
Nontraditional investments, §8.1(a)
Nonvoting stock, usage, §§ 7.1(d),
  7.2(b)
No-rent lease, offering, §5.3
North American Industry Classification
  System (NAICS) code, digits
  (usage), §11.5(b)
"No rule" list, §12.5(b)
Notification requirement, supporting
  organization, §15.6(g)(ii)

INDEX

Notional principal contracts, income, §10.4(a)
Not-profit corporation, choice of form, §7.3(d)

O

Office space/personnel, sharing (approval), §5.9(b)
Official Catholic Directory, The, §6.4(d)(iii)
Operating expenses, deduction allowance, §10.5
Operating foundations
  activities, §3.1(a)
  exempt operating foundations, §§3.2, 10.7
Operational test, §§1.6, 15.6(b)
Ordering rule, qualifying distributions, §6.5(b)
Ordinary business care and prudence, §8.1(a)
  exercise, §8.2(g)
Organizational form, choice, §2.3
Organizational rules, §1.7
Organizational test
  private foundations, §1.7
  supporting organizations, §15.6(a)
Organizations
  Canadian organizations, private foundation grants, §9.6(c)
  compensation, §5.6(e)(ii)
    package, comparison, §5.6(c)
  donative publicly supported charities qualification, §15.4(a)
  formal instruction, presentation, §15.3(b)
  fundraising efforts, §15.4(d)
  inter vivos gift, receipt (IRS unusual grant rule), §15.5(c)(i)
  Mexican organizations, private foundation grants, §9.6(c)
  non-exempt-use assets, aggregate fair market value, §15.6(c)(vi)
  operation, connection, §15.6(c)
  quarterly estimated tax payment, §11.5(e)
  service provider qualification, §15.9
  tax-exempt purposes, trade/business (relationship), §11.1(c)
Organizations that test for public safety, §15.2
"Other adjustment, organization, or reorganization" (terms), §13.5(1)
Outside advisors, reliance, §8.5(c)
Overall return method, §8.2(e)
Overlapping taxes, potential, §1.8(e)
Over The Counter Bulletin Board (OTCBB), market quotation availability, §14.5

P

Paid, meaning (departure), 6.4(g)(i)
Parachute payment, §5.6(e)(i)
Parking lot rental, rent situation, §11.2(b)
Partial interest (gift), §14.2
Partial ownership, §7.3
Participation, constituting (political campaign activity), §9.2(a)
Partnerships, §7.2(b)
  agreement, investment prohibition, §7.1(c)
  disqualified persons, relationship, §4.5
  income, capital gains/losses, §10.4(h)
  unrelated business activity, §11.3(c)
Passive business operations, usage, §7.1(b)
Passive income, §11.2
  businesses, §7.1(b)
  modification s, unrelated business income, §11.2
Passive sources, §11.3(a)
  income, concept, §7.1(b)
Past achievement, award (private foundation earmarking), §9.3(d)(iii)
Payor, identification, §15.5(a)
Payout rules, revision, §6.6
Pending regulation projects, supporting organizations, §15.6(g)(vii)

■ 759 ■

INDEX

Pension Protection Act of 2006, §§ 16.7, 16.8(a)
People, sharing, §5.9
Percentage interest, determination, §11.5(b)
Percentage limitations, §7.1(d)
Percentage test, satisfaction, §9.3(d)(ii)
Permitted businesses, §11.3(b)
Permitted business holdings, §7.2
    general rules, §7.2(a)
Personal services, definition, §5.6(a)
Person, term (meaning), §4.1(a)
Philanthropic businesses, §7.4
Philanthropy Roundtable, §16.10
    letter, §16.9(c)
Physical facilities, usage, §6.2(d)
Pigouvian taxes, §1.8(b)
Planned giving, §2.6
    charitable remainder trusts, §2.6(b)
    in general, §2.6(a)
    vehicles, §2.6(c)
Pledge, §6.4(a)
Political activities, engagement, §9.2(a)
Political campaign activities, §9.2
Political subdivision, instrumentality, §15.3(g)
Ponzi scheme, §8.4(a), §9.8
    foundations, participation, §8.4(b)
    investment, §8.4(b)
        jeopardizing investment, comparison, §8.4(b)
        losses (capital gains/losses), §10.4(b)(iv)
    private foundation investor confrontation, §8.4(b)
Pooled income funds, §11.3(d)
Positive results, achievement (IRS examination), §12.6(c)
Preferred written advice, §6.4(e)
Pre-grant inquiry, §9.7(b)
Premium, §8.2(f)
Pre-selected funds, §16.4(b)
Present holdings, §7.2(a)
Primarily, term (meaning), §15.6(b)
Principal (investment), §8.2(a)

Private benefit doctrine, §§ 5.2, 17.4
    IRS use, §2.8(f)
Private benefit forms, shielding, §17.6(e)
Private benefit, permission, §17.4
Private foundations
    accounts receivable, §11.2
    adjusted net income determination, §6.6
    advantages, §2.2
    alternatives, §2.1
    assets investment, §8.1(a)
        total return purpose, §10.3
    assets transfer, §13.5(b)
        significant but not all assets, transfer, §13.5(d)
        tax return filing obligations, §13.5(b)
    bank fees, §5.6(g)
    board of trustees, components, §8.5(b)
    budget document reliance, §9.1(c)
    Canadian/Mexican organization grants, §9.6(c)
    capital endowment grant, §9.7(d)
    charitable purposes, §8.1
    compensation, §5.3
    corporate liquidation/merger/redemption/recapitalization, proceeds, §5.3
    corporate status, suspension, §12.7(d)
    costs, absorption, §11.3(e)
    definition, §1.2
    disqualified persons. *See* Disqualified persons.
    employer-related grant/loan program, publicizing, §9.3(d)(ii)
    EO examinations, §12.6(a)
    estate planning principles, §2.5
    examinations, §12.6(b)
        types, §12.6(a)
    foreign private foundations, §3.8
    Form 872-B submission, §13.4(c)
    Form 990-PF disclosure, §12.1(b)
    Form 990-PF filing failure (electronic form), §12.2(a)

INDEX

formation, §16.1
founder, liability, §9.2(b)
functionally related business, partial ownership form, §7.3
funding, §2.4
  sources, security, §8.2(a)
general operational requirements, §1.4(b)
good-faith determination, §9.6(b)
government officials, payments (prohibition), §5.10
grant-making activity records, electronic maintenance, §9.7(g)
grants, §§6.4, 8.3, 9.3(b), 9.3(f)(iii), 9.4(c), 9.5, 9.6
  anti-terrorist financing guidelines, §9.6(d)
  expenditure responsibility, §9.7(a)
  foreign organizations, §§6.4(e), 9.6
  IRS ruling, §9.8
  making, §15.4(e)
  public charities, §9.4
gross income, net short-term capital gains (inclusion), §6.6
group insurance policies, usage, §5.9(c)
historical background/evolution, §§1.3, 1.10
holdings, sale (assistance), §7.2(d)
indebted real/personal property, transfer, §5.3
influence, considerations, §9.2(b)
interest, disposition, §7.2(d)
investments, §8.3
IRS examinations, §12.6
IRS letter rulings, receiving, §12.5(b)
law
  applicability, §§ 9.1(b), 9.2(b)
  changes, §1.10
  primer, §1.4
  sanctions, §1.8
lobbying activity, prohibition, §9.1
long-term financial needs, §8.5(c)
managed commodity trading program, §8.1(a)

managers
  knowledge, §§8.5(b), 9.9(b)
  participation, §§8.5(b), 9.9(b)
mergers/split-ups/transfers, §13.5
  general rules, §13.5(a)
minimum investment return, determination, §6.6
need-based distributions (IRS guidelines), §9.3(c)
net assets
  distribution, §13.3(a)
  transfer, §13.5(a)
  value, computation, §13.7
office space/personnel, sharing (approval), §5.9(b)
operational test, §1.6
organizational test, §1.7
overlapping taxes, potential, §1.8(e)
partnership, §11.4(a)
payments, determination, §5.9(a)
percentage interest, determination, §11.5(b)
portfolio, options (sale), §8.1(a)
principal, loss, §8.2(a)
profits interest, determination, §11.5(b)
program-related investment, §8.3
property use, correction
  disqualified person, §5.15(d)(iv)
  foundation, §5.15(d)(v)
proposed loan, §8.3
purposes, §7.3
qualifying distribution, need, §§6.4, 10.3
reasonable cause, §12.4(c)
recordkeeping requirements, §9.7(g)
records, reliance, §9.7(f)
reformation rule, §§ 13.5(a), 13.5(b)
rules
  interrelationships, §§ 2.6(d), 16.6
  subsequent law, influence, 1.8(f)
sanctions, §1.8(a)
securities investments, §11.3(a)
self-dealing
  membership payments, §5.8(f)

INDEX

Private foundations (*Continued*)
    Pigouvian taxes, §1.8(b)
    taxes/penalties, contrast, §1.8(c)
    short-term financial needs, §8.5(c)
    space/people/expenses, sharing, §5.9
    staff, investment control, §8.2(a)
    statistical profile, §1.9
    status, termination
        general overview, §1.4(j)
        involuntary termination, §13.2
        operation as public charity, §13.4
        transfer to public charity, §13.3(a)
        trusts treated as private foundations, §13.6
        voluntary termination, §13.1
    stock holdings, usage, §7.1
    taxable expenditures, making (absence), §9.1(c)
    expenditures for noncharitable purposes, §9.8
    grants
        exempt operating foundations, §9.5
        foreign organizations, §9.6
        individuals, §9.3
        legislative activities, §9.1
        political campaign activities, §9.2
    tax-exempt status, revocation, §12.7(a)
    tax law primer, §1.4
    third-party website reliance, §12.3(a)
    total assets/liabilities, analysis, §12.2(b)
    total revenues/expenses, analysis, §12.2(b)
    unique nature, §1.1
    unrelated business activity rules, §11.3
    use, incidental/tenuous benefits, §5.8(e)
    voting stock ownership, §7.1(d)
Private inurement doctrine, §§ 5.1, 17.3
Private letter rulings, §§12.5(b), 16.5
Private operating foundations, §§ 3.1, 14.2(a)
    advantages/disadvantages, §3.1(g)
    asset, endowment, or support test, §3.1(e)
        asset test, §3.1(e)(i)
        endowment test, §3.1(e)(ii)
        support test, §3.1(e)(iii)
    compliance period, §3.1(f)
    direct charitable distributions, §3.1(a)
    grants, §3.1(b)
    income test, §3.1(d)
    individual grant programs, §3.1(c)
    status, conversion, §3.1(h)
    technical assistance, providing, §11.3(e)
Prizes, §9.3(d)(iii)
Profit motive, §11.1(b)
Profits interest, §11.5(b)
    meaning, §4.3
    substitution, stock, §8.3
Program-related investment, §8.3
    accountability, ensuring, §9.7(a)
    business enterprise, exclusion, §7.2(d)
    business holding inclusion, §11.3(b)
    impact, §15.6(g)(vii)
    reporting, §9.7(f)
Prohibited transaction, meaning, §10.6
Property
    agents, transactions, §5.4(b)
    charitable contribution, §14.3
    co-investments, §5.4(g)
    co-owned property, §5.4(f)
    costs, deduction allowance, §10.5
    disqualified person use, §5.15(d)(iv)
    dual-use property, allocation, §6.2(d)
    estate administration exception, §5.12
    exchanges, §5.4(c)
    furnishing, §§ 5.4, 5.4(e)
    gift, charitable deduction, §14.3
    indebted property, gifts, §5.5(a)
    interest, holding, §7.2(d)
    lease/leasing, §§ 5.4, 5.4(d), 6.2(d)
    private foundation
        acquisition, §11.4(a)
        purchase/sale, prohibition, §15.1
    private foundation use, §5.15(d)(v)
    sale, §§ 5.4, 5.4(a)

INDEX

usage, absence, §11.1(e)
use, §5.15(b)(i)
gift, §14.6(e)
Proprietorships, §7.2(b)
Prudent investments, §8.2
Prudent investor rules, §8.2
Prudent man rules, §8.2
Prudent trustee approach, §8.2
Public charity (public charities)
  assets, transfer, §13.3
    acceptable restrictions/conditions, §13.3(b)(i)
    general rules, §13.3(a)
    restrictions/conditions, §13.3(b)
    unacceptable restrictions/conditions, §13.3(b)(ii)
  category, change, §15.7(a)–(c)
  distributions, directing right (reservation), §13.3(c)
  grantee, tax exemption status (loss), §9.1(c)
  grantee, types, §9.4(a)
  grants, §9.4
  guidance, §9.3(c)
  private foundation grant, earmarking, §9.3(g)
  private foundation operation as, termination of private foundation status, §13.4
    advance ruling requests, §13.4(c)
    general rules, §13.4(a)
    termination, failure, §13.4(a)
    termination, final notice, §13.4(d)
    termination, initial notice, §13.4(b)
  status
    advantages, §15.1
    change, IRS recognition, §15.7(d)
    termination, §15.8
  status of donor-advised funds, §16.5
  statutory categories, §15.2
Public college support foundations, public charity status, §15.3(f)
Public disclosure of returns, §12.3(a)
Public facilities, disqualified person use, §5.9(d)

Public inspection requirement, §12.3(a)
Public institutions, §15.3
Publicly supported charities, §15.2
  donative, §15.4
  service provider, §15.5
Publicly traded partnership, §11.3(c)
Publicly traded stock, short sale income, §11.4(a)
Public office
  candidate, §9.2(a)
  term, defining, §§ 4.8, 9.2(a)
Public support
  attraction, §15.1(c)(i)
  determination, §§15.4(c), 15.5(a)

Q

Qualified appraisal, §14.7(d)
Qualified appraiser, definition, §14.7(d)
Qualified appreciated stock
  exclusions, §14.5
  rule, §14.5
  term, meaning, §14.5
Qualified bingo games, income, §11.2(d)
Qualified charitable gift annuity, payment, §11.4(b)
Qualified disasters, §9.3(c)
  private foundation payments, §9.3(c)
Qualified first-tier taxes, §12.4(c)
Qualified investment counsel, foundation manager disclosure, §8.5(c)
Qualified organization
  conservation easement contributions, §14.6(g)
  research and experimentation credit, §3.5
Qualified tax practitioner, definition, §§6.4(e), 9.6(b)
Qualifying distributions, §§ 3.1(d), 6.4
  administrative expenses, §6.4(f)(ii)
  cash distribution test set-asides, §6.4(g)(ii)
  charitable grants, in general, §6.4(b)
  charities, group ruling, §6.4(d)(iv)

Qualifying distributions (*Continued*)
  controlled organizations, grants, §6.4(c)
    control, definition, §6.4(c)(i)
    court order set-asides, §6.4(g)(iii)
    foreign organizations, grants, §6.4(e)
    foundations, grants, §6.4(c)
    general definition/rules, §6.4(a)
    grantor reliance standards, §6.4(d)
      general rules, §6.4(d)(i)
      good faith (equivalency) determinations, §6.4(e)
      IRS determination letter, absence, §6.4(d)(iii)
    ordering rule, §6.5(b)
    redistribution rule, §6.4(c)(ii)
    set-asides, §6.4(g)
    suitability test set-asides, §6.4(g)(i)
    supporting organizations, grants, §6.4(d)(ii)
Qualifying partnership interest (QPI), definition, §11.5(b)
Qualifying public charity, good faith determinations, §§6.4(e), 9.6(b)
Qualifying S corporation interest, definition, §11.5(b)
Quarterly estimated tax, organization payment, §11.5(e)
Quid pro quo contribution, §14.7(c)
Quid pro quo exchange, §14.1

R
Readily marketable securities, §6.3(b)
  distribution, §10.3
Real estate, §6.2(d)
  activities, unrelated business, §11.1(e)
  charitable organization purchase, §11.1(e)
  as exempt-function asset, §6.2(d)
Realized, term (usage), 8.2(e)
Reasonable basis, expense allocations, §§3.1(b), 10.5(b), 11.5(a)
Reasonable cash balances, §6.2(d)
Reasonable cause, §§ 9.9(b), 12.2(c)
  abatement of excise taxes, §12.4(c)
  existence, evaluation, §12.2(c)
  presumption, §12.4(b)
  professional advice, reliance, §12.2(c)
Reasonable compensation, §5.6(c)
Reasonable judgment, term (usage), §§6.4(e), 9.8
Recapture rule, §14.4(b)
Recoverable grants, interest-free loan function, §8.3
Redistribution rule, §§ 6.4(c)(ii), 6.5(c)
Reformation rule (private foundations), §§ 13.5(a), 13.5(b)
Regular faculty, absence, §15.3
Regularly carried on, §11.1(d)
Reimbursements, §5.6(g)
  payment, §17.6(a)
Related trade/business, conduct, §11.1(c)
Related-use exceptions, unrelated debt-financed income, §11.4(b)
Remote contingency, §15.6(c)
Rent
  exceptions, unrelated business income, §11.2(b)
  taxable investment income, §10.4(e)
Reporting rules, unrelated business income, §11.5(d)
Required relationships, supporting organizations, §15.6(d)
Research
  exclusion from unrelated business income, §11.2(c)
  nonpartisan, §9.1(d)
Research and experimentation funds, §3.5
Responsiveness test, supporting organizations, §15.6(g)(iii)
  revision, §15.6(g)(vii)
Restatement of the Law, Trust—Prudent Investor Rule, revision, §8.1(a)
Retroactive revocation, §12.7(b)
Returns, inspection, §12.3
Revocation
  consequences, §12.7(e)
  contesting, §12.7(d)
  retroactive revocation, §12.7(b)

INDEX

Risk, investment return (correlation), §8.2(c)
Royalties
　exclusion, unrelated business income, §11.2(a)
　net investment income, §10.4(f)
Royalty interest, as program-related investment, §8.3

S

Safe harbor criteria, unusual grant, §15.5(c)(ii)
Safekeeping activities (general banking services), §5.6(g)
Salary
　increases, payments (casting), §5.6(c)
　statistics, finding, §5.6(d)
Savings
　accounts (general banking service), §5.6(g)
　provisions, §5.14(b)
Schedule A
　Form 990, §§ 2.7(a), 13.4(a), 15.6(g)(v), 15.6(j), 15.8
　Form 990-T, §11.5(e)
　Form 4720, §12.4(a)
　Form 8940, §6.4(g)(i), (iii)
Schedule B
　Form 4720, §12.4(a)
　Form 8940, §9.2(c)
Schedule C
　Form 4720, §§12.4(a), 16.7
　Form 8940, §9.3(f)(i)
Schedule D, Form 4720, §12.4(a)
Schedule E
　Form 1023, §2.7(b)
　Form 4720, §12.4(a)
　Form 8940, §15.5(c)(iii)
Schedule F
　Form1023, §2.7(a)
　Form 4720, §12.4(a)
　Form 8940, §§12.5(a), 13.4(c), 13.4(d)
Schedule G
　Form 4720, §12.4(a)
　Form 8940, §§3.1(h), 10.7, 13.1, 15.7(c), 15.8
Schedule H
　Form 1023, §§2.7(a), 9.3(f)(i), (ii)
　Form 4720, §12.4(a)
　Form 8940, §13.4(c)
Schedule I
　Form 4720, §§12.4(a), 16.7
　Form 8940, §13.4(b)
Schedule J
　Form 4720, §12.4(a)
　Form 8940, §13.4(d)
Schedule K
　Form 4720, §§12.4(a), 16.7
　Form 8940, §2.7(f)
Schedule K-1, Form 1065, §11.5(b)
Schedule L
　Form 4720, §§ 12.4(a), 16.7
　Form 8940, §§13.4(c), 13.4(d)
Schedule M
　Form 4720, § 12.4(a)
　Form 8940, §§13.4(c), 13.4(d)
Schedule N
　Form 4720, §12.4(a)
　Form 8940, §§13.4(c), 13.4(d)
Schedule O
　Form 4720, § 12.4(a)
　Form 8940, §§13.4(c), 13.4(d)
Schedule P, Form 8940, §§ 13.4(c), 13.4(d)
Scholarships, §9.3(d)(i)
　employer-related programs, §9.3(d)(ii)
　grant procedures
　　IRS pre-approval, §9.3(f)
　　requirements, §9.3(e)
　selection, objective/nondiscriminatory basis, §9.3(e)(i)
S Corporation
　income, capital gains/losses, §10.4(h)
　stock, private foundation ownership, §11.5(b)
　unrelated business activity, §11.3(c)
Secondary grantees, §9.4(c)
Second-tier tax. *See* Additional (second-tier) excise tax

INDEX

Securities transactions, §5.8(a)
   law, summary, §5.8(a)(i)
Selection criteria, objective/
      nondiscriminatory, §9.3(e)(i)
Self-dealing excise taxes, §5.15(a)
   abatement, limitation, §5.15(a)(iv)
   additional (second-tier) taxes,
      §§5.15(a)(ii), 12.4(c)
   amount, involved, §5.15(b)
     compensation, §5.15(b)(ii)
     date of valuation, §5.15(c)
     exceptions based on fair market
       value, §5.15(b)(iii)
     use of money, §5.15(b)(i)
     use of other property, §5.15(b)(i)
   correction, §5.15(d)
     loans, §5.15(d)(iii)
     sales by the foundation, §5.15(d)(i)
     sales to the foundation, §5.15(d)(ii)
     unreasonable compensation,
       §5.15(d)(vi)
     use of property
       by disqualified persons,
        §5.15(d)(iv)
       by foundation, §5.15(d)(v)
   counsel, advice, §5.15(a)(v)
   initial (first-tier) taxes, §§5.15(a)
      (i), 12.4(e)
   as penalties, §1.8(c)
   as Pigouvian taxes, §1.8(b)
   termination tax, §5.15(a)(iii)
Self-dealing rules
   application, absence, §4.1(b)
   benefit tickets, joint purchase, §5.8(g)
   charitable pledges, payment, §5.8(c)
   and company foundations, §17.6
   compensation, §§5.6, 17.6(a)
   compensatory indemnification/
      insurance, §5.7(b)
   corporate organizations/
      reorganizations, exceptions,
      §§5.14(a), 17.6(f)
   estate administration exception, §5.12
   expense advances, §5.6(g)
   facilities, sharing, §17.6(b)
   fair market value, exceptions,
      §5.15(b)(iii)
   in general, §1.4(d)
   general definition, §5.3
   grantmaking, §17.6(c)
   incidental and tenuous benefits,
      §§5.8(e), 17.6(e)
     public recognition, §17.6(e)
   indirect self-dealing, §§ 5.3, 5.11
   memberships, payment, §5.8(f)
   noncompensatory indemnification/
      insurance, §5.7(a)
   other acts, §5.8(h)
   reimbursements, payment,
      §§5.6(g), 17.6(a)
   securities transactions, §5.8(a)
   stock transfers, §17.6(f)
   tax, court jurisdiction, §5.15(e)
   transitional rules (savings
      provisions), §5.14(b)
   valuation date, §5.15(c)
Self-defense exception, influencing
      legislation, §9.1(e)
Service provider publicly supported
      charity, §15.5
   investment income test, §15.5(b)
   support test, §15.5(a)
Services
   compensation, exclusion, §11.2(a)
   furnishing, §5.4(e)
   prohibition, §5.9(a)
   gift, nondeductibility, §14.6(f)
Set-asides, §§ 3.1(a), 6.4(g)
   cash distribution test set-asides,
      §6.4(g)(ii)
   court-order set-asides, §6.4(g)(iii)
   suitability test set-asides, §6.4(g)(i)
Short-term capital gain,
      realization, §11.3(c)
Short-term emergency aid (IRS
      guidelines), §9.3(c)
Single-member limited liability
      company, holdings, §7.3
Skills enhancement, grants
      (relationship), §9.3(d)(iv)

INDEX

Social issues, nonpartisan study, §9.1(d)
Societal problems, examinations/
discussions, §9.1(d)
Space, sharing, §5.9
Special corporation deductions, §10.5(b)
Special gift situations, §14.6
Specific legislation, meaning, §9.1(b)
Specific objectives, grants, §9.3(d)(iv)
Split-interest trust, §§ 7.2(c),
11.3(d), 15.5(b)
  distributions from, §10.4(g)
  private foundation treatment, §3.7
Sponsoring organization, donor-advised
fund, §16.7
  average payout rate, §16.8(b)
  grants payment, §16.8(b)
Sponsorship payments, as public
support, §15.4(c)
Start-up period minimum amount,
§6.4(g)(ii)
State fundraising regulation, §14.7(g)
State law, tax exemption, §2.7(g)
State officials, disclosure of
returns, §12.3(b)
Statute of limitations, §11.5(f)
  Form 990-PF, §12.2(b)
  Form 990-T, §12.2(b)
  Form 4720, §12.4(d)
Statutory criteria, donor-advised
funds, §16.7
Stock transfers, §17.6(f)
Straight-line depreciation, allowance
  adjusted net income, calculation,
§3.1
  net investment income,
calculation, §10.5(a)
  unrelated business income,
calculation, §11.4(c)
Straight-line method, usage, §10.5(a)
Subpart F income
  passive income, treatment, §7.1(b)
  unrelated business income,
treatment, §11.2
Substantial compliance,
doctrine, §14.7(d)

fatal mistakes, categories, §14.7(e)
Substantial contributor
  2 percent test, §4.1(b)
  §509(a)(2) support test and, §15.5(a)
  general rules, §4.1(a)
  status, termination, §4.1(c)
Substantiality, general test, §9.1(b)
Substantially related activity, §11.1(c)
Substantiation, charitable
contribution deduction
  requirements, application, §14.7(b)
  rules, §14.7(b)
Successor foundations, reporting
requirements/factors,
§13.5(b)
Suitability test set-asides, §6.4(g)(I)
Supported organization
  attentiveness, §15.6(g)(vi)
  governmental entities, §15.6(g)(v)
  noncharitable entities, §15.6(l)
  parent, §15.6(g)(v)
Support fraction, construction, §§15.4(b),
15.4(c), 15.5(a)
Supporting organizations, §§ 15.2, 15.6
  characteristics, §15.6(b)
  control by disqualified persons,
prohibition, §15.6(j)
  designations, §15.6(c)
  excess benefit transaction rules,
application, §15.6(i)
  excess business holdings rules,
application, §15.6(k)
  grants, §6.4(d)(ii)
  minimum asset amount, §15.6(g)(vi)
  non-exempt-use assets, §15.6(g)(vi)
  operational test, §15.6(b)
  organization, §15.6
  organizational test, §15.6(a)
  required relationships, §15.6(d)
  specified public charities, §15.6(c)
  support, amount, §15.6(g)(vi)
  supported organization parent,
§15.6(g)(v)
  use of for-profit subsidiaries
by, §15.6(m)

INDEX

Support, term (meaning)
  donative publicly supported charities, §15.4(c)
  private operating foundations, §3.1(e)(iii)
  service provider publicly supported charities, §15.5(a)

Support test
  donative publicly supported charities, §15.4(c)
  private operating foundations, §3.1(e)(iii)
    compliance period, §3.1(f)
  service provider publicly supported charities, §15.5(a)

T

Tangible personal property, charitable contributions (tax benefit), §14.4(b)

Taxable distribution, donor-advised funds
  amount, tax, §16.7
  DAF distribution, §16.7

Taxable expenditures
  additional (second-tier) taxes, §9.9(a)
  and company foundations, §17.7(d)
  corrections, §9.9(d)
  exception, transfer to non-controlled foundation, §13.5(c)
  excise taxes, §9.9.
  expenditures for noncharitable purposes, §9.8
  general overview, §1.4(h)
  initial (first-tier) taxes, §9.9(a)
    payment, §9.9(c)
  legislative activities, §9.1
  managers, tax, §9.9(b)
  political campaign activities, §9.2

Taxable net investment income
  calculation, §10.3
  gross investment income, §10.4(a)

Taxable period
  excess business holdings, §7.7
  jeopardizing investments, §8.5(a)

  self-dealing transactions, §5.15(a)(i)
  taxable expenditures, §9.9(b)
  undistributed income, §6.5(d)

Tax Exempt and Government Entities (TE/GE) Division, §13.1

Tax Exempt Organization Search (database), §§ 6.4(d)(i), 6.4(d)(ii), 9.4(b), 12.3(a)

Tax-Exempt Organizations Examination Procedures (IRS), §12.6(b)

Tax-exempt private foundation grantee, grant funds segregation, §9.7(e)

Tax-exempt social club, private foundation grant, §9.7(a)

Tax-exempt status
  27-month rule, §2.7(b)
  exemption, state purposes, §2.7(g)
  foreign organizations, recognition of, §2.7(f)
  Form 1023, §2.7(a)
  initial determination, §12.7(d)
  non-filing, automatic revocation, §12.7(a)
  revocation, §§ 12.5(c), 12.7, 12.7(d)

Tax-exempt status, recognition of
  acquisition, §2.7
  denial, administrative procedures, §2.7(d)
  denial, declaratory judgment procedures, §2.7(e)
  IRS determination letters, §2.7(c)

Tax-exempt title-holding companies, usage, §7.1(b)

Taxpayer (professional advice reliance), three-part test (U.S. Tax Court adoption), §12.4(c)

Tax Reform Act (1969), §6.5(f)
Tax Reform Act (1976), §6.6
Tax Reform Act (1984), §9.7(h)

Team Examination Program (TEP) examination, §12.6(a)

Technical assistance, provision, as related business, §11.3(e)

Technical Guides (TGs), §12.6(b)

INDEX

Termination of private foundation status.
See Private foundations, status
Termination (third-tier) tax, §§5.15(a)(iii), 6.5(d), 7.7, 8.5(d), 9.9(a), 13.7
abatement, §13.8
Total return, §§ 8.2(a), 10.3
concept, §8.2(d)
investing, §8.2(d)
investment policy, foundation usage, §8.2(a)
method, §8.2(e)
Trade or business
definition, §11.1(a)
income, §§ 11.1(b), 11.3(a)
related trade/business, conduct, §11.1(c)
Transferee private foundation
aggregate tax benefit, §13.5(c)
effective control, §13.5(a)
Transferee public charity, termination requirements, §13.3(b)(ii)
Transferor private foundation
aggregate tax benefit, §13.5(d)
leases/contractual obligations/liabilities, public charity assumption, §13.3(b)(ii)
liability, incurring, §13.5(d)
liquidation/dissolution/termination/contraction, statement attachment, §13.5(b)
property transfer, §13.3(b)(i)
transferee public charity distribution right, §13.3(b)(ii)
Transitional rules, savings provisions (self-dealing), §5.14(b)
Transitory indebtedness, obtaining, §11.4(a)
Travel, individual grants, §9.3(d)
Treasury/IRS Priority Guidance Plan, §§5.4(g), 11.5(b), 16.9(a)
Trusts
beneficial interest, §4.3
charitable remainder trusts, early terminations, §5.13
disqualified persons, relationship, §4.6
distributions, capital gains/losses, §10.4(g)
and excess business holdings, §7.2(b)
nonexempt charitable trusts, §3.6
private foundation payments, IRS ruling, §9.8
split-interest trusts, §§2.6(a), 3.7
termination (private foundation treatment), §13.6
Two-part support test, meeting, §15.5
Two-percent limitation, §§ 15.4(b), 15.4(c)
Type I supporting organization, §§ 15.6, 15.6(a), 15.6(d)
contributions from controlling donors, limitation, §15.6(h)
designation of supported organizations, §15.6(c)
operation/supervision/control relationship, §15.6(e)
Type II supporting organization, §§ 15.6, 15.6(a), 15.6(d)
designation of supported organizations, §15.6(c)
excess business holdings rules, application, §15.6(k)
supervision/control, §15.6(f)
Type III supporting organization, §§15.6, 15.6(a), 15.6(d)
contributions from controlling donors, limitation, §15.6(h)
excess business holdings rules, §15.6(k)
foreign supported organizations, prohibition, §15.6(g)(i)
functionally integrated Type III organizations, integral part test, §15.6(g)(v)
activities directly furthering exempt purposes, meaning, §15.6(g)(v)
supporting governmental entities, §15.6(g)(v)
nonfunctionally integrated Type III organizations, integral part test, §15.6(g)(vi)

INDEX

Type III supporting organization (*Continued*)
    attentiveness requirement, §15.6(g)(vi)
    distribution requirement, §15.6(g)(vi)
        adjusted net income, §15.6(g)(vi)
        determining fair market value of assets, §15.6(g)(vi)
        distributable amount, §15.6(g)(vi)
        excess amounts, treatment, §15.6(g)(vi)
        minimum asset amount, §15.6(g)(vi)
    notification requirement, §15.6(g)(ii)
    operated in connection with relationship, §15.6(g)
    overview, §15.6(g)(i)
    pending regulation projects, §15.6(g)(vii)
    relationship, §15.6(c)
    responsiveness test, §15.6(g)(iii)
    types, §15.6(g)(iv)

U

Undistributed income, §6.5(a)
    excise taxes, §6.5(d)
Uniform Management of Institutional Funds Act (UMIFA), §8.2
Uniform Prudent Investor Act, finalization, §8.2
Uniform Prudent Management of Institutional Funda Act (UPMIFA), §8.2
Unreasonable compensation. *See* Compensation
Unrelated business activity
    business enterprise, passive income exclusion, §11.3(a)
    community foundations, grant-making services, §11.3(d)
    exceptions, §11.2
        nonbusiness activities, §11.2(d)
        rents, §11.2(b)
        research, §11.2(c)
        royalties, §11.2(a)
    excess business holdings rules, limitations, §11.3
    general rules, §11.1
    overview, definition, §11.1(a)
    partnerships, §11.3(c)
    private foundations
        permitted businesses, §11.3(b)
        providing technical assistance, §11.3(e)
    real estate activities, §11.1(e)
    regularly carried on, meaning, §11.1(d)
    research, §11.2(c)
    rules, §11.3
    S Corporation, §11.3(c)
    statute of limitations, §11.5(e)
    substantially related activity, §11.1(c)
    trade or business, definition, §§11.1(a), 11.1(b)
Unrelated business income tax
    additions to tax, §11.5(e)
    bucketing (silo) rule, §11.5(b)
    computation of tax, §11.5(d)
    deductions, §11.5(a)
    inclusion of debt-financed income, §11.4(c)
    penalties, §11.5(e)
    reporting requirements, §11.5(d)
    statute of limitations, §11.5(f)
    tax rates, §11.5(c)
    unrelated business taxable income, meaning, §11.5
Unrelated debt-financed income rules, §11.4
    acquisition indebtedness, §11.4(a)
    related-use exception, §11.4(c)
Unrelated trade or business
    regularly carried on, meaning, §11.1(d)
    term, meaning, §§11.1(a), 11.1(b)
Unusual grants, §15.5(c)
    advanced IRS ruling requests, §15.5(c)(iii)